HANDBOOK OF RELATIONSHIP

Initiation

HANDBOOK OF RELATIONSHIP

Initiation

Edited by

SUSAN SPRECHER
AMY WENZEL
JOHN HARVEY

Psychology Press
Taylor & Francis Group
New York   Hove

Psychology Press
Taylor & Francis Group
270 Madison Avenue
New York, NY 10016

Psychology Press
Taylor & Francis Group
27 Church Road
Hove, East Sussex BN3 2FA

Printed in the United States of America on acid-free paper
10 9 8 7 6 5 4 3 2 1

International Standard Book Number-13: 978-0-8058-6160-0 (Softcover) 978-0-8058-6159-4 (Hardcover)

Library of Congress Cataloging-in-Publication Data

Library of Congress Cataloging-in-Publication Data
   Sprecher, Susan, 1955-
   Handbook of relationship initiation / Susan Sprecher, Amy Wenzel, and John Harvey.
      p. cm.
   Includes bibliographical references and index.
   ISBN 978-0-8058-6160-0 (alk. paper) -- ISBN 978-0-8058-6159-4 (alk. paper) 1. Interpersonal relations. 2. Man-woman relationships. I. Wenzel, Amy. II. Title.

HM1106.S67 2008
305.3--dc22   2008012956

Visit the Taylor & Francis Web site at
http://www.taylorandfrancis.com

and the Psychology Press Web site at
http://www.psypress.com

Contents

Preface   ix

List of Contributors   xi

SECTION I   INTRODUCTION

1   Have We Met Before?: A Conceptual Model of First Romantic Encounters   3

Carrie A. Bredow, Rodney M. Cate, and Ted L. Huston

2   Friendship Formation   29

Beverley Fehr

3   An Evolutionary Perspective on Mate Choice and Relationship Initiation   55

David P. Schmitt

4   Attachment Theory and Research: A Special Focus on Relationship Initiation   75

Gary Creasey and Patricia Jarvis

SECTION II   THE PROCESS OF RELATIONSHIP INITIATION

5   Prelude to a Kiss: Nonverbal Flirting, Opening Gambits, and Other Communication Dynamics in the Initiation of Romantic Relationships   97

Michael R. Cunningham and Anita P. Barbee

6   Uncertainty and Relationship Initiation   121

Leanne K. Knobloch and Laura E. Miller

7   Information Seeking in the Initial Stages of Relational Development   135

Walid A. Afifi and Alysa A. Lucas

8   Self-Disclosure and Starting a Close Relationship   153

Valerian J. Derlega, Barbara A. Winstead, and Kathryn Greene

9   On Becoming "More Than Friends": The Transition from Friendship to Romantic
     Relationship   **175**

     Laura K. Guerrero and Paul A. Mongeau

SECTION III   DIVERSE CONTEXTS OF RELATIONSHIP INITIATION

10   The Social and Physical Environment of Relationship Initiation: An Interdependence
     Analysis   197

     Ximena B. Arriaga, Christopher R. Agnew, Nicole M. Capezza, and Justin J. Lehmiller

11   Speed-Dating: A Powerful and Flexible Paradigm for Studying Romantic Relationship
     Initiation   217

     Paul W. Eastwick and Eli J. Finkel

12   MySpace or Your Place: Relationship Initiation and Development in the Wired and
     Wireless World   235

     Katelyn Y. A. McKenna (Yael Kaynan)

13   TheBusinessofLove.com: Relationship Initiation at Internet Matchmaking Services 249

     Susan Sprecher, Pepper Schwartz, John Harvey, and Elaine Hatfield

SECTION IV   ATTRACTION AND OTHER EMOTIONS
IN RELATIONSHIP INITIATION

14   Attraction and the Initiation of Relationships: A Review of the Empirical Literature 269

     William G. Graziano and Jennifer Weisho Bruce

15   Insider Perspectives on Attraction   297

     Susan Sprecher and Diane Felmlee

16   Falling in Love   315

     Arthur Aron, Helen E. Fisher, Greg Strong, Bianca Acevedo, Suzanne Riela, and Irene Tsapelas

17   Satisfaction, Love, and Respect in the Initiation of Romantic Relationships   337

     Susan S. Hendrick and Clyde Hendrick

18   The Emotional Landscape of Romantic Relationship Initiation   353

     Sandra Metts and Sylvia L. Mikucki

SECTION V   CHALLENGES AND PROBLEMATIC RELATIONSHIP INITIATION

19   Hookups: A Facilitator or a Barrier to Relationship Initiation and Intimacy Development?   375

Elizabeth L. Paul, Amy Wenzel, and John Harvey

20   Romantic Relationship Initiation Following Relationship Dissolution   391

Mark A. Fine, Tina A. Coffelt, and Loreen N. Olson

21   "Thanks, but No Thanks ..." The Occurrence and Management of Unwanted Relationship Pursuit   409

William R. Cupach and Brian H. Spitzberg

22   Emotional Disturbances and the Initial Stages of Relationship Development: Processes and Consequences of Social Anxiety and Depression   425

Amy Wenzel and Todd B. Kashdan

SECTION VI   COGNITIONS, BELIEFS, AND MEMORIES ABOUT RELATIONSHIP INITIATION

23   "So How Did You Two Meet?" Narratives of Relationship Initiation   453

Lindsay Custer, Diane Holmberg, Karen Blair, and Terri L. Orbuch

24   Relationship Beliefs and Their Role in Romantic Relationship Initiation   471

C. Raymond Knee and Amber L. Bush

25   The Role of Ideal Standards in Relationship Initiation Processes   487

SiSi Tran, Jeffry A. Simpson, and Garth J. O. Fletcher

26   Perceptions of Goals and Motives in Romantic Relationships   499

Glenn D. Reeder

SECTION VII   COMMENTARY

27   Ending the Beginning of Relationships   517

Daniel Perlman

Name Index   541

Subject Index   567

Preface

In 2004, we published *The Handbook of Sexuality in Close Relationships*. Working together as editors and with Debra Riegert, then senior editor at Lawrence Erlbaum Associates, was a very positive experience. It did not take us long to identify another topic about personal relationships that interested us and that we viewed as being relatively neglected in the growing collection of edited and authored books in the personal relationships literature. This was the topic of relationship initiation.

We were aware of books that had focused on the relationship stages of maintenance and dissolution, and on the topics of satisfaction, love, commitment, sexuality, and many other relationship phenomena. However, none had focused exclusively on the birth of relationships. Even the two most recent sourcebooks on relationships (*The Cambridge Handbook of Personal Relationships*, edited by Anita L. Vangelisti and Daniel Perlman; and *Close Relationships: A Sourcebook*, edited by Susan and Clyde Hendrick) give scant attention to the beginning stage of relationships. This stage, however, is critically important. Before relationships can reach the development, maintenance, and dissolution stages—and before partners can experience love, commitment, sex, and disenchantment—two people must meet, communicate for the first time, and begin to define themselves as being in a relationship.

Neglect of the initiation stage, however, was not the case during the birth of the field of personal relationships in the 1960s and 1970s. The field's early focus, particularly by social psychologists, was on initial attraction, often between strangers. Research examined the question of what led to initial attraction and identified the importance of familiarity, proximity, similarity, reciprocity of liking, and physical attractiveness. It has sometimes been assumed that research on relationships shifted completely away from the topic of attraction in the laboratory to naturalistic phenomena that occur in real relationships that have a history and a future. Although it is true that the focus shifted, research on relationship initiation and early attraction continued in various research labs and in multiple disciplines. It is time that this research and theory are highlighted and synthesized in one volume. This was our major goal for *The Handbook of Relationship Initiation*. A second goal was that the volume would stimulate new directions for research. One of our requests to the authors was that they offer suggestions for future research.

This volume is timely not only by providing an overdue synthesis of literature on relationship initiation but also because the topics of relationship initiation and science's contribution to understanding this process have received media and laypeople's attention in recent years. With the increasing popularity of relationship initiation on the Internet, particularly through matchmaking services, awareness has become more widespread that science can be used to create and facilitate compatible matching.

Once the idea for this edited volume was articulated in a book prospectus, and potential authors were contacted, the interest and enthusiasm for this project were contagious. Almost every scholar we invited to write a chapter quickly agreed. Many expressed upon completing their chapters that they thoroughly enjoyed the opportunity to focus specifically on the beginning stage of the relationship. Debra Riegert at Erlbaum was unwavering in her support for this project, and when we put the idea on the back burner after initially proposing it, she encouraged us to move forward on it. When Taylor & Francis combined with Erlbaum, our new editor, Paul Dukes, was equally enthusiastic about the project.

What is meant by relationship initiation? Is it one of those terms that everyone just knows, and a definition is not necessary? What characteristics define a relationship to be in the initiation stage versus a postinitiation developing stage? In the most expansive view, relationship initiation may span from the time of first awareness between two people to the time when the two begin to think of themselves as in a relationship, whether that's a romantic bond or a friendship. It is a process that might occur over days or weeks, and it involves cognitions, feelings, and behaviors. Each chapter discusses a distinct aspect of the process or context of relationship initiation.

This volume includes 61 authors writing 27 chapters, divided into seven sections. Our sections focus on introductory issues including theory (4 chapters); the process of relationship initiation (5 chapters); the diverse contexts of relationship initiation (4 chapters); attraction and other emotions in relationship initiation (5 chapters); challenges and problematic relationship initiation (4 chapters); and cognitions, beliefs, and memories about relationship initiation (4 chapters). In the final section, distinguished scholar Daniel Perlman presents a commentary and synthesis of the entire volume.

We are very pleased with the quality of the chapters in this volume. All of the authors are experts on their topics. In addition, each chapter was reviewed not only by the three editors (and multiple times) but also by another author who contributed to this book. We thank the authors for their cooperation in being challenged to revise and extend their chapters.

We learned a tremendous amount from our chapter contributors, and we hope that the reader of this volume will have the same experience. Several chapters present rich theoretical paradigms that can account for the mechanism by which relationship initiation occurs. Other chapters describe innovative experimental designs and methodologies that allow for relationships to unfold naturally but for their characteristics to be measured with precision. One theme that was evident in most chapters is that more research is needed to determine the extent to which our theories and empirical findings apply to individuals of different racial and ethnic backgrounds, ages, and sexual orientations. We encourage readers of this handbook to continue the exploration of processes associated with relationship initiation, using the theories, constructs, methodologies, and previous findings described in these chapters as a springboard to investigate the development of close relationships in diverse populations.

Susan Sprecher
Amy Wenzel
John Harvey

List of Contributors

EDITORS

Susan Sprecher
Department of Sociology & Anthropology, and
  Department of Psychology
Illinois State University
Normal, IL 61790-4660
Phone: (309) 438-8357
E-mail: sprecher@ilstu.edu

Amy Wenzel
Psychopathology Research Unit
Department of Psychiatry
University of Pennsylvania
3535 Market St., Room 2029
Philadelphia, PA 19104
Phone: (215) 898-4103
E-mail: awenzel@mail.med.upenn.edu

John Harvey
Department of Psychology
E11 Seashore Hall
University of Iowa
Iowa City, IA 52242
Phone: (319) 335-2473
E-mail: john-harvey@uiowa.edu

CONTRIBUTORS

Carrie A. Bredow
Department of Human Ecology
College of Natural Sciences
1 University Station A2700
University of Texas at Austin
Austin, TX 78712
Phone: (512) 706-5799
E-mail: Carrie.bredow@mail.utexas.edu

Rodney M. Cate
Division of Family Studies and Human
  Development
University of Arizona
Tucson, AZ 85721
Phone: (360) 485-3922
E-mail: Rcate@ag.arizona.edu and rnpcate@
  comcast.net

Ted L. Huston
Department of Human Ecology
College of Natural Sciences
1 University Station A2700
University of Texas at Austin
Austin, TX 78712
Phone: (512) 471-5606
E-mail: huston@mail.utexas.edu

Beverley Fehr
Department of Psychology
University of Winnipeg
515 Portage Avenue
Winnipeg, MB Canada R3T 2N2
Phone: (204) 786-9864
E-mail: bfehr@uwinnipeg.ca

David P. Schmitt
Department of Psychology
Bradley University
105 Comstock Hall
Peoria, IL 61625
Phone: (309) 677-2588
E-mail: dps@bradley.edu

Gary Creasey
4620 Psychology Department
Illinois State University
Normal, IL 61790-4620
Phone: (309) 438-8139
E-mail: glcrease@ilstu.edu

Patricia Jarvis
4620 Psychology Department
Illinois State University
Normal, IL 61790-4620
Phone: (309) 438-8425
E-mail: pajarvis@ilstu.edu

Michael R. Cunningham
Department of Communication
University of Louisville
Louisville, KY 40292
Phone: (502) 852-5953
E-mail: michael.cunningham@louisville.edu

Anita P. Barbee
Kent School of Social Work
University of Louisville
Louisville, KY 40292
Phone: (502) 852-0416
E-mail: anita.barbee@louisville.edu

Leanne K. Knobloch
Department of Speech Communication
University of Illinois
244 Lincoln Hall, 702 S. Wright St.
Urbana, IL 61801
Phone: (217) 333-8913
E-mail: knobl@uiuc.edu

Laura E. Miller
Department of Speech Communication
University of Illinois
244 Lincoln Hall, 702 S. Wright St.
Urbana, IL 61801
Phone: (217) 333-9106
E-mail: lemillr1@uiuc.edu

Walid A. Afifi
Department of Communication
University of California, Santa Barbara
4814 Ellison Hall
Santa Barbara, CA 93106
Phone: (805) 893-7105
E-mail: w-afifi@comm.ucsb.edu

Alysa A. Lucas
The Pennsylvania State University
Department of Communication Arts &
    Sciences
234 Sparks Bldg.
University Park, PA 16802
Phone: (814) 308-2786
E-mail: aal150@psu.edu

Valerian J. Derlega
Department of Psychology
Old Dominion University
Norfolk, VA 23529-0267
Phone: (757) 683-3118
E-mail: vderlega@odu.edu

Barbara A. Winstead
Department of Psychology
Old Dominion University
Norfolk, VA 23529-0267
Phone: (757) 683-4239
E-mail: bwinstea@odu.edu

Kathryn Greene
Department of Communication
Rutgers University
New Brunswick, NJ 08091-1071
Phone: (732) 932-7500, ext. 8115
E-mail: kgreene@scils.rutgers.edu

Laura K. Guerrero
Hugh Downs School of Human Communication
Arizona State University
Tempe, AZ 85287-1205
Phone: (480) 965-3730
E-mail: laura.guerrero@asu.edu

Paul A. Mongeau
Hugh Downs School of Human Communication
Arizona State University
Tempe, AZ 85287-1205
Phone: (480) 965-3773
E-mail: Paul.Mongeau@asu.edu

Ximena B. Arriaga
Department of Psychological Sciences
Purdue University
703 Third Street
West Lafayette, IN 47907-2081
Phone: (765) 494-6888
E-mail: arriaga@purdue.edu

Christopher R. Agnew
Department of Psychological Sciences
Purdue University
703 Third Street
West Lafayette, IN 47907-2081
Phone: (765) 494-6254
E-mail: agnew@purdue.edu

Nicole M. Capezza
Department of Psychological Sciences
Purdue University
703 Third Street
West Lafayette, IN 47907-2081
Phone: (765) 494-6892
E-mail: ncapezza@purdue.edu

Justin J. Lehmiller
Department of Psychological Sciences
Purdue University
703 Third Street
West Lafayette, IN 47907-2081
Phone: (765) 494-6892
E-mail: justin@purdue.edu

Paul W. Eastwick
Department of Psychology
Northwestern University
2029 Sheridan Road
Evanston, IL 60208
Phone: (773) 484-3878
E-mail: p-eastwick@northwestern.edu

Eli J. Finkel
Department of Psychology
Northwestern University
2029 Sheridan Road
Evanston, IL 60208
Phone: (847) 491-3212
E-mail: finkel@northwestern.edu

Katelyn Y. A. McKenna (Yael Kaynan)
Sammy Ofer School of Communication
Interdisciplinary Center Herzliya
Herzliya 46150, Israel
Phone: 011 + 972-54-255-6837
E-mail: yaeli.kaynan@gmail.com

Pepper Schwartz
Department of Sociology
University of Washington
Seattle, WA 98195
Phone: (206) 465-6573
E-mail: pepperschwartz@hotmail.com

Elaine Hatfield
Department of Psychology
University of Hawaii
2430 Campus Road
Honolulu, HI 96822-2216
Phone: (808) 956-6276
E-mail: Elaineh1@aol.com

William G. Graziano
Purdue University
Department of Psychological Sciences
703 Third St.
Room PSYC 2170
West Lafayette, IN 47907-2081
Phone: (765) 494-7224
E-mail: graziano@purdue.edu

Jennifer Weisho Bruce
Purdue University
Department of Psychological Sciences
703 Third St.
West Lafayette, IN 47907-2081
Phone: (765) 494-6892
E-mail: jenbruce@psych.purdue.edu

Diane Felmlee
Department of Sociology
One Shields Avenue
University of California, Davis
Davis, CA 95616
Phone: (530) 752-5430
E-mail: dhfelmlee@ucdavis.edu

Arthur Aron
Department of Psychology
Stony Brook University
Stony Brook, NY 11794-2520
Phone: (631) 632-7007
E-mail: Arthur.Aron@stonybrook.edu

Helen E. Fisher
Department of Anthropology
Rutgers University
131 George St.
New Brunswick, NJ 08901-1414
Phone: (212) 744-9870
E-mail: HeFisher@worldnet.att.net

Greg Strong
Department of Psychology
Stony Brook University
Stony Brook, NY 11794-2520
Phone: (631) 632-9601
E-mail: gregjstrong@hotmail.com

Bianca Acevedo
Department of Psychology
Stony Brook University
Stony Brook, NY 11794-2520
Phone: (631) 632-9601
E-mail: bianca1127@aol.com

Suzanne Riela
Department of Psychology
Stony Brook University
Stony Brook, NY 11794-2520
Phone: (631) 632-9601
E-mail: sriela@ic.sunysb.edu

Irene Tsapelas
Department of Psychology
Stony Brook University
Stony Brook, NY 11794-2520
Phone: (631) 632-9601
E-mail: itsapelas@notes.cc.sunysb.edu

Susan S. Hendrick
Department of Psychology
Texas Tech University
Lubbock, TX 79409-2051
Phone: (806) 742-3711, ext. 244
E-mail: s.hendrick@ttu.edu

Clyde Hendrick
Department of Psychology
Texas Tech University
Lubbock, TX 79409-2051
Phone: (806) 742-3711, ext. 248
E-mail: clyde.hendrick@ttu.edu

Sandra Metts
Illinois State University
Fell 423
Normal, IL 61790-4480
Phone: (309) 438-7883
E-mail: smmetts@ilstu.edu

Sylvia L. Mikucki
Department of Communication
University of Illinois
244 Lincoln Hall, 702 S. Wright Street
Urbana, IL 61801
Phone: (217) 333-9107
E-mail: mikucki2@uiuc.edu or smikucki@
    hotmail.com

Elizabeth L. Paul
Psychology Department
Social Sciences Building
The College of New Jersey
P.O. Box 7718
2000 Pennington Rd.
Ewing, NJ 08628
Phone: (609) 771-2651
E-mail: bethpaul@tcnj.edu

Mark A. Fine
Department of Human Development and
    Family Studies
410 Gentry Hall
University of Missouri–Columbia
Columbia, MO 65211
Phone: (573) 884-6301
E-mail: finem@missouri.edu

Tina A. Coffelt
Department of Communication Studies
Switzler Hall
University of Missouri–Columbia
Columbia, MO 65211
Phone: (573) 673-6792
E-mail: tac244@mizzou.edu

Loreen N. Olson
Department of Communication Studies
Switzler Hall
University of Missouri–Columbia
Columbia, MO 65211
Phone: (573) 882-3667
E-mail: olsonln@missouri.edu

William R. Cupach
School of Communication
Illinois State University
Normal, IL 61790-4480
Phone: (309) 438-7110
E-mail: wrcupac@ilstu.edu

Brian H. Spitzberg
School of Communication
San Diego State University
San Diego, CA 92182-4561
Phone: (619) 594-7097
E-mail: spitz@mail.sdsu.edu

Todd B. Kashdan
Department of Psychology
George Mason University
Mail Stop 3F5
Fairfax, VA 22030
Phone: (703) 993-9486
E-mail: tkashdan@gmu.edu

Lindsay Custer
Cascadia Community College
18345 Campus Way NE
Bothell, WA 98007
Phone: (425) 352-8214
E-mail: lcuster@cascadia.ctc.edu and
  lindcust5@msn.com

Diane Holmberg
Department of Psychology
313 Horton Hall
18 University Avenue
Acadia University
Wolfville, NS B4P 2R6 Canada
Phone: (902) 585-1226
E-mail: diane.holmberg@acadiau.ca

Karen Blair
Department of Psychology
117 Horton Hall
Acadia University
Wolfville, NS B4P 2R6 Canada
Phone: (902) 585-1745
E-mail: Karen@klbresearch.com

Terri L. Orbuch
Department of Sociology
Oakland University
Rochester Hills, MI 48309
Phone: (248)709-1939
E-mail: orbuch@umich.edu

C. Raymond Knee
Department of Psychology
University of Houston
Houston, TX 77294-5022
Phone: (713) 743-8524
E-mail: knee@uh.edu

Amber L. Bush
Department of Psychology
University of Houston
Houston, TX 77204-5022
Phone: (713) 743-8500
E-mail: albush@mail.uh.edu

SiSi Tran
Department of Psychology
Vassar College
124 Raymond Avenue
Poughkeepsie, NY 12604-0205
Phone: (845) 437-7934
E-mail: sitran@vassar.edu

Jeffry A. Simpson
N218 Elliot Hall
75 East River Rd.
University of Minnesota
Minneapolis, MN 55455-0344
Phone: (612) 626-0025
E-mail: simps108@umn.edu

Garth J. O. Fletcher
Department of Psychology
University of Canterbury
Private Bag 4800
Christchurch, New Zealand
Phone: 011 643 364 2970
E-mail: garth.fletcher@canterbury.ac.nz

Glenn D. Reeder
Department of Psychology
Illinois State University
Normal, IL 61790-4620
Phone: (309) 438-7140
E-mail: gdreeder@ilstu.edu

Daniel Perlman
Human Development and Family Studies
School of Human Environmental Sciences
University of North Carolina at Greensboro
P.O. Box 26170
Greensboro, NC 27402-6170
Phone: (336) 256-0134
E-mail: d_perlma@uncg.edu

Section I

Introduction

1

Have We Met Before?
A Conceptual Model of First Romantic Encounters

CARRIE A. BREDOW, RODNEY M. CATE, and TED L. HUSTON

*P*eople often take much pleasure and satisfaction in reminiscing about how an intimate relationship began (see Custer, Holmberg, Blair, & Orbuch, this volume). *New Yorker* writer Calvin Trillin (2006) recalled his first impression of Alice, his future wife:

> … she was wearing a hat. At least, I've always remembered her as wearing a hat. She later insisted that she'd never owned a hat of the sort I described. Maybe, but I can still see her in the hat—a white hat, cocked a bit to the side. Her cheeks were slightly flushed. She had blond hair, worn straight in those days, and a brow, just a shade darker than her hair. She was … so very pretty, but that wasn't the first thing that struck me about her; it might have come as much as two or three seconds later. My first impression was that she looked more alive than anyone I'd ever seen. She seemed to glow. (pp. 12–13)

Trillin spotted Alice at a party organized by a mutual friend. Others meet by happenstance. Friendships can blossom into romances, at times in highly unorthodox ways. John Fowles initially befriended a young couple, Elizabeth and Roy Christy, when the three found themselves together on a remote Greek island—the setting for his novel, *The Magus*—with little to do but drink. When Roy fell into a drunken stupor, a regular occurrence, John and Elizabeth were left to wile away the hours together. Over a period of months, a growing tenderness developed between them, but Fowles (2003) held his feelings in check, reasoning that as long as he did not touch her, or kiss her when she offered, he was not transgressing. When his resistance weakened, they kissed, and the romance flowered.

In this chapter, we offer a descriptive analysis of the beginnings of relationships and situate them within a broader historical context, focusing on the development of the "dating system" and its evolution over the course of the 20th century. We then present a conceptual model of the dynamics of first encounters. We examine the motives that underlie relationship formation and discuss (a) the connection between a person's motives and initial attraction, (b) the decision to make an overture, (c) strategic self-presentation, and (d) the buildup of rapport. The chapter concludes with a consideration of theories relevant to our model.

THE SIX TASKS OF SUCCESSFUL ENCOUNTERS

Sociologist Murray Davis (1973), writing in the symbolic interactionist tradition, was the first to provide a systematic breakdown of the steps involved in making a successful overture. Both Trillin's (2006) and Fowles' (2003) accounts offer a sense of the tension and excitement involved in starting a relationship, but their accounts lack the "he said, she said" detail necessary to explicate the process delineated by Davis. The following hypothetical scenario, though it lacks nuance, serves this purpose:

> Amy has decided to have her bag lunch outside in the plaza of her office building. There are several options: She can sit by herself, eat with a group of female coworkers, or sit near a man who is eating alone and reading *Variety*. Amy notes that the guy is "hot," and that he looks "so good" in his business suit. Would he be open to talking with her? Amy takes the seat across from the man. She notices that his posture changes subtly toward her. She sees that he is not wearing a wedding band. Amy says, "It's such a nice day, I couldn't resist having lunch outside." He smiles, and replies, "It couldn't be nicer. It's supposed to be like this for the next week or so." Amy notices his smile, and then says, "I see you're reading *Variety*. What type of entertainment do you like?" He responds, "I love music, especially musical theater! In fact, I just saw *Mama Mia* last night. Have you seen it?" Amy says that she has. They soon discover that they share a taste for jazz and bluesy rock-and-roll. Finally, Amy says, "By the way, my name is Amy." He responds, "I'm Michael." Before she returns to work, Amy asks, "Would you like to have lunch again tomorrow?" Michael replies, "That would be great. I'll see you at noon."

Davis (1973) proposed that six core tasks are involved in starting a relationship [see the initiating and experimenting stages of Knapp's (1984) model of interaction stages for an additional account of Davis' sequence].

- First, the would-be initiator must determine whether the potential partner possesses the *qualifiers* that make it likely that an encounter will be worthwhile. The qualifiers that push Amy toward Michael are his good looks—a usual draw—and his business attire, perhaps a sign of success.
- Second, the would-be initiator must determine whether the other is *cleared* for an encounter and a relationship. Amy sees that Michael is not wearing a wedding ring, and she reads his posture as suggesting that he is open to her overture.
- Third, the initiator must find an *opener* to secure the other person's attention and provide the person with an opportunity to make a preliminary appraisal of the initiator's appeal. Amy comments on the weather, a generally safe conversational opener. Michael's smile and response signal his willingness to continue the conversation.
- Fourth, the initiator must seek an *integrating topic*, one that engages both partners. Often in such a situation, the initiator will ask questions, hoping to uncover a common interest. Amy had the benefit of a cue—Michael's perusal of *Variety*. His expressed interest in musicals, and his query as to whether she had seen *Mama Mia*, shows his interest in continuing the conversation and the encounter.
- Fifth, the initiator seeks to present a self that will be attractive to the other, which Davis (1973) referred to as the *come-on self*. This come-on self creates a first impression that the other can use to determine the desirability of continuing the dialogue. During Amy and Michael's ongoing conversation about music, Amy seeks to be appealing.
- Finally, the initiator or the other must schedule a *second encounter*. After Amy and Michael exchange names, Amy proposes they have lunch together the next day—and Michael agrees.

This contemporary scenario is but one example of the ways relationships get started today. The scene, with Amy taking the lead, is a modern version of a pattern that started during the first third of the 20th century and, in modified form, continues to the present day. However, an initial encounter with a potential romantic partner in the early to mid-1900s would have been situated much differently than is the case today.

A HISTORICAL PERSPECTIVE ON RELATIONSHIP INITIATION

Three broad periods frame the historical shifts in how relationships in the United States and other Western societies are initiated. The first, which we label *closed-field partnering* (Murstein, 1970), ranges from approximately the late 1800s to the early 1920s, when partnering was regulated and supervised by parents, and mates were often drawn from a pool of family acquaintances. The second period, the *dating system*, began in the early 1920s and quickly took hold, particularly among the middle class and the nouveau riche—as personified in F. Scott Fitzgerald's novel of the flapper era, *The Great Gatsby* (Fitzgerald, 1925). Young men and women "played the field" until they found a suitable partner. The third period, which we call *modern partnering*, can be dated from the early 1970s to the present day. Phrases such as *recreational sex*, *hanging out*, and *hooking up* entered public discourse during this time. This period also saw the development of commercialized methods of finding a partner (e.g., personal ads and Internet dating), as well as the emergence of open dating among gays and lesbians.

Closed-Field Partnering

Naturalist John Muir was introduced to his future wife, Louie Strentzel, by a friend who wrote, "I want you to know my John Muir. … I wish I could give him some noble young woman 'for keeps' and so take him out of the wilderness into the society of his peers" (Turner, 1985, p. 250). After some encouragement, Muir began to correspond with Louie's family. The letters were addressed to "Dr. and Mrs. Strentzel," and though they contained but a single reference to Louie, Muir's biographer reported that the letters leave "little doubt that he meant them more for her eyes than theirs … in them he was at his engaging best—jocular, witty … telling them tales of desert adventure [and] … waxing lyrical about … the virtues of anything wild" (Turner, 1985, p. 250).

This kind of introduction was typical of the time. School curricula were segregated by gender, and the separate spheres of men and women made the kinds of chance meetings that could result in the independent development of intimacy rare (Bailey, 1988; Degler, 1980). Muir and his peers operated in what was known as the *calling system*, wherein a man visited the home of a woman and socialized there under the supervision of her parents (Bailey, 1988). Usually, when a woman came of age, suitors were invited by the mother to call on her daughter. Women largely controlled this calling system. Consequently, it was initially the mother who determined whether a man possessed the requisite qualities for marriage. When individuals were beyond what was then considered a marriageable age—Muir was 40 and Strentzel was 30 when they married—accommodations were common. Although the Muir–Strentzel courtship was conventional in many ways, women Louie's age often were given more freedom to invite men to call and to decide if a man possessed the qualifiers she desired.

The Dating System

The calling system gradually eroded during the last of the 19th century and the beginning of the 20th century. American society was changing greatly (Bailey, 1988). Many people were migrating into the cities. The automobile was becoming more available to the average person. Women were enjoying more freedom, an increased presence in schools, and greater participation in the paid workforce. These changes resulted in both men and women having the opportunity to "play the field," and the dating system came into being. Social initiations and activities moved from the female-dominated home to an external world that was dominated by men. Moreover, magazines, popular novels, and radio shows helped establish rules of dating etiquette. These rules specified that men, rather than women, were to initiate dates. The new arrangement also required money for socializing, thus further strengthening male control of the process.

Men were responsible for the majority of Davis' (1973) tasks, including determining whether the potential other was cleared for an encounter, selecting an opener, and setting up a second encounter. Women were shifted largely to a "gatekeeping" role, in which they accepted or rejected overtures according to their interest in the potential suitor. Women were not always passive, of course, as Wolfenstein and Leites (1950) illustrate with scenes from the movie, *Casablanca*:

> When Lauren Bacall appeared in the doorway of a shabby hotel, gave Humphrey Bogart a long level look, and asked in a deliberate throaty voice—"Got a match?" [and] … in a later episode, she kissed him, and commenting on his passive reaction, taunted: "It's even better when you help"—she became a new type of movie heroine … a woman who approaches a man with a man's technique. (p. 76)

Modern Partnering

The dating system was firmly established by the 1930s and remained relatively unchanged through the 1950s and into the 1960s. At that time, men promised commitment with the hope of having sex (Fleming & Fleming, 1975), whereas in the 1970s, when birth control became relatively safe and widely available, sex came to be openly pursued outside of marriage, not only by men but also by women. A romantic and sexually hungry Nora Ephron captured the spirit of the times when she wrote that

> you didn't sleep with people unless you were in love with them. So I went through a period of trying to fall in love with people just to go to bed with them, and then a period of thinking I would eventually fall in love with whoever I was going to bed with. (Quoted in Fleming & Fleming, 1975, p. 81)

Since the 1970s, it has become more acceptable for women to initiate relationships and assume some responsibility for the economics of a date (Mongeau & Carey, 1996). In recent years, there has also been a movement toward *group dating* or "getting together." This involves mixed-sex groups of individuals, most commonly adolescents or young adults, meeting at common gathering places (e.g., movies, dances, parties, and malls) for the primary purpose of having fun. There has been little formal study of these groups, but group dating may facilitate relationship initiation in at least two ways. First, it gives people more time to determine if others in the group have the qualities they desire before they signal an interest. Second, group activities also provide people with clues useful to identifying integrating topics should they decide to move forward with someone in the group.

The late 20th and early 21st centuries ushered in several new methods for beginning relationships. *Speed dating*—an organized event that brings together people who are seeking dates—has gained popularity in recent years, particularly in large cities (see Eastwick & Finkel, this volume). Whereas some speed-dating events are open to anyone within a particular age range, many target specific groups (e.g., gays, lesbians, Jews, or Catholics), thus bringing together potential relationship partners who are likely to share at least one major qualifier. Moreover, speed-dating participants benefit from knowing that, at least in principle, other participants are cleared for an encounter. In a typical speed-dating session, potential dating partners rotate to meet each other in a series of short "dates," each lasting from 3 to 8 minutes. During these brief interactions, people exchange personal information. Following each of these mini-dates, participants fill out cards indicating whether they would be interested in further contact with the other person. Participants then leave the cards with the organizers or transmit their interest over the Internet. Therefore, instead of one or both individuals verbally requesting a second encounter on the spot, as was necessary for Amy and Michael, speed-dating participants do not need to set up a second meeting until after they have been informed that the potential other is interested.

Internet dating, sometimes referred to as *online dating*, also has become very popular, both in the United States and in many parts of the world. Although many Internet daters meet by means other than Internet dating services (e.g., chat rooms, blogs, and special interest groups), online dating services such as Match.com and eHarmony.com have quickly become household names. In the United States alone, individuals spent over $450 million on online dating services in 2003, the largest segment of "paid content" on the Internet at that time (Online Publishers Association, 2004). Traditionally, Internet dating services have assisted individuals in locating potential partners by providing a medium for electronic personal advertisements that can be posted and searched using criteria such as age, gender, location, and interests. Some commercial dating sites (e.g., eHarmony.com) claim to use a "scientific formula" to match members according to their preferences and calculated compatibility (see Sprecher, Schwartz, Harvey, & Hatfield, this volume). Once individuals have found or been "matched" with a person who seems to possess the qualifiers they desire, the dating service provides a way for them to make contact. If the interest is mutual, they may establish an e-mail correspondence, which then may or may not progress to face-to-face contact.

Internet dating services appear to facilitate the tasks of relationship initiation in a variety of ways (see McKenna, this volume). First, they greatly increase the pool of potential partners who can be approached. This increases the number of people encountered who possess the qualifiers desired in a potential relationship and who are cleared for an "encounter." Second, the availability of information on people's interests, occupations, and other preferences should facilitate finding openers and integrating topics that maximize the likelihood of a positive response from the person who is contacted. Finally, because face-to-face interaction is not immediate, individuals have time to cultivate a more attractive come-on self. For example, if Amy were a less physically attractive individual, she may be able to partially overcome attractiveness stereotypes by constructing an online profile that emphasizes her desirable attributes. On the downside, it is worth noting that Internet dating opens the naïve and emotionally vulnerable to predators who may take advantage of the ease with which they can put forth an appealing face and portray their motives as honorable.

Despite the growing popularity of commercialized methods for meeting potential partners, the majority of first encounters are still arranged noncommercially. Most people continue to meet others both on their own and with the assistance of family members and friends who help them identify people who are available and interested, encourage their interest in potential partners, and arrange introductions (Clark, Shaver, & Abrahams, 1999). Of a sample of 437 students enrolled at the University of Washington, 64% of the respondents who had started a new romantic relationship in the past year indicated that they had received assistance from one or more people (Parks, 2007).

Up to this point, we have described how the process of beginning relationships has changed since the 1800s. The tasks that Davis (1973) identified have remained largely the same, though the contexts within which relationships begin have changed. Davis' description does not account, however, for the varied, and often complex, means by which the tasks are accomplished. Moreover, Davis presumes that the tasks of relationship initiation are discrete and sequential, whereas in reality people consider whether a potential partner is both desirable (that is, has the necessary qualifiers) and available (that is, cleared) on a continuous basis as the interaction unfolds. Regardless of whether people are speed dating, sorting through prospects on the Internet, or hoping to start a relationship with someone in a bar, they must choose whom to pursue. In making that decision, today's "suitors" must assess not only the other's appeal but also the likelihood the other will be open to the kind of relationship they are interested in forming.

MOTIVES FOR FORMING RELATIONSHIPS

The motives behind establishing personal relationships have evolved considerably over the years. In the days of institutionalized marriage that preceded the dating system, individuals partnered to fulfill a variety of political, social, and economic ends, such as the merger of property and families and the attainment of social position (Coontz, 2004). It was only after the emergence of the dating system in the 1920s that the revolutionary idea of forming personal relationships on the basis of love and attraction was widely embraced in Western culture. Even within the dating system, obtaining relational goals such as personal satisfaction, intimacy, companionship, and sexual gratification was still inextricably linked to marriage. The entrance into marriage remained largely synonymous with the entrance into "adulthood" (Coontz, 2005). Consequently, analyses of relationship initiation during this period—including that of Davis (1973)—presumed that the subtext of partnering, even among teenagers, involved finding a desirable lifelong mate. Davis' qualifiers thus generally pertained to a prospect's suitability and desirability as a marriage partner, whereas being "cleared" typically meant that the person was unmarried, not otherwise involved, and of a suitable age. Even as late as the early 1980s, the relationship histories of newlywed men and women in rural Pennsylvania largely supported Davis' assumption that finding a spouse was the primary motive behind relationship formation. Data from the Processes of Adaptation in Intimate Relationships (PAIR) Project revealed, for example, that newlywed husbands and wives in this environment married young (23.6 and 21 years, respectively) and dated an average of only two other individuals on a more than casual basis before marrying (Huston, 1982). In more urban areas, however, the changes that would undermine the primacy of finding a marriage partner were already underway.

Over the last third of the 20th century and into the 21st century, two broad trends in sexuality and marriage have transformed the landscape of unmarried intimacy and significantly increased the number of socially legitimate motives for forming relationships. First, as the stigma against premarital and nonmarital sexual behavior has decreased, teenagers and young adults have become more sexually active in relationships with little or no long-term commitment (Coontz, 2004; Luker, 1996). Accordingly, the sexual desire that once served as a strong impetus for young adults' entrance into marriage has become an acceptable motive for forming premarital relationships without the intent of marriage. Second, as the idea of marriage as a "bridge to adulthood" has broken down over the past 30 years, the age of men and women when they first marry has increased significantly to an average age of 27 for men and 25 for women (U.S. Census Bureau, 2003); the proportion of 25 to 29 year olds who have never been married tripled for women (to 38%) and doubled for men (to 52%) between 1970 and 1996 (Saluter & Lugaila, 1998). Correspondingly, multiple alternatives to marriage, such as serial casual dating and cohabitation, have become more prominent. Just as sexual profligacy separated the quest for sexual gratification from the quest for a marriage partner, the postponement of marriage and the adoption of alternative lifestyles have legitimized relational goals that previously were sought primarily in the context of marriage (e.g., companionship, intimacy, or economic partnership).

Notably, Americans are no less interested in marriage and the ideal of lifelong commitment today than they were in the past. An overwhelming majority still believe that marriage affords them the best opportunity to enjoy a good life, and they continue to express the desire to marry (Axinn & Thornton, 2000). Rather than devaluing marriage as a legitimate motive for partnering, the predominant ideology in much of Western society today is that marriage is a special union that one is prepared to enter into only after ample relational and life experiences have been acquired (Cherlin, 2004). Consequently, although most people will, at some point in their lives, form a relationship with the objective of finding a marriageable partner, the salience of this motive for a particular person at a particular time cannot be assumed. It is not uncommon for an individual to fall "in love" many times, to have multiple sexual partners, and to live with at least one romantic partner before deciding to pursue a relationship that will lead to marriage (Coontz, 2005). During this time—which most frequently occurs between one's late teens and late 20s to early 30s—motives for partnering such as companionship and sexual intimacy may often be more salient than those of lifelong commitment.

Although Davis' (1973) model of relationship initiation presumed that individuals generally share similar motivations for forming personal relationships, it is evident that, in the forum of modern partnering, such motivational congruency can no longer be taken for granted. The task of assessing a prospective partner's motives has become an important element of evaluating a partner's desirability. Indeed, failing to consider a potential partner's motives, and his or her likely openness to one's own motives, can lead to embarrassing, hurtful, and at times dangerous situations. In contrast, being conscious of cues that suggest an incongruity of motives may prevent an individual who is seeking a long-term relationship partner from getting involved with someone who is interested in only a one-night stand (see Reeder, this volume). The importance of correctly perceiving others' relational motives and goals likely depends on the nature of one's own motives for forming a relationship. An individual whose sole aim is to find a marriageable partner has much more to lose by misperceiving the intentions of a "player" than does an individual who is seeking a casual romantic encounter. Individuals' most salient motive(s) influence, to some degree, what attributes they consider to be attractive, the cues to which they are most attentive, their perception of the likelihood that their overture will be accepted, and the ways in which they choose to strategically present themselves to others.

A MODEL OF RELATIONSHIP BEGINNINGS

In this section, we present a conceptual model of relationship formation that elaborates upon and updates Davis' (1973) insights. We employ the open field encounter between Amy and Michael for illustration purposes. We detail the model's main components, and consider, in turn, the factors that affect a person's decision to initiate an encounter, the use of strategic self-presentation, and the buildup of rapport, as they pertain to whether an encounter moves forward.

An Overview of the Model

Our conceptual model of relationship beginnings seeks to rectify several of the analytical shortcomings in Davis' (1973) characterization of the tasks constituting a successful relationship initiation (see Figure 1.1). First and foremost, our model suggests that an analysis of relationship initiations should begin with a consideration of the motives that people have for forming relationships and should recognize that these motives shape how people view potential partners who come "under their radar." Second, we propose that, in addition to Davis' tasks of determining if a potential partner

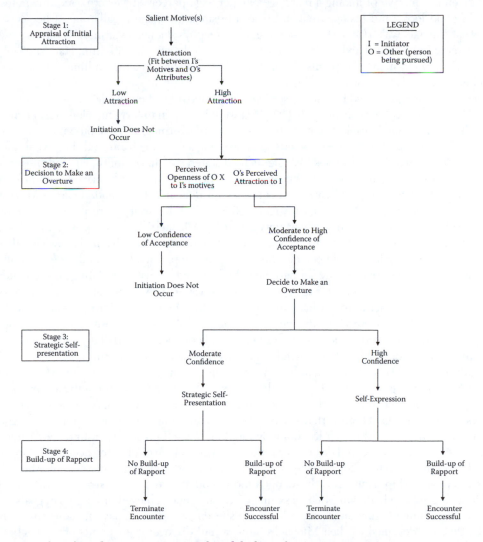

Figure 1.1   Flow chart depicting a conceptual model of initial romantic encounters.

has important qualifiers and is cleared for an encounter, individuals also weigh a number of other considerations—such as the other's likely attraction to them—before deciding to make an overture. Third, our model acknowledges and elucidates the various factors that influence individuals' use (or lack thereof) of strategic self-presentation to curry the favor of a potential partner. Fourth, we examine the dialectical nature of the process of building rapport after an encounter has begun. Our approach assumes that the cognitions, observations, and experiences occurring during each stage of the initiation process influence and shape the stages that follow (e.g., the degree to which an individual perceives the decision to make an overture as "risky" influences the degree to which strategic self-presentation is utilized). Moreover, although our model is illustrated sequentially, individuals may often "cycle back" to earlier stages in the model, such as when initiators are received much more enthusiastically than expected and reevaluate their options for self-presentation.

The four-stage model of relationship initiation illustrated in Figure 1.1 portrays the sequence of appraisals and events that bear upon whether an encounter is successful. Imagine, for example, that Amy is a 33-year-old career woman whose primary goal (i.e., her "salient motive") is to find a suitable marriage partner. When Amy spots Michael from across the plaza, she first appraises her level of attraction to him (Stage 1 in Figure 1.1) by assessing the degree to which he possesses both generally desired qualifiers (e.g., physical attractiveness) as well as qualifiers that are likely to be particularly salient given her motive of finding a marriage partner (e.g., perceived warmth). As Amy notes both Michael's good looks and his apparent status as a businessman, she recalls one of her coworkers stating that Michael was "one of the most genuinely nice guys she had ever met." Overall, Amy feels highly attracted to Michael and decides to try to initiate a relationship with him. Had Michael had a reputation as a "cold-hearted capitalist," Amy very likely may have dismissed him as a prospect and joined her girlfriends for lunch.

Once Amy has established that she is sufficiently attracted to Michael, she also considers various other factors—such as the probability that Michael would be open to forming a long-term committed relationship and Michael's likely attraction to her—to help determine if she should make an overture (Stage 2 in Figure 1.1). The fact that Michael is not wearing a wedding band leads her to consider why such a handsome man in his late 30s is single. Is he disinterested in commitment, and thus probably not very open to starting a serious relationship, or is he divorced and just hasn't yet found the "right" woman with whom to start over? Given her success with men and the extended glance Michael had given her when she entered the plaza, Amy feels confident that he would be responsive if she were to initiate an encounter. Thus, despite uncertainty regarding Michael's likely receptiveness to forming a long-term relationship, Amy decides to make an overture. Note, however, that had Amy felt only somewhat confident that Michael would perceive her as a desirable partner, her overall level of confidence regarding Michael's acceptance may not have been high enough to justify initiating an encounter.

After Amy decides to approach Michael, she then considers how to present herself in a way that is likely to be both attractive to Michael and conducive to achieving her interpersonal goals (Stage 3 in Figure 1.1). Because Amy's confidence that Michael will respond positively to her long-term relational objectives is relatively low (and thus her overall confidence in Michael's acceptance is only moderate), Amy recognizes that being self-expressive and showing her true motives and self are not certain to elicit Michael's favorable reception. Consequently, Amy approaches Michael's table, and, rather than being forthright about her disinterest in having a casual romantic affair, she steers the conversation largely toward neutral topics, such as the weather and music. Amy simultaneously attempts to reveal parts of herself that she believes Michael would find most attractive, such as her wit and her intelligence. Although fraudulently molding her self-presentation to be congruent with Michael's perceived motives and desires may increase Amy's chances of being accepted, Amy knows that such deception would likely be detected in the future and undermine her goal of establishing a committed relationship. Thus, Amy draws upon more moderate and subtle strategies of self-presentation in an attempt to both win Michael's immediate favor and achieve her long-term goals.

From the moment Amy approaches Michael, she enacts social behaviors, sometimes unconsciously, that are designed to elicit Michael's interest and discover their points of connection, and thus build rapport (Stage 4 in Figure 1.1). Amy begins by questioning Michael about his apparent interest in entertainment, imagining that Michael may be interested in talking about movies, one of her passions. Michael, pleased by Amy's query, amiably replies that he loves music and musical theater, and inquires about her interest in such. Amy is an adept conversationalist and is able to connect with Michael about music despite her more limited knowledge. Her interest in jazz and bluesy rock piques Michael's interest. Amy perceives that her stock with him is rising. By the end of lunch, Amy also feels increasingly attracted to Michael and suggests they have lunch the next day. This encounter could have gone awry, however, at any point in the conversation, as might have happened, for example, had Amy abruptly changed the topic to movies or had Michael been overly talkative and self-referent.

Motives and Initial Attraction

Attraction is rooted in the motives and goals that people have for forming relationships. Whereas some attributes (e.g., physical attractiveness or kindness) are desirable regardless of the specific motives involved, many of the qualities that make a potential partner attractive are tied to a person's motive(s) for the relationship. Considerable research supports the notion that the salience of particular attributes is different for individuals seeking short-term rather than long-term engagements. Those with short-term motives generally place greater emphasis on qualities such as physical attractiveness, sex appeal, and munificence, whereas those who hold long-term goals are more likely to emphasize the importance of commitment, dependability, emotional stability, and the capacity to love (Buss & Schmitt, 1993; Shackelford, Schmitt, & Buss, 2005).

Women are more likely than men to seek long-term, committed relationships, whereas men are more likely than women to desire short-term, recreational involvements (Simpson & Gangestad, 1991, 1992; also see Tran, Simpson, & Fletcher, this volume). From an evolutionary perspective, these gender differences in motives for forming relationships are rooted in Darwinian principles and are evolutionarily functional (e.g., Buss, 1999; Buss & Barnes, 1986). Men are thus more likely than women to value physical beauty and vitality—indicators of "good genes" and reproductive potential—whereas women are more prone to value economic status, warmth, and trustworthiness—indicators of men's potential to invest in possible offspring (Fletcher, Tither, O'Loughlin, Friesen, & Overall, 2004; Schmitt, this volume). However, gender is not always a reliable indicator of the attributes people desire in a partner. Although a common scenario is one in which a man seeking a casual, sexual, relationship encounters a woman who is looking for a committed partnership, the pursuit of committed relationships is by no means exclusive to women, and many women, especially those who are not seeking marriage, are interested in casual involvements (e.g., Buss & Schmitt, 1993).

Additionally, although men are more likely to seek short-term sexual relationships than are women, both men and women still look for the same kinds of qualities in short-term mates (Li & Kenrick, 2006). Multiple studies have shown that although men, in general, still place more value on good looks than women, both men and women prioritize physical attractiveness over other attributes (e.g., social status, generosity, and kindness) in a short-term partner (Li & Kenrick; Wiederman & Dubois, 1998). Although physical attractiveness remains an important attribute in the context of long-term partnering, with men still valuing good looks more than women (see Li, Bailey, Kenrick, & Linsenmeier, 2002), the importance attached to physical beauty is much less than in short-term contexts. Indeed, a recent study found that physical attractiveness was not among the five most important qualities men and women seek in a long-term relationship (Buss, Shackelford, Kirkpatrick, & Larsen, 2001). The top five were (a) mutual attraction and/or love, (b) emotional stability and/or maturity, (c) dependable character, (d) pleasing disposition, and (e) education and/or intelligence.

Although much of the research associating motives and attraction has focused on the broad, categorical goals of forming short-term and long-term relationships, the motives that prime individuals to look for certain attributes in a partner are often complex and cannot always be discretely classified. Many individuals have relational motives that are not inextricably tied to a specific short-term or long-term context, such as forming a relationship to promote personal growth or to enlarge one's social network (see Reeder, this volume). Some people may seek to experience a particular type of "love experience." Whereas both erotic love and playful love are commonly sought in short-term relationships, an individual seeking an intense, erotic love relationship is likely to desire different qualities in a partner than a person looking for a light, playful encounter (Lee, 1977, 1988; see also Hendrick & Hendrick, this volume). People are not necessarily mindful of their motives, as is illustrated by a short story

> in which a man and a woman, drunk on the eve of [Israel's] Independence Day, and finding themselves in an apartment belonging to one of them, go to bed and make love; in the morning ... they behave with scrupulous politeness, introducing themselves to each other, and part with a handshake but no exchange of addresses. (Beilin, 2000, p. 135)

In the prototypical open-field situation, would-be suitors commonly know little about whether the other possesses the qualifiers that are most important to their relational goals. In such a situation, reason usually argues for caution, but caution does not necessarily prevail. An attractive face, coupled with a sexy body, for example, can often animate a person's interest with little thought to other qualifiers (Dion, Berscheid, & Walster [now Hatfield], 1972; Langlois et al., 2000). Additionally, some people are prone to leap to conclusions about a person's inner qualities based on outward appearances (see Bruce & Graziano, this volume; Livingston, 2001; Snyder, Berscheid, & Glick, 1985). Even people who are ordinarily cautious can experience strong attraction for a person whom they hardly know—and for reasons they do not fully understand. It is unlikely that many women appreciate how their attraction toward various types of men often changes during different phases of their menstrual cycle. Yet, when women were asked to think about men as short-term sexual partners rather than long-term mates, a recent study found that women in the fertile phase of their menstrual cycle were more attracted to men who were competitive with other men and eschewed being a "nice guy" than women in infertile stages (Gangestad, Garver-Apgar, Simpson, & Cousins, 2007). Similarly, women in the fertile phase of their cycle have been shown to rate masculine male faces as more attractive than feminized male faces, a preference that often does not persist during other stages of the menstrual cycle (Little, Penton-Voak, Burt, & Perrett, 2002). Adrenaline also covertly primes attraction, particularly when people who are "pumped up" encounter someone who is good-looking (Dutton & Aron, 1974; White, Fishbein, & Rutstin, 1981). These findings, taken together, suggest that both motives and physiological states combine to affect the likelihood that an individual will become attracted to another.

The Decision to Make an Overture: From Attraction to Affiliation

Relationships are initiated and take shape within what Kerckhoff (1974) described as people's "field of availables." This field consists of people individuals are likely to come across in their day-to-day lives, or learn about through a mutual acquaintance. Would-be partners may work in the same building, as did Amy and Michael; they may be coworkers, friends of friends, or people who are part of the landscape of one's daily rounds. Regardless of the context from which a personal or romantic relationship emerges, someone has to make the first move. Someone has to say, "Have we met before?" or "I've really enjoyed working with you on this project. Would you like to go to dinner sometime?"

The decision to make a bid for another's attention is driven by attraction. But, of course, people do not always try to affiliate with those they find attractive, even if their attraction is strong and they have time on their hands. Why is this so? The main reason, we believe, is that the decision to make an overture is rooted in both attraction and individuals' beliefs about whether the object of their affection is likely to be open to their overture (Huston & Levinger, 1978). When people fail to act on their romantic attraction, they generally explain their inaction in terms of fears of rejection (Vorauer & Ratner, 1996). The dual importance of attraction and concerns about reciprocation, as they combine to affect a person's propensity to make an overture, can be represented formally as follows (for similar formulations, see Huston, 1972; Shanteau & Nagy, 1979):

$$V = f(A \times P)$$

where V is the strength of the valence of making an overture, A is the individual's attraction toward the other, and P is the would-be initiator's estimate of the probability that an overture will be accepted rather than rejected by the person. The probability of acceptance, in turn, is a joint function of the potential initiators' perceptions of the other's openness to their motives for affiliation and their estimate of the likelihood the other will return their attraction.

This formulation has several important ramifications with regard to the decision to initiate a relationship. First, it takes as axiomatic the idea that attraction provides the incentive for making a bid for another's interest. Second, it suggests that when people are tipped off in advance, or are otherwise convinced that a person is interested in them, the decision about whether to approach the individual rests entirely on whether the prospect is sufficiently attractive to make it worth their while to proceed. This assessment involves two comparisons (Thibaut & Kelley, 1959). The first is the person's standards for a partner based on their past experiences, or how the prospect stacks up against the person's comparison level (CL); the second is whether the other is more attractive than available alternatives, or the comparison level for alternatives (CL_{alt}). The more a prospect exceeds a person's CL and CL_{alt}, the more inclined the individual will be to initiate an encounter (our later theory section will discuss the intersection of interdependence theory and our model in more detail).

The two-factor model of affiliation, as set forth above, was first tested by Huston (1973), who asked men interested in dating to choose a date from an array of six women varying in physical attractiveness from beautiful to above average in looks. In one condition, the men were led to believe all six of the women had expressed an interest in dating them; in a second condition, the women's interest was left to the men's imagination. When men believed that all of the women wanted to date them, nearly all of them picked either a beautiful (78%) or a highly attractive (19%) woman, whereas when the men were not provided any information about whether any of the women would accept them, most chose one of the less attractive women. They appeared not to want to lose out by shooting too high.

The $A \times P$ interactive term in the model indicates that interest in making an overture (V) is low unless the individual is strongly attracted to the person *and* the probability of acceptance is high enough to be promising. This was documented in a series of experiments carried out by Shanteau and Nagy (1976, 1979) that showed that attraction and considerations of reciprocity operate in tandem, rather than additively, such that when the probability of acceptance is low, people's interest in pursuing a relationship is nil, or nearly nil, regardless of how attracted they are to the person. As the probability of acceptance increases, however, the desire to affiliate with someone who has attractive qualities over someone less attractive is amplified.

Would-be initiators often have little information about whether another person is likely to reciprocate their interest. They will seek out information about the prospect and look for signs of openness, provided they are able to imagine that an overture might be welcomed. Before proceeding, they may gather information over an extended period of time, all the while revising and refining their impressions and ideas about their chances of making a successful overture (see Afifi & Lucas, this volume, for a discussion of information-seeking in initial interactions). Along the way, they may rehearse hypothetical sequences in their minds as they imagine how the other might react.

The first order of business in assessing the chances of acceptance often is to determine whether a prospect is "cleared" for the kind of encounter or relationship being sought. If an individual is looking for a marriage partner, the person may rule out those who are married or who are already involved with someone else. But if the individual hopes for a sexual tryst, the person might not immediately rule out such people, but continue to gather information about the other's likely interest.

The fact that a prospect is thought to have an interest in the type of relationship the would-be initiator wants to pursue is, of course, not enough. As shown in Figure 1.1, initiators also must gauge whether the other would likely reciprocate their attraction if they were to make an approach. People may signal their interest in being approached, for example, by how they orient to the person, by their bodily posture, by physical displays, by establishing and maintaining eye contact, or by smiling and moving closer or into a person's line of sight (see Cunningham & Barbee, this volume; also see McCormick & Jones, 1989).

When people come across someone who is handsome or beautiful, they typically assume that the attractive person is likely to be sought after and therefore is in a position to be highly selective (Huston, 1973). However, people who themselves are good-looking, or who possess obvious bankable assets (e.g., status and wealth), may believe that even though the competition is stiff, they have a good chance of success with an attractive other (Huston, 1973). Within a broader context, these observations point to the idea that partnering is, at least in part, an exchange of assets—a social exchange—and that people appreciate that what they have to offer will affect what they are able to get in return (see Huston & Burgess, 1979; see also our later discussion of exchange theory).

When people are drawn to others because they have something important in common, the common interest also signifies a greater chance of acceptance should they make a direct overture (see Condon & Crano, 1988). A strong interest in any activity—whether it be bicycling, break-dancing, music, the outdoors, wine, movies, or Chinese food—can lead people to assume that those of like mind will be interested in their overture. All it may take to get a relationship underway is for one person to act on the sense that they may be "soul mates." In such situations, the "integrative topic," to use Davis' (1973) term, is both a source of attraction and a reason for confidence that the attraction will be mutual.

A person's confidence also is rooted to some extent in his or her own personality, and this confidence (or lack thereof) may reveal itself particularly often in situations where the chances of acceptance are unknown or ambiguous. Most people are confident of acceptance if they receive an unmistakable signal of another's interest, but an unmistakable sign for some may be an ambiguous message for others. People who have a secure attachment style are likely to read cues of acceptance or rejection accurately and to calibrate their interest according to the prospect of success (Hazan & Shaver, 1987). In contrast, people who are fearful (Bartholomew & Horowitz, 1991), those who have low self-esteem (Baldwin & Keelan, 1999; Leary, 2004), and those who are particularly sensitive to rejection (Downey, Freitas, Michaelis, & Khouri, 1998) are less likely to make an overture because they are slow to entertain the hypothesis that others are interested in having a relationship with them. Such people read ambiguous cues negatively. People with a "dismissing" or "avoidant" attachment style also often appear to give up hope of attracting another's interest. Rather than trying to make relationships happen and risk failing, such people are prone to take a passive approach, and to invest little of themselves in trying to establish a relationship (see Metts & Mikucki, this volume; also see Creasey & Jarvis, this volume, and our later theory section for a more detailed discussion of attachment theory).

The Presentation of Self in First Encounters

When people decide to initiate a relationship, they often experience a tension between wanting to be known and wanting to be liked (Baumeister, 1998). Most individuals have a sense of who they are—that is, a strong core identity—and would prefer, at least when they are looking for a long-term relationship, to express themselves openly and to be liked for the virtues they possess and forgiven for their limitations (Chambliss, 1965; Swann, Griffin, Predmore, & Gaines, 1987). Even individuals seeking short-term relationships may likely derive more satisfaction from being liked after expressing their true selves than from being liked after expressing a side of themselves that had been strategically crafted.

In first encounters, people are likely to be self-expressive rather than strategic only if they are both strongly attracted to the other and very confident that their overture will be accepted. This "incentive" model, with its focus on the dual importance of attraction and probability, parallels the formulation we used to account for the decision to initiate an overture, except now our focus is on the relative valence of self-expressive versus strategic motives in the presentation of self. This formulation is hardly new (cf. Figley, 1974, 1979; Jones & Pittman, 1982) and is consistent with an analysis set forth by the sociologist Peter Blau (1964), who more than 40 years ago stated that "[n] ew social situations typically pose a challenge, since there is the risk of failure to impress others" (p. 41). Blau went on to write,

> For a social situation to be experienced as a challenge by an individual, the others present must be sufficiently significant for him to be concerned with impressing them and winning their approval. For it to be experienced as a stimulating challenge rather than a debilitating threat, he must be fairly confident in his ability to earn their acceptance, if not their respect. Insufficient challenge makes a social occasion boring, and excessive challenge makes it distressing. It is the social gathering in which individuals cannot take their success in impressing others for granted but have reasonable chances of success that animates their spirit and stimulates their involvement in social intercourse. (pp. 41–42)

Suppose, for purposes of illustration, that Amy has inside information about Michael's interest in her. Perhaps a common friend has told her that Michael is both attracted to her and interested in a long-term relationship (see Arriaga, Agnew, Capezza, & Lehmiller, this volume, for a discussion of how social networks can affect the relationship initiation process). Armed with confidence, Amy will likely feel comfortable being herself and may have little need to draw special attention to her desirable attributes or to otherwise try to ingratiate herself. She may be so confident that she can be self-expressive (have her cake) and be liked (and eat it too). Now suppose that Michael has also been tipped off about Amy—that he knows that she thinks he is "hot" and is interested in a serious relationship. In such a situation, Amy and Michael may both feel comfortable being relatively self-expressive, and their first encounter might resemble that of old friends conversing.

Figley (1974, 1979) set up a situation much like the one Amy would have faced had she been informed of Michael's attraction toward her. He found that when people are highly attracted to a potential partner and strongly assured that the individual is interested in them, they typically present themselves much as they see themselves, showing little, if any, tendency to overstate their positive qualities or downplay their shortcomings. However, it is common for individuals to lack total confidence that they will be able to arouse a prospect's interest solely by being themselves. In such situations, concerns about acceptance become more salient and may lead people to try to cultivate the other's interest by presenting a self that they think the other will find attractive. Figley (1974, 1979) demonstrated that when people are highly attracted to a prospect, but are provided with only moderate assurance of the other's interest, they are likely to embellish their positive qualities and minimize their shortcomings. This tendency to enhance one's image was not found in situations where individuals were not attracted to the potential partner or when they were informed that there was no chance of acceptance by the other.

At the beginning of an encounter the other's interest is often not clear, thus the primary objective typically is to secure the other's initial approval (cf. Swann et al., 1987; Swann, De La Ronde, & Hixon, 1994). In situations where a strong incentive to engage in strategic self-presentation exists, to be successful, would-be ingratiators must cultivate the other's interest in them while appearing to be genuine. This may be more easily said than done. Gordon's (1996) meta-analysis of ingratiation found that the more obvious the stake a person has in attracting a prospect's favor, the less effective an ingratiation tactic is in securing the other's interest.

There are three primary ways people can strategically attempt to build a prospect's interest in them, each carrying different kinds of risks: (a) They can try to make themselves appear *likable*, (b) they can attempt to appear competent or *capable*, and (c) they can seek to come across as morally *virtuous* (i.e., as having integrity). People try to make themselves likable by drawing attention to positive aspects of their personality, by expressing attitudes or interests they believe conform to those of the other, or by flattering the other by commenting favorably on the other's qualities (see Jones, 1964; Jones & Pittman, 1982). Had Amy offered a flattering comment on Michael's knowledge of music, her appeal might have been enhanced. According to Gordon's (1966) meta-analysis of the success rates of various ingratiation strategies, flattery is a particularly effective tactic because people like to be liked, and thus perceive the flatterer to be credible (Vonk, 2002). On the other hand, there are significant risks to drawing attention to one's good qualities or trying to find points of agreement; the ingratiator may seem too eager to please and may be seen as obsequious or needy (Jones & Pittman, 1982).

People admire and respect—and hence are attracted to—others who are capable, talented, accomplished, and resourceful (see Tran, Simpson, & Fletcher, this volume). Would-be ingratiators may seek to attract interest by promoting their talents or drawing attention to their athleticism, their knowledge, or their pedigree. If they are not careful, however, they run the risk of seeming conceited, narcissistic, or self-important, all of which might undermine their appeal. Although Gordon's (1996) meta-analysis did not distinguish between self-promotion as embellishing one's likableness and self-promotion of one's talents or virtues, he found evidence that obvious self-promotion, in the service of whatever positive impression, generally boomerangs. It is far better to have someone else brag about one than to do the bragging oneself.

People are also drawn to individuals who have integrity; are honest, sincere, and moral; and have a strong sense of humanitarianism. Some people, knowing this, put themselves forth as possessing such qualities when they do not, particularly when they have little at stake beyond the here and now of an encounter (see Cunningham & Barbee, this volume). The risk of drawing attention to one's virtues is that the self-promoter may seem sanctimonious, or, if the would-be ingratiator's motives are already suspect, the effort may raise suspicion that the person is trying to take advantage of the other's desire to connect with a worthy individual.

Cunningham and Barbee (this volume) found that individuals who are seeking short-term relationships are particularly likely to be disingenuous—if need be—in order to attract another's interest. Both those who pursue others by being emotionally warm with little interest in long-term commitment ("players") and those who try to get what they want while remaining emotionally distant and uncommitted ("predators") endorse using charm and manipulation to secure a potential partner's interest. Players are also likely to report being willing to seduce a prospect by lying and being flashy (Cunningham & Barbee, this volume). In contrast, individuals who have a long-term orientation are more likely to try to attract a partner through supportive ingratiating behaviors, such as helping a potential partner accomplish something, being honest, and providing sincere compliments. Such partner-oriented individuals typically eschew the use of deceptive, manipulative ingratiation tactics, seeing them as illegitimate ways to elicit the other's attraction.

The way initiators frame their experience in an encounter may shift as the encounter unfolds. At first, initiators center their attention on reassessing their own attraction toward the other, gauging the other's interest in them, and priming that interest, if need be. If they come to gain confidence in the other's positive regard, they may open up and reveal more of their inner self, or core identity (Baumeister, 1998). Such self-expressive behaviors provide the other with an opportunity to understand and acknowledge aspects of the initiator's core identity in a way that is not possible when self-presentation is primarily strategic. Of course, self-revelation is not always acknowledged or responded to favorably. But when people reveal something of their core being, and find that they are understood and appreciated as a result, they are likely to be more gratified by the exchange than when others like them based on minimal self-revelation or like them without really knowing them (Chambliss, 1965; Katz & Beach, 2000; Swann, Pelham, & Krull, 1989; Swann et al., 1987). However, people still prefer, at least early on, that others be overly generous rather than overly critical in their evaluations (see Murray, Holmes, & Griffin, 2003). Not surprisingly, the desire to be seen and liked for one's good qualities, or in spite of knowing one's shortcomings, is greater for those who are seeking long-term relationships rather than short-term involvements (Campbell, Lackenbauer, & Muise, 2006).

Building Rapport in Initial Encounters

For an encounter to be successful, people must build rapport. This goal is salient regardless of whether a person seeks a friend, a casual sex partner, a romantic partner, or a mate. In all such situations, the relationship seeker must use an effective opener, build an affinity, and, if in the end the partners wish to meet again, set the stage for another encounter. We will treat these tasks sequentially. Once an individual opens a conversation, however, the dialogue between the partners proceeds dialectically, with the outcome depending on how both partners act and react to each other as the encounter unfolds.

To build rapport with a potential partner, the initiator must first open the conversation, typically by putting forth an opening line designed to persuade the other to continue the interaction. Socially confident people may put little thought into how to open a conversation because they find it easy to attract the initial interest of others. In contrast, individuals who lack such social confidence—those who are shy, insecure, or fearful of rejection—may not seriously consider making an overture in the first place (e.g., Downey et al., 1998; Park, 2007). However, according to our model, those who are attracted to someone and moderately confident of acceptance, should give considerable thought to the likely effectiveness of various opening approaches before making an overture.

What approaches work best as conversational openers? Much of the research examining the effectiveness of openers has focused on those deployed to initiate male–female encounters in meeting places. The best openers for men, this research shows, appear to be those that are not seen as "lines" by women: Confident, direct, or innocuous overtures are more likely to get a conversation off to a good start than are indirect, cute, or clever gambits (Clark et al., 1999; Cunningham, 1989; Kleinke & Dean, 1990). In contrast, women interested in getting a conversation off the ground, at least in a singles bar, can open pretty much any way they please. They can be direct, cutesy, or coy when approaching an opposite-sex prospect—all starters work about equally well (Cunningham, 1989). Perper (1985) further suggested that the intensity of an opener should mirror the intensity of the potential partner's signal—if, in fact, there is one (see Cunningham & Barbee, this volume, for further discussion of opening gambits).

Once the conversation has been successfully opened, two things can be assumed. First, the initiator is at least reasonably attracted to the other, as evidenced by the fact that an overture was actually made. Second, the initiator is reasonably confident that his or her feelings of attraction will be reciprocated. The combination of these two factors sets the stage for the development of rapport. The classic study carried out by Snyder, Tanke, and Berscheid (1977) showed that when individuals are attracted to others, they behave in ways that elicit the other's attraction, which, in turn, then builds their own affinity for the partner. When men were led to believe that a woman they were talking to on the phone was physically attractive, they acted more sociable, sexually warm, interesting, outgoing, and humorous than when they were led to believe their conversation partner was unattractive. In turn, these supposedly physically attractive women reciprocated the men's apparent interest, conveying more confidence, animation, enjoyment of the conversation, and liking for the other than women who were assumed to be unattractive. A study conducted by Curtis and Miller (1986) complements Snyder and colleagues' (1977) findings and provides further support for the notion that attraction begets attraction. Individuals, when led to believe that they were liked by another person, engaged in more self-disclosure, expressed less dissimilarity, and had a more positive attitude and tone of voice than those who did not believe the other person liked them, and, not surprisingly, they actually elicited more liking in return.

The literature on building rapport within interpersonal relationships has identified a variety of behaviors that are integral to the development of mutual affinity in both initial encounters and continuing relationships. Among the most effective of these strategies are self-disclosure (particularly emotional disclosure), attentiveness, and clearly expressing interest in the other (Clark et al., 1999; Hess, Fannin, & Pollom, 2007; Kenny & La Voie, 1984). When individuals are very interested in another person, they are likely to disclose more information about themselves, thus accelerating the development of the relationship (see Derlega, Winstead, & Greene, this volume, for a discussion of disclosure in initial encounters). Such expressions are a proficient way to build rapport due to the tendency for attraction to be reciprocated in social interactions (Kenny & La Voie, 1984). Notably, an additional key task in the buildup of rapport is what Davis (1973) referred to as finding an integrating topic. Individuals who are able to discover common interests, experiences, or attitudes—particularly those that are subjective, such as a common love for an obscure band—often experience greater liking and rapport than do individuals who do not possess or uncover these similarities (Pinel, Long, Landau, Alexander, & Pyszczynski, 2006). Even sharing a humorous experience can contribute to the development of affinity in a budding relationship (Fraley & Aron, 2004). This is not to say that the development of rapport in a relationship is contingent upon the partners being clones of one another. Rather, once partners develop a sense that they are compatible, discovering key differences may also become important to the buildup of rapport (Aron, Steele, Kashdan, & Perez, 2006).

Not all individuals are equally successful at fostering affinity in their interactions. Some individuals—such as those who are shy, insecure, or fearful of rejection—have difficulty initiating encounters because they are reluctant to believe that others will like them (see Metts & Mikucki, this volume). When people believe that others in general (Downey et al., 1998), or a particular other (Curtis & Miller, 1986), will not like them, they tend to behave cautiously and defensively. They are also less forthcoming and more disagreeable than individuals who believe that they are likable. Accordingly, these initial expectations set up an interpersonal dynamic that is self-fulfilling, leading them to behave in ways that actually induce the awkward social situations and rejection that they fear. Similarly, individuals who are high in global uncertainty (the tendency to be uncertain about social contact in general) often experience more anxiety in new social situations than those who are low in global uncertainty, and tend to communicate less effectively during initial interactions (Douglas, 1991; see also Knobloch & Miller, this volume). The more individuals who are high in attachment anxiety are romantically attracted to a prospect, the less romantic interest they actually communicate to the other during an interaction, thus undermining the development of rapport in the exchange (Vorauer, Cameron, Holmes, & Pearce, 2003). Not surprisingly, if initiators possess traits or propensities that cause them to undercut the buildup of rapport in initial encounters—or if the potential partner they approach has such tendencies—the interaction is unlikely to progress to the point where a second meeting is proposed.

THEORETICAL PERSPECTIVES ON THE CONCEPTUAL MODEL

The conceptual model presented in this chapter is not based on a single theory. Rather, the model is able to accommodate research from various theoretical perspectives. In this section, we briefly discuss several of these theories and show how they contribute to our model of initial romantic encounters.

Social Exchange Theory

Exchange theory derives from social learning and marketplace economic theories of human behavior (Blau, 1964; Homans, 1961; Thibaut & Kelley, 1959). The starting assumption, which is taken as axiomatic by exchange theorists, is that people operate under the "pleasure principal," and, as such, they seek to identify prospective partners with whom interaction promises to be rewarding rather than costly. The main currency of exchange, according to Homans, is the expression of positive and negative sentiment: Another person's esteem is rewarding, whereas rejection is costly.

The exchange logic is reflected succinctly in the idea that "[p]eople join together only insofar as they believe and subsequently find it in their mutual interest to do so" (Huston & Burgess, 1979, p. 4). Exchange theorists apply this logic to understanding the initial bids that people make to others for attention. The model we presented in this chapter is clearly rooted in exchange principles. The decision to make an overture, as we portrayed it, is the product of the initiator's attraction, or in exchange terms, the value of the other's acceptance, and the probability that the other will provide acceptance, or express a mutual interest. Consistent with exchange theory, we argued that the risks attendant to overplaying one's hand, or of miscalculating one's value in the marketplace, should lead people to seek out partners whose social standing is similar to their own (Huston, 1973; cf. Ellis & Kelley, 2000).

Exchange theory also draws attention to the idea that, even at the outset of a relationship, people may think about what might happen down the road. People contemplating the initiation of a relationship that they hope will be long-term attend both to the likelihood of immediate acceptance and to the likelihood of long-term mutual interest, should a relationship become established. They know that it is one matter for a person to say "yes" to an overture, and quite another matter for a person to say "yes" to an ongoing relationship. Goffman (1959) summed up the idea of exchange as it pertains to commitment:

> A proposal of marriage in our society tends to be a way in which a man sums up his social attributes and suggests to a woman that hers are not so much better as to preclude a merger in these matters. (p. 456)

Such a proposal can be seen as the culmination of an extended two-way dialogue as the partners negotiate and renegotiate their level of involvement based on their interest in each other and the mutuality of that interest. Social exchange theory does not assume, however, that the participants are necessarily mindful of the negotiation dynamic involved. One partner may put out a tentative feeler, and, with the other taking it up, the progression may proceed, almost as if the changes were meant to be. People become mindful when they begin to think about escalating or deescalating the relationship without knowing how the other will respond, or alternatively, when one person initiates a change that is resisted.

Exchange theorists also have suggested that concerns about issues of reciprocity underlie strategic self-presentation in initial encounters (e.g., Blau, 1964). People fashion a come-on self based on their assessment of whether a hoped-for partner will accept their overture, and try to show themselves as having qualities valued in the marketplace (Figley, 1974, 1979). Social exchange principles also underlie the success of many ingratiation strategies—such as opinion conformity and flattery—that rely on offering another person rewards (e.g., compliments) to increase the probability that the other will reciprocate in kind (Jones, 1964; Jones & Pittman, 1982).

Finally, self-disclosure—an important element in the promotion of rapport—has also long been viewed as a process of social exchange (Altman & Taylor, 1973; Worthy, Gary, & Kahn, 1969). From an exchange perspective, rewards can accrue to both the discloser and the recipient of disclosure. Disclosers may feel rewarded when their disclosures are met with understanding or empathy. Recipients of disclosures may experience rewards from being trusted with personal information concerning the discloser (Worthy et al., 1969) or through the reduction of ambiguity regarding the encounter (e.g., Berger & Kellermann, 1983). This mutual rewardingness leads to a cycle of increasingly intimate disclosures that promotes rapport between the partners (Laurenceau, Barrett, & Pietromonaco, 1998).

Interdependence Theory

Interdependence theory (Kelley, 1979; Kelley et al., 2003) is built partly on principles of exchange (see Arriaga et al., this volume, for a fuller discussion of interdependence theory). The theory takes as its starting point the "situation" in which two individuals find themselves. Situations differ in the extent to which the partners' interests are correspondent, in how the partners communicate and share information, and in the serial ordering of their actions (Kelley et al., 2003). The prototypical situation we have used in this chapter is one in which a person is faced with deciding whether or not to make an overture to another individual. The interdependence theorist would break down the situation much like we have, first by representing the would-be initiator as choosing between two options, *make an overture* or *not make an overture*, and then identifying two possible responses to the overture on the part of the other, *accept* or *reject*. The initiator does not know in advance whether the other will be pleased and accept an overture, or if the other will be displeased or indifferent and turn an overture aside. According to the principles of interdependence theory, this situation poses a dilemma for would-be initiators if their stake is great—as it would be if an initiator was strongly attracted to the target person. Initiators in such a situation may feel particularly vulnerable because their "fate" is under the control of the other individual. The underlying reality, however, may be quite different because the other may have just as much stake in the overture being made as the initiator has in the overture being accepted. Their mutual attraction will be revealed, however, only if the initiator makes a move, or if the other takes the situation in hand.

Interdependence theory and exchange theory are close cousins, and, indeed, exchange ideas were built into interdependence theory from the outset. A core idea of exchange theory is that the "outcomes" of the combinations of the partners' choices (e.g., making an overture, followed by rejection) can affect both partners. Both theories presume that people stay engaged in an encounter, or want to continue a relationship, if the outcomes they experience are above their CL and their CL_{alt}. The two theories also are able to incorporate the idea that the outcomes partners experience reflect, in part, the strength of their attraction. However, because interdependence theory is concerned more with situated actions, it provides better analytic tools for conceptualizing the cognitions that underlie the choices an initiator might make between options. The theory also can be used to map changes in the structure of the situations the partners encounter as their interaction unfolds, as well as the movements of the partners from one situation to another as their relationship develops over time (see Kelley et al., 2003).

In the early stages of relationships—particularly in first encounters—the partners have little information about each other's preferences, which makes it difficult for them to know what kind of self-presentation will be appealing. Unlike exchange theory, interdependence theory draws attention to the idea that people often have an investment in being seen as possessing particular dispositions—as being honest, loyal, or compassionate, for instance—and it pays as much attention to the actors' motives and dispositions as it does to the direct outcomes experienced in the exchange. People derive pleasure from being seen as having sterling qualities, such as when a partner sees them as sincere.

Attracting an individual's interest—and then sustaining a relationship—requires finding common ground. The likelihood of finding such common ground, from the perspective of interdependence theory, depends on the "correspondence of outcomes," which generally prevails when people have similar points of view, interests, values, and hopes. People who have a broad range of interests, particularly interests that are widely shared among friends and acquaintances in their circle, may have little trouble finding nodes of connection with most of those they encounter and thus may be attractive companions to many individuals. Whereas exchange theory tends to focus on the idea that people's value in the marketplace is closely tied to their social status—for example, their looks, education, or income—interdependence theory lends itself to the idea that people value partners for reasons that often have little connection to such attributes.

It is important, as well, to recognize that marketplace considerations are likely to be less salient when relationships have a "running start," as when people know each other through family or mutual friends, or when they have engaged in some joint activity in a group setting prior to one of them trying to start a personal relationship. A person may show kindness to another at some personal cost in a group setting or may behave benevolently toward a person who could easily be exploited. People in the group or circle may perceive a capacity for love reflected in the other's willingness to sacrifice or trustworthiness reflected in his or her benevolence. These attributions, in turn, may pique their interest in making an overture because such qualities are highly valued in partners, particularly when individuals are seeking a long-term relationship (cf. Kelley et al., 2003; Rusbult & Van Lange, 2003).

Evolutionary Social Psychological Theory

Evolutionary social psychological theory posits that preferences for potential partners have evolved, according to Darwinian principles, over evolutionary time (Buss, 1988). Specifically, evolutionary theorists believe that the human mind is a set of information-processing machines that have evolved through natural selection to solve adaptive problems related to survival and reproduction (Cosmides & Tooby, 1992). Parental investment–based models (e.g., Buss & Schmitt, 1993; Kenrick, Sadalla,

Groth, & Trost, 1990) presuppose that men and women have differential investments in their off-spring and that individuals' reproductive success is dependent upon pairing with mates who optimize the chances that their investments will pay off. Ancestral men who preferred and mated with healthy as opposed to unhealthy women, and ancestral women who preferred and mated with men who had sufficient as opposed to insufficient resources, were more successful in producing offspring and passing on their genes. Over time, these preferences have become basic human tendencies (see Schmitt, this volume, for a more complete discussion of evolutionary theory).

Early theorizing and research from the evolutionary perspective suggested that men (rather than women) are attracted to physical attractiveness in a mate, whereas women (rather than men) are attracted to status and resources in a mate (Buss & Barnes, 1986). These characteristics serve the reproductive purposes of each sex (see Schmitt, this volume). However, the model presented in this chapter relies on further refinements of evolutionary theory. These refinements posit that the perceived attractiveness of partner characteristics depends on whether a person is seeking a short-term liaison or a long-term relationship (Buss & Schmitt, 1993). Although these differing sexual strategies may have been strictly sex-typed among our ancestors, one can no longer safely presume to know a prospect's relational motives—and thus partner preferences—solely based upon his or her gender.

After initial attraction is determined, people seek information about the probability that a desired other is likely to reciprocate that attraction before making a decision on whether to approach. Evolutionary theory suggests that these assessments are partially based on a would-be initiator's sensitivity to the desired other's nonverbal behaviors (see Cunningham & Barbee, this volume). Research shows that smiling, eye contact, and moving closer to the initiator are often interpreted as signs that the other is likely to be receptive to an overture (McCormick & Jones, 1989). From an evolutionary perspective, modern humans are sensitive to these nonverbal cues because they resulted in reproductive success in the past.

Evolutionary theory (Buss, 1988) posits specific strategies that people use to maximize the probability that a desired other will provide them with rewards. These strategies are proposed to differ by sex and the type of relationship being pursued (Schmitt & Buss, 1996). Strategic self-presentation can take the form of directly promoting oneself or derogating competing potential partners (Schmitt & Buss, 2001). For example, when the goal is to attract a short-term mate, women are believed to present themselves as sexually available through flirting, sexualizing their appearance, and acting seductively, or by derogating other women's appearances and hinting that rivals are sexually unavailable or unclean. In contrast, women seeking to attract a long-term mate are posited to present themselves as willing to be sexually exclusive, or to belittle potential rivals as promiscuous. On the other hand, men seeking short-term versus long-term mates are predicted to enact differing strategies that show off their present or future resources and status (e.g., wearing expensive clothes versus talking about their willingness to commit and ability to acquire long-term resources) and/or derogate their rivals' resources or ability to provide (see Schmitt, this volume; Schmitt & Buss, 2001).

Although the strategic process of determining whether a prospect can provide desirable outcomes may build rapport, nonstrategic behavior in initial encounters can also induce rapport between potential partners. It is well established that as initial interactions progress, people begin to unconsciously mimic each other's behaviors (e.g., speech patterns, posture, and gestures; see Chartrand & Bargh, 1999, for a review). Further experimental work has shown that behavioral mimicry induces increased rapport, and increasing rapport during interaction, in turn, induces higher levels of mimicry (Chartrand & Bargh). This reciprocal process of nonconscious behavioral mimicry is posited to serve the evolutionary function of facilitating communication and the development of social bonds (Lakin, Jefferis, Cheng, & Chartrand, 2003; also see Cunningham & Barbee, this volume).

Adult Attachment Theory

The attachment literature is voluminous, and many classification schemes have been developed to characterize adult attachment phenomena (Cassidy & Shaver, 1999; Mikulincer & Goodman, 2006). Adult attachment theory, at its core, posits that people possess different interpersonal predispositions as a result of their early experiences with caregivers and other personal relationships (Hazan & Shaver, 1987). These past experiences result in differences between people in how comfortable they are with being close to others and how anxious they are about being abandoned (Brennan, Clark, & Shaver, 1998). The extent to which people possess these two characteristics can be used to classify them into attachment orientations: secure (e.g., those comfortable with trusting and depending on others), avoidant (e.g., those distrustful and uncomfortable with being close to and depending on others), and anxious (e.g., those who worry that others will leave them and feel that others are reluctant to get close to them) (Shaver, Hazan, & Bradshaw, 1988; also see Creasey & Jarvis, this volume, for a discussion of each attachment style). Other researchers have taken a more dimensional approach to adult attachment, discovering, for example, that three dimensions—comfort with depending on others, anxiety or fear of being abandoned or unloved, and comfort with closeness—underlie the traditional adult attachment orientations (Collins & Read, 1990). Alternatively, Bartholomew's (1990) classification presumes that two dimensions underlie adult attachment patterns—the self and the other—thus resulting in four attachment patterns: secure (low anxiety and low avoidance), preoccupied (high anxiety and low avoidance), dismissing (low anxiety and high avoidance), and fearful (high anxiety and high avoidance) (Griffin & Bartholomew, 1994).

The expectations that individuals hold for potential partners differ according to their attachment classification and are posited to influence how people appraise the potential rewardingness of a prospect (Mikulincer, 1998). For example, avoidant individuals—those who expect others to be untrustworthy—are more likely than secure individuals to project their own perceived interpersonal deficiencies onto potential partners (Mikulincer & Horesh, 1999), thus reducing the other's perceived reward value. Additionally, extremely avoidant individuals may choose to remove themselves altogether from situations that could lead to receiving rewards from others. The relational expectations that influence initial attraction also play a role in a would-be initiator's evaluation that a potential partner is likely to reciprocate the initiator's attraction (Hazan & Shaver, 1987). Secure individuals are likely to be trusting of others and expect that others will act benevolently and accept their overtures, whereas anxious and avoidant individuals tend to expect that a perceived other will not be responsive (Hazan & Shaver, 1987; also see Metts & Mikucki, this volume).

Once an approach has been made, people's attachment orientations also influence the effectiveness of their tactics in eliciting acceptance (Shaver & Mikulincer, 2006). Avoidant people tend to present an inflated view of themselves to others in order to appear strong and self-sufficient, an approach that often impairs, rather than promotes, the development of intimacy (Mikulincer, 1998). Anxious people tend to devalue themselves to others—possibly in an attempt to receive the compassion and love that they fear others will not give them—a strategy that also is not very effective. Secure individuals, in contrast, are less likely than both avoidant and anxious individuals to be biased or self-destructive in their self-presentations.

Attachment-related conceptions of self and others also are important in the rapport-building phase of first encounters (Shaver & Mikulincer, 2006). Secure persons, who trust others and are comfortable with closeness, openly disclose to would-be partners and are responsive to the reciprocal disclosures of others (Keelan, Dion, & Dion, 1998), thus facilitating the development of relationships. In contrast, avoidant individuals tend to engage in low levels of self-disclosure, which reflects their fear of dependence and lack of trust in others. Anxious people, who frequently worry about how others regard them, often attempt to rush disclosure, thus halting the buildup of rapport because the other is not ready for such intimacy (Mikulincer & Nachshon, 1991; also see Derlega et al., this volume).

CONCLUSION

Our analysis of the initiation of relationships provides yet another example of the centrality of the principle of reciprocity in understanding human affairs. People care about how others respond to them: They make overtures with the hope that their interest will be reciprocated; they put out feelers for sex with the hope that their offer will be taken up; they reveal parts of their identity with the hope that others will like what they see, or like them in spite of what they see; they commit their time and energy, and sacrifice their immediate interests, with the hope that their partner will do the same; and they love with the hope that their love will be returned in kind.

We have emphasized the idea that the decision to begin an encounter is discrete, that it is based on a more or less objective, strategic appraisal of the likely balance between what a person has to offer and what others have to offer—and are likely to offer—in return. In so doing, we may have inadvertently overplayed the mindfulness involved. When people are strongly attracted to another—as Calvin Trillin was to Alice—their fluttering hearts may lead them to throw caution to the wind and approach someone even though they believe the odds of acceptance are not high. Moreover, many freely initiated encounters are low-key, with neither party investing much (i.e., strategizing) or expecting much in return. Indeed, even when would-be initiators appear to carefully assess the probable outcomes of an approach or encounter—as was the case with Amy's assessment of Michael upon entering the plaza—it is likely that much of the information upon which they base their appraisal is acquired nonstrategically and out of conscious awareness. Research has demonstrated that behavior can be influenced by unconscious priming in immediately previous encounters (Bargh, Chen, & Burrows, 1996). For example, a person who has experienced a negative interaction just before encountering a desired other may be particularly attuned, albeit unconsciously, to the negative attributes of the potential partner. Future research on relationship initiation in romantic relationships should address these nonstrategic, often nonconscious, processes.

Regardless of how much forethought initiators give to their chances, they are faced soon enough with a reaction, and they use the new information to recalibrate their interest in continuing further pursuit. The reactions, of course, are often muted—a subtle turning aside, a weak smile, or a lack of enthusiasm may indicate rejection, and an open, friendly face may signal acceptance. If the interest is mutual, however, the interaction will liven up, for reciprocity is the energy that fuels engagement. Overture makers may initially seek little more than a flirtation, but when their flirtation is taken up, they may begin to think about romance, a sexual encounter, or even a long-term relationship. The progression of encounters, as we characterized them, involves an effort to build rapport, and if there is mutual interest, an agreement of sorts is made about the next step.

We also emphasized that in today's marketplace, where romantic overtures are made with varied end-goals in mind, individuals may or may not be thinking in terms of how their first encounter might shape later encounters, or that how they proceed in a first encounter may set the stage for a long-term relationship. Social scientists know little about whether "love at first sight" typically sets in motion a process that creates mutual love, or whether it sets people up for disappointment when they discover that their initial excitement was more fictional than reality-based. Do people who carefully gather information about the likelihood that establishing a bond will be in both partners' rational self-interests make better choices at the outset? Are some people more able than others to present themselves in attractive ways without being deceptive? These are only a sampling of the questions that remain to be answered.

As the chapters in this volume attest, considerable knowledge has accumulated about the motives behind relationships, the bases of attraction, the ways people attract another's interest, and the buildup of rapport. This knowledge, however, is built largely on studies of young college students, and the scenes and scenarios have been primarily of a heterosexual nature. Nevertheless, we believe that the framework we have introduced and the issues we have addressed are salient whether the individuals are teenagers, middle-aged adults, or senior citizens; rich or poor; straight or gay; and Black, White, or some other color. The fact that we must speculate, however, suggests the importance of examining relationship initiation among various subpopulations. This expansion will likely reveal, for example, that for a gay individual interested in romance, identifying someone as "cleared" requires much more than a quick check for a wedding band. A 40-year-old widowed father may look for very different qualifiers in a mate and perceive his own market value very differently than would a single man half or twice his age. An individual with little "human capital" (e.g., education, work skills, and income) may be forced to think about partnering with a person who has little to offer or consider not partnering at all.

AUTHOR NOTE

The coauthors contributed equally to the production of the chapter and are listed alphabetically. We thank Gilbert Geis and Elizabeth Schoenfeld for their helpful comments on an earlier draft of the chapter.

REFERENCES

Altman, I., & Taylor, D. A. (1973). *Social penetration: The development of interpersonal relationships*. New York: Holt, Rinehart & Winston.

Aron, A., Steele, J. L., Kashdan, T. B., & Perez, M. (2006). When similars do not attract: Tests of a prediction from the self expansion model. *Personal Relationships, 13*, 387–396.

Axinn, W. G., & Thornton, A. (2000). The transformation in the meaning of marriage. In L. J. Waite (Ed.), *The ties that bind: Perspectives on marriage and cohabitation* (pp. 147–165). New York: Aldine de Gruyter.

Bailey, B. L. (1988). *From front porch to back seat: Courtship in twentieth-century America*. Baltimore: John Hopkins University Press.

Baldwin, M. W., & Keelan, J. P. R. (1999). Interpersonal expectations as a function of self-esteem and sex. *Journal of Social and Personal Relationships, 16*, 822–833.

Bargh, J. A., Chen, M., & Burrows, L. (1996). Automaticity of social behavior: Direct effects of trait construct and stereotype activation on action. *Journal of Personality and Social Psychology, 71*, 230–244.

Bartholomew, K. (1990). Avoidance of intimacy: An attachment perspective. *Journal of Social and Personal Relationships, 7*, 147–178.

Bartholomew, K., & Horowitz, L. M. (1991). Attachment styles among young adults: A test of a four-category model. *Journal of Personality and Social Psychology, 61*, 226–244.

Baumeister, R. F. (1998). The self. In D. Gilbert, S. Fiske, & G. Lindzey (Eds.), *The handbook of social psychology* (Vol. 1, 4th ed., pp. 680–740). Oxford: Oxford University Press.

Beilin, Y. (2000). *His brother's keeper: Israel and Diaspora Jewry in the twenty-first century*. New York: Schoken.

Berger, C. R., & Kellermann, K. (1983). To ask or not to ask: Is that a question? In R. N. Bostrom (Ed.), *Communication Yearbook 7* (pp. 342–368). Newbury Park, CA: Sage.

Blau, P. (1964). *Exchange and power in social life*. New York: Wiley.

Brennan, K. A., Clark, C. L., & Shaver, P. R. (1998). Self-report measurement of adult attachment: An integrative overview. In J. A. Simpson & W. S. Rholes (Eds.), *Attachment theory and close relationships* (pp. 46–76). New York: Guilford Press.

Buss, D. M. (1988). The evolution of human intrasexual competition: Tactics of mate attraction. *Journal of Personality and Social Psychology, 54*, 616–628.

Buss, D. M. (1999). *Evolutionary psychology*. Boston: Allyn & Bacon.

Buss, D. M., & Barnes, M. (1986). Preferences in human mate selection. *Journal of Personality and Social Psychology, 50*, 559–570.

Buss, D. M., & Schmitt, D. P. (1993). Sexual strategies theory: An evolutionary perspective on human mating. *Psychological Review, 100*, 204–232.

Buss, D. M., Shackelford, T. K., Kirkpatrick, L. A., & Larsen, R. J. (2001). A half century of mate preferences: The cultural evolution of values. *Journal of Marriage and the Family, 63*, 491–503.

Campbell, L., Lackenbauer, S. D., & Muise, A. (2006). When is being known or adored by romantic partners most beneficial? Self-perceptions, relationship length, and response to verifying and enhancing appraisals. *Personality and Social Psychology Bulletin, 32*, 1283–1294.

Cassidy, J., & Shaver, P. R. (Eds.). (1999). *Handbook of attachment: Theory, research, and clinical applications*. New York: Guilford Press.

Chambliss, W. J. (1965). The selection of friends. *Social Forces, 43*, 370–380.

Chartrand, T. L., & Bargh, J. A. (1999). The chameleon effect: The perception-behavior link and social interaction. *Journal of Personality and Social Psychology, 76*, 893–910.

Cherlin, A. (2004). The deinstitutionalization of American marriage. *Journal of Marriage and Family, 66*, 848–861.

Clark, C. L., Shaver, P. R., & Abrahams, M. F. (1999). Strategic behaviors in romantic relationship initiation. *Personality and Social Psychology Bulletin, 25*, 707–720.

Collins, N. L., & Read, S. J. (1990). Adult attachment, working models, and relationship quality in dating couples. *Journal of Personality and Social Psychology, 58,* 644–663.

Condon, J. W., & Crano, W. D. (1988). Inferred evaluation and the relation between attitude similarity and interpersonal attraction. *Journal of Personality and Social Psychology, 54,* 789–797.

Coontz, S. (2004). The world historical transformation of marriage. *Journal of Marriage and Family, 66,* 974–979.

Coontz, S. (2005). *Marriage, a history.* New York: Viking.

Cosmides, L., & Tooby, J. (1992). Cognitive adaptations for social exchange. In J. H. Barkow, L. Cosmides, & J. Tooby (Eds.), *The adapted mind: Evolutionary psychology and the generation of culture* (pp. 163–228). New York: Oxford University Press.

Cunningham, M. R. (1989). Reactions to heterosexual opening gambits: Female selectivity and male responsiveness. *Personality and Social Psychology Bulletin, 15,* 27–41.

Curtis, R. C., & Miller, K. (1986). Believing another likes or dislikes you: Behaviors making the beliefs come true. *Journal of Personality and Social Psychology, 51,* 284–290.

Davis, M. S. (1973). *Intimate relations.* New York: Free Press.

Degler, C. A. (1980). *At odds: Women and the family in America from the revolution to the present.* Oxford: Oxford University Press.

Dion, K. K., Berscheid, E., & Walster, E. (1972). What is beautiful is good. *Journal of Personality and Social Psychology, 24,* 285–290.

Douglas, W. (1991). Expectations about initial interaction: An examination of the effects of global uncertainty. *Human Communication Research, 17,* 355–384.

Downey, G., Freitas, A. L., Michaelis, B., & Khouri, H. (1998). The self-fulfilling prophecy in close relationships: Rejection sensitivity and rejection by romantic partners. *Journal of Personality and Social Psychology, 75,* 545–560.

Dutton, D. G., & Aron, A. P. (1974). Some evidence for heightened sexual attraction under conditions of high anxiety. *Journal of Personality and Social Psychology, 30,* 510–517.

Ellis, B. J., & Kelley, H. H. (2000). The pairing game: A classroom demonstration of the matching phenomenon. *Teaching of Psychology, 26,* 119–121.

Figley, C. R. (1974). *Tactical self-presentation in a dating decision-making context.* Unpublished doctoral dissertation, Pennsylvania State University.

Figley, C. R. (1979). Tactical self-presentation and interpersonal attraction. In M. Cook & G. Wilson (Eds.), *Love and attraction* (pp. 91–99). Oxford: Pergamon Press.

Fitzgerald, F. S. (1925). *The great Gatsby.* New York: Scribner.

Fleming, K., & Fleming, A. T. (1975). *The first time.* New York: Simon & Schuster.

Fletcher, G. O., Tither, J. M., O'Loughlin, C., Friesen, M., & Overall, N. (2004). Warm and homely or cold and beautiful? Sex differences in trading off traits in mate selection. *Personality and Social Psychology Bulletin, 30,* 659–672.

Fowles, J. (2003). *The journals: Vol. 1. 1949–1965.* New York: Knopf.

Fraley, B., & Aron, A. (2004). The effect of a shared humorous experience on closeness in initial encounters. *Personal Relationships, 11,* 61–78.

Gangestad, S. W., Garver-Apgar, C. E., Simpson, J. A., & Cousins, A. J. (2007). Changes in women's mate preferences across the ovulatory cycle. *Journal of Personality and Social Psychology, 92,* 151–163.

Goffman, E. (1959). *The presentation of self in everyday life.* Garden City, NY: Doubleday Anchor.

Gordon, R. A. (1996). Impact of ingratiation on judgments and evaluations: A meta-analytic investigation. *Journal of Personality and Social Psychology, 71,* 54–70.

Griffin, D., & Bartholomew, K. (1994). Models of the self and other: Fundamental dimensions underlying measures of adult attachment. *Journal of Personality and Social Psychology, 67,* 430–445.

Hazan, C., & Shaver, P. (1987). Romantic love conceptualized as an attachment process. *Journal of Personality and Social Psychology, 52,* 511–524.

Hess, J. A., Fannin, A. D., & Pollom, L. H. (2007). Creating closeness: Discerning and measuring strategies for fostering close relationships. *Personal Relationships, 14,* 25–44.

Homans, G. C. (1961). *Social behavior: Its elementary forms* (Rev. ed.). New York: Harcourt, Brace, & World.

Huston, T. L. (1972). *From liking to affiliation: Empirical tests of a two-factor model of social choice.* Unpublished doctoral dissertation, State University of New York at Albany.

Huston, T. L. (1973). Ambiguity of acceptance, social desirability, and dating choice. *Journal of Experimental Social Psychology, 9,* 32–42.

Huston, T. L. (1982, January). *The Penn State PAIR Project Newsletter, 1,* 1–4.

Huston, T. L., & Burgess, R. L. (1979). Social exchange in developing relationships. In R. L. Burgess & T. L. Huston (Eds.), *Social exchange and developing relationships* (pp. 3–28). New York: Academic Press.

Huston, T. L., & Levinger, G. A. (1978). Interpersonal attraction and relationships. *Annual Review of Psychology*, 29, 115–156.

Jones, E. E. (1964). *Ingratiation*. East Norwalk, CT: Appleton-Century-Croft.

Jones, E. E., & Pittman, T. S. (1982). Toward a general theory of strategic self-presentation. In J. Suls (Ed.), *Psychological perspectives on the self* (Vol. 1, pp. 231–262). Hillsdale, NJ: Lawrence Erlbaum.

Katz, J., & Beach, S. R. H. (2000). Looking for love? Self-verification and self-enhancement effects on initial romantic attraction. *Personality and Social Psychology Bulletin*, 26, 1476–1489.

Keelan, J. P., Dion, K. K., & Dion, K. L. (1998). Attachment style and relationship satisfaction: Test of a self-disclosure explanation. *Canadian Journal of Behavioural Science*, 30, 24–35.

Kelley, H. H. (1979). *Personal relationships: Their structures and processes*. Hillsdale, NJ: Lawrence Erlbaum.

Kelley, H. H., Holmes, J. G., Kerr, N. L., Reis, H. T., Rusbult, C. E., & Van Lange, P. A. M. (2003). *An atlas of interpersonal situations*. New York: Cambridge University Press.

Kenny, D. A., & La Voie, L. (1984). The social relations model. *Advances in Experimental Social Psychology*, 18, 142–182.

Kenrick, D. T., Sadalla, E. K., Groth, G., & Trost, M. R. (1990). Evolution, traits, and the stages of human courtship: Qualifying the parental investment model. *Journal of Personality*, 58, 97–116.

Kerckhoff, A. C. (1974). The social context of interpersonal attraction. In. T. L. Huston (Ed.), *Foundations of interpersonal attraction* (pp. 61–78). New York: Academic Press.

Kleinke, C. L., & Dean, G. O. (1990). Evaluation of men and women receiving positive and negative responses with various acquaintance strategies. *Journal of Social Behavior and Personality*, 5, 369–377.

Knapp, M. L. (1984). *Interpersonal communication and human relationships*. Boston: Allyn & Bacon.

Lakin, J. L., Jefferis, V. E., Cheng, C. M., & Chartrand, T. L. (2003). The chameleon effect as social glue: Evidence for the evolutionary significance of nonconscious mimicry. *Journal of Nonverbal Behavior*, 27, 145–162.

Langlois, J. H., Kalakanis, L., Rubenstein, A. J., Larson, A., Hallam, M., & Smoot, M. (2000). Maxims or myths of beauty? A meta-analytic and theoretical review. *Psychological Bulletin*, 126, 390–423.

Laurenceau, J., Barrett, L. F., & Pietromonaco, P. R. (1998). Intimacy as an interpersonal process: The importance of self-disclosure, partner disclosure, and perceived partner responsiveness in interpersonal exchanges. *Journal of Personality & Social Psychology*, 74, 1239–1251.

Leary, M. R. (2004). The sociometer, self-esteem, and the regulation of interpersonal behavior. In K. D. Vohs & R. F. Baumeister (Eds.), *Handbook of self-regulation: Research, theory, and applications* (pp. 373–391). New York: Guilford Press.

Lee, J. A. (1977). A typology of styles of loving. *Personality and Social Psychology Bulletin*, 3, 173–182.

Lee, J. A. (1988). Love styles. In R. J. Sternberg & M. L. Barnes (Eds.), *The psychology of love* (pp. 38–67). New Haven, CT: Yale University Press.

Li, N., Bailey, M., Kenrick, D., & Linsenmeier, J. (2002). The necessities and luxuries of mate preference: Testing the tradeoffs. *Journal of Personality and Social Psychology*, 82, 947–955.

Li, N. P., & Kenrick, D. T. (2006). Sex similarities and differences in preferences for short-term mates: What, whether, and why. *Journal of Personality and Social Psychology*, 90, 468–489.

Little, A. C., Penton-Voak, I. S., Burt, M., & Perrett, D. I. (2002). Evolution and individual differences in the perception of attractiveness: How cyclic hormonal changes and self-perceived attractiveness influence male preferences for male faces. In G. Rhodes & L. A. Zebrowitz (Eds.), *Facial attractiveness: Evolutionary, cognitive, and social perspectives* (pp. 59–90). Westport, CT: Ablex.

Livingston, R. W. (2001). What you see is what you get: Systematic variability in perceptual-based social judgment. *Personality and Social Psychology Bulletin*, 27, 1086–1096.

Luker, K. (1996). *Dubious conceptions: The politics of teenage pregnancy*. Cambridge, MA: Harvard University Press.

McCormick, N. B., & Jones, A. J. (1989). Gender differences in nonverbal flirting. *Journal of Sex Education and Therapy*, 15, 271–282.

Mikulincer, M. (1998). Attachment working models and the sense of trust: An exploration of interaction goals and affect regulation. *Journal of Personality and Social Psychology*, 74, 1209–1224.

Mikulincer, M., & Goodman, G. S. (Eds.). (2006). *Dynamics of romantic love: Attachment, caregiving, and sex*. New York: Guilford Press.

Mikulincer, M., & Horesh, N. (1999). Adult attachment style and perception of others: The role of projective mechanisms. *Journal of Personality and Social Psychology*, 76, 1022–1034.

Mikulincer, M., & Nachshon, O. (1991). Attachment styles and patterns of self-disclosure. *Journal of Personality and Social Psychology, 61*, 321–331.

Mongeau, P. A., & Carey, C. M. (1996). Who's wooing whom II? An experimental investigation of date-initiation and expectancy violation. *Western Journal of Communication, 60*, 195–213.

Murray, S. L., Holmes, J. G., & Griffin, D. W. (2003). Reflections on the self-fulfilling effects of positive illusions. *Psychological Inquiry, 14*, 289–295.

Murstein, B. (1970). Stimulus-value-role: A theory of marital choice. *Journal of Marriage and the Family, 32*, 465–481.

Online Publishers Association. (2004, May 11). U.S. consumer spending for online content totals nearly $1.6 billion in 2003, according to Online Publishers Association report [*Press release*]. **Online Publishers Association**. Retrieved October 12, 2006, from http://www.online-publishers.org/?pg=press&dt=051104

Park, L. E. (2007). Appearance-based rejection sensitivity: Implications for mental and physical health, affect, and motivation. *Personality and Social Psychology Bulletin, 33*, 490–504.

Parks, M. R. (2007). *Personal relationships and personal networks*. Mahwah, NJ: Lawrence Erlbaum.

Perper, T. (1985). *Sex signs: The biology of love*. Philadelphia: ISI Press.

Pinel, E. C., Long, A. E., Landau, M. J., Alexander, K., & Pyszczynski, T. (2006). Seeing I to I: A pathway to interpersonal connectedness. *Journal of Personality and Social Psychology, 90*, 243–257.

Rusbult, C. E., & Van Lange, P. A. M. (2003). Interdependence, interaction, and relationships. *Annual Review of Psychology, 54*, 351–375.

Saluter, A. F., & Lugaila, T. A. (1998). *Marital status and living arrangements: March 1996* (Current Population Reports, P20–496). Washington, DC: U.S. Census Bureau.

Schmitt, D. P., & Buss, D. M. (1996). Strategic self-promotion and competitor derogation: Sex and context effects on the perceived effectiveness of mate attraction tactics. *Journal of Personality and Social Psychology, 70*, 1185–1204.

Schmitt, D. P., & Buss, D. M. (2001). Human mate poaching: Tactics and temptations for infiltrating existing mateships. *Journal of Personality and Social Psychology, 80*, 894–917.

Shackelford, T. K., Schmitt, D. P., & Buss, D. M. (2005). Universal dimensions of human mate preferences. *Personality and Individual Differences, 39*, 447–458.

Shanteau, J., & Nagy, G. (1976). Decisions made about other people: A human judgment analysis of dating choice. In J. Carroll & J. Payne (Eds.), *Cognition and social behavior* (pp. 221–242). Hillsdale, NJ: Lawrence Erlbaum.

Shanteau, J., & Nagy, G. F. (1979). Probability of acceptance in dating choice. *Journal of Personality and Social Psychology, 37*, 522–533.

Shaver, P., Hazan, C., & Bradshaw, D. (1988). Love as attachment. In R. J. Sternberg & M. L. Barnes (Eds.), *The psychology of love* (pp. 68–99). New Haven, CT: Yale University Press.

Shaver, P., & Mikulincer, M. (2006). Attachment theory, individual psychodynamics, and relationship functioning. In A. Vangelisti & D. Perlman (Eds.), *The Cambridge handbook of personal relationships* (pp. 251–271). Cambridge: Cambridge University Press.

Simpson, J. A., & Gangestad, S. W. (1991). Individual differences in sociosexuality: Evidence for convergent and discriminant validity. *Journal of Personality and Social Psychology, 60*, 870–883.

Simpson, J. A., & Gangestad, S. W. (1992). Sociosexuality and romantic partner choice. *Journal of Personality, 60*, 31–51.

Snyder, M., Berscheid, E., & Glick, P. (1985). Focusing on the exterior and the interior: Two investigations of the initiation of personal relationships. *Journal of Personality and Social Psychology, 48*, 1427–1439.

Snyder, M., Tanke, E. D., & Berscheid, E. (1977). Social perception and interpersonal behavior: On the self-fulfilling nature of social stereotypes. *Journal of Personality and Social Psychology, 35*, 656–666.

Swann, W. B., Jr., De La Ronde, C., & Hixon, G. (1994). Authenticity and positivity strivings in marriage and courtship. *Journal of Personality and Social Psychology, 66*, 857–869.

Swann, W. B., Jr., Griffin, J. J., Jr., Predmore, S. C., & Gaines, B. (1987). The cognitive-affective crossfire: When self-consistency confronts self-enhancement. *Journal of Personality and Social Psychology, 52*, 881–889.

Swann, W. B., Jr., Pelham, B. W., & Krull, D. S. (1989). Agreeable fancy or disagreeable truth? Reconciling self-enhancement and self-verification. *Journal of Personality and Social Psychology, 57*, 782–791.

Thibaut, J., & Kelley, H. (1959). *The social psychology of groups*. New York: Wiley.

Trillin, C. (2006). *About Alice*. New York: Random House.

Turner, F. (1985). *John Muir: Rediscovering America*. New York: Perseus.

U.S. Census Bureau. (2003). *Estimated median age at first marriage, by sex: 1980 to present*. Retrieved July 13, 2007, from http://www.census.gov/population/www/socdemo/hh-fam.html

Vonk, R. (2002). Self-serving interpretations of flattery. Why ingratiation works. *Journal of Personality and Social Psychology, 82,* 515–526.

Vorauer, J. D., Cameron, J. J., Holmes, J. G., & Pearce, D. G. (2003). Invisible overtures: Fears of rejection and the signal amplification bias. *Journal of Personality and Social Psychology, 84,* 793–812.

Vorauer, J. D., & Ratner, R. K. (1996). Who's going to make the first move? Pluralistic ignorance as an impediment to relationship formation. *Journal of Social and Personal Relationships, 13,* 483–506.

Wiederman, M. W., & Dubois, S. L. (1998). Evolution and sex differences in preferences for short-term mates: Results from a policy capturing study. *Evolution and Human Behavior, 19,* 153–170.

White, G. L., Fishbein, S., & Rutstin, J. (1981). Passionate love: The misattribution of arousal. *Journal of Personality and Social Psychology, 41,* 56–62.

Wolfenstein, M., & Leites, N. (1950). *Movies: A psychological study.* Glencoe, IL: Free Press.

Worthy, M., Gary, A. L., & Kahn, G. M. (1969). Self-disclosure as an exchange process. *Journal of Personality and Social Psychology, 13,* 59–63.

2

Friendship Formation

BEVERLEY FEHR

Yes' m, old friends is always best, 'less you can catch a new one that's fit to make an old one out of.

—Sarah Orne Jewett

The basic question to be addressed in this chapter is, how do people "catch" new friends? Research to address this question is somewhat limited, given that, as the present volume attests, relationship initiation research has overwhelmingly targeted romantic relationships. Friendship is still branded as the "under-studied" relationship (Rawlins, 1992), which may, in part, reflect the greater importance granted to romantic and familial relationships in our society (see e.g., Fehr & Harasymchuk, 2005). Interestingly, however, when people are asked what gives their lives happiness, joy, and meaning, friendships are near the top, or at the top, of the list (see Fehr, 1996, for a review). These perceptions are corroborated by research on daily experiences. Larson and Bradney (1988), for example, tracked the day-to-day interactions of teenagers and adults and found that the greatest enjoyment and excitement were reported when in the presence of friends—more so than when alone or in the presence of spouse or family. Given how important friendships actually are in people's lives, it becomes critical to understand how people form this kind of relationship.

As will be seen, friendship formation is a complex process in which a number of factors must converge. I will focus on four major factors identified in the literature: environmental factors, situational factors, individual factors, and, finally, dyadic factors. Each of these will be discussed, along with supporting research, followed by research that has examined these factors in conjunction. The chapter ends with a consideration of future directions as well as speculation on the state of friendship initiation research, including whether extant work points to a "grand model" of friendship formation.

Before delving into how friendships are formed, it is necessary to define what friendship is. Although relationships scholars have yet to agree on a specific definition, there is consensus that friendship is, first and foremost, a type of *relationship*. According to Allan (1989),

> "[F]riend" is not just a categorical label, like "colleague" or "cousin," indicating the social position of each individual relative to the other. Rather it is a relational term which signifies something about the quality and character of the relationship involved. (p. 16)

Exactly what qualities and characteristics should be included in definitions of friendship remains a matter of debate. However, some common themes that can be extracted from extant definitions include the following: Friendship is a voluntary, personal relationship, characterized by equality and mutual involvement, reciprocal liking, self-disclosure, and the provision of various kinds of support (see Fehr, 1996, for a review). Friendships in the early, formative stages—the focus of the present chapter—are not likely to instantiate all of the aforementioned characteristics. For example, as will be discussed later in this chapter, research has shown that self-disclosure tends to be more super-ficial and circumscribed in acquaintanceships and newly formed friendships than in close or best friendships (see, e.g., Altman & Taylor, 1973; Knapp, Ellis, & Williams, 1980). Newly formed friend-ships are not likely to entail high levels of mutual assistance and emotional support. On the other hand, qualities such as voluntariness, reciprocal liking, and equality are likely to be evident even in nascent friendships. The focus of the present chapter is on these budding relationships. More specifi-cally, the purpose is to examine the factors that promote the formation of friendships.

ENVIRONMENTAL FACTORS

It has been assumed that a prerequisite for the development of friendships is that the two people must be brought into contact with one another through physical proximity or *propinquity*. First, I will examine the larger environmental context, namely, whether greater or lesser population density is more conducive to friendship formation. The focus will then narrow to an examination of the effects of residential proximity and proximity in workplace and school settings. As will be seen, there is considerable evidence that people who inhabit the same physical space are more likely to become friends than those who do not. However, the current availability of computer-mediated communica-tion (CMC) calls into question whether physical proximity is still a necessary condition for friendship development. This issue will be discussed, along with the findings of studies investigating friendship formation over the Internet. The section will end with an examination of the role of social networks in friendship formation.

Population Density

A commonly held stereotype is that urban dwellers are less friendly than their rural counterparts. Does living in a large city actually impede the formation of friendships? Some researchers have found that adults living in urban areas have more friends than their rural counterparts (Fischer, 1982) and that teenagers living in urban areas actually report more friends, particularly neighbor-hood friends, than those living in less densely populated suburbs (Van Vliet, 1981). Others have found just the opposite. For example, Oppong, Ironside, and Kennedy (1988) found that people in small towns reported more friendships than people in big cities. Similar findings were obtained in a study conducted in France (Moser, Legendre, & Ratiu, 2003). These researchers compared the friendships of adults living in central Paris, the suburbs of Paris, and a smaller provincial city. The small-city residents reported significantly more friendships ($M = 8.13$) than the large-city and subur-ban residents ($M = 7.53$ and 6.80, respectively; the latter did not differ significantly).

To present a final study, Franck (1980) tracked the friendship patterns of students who moved to either a large city or a small town to attend graduate school and found that it took longer to make friends in the city. Specifically, within 2 months of their arrival, students who had moved to a city reported an average of 3.51 friends compared to 6.32 reported by the small-town group. Those who moved to a city also reported that they found their new environment difficult for friendship forma-tion. However, when interviewed 7 or 8 months later, both groups named approximately the same number of friends ($M = 5.34$ for the city group, and $M = 5.12$ for the small-town group).

These conflicting sets of findings make it difficult to draw clear conclusions about the effects of urban versus nonurban settings on friendship formation. Part of the difficulty is that studies vary in terms of whether participants are asked to report on friends in general, close friends, neighborhood friends, and so on. In addition, urban environments have been compared to a number of different targets: suburbs, small cities, small towns, or rural areas. These are obviously not equivalent. It may also be the case that it is not an urban versus nonurban setting, per se, that influences friendship formation, but rather the opportunities for friendship formation that are present in each of these settings. For example, cities may be more conducive to friendship formation because of the greater pool of potential friendship choices and enhanced opportunities for informal interaction (see Creekmore, 1985). Consistent with this view, Dugan and Kivett (1998) found that among retired adults, urban dwellers had more frequent contact with friends than those living in rural areas. Presumably, the availability of public transportation made it easier for city folks to see their friends. On the other hand, Moser et al. (2003) found that for those in the workforce, living in a city reduced opportunities for friendship formation because of the time spent commuting to and from work.

Thus, it would appear that whether one lives in a more or less densely populated area has little direct effect on the formation of friendships. What seems critical is whether there are opportunities for friendship formation in a given setting and whether people are able to take advantage of them. Population density can facilitate friendship formation because of the greater availability of potential friends, easier access to friends afforded by public transportation, and so on. On the other hand, it may take more time to commute to a friend's house in a large city than in a small town. For those in the workforce, opportunities for interaction with friends may be limited because of time spent commuting to and from work. Thus, situational factors (e.g., distance to a friend's house or availability of transportation) and life stage factors (e.g., retired versus in the workforce) seem to play a role in determining whether population density is a hindrance or a help.

Residential Proximity

In a classic study, Festinger, Schachter, and Back (1950) documented the important role of residential proximity in friendship formation. They asked residents of a married student housing complex to name the three people in the complex with whom they socialized most. Two thirds of the people named lived in the same building, and two thirds of these people lived on the same floor. The person next door was named most frequently, followed by the person who lived two doors down, and so on. Festinger and colleagues (1950) also discovered that people on different floors were much less likely to become friends than those who lived on the same floor—even if the distance between them was the same. To account for this phenomenon, the researchers coined the term *functional distance*, meaning that the probability of two people interacting is a function of both the design of the environment and the actual physical distance.

Similar findings have been reported in other studies of student residences. For example, in a longitudinal investigation of friendship formation among new university students, Hays (1985) found that the physical distance between the students' residences (ranging from dormitory residence to living across town) was inversely related to friendship development. In the same vein, Holahan and colleagues (Holahan & Wilcox, 1978; Holahan, Wilcox, Burnam, & Culler, 1978) found that students living in high-rise megadormitories reported greater dissatisfaction with opportunities for friendship formation than students living in smaller, low-rise dormitories. In high-rise dormitories, those who lived on lower floors—the floors that are most accessible—reported a greater number of dormitory-based friendships than those living on middle or upper floors (Holahan & Wilcox; Holahan et al., 1978).

A number of studies have documented that friendship formation within dormitories is linked to room proximity; the closer two people's dormitory rooms are, the greater the probability that they will become friends (e.g., Cadiz Menne & Sinnett, 1971; Caplow & Forman, 1950). Griffin and Sparks (1990) found that, at least among men, having been college roommates—an instance of extreme residential proximity—predicted friendship closeness 4 years later (when they were no longer attending college).

The effects of residential proximity have also been documented in nonuniversity settings. For example, in a study conducted in Taiwan, Tsai (2006) found that residential proximity was the most important predictor of contact with close others. However, people's resources also played a role. For example, those with less education and lower income (referred to as *status resources*) were more likely to report that their closest relationships were with local residents compared to those who were better educated and more affluent. Presumably, those with greater resources had the means to maintain ties with those who lived farther away.

Finally, there is also evidence of proximity effects within residential dwellings. Ebbesen, Kjos, and Konecni (1976) found that residents of a condominium complex in California were more likely to become friends (and, incidentally, enemies) with those who lived closest to them. In fact, in one study of residents of a public housing project, it was found that 88% of people's best friends in the complex lived in the same building; nearly half lived on the same floor (Nahemow & Lawton, 1975). Proximity was an especially important variable in friendship formation between dissimilar people. In the words of the authors, "[F]riendships between people of different ages and races existed almost exclusively among those who lived very close to one another. These people resided on the same floor 70% of the time" (Nahemow & Lawton, 1975, p. 210).

Workplace and School Settings

The workplace is another important setting for the formation of friendships (e.g., Riordan & Griffeth, 1995; Roberto & Scott, 1987; Shulman, 1975). More than 30 years ago, nearly 1,000 men living in the Detroit area were asked about the source of their closest friendships (Fischer et al., 1977; Fischer & Phillips, 1982). The largest percentage of friendships were made at work (26%), followed by the neighborhood (23%). Other categories included childhood and juvenile friends (20%), kinship (7%), and voluntary organizations (7%). The workplace and neighborhood were especially important in the formation of new friendships: 79% of these men's most recent friendship ties were formed there, compared to 35% of their longest ties.

The role of the workplace in the formation of women's friendships has received less attention. It has been suggested that for women who do not work outside of the home, the neighborhood may play a role analogous to the workplace for men (O'Connor, 1992). Indeed, some studies have found evidence of neighborhood-based friendships among women (e.g., Jerrome, 1984), although others have not (Oliker, 1989). For employed women with family responsibilities, the demands of work and domestic duties tend to inhibit the development of workplace friendships (e.g., Allan, 1989; Wellman, 1985). For example, women may use their lunch hour to run household errands rather than socialize with coworkers. An exception may be divorced women. One study found that among divorced mothers, the workplace was second only to kin as a source of relationships (Leslie & Grady, 1985).

Proximity is also important within workplace or school settings. In a classic study, Segal (1974) examined the friendship choices of state police trainees who were assigned to dormitory rooms and classroom seats alphabetically by surname. Friendships were most likely to form between those whose surnames began with the same, or a nearby, letter of the alphabet. In a conceptually similar study, Skyes (1983) observed the interaction patterns of naval apprentice trainees who lived together over a 2-week period. The best predictor of who was chosen as a conversation partner during unstructured free time was past membership in the same recruit company. Thus, these men preferred to interact with someone who was familiar to them (the importance of familiarity is discussed in greater detail in a later section), even though pretest measures showed that they had not been close friends in their earlier, shared environment. The second best predictor was current proximity: Those whose bunks were close together and who sat near one another in their classroom were most likely to spend time talking together.

Proximity effects also have been documented in research on children's friendships. For example, children are more likely to nominate classmates as close friends than nonclassmates (see Gifford-Smith & Brownell, 2003, for a review; see Foster, 2005, for similar findings with university students). The physical structure of the classroom environment also influences friendship formation. In traditionally organized classrooms, children are less likely to form friendships than in less traditional, more open classrooms (see Gifford-Smith & Brownell, 2003). Within classrooms, various grouping arrangements bring children into greater contact with some classmates than others, and this also affects friendship formation. For example, Kubitschek and Hallinan (1998) explored the implications of tracking—grouping students in terms of academic ability—for friendship formation. Tracking was found to influence the formation of friendships through the processes of propinquity, similarity, and status. For example, students in the same track were more likely to have frequent contact with one another. There was also evidence that being in the same track led to perceptions of similarity. Finally, children in higher status tracks were more likely to be sought out for friendships than children in lower status tracks. The authors pointed out that "students have no control over which other students will be in their classroom. Through the effects of propinquity, similarity, and status caused by placement, however, these involuntary classroom associations lead to voluntary positive sentiment relations" (p. 13). Related research has shown that if classroom groupings are competitive and ability based, children's friendships will form on the basis of similar ability. If groupings are cooperative and interest based, children will form friendships based on shared interests (see review by Gifford-Smith & Brownell, 2003).

What is it about workplace and school settings that promotes friendship formation? First, these settings provide opportunities for contact. The greater the amount of contact that is afforded by the environment, the greater the likelihood of friendship formation. Second, as Fine (1986) documented in his research on restaurants as work settings, many tasks require, or even encourage, friendly cooperative behaviors between coworkers. Thus, to the extent that the work or school environment fosters interaction, noncompetitiveness, and interdependence, friendships will be more likely to form (e.g., Aronson & Bridgeman, 1979; Farrell, 1986). Consistent with this notion, Parker (1964) found that women and men in service occupations (e.g., child care and social services) were more likely to have friends in the same line of work than were businesspeople.

Making Friends Online

The research discussed so far demonstrates the importance of proximity—residential, workplace, or classroom—in promoting the formation of friendships. However, computer-mediated communication has opened up a world of new possibilities for friendship formation in the absence of physical proximity. How effective and important an avenue is CMC for the development of friendships? Has CMC replaced face-to-face contact as the primary medium for friendship formation? Unfortunately, research on these questions is relatively sparse. There is an increasing body of literature on online relationships, but most of these investigations have focused on the formation of romantic relationships (see reviews by McKenna, this volume; McKenna & Bargh, 2000; Sprecher, Schwartz, Harvey, & Hatfield, this volume). Studies on friendship have tended to examine the quality of online friendships (e.g., intimacy, satisfaction, and trust) rather than their formation (e.g., Chan & Cheng, 2004; Cheng, Chan, & Tong, 2006; Henderson & Gilding, 2004; Hu, Wood, Smith, & Westbrook, 2004).

There are a few exceptions. In a study of why people join virtual communities, Ridings and Gefen (2004) asked members of bulletin board groups to respond to the question "Why did you join this virtual community?" The responses given included information exchange, followed by "to make friends," exchange of social support, and so on. Moreover, the frequency with which these responses were given varied, depending on the nature of the virtual community. For example, "making friends" was not a prominent reason for joining health and professional groups, but it ranked second for interest, pet, and recreation groups. (Exchange of information was the most common reason given by these groups.) McCown, Fischer, Page, and Homant (2001) administered a questionnaire to a small group of undergraduate students who reported having used the Internet as a way of meeting people. Eighty percent of the participants had formed casual or friendly relationships through the Internet, whereas only 6% reported that they had formed romantic or intimate relationships. Approximately one third of the participants subsequently made offline contact (e.g., telephone conversations or a face-to-face meeting). In their study of Internet newsgroups, McKenna, Green and Gleason (2002) found that half to two-thirds of their sample reported having made some form of off-line contact.

Other researchers have focused on identifying the profile of individuals most likely to rely on CMC for friendship formation. The hypothesis most commonly tested is whether those who are lonely, low in self-esteem, or lacking in social skills are likely to form friendships over the Internet. There is some support for this hypothesis, although the findings are mixed. Donchi and Moore (2004) found that among high school and university students, a greater number of online friendships was associated with lower self-esteem and loneliness, but only for male participants. Female participants showed the opposite pattern. Interestingly, for both genders, a greater number of face-to-face friendships was associated with higher self-esteem and less loneliness. Morahan-Martin and Schumacher (2003) found that lonely undergraduates spent more hours on the Internet, including using e-mail, than nonlonely participants. Lonely users were more likely than nonlonely ones to report using the Internet to meet new people and to interact with others with similar interests. They claimed that going online had made it easier for them to make friends, that they had a network of online friends, and that most of their friends were online. Lonely users also reported that they had more fun with their online than their offline friends. The researchers concluded that the anonymity and lack of face-to-face communication in online interactions may decrease self-consciousness and social anxiety, which can facilitate the formation of online friendships (see McKenna & Bargh, 2000, for a similar argument). However, they also cautioned that normal social functioning may be compromised when social needs are met exclusively through the Internet. Consistent with this cautionary note, Caplan (2005) found that individuals who lacked self-presentation skills preferred online interaction to face-to-face interaction. Moreover, the preference for online interaction was correlated with negative outcomes such as compulsive Internet use.

Other researchers have found that those who are socially competent are more likely to form online friendships, presumably because the Internet offers another domain in which to employ their social skills (e.g., Tyler, 2002). For example, based on their research, McCown and colleagues (2001) concluded that "people who use the Internet to meet people tend to be socially skilled—having strong verbal skills, demonstrating empathy for others, and enjoying close, genuine relationships" (p. 595). Similarly, Peter, Valkenburg, and Schouten (2005) found that in a sample of adolescents, extroverts communicated online more frequently than did introverts. Extroverts also engaged in greater self-disclosure, thereby facilitating the formation of online friendships. Introversion was negatively correlated with frequency of online communication in this study. The exception was introverts who reported that they used the Internet to compensate for social skills deficits—these participants were more likely to form friendships online than introverts who were not motivated to compensate for skills deficits (Peter et al., 2005).

In summary, the small number of studies, coupled with conflicting sets of findings, make it difficult to draw clear conclusions about the role of the Internet in friendship formation. There is some evidence that the "rich get richer" in the sense that the Internet provides socially competent individuals with yet another arena in which to exercise their friendship-making skills. For those who are socially isolated or lacking social competencies, it is not clear whether CMC facilitates or impedes friendship formation. CMC could be construed as a less threatening venue in which social skills can be practiced and rehearsed, thereby providing preparation for face-to-face encounters. On the other hand, CMC may inhibit socially isolated individuals from making the effort to initiate "real-world" friendships. What is clear is that computer-mediated communication is offering another venue for friendship formation— one that may not involve any face-to-face proximity. As Adams (1998) pointed out, one implication is that theories of friendship formation "need to be freed conceptually from grounding in face-to-face contexts so that they can be applied equally as productively to non-proximate contexts" (p. 176).

Social Networks

When people are asked how they met their current friends, a common response is "through other friends and relatives" (Parks & Eggert, 1991; see also Roberto & Scott, 1987; Shulman, 1975). According to Parks and Eggert, an important variable in predicting friendship formation is *communication network proximity*. As the authors put it, "I am more likely to meet the friends of those who are already my friends than to meet the friends of those who are not already my friends" (p. 6). These researchers predicted that pairs of friends would already have been connected through network proximity prior to actually meeting one another. To test this, they had high school and university students nominate a same-sex friend and then list their friend's 12 closest network members. Next, participants were asked to indicate how many of these network members they had met before ever meeting their friend. Approximately two thirds of the participants had been acquainted with at least one person in their friend's network prior to meeting their friend. Nearly half (47.3%) had prior contact with one to three members. The converse is also true; Salzinger (1982) found that people who were in a social network that did not have many connections to other networks had fewer friends.

Social networks also influence friendship formation through members' reactions to friendship choices. In one study, high school students were asked to report on the extent to which their own and their friend's network of family and friends supported the friendship (see Parks & Eggert, 1991). As expected, friendship development was positively correlated with the perceived level of support from these networks. Even adults' friendship choices are governed by the reactions of network members (Allan, 1989). For example, one's romantic partner may discourage the formation of a particular cross-sex friendship. As Allan put it, "[P]atterns of existing ties can push the individual toward some relationships … while more or less subtly discouraging participation in others" (p. 44). Thus, not only are social networks sources of potential friends, but they also influence which friendship ties are most likely to be cultivated.

In summary, a number of environmental factors affect the formation of friendships, including population density; residential, workplace, and school proximity; as well as social network influences. So far, there is little evidence that computer-mediated communication is supplanting face-to-face contact as a source of friendships. As long as people rub shoulders with neighbors, coworkers, classmates, and the like, it seems likely that physical proximity will continue to be important in facilitating friendships.

SITUATIONAL FACTORS

The role of serendipity in the formation of relationships is generally not acknowledged. However, there are a number of "chance" factors that influence whether or not friendships are formed. For example, as will be seen, a friendship will not develop unless both individuals happen to be available for this kind of relationship. A number of other situational factors also play a role in friendship formation. These include the probability of future interaction, the frequency of exposure to a potential friend, and whether the other person has some control over one's outcomes.

Probability of Future Interaction

When two people are engaged in an interaction, they usually know whether it is likely to be a onetime occurrence (e.g., a conversation with a fellow passenger on an airplane) or whether their interactions will be ongoing (e.g., a conversation with a new colleague). Does the expectation of future interaction influence friendship formation? To find out, Darley and Berscheid (1967) presented female participants with neutral information about two female students. They were led to believe that they would be engaging in an intimate conversation with one of the students. Consistent with predictions, participants reported greater liking for the person with whom they expected to interact.

In other classic research, participants were led to expect, or not to expect (depending on the condition), future encounters with an interaction partner (Tyler & Sears, 1977). Pleasant, likable interaction partners were evaluated positively, regardless of the probability of future interaction. However, those who were not as likable were perceived more positively when future interaction was anticipated than when it was not. Subsequent studies have shown that when we expect to have ongoing interactions with another person, we accentuate the positive and downplay the negative to increase the probability that our future encounters will be smooth and enjoyable (Knight & Vallacher, 1981; Lassiter & Briggs, 1990; Miller & Marks, 1982).

Frequency of Exposure and Familiarity

As just discussed, if we anticipate future interactions with a person, we evaluate him or her more positively than if we do not. A question that follows is, does the frequency of interactions actually influence friendship formation? According to Zajonc's (1968) seminal studies on the *mere exposure* effect, the answer is yes. The more often we come in contact with another person, the more we like him or her. Indeed, hundreds of studies have shown that the greater our exposure to another person (or even a photograph), the greater our attraction—even if no interaction actually takes place (see review by Bornstein, 1989; see also Bornstein & D'Agostino, 1992). However, there are some limiting conditions. For example, if we initially dislike someone, repeated exposure can actually lead to less, rather than more, liking (Perlman & Oskamp, 1971).

Research on children's friendships confirms the role of familiarity in friendship formation. For example, there is evidence that children are more likely to form friendships with classmates whom they have previously encountered in another class (see Gifford-Smith & Brownell, 2001, for a review).

Outcome Dependency

Another situational variable that influences friendship formation is outcome dependency—namely, whether another person is in a position to reward or punish us (Berscheid & Graziano, 1979). The classic study in this area, conducted by Berscheid and colleagues (Berscheid, Graziano, Monson, & Dermer, 1976), focused on attraction to potential romantic partners, although the findings are applicable to friendships. These researchers conducted an experiment in which participants watched a videotape of three people having a discussion. Some participants were led to believe that they would be dating one of the individuals in the videotape for a period of 5 weeks. Others were told that they would date the target person once. Still others did not expect to date any of the people on the videotape. Consistent with predictions, attraction and liking increased as outcome dependency increased. In other words, participants who expected that the target individual would affect their lives for the next 5 weeks evaluated the person most positively, followed by those who expected to have only one date, with the least positive ratings assigned by those who did not expect to date any of the target individuals.

More recently, Sunnafrank and Ramirez (2004) developed a model labeled *predicted outcome value theory* in which the central assumption is that people seek to maximize their outcomes. Consequently, they pursue relationships that promise to be most rewarding and restrict the development of relationships with lower reward potential. Moreover, it is posited that decisions about the rewardingness of potential relationships are made very quickly—often in the beginning moments of an encounter. To test these hypotheses, the researchers had participants engage in a short "get-acquainted" interaction with a same-sex classmate. To assess predicted outcome value, participants were asked to forecast how positive a future relationship with their interaction partner would be. As hypothesized, predicted outcome value was positively associated with proximity in the classroom (i.e., choosing a desk close to that of the interaction partner), continued communication with the partner over the semester, long-term attraction, and friendship development. These findings suggest that laboratory-based demonstrations of outcome dependency leading to greater liking or attraction actually translate into "real-world" friendship formation.

Availability

The research presented so far suggests that we are likely to form a friendship with another person if we expect to have ongoing interactions, if there is frequent contact, and if we are dependent on the other person for our outcomes. Yet, these factors do not ensure that a friendship will develop. A pivotal situational variable that comes into play is whether both individuals are available for a friendship—in other words, whether each person has room in his or her life for a new friendship, given each person's preexisting relationships and commitments. According to Berg and Clark (1986), judgments of availability include assessments of accessibility as well as assessments of one's other commitments and alternatives. The former entails judgments about whether there will be opportunities for frequent interacting and engaging in activities together. With regard to the latter, if we already have a full store of friendships or have other time-consuming commitments (e.g., family, work, or studies), we will be less available for new friendships.

Although the role of availability has not received much empirical examination, interview data support the idea that people's level of availability influences the formation of friendships. For example, the middle-aged women interviewed by Gouldner and Strong (1987) reported that there were practical limitations on the number of friendships they could form (see also Allan, 1989). An individual's "friendship budget" depended on how many new friends were desired as well as how many new friendships she thought could be maintained, given the demands of work and family. These kinds of constraints on friendships prompted Brenton's (1974) wry observation that "the graveyard of social relationships is littered with the bones of friendships that might have been" (p. 61).

In short, a friendship will not develop unless a number of situational factors are favorably aligned. However, the convergence of situational factors alone does not guarantee friendship formation. As discussed next, the individuals involved must possess the kinds of characteristics that are considered desirable in a friend.

INDIVIDUAL FACTORS

People obviously do not pursue friendships with everyone they meet. In determining which acquaintanceships will develop into friendships and which will remain acquaintanceships, another class of variables must be considered, namely, individual-level factors. Interestingly, friendship selection appears to be a two-stage process. The first is an exclusion process in which undesirable candidates are eliminated from the pool of possibilities (Rodin, 1982). The second stage is an inclusion process that entails deciding which candidates meet one's friendship criteria. As shall be seen, people who possess particular characteristics (e.g., attractiveness and social skills) are more likely to be selected as friends than those who do not.

Exclusion Criteria: Deciding Who We Do Not Want as a Friend

According to Rodin (1982), exclusion judgments precede inclusion judgments; we decide who we do not want as a friend before deciding who we do want. Rodin identified two kinds of exclusion criteria: dislike and disregard. As she pointed out, "We never like people who meet our dislike criteria regardless of what likable qualities they may also possess" (Rodin, p. 32). In fact, judgments about liking and disliking are asymmetrical. People may attribute likable qualities to disliked people (e.g., we might admit that a disliked colleague has a good sense of humor), but they do not attribute disliked qualities to people who are liked (e.g., we would not describe a liked colleague as obnoxious). According to this view, if an acquaintance exhibits qualities that we dislike, he or she is immediately stricken from the list of potential friends.

The other exclusion criterion is disregard. In this case, people are eliminated from the friendship pool, not because they are disliked, but because they are judged to be unsuitable friendship candidates. People may be disregarded because of their race, education level, age, physical attractiveness, manner of dress, and so on. Rodin (1982) suggested that we use disregard criteria because they "enable us to operate on actuarial or 'best guess' strategies so that our energy and attention are not expended fruitlessly on people we are unlikely to like" (p. 37).

Although it is difficult to test these ideas empirically, interview data are consistent with Rodin's (1982) model. For example, Gouldner and Strong (1987) found evidence of the use of dislike and disregard criteria to narrow down the set of possible friends. More specifically, the women they interviewed reported that they had disregarded potential friends on the basis of dissimilarity of race, education, mode of dress, and, especially, age.

More recent theorizing and research provide insight into how the process of exclusion "works" in thwarting the formation of relationships. According to Denrell's (2005) experience sampling model, once a negative impression of a person has been formed, the probability of future contact (further "experience sampling") is reduced. Consequently, false initial impressions are unlikely to be corrected. On the other hand, positive first impressions increase the probability of future contact, with the result that first impressions are ultimately confirmed or disconfirmed. In an empirical test of these predictions, Denrell (2005) provided participants with information about the friendliness of a hypothetical fellow student, ranging from much unfriendlier than other students on campus to much friendlier than other students. Next, they were asked whether they would want to initiate a conversation with the student, invite the student out for coffee, and so on. Participants were less likely to desire future interaction when their initial impression was negative rather than positive (see Shaw & Steers, 1996, for a conceptually similar study).

Inclusion Criteria: Deciding Who We Want as a Friend

Once the candidates who are judged as unsuitable have been culled, the focus shifts to inclusion criteria, namely, whether the person in question possesses qualities that we desire in a friend. Of course, this is a two-way process—not only do we assess whether a potential friend has desirable qualities, but the other person also assesses whether he or she perceives those same qualities in us. There are a number of characteristics that are associated with friendship desirability, including physical attractiveness, social skills, and responsiveness.

Physical Attractiveness   Although physical attractiveness plays a greater role in the selection of romantic partners than friends (e.g., Shaw & Steers, 1996), there is considerable evidence that attractiveness matters in the formation of same- and other-sex friendships (e.g., Friedman, Riggio, & Casella, 1988; Patzer, 1985). Interestingly, these effects have even been observed in children's friendships. In a classic study, Dion, Berscheid, and Walster (now Hatfield) (1972) found that among nursery school children, the most physically attractive children also were the most popular. Similarly, Kleck, Richardson, and Ronald (1974) found that the friendship choices of children after 2 weeks of intensive social interaction were strongly related to physical attractiveness. A recent meta-analysis confirms that among both adults and children, facial attractiveness is correlated with popularity (Langlois et al., 2000).

Why do we want to form friendships with physically attractive people? There are a number of reasons. According to the "what is beautiful is good" stereotype (Dion, Berscheid, & Walster, 1972), people assume that those who are physically attractive also possess desirable traits (for meta-analytic reviews, see Eagly, Ashmore, Makhijani, & Longo, 1991; Feingold, 1992; Langlois et al., 2000). Recent research shows that this stereotype operates at an implicit, unconscious level (van Leeuwen & Macrae, 2004). That is, people automatically tend to attribute positive qualities to good-looking people and negative qualities to those who are not good-looking.

We also assume that physically attractive people are similar to us in terms of personality and attitudes (e.g., Horton, 2003; Patzer, 1985). As will be discussed later, similarity is a major determinant of friendship formation. Finally, it has been suggested that attractive people tend to experience positive reactions from others, which contributes to the development of self-confidence and competent social skills. As a result, interactions with physically attractive people are more pleasant and enjoyable than with those who are physically unattractive (e.g., Zakahi & Duran, 1984). Not all research has supported this view (see Brehm, 1985). However, the conclusion reached in a recent meta-analysis was that physically attractive adults are, in fact, more extroverted, popular, intelligent, and self-confident, and have more dating experience, than their less attractive counterparts (Langlois et al., 2000). Similarly, attractive children are more popular and intelligent, and score higher on measures of adjustment, than less attractive children. Thus, when it comes to forming friendships, physically attractive people are at an advantage for a number of reasons.

Social Skills   According to Cook (1977), making friends is a skilled performance much like learning to play a sport or drive a car. Indeed, studies conducted with children and adults have consistently found that those with good social skills have more friends and interact more positively with others compared to those whose skills are deficient (e.g., Argyle, Lefebvre, & Cook, 1974; Asher, Renshaw, & Geraci, 1980; Blieszner & Roberto, 2004; Gest, Graham-Bermann, & Hartup, 2001; Gifford-Smith & Brownell, 2003; Gottman, Gonso, & Rasmussen, 1975; Samter, 2003). For example, Riggio (1986) found that socially skilled university students reported a greater number of daily school acquaintances and close friends than did those who were less socially skilled. In a follow-up laboratory study, students had a brief conversation with two confederates. Once again, the better a participant's social skills, the more the confederates liked him or her.

Interestingly, social skills may be most important in the early stages of friendship formation. Shaver, Furman, and Buhrmester (1985) administered a social skills scale to university students shortly before they entered university and several times throughout their first year. Social skills emerged as an important determinant of relationship satisfaction upon arrival at university. Later in the year, as the students' social networks stabilized, social skills did not predict satisfaction with relationships as strongly. Shaver and colleagues (1985) also found that different kinds of social skills were important at different phases of friendship development. Skills at initiating interactions (e.g., introducing yourself) were most important in the early stages, when the students were unacquainted with their peers; self-disclosure skills were most important once friendships had been established. Other researchers have reported similar findings (e.g., Buhrmester, Furman, Wittenberg, & Reis, 1988; Cook, 1977; Spitzberg & Cupach, 1989). In the words of Buhrmester et al. (1988), "[I]nitiation competence may be important in the beginning of relationships, but may lessen in impact once a relationship is well-established; instead competence in providing warmth and support becomes important" (p. 1006).

Responsiveness   An individual characteristic that is closely related to social skill competence is responsiveness. Research on responsiveness generally takes the form of having participants interact with a confederate who behaves either responsively or nonresponsively. The dependent variable is typically liking or ratings of the confederate's desirability as a friend. For example, Davis and Perkowitz (1979) trained a confederate to either answer (responsive condition) or not answer (nonresponsive condition) most of the questions asked by the participants, or, in a variation, provide a response that was either related (responsive condition) or unrelated (nonresponsive condition) to the topic that the participant had chosen for discussion. Participants reported greater liking for the confederate and saw greater prospects for a friendship in the responsive than the nonresponsive conditions. Interestingly, in the responsive conditions, participants also believed that the confederate liked them more and was more interested in them.

In other studies, responsiveness has been operationalized as showing interest and concern during an interaction. Again, these studies show that responsive interaction partners are liked more than nonresponsive partners (e.g., Berg & Archer, 1983; Godfrey, Jones, & Lord, 1986; Miller, Berg, & Archer, 1983). According to Berg (1987), responsiveness conveys liking and an interest and concern in the other, which has the effect of eliciting self-disclosure from the other. (As will be discussed later, self-disclosure is one of the critical factors in friendship formation.)

More than 70 years ago, Dale Carnegie (1936) observed that "you can make more friends in two months by becoming interested in other people than you can in two years by trying to get other people interested in you" (p. 58). The research suggests that those who are seeking friendships would do well to heed Carnegie's advice!

In conclusion, there are a number of characteristics that are associated with friendship desirability. To the extent that another person is physically attractive, socially skilled, and responsive, we will be motivated to seek out a friendship with him or her. Conversely, other people will be inclined to seek us out as potential friends if we possess these qualities.

DYADIC FACTORS

Friendships are dyadic relationships. Thus, analyses of friendship formation must take into account not only the individual characteristics of each person but also the interplay between them. As shall be seen, friendships are more likely to form when liking is reciprocal, when self-disclosure is mutual, and when the two individuals are similar to one another. Recent research also suggests that friendships are more likely to "get off the ground" if the two people share a humorous experience.

Reciprocity of Liking

"How I like to be liked, and what I do to be liked!" These words, penned by the 19th-century English writer Charles Lamb, are as applicable today as they were 200 years ago. In a classic experiment, Backman and Secord (1959) had groups of same-sex strangers engage in weekly discussions over a 6-week period. Before the first meeting, participants were told that based on personality information gathered earlier, the researchers could predict which group members would like him or her. (The names of the group members were actually randomly selected.) As expected, participants most liked the group members who they believed liked them. However, this effect held only for the first discussion. Presumably, subsequent discussions provided participants with more veridical information about which group members actually did or did not like them. These findings were replicated in subsequent research, and limiting conditions have been identified (see Berscheid & Walster, 1978). For example, reciprocity of liking is most pronounced when one is making initial judgments about another person.

Interestingly, the perception that another person likes us may cause us to behave in ways that confirm that expectation. Curtis and Miller (1986) conducted a landmark study in which participants were led to believe that their interaction partner either liked or disliked them. Those who believed they were liked engaged in more intimate self-disclosure, were more pleasant, and demonstrated fewer distancing behaviors than those who believed they were disliked. Importantly, these behaviors had the effect of eliciting liking from the interaction partner. Thus, when another person likes us, we tend to like them in return. Even the belief that another person may like us produces liking because it puts in motion a self-fulfilling prophecy whereby we behave in ways that produce the liking that we initially expected.

Self-Disclosure

According to social penetration theory (Altman & Taylor, 1973; see also Derlega, Winstead, & Greene, this volume), when we first meet another person, we typically disclose only superficial information about ourselves. If an interaction is pleasant and rewarding, we will continue to increase the breadth and depth of our disclosures until we eventually reveal virtually everything about ourselves on virtually every topic. On the other hand, if exchanges become unpleasant or uncomfortable, we will return to our earlier, more superficial level of disclosure.

One implication of this theory is that we should be attracted to people who engage in intimate self-disclosure because revealing personal information indicates that they like us and desire intimacy with us. Indeed, many studies have demonstrated that people who engage in intimate self-disclosure are liked more than those who disclose nonintimately (see Collins & Miller, 1994, for a review). To give a recent example, Clark and colleagues (Clark et al., 2004) had opposite-sex strangers engage in an 8-minute conversation about life as an undergraduate. The greater the self-disclosure from the interaction partner, the greater the attraction (e.g., liking, and belief that the other could become a friend) reported by the participants (Clark et al., 2004). Interestingly, research by Aron, Melinat, Aron, Vallone, and Bator (1997) has shown that even "forced" self-disclosure leads to feelings of closeness. In this research, stranger dyads engaged in a structured self-disclosure process in which each person was required to reveal increasingly more intimate information about him or herself. Participants in the control group disclosed only neutral information. Those who engaged in intimate self-disclosure subsequently reported feeling closer to their partner than those who engaged in nonintimate disclosure (Aron et al., 1997).

Aron and colleagues' (1997) findings imply that not only do we like those who self-disclose to us, but we also like those to whom we have self-disclosed. The effect of engaging in self-disclosure (rather than being on the receiving end) was examined in a study by Vittengl and Holt (2000). They had same-sex strangers participate in a 10-minute "get-acquainted" discussion. Self-disclosure on the part of self was positively correlated with attraction to the other (e.g., "I think he or she could be a friend of mine"). Thus, in general, the greater another person's self-disclosure, the more we like him or her. We also like those to whom we have self-disclosed.

At the early stages of relationships, it is also important for disclosures to be reciprocal. If Person A reveals something intimate about herself, Person B needs to reciprocate with an equally intimate disclosure. Indeed, there is evidence that reciprocity of disclosure is associated with greater liking for an interaction partner (Berg & Archer, 1980). Rotenberg and Mann (1986) found that the relation between disclosure reciprocity and liking was already evident among sixth graders, although not in younger children (i.e., second and fourth graders).

Reciprocity is considered important in establishing trust in a relationship (Altman, 1973). Once trust is established, it is not necessary for each self-disclosure to be reciprocated in kind, as demonstrated in a classic study by Derlega, Wilson, and Chaikin (1976). In this study, participants received notes varying in their degree of intimacy from either a friend or a stranger. The intimacy of disclosures from a stranger tended to be reciprocated, but not the intimacy of disclosures from a friend (although see Levesque, Steciuk, & Ledley, 2002, for somewhat different findings). Derlega and colleagues (1976) suggested that when a friendship is established, there is an assumption of reciprocity over the long haul. It therefore becomes less important that reciprocity occur in each specific interaction.

Finally, there is evidence that disclosures that are too intimate—revealing "too much too soon"—are not likely to be reciprocated and can result in dislike for the discloser (e.g., Archer & Berg, 1978; Archer & Burleson, 1980; Cozby, 1972; Rubin, 1975; Wortman, Adesman, Herman, & Greenberg, 1976).

Thus, the results of countless laboratory studies support the idea that self-disclosure that is reciprocal and gradually increases intimacy is associated with closeness and liking. Does real-life friendship formation mirror the processes that have been identified as important in laboratory studies? To find out, Miell and Duck (1986) conducted in-depth interviews with first-term university students, asking them questions such as "How would you gather information about a new partner?" and "How would you decide whether or not to develop a friendship?" Participants reported reciprocating self-disclosures, increasing the breadth and depth of interactions if early signs look promising, being careful not to reveal "too much too soon," and so on. The findings from these accounts of friendship formation were corroborated in a study of actual friendship formation (Duck & Miell, 1986). In this study, participants kept daily records of their most significant interactions with friends or acquaintances for the first two semesters of the academic year (an 18-week period). Early on, topics of conversation tended to be superficial. Later in the year, the frequency of personal self-disclosures increased. Thus, the self-disclosure processes that have been demonstrated as facilitative of friendship formation in the laboratory are confirmed in people's reports of the strategies that they use to form friendships (Miell & Duck, 1986) as well as in their "real-world" experiences of friendship formation (Duck & Miell, 1986). Recent evidence suggests that self-disclosure also follows a process of increasing in depth and breadth in the formation of online relationships (see Derlega et al., this volume).

Shared Fun and Humor

In a review of the literature on friendship interaction skills across the life span, Samter (2003) noted that among children, two of the communicative competencies that facilitate friendship formation and maintenance are being fun and entertaining and having a good sense of humor. Having fun and playing together also comprise a criterion used to identify friendships among toddlers and preschoolers (see Howes, 1996). The importance of humor and fun in adult friendships has received little attention. There are a few exceptions, however. Planalp and Benson (1992) examined the dimensions that people use to discriminate between the conversations of acquaintances versus those of friends. Friends' conversations were more informal, relaxed, and friendly than acquaintances' conversations. Friends were also more likely to engage in joking and teasing. Jerrome (1984) observed the interactions of a friendship group composed of middle-aged and older women, and was struck by the amount of joking and laughing. Other studies have shown that the amount of fun and enjoyment experienced is a significant predictor of friendship satisfaction for women and men (Hays & Oxley, 1986; Jones, 1991).

Thus, there is some evidence that once friendships are established, shared laughter and fun are important in maintaining the relationship. However, these studies do not speak to the issue of whether humor and fun are important in establishing friendships. This issue was examined in a recent study by Fraley and Aron (2004), who hypothesized that a shared humorous experience during a first encounter between strangers would promote feelings of closeness. To test this idea, pairs of same-sex strangers engaged in a variety of activities that were intended to either evoke humor or not. For example, participants in the nonhumor condition played catch. Those in the humor condition did so while one person of the pair was blindfolded. Consistent with predictions, those who shared a humorous experience reported greater closeness to their partner than those who did not. The authors also examined several mediators of this relation, including self-disclosure and acceptance, self-expansion (e.g., sense of awareness, and feeling one has a new perspective because of the partner), and the distraction from the initial awkwardness that typically occurs during first encounters. Self-expansion and distraction were found to at least partly account for the relation between shared humor and closeness.

Similarity

One of the most widely researched predictors of friendship formation is similarity. Indeed, the "rule of homogamy" has been described as "one of the most basic principles that has come from the study of interpersonal attraction" (Brehm, 1985, p. 70). As shown in Table 2.1, similarity effects have been examined in a number of different domains. There is considerable evidence that people are likely to become friends with those who are similar to them in terms of demographic characteristics (e.g., age, physical health, education, religion, and family background), residential proximity, social status, physical attractiveness, and so on. Most of these effects have been obtained in studies with children and adolescents as well (see, e.g., Bleiszner & Roberts, 2004; Kandel, 1978a, 1978b).

The classic domain in which similarity effects have been investigated is attitude similarity (Byrne, 1971; Byrne & Clore, 1970). Strong similarity effects have been found in this area and for the related construct of value similarity (see Table 2.1). Similarity effects also are pronounced for activity preferences (e.g., Davis, 1981; Erwin, 1985; Werner & Parmelee, 1979). In fact, Werner and Parmelee found that friends were more similar in terms of activity preferences than attitudes. In the same vein, Davis found that the similarity–attraction relation was stronger for interests and hobbies than political views. Davis' explanation was that similarity in these areas has greater implications for interaction (i.e., interactions will be pleasant and enjoyable if friends have similar interests).

Interestingly, there is little evidence that people become friends on the basis of personality similarity, although Haselager, Hartup, van Lieshout, and Riksen-Walraven (1998) found evidence of similarity in terms of shyness and depressive symptoms among schoolchildren. However, similarity effects have been found for more relationally oriented traits such as the application of personal constructs, cognitive complexity (e.g., emphasizing the affective and relational aspects of interactions, and valuing affective expression skill), and social and communication skills (see Table 2.1).

There is one domain in which similarity is important for children's and adolescents' friendships, namely, similarity in terms of prosocial and antisocial behaviors, particularly the latter (Haselager et al., 1998). In fact, one of the major differences between adults' and children's friendships is that children are more likely than adults to form friendships based on similarity in terms of aggression and antisocial behavior (e.g., drug and alcohol use). For example, there is evidence that aggressive children seek out other aggressive children as early as preschool and that this tendency becomes stronger with age (see e.g., Gifford-Smith & Brownell, 2003; Haselager et al., 1998). In adolescence, friends' similarity in terms of deviant or antisocial behavior is a strong predictor of friendship (see Fehr, 1996; Gifford-Smith & Brownell, 2003; Haselager et al., 1998; Kandel, 1978a, 1978b). These findings have been interpreted in terms of Hartup's

TABLE 2.1   Relation Between Similarity and Friendship

Type of Similarity	Study	Participants	Results
Demographic Variables	Johnson (1989)	Middle-class adults and two of their close friends, two acquaintances, and two nonfriends	Nonfriends were less similar than acquaintances and friends in terms of income, parental status, and age.
	Lederberg, Rosenblatt, Vandell, and Chapin (1987)	Hearing and deaf children (ages 3–5)	Acquaintances were less similar in age than long-term friends. Acquaintances were less similar than temporary and long-term friends in terms of ethnicity and gender.
	Hill and Stull (1981)	Same-sex college roommates	Roommates who chose one another were more similar in terms of year in college than those who were assigned to one another.
			Among male roommate pairs who chose one another, similarity in year of college was correlated with liking and staying together as roommates.
			No significant effects for similarity of major area of study, religious background, age, race, and father's education.
	Verbrugge (1977)	1966 Detroit Area Survey study sample (adult men) and 1971 Altneustadt Survey (West Germany; adult women and men)	Of participants' three closest friends, greatest similarity was found in terms of age, marital status, sex, political preference (Altneustadt sample), religious preference, education, and residential mobility for first-named (best) friends, followed by second- and then third-named friend.
			Similarity in terms of occupation, employment status, and occupational prestige relatively equal across the three friends.
	Hamm (2000)	European American, African American, and Asian American high school students	Similarity in terms of academic orientation (especially for African Americans). Some evidence of similarity in terms of ethnic identity.
	Foster (2005)	College students	Students who were similar in terms of academic ability were more likely to become friends. Students who were originally from the same geographic region were more likely to become friends.
	Haselager, Hartup, van Lieshout, and Riksen-Walraven (1998)	Children (grades 4–8)	Friends were more similar than nonfriends in terms of social status (acceptance and rejection).
Physical Attractiveness	Cash and Derlega (1978)	College students	Friends were more similar than nonfriends in terms of physical attractiveness.
Attitude Similarity	Byrne (1971)	College students	Greater attraction was reported to a hypothetical target whose attitudes were portrayed as similar, rather than dissimilar, to those of the participant.
	Werner and Parmelee (1979)	Same-sex pairs (college students)	Friends and strangers did not differ in terms of attitude similarity.
Values	Hill and Stull (1981)	College roommate pairs	Female roommates (chosen and assigned) high in value similarity were more likely to remain roommates (not significant for male pairs).
	Curry and Kenny (1974)	8-person groups of college residents	Both actual and perceived value similarity were correlated with attraction over time.

(continued)

TABLE 2.1 (CONTINUED)   Relation Between Similarity and Friendship

Type of Similarity	Study	Participants	Results
			Perceived value similarity had the greatest effect on attraction early on; actual similarity assumed a greater importance in later interactions.
	Davis (1981)	College students	Participants were more attracted to a hypothetical person portrayed as similar to them in terms of *interests and hobbies* and *basic values (e.g., morals, religion)* than someone similar to them in terms of *political opinions* and *opinions about matters of fact.*
Leisure and Activity Preferences	Werner and Parmelee (1979)	Same-sex pairs (college students)	Friends were more similar than strangers in terms of activity preferences.
	Johnson (1989)	Middle-aged adults	Nonfriends were more similar than acquaintances and friends in terms of leisure activities.
	Davis (1981)	College students	Participants were more attracted to a hypothetical person portrayed as similar to them in terms of *interests and hobbies* and *basic values (e.g., morals, religion)* than someone similar to them in terms of *political opinions* and *opinions about matters of fact.*
Personality	Curry and Kenny (1974)	8-person groups of college residents, initially unacquainted	No relationship between personality similarity and attraction over time.
Personal Constructs	Neimeyer and Neimeyer (1981)	10-person groups of college students, initially unacquainted	Dyads high in functional similarity (i.e., who applied constructs in a similar way when rating other group members) were more attracted to one another than dyads low in functional similarity.
	Neimeyer and Neimeyer (1983)	10-person groups of adults arrested for drunken driving, initially unacquainted	Dyads high in structural similarity (i.e., who showed similar differentiation and organization of personal constructs when rating group members) were more attracted to one another than medium- or low-similarity dyads (when tested after 18 weeks of interaction; these effects were not evident after 4 weeks).
	Haselager et al. (1998)	Children (grades 4–8)	Friends used more similar systems of interpersonal constructs than nonfriends.
Cognitive Complexity	Burleson, Kunkel, and Birch (1994, Study 1)	College students	Some evidence that participants were more attracted to a hypothetical target person who was similar versus dissimilar to them in cognitive complexity.
	Burleson, Kunkel, and Szolwinski (1997)	College students	Same results as Burleson et al. (1994), reported above.
Social Skills	Burleson (1994)	Children (grades 1 and 3)	Some evidence that children were more attracted to peers who were similar versus dissimilar to them in terms of social skills (especially skills reflecting emotional sensitivity and responsiveness).
	Howes (1996)	Children (preschoolers and toddlers) in child care	Toddler-age friends were more similar in terms of social skills than preschool friends or nonfriend dyads

Note: Portions of this table are based on Fehr (1996, Table 4.3 and Table 4.4).

(1996) normative salience hypothesis, namely, the idea that similarities between friends are governed by the importance of an attribute in determining reference group membership or social reputations. As Haselager et al. (1998) explained, "[A]ntisocial behavior probably has more to do with determining who a child associates with and the nature of the child's reputation than any other attribute" (p. 1206). Also consistent with the normative salience hypothesis, Hamm (2000) found that among ethnically diverse high school students, participants selected more similar friends when they more strongly endorsed the dimension in question (e.g., high academic orientation or low substance use). Overall, there is substantial evidence that in many domains, similarity is associated with the development of friendships. The only area in which similarity effects seem to be weak or nonexistent is personality similarity. It seems to matter less that our friends share our traits than that they share our attitudes, values, social competencies, and leisure preferences. Finally, the kind of similarity that matters most is at least somewhat dependent on the friends' life stages.

Why are we more likely to form friendships with similar, rather than dissimilar, others? The most common explanation is that our views are validated by interacting with someone who shares them (e.g., Berscheid & Walster, 1978; Byrne, 1971). Put another way, we feel more confident that we are "right" in our thinking if we encounter someone else who thinks just like us. Another explanation focuses on the rewards of interaction. As Berscheid and Walster explained, "If a person feels as we do about things, we feel fairly confident that it would be rewarding to spend some time with that person; if a person despises everything we cherish, we might well be apprehensive about associating with the person" (p. 66). As already mentioned, the finding that we are likely to be similar to friends in terms of activity preferences is consistent with this view. Similarly, Burleson and colleagues (Burleson, 1994; Burleson, Kunkel, & Szolwinski, 1997; see Table 2.1) maintained that interaction is more likely to be pleasurable when partners are similar in terms of social and communication skills. It should be noted that the self-validation and the rewards-of-interaction explanations are generally both accepted in the literature, although they have not been exempt from criticism (see Aboud & Mendelson, 1996).

Recently, two other explanations have been proposed for similarity effects in friendship formation, namely, an existential and an evolutionary account. To begin with the former, Pinel, Long, Landau, Alexander, and Pyszczynski (2006) recently introduced the concept of *I-sharing*, defined as the "subjective experience of having one's self-as-subject (i.e., one's I) merge with that of at least one other person" (p. 244). They posited that I-sharing contributes to feelings of attraction and connectedness to others via the alleviation of existential isolation. These researchers conducted a series of studies in which they manipulated I-sharing and similarity. To create I-sharing, participants were led to believe that their interaction partner shared their opinion of a particular band. In the non-I-sharing condition, the partner was presented as not sharing the participant's opinion. To create similarity, participants were told that their interaction partner came from their hometown; in the dissimilarity condition, the partner was described as a student from another country. Consistent with predictions, I-sharing promoted liking for the interaction partner. Moreover, this effect was strong enough to override similarity effects, such that participants expressed greater liking for a dissimilar I-sharer than for a similar non-I-sharer.

Rushton and Bons (2005) recently proposed an evolutionary explanation for similarity effects. They administered demographic, attitudinal, and personality scales to twin pairs who completed the scales for self, spouse, and same-sex best friend. As expected, twins showed evidence of similarity on these measures. However, remarkably, it was found that spouses and friends were just as similar to the target as his or her twin. The authors concluded that people are genetically inclined to choose as social partners those who resemble themselves at a genetic level. In their words:

> If you like, become friends with, come to the aid of, and mate with those people who are most genetically similar to yourself, you are simply trying to ensure that your own segment of the gene pool will be safely maintained and eventually transmitted to future generations. (Rushton & Bons, p. 559)

In conclusion, there are a number of dyadic factors that promote the formation of friendships. Potential friends must like each other. Potential friends must engage in a process of mutual self-disclosure in which the intimacy information revealed gradually increases over time. Potential friends also should have fun together. And, finally, potential friends should be similar in myriad ways.

CONVERGENCE OF ENVIRONMENTAL, SITUATIONAL, INDIVIDUAL, AND DYADIC FACTORS

The central thesis of this chapter is that multiple factors converge in the formation of friendships. In this last section, I present studies that have included some, if not all, of the categories of friendship formation factors discussed thus far. The advantage of including multiple factors in a single study is that it enables conclusions about which factors are most important in the friendship formation process. In a large-scale study, Knapp and Harwood (1977) combed the friendship literature for predictors of friendship formation and identified 39 variables. These included environmental factors (e.g., proximity), situational factors (i.e., willingness to spend time together [accessibility]), individual factors (e.g., being considerate and understanding), and dyadic factors (e.g., attitudinal similarity, demographic similarity, reciprocal self-disclosure, and the expectation of being liked). Five hundred participants rated the importance of these variables in the formation of an intimate, same-sex friendship. The variables that were regarded as most critical were largely dyadic in nature, namely, attitudinal similarity, the expectation of being liked, and reciprocal intimate disclosure. The situational factor of accessibility also received high ratings. In a conceptually similar study, Sprecher (1998; see also Sprecher & Felmlee, this volume) extracted a list of predictors of attraction from the literature and asked participants to rate the extent to which these factors applied to the initial attraction that they experienced in either a romantic relationship or a friendship. The predictors included environmental factors (e.g., proximity, and support from significant others), situational factors (familiarity), individual characteristics (e.g., other's warmth and kindness, desirable personality, and physical attractiveness), and dyadic factors (e.g., similarity of attitudes and values, similarity of interests and leisure activities, and reciprocal liking). All four categories of variables were rated as important, with the highest weighting given to individual-level factors (e.g., other's warmth and kindness) and dyadic qualities (e.g., similarity and reciprocal liking). Environmental factors were rated as least important. Sprecher (1998) noted that "these factors (e.g., proximity, reactions of friends and family) may be more important for attraction than suggested by 'insider' reports if their effects occur outside of people's awareness" (p. 297).

Aron, Dutton, Aron, and Iverson (1989) also relied on retrospective accounts of friendship development, but in their research, participants provided open-ended accounts of a "falling in friendship" experience. These accounts were coded for the presence of 11 predictors of attraction, taken from the literature (Aron et al., 1989). Dyadic factors (e.g., reciprocal liking, and similarity) were paramount. The individual-level factor "desirable characteristics" (e.g., physical attractiveness) also was mentioned frequently, as was the environmental factor "proximity".

Other researchers have tracked the formation of real-world friendships in order to examine which factors are most predictive (e.g., Berg, 1984; Hays, 1984, 1985). Participants in these studies are typically university students whose friendship formation patterns are followed over the course of their first year. A consistent finding in these studies is that dyadic factors (e.g., self-disclosure and similarity) play a crucial role in friendship formation. However, environmental factors (e.g., proximity) and situational factors (e.g., availability) are also important in facilitating the formation of friendships. To give a recent example, Foster (2005) conducted a complex analysis of the role of environmental factors (e.g., same residence or same class) and dyadic factors (e.g., similarity in terms of academic ability, or race) in the formation of friendships among first-year university students. Based on her findings, she concluded that "unobserved proclivities and luck (including initial campus location) play a starring role in determining whether friendships form, but … observable social similarities and ability similarity are also significant factors" (Foster, 2005, p. 1462).

Thus, multivariate studies support the importance of environmental, situational, individual, and, especially, dyadic factors in the formation of friendships. When all of these factors converge, not only is it likely that we will "catch" a new friend, but it is also likely that this new friend will be "one that's fit to make an old one out of."

FUTURE DIRECTIONS

There is still much to be learned about the process of friendship formation. In terms of environmental influences, perhaps the most pressing issue is to better understand the importance of physical proximity. The advent of computer-mediated communication calls into question what has been regarded a major prerequisite of friendship formation, namely, face-to-face contact. Although there is some research on the formation of online friendships, the most fundamental question has not been addressed: Does the process of forming friendships online differ from the process of forming "real-life" friendships? Several other questions merit investigation: Is it necessary for people to eventually meet face-to-face, or can friendships be developed and maintained exclusively online? A related question is whether the quality of friendships formed online differs from that of friendships that have been formed through face-to-face contact. Research to address these questions seems crucial, given the access to potential friends that is afforded by computer-mediated communication.

With regard to individual-level factors, it would be worthwhile to direct future research attention to the issue of how friendship formation differs throughout the life course. Although this question has received some attention (see, e.g., review by Blieszner & Roberto, 2004), there is much to be learned about how a retired person, for example, goes about forming friendships and how that might differ from how an entering university student goes about making friends. It also will be important in future research to explore whether the characteristics that are considered desirable in a friend (e.g., physical attractiveness, and social skills) are dependent on sociohistorical and cultural contexts. Interestingly, recent reviews of the facial attractiveness literature have shown that there is greater agreement across cultures on what constitutes beauty than had been previously thought (see, e.g., review by Dion, 2002, and meta-analysis by Langlois et al., 2000). However, this research does not speak to the issue of whether attractiveness is valued equally in friends, across cultures. More generally, a goal for future research is to determine which, if any, desired qualities in a friend are universal and which are more culturally specific.

There are also a number of dyadic issues that merit further investigation. The role of shared humor and fun in facilitating friendship formation is a particularly promising avenue for future research. For example, it would seem important to determine whether the closeness reported by participants in Fraley and Aron's (2004) study would actually translate into the development of a friendship. On another note, in their daily diary study of friendship formation, Miell and Duck (1986) observed a number of phenomena that have not been addressed in theories of friendship formation. One of their findings was that friendship development was marked by periods of uncertainty and doubt, rather than following a neat, linear progression. This is a topic that should be probed further, including formally tracking friendship trajectories, gathering data on periods of uncertainty, noting "turning points" in the development of the friendship, and so on. Recent research by Johnson, Wittenberg, Villagran, Mazur, and Villagran (2003) on turning points in communication among casual, close, and best friendships provides a promising starting point. Miell and Duck also found that participants seemed to underestimate the extent to which they could control the course of a friendship, perceiving that the fate of their relationship is in the hands of the other. Such findings beg for further conceptual development on friendship formation, and, of course, further research to refine and inform theoretical formulations.

Finally, although it is assumed that friendship formation is a dyadic processes, research in this area has yet to adopt the kind of methodology (e.g., gathering data from both members of a friendship pair) and statistical analyses that would allow more definitive conclusions to be drawn. The application of Kenny, Kashy, and Cook's (2006) actor-partner interdependence (applicable to dyads) and social relations models (applicable to dyadic interactions that occur in a group context) seems particularly promising. These models allow researchers to determine which effects are attributable to the actor (the self), to the partner, and to the actor-partner interaction (Kenny et al., 2006). Levesque et al.'s (2002) analysis of self-disclosure illustrates the fruitfulness of this approach.

Kenny and colleagues (2006) also have developed sophisticated analyses that can disentangle sources of interdependence between friends—whether dyadic effects are due to compositional effects (i.e., the two individuals may already have been similar prior to forming a friendship), partner effects (the traits or behaviors of one friend affect the other's outcomes), mutual influence (both friends' outcomes directly influence each other), or common fate (the two friends are exposed to the same causal factors, such as living in a crowded dormitory; see Kenny et al., 2006). The use of dyadic data analytic techniques will allow this area of research to take significant strides forward.

CONCLUSION

In conclusion, friendship formation is a complex, multifaceted process. The physical environment determines whether or not people come into contact with one another. Situational factors, such as the frequency of interactions and one's availability for friendships, are also important determinants. In addition, friendship formation is governed by the characteristics of each of the individuals involved. Those who possess desirable qualities, particularly those pertaining to social competence, are more likely to successfully develop friendships than those who do not. Finally, given that a friendship is, by definition, a relationship, it is perhaps not surprising that the lion's share of the variance in friendship formation is accounted for by dyadic-level variables. People are more likely to become friends when they like each other, when they engage in reciprocal self-disclosure that gradually increases in intimacy, when they have fun together, and when they are similar to one another in a number of ways.

A final question that might be asked is whether the research reviewed in this chapter points the way to a "grand theory" of friendship formation. Although a grand theory is still premature, the research that has been conducted offers some promising leads. Turning first to environmental factors, these might best be conceptualized as exogenous factors that "set the stage" for the formation of friendships. The worlds of two individuals have to intersect in order for a friendship to develop. This intersection occurs when people inhabit the same workplace or residence hall or have social network members in common. It can also occur when two people navigate the same websites (*cyberspace proximity*). Thus, coming into contact with another person—either in person or via computer-mediated communication—is a necessary condition for friendship. However, it is not sufficient.

The same holds true for situational factors, which can be thought of as another class of exogenous variable. Friendships are likely to form when the situation affords frequent contact, when one person's outcomes are dependent on the other, and when each individual "happens" to have the time and resources to invest in a new friendship. In other words, the circumstances in which potential friends find themselves play a role in determining whether or not a friendship is formed. Thus, the optimal alignment of situational factors also is a necessary—but, once again, not sufficient—condition for the development of friendship.

Individual-level factors can be construed as endogenous. The display of desirable personal characteristics may not be absolutely necessary for the formation of friendships—some unattractive, socially unskilled, unresponsive people seem to have friends. However, individual factors certainly can facilitate the formation of friendships. The research is clear that friendships are much more likely to be formed with those who are attractive and socially competent than with those who are not.

Finally, the most critical ingredient in friendship formation is another endogenous factor, namely, the nature of the interaction between the two individuals. Indeed, dyadic factors emerge as most important both in retrospective reports and in studies of actual friendship formation (cited earlier). It takes two to have a friendship. One can imagine a situation in which environmental factors bring two people into contact with one another, the circumstances in which they interact are salutary, and they are both very nice. However, unless these people share important similarities, like each other, enjoy being together, and engage in the kind of self-disclosure that promotes intimacy, it seems unlikely that a friendship will form. Thus, in order for a friendship to develop, exogenous factors are necessary to set the stage, but it is the endogenous factors that determine whether or not there are actors, engaged with one another, on it.

AUTHOR NOTE

Preparation of this chapter was supported by a grant from the Social Sciences and Humanities Research Council of Canada. I am grateful to Cheryl Harasymchuk, Justin Friesen, and Lorissa Martens for their assistance. Thank you also to the editors and an anonymous reviewer for their incisive feedback on an earlier version of this piece.

REFERENCES

Aboud, F. E., & Mendelson, M. J. (1996). Determinants of friendship selection and quality: Developmental perspectives. In W. M. Bukowski, A. F. Newcomb, & W. W. Hartup (Eds.), *The company they keep: Friendship in childhood and adolescence* (pp. 87–112). New York: Cambridge University Press.

Adams, R. G. (1998). The demise of territorial determinism: Online friendships. In R. G. Adams & G. Allan (Eds.), *Placing friendship in context* (pp. 153–182). Cambridge: Cambridge University Press.

Allan, G. (1989). *Friendship: Developing a sociological perspective.* London: Harvester Wheatsheaf.

Altman, I. (1973). Reciprocity of interpersonal exchange. *Journal for the Theory of Social Behaviour, 3,* 249–261.

Altman, I., & Taylor, D. A. (1973). *Social penetration: The development of interpersonal relationships.* New York: Holt, Rinehart & Winston.

Archer, R. L., & Berg, J. H. (1978). Disclosure reciprocity and its limits: A reactance analysis. *Journal of Experimental Social Psychology, 14,* 527–540.

Archer, R. L., & Burleson, J. A. (1980). The effects of timing of self-disclosure on attraction and reciprocity. *Journal of Personality and Social Psychology, 38,* 120–130.

Argyle, M., Lefebvre, L., & Cook, M. (1974). The meaning of five patterns of gaze. *European Journal of Social Psychology, 4,* 125–136.

Aron, A. P., Dutton, D. G., Aron, E. N., & Iverson, A. (1989). Experiences of falling in love. *Journal of Social and Personal Relationships, 6,* 243–257.

Aron, A. P., Melinat, E., Aron, E. N., Vallone, R. D., & Bator, R. J. (1997). The experimental generation of interpersonal closeness: A procedure and some preliminary findings. *Personality and Social Psychology Bulletin, 23,* 363–377.

Aronson, E., & Bridgeman, D. (1979). Jigsaw groups and the desegregated classroom: In pursuit of common goals. *Personality and Social Psychology Bulletin, 5,* 438–446.

Asher, S. R., Renshaw, P. D., & Geraci, R. L. (1980). Children's friendships and social competence. *International Journal of Psycholinguistics, 7,* 27–39.

Backman, C. W., & Secord, P. F. (1959). The effect of perceived liking on interpersonal attraction. *Human Relations, 12,* 379–384.

Berg, J. H. (1984). Development of friendship between roommates. *Journal of Personality and Social Psychology, 46,* 346–356.

Berg, J. H. (1987). Responsiveness and self-disclosure. In V. J. Derlega & J. H. Berg (Eds.), *Self-disclosure: Theory, research, and therapy* (pp. 101–130). New York: Plenum.

Berg, J. H., & Archer, R. L. (1980). Disclosure or concern: A second look at liking for the norm breaker. *Journal of Personality, 48,* 245–257.

Berg, J. H., & Archer, R. L. (1983). The disclosure-liking relationship: Effects of self-perception, order of disclosure, and topical similarity. *Human Communication Research, 10,* 269–281.

Berg, J. H., & Clark, M. S. (1986). Differences in social exchange between intimate and other relationships: Gradually evolving or quickly apparent? In V. J. Derlega & B. A. Winstead (Eds.), *Friendship and social interaction* (pp. 101–128). New York: Springer-Verlag.

Berscheid, E., & Graziano, W. G. (1979). The initiation of social relationships and interpersonal attraction. In R. L. Burgess & T. L. Huston (Eds.), *Social exchange in developing relationships* (pp. 31–60). New York: Academic Press.

Berscheid, E., Graziano, W., Monson, T., & Dermer, M. (1976). Outcome dependency: Attention, attribution, and attraction. *Journal of Personality and Social Psychology, 34*, 978–989.

Berscheid, E., & Walster, E. H. (1978). *Interpersonal attraction* (2nd ed.). Reading, MA: Addison-Wesley.

Blieszner, R., & Roberto, K. A. (2004). Friendship across the life span: Reciprocity in individual and relationship development. In F. R. Lang & K. L. Fingerman (Eds.), *Growing together: Personal relationships across the lifespan* (pp. 159–182). New York: Cambridge University Press.

Bornstein, R. F. (1989). Exposure and affect: Overview and meta-analysis of research, 1968–1987. *Psychological Bulletin, 106*, 265–289.

Bornstein, R. F., & D'Agostino, P. R. (1992). Stimulus recognition and the mere exposure effect. *Journal of Personality and Social Psychology, 63*, 545–552.

Brehm, S. S. (1985). *Intimate relationships*. New York: Crown/Random House.

Brenton, M. (1974). *Friendship*. New York: Stein & Day.

Buhrmester, D., Furman, W., Wittenberg, M. T., & Reis, H. T. (1988). Five domains of interpersonal competence in peer relationships. *Journal of Personality and Social Psychology, 55*, 991–1008.

Burleson, B. R. (1994). Friendship and similarities in social-cognitive and communication abilities: Social skill bases of interpersonal attraction in childhood. *Personal Relationships, 1*, 371–389.

Burleson, B. R., Kunkel, A. W., & Birch, J. D. (1994, July). *How similarities in cognitive complexity influence attraction to friends and lovers: Experimental and correlational studies*. Paper presented at the International Conference on Personal Relationships, Groningen, Netherlands.

Burleson, B. R., Kunkel, A. W., & Szolwinski, J. B. (1997). Similarity in cognitive complexity and attraction to friends and lovers: Experimental and correlational studies. *Journal of Constructivist Psychology, 10*, 221–248.

Byrne, D. (1971). *The attraction paradigm*. New York: Academic Press.

Byrne, D., & Clore, G. L. (1970). A reinforcement model of evaluative responses. *Personality: An International Journal, 1*, 103–128.

Cadiz Menne, J. M., & Sinnett, E. R. (1971). Proximity and social interaction in residence halls. *Journal of College Student Personnel, 12*, 26–31.

Caplan, S. E. (2005). A social skill account of problematic Internet use. *Journal of Communication, 55*, 721–736.

Caplow, T., & Forman, R. (1950). Neighborhood interaction in a homogeneous community. *American Sociological Review, 15*, 357–366.

Carnegie, D. (1936). *How to win friends and influence people*. New York: Pocket Books.

Cash, T. F., & Derlega, V. J. (1976). The matching hypothesis: Physical attractivness among same-sexed friends. *Personality and Social Psychology Bulletin, 4*, 240–243.

Chan, D. K-S., & Cheng, G. H-L. (2004). A comparison of offline and online friendship qualities at different stages of relationship development. *Journal of Social and Personal Relationships, 21*, 305–320.

Cheng, G. H. L., Chan, D. K. S., & Tong, P. Y. (2006). Qualities of online friendships with different gender compositions and durations. *CyberPsychology and Behavior, 9*, 14–21.

Clark, R. A., Dockum, M., Hazeu, H., Huang, M., Luo, N., Ramsey, J., et al. (2004). Initial encounters of young men and women: Impressions and disclosure estimates. *Sex Roles, 50*, 699–709.

Collins, N. L., & Miller, L. C. (1994). Self-disclosure and liking: A meta-analytic review. *Psychological Bulletin, 116*, 457–475.

Cook, M. (1977). The social skill model and interpersonal attraction. In S. W. Duck (Ed.), *Theory and practice in interpersonal attraction* (pp. 319–338). New York: Academic Press.

Cozby, P. C. (1972). Self-disclosure, reciprocity and liking. *Sociometry, 35*, 151–160.

Creekmore, C. R. (1985). Cities won't drive you crazy. *Psychology Today, 19*(1), 46–53.

Curry, T. J., & Kenny, D. A. (1974). The effects of perceived and actual similarity in values and personality in the process of interpersonal attraction. *Quality and Quantity, 8*, 27–44.

Curtis, R. C., & Miller, K. (1986). Believing another likes or dislikes you: Behaviors making the beliefs come true. *Journal of Personality and Social Psychology, 51*, 284–290.

Darley, J. M., & Berscheid, E. (1967). Increased liking as a result of the anticipation of personal contact. *Human Relations, 20*, 29–40.

Davis, D. (1981). Implications for interaction versus effectance as mediators of the similarity-attraction relationship. *Journal of Experimental Social Psychology, 17*, 96–117.

Davis, D., & Perkowitz, W. T. (1979). Consequences of responsiveness in dyadic interaction: Effects of probability of response and proportion of content-related responses on interpersonal attraction. *Journal of Personality and Social Psychology, 37*, 534–550.

Denrell, J. (2005). Why most people disapprove of me: Experience sampling in impression formation. *Psychological Review, 112*, 951–978.

Derlega, V. J., Wilson, M., & Chaikin, A. L. (1976). Friendship and disclosure reciprocity. *Journal of Personality and Social Psychology, 34*, 578–582.

Dion, K., Berscheid, E., & Walster, E. (1972). What is beautiful is good. *Journal of Personality and Social Psychology, 24*, 285–290.

Dion, K. K. (2002). Cultural perspectives on facial attractiveness. In G. Rhodes & L. A. Zebrowitz (Eds.), *Facial attractiveness: Evolutionary, cognitive, and social perspectives* (pp. 239–259). Westport, CT: Ablex.

Donchi, L., & Moore, S. (2004). It's a boy thing: The role of the Internet in young people's psychological well-being. *Behaviour Change, 21*, 76–89.

Duck, S., & Miell, D. (1986). Charting the development of personal relationships. In R. Gilmour & S. Duck (Eds.), *The emerging field of personal relationships* (pp. 133–143). Hillsdale, NJ: Lawrence Erlbaum.

Dugan, E., & Kivett, V. R. (1998). Implementing the Adams and Blieszner conceptual model: Predicting interactive friendship processes of older adults. *Journal of Social and Personal Relationships, 15*, 607–622.

Eagly, A. H., Ashmore, R. D., Makhijani, M. G., & Longo, L. C. (1991). What is beautiful is good, but … . A meta-analytic review of research on the physical attractiveness stereotype. *Psychological Bulletin, 110*, 109–128.

Ebbesen, E. B., Kjos, G. L., & Konecni, V. J. (1976). Spatial ecology: Its effects on the choice of friends and enemies. *Journal of Experimental Social Psychology, 12*, 505–518.

Erwin, P. G. (1985). Similarity of attitudes and constructs in children's friendships. *Journal of Experimental Child Psychology, 40*, 470–485.

Farrell, M. P. (1986). Friendship between men. *Marriage and Family Review, 9*, 163–197.

Fehr, B. (1996). *Friendship processes*. Newbury Park, CA: Sage.

Fehr, B., & Harasymchuk, C. (2005). The experience of emotion in close relationships: Toward an integration of the emotion-in-relationships and interpersonal scripts models. *Personal Relationships, 12*, 181–196.

Feingold, A. (1992). Good-looking people are not what we think. *Psychological Bulletin, 111*, 304–341.

Festinger, L., Schachter, S., & Back, K. (1950). *Social pressures in informal groups: A study of human factors in housing*. New York: Harper.

Fine, G. A. (1986). Friendships in the work place. In V. J. Derlega & B. A. Winstead (Eds.), *Friendship and social interaction* (pp. 185–206). New York: Springer.

Fischer, C. S. (1982). *To dwell among friends: Personal networks in town and city*. Chicago: University of Chicago Press.

Fischer, C. S., Jackson, R. M., Stueve, C. A., Gerson, K., Jones, L. M., & Baldassare, M. (1977). *Network and places: Social relations in the urban setting*. New York: Free Press.

Fischer, C. S., & Phillips S. (1982). Who is alone: Social characteristics of people with small networks. In L. A. Peplau & D. Perlman (Eds.), *Loneliness: A sourcebook of current research* (pp. 21–23). New York: Wiley.

Foster, G. (2005). Making friends: A nonexperimental analysis of social pair formation. *Human Relations, 58*, 1443–1465.

Fraley, B., & Aron, A. (2004). The effect of a shared humorous experience on closeness in initial encounters. *Personal Relationships, 11*, 61–78.

Franck, K. A. (1980). Friends and strangers: The social experience of living in urban and non-urban settings. *Journal of Social Issues, 36*, 52–71.

Friedman, H. S., Riggio, R. E., & Casella, D. F. (1988). Nonverbal skill, personal charisma, and initial attraction. *Personality and Social Psychology Bulletin, 14*, 203–211.

Gest, S. D., Graham-Bermann, S. A., & Hartup, W. W. (2001). Peer experience: Common and unique features of number of friendships, social network centrality, and sociometric status. *Social Development, 10*, 23–40.

Gifford-Smith, M. E., & Brownell, C. A. (2003). Childhood peer relationships: Social acceptance, friendships, and peer networks. *Journal of School Psychology, 41*, 235–284.

Godfrey, D. K., Jones, E. E., & Lord, C. G. (1986). Self-promotion is not ingratiating. *Journal of Personality and Social Psychology, 50*, 106–115.

Gottman, J., Gonso, J., & Rasmussen, B. (1975). Social interaction, social competence, and friendship in children. *Child Development, 46*, 709–718.

Gouldner, H., & Strong, M. S. (1987). *Speaking of friendship: Middle-class women and their friends*. New York: Greenwood Press.

Griffin, E., & Sparks, G. G. (1990). Friends forever: A longitudinal exploration of intimacy in same-sex friends and platonic pairs. *Journal of Social and Personal Relationships, 7,* 29–46.

Hamm, J. V. (2000). Do birds of a feather flock together? The variable bases for African American, Asian American, and European American adolescents' selection of similar friends. *Developmental Psychology, 36,* 209–219.

Hartup, W. W. (1996). The company they keep: Friendships and their developmental significance. *Child Development, 67,* 1–13.

Haselager, G. J. T., Hartup, W. W., van Lieshout, C. F. M., & Riksen-Walraven, J. M. A. (1998). Similarities between friends and nonfriends in middle childhood. *Child Development, 69,* 1198–1208.

Hays, R. B. (1984). The development and maintenance of friendship. *Journal of Social and Personal Relationships, 1,* 75–98.

Hays, R. B. (1985). A longitudinal study of friendship development. *Journal of Personality and Social Psychology, 48,* 909–924.

Hays, R. B., & Oxley, D. (1986). Social network development and functioning during a life transition. *Journal of Personality and Social Psychology, 50,* 305–313.

Henderson, S., & Gilding, M. (2004). "I've never clicked this much with anyone in my life": Trust and hyperpersonal communication in online friendships. *New Media and Society, 6,* 487–506.

Hill, C. T., & Stull, D. E. (1981). Sex differences in effects of social and value similarity in same-sex friendship. *Journal of Personality and Social Psychology, 41,* 488–502.

Holahan, C. J., & Wilcox, B. L. (1978). Residential satisfaction and friendship formation in high- and low-rise student housing: An interactional analysis. *Journal of Educational Psychology, 70,* 237–241.

Holahan, C. J., Wilcox, B. L., Burnam, M. A., & Culler, R. E. (1978). Social satisfaction and friendship formation as a function of floor level in high-rise student housing. *Journal of Applied Psychology, 63,* 527–529.

Horton, R. S. (2003). Similarity and attractiveness in social perception: Differentiating between biases for the self and the beautiful. *Self and Identity, 2,* 137–152.

Howes, C. (1996). The earliest friendships. In W. M. Bukowski, A. F. Newcomb, & W. W. Hartup (Eds.), *The company they keep: Friendship in childhood and adolescence* (pp. 87–112). New York: Cambridge University Press.

Hu, Y., Wood, J. F., Smith, V., & Westbrook, N. (2004). Friendships through IM: Examining the relationship between instant messaging and intimacy. *Journal of Computer-Mediated Communication, 10*(1), Article 6.

Jerrome, D. (1984). Good company: The sociological implications of friendship. *Sociological Review, 32,* 696–715.

Johnson, A. J., Wittenberg, E., Villagran, M. M., Mazur, M., & Villagran, P. (2003). Relational progression as a dialectic: Examining turning points in communication among friends. *Communication Monographs, 70,* 230–249.

Johnson, M. A. (1989). Variables associated with friendship in an adult population. *Journal of Social Psychology, 129,* 379–390.

Jones, D. C. (1991). Friendship satisfaction and gender: An examination of sex differences in contributors to friendship satisfaction. *Journal of Social and Personal Relationships, 8,* 167–185.

Kandel, D. B. (1978a). Homophily, selection, and socialization in adolescent friendships. *American Journal of Sociology, 84,* 427–436.

Kandel, D. B. (1978b). Similarity in real-life adolescent friendship pairs. *Journal of Personality and Social Psychology, 36,* 306–312.

Kenny, D. A., Kashy, D. A., & Cook, W. L. (2006). *Dyadic data analysis.* New York: Guilford.

Kleck, R. E., Richardson, S. A., & Ronald, L. (1974). Physical appearance cues and interpersonal attraction in children. *Child Development, 45,* 305–310.

Knapp, C. W., & Harwood, B. T. (1977). Factors in the determination of intimate same-sex friendship. *Journal of Genetic Psychology, 131,* 83–90.

Knapp, M. L., Ellis, D. G., & Williams, B. A. (1980). Perceptions of communication behavior associated with relationship terms. *Communication Monographs, 47,* 262–278.

Knight, J. A., & Vallacher, R. R. (1981). Interpersonal engagement in social perception: The consequences of getting into the action. *Journal of Personality and Social Psychology, 40,* 990–999.

Kubitschek, W. N., & Hallinan, M. T. (1998). Tracking and students' friendships. *Social Psychology Quarterly, 61,* 1–15.

Langlois, J. H., Kalakanis, L., Rubenstein, A. J., Larson, A., Hallam, M., & Smoot, M. (2000). Maxims or myths of beauty? A meta-analytic and theoretical review. *Psychological Bulletin, 126,* 390–423.

Larson, R. W., & Bradney, N. (1988). Precious moments with family members and friends. In R. M. Milardo (Ed.), *Families and social networks* (pp. 107–126). Thousand Oaks, CA: Sage.

Lassiter, G. D., & Briggs, M. A. (1990). Effect of anticipated interaction on liking: An individual difference analysis. *Journal of Social Behavior and Personality, 5,* 357–367.

Leslie, L. A., & Grady, K. (1985). Changes in mothers' social networks and social support following divorce. *Journal of Marriage and Family, 47,* 663–673.

Levesque, M. J., Steciuk, M., & Ledley, C. (2002). Self-disclosure patterns among well-acquainted individuals: Disclosers, confidants and unique relationships. *Social Behavior and Personality, 30,* 579–592.

McCown, J. A., Fischer, D., Page, R., & Homant, M. (2001). Internet relationships: People who meet people. *CyberPsychology & Behavior, 4,* 593–596.

McKenna, K., & Bargh, J. A. (2000). Plan 9 from cyberspace: The implications of the Internet for personality and social psychology. *Personality and Social Psychology Review, 4,* 57–75.

McKenna, K. Y., Green, A. S., & Gleason, M. F. J. (2002). Relationship formation on the Internet: What's the big attraction? *Journal of Social Issues, 58,* 9–31.

Miell, D. E., & Duck, S. (1986). Strategies in developing friendships. In V. J. Derlega & B. A. Winstead (Eds.), *Friends and social interaction* (pp. 129–143). New York: Springer.

Miller, L. C., Berg, J. H., & Archer, R. L. (1983). Openers: Individuals who elicit intimate self-disclosure. *Journal of Personality and Social Psychology, 44,* 1234–1244.

Miller, N., & Marks, G. (1982). Assumed similarity between self and other: Effect of expectation of future interaction with that other. *Social Psychology Quarterly, 45,* 100–105.

Morahan-Martin, J., & Schumacher, P. (2003). Loneliness and social uses of the Internet. *Computers in Human Behavior, 19,* 659–671.

Moser, G., Legendre, A., & Ratiu, E. (2003). City dwellers' relationship networks: Patterns of adjustment to urban constraints. In R. Garcia Mira, J. M. Sabucedo Cameselle, & J. Romay Martinez (Eds.), *Culture, environmental action and sustainability* (pp. 161–170). Ashland, OH: Hogrefe & Huber.

Nahemow, L., & Lawton, M. P. (1975). Similarity and propinquity in friendship formation. *Journal of Personality and Social Psychology, 32,* 205–213.

Neimeyer, G. J., & Neimeyer, R. A. (1981). Functional similiarity and interpersonal attraction. *Journal of Research in Personality, 15,* 427–435.

Neimeyer, R. A., & Neimeyer, G. J. (1983). Structural similiarity in the acquaintance process. *Journal of Social and Clinical Psychology, 1,* 146–154.

Oppong, J. R., Ironside, R. G., & Kennedy, L. W. (1988). Perceived quality of life in a centre-periphery framework. *Social Indicators Research, 20,* 605–620.

Parker, S. R. (1964). Type of work, friendship patterns, and leisure. *Human Relations, 17,* 215–219.

Parks, M. R., & Eggert, L. L. (1991). The role of social context in the dynamics of personal relationships. In W. H. Jones & D. Perlman (Eds.), *Advances in personal relationship: A research annual* (Vol. 2, pp. 1–34). London: Jessica Kingsley.

Patzer, G. (1985). *The physical attractiveness phenomena.* New York: Plenum.

Perlman, D., & Oskamp, S. (1971). The effects of picture content and exposure frequency on evaluations of Negroes and Whites. *Journal of Experimental Social Psychology, 7,* 503–514.

Peter, J., Valkenburg, P. M., & Schouten, A. P. (2005). Developing a model of adolescent friendship formation on the Internet. *CyberPsychology & Behavior, 8,* 423–430.

Pinel, E. C., Long, A. E., Landau, M. J., Alexander, K., & Pyszczynski, T. (2006). Seeing I to I: A pathway to interpersonal connectedness. *Journal of Personality and Social Psychology, 90,* 243–257.

Planalp, S., & Benson, A. (1992). Friends' and acquaintances' conversations: I. Perceived differences. *Journal of Social and Personal Relationships, 9,* 483–506.

Rawlins, W. K. (1992). *Friendship matters: Communication, dialectics, and the life course.* Hawthorne, NY: Aldine de Gruyter.

Ridings, C. M., & Gefen, D. (2004). Virtual community attraction: Why people hang out online. *Journal of Computer-Mediated Communication, 10*(1), Article 4.

Riggio, R. E. (1986). Assessment of basic social skills. *Journal of Personality and Social Psychology, 51,* 649–660.

Riordan, C. M., & Griffeth, R. W. (1995). The opportunity for friendship in the workplace: An underexplored construct. *Journal of Business and Psychology, 10,* 141–154.

Roberto, K. A., & Scott, J. P. (1987). Friendships in late life: A rural-urban comparison. *Lifestyles, 8*(3–4), 16–26, 146–156.

Rodin, M. J. (1982). Non-engagement, failure to engage, and disengagement. In S. Duck (Ed.), *Personal relationships: Vol. 4. Dissolving personal relationships* (pp. 31–49). London: Academic Press.

Rotenberg, K. J., & Mann, L. (1986). The development of the norm of the reciprocity of self-disclosure and its function in children's attraction to peers. *Child Development, 57,* 1349–1357.

Rubin, Z. (1975). Disclosing oneself to a stranger: Reciprocity and its limits. *Journal of Experimental Social Psychology, 11,* 233–260.

Rushton, J. P., & Bons, T. A. (2005). Mate choice and friendship in twins: Evidence for genetic similarity. *Psychological Science, 16,* 555–559.

Salzinger, L. L. (1982). The ties that bind: The effects of clustering on dyadic relationships. *Social Networks, 4,* 117–145.

Samter, W. (2003). Friendship interaction skills across the life-span. In J. O. Greene & B. R. Burleson (Eds.), *Handbook of communication and social interaction skills* (pp. 637–684). Mahwah, NJ: Lawrence Erlbaum.

Segal, M. W. (1974). Alphabet and attraction: An unobtrusive measure of the effect of propinquity in field setting. *Journal of Personality and Social Psychology, 30,* 654–657.

Shaver, P., Furman, W., & Buhrmester, D. (1985). Transition to college: Network changes, social skills, and loneliness. In S. Duck & D. Perlman (Eds.), *Understanding personal relationships: An interdisciplinary approach* (pp. 193–219). Thousand Oaks, CA: Sage.

Shaw, J. I., & Steers, W. N. (1996). Effects of perceiver sex, search goal, and target person attributes on information search in impression formation. *Journal of Social Behavior and Personality, 11,* 209–227.

Shulman, N. (1975). Life-cycle variations in patterns of close relationships. *Journal of Marriage and the Family, 37,* 813–821.

Spitzberg, B. H., & Cupach, W. R (1989). *Handbook of interpersonal competence research.* New York: Springer-Verlag.

Sprecher, S. (1998). Insiders' perspectives on reasons for attraction to a close other. *Social Psychology Quarterly, 61,* 287–300.

Sunnafrank, M., & Ramirez, A. (2004). At first sight: Persistent relational effects of get-acquainted conversations. *Journal of Social and Personal Relationships, 21,* 361–379.

Sykes, R. E. (1983). Initial interaction between strangers and acquaintances: A multivariate analysis of factors affecting choice of communication partners. *Human Communication Research, 10,* 27–53.

Tsai, M. (2006). Sociable resources and close relationships: Intimate relatives and friends in Taiwan. *Journal of Social and Personal Relationships, 23,* 151–169.

Tyler, T. R. (2002). Is the Internet changing social life? It seems the more things change, the more they stay the same. *Journal of Social Issues, 58,* 195–205.

Tyler, T. R., & Sears, D. O. (1977). Coming to like obnoxious people when we must live with them. *Journal of Personality and Social Psychology, 35,* 200–211.

van Leeuwen, M. L., & Macrae, C. N. (2004). Is beautiful always good? Implicit benefits of facial attractiveness. *Social Cognition, 22,* 637–649.

Van Vliet, W. (1981). The environmental context of children's friendships: An empirical and conceptual examination of the role of child density. *EDRA: Environmental Design Research Association, 12,* 216–224.

Verbrugge, L. M. (1977). The structure of adult friendship choices. *Social Forces, 56,* 576–597.

Vittengl, J. R., & Holt, C. S. (2000). Getting acquainted: The relationship of self-disclosure and social attraction to positive affect. *Journal of Social and Personal Relationships, 17,* 53–66.

Wellman, B. (1985). Domestic work, paid work, and net work. In S. Duck & D. Perlman (Eds.). *Understanding personal relationships* (pp. 159–191). London: Sage.

Werner, C., & Parmelee, P. (1979). Similarity of activity preferences among friends: Those who play together stay together. *Social Psychology Quarterly, 42,* 62–66.

Wortman, C. B., Adesman, P., Herman, E., & Greenberg, R. (1976). Self-disclosure: An attributional perspective. *Journal of Personality and Social Psychology, 33,* 184–191.

Zajonc, R. B. (1968). Attitudinal effects of mere exposure. *Journal of Personality and Social Psychology, 9(2),* 1–27.

Zakahi, W. R., & Duran, R. L. (1984) Attraction, communicative competence and communication satisfaction. *Communication Research Reports, 1,* 54–57.

3

An Evolutionary Perspective on Mate Choice and Relationship Initiation

DAVID P. SCHMITT

*F*rom an evolutionary perspective, animal mate choice and relationship initiation depend in large part on the natural mating system of a species. Mating systems can vary widely both within and across species, and differences in mating systems fundamentally influence the degree of sexual differentiation and population variability in mate choice and courtship-related behavior (Shuster & Wade, 2003). In humans, there are several indications that we have a monogamous mating system. For example, humans are highly altricial—we have prolonged childhoods and rely heavily on extended families throughout our life spans (Alexander & Noonan, 1979). We also appear designed to form romantic pairbonds, having a dedicated neurochemistry of attachment associated with monogamy across mammalian species (Fisher, 1998; Young, 2003). This evidence would suggest humans are designed to choose romantic partners who possess qualities advantageous to a monogamous mating system (e.g., fidelity), and according to sexual selection theory (Darwin, 1871), men and women who displayed cues to qualities such as fidelity would be especially effective at initiating and maintaining romantic relationships.

At the same time, however, humans appear to possess evolved design features associated with multimale or multifemale, or "promiscuous," mating. For example, humans may possess psychological and physiological adaptations for sperm competition (Baker & Bellis, 1995; Shackelford & LeBlanc, 2001), such as women's adaptive timing of extrapair copulations (i.e., infidelities; Gangestad & Thornhill, 1998; Haselton & Miller, 2006), men's specialized expressions of sexual jealousy (Buss, 2000; Schützwohl, 2006), and the physical structure of the human penis serving as a semen displacement device (Gallup et al., 2003). Among men, casual sex with multiple partners is often viewed as desirable (Oliver & Hyde, 1993; Symons & Ellis, 1989), with most men agreeing to have sex with complete strangers when asked in field experiments (Clark & Hatfield, 1989). Patterns of premarital sex, extramarital sex, and mate poaching by both men and women (i.e., adaptive patterns suggesting these are evolved sexual strategies) have been documented across cultures (Broude & Greene, 1976; Schmitt, Alcalay, Allik, et al., 2004).

There is also evidence that humans are designed, at least in part, for polygynous mating. For example, men and women have sexually dimorphic life history traits such as men's tendencies to be more physically aggressive, to die much earlier, and to physically mature much later than women across all known cultures (Archer & Lloyd, 2002; Kaplan & Gangestad, 2005). Such sex differences are usually not seen among truly monogamous species, especially primates (Alexander, Hoogland, Howard, Noonan, & Sherman, 1979). Moreover, across foraging cultures—the predominantly polygynous cultures in which humans have spent most of our evolutionary history (Brown, 1991; Frayser, 1985; Pasternak, Ember, & Ember, 1997)—there are ethnographically pervasive links among men's status, polygynous marriage, and reproductive success (Low, 2000;

Turke & Betzig, 1985). In contrast, very few cultures (less than 1%) have polyandrous marriage systems (Broude & Greene, 1976).

EVOLUTIONARY THEORIES OF MATE CHOICE AND RELATIONSHIP INITIATION

Evolutionary psychologists tend to reconcile these seemingly contradictory findings by acknowledging that humans, like many other species, are probably designed and adapted for more than one mating strategy (Barash & Lipton, 2001; Mealey, 2000). Specifically, most evolutionary psychologists view humans as coming equipped with specialized mate choice adaptations for both *long-term mating* (i.e., marriage and extended pairbonding) and *short-term mating* (i.e., promiscuity and infidelity; see Buss & Schmitt, 1993; Kenrick, Sadalla, Groth, & Trost, 1990). Not all people try to initiate both types of mating relationships at all times. Instead, humans possess adaptive desires, preferences, and behavioral tactics that are differentially activated depending on whether a long-term or short-term mating strategy is actively being pursued at the time (Gangestad & Simpson, 2000; Schmitt, 2005a; Schmitt et al., 2003; Simpson, Wilson, & Winterheld, 2004).

Most evolutionary theories of human mating argue that such a flexible mating design—composed of both long-term monogamous adaptations and short-term promiscuous adaptations—would have provided important reproductive benefits to humans in our ancestral past, allowing individuals to functionally respond to a wide range of familial, cultural, and ecological contexts (Belsky, 1999; Buss & Schmitt, 1993; Lancaster, 1994; Pedersen, 1991). Evolutionary theories further acknowledge that humans can benefit from shifting between long-term and short-term mating strategies during their life span, when in different stages of romantic relationships, and across the ovulatory cycle (Gangestad, 2001; Klusmann, 2002; Schmitt et al., 2002). Thus, humans have evolved the capacity to initiate a mix of mating relationship types—both long-term and short-term—depending on fitness-related circumstances.

Most evolutionary psychology approaches further postulate that men and women possess design features that cause sex differences within long-term and short-term mating contexts. For example, when men seek short-term mates they appear motivated by adaptive desires for sexual variety—desires that lead them to functionally pursue numerous mating partners and to consent to sex relatively quickly compared to women (Clark & Hatfield, 1989; Okami & Shackelford, 2001; Schmitt et al., 2003; Symons & Ellis, 1989). Women's short-term mating motivations appear not to be rooted in the desire for numerous sexual partners and seem focused, instead, on other factors such as obtaining select men who display dominance, intelligence, or creativity (i.e., show high genetic quality; see Gangestad & Thornhill, 1997; Penton-Voak et al., 2003; Regan, Levin, Sprecher, Christopher, & Cate, 2000). As a consequence, evolutionary approaches predict that men's and women's mate choices and relationship initiation tactics will differ in important ways, especially within the context of short-term mating. Most evolutionary theories of human mate choice are based on the assumption that the sexes will differ in some ways, an assumption that can be traced to the logic of parental investment theory (Trivers, 1972).

Parental Investment Theory

According to parental investment theory (Trivers, 1972), the relative proportion of parental investment—the time and energy devoted to the care of individual offspring (at the expense of other offspring)—varies across the males and females of different species. In some species, males provide more parental investment than females (e.g., the Mormon cricket). In other species, females possess the heavy-investing burdens (e.g., most mammals; Clutton-Brock, 1991). Sex differences in parental investment burdens are systematically linked to processes of sexual selection (Darwin, 1871) in ways that influence mate choice and relationship initiation. The sex that invests less in offspring is *intrasexually* more competitive, especially over gaining reproductive access to members of the opposite sex, in part because the opposite sex is reluctant to make bad decisions in committing its typically heavier investment. This normally results in the lesser investing sex being reliably more aggressive with his or her own sex, and tending to die earlier, to mature later, and generally to compete for mates with more vigor, than does the heavier investing sex (Alcock, 2001). Furthermore, the lesser investing sex of a species is *intersexually* less discriminating in mate choice than the heavier investing sex. The lesser investing sex is willing to mate more quickly and at lower cost, and will initiate relationships with more partners than the heavier investing parent (Bateson, 1983). Again, this is largely because members of the heavier investing sex face higher reproductive costs associated with poor mating decisions and also have fewer mating decisions with which to gamble over their reproductive life spans.

Much of the evidence in favor of parental investment theory (Trivers, 1972) has come from species where females happen to be the heavy-investing sex (see Clutton-Brock, 1991). In such species, parental investment theory leads to the prediction that sexual selection has been more potent among males. Upon empirical examination, males of these species tend to display more competitiveness with each other over sexual access to heavier investing females, and to exhibit more intrasexual competition through greater aggressiveness, riskier life history strategies, and earlier death than females (Archer & Lloyd, 2002; Trivers, 1985). Lesser investing males are also less discriminate through intersexual mate choice, often seeking multiple partners and requiring less time before initiating sex than females do (see Geary, 1998).

Perhaps the most compelling support for parental investment theory (Trivers, 1972), however, has come from "sex-role-reversed" species. In species where males are the heavy-investing parent, the processes of sexual selection are thought to have been more potent among females. Females of these species vie more ferociously for sexual access to heavy-investing males and require little from males before consenting to sex. Evidence of this form of sexual differentiation has been documented among such "sex-role-reversed" species as the red-necked phalarope, the Mormon cricket, katydids, dance flies, water bugs, seahorses, and a variety of fish species (Alcock, 2001). Parental investment theory, therefore, is not a theory about males always having more interest in indiscriminate sex than females. Instead, it is a theory about differences in parental investment *obligations* systematically relating to sex differences in mate choice and relationship initiation.

Among humans, many men invest heavily in their children, teaching them social skills, emotionally nurturing them, and investing both resources and prestige in them. Nevertheless, men incur much lower levels of obligatory or "minimum" parental investment in offspring than women do (Symons, 1979). Women are obligated, for example, to incur the costs of internal fertilization, placentation, and gestation in order to reproduce. The minimum physiological obligations of men are considerably less—requiring only the contribution of sperm. Furthermore, all female mammals, including ancestral women, carried the obligatory investments associated with lactation. Lactation can last several years in human foraging environments (Kelly, 1995), years during which it is harder for women than men to reproduce and invest in additional offspring (Blurton Jones, 1986). Finally, across all known cultures human males typically invest less in active parenting efforts than females (Low, 1989; Munroe & Munroe, 1997).

This human asymmetry in parental investment should affect mate choice and relationship initiation, with the lesser investing sex (i.e., men) displaying greater intrasexual competitiveness and lower intersexual "choosiness" in mate preferences. Numerous studies have shown that men exhibit greater physical size and competitive aggression (Archer & Lloyd, 2002), riskier life history strategies (Daly & Wilson, 1988), relatively delayed maturation (Geary, 1998), and earlier death than women do across cultures (Alexander & Noonan, 1979). In addition, men's mate preferences are, as predicted, almost always less "choosy" or discriminating than women's, especially in the context of short-term mating (Kenrick et al., 1990; Regan et al., 2000).

Because men are the lesser investing sex of our species, they also should be more inclined toward initiating low-cost, short-term mating than women. Human sex differences in the desire for short-term sex have been observed in studies of sociosexuality (Jones, 1998; Schmitt, 2005a; Simpson

& Gangestad, 1991), motivations for and prevalence of extramarital mating (Seal, Agostinelli, & Hannett, 1994; Wiederman, 1997), quality and quantity of sexual fantasies (Ellis & Symons, 1990), quality and quantity of pornography consumption (Malamuth, 1996), motivations for and use of prostitution (McGuire & Gruter, 2003), willingness to have sex without commitment (Townsend, 1995), willingness to have sex with strangers (Clark, 1990; Clark & Hatfield, 1989), and the fundamental differences between the short-term mating psychology of gay males and lesbians (Bailey, Gaulin, Agyei, & Gladue, 1994). Clearly, sex differences in parental investment obligations have an influence on men's and women's fundamental mate choices and relationship initiation strategies.

Sexual Strategies Theory

Buss and Schmitt (1993) expanded on parental investment theory (Trivers, 1972) by proposing sexual strategies theory (SST). According to SST, men and women have evolved a pluralistic repertoire of mating strategies. One strategy within this repertoire is "long-term" mating. Long-term mating is usually marked by extended courtship, heavy investment, pairbonding, the emotion of love, and the dedication of resources over a long temporal span to the mating relationship and any offspring that ensue. Another strategy within the human mating repertoire is "short-term" mating, defined as a relatively fleeting sexual encounter such as a brief affair, a hookup, or a one-night stand. Which sexual strategy or mix of strategies an individual pursues is predicted to be contingent on factors such as opportunity, personal mate value, sex ratio in the relevant mating pool, parental influences, regnant cultural norms, and other features of social and personal contexts (see also Gangestad & Simpson, 2000; Schmitt, 2005a, 2005b).

EVOLUTION OF SEX DIFFERENCES IN MATE CHOICE AND RELATIONSHIP INITIATION

Sex Differences in Long-Term Mating

Although SST views both sexes as having long-term and short-term mating strategies within their repertoire, men and women are predicted to differ psychologically in what they desire (i.e., mate choice) and in how they tactically pursue (i.e., initiate) romantic relationships. In long-term mate choice, the sexes are predicted to differ in several respects. Men are hypothesized to possess adaptations that lead them to place a greater mate choice premium during long-term mating on signals of fertility and reproductive value, such as a woman's youth and physical appearance (Buss, 1989; Jones, 1995; Kenrick & Keefe, 1992; Singh, 1993; Symons, 1979). Men also prefer long-term mates who are sexually faithful and are capable of good parenting (see Table 3.1). Women, in contrast, are hypothesized to place a greater premium during long-term mating on a man's status, resources, ambition, and maturity (cues relevant to his *ability* for long-term provisioning), as well as his kindness, generosity, and emotional openness (cues to his *willingness* to provide for women and their children) (Buunk, Dijkstra, Kenrick, & Warntjes, 2001; Cashdan, 1993; Ellis, 1992; Feingold, 1992; Townsend & Wasserman, 1998).

Conversely, men who display cues to long-term provisioning, and women who display youthfulness, tend to be the ones who are most effective at initiating, enhancing, and preserving monogamous mating relationships (Buss, 1988; Hirsch & Paul, 1996; Landolt, Lalumiere, & Quinsey, 1995; Schmitt, 2002; Tooke & Camire, 1991; Walters & Crawford, 1994). From an evolutionary perspective, the differing qualities that men and women preferentially respond to are thought to help solve the adaptive problems that men and women had to overcome throughout human evolutionary history (Schmitt & Buss, 1996). Of course, in our ancestral past men and women also faced similar problems of mate choice, leading to little or no sex differences in some domains (see Buss & Schmitt, 1993).

Numerous survey and meta-analytic studies have confirmed many of the major tenets of SST, including the fact that men and women seeking long-term mates desire different attributes in potential partners (e.g., Cunningham, Roberts, Barbee, Druen, & Wu, 1995; Graziano, Jensen-Campbell, Todd, & Finch, 1997; Jensen-Campbell, Graziano, & West, 1995; Kruger, Fisher, & Jobling, 2003; Li, Bailey, Kenrick, & Linsenmeier, 2002; Regan, 1998a, 1998b; Regan & Berscheid, 1997; Urbaniak & Kilmann, 2003). Several investigators have replicated or confirmed SST-related findings using nationally representative, cross-cultural, or multicultural samples (Feingold, 1992; Knodel, Low, Saengtienchai, & Lucas, 1997; Schmitt et al., 2003; Sprecher, Sullivan, & Hatfield, 1994; Walter, 1997). For example, in a recent Internet study of 119,733 men and 98,462 women across 53 nations, Lippa (2007) replicated the classic evolutionary finding of men's greater desires, relative to women, for long-term mates who are physically attractive. Women, in contrast to men, tended to report greater preferences for long-term mates who display cues to the ability and willingness to provide resources (e.g., intelligence, kindness, and dependability; see Lippa, 2007). Other investigators have validated key SST hypotheses concerning sex differences in long-term mate choice using nonsurvey techniques such as studying actual mate attraction, marital choice, spousal conflict, and divorce (Betzig, 1989; Dawson & McIntosh, 2006; Kenrick, Neuberg, Zierk, & Krones, 1994; Salmon & Symons, 2001; Schmitt, Couden, & Baker, 2001; Townsend & Wasserman, 1998; Wiederman, 1993). These experimental, behavioral, and naturalistic methodologies suggest that evolutionary-supportive findings are not merely stereotype artifacts or social desirability biases limited to self-reported mate choice.

Kenrick and his colleagues (1994), for example, demonstrated using the "contrast effect" that experimental exposure to physically attractive women tended to lessen a man's commitment to his current relationship partner. However, exposure to physically attractive men had no effect on women's commitment to their current partners. Conversely, when women were exposed to targets who had high status- and resource-related attributes, this lessened women's (but not men's) commitment to their current romantic partners. Kenrick and others argued that this indirect research method not only confirms self-reported mate preference findings but also further shows that men's and women's evolved mate preferences unconsciously influence men's and women's satisfaction and commitment over the long-term course of relationships (see also Buss & Shackelford, 1997; Little & Mannion, 2006).

Another indirect effect of sex-differentiated mating desires can be found in the context of relationship initiation and romantic attraction. According to sexual selection theory (Darwin, 1871), the evolved mate preferences of one sex should have a substantive impact on the effectiveness of attraction tactics used by the opposite sex. If men possess an evolved preference for physical attractiveness, the argument goes, women should be more effective than men at using mate initiation and attraction tactics that manipulate physical attractiveness (e.g., by appearing youthful). Conversely, if women prefer resource-related attributes more than men do, men should be seen as more effective than women at using resource-related tactics of initiation and attraction (e.g., by demonstrating intelligence, kindness, and dependability). Empirical evaluations of this aspect of sexual selection in humans have been supportive. For example, Buss (1988), Tooke and Camire (1991), and Walters and Crawford (1994) all demonstrated that women are judged more effective than men when using appearance-related tactics of initiation and attraction, whereas men are judged more effective than women when using resource-related tactics of romantic initiation and attraction (for a meta-analysis of attraction results, see Schmitt, 2002).

Perceived sex differences in physical appearance and resource-related tactic effectiveness have also been documented within more specialized rating contexts of romantic attraction. Buss (1988) found sex differences in effectiveness ratings of appearance and resource-related tactics when used by men and women to both *attract* and *retain* a long-term marital partner (see also Bleske-Rechek & Buss, 2001; Flinn, 1985). Schmitt and Buss (1996) documented sex differences in perceived tactic effectiveness across both *self-promotion* and *competitor derogation* forms of mate attraction (i.e., when people highlight their own positive qualities and tear down their rivals' perceived qualities; see also Greer & Buss, 1994; Walters & Crawford, 1994). Schmitt and Buss (2001) found sex differences in perceived appearance and resource-related mate attraction within the specialized context of obtaining a long-term mating partner who is already in a relationship, what they called the context of *mate poaching* (see also Bleske & Shackelford, 2001; Schmitt & Shackelford, 2003). Whether researchers ask people directly, observe their real-life behavior, or subtly look for indirect effects, the pervasive range of sex differences in long-term mating psychology supports the evolutionary perspective on mate choice and relationship initiation.

Sex Differences in Short-Term Mating

According to SST, both sexes are hypothesized to pursue short-term mateships in certain contexts, but for different reproductive reasons that reflect sex-specific adaptive problems (Buss & Schmitt, 1993). For women, the asymmetry in obligatory parental investment (Symons, 1979; Trivers, 1972) leaves them little to gain in reproductive output by engaging in indiscriminate, short-term sex with high numbers of partners. Women can reap evolutionary benefits from short-term mating (Greiling & Buss, 2000; Hrdy, 1981). However, women's psychology of short-term mate choice appears to center on obtaining men of high genetic quality rather than numerous men in high-volume quantity (Banfield & McCabe, 2001; Gangestad & Thornhill, 1998; Li & Kenrick, 2006; Smith, 1984).

For men, the potential reproductive benefits from short-term mating with numerous partners can be profound. A man can produce as many as 100 offspring by mating with 100 women over the course of a year, whereas a man who is monogamous will tend to have only one child with his partner during that same time period. In evolutionary currencies, this represents a strong selective pressure—and a potent adaptive problem—for men's short-term mating strategy to center on obtaining large numbers of partners (Schmitt et al., 2003). Obviously, 100 instances of only onetime mating would rarely produce precisely 100 offspring. However, a man mating with 100 women over the course of a year—particularly repeated matings when the women are nearing ovulation and are especially interested in short-term mating (Gangestad, 2001)—would likely have significantly more offspring than a woman mating repeatedly with 100 interested men over the course of a year.

According to SST, three of the specific design features of men's short-term mating psychology are that (a) men possess a greater desire than women do for a variety of sexual partners, (b) men require less time to elapse than women do before consenting to sexual intercourse, and (c) men tend to more actively seek short-term mateships than women do (Buss & Schmitt, 1993). This suite of hypothesized sex differences has been well supported empirically. For example, Schmitt and his colleagues (2003) documented these fundamental sex differences across 10 major regions of the world. When people from North America were asked, "Ideally, how many different sexual partners would you like to have in the next month?" over 23% of men, but only 3% of women, indicated that they would like *more than one* sexual partner in the next month. This finding confirmed that many men, and few women, desire sexual variety in the form of multiple sexual partners over short time intervals. Similar degrees of sexual differentiation were found in South America (35.0% versus 6.1%), Western Europe (22.6% versus 5.5%), Eastern Europe (31.7% versus 7.1%), Southern Europe (31.0% versus 6.0%), the Middle East (33.1% versus 5.9%), Africa (18.2% versus 4.2%), Oceania (25.3% versus 5.8%), South and Southeast Asia (32.4% versus 6.4%), and East Asia (17.9% versus 2.6%). These sex differences also persisted across a variety of demographic statuses, including age, socioeconomic status, and sexual orientation. Moreover, when men and women who reported actively pursuing a short-term mating strategy were asked whether they wanted more than one partner in the next month, over 50% of men, but less than 20% of women, expressed desires for multiple sexual partners (Schmitt et al., 2003). This finding supports the key SST hypothesis that men's short-term mating strategy is very different from women's and is based, in part, on obtaining large numbers of sexual partners.

Other findings from the cross-cultural study by Schmitt and his colleagues (2003) documented that men universally agree to have sex after less time has elapsed than women do, and that men from all world regions expend more effort on seeking brief sexual relationships than women do. For example, across all cultures nearly 25% of married men, but only 10% of married women, reported that they are actively seeking short-term, extramarital relationships (see also Wiederman, 1997). These culturally universal findings support the view that men evolved to seek large numbers of sex partners when they pursue a short-term mating strategy. Some women also pursue short-term mates. However, when women seek short-term mates they are more selective and tend to seek out men who are physically attractive, are intelligent, and otherwise possess high-quality genes (Buss & Schmitt, 1993; Gangestad & Thornhill, 1997, 2003).

EVOLUTION OF INDIVIDUAL DIFFERENCES IN MATE CHOICE AND RELATIONSHIP INITIATION

The previous section addressed the evolutionary psychology of *how* men and women choose and initiate short-term and long-term mating relationships. Another important question is *when* and *why* an individual man or woman would choose to pursue a long-term mateship versus a short-term mateship. Several theories have suggested that personal circumstances—including stage of life, personal characteristics, and physical attributes—play an adaptive role in shaping or evoking people's strategic mating choices (Buss & Schmitt, 1993; Gangestad & Simpson, 2000). Among the more important sex-specific features that affect mating strategies are men's overall mate value and women's ovulatory status.

Mating Differences within Men

According to SST (Buss & Schmitt, 1993), men possess a menu of alternative mating strategies that they can follow. Whether a man chooses to pursue a short-term or long-term mating strategy (or both) may depend, in part, on his status and prestige. In foraging cultures, men with higher status and prestige tend to possess multiple wives (Betzig, 1986; Borgerhoff Mulder, 1987, 1990; Cronk, 1991; Heath & Hadley, 1998), and in so doing polygynous men are able to satisfy aspects of both their long-term pairbonding desires and short-term "numerous partner" desires. In most modern cultures, men with high status are unable to legally marry more than one woman. However, high-status men are more likely to successfully pursue extramarital affairs and to practice de facto or "effective" polygyny in the form of serial divorce and remarriage compared to others (Brown & Hotra, 1988; Buss, 2000; Fisher, 1992). Given an equal sex ratio of men and women in a given culture, this results in other men—namely, those with low status and prestige—being limited to monogamy in the form of one wife. Some low-status men are left with no wives at all, and may choose to resort to coercive, low-investment mating strategies (Thornhill & Palmer, 2000). Consequently, important sources of individual variation in men's mate choice and relationship initiation tactics are status and prestige.

Whether a man follows a more short-term- or long-term-oriented mating strategy depends on other factors as well, many of which relate to the man's overall value in the mating marketplace (Gangestad & Simpson, 2000). A man's "mate value" is determined, in part, by his status and prestige. It is also affected by his current resource holdings, long-term ambition, intelligence, interpersonal dominance, social popularity, sense of humor, reputation for kindness, maturity, height, strength, and athleticism (Chagnon, 1988; Ellis, 1992; Miller, 2000; Nettle, 2002; Pierce, 1996).

Most studies of men in modern cultures find that, when they are able to do so as a result of high mate value, men choose to engage in multiple mating relationships. For example, Lalumiere, Seto, and Quinsey (1995) designed a scale to measure overall mating opportunities. The scale, similar to overall mate value, included items such as "Relative to my peer group, I can get dates with ease." They found that men with higher mate value tended to have sex at an earlier age, to have a larger number of sexual partners, and to follow a more promiscuous mating strategy overall (see also James, 2003; Landolt et al., 1995).

Another potential indicator of mate value is the social barometer of self-esteem (Kirkpatrick, Waugh, Valencia, & Webster, 2002). Similar to the results with mating opportunities, men who score higher on self-esteem scales tend to choose and to successfully engage in more short-term mating relationships (Baumeister & Tice, 2001; Walsh, 1991). Indeed, in a recent cross-cultural study by Schmitt (2005b), this revealing trend was evident across several world regions. The same relationship was usually not evident, and was often reversed, among women in modern nations (see also Mikach

& Bailey, 1999). That is, women with high self-esteem were more likely to pursue monogamous, long-term mating strategies. These findings would seem to support parental investment theory (Trivers, 1972), in that when mate value is high and people are given a choice, men prefer short-term mating (sometimes in addition to long-term mating), whereas women strategically prefer a single monogamous mateship. An important determinant of individual mate choice, therefore, is overall mate value in the mating marketplace, with men of high mate value and women of low mate value more likely to pursue short-term mating strategies (see Table 3.1).

According to strategic pluralism theory (Gangestad & Simpson, 2000), men should also be more likely to engage in short-term mating when they exhibit the physical characteristics most preferred by women who desire a short-term mate, especially those traits indicative of high genetic quality. Higher facial symmetry, for example, is indicative of low genetic mutation load in men, and women adaptively prefer facial symmetry when pursing short-term mates (Gangestad & Thornhill, 1997). This is because one of the key benefits women can reap from short-term mating is to gain access to high-quality genes that they might not be able to secure from a long-term partner (Gangestad, 2001).

TABLE 3.1   Fundamental Features of Long-Term and Short-Term Mating Strategies in Men and Women

Men's Long-Term Mating Strategy

Key mate choice adaptations	Prefer cues to youth and fertility, prefer sexual fidelity, and prefer good parenting skills
Effective relationship initiation tactics	Demonstrate ability and willingness to invest, and demonstrate emotional commitment
Associated personal characteristics	Low mate value, feminine and asymmetrical facial features, and low testosterone
Eliciting cultural and familial factors	High sex ratio (more men than women), and secure parent–child attachment

Women's Long-Term Mating Strategy

Key mate choice adaptations	Prefer attributes that indicate ability and willingness to invest in self and offspring
Effective relationship initiation tactics	Provide cues to youth and fertility, suggest sexual fidelity, and suggest good parenting skills
Associated personal characteristics	High mate value, high self-esteem, and luteal phase of ovulatory cycle
Eliciting cultural and familial factors	High sex ratio, and secure parent–child attachment

Men's Short-Term Mating Strategy

Key mate choice adaptations	Prefer large number of partners, prefer easy sexual access, and minimize commitment
Effective relationship initiation tactics	Provide immediate resources, demonstrate intelligence, and feign long-term interests
Associated personal characteristics	High mate value, masculine and symmetrical facial features, and high testosterone
Eliciting cultural and familial factors	Low sex ratio (more women than men), and insecure-dismissing parent–child attachment

Women's Short-Term Mating Strategy

Key mate choice adaptations	Prefer immediate resources, and prefer genetic quality (intelligence, masculinity, and symmetry)
Effective relationship initiation tactics	Provide easy sexual access, and limit future commitment
Associated personal characteristics	Low mate value, low self-esteem, and late follicular phase of ovulatory cycle
Eliciting cultural and familial factors	Low sex ratio, and insecure-fearful and insecure-preoccupied parent–child attachment

Evidence that physically attractive men adaptively respond to women's desires and become more promiscuous comes from other sources, as well. For example, men who possess broad and muscular shoulders, a physical attribute preferred by short-term-oriented women (Frederick, Haselton, Buchanan, & Gallup, 2003), tend toward short-term mating as reflected in an earlier age of first intercourse, more sexual partners, and more extrapair copulations (Hughes & Gallup, 2003). In numerous studies, Gangestad and his colleagues have shown that women who seek short-term mates place special importance on the physical attractiveness of their partners, and that physically attractive men are more likely to pursue short-term mating strategies (Gangestad & Cousins, 2001; Gangestad & Thornhill, 1997; Thornhill & Gangestad, 1994, 1999).

Some research suggests that genetic and hormonal predispositions may affect men's mate choice and relationship initiation strategies (Bailey, Kirk, Zhu, Dunne, & Martin, 2000). Much of this research focuses on the moderating effects of testosterone (Dabbs & Dabbs, 2000). For example, married men, compared to their same-age single peers, tend to have lower levels of testosterone (Burnham et al., 2003), though this is not true among married men who are also interested in concurrent extrapair copulations or short-term mateships (McIntyre et al., 2006). Men who are expectant fathers and hope to have children only with their current partner have relatively low testosterone (Gray, Kahlenberg, Barrett, Lipson, & Ellison, 2002), whereas men possessing high testosterone tend to have more sexual partners, to start having sex earlier, to have higher sperm counts, to be more interested in sex, and to divorce more frequently, and are more likely to have affairs (Alexander & Sherwin, 1991; Manning, 2002; Mazur & Booth, 1998; Udry & Campbell, 1994). The root cause of this mate choice variability may lie in early testosterone exposure and its effects on the activation of men's short-term mating psychology. Exposure to high testosterone levels in utero causes increased masculinization of the human brain and increased testosterone in adulthood (Manning; Ridley, 2003). If men's brains are programmed for greater short-term mating in general (Symons, 1979; Trivers, 1972), this would lead to the hypothesis that those who are exposed to higher testosterone levels in utero would be more likely to develop short-term mating strategies in adulthood. In women, though, other factors appear to adaptively influence mating strategy choice.

Mating Differences within Women

Women's desires for engaging in sexual intercourse tend to vary across their ovulatory cycles. On average, women's desires for sex peak during the late follicular phase, just before ovulation, when the odds of becoming pregnant would be maximized (Regan, 1996). It was once thought that this shift in sexual desire evolved because it increased the probability of having conceptive intercourse in our monogamous female ancestors. However, several studies have now documented that women's short-term desires for men with high-quality genes actually peak in the highly fertile days just before ovulation (Gangestad, 2001; Gangestad, Garver-Apgar, & Simpson, 2007; Gangestad & Thornhill, 1997; Haselton & Miller, 2006).

For example, women who are interested in short-term mating tend to prefer men who are high in dominance and masculinity (Buss & Schmitt, 1993), as indicated by testosterone-related attributes such as prominent brows, large chins, and other features of facial masculinity (Mueller & Mazur, 1997; Penton-Voak & Chen, 2004; Perrett et al., 1998). Short-term-oriented women may prefer these attributes because facial markers of testosterone are honest indicators of immunocompetence quality in men (Gangestad & Thornhill, 2003). During the late follicular phase, women's preferences for men with masculine faces conspicuously increase (Johnston, Hagel, Franklin, Fink, & Grammer, 2001; Penton-Voak et al., 2003), as do their preferences for masculine voices (Puts, 2006), precisely as though women are shifting their mating psychology to follow a more short-term-oriented strategy around ovulation.

A similar ovulatory shift can be seen in women's preference for symmetrical faces. Women who generally pursue a short-term mating strategy express strong preferences for male faces that are symmetrical, perhaps because facial symmetry is indicative of low mutation load (Gangestad & Thornhill, 1997). During the late follicular phase, women's preference for symmetrical faces increases even further (Gangestad & Cousins, 2001), again as though they have shifted their psychology to that of a short-term mating strategist. It has also been shown that women who are nearing ovulation find the pheromonal smell of symmetrical men more appealing than when women are less fertile (Gangestad & Thornhill, 1998; Rikowski & Grammer, 1999), that women who mate with more symmetrical men have more frequent and intense orgasms (Thornhill, Gangestad, & Comer, 1995), and that men with attractive faces have qualitatively better health (Shackelford & Larsen, 1999) and semen characteristics (Soler et al., 2003). Finally, women appear to dress more provocatively when nearing ovulation (Grammer, Renninger, & Fischer, 2004), though women near ovulation also reduce risky behaviors associated with being raped, especially if they are not taking contraception (Bröder & Hohmann, 2003).

Overall, there is compelling evidence that women's mating strategies shift at the within-person level from a long-term mating psychology to a more short-term-oriented mating psychology, precisely when they are the most fertile. It is possible that these shifts reflect women seeking high-quality genes from extrapair copulations while maintaining a long-term relationship with a heavily investing partner (Gangestad, 2001; Haselton & Miller, 2006).

Additional individual differences and personal situations may be linked to adaptive variability in women's mate choices and relationship initiation strategies. For example, short-term mating strategies are more likely to occur during adolescence, when one's partner is of low mate value, when one desires to get rid of a mate, and after divorce—all situations where short-term mating may serve adaptive functions (Cashdan, 1996; Greiling & Buss, 2000). In some cases, short-term mating seems to emerge as an adaptive reaction to early developmental experiences within the family (Michalski & Shackelford, 2002). For example, short-term mating strategies are more likely to occur among women growing up in father-absent homes (Moffit, Caspi, Belsky, & Silva, 1992; Quinlan, 2003), especially in homes where a stepfather is present (Ellis & Garber, 2000). In these cases, the absence of a father and presence of a stepfather may indicate to young women that mating-age men are unreliable. In such environments, short-term mating may serve as the more viable mating strategy choice once in adulthood (see also Belsky, 1999).

Finally, some have argued that frequency-dependent or other forms of selection have resulted in different heritable tendencies toward long-term versus short-term mating (Gangestad & Simpson, 1990). There is behavioral genetic evidence that age at first intercourse, lifetime number of sex partners, and sociosexuality—a general trait that varies from restricted long-term mating to unrestricted short-term mating—are somewhat heritable (Bailey et al., 2000; Rowe, 2002). However, most findings suggest that heritability in mate choice and mating strategy is stronger in men than in women (Dunne et al., 1997).

EVOLUTION OF CULTURAL DIFFERENCES IN MATE CHOICE AND RELATIONSHIP INITIATION

Sex Ratios and Human Mating

In addition to sex and individual differences in mating strategies, mate choices and relationship initiation behaviors appear to vary in evolutionary-relevant ways across cultures (Frayser, 1985; Kelly, 1995; Pasternak et al., 1997). Pedersen (1991) has speculated that the relative number of men versus women in a given culture should influence mating behavior. Operational sex ratio can be defined as the relative balance of marriage-age men versus marriage-age women in the local mating pool (Secord, 1983). Sex ratios are considered "high" when the number of men significantly outsizes the number of women in a local culture. Sex ratios are considered "low" when there are relatively more women than men in the mating market. In most cultures women tend to slightly outnumber men, largely because of men's polygynous tendency to have a higher mortality rate (Daly & Wilson, 1988). Nevertheless, significant variation often exists in sex ratios across cultures, and within cultures when viewed over historical time (Grant, 1998; Guttentag & Secord, 1983).

Pedersen (1991) argued that a combination of sexual selection theory (Darwin, 1871) and parental investment theory (Trivers, 1972) leads to a series of predictions concerning the effects of sex ratios on human mating strategies. According to sexual selection theory, when males desire a particular attribute in potential mating partners, females of that species tend to respond by competing in the expression and provision of that desired attribute. Among humans, when sex ratios are especially low and there are many more women than men, men should become an especially scarce resource that women compete for with even more intensity than normal (see also Guttentag & Secord, 1983).

When combined with the parental investment notion described earlier in which men tend to desire short-term mating (Trivers, 1972), this leads to the hypothesis that humans in cultures with lower sex ratios (i.e., more women than men) should possess more short-term-oriented mating strategies. Conversely, when sex ratios are high and men greatly outnumber women, men must enter into more intense competition for the limited number of potential female partners. Women's preferences for long-term monogamous relationships become the key desires that must be responded to if men are to remain competitive in the courtship marketplace.

Using data from sex ratio fluctuations over time within the United States, Pedersen (1991) marshaled a compelling case for a causal link between sex ratios and human mating strategies (see also Guttentag & Secord, 1983). For example, high sex ratio fluctuations have been historically associated with increases in monogamy, as evidenced by lower divorce rates and men's greater willingness to invest in their children. Low sex ratios have been historically associated with indexes of short-term mating, such as an increase in divorce rates and a reduction in what he termed female "sexual coyness." In a recent cross-cultural study (Schmitt, 2005a), national sex ratios were correlated with direct measures of basic human mating strategies across 48 nations in an attempt to test Pedersen's theory. As expected, cultures with more men than women tended toward long-term mating, whereas cultures with more women than men tended toward short-term mating (see also Barber, 2000).

Attachment and Human Mating

Several combinations of life history theory (Low, 1998) and attachment theory (Bowlby, 1982) have suggested that certain critical experiences during childhood play a role in the development of human mating strategies (Belsky, 1999). Perhaps the most prominent of these theories is a life span model developed by Belsky, Steinberg, and Draper (1991). According to this model, early social experiences adaptively channel children down one of two reproductive pathways. Children who are socially exposed to high levels of stress—especially insensitive or inconsistent parenting, harsh physical environments, and economic hardship—tend to develop insecure attachment styles. These children also tend to physically mature earlier than those children who are exposed to less stress. According to Belsky and his colleagues (1991), attachment insecurity and early physical maturity subsequently lead to the evolutionary-adaptive development of what is called an "opportunistic" reproductive strategy in adulthood (i.e., short-term mating). In cultures with unpredictable social environments, it is therefore argued, children adaptively respond to stressful cues by developing the more viable strategy of short-term mating.

Conversely, those children exposed to lower levels of stress and less environmental hardship tend to be more emotionally secure and to physically mature later. These children are thought to develop a more "investing" reproductive strategy in adulthood (i.e., long-term mating) that pays evolutionary dividends in low-stress environments. Although the causal mechanisms that influence strategic mating are most prominently located within the family, this model also suggests that certain aspects of culture may be related to mating strategy variation (see also Belsky, 1999).

A closely related theory has been proposed by Chisholm (1996). Chisholm argued that local mortality rates—presumably related to high stress and inadequate resources—act as cues that facultatively shift human mating strategies in evolutionary-adaptive ways. In cultures with high mortality rates and unpredictable resources, the optimal mating strategy is to reproduce early and often, a strategy related to insecure attachment, short-term temporal orientations, and promiscuous mating strategies. In cultures that are physically safe and have abundant resources, mortality rates are lower and the optimal strategy is to invest heavily in fewer numbers of offspring. In safer environments, therefore, one should pursue a long-term strategy associated with more monogamous mating. Collectively, the Belsky et al. (1991) and Chisholm (1996) theories can be referred to as a "developmental-attachment theory" of human mating strategies.

Numerous studies have provided support for developmental-attachment theory (Barber, 2003; Belsky, 1999; Ellis & Garber, 2000; Moffit et al., 1992; Quinlan, 2003). In a recent attempt to test developmental-attachment theory, Schmitt and his colleagues (Schmitt, Alcalay, Allensworth, et al., 2004) measured the romantic attachment styles of over 17,000 people from 56 nations. They related insecure attachment styles to various indexes of familial stress, economic resources, mortality, and fertility. They found overwhelming support for developmental-attachment theory. For example, nations with higher fertility rates, higher mortality rates, higher levels of stress (e.g., poor health and education), and lower levels of resources tended to have higher levels of insecure romantic attachment. Schmitt (2005a) also found that short-term mating was related to insecure attachment across cultures. As expected, the dismissing form of insecure attachment was linked to short-term mating in men, and fearful or preoccupied forms of insecure attachment were linked to short-term mating in women. These findings support the view that stressful environments cause increases in insecure romantic attachment, increases presumably linked to short-term mating strategies (see also Kirkpatrick, 1998).

LIMITATIONS AND FUTURE RESEARCH DIRECTIONS

Evolutionary psychology is but one perspective from which to view the special psychology of human romance, and relying solely on the perspective presented here would be a mistake. For example, religion has been shown to have a strong influence on mate choice and relationship initiation (Pasternak et al., 1997; Reynolds & Tanner, 1983), particularly among women (Baumeister & Twenge, 2002). The same appears true for political ideology, education level, and other sociopolitical facets of the modern human condition (Laumann, Gagnon, Michael, & Michaels, 1994; Pratto, 1996). None of these factors have been fully integrated into the current review.

Future research on human mate choice and relationship initiation should attempt to integrate evolutionary perspectives with other theories and viewpoints on human sexuality, particularly social role theories (e.g., see Kenrick, 2006; Kenrick, Trost, & Sundie, 2004; Schmitt, 2005a). It can be tempting to contrast evolutionary and social role theories as either-or explanations of human mate choice and relationship initiation. However, an increasing number of investigators have focused on integrating these perspectives into coherent accounts of how biology and culture interact to produce the patterns of human sexuality we see across sexes, individuals, and cultures (Gangestad, Haselton, & Buss, 2006; Lippa, 2007).

The current chapter, in which mate choice and relationship initiation were viewed as resulting from a collection of evolved psychological adaptations, focused primarily on the evolutionary perspective and, as a result, may appear quite limited. Still, any comprehensive theory of mate choice and relationship initiation must first take into account the most fundamental evolutionary questions: As a species, what is our natural mating system, and how does our resulting evolved psychology influence modern human sexuality? Based on the evidence reviewed here, humans appear to possess psychological adaptations related to several mating systems, including monogamy, polygyny, and promiscuity. Our pluralistic human mating repertoire may be fundamentally organized in terms of basic long-term and short-term mating psychologies. The activation and pursuit of these mating psychologies—including concomitant patterns of mate choice and relationship initiation—differ in adaptive ways across sex, individual circumstance, and cultural context.

The sexes differ significantly in their adaptations for short-term mate choice. Men's short-term mating strategy is based primarily on obtaining large numbers of partners, being quick to consent to sex, and more actively seeking brief sexual encounters. Women's short-term strategy seems more heavily rooted in obtaining partners of high genetic quality, including men who possess masculine and symmetrical faces. Both sexes desire long-term monogamous partners who are kind and understanding, but men place more emphasis on youth, and women on social status and resource ability, when considering a long-term mate (see Table 3.1).

According to sexual selection theory (Darwin, 1871), evolved mate choice adaptations in one sex should impact on the effectiveness of relationship initiation tactics used by the opposite sex. If men possess an evolved preference for long-term mates who are relatively youthful, for example, women should be effective at using relationship initiation and mate attraction tactics that manipulate the appearance of youthfulness. Evidence suggests this is, indeed, the case (Schmitt, 2002). Conversely, if women prefer long-term mates who are able and willing to provide resources and emotional investment in offspring, men should be effective at using these tactics of initiation and attraction when seeking long-term mates (see Table 3.1).

Individual differences in mate choice and relationship initiation are also important from an evolutionary perspective, and *within-sex* differences in human mating appear to sometimes emerge as adaptive responses to key personal circumstances (e.g., one's physical characteristics). Men high in social status and mate value, for example, tend to pursue more short-term-oriented mating strategies than other men, and where possible highly valued men strive for polygynous marriages (or serial marriages). Women nearing ovulation tend to manifest desires indicative of their short-term mating psychology, expressing more potent mate choice for masculine and dominant men and being more sensitive to the pheromones of symmetrical men (Gangestad et al., 2007).

Features of culture and local ecology may influence the differential pursuit of long-term versus short-term mating strategies. In cultures with high stress levels and high fertility rates, insecure attachment and resulting short-term mating psychologies in men and women may be more common. As a result, in these cultures evolutionary psychologists expect men to emphasize obtaining large numbers of partners and women to emphasize physical features associated with masculinity and symmetry in potential mates (see Schmitt, 2005a). Finally, the relative sex ratio of men versus women in the local mating pool may play a causal role in generating differences in mate choice and relationship initiation behavior both over historical time and across the many diverse forms of human culture. Ultimately, any complete theory of human mate choice and relationship initiation will need to take account of the pluralistic mating system of humans and the accompanying psychological adaptations that lead to the sex, individual, and cultural differences reviewed here.

REFERENCES

Alcock, J. (2001). *Animal behavior* (7th ed.). Sunderland, MA: Sinauer.

Alexander, G. M., & Sherwin, B. B. (1991). The association between testosterone, sexual arousal, and selective attention for erotic stimuli in men. *Hormones and Behavior, 25,* 367–381.

Alexander, R. D., Hoogland, J. L., Howard, R. D., Noonan, K. M., & Sherman, P. W. (1979). Sexual dimorphism and breeding systems in pinnipeds, ungulates, primates, and humans. In N. A. Chagnon & W. Irons (Eds.), *Evolutionary biology and human social behavior: An anthropological perspective* (pp. 402–435). North Scituate, MA: Duxbury.

Alexander, R. D., & Noonan, K. M. (1979). Concealment of ovulation, parental care, and human social interaction. In N. A. Chagnon & W. Irons (Eds.), *Evolutionary biology and human social behavior: An anthropological perspective* (pp. 436–453). North Scituate, MA: Duxbury.

Archer, J., & Lloyd, B. B. (2002). *Sex and gender* (2nd ed.). New York: Cambridge University Press.

Bailey, J. M., Gaulin, S., Agyei, Y., & Gladue, B. A. (1994). Effects of gender and sexual orientation on evolutionary relevant aspects of human mating psychology. *Journal of Personality and Social Psychology, 66,* 1081–1093.

Bailey, J. M., Kirk, K. M., Zhu, G., Dunne, M. P., & Martin, N. G. (2000). Do individual differences in sociosexuality represent genetic or environmentally contingent strategies? Evidence from the Australian twin registry. *Journal of Personality and Social Psychology, 78,* 537–545.

Baker, R. R., & Bellis, M. A. (1995). *Human sperm competition.* London: Chapman & Hall.

Banfield, S., & McCabe, M. P. (2001). Extra relationship involvement among women: Are they different from men? *Archives of Sexual Behavior, 30,* 119–142.

Barash, D. P., & Lipton, J. E. (2001). *The myth of monogamy*. New York: W.H. Freeman.

Barber, N. (2000). On the relationship between country sex ratios and teen pregnancy rates: A replication. *Cross-Cultural Research, 34*, 26–37.

Barber, N. (2003). Paternal investment prospects and cross-national differences in single parenthood. *Cross-Cultural Research, 37*, 163–177.

Bateson, P. (Ed.). (1983). *Mate choice*. Cambridge: Cambridge University Press.

Baumeister, R. F., & Tice, D. M. (2001). *The social dimension of sex*. Needham Heights, MA: Allyn & Bacon.

Baumeister, R. F., & Twenge, J. M. (2002). Cultural suppression of female sexuality. *Review of General Psychology, 6*, 166–203.

Belsky, J. (1999). Modern evolutionary theory and patterns of attachment. In J. Cassidy & P. R. Shaver (Eds.), *Handbook of attachment* (pp. 141–161). New York: Guilford.

Belsky, J., Steinberg, L., & Draper, P. (1991). Childhood experience, interpersonal development, and reproductive strategy: An evolutionary theory of socialization. *Child Development, 62*, 647–670.

Betzig, L. (1986). *Despotism and differential reproduction: A Darwinian view of history*. New York: Aldine.

Betzig, L. (1989). Causes of conjugal dissolution: A cross-cultural study. *Current Anthropology, 30*, 654–676.

Bleske, A. L., & Shackelford, T. K. (2001). Poaching, promiscuity, and deceit: Combating mating rivalry in same-sex friendships. *Personal Relationships, 8*, 407–424.

Bleske-Rechek, A. L., & Buss, D. M. (2001). Opposite-sex friendship: Sex differences and similarities in initiation, selection, and dissolution. *Personality & Social Psychology Bulletin, 27*, 1310–1323.

Blurton Jones, N. (1986). Bushman birth spacing: A test for optimal interbirth intervals. *Ethology and Sociobiology, 7*, 91–105.

Borgerhoff Mulder, M. (1987). Cultural and reproductive success: Kipsigis evidence. *American Anthropologist, 89*, 617–634.

Borgerhoff Mulder, M. (1990). Kipsigis women's preferences for wealthy men: Evidence for female choice in mammals. *Behavioral Ecology and Sociobiology, 27*, 255–264.

Bowlby, J. (1982). *Attachment and loss: Vol. I. Attachment*. New York: Basic Books. (Original work published 1969.)

Bröder, A., & Hohmann, N. (2003). Variations in risk taking over the menstrual cycle: An improved replication. *Evolution and Human Behavior, 24*, 391–398.

Broude, G. J., & Greene, S. J. (1976). Cross-cultural codes on twenty sexual attitudes and practices. *Ethnology, 15*, 409–403.

Brown, D. E. (1991). *Human universals*. New York: McGraw-Hill.

Brown, D. E., & Hotra, D. (1988). Are prescriptively monogamous societies effectively monogamous? In L. Betzig, M. Borgerhoff Mulder, & P. Turke (Eds.), *Human reproductive behavior: A Darwinian perceptive* (pp. 153–159). Cambridge: Cambridge University Press.

Burnham, T. C., Chapman, J. F., Gray, P. B., McIntyre, M. H., Lipson, S. F., & Ellison, P. T. (2003). Men in committed, romantic relationships have lower testosterone. *Hormones and Behavior, 44*, 119–122.

Buss, D. M. (1988). From vigilance to violence: Tactics of mate retention in American undergraduates. *Ethology and Sociobiology, 9*, 291–317.

Buss, D. M. (1989). Sex differences in human mate preferences: Evolutionary hypotheses tested in 37 cultures. *Behavioral and Brain Sciences, 12*, 1–49.

Buss, D. M. (2000). *The dangerous passion*. New York: Free Press.

Buss, D. M., & Schmitt, D. P. (1993). Sexual strategies theory: An evolutionary perspective on human mating. *Psychological Review, 100*, 204–232.

Buss, D. M., & Shackelford, T. K. (1997). From vigilance to violence: Mate retention tactics in married couples. *Journal of Personality and Social Psychology, 72*, 346–361.

Buunk, A. P., Dijkstra, P., Kenrick, D. T., & Warntjes, A. (2001). Age preferences for mates as related to gender, own age, and involvement level. *Evolution and Human Behavior, 22*, 241–250.

Cashdan, E. (1993). Attracting mates: Effects of paternal investment on mate attraction strategies. *Ethology and Sociobiology, 14*, 1–24.

Cashdan, E. (1996). Women's mating strategies. *Evolutionary Anthropology, 5*, 134–143.

Chagnon, N. A. (1988). Life histories, blood revenge, and warfare in a tribal population. *Science, 239*, 985–992.

Chisholm, J. S. (1996). The evolutionary ecology of attachment organization. *Human Nature, 7*, 1–38.

Clark, R. D. (1990). The impact of AIDS on gender differences in willingness to engage in casual sex. *Journal of Applied Social Psychology, 20*, 771–782.

Clark, R. D., & Hatfield, E. (1989). Gender differences in receptivity to sexual offers. *Journal of Psychology and Human Sexuality, 2*, 39–55.

Clutton-Brock, T. H. (1991). *The evolution of parental care*. Princeton, NJ: Princeton University Press.

Cronk, L. (1991). Wealth, status, and reproductive success among the Mukogodo of Kenya. *American Anthropologist*, 93, 345–360.

Cunningham, M. R., Roberts, R., Barbee, A. P., Druen, P. B., & Wu, C. (1995). Their ideas of attractiveness are, on the whole, the same as ours: Consistency and variability in the cross-cultural perception of female attractiveness. *Journal of Personality and Social Psychology*, 68, 261–279.

Dabbs, J. M., & Dabbs, M. G. (2000). *Heroes, rogues, and lovers: Testosterone and behavior*. New York: McGraw-Hill.

Daly, M., & Wilson, M. (1988). *Homicide*. New York: Aldine de Gruyter.

Darwin, C. R. (1871). *The descent of man and selection in relation to sex*. London: Murray.

Dawson, B. L., & McIntosh, W. D. (2006). Sexual strategies theory and internet personal advertisements. *CyberPsychology and Behavior*, 9, 614–617.

Dunne, M. P., Martin, N. G., Statham, D. J., Slutske, W. S., Dinwiddie, S. H., Bucholz, K. K., et al. (1997). Genetic and environmental contributions to variance in age at first intercourse. *Psychological Science*, 8, 211–216.

Ellis, B. J. (1992). The evolution of sexual attraction: Evaluative mechanisms in women. In J. H. Barkow, L. Cosmides, & J. Tooby (Eds.), *The adapted mind* (pp. 267–288). New York: Oxford University Press.

Ellis, B. J., & Garber, J. (2000). Psychosocial antecedents of variation in girl's pubertal timing: Maternal depression, stepfather presence, and marital and family stress. *Child Development*, 71, 485–501.

Ellis, B. J., & Symons, D. (1990). Sex differences in sexual fantasy: An evolutionary psychological approach. *Journal of Sex Research*, 27, 527–556.

Feingold, A. (1992). Gender differences in mate selection preferences: A test of the parental investment model. *Psychological Bulletin*, 112, 125–139.

Fisher, H. E. (1992). *Anatomy of love: The natural history of monogamy, adultery, and divorce*. New York: Norton.

Fisher, H. E. (1998). Lust, attraction, and attachment in mammalian reproduction. *Human Nature*, 9, 23–52.

Flinn, M. V. (1985). Mate guarding in a Caribbean village. *Ethology and Sociobiology*, 9, 1–28.

Frayser, S. (1985). *Varieties of sexual experience: An anthropological perspective*. New Haven, CT: HRAF Press.

Frederick, D., Haselton, M. G., Buchanan, G. M., & Gallup, G. G. (2003, June). *Male muscularity as a good-genes indicator: Evidence from women's preferences for short-term and long-term mates*. Paper presented at the 15th annual meeting of Human Behavior and Evolution Society, Lincoln, Nebraska.

Gallup, G. G., Burch, R. L., Zappieri, M. L., Parvez, R. A., Stockwell, M. L., & Davis, J. A. (2003). The human penis as a semen displacement device. *Evolution and Human Behavior*, 24, 277–289.

Gangestad, S. W. (2001). Adaptive design, selective history, and women's sexual motivations. In J. A. French, A. C. Kamil, & D. W. Leger (Eds.), *Evolutionary psychology and motivation* (pp. 37–74). Lincoln: University of Nebraska Press.

Gangestad, S. W., & Cousins, A. J. (2001). Adaptive design, female mate preferences, and shifts across the menstrual cycle. *Annual Review of Sex Research*, 12, 145–185.

Gangestad, S. W., Garver-Apgar, C. E., & Simpson, J. A. (2007). Changes in women's mate preferences across the ovulatory cycle. *Journal of Personality and Social Psychology*, 92, 151–163.

Gangestad, S. W., Haselton, M. G., & Buss, D. M. (2006). Evolutionary foundations of cultural variation: Evoked culture and mate preferences. *Psychological Inquiry*, 17, 75–95.

Gangestad, S. W., & Simpson, J. A. (1990). Toward an evolutionary history of female sociosexual variation [Special issue: Biological foundations of personality: Evolution, behavioral genetics, and psychophysiology]. *Journal of Personality*, 58, 69–96.

Gangestad, S. W., & Simpson, J. A. (2000). The evolution of human mating: Trade-offs and strategic pluralism. *Behavioral and Brain Sciences*, 23, 573–644.

Gangestad, S. W., & Thornhill, R. (1997). The evolutionary psychology of extrapair sex: The role of fluctuating asymmetry. *Evolution and Human Behavior*, 18, 69–88.

Gangestad, S. W., & Thornhill, R. (1998). Menstrual cycle variation in women's preferences for the scent of symmetrical men. *Proceedings of the Royal Society of London B*, 265, 927–933.

Gangestad, S. W., & Thornhill, R. (2003). Facial masculinity and fluctuating asymmetry. *Evolution and Human Behavior*, 24, 231–241.

Geary, D. C. (1998). *Male, female: The evolution of human sex differences*. Washington, DC: American Psychological Association.

Grammer, K., Renninger, L., & Fischer, B. (2004). Disco clothing, female sexual motivation, and relationship status: Is she dressed to impress? *Journal of Sex Research*, 41, 66–74.

Grant, V. J. (1998). *Maternal personality, evolution and the sex ratio.* London: Routledge.

Gray, P. B., Kahlenberg, S. M., Barrett, E. S., Lipson, S. F., & Ellison, P. T. (2002). Marriage and fatherhood are associated with lower testosterone in males. *Evolution and Human Behavior, 23,* 193–201.

Graziano, W. G., Jensen-Campbell, L. A., Todd, M., & Finch, J. F. (1997). Interpersonal attraction from an evolutionary perspective: Women's reactions to dominant and prosocial men. In J. A. Simpson & D. T. Kenrick (Eds.), *Evolutionary social psychology* (pp. 141–167). Mahwah, NJ: Lawrence Erlbaum.

Greer, A. E., & Buss, D. M. (1994). Tactics for promoting sexual encounters. *Journal of Sex Research, 31,* 185–201.

Greiling, H., & Buss, D. M. (2000). Women's sexual strategies: The hidden dimension of short-term mating. *Personality and Individual Differences, 28,* 929–963.

Guttentag, M., & Secord, P. F. (1983). *Too many women? The sex ratio question.* Beverly Hills, CA: Sage.

Haselton, M. G., & Miller, G. F. (2006). Women's fertility across the cycle increases the short-term attractiveness of creative intelligence. *Human Nature, 17,* 50–73.

Heath, K. M., & Hadley, C. (1998). Dichotomous male reproductive strategies in a polygynous human society: Mating versus parental effort. *Current Anthropology, 39,* 369–374.

Hirsch, L. R., & Paul, L. (1996). Human male mating strategies, I. Courtship tactics of the "quality" and "quantity" alternatives. *Ethology and Sociobiology, 17,* 55–70.

Hrdy, S. B. (1981). *The woman that never evolved.* Cambridge, MA: Harvard University Press.

Hughes, S. M., & Gallup, G. G. (2003). Sex differences in morphological predictors of sexual behavior: Shoulder to hip and waist to hip ratios. *Evolution and Human Behavior, 24,* 173–178.

James, J. (2003, June). *Sociosexuality and self-perceived mate value: A multidimensional approach.* Poster presentation to the 15th annual meeting of Human Behavior and Evolution Society, Lincoln, Nebraska.

Jensen-Campbell, L. A., Graziano, W. G., & West, S. G. (1995). Dominance, prosocial orientation, and female preferences: Do nice guys really finish last? *Journal of Personality and Social Psychology, 68,* 427–440.

Johnston, V., Hagel, R., Franklin, M., Fink, B., & Grammer, K. (2001). Male facial attractiveness: Evidence for hormone-mediated adaptive design. *Evolution and Human Behavior, 22,* 251–267.

Jones, D. (1995). Sexual selection, physical attractiveness, and facial neoteny: Cross-cultural evidence and implications. *Current Anthropology, 36,* 723–748.

Jones, M. (1998). Sociosexuality and motivations for romantic involvement. *Journal of Research in Personality, 32,* 173–182.

Kaplan, H. S., & Gangestad, S. W. (2005). Life history theory and evolutionary psychology. In D. M. Buss (Ed.), *The handbook of evolutionary psychology* (pp. 68–95). Hoboken, NJ: Wiley.

Kelly, R. L. (1995). *The foraging spectrum: Diversity in hunter-gatherer lifeways.* Washington, DC: Smithsonian Institution Press.

Kenrick, D. T. (2006). Evolutionary psychology: Resistance is futile. *Psychological Inquiry, 17,* 102–109.

Kenrick, D. T., & Keefe, R. C. (1992). Age preferences in mates reflect sex differences in human reproductive strategies. *Behavioral and Brain Sciences, 15,* 75–133.

Kenrick, D. T., Neuberg, S. L., Zierk, K. L., & Krones, J. M. (1994). Evolution and social cognition: Contrast effects as a function of sex, dominance, and physical attractiveness. *Personality and Social Psychology Bulletin, 20,* 210–217.

Kenrick, D. T., Sadalla, E. K., Groth, G., & Trost, M. R. (1990). Evolution, traits, and the stages of human courtship: Qualifying the parental investment model [Special issue: Biological foundations of personality: evolution, behavioral genetics, and psychophysiology]. *Journal of Personality, 58,* 97–116.

Kenrick, D. T., Trost, M. R., & Sundie, J. M. (2004). Sex roles as adaptations: An evolutionary perspective on gender differences and similarities. In A. H. Eagly, A. E. Beall, & R. J. Sternberg (Eds.), *The psychology of gender* (2nd ed.; pp. 65–91). New York: Guilford Press.

Kirkpatrick, L. A. (1998). Evolution, pair-bonding, and reproductive strategies: A reconceptualization of adult attachment. In J. A. Simpson & W. S. Rholes (Eds.), *Attachment theory and close relationships* (pp. 353–393). New York: Guilford.

Kirkpatrick, L. A., Waugh, C. E., Valencia, A., & Webster, G. D. (2002). The functional domain specificity of self-esteem and the differential prediction of aggression. *Journal of Personality and Social Psychology, 82,* 756–767.

Klusmann, D. (2002). Sexual motivation and the duration of partnership. *Archives of Sexual Behavior, 31,* 275–287.

Knodel, J., Low, B., Saengtienchai, C., & Lucas, R. (1997). An evolutionary perspective on Thai sexual attitudes and behavior. *Journal of Sex Research, 34,* 292–303.

Kruger, D. J., Fisher, M., & Jobling, I. (2003). Proper and dark heroes as dads and cads: Alternative mating strategies in British romantic literature. *Human Nature, 14,* 305–317.

Lalumiere, M. L., Seto, M. C., & Quinsey, V. L. (1995). *Self-perceived mating success and the mating choices of males and females.* Unpublished manuscript.

Lancaster, J. B. (1994). Human sexuality, life histories, and evolutionary ecology. In A. S. Rossi (Ed.), *Sexuality across the life course* (pp. 39–62). Chicago: University of Chicago Press.

Landolt, M. A., Lalumiere, M. L., & Quinsey, V. L. (1995). Sex differences in intra-sex variations in human mating tactics: An evolutionary approach. *Ethology and Sociobiology, 16,* 3–23.

Laumann, E. O., Gagnon, J. H., Michael, R. T., & Michaels, S. (1994). *The social organization of sexuality.* Chicago: University of Chicago Press.

Li, N. P., Bailey, M. J., Kenrick, D. T., & Linsenmeier, J. A. (2002). The necessities and luxuries of mate preferences: Testing the tradeoffs. *Journal of Personality and Social Psychology, 82,* 947–955.

Li, N. P., & Kenrick, D. T. (2006). Sex similarities and differences in preferences for short-term mates: What, whether, and why. *Journal of Personality and Social Psychology, 90,* 468–489.

Lippa, R. A. (2007). The preferred traits of mates in a cross-national study of heterosexual and homosexual men and women: An examination of biological and cultural influences. *Archives of Sexual Behavior, 36,* 193–208.

Little, A. C., & Mannion, H. (2006). Viewing attractive or unattractive same-sex individuals changes self-rated attractiveness and face preferences in women. *Animal Behavior, 72,* 981–987.

Low, B. S. (1989). Cross-cultural patterns in the training of children: An evolutionary perspective. *Journal of Comparative Psychology, 103,* 313–319.

Low, B. S. (1998). The evolution of human life histories. In C. Crawford & D. L. Krebs (Eds.), *Handbook of evolutionary psychology* (pp. 131–161). Mahwah, NJ: Lawrence Erlbaum.

Low, B. S. (2000). *Why sex matters.* Princeton, NJ: Princeton University Press.

Malamuth, N. M. (1996). Sexually explicit media, gender differences, and evolutionary theory. *Journal of Communication, 46,* 8–31.

Manning, J. T. (2002). *Digit ratio: A pointer to fertility, behavior, and health.* New Brunswick, NJ: Rutgers University Press.

Mazur, A., & Booth, A. (1998). Testosterone and dominance in men. *Behavioral and Brain Sciences, 21,* 353–397.

McGuire, M., & Gruter, M. (2003). Prostitution: An evolutionary perspective. In A. Somit & S. Peterson (Eds.), *Human nature and public policy: An evolutionary approach* (pp. 29–40). New York: Palgrave Macmillan.

McIntyre, M., Gangestad, S. W., Gray, P. B., Chapman, J. F., Burnham, T. C., O'Rourke, M. T., et al. (2006). Romantic involvement often reduces men's testosterone levels—but not always: The moderating role of extrapair sexual interest. *Journal of Personality and Social Psychology, 91,* 642–651.

Mealey, L. (2000). *Sex differences: Developmental and evolutionary strategies.* San Diego, CA: Academic Press.

Michalski, R. L., & Shackelford, T. K. (2002). Birth order and sexual strategy. *Personality and Individual Differences, 33,* 661–667.

Mikach, S. M., & Bailey, J. M. (1999). What distinguishes women with unusually high numbers of sex partners? *Evolution and Human Behavior, 20,* 141–150.

Miller, G. F. (2000). *The mating mind.* New York: Doubleday.

Moffit, T. E., Caspi, A., Belsky, J., & Silva, P. A. (1992). Childhood experience and the onset of menarche: A test of a sociobiological model. *Child Development, 63,* 47–58.

Mueller, U., & Mazur, A. (1997). Facial dominance in *Homo sapiens* as honest signaling of male quality. *Behavioral Ecology, 8,* 569–579.

Munroe, R. L., & Munroe, R. H. (1997). A comparative anthropological perspective. In J. W. Berry, Y. H. Poortinga, & J. Pandey (Eds.), *Handbook of cross-cultural psychology* (2nd ed., Vol. 1, pp. 171–213). Boston: Allyn & Bacon.

Nettle, D. (2002). Height and reproductive success in a cohort of British men. *Human Nature, 13,* 473–491.

Okami, P., & Shackelford, T. K. (2001). Human sex differences in sexual psychology and behavior. *Annual Review of Sex Research, 12,* 186–241.

Oliver, M. B., & Hyde, J. S. (1993). Gender differences in sexuality: A meta-analysis. *Psychological Bulletin, 114,* 29–51.

Pasternak, B., Ember, C., & Ember, M. (1997). *Sex, gender, and kinship: A cross-cultural perspective.* Upper Saddle River, NJ: Prentice Hall.

Pedersen, F. A. (1991). Secular trends in human sex ratios: Their influence on individual and family behavior. *Human Nature, 2,* 271–291.

Penton-Voak, I. S., & Chen, J. Y. (2004). High salivary testosterone is linked to masculine male facial appearance in humans. *Evolution and Human Behavior, 25,* 229–241.

Penton-Voak, I. S., Little, A. C., Jones, B. C., Burt, D. M., Tiddeman, B. P., & Perrett, D. I. (2003). Female condition influences preferences for sexual dimorphism in faces of male humans (*Homo sapiens*). *Journal of Comparative Psychology, 117,* 264–271.

Perrett, D. I., Lee, K. J., Penton-Voak, I. S., Rowland, D. R., Yoshikawa, S., Burt, D. M., et al. (1998). Effects of sexual dimorphism on facial attractiveness. *Nature, 394,* 884–887.

Pierce, C. A. (1996). Body height and romantic attraction: A meta-analytic test of the male-taller norm. *Social Behavior & Personality, 24,* 143–149.

Pratto, F. (1996). Sexual politics: The gender gap in the bedroom, the cupboard, and the cabinet. In D. M. Buss & N. M. Malamuth (Eds.), *Sex, power, and conflict: Evolutionary and feminist perspectives* (pp. 179–230). New York: Oxford University Press.

Puts, D. A. (2006). Cyclic variation in women's preferences for masculine traits: Potential hormonal causes. *Human Nature, 17,* 114–127.

Quinlan, R. J. (2003). Father absence, parental care, and female reproductive development. *Evolution and Human Behavior, 24,* 376–390.

Regan, P. C. (1996). Rhythms of desire: The association between menstrual cycle phases and female sexual desire. *Canadian Journal of Human Sexuality, 5,* 145–156.

Regan, P. C. (1998a). Minimum mate selection standards as a function of perceived mate value, relationship context, and gender. *Journal of Psychology and Human Sexuality, 10,* 53–73.

Regan, P. C. (1998b). What if you can't get what you want? Willingness to compromise ideal mate selection standards as a function of sex, mate value, and relationship context. *Personality and Social Psychology Bulletin, 24,* 1294–1303.

Regan, P. C., & Berscheid, E. (1997). Gender differences in characteristics desired in a potential sexual and marriage partner. *Journal of Psychology and Human Sexuality, 9,* 25–37.

Regan, P. C., Levin, L., Sprecher, S., Christopher, F. S., & Cate, R. (2000). Partner preferences: What characteristics do men and women desire in their short-term and long-term romantic partners? *Journal of Psychology and Human Sexuality, 12,* 1–21.

Reynolds, V., & Tanner, R. E. S. (1983). *The biology of religion.* London: Longman.

Ridley, M. (2003). *Nature via nurture.* New York: HarperCollins.

Rikowski, A., & Grammer, K. (1999). Human body odor, symmetry, and attractiveness. *Proceedings of the Royal Academy of London B, 266,* 869–874.

Rowe, D. C. (2002). On genetic variation in menarche and age at first intercourse: A critique of the Belsky-Draper hypothesis. *Evolution and Human Behavior, 23,* 365–372.

Salmon, C., & Symons, D. (2001). *Warrior lovers: Erotic fiction, evolution, and female sexuality.* London: Weidenfeld & Nicolson.

Schmitt, D. P. (2002). A meta-analysis of sex differences in romantic attraction: Do rating contexts affect tactic effectiveness judgments? *British Journal of Social Psychology, 41,* 387–402.

Schmitt, D. P. (2005a). Sociosexuality from Argentina to Zimbabwe: A 48-nation study of sex, culture, and strategies of human mating. *Behavioral and Brain Sciences, 28,* 247–275.

Schmitt, D. P. (2005b). Is short-term mating the maladaptive result of insecure attachment? A test of competing evolutionary perspectives. *Personality and Social Psychology Bulletin, 31,* 747–768.

Schmitt, D. P., Alcalay, L., Allik, J., Ault, L., Austers, I., Bennett, K. L., et al. (2003). Universal sex differences in the desire for sexual variety: Tests from 52 nations, 6 continents, and 13 islands. *Journal of Personality and Social Psychology, 85,* 85–104.

Schmitt, D. P., Alcalay, L., Allensworth, M., Allik, J., Ault, L., Austers, I., et al. (2004). Patterns and universals of adult romantic attachment across 62 cultural regions: Are models of self and other pancultural constructs? *Journal of Cross-Cultural Psychology, 35,* 367–402.

Schmitt, D. P., Alcalay, L., Allik, J., Angleiter, A., Ault, L., Austers, I., et al. (2004). Patterns and universals of mate poaching across 53 nations: The effects of sex, culture, and personality on romantically attracting another person's partner. *Journal of Personality and Social Psychology, 86,* 560–584.

Schmitt, D. P., & Buss, D. M. (1996). Strategic self-enhancement and competitor derogation: Sex and context effects on the perceived effectiveness of mate attraction tactics. *Journal of Personality and Social Psychology, 70,* 1185–1204.

Schmitt, D. P., & Buss, D. M. (2001). Human mate poaching: Tactics and temptations for infiltrating existing mateships. *Journal of Personality and Social Psychology, 80,* 894–917.

Schmitt, D. P., Couden, A., & Baker, M. (2001). Sex, temporal context, and romantic desire: An experimental evaluation of sexual strategies theory. *Personality and Social Psychology Bulletin, 27,* 833–847.

Schmitt, D. P., & Shackelford, T. K. (2003). Nifty ways to leave your lover: The tactics people use to entice and disguise the process of human mate poaching. *Personality and Social Psychology Bulletin, 29,* 1018–1035.

Schmitt, D. P., Shackelford, T. K., Duntely, J., Tooke, W., Buss, D. M., Fisher, M. L., et al. (2002). Is there an early-30's peak in female sexual desire? Cross-sectional evidence from the United States and Canada. *Canadian Journal of Human Sexuality, 11,* 1–18.

Schützwohl, A. (2006). Sex difference in jealousy: Information search and cognitive preoccupation. *Personality and Individual Differences, 40,* 285–292.

Seal, D. W., Agostinelli, G., & Hannett, C. A. (1994). Extradyadic romantic involvement: Moderating effects of sociosexuality and gender. *Sex Roles, 31,* 1–22.

Secord, P. F. (1983). Imbalanced sex ratios: The social consequences. *Personality and Social Psychology Bulletin, 9,* 525–543.

Shackelford, T. K., & Larsen, R. J. (1999). Facial attractiveness and physical health. *Evolution and Human Behavior, 20,* 71–76.

Shackelford, T. K., & LeBlanc, G. J. (2001). Sperm competition in insects, birds, and humans: Insights from a comparative evolutionary perspective. *Evolution and Cognition, 7,* 194–202.

Shuster, S. M., & Wade, M. J. (2003). *Mating systems and strategies.* Princeton, NJ: Princeton University Press.

Simpson, J. A., & Gangestad, S. W. (1991). Individual differences in sociosexuality: Evidence for convergent and discriminant validity. *Journal of Personality and Social Psychology, 60,* 870–883.

Simpson, J. A., Wilson, C. L., & Winterheld, H. A. (2004). Sociosexuality and romantic relationships. In J. H. Harvey, A. Wenzel, & S. Sprecher (Eds.), *Handbook of sexuality in close relationships* (pp. 87–111). Mahwah, NJ: Lawrence Erlbaum.

Singh, D. (1993). Adaptive significance of female physical attractiveness: Role of waist-to-hip ratio. *Journal of Personality and Social Psychology, 65,* 293–307.

Smith, R. L. (1984). Human sperm competition. In R. L. Smith (Ed.), *Sperm competition and the evolution of animal mating systems* (pp. 601–659). New York: Academic Press.

Soler, C., Nunez, M., Gutierrez, R., Nunez, J., Medina, P., Sancho, M., et al. (2003). Facial attractiveness in men provides clues to semen quality. *Evolution and Human Behavior, 24,* 199–207.

Sprecher, S., Sullivan, Q., & Hatfield, E. (1994). Mate selection preferences: Gender differences examined in a national sample. *Journal of Personality and Social Psychology, 66,* 1074–1080.

Symons, D. (1979). *The evolution of human sexuality.* New York: Oxford University Press.

Symons, D., & Ellis, B. J. (1989). Human male-female differences in sexual desire. In A. Rasa, C. Vogel, & E. Voland (Eds.), *Sociobiology of sexual and reproductive strategies* (pp. 131–147). London: Chapman and Hall.

Thornhill, R., & Gangestad, S. W. (1994). Human fluctuating asymmetry and sexual behavior. *Psychological Science, 5,* 297–302.

Thornhill, R., & Gangestad, S. W. (1999). The scent of symmetry: A human sex pheromone that signals fitness? *Evolution and Human Behavior, 20,* 175–201.

Thornhill, R., Gangestad, S. W., & Comer, R. (1995). Human female orgasm and mate fluctuating asymmetry. *Animal Behaviour, 50,* 1601–1615.

Thornhill, R., & Palmer, C. T. (2000). *A natural history of rape.* Cambridge, MA: MIT Press.

Tooke, W., & Camire, L. (1991). Patterns of deception in intersexual and intrasexual mating strategies. *Ethology and Sociobiology, 12,* 345–364.

Townsend, J. M. (1995). Sex without emotional involvement: An evolutionary interpretation of sex differences. *Archives of Sexual Behavior, 24,* 173–205.

Townsend, J. M., & Wasserman, T. (1998). Sexual attractiveness: Sex differences in assessment and criteria. *Evolution and Human Behavior, 19,* 171–191.

Trivers, R. (1972). Parental investment and sexual selection. In B. Campbell (Ed.), *Sexual selection and the descent of man: 1871–1971* (pp. 136–179). Chicago: Aldine.

Trivers, R. (1985). *Social evolution.* Menlo Park, CA: Benjamin/Cummings.

Turke, P., & Betzig, L. (1985). Those who can do: Wealth, status, and reproductive success on Ifaluk. *Ethology and Sociobiology, 6,* 79–87.

Udry, J. R., & Campbell, B. C. (1994). Getting started on sexual behavior. In A. S. Rossi (Ed.), *Sexuality over the life course* (pp. 187–207). Chicago: University of Chicago Press.

Urbaniak, G. C., & Kilmann, P. R. (2003). Physical attractiveness and the "nice guy paradox": Do nice guys really finish last? *Sex Roles, 49,* 413–426.

Walsh, A. (1991). Self-esteem and sexual behavior: Exploring gender differences. *Sex Roles, 25,* 441–450.

Walter, A. (1997). The evolutionary psychology of mate selection in Morocco: A multivariate analysis. *Human Nature, 8,* 113–137.

Walters, S., & Crawford, C. B. (1994). The importance of mate attraction for intrasexual competition in men and women. *Ethology and Sociobiology, 15,* 5–30.

Wiederman, M. W. (1993). Evolved gender differences in mate preferences: Evidence from personal advertisements. *Ethological and Sociobiology, 14,* 331–352.

Wiederman, M. W. (1997). Extramarital sex: Prevalence and correlates in a national survey. *Journal of Sex Research, 34,* 167–174.

Young, L. J. (2003). The neural basis of pair bonding in a monogamous species: A model for understanding the biological basis of human behavior. In K. W. Wachter & R. A. Bulatao (Eds.), *Offspring: Human fertility behavior in biodemographic perspective* (pp. 91–103). Washington, DC: National Academies Press.

4

Attachment Theory and Research
A Special Focus on Relationship Initiation

GARY CREASEY and PATRICIA JARVIS

*T*he importance of very close relationships to adult functioning is underscored by the finding that many adults seeking mental health services cannot form or effectively maintain close affiliations in general (Creasey & Hesson-McInnis, 2001). Given this aforementioned finding, and that our network of close relationships has been shrinking over time (McPherson, Smith-Lovin, & Brashears, 2006), predicting the successful initiation of these affiliations holds important theoretical and practical value. However, the quest to identify a unifying theory to forecast relationship initiation across different types of affiliations is difficult because the motives to establish new relationships are often dependent on personal needs and relationship provisions. For example, a young adult may initiate a dating relationship based on physical attributes, but instigate a close relationship with a coworker because the affiliation may enhance career development. However, we suggest herein that attachment theory provides a useful perspective for explaining the successful initiation of relationships that have the potential to become very close and intimate.

This chapter opens with a description of attachment theory, a conceptualization of an attachment relationship, as well as information on recent advances in attachment theory and research. Next, research that has associated attachment functioning with relationship initiation across a number of important affiliations will be described. Studies that have examined the role of attachment functioning in dating and newlywed relationships will be delineated, followed by a discussion on how emerging attachment processes may influence the behavior of new parents, the development of attachment stances in their infants, and the ability of caregivers to work together as a team to care for the newborn. This latter phenomenon is known as co-parenting and marks a reorganization of the marital relationship. Next, we examine the association between attachment and grandparent–grandchildren relationships, and how attachment processes predict the initiation of family caregiving.

Because attachment functioning predicts the quality of affiliations outside the family, we next specify the role of attachment in friendship initiation and worker–mentor relationships. Further, much has been written regarding the clinical implications of attachment theory (e.g., Slade, 1999); thus, we turn to work that has examined the role of attachment processes in the initiation of client–therapist relationships. Finally, theorists have provided accounts for the role of attachment functioning in forecasting relationship initiation after a loss (Bowlby, 1980); therefore, this issue is discussed as well. The chapter concludes with a summary regarding future research directions.

Although there has been some excellent research connecting attachment processes to relationship initiation, there are some thorny issues that we will reflect on throughout this chapter. First, a considerable amount of research on the topic of relationship initiation, in general, includes traditional-aged college student samples. It is highly debated in the social sciences whether data gleaned from such samples can be generalized because college students are generally viewed as higher functioning (in terms of most abilities) than the broader population. The second issue is related to the first and concerns the paucity of research involving attachment and relationship initiation at different phases of life. For example, the role of attachment functioning in motivating relationship initiation may shift as adults change the manner in which they think about social and emotional relationships (Carstensen, 1991). Third, much of the current research concerning attachment and relationship functioning has been conducted on dyads that have been in a relationship for some time, and there is much less work involving affiliations that are newly evolving (i.e., in the initiation phase). Thus, we acknowledge that some of the relationships discussed in this chapter are not necessarily "new" affiliations but, rather, are newly transformed relationships that are influenced by attachment issues. For example, whereas parenthood involves the initiation of an attachment relationship with the infant, the marital relationship also undergoes important transformations with the initiation of co-parenting that are touched by attachment processes. In such cases, both types of relationships (new and transformed) will be discussed because of their reciprocal influences.

CONTEMPORARY ATTACHMENT THEORY

The catalyst for modern attachment research is based primarily on Bowlby's (1969/1982) ethological attachment theory; thus, his work should be broached first. Bowlby (1969/1982) asserted that attachment affiliations between infants and caregivers were necessary from a survival standpoint. The development of emotional bonds between infants and caregivers was theorized as a major reason our species has become successful (Bowlby, 1988). However, although all infants become attached to caregivers, the caregiving environment produces differences in the quality of this attachment, and to capture such diversity, Ainsworth developed the *strange situation* procedure (Ainsworth, Blehar, Waters, & Wall, 1978). In this method, infants are separated from, and reunited with, their caregiver as well as a "stranger" over brief observational segments. To assess attachment quality, Ainsworth developed a classification system that identified three *organized* patterns of attachment. *Secure* infants can receive comfort from caregivers when distressed, yet are prone to exploration when content. *Avoidant* infants distance themselves from caregivers and rely on themselves (or focus on the environment) for comfort. When distressed, infants may focus on toys instead of the caregiver. *Ambivalent* or *resistant* infants have difficulties with receiving comfort from caregivers and display limited exploration when content (Ainsworth et al., 1978). The latter two classifications are signs of *attachment insecurity*.

Attachment security is considered the modal attachment classification and is closely linked with healthy development across cultures. Further, in Ainsworth's (Ainsworth et al., 1978) original classification scheme, some infants could not be classified. Main and Solomon (1990) concluded that these infants did not have an organized attachment system and rated them as *disorganized-disoriented*. Such infants often display contradictory, bizarre behavior. For example, these infants, upon seeing the parent return to the room, may approach the caregiver and then suddenly back away.

The validity of infant attachment is accentuated by the finding that attachment classifications modestly predict later social competence, psychological health, and academic adjustment (Thompson, 1999). Further, attachment experiences with principal caregivers become internalized as working models of attachment or *generalized attachment representations* (Bowlby, 1988). Generalized representations are conceptualized as "operable" models of self and attachment partners, and serve to "regulate, interpret, and predict both the attachment figure's and the self's attachment-related behaviors, thoughts, and feelings" (Bretherton & Munholland, 1999, p. 89). Thus, generalized attachment representations are stable, deeply ingrained mental schemes regarding relationships that we import to emerging affiliations. In this vein, these representations may have important implications for relationship initiation.

However, Bowlby never projected that generalized attachment representations predict functioning in every adult "close" or personal relationship. Rather, attachment theory forecasts interpersonal functioning in our *closest relationships* or, as proposed by Waters, Corcoran, and Anafarta (2005), "affairs of the heart" (p. 81). Thus, because not all close or personal relationships necessarily qualify as attachment relationships, certain standards for these latter affiliations have been set forth. For example, attachment relationships tend to be enduring and emotionally salient, and attachment figures are not easily interchangeable with other people when an individual is distressed (Ainsworth, 1989; Cassidy, 1999). Thus, whereas these tenets were first applied as a way to conceptualize attachment relationships between parents and their offspring (and eventually marital partners), such criteria also pertain to other relationships (Creasey & Jarvis, 2008). Nonfamilial affiliations, such as close friendships, workplace relationships, and relationships with mental health professionals, could be considered attachment-like. Thus, in adhering to the aforementioned conceptualization of an attachment relationship, we herein focus on the role of attachment in predicting relationship initiation within potentially close affiliations.

Advances in Attachment Theory and Research

Bowlby's (1988) conceptualization of generalized attachment representations was supported by the development of the Adult Attachment Interview (AAI; George, Kaplan, & Main, 1996). This interview assesses one's *state of mind* regarding attachment to principal caregivers, and measures "the security of attachment in its generality rather than in relation to any particular present or past relationship" (Main, Kaplan, & Cassidy, 1985, p. 78). Although the AAI inquires about past relationships, the interview discourse is thought to reflect a stable "state of mind" that is reflective of broad, generalized representations of very close relationships rather than a relationship to any one person. Like the infant strange situation, the AAI coding system yields three organized attachment classifications, but these evaluations are based primarily on the person's state of mind regarding attachment. Thus, it is possible for adults who report childhood negative experiences to be rated as secure, given that they are objective and collaborative regarding these experiences.

Individuals classified as *secure* are coherent throughout the interview and objectively discuss positive and negative experiences. *Dismissing* adults provide highly idealized representations of attachment experiences, which are unsupported throughout the interview. They are often dismissive of unfavorable attachment experiences and display a highly defensive stance during the interview. Finally, *preoccupied* adults provide excessive discourse when describing attachment experiences and show strong negative (e.g., anger) responses when discussing these memories (Main, Goldwyn, & Hesse, 2002).

After these classifications are derived, interviews can be classified as *unresolved-disorganized* with respect to trauma. During discussion of loss or maltreatment, the adult may display sudden lapses in monitoring of discourse, such as unusual attention to a traumatic event, sudden changes of topic, or invasions of other topics of information (Main et al., 2002). Although secure people have experienced such events, they can speak about them in a lucid manner. In contrast, unresolved adults *remain* traumatized, as evidenced by their peculiar patterns of linguistic discourse as they discuss these experiences.

Although generalized attachment representations captured via the AAI forecast the development of marital relationships, parenting behavior, and adult child–parent caregiving relationships (Waters et al., 2005), the dynamics and needs in the relationships also differ. For example, although infants are dependent on parents, the support or encouragement of such one-sided dependence would be unhealthy in adult relationships. Thus, parent–infant and adult romantic partners qualify as attachment figures; however, the perceptions of closeness, dependability, anxiety, and trust in these affiliations depend on the nature and maturity of the relationship (Collins & Read, 1994; Hazan & Shaver, 1987). As a result, adults not only possess generalized representations but acquire *relationship-specific representations* as well (Creasey & Ladd, 2005; Furman & Simon, 2006; Roisman, Collins, Sroufe, & Egeland, 2005; Treboux, Crowell, & Waters, 2004).

As an example, romantic love has been conceptualized as an attachment process, and various attachment styles of romantic couples have been proposed that mirror Ainsworth's (Ainsworth et al., 1978) depiction of infant attachment (Bartholomew, 1990; Hazan & Shaver, 1987). A *secure* adult feels emotionally close to partners, is trusting, and is comfortable depending on partners (and vice versa). *Avoidant* adults are uncomfortable with closeness and dislike depending on partners, and *anxious* or *ambivalent* adults express concerns over partner availability and are distrusting of romantic partners. Further, *fearful* adults view themselves as nonviable partners and are generally fearful of close relationships (Bartholomew & Horowitz, 1991).

Two key points should be made at this juncture. First, a generalized attachment representation signifies a broad way of thinking about close relationships that is based on years of attachment experiences. Thus, it is straightforward to posit that these representations play an important role in the relationship initiation process and relationship development. Secondly, a relationship-specific schema is more targeted; this representation may be about a particular relationship (e.g., a romantic relationship), or even a particular person (e.g., a marital partner). Because more targeted attachment representations take time to develop, it could be argued that research pertaining to this construct may have little relevance for relationship initiation.

Indeed, much of the work that is cited in this chapter concerns associations between generalized attachment representations and relationship initiation success. However, there is some debate regarding the conceptualization of specific attachment representations. Some researchers instruct their participants to think about their relationship with one person when conducting assessments (e.g., a marital partner; Treboux et al., 2004), whereas others ask adults to consider their broad thinking regarding one type of relationship across different attachment partners (e.g., history of romantic relationships). When construed in the latter fashion, more specific representations might have some bearing in relationship initiation. For example, an adult who has had harmonious relationships with previous romantic partners may feel very comfortable initiating new dating relationships (Carnelley & Janoff-Bulman, 1992).

In sum, attachment theory represents a viable perspective to consider in predicting relationship initiation. Indeed, there are fundamental correlates of general attachment security that have important implications for such relationship initiation. Secure people of all ages are curious, socially competent, persistent, open to experience, and autonomous, and possess good social information–processing skills (e.g., Allen & Land, 1999; Sroufe, Egeland, Carlson, & Collins, 2005). These are qualities that theoretically could spur relationship initiation and, as importantly, might mark just the type of individuals with whom one would like to initiate a close relationship.

Further, there are correlates of insecure attachment stances that are socially ineffective. For example, more dismissing adults are viewed as hostile, aloof, and domineering (Kobak & Sceery, 1988). Similarly, there are qualities of attachment anxiety that might be viewed as undesirable; for example, these adults have high emotional needs, are moody, lack general self-confidence (Sroufe et al., 2005), and are impulsive in their "emotional decisions." To illustrate, preoccupied adults make errors in judging the emotions of others (e.g., attributing anger to a neutral facial expression) as well as the motives behind the emotion (Fraley, Niedenthal, Marks, Brumbaugh, & Vicary, 2006). Thus, the tendency for dismissing adults to express discomfort with relationships and the proneness of preoccupied people to have poor "people-reading" skills could conceivably dampen their ability to competently initiate relationships and could make them undesirable relationship targets. These are themes that will be revisited throughout this chapter. We now turn to a discussion of the role of attachment processes in relationship initiation across different affiliations.

Dating and Newlywed Relationships

There are many studies that have linked attachment functioning to success in romantic relationships; however, most of this research involves college students who have been involved in dating relationships for some time. In adherence to the central theme of this volume, we concentrate our efforts on two important relationship events—the initiation of dating relationships and the transition to marriage. Although the former relationship is clearly one that has an "initiation" phase, it is also true that newlywed relationships mark a transition in a romantic relationship. That is, the adult is no longer dating; rather, the adult is now initiating or negotiating a new, potentially long-term, legal, committed relationship.

Dating Relationships   Researchers have examined demographic, psychosocial, emotional, and physical characteristics that facilitate or dampen the pursuit of such affiliations. For example, young adults who consider themselves physically attractive are more likely to initiate dating relationships than their counterparts who consider themselves less attractive, whereas adults who are shy or inhibited display more hesitancy in initiating such relationships than their less inhibited counterparts (Clark, Shaver, & Abrahams, 1999; Simpson, Rholes, & Phillips, 1996; Snyder, Berscheid, & Glick, 1985). Further, adults tend to value physical attractiveness in a potential partner as a motivator to initiate dating relationships (Hazan & Diamond, 2000). There are also variables that moderate or mediate these aforementioned findings; for example, inhibited adults are more comfortable initiating these relationships via online dating services than in person (Scharlott & Christ, 1995).

What role may attachment processes play in the initiation of dating relationships? Secure and insecure adults demonstrate first impressions that could have an influence on their relative success as potential viable dating partners. For example, in first-time meetings *with unfamiliar people*, secure adults are rated as more emotionally engaging than their insecure counterparts. Further, dismissing adults display more indifference or aloofness, and preoccupied people exhibit more conversation dominance (Roisman, 2006). These compelling data raise two important issues. First, the fact that attachment stances predict interactions with unfamiliar adults contradicts the notion that attachment functioning is relevant for only very close relationships. Second, the initial, somewhat pushy behavior of preoccupied adults toward unfamiliar adults seems at odds with the notion that they have little confidence in their relationship adeptness. However, this initial aggressive posture of preoccupied adults reminds us of a familiar theme in the child development literature. Children who are disliked in their peer group are prone to very high approach behavior when they are introduced to new peers (Dodge, Pettit, McClasky, & Brown, 1986). However, this approach behavior is not competent and typically results in eventual rejection in the new peer group. Thus, such research findings suggest that we need to better examine "the way" people initiate relationships in conjunction with whether they do so or not. Indeed, given that secure people have more lasting relationships than their insecure counterparts (Hazan & Shaver, 1987), it is possible that more insecure adults attempt more relationship initiation over their life span. This premise supports our contention that "how" adults initiate relationships may be a more important consideration than "how much" or "how little" adults conduct such social business.

However, do the general positive social and emotional qualities of secure people translate to the successful initiation of dating relationships? It appears so, because adults highly value characteristics of potential dating partners that are consistent with a secure attachment style. Most adults view potential dating partners as more attractive if they are portrayed as trustworthy, dependable, and emotionally open, and are less inclined to date someone if he or she is portrayed as emotionally vulnerable (or emotionally unavailable), undependable, or dishonest (Chappell & Davis, 1998; Frazier, Byer, Fischer, Wright, & DeBord, 1996; Pietromonaco & Carnelley, 1994). Thus, when considering the viability of potential dating partners, most adults desire the attributes that define a secure attachment stance.

Furthermore, adults who are portrayed as more anxious or preoccupied are viewed as more viable dating partners than individuals viewed as more dismissing-avoidant or unresolved-fearful (Klohnen & Luo, 2003). Thus, adults are more likely to accept emotional vulnerability in their potential dating partners than a partner who is undependable, uncomfortable with close relationships, or fearful regarding romantic attachments. Whereas adults are more attracted to potential dating partners who are more secure, the viability of potential dating partners with insecure attachment stances is dependent on the individual's attachment representation as well. For example, adults who are more preoccupied or anxious about romantic relationships voice strong displeasure when confronted with potential dating partners who are portrayed as more avoidant or dismissing (Klohnen & Luo, 2003). Such a reaction is understandable, given that more anxious or preoccupied people express very strong emotional needs that are unlikely to be met by this potential partner.

Although secure people are viewed as desirable dating partners, does one's *own* attachment stance influence dating initiation? Because secure adults exhibit the types of thinking (e.g., good social information–processing skills) and behaviors that maintain close relationships (Allen & Land, 1999; Creasey & Jarvis, 2008), they may be adept at pursuing and initiating potential romantic relationships they judge to be potentially viable. Also, because more secure people are curious as well as confident in their social abilities (Sroufe et al., 2005), such competency should forecast successful relationship initiation. For example, the curiosity of more secure adults may translate to competent, well-reasoned, dating initiation behavior, in that these individuals, when confronted with hypothetical dating partners, request a lot of information about these potential partners before selecting one for a "date" (Aspelmeier & Kerns, 2003).

Whereas even insecure adults may initiate romantic relationships, the very nature of certain insecure attachment stances may also inhibit relationship initiation. Fearful adults, who may be traumatized over some form of abuse or loss, may be very inhibited regarding close relationships and less likely to initiate such relationships (Scharlott & Christ, 1995). Further, more avoidant or dismissing adults tend to eschew close relationships (Allen & Land, 1999), whereas more anxious or preoccupied individuals have received the lifelong message that they are not worthy of love or attachment. Thus, more insecure adults may be more inhibited than their secure counterparts in initiating dating relationships, or not be as choosy about whom to go out with on an initial date. For example, more dismissing adults, when confronted with an array of potential dating partners, ask for less social information about these individuals than secure individuals in deciding which one to ask out for a date (Aspelmeier & Kerns, 2003). Further, when presented hypothetical dating partners, more anxious adults are more likely to anticipate rejection than more secure adults; that is, they anticipate initial interactions that map onto their working model of relationships (Mikulincer & Shaver, 2006).

In sum, research has examined the role of attachment processes in predicting the potential viability or attractiveness of dating partners. It appears that most adults prefer their potential dating partner to be secure; yet they anticipate that new dating partners will display the types of behavior and thinking that mirror their own working model of attachment (Hazan & Zeifman, 1994; Mikulincer & Shaver, 2006). However, it should be pointed out that most studies in this area are contrived in a hypothetical manner. That is, in most studies, young adults are asked to *think about* who they would like to date, as opposed to whether or not they *actually* initiate relationships with people they view as secure or insecure. Furthermore, although it seems prudent to theorize that secure adults are more likely to successfully initiate potential romantic relationships, this idea has not been tested well.

Newlywed Relationships   Although more work is needed to better understand how attachment processes are linked to romantic relationship initiation, there exist a number of studies that have specified how attachment relates to newlywed relationships. One of the more interesting findings concerns associative mating, or the tendency for individuals to select marital partners based on a "match" between the attachment stances of both partners. Initial research on this topic appeared to suggest a high degree of compatibility, for instance, adults who consider themselves secure often marry partners who perceive themselves to be secure (e.g., Senchak & Leonard, 1992). However, when attachment functioning is assessed via trained experts using intensive interview methods, there is a strong suggestion that adults do not necessarily marry partners with compatible levels of attachment security (Dickstein, Seifer, St. Andre, & Schiller, 2001; Paley, Cox, Burchinal, & Payne, 1999).

These discrepant findings are debatable; however, they may also explain why negotiating a long-term committed relationship is not a simple task. There is growing evidence that an adult's self-diagnosis of attachment functioning is not always congruent with how he or she is evaluated by others (Treboux et al., 2004); for instance, dismissing adults identified via interview methods almost always rate themselves "secure" on attachment questionnaires (Creasey & Ladd, 2005). If it is difficult to self-diagnose our own attachment stance, then it is probably equally difficult for an adult to "diagnose" the attachment functioning of a prospective marital partner because attachment processes are deeply internalized and difficult to activate (Simpson et al., 1996). The contextual and interpersonal variables that are thought to activate the attachment system may not occur frequently enough in some couples contemplating marriage (or at least in couples who have not dated over a lengthy time period), and thus attachment problems (and the emotions and behaviors that accompany them) of one or both partners may not manifest themselves until the relationship becomes more evolved. Thus, although many adults desire to date and eventually marry partners who are trustworthy, dependable, and emotionally close, it may take some time to unite these ideas into a consolidated working model of the romantic partner (Crowell, Treboux, & Waters, 2002). To sum up, many adults may think they are marrying a partner with a desirable or compatible attachment style, but in reality, it may take some time to develop an accurate attachment representation of the partner. Further, it is also possible that some adults do have a high degree of insight regarding the attachment functioning of their partner, but weigh this variable along with other factors that they deem important to a relationship (e.g., attractiveness, socioeconomic status, and similar values and goals; Luo & Klohnen, 2005) when contemplating marriage.

Whereas a secure person may not necessarily marry another secure adult, the attachment security of both partners does seem to forecast the successful beginnings of a marital relationship. However, although it is tempting to suggest that adults with more secure attachment stances have better "early-stage" marriages than their insecure counterparts (Cohn, Silver, Cowan, Cowan, & Pearson, 1992; Senchak & Leonard, 1992), such explanations are too simplistic to explain the complexities of marital functioning over time. Indeed, some secure adults have extremely poor marriages (even in the early phases) and are at a high risk for later divorce (Treboux et al., 2004).

At this juncture, it is prudent to emphasize again that adults possess multiple working models of attachment. Adults bring into new marriages a deeply internalized generalized attachment representation of very close relationships, yet they develop specific representations of their new marital partner. Among other things, we can examine how the *compatibility* of these models affects the well-being of newly married couples and examine variables within the marital context that might alter the development of attachment representations. That is, in terms of the latter concern, attachment representations of marital partners might not remain highly stable and can be influenced by the behavior of one's partner over time (Davila, Karney, & Bradbury, 1999).

Let us turn to research that has examined the compatibility of attachment representations in newly married couples. Crowell and colleagues (Crowell et al., 2002; Treboux et al., 2004) examined the relative impact of generalized and partner-specific representations over a 6-year period from the engagement period through the early years of marriage. Quite predictably, couples consisting of an adult who possessed secure generalized *and* secure partner-specific representations (or *secure-secure*) possessed better marital functioning than their counterparts who had alternative models of relationships. Thus, such thinking represents an adult who values attachment, has a history of positive attachment experiences, trusts others, and possesses a partner who confirms this representation. Individuals who possess such *secure-secure* representations report positive appraisals regarding their marriage and low levels of relationship conflict, and they function as effective support figures to their partner during stressful time periods.

Further, the suggestion that an insecure generalized attachment representation and an insecure partner-specific representation (or *insecure-insecure*) spells doom to marital health would be challenged by the results of this work. *Insecure-insecure* adults display low rates of socially supportive behavior and evidence more relationship conflict; however, they do not report unusually high amounts of marital dissatisfaction. Perhaps these adults are comfortable with having their attachment representations confirmed and have learned to somehow live with interpersonal problems (Treboux et al., 2004). Further, these results confirm what has been demonstrated in the dating literature. For example, dating couples in which both partners are insecure show high rates of relationship problems, but are more likely to remain together than couples containing a secure and insecure partner (Creasey, Ladd, Dransfield, Giaudrone, & Johnson, 2005).

In support of this latter finding, newly married couples are more likely to divorce if one member of the couple displays a secure representation, but has an insecure representation of his or her marital partner (or *secure-insecure*; Crowell et al., 2002). Further, *secure-insecure* individuals report the most relationship distress and exhibit some of the worst relationship behavior when they report major stress in their lives (Treboux et al., 2004). This incompatibility in attachment representations is problematic because the partner's behavior, which is viewed as the chief force behind the development of partner-specific representations (e.g., Davila et al., 1999), is inconsistent with the way the adult generally has come to think about attachment relationships. Although this is not something the *secure-insecure* adults may routinely think about, perhaps this idea becomes more apparent when an adult needs the support of a partner during times of stress and does not receive it.

Another intriguing finding concerns adults who possess an insecure generalized attachment representation, yet have developed a secure representation of their marital partner (*insecure-secure*). Treboux and colleagues (2004) noted that *insecure-secure* individuals reported more relationship problems than adults with *secure-secure* attachment representations, yet hold positive feelings of their spouses and report relatively low levels of conflict. This particular finding suggests that a secure attachment representation of one's marital partner may mitigate the effects of an insecure generalized attachment representation (cf. Alexandrov, Cowan, & Cowan, 2005).

Thus, adults develop multiple mental models of relationships. A generalized representation is based on years of experience with principal attachment figures, whereas a relationship-specific representation is based on lengthy experiences with one person. Although these models can be compatible, incompatibility is not necessarily negative, at least in cases when the adult possesses an insecure generalized attachment representation yet possesses a secure representation of his or her partner. What is very intriguing about this finding is that this generally insecure adult may have developed a secure representation of his or her partner, even in cases when that partner is not necessarily secure (Crowell et al., 2002). Perhaps the attachment-related behavior of that partner is "good enough" and may represent some type of improvement over the way the adult has been treated in the past by other attachment figures.

Parenthood, Infant–Parent Attachment Relationships, and Co-parenting

Theoretically, generalized attachment representations should influence early parenting behavior and the development of the infant–parent attachment relationship. Quite naturally, because the caregiver's responsiveness and trustworthiness play major roles in the initial development of the infant's attachment formation (Ainsworth et al., 1978), the caregiver's internal working model of relationships should forecast the treatment of the infant (Main et al., 1985). As suggested by Fonagy, Steele, Steele, Moran, and Higgitt (1991), a caregiver who is able to coherently reflect on his or her own experiences with parents should be able to understand the motives and intentions of his or her own infant's thinking, emotions, and behavior.

In support of the contention that caregiver attachment representations are linked to infant attachment, a number of studies have linked parent attachment stances, as assessed via the Adult Attachment Interview, with infant attachment security. In a classic meta-analysis of existing studies across several cultures, van IJzendoorn (1995) documented significant associations between AAI and strange situation classifications. In addition to secure infants having secure parents, avoidant and anxious-resistant infants had dismissing and preoccupied parents, respectively. Further, caregivers who were unresolved due to trauma were likely to have an infant with a disorganized attachment stance (Main & Solomon, 1990). The fact that many of the caregivers in these studies were administered AAIs *before* the birth of these babies makes these results even more compelling.

Associations between AAI classifications and subsequent infant–parent attachment are thought to be due to the impact of generalized attachment representations on emerging parenting behavior during the newborn period. However, in such studies, associations between AAI classification, parent sensitivity, and infant classifications are only "modest" (Pederson, Gleason, Moran, & Bento, 1998). These modest associations could be due to difficulties with assessing complex constructs such as caregiver sensitivity, or van IJzendoorn's (1995) transmission gap hypothesis. This latter suggestion means that there may be other variables, such as parental mental health or infant characteristics (e.g., temperament), that help solidify associations between adult and infant attachment.

Beyond the infant–parent relationship, marital relationships must be renegotiated during the transition to parenthood. Predictably, adults with secure attachment representations report more marital satisfaction during this transition than insecure adults (Simpson & Rholes, 2002; Simpson, Rholes,

Campbell, Tran, & Wilson, 2003). In particular, more insecure adults who report low levels of marital satisfaction or high levels of conflict in their relationships during the prenatal period report the most problems following the birth of the infant (Paley et al., 2005). Also, the interpersonal mechanisms that account for changes in marital satisfaction are clearer. More anxious or preoccupied women report the most marital difficulties when they perceive a lack of support from their spouses (Simpson et al., 2003), and more dismissing partners report less "marital maintenance" (i.e., attempts to make a marriage more satisfying) during this transition (Curran, Hazen, Jacobvitz, & Feldman, 2005).

Thus, the transition to parenthood may activate thoughts and behaviors in couples that map onto, or reaffirm, their working models of attachment. That is, because more anxious or preoccupied adults are thought to be hypervigilant regarding relationships, it is not surprising that they report more serious declines in marital satisfaction when they perceive their partners to be nonsupportive. Further, more avoidant or dismissing adults appear to neglect important aspects of one relationship (their marriage) as they make the transition to a new one (becoming a parent).

Another promising direction concerns the beginnings of co-parenting behaviors that occur with the birth of a new child. *Co-parenting* refers to the ability of the new parents to cohesively "work together" in rearing their infant. Some couples "work together" better than others—some display almost hostile, competitive exchanges (e.g., criticizing the partner's parenting behavior), whereas others display co-parenting discrepancies, or direct, highly asynchronous behaviors or emotions toward their offspring (McHale, 1995). Surprisingly, various aspects of the marital relationship are not powerful predictors of this co-parenting phenomenon; high marital satisfaction does not reliably predict harmonious co-parenting behaviors (Gable, Belsky, & Crnic, 1992; Van Egeren, 2004).

Although little work has examined the role of attachment processes in co-parenting, generalized attachment representations might play an important role in its successful initiation. Adults with a secure attachment representation might be motivated to work harder at developing a harmonious co-parenting relationship with their partner, even in cases when marital satisfaction is low. This premise could explain why some couples who report low levels of marital satisfaction nevertheless exhibit very strong co-parenting tendencies (Van Egeren, 2004). This area of research is underdeveloped, but nevertheless, the implications for attachment in the development of co-parenting seem theoretically tenable.

In conclusion, the birth of a child marks the initiation as well as the transformation of relationships in several ways. First, adults must develop a new relationship with their son or daughter. Second, they must renegotiate or essentially initiate a new relationship with their partner. Finally, the couple must work together in a coherent manner to optimize the caregiving context. In all instances, attachment functioning plays an important role in the negotiation of these new or newly transformed relationships, but more research on these ideas is needed.

INTERGENERATIONAL RELATIONSHIPS

Although considerable work has been devoted to the influence of adult attachment in the development of infant–parent relationships, little research has examined its role in facilitating the grandparent–grandchild relationship. Further, in some families, relationships between adult children and their own parents may transform. For instance, in the case of parent caregiving, the role of the child and parents is reversed so that adult children must provide support and care for their own parents. The history of this attachment relationship might play a role in the willingness of adult children to provide care for their parents, or for the parents to receive such care.

Grandparent–Grandchild Relationships

We next explore how attachment processes may influence the emerging grandparent–grandchild relationship. If the grandparent is also the grandchild's primary caregiver, then one could logically conclude that the grandparent's generalized attachment representation would play a role in his or her initial interactions with the grandchild. Indeed, even when the grandparent is not the primary caregiver, infants treat their mother and her mother interchangeably as attachment figures. Infants who direct behaviors toward their mothers that are indicative of a secure attachment relationship display almost identical behaviors toward their maternal grandmothers when observed using the same method (Myers, Jarvis, & Creasey, 1987). This finding suggests that grandparents might initially display certain caregiving behaviors toward infants that have implications for the development of infant attachment, or may affect early infant social development in more indirect ways.

For example, some researchers have examined interrelationships between the generalized attachment representations of grandmothers and their own daughters, and the development of infant attachment status in the weeks or months following these initial assessments. In most cases (about 70% of the time), the attachment functioning of maternal grandmothers, their daughters, and infant grandchildren is congruent (Benoit & Parker, 1994), supporting Bowlby's (1969/1982) position that attachment representations display stability across generations. These data also support the contention that the initial parenting behavior of the adult may be somewhat guided by the way he or she was parented, or at least via his or her representation of these caregiving experiences.

The studies that have examined associations between grandparent attachment functioning and its relative influence on infant attachment have been primarily limited to maternal grandmothers. However, a case could be made that attachment functioning may influence the behavior of most new grandparents, regardless of gender or kinship status. There are large individual differences in the amount of initial involvement of new grandparents (Cherlin & Furstenberg, 1986), and the grandparent's attachment security may forecast such involvement and desire for contact. However, the impact of the grandparents' attachment stances on their grandparenting behavior and their grandchildren is probably mitigated by the grandchildren's own parents. For example, the role of the grandparent in the life of the grandchild is somewhat regulated by the grandchild's mother, an individual often referred to as the "gatekeeper" (Tinsley & Parke, 1987). Thus, the relationship of the grandparent with the child's mother may play a major role in whether or not the grandparent has access to the grandchild. If this access were blocked, then such a barrier would have major implications for the successful initiation of a relationship between grandparent and grandchild.

Family Caregiving

Attachment processes may forecast other patterns of family caregiving, such as when an older family member becomes ill. In terms of caregiving roles, the spouse or adult daughter often volunteers to be a primary caregiver. Further, adults who have secure attachment stances and/or report a positive relationship history with the care receiver provide better care and experience less caregiver burden than their counterparts with more insecure attachment functioning (Crispi, Schiaffano, & Berman, 1997; Magai & Cohen, 1998). Indeed, more secure adults express fewer concerns *over the idea* of becoming a caregiver (Fenney & Hohaus, 2001; LoboPrabhu, Molinari, Arlinghaus, Barr, & Lomax, 2005); thus, one could posit that they are more likely to initiate this role should it be needed.

The latter research provides an impetus for a more general discussion on exactly who chooses to initiate the caregiving role—this is a concern because professionals know that these caregivers will differ greatly in their eventual investment in this role. That is, some caregivers are extremely neglectful, others totally immerse themselves in the responsibility (at the sake of their own health), and still others possess more balance in this role. The association between the effort that caregivers put into their role, their health, and the well-being of the care receiver is not always in a positive, linear direction. That is, some adults could be considered "expert caregivers" yet develop health problems associated with caregiver burnout (e.g., Coyne & Smith, 1991). In this instance, caregivers may put the care receiver's concerns ahead of those of other people, including themselves.

Although research is lacking on the initiation process of family caregiving, there is considerable theory that would suggest that attachment functioning plays a role in this process. That is, dismissing adults would not volunteer to take care of a parent due to their concern that the caregiving role would impede their own lives, and due to their general aloofness concerning the needs of others. Further, perhaps avoidant people shun such a responsibility because the weakness and vulnerability of the care receiver parallel their own deeply suppressed frailties (Mikulincer & Shaver, 2006). In all likelihood, this is just the type of person that we would like to see successfully beg off caregiving responsibilities, in that more dismissing caregivers may ignore the emotional and physical needs of the care receiver in favor of their own well-being.

Because more preoccupied people are highly motivated to care for others (Mikulincer & Shaver, 2006), such adults may quickly, and sometimes impulsively, volunteer to assume major caregiving roles. We have noted in our professional work with family caregivers that adults who fit this profile often are quite enthusiastic about acquiring this role; in fact, they sometimes profess to know as much about the prevailing disorder of the client as trained experts. Indeed, attachment theory, when integrated with theories involving the ethics of care (e.g., Gilligan, 1982), would suggest that these individuals might quickly volunteer to provide care yet create difficulties for themselves in the process. It is not surprising that more preoccupied attachment stances are associated with more caregiver strain and psychological symptoms (Magai & Cohen, 1998); and given the finding that preoccupied people are very uncertain of themselves in parenting roles (Main et al., 2002), the effectiveness of these adults at providing care for their own parents or spouses is questionable. Thus, one would speculate that the initial enthusiasm over the idea of caring for a loved one would be quickly replaced with feelings of exhaustion and burnout.

As stated earlier, secure adults frequently express comfort over the idea of caring for another family member, and because secure adults are objective about relationships, they may approach caregiving in a highly interdependent manner (e.g., Gilligan, 1982). That is, they not only are capable of providing excellent care but also find ways to maintain their own health. Indeed, secure adults report low levels of caregiving strain (Magai & Cohen, 1998).

Of course, attachment is not the only variable that forecasts care initiation. The caregiver's relationship to the care receiver (e.g., spouse versus adult child), the nature of the care receiver's disability, and the caregiver's gender are other variables that predict caregiving initiation (Hooker, Manoogian-O'Dell, Monahan, Frazier, & Shifren, 2000) and may moderate or mediate associations between attachment, caregiver initiation, and eventual quality of care. The dynamics of caregiving are further complicated because the caregiver and care receiver often have an attachment history and bring competing or complementary working models of attachment into this new relationship. Thus, although there is promising theory that could be used to guide predictions in this area, there are probably multiple variables worthy of study that explain how an effective caregiving relationship is initiated and maintained.

ATTACHMENT AND FRIENDSHIPS

Although there are some experts who hold a relatively "narrow" view of the role of attachment in interpersonal functioning—and thus concentrate their efforts on specifying how attachment functioning may influence relationship development within the family system—there are others who believe that attachment processes may impact the evolution of relationships beyond the family. One such case pertains to links between adult attachment and friendship development—a prevailing theory is that attachment security garnered via interactions with family members should somewhat "transfer" and have implications for such development (Hazan & Shaver, 1994; Kamenov & Jelic, 2005). As suggested by Allen and Land (1999), generalized attachment representations based on family experiences may relate to friendship initiation in predictable ways. Generalized attachment security, which is marked by the ability to comfortably, accurately, and coherently think about attachment relationships, should be related to the ability to accurately and lucidly think about the importance of close friends. Adults with insecure attachment stances may develop distorted ways of thinking about relationships that in turn lead to difficulties with social competence and unrealistic expectancies of others. As an example, because of his or her discomfort with close relationships, a more avoidant person may abstain from relationships with people who could potentially become friends.

Not surprisingly, a secure, generalized attachment representation that reflects a general, positive history with attachment figures over time is related to higher quality friendships and marked by more intimacy, more support, and less conflict (Furman, 2001; Saferstein, Neimeyer, & Hagans, 2005; Sibley & Liu, 2006). Further, friends are better able to use each other as support figures when both members are secure (Weimer, Kerns, & Oldenburg, 2004), and they display more problems in the relationship when one or both partners are insecure (Weimer et al., 2004). For instance, there is some evidence to suggest that more avoidant or dismissing people are less supportive of their friends, and that more anxious or preoccupied individuals are more demanding in their relationships (Furman, 2001).

However, literature concerning links between attachment processes and friendship qualities is similar to that involving romantic couples—almost all of the research involves young adult samples. Thus, it would also be refreshing to study how attachment functioning influences friendship initiation at other times of life. For example, how do attachment processes affect such initiation during key adult transition points, such as during the transition to adult work settings or after the loss of a spouse? Attachment theory would predict that more secure people would acknowledge their vulnerabilities and express comfort over the idea of approaching others who could provide support during times of need or major transitions. Further, it would be expected that more dismissing adults would avoid close relationships during vulnerable transition periods, whereas more preoccupied people, due to their need to express pain and suffering to others (Mikulincer & Shaver, 2006), may initiate friendships in an overly intrusive or pushy manner. It is probable that these adults present a highly vulnerable side during times of need and may initiate relationships with whoever will listen.

A final concern with the friendship literature pertains to the fact that most of the available research involves dyads that have been in these relationships for some time; thus, we are unaware of research that has linked attachment processes with actual friendship initiation. However, we are reminded that secure adults tend to make very positive first impressions when meeting new people (Roisman, 2006); thus, we envision them as the type of people who are good at initiating relationships that could potentially become friendships, and as likely to be viewed by others as having the types of qualities (e.g., a positive demeanor) that would make up a good friend.

ATTACHMENT AND MENTORING RELATIONSHIPS

Perhaps one of the more relevant exemplars concerning the role of attachment in predicting adult transitions pertains to the development of workplace-based protégé–mentor relationships. Like associations with friends, these relationships are attachment-like, and these affiliations are emotionally charged between the mentor and protégé as they negotiate this relationship (Scandura & Williams, 2001). Further, much like a parent, the mentor assumes an "older and wiser role." Although some studies have identified variables that may facilitate or impede mentor–protégé relationships, such as the gender of both parties (Scandura & Williams), the role of attachment in the development of this relationship is relatively unknown.

Nevertheless, there is some research that provides insight into how attachment processes may encourage the initiation of mentoring relationships. For instance, secure people have higher career self-efficacy and self-direction than more insecure people (Blustein, Prezioso, & Schultheiss, 1995; O'Brien, 1996). Following attachment theory, secure people of all ages are open to experience, confident, and comfortable with exploration. These are relevant findings because career self-efficacy and self-direction are likely mechanisms that explain the relation between attachment and the initiation of mentoring relationships.

Of course, confidence and self-direction may not be the only psychological variables that mediate associations between attachment functioning and mentorship initiation. For example, more secure people are more trusting of mentors and more open to their advice than more insecure people (Larose, Bernier, & Soucy, 2005; Levesque, Larose, & Bernier, 2002). These are important findings because the pursuit of a mentoring relationship may not automatically be tied to career success. For example, as collegiate professors, we know that there are some students who heed our advice and guidance, whereas others ignore or reject it. Thus, beyond studying mechanisms that explain the relation between attachment and the initiation of mentoring relationships, more research is needed to determine how attachment functioning predicts whether adults "follow through" with the advice and support they receive from this valuable affiliation.

ATTACHMENT AND CLIENT–THERAPIST RELATIONSHIPS

Another adult relationship influenced by attachment processes is that of the client and therapist. Bowlby (1988) proposed that a close, trusting relationship with a therapist is paramount for successful treatment. Indeed, much empirical work has been conducted that suggests that a strong therapeutic alliance is related to successful treatment outcomes (Martin, Garske, & Davis, 2000). Because the therapist is an attachment-like figure, the client's generalized attachment representation has implications for therapy initiation. Secure adults are more likely to have shorter, more successful interventions with therapists than their insecure counterparts (Dozier, 1990). Further, secure and preoccupied adults are more likely to seek psychological services, whereas more dismissing-avoidant or fearful adults are more likely to eschew them (Slade, 1999). Given their highly defensive posture, dismissing adults are unlikely to self-refer to treatment.

Once the client steps into the therapist's office, the relationship then must be initiated. It is in this regard that attachment representations play a key role in the initial relationship between the client and therapist. Secure adults are more likely to feel comfortable establishing this relationship, whereas more insecure adults may utilize their working model of relationships in detrimental ways. Slade (1999) proposed that both dismissing and preoccupied stances pose certain obstacles for the initial client–therapist relationship. For example, dismissing adults may deny the importance of the association, are less likely to ask for help, might miss appointments, and so on (cf. Dozier, 1990). In contrast, preoccupied adults are more likely to demand extra appointments, contact therapists between sessions, and demand more support and advice (Slade), yet seem unwilling to make progress in their psychological treatment.

Some of the aforementioned findings in the therapy domain may be applicable to the development of close relationships between adults and mentors in occupational settings, which was alluded to in the previous section. Both a mentor and therapist are in positions of power—almost in caretaker roles—that may have a potent influence on the outcomes of both protégé and client. Further, the relative success of the therapist or mentor in establishing a competent attachment relationship with a client or protégé may require more than an assessment of the latter adult. For example, in therapeutic settings, there is no guarantee that the mental health professional is secure in his or her attachment stance (Dozier, Cue, & Barnett, 1994). Thus, more work is needed in both therapeutic and workplace settings to determine if the attachment representation of mentors or therapists plays a role in the initiation of these relationships.

COPING WITH LOSS AND SUBSEQUENT RELATIONSHIP INITIATION

One major life event that has significant attachment ramifications concerns the loss of an attachment figure. According to Bowlby (1980), such a loss during adulthood is marked by a series of phases, beginning with a state of disbelief and then eventual yearning for or preoccupation with the deceased. In this latter phase, the attachment system motivates the adult to try to stay physically and/or psychologically close to the lost loved one, and when this effort fails, the adult moves into a stage of despair and mourning (Bowlby, 1988). Finally, the adult comes to accept the loss, and reorganizes his or her working model of relationships in such a manner that allows for a return to a more normal life and allows him or her "to seek out or renew social relationships" (Fraley & Shaver, 1999, p. 737). Thus, Bowlby (1980) posited that attachment functioning predicts both psychological and interpersonal adjustment following the loss.

Whereas studies support Bowlby's (1980) contention that adults, after a significant loss, experience feelings of yearning, numbness, and depression (Lindstrom, 1995), adjustment to loss is dependent on additional variables. For example, personality functioning (Bonanno et al., 2002), situational factors (e.g., loss of a spouse versus child; Stillion, 1995), coping styles (Stoebe & Schut, 1999), and gender (Stoebe, Stoebe, & Abakoumkin, 1999) predict the intensity and duration of psychological symptoms after a significant loss. Also, and relevant to the present chapter, women display fewer adjustment problems and are more likely to initiate new friendships compared to men (Lamme, Dykstra, & Broese van Groeou, 1996).

However, because the death of a close person triggers the attachment system, attachment functioning is nevertheless important for adjustment. Adults who are secure adjust better to losses in general (whether due to death or the case of romantic relationship breakup) than individuals who are generally anxious or fearful (Fraley & Shaver, 1999). In particular, adults who are highly preoccupied are more likely to report intense feelings of yearning and depression or anxiety than do adults who are more secure (Parkes & Weiss, 1983).

Although general attachment insecurity may lead to more difficulties in coping with an important loss, some promising work from a practical level concerns the research of Mary Main and colleagues (2002). Specifically, through the use of the AAI, a classification expert can determine if the adult *remains* traumatized or unresolved regarding a significant loss. Adults can be classified as *unresolved-disorganized* with respect to loss, in which respondents (a) display lapses in the monitoring of reasoning surrounding the loss, such as fears of being taken over mentally by the deceased attachment figure; (b) highly incoherent speech; (c) disbelief that the loss has occurred; and/or (d) lapses in the monitoring of discourse, such as unusual attention to detail of loss, sudden changes of topic, or sudden invasions of other topics of information (Main et al., 2002).

Further, any adult who is assigned the unresolved-disorganized classification is also assigned a *secondary, best fitting*, organized classification (e.g., secure, dismissing, or preoccupied; Main et al., 2002). For example, there are adults who are generally secure, yet remain traumatized regarding a significant loss, and there are adults who are traumatized and are generally dismissing or preoccupied. The logical question concerns whether an underlying attachment security moderates associations between unresolved loss (i.e., chronic bereavement), psychological adjustment, and relationship initiation and functioning following the loss.

Most of the research regarding unresolved attachment status as assessed via the AAI concerns the role of unresolved loss in predicting parent–infant and romantic relationship functioning. In both instances, individuals who display unresolved thinking, and also display other indices of attachment insecurity (e.g., they are more preoccupied or dismissing), display especially problematic behaviors in these existing relationships (Creasey, 2002; Main & Solomon 1990). The fact that unresolved adults who are otherwise generally secure on attachment measures do not display such problems has important implications for initial treatment approaches that therapists may use with new clients. That is, the goal of treatment might not be to resolve every loss or trauma for a client; rather, alteration of general attachment insecurity (dismissing or preoccupied) may represent the first important outcome.

One of the more interesting outcomes pertaining to this research area concerns the finding that both dismissing and preoccupied adults who are unresolved regarding a major loss face major relationship challenges following the loss. Indeed, the finding that unresolved yet dismissing adults also display subsequent problems in parent–infant and romantic relationships provides important evidence for Bowlby's (1980) contention that major suppression or dampening of grief by more dismissing adults is not an adaptive response. As suggested by Fraley and Shaver (1999), another cost to a more dismissing stance is that a more dismissing person may need psychological assistance after a loss, yet may not initiate close relationships after a loss and/or may avoid the assistance of others. Further, because dismissing people are viewed as aloof and hostile by people close to them (Kobak

& Sceery, 1988), they may not be the type of person with whom one would voluntarily initiate a relationship in the first place.

In sum, Bowlby (1980) suggested that secure adults are the individuals most likely to successfully forge new and existing relationships after a significant loss, particularly if such adults hold secure representations regarding the deceased. Although even secure people go through a grieving process, Bowlby (1980) speculated that such adults might be made even stronger in terms of forging new relationships because their secure relationship with the deceased provokes self-reliance and "an abiding sense of the lost person's continuing and benevolent presence" (as cited in Fraley & Shaver, 1999, p. 750). The difficulty is when the attachment representation of the deceased prompts overwhelming fear or anger on the part of the adult that encourages chronic bereavement and relationship problems. An added challenge is that some adults may not easily interpret the root of these strong emotions; for example, some adults may be unresolved regarding a loss, not realize this, and believe their emotional difficulties stem from another loss that might very well be resolved (at least from the standpoint of a clinician).

CONCLUSION

In this chapter, it was acknowledged that variables such as maturity, gender, personality, and loss encourage relationship initiation. Recognizing this point, an attempt was made to delineate the importance of attachment theory in the initiation process. However, as repeatedly reiterated, most of the extant research on close, interpersonal relationships involves couples, friends, coworkers, parents, and so on who have had existing relationships for some time. In addition, an attachment relationship is just that, that is, by definition, it is a relationship that takes time to develop. However, many readers probably view the relationships discussed in this chapter as affiliations that potentially could become legitimate attachment relationships. It is probable in such cases that attachment functioning plays a more predominant role than in the pursuit of relationships that are less emotionally charged and/or are appraised as more temporary. In addition, some relationships that are initiated are actually existing attachment relationships—consider how attachment functioning may be reorganized in romantic relationships upon the birth of a new baby.

A predominant finding is that secure people negotiate new and transformed attachment relationships better than insecure adults. This result is not surprising; secure people are curious, likable, persistent, and emotionally mature, and they can effectively provide and receive support (Crowell et al., 2002; Kobak & Sceery, 1988; Thompson, 1999). Indeed, secure and insecure adults admire the qualities of secure people (Kirkpatrick & Davis, 1994). One might be hard-pressed to find someone who would not prefer a potential attachment figure who emits a confident, supportive presence. Further, there is emerging evidence that secure people are more likely to competently seek out information about new relationships than their counterparts. They are more likely to seek important social information about an individual before considering a date with a person (Aspelmeier & Kerns, 2003), and we believe this premise applies to other affiliations discussed in this chapter as well. For example, it would be understandable that a secure, confident adult would more likely seek out important information on caregiving before stepping into this role. This is a very important consideration because, as stipulated earlier in this chapter, relationship initiation may not behoove one if it is not performed in an informed, competent manner.

The evidence suggests that insecure people have more difficulties initiating and maintaining close relationships. More avoidant people dismiss the value of relationships, and others find such people aloof and difficult to get close to (Kobak & Sceery, 1988). In addition, these adults display emotions and behaviors that are unlikable (Creasey & Ladd, 2005). Further, preoccupied people also appear to have difficulties initiating relationships. These adults harbor unrealistic expectancies of others, are often demanding in relationships, are overly emotional, and cannot be easily comforted by others (Slade, 1999). Also, in attachment relationships where they have more power, such as parent–infant relationships, or in cases where they must take care of their own parent, they seem to want to provide care but are exceedingly ineffective (Main et al., 2002). It seems that preoccupied adults have a high need to affiliate and forge new relationships, yet engage in self-defeating behaviors that could drive others away. Further, the correlates of a preoccupied attachment stance, such as high emotional needs, are not the relationship traits that most potential attachment figures would find desirable. This idea suggests that others will be less likely to initiate relationships with them, which reinforces their model that they are unworthy as attachment figures.

Much of the work that has examined associations between unresolved attachment status and relationship initiation has examined correlates of this stance with parenting behavior, the development of parent–infant attachment, and dating relationships in young couples. The prognosis for these relationships does not appear to be a good one, particularly if the unresolved adult also is preoccupied or dismissing (Heese, 1999). Of particular interest concerns the emerging finding that the behavior of insecure, unresolved adults—whether they are parents or romantic partners—is distinctly different from that of adults who are dismissing or preoccupied and not unresolved due to loss (Creasey, 2002). In addition, although it is tempting to suggest that highly unresolved adults are "fearful" of relationships, this finding does not seem to translate into low relationship initiation. For example, almost 20% of community-residing adults in large, meta-analytic studies have been identified as unresolved due to loss or trauma (van IJzendoorn & Bakermans-Kranenburg, 1996), and similar percentages of adults in close relationships (e.g., romantic relationships) have been documented (Creasey, 2002). Although it is surprising that such a high percentage of these adults would be found in close, emotional relationships, it has been theorized that an unresolved working model of attachment only occasionally manifests itself. That is, the fearful or angry affect and problematic relationship behaviors associated with this attachment stance are most likely to emerge when the adult is highly stressed and the attachment system is activated (Lyons-Ruth & Jacobvitz, 1999). As suggested earlier, this behavior is likely to alarm or concern the attachment partner but may not occur enough to dampen the emergence of the relationship. Nevertheless, unresolved attachment status is a significant risk for both personal and interpersonal adjustment and is highly prevalent in treatment settings (Dozier, Stovall, & Albus, 1999).

Although relationships that emerge at different periods of the life span were discussed, one of the most important research gaps concerns how attachment functioning may play different roles in new and existing relationships across the life course. For example, because the evolutionary significance of attachment is rooted in parenting and mate selection (Hazan & Diamond, 2000), the relative influence of attachment processes in predicting relationship initiation may be stronger for select relationships and more potent at certain times of our life (Allen & Land, 1999). On the other hand, Bowlby viewed attachment as a "cradle to death" issue (Bretherton & Munholland, 1999); thus, attachment functioning would appear to be an important resource throughout our life span. Indeed, whereas it could be readily asserted that attachment functioning plays a role in parenting and romantic relationships, the research reviewed suggests that it is important for existing and new relationships in later life as well.

There is evidence that supports more consideration of later-life relationship initiation. For example, there is some verification that older adults parse their affiliations down to their closest attachment figures (Carstensen, 1991). In addition, older adults continue to revisit their relationships with existing attachment figures, such as adult children and grandchildren, and must grapple with their own mortality and that of others around them. Thus, attachment functioning plays an important role in relationship functioning throughout the life span, and a coherent, secure attachment representation may allow adults to successfully formulate not only a healthy view of relationships but also a lucid picture of their identity over the life cycle. In any case, an important, final suggestion pertains to the need for more attachment-based research with older adults. This research would highlight the importance of attachment in the later years and provide more insight into how working models of attachment develop over the life course.

REFERENCES

Ainsworth, M. (1989). Attachments beyond infancy. *American Psychologist, 44,* 709–716.

Ainsworth, M., Blehar, M., Waters, E., & Wall, S. (1978). *Patterns of attachment: A psychological study of the strange situation.* Hillsdale, NJ: Lawrence Erlbaum.

Alexandrov, E., Cowan, P., & Cowan, C. (2005). Couple attachment and quality of marital relationships: Method and concept in the validation of the new couple attachment interview and coding system. *Attachment and Human Development, 7,* 123–152.

Allen, J., & Land, D. (1999). Attachment in adolescence. In J. Cassidy & P. Shaver (Eds.), *Handbook of attachment* (pp. 319–335). New York: Guilford.

Aspelmeier, J., & Kerns, K. (2003). Love and school: Attachment/exploration dynamics in college. *Journal of Social and Personal Relationships, 20,* 5–30.

Bartholomew, K. (1990). Avoidance of intimacy: An attachment perspective. *Journal of Social and Personal Relationships, 7,* 147–178.

Bartholomew, K., & Horowitz, L. (1991). Attachment styles among young adults: A test of a four-category model. *Journal of Personality and Social Psychology, 61,* 226–244.

Benoit, D., & Parker, K. (1994). Stability and transmission of attachment across three generations. *Child Development, 65,* 1444–1456.

Blustein, D., Prezioso, M., & Schultheiss, D. (1995). Attachment theory and career development: Current status and future directions. *Counseling Psychologist, 23,* 416–432.

Bonanno, G., Wortman, C., Lehman, D., Tweed, R., Haring, M., Sonnega, J., et al. (2002). Resilience to loss and chronic grief: A prospective study from preloss to 18-months postloss. *Journal of Personality and Social Psychology, 83,* 1150–1164.

Bowlby, J. (1982). *Attachment and loss: Vol. 1. Attachment* (2nd ed.). New York: Basic. (Original work published 1969.)

Bowlby, J. (1980). *Attachment and loss: Vol. 3. Loss: Sadness and depression.* New York: Basic.

Bowlby, J. (1988). *A secure base: Clinical applications of attachment theory.* London: Routledge.

Bretherton, I., & Munholland, K. (1999). Internal working models in attachment relationships: A construct revisited. In J. Cassidy & P. Shaver (Eds.), *Handbook of attachment: Theory, research, and clinical applications* (pp. 89–111). New York: Guilford Press.

Carnelley, K., & Janoff-Bulman, R. (1992). Optimism about love relationships: General vs. specific lessons from one's personal experiences. *Journal of Social and Personal Relationships, 9,* 5–20.

Carstensen, L. (1991). Selectivity theory: Social activity in life-span context. In K. Schaie (Ed.), *Annual review of gerontology and geriatrics* (Vol. 11, pp. 195–217). New York: Springer.

Cassidy, J. (1999). The nature of the child's ties. In J. Cassidy & P. Shaver (Eds.), *Handbook of attachment: Theory, research, and clinical applications* (pp. 3–20). New York: Guilford Press.

Chappell, K., & Davis, K. (1998). Attachment, partner choice, and perception of romantic partners: An experimental test of the attachment-security hypothesis. *Personal Relationships, 5,* 327–342.

Cherlin, A., & Furstenberg, F. (1986). *The new American grandparent.* New York: Basic Books.

Clark, C., Shaver, P., & Abrahams, M. (1999). Strategic behavior in romantic relationship initiation. *Personality and Social Psychology Bulletin, 25,* 707–720.

Cohn, D., Silver, D., Cowan, C., Cowan, P., & Pearson, J. (1992). Working models of childhood attachment and couple relationships. *Journal of Family Issues, 13,* 432–449.

Collins, N., & Read, S. (1994). Cognitive representations of adult attachment: The structure and function of working models. In K. Bartholomew & D. Perlman (Eds.), *Advances in personal relationships: Vol. 5. Attachment processes in adulthood* (pp. 53–90). London: Jessica Kingsley.

Coyne, J., & Smith, D. (1991). Couples coping with a myocardial infarction: A contextual perspective on wives' distress. *Journal of Personality and Social Psychology, 61,* 404–412.

Creasey, G. (2002). Associations between working models of attachment and conflict management behavior in romantic couples. *Journal of Counseling Psychology, 49,* 365–375.

Creasey, G., & Hesson-McInnis, M. (2001). Affective responses, cognitive appraisals, and conflict tactics in late adolescent romantic relationships: Associations with attachment orientations. *Journal of Counseling Psychology, 48,* 85–96.

Creasey, G., & Jarvis, P. (2008). Attachment and marriage. Invited chapter to appear in M. Cecil Smith & T. Reio (Eds.), *Handbook of adult development and learning.* Hillsdale, NJ: Lawrence Erlbaum.

Creasey, G., & Ladd, A. (2005). Generalized and specific attachment representations: Unique and interactive roles in predicting conflict behaviors in close relationships. *Personality and Social Psychology Bulletin, 31,* 1026–1038.

Creasey, G., Ladd, A., Dransfield, M., Giaudrone, L., & Johnson, K. (2005, April). *Predicting romantic relationship status: The role of attachment representations and conflict tactics*. Paper presented at the biennial meeting of the Society for Research in Child Development, Atlanta, GA.

Crispi, E., Schiaffano, K., & Berman, W. (1997). The contribution of attachment to burden in adult children of institutionalized parents with dementia. *Gerontologist, 37*, 52–60.

Crowell, J., Treboux, D., & Waters, E. (2002). Stability of attachment representations: The transition to marriage. *Developmental Psychology, 38*, 467–479.

Curran, M., Hazen, N., Jacobvitz, D., & Feldman, A. (2005). Representations of early family relationships predict marital maintenance during the transition to parenthood. *Journal of Family Psychology, 19*, 189–197.

Davila, J., Karney, B., & Bradbury, T. (1999). Attachment change processes in the early years of marriage. *Journal of Personality and Social Psychology, 76*, 783–802.

Dickstein, S., Seifer, R., St. Andre, M., & Schiller, M. (2001). Marital Attachment Interview: Adult attachment assessment of marriage. *Journal of Social and Personal Relationships, 18*, 651–672.

Dodge, K., Pettit, G., McClasky, C., & Brown, M. (1986). Social competence in children. *Monographs of the Society for Research in Child Development, 51*(2, Serial No. 213), 1–85.

Dozier, M. (1990). Attachment organization and treatment use for adults with serious psychopathological disorders. *Development and Psychopathology, 2*, 47–60.

Dozier, M., Cue, K., & Barnett, L. (1994). Clinicians as caregivers: Role of attachment organization in treatment. *Journal of Consulting and Clinical Psychology, 62*, 794–800.

Dozier, M., Stovall, K. C., & Albus, K. (1999). Attachment and psychopathology in adulthood. In J. Cassidy & P. Shaver (Eds.), *Handbook of attachment* (pp. 497–519). New York: Guilford.

Fenney, J., & Hohaus, L. (2001). Attachment and spousal caregiving. *Personal Relationships, 8*, 21–39.

Fonagy, P., Steele, M., Steele, H., Moran, G., & Higgitt, A. (1991). The capacity for understanding mental states: The reflective self in parent and child and its significance for security of attachment. *Infant Mental Health Journal, 12*, 201–218.

Fraley, R. C., Niedenthal, P., Marks, M., Brumbaugh, C., & Vicary, A. (2006). Adult attachment and the perception of emotional expressions: Probing the hyperactivating strategies underlying anxious attachment. *Journal of Personality, 74*, 1163–1190.

Fraley, R. C., & Shaver, P. (1999). Loss and bereavement: Attachment theory and recent controversies concerning "grief work" and the nature of detachment. In J. Cassidy & P. Shaver (Eds.), *Handbook of attachment* (pp. 735–759). New York: Guilford.

Frazier, P., Byer, A., Fischer, A., Wright, D., & DeBord, K. (1996). Adult attachment style and partner choice: Correlational and experimental findings. *Personal Relationships, 3*, 117–136.

Furman, W. (2001). Working models of friendships. *Journal of Social and Personal Relationships, 18*, 583–602.

Furman, W., & Simon, V. (2006). Actor and partner of adolescents' romantic working models and styles of interactions with romantic partners. *Child Development, 77*, 588–604.

Gable, S., Belsky, J., & Crnic, K. (1992). Marriage, parenting, and child development: Progress and prospects. *Journal of Family Psychology, 5*, 276–294.

George, C., Kaplan, N., & Main, M. (1996). *Adult Attachment Interview* (3rd ed.). Unpublished manuscript, Department of Psychology, University of California, Berkeley.

Gilligan, C. (1982). *In a different voice*. Cambridge, MA: Harvard University Press.

Hazan, C., & Diamond, L. (2000). The place of attachment in human mating. *Review of General Psychology, 4*, 186–204.

Hazan, C., & Shaver, P. (1987). Romantic love conceptualized as an attachment process. *Journal of Personality and Social Psychology, 52*, 511–524.

Hazan, C., & Shaver, P. (1994). Attachment as an organizational framework for research on close relationships. *Psychological Inquiry, 5*, 1–22.

Hazan, C., & Zeifman, D. (1994). Sex and the psychological tether. In K. Bartholomew & D. Perlman (Eds.), *Advances in personal relationships: Attachment processes in adulthood* (Vol. 5, pp. 151–177). London: Jessica Kingsley.

Hesse, E. (1999). The adult attachment interview: Historical and current perspectives. In J. Cassidy & D. Shaver (Eds.), *Handbook of Attachment* (pp. 395–433) New York: Guilford.

Hooker, K., Manoogian-O'Dell, M., Monahan, D., Frazier, L., & Shifren, K. (2000). Does type of disease matter? Gender differences amongst Alzheimer's and Parkinson's disease spouse caregivers. *The Gerontologist, 40*, 568–573.

Kamenov, Z., & Jelic, M. (2005). Stability of attachment styles across students' romantic relationships, friendships, and family relationships. *Review of Psychology, 12,* 115–123.

Kirkpatrick, L., & Davis, K. (1994). Attachment style, gender, and relationship stability: A longitudinal analysis. *Journal of Personality and Social Psychology, 66,* 502–512.

Klohnen, E., & Luo, S. (2003). Interpersonal attraction and personality: What is attractive—self similarity, complementarity, or attachment security? *Journal of Personality and Social Psychology, 85,* 709–722.

Kobak, R., & Sceery, A. (1988). Attachment in late adolescence: Working models, affect regulation, and representations of self and others. *Child Development, 59,* 135–146.

Lamme, S., Dykstra, P., & Broese van Groeou, M. (1996). Rebuilding the network: New relationships in widowhood. *Personal Relationships, 3,* 337–349.

Larose, S., Bernier, A., & Soucy, N. (2005). Attachment as a moderator of the effect of security in mentoring on subsequent perceptions of mentoring and relationship quality with college teachers. *Journal of Social and Personal Relationships, 22,* 399–415.

Levesque, G., Larose, S., & Bernier, A. (2002). The cognitive organization of adolescents' attachment and their perceptions of dyadic mentoring relationships. *Canadian Journal of Behavioural Science, 34,* 186–200.

Lindstrom, T. (1995). Anxiety and adaptation in bereavement. *Anxiety, Stress and Coping: An International Journal, 8,* 251–261.

LoboPrabhu, S., Molinari, V., Arlinghaus, K., Barr, E., & Lomax, J. (2005). Spouses of patients with dementia: How do they stay together "Till death do us part"? *Journal of Gerontological Social Work, 44,* 161–174.

Luo, S., & Klohnen, E. (2005). Associative mating and marital quality in newlyweds: A couple-centered approach. *Journal of Personality and Social Psychology, 88,* 304–326.

Lyons-Ruth, K., & Jacobvitz, D. (1999). Attachment disorganization: Unresolved loss, relational violence, and lapses in behavioral and attentional strategies. In J. Cassidy & P. Shaver (Eds.), *Handbook of attachment: Theory, research, and clinical applications* (pp. 520–554). New York: Guilford.

Magai, C., & Cohen, C. (1998). Attachment style and emotion regulation in dementia patients and their relation to caregiver burden. *Journals of Gerontology: Series B: Psychological and Social Sciences, 53B,* 147–164.

Main, M., Goldwyn, R., & Hesse, E. (2002). *Adult attachment scoring and classification systems* (Version 7.1). Unpublished manuscript, University of California, Berkeley.

Main, M., Kaplan, N., & Cassidy, J. (1985). Security in infancy, childhood, and adulthood: A move to the level of representation. In I. Bretherton & E. Waters (Eds.), *Growing points of attachment theory and research. Monographs of the Society for Research in Child Development, 50*(1–2, Serial No. 209), 66–106.

Main, M., & Solomon, J. (1990). Procedures for identifying infants as disorganized/disoriented during the Ainsworth strange situation. In M. Greenberg, D. Cicchetti, & E. Cummings (Eds.), *Attachment in the preschool years: Theory, research, and intervention* (pp. 121–160). Chicago: University of Chicago Press.

Martin, D., Garske, J., & Davis, M. K. (2000). Relation of the therapeutic alliance with outcome and other variables: A meta-analytic review. *Journal of Consulting and Clinical Psychology, 68,* 438–450.

McHale, J. (1995). Coparenting and triadic interactions during infancy: The role of marital distress and child gender. *Developmental Psychology, 31,* 985–996.

McPherson, M., Smith-Lovin, L., & Brashears, M. (2006). Social isolation in America: Changes in core discussion networks over two decades. *American Sociological Review, 71,* 353–375.

Mikulincer, M., & Shaver, P. (2006). *Attachment in adulthood: Structure, dynamics and change.* New York: Guilford Press.

Myers, B. J., Jarvis, P., & Creasey, G. (1987). Infants' behavior with their mothers and grandmothers. *Infant Behavior and Development, 10,* 245–259.

O'Brien, K. (1996). The influence of psychological separation and parental attachment on the career development of adolescent women. *Journal of Vocational Behavior, 48,* 257–274.

Paley, B., Cox, M., Burchinal, M., & Payne, C. (1999). Attachment and marital functioning: Comparison of spouses with continuous secure, earned-secure, dismissing, and preoccupied attachment stance. *Journal of Family Psychology, 13,* 580–597.

Paley, B., Cox, M., Kanoy, K., Harter, K., Burchinal, M., & Margand, N. (2005). Adult attachment and marital interaction as predictors of whole family interactions during the transition to parenthood. *Journal of Family Psychology, 19,* 420–429.

Parkes, C., & Weiss, R. (1983). *Recovery from bereavement.* New York: Basic Books.

Pederson, D., Gleason, K., Moran, G., & Bento, S. (1998). Maternal attachment representations, maternal sensitivity, and the infant-mother attachment relationship. *Developmental Psychology, 34,* 925–933.

Pietromonaco, P., & Carnelley, K. (1994). Gender and working models of attachment: Consequences for perceptions of self and romantic relationships. *Personal Relationships, 1,* 23–43.

Roisman, G. (2006). The role of adult attachment security in non-romantic, non-attachment-related first inter-actions between same-sex strangers. *Attachment and Human Development, 8,* 341–352.

Roisman, G., Collins, W., Sroufe, L. A., & Egeland, B. (2005). Predictors of young adults' representations of and behavior in their current romantic relationship: Prospective tests of the prototype hypothesis. *Attachment and Human Development, 7,* 105–121.

Saferstein, J., Neimeyer, G., & Hagans, C. (2005). Attachment as a predictor of friendship qualities in college youth. *Social Behavior and Personality, 33,* 767–776.

Scandura, T., & Williams, E. (2001). An investigation of the moderating effects of gender on the relationships between mentorship initiation and protégé perceptions of mentoring functions. *Journal of Vocational Behavior, 59,* 342–363.

Scharlott, B., & Christ, W. (1995). Overcoming relationship-initiation barriers: The impact of a computer-dating system on sex role, shyness, and appearance inhibitions. *Computers in Human Behavior, 11,* 191–204.

Senchak, M., & Leonard, K. (1992). Attachment styles and marital adjustment among newlywed couples. *Journal of Social and Personal Relationships, 9,* 51–64.

Sibley, C., & Liu, J. (2006). Working models of romantic relationships and the subjective quality of social inter-actions across relational contexts. *Personal Relationships, 13,* 243–259.

Simpson, J., & Rholes, W. (2002). Attachment orientations, marriage, and the transition to parenthood. *Journal of Research in Personality, 36,* 622–628.

Simpson, J., Rholes, W., Campbell, L., Tran, S., & Wilson, C. (2003). Adult attachment, the transition to par-enthood, and depressive symptoms. *Journal of Personality and Social Psychology, 84,* 1172–1187.

Simpson, J., & Rholes, W., & Phillips, D. (1996). Conflict in close relationships: An attachment perspective. *Journal of Personality and Social Psychology, 71,* 899–914.

Slade, A. (1999). Attachment theory and research: Implications for the theory and practice of individual psy-chotherapy with adults. In J. Cassidy & P. Shaver (Eds.), *Handbook of attachment* (pp. 575–594). New York: Guilford.

Snyder, M., Berscheid, E., & Glick, P. (1985). Focusing on the exterior and interior: Two investigations of the initiation of personal relationships. *Journal of Personality and Social Psychology, 48,* 1427–1439.

Sroufe, L. A., Egeland, B., Carlson, E., & Collins, W. (2005). *The development of the person: The Minnesota study of risk and adaptation from birth to adulthood.* New York: Guilford.

Stillion, J. (1995). Death in the lives of adults: Responding to the tolling of the bell. In H. Wass & R. Neimeyer (Eds.), *Dying: Facing the facts* (pp. 303–322). New York: Taylor & Francis.

Stoebe, M., & Schut, H. (1999). The dual process model of coping with bereavement. *Death Studies, 23,* 197–224.

Stoebe, W., Stoebe, M., & Abakoumkin, G. (1999). Does differential spouse support cause sex differences in bereavement outcome? *Journal of Community and Applied Social Psychology, 9,* 1–12.

Thompson, R. (1999). Early attachment and later development. In J. Cassidy & P. Shaver (Eds.), *Handbook of attachment: Theory, research, and clinical applications* (pp. 265–286). New York: Guilford Press.

Tinsley, B., & Parke, R. (1987). Grandparents as interactive and social support agents for families with young infants. *International Journal of Aging & Human Development, 25,* 259–277.

Treboux, D., Crowell, J., & Waters, E. (2004). When "new" meets "old": Configurations of adult attachment rep-resentations and their implications for marital functioning. *Developmental Psychology, 40,* 295–314.

Van Egeren, L. (2004). The development of the coparenting relationship over the transition to parenthood. *Infant Mental Health Journal, 25,* 453–477.

van IJzendoorn, M. (1995). Adult attachment representations, parental responsiveness, and infant attachment: A meta-analysis on the predictive validity of the Adult Attachment Interview. *Psychological Bulletin, 117,* 387–403.

van IJzendoorn, M., & Bakermans-Kranenburg, M. (1996). Attachment representations in mothers, fathers, adolescents and clinical groups: A meta-analytic search for normative data. *Journal of Consulting and Clinical Psychology, 64,* 8–21.

Waters, E., Corcoran, D., & Anafarta, M. (2005). Attachment, other relationships, and the theory that all good things go together. *Human Development, 48,* 80–84.

Weimer, B., Kerns, K., & Oldenburg, C. (2004). Adolescents' interactions with a best friend: Associations with attachment styles. *Journal of Experimental Child Psychology, 88,* 102–120.

Section II

The Process of Relationship Initiation

5

Prelude to a Kiss
Nonverbal Flirting, Opening Gambits, and Other Communication Dynamics in the Initiation of Romantic Relationships

MICHAEL R. CUNNINGHAM and ANITA P. BARBEE

I was alarmed. I said to myself, "Don't beautiful women travel anymore?" And then I saw you and I was saved, I hope.

Cary Grant (as Nickie Ferrante) in *An Affair to Remember* (Wald & McCary, 1957)

PRELUDE: THE LEGACY OF CARY GRANT AND WILL SMITH

*I*n films, romance often begins with the leading man offering a clever conversational opening gambit to the leading lady. The woman may not be immediately smitten. In *An Affair to Remember* (Wald & McCary, 1957), Terry McKay, played by Deborah Kerr, responded to Nickie Ferrante with the sarcastic comeback "Tell me, have you been getting results with a line like that?" Nonetheless, her interest was piqued, and the scene ended with the two going to dinner together, which ultimately escalated into a love affair. As a result of such media scripts, many males believe that the secret to romance is to use a good pickup line. Or, as stated with boundless optimism by Will Smith as Alex Hitchens in Tennant's (2005) *Hitch*, almost half a century after Cary Grant, "No matter what, no matter when, no matter who, any man has a chance to sweep any woman off her feet. He just needs the right broom."

Hitch's approach to attraction emphasizes the clever opening gambit as a key to success, but current social science research suggests that the dynamics of attraction commence well before the first words are spoken. This chapter will organize relevant observations using a multistage flirtation and courtship process model inspired by Scheflen (1965), Perper (1985), Perper & Weiss (1987), and Givens (2005). In this perspective, relationship initiation begins with the biology (such as gender and temperament), background (such as culture), motives, and expectations of each person. Similarly, our model begins with *prioritize desires*, which focuses on how salient motives and expectations affect the courtship sequence as a function of a variety of individual and social variables. This first stage has an impact on subsequent flirtation and courtship stages, which we term (b) *attract attention*, (c) *notice and approach*, (d) *talk and reevaluate*, and (e) *touch and synchronize*, that follow in the dance of courtship. The model is offered as an organizational heuristic rather than as a fixed sequence of actions. The chapter will review the nonverbal and verbal communication literatures, and other relevant observations relevant to these hypothetical phases of relationship initiation.

PRIORITIZE DESIRES: COURTSHIP BEHAVIOR AS A FUNCTION OF CULTURE, GENDER, RELATIONSHIP ASPIRATIONS, AND PERSONALITY

Although opening gambits and other heterosexual attraction behaviors serve the goal of furthering biological reproduction, cultural norms and individual differences influence the performance and meaning of the behaviors. Behaviors to initiate a romantic relationship primarily occur in cultures that permit individual autonomy in the choice of a mating partner, which is not always the case.

Even cultures that do not have the institution of arranged marriages may have limited courtship activity. In the Irish island community of the Gaeltacht, which Messenger (1971) called Inis Beag, the 350 inhabitants were quite poor, and marriage was delayed until an average age of 36 for males and 25 for females. Consistent with the demands of strict Catholicism and local tradition, the sexes were largely kept apart, and there was no dating or premarital sexual behavior. Consequently, the inhabitants of Inis Beag, like those of some other religious cultures, may show little of the verbal and nonverbal courtship behavior described later in this chapter.

Similar to Inis Beag, single people in the bountiful community of Mangaia, in the lush southern Pacific Cook Islands, were segregated by gender. But, in contrast to Inis Beag, they were encouraged by their elders and peers to have sex frequently, within the boundaries of Polynesian discretion. There was no formal dating, but the sexes flirted with each other very subtly, leading to private trysts:

> The slight pressure of a finger or arm in dancing, the raising of an eyebrow, the showing of a seed pod or flower cupped in the hand so as to provide a sexually suggestive sign are all that is required to raise the question in this society where boy is not seen with girl in public. (Marshall, 1971, p. 117)

The Mangaian ecology provided ample food, and an unexpected pregnancy did not cause economic hardship or stigma, which may be one reason why females displayed a relatively uninhibited approach to sex compared to in Inis Beag or other harsh environments. Both Inis Beag and Mangaia, however, were exceptions to a general trend that resource-poor environments were associated with higher rates of teen reproduction and lower rates of nonmarried parents (Barber, 2003; Ellis, McFadyen-Ketchum, Dodge, Pettit, & Bates, 1999). The larger point is that relationship initiation occurs in the context of parameters influenced by the ecology, reified by the culture, and expressed in individual standards of propriety.

Gender

The genders generally differ in their motives for courtship behaviors. Understanding the differences in motives requires a brief recounting of evolutionary theory. The reader is directed to Schmitt's chapter in this volume for more details, but some highlights must be mentioned with respect to the initial dance of courtship. Darwin's (1871) theory of sexual selection suggested that whatever trait is associated with reproductive success will increase in the population and evolve over time. Trivers (1972) proposed that sex differences in mating dynamics stemmed from differential parental investment, such that the gender that made the most investment in offspring would be relatively selective in the choice of a partner, and compete with other members of that gender to attract the best mate. Because human females invest more resources in fetal development and infancy than do human males, Cunningham (1981) noted that physical attractiveness is particularly important in evaluations of females, while males tend to be evaluated on their social status and competence ... since females have more to lose by making a poor mate selection, there may also have been selection pressure for females who were discriminating of males with the best genetic combinations and who were not deceived by false displays of fitness. (pp. 78–79)

Relationship Aspirations

A quarter century of research supported, and qualified, those predictions. Kenrick, Sadalla, Groth, and Trost (1990) argued that not only does gender influence mate selection criteria but so does the nature of the intended relationship. They found that individuals had different priorities and standards when they were seeking to meet someone for a single date, a sexual encounter, a steady dating relationship, or marriage. Females had higher standards for sexual relations (which involve pregnancy and disease risks) than they had for a single date, whereas males had higher standards to go out on a date (in which they generally pay the costs) than they had for a sexual fling. Females expressed higher standards than males overall, particularly for their mate's status and earning capacity, whereas males tended to have higher standards for their mate's physical attractiveness than females.

Li, Bailey, Kenrick, and Linsenmeier (2002) used several creative methodologies to extend the finding that female physical attractiveness was a necessity for males in long-term relationships, whereas male resources and status were necessities for females. Giving research participants a limited number of "mate dollars" to spend, females were found to spend more of their low budget on male intelligence, followed by male yearly income. Men spent the highest proportion of their low budget on female physical attractiveness, followed by female intelligence. In another study, these investigators examined whether participants looked first at ratings of a potential long-term marriage partner's physical attractiveness, kindness, creativity, liveliness, or social level. Males checked physical attractiveness first, but kindness was not significantly lower. Females checked social level first, but kindness was a very close second. Thus, although there is support for the principle that "males want physical attractiveness, and females want status and money," neither beauty nor wealth was the consistently dominant priority for either gender, and even those preferences were not universally apparent (cf. Buss, 1988).

People are not always looking for lasting love. Buss and Schmitt (1993) reported that males expressed a greater desire for short-term mates, desired more partners, and were willing to engage in intercourse after knowing the partner for less time than did females. Consistent with that observation, males in Mangaia prided themselves on the number of their sexual partners, and averaged eight such relationships before marriage. But females averaged three to four, suggesting that the genders had different motives, even in a permissive society (Messenger, 1971).

Although males may be more interested in short-term relationships than females, Miller and Fishkin (1997) reported that most single college-age males sought just one or two partners in a year, rather than multiple sexual partners (cf. Schmitt, 2005a). Further, Gangestad and Simpson (2000) noted that prior research's

focus on sex differences in human mating has been criticized ... for not explaining why there is more variation in mating-related behaviors within sexes than between [them] ... and for not considering how ... control of resources may have influenced the mating strategies of both sexes. (p. 574)

For some males to have a large number of sexual partners, there must be some females who are willing to have relations with them. According to strategic pluralism theory, some females see short-term relationships with highly desirable males as a fallback strategy to insure that their offspring possess adaptive heritable traits (Gangestad & Simpson, 2000). Females also may use short-term relationships as a means of evaluating a male's suitability for a long-term relationship or securing his interest so he will commit to a long-term relationship (Buss & Schmitt, 1993).

To explore such issues, Greitemeyer (2005) conducted experiments in the United States and Germany in which individuals had the opportunity to choose between three hypothetical romantic partners for a variety of romantic activities. Regardless of the type of relationship or romantic activity, males consistently showed the greatest interest in a highly physically attractive partner, followed by a moderately physically attractive partner, followed by a high socioeconomic status (SES) partner. Females, by contrast, were most interested in a physically attractive partner for a short-term relationship and for dating, kissing, making out, and having sexual intercourse, but were equally interested in the high SES partner and high physical attractiveness partner for a longer term relationship. Similarly, Li and Kenrick (2006) reported that both males and females treated physical attractiveness as a necessity in a short-term relationship, but both genders treated warmth and trustworthiness as necessities in long-term mates. The majority of their research participants reported never having had a short-term sexual relationship.

Sociosexuality

People vary in their willingness to ask a stranger to visit their apartment, or accept an invitation to go to bed. Not only are shyness and a fear of rejection factors, but also some people are simply not interested in short-term romantic relationships. Such individual differences can have a decisive influence on communication during relationship initiation. Simpson and Gangestad (1991) offered the Sociosexuality Orientation Inventory (SOI) to assess willingness to engage in uncommitted sexual relations. The SOI focused on number of partners, one-night stands, and sexual attitudes. People who desired casual, short-term relationships were termed *unrestricted*, and their incidence varied cross-culturally. In cultures with relatively benign ecologies, those in which males are in relatively short supply, or those in which women possess more political, economic, and relational power, there is a tendency toward more unrestricted sociosexuality, compared to cultures in which the ecology is more stressful, females are in short supply, or females are relatively powerless (Schmitt, 2005a, 2005b).

Unrestricted individuals sometimes appeared selfish; they displayed less investment, commitment, dependency, and love than more traditional "restricted" individuals (Simpson & Gangestad, 1991). Unrestricted females reported more negative interactions with their romantic partners (Hebl & Kashy, 1995), and unrestricted males described themselves as irresponsible, cold, and narcissistic (Reise & Wright, 1996). But unrestricted individuals sometimes seemed more sociable than restricted individuals. Unrestricted females were adventurous and pleasure seeking, whereas restricted females were compliant and dysphoric (Wright, 1999). Unrestricted individuals also were less instrumental, or ends oriented, in their current relationships than restricted individuals (Jones, 1998). Of relevance to initial encounters, unrestricted males smiled more, laughed more, and displayed more flirtatious glances than restricted males in a lab study of nonverbal behavior and interaction. Unrestricted females were more likely to lean forward and cant their heads than were restricted females (Simpson, Gangestad, & Biek, 1993).

Mating and Attachment Styles

Rather than attempting to judge whether sexually unrestricted individuals are really warm and playful, or truly cold and manipulative, our lab suggested that unrestricted sociosexuality may be found in two varieties. We proposed that the specific manifestation of SOI was dependent on other aspects of the individual's personality, such as agreeableness, and that the combination of two personality dimensions can have a substantial impact on mating strategies (Cunningham, Barbee, & Philhower, 2002). Individuals who possess the personality trait of agreeableness tended to be warm, cooperative, sympathetic, and helpful, whereas people who possess the opposite tendency of disagreeableness tended to be hostile and uncooperative. In addition, agreeable people expend some effort to control their negative, prejudicial, or antisocial impulses, whereas disagreeable people do not (Jensen-Campbell et al., 2002). People who were unrestricted in their sociosexuality tended to be slightly less agreeable than others ($r = -.25$ in three samples, $n = 1,230$), but those who were unrestricted or restricted in their sociosexuality may be found with both agreeable and disagreeable personalities. The combination of the two dimensions leads to four different approaches to mate attraction.

We created four new scales to measure those mating styles, using SOI, Saucier's (1994) measure of agreeableness, and Bartholomew and Horowitz's (1991) attachment prototypes to validate them. The four dimensions were labeled *partner, player, parasite,* and *predator.* The **partner** is caring, responsive, communal, and intrinsically interested in a romantic relationship. A higher score on the partner dimension was positively correlated with agreeableness and a secure attachment style, and negatively correlated with sociosexuality and the three insecure attachment styles. Partners were more likely to be female than male. The **player** pursues a mixed reproductive strategy of being moderately warm while eschewing commitment. High scores on the player dimension were strongly correlated with sociosexuality and somewhat negatively correlated with agreeableness, and correlated with all three of the insecure attachment prototypes, most strongly with *dismissive.* The **parasite** pursues a long-term relationship strategy apparently to address personal needs or deficiencies. The parasite is passionate and intense, and may engage in stalking if the partner decides to leave. High scores on the parasite dimension were negatively correlated with agreeableness, positively correlated with the preoccupied attachment style, and uncorrelated with sociosexuality. Finally, a disagreeable unrestricted individual may be an unscrupulous **predator**, who exploits and then abandons the date. High scores on the predator dimension were negatively correlated with agreeableness, and positively correlated with sociosexuality and a fearful attachment style. We will return to these dimensions when discussing *mating tactics* in the *talk and reevaluate* stage of initial encounters.

The foregoing section indicated that individual differences in such variables as culture, gender, desired type of relationship, sociosexuality, mating style, and attachment prototype all may have a substantial impact on a person's approach to, and responsiveness in, an initial romantic encounter. Consequently, at any given moment, an individual may be operating from any one of a dizzying variety of priorities. In light of such between- and within-person variability, having the right broom at the right time to sweep a person off his or her feet can be challenging.

ATTRACT ATTENTION

Before a romantic relationship can form, people have to become aware of each other. One of the primary nonverbal stimuli that capture the attention of others is physical appearance. The presentation of physical attractiveness is a nonverbal behavior that is forbidden to females in some Islamic cultures, which require head-to-toe clothing. Elsewhere, both males and females pay attention to and remember physically attractive people more so than unattractive people (Maner et al., 2003). Attention to physical attractiveness may have evolved because it provided a clue to healthy mates (Symons, 1979), but evidence for the relation of physical attractiveness to health and fertility is mixed (Weeden & Sabini, 2005). One reason for such inconsistent findings is that physical attractiveness is not a single dimension, such as being curvaceous, possessing symmetry, or matching the population average, but a combination of several desirable qualities.

In the multiple fitness model (Cunningham et al., 2002), physical attractiveness involves the display of attributes from four categories of features: *neonate, mature, expressive,* and *grooming.* Attributes from each of these categories convey different desirable qualities of the person who possesses them.

Neonate and Sexually Mature Features

Neoteny is based on Konrad Lorenz's observation (1943) that humans are drawn to mammals with cute, babyish features. Neonate features include large eyes, a small nose, smooth skin, glossy hair, and light coloration. Each of these stimuli suggests youthfulness and fitness as a beneficiary of resources.

Although neonate cuteness is desirable, physically attractive adults possess striking postpubescent *sexually mature* features, which convey the fitness of a mating partner. Female sexual maturity features include high cheekbones, narrow cheeks, prominent breasts, a .7 waist-to-hip ratio, long legs, and symmetrical features. Male sexual maturity, by contrast, is conveyed by a broad chin, thick eyebrows, visible facial hair, broad shoulders, tall height, and a 1.0 waist-to-hip ratio. A deep voice (Berry, 1992) and male pheromones (Rantala, Eriksson, Vainikka, & Kortet, 2006) also may be classified as maturity features.

Male sexual maturation of the face causes changes to the eyebrows, brow ridge, nose, chin, and facial hair that intrude on neonate features to a greater extent than the changes caused by female sexual maturation. As a consequence, babyish facial features tend to be perceived as feminine, whereas many sexual maturity facial features tend to be perceived as masculine (Berry, 1990). But both males and females are seen as more attractive if they possess a blend of desirable neonate–feminine and sexual maturity–masculine features (Berry, 1991; Cunningham, 1985; Cunningham, Barbee, & Pike, 1986; Cunningham, Roberts, Barbee, Druen, & Wu, 1995), thereby conveying both youthfulness and the good genes that afford effective maturation and reproduction.

Expressive Features

Not only is the display of physical attractiveness a nonverbal courting behavior, but also nonverbal behavior is a component of physical attractiveness. Individuals convey positive emotion and social interest through expressive features, such as a large smile, dilated pupils, highly set eyebrows, full lips, and a confident posture. Such features cause the person to look friendly, helpful, and responsive, independently of his or her apparent biological fitness. Such personally controllable variables can be as influential as the biological-structural variables (Osborn, 1996, 2006). Indeed, sometimes expressiveness is more important than biological fitness in attraction. Wong and Cunningham (1990; reported in Cunningham, Druen, & Barbee, 1997) induced males to feel a bit depressed in an experiment. Those males reported greater attraction to a *girl next door* type of female, who was high in warm expressiveness and low in sexual maturity, compared to an *ice princess*, who was high in sexual maturity and low in expressiveness. But, males who were induced to feel elated showed the opposite pattern. They preferred a sexually mature but coolly inexpressive ice princess over a girl next door. Males in a neutral mood were equally divided in their preferences.

These results should not be misconstrued to indicate that beauty is solely in the mind of the beholder. Both elated and depressed males preferred females who displayed an ideal combination of both expressive and sexual maturity features over either the girl next door or the ice princess, who displayed only one of the two desirable attributes. Females, by contrast, may generally prefer a warm, expressive male appearance to a cool, sexually mature appearance (Fletcher, Tither, O'Loughlin, Friesen, & Overall, 2004). When females are ovulating, however, they prefer more sexual maturity in the ideal male face than at other times (Little, Penton-Voak, Burt, & Perrett, 2002).

Grooming

The fourth dimension of physical attractiveness, grooming, also involves nonverbal behavior. Grooming includes hairstyle, cosmetics, body weight, possessions, and clothing. Grooming can be used to accentuate other dimensions of attractiveness. For example, a woman may use her hairstyle to convey healthy youthfulness (Hinsz, Matz, & Patience, 2001), flattering clothing can reveal maturity, and lipstick and eye shadow can accentuate expressiveness (Osborn, 1996).

Grooming, especially in terms of clothing and jewelry, also can be used to convey the woman's sense of style, intelligence, and creativity, and the subcultural group with which she identifies, including access to personal and social resources. A specific biological resource is body weight. Females can modify their body weight to optimize their response to the local ecology, and meet the expectations of their society. Females tend to carry more body weight in resource-poor environments and display more slenderness in abundant ecologies (Cunningham & Shamblen, 2003). Females also display more curvaciousness in historical periods when childbearing is valued, and more slenderness when males are scarce and careers are valued (Barber, 2002).

Females may modify their grooming depending on the type of relationship that they are seeking. In a study in Austrian discotheques, Grammer, Renninger, and Fischer (2004) found that females who wore sheer and tight clothing reported stronger motivation to have sex than their peers. Males also can modify their grooming to meet local demands. Males may allow their facial hair to grow into a mustache and beard to convey maturity and dominance, which is more common during wartime, or shave it to suggest youthfulness and cooperation (Muscarella & Cunningham, 1996).

Possessions and Extrapersonal Displays

In the multiple fitness analysis of physical attractiveness, grooming also includes tanning, dieting, bodybuilding, and wearing perfume and cologne. But grooming does not stop there. If an individual looks better in a new suit (Cunningham et al., 1994), he or she can also look better in a new car or spacious apartment. Males were more likely than females to use an expensive car as an attraction tactic (Buss, 1988), but either gender may look good when surrounded by sparkling paint, soft leather, or nice real estate. Possessions can serve as a display of valuable resources (Buss & Schmitt, 1993), but property also can be informative as an indicator of taste, personality, and group membership. Carefully chosen possessions, such as a pen, a cell phone, or car keys, can serve as extensions and reflections of the self (Beggan, 1992; Given, 2005). For example, a Hummer 3 sport utility vehicle costs about the same as a Volvo S80 sedan, so the two would convey comparable levels of monetary resources. But the Hummer currently conveys a love of adventure and a degree of aggressiveness, whereas the Volvo suggests safety and reliability, so they might convey different impressions of their owners. Interpersonal researchers have been hesitant to conduct studies on the attraction to individuals as a function of specific types of merchandise, perhaps because of frequent changes in model designations and marketing campaigns. A larger question is whether individuals actually increase their romantic success when they display resources such as their cars, sports trophies, or diplomas, versus seeming insecurely competitive (cf. Buss, 1988).

Peer Esteem and Mate Copying

Attention is often stimulated by the contagious enthusiasm of other people. Sports teams use cheerleaders to drum up spirit in stadiums, whereas television comedies have laugh tracks to model chuckling for viewers. Modeling may facilitate copying in some domains, but does peer behavior influence important decisions, such as the selection of a mate? Biologists have studied mate copying (Pruett-Jones, 1992), in which the probability of the choice of a given mate by a member of the opposite sex is either greater or less than it otherwise would be, depending on whether that mate was courted or avoided by a conspecific. Female guppies, for example, ignored a physically attractive male in favor of a moderately attractive male who received more female attention, although such mate copying did not occur when the male was very unattractive (Dugatkin, 2000; Gibson & Hoeglund, 1992).

The human custom of critical evaluation before sexual involvement and long-term pair bonding differs from the activities of mate-copying species. But, the complexity of mate selection could activate a simple heuristic to increase decision speed and efficiency by copying others (Asch, 1955; Festinger, 1954; Sherif, 1935). If speed and efficiency are the motives, then males might use mate copying more than females, because of males' lower reproductive costs and lower selectivity (Clark & Hatfield, 1989). Alternately, a model's preferences could provide unique information about the social attributes of the target, which could be systematically processed. Females tend to be sensitive to a male's social status, presumably because such information provides cues to the male's capacity to contribute resources for child care (Cunningham, 1981; Eagly & Woods, 1999). If peer attention provides information about a target's social attributes, then females may show more mate copying than males. Graziano et al. (1993) reported that peer ratings influenced females' ratings of physical attractiveness more than males', even when the individual had the opportunity to independently judge photos of the targets. Copying attractiveness ratings is not quite the same as copying mating choices, but such results were suggestive.

Our research team (Cunningham, Dugatkin, Lundy, Druen, & Barbee, 2006) conducted several studies on mate copying. Study 1 examined the impact of sex, peer acceptance or rejection of the target, and the target's physical attractiveness on participants' interest in short-term and long-term mating. Participants were informed that targets were interviewed independently by five females, who rated several characteristics, for 20 to 30 minutes in a previous experiment. Six scenarios combined two levels of physical attractiveness with three levels of peer attention. Respondents rated how interested they would be in the short-term, relatively low-cost behavior of dating the target, and in a long-term, high-cost relationship, such as marriage. We found that both males' and females' mating interest was influenced by peer attention to a target. An interaction of peer attention with physical attractiveness was found, such that high peer attention compensated for low physical attractiveness. Females were more influenced than males by levels of peer attention, especially by negative information, supporting the social attributes hypothesis. A second study used the variables of the first and also manipulated the potential mate's wealth. High wealth was based on a yearly income of $520,000, which was due to the parent's luck rather than either the hard work or luck of the target. Low wealth involved an income of $20,000. Again, both males' and especially females' mating interest was influenced by peer attention to a target. In Study 2, peer attention increased attraction independently of wealth. Thus, peer esteem can be a personal asset that is as desirable as physical attractiveness or wealth, a result that we call the *celebrity effect*.

Many questions remain. If a male sees another male being attracted to a female with a specific look in the mass media, will that increase his attraction to other females with a similar appearance? Conversely, do females who copy the hairstyle, makeup, clothing, or mannerisms of current female celebrities thereby enhance their own attractiveness to males? We suspect so, but it remains to be demonstrated. It is also possible that males could resist copying through strategic nonconformity, but that seems to require the incentive of an approving female onlooker (cf. Griskevicius, Goldstein, Mortensen, Cialdini, & Kenrick, 2006).

As the foregoing section indicated, a variety of personal stimuli, ranging from structural-biological qualities such as large eyes and curvaceous hips to controllable nonverbal displays such as smiling and hairstyle, serves to attract the interest and romantic attention of onlookers. Individuals' attention in a prospective date also may be piqued by romantic overtures made by other people toward that prospect.

DECIDE AND APPROACH

It is one thing to become aware of an attractive stranger; it is another thing to decide to bridge the gap and initiate interaction. Females, who generally control the early stages of courting (Givens, 1978), may simply approach the male themselves or, more commonly, may engage in a wide range of behaviors to increase the chance of males approaching them.

Nonverbal Solicitation

The nonverbal behavior displayed by a prospective date can have a significant impact on the likelihood that an onlooker will approach. Walsh and Hewitt (1985) found that males were significantly more likely to approach females who displayed both repeated eye contact and smiling than females displaying other nonverbal behaviors. But, eye contact and smiling are only a small part of the female solicitation repertoire. Moore (1985) observed over 200 females at a singles bar, and cataloged the frequency with which they engaged in 52 behaviors. The most frequent solicitation behaviors included smiling, glancing around the room, solitary dancing, laughing, and hair flipping. To justify the claim that those were solicitation behaviors, Moore conducted a second study to observe the frequency of the behaviors displayed by 40 subjects at four locations—a singles bar, a university snack bar, a university library, and a university women's center meeting where no males were present. In the singles bar, the females expressed an average of 70.6 solicitation displays in a one-hour period, or a little over one display per minute, selected from an average of 12.8 categories of behavior. By contrast, the frequency and diversity of displays in the snack bar (18.6 behaviors drawn from 4.0 categories), library (7.5 from 4.7), and women's meeting (9.6 from 2.1) were lower.

These results indicate that when females are interested in attracting males, they increase both the frequency and the diversity of their solicitation behaviors. Such displays appear to be effective, in that there was a strong correlation ($r = .89$) between the number of female solicitation displays and the number of approaches made by males. In a study of 100 females ages 13 to 16 in a mixed-sex setting, Moore (1995) reported that the younger girls used many of the same solicitation signals commonly exhibited by women. But, girls made more frequent use of play and teasing behavior, and displayed an exaggerated form of many signals. No doubt, the girls learned subtlety with time. Unfortunately, Moore did not reveal which specific female solicitation behavior, if any, was most effective in stimulating male approach (Moore & Butler, 1989).

It is possible that the total volume of a person's activity, rather than any specific nonverbal signal, reveals mating interest. Grammer, Honda, Juette, and Schmitt (1999) used computerized motion energy detection to study the behavior of opposite-sex strangers in both Germany and Japan. The analysis of both form of movement and gaze did not reveal a consistent repertoire of courtship behavior. But a movement quality score, based on the number of female movements plus their duration, size, speed, and complexity, correlated with the females' interest in the males.

Although cross-cultural studies of courtship behaviors are rare, Eibl-Eibesfeldt (1989) documented the use of the eyebrow flash and the coy smile in several nonindustrialized cultures. The eyebrow flash consists of a rapid raising and lowering of the eyebrows, accompanied by a quick smile and head nod. The coy smile consists of a female making brief eye contact, showing a fleeting smile, then looking away. But Moore's (1985) U.S. study recorded few instances of the eyebrow flash or the coy smile. She suggested that American females may be more inclined to use the full smile and direct eye contact, rather than more subtle flirting behaviors.

Signal (Mis)perception

Givens (1978, 2005) suggested that females often control the early phases of an opposite-sex encounter. In his view, a male who approaches a female without the female noticing him and displaying solicitation behavior is unlikely to be successful. Conversely, males who fail to notice females' signals miss fleeting opportunities. Thus, in the dance of courtship, one gender must solicit an approach without appearing to promise too much, whereas the other gender must learn to recognize the subtle nonverbal cues indicating such solicitation. From an evolutionary perspective, males suffer more reproductive costs if they miss a signal that is intended by a female to solicit his approach than if they misinterpret female nonverbal behavior as solicitation when it is not. Consequently, males may be biased toward the overperception of female solicitation cues.

Abbey (1982) conducted an intriguing experiment in which a male and female participated in a 5-minute conversation while another male and female remotely observed the interaction. Males, regardless of whether they were interacting or just observing, rated the female who was interacting as being more promiscuous and seductive than did the female interaction participants themselves or the female observers. Males were also more sexually attracted to the opposite-sex person than were females. Such results suggest that males may interpret female behavior as romantic solicitation when it is simply friendliness. Males' biased evaluation of female nonverbal behavior has been reported by other observers (Moore, 2002; Shotland & Craig, 1988).

An important distinction is that males and females generally agree about a female's motives if her nonverbal behaviors, such as interpersonal distance, eye contact, and touch, are clearly seductive or clearly cool. In addition, when the female wore revealing clothing (Abbey, Cozzarelli, McLaughlin, & Harnish, 1987) or consumed alcohol (Abbey & Harnish, 1995), both genders saw her as more sexually motivated than when she wore modest clothing or consumed nonalcoholic beverages. But, the genders diverge when the behavior is ambiguous, with males more likely to see the female target as being sexually interested than females perceive her to be (Abbey & Melby, 1986), especially when the male is consuming alcohol (Abbey, Zawacki, & Buck, 2005).

In a pair of surveys of 985 college students, females personally experienced misperceptions of friendliness as sexual interest more often than did males, but such misunderstandings happened to both genders. Most of these encounters were resolved without a problem, but some incidents involved a degree of coerced sexual activity, which left the individual feeling angry, humiliated, and depressed (Abbey, 1987). Consequently, it would be helpful to know the specific actions that are most likely to be misperceived as seductive, so that people can be aware of their ambiguous behaviors. Conversely, shy people may be aided by learning the subtle solicitation signals that convey that they are unlikely to be rejected if they will simply decide to go for it and approach someone.

Moving Closer

When one person is introduced to another, he or she is already in a position to begin a conversation. But, in a setting like a classroom, party, or bar, an individual may develop the impression that a stranger shares a mutual romantic interest, and have that perception confirmed by nonverbal solicitation behaviors, but someone still must make the first move and reduce the distance. In some cases, a particularly fetching come-hither look may be necessary to reduce possible fears of rejection (or entrapment). In other cases, it may require only the repetition of a mundane flirting gesture for the other party to bridge the gap.

In Moore's (1985) study, males made the approach 80% of the time, but approaches by females to males accounted for nearly 20% of the opposite-sex encounters. Although it is the subject of many men's anxieties, there is very little research guidance on the timing and proper way to cross a room to engage a person with whom one has been nonverbally flirting. Perper (1985), however, recommended that the intensity of the male's response should match the intensity of the woman's signal. He should be cool and casual if that is what she is exuding. Givens (2005) advised that males should show vulnerability and reduce the appearance of threat when they approach a female. If the female begins to show signs of nervousness, the male should make appeasing gestures, such as lowering his shoulders and tilting his head to show his neck. The male also might appear less threatening if he uses self-deprecating humor (Lundy, Tan, & Cunningham, 1998) or even commits a minor pratfall (Helmreich, Aronson, & Lefan, 1970).

The complex nonverbal signaling involved in *decide and approach* presumes that two people are strangers and lack a mutual acquaintance to introduce them. If someone introduces them, they might skip both *attract attention* and *decide and approach* and move directly into a conversation.

TALK AND REEVALUATE

When you first came in to breakfast, when I first saw you, I thought you were handsome. Then, of course, you spoke.

Helen Hunt (as Carol Connelly) in *As Good as It Gets* (Sakai & Brooks, 1997)

Physical attractiveness and congenial nonverbal behavior can help to move two people into closer proximity with one another, but verbal interaction either bonds the people together or repels them (Reyes et al., 1999). As Jack Nicholson (as Melvin Udall) was informed in *As Good as It Gets*, his obnoxious verbal style undermined the positive first impression created by his nonverbal qualities. Conversely, vocal attractiveness may be just as potent an influence on liking as physical attractiveness (Zuckerman, Miyake, & Hodgins, 1991), and just as multidimensional (Zuckerman & Miyake, 1993). With so much riding on the first few seconds of conversation, many people have communication apprehension when it comes time to speak.

Opening Gambits

Some people search for a magically charming opening conversational gambit, or pickup line, that will break the ice and melt the heart of the stranger. Kleinke, Meeker, and Staneski (1986) collected approximately 100 opening gambits from advice books, magazines, and other sources. They had males and females rate opening lines used by men for meeting women in general situations, and for specific situations, such as a bar, restaurant, and laundromat. In Study 2, university students and employees rated opening lines used by women for meeting men in general situations. Factor analysis of ratings of the lines across studies revealed three basic types. The *direct approach* involved an overt statement of interest, sometimes with elements of self-disclosure, flattery, or self-effacement, such as "I feel a little embarrassed about this, but I'd really like to meet you." The *innocuous approach* elicited conversation through a pleasantry, such as "How are you?" The *cute-flippant approach* involves humor, sometimes of a sexual nature, such as "I'm easy, are you?" The investigators reported that direct and innocuous approaches were about equally represented among the preferred opening lines, but nearly all of the least preferred approaches were of the cute-flippant type. Kleinke et al. (1986) also reported a tendency for females to dislike cute-flippant opening lines, and to prefer innocuous lines, more than did males. The authors suggested that "these findings support expectations from research on sex role socialization that men prefer more direct and aggressive approach[es] toward social encounters whereas women are inclined toward approaches that are nonthreatening and benign" (pp. 597–598).

Cunningham (1989) tested the effectiveness of the direct, innocuous, and cute-flippant opening lines in the field. In Experiment 1, a male approached 63 female singles bar patrons, using one of six opening lines, classified as direct, innocuous, or cute-flippant. Females were much more likely to respond positively if the male used a direct (67%) or innocuous line (62%) instead of a flippant approach (19%). In Experiment 2, both male and female experimenters delivered direct, innocuous, and cute-flippant lines to 212 opposite-sex bar patrons. The experimenters also touched half of the respondents on the forearm while delivering the opening lines. The outcome for males approaching females was comparable to that of Experiment 1 (direct approach, 69% positive; innocuous, 71%; and flippant, 25%). Forearm touching had no impact, perhaps because it was seen as an attention-getting, rather than intimate, gesture. When a female approached a male, however, the response was remarkably positive. There was no difference in the males' responses to the three approaches, including no aversion to the flippant lines (direct, 81%; innocuous, 100%; flippant, 89%). Experiment 3 examined whether gender differences in personality inference processes accounted for the differences in responsiveness. Both males and females derived information about the targets' qualities, such as sociability, from the various opening lines, which influenced their interest. But, the males' judgments of sexiness were closely related to males' interest in the female target but not to females' interest in the male. Females were more influenced by the male targets' perceived intelligence than by their sexiness.

The foregoing suggests that opening lines are effective to the extent that the sender meets the receiver's needs and expectations, such as females' desire for intelligence or males' desire for sexiness. If the recipient has other priorities, different opening gambits may be required. Rowatt (2001) demonstrated that the same approach produced a different reaction depending on both the social context and whether the initiator was a friend versus a stranger. Similarly, different opening lines might be necessary to address new needs and concerns that emerge at later stages of life.

Humor

Cute-flippant opening lines are intended to be provocative and humorous. A sense of humor is a characteristic that people often seek in a mate. Hewitt (1958) reported that 90% of male and 81% of female college students said that a sense of humor was crucial in a dating partner, with similar percentages for marriage partners. Comparable findings were reported by Hansen (1977) and Goodwin (1990). Smith, Waldorf, and Trembath (1990) examined personal advertisements in a singles magazine and found that 41% of females desired a male who was humorous (a desire that was mentioned second only to *understanding*), and 21% of males desired a female who was humorous (the seventh most nominated attribute). Kenrick et al. (1990) reported that college students preferred a prospective marriage partner to be above average in sense of humor. No other single attribute had a consistently higher minimum standard than did humor, and most attributes were consistently lower. In addition, humor became more important to both males and females as the level of commitment of the relationship increased.

Felmlee (1995) asked male and female participants to reflect on the personal quality that most attracted them to their partners in their most recently terminated romantic relationship. She reported that the category of *fun qualities* was the second most nominated as responsible for initial attraction. The most common attribute comprising this category was *a good sense of humor*. Interestingly, this category of initial attraction was also associated with a *fatal attraction*, a quality that eventually became strongly disliked, perhaps by being too much of a good thing.

Lundy et al. (1998) examined the effects of expressions of humor and physical attractiveness on attraction for various types of heterosexual relationships. Humor was manipulated using interview transcripts containing humorously self-deprecating responses; physical attractiveness was manipulated using photographs. Males were found to emphasize physical attractiveness more than did females for dating, sexual intercourse, and a serious relationship. Individuals who expressed humor, particularly males, were rated as more desirable for a serious relationship and marriage, but only when those individuals were physically attractive. Humorous individuals were perceived to be more cheerful but less intellectual than nonhumorous individuals. It appeared that conveying a sense of humor served to humanize the good-looking person, and reduced the intimidation caused by high physical attractiveness.

Humor can be created by the situation, rather than by individual wit. Fraley and Aron (2004) randomly paired same-sex strangers ($n = 96$) in a series of structured interactions systematically manipulated to either create or not create a shared humorous experience. Participants then completed measures of feelings of closeness to their interaction partner. There was a significant effect of humor on closeness. This effect was partially mediated by self-expansion and distraction from the discomfort of the first encounter. The effect was significantly moderated by trait sense of humor and marginally moderated by anxious attachment style, such that the effect was greater for those high in trait sense of humor and high in anxious attachment. Put simply, being involved in humorous situations can help to break the ice and reduce tension among strangers.

Direct Propositions

Humorous opening lines are one way to start a conversation leading to romance. Another tactic is to come right to the point. In 1978 and 1982, Clark and Hatfield (1989) had male and female confederates of average attractiveness approach potential partners with one of three opening lines: "Would you go out with me tonight?" "Will you come over to my apartment tonight?" or "Would you go to bed with me tonight?" Male responses to the date offer were identical in the two studies (Experiments 1 and 2: 50%). Males were even more interested in going to the females' apartment (Experiments 1 and 2: 69%), which was comparable to their willingness to have sex (Experiment 1: 75%; and Experiment 2: 69%). Females were as willing as males to go out on a date (Experiment 1: 56%; and Experiment 2: 50%), but none agreed to go to the apartment or to have sex. Those results were obtained before awareness of Acquired Immune Deficiency Syndrome (AIDS), so Clark (1990) conducted a follow-up study. Male responsiveness to romantic opportunities remained evident despite the increased risk (date: 69%; apartment: 50%; and bed: 69%), as was female selectivity (date: 44%; apartment: 14%; and bed: 0%). Clark's finding that 14% of females were willing to go to the males' apartment represented only two respondents, which is not significantly different from the zero reported earlier.

It is conceivable that females who are unrestricted, acutely lonely, or at the midpoint of their menstrual cycles could respond positively to a stranger who offered a suggestive cute-flippant line, or a direct proposition, provided that the male meets the females' minimum standard for attractiveness. Voracek, Hofhansl, and Fisher (2005) reported the results of an Austrian magazine project that followed up the Clark and Hatfield (1989) studies. That study reported that 6.1% of 100 females of unspecified ages accepted immediate sexual involvement with a complete stranger. The authors suggested that various contextual factors "such as setting, subjects' age and attractiveness, and age differences between requestor and receiver, probably contributed to the observed difference in outcome between the journalistic project and the original experiments" (p. 11). Although 0% may be too low an estimate for female responsiveness to a one-night stand opportunity, the 6% to 14% range is so much higher that replication with a true population sample seems needed.

Mating Tactics

Humorous opening gambits and direct propositions are a subset of mating tactics, or behaviors designed to increase the attraction of a potential partner. Work in our lab focused on the determinants of prosocial and antisocial mate tactics to foster long- or short-term relationships. The 747 participants in Cunningham et al. (2002) were asked to respond to 65 questions about their mating tactics, including whether they would perform specific behaviors to attract and retain a dating partner, using a 9-point scale. The mating tactics inventory focused on the display of care and material characteristics, as well as the use of romanticism, exploitation, and honesty versus deception. The items were inspired by diverse sources ranging from Buss (1988) to Fein and Schneider's (1995) popular neotraditional book, *The Rules*. Four types of mating tactics emerged: *support*, *charm*, *manipulate*, and *seduce*. These behaviors showed coherent relationships with the four mating styles described previously, and with attachment styles.

Support mating behaviors emphasize care and honesty toward the partner. The partner mating style was the best predictor of the use of *support*, followed by agreeableness, and a secure attachment style. An emphasis on creating a light but sensual mood is the hallmark of the **charm** behavior. The player mating style was the best predictor of the use of *charm* behavior, followed by the parasite mating style, and a preoccupied attachment style. The **manipulate** mating style emphasizes subtle control and demands, and has many items inspired by "the rules." The parasite mating style was the best predictor of the use of *manipulate* behavior, followed by the predator mating style, and a preoccupied attachment style. The **seduce** behavior emphasizes the use of deception, and display of resources, for sexual conquest. The predator mating style was the best predictor of the use of *seduce* behavior, followed by the player mating style. Other predictors of seduce behavior were sociosexuality and a fearful attachment style. Males were more likely to use seduce tactics than females, but the genders did not differ on support, charm, or manipulate behaviors.

Just as mating styles predict the use of mating tactics, a person's use of specific mating tactics may allow a recipient to deduce that person's mating style and romantic intentions. A person who offers only sincere compliments and does not brag is likely to be a partner, and may be looking for a long-term relationship. But, someone who lights candles, puts on quiet jazz, and changes into something flattering on the first date might be a player, and interested in a mutually satisfying but short-term encounter. By contrast, a person who wishes to be pursued while playing hard to get, and is always the first to end a phone call, might be a parasite, who is more interested in the material benefits of marriage than in the discoveries of dating. Finally, an individual who displays the keys to an expensive car while plying a potential date with liquor could be a predator who will say anything to get lucky and whose interest will be gone by dawn.

Lying to Get a Date

Although predators are those most likely to be deceptive, lying is common in social interactions (DePaulo & Kashy, 1998). Deception is often used to enhance self-promotion (Tooke & Camire, 1991). Indeed, the most common tactic that people reported using to attract a date involves making the self appear to be more attractive or able than a competitor (Buss, 1988). In some cases, the deceit may consist of a subtle exaggeration, such as feigning agreement with a prospective date's opinion. In other cases, the lie may be an absolute falsification, like saying one's income is twice as much as it really is (cf. Walters & Crawford, 1994).

Rowatt, Cunningham, and Druen (1998) examined whether high self-monitors, who are dispositionally inclined to manage their self-presentations to meet the expectations of other people, use more deceptive self-presentation than others to initiate a dating relationship. In Experiment 1, males reviewed the photograph, personality, background, and "My Ideal Man" ratings made by physically attractive and unattractive females who were potential dates. Half of the time, the physically attractive female desired instrumental traits in a date, such as being independent, active, and decisive. In that condition, the unattractive female sought expressive traits, such as being gentle, kind, and emotional. The other half of the time, preferences were reversed. Males had the opportunity to create separate self-descriptions, including ratings of their instrumentality–expressivity, for both females. As expected, males who possessed the personality trait of high self-monitoring presented themselves as more instrumental or more expressive as a function of what would match the desires of the attractive female. Such self-presentations were clearly deceptive, because they differed from the self-presentations that the same males made to the unattractive female. Experiment 2 in this series used both males and females, and measured their self-reported instrumentality–expressivity, love attitudes, and physical attractiveness 2 weeks before they were given an opportunity to describe themselves to two potential dates. Males and females did not differ in their willingness to deceive, but high self-monitors again changed their self-descriptions to match the expectations of the attractive potential dates. These outcomes suggest that high self-monitors behave in a chameleon-like fashion during dating initiation, strategically changing their self-presentation in an attempt to appear more desirable to the person they wish to date.

Rowatt, Cunningham, and Druen (1999) continued this research by asking participants to report how much they would lie to get a date with each of four people, two of whom were physically attractive based on their photographs, and two of whom were physically unattractive. Individuals reported being quite willing to lie to the facially attractive prospective dates, particularly about their personal appearance, personality, income, past relationship outcomes, career skills, and course grades. Males were marginally more willing than females to lie to a prospective date about their career skills and course grades, perhaps because males' intellectual potential and career prospects have somewhat more influence on the quality of the females' lives than the reverse. Males were no less willing than females to lie about their personal appearance, perhaps because male physical attractiveness affects females' decisions about short-term relationships. Other analyses indicated that subjects were particularly willing to tell lies to maximize their apparent similarity with the attractive potential dates.

Self-Presentation in Newspaper Ads and Online

Newspaper and online ads for romantic partners have no mechanism to regulate veracity. Some advertisers might post personal photos that are 10 years out of date or borrowed from a magazine model, or even invent careers that are fabrications. Gibbs, Ellison, and Heino (2006) surveyed 349 users of the online dating service Match.com. They found that 86% of respondents felt that other users misrepresented their physical appearance, 49% were suspicious that others misstated their relationship goals, 45% doubted reported age, 45% questioned reported income, and 40% were suspicious of stated marital status. Yet, although many users of online dating services had suspicions about the veracity of their peers, we do not have data on the actual frequency of deception. It would be interesting to know how many online daters could pass a credential verification process based on a birth certificate, diploma, pay stub, and personal photo holding that day's newspaper. It also would be interesting to know what cues people use to suspect misrepresentations in online encounters (cf. Burgoon, Buller, White, Afifi, & Buslig, 1999; DePaulo et al., 2003).

In the Gibbs et al. (2006) survey, 94% strongly disagreed with the idea that they had intentionally misrepresented themselves, and 87% strongly disagreed that misrepresentation was acceptable, leaving only 6 to 13% who may be willing to lie. But, although the survey respondents regarded intentional misrepresentation as wrong, they were not convinced that honesty was the best policy. The more that the online daters said that they had been honest in their profiles, the less romantically successful that they reported having been.

Dissatisfaction with honesty as an online policy could result in some selective editing of one's profile, to minimize the negative and exaggerate the positive. In qualitative interviews of 11 individuals, respondents reported projecting a self-image in their online descriptions that was more self-confident, outgoing, or desirable than was the case in real life (Yurchisin, Watchravesrinkan, & McCabe, 2005). But, this was not so much a dishonest self as a potential self to which the person aspired to grow. After receiving positive feedback from respondents to the ads, the authors felt encouraged to move toward achieving their potential selves. So, a certain level of online self-idealization may become a self-fulfilling prophecy, benefiting both the advertiser and the respondent.

But, honesty may be the best policy, because falsely managing one's impression to meet the presumed preferences of potential partners may simply miss the target audience. Strassberg and Holty (2003) posted four "female seeking male" advertisements on U.S. Internet sites in 1997. In the most popular ad, the female described herself as financially independent, successful, and ambitious. This ad generated 50% more male responses than the next most popular ad, in which the female described herself as being lovely, very attractive, and slim. It is possible that Internet users were more mature and career oriented than the college students used in most studies, and were more interested in kindred spirits rather than eye candy. Nonetheless, it was interesting that the most (self-described) beautiful woman may not always be the most *attractive* woman to some men.

Rhetoric of Responses

A common script evolved for newspaper personal ads for those seeking mates, which carried over to online profiles. For example, individuals placing ads generally specify their own demographics (DWM, 32) and those of the type of person whom they are seeking (S/DWF 25–32), plus some self-descriptive characteristics (e.g., literate, fun loving), and some specific preferences for qualities in a partner (e.g., nonsmoker, must love dogs). Individuals placing ads for the first time have the opportunity to study prior submissions, gain inspiration, and even borrow phrases that seem personally accurate.

Strategies for a response to a personal ad or profile are less scripted. Should the opening sentence seem tentative ("I've never done this before …") or bold ("I think you and I would hit it off … .")? Should the responder compliment the advertiser first, or first mention the responder's own desirable qualities? Does the lyricism, graciousness, or boldness of the written response have any impact on the advertiser, or is that less influential than the responder's demographics and photograph? How many rounds of correspondence should there be before inviting a face-to-face meeting? Should the male or the female make that request?

A few studies examined responses to personal ads, but such studies tended to focus on resource-exchange dynamics rather than rhetoric. Strassberg and Holty (2003), for example, examined if the female stated that she was ambitious, the male's likelihood of mentioning his education (34%), or, if the female reported that she was slim and attractive, the male's likelihood of mentioning his height (63%) and appearance (31%). Such exchanges are interesting, but interpersonal scholars also are interested in the style and form of replies to the advertisement. What seem to be needed are Markovian analyses, which examine tit-for-tat interactions between the advertiser and the responder over a sequence of messages. Does the length of the messages, and the depth and breadth of self-disclosure, converge in successful online relationships? How often does the male play the role of the pursuer and the female play hard to get, and how often are those roles reversed? In this context, it is interesting to note that Strassberg and Holty received 507 responses to online ads involving females seeking males, but fewer than 25 responses to online ads involving males seeking females. Consequently, the rhetorical content of female responses to male ads is a largely undocumented domain.

As the foregoing section suggested, communication during initial romantic encounters can go in many different directions after the initial pleasantries. The timing and impact of demographics, self-disclosure, similarity of interests, humor, and requests to move the relationship to the next level are hard to disentangle, but might be advanced through data mining of the rich corpus of material accumulating in online chat rooms.

TOUCH AND SYNCHRONIZE

Assuming that both parties like what they hear during the first few rounds of communication and do not detect any outrageous deceptions, then behavior may escalate from casual flirtation to romantic courtship. Eye contact becomes more intense and prolonged, self-disclosure becomes deeper and broader, and physical contact may occur.

Perper (1985) observed that the female often makes the first touch, which is typically light and fleeting such as fingertips on the male's hand, or the palm placed on the forearm. Extended eye contact and a physical touch can be arousing and can increase romantic feelings, at least among those who are already romantically inclined (Williams & Kleinke, 1993). On some occasions, Perper (1985) noticed males making the first move by putting his arm around the female's shoulders or touching her hair. But, such a pass implicitly requires the female to reject or reciprocate it, which may precipitate a premature stay versus go decision. Exploring such issues, McCormick and Jones (1989) conducted an observational study of 70 cross-sex couples. Females were more likely than males to gaze at and briefly touch their partners, display positive facial expressions, and groom themselves, but males used more intimate touches than did females. They also noticed that females deescalated flirtation more in the beginning of the interaction, whereas males deescalated more later, suggesting that females take less time to be decisive about a mate.

Maxwell, Cook, and Burr (1985) confirmed an early observation by Scheflen (1965) that couples in an emerging relationship engage in nonverbal synchrony. They videotaped pairs of 50 high school students meeting over coffee in a lab that resembled a comfortable living room. The subjects' liking was predicted by their mutual gaze, their self-disclosure, the expressiveness of their faces, the liveliness of the voices, and their synchrony in movement and gesture.

Music

Although the outside world may distract a couple, it also may facilitate synchronization through cultural institutions such as music. Pleasing music often creates a pleasant mood in the listener, and May and Hamilton (1980) demonstrated that positive affect–evoking rock music increased females' ratings of the physical attractiveness of males, compared to females who listened to negative affect–evoking avant-garde music or no music. Unfortunately, the precise stimuli in music that are responsible for the positive effects, such as the lyrics, harmony, or rhythm, are unknown. Merker (2000), however, suggested that the rhythmic pulse of music allows the listener to predict where the next beat is going to fall, which allows two or more people to synchronize their performances. This predictability allows coordinated choral singing, dancing, and manual labor, which may increase group cohesion and productivity.

Humans' interest in synchronizing their vocal expressions is not only evident when music is present, such as in choral singing and rock concerts, but also evident without music, such as in sports cheers, protest chants, and church prayers. A portion of the impulse to synchronize may be a desire to bask in reflected glory or derive self-esteem from affiliating with a high-status group, such as a winning sports team or prestigious institution (Cialdini et al., 1976). But, another influence may be the inclination to be swept along with another person or the tide of humanity, behaving in coordination with others rather than acting autonomously. Such an inclination may be implicated in hypnotic susceptibility, in mate copying, and in the tendency of some individuals to suppress their doubts and synchronize with the romantic inclinations of an attractive stranger. Zillman and Bhatia (1989) reported that individuals were more attracted to potential partners who shared their musical tastes than those who did not, perhaps because it would allow them to synchronize to the same music, and thereby to each other.

Dance

An organized dance event, such as a high school mixer, allows for the expression of the full range of flirtation and courtship stages: *prioritize desires, attract attention, notice and approach, talk and reevaluate*, and *touch and synchronize*. Indeed, some of the earliest studies of romantic attraction were conducted at college dances (Brislin & Lewis, 1968; Tesser & Brodie, 1971; Walster [now Hatfield], Aronson, Abrahams, & Rottman, 1966), which may have served to emphasize the impact of variables such as physical attractiveness (cf. May & Hamilton, 1980). Slow dances provide a justification for physical touching, whereas faster dances allow for the demonstration of physical fitness and grace of movement (cf. Berry et al., 1991), and the ability to coordinate complex moves with the partner. Such coordination may be a prerequisite for affectionate activities, such as holding hands, hugging, kissing, cuddling and holding, backrubs and massages, caressing and stroking, and sexual intercourse (Gulledge, Gulledge, & Stahmann, 2003).

Unfortunately, no studies were located that demonstrated that couples that danced well together were more likely to move on to other forms of synchrony. Nor is it clear what verbal or nonverbal signals are involved in transitioning from one form of touch to the next, such as from hand-holding to kissing (cf. Brook, Balka, Abernathy, & Hamburg, 1994). But once a couple has developed synchrony, they are in a good position to live happily ever after … at least until morning.

UNANSWERED QUESTIONS AND FUTURE DIRECTIONS

This review of nonverbal and verbal communication dynamics in the initiation of romantic relationships was facilitated by a strong empirical foundation, contributed by many creative researchers, offering reliable observations of both the macro and micro variables that contribute to initial attraction. At that same time, close examination of each phase of the dance of courtship revealed many unanswered questions (see Table 5.1).

TABLE 5.1   Some Unanswered Questions Concerning Verbal and Nonverbal Dynamics in Courtship Initiation

1. Prioritize desires.
   - What are the social norms specifying courtship dynamics in each culture, and what ecological and historical factors influence them?
   - How can a potential suitor quickly determine if a potential date is seeking a short-term versus a long-term relationship? Which nonverbal and verbal approaches appeal to each desire?
   - How do early attachment experiences and temperament differentially contribute to the development of *partner, player, parasite*, and *predator* mating styles?

2. Attract attention.
   - Are individuals more successful in attracting dates when their self-presentation matches their physical appearance? For example, do males with babyish features do better by presenting innocence and vulnerability, and females people who look mature and angular do better by conveying independence and aloofness, as opposed to working against their physical types? Or, do people do better by exemplifying sex role stereotypes, with males conveying independence and females conveying vulnerability, regardless of their own personal appearance?
   - Are individuals generally successful when they attempt to enhance their attractiveness by mentioning their resources, such as their social connections, cars, sports trophies, or education, or do they usually seem bragging and desperate?
   - Extending mate copying to the mass media, if a male sees another male be attracted to a female with a specific look in the mass media, does that increase his attraction to other females with that look? Conversely, do females who copy the hairstyle, makeup, clothing, and mannerisms of current celebrities thereby enhance their attractiveness to males?

(continued)

TABLE 5.1 (CONTINUED)   Some Unanswered Questions Concerning Verbal and Nonverbal Dynamics in Courtship Initiation

3. Decide and approach.

- Which specific female solicitation behaviors, if any, are most effective in stimulating male approach for dating and for a long-term relationship?
- What specific actions are most likely to be misperceived as seductive, so that individuals can deter potential misunderstandings?
- How long should nonverbal flirting continue before someone makes a move, and what is the best way to cross a room to engage the person with whom one has been nonverbally flirting?
- Which opening lines are effective in initiating relationships in later life stages, or in escalating relations among current friends?
- What percentage of males and females, of different ages, in different cultures, would be receptive to overt offers of sexual activity with minimal acquaintance?

4. Talk and reevaluate.

- What percentage of online daters engage in major deceptions about their age, education, income, and physical appearance?
- What is the relative impact of a respondent's literary style, compared to his or her demographics, income, and physical attractiveness, on acceptance by an advertiser?
- Does the length of the messages, and the depth and breadth of self-disclosure, converge in successful online relationships?
- How often does the male play the role of the pursuer and the female play hard to get, and how often are those roles reversed?
- What is the content of female responses to male ads, and how do the relationships progress?

5. Touch and synchronize.

- Which stimuli are responsible for the positive impact of music on attraction?
- Are couples that dance well together more likely to move on to other forms of synchrony?
- What verbal or nonverbal signals are involved in transitioning from one form of touch to the next, such as from hand-holding to kissing?

The model of initial attraction described above implicitly suggests a courtly minuet between the prospective partners. This script may be more descriptive of partners and parasites seeking dating and long-term relationships than players and predators seeking one-night stands. A predator who is seeking a short-term partner might deceptively follow the standard courting ritual. But, a player who is looking for a short-term partner might streamline the process by systematically approaching each prospective partner that he or she finds attractive until one reciprocates the sentiment (cf. Clark & Hatfield, 1989).

A major theme of this review was the dialectical tension between biologically driven processes and social influence dynamics. This was evident in the perception of physical attractiveness, which involves both biological-structural and social-style components. It also was evident in the finding that social influence in the form of mate copying can be at least as powerful as physical attractiveness in initial attraction. Current cross-cultural research indicates some universals in attractiveness dynamics, but humans' response to social influence means that the impact of age, class, ethnicity, and the specific content of verbal and nonverbal communication will be a perennial topic of study. We eagerly look forward to the next generation of research on these provocative issues!

AUTHOR NOTE

Preparation of this chapter was supported by the National Institute of Child Health and Development (HD042245-01A2). Thanks to Lorraine H. Cunningham for her helpful comments on an earlier draft.

REFERENCES

Abbey, A. (1982). Sex differences in attributions for friendly behavior: Do males misperceive females' friendliness? *Journal of Personality and Social Psychology, 42,* 830–838.

Abbey, A. (1987). Misperceptions of friendly behavior as sexual interest: A survey of naturally occurring incidents. *Psychology of Women Quarterly, 11,* 173–194.

Abbey, A., Cozzarelli, C., McLaughlin, K., & Harnish, R. J. (1987). The effects of clothing and dyad sex composition on perceptions of sexual intent: Do women and men evaluate these cues differently? *Journal of Applied Social Psychology, 17,* 108–126.

Abbey, A., & Harnish, R. J. (1995). Perception of sexual intent: The role of gender, alcohol consumption, and rape supportive attitudes. *Sex Roles, 32,* 297–313.

Abbey, A., & Melby, C. (1986). The effects of nonverbal cues on gender differences in perceptions of sexual intent. *Sex Roles, 15,* 283–298.

Abbey, A., Zawacki, T., & Buck, P. O. (2005). The effects of past sexual assault perpetration and alcohol consumption on men's reactions to women's mixed signals. *Journal of Social and Clinical Psychology, 24,* 129–155.

Asch, S. E. (1955). Opinions and social pressure. *Scientific American, 193,* 31–35.

Bailey, J. M., Gaulin, S., Agyei, Y., & Gladue, B. A. (1994). Effects of gender and sexual orientation on evolutionarily relevant aspects of human mating psychology. *Journal of Personality and Social Psychology, 66,* 1081–1093.

Barber, N. (2002). *The science of romance: Secrets of the sexual brain.* New York: Prometheus Books.

Barber, N. (2003). Paternal investment prospects and cross-national differences in single parenthood. *Cross-Cultural Research, 37,* 163–177.

Bartholomew, K., & Horowitz, L. M. (1991). Attachment styles among young adults: A test of a four-category model. *Journal of Personality and Social Psychology, 61,* 226–244.

Beggan, J. K (1992). On the social nature of nonsocial perception: The mere ownership effect. *Journal of Personality and Social Psychology, 62,* 229–237.

Berry, D. S. (1990). Taking people at face value: Evidence for the kernel of truth hypothesis. *Social Cognition.* 8, 343–361.

Berry, D. S. (1991). Attractive faces are not all created equal: Joint effects of facial babyishness and attractiveness on social perception. *Personality and Social Psychology Bulletin.* 17, 523–531.

Berry, D. S. (1992). Vocal types and stereotypes: Joint effects of vocal attractiveness and vocal maturity on person perception. *Journal of Nonverbal Behavior.* Vol. 16(1). 41–54.

Berry, D. S., Kean, K. J., Misovich, S. J., & Baron, R. M., (1991). Quantized displays of human movement: A methodological alternative to the point-light display. *Journal of Nonverbal Behavior.* Vol. 15(2) Sum 1991, 81–97.

Birkhead, T. R., & Møller, A. P. (1996). Monogamy and sperm competition in birds. In J. M. Black (Ed.), *Partnerships in birds: The ecology of monogamy* (pp. 323–343). New York: Oxford University Press.

Brislin, R. W., & Lewis, S. A. (1968). Dating and physical attractiveness: Replication. *Psychological Reports, 22,* 976.

Brook, J. S., Balka, E. B., Abernathy, T., & Hamburg, B. A. (1994). Sequence of sexual behavior and its relationship to other problem behaviors in African American and Puerto Rican adolescents. *Journal of Genetic Psychology, 155,* 107–114.

Burgoon, J. K., Buller, D., White, C. H., Afifi, W., & Buslig, A. L. S. (1999). The role of conversational involvement in deceptive interpersonal interactions. *Personality and Social Psychology Bulletin, 25,* 669–685.

Buss, D. M. (1988). The evolution of human intrasexual competition: Tactics of mate attraction. *Journal of Personality and Social Psychology, 54,* 616–628.

Buss, D. M. (1994). *The evolution of desire: Strategies of human mating.* New York: Basic Books.

Buss, D. M., & Schmitt, D. P. (1993). Sexual strategies theory: An evolutionary perspective on human mating. *Psychological Review, 100,* 204–232.

Cialdini, R. B., Thorne, A., Borden, R. J., Walker, M. R., Freeman, S., & Sloan, L. R. (1976). Basking in reflected glory: Three (football) field studies. *Journal of Personality and Social Psychology.* Vol. 34(3) Sep. 1976, 366–375.

Clark, R. D. (1990). The impact of AIDS on gender differences in willingness to engage in casual sex. *Journal of Applied Social Psychology, 20,* 771–782.

Clark, R. D., & Hatfield, E. (1989). Gender differences in receptivity to sexual offers. *Journal of Psychology and Human Sexuality, 2,* 39–55.

Cunningham, M. R. (1981). Sociobiology as a supplementary paradigm for social psychological research. In L. Wheeler (Ed.), *Review of personality and social psychology* (Vol. 2, pp. 69–106). Beverly Hills, CA: Sage.

Cunningham, M. R. (1986). Measuring the physical in physical attractiveness: Quasi-experiments on the sociobiology of female facial beauty. *Journal of Personality and Social Psychology, 50,* 925–935.

Cunningham, M. R. (1989). Reactions to heterosexual opening gambits: Female selectivity and male responsiveness. *Personality and Social Psychology Bulletin, 15,* 27–41.

Cunningham, M. R., Barbee, A. P., Graves, C. R., Lundy, D. E., Lister, S. C., & Rowatt, W. (2005). *Can't buy me love: The effects of male wealth and personal qualities on female attraction.* Unpublished manuscript, University of Louisville.

Cunningham, M. R., Barbee, A. P., & Philhower, C. (2002). Dimensions of facial physical attractiveness: The intersection of biology and culture. In G. Rhodes & L. Zebrowitz (Eds.), *Advances in visual cognition: Vol. 1. Facial attractiveness* (pp. 193–238). Stamford, CT: JAI/Ablex.

Cunningham, M. R., Barbee, A. P., & Pike, C. L. (1990). What do women want? Facialmetric assessment of multiple motives in the perception of male facial attractiveness. *Journal of Personality and Social Psychology, 59,* 61–72.

Cunningham, M. R., Druen, P. B., & Barbee, A. P (1997). Angels, mentors, and friends: Trade-offs among evolutionary, social, and individual variables in physical appearance. In J. A. Simpson & D. T. Kenrick (Eds.), *Evolutionary social psychology* (pp. 109–140). Hillsdale, NJ: Lawrence Erlbaum.

Cunningham, M. R., Dugatkin, L. A., Lundy, D. E., Druen, P., & Barbee, A. P. (2006, July). *The celebrity effect: Peer attention and target qualities affect human mate-copying.* Paper presented at the International Association for Relationship Research Conference, Rethymnon, Greece.

Cunningham, M. R., Roberts, A. R., Barbee, A. P., Druen, P. B., & Wu, C. H. (1995). "Their ideas of beauty are, on the whole, the same as ours": Consistency and variability in the cross-cultural perception of female physical attractiveness. *Journal of Personality and Social Psychology, 68,* 261–279.

Cunningham, M. R., Rowatt, T. J., Shamblen, S., Rowatt, W. C., Ault, L. K., Bettler, R., et al. (2005). *Men and women are from Earth: Life-trajectory dynamics in mate choices.* Manuscript in preparation, University of Louisville.

Cunningham, M. R., & Shamblen, S. R. (2003). Beyond nature versus culture: A multiple fitness analysis of variations in grooming. In V. Eckert (Ed.), *Evolutionary aesthetics* (pp. 201–238). New York: Springer-Verlag.

Cunningham, M. R., Shamblen, S. R., Barbee, A. P., & Ault, L. K. (2005). Social allergies in romantic relationships: Behavioral repetition, emotional sensitization, and dissatisfaction in dating couples. *Personal Relationships, 12,* 273–295.

Darwin, C. (1871). *The descent of man and selection in relation to sex.* London: Murray.

DePaulo, B. M., & Kashy, D. A. (1998). Everyday lies in close and casual relationships. *Journal of Personality and Social Psychology, 74,* 63–79.

DePaulo, B. M., Lindsay, J. J., Malone, B. E., Muhlenbruck, L., Charlton, K., & Cooper, H. (2003). Cues to deception. *Psychological Bulletin, 129,* 74–118.

Druen, P. B., Scheirer, J., & Perez, C. (2004). *I'll take your partner, please! Human date/mate-copying.* Unpublished manuscript, York College of Pennsylvania.

Dugatkin, L. A. (2000). *The imitation factor: Evolution beyond the gene.* New York: Free Press.

Eagly, A., & Woods, W. (1999). The origins of sex differences in human behavior: Evolved dispositions versus social roles. *American Psychologist, 54,* 408–423.

Eibl-Eibesfeldt, I. (1989). *Human ethology.* New York: Aldine de Gruyter.

Ellis, B. J., McFadyen-Ketchum, S., Dodge, K. A., Pettit, G. S., & Bates, J. E. (1999). Quality of early family relationships and individual differences in the timing of pubertal maturation in girls: A longitudinal test of an evolutionary model. *Journal of Personality and Social Psychology, 77,* 387–401.

Fein, E., & Schneider, S. (1995). *The rules: Time-tested secrets for capturing the heart of Mr. Right.* New York: Warner Books.

Felmlee, D. H. (1995). Social norms in same- and cross-gender friendships. *Social Psychology Quarterly, 62,* 53–67.

Festinger, L. (1954). A theory of social comparison processes. *Human Relations, 7,* 117–140.

Fisher, R. A. (1930). *The genetic theory of natural selection.* New York: Dover.

Fletcher, G. J. O., Tither, J. M., O'Loughlin, C., Friesen, M., & Overall, N. (2004). Warm and homely or cold and beautiful? Sex differences in trading off traits in mate selection. *Personality and Social Psychology Bulletin, 30,* 659–672.

Flinn, M. V. (1988). Mate guarding in a Caribbean village. *Ethology & Sociobiology, 9,* 1–28.

Fraley, B., & Aron, A. (2004). The effect of a shared humorous experience on closeness in initial encounters. *Personal Relationships, 11*, 61–78.

Gangestad, S. W., & Simpson, J. A. (1990). Towards an evolutionary history of female sociosexual variation. *Journal of Personality, 58*, 69–96.

Gangestad, S. W., & Simpson, J. A. (2000). The evolution of human mating: Trade-offs and strategic pluralism. *Behavioral and Brain Sciences, 23*, 573–587.

Gangestad, S. W., & Thornhill, R. (1997a). The evolutionary psychology of extrapair sex: The role of fluctuating asymmetry. *Evolution and Human Behavior, 18*, 69–88.

Gangestad, S. W., & Thornhill, R. (1997b). Human sexual selection and developmental stability. In J. A. Simpson & D. T. Kenrick (Eds.), *Evolutionary personality and social psychology* (pp. 169–195). Hillsdale, NJ: Lawrence Erlbaum.

Gangestad, S. W., & Thornhill, R. (1998). Menstrual cycle variation in women's preferences for the scent of symmetrical men. *Proceedings of the Royal Society of London B, 265*, 927–933.

Gangestad, S. W., Thornhill, R., & Garver, C. E. (2002). Changes in women's sexual interests and their partners' mate retention tactics across the menstrual cycle: Evidence for shifting conflicts of interest. *Proceedings of the Royal Society of London B, 269*, 975–982.

Gibbs, J. L., Ellison, N. B., & Heino, R. D. (2006). Self-presentation in online personals: The role of anticipated future interaction, self-disclosure, and perceived success in Internet dating. *Communication Research, 33*, 152–177.

Gibson, R., Bradbury, J. S., & Vehrencamp, S. L. (1991). Mate choice in lekking sage grouse: The roles of vocal display, female site fidelity and copying. *Behavioral Ecology, 2*, 165–180.

Gibson, R. M., & Hoeglund, J. (1992). Copying and sexual selection. *Trends in Ecology and Evolution, 7*, 229–232.

Givens, D. B. (1978). The nonverbal basis of attraction: Flirtation, courtship and seduction. *Journal for the Study of Interpersonal Processes, 41*, 346–359.

Givens, D. B. (2005). *Love signals: A practical field guide to the body language of courtship*. New York: St. Martin's.

Goodwin, R. (1990). Sex differences among partner preferences: Are the sexes really very similar? *Sex Roles, 23*, 501–513.

Gosling, S. D., Ko, S. J., Mannarelli, T., & Morris, M. E. (2002). A room with a cue: Personality judgments based on offices and bedrooms. *Journal of Personality and Social Psychology, 82*, 379–398.

Gosling, S. D., Kwan, V. S. Y., & John, O. P. (2003). A dog's got personality: A cross-species comparative approach to personality judgments in dogs and humans. *Journal of Personality and Social Psychology, 85*, 1161–1169.

Grammer, K. (1990). Strangers meet: Laughter and nonverbal signs of interest in opposite-sex encounters. *Journal of Nonverbal Behavior, 14*, 209–236.

Grammer, K., Honda, M., Juette, A., & Schmitt, A. (1999). Fuzziness of nonverbal courtship communication unblurred by motion energy detection. *Journal of Personality and Social Psychology, 77*, 487–508.

Grammer, K., Renninger, L. A., & Fischer, B. (2004). Disco clothing, female sexual motivation, and relationship status: Is she dressed to impress? *Journal of Sex Research, 41*, 66–74.

Grammer, K., & Thornhill, R. (1999). The body and face of woman: One ornament that signals quality? *Evolution and Human Behavior, 20*, 105–120.

Graziano, W. G., & Eisenberg, N. (1997). Agreeableness: A dimension of personality. In R. Hogan, J. Johnson, & S. Briggs (Eds.), *Handbook of personality psychology* (pp. 795–824). San Diego, CA: Academic Press.

Graziano, W. G., Jensen-Campbell, L., Shebilski, L., & Lundgren, S. (1993). Social influence, sex differences and judgments of beauty. Putting the "interpersonal" back in interpersonal attraction. *Journal of Personality and Social Psychology, 65*, 522–531.

Greitemeyer, T. (2005). Receptivity to sexual offers as a function of sex, socioeconomic status, physical attractiveness, and intimacy of the offer. *Personal Relationships, 12*, 373–386.

Griskevicius, V., Goldstein, N. J., Mortensen, C. R., Cialdini, R. B., & Kenrick, D. T. (2006). Going along versus going alone: When fundamental motives facilitate strategic (non)conformity. *Journal of Personality and Social Psychology, 91*, 281–294.

Gulledge, A., Gulledge, M., & Stahmann, R. (2003). Romantic physical affection types and relationship satisfaction. *American Journal of Family Therapy, 31*(4), 233–242.

Hansen, S. L. (1977). Dating choices of high school students. *The Family Coordinator, 26*(2), 133–138.

Hebl, M. R., & Kashy, D. A. (1995). Sociosexuality and everyday social interaction. *Personal Relationships, 2*, 371–383.

Helmreich, R., Aronson, E., & LeFan, J. (1970). To err is humanizing sometimes: Effects of self-esteem, competence, and pratfall on interpersonal attraction. *Journal of Personality and Social Psychology*. 16, 259–264.

Hewitt, L. E. (1958). Student perceptions of traits desired in themselves as dating and marriage partners. *Marriage & Family Living*. Nov. 20, 344–349.

Hinsz, V. B., Matz, D. C, & Patience, R. A. (2001). Does women's hair signal reproductive potential? *Journal of Experimental Social Psychology*, 37, 166–172.

Jensen-Campbell, L. A., Rosselli, M., Workman, K. A., Santisi, M., Rios, J. D., & Bojan, D. (2002). Agreeableness, conscientiousness and effortful control processes. *Journal of Research in Personality*, 36, 476–489.

Jones, M. (1998). Sociosexuality and motivations for romantic involvement. *Journal of Research in Personality*, 32, 173–182.

Kenrick, D. T., Sadalla, E. K., Groth, G., & Trost, M. R. (1990). Evolution, traits, and the stages of human courtship: Qualifying the parental investment model. *Journal of Personality*, 58, 97–116.

Kleinke, C. L, Meeker, F. B., & Staneski, R. A. (1986). Preference for opening lines: Comparing ratings by men and women. *Sex Roles*, 15, 585–600.

Li, N. P., Bailey, J. M., Kenrick, D. T., & Linsenmeier, J. A. W. (2002). The necessities and luxuries of mate preferences: Testing the tradeoffs. *Journal of Personality and Social Psychology*, 82, 947–955.

Li, N. P., & Kenrick, D. T. (2006). Sex similarities and differences in preferences for short-term mates: What, whether, and why. *Journal of Personality and Social Psychology*, 90, 468–489.

Little, A. C., & Mannion, H. (2006). Viewing attractive or unattractive same-sex individuals changes self-rated attractiveness and face preferences in women. *Animal Behavior*, 72, 981–987.

Little, A. C., Penton-Voak, I. S., Burt, D. M., & Perrett, D. I. (2002). Evolution and individual differences in the perception of attractiveness: How cyclic hormonal changes and self-perceived attractiveness influence female preferences for male faces. In G. Rhodes & L. A. Zebrowitz (Eds.), *Facial attractiveness: Evolutionary, cognitive, and social perspectives* (pp. 59–90). Westport, CT: Ablex.

Lorenz, K. (1943). Di angeborenen Formen moglicher Arfahrung [The innate forms of potential experience]. *Zietschrift fur Tierpsychologie*, 5, 234–409.

Lundy, D. E., Tan, J., & Cunningham, M. R. (1998). Heterosexual romantic preferences: The importance of humor and physical attractiveness for different types of relationships. *Personal Relationships*, 5, 311–325.

Maner, J. K., Kenrick, D. T., Becker, D. V., Delton, A. W., Hofer, B., Wilbur, C. J., et al. (2003). Sexually selective cognition: Beauty captures the mind of the beholder. *Journal of Personality and Social Psychology*, 85, 1107–1120.

Marshall, D. S. (1971). Sexual behavior on Mangaia. In D. S. Marshall & R. C. Suggs (Eds.), *Human sexual behavior* (pp. 103–162). New York: Basic Books.

Maxwell, G. M., Cook, M. W., & Burr, R. (1985). The encoding and decoding of liking from behavioral cues in both auditory and visual channels. *Journal of Nonverbal Behavior*, 9, 239–263.

May, J. L., & Hamilton, P. A. (1980). Effects of musically evoked affect on women's interpersonal attraction toward and perceptual judgments of physical attractiveness of men. *Motivation and Emotion*, 4, 217–228.

McCormick, N. B. (1979). Come-ons and put-offs: Unmarried students' strategies for having and avoiding intercourse. *Psychology of Women Quarterly*, 4, 194–211.

McCormick, N. B., & Jones, A. J. (1989). Gender differences in nonverbal flirtation. *Journal of Sex Education and Therapy*, 15, 271–282.

Merker, B. (2000). Synchronous chorusing and human origins. In N. L. Wallin, B. Merker, & S. Brown (Eds.), *The origins of music* (pp. 315–327). Cambridge, MA: MIT Press.

Messenger, J. C. (1971). Sex and repression in an Irish folk community. In D. Marshall & R. Suggs (Eds.), *Human sexual behavior* (pp. 3–37). Englewood Cliffs, NJ: Prentice Hall.

Miller, L. C., & Fishkin, S. A. (1997). On the dynamics of human bonding and reproductive success: Seeking windows on the adapted-for human-environment interface. In J. Simpson & D. Kenrick (Eds.), *Evolutionary social psychology* (pp. 197–235). Mahwah, NJ: Lawrence Erlbaum.

Moore, M. M. (1985). Nonverbal courtship patterns in women: Context and consequences. *Ethology and Sociobiology*, 6, 237–247.

Moore, M. M. (1995). Courtship signaling and adolescents: "Girls just wanna have fun"? *Journal of Sex Research*. 32, 319–328.

Moore, M. M. (2002) Courtship communication and perception. *Perceptual and Motor Skills*. 94, 97–105.

Moore, M. M. (1998). Nonverbal courtship patterns in women: Rejection signaling—an empirical investigation. *Semiotica*, 3, 201–214.

Moore, M. M., & Butler, D. L. (1989). Predictive aspects of nonverbal courtship behavior in women. *Semiotica*, *3*, 205–215.

Muscarella, F., & Cunningham, M. R. (1996). The evolutionary significance and social perception of male pattern baldness and facial hair. *Ethology and Sociobiology*, *17*, 99–117.

Osborn, D. R. (1996). Beauty is as beauty does? Makeup and posture effects on physical attractiveness judgments. *Journal of Applied Social Psychology*, *26*, 31–51.

Osborn, D. R. (2006). *Renaissance beauty = today's ugly: The size and significance of historico-cultural differences in physical attractiveness judgments.* Manuscript under editorial review.

Perper, T. (1985). *Sex signals: The biology of love.* Philadelphia: ISI Press.

Perper, T., & Weis, D. (1987). Proceptive and rejective strategies of U.S. and Canadian college women. *Journal of Sex Research*, *23*, 455–480.

Pruett-Jones, S. (1992). Independent versus non-independent mate choice: Do females copy each other? *American Naturalist*, *140*, 1000–1009.

Rantala, M. J., Eriksson, C. J. P., Vainikka, A., & Kortet, R. (2006). Male steroid hormones and female preference for male body odor. *Evolution and Human Behavior*, *27*, 259–269.

Reise, S. P., & Wright, T. M. (1996). Personality traits, Cluster B personality disorders and sociosexuality. *Journal of Research in Personality*, *30*, 128–136.

Rentfrow, P. S., & Gosling, S. D. (2003). The do re mi's of everyday life: The structure and personality correlates of music preferences. *Journal of Personality and Social Psychology*, *84*, 1236–1256.

Reyes, M., Afifi, W., Krawchuk, A., Imperato, N., Shelley, D., & Lee, J. (1999, June). *Just (don't) talk: Comparing the impact of interaction style on sexual desire and social interaction.* Paper presented at the Joint Conference of the International Network on Personal Relationships and the International Association for the Study of Personal Relationships, Louisville, KY.

Rowatt, T. J. (2001). "Let's just be friends": Relationship negotiation and the communication of social rejection in unrequited love. *Dissertation Abstracts International: Section B: The Sciences and Engineering*, *62*, 2538.

Rowatt, W. C., Cunningham, M. R., & Druen, P. B. (1998). Deception to get a date. *Personality and Social Psychology Bulletin*, *24*, 1228–1242.

Rowatt, W. C., Cunningham, M. R., & Druen, P. B. (1999). Lying to get a date: The effect of facial physical attractiveness on the willingness to deceive prospective dating partners. *Journal of Social and Personal Relationships*, *16*, 209–223.

Sakai, R., & Brooks, J. L. (1997). *As good as it gets* [Motion picture]. United States TriStar Pictures.

Saucier, G. (1994). Mini-markers: A brief version of Goldberg's unipolar big-five markers. *Journal of Personality Assessment*, *63*, 506–516.

Scheflen, A. E. (1965). Quasi-courtship behavior in psychotherapy. *Psychiatry Interpersonal and Biological Processes*, *28*, 245–257.

Schmitt, D. P. (2005a). Sociosexuality from Argentina to Zimbabwe: A 48-nation study of sex, culture, and strategies of human mating. *Behavioral and Brain Sciences*, *28*, 247–275.

Schmitt, D. P. (2005b). Is short-term mating the maladaptive result of insecure attachment? A test of competing evolutionary perspectives. *Personality and Social Psychology Bulletin*, *31*, 747–768.

Sherif, M. (1935). A study of some social factors in perception. *Archives of Psychology*, *60*.

Shotland, R. L., & Craig, J. M. (1988). Can men and women differentiate between friendly and sexually interested behavior? *Social Psychology Quarterly*, *51*, 66–73.

Simpson, J. A., & Gangestad, S. W. (1991). Individual differences in sociosexuality: Evidence for convergent and discriminant validity. *Journal of Personality and Social Psychology*, *60*, 870–883.

Simpson, J. A., Gangestad, S. W., & Biek, M. (1993). Personality and nonverbal social behavior: An ethological perspective of relationship initiation. *Journal of Experimental Social Psychology*, *29*, 434–461.

Simpson, J. A, Green, S. W., Christensen, P., & Niels, L. K. (1999). Fluctuating asymmetry, sociosexuality, and intrasexual competitive tactics. *Journal of Personality and Social Psychology*, *76*, 159–172.

Smith, J. E., Waldorf, V. A., & Trembath, D. L. (1990). "Single white male looking for thin, very attractive …" *Sex Roles*, *23*, 475–485.

Snyder, M., Tanke, E. D., & Berscheid, E. (1977). Social perception and interpersonal behavior: On the self-fulfilling nature of social stereotypes. *Journal of Personality and Social Psychology*, *35*, 656–666.

Sprecher, S. (1989). The importance to males and females of physical attractiveness, earning potential, and expressiveness in initial attraction. *Sex Roles*, *21*, 591–607.

Strassberg, D. S., & Holty, S. (2003). An experimental study of women's Internet personal ads. *Archives of Sexual Behavior*, *32*, 253–260.

Sunnafrank, M. (1992). On debunking the attitude similarity myth. *Communication Monographs*, *59*, 164–179.

Symons, D. (1979). *The evolution of human sexuality.* New York: Oxford University Press.

Tennant, A. (2005). *Hitch* [Motion picture]. United States: Columbia Pictures.

Tesser, A., & Brodie, M. (1971). A note on the evaluation of a "computer date." *Psychonomic Science, 23,* 300.

Thornhill, R., & Gangestad, S. W. (1994). Human fluctuating asymmetry and sexual behavior. *Psychological Science, 5,* 297–302.

Tooke, W., & Camire, L. (1991). Patterns of deception in intersexual and intrasexual mating strategies. *Ethology and Sociobiology, 12,* 345–364.

Trivers, R. L. (1972). Parental investment and sexual selection. In B. Campbell (Ed.), *Sexual selection and the descent of man: 1871–1971* (pp. 136–179). Chicago: Aldine.

Voracek, M., Hofhansl, A., & Fisher, M. L. (2005). Clark and Hatfield's X revisited. *Psychological Reports, 97,* 11–20.

Wald, J., & McCary, L. (1957). *An affair to remember* [Motion picture]. United States: Twentieth-Century Fox.

Walsh, D. G., & Hewitt, J. (1985). Giving men the come on: Effect of eye contact and smiling in a bar environment. *Perceptual and Motor Skills, 61,* 873 774.

Walster, E., Aronson, V., Abrahams, D., & Rottman, L. (1966). Importance of physical attractiveness in dating behavior. *Journal of Personality and Social Psychology, 4,* 508–516.

Walster, E., Walster, G. W., Piliavin, J., & Schmidt, L. (1973). "Playing hard to get": Understanding an elusive phenomenon. *Journal of Personality and Social Psychology, 26,* 113–121.

Walters, S., & Crawford, C. B. (1994). The importance of mate attraction for intrasexual competition in men and women. *Ethology and Sociobiology, 15,* 5–30.

Weeden, J., & Sabini, J. (2005). Physical attractiveness and health in western societies: A review. *Psychological Bulletin, 131,* 635–653.

Williams, G. P., & Kleinke, C. L. (1993). Effects of mutual gaze and touch on attraction, mood, and cardiovascular reactivity. *Journal of Research in Personality, 27,* 170–183.

Wong, D. T., & Cunningham, M. R. (1990, April). *Interior versus exterior beauty: The effects of mood on dating preferences for different types of physically attractive women.* Paper presented at the Southeastern Psychological Association, Atlanta. Data reported in Cunningham, M., Druen, P. & Barbee, A. (1997). Evolutionary, social and personality variables in the evaluation of physical attractiveness. In J. Simpson & D. Kenrick (Eds.), *Evolutionary social psychology* (ch. 5, pp. 109–140). Hillsdale, NJ: Lawrence Erlbaum.

Wright, T. M. (1999). Female sexual behavior: Analysis of big five trait facets and domains in the prediction of sociosexuality (Doctoral dissertation, University of California, Riverside, 1999). *Dissertation Abstracts International, 59*(10-B).

Yurchisin, J., Watchravesringkan, K., & McCabe, D. B. (2005). An exploration of identity re-creation in the context of Internet dating. *Social Behavior and Personality, 33,* 735–750.

Zillman, D., & Bhatia, A. (1989). Effects of associating with musical genres on heterosexual attraction. *Communication Research, 16,* 263–288.

Zuckerman, M., & Miyake, K. (1993). The attractive voice: What makes it so? *Journal of Nonverbal Behavior. 17,* 119–135.

Zuckerman, M., Miyake, K., & Hodgins, H. S. (1991). Cross-channel effects of vocal and physical attractiveness and their implications for interpersonal perception. *Journal of Personality and Social Psychology, 60,* 545–554.

6

Uncertainty and Relationship Initiation

LEANNE K. KNOBLOCH and LAURA E. MILLER

*U*ncertainty is an intrinsic part of forming relationships (Berger & Calabrese, 1975; Sunnafrank, 1986a). Acquaintances grapple with questions about their own behavior (e.g., "How should I respond?"), their partner's behavior (e.g., "Why did he say that?"), and the nature of the relationship itself (e.g., "What is the status of this relationship?"). Uncertainty during the early stages of relationship development merits study for two reasons. First, uncertainty is a powerful predictor of people's verbal and nonverbal communication behavior (Afifi & Burgoon, 1998; Berger & Gudykunst, 1991; Knobloch, 2006). Second, uncertainty shares a close connection with dyadic well-being. Individuals experiencing uncertainty tend to evaluate their partner more negatively (Gudykunst, Yang, & Nishida, 1985; Kellermann & Reynolds, 1990; Solomon & Knobloch, 2004), experience more negative emotion (Afifi & Reichert, 1996; Knobloch, Miller, & Carpenter, 2007; Theiss & Solomon, 2006a), and perceive their relationship to be more turbulent (Knobloch, 2007b). Hence, uncertainty during acquaintance is important to understand because it predicts both the behavior of individuals and the health of relationships.

Our goal in this chapter is to organize, integrate, and critique the literature on uncertainty during the initial phases of relationship progression. We begin by explicating uncertainty. Next, we describe the logic and research of two dominant theories on the topic: uncertainty reduction theory (URT) and predicted outcome value theory (POV). We then question three assumptions entrenched in the literature, and we propose a broader conceptualization of uncertainty to further illuminate the initiation of relationships. Finally, we identify directions for future research to spark continued growth in this area.

THE NATURE OF UNCERTAINTY

Uncertainty exists when people lack confidence in their ability to understand their surroundings (Berger & Bradac, 1982; Berger & Calabrese, 1975). More formally, uncertainty stems from the number and likelihood of alternatives that may occur in social situations (Shannon & Weaver, 1949). Uncertainty is low when only a single outcome is plausible; uncertainty is high when multiple outcomes are equally probable. Uncertainty is a function of people's ability both to predict future events and to explain past events (Berger & Bradac, 1982). Individuals lack predictive power when they are unable to proactively identify the most likely outcome. Similarly, they lack explanatory power when they are unable to retroactively determine the cause of an occurrence. Uncertainty increases as people's ability to predict and explain decreases (Berger & Calabrese, 1975).

Uncertainty arises from both cognitive questions and behavioral questions (Berger & Bradac, 1982). *Cognitive uncertainty* refers to the ambiguity individuals experience about their own attitudes and the attitudes of others. Cognitive uncertainty encompasses questions such as "Is he sincere?"

"Do I like spending time with her?" and "Why is he annoyed?" *Behavioral uncertainty* indexes the questions people have about their own actions and the actions of others. Behavioral uncertainty entails questions such as "What is she going to do next?" "How should I respond?" and "Is he about to laugh or cry?" In sum, individuals experience uncertainty when they lack information about themselves and others.

Uncertainty, according to this broad definition, is relevant to a range of dyadic relationships. It transpires within acquaintance (Berger & Gudykunst, 1991), friendship (Afifi & Burgoon, 1998; Planalp, Rutherford, & Honeycutt, 1988), courtship (Knobloch, 2006; Knobloch & Carpenter-Theune, 2004), marriage (Knobloch, Miller, Bond, & Mannone, 2007; Turner, 1990), and family (Afifi & Schrodt, 2003; Bevan, Stetzenbach, Batson, & Bullo, 2006) relationships. Of course, the beginning stages of relationship formation are rife with uncertainty because people lack basic information about a partner's personality characteristics and preferences (Berger & Calabrese, 1975).

Perhaps because uncertainty is so salient within human interaction, the construct has garnered considerable scholarly attention. Almost six decades ago, information theory first introduced uncertainty to the field of interpersonal communication (Shannon & Weaver, 1949). Information theory provided a mathematical model designed to maximize the amount of information that messages can carry with minimal distortion. According to the theory, messages that contain new information reduce the entropy, randomness, and uncertainty of social situations. In other words, messages that convey nonredundant data are most effective for reducing uncertainty. Information theory offered a foundation for conceptualizing uncertainty during the early phases of relationship development.

Uncertainty reduction theory extended information theory by considering how ambiguity shapes people's behavior within initial interaction (Berger & Bradac, 1982; Berger & Calabrese, 1975). URT also drew on theories of attribution (e.g., Heider, 1958; Kelley, 1973) to argue that individuals strive to make sense of their social environment. According to URT, uncertainty is prominent when people meet for the first time because strangers are not familiar with each other's personality characteristics, attitudes, and preferences.

A decade later, predicted outcome value theory challenged URT's assumption that uncertainty is the driving force behind people's communication behavior within acquaintance (Sunnafrank, 1986a, 1990). POV adopted a social exchange perspective (e.g., Altman & Taylor, 1973; Kelley & Thibaut, 1978; Thibaut & Kelley, 1959) to argue that individuals are fundamentally motivated to maximize the rewards of social interaction. Sunnafrank (1986a, 1990) proposed that people work to reduce uncertainty to ascertain whether continued interaction with a partner will be advantageous or disadvantageous. According to POV, uncertainty reduction is subordinate to the more primary goal of forecasting the rewards and costs of relationship progression. Berger (1986) countered with the claim that uncertainty reduction is a prerequisite to predicting the rewards and costs of future interaction. Debate about the merits of the two theories ensued (Berger, 1986; Sunnafrank, 1986b) and is still apparent in the literature (e.g., Grove & Werkman, 1991; Sunnafrank & Ramirez, 2004).

URT and POV remain the leading theories of uncertainty during the initial stages of relationship development, so they figure prominently in our chapter. We devote the following sections to describing each theory and its corresponding research. Then, we critique some of the long held assumptions ingrained in the literature since the inception of URT and POV.

UNCERTAINTY REDUCTION THEORY

Assumptions

URT seeks to explain how individuals communicate under conditions of uncertainty (Berger & Bradac, 1982; Berger & Calabrese, 1975). A main premise of URT is that people are motivated to predict and explain their surroundings (Berger & Bradac, 1982; Berger & Calabrese, 1975). Hence, individuals communicate to reduce uncertainty about their environment. According to URT, uncertainty is high when people meet for the first time but decreases as relationships develop. The original formulation of URT focused on communication between strangers (Berger & Calabrese, 1975). Subsequent scholarship has extended URT beyond acquaintance to more advanced stages of relationship development (Gudykunst, 1985; Parks & Adelman, 1983).

Several conditions increase people's drive to reduce uncertainty during acquaintance (Berger, 1979). One is *deviance*. Individuals are especially motivated to reduce uncertainty when a partner behaves in nonnormative ways. A second is *anticipation of future interaction*. People are particularly interested in gaining information if they are likely to interact with a partner again in the future. A third is *incentive value*. Individuals are especially eager to alleviate doubts when a partner controls the rewards and costs they receive.

According to URT, communication is a tool for gaining knowledge and creating understanding (Berger & Calabrese, 1975). Communication can play two roles within interaction. First, communication can produce uncertainty. For example, people may question what to disclose, why a behavior occurred, or how to seek information. Second, uncertainty can be reduced through communication. For instance, individuals may obtain insight through observation, glean information from nonverbal cues, or gain knowledge from conversation. URT posits that communication can both escalate and diminish uncertainty.

In their original formulation of URT, Berger and Calabrese (1975, pp. 101–107) proposed seven axioms to explain the connection between uncertainty and communication:

Axiom 1:   Given the high level of uncertainty present at the onset of the entry phase, as the amount of verbal communication between strangers increases, the level of uncertainty will decrease. As uncertainty is further reduced, the amount of verbal communication will increase.

Axiom 2:   As nonverbal affiliative expressiveness increases, uncertainty levels will decrease. In addition, decreases in uncertainty levels will cause increases in nonverbal affiliative expressiveness.

Axiom 3:   High levels of uncertainty cause increases in information-seeking behavior. As uncertainty levels decline, information-seeking behavior decreases.

Axiom 4:   High levels of uncertainty cause decreases in the intimacy level of communication content. Low levels of uncertainty produce high levels of intimacy of communication content.

Axiom 5:   High levels of uncertainty produce high rates of reciprocity. Low levels of uncertainty produce low reciprocity rates.

Axiom 6:   Similarities between persons reduce uncertainty, while dissimilarities produce increases in uncertainty.

Axiom 7:   Increases in uncertainty level produce decreases in liking. Decreases in uncertainty level produce increases in liking.

An eighth axiom was adopted after Parks and Adelman (1983) extended the theory's scope to the context of courtship. Their longitudinal research indicated that individuals experience less uncertainty when they communicate more with their partner's friends and family members.

Axiom 8:   Shared communication networks reduce uncertainty, while lack of shared networks increases uncertainty.

Consider the example of Jerry and Elaine, who are introduced by a mutual friend at a party. They engage in small talk about the weather (Axiom 4), inquire about each other's hobbies (Axiom 3), and reciprocate disclosures about their favorite restaurants (Axiom 5). The longer they chat, the less uncertainty they feel (Axiom 1), the more they smile and nod (Axiom 2), and the more they like each other (Axiom 7). Their uncertainty diminishes even more when they realize that they live in the same apartment complex (Axiom 6) and that they are acquainted with some of the same neighbors (Axiom 8).

Strategies for Managing Uncertainty

Scholars working under the rubric of URT have delineated a trio of ways people manage uncertainty in social situations: (a) *seeking information*, (b) *planning*, and (c) *hedging* (Berger, 1997; Berger & Bradac, 1982). We describe these strategies in the following subsections.

Seeking Information   According to URT, people employ passive, active, and interactive strategies for seeking information (Berger & Bradac, 1982; Berger & Kellermann, 1994). *Passive strategies* entail unobtrusively observing the target person. This "fly-on-the-wall" behavior allows an individual to gather information while the target person remains unaware of the scrutiny. *Active strategies* are behaviors that require direct action but do not involve communicating with the target person. Examples include asking questions of a third party and manipulating the target person's environment to see how he or she will respond. *Interactive strategies* require communicating with the target person. This category encompasses behaviors such as asking questions, disclosing information in the hopes that the target person will reciprocate, and relaxing the target person in the hopes that he or she will open up.

The categories of information-seeking behavior vary in their degree of face threat, efficiency, and social appropriateness (e.g., Berger & Kellermann, 1983, 1994; Douglas, 1987). For example, passive strategies incur only minimal face threat because an individual observes from a distance. On the other hand, passive strategies may not generate the specific information the observer is hoping to discover. Active strategies give an individual more latitude over the kind of information obtained, but they may backfire if the third party lacks information and/or alerts the target person. Interactive strategies offer the most direct way of acquiring information, but they also furnish the most face threat. A person could violate social norms, appear pushy, and/or offend the target person within conversation. URT does not advance hypotheses about how people select an information-seeking strategy, but they probably weigh the risks against the likelihood of success (Berger & Kellermann, 1994).

Planning   A second method of managing uncertainty is planning (Berger, 1997). Individuals develop a *plan*, or a cognitive representation of goal-directed action, to help them communicate in ambiguous surroundings. People formulate a plan by relying on the knowledge they possess about similar situations (Berger & Jordan, 1992). A plan is most valuable when it contains an optimal level of complexity: It should be comprehensive enough to help individuals anticipate contingencies (Berger & Bell, 1988), but it should be simple enough to allow them the freedom to improvise (Berger, Karol, & Jordan, 1989). When a plan fails to achieve its objective, people typically conserve their cognitive resources by altering low-level tactics rather than expending mental energy to alter higher order tactics (Berger & diBattista, 1993). Individuals communicate most effectively when they are able to plan for uncertain circumstances (Berger, 1997).

Hedging   A third strategy for managing uncertainty is to hedge against the negative outcomes that could occur within conversation. Berger (1997) identified several ways of crafting messages to hedge against face threat, embarrassment, and anxiety under conditions of uncertainty. One option is to *frame* messages by using humor (e.g., "I'll bet you're dying to go out with me on Saturday night.") or inserting other plausible interpretations so backtracking is possible (e.g., "I'm just kidding." or "You're confused—that's not what I meant."). Individuals can also rely on *ambiguous language* to hide the actual purpose of the message (e.g., "What are you up to this weekend?"). People can employ *disclaimers* to guard against an unfavorable response (e.g., "I don't want to move too fast, but would you like to go out with me on Saturday night?"). Individuals can engage in *retroactive discounting* to tone down a message (e.g., "We could go out for dinner on Saturday night; I don't know if you'd want to do that, though."). Finally, people can *control the floor* by assigning the other person to lead the conversation (e.g., "Tell me about your plans for the weekend."). All of these hedging devices can be effective for avoiding negative outcomes in ambiguous situations (Berger, 1997).

Empirical Tests

Thus far in this section, we have explicated URT and discussed three strategies for managing uncertainty. Now, we turn our attention to reviewing empirical research that has tested the logic of URT. One line of work has investigated predictors of uncertainty; we organize this literature into individual, dyadic, and cultural categories of predictors. Other research has examined communicative outcomes of uncertainty; we divide this work into behavioral strategies versus linguistic features of messages.

Predictors of Uncertainty   Research on URT suggests that individual differences play a role in people's experience of uncertainty (Douglas, 1991, 1994). For example, Douglas (1991) worked to extend URT by examining a personality characteristic he labeled *global uncertainty*. He defined global uncertainty as people's tendency to be uncertain about acquaintance in general (e.g., "How confident are you of your general ability to predict how strangers will behave?" and "In general, how well do you think you know other people after you meet them for the first time?"). He found that individuals high in global uncertainty are more apprehensive when meeting strangers, communicate less effectively during initial interaction, and develop less satisfying long-term relationships. Although these results suggest that people's experience of uncertainty may be at least partially governed by individual differences, URT has not been formally updated to encompass personality characteristics.

Other investigations of URT have delineated the features of relationships that contribute to uncertainty. As previously noted, Parks and Adelman (1983) found that dating partners who communicated more frequently with their partner's social networks reported experiencing less uncertainty. Gudykunst (1985), who solicited college students' perceptions of their relationship with either an acquaintance or a friend, observed that liking for a partner was negatively associated with uncertainty in both types of relationships. In a second study, Gudykunst et al. (1985) asked college students in Japan, Korea, and the United States to report on a relationship with an acquaintance, friend, or dating partner. They discovered that liking for a partner corresponded with less uncertainty across all of the relationship conditions. Moreover, they found that friends who were more similar to each other experienced less uncertainty across all three cultures. Taken together, these studies support URT's logic about how characteristics of relationships such as shared social networks (Axiom 8), liking (Axiom 7), and similarity (Axiom 6) coincide with uncertainty.

Scholars have also identified cultural factors that predict people's experience of uncertainty. In fact, URT provided a foundation for Gudykunst's (1995) anxiety/uncertainty management theory (AUM). AUM theorizes that individuals experience both anxiety (an emotion) and uncertainty (a cognition) when they communicate with a person from a different cultural group. The theory contains 94 axioms about the roles of culture, anxiety, and uncertainty in cross-cultural interactions (Gudykunst, 1995). Empirical findings support AUM's starting premise that URT is useful for understanding people's experience of uncertainty across cultures (Gudykunst & Hammer, 1988; Gudykunst, Nishida, & Schmidt, 1989). In fact, in their review of self-report studies involving participants from minority and majority groups in Japan, Korea, and the United States, Berger and Gudykunst (1991) concluded,

> [Results] suggest that even though there are cultural differences in mean scores for variables associated with URT, there is a high level of consistency in the relationships among the variables across cultures and ethnic groups studied to date. It, therefore, appears that culture is *not* a scope / boundary condition for URT. (p. 46)

See Gudykunst (1995) for a detailed description of AUM.

Effects of Uncertainty on Communication   A second body of work conducted under the rubric of URT has documented the effects of uncertainty on communication. Notably, research has failed to corroborate the theory's prediction that individuals experiencing uncertainty seek information to reduce their ambiguity (Axiom 3). Gudykunst (1985) did not document a link between uncertainty and information seeking within people's reports of their relationship with an acquaintance or a friend. Kellermann and Reynolds (1990) asked college students to (a) read a hypothetical scenario about meeting someone new, and (b) report the degree of uncertainty they would experience and the amount of information they would seek. Like Gudykunst (1985), Kellermann and Reynolds did not observe an association between uncertainty and information seeking. One explanation for the lack of support for Axiom 3 is that people's motivation to gain knowledge is contingent on the valence of information they expect to receive. Individuals may gather information only when they expect to receive good news (e.g., Bell & Buerkel-Rothfuss, 1990; Knobloch & Solomon, 2002a; Sunnafrank, 1990). This reasoning implies that the link between uncertainty and information seeking is more complex than was originally anticipated by URT.

Findings offer more consistent support for URT's premise that uncertainty predicts linguistic features of messages. For example, Ayers (1979) reported that both strangers and friends tended to ask fewer questions as conversations progressed, presumably after their uncertainty had declined. Sherblom and Van Rheenen (1984) found that participants in radio interviews used a more diverse vocabulary during later segments of the interviews, again presumably after their uncertainty had decreased. In a direct test of the axioms of URT, Gudykunst (1985) solicited people's perceptions of their relationship with either an acquaintance or a friend. He found that individuals experiencing high levels of uncertainty reported engaging in less communication with their partner and discussing less intimate topics with him or her; these results were robust for both acquaintances and friends. Gudykunst's (1985) findings support Axiom 1 and Axiom 4. More recently, Knobloch (2006) reported that individuals who simulated leaving a date request voice mail message for their partner communicated less fluently when they were unsure about the status of their courtship. These findings, examined as a set, bolster URT's logic that uncertainty shapes micro facets of conversation as people form and maintain relationships.

PREDICTED OUTCOME VALUE THEORY

Assumptions

Whereas URT posits that people's central concern is reducing uncertainty, POV proposes that their more primary goal is maximizing rewards and minimizing costs. Sunnafrank (1986a) advanced POV as a reformulation of URT by arguing, "Empirical research provides inconsistent and generally weak support for the posited role of uncertainty reduction, suggesting that major theoretical modifications are needed. Predicted outcome value theory attempts to provide these modifications" (pp. 28–29). POV uses a social exchange perspective (e.g., Altman & Taylor, 1973; Kelley & Thibaut, 1978; Thibaut & Kelley, 1959) to explain the link between uncertainty and communication within acquaintance. In particular, POV claims that individuals engage in uncertainty reduction only in the service of forecasting relational outcomes (Sunnafrank, 1986a, 1986b, 1990).

According to POV, individuals gather information to predict whether future interaction with a partner is likely to be rewarding or costly, and then they decide whether to pursue or avoid further contact (Sunnafrank, 1986a, 1990). This overarching logic suggests three claims about relationship formation. First, individuals should be attracted to a partner when they expect future interaction with him or her to be advantageous. Second, people should be motivated to develop relationships that correspond with favorable predicted outcome values, and they should seek to terminate relationships that correspond with unfavorable predicted outcome values. Third, individuals should steer conversation toward topics that they expect will produce rewards, and they should avoid topics that they expect will incur costs. Sunnafrank (1986a, 1990) built on these premises to argue that the impressions people form during initial encounters should have a strong influence on relationship formation.

An example may help clarify the logic of the theory. Again, consider the case of Jerry and Elaine. They are strangers when they cross paths at a party hosted by a mutual friend. According to POV, Jerry and Elaine are not motivated to communicate merely to reduce uncertainty; instead, they want to learn whether forming a relationship would be worthwhile. Jerry finds the conversation to be rewarding because Elaine is easy to talk to. Elaine is attracted to Jerry because he is interested in her hobbies. They chat about their favorite restaurants, hoping that the conversation will furnish an opportunity to make future plans, but they avoid discussing the leaky roof of their apartment complex because both are frustrated with their landlord's inactivity. By the end of the party, Jerry and Elaine suspect that future interaction would be satisfying, so they exchange telephone numbers with the goal of spending time together the following week.

Empirical Tests

Investigations of POV are consistent with the theory. Sunnafrank (1990) evaluated competing predictions from URT versus POV by asking undergraduate students to interact with a peer on the first day of class. When participants forecasted positive outcomes, uncertainty was negatively associated with amount of verbal communication, nonverbal affiliative expressiveness, and liking. When participants forecasted negative outcomes, uncertainty did not predict amount of verbal communication, nonverbal affiliative expressiveness, or liking. These results are consistent with POV rather than URT because the predictive power of uncertainty was limited to situations in which individuals anticipated positive outcomes. Accordingly, Sunnafrank (1990) concluded that the goal of uncertainty reduction is secondary to the goal of maximizing rewards within the initial interaction.

In a more recent test of POV, Sunnafrank and Ramirez (2004) invited undergraduate students to have a short conversation with a new acquaintance and report on the status of that relationship nine weeks later. They found that individuals who anticipated favorable outcomes after the first conversation reported more communication with and more attraction to their partner nine weeks later. Uncertainty was not associated with amount of communication or attraction after predicted outcome value was covaried. The results of this second study are consistent with POV's premise that people's first impressions of rewards and costs have long-term effects on relationship development.

TOWARD A BROADER CONCEPTUALIZATION OF UNCERTAINTY WITHIN RELATIONSHIP INITIATION

In decades past, researchers turned to URT or POV when investigating the link between uncertainty and interpersonal communication. More recently, scholars have moved beyond the foundation laid by URT and POV to craft other frameworks for understanding how individuals communicate under conditions of uncertainty. Problematic integration theory, for example, argues that communication helps people integrate the probability and valence of projected outcomes (Babrow, 2001). Uncertainty management theory proposes that individuals actively cultivate uncertainty rather than seek information about an impending negative outcome (Brashers, 2001). The theory of motivated information management posits that when people experience a mismatch between their desired and actual levels of uncertainty, they interpret and evaluate their situation to decide whether to seek information (Afifi & Weiner, 2006). Unlike URT and POV, which were designed to predict how individuals communicate during relationship formation, these theories have shed light on how people communicate about health issues (e.g., Afifi & Weiner, 2006; Babrow, Kasch, & Ford, 1998; Brashers et al., 2000).

Another trend is a growing interest in personality predictors of uncertainty. This research has investigated individual differences in how people experience uncertainty outside the context of close relationships. Scholars have examined uncertainty as a personality trait using labels such as *tolerance for uncertainty* (Teboul, 1995), *need for closure* (Kruglanski, 1989; Kruglanski & Webster, 1996), and *uncertainty orientation* (Shuper, Sorrentino, Otsubo, Hodson, & Walker, 2004; Sorrentino & Roney, 2000). Although these constructs diverge in significant ways, they all predict how people experience social situations. For instance, individuals who have a low tolerance for ambiguity often experience anxiety about ambiguous circumstances (Dugas et al., 2005). Those with a high need for closure tend to express elevated (and sometimes unfounded) confidence in the judgments they make about their surroundings (Kruglanski & Webster, 1996). People who are certainty oriented usually strive to preserve clarity in their interpersonal relationships (Driscoll, Hamilton, & Sorrentino, 1991; Sorrentino, Holmes, Hanna, & Sharp, 1995). These programs of research stand in marked contrast to URT and POV, which do not address how individual differences in uncertainty may guide relationship formation.

We are intrigued that this recent work within the communication and psychology disciplines has ignored, jettisoned, updated, and/or disputed the assumptions of URT and POV. Scholars of relationship initiation, in contrast, have not been similarly bold in moving beyond the foundation laid by the theories. Of course, URT and POV set the agenda for decades of research, so the literature on acquaintance quite naturally resembles the contours of those theories. At the same time, we believe it is important to step back for a moment to critically evaluate the assumptions lodged in the literature. We offer a broader conceptualization of uncertainty within relationship initiation to expand the prevailing view.

Uncertainty Is Broader Than Just Questions about Partners

Early in the development of URT, Berger and Bradac (1982) noted that "for a relationship to continue, it is important that the persons involved in the relationship consistently update their fund of knowledge about themselves, their relational partner, and their relationship" (pp. 12–13). Berger and Bradac's passing observation garnered little attention. Instead, most scholarship on uncertainty within acquaintance has focused on questions about partners. The most widely used measure of uncertainty, Clatterbuck's (1979) CLUES scale, asks people to report their ability to predict an acquaintance's behaviors, values, attitudes, and feelings (e.g., "How well do you think you know the person?" "How accurate do you think you are at predicting the person's attitudes?" and "How well do you think you can predict the person's feelings and emotions?"). As we noted previously, research employing this measure has shed light on how uncertainty about partners corresponds with diverse outcomes such as liking (Gudykunst, 1985; Gudykunst et al., 1985; Kellermann & Reynolds, 1990), the amount of communication between people (Sunnafrank & Ramirez, 2004), and the intimacy of communication content (Gudykunst, 1985).

In retrospect, the tendency for scholars to have emphasized partner predictability issues is reasonable given the acquaintance context. The beginning stages of relationship formation are filled with ambiguity about a partner's thoughts and feelings, likes and dislikes, and past history and future goals. Because partners are such a prominent source of uncertainty in initial interaction, scholars quite logically attended to questions about a partner's attributes as a focal point (Knobloch & Solomon, 2002a). The downside of privileging questions about a partner's characteristics, however, is that the full breadth of the construct has been overlooked.

We emphasize the importance of conceptualizing uncertainty in ways that go beyond ambiguity about a partner's personality characteristics. Our own work demonstrates that uncertainty in ongoing associations often stems from questions about participating in the relationship (Knobloch, 2006; Knobloch & Donovan-Kicken, 2006; Knobloch & Solomon, 1999). We define *relational uncertainty* as the degree of confidence people have in their perceptions of involvement within interpersonal relationships (Knobloch & Solomon, 1999, 2002a). Relational uncertainty stems from self, partner, and relationship sources. *Self uncertainty* refers to the questions people have about their own participation in a relationship (e.g., "How certain am I about how much I want to pursue this relationship?"). *Partner uncertainty* refers to the ambiguity individuals experience about their partner's participation in a relationship (e.g., "How certain am I about how much my partner wants to pursue this relationship?"). *Relationship uncertainty* encompasses the questions people have about the relationship as a whole (e.g., "How certain am I about the definition of this relationship?"). Accordingly, relational uncertainty is an umbrella construct that encompasses three sources of ambiguity.

We see value in employing this broader view of uncertainty in the context of acquaintance. Work on relational uncertainty has focused on courtship and marriage (for review, see Knobloch, 2007a), but relational uncertainty should also be relevant to the early stages of relationship formation (e.g., "Will this first encounter lead to more regular interaction?" "Am I ready, willing, and able to develop this relationship further?" "Is this person interested in pursuing a relationship with me?" and "How likely is a new relationship to succeed?"). We call for additional work examining self and relationship uncertainty issues to complement the literature replete with studies about partner uncertainty issues. Attending to self uncertainty (e.g., "How certain am I about how much I like this person?") and relationship uncertainty (e.g., "How certain am I about where this relationship is going?") would provide insight into how people form relationships when they are grappling with questions about their own involvement in the relationship and questions about the dyad as a whole.

Uncertainty Is Rewarding as Well as Costly

Both URT and POV suggest that uncertainty is problematic for participants in initial interaction. According to URT, uncertainty makes it harder for people to formulate plans, anticipate contingencies, and make sense of their surroundings (Berger, 1997; Berger & Bradac, 1982). According to POV, uncertainty makes it difficult for individuals to anticipate whether future interactions will be advantageous or disadvantageous (Sunnafrank, 1986a). Most scholarship has proceeded in this vein by conceptualizing uncertainty as costly for participants during the early stages of relationship development.

Empirical research bolsters the view that uncertainty poses challenges to relationship formation. As previously noted, studies of acquaintance suggest that uncertainty corresponds with less liking (Gudykunst, 1985; Gudykunst et al., 1985; Kellermann & Reynolds, 1990; but see Norton, Frost, & Ariely, 2007). Similarly, investigations of established relationships demonstrate that relational uncertainty coincides with unfavorable appraisals of a partner's behavior (Solomon & Knobloch, 2004; Theiss & Solomon, 2006b), negative emotion (Knobloch, Miller, & Carpenter, 2007; Knobloch & Solomon, 2002b; Theiss & Solomon, 2006a), perceived relationship turmoil (Knobloch, 2007b), difficulty gleaning information from messages (Knobloch & Solomon, 2005), and pessimistic judgments of conversation (Knobloch, Miller, Bond, et al., 2007). These findings imply that uncertainty can impede the initiation, development, and maintenance of interpersonal relationships.

We wonder, however, about the utility of characterizing uncertainty as uniformly negative within acquaintance. We suspect that uncertainty can add curiosity, excitement, and energy to the initial phases of relationship progression. For example, scholars adopting a relational dialectics approach have argued that too much certainty can make relationships monotonous (Baxter & Montgomery, 1996). Similarly, Livingston (1980) theorized that ambiguity can heighten attraction and escalate romance within romantic relationships (see also Norton et al., 2007). Two sets of empirical findings are consistent with this logic. First, 25% of the college students who participated in Planalp et al.'s (1988) study of uncertainty-increasing events reported that their friendship or romantic relationship became closer after they had experienced such an event. Moreover, 12% of the undergraduates in Afifi and Weiner's (2006) study of information seeking wished they were more uncertain about their romantic partner's sexual health. We interpret these lines of scholarship to underscore the importance of attending to both the costs *and* rewards that uncertainty may furnish within initial interaction.

Uncertainty Is Strategically Increased and Maintained (as Well as Reduced)

A third assumption of both theories is that individuals are motivated to reduce their uncertainty. URT contains this premise as a central tenet (Berger, 1979; Berger & Calabrese, 1975). In a similar vein, POV argues that people seek to reduce uncertainty in order to forecast the rewards and costs of relationship formation (Sunnafrank, 1986a). Together, the theories have generated a voluminous literature on the strategies individuals use to reduce uncertainty within initial interaction (e.g., Berger, 1979; Berger & Kellermann, 1994).

A more complex view suggests that people do not always strive to reduce uncertainty. Rather, individuals may be motivated to increase or maintain uncertainty rather than diminish it. Recent theorizing argues that people may cultivate or preserve ambiguity if they believe doing so will lead to more favorable outcomes (e.g., Babrow, 2001; Brashers, 2001). For example, individuals may foster uncertainty in the early stages of relationship development as a way of piquing a partner's interest (e.g., Brainerd, Hunter, Moore, & Thompson, 1996; White, 1980). People may also refrain from engaging in direct information seeking if they anticipate receiving undesirable information (e.g., discovering that a prospective friend does not share similar interests, or learning that a prospective dating partner is not interested in pursuing a romantic relationship; Knobloch & Solomon, 2002a). Hence, individuals may have other motives than engaging in uncertainty reduction.

Recent research verifies the claim that individuals strategically foster and sustain uncertainty. Studies show that uncertainty is positively associated with topic avoidance in cross-sex friendships (Afifi & Burgoon, 1998), dating relationships (Knobloch & Carpenter-Theune, 2004), and family relationships (Afifi & Schrodt, 2003). Other work demonstrates that people refrain from talking about the status of their relationship when they are experiencing uncertainty about mutual commitment between partners (Baxter & Wilmot, 1985). Findings also suggest that individuals who are unsure about the nature of their courtship tend to avoid expressing jealousy to their partner (Afifi & Reichert, 1996). Although all of this work has been conducted within the context of established relationships, it may foreshadow an analogous motivation among individuals within acquaintance. We suspect that people in the throes of relationship formation may similarly seek to evade talking about unpleasant topics (e.g., Sunnafrank, 1986a), avoid defining the nature of the relationship prematurely, and refrain from displaying attachment when they are unsure how a new acquaintanceship may unfold.

Directions for Future Research

To this point, we have explicated URT and POV as leading theories of uncertainty within initial interaction. We coupled our review with a critical examination of three widely accepted premises that have emerged from the legacies of URT and POV. Now, we identify avenues for future work that are important for continuing to accumulate knowledge on the topic.

Of course, a first agenda item is to test our reconceptualization of uncertainty within acquaintance. We questioned the assumptions that (a) uncertainty is limited to ambiguity about partners, (b) uncertainty is universally problematic, and (c) uncertainty is always paired with a desire to gain information. Although preliminary evidence supports the debunking of these assumptions, we note that tests of our logic have been conducted against the backdrop of intimate associations rather than initial interactions. Accordingly, we see a need for research that evaluates our theorizing within the context of acquaintance.

Another agenda item is to document conversational manifestations of uncertainty. Although URT and POV imply that uncertainty shapes the messages people produce (Berger & Calabrese, 1975; Sunnafrank, 1986a), studies of established relationships have privileged the global strategies individuals use to gain information (e.g., Afifi & Burgoon, 1998; Knobloch & Carpenter-Theune, 2004; Knobloch & Solomon, 2002b; Planalp et al., 1988). As a result, we know more about how people employ passive, active, and interactive information-seeking strategies to develop and maintain relationships than we know about how they craft messages to manage uncertainty in conversation (e.g., Knobloch, 2006, 2007a). A variety of questions remain to be answered. For example, what are the most and least effective ways of managing uncertainty in conversation during the early stages of relationship formation? Which verbal and nonverbal cues help acquaintances make sense of conversation? Which linguistic features of messages allow acquaintances to preserve uncertainty? We call for future work to shed light on these issues by attending to the link between uncertainty and message production.

Finally, we emphasize the importance of investigating uncertainty in diverse relationship contexts. Work on uncertainty beyond initial interaction has tended to privilege romantic relationships, especially courtship (for review, see Knobloch, 2007a). The focus on romantic associations has left a gap in our understanding of how ambiguity operates within the early stages of platonic relationships. Whereas romantic partners grapple with questions about the current status and future progression of the relationship (Knobloch & Solomon, 1999, 2002a), participants in platonic relationships are probably concerned with other uncertainty issues. For example, questions about shared interests may be especially relevant to friendship (e.g., Afifi & Burgoon, 1998; Parks & Floyd, 1996), questions about prognosis may be particularly salient within doctor–patient interaction (e.g., Brashers, Goldsmith, & Hsieh, 2002; Robinson & Stivers, 2001), and questions about job performance may be especially germane to supervisor–subordinate relationships (e.g., Kramer, 1999, 2004). If the content of uncertainty differs according to the relationship context, then the foundations and outcomes of uncertainty may differ as well. Thus, we encourage scholars of uncertainty to broaden their focus beyond the initiation of romantic relationships.

CONCLUSION

After three decades of research, Babrow (2001) characterized the study of uncertainty as a still fledgling area of inquiry: "Whereas the concept is a focal point in a few theories, it has received insufficient direct and sustained interest, particularly of the sort likely to generate broad, inclusive, and enriching dialogue" (p. 453). His comment challenges scholars to investigate uncertainty in ways that span disciplinary boundaries and dyadic contexts. With respect to the domain of relationship formation, we believe the time is right for a new generation of scholarship to consider how individuals experience uncertainty during the early stages of relationship development. We propose that the next wave of work attend to (a) self and relationship sources of uncertainty as well as partner sources, (b) the rewards as well as the costs of uncertainty, and (c) the behaviors people use to preserve as well as dispel uncertainty. Along the way, we encourage scholars to appreciate *and* question the premises of the dominant paradigms that become embedded in the literature over time.

AUTHOR NOTE

Leanne K. Knobloch (Ph.D., University of Wisconsin–Madison, 2001) is an assistant professor in the Department of Communication at the University of Illinois. Laura E. Miller (M.A., University of Illinois, 2005) is a doctoral candidate in the Department of Communication at the University of Illinois.

REFERENCES

Afifi, T. D., & Schrodt, P. (2003). Uncertainty and the avoidance of the state of one's family in stepfamilies, post divorce single-parent families, and first-marriage families. *Human Communication Research, 29,* 516–532.

Afifi, W. A., & Burgoon, J. K. (1998). "We never talk about that": A comparison of cross-sex friendships and dating relationships on uncertainty and topic avoidance. *Personal Relationships, 5,* 255–272.

Afifi, W. A., & Reichert, T. (1996). Understanding the role of uncertainty in jealousy experience and expression. *Communication Reports, 9,* 93–103.

Afifi, W. A., & Weiner, J. L. (2006). Seeking information about sexual health: Applying the theory of motivated information management. *Human Communication Research, 32,* 35–57.

Altman, I., & Taylor, D. A. (1973). *Social penetration: The development of interpersonal relationships.* New York: Holt, Rinehart & Winston.

Ayers, J. (1979). Uncertainty and social penetration theory expectations about relationship communication: A comparative test. *Western Journal of Speech Communication, 43,* 192–200.

Babrow, A. S. (2001). Uncertainty, value, communication, and problematic integration. *Journal of Communication, 51,* 553–573.

Babrow, A. S., Kasch, C. R., & Ford, L. A. (1998). From "reducing" to "managing" uncertainty: Reconceptualizing the central challenge in breast self-exams. *Social Science and Medicine, 51,* 1805–1816.

Baxter, L. A., & Montgomery, B. M. (1996). *Relating: Dialogues and dialectics.* New York: Guilford.

Baxter, L. A., & Wilmot, W. W. (1985). Taboo topics in close relationships. *Journal of Social and Personal Relationships, 2,* 253–269.

Bell, R. A., & Buerkel-Rothfuss, N. L. (1990). S(he) loves me, S(he) loves me not: Predictors of relational information-seeking in courtship and beyond. *Communication Quarterly, 38,* 64–82.

Berger, C. R. (1979). Beyond initial interaction: Uncertainty, understanding, and the development of interpersonal relationships. In H. Giles & R. St. Clair (Eds.), *Language and social psychology* (pp. 122–144). Oxford: Basil Blackwell.

Berger, C. R. (1986). Uncertain outcome values in predicted relationships: Uncertainty reduction theory then and now. *Human Communication Research, 13,* 34–38.

Berger, C. R. (1997). Producing messages under uncertainty. In J. O. Greene (Ed.), *Message production: Advances in communication theory* (pp. 221–244). Mahwah, NJ: Lawrence Erlbaum.

Berger, C. R., & Bell, R. A. (1988). Plans and the initiation of social relationships. *Human Communication Research, 15,* 217–235.

Berger, C. R., & Bradac, J. J. (1982). *Language and social knowledge: Uncertainty in interpersonal relationships.* London: Edward Arnold.

Berger, C. R., & Calabrese, R. J. (1975). Some explorations in initial interaction and beyond: Toward a developmental theory of interpersonal communication. *Human Communication Research, 1,* 99–112.

Berger, C. R., & diBattista, P. (1993). Communication failure and plan adaptation: If at first you don't succeed, say it louder and slower. *Communication Monographs, 60,* 222–238.

Berger, C. R., & Gudykunst, W. B. (1991). Uncertainty and communication. In B. Dervin & M. J. Voight (Eds.), *Progress in communication sciences* (Vol. 10, pp. 21–66). Norwood, NJ: Ablex.

Berger, C. R., & Jordan, J. M. (1992). Planning sources, planning difficulty and verbal fluency. *Communication Monographs, 59,* 130–149.

Berger, C. R., Karol, S. H., & Jordan, J. M. (1989). When a lot of knowledge is a dangerous thing: The debilitating effects of plan complexity on verbal fluency. *Human Communication Research, 16,* 91–119.

Berger, C. R., & Kellermann, K. A. (1983). To ask or not to ask: Is that a question? In R. Bostrom (Ed.), *Communication yearbook 7* (pp. 342–368). Newbury Park, CA: Sage.

Berger, C. R., & Kellermann, K. A. (1994). Acquiring social information. In J. A. Daly & J. M. Weimann (Eds.), *Strategic interpersonal communication* (pp. 1–31). Hillsdale, NJ: Lawrence Erlbaum.

Bevan, J. L., Stetzenbach, K. A., Batson, E., & Bullo, K. (2006). Factors associated with general partner uncertainty and relational uncertainty within early adulthood sibling relationships. *Communication Quarterly, 54,* 367–381.

Brainerd, E. G., Hunter, P. A., Moore, D., & Thompson, T. R. (1996). Jealousy induction as a predictor of power and the use of other control methods in heterosexual relationships. *Psychological Reports, 79,* 1319–1325.

Brashers, D. E. (2001). Communication and uncertainty management. *Journal of Communication, 51,* 477–497.

Brashers, D. E., Goldsmith, D. J., & Hsieh, E. (2002). Information seeking and avoiding in health contexts. *Human Communication Research, 28,* 258–271.

Brashers, D. E., Neidig, J. L., Haas, S. M., Dobbs, L. K., Cardillo, L. W., & Russell, J. A. (2000). Communication in the management of uncertainty: The case of persons living with HIV or AIDS. *Communication Monographs, 67,* 63–84.

Clatterbuck, G. W. (1979). Attributional confidence and uncertainty in initial interaction. *Human Communication Research, 5,* 147–157.

Douglas, W. (1987). Affinity-testing in initial interactions. *Journal of Social and Personal Relationships, 4,* 3–15.

Douglas, W. (1991). Expectations about initial interaction: An examination of the effects of global uncertainty. *Human Communication Research, 17,* 355–384.

Douglas, W. (1994). The acquaintanceship process: An examination of uncertainty, information seeking, and social attraction during initial conversation. *Communication Research, 21,* 154–176.

Driscoll, D. M., Hamilton, D. L., & Sorrentino, R. M. (1991). Uncertainty orientation and recall of person-descriptive information. *Personality and Social Psychology Bulletin, 17,* 494–500.

Dugas, M. J., Hedayati, M., Karavidas, A., Buhr, K., Francis, K., & Phillips, N. A. (2005). Intolerance of uncertainty and information processing: Evidence of biased recall and interpretations. *Cognitive Therapy and Research, 29,* 57–70.

Grove, T. G., & Werkman, D. L. (1991). Conversations with able-bodied and visibly disabled strangers: An adversarial test of predicted outcome value and uncertainty reduction theories. *Human Communication Research, 17,* 507–534.

Gudykunst, W. B. (1985). The influence of similarity, type of relationship, and self-monitoring on uncertainty reduction processes. *Communication Monographs, 52,* 203–217.

Gudykunst, W. B. (1995). Anxiety/uncertainty management (AUM) theory: Current status. In R. L. Wiseman (Ed.), *Intercultural communication theory* (pp. 8–58). Thousand Oaks, CA: Sage.

Gudykunst, W. B., & Hammer, M. R. (1988). The influence of social identity and intimacy of interethnic relationships on uncertainty reduction processes. *Human Communication Research, 14,* 569–601.

Gudykunst, W. B., Nishida, T., & Schmidt, K. L. (1989). The influence of cultural, relational, and personality factors on uncertainty reduction processes. *Western Journal of Speech Communication, 53,* 13–29.

Gudykunst, W. B., Yang, S. M., & Nishida, T. (1985). A cross-cultural test of uncertainty reduction theory: Comparisons of acquaintance, friend, and dating relationships in Japan, Korea, and the United States. *Human Communication Research, 11,* 407–455.

Heider, F. (1958). *The psychology of interpersonal relations.* New York: Wiley.

Kellermann, K. A., & Reynolds, R. (1990). When ignorance is bliss: The role of motivation to reduce uncertainty in uncertainty reduction theory. *Human Communication Research, 17,* 5–75.

Kelley, H. H. (1973). The process of causal attribution. *American Psychologist, 28,* 107–128.

Kelley, H. H., & Thibaut, J. W. (1978). *Interpersonal relations: A theory of interdependence.* New York: Wiley.

Knobloch, L. K. (2006). Relational uncertainty and message production within courtship: Features of date request messages. *Human Communication Research, 32,* 244–273.

Knobloch, L. K. (2007a). The dark side of relational uncertainty: Obstacle or opportunity? In B. H. Spitzberg & W. R. Cupach (Eds.), *The dark side of interpersonal communication* (2nd ed., pp. 31–59). Mahwah, NJ: Lawrence Erlbaum.

Knobloch, L. K. (2007b). Perceptions of turmoil within courtship: Associations with intimacy, relational uncertainty, and interference from partners. *Journal of Social and Personal Relationships, 24,* 363–384.

Knobloch, L. K., & Carpenter-Theune, K. E. (2004). Topic avoidance in developing romantic relationships: Associations with intimacy and relational uncertainty. *Communication Research, 31,* 173–205.

Knobloch, L. K., & Donovan-Kicken, E. (2006). Perceived involvement of network members in courtships: A test of the relational turbulence model. *Personal Relationships, 13,* 281–302.

Knobloch, L. K., Miller, L. E., Bond, B. J., & Mannone, S. E. (2007). Relational uncertainty and message processing in marriage. *Communication Monographs, 74,* 154–180.

Knobloch, L. K., Miller, L. E., & Carpenter, K. E. (2007). Using the relational turbulence model to understand negative emotion within courtship. *Personal Relationships, 14,* 91–112.

Knobloch, L. K., & Solomon, D. H. (1999). Measuring the sources and content of relational uncertainty. *Communication Studies, 50,* 261–278.

Knobloch, L. K., & Solomon, D. H. (2002a). Information seeking beyond initial interaction: Negotiating relational uncertainty within close relationships. *Human Communication Research, 28,* 243–257.

Knobloch, L. K., & Solomon, D. H. (2002b). Intimacy and the magnitude and experience of episodic relational uncertainty within romantic relationships. *Personal Relationships, 9,* 457–478.

Knobloch, L. K., & Solomon, D. H. (2005). Relational uncertainty and relational information processing: Questions without answers? *Communication Research, 32,* 349–388.

Kramer, M. W. (1999). Motivation to reduce uncertainty: A reconceptualization of uncertainty reduction theory. *Management Communication Quarterly, 13,* 305–316.

Kramer, M. W. (2004). *Managing uncertainty in organizational communication.* Mahwah, NJ: Lawrence Erlbaum.

Kruglanski, A. W. (1989). *Lay epistemics and human knowledge: Cognitive and motivational bases.* New York: Plenum.

Kruglanski, A. W., & Webster, D. M. (1996). Motivated closing of the mind: "Seizing" and "freezing." *Psychological Review, 103,* 263–283.

Livingston, K. R. (1980). Love as a process of reducing uncertainty: Cognitive theory. In K. S. Pope (Ed.), *On love and loving* (pp. 133–151). San Francisco: Jossey-Bass.

Norton, M. I., Frost, J. H., & Ariely, D. (2007). Less is more: The lure of ambiguity, or why familiarity breeds contempt. *Journal of Personality and Social Psychology, 92,* 97–105.

Parks, M. R., & Adelman, M. B. (1983). Communication networks and the development of romantic relationships: An expansion of uncertainty reduction theory. *Human Communication Research, 10,* 55–79.

Parks, M. R., & Floyd, K. (1996). Meanings for closeness and intimacy in friendship. *Journal of Social and Personal Relationships, 13,* 85–107.

Planalp, S., Rutherford, D. K., & Honeycutt, J. M. (1988). Events that increase uncertainty in personal relationships II: Replication and extension. *Human Communication Research, 14,* 516–547.

Robinson, J. D., & Stivers, T. (2001). Achieving activity transitions in physician-patient encounters: From history taking to physical examination. *Human Communication Research, 27*, 253–298.

Shannon, C. E., & Weaver, W. (1949). *The mathematical theory of communication*. Champaign: University of Illinois.

Sherblom, J., & Van Rheenen, D. D. (1984). Spoken language indices of uncertainty. *Human Communication Research, 11*, 221–230.

Shuper, P. A., Sorrentino, R. M., Otsubo, Y., Hodson, G., & Walker, A. M. (2004). A theory of uncertainty orientation: Implications for the study of individual differences within and across cultures. *Journal of Cross-Cultural Psychology, 35*, 460–480.

Solomon, D. H., & Knobloch, L. K. (2004). A model of relational turbulence: The role of intimacy, relational uncertainty, and interference from partners in appraisals of irritations. *Journal of Social and Personal Relationships, 21*, 795–816.

Sorrentino, R. M., Holmes, J. G., Hanna, S. E., & Sharp, A. (1995). Uncertainty orientation and trust in close relationships: Individual differences in cognitive styles. *Journal of Personality and Social Psychology, 68*, 314–327.

Sorrentino, R. M., & Roney, C. J. R. (2000). *The uncertain mind: Individual differences in facing the unknown*. Philadelphia: Psychology Press.

Sunnafrank, M. (1986a). Predicted outcome value during initial interactions: A reformulation of uncertainty reduction theory. *Human Communication Research, 13*, 3–33.

Sunnafrank, M. (1986b). Predicted outcome values: Just now and then? *Human Communication Research, 13*, 39–40.

Sunnafrank, M. (1990). Predicted outcome value and uncertainty reduction theories: A test of competing perspectives. *Human Communication Research, 17*, 76–103.

Sunnafrank, M., & Ramirez, A., Jr. (2004). At first sight: Persistent relational effects of get-acquainted conversations. *Journal of Social and Personal Relationships, 21*, 361–379.

Teboul, J. B. (1995). Determinants of new hire information-seeking during organizational encounter. *Western Journal of Communication, 59*, 305–325.

Theiss, J. A., & Solomon, D. H. (2006a). Coupling longitudinal data and multilevel modeling to examine the antecedents and consequences of jealousy experiences in romantic relationships: A test of the relational turbulence model. *Human Communication Research, 32*, 469–503.

Theiss, J. A., & Solomon, D. H. (2006b). A relational turbulence model of communication about irritations in romantic relationships. *Communication Research, 33*, 391–418.

Thibaut, J. W., & Kelley, H. H. (1959). *The social psychology of groups*. New York: Wiley.

Turner, L. H. (1990). The relationship between communication and marital uncertainty: Is "her" marriage different from "his" marriage? *Women's Studies in Communication, 13*, 57–83.

White, G. L. (1980). Inducing jealousy: A power perspective. *Personality and Social Psychology Bulletin, 6*, 222–227.

7

Information Seeking in the Initial Stages of Relational Development

WALID A. AFIFI and ALYSA A. LUCAS

SWF ISO career-minded but not a workaholic male … should also be similar to me but different, attractive but not gorgeous, clean cut and fashion-conscious but not obsessed with looks, good conversationalist but not phony, family man but not mama's boy, independent but interdependent, committed but not smothering, loving but not possessive, sexually experienced but not overly willing, kind to others but stands up for himself, polite but not sappy, expressive but not emotional, stable and able to be fragile, fragile but able to be strong, listener but not silent.

Based on what we know about attraction, the completely truthful singles ad would look a lot like the above for many people. However, relational partners do not come to us having responded to a detailed wish list such as the one above. We rarely initiate relationships with an already established and detailed base of knowledge about the other person. Instead, we typically start with very little information about the thousands of people with whom we interact over a lifetime. Ultimately, we make decisions to pursue close relationships with a tiny percentage of those people. So how is it that we know whether someone is a good fit for us? It may be best to view relationships as a series of discovery journeys during which we learn about the other's traits (and often our own). This chapter explores the journeys that start us off. Given its centrality to our decision about whether to pursue a close relationship or not, there may be no more important aspect of relationship formation than the ways in which we gather information about potential romantic partners.

The research on attraction is based on the premise that we know certain things about someone else (e.g., physical appearance, attitudes, and communication skill). Indeed, it is the knowledge about these things that results in attraction. But how is it that we gather that information about these people and, thereby, know these things? Curiously, most of the attraction research has ignored that question. Scholarship in related domains, though, allows us to (at least partly) answer it. The literature on information seeking in interpersonal settings is divided into two general categories: (a) the communication strategies that people use to gather information about others, and (b) the cognitive and affective biases that shape information retrieval and processing (for review of the latter category, see Forgas, 2001; Wyer & Gruenfeld, 1995). To focus the chapter, we will attend primarily to the former of these two research areas.

Although the ideal for our purposes would be a plethora of studies that answered the question of how it is that people seek attraction-related information in *early stages* of relational development, such a research corpus does not seem to exist. Instead, the literature on information-seeking strategies mostly addresses behavior during initial interactions or in well-developed relationships. Fortunately, those studies are still helpful for our goal. After all, the "initiation" of relationships *begins* in initial interactions and may *reemerge* during transition stages in well-developed relationships, as people move from one relational state (e.g., friendship) to another (e.g., romantic relationship; see Creasey & Jarvis, this volume; Guerrero & Mongeau, this volume). So, this chapter will start with a review of what we can extrapolate about early-stage information seeking from studies of initial interactions and well-developed relationships. We will then narrow the focus to a specific target of knowledge acquisition that is of common concern for relational members in the initial stages of relational development—information about the partner's sexual health.

INFORMATION SEEKING IN INITIAL INTERACTIONS

Seeking General Information

Berger and Calabrese (1975) introduced uncertainty reduction theory in hopes of understanding individuals' behavior during initial interactions among strangers. The theory encouraged considerable attention to the information-seeking process during these interactions and led to a burgeoning of knowledge about the ways in which we gather information about others—not only in initial interactions but also beyond. At a general level, the literature suggests that information is sought in one of three ways: passive, active, or interactive. As with any communication behavior, these three categories and related communication strategies may be mapped on two-dimensional space reflecting variance on efficiency, on the one hand, and social appropriateness, on the other (see Berger & Kellermann, 1983, 1994; Knobloch & Miller, this volume).

Several studies have tested the conditions that promote the use of each of these information-seeking strategies. In general, the available evidence suggests that individuals start their information searches through passive means (see Berger, 1979). The low cost of unobtrusively observing another person makes it especially appealing as an initial information-gathering strategy. Of course, not all observational situations provide equally rich "data." Instead, Berger and his colleagues have shown that the most information-rich environments for observing others are those in which the target person is interacting with others, rather than being isolated or silent (Berger & Perkins, 1978), and those that present relatively few social constraints on behavior (e.g., informal social settings; Berger & Douglas, 1981). The informational value of these settings comes from the sense that they offer a much more insightful peek into the uninhibited (i.e., real) nature of the target person than does his or her physical appearance alone or interactions in a more strictly rules-guided formal setting. However, this literature also shows that individuals rely on a host of interactive strategies once interaction begins.

Berger and Kellermann (1983) identified three specific interactive strategies that individuals use during initial interactions to gather information about the target person: interrogation (i.e., question asking), disclosure (i.e., talking about one's self in hopes of eliciting reciprocity by the other), and relaxing the target (i.e., creating a conversational atmosphere that encourages disclosure on the other's part). Each of these interactive strategies has been shown to have its place in interactions. The first few seconds of stranger interactions are typically littered with questions—most are focused on biographic and demographic characteristics. In fact, estimates for the number of questions asked range from 10 in the first 4 minutes (Douglas, 1994) to 22 in the first 5 minutes of conversation (Berger & Kellermann, 1983). Moreover, an exponential decrease in interrogation seems to occur after only the first minute of initial interactions (for review, see Berger & Kellermann, 1994; Douglas, 1994). It is clear that the initial moments of the first interaction between strangers are question laden. When combined with evidence from the attraction literature that many of our relationship-initiation decisions are based on biographic and demographic information (e.g., similarity; see Bruce & Graziano, this volume; see also Sprecher & Felmlee, this volume), a picture develops of nearly instantaneous assessments about relationship fit. In other words, it seems that we have often gathered sufficient information *within the first minute of conversation* to determine whether the target person is someone with whom we may be interested in pursuing a relationship. So, the first information-gathering journey seems to take a turn within seconds of the initial interaction.

   Question asking is the most efficient but also the most intrusive way of gathering information and is often considered the least appropriate. As a result, individuals often turn to other forms of interactive information seeking during initial interactions. As noted above, two less efficient but also less intrusive forms are disclosure and target relaxation efforts. The disclosure strategy—the second most common form of information seeking in initial interactions (Berger & Kellermann, 1983)—relies on the norm of reciprocity (see Gouldner, 1960). Specifically, individuals manipulate social rules for their ends by offering a disclosure, thereby putting pressure on others to reveal information about themselves in return. Although this is a relatively common strategy, according to Berger and Kellermann (1983), it is also one full of potholes. Individual differences in willingness to offer immediate reciprocity and variance in perceptions of what it means to reciprocate (e.g., return disclosure on topic, but not on intimacy of information) translate to the limited success of such a strategy for information acquisition.

   Efforts to relax the target are similarly restricted as successful information-gathering tools. The notion is that enacting the sort of verbal and nonverbal behavior that makes the target comfortable in the interaction (e.g., head nods, forward body lean, and skilled support messages) is likely to increase his or her willingness to be vulnerable by offering information about him or herself. Indeed, Kellermann and Berger (1984) showed that individuals who were motivated to seek information were more likely to engage in partner relaxation behaviors than those who were not. Unfortunately, we know relatively little about the success of these strategies. For one, the evidence suggests that such behaviors often accompany other interactive information-seeking strategies (e.g., interrogation; Kellermann & Berger, 1984). Moreover, relaxation may indeed increase the likelihood of disclosure, but does not guide such revelations in directions that are consonant with the seeker's information needs (Berger & Kellermann, 1994). So, although sometimes inappropriate, question asking is also the only strategy in initial interactions that is reliably efficient for the task at hand (i.e., gathering information).

Seeking Attraction-Related Information

The findings reported so far speak to the information-seeking behavior used during initial interactions—the starting point of all relationships. Other than some studies that manipulated participants' desire for information seeking, the methodological paradigm applied in the above cited studies does not vary the topical target of participants' information-seeking goals. Given the diverse nature of initial interactions, it is not clear whether the strategies that are used when participants are asked to get acquainted with a stranger generalize to situations when individuals are motivated to gather information about the other's attraction to them. Douglas (1987) performed the only published study (to our knowledge) of affinity-*testing* strategies in initial interactions. Given the centrality of information regarding the other's *perceived affinity* (aka *perceived attraction*) for guiding relationship initiation and development decisions, Douglas' findings are central to this chapter. In contrast to the tripartite distinction of passive, active, and interactive strategies, his results reveal a much more intricate menu of information-seeking options from which individuals choose.

   Through a series of studies, Douglas (1987, pp. 7–8) discovered eight general strategies that individuals reported using to gain affinity-related information from opposite-sex others in initial interactions: *confronting* (i.e., "actions that required a partner to provide immediate and generally public evidence of his or her liking"), *withdrawing* (i.e., "actions that required a partner to sustain the interaction"), *sustaining* (i.e., "actions designed to maintain the interaction without affecting its apparent intimacy"), *hazing* (i.e., "actions that required a partner to provide a commodity or service to the actor at some cost to him or herself"), *diminishing self* (i.e., "actions that lowered the value of self, either directly by self-deprecation or indirectly by identifying alternative reward sources for a partner"), *approaching* (i.e., "actions that implied increased intimacy to which the only disconfirming partner response is compensatory activity"), *offering* (i.e., "actions that generated conditions favorable for approach by a partner"), and *networking* (i.e., "actions that included third parties, either to acquire or [to] transmit information"). Each category was operationalized by two to four specific examples taken from participant reports.

Based on Kellermann and Berger's (1984) suggestion that individuals struggle between being efficient and being socially appropriate, Douglas (1987) had each strategy rated on those two dimensions.
Not surprisingly, *confronting* (e.g., "I asked her if she liked me") and *approaching* (e.g., "I would touch
his shoulder or move close to see if he would react by staying where he was or moving closer.") were
rated as the most efficient forms of affinity testing, whereas *withdrawing* (e.g., "I would be silent sometimes to see if he would start the conversation again"), *hazing* (e.g., "I told him I lived 16 miles away ... .
I wanted to see if he would try and back out"), and *diminishing self* (e.g., "I told him I wasn't very interesting. Waiting for him to say, 'Oh, no.'") were perceived as the most *inefficient*. It is also worth noting,
though, that these were also perceived to be three of the most *inappropriate* strategies for gathering
information about the person's attraction. Their ineffectiveness (they are seen as both inefficient and
inappropriate strategies for affinity testing) makes them unlikely information-seeking strategies for
those who are skilled at relational development. Interestingly, the strategy labeled *sustaining* (e.g.,
"I kept asking questions. You know, like, 'where was she from?' 'What music did she like?'") most
closely approximates Berger and colleagues' *interrogation* strategy and was perceived to be the most
appropriate of the strategies by far, although not as efficient in terms of affinity testing as confronting
and approaching strategies. Overall, Douglas' results show that individuals interacting with strangers
gather information about the person's attraction to them in a variety of ways. Consistent with Berger
and Kellermann's findings, though, biographical and demographic questions served as the information-
seeking strategy deemed most appropriate in such situations. Yet it is also worth noting that the most
relevant strategy in this context, which the authors labeled as *confronting* (e.g., "I asked her if she liked
me"), although appropriately rated as the most efficient was also seen as relatively inappropriate—a
finding that seems to put a particularly fine point on the challenges that individuals face when seeking
information about someone's attraction to them.

Sending Attraction-Related Information

The literature on the ways in which we *signal* affiliation is not of central interest in this chapter,
given our attention to information-*seeking* efforts. Nevertheless, at least some mention of the ways
in which individuals may show romantic interest is warranted because it has implications for whether
such information will be pursued. So, how is affiliation expressed? Research on nonverbal communication shows that intimacy and liking are conveyed through forward body lean, smiling, eye contact,
close proximity, direct body orientation, and frequent gesturing, among other signals (see Burgoon,
1985). Tie signs like hugging, hand-holding, kissing, and the like are also clear ways in which we
send relational signals (see Afifi & Johnson, 1999), and a vast repertoire of behaviors is used with the
specific intent to flirt (Egland, Spitzberg, & Zormeier, 1996).

Not surprisingly, studies have shown that individuals who are sexually interested in a target display more nonverbal signals of affection than less interested others. Specifically, Simpson, Gangestad, and Biek (1993) found that "head canting" among women and "flirtatious glances" by men were
positively associated with their willingness to engage in uncommitted sexual relations (i.e., their
level of sociosexual orientation). But, in the end, it is the receiver's ability to correctly *interpret* these
messages and follow up with a search for additional information that determines the interaction's
ultimate outcome. So, what do we know about perceptual filters that might guide this process?

The Role of Perceived Romantic Interest

One obvious candidate for predicting a willingness to aggressively seek information in early stages of
relationship development is the extent to which individuals are likely to perceive romantic or sexual
(dis)interest in the other. Two programs of research seem especially relevant to that domain: Vorauer
and Ratner's (1996) investigation of relationship initiation, and Abbey and colleagues' work on perception of sexual interest (for review, see Abbey, 1987).

Vorauer and Ratner (1996) tested the extent to which perceived *dis*interest on the other's part
served as an impediment to relationship development. In a creative set of six studies, the authors

concluded that individuals interested in developing a romantic relationship often fail to initiate a date request because of fears that they will be rejected. However, in an interesting perceptual twist, participants did not consider that same fear as motivating the other's inaction (i.e., why the other person didn't initiate a date request). Instead, they accounted for it as being a reflection of disinterest. In other words, individuals interpret the other's inaction from a pessimistic frame. Although the authors often did not have the statistical power to adequately test for sex differences, they did report that male and female responses followed the same pattern.

Both the pessimistic bias and the apparent failure to find sex differences are especially interesting because they clash somewhat with other research on the perception of sexual interest after brief interactions. For example, Abbey and colleagues have repeatedly shown that men "oversexualize" the behavior of women (for review, see Abbey, 1987). Consistent with this notion, Henningsen (2004) found that men are more likely than women to interpret flirtation as being motivated by sexual interest. Indeed, a review in this area leaves little doubt that men, more than women, perceive sexual interest in its absence (Levesque, Nave, & Lowe, 2006). The general argument is that men's elevated sexual appetite (see Baumeister, Catanese, & Vohs, 2001) results in a significantly lower threshold for perceiving sexual interest than women. That perceptual lens is then argued to serve as "a model for the attribution of the appetite of others" (Shotland & Craig, 1988, p. 66). In other words, men often perceive behavior as sexual and mistakenly believe that women share that perceptual filter. The crux of these findings is that women often send signals that men interpret as sexual when women do not intend them as such. Indeed, 72% of women in one of Abbey's studies on the issue reported that their friendly behavior had been misinterpreted as sexual on at least one occasion. Although the consequence is sometimes trivial (e.g., men's embarrassment for misinterpreting intent), it can also lead to devastating results (e.g., sexual aggression; Abbey, McAuslan, & Ross, 1998; Shotland, 1992).

When compared, Vorauer and Ratner (1996) and Abbey and colleagues' (see Abbey, 1987) findings offer strikingly divergent conclusions regarding male perceptions during early stages of relationship development. The former suggest that men *underestimate* the other's interest in them, whereas the latter suggest they *overestimate* that interest. However, close inspection suggests that the implications may not be particularly disparate. One possibility, for example, is that men may indeed perceive sexual interest but still hold a pessimistic bias that leads them to be expect rejection. Alternatively, the two findings may reflect shifts in the dominant perceptual paradigm across stages of relationship initiation. So, after repeated instances of perceptual correction with the same target, men's oversexualization trend may be gradually replaced by a pessimistic bias. Unfortunately, the available evidence does not allow for more than conjectures on the matter—conjectures that call for future empirical testing.

INFORMATION SEEKING IN DEVELOPING RELATIONSHIPS

Typologies of Information-Seeking Strategies

The initial stage of relationship development typically goes well beyond the first interaction. As such, it is important to ask how individuals seek relationally relevant information beyond that first encounter. Although the research domain that guides the answer to that question is not large, several studies do provide insight on the issue. To our knowledge, the first scholars to address the question were Baxter and Wilmot (1984). They embarked with a goal to study "the social strategies that people use to acquire knowledge about the state of their opposite-sex relationships" (Baxter & Wilmot, p. 171). Their efforts revealed seven types of what they labeled "secret tests": (a) *directness tests*, which involved direct questioning or disclosure about the relationship; (b) *endurance tests*, which were characterized by behaviors that tested the lengths to which the person would go for the relationship; (c) *indirect suggestion*, which included hints or jokes about a relational matter (e.g., making fun of a friend's decision to move in with his partner to see how the other reacted to the idea); (d) *public presentation*, which involved attending to the way that the partner responded to a particular form of introduction (e.g., introducing him as your "boyfriend"); (e) *third party*, which consisted of gathering information from the partner's friends or family; (f) *separation*, which meant not seeing one another for a while as a way to gather information about his or her commitment to the relationship; and (g) *triangle tests*, which introduced third parties into the mix as possible romantic threats (e.g., flirting with someone else to see if one's partner got jealous or testing the partner's commitment by having someone else flirt with him or her and testing his or her reaction).

In contrast to the findings from the work on information seeking during initial interactions—when question asking dominated the landscape—the results from this investigation showed *directness tests* to be the third *least* frequent strategy. Instead, participants relied on such behaviors as *endurance tests*, *triangle tests*, and other highly indirect methods of information acquisition. Moreover, a comparison of relationship types showed that those in relationships with romantic potential (i.e., those relationships described as "more than friends" but not yet romantic) engaged in more secret tests and did so in more indirect ways than those in either romantic relationships or already established platonic friendships.

Planalp and colleagues' (Planalp & Honeycutt, 1985; Planalp, Rutherford, & Honeycutt, 1988) investigation of responses to uncertainty-increasing events in close relationships also shows a preference for indirectness under conditions of uncertainty—a state that reflects early stages of relational development. Events such as an unexplained loss of contact, the discovery of a competing relationship, or a change in personality were typically followed by efforts to seek information by "talking over" or "talking around" the issue, hardly direct strategies.

Bell and Buerkel-Rothfuss (1990) supported and extended this work. Their study of 226 college students in romantic relationships showed that this population frequently engages in secret tests (participants averaged 4.5 secret tests in their current relationship) and confirmed Baxter and Wilmot's (1984) finding that the number of secret tests generally decreases over the stages of courtship. However, separate analyses by type of "secret test" revealed an important caveat to that pattern: Directness tests, the one direct and nonsecretive information-seeking strategy, *increased* across courtship stages for both males and females. In other words, we become increasingly direct in our information-seeking efforts as we move from initial to late stages of relational development.

Another finding of note is the role played by third parties in individuals' information-seeking efforts. Although reported relatively infrequently by participants in Baxter and Wilmot's (1984) original study, the data from both Bell and Buerkel-Rothfuss (1990) and from Parks and Adelman's (1983) longitudinal study of information seeking in developing relationships suggest that third parties played a crucial role as information sources. In fact, Parks and Adelman found that the level of relational uncertainty was more significantly reduced across time by the amount of communication with the partner's network members than by communication with the partner him or herself.

Although these typologies of information-seeking strategies in relationships have been tremendously useful, the methodological reliance on interviews or self-reports rather than on behavioral coding inherently limited precision about certain features of the communication process in information-seeking exchanges. Toward that end, Knobloch (2006) recently completed a novel test that was able to capture the quality of information acquisition within developing romantic relationships (the participants' median length of reported romantic interest in their partner was 9.25 months). She asked participants to call their dating partners and leave a message on an answering machine (set up for the study) to request spending time together on a date. Subsequent analysis of the messages revealed that the level of relational uncertainty was negatively associated with fluency, affiliativeness, relationship focus, explicitness, and perceived effectiveness of the date requests (see Knobloch & Miller, this volume). In other words, those whose desire for relational information was the highest were also the least competent in their date requests. The results highlight the anxiety that undoubtedly comes with relationally focused information-seeking efforts in initial relationships. The process is more difficult than simply deciding among a host of information-seeking strategies; the actual enactment of the strategy may present the most significant challenge to successful information seeking and can dramatically influence the information one receives. Asking someone out in a communicatively inept manner may successfully produce relational information, but not of the sort being sought. In those cases, passive observation or other forms of information seeking may be more appropriate. Unfortunately, the literature on relational information seeking remains in its infancy and leaves several questions unanswered. Yet, recent theoretical accounts offer promise.

Theoretical Accounts

One factor that seems to play a strong role in the individuals' information-seeking decisions is the valence of the information they expect to receive. For example, Holton and Pyszcynski (1989) showed that participants most thoroughly sought attraction-related information about a male confederate when "it was apparent that the available information would be supportive of their self-serving impressions of [the person]" (p. 50). In other words, participants who were previously *critiqued* by the confederate were motivated to find *negative* information about him and refrained from information seeking when it seemed that they might conclude that he was a likeable person, whereas the reverse was true for those whom he praised. Consistent with this notion, Knobloch and Solomon (2002) advanced a model of information seeking in close relationships in which the expected outcome of the information search plays a central role (see also Sunnafrank, 1990).

Most recently, Afifi and Weiner (2004) developed the theory of motivated information management (TMIM), a framework to help understand information-seeking decisions in interpersonal encounters. The theory was developed in response to dissatisfaction with the comprehensiveness of existing uncertainty frameworks. It started by explicitly narrowing its scope to interpersonal encounters and to issues of import to the potential information seeker. It then brought to the area of uncertainty management two significant components: first, a focus on the role of efficacy in the information-seeking process, and, second, explicit recognition of the interactive role played by the information provider during the exchange.

Afifi and Weiner (2004) proposed a three-phase information management process (see Figure 7.1) that starts with a discrepancy between the amount of actual and desired uncertainty about an issue and the resultant anxiety (labeled the "interpretation phase"), moves to an evaluation phase that includes an assessment about the expected outcome of the information search (i.e., outcome expectancies) and an assessment of efficacy, and ends with a decision phase. In the evaluation phase, individuals first consider the rewards and costs expected from a search for information from a particular source, and then make three efficacy determinations: (a) whether they are able to communicate with sufficient skill to gather the information sought (i.e., communication efficacy), (b) whether they can cope with the information they expect to receive (i.e., coping efficacy), and (c) whether the source is willing and able to provide the information being sought (i.e., target efficacy). TMIM argues that individuals are increasingly likely to seek information directly to the extent that the outcome expectancy is positive (i.e., they expect a relatively positive outcome of an information search) and the three perceptions of efficacy are high.

TMIM is particularly well suited to study information seeking in early stages of relationships for several reasons. First, it considers uncertainty states—a primary feature of individuals' experiences in relationship beginnings (see Knobloch & Miller, this volume)—as the engine that drives the process. Second, it accounts for expectations regarding the outcome of an information search—a variable that has been shown to impact information-seeking decisions in contexts where information about attraction is salient. Third, it recognizes the diversity of information-seeking options. The theory proposes that individuals may choose to seek information either directly or indirectly, avoid information either actively or passively, or cognitively reassess the degree of uncertainty discrepancy (see Afifi & Weiner, 2004). Fourth, it explicitly takes into account the information provider in the process. In that sense, it recognizes that information exchange is an interactive process in which both sender and receiver are assessing the value and feasibility of various communication choices and acting accordingly. Finally, it adopts a bounded rationality approach (see

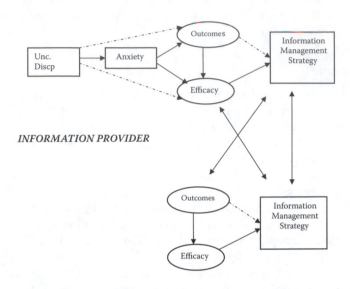

INFORMATION SEEKER

Interpretation Phase   **Evaluation Phase**   **Decision Phase**

INFORMATION PROVIDER

Evaluation Phase   Decision Phase

Figure 7.1 The information management process as proposed in the theory of motivated information management. *Note*: The dashed paths reflect paths that are partly mediated by other variables with which the relevant variable has associations. The figure is intended as a visual simplification of the general theoretical framework.

Kahneman, 2003) and, as such, recognizes the role that emotions play both in the perceived outcomes of various communicative decisions and in the particular enactment of strategies for both interactants. These five properties are all central to the search for affinity-related information in relationship beginnings, thereby making the theory uniquely suited for understanding information seeking in this context.

Preliminary tests have generally supported the framework. For example, Afifi, Dillow, and Morse (2004) asked college students who were romantically involved to think about a partner-related issue for which they wanted more information. Participants then returned 3 weeks later to report on any information-seeking efforts on that topic since the first survey. Consistent with the theory's predictions, results showed that individuals used increasingly direct information-seeking strategies to the extent that the issue in question was important, the expected outcome of the search was positive, and their perceptions of efficacy were high. They also found that participants actively avoided relational information when they expected the outcome of an information search to be negative. Moreover, those who expected negative information and searched for it experienced a drop in relational commitment across the study's 3-week time frame. In other words, it confirmed the functional importance of being selective in the type of information one seeks (of course, there are also known biases in our perception of the positivity of information being sought; see Murray, 1999).

Afifi and Weiner (2006) followed up on the Afifi et al. (2004) test of TMIM by applying the framework to a domain of relational inquiry that has significant implications for college students' well-being—the partner's sexual health. Given the relevance of sexual health information to sexual decisions and the common occurrence of sexual activity in beginning stages of relationship development, it is a locale for information seeking that seems especially appropriate for this chapter.

SEEKING SEXUALLY RELATED INFORMATION FROM PARTNERS

The cost of unprotected sexual activity is very high. For example, estimates are that as many as 40% of college students are infected with human papilloma virus (HPV; Academy for Educational Development, 2000). Increasingly, scholars and health professionals are recognizing the importance of examining safe sex behavior from a relational lens (for review, see Noar, Zimmerman, & Atwood, 2004) and strongly encouraging individuals to seek information about their partner's sexual health (e.g., talk about condom use, birth control, and previous sexual history) before engaging in sexual activity (for review, see Afifi & Weiner, 2006; Cline, Freeman, & Johnson, 1990). Unfortunately, although efforts to examine sexual history discussions and related sexual information seeking have increased, the literature remains small. A recent study offers a glimpse into the experience of college students on this front. Afifi and Weiner (2006) found that a mere 2% of participants believed that their partner had a sexually transmitted infection (STI)—quite a contrast from the 40% infection rate estimate made by health professionals. What may be especially striking, though, is that this prediction was almost universally made with complete certainty. Seventy-four percent of participants rated their certainty as a 6 or 7 on a 7-point scale (with 7 indicating complete certainty). So what information-seeking strategies lead to such flawed information, and how do they gain this sort of (mistaken) certainty? The available literature lends itself nicely to Berger and colleagues' (e.g., Berger & Bradac, 1982) information-seeking typology of passive, active, and interactive strategies as an organizational framework.

Passive Sexual Information Seeking

Baxter and Wilmot (1985) summarized what they noted as "taboo topics" in close relationships. High among that list of avoided topics was sex. As such, it should come as no surprise that individuals often rely on observable outward signals to assess a partner's sexual health (Cleary, Barhman, MacCormack, & Herold, 2002). For example, Williams et al. (1992) found that college students determine the riskiness of a potential sexual partner by how they look or where they are socializing. Specifically, participants indicated that individuals would be perceived as risky if they dressed "slutty," were met at a bar, or were older. Edgar, Freimuth, Hammond, McDonald, and Fink (1992) noted a common belief among their participants that they could tell from someone's appearance whether or not engaging in sexual activity with that person would put themselves in danger of a sexually transmitted infection. Other studies (for review, see Afifi, 1999) have shown that information that should connote sexual responsibility (e.g., carrying a condom in a wallet and having ready access to a condom in the bedroom) was instead perceived to communicate negative impressions of the person (e.g., has a sexually transmitted illness and is "loose"). Cline and Freeman (as cited in Cline, Johnson, & Freeman, 1992) referred to this manner of information seeking as individuals' reliance on their "relational radar"—an intuition-based, yet typically flawed, gauge about the sexual riskiness of a partner that stems from relatively superficial cues. Particularly worrisome is that this sort of passive information acquisition apparently trumps the need for sexual history discussions and guides safe-sex decisions (Cleary et al., 2002; Williams et al., 1992).

Active Sexual Information Seeking

Curiously, we were able to find only one study that examined active efforts at seeking information about a partner's sexual health. Edgar et al. (1992) found that only 7% of their participants acquired sexual health information from a third person, went through the target's personal belongings for sexual health information, or used other active information-seeking strategies. Because the topic is both immensely personal (and, as such, others may be a poor source for information) and sensitive, it presents an interesting dilemma for information seekers. On the one hand, the indirect information-seeking efforts represented by active efforts (e.g., asking third parties) are attractive because they bypass the need for intimate discussion with a partner at an early relational stage. On the other hand, they are limiting because asking for such information from third parties may be both awkward and of limited utility.

Interactive Sexual Information Seeking

Interactive information-seeking efforts surrounding sexual health have long been recommended by health officials (see Cline et al., 1990). Yet, there are few studies that explicate the communication that occurs between partners on this topic. In one exception, Cline et al. (1992) asked participants about the sexual health topics they discussed with their partner. The analysis of general topics showed that the most commonly discussed sexual topics are sexual history (e.g., "Who/how many and what type of guys she'd been with"; 16% reported discussion), general conversation (12%), and general clinical topics (e.g., "How exactly it is transmitted between male/female contact"; discussed by 12% of participants). An analysis of specific issues revealed that indirect questions about the partner's sexual health (16%) and condom use intentions (10%) most commonly represented information-seeking efforts in this domain.

In another study describing the nature of sexual health–related talk among partners, participants received a list of questions and were asked to note the ones that they thought of prior to having intercourse (Edgar et al., 1992). Results indicated that the most salient concerns were questions regarding sexual experience and commitment (e.g., "The number of previous sexual partners she or he had before me," 77%; "When she or he last had a new sex partner," 64%; and "Whether or not she or he was currently involved sexually with someone else," 55%) and concerns with the partner's sexual health (e.g., "His or her feelings about using condoms with previous sex partners," 66%; "Whether or not she or he was infected with [the] AIDS virus," 53%; and "Whether or not she or he has a sexually transmitted disease," 44%). In the cases when there was discussion of these topics, Edgar et al. noted that communication about these issues was marked by self-disclosure, joking, indirect suggestion, and direct questions.

Finally, Cline et al. (1990, 1992) identified four groups of sexual health "talkers": safer-sex talkers, general AIDS talkers, nontalkers, and want-to-be talkers. *Safer-sex talkers* discuss the majority of topics with their partners, including AIDS, condoms, sexual history, and relationship exclusivity. *General AIDS talkers* focus on AIDS discussion, but in a global sense not specific to their relationship. Moreover, safer-sex talkers' conversations are initiated by the imminent possibility of engaging in sex, whereas general AIDS talkers discuss topics in response to such things as the media and casual conversation (Cline et al., 1992). In contrast to these groups of "talkers," a full one third of participants avoided discussion of sexually transmitted infections with their partners. *Nontalkers* were described as avoiding such discussions altogether, whereas *want-to-be talkers* are also avoiders but are willing to initiate discussion under the right circumstances. In both cases, avoidance is typically motivated by embarrassment, lack of intimacy, concern that discussion would ruin the mood, or anxiety. Consistent with these data, Coleman and Ingham (1999) found that one fourth of their sample experienced at least one instance when they wanted to initiate a discussion about condom use with their sexual partner but lacked the skill or confidence to do so. These authors also found that fear of a partner's negative response to condom requests motivated much of the avoidance on the issue.

A Study of Information Seeking about Sexual Health

In order to contribute empirically to the literature on information seeking in relationship beginnings, we will summarize previously unreported descriptive data on the strategies that participants in initial stages of relationship development use to seek information about their partner's sexual health (for a detailed summary of the study and an analysis of the entire sample, see Afifi & Weiner, 2006).

Procedures and Results   One-hundred and eighty-nine participants completed a host of measures at two times across a 3-week interval. Data from the first phase of data collection are reported here. Forty-one of these participants reported on an ongoing romantic relationship that was 3 months old or less and will be the subsample analyzed here. They consisted of 22 males and 19 females, varied in age from 18 to 21 ($M = 19.76$, $SD = 0.73$), and mostly included Caucasians (90%). Interestingly,

TABLE 7.1   Participant Response to Information-Seeking Items by Target Other

Item	Partner	Close Friend	Others
	Target Other		
I have sought _____ information from [target other] about [my partner's] sexual health.	3.90 (2.20; 80%)	1.81 (1.55; 38%)	2.23 (1.59; 45%)
How many questions have you asked [target other] about [your partner's] sexual health?	4.02 (1.97; 88%)	2.00 (1.83; 34%)	2.03 (1.33; 54%)

Note: The data represent means on a 7-point scale ranging from 0 = *no* to 7 = *a lot of*, with standard deviation in parentheses, followed by the percentage of participants who reported engaging in at least some of the behavior.

only two participants from this subsample (i.e., 5%) expected that a search for information about their partner's sexual health would reveal that he or she had a sexually transmitted infection.

The first set of items of interest for this investigation are two assessments of information seeking about their partner's sexual health—one that asked participants how much information they sought and one that asked about the numbers of questions they asked on the topic. The participants reported on their information seeking on this topic from three sources: (a) their partner, (b) a close friend of the participant's, and (c) other people. The results are reported in Table 7.1. The frequency of self-reported information seeking from partners on this issue is quite high, with 80% of participants reporting at least some information seeking from their partner within the first 3 months of their romantic involvement. The results also show that about 50% of participants sought information about their partner's sexual health from third parties. However, it is the particulars of those third parties that are especially intriguing. Participants were more likely to seek this information from people other than their close friends. Without additional data on the identity of those other third parties, the best explanation for this finding is that individuals may correctly consider *the partner's* friends as a more accurate source for that information and rely on their knowledge more than that of *their own* friends—people who may know little about their partner's past sexual activity. Still, the finding is intriguing given all we know about boundary management and disclosure (for review, see Petronio, 2002).

The second set of questions asked participants to rate the extent to which they sought the information in a direct manner or indirect manner. First, they were asked, "To what extent have you tried to get information from your partner about her/his sexual health in an *indirect* manner (e.g., through hinting, jokes, games)?" The data showed moderate frequency of indirect question asking from partners (M = 3.75 on a 7-point scale ranging from *not at all* to *a lot*; SD = 2.16; 80% reported at least some indirect questioning of their partner). Participants were then given the same item kernel, with "*direct* manner (e.g., direct questions & discussions)" replacing the reference to indirectness. The data revealed moderate amounts of direct information seeking as well (M = 3.53 on a 7-point scale ranging from *not at all* to *a lot*; SD = 2.11; 75% reported at least some direct questioning of their partner). Participants were also asked to indicate the number of people who they had asked directly (M = 1.98 on a 7-point scale ranging from *nobody* to *a lot of people*; SD = 1.12; 53% reported asking at least one other person directly) and indirectly (M = 1.88 on a 7-point scale ranging from *nobody* to *a lot of people*; SD = 1.27; 50% reported asking at least one other person indirectly) about their partner's sexual health. So again we see that the romantic partner is the primary target of information seeking on this issue, but that a considerable number of people also seek such intimate information from third parties.

Summary and Implications   Three contributions from these analyses are especially worth noting. First, the data suggest that a vast majority of college students seek sexual health information from their partners in early stages of relationship development. This conclusion seems to stand in stark contrast to the widely held notions that sexual topics are taboo and that college students are unaware of the threat posed by sexually transmitted infections. If this finding is replicated with a larger sample, it would suggest that public health messages encouraging these talks may have reached their audience. However, it would also imply the need to reexamine the content of these campaigns to recognize the new on-the-ground realities.

The second contribution of note from these descriptive data is that approximately half of the participants sought information about their partner's sexual health *from third parties*. This finding is noteworthy for two reasons. First, such a multiple-source hunt for information shows the fervor with which many college students are searching for this information—a conclusion that is at odds with past scholarly beliefs. Second, the data contradict past studies suggesting that reliance on active information-seeking efforts in such cases is exceedingly rare. Unfortunately, we know almost nothing outside of this study about the role of third parties in the accumulation of sexual health information, we do not know the particular communication strategies used with these sources, and we do not have details about the relative weight given to this information over that derived from the partners themselves. To our knowledge, these data are the first to suggest an important role for third parties in this context. However, because we originally did not expect that they would play such a role, we gathered very limited data on the issue. Clearly, additional inquiry is needed. If these findings are replicated, then public health campaigns must account for the role of these third parties in the information exchange—something they currently do not do.

The third contribution worth noting relies on a comparison of two data points in the investigation. The first is that a mere 5% of the subsample believed that a search for information about their partner's sexual health status would reveal that she or he had an STI. In stark contrast is the second data point—government sources (Centers for Disease Control and Prevention, 2002) that estimate, rightly or wrongly, that 40% of college students are infected with HPV (not to mention infection rates for other STIs). Regardless of the exact infection rate data, the reality is that a far greater percentage of our sample likely had an infected romantic partner than believed so. We reach a troubling conclusion when we combine evidence that our participants were voracious information seekers with the knowledge that only 5% perceived their partner to be infected. Unlike what current scholarly belief indicates, the participants' perception was not a function of putting their head in the sand, so to speak, but, somewhat more dangerously, was based on considerable efforts at information seeking. As a result, their confidence in the validity of their conclusion is high, as our data show.

So what explains their mistaken perception? Three candidate explanations emerge. First, it could be that the information they are receiving is incomplete—their partner lied and/or the third-party sources were unaware of the STI. Past studies have certainly shown the former possibility to be a real one (e.g., Williams et al., 1992). Second, the partner may be unaware of his or her own infection. For example, we know that some infections remain undetected for a prolonged period. Finally, individuals may be intentionally misperceiving the information they receive so that they can reach the conclusion that their partner is "safe." A vast literature shows the processing biases in which people in close relationships engage (e.g., for review, see Baldwin, 2005). Each of these possibilities offers unique challenges to public health professionals interested in decreasing the incidence of STIs. However, regardless of the explanation, we are left with a troubling current state in which individuals seem to be confident in their assessment of their partner's sexual health—and have reached that state based on their information-seeking efforts—but are likely to be holding knowledge that is critically flawed.

Of course, it is important to keep in mind the limitations of this study. It is based on self-report measures, a notoriously biased method of assessment for issues with salient social desirability pressures (see Wiederman & Whitley, 2002), and reflects the behavior of only 41 participants. Still, the data certainly have their strengths (e.g., ongoing relationships, and asking about recent behaviors) and do suggest the need to more carefully examine past conclusions about the information-seeking landscape in early stages of relational development surrounding the partner's sexual health.

FUTURE DIRECTIONS

Implied in almost all studies of relationship initiation is that individuals gather information about their partner. How else would they know anything about the person, decide that it is a relationship worth pursuing, or decide on the sorts of relational behaviors in which they engage? Curiously, though, very few studies have focused on the information-seeking strategies that individuals use in these early stages of relationship development. As we have seen in this chapter, the literature addresses information-seeking behavior in initial interactions and in developed relationships. The evidence we have offers a glimpse into the ways that people gather this important information in relationship beginnings. Yet there are still significant holes to fill.

The avenues available for future inquiry in this area are vast. We will highlight three substantive areas in particular: the role of emotion, the influence of efficacy, and the impact of technology. In addition, the area poses methodological challenges that have not yet been adequately met. We will begin with a brief discussion of the substantive areas where this literature could easily grow.

Role of Emotion

We know that relationship beginnings are emotionally laden times, yet, to our knowledge, there are no studies of the ways in which these emotions impact the information-seeking process during that time. Research at the general level has increasingly recognized the ways in which affect influences both information processing and seeking in important ways. For example, the affect-as-information model (for review, see Schwarz, 2000) argues that affective states impact individuals' cognitive processing when the emotion is deemed relevant to the task at hand. Moreover, emotions are characterized by a complex system of brain region activities that dramatically impact information processing (for a review, see Lane & Nadel, 2000). Relatively few studies, however, have applied this model to information *seeking* as opposed to *processing*. One exception is Isbell, Burns, and Haar (2005), who found that participants in the sad induction condition sought out very different types of information about a target than their counterparts in the happy induction group.

One could surmise that the elation of relationship beginnings encourages the pursuit of information that reifies the rose-colored perception of the partner while simultaneously discouraging the search for threatening information. Indeed, Isbell, Burns, and James (as cited in Gasper & Isbell, 2007) found that happy moods encouraged efforts to seek confirmatory information. On the other hand, these same positive emotions may also lead us to drop the protective mechanisms that shield us from disappointment. For example, researchers have found that we often engage in pessimistic forecasting as a way to "brace for loss" rather than being sideswiped by a wholly unexpected negative blow (e.g., Shepperd, Findley-Klein, Kwavnick, Walker, & Perez, 2000). How might the emotional wave of relationship beginnings impact this protective tendency to "brace for loss" and its functional impact on coping? And which of these frameworks offers the most predictive accuracy in the context of information seeking during this stage of relationship development?

Influence of Efficacy

Another front that is rich for the attention of scholars interested in information seeking during relationship beginnings is the literature on efficacy. The evidence for the role of efficacy in decisions is extensive (for review, see Bandura, 1997), and we know that information seeking is impacted in important ways by efficacy assessments (see Afifi & Weiner, 2004). Yet, with the exception of research on safe-sex decisions (e.g., Bandura, 1992), there is very little attention to efficacy as an important predictor of day-to-day relational behavior. The earlier-discussed TMIM framework offers promise as a guiding framework for scholars hoping to better understand the ways in which efficacy perceptions impact information-seeking and -giving decisions in relationship beginnings. The theory envisions a transactional process between information seeker and provider that is shaped, for both actors, by assessments of efficacy. The specific type of efficacy that may be of most direct relevance to information seeking in relationship beginnings may be communication efficacy—the perceived ability to competently seek information from the target (Afifi & Weiner, 2004). To date, two studies have tested the role of communication efficacy in romantic relationships. The first examined its utility as a predictor of general information seeking from a partner (Afifi et al., 2004), and the second narrowed the focus to information seeking about the partner's sexual health (Afifi & Weiner, 2006). In both cases, communication efficacy emerged as a significant predictor of the directness with which individuals sought information from their partners. Although neither study targeted relationship beginnings, the data support the utility of this type of efficacy as an influence on information-seeking decisions. Future investigations utilizing the framework could help reveal the ways in which both relational partners manage the tricky waters of relationship beginnings while either cuffed or freed by efficacy perceptions that ultimately control the nature of the information exchanges.

We can find some correlates to this notion in other literatures. For example, research on individual differences in rejection sensitivity has shown that individuals who are especially fearful of rejection "behave in ways that elicit rejection from their dating partners" (Downey, Freitas, Michaelis, & Khouri, 1998, p. 545). Not surprisingly, such fears also erode self-efficacy perceptions over time (Ayduk et al., 2000), making individuals more doubtful of their ability to succeed in relationships or first date requests. So, although efficacy has not received much attention in either the literature on relational beginnings or the literature on information seeking, it appears to be a construct that holds considerable promise for future scholars interested in examining the intersection of these areas.

Impact of Technology

A recent method of information seeking in relationship beginnings that has received increasing scholarly attention is the reliance on social networking sites like Facebook and MySpace. Social networking sites are web-based profiles that individuals can easily create to serve as reflections of themselves to others (boyd & Ellison, 2007). The explosion in the creation of these profiles is astounding. In 2005, only one year after its launch, 85% of college students had initiated a profile on Facebook, with 60% logging in *daily* (Arrington, 2005).

Investigations into the content of profiles helps explain their widespread use. Changes that the site made to access restrictions continued the rapid diffusion of the site. The site reports that the majority of its users are now outside the college population, but that it still maintains near saturation of that latter group (http:/www.facebook.com/press/info.php?statistics). It also reports "more than 64 million active users" and an "average of 250,000 new registrations per day since January of 2007" (http://www.facebook.com/press/info.php?statistics). Its reach is global and its use is heavy — recent estimates suggest that the site receives more than 2 billion page views per day (http://www.facebook.com/press/info.php?statistics). Perhaps most importantly, the profiles typically included a litany of personal information: 91% included at least one photographic image of themselves, 63% identified their relational status (e.g., single or dating), 51% revealed their address, and 40% listed a phone number. In addition, most profiles disclosed such information as their hometown; their favorite movies, books, and music; their political views; and their interests. Other information that can be gleaned from the profiles includes their major, the classes in which they are currently enrolled, the groups to which they belong, and the friends they have (Ellison et al., 2007).

Given this sort of access to information, it should come as no surprise that "check[ing] out a facebook profile of someone I met socially" was the second most likely reason given for using Facebook, after "keep[ing] in touch with an old friend" (Lampe, Ellison, & Steinfield, 2006). Moreover, "get[ing] information about people that live in my dorm, fraternity, or sorority" and "get[ing] information about people in my classes" were the third and fourth most likely reasons, respectively— all reasons that were rated above the midpoint of the likelihood scale. In other words, millions of students are using social networking sites daily to gather information that was otherwise restricted to face-to-face interpersonal channels (see also Ellison et al., 2007). This sort of preinteraction information-gathering system has clear implications for traditional information-seeking efforts during relationship beginnings. To adequately capture the process of information seeking early in relationships, it is critical that future empirical studies recognize the role played by social network sites in this process.

In sum, the domain of interest for this chapter is ripe for research pursuits. It involves the scholarly holy grail: a woefully understudied phenomenon that involves a behavior that has otherwise been shown to be both frequent and important (i.e., information seeking) in a context that is central to people's lives and motivations (i.e., relationship development). In this chapter we have summarized existing typologies that should guide future efforts, have identified heuristic theoretical frameworks that provide causal explanations for the process, and have noted variables that offer special promise for advancing knowledge.

REFERENCES

Abbey, A. (1987). Misperceptions of friendly behavior as sexual interest: A survey of naturally occurring instances. *Psychology of Women Quarterly, 11*, 173–194.

Abbey, A., McAuslan, P., & Ross, L. T. (1998). Sexual assault perpetration by college men: The role of alcohol, misperception of sexual intent, and sexual beliefs and experiences. *Journal of Social and Clinical Psychology, 17*, 167–195.

Academy for Educational Development. (2000, May). *Sexually transmitted diseases: An overview* (Report prepared by the Center for Community-Based Health Strategies). Washington, DC: Author.

Afifi, W. A. (1999). Harming the ones we love: Relational attachment and perceived consequences as predictors of safe-sex behavior. *Journal of Sex Research, 36*, 198–206.

Afifi, W. A., Dillow, M., & Morse, C. (2004). Seeking information in relational contexts: A test of the theory of motivated information management. *Personal Relationships, 11*, 429–450.

Afifi, W. A., & Johnson, M. L. (1999). The use and interpretation of affection displays in a public setting: Relationship and sex differences. *Journal of Social and Personal Relationships, 16*, 9–38.

Afifi, W. A., & Weiner, J. L. (2004). Toward a theory of motivated information management. *Communication Theory, 14*, 167–190.

Afifi, W. A., & Weiner, J. L. (2006). Seeking information about sexual health: Applying the theory of motivated information management. *Human Communication Research, 32*, 35–57.

Arrington, M. (2005). *85% of college students use Facebook*. Retrieved March 3, 2006, from http://www.techcrunch.com/2005/09/07/85-of-college-students-use-facebook/

Ayduk, O., Mendoza-Denton, R., Mischel, W., Downey, G., Peake, P. K., & Rodriguez, M. (2000). Regulating the interpersonal self: Strategic self-regulation for coping with rejection sensitivity. *Journal of Personality and Social Psychology, 79*, 776–792.

Baldwin, M. W. (Ed.). (2005). *Interpersonal cognition*. New York: Guilford.

Bandura, A. (1992). A social cognitive approach to the exercise of control over AIDS infection. In R. J. DiClemente (Ed.), *Adolescents and AIDS: A generation in jeopardy* (pp. 89–116). Newbury Park, CA: Sage.

Bandura, A. (1997). *Self-efficacy: The exercise of control*. New York: Freeman.

Baumeister, R. F., Catanese, K. R., & Vohs, K. D. (2001). Is there a gender difference in strength of sex drive? Theoretical views, conceptual distinctions, and a review of relevant evidence. *Personality and Social Psychology Review, 5*, 242–273.

Baxter, L. A., & Wilmot, W. W. (1984). "Secret tests": Social strategies for acquiring information about the state of the relationship. *Human Communication Research, 2*, 171–201.

Baxter, L. A., & Wilmot, W. W. (1985). Taboo topics in close relationships. *Journal of Social and Personal Relationships, 2*, 253–269.

Bell, R. A., & Buerkel-Rothfuss, N. L. (1990). S(he) loves me, s(he) loves me not: Predictors of relational information-seeking in courtship and beyond. *Communication Quarterly, 38*, 64–82.

Berger, C. R. (1979). Beyond initial interaction: Uncertainty, understanding, and the development of interpersonal relationships. In H. Giles & R. N. St. Clair (Eds.), *Language and social psychology* (pp. 122–144). Oxford: Basil Blackwell.

Berger, C. R., & Bradac, J. J. (1982). *Language and social knowledge: Uncertainty in interpersonal relations*. London: Edward Arnold.

Berger, C. R., & Calabrese, R. J. (1975). Some explorations in initial interactions and beyond: Toward a developmental theory of interpersonal communication. *Human Communication Research, 1*, 99–112.

Berger, C. R., & Douglas, W. (1981). Studies in interpersonal epistemology III: Anticipated interaction, self-monitoring, and observational context selection. *Communication Monographs, 48*, 183–196.

Berger, C. R., & Kellermann, K. (1983). To ask or not to ask: Is that a question? In R. N. Bostrom (Ed.), *Communication Yearbook 7* (pp. 342–368). Newbury Park, CA: Sage.

Berger, C. R., & Kellermann, K. (1994). Acquiring social information. In J. A. Daly & J. M. Wiemann (Eds.), *Strategic interpersonal communication* (pp. 1–32). Hillsdale, NJ: Lawrence Erlbaum.

Berger, C. R., & Perkins, J. W. (1978). Studies in interpersonal epistemology 1: Situational attributes in observational context selection. In B. D. Ruben (Ed.), *Communication Yearbook 2* (pp. 171–184). New Brunswick, NJ: Transaction Press.

boyd, d. m., & Ellison, N. B. (2007). Social networking sites: Definition, history, and scholarship. *Journal of Computer-Mediated Communication, 13,* 210–230.

Burgoon, J. K. (1985). Nonverbal signals. In M. L. Knapp & G. R. Miller (Eds.), *Handbook of interpersonal communication* (pp. 344–390). Beverly Hills, CA: Sage.

Centers for Disease Control and Prevention. (2002, September). *Sexually transmitted diseases surveillance 2001* (Report prepared by the Division of STD Prevention). Washington, DC: Author.

Cleary, J., Barhman, R., MacCormack, T., & Herold, E. (2002). Discussing sexual health with a partner: A qualitative study with young women. *Canadian Journal of Human Sexuality, 11,* 117–132.

Cline, R. J. W., Freeman, K. E., & Johnson, S. J. (1990). Talk among sexual partners about AIDS: Factors differentiating those who talk from those who do not. *Communication Research, 17,* 792–808.

Cline, R. J. W., Johnson, S. J., & Freeman, K. E. (1992). Talk among sexual partners about AIDS: Interpersonal communication for risk reduction or risk enhancement? *Health Communication, 4,* 39–56.

Coleman, L. M., & Ingham, R. (1999). Exploring young people's difficulties in talking about contraception: How can we encourage discussion between partners? *Health Education Research, 14,* 741–750.

Douglas, W. (1987). Affinity testing in initial interactions. *Journal of Social and Personal Relationships, 4,* 3–15.

Douglas, W. (1994). The acquaintanceship process: An examination of uncertainty, information seeking, and social attraction during initial conversation. *Communication Research, 21,* 154–176.

Downey, G., Freitas, A. L., Michaelis, B., & Khouri, H. (1998). The self-fulfilling prophecy in close relationships: Rejection sensitivity and rejection by romantic partners. *Journal of Personality and Social Psychology, 75,* 545–560.

Edgar, T., Freimuth, V. S., Hammond, S. L., McDonald, D. A., & Fink, E. L. (1992). Strategic sexual communication: Condom use resistance and response. *Health Communication, 4,* 83–104.

Egland, K. L., Spitzberg, B. H., & Zormeier, M. M. (1996). Flirtation and conversational competence in cross-sex platonic and romantic relationships. *Communication Reports, 9,* 105–117.

Ellison, N. B., Steinfield, C., & Lampe, C. (2007). The benefits of Facebook "friends;" Social capital and college students' use of onling social networking sites. *Journal of Computer-Mediated Communication, 12,* 1143–1168.

Forgas, J. P. (2001). Affect, cognition, and interpersonal behavior: The mediating role of processing strategies. In J. P. Forgas (Ed.), *Handbook of affect and social cognition* (pp. 293–318). Mahwah, NJ: Lawrence Erlbaum.

Gasper, K., & Isbell, L. M. (2007). Feeling, searching, and preparing: How affective states alter information seeking. In Vohs, K. D., Baumeister, R. F., & Loewenstein, G. *Do emotions help or hurt decision making? A Hedgefoxian perspective* (pp. 93–116). New York: Russel Sage Foundation Press.

Gouldner, A. W. (1960). The norm of reciprocity: A preliminary statement. *American Sociological Review, 25,* 161–178.

Gross, R., & Acquisti, A. (2005). Information revelation and privacy in online social networks. *Proceedings of the 2005 ACM Workshop on Privacy in the Electronic Society, '05,* 71–80.

Henningsen, D. D. (2004). Flirting with meaning: An examination of miscommunication in flirting interactions. *Sex Roles, 50,* 481–489.

Holton, B., & Pyszcynski, T. (1989). Biased information search in the interpersonal domain. *Personality and Social Psychology Bulletin, 15,* 42–51.

Isbell, L. M., Burns, K. C., & Haar, T. (2005). The role of affect on the search for global and specific target information. *Social Cognition, 23,* 529–552.

Kahneman, D. (2003). A perspective on judgment and choice: Mapping bounded rationality. *American Psychologist, 58,* 697–720.

Kellermann, K. A., & Berger, C. R. (1984). Affect and the acquisition of social information: Sit back, relax, and tell me about yourself. In R. N. Bostrom (Ed.), *Communication yearbook 8* (pp. 412–445). Newbury Park, CA: Sage.

Knobloch, L. K. (2006). Relational uncertainty and message production within courtship. *Human Communication Research, 32,* 244–273.

Knobloch, L. K., & Solomon, D. H. (2002). Information seeking beyond initial interactions: Negotiating relational uncertainty within close relationships. *Human Communication Research, 28,* 243–257.

Lampe, C., Ellison, N., & Steinfield, C. (2006). A Face(book) in the crowd: Social searching vs. social browsing. *Proceedings of the Conference on Computer Supported Cooperative Work, '06,* 167–170.

Lane, R. D., & Nadel, L. (Eds.) (2000). *Cognitive neuroscience of emotion.* Oxford: Oxford University Press.

Levesque, M. J., Nave, C. S., & Lowe, C. A. (2006). Toward an understanding of gender differences in inferring sexual interest. *Psychology of Women Quarterly, 30,* 150–158.

Murray, S. L. (1999). The quest for conviction: Motivated cognition in romantic relationships. *Psychological Inquiry,* 10, 23–34.

Noar, S. M., Zimmerman, R. S., & Atwood, K. A. (2004). Safer sex and sexually transmitted infections from a relationship perspective. In J. H. Harvey, A. Wenzel, & S. Sprecher (Eds.), *The handbook of sexuality in close relationships* (pp. 519–544). Mahwah, NJ: Lawrence Erlbaum.

Parks, M. R., & Adelman, M. B. (1983). Communication networks and the development of romantic relationships: An expansion of uncertainty reduction theory. *Human Communication Research, 10,* 55–80.

Petronio, S. (2002). *Boundaries of privacy: Dialectics of disclosure.* Albany: State University of New York Press.

Planalp, S., & Honeycutt, J. M. (1985). Events that increase uncertainty in personal relationships. *Human Communication Research, 11,* 593–604.

Planalp, S., Rutherford, D. K., & Honeycutt, J. M. (1988). Events that increase uncertainty in personal relationships II: Replication and extension. *Human Communication Research, 14,* 516–547.

Schwarz, N. (2000). Emotion, cognition, and decision making. *Cognition & Emotion, 14,* 433–440.

Shepperd, J. A., Findley-Klein, C., Kwavnick, K. D., Walker, D., & Perez, S. (2000). Bracing for loss. *Journal of Personality and Social Psychology, 78,* 620–634.

Shotland, R. L. (1992). A theory of the causes of courtship rape: Part 2. *Journal of Social Issues, 48,* 127–143.

Shotland, R. L., & Craig, J. M. (1988). Can men and women differentiate between friendly and sexually interested behavior? *Social Psychology Quarterly, 51,* 66–73.

Simpson, J. A., Gangestad, S. W., & Biek, M. (1993). Personality and nonverbal social behavior: An ethological perspective of relationship initiation. *Journal of Experimental Social Psychology, 29,* 434–461.

Sunnafrank, M. (1990). Predicted outcome value and uncertainty reduction theories: A test of competing perspectives. *Human Communication Research, 17,* 76–103.

Vorauer, J. D., & Ratner, R. K. (1996). Who's going to make the first move? Pluralistic ignorance as an impediment to relationship formation. *Journal of Social and Personal Relationships, 13,* 483–506.

Wiederman, M. W., & Whitley, B. E., Jr. (Eds.). (2002). *Handbook for conducting research on human sexuality.* Mahwah, NJ: Lawrence Erlbaum.

Williams, S. S., Kimble, D. L., Covell, N. H., Weiss, L. H., Newton, K. J., Fisher, J. D., & Fisher, W. A. (1992). College students use implicit personality theory instead of safer sex. *Journal of Applied Social Psychology, 22,* 921–933.

Wyer, R. S., Jr., & Gruenfeld, D. H. (1995). Information processing in interpersonal communication. In D. E. Hewes (Ed.), *The cognitive bases of interpersonal communication* (pp. 7–50). Hillsdale, NJ: Lawrence Erlbaum.

8

Self-Disclosure and Starting a Close Relationship

VALERIAN J. DERLEGA, BARBARA A. WINSTEAD, and KATHRYN GREENE

The self-disclosure transaction provides an important context in which decisions are made in beginning a relationship with a new acquaintance. People use "self-disclosure" (including what, when, and how thoughts and feelings are disclosed or not disclosed) as well as reactions by the disclosure recipient and the initial discloser to collect information about a prospective partner and to make forecasts about the possibility for a future relationship. It is also used by new acquaintances to infer how much they like and trust one another and whether they might identify themselves as friends or as an intimate couple.

In this chapter we examine various topics about self-disclosure and starting a relationship. We examine how background factors (e.g., culture, personality, and gender) and communication medium (e.g., face-to-face versus Internet communication) influence self-disclosure at the start of a relationship. We show how self-disclosure is incorporated into conversations to intensify or restrict intimacy and closeness between new acquaintances. We describe how the reactions of the disclosure recipient *and* the discloser to self-disclosure input assist new acquaintances to assess feelings of intimacy for one another and whether or not to seek a closer relationship. We also illustrate how a relationship-building exercise incorporating self-disclosure may increase feelings of closeness between new acquaintances. First, let us define self-disclosure and review influential, early approaches about the role of self-disclosure at the start of a relationship.

WHAT IS SELF-DISCLOSURE?

People may loosely define *self-disclosure* as anything intentional or unintentional that informs us about what someone is like. However, theory and research on self-disclosure—and this chapter—focus on self-disclosure as a deliberate or voluntary activity whereby people reveal information, thoughts, and feelings about themselves to at least one other person during an interaction (Greene, Derlega, & Mathews, 2006). There are a number of dimensions of self-disclosure that should be considered (Archer, 1980; Derlega & Grzelak, 1979; Dindia, 1998; Rosenfeld, 1979). Although self-disclosure is usually studied as a *verbal* activity (e.g., "I think …" or "I feel …"), it may also refer to *nonverbal* messages that are intended to communicate information (e.g., indicating relationship commitment by wearing a wedding ring or wearing a tattoo on one's arm that says, "I love Maisie"). Self-disclosure is a *transaction* that occurs between two or more persons in the roles of "discloser" and "disclosure recipient" or "listener" at cognitive, emotional, and behavioral levels. What, when, and how self-disclosure occurs on one occasion or over time influence and are influenced by the interaction and/or the relationship that unfolds between the participants (Bavelas, Coates, & Johnson, 2000; Dindia, 1998; Greene et al., 2006; Pearce & Sharp, 1973).

There are other aspects of disclosure or nondisclosure that may influence how a close relationship begins, including *privacy regulation* (how much control the discloser and the disclosure recipient have over the process of what is said and heard, as well as who owns the information and how "it" will be protected; Altman, Vinsel, & Brown, 1981; Derlega & Chaikin, 1977; Petronio, 1991, 2002), *truthfulness* (the extent to which the discloser conveys information that he or she subjectively perceives to be about the "true" or "authentic self"), *informativeness* (how much information is conveyed from the discloser's and the disclosure recipient's behavior, contributing to attributions about the reasons underlying each person's behavior), and *effectiveness* (how successful the discloser *and* the disclosure recipient are in accomplishing important goals via their behaviors, e.g., developing a closer relationship or keeping a social distance from the other person).

Self-disclosure varies in *content*. It may focus on facts about one's self (*descriptive disclosures* such as "I listen to talk radio programs") or subjective opinions and feelings (*evaluative disclosures* such as "I enjoyed Dan Brown's book, *The Da Vinci Code*, but I felt let down by the movie"; Berg & Archer, 1982; Morton, 1976, 1978). The content of disclosure may also focus entirely on the self (*personal disclosure* such as "I feel good about winning the lottery") or on one's relationship and/or interactions with others (*relational self-disclosure* such as "I enjoyed the time I spent with you this weekend"; Baxter, 1987; Waring, 1987).

Self-disclosure may be perceived as *personalistic* (i.e., uniquely intended for a recipient) or *nonpersonalistic* (i.e., intended for anyone) (Taylor, Gould, & Brounstein, 1981). The behavior of the disclosure recipient and/or the discloser may also vary in *responsiveness*, reflecting how much each person's reactions are perceived as understanding, validating, and caring (Reis & Patrick, 1996; Reis & Shaver, 1988). Judgments about responsiveness, based on perceptions about how the disclosure recipient and the discloser responded during and across disclosure episodes, are used to infer intimacy in an interaction and in a relationship (Laurenceau, Barrett, & Pietromonaco, 1998).

SELF-DISCLOSURE AT THE START OF A RELATIONSHIP: HISTORICALLY IMPORTANT APPROACHES

Let us consider historically important theories and research about the role of self-disclosure at the start of a close relationship, including social penetration theory (Altman & Taylor, 1973), the "clicking model" (Berg & Clark, 1986), and dialectical and privacy models (Altman et al., 1981; Petronio, 2002). Each approach proposes a somewhat different role for self-disclosure in beginning a relationship.

Social Penetration Theory

Social penetration theory (proposed by Irwin Altman and Dalmas Taylor in 1973) provided an important, early perspective about self-disclosure and the development of a close relationship. According to this theory, at the start of a relationship, prospective partners may be limited to fairly stereotyped and superficial behaviors. But as a relationship progresses, individuals are predicted to increase the range of activities they share with one another, including disclosing more personal information to one another. Prospective partners also compose a mental picture of one another based on positive and negative experiences with the current partner and their value in comparison to prior relationship experiences. If this picture is favorable, based on a favorable benefit–cost ratio from previous interactions and based on a favorable forecast for the future, then the budding relationship progresses. If this picture is unfavorable, then the budding relationship stops or slows down in development (Altman & Taylor, 1973, pp. 46–47). Although self-disclosure is a behavioral component of the social penetration process, *social penetration* includes *any* behavior that is interpersonal—verbal (e.g., self-disclosure), nonverbal (e.g., frowns, smiling, handshakes, hugs, and kissing), or environmental (e.g., moving chairs to sit closer to or farther away from one another)—and that affects relationship development.

Close relationships develop in variable ways. But whatever the specific pattern, social penetration theory gives a distinctive emphasis to self-disclosing behaviors because a relationship begins and is maintained by the "the gradual overlapping and exploration of their mutual selves by parties to a relationship" (Altman & Taylor, 1973, p. 15). Social penetration theory identified several dimensions of self-disclosure that are associated with the development of a close relationship: how many different topics are disclosed (topic breadth), how much information is disclosed about a particular topic (breadth frequency), how much time is spent talking about a particular topic (topic time), and how intimate the level of disclosure is (topic depth).

Social penetration theory generates a number of predictions about the pattern of self-disclosure that may occur as a relationship progresses: At each stage of relationship development, there is a distinctive "wedge-shaped pattern" to disclosure associated with greater disclosure at superficial than at intimate levels, there is a gradual increase in disclosure from superficial to intimate levels of exchange as a relationship develops, there is a gradual widening of information being exchanged at a particular level of intimacy as a relationship develops, and there is a slowing down of self-disclosure (in the manner of a negatively accelerated curve) as it moves into more intimate topic areas. Although self-disclosure is predicted to be generally linear as a relationship develops, there are also certain topics that may be identified unilaterally or mutually as off-limits to talk about, including family secrets and topics that are perceived as too personal (see Baxter & Wilmot, 1985, who distinguished between taboo and disclosive topics).

An early study by Taylor (1968) illustrates how self-disclosure progresses during the early stages of a relationship—as predicted by social penetration theory. College students, who were originally strangers, were assigned as dormitory roommates at the beginning of an academic semester. They were administered self-disclosure questionnaires several times during the semester to measure how much information the roommates had shared with one another. Results indicated that breadth of disclosure at various levels of intimacy increased over the semester for the roommates. Breadth of disclosure also occurred at a higher level and at a faster rate for superficial than for more intimate topics, supporting the notion that people may be cautious in revealing personal information at the beginning of a relationship. These results are also consistent with the wedge-shaped pattern predicted by social penetration theory for disclosure at different stages in a relationship: Breadth of disclosure was always greater at superficial than at more intimate levels of disclosure regardless of how long the college roommates knew one another.

It is interesting to note a renaissance of interest in social penetration theory in studying relationships that begin on the Internet. For instance, based in part on social penetration theory, Parks and Floyd (1996) constructed straightforward measures of social communications and relationship development on the Internet. Two measures overlap with indices of breadth (e.g., "Our communication is limited to just a few specific topics") and depth (e.g., "I usually tell this person exactly how I feel") of self-disclosure. Other measures constructed by Parks and Floyd focus on relationship commitment (e.g., "The two of us depend on each other"), code change (e.g., "We have special nicknames that we just use with each other"), predictability (e.g., "I do not know this person very well"), commitment (e.g., "The relationship is a big part of who I am"), and network covergence (e.g., "We have overlapping social circles on the Net"). Parks and Floyd found that people reported "moderate to high levels of breadth and depth" (p. 88) in relationships started online. Note, though, that the majority of the participants in Parks and Floyd's study had been in an online relationship for an average of 9.62 months when they completed the survey. Parks and Floyd did not examine breadth and depth of disclosure when participants first met online.

Using a version of the online questionnaire devised by Parks and Floyd (1996), Chan and Cheng (2004) found that online communications tend to increase gradually in breadth and depth of disclosure over the length of time in an online relationship—consistent with social penetration theory's predictions. Yum and Hara (2005) also reported that increases in breadth and depth of self-disclosure in Internet communications were associated with increased feelings of liking, love, and interdependence with one's partner, based on a survey of Japanese, American, and South Korean Internet users. These results are consistent with social penetration's prediction that changes in self-disclosure are associated with the development of a close relationship.

The Clicking Model

Social penetration theory predicts that relationship development is a continuous and usually a gradual process. Self-disclosure in social interactions moves from superficial to more personal levels (i.e., increases in topic depth) and the partners divulge information about a wider range of topics (i.e., increases in topic breadth) as a relationship progresses. In contrast, John Berg and Margaret Clark (1986) proposed a "clicking model" of relationship development, suggesting that relatively high levels of self-disclosure and the development of close relationships may occur quickly rather than gradually over time. The clicking model assumes that relationship partners make an assessment rather soon after meeting someone that the other person fits (or may fit) the prototype for a friend or intimate dating partner. In turn, these rapid assessments about the "new relationship" fitting the picture of a "close relationship" lead to an acceleration of intimacy-linked behaviors—including greater breadth and depth of self-disclosure, spending lots of time in social activities together, accommodation to one another's needs, and identifying each other as a "partner" or "close friend."

Several studies in the literature on self-disclosure and close relationships support the clicking model (Berg, 1984; Berg & McQuinn, 1986; Hays, 1984, 1985). For instance, Hays (1985) asked undergraduate students to complete questionnaires every 3 weeks about their interactions with two persons of the same sex "whom they did not know before the school term began and with whom they thought they 'might become good friends as the school year progress[es]'" (p. 911). Ratings were obtained on a variety of behaviors, including the breadth and depth of communication (i.e., self-disclosure), companionship, affection, and consideration. Partners who later became "friends" versus "not friends" differed in the number of these behaviors they engaged in during the length of the study, all of which appeared quickly. At the time of the first assessment, during the third week of the semester, individuals who at the end of the semester described themselves as close rather than not close were more likely to engage in a variety of behaviors—at superficial, casual, and intimate levels—associated with communication, companionship, consideration, and affection. Partners who reported being "friends" by the end of the semester also increased their interaction rates on most of the behavioral measures from the third to the ninth week of the study; in fact, partners reached a peak in intimate communications at 9 weeks.

Berg and Clark's (1986) clicking model is supported by recent research. For instance, Sunnafrank and Ramirez (2004) found that college classmates make decisions about "how positive a future relationship with a new acquaintance would be" (p. 370) after talking with someone for just 3 to 10 minutes. These short, initial impressions are, in turn, associated with how frequently the classmates communicate with one another as well as with how close their relationship becomes after 9 weeks have elapsed. This research is based on predicted outcome value theory (POVT; Sunnafrank, 1986, 1988; Sunnafrank & Ramirez, 2004). This theory, like the clicking model, predicts that new acquaintances will organize their interactions (including self-disclosure) to promote the development of a close relationship with someone with whom they expect positive outcomes in the future.

Dialectical and Privacy Perspectives about Self-Disclosure at the Beginning of a Relationship

Self-disclosure in the development of a close relationship may accelerate quickly, as the clicking model argues. But it is also not inevitable that self-disclosure and close relationships will evolve or progress in a linear fashion. Altman and his colleagues (Altman et al., 1981) elaborated on the notion that there may be different patterns of self-disclosure that occur between relationship partners as they negotiate how accessible (open) or closed they decide to be with one another. Relationship partners may "ebb and flow" between the disclosure of superficial versus personal information; partners may not move into more personal areas of disclosure with one another, and may simply exchange information at superficial or maybe moderately personal levels of disclosure; or partners may decide to restrict disclosure to certain topic areas and maintain other topic areas as off-limits. Hence, Altman's theory of privacy regulation emphasizes that at every stage in a relationship's growth, there are dialectical or oppositional forces that lead to getting close to or keeping a distance from the other person. For instance, there may be pushes for self-disclosure (e.g., nurturing a friendship, gaining social support, and acquiring a confidant). But there are also pulls against self-disclosure (e.g., concerns about being rejected, being ridiculed, hurting someone else's feelings, or burdening someone with sharing one's emotional problems).

Altman (Altman et al., 1981) assumed that partners in a relationship will have to balance the oppositional tendencies to be open versus closed with one another. But there will also be changes in frequency, amplitude, relative duration, and regularity of occurrence of these cyclical tendencies toward openness and closedness based on the partners' needs, situational requirements, and the nature of each relationship. There may also be an intrinsic opposition between openness and closedness: The more open that partners are with one another (associated with concerns about being rejected or losing independence), the more they may be drawn in the opposite direction to be more closed with one another.

There is considerable support for the notion of the openness–closedness contradiction as an important issue as couples start and manage their relationships. For instance, Baxter and Erbert (1999) found that many romantic couples retrospectively report that dealing with contradictory pressures to be open versus closed was an important consideration at a number of "turning points" in their relationship, including when they were getting to know one another. The dialectical notion of openness and closedness in self-disclosure is also consistent with research documenting the occurrence of cycling in self-disclosure when conversations between new acquaintances are recorded and coded. Vanlear (1991; also see Vanlear, 1998) coded conversations between new acquaintances who met once a week to talk with one another for 30 minutes over a 4-week period. Although conversations were more open over time (indicating a linear trend), there were also cyclical patterns of openness and closedness (reflecting changes in the personalness of self-disclosure) within and across conversations. The new acquaintances in Vanlear's (1991) research also tended to match one another in the timing and frequency of their cycles of openness and closedness.

The notion of "privacy boundaries" is another component in Altman's (1975, 1977; Altman et al., 1981) theory of privacy regulation, and it illustrates how prospective partners regulate privacy and openness–closedness at the beginning of a relationship. For instance, when partners disclose or do not disclose, they are adjusting a self or personal boundary regulating how open or closed they want to be with the other person (Altman, 1977; also see Derlega & Chaikin, 1977). There is also a collective boundary that surrounds the information that relationship partners reveal to one another (Petronio, 2002). Partners may share similar perceptions of a collective boundary within which the information is safe and protected and both may feel secure that the information will not be leaked to unwanted third parties. Prospective partners' willingness to share co-ownership and mutual responsibility for protecting and managing this collective boundary is an important milestone in transitioning from being strangers or new acquaintances to being friends and/or romantic partners (Levinger & Snoek, 1972; Petronio, 2002).

The dialectical and privacy perspective pioneered by Altman et al. (1981) has been important and influential in theory and research on relationship development (see Margulis, 2003, for a recent critique). It has contributed to a number of dialectical models that examine basic contradictions (including openness–closedness) that partners experience in starting and maintaining a relationship (e.g., Baxter, 1990, 2004; Montgomery & Baxter, 1998; Petronio, 2002). It has encouraged researchers to consider how and why self-disclosure may cycle up and down over time, and how and why decisions are made in a new relationship about what thoughts and feelings to disclose versus not to disclose (Afifi & Guerrero, 2000; Knobloch & Carpenter-Theune, 2004). The notion of boundaries in Altman's (1975, 1977) theory of privacy has also proved useful in conceptualizing how people make adjustments in disclosure to a new acquaintance (based on regulating the self boundary) and in understanding how individuals come to identify themselves as a "couple" as they accept "shared ownership" over mutually disclosed information (based on mutually regulating the collective boundary; Petronio, 2002).

Comments on Social Penetration, Clicking, and Dialectical Privacy Theories

Although levels of self-disclosure are often associated with the status of a close relationship, social penetration, clicking, and dialectical-privacy theories do not assume that changes in self-disclosure per se are equivalent to changes in the development of a relationship. Instead, self-disclosure input, along with the initial discloser's and the disclosure recipient's reactions, is expected to provide a context for new acquaintances to get to know one another, to make assessments about the future of a possible relationship, to infer how they feel about one another, and to decide whether or not they want to construct a closer relationship. Partners who begin to identify as friends or intimate partners have other ways besides self-disclosure to demonstrate closeness, including sharing time together, doing favors for one another, and being companions (e.g., Berg, 1984; Hays, 1984, 1985). Especially in social penetration and dialectical-privacy theories, it is also expected that partners will avoid talking about certain topics or keep certain secrets from one another to maintain privacy and/or to protect the relationship from deteriorating (cf. Caughlin & Afifi, 2004; Finkenauer & Hazam, 2000).

More research is necessary on when self-disclosure progresses gradually (as social penetration theory might predict), quickly (as the clicking model might predict), or in a cyclical or spiraling manner (as dialectical-privacy models might predict) as a relationship develops. Based on differences in personality (e.g., a predisposition to be a high versus a low discloser or high versus low in avoidance and/or anxiety attachment; Taylor, Wheeler, & Altman, 1973; Wei, Russell, & Zakalik, 2005), dyadic factors (e.g., partners "feeling connected" or not when they first meet), and situational factors (e.g., face-to-face versus computer-mediated communication), different patterns of self-disclosure and possibly relationship development may occur. The availability of statistics to examine distinct developmental trajectories (based on latent growth mixture models) will be useful in identifying patterns of change in self-disclosure and in relationship growth (e.g., Muthén & Muthén, 2000) as well as variables that predict the likelihood of different trajectories.

BACKGROUND FACTORS AFFECTING SELF-DISCLOSURE BETWEEN INITIAL STRANGERS OR ACQUAINTANCES

A number of background factors influence if, when, and how disclosure occurs between strangers or new acquaintances, including cultural norms and expectations, prior access to a social network of friends and/or an intimate partner, and personality and individual characteristics of the prospective relationship partners. For instance, although there may be certain cross-cultural differences, many societies share rules and scripts that regulate self-disclosure and intimate conversations generally between strangers or new acquaintances as opposed to, say, close friends or romantic partners. People in different cultures (e.g., in the United States and in Japan) may expect to limit their talk to polite and superficial conversation with a stranger or new acquaintance; they do not expect to reveal moderately or highly personal information to this person, and they may also risk social rejection if they do disclose at a personal level (Chaikin & Derlega, 1974; Nakanishi, 1986; Petronio, 2002).

Parenthetically, abiding by cultural sanctions restricting self-disclosure between new acquaintances does not mean that individuals are not gathering information about one another. In conversations between new partners (Miell & Duck, 1986), individuals are gathering information based on one another's body language and verbal behavior as they talk about general topics (e.g., about mutual interests, biographical information, and temperament). Disclosing about superficial topics has an additional bonus for the participants—it eases the flow of conversation between individuals who are previously unacquainted (Miell & Duck, 1986).

Cultural rules are likely to inhibit high levels of self-disclosure between strangers or new acquaintances. But cultural expectations internalized as "relationship prototypes" or "interaction scripts" that support self-disclosure between friends and romantic partners (Baxter, Dun, & Sahlstein, 2001; Fehr, 2004a, 2004b; Hassebrauck & Fehr, 2002; Rose & Frieze, 1993) may actually increase self-disclosure between strangers or new acquaintances. If a stranger or new acquaintance resembles a mental representation for a "positive significant other," such as a parent, close friend, or previous dating partner, then unconscious processes via transference are activated that increase liking for and possibly self-disclosure to this person (Andersen & Adil Saribay, 2005).

Whether or not someone already has a network of friends and/or an intimate partner may also affect if and how self-disclosure occurs with a prospective relationship partner: If someone has close friends or an intimate partner, she or he may be less motivated to initiate another relationship compared to someone who has no friends or relationship partners (McPherson, Smith-Lovin, & Brashears, 2006). A lack of interest in starting a new relationship may cause someone to restrict self-disclosure with a new acquaintance or to act unresponsive to the other person's disclosure input. On the other hand, friends and family may affect relationship development, including self-disclosure, in other ways, too. In particular, if they support the budding relationship, we speculate that the relationship is more likely to develop.

There are individual differences in traits that influence the desire to start a new relationship and one's willingness to disclose. People with a secure attachment—who combine low attachment anxiety (i.e., those with high self-worth) and low attachment avoidance (i.e., those with high regard for others)—are motivated to have close and intimate relationships, and they perceive new acquaintances as "safe" to get to know and as trustworthy (Mikulincer, 1998; Mikulincer & Erev, 1991). This high level of trust that "secure" persons feel toward a prospective partner is, in turn, associated with increased self-disclosure to new acquaintances (Mikulincer & Nachshon, 1991; Wei et al., 2005).

There are also individual differences in interpersonal skills that influence the likelihood of self-disclosure occurring in a conversation between new acquaintances. For instance, *high openers* (measured by the Opener Scale; Miller, Berg, & Archer, 1983) are people who encourage others to self-disclose and to engage in intimate conversations because they are attentive and responsive to what the other person is saying. Miller et al. (1983; also see Purvis, Dabbs, & Hopper, 1984) found that high openers (who endorse statements such as "I enjoy listening to people," "I encourage people to tell me how they are feeling," and "I'm very accepting of others"), compared to *low openers*, were more successful in stimulating *low disclosers* (that is, someone who scored low on a scale measuring willingness to self-disclose to a same-sex stranger) to reveal personal information about themselves during a "getting acquainted" exercise.

Gender differences may occur in comfort with self-disclosure—especially among adolescent boys and girls who have limited experiences with dating and/or romantic relationships. A recent survey of adolescents in the United States (Giordano, Longmore, & Manning, 2006) found that boys, compared to girls, felt more awkward in talking about their feelings to a prospective or actual dating partner (e.g., "I would be uncomfortable having intimate conversations with X," or "Sometimes I feel I need to watch what I say to X") and have lower confidence in communicating about relationship-based concerns to the partner (e.g., "How confident are you that you could … refuse a date?" or "… tell your girlfriend/boyfriend how to treat you?"; p. 268). Giordano et al. (2006) suggested that young men's awkwardness in talking to their female partners about relationship-based dilemmas may be due, in part, to a discomfort and sense of inadequacy in fulfilling gender stereotypes about the "male as initiator" at the beginning of a dating and/or romantic relationship. These findings reflect heterosexual assumptions about gender roles influencing self-disclosure at the start of an intimate relationship between men and women. Heterosexual assumptions about "who initiates" may not necessarily be a barrier to self-disclosure and/or starting a relationship for lesbian and gay male couples (Klineberg & Rose, 1994; Rose, 2000; Rose & Zand, 2000). For a further description of gender roles and self-disclosure, see a later section in this chapter on the different use of self-disclosure by men and women to initiate a relationship.

SELF-DISCLOSURE AND "INTENSIFYING" VERSUS "RESTRICTING" SCRIPTS FOR INCREASING OR DECREASING THE PACE OF AN INTERACTION AND/OR A RELATIONSHIP

There are a number of interactional strategies for assessing and making forecasts about the suitability of a new acquaintance for a possible relationship (see Baxter & Wilmot, 1984; Berger & Bradac, 1982;

Berger & Calabrese, 1975; Miell & Duck, 1986; Tolhuizen, 1989). Information-seeking strategies may initially focus on gathering general information about the new acquaintance—perhaps asking direct questions about the other person's interests and recent activities as well as observing the other's (and one's own) reactions during conversations. People may also draw inferences about someone's potential as a relationship partner from the general tone of a conversation (e.g., "Does the other person seem friendly and responsive?"). But people may also hold back and show a desire to play safe in talking initially with the new partner (e.g., acting reserved and polite, exchanging superficial disclosures, and limiting social contact) to avoid appearing "inappropriate." However, when individuals identify some-one who is potentially interesting to get to know, they may adopt an "intensifying script" (Miell & Duck, 1986; also see Klineberg & Rose, 1994) that includes a willingness to talk about a wide range of disclosure topics as well as a more intimate level of self-disclosure to accelerate the level of intimacy in the relationship. The new partners may also decide to spend more time together (Miell & Duck, 1986; Tolhuizen, 1989). How the partners react to the intensification of the relationship will in turn be used to further assess the partner and forecast the future of the relationship.

On the other hand, individuals may decide, after interacting with someone, that they do not want a relationship with the new partner. The new partner may be perceived as "unacceptable" for any of a variety of reasons, including having different interests and attitudes, already being in an exclusive dating relationship, or being difficult to get along with (Miell & Duck, 1986). If partners want to "end" a budding relationship, they may engage in behaviors that are designed to restrict closeness (Miell & Duck, 1986). The "restricting script" may include behaviors that are viewed as appropriate with a new partner (e.g., limiting the range of topics in a conversation, disclosing at a superficial level, and infrequent or limited social contacts)—at least when the new partners are trying to be polite and not too revealing. But it also may include behaviors that are viewed as inappropriate with a new partner (e.g., acting disinterested, distancing, and nonresponsive). The restricting script is designed to "trivialize" the partners' social interactions and conversations and to convey the message that the relationship has no future (Miell & Duck). Hays (1985) reported research consistent with the notion of a restricting script in social interactions. New acquaintances who did not become close friends by the end of the first semester in college restricted interactions (including intimate communication) with their partner as early as the third week of school.

MANAGING THE RISKS (INCLUDING SELF-DISCLOSURE) IN STARTING A RELATIONSHIP

Despite the usefulness of self-disclosure in beginning a relationship, people must weigh the benefits of self-disclosure against its risks, including uncertainty about the other's reaction, and concerns about trusting the other not to divulge sensitive information to unwanted third parties (i.e., gossip). A study by Boon and Pasveer (1999) illustrates, based on college students' accounts of past dating experiences, concerns that were reported ("in which [they] felt somehow at risk"; p. 320) in starting and/or being in a dating relationship. Based on a content analysis of the risk accounts, participants described many fears that were not directly related to self-disclosure, including the following: Is the partner going to judge me negatively? Is my partner trustworthy, caring, and reliable? Should I be concerned about being romantically involved with someone whom I do not know very well? But participants also frequently reported risks that were directly associated with self-disclosure to a relationship partner, including "[c]oncerns about the unpleasant consequences that arise when con-fidences are betrayed; [and] fears about disclosing feelings for the partner" (Boon & Pasveer, 1999, p. 322). Participants also reported risks linked to deception and/or lack of honesty in their dating relationships, including "[f]ear that the partner is withholding information. Fear of the consequences if the partner detects the respondent's dishonesty" (Boon & Pasveer, 1999, p. 323).

Research by Baxter (1990) indicates how partners may choose different strategies to address the risks associated with disclosure as well as to resolve contradictory demands about "telling everything to a partner" versus "being discreet and not divulging anything personal about oneself." For instance, prospective partners frequently rely on the strategy of "separation/segmentation" to select topic areas that are acceptable for disclosure and other topic areas that are considered to be "taboo" or "off-limits" for disclosure. Partners may also use "neutralization through moderation," where there is reliance on lots of small talk while maintaining discretion in disclosing about certain topic areas. Another strategy called "selection" involves choosing a strategy focusing on being "totally open" with a prospective partner versus "totally withholding."

Given concerns about possible rejection by disclosing potentially sensitive information (e.g., "I had an abortion" or "I have low self-esteem"), prospective partners may also make the decision fairly early to "plunge in" and reveal personal information as a sort of "relationship test." Consider someone who is diagnosed with HIV. She or he may disclose information about the seropositive diagnosis at the beginning of a relationship to test the other's reactions (e.g., "Does this person want to begin or to have a relationship with me?"). Disclosure of the HIV diagnosis early in the relationship will allow the person with the disease to find out how the other feels about him or her before either has made a substantial investment in the relationship (Derlega & Winstead, 2001; Greene, Derlega, Yep, & Petronio, 2003; Winstead et al., 2002). An "up-front" strategy of disclosure about the diagnosis is also consistent with laboratory research indicating that people who delay disclosure of discreditable information (meaning that the stigmatizing characteristic is not visible or known) are liked less than those who reveal this information early in a conversation with a new acquaintance (Jones & Archer, 1976; Jones & Gordon, 1972; also see Goffman, 1963).

RESPONSIVENESS IN CONVERSATIONS AND PERCEPTIONS OF RELATIONSHIP INTIMACY

The term *relational responsiveness* refers to partners' perceptions that each person "demonstrates that he or she is taking another's outcomes, needs, or wishes into consideration" (Miller & Berg, 1984, p. 197). Rather than just providing "rewards" or benefits for one's partner to repay that partner for benefits previously given or expected to be given (reflecting an exchange orientation), "developing a close relationship" is associated with partners' perceptions that each is doing what is most helpful to meet the other person's needs (reflecting a communal orientation; Clark & Mills, 1979). How each partner reacts to the self-disclosure input in an interaction (e.g., is the listener acting supportive and caring, and/or does the discloser perceive her or himself to be understood and supported by the listener's response?) contributes to the perception of responsiveness in a conversation and, over a number of interactions, to perceptions of relational responsiveness and intimacy (Reis, Clark, & Holmes, 2004; Reis & Patrick, 1996; Reis & Shaver, 1988). Let us review the evidence linking self-disclosure with responsiveness in conversations between new acquaintances and how this interaction process may influence the development of an intimate relationship.

Partners may use responsiveness in initial interactions with a new acquaintance to assess whether or not they and/or their partner want to start a relationship. This conversational responsiveness "refers to behaviors made by the recipient of another's communications through which the recipient indicates interest in and understanding of that communication" (Miller & Berg, 1984, p. 193). It includes three components: content, style, and timing (Berg, 1987; Davis, 1982; Davis & Perkowitz, 1979; Miller & Berg, 1984). *Content* refers to the extent to which the disclosure recipient's response addresses the discloser's previous communication (e.g., expressing concern about what the speaker said, matching disclosure topics, matching intimacy, or elaborating on what the initial discloser said). *Style* refers to showing enthusiasm and interest in what the other person said as opposed to acting disengaged or uninterested (e.g., involving "immediacy" cues such as direct eye contact, head nods, standing close to the speaker, longer speech responses to the discloser's input, and saying, "I see"). *Timing* refers to how quickly a response occurs to the discloser's input (e.g., responding immediately or delaying one's response).

Research by Deborah Davis and William Perkowitz (1979) documents that content responsiveness in a conversation affects liking in interactions involving strangers. Davis and Perkowitz (Study 2) arranged for a confederate (a stranger) to answer the same questions as a research participant in what was described as a study of the "acquaintanceship process." Based on prearranged responses, the confederate answered the same questions as the research participant either 80% or 20% of the time. The topics of the questions were generally superficial in content (e.g., "What would you do if you suddenly inherited a million dollars?"), but the proportion of content-related responses by the confederate affected liking and how much participants felt that they had become acquainted with the confederate. Davis and Perkowitz concluded that the proportion of content-related responsiveness (or conversational responsiveness) "affected something more basic than attraction, namely the perception of a 'bond' or 'relationship' between the subject and the confederate" (p. 546).

Davis and Perkowitz's (1979) research on conversational responsiveness supports the notion that self-disclosure is part of a transactional process in the development of a relationship. The disclosure recipient's reactions are as important as the disclosure input from an initial discloser in influencing what happens in a conversation and perhaps in influencing a relationship's development. But this research does not necessarily support an often held assumption in the self-disclosure literature that there is a "norm of disclosure reciprocity" in initial conversations between new acquaintances, whereby self-disclosure input by one partner must be matched by self-disclosure output from the other partner (Altman, 1973; Chaikin & Derlega, 1974; Derlega, Wilson, & Chaikin, 1976; Won-Doornik, 1979, 1985). For instance, Berg and Archer (1980) found that people react more favorably to expressions of concern and interest in what is said in a conversation and/or social interaction than to reciprocation of intimacy of disclosure. Berg and Archer presented research participants with a description of an initial meeting between two women in a student union, where one person revealed either low- or high-intimacy information. The second person responded by revealing either low- or high-intimacy information, by expressing concern about what the first person said, or by combining low- or high-intimacy disclosure output along with expressions of concern. Liking for the second person was higher when the intimacy of the response matched the intimacy of the disclosure input. But regardless of disclosure input, the highest level of liking for the second person occurred in the condition where she simply expressed concern for what the first person had said.

The results of Berg and Archer's (1980) research are theoretically important because they indicate that the initial bond between new acquaintances may depend not so much on a "tit-for-tat" matching of disclosure input, but in enacting an appropriate expression of concern and/or social support in response to someone's disclosure input. The recipient of disclosure intimacy can best communicate interest in a possible relationship by tailoring his or her response to the needs of the initial discloser—maybe by matching disclosure input, if that is perceived to be appropriate, or by listening supportively (Berg, 1987; Miller & Berg, 1984).

The interpersonal process model of intimacy (Reis et al., 2004; Reis & Patrick, 1996; Reis & Shaver, 1988; also see Prager, 1995; Prager & Roberts, 2004) integrates research on self-disclosure and responsiveness to describe the development of intimacy in interactions and in a close relationship generally. In the interpersonal model, *intimacy* is an emergent feature in a conversation and/or close relationship based on one person's self-disclosure input and the other's reactions: The first person (in the role of discloser) reveals or, more generally, "self-expresses" thoughts and feelings to a second person (in the role of listener). The term *self-expression* most often refers to voluntary self-disclosures, but it also encompasses any involuntary and/or unconscious behaviors that reveal someone's thoughts and feelings. The intimacy process continues based on the listener's behavioral and emotional responses that may convey either interest or disinterest in the initial disclosure. According to Reis and Patrick, if the discloser based on the listener's response "feels understood, validated, and cared for, then the interaction is likely to be experienced as intimate" (p. 537). On the other hand, if the discloser feels misunderstood, invalidated, and nonsupported—or if the listener's response is inappropriate—then the interaction may be seen as nonintimate, and the budding relationship discontinued. Also, if the listener feels appreciated because "his or her response allowed ... [the initial discloser] to feel understood, validated, and cared for" (Reis & Patrick, 1996, p. 537), then the listener may also experience the interaction as more intimate, leading him or her to self-disclose and/or self-express. On the other hand, if the "listener" does not feel appreciated, he or she may choose to end the conversation as well as the budding relationship (Miell & Duck, 1986).

The intimacy process model predicts that emotional disclosures (revealing feelings and opinions) have more impact than descriptive disclosures (revealing facts and information about oneself) in accelerating perceptions of intimacy in a social interaction. Emotional or evaluative disclosures are considered to represent the "innermost aspects of the self" (Reis & Patrick, 1996, p. 544) and reflect individuals' desires to have an authentic and/or honest relationship with another person. Reactions by a listener to these emotional as opposed to descriptive disclosures have been found to influence among college students and married couples keeping a diary of their social interactions how much the discloser feels understood, validated, and cared for and, in turn, if the conversation is perceived to be intimate (Laurenceau et al., 1998; Laurenceau, Barrett, & Rovine, 2005).

Research by Susan Cross and her colleagues illustrates how individual differences in a personality variable (i.e., relational self-construal) influence via self-disclosure perceptions of responsiveness in interactions and in the development of intimate relationships—especially among persons who are initially unacquainted or do not know one another very well before being in the research. The Relational Interdependent Self-Construal Scale taps "individual differences in the extent to which people define themselves in terms of close relationships" (Gore, Cross, & Morris, 2006, p. 84). Persons who are high in relational interdependent self-construal identify themselves in terms of being connected with others, especially in valuing the development and maintenance of close relationships. Typical items on the Relational Interdependent Self-Construal Scale (Cross, Bacon, & Morris, 2000, p. 795) include the following: "My close relationships are an important reflection of who I am" and "When I establish a close friendship with someone, I usually develop a strong sense of identification with that person." Someone scoring high, compared to low, in relational self-construal is perceived by new acquaintances as being more disclosing and as being especially caring and responsive to his or her partner's concerns (Cross et al., 2000, Study 3).

A recent longitudinal study among previously unacquainted dormitory roommates (Gore et al., 2006) documents how self-disclosure by persons high in relational self-construal accelerates relationship development. Time 1 results demonstrated that persons who were high, compared to low, in relational self-construal were more likely to engage in emotional disclosure to their new roommate at the beginning of the academic semester. Higher emotional disclosure predicted higher perceptions of responsiveness (e.g., "My roommate seems sensitive to my feelings") by the disclosure recipient that, in turn, predicted the recipient's perception of a higher quality relationship (based on measures of relationship strength, commitment, depth, liking, closeness, and conflict) and the recipient's own higher emotional disclosure. Time 2 results indicated, after one month had elapsed in the roommates' relationship, how the intimacy process sustains itself over time: The disclosure recipient's own emotional disclosure at Time 1 was associated with the initial discloser's perceptions of his or her partner's responsiveness at Time 2, predicting in turn the initial discloser's perceptions of the quality of the relationship at Time 2 as well as the initial discloser's own emotional disclosure at Time 2.

Cross and her colleagues' research (Cross et al., 2000; Gore et al., 2006) is impressive in documenting the roles of self-disclosure and responsiveness at the beginning of a relationship. It also provides an interesting "twist" on the original intimacy process model of Reis and Shaver (1988): High levels of emotional disclosure by itself (associated with an individual difference variable such as scoring high on the Relational Construal Scale) may increase perceptions of responsiveness (e.g., "My partner cares about me") by disclosure recipients that, in turn, strengthen perceptions of intimacy in an interaction and in a close relationship. If the disclosure recipient feels closer to the initial discloser, then he or she may increase disclosure to the new partner. The disclosure recipient's own emotional disclosure may, in turn, lead the initial discloser to reciprocate inferences about her or his partner's responsiveness and likeability—leading to the initial discloser's further emotional disclosure on a later occasion and to the development of intimacy between the new acquaintances.

GENDER'S IMPACT ON SELF-DISCLOSURE AT THE START OF A RELATIONSHIP

Prior research on gender differences in self-disclosure (summarized in a meta-analysis by Dindia & Allen, 1992) has found statistically reliable, albeit small, gender differences in disclosure: Women generally disclose more about themselves than men in various kinds of relationships. But the gender difference in self-disclosure to a relationship partner is also greater in close relationships (e.g., a friend, spouse, or parent) than in interactions with a stranger or new acquaintance (Dindia, 2002; Dindia & Allen; Reis, 1998; also see Giordano et al., 2006). Researchers should not exaggerate the magnitude of gender differences in self-disclosure in either beginning or ongoing relationships (Dindia & Allen, 1992; Reis, 1998; Rubin, Hill, Peplau, & Dunkel-Schetter, 1980). But the literature on gender differences in self-disclosure is consistent with earlier findings in "impression rating" studies (Chelune, 1976; Derlega & Chaikin, 1976; Kleinke & Kahn, 1980) that self-disclosure is perceived as more appropriate for women than for men among new acquaintances.

We want to focus briefly on several studies cited in Dindia and Allen's (1992) meta-analysis that suggest an exception to the finding that women tend to exceed men in self-disclosure. These "exceptions" are studies that have focused on initial interactions between men and women in an acquaintance exercise, and they found that men either equaled or exceeded women in self-disclosure. These studies suggest a strategic role for self-disclosure in the first encounter between a man and woman as the partners abide by gender-related expectations about the role of initiator and reactor. When someone has the goal of becoming better acquainted with their opposite-sex partner, then the man may be more likely than the woman to use "his" self-disclosure input to accelerate "getting to know one another"—to let his partner know more about himself and to find out more about his partner by encouraging disclosure reciprocity.

Consider the following study by Derlega, Winstead, Wong, and Hunter (1985): Male and female research participants who did not previously know one another first met in small groups to get acquainted during a group conversation. Then they were assigned to a bogus partner (either a man or woman) for the second phase—someone who purportedly had expressed an interest in getting to know them based on the group conversation. The research participant was asked to prepare a self-description for the partner. The results indicated that men disclosed more intimately than women to an opposite-sex partner. The men with a female partner also disclosed more than women paired with a female partner or men with a male partner. Consistent with the idea of the men in the role of initiator, the men's intimacy of disclosure in the opposite-sex pairs was positively correlated with how much they perceived that their female partner liked and trusted them; but there was no correlation between the women's intimacy of disclosure and how much they thought their male partner liked or trusted them.

Davis (1978) found similar results in a study with male and female college students engaged in an acquaintance exercise with opposite-sex classmates: Consistent with the idea that men take the initiator role in an initial meeting with an opposite-sex partner, the men selected more intimate topics than the women to talk about, and they reported exercising more influence on the course of the interaction. On the other hand, the women took on a reactive role. For instance, the women were more likely than the men to reciprocate the level of intimacy of their partner's disclosure input, and the women took on a (sort of) "consensus role" by going along with the intimacy of topics selected by the male partner. The women may have been "a shade reluctant" (Davis, 1978, p. 691) compared to the men to participate in this acquaintanceship exercise: The women enjoyed the acquaintance exercise less than the men in these mixed-gender pairs. There was also no significant association between the women's enjoyment of the mixed-sex encounters and their male partner's intimacy of disclosure, whereas there was a significant positive correlation between the men's enjoyment and their female partner's intimacy of disclosure.

Gender differences in self-disclosure may be more likely to occur when the man and woman in an opposite-sex interaction anticipate meeting again in a future interaction. Shaffer and Ogden

(1986; also see Shaffer, Pegalis, & Bazzini, 1996) conducted an experimental study where partners who met in an acquaintance exercise either expected or did not expect to interact subsequently. Over a series of trials, the research participant (a man or woman) provided self-disclosures in response to high- or low-disclosure input from a confederate of the opposite sex. The results indicated that the men disclosed more intimately, albeit nonsignificantly, when future interaction with the female partner was anticipated (i.e., working together on a decision-making task after an initial acquaintanceship exercise was finished) versus not anticipated. On the other hand, the women disclosed less intimately when future interaction with the male partner was anticipated versus not anticipated. Consistent with the idea that men—in the role of initiator—use self-disclosure to get acquainted with a woman who they liked initially, there was a positive correlation between the men's attraction for the female partner and how much they disclosed to her (based on judges' ratings of disclosure intimacy and emotional investment in communicating about a topic) when they expected future interaction compared to when they did not expect future interaction. For the women, interestingly, there was a negative correlation between their attraction for the male partner and how much they disclosed to him, but there was no correlation between their attraction and disclosure when no future interaction was anticipated. Shaffer and Ogden (1986) speculated that the women who expected future interaction may have been more concerned than the men about maintaining a "professional relationship" during the acquaintance exercise and in the follow-up study in which they were both participating. The women, compared to the men, may have reduced self-disclosure during the acquaintance exercise to maintain an emotional distance with a future work partner.

A comment is worthwhile about the contemporary relevance of this research on gender differences in self-disclosure. The findings that men may exceed (or at least equal) women in self-disclosure at the beginning of a relationship between a man and woman are generally unexpected given the weight of studies indicating that women (compared to men) disclose more. But the findings highlight the strategic role of self-disclosure in regulating topic intimacy in a conversation (see Goffman, 1969) and in the development of closeness in a relationship: Men more than women in a first encounter may increase self-disclosure to accelerate getting to know an attractive opposite-sex partner; women more than men in an initial encounter with a man (especially if there is a future prospect of a "professional relationship") may restrict their own self-disclosure to establish a harmonious, albeit somewhat emotionally distant, relationship with their opposite-sex partner (Shaffer & Ogden, 1986).

The studies cited in this section on gender differences in disclosure in an initial acquaintance exercise involving opposite-sex partners were mostly published in the 1970s and 1980s, but they are consistent with current gender-related stereotypes about men's and women's roles in initiating a heterosexual dating and/or romantic relationship (Baxter et al., 2001). Nevertheless, it is not inevitable that the man in the role of initiator will accelerate "getting to know his partner" by self-disclosing to an attractive opposite-sex partner. If the man lacks the social skills or the confidence to intensify closeness via self-disclosure and/or other immediacy behaviors (Garcia, Stinson, Ickes, Bissonnette, & Briggs, 1991; Giordano et al., 2006), or if a "responsive" partner is unavailable (Miller et al., 1983), then the potential relationship may fail from the start.

SELF-DISCLOSURE AND "JUMP STARTING" A RELATIONSHIP ON THE INTERNET

Today, many people use the Internet as a medium for communicating with friends, family, and romantic partners (Jones, 2002). But they may also use the Internet to start a personal relationship (Bargh, McKenna, & Fitzsimons, 2002; Chan & Cheng, 2004; McKenna, Green, & Gleason, 2002; Parks & Floyd, 1996; Parks & Roberts, 1998; Ward & Tracey, 2004; also see the chapters by McKenna [chapter 12] and Sprecher, Schwartz, Harvey, & Hatfield [chapter 13] in this *Handbook* about starting relationships online). There are features of the Internet that may increase self disclo sure between online, compared to face-to-face, partners in an initial interaction and accelerate the development of a close online relationship (McKenna et al., 2002). First, the relative anonymity of many forms of Internet-based, compared to face-to-face, communications reduces the risk of rejec- tion. People might disclose fairly intimate information to "strangers on the Internet" (Bargh et al., 2002), based on the expectation that they are unlikely to interact with their online partners ever again. Second, Internet venues may lack and/or filter out the sorts of "gating features" (e.g., physical appearance and/or social skill deficits such as behavioral shyness and nervousness) that may inhibit self-disclosure between new acquaintances in a face-to-face encounter (Garcia et al., 1991; McKenna et al., 2002; Parks & Floyd, 1996; Ward & Tracey, 2004). Third, individuals may select Internet sites where they are likely to meet others who share similar interests and/or opinions. For instance, if someone joins a newsgroup focusing on, say, climate change, he or she knows that other persons who access the site are likely to have common interests. The perception of common interests may, in turn, increase self-disclosure (McKenna et al., 2002).

If people believe that they are disclosing their "authentic self" on the Internet and that the other person has the qualities of an "ideal" friend, then the partners in an online encounter may move more quickly in developing a relationship. Bargh et al. (2002) collected data consistent with these predictions. Bargh et al. (2002, Studies 1 and 2) first demonstrated that an online, compared to face-to-face, interaction is more likely to activate cognitions associated with what research participants perceive to be their "true" or "authentic" self. At the beginning of these two studies, participants were asked to list characteristics associated with their "actual self" (i.e., how they typically present themselves in social settings) as opposed to their "true self" (i.e., how they see themselves but what they usually do not express in social settings). Next, participants interacted with another person either in an Internet chat room or in a face-to-face condition. The results found that the "true self" was more accessible cognitively, based on responses to a reaction time, self-description task, after interacting in an Internet chat room versus a face-to-face condition. On the other hand, the actual self was more accessible after interacting in a face-to-face condition than in an Internet chat room. In the next study, Bargh et al. (2002, Study 3) found that research participants were more likely to disclose information about attributes associated with their "true self" in an Internet chat room than in a face-to-face condition (based on the level of match after the interaction between the other person's description of the participant's "true self" and the participant's self-description of his or her "true self"). Participants also expressed greater liking for their partner after meeting in the Internet chat room than in person. Greater liking for the partner in the Internet chat room but not in the face-to-face condition was also associated with a greater tendency to project ideal or hoped-for qualities of a close friend onto the partner. Bargh et al. argued that "this projection tendency over the Internet, facilitated by the absence of the traditional gating features that dominate initial liking and relation formation, is a contributor to the establishment of close relationships over the internet" (p. 45).

Other research by McKenna et al. (2002, Study 1) found that the tendency to disclose the "real self" over the Internet and, in turn, to accelerate the development of personal relationships via online versus offline interactions is greater among those who lack the social skills to communicate effectively in face-to-face interactions. The participants for this research were recruited from Usenet newsgroups. Individuals who were more, compared to less, lonely and anxious reported that it was easier to disclose personal information to someone they knew on the Internet than in "real life." In turn, if participants found that it was easier to disclose to someone on the Internet than in real life (locating the "real me" online versus offline), then they also reported greater intimacy and greater speed of developing intimacy in these online relationships. These online interactions increased to include interactions in offline settings (also see Parks & Floyd, 1996). The more participants reported interacting with someone online (e.g., via Internet Relay Chat), the more likely they were to engage in offline activities with these acquaintances such as writing postal letters, talking on the telephone, and eventually meeting the other person. In a follow-up study, McKenna et al. (2002, Study 2; also see Chan & Cheng, 2004) reported that friendships and romantic relationships started on the Internet were durable over time. After a 2-year period, relationships started online remained relatively stable: 79% of the friendships started on the Internet were intact, and 71% of the romantic partnerships started on the Internet were still intact.

A word of caution is appropriate about the role of self-disclosure in starting a close relationship over the Internet. As Bargh et al. (2002) indicated, the self-disclosure transaction may begin in relative anonymity on the Internet; and the "projection bias" associated with the tendency to perceive idealized qualities in those initially liked on the Internet may intensify an online relationship before the "real" qualities of the partner are revealed. Given a high motivation to find friends and romantic partners in an online setting, important questions need to be addressed about the link between satisfaction and stability in relationships that begin online and how individuals address boundary and privacy issues about the control, protection, and ownership of information disclosed in these settings (see Irvine, 2006; Petronio, 2002).

THE ACQUAINTANCE EXERCISE: A LABORATORY-BASED PROCEDURE (INCORPORATING SELF-DISCLOSURE) FOR DEVELOPING TEMPORARY CLOSENESS

Not surprisingly, research on new dormitory roommates (e.g., Gore et al., 2006; Hays, 1985) and new dating couples (e.g., Berg & McQuinn, 1986) has contributed significantly to understanding the development of relationships. This focus on "real" relationship partners at the beginning of a relationship avoids the pitfalls of studying relationship processes in laboratory settings—where strangers and/or new acquaintances may have limited expectations about being in a relationship, given that they expect to interact for (usually) one session or (less frequently) over several sessions. Nevertheless, there are benefits to studying closeness in a laboratory setting, especially by manipulating the level of disclosure input. For instance, Aron, Melinat, Aron, Vallone, and Bator (1997) have constructed an acquaintance-building exercise that generates in new partners "a temporary feeling of closeness, not an actual ongoing relationship" (p. 364), using self-disclosure and relationship-building tasks. Pairs of individuals who do not know one another are assigned a series of tasks involving either self-disclosure and relationship building (the "closeness condition") or superficial talk (the "small talk condition"). The interaction takes about 45 minutes.

The instructions for the acquaintance exercise involve the two partners completing three sets of tasks. In the closeness condition, the depth of disclosure expected from participants increases within a set and across the three sets of tasks. For instance, task slips to be completed by each participant in Set I of the closeness condition include the following: "Given the choice of anyone in the world, whom would you want as a dinner guest?" "Do you have a secret hunch about how you will die?" "Take 4 minutes and tell your partner your life story in as much detail as possible." Set II task slips include the following: "If a crystal ball could tell you the truth about yourself, your life, the future, or anything else, what would you want to know?" and "How close and warm is your family? Do you feel your childhood was happier than most other people's?" Set III task slips include the following: "Make 3 true 'we' statements each. For instance, 'We are both in this room feeling …'" In the small talk condition, participants complete activities that, according to Aron et al. (1997, p. 366) "involved minimal disclosure or focus on partner or relationship" across the three sets of tasks. Typical task slips to be completed in the small talk condition include the following: "What is the best restaurant you've been to in the last month that your partner hasn't been to? Tell your partner about it" in Set I; "What did you do this summer?" in Set II; and "Do you subscribe to any magazines? Which ones? What have you subscribed to in the past?" in Set III.

Aron et al. (1997, Study 1) found that partners in the closeness, compared to the small talk, condition reported feeling closer to one another. "Closeness" was measured by a composite score derived from responses to the Inclusion of Other in the Self Scale (Aron, Aron, & Smollan, 1992) and the Subjective Closeness Index (Berscheid, Snyder, & Omoto, 1989). Additional results found that generating feelings of closeness, based on what happened in the closeness condition, was not moderated by the attachment styles of the participants, whether or not participants disagreed on issues rated as important, or explicit instructions about making closeness a goal for the interaction (Aron et al., 1997, Studies 1, 2 and 3). Aron et al. (1997) also found that participants in the closeness condition adopted a more favorable working model of a relationship partner, from pre- to posttest, based on responses to Bartholomew and Horowitz's (1991) fourfold classification of attachment styles (i.e., secure and avoidant/dismissive attachment versus preoccupied and avoidant/fearful attachment). Hence, interacting with someone in an acquaintance exercise that incorporates self-disclosure and relationship-building tasks—especially when cautions are in place to create a "safe setting" for participants (see Aron et al., 1997, n. 9)—may diminish concerns about rejection by any partner (Edelstein & Shaver, 2004) as well as increase feelings of closeness with the particular partner.

There are methodological limitations in using the acquaintance exercise to study processes involved in the beginning of a close relationship. Researching "temporary closeness" in the laboratory definitely may not compare to studying new roommates or new dating partners (see Aron et al., 1997; Duck, 1988). For instance, research participants may memorize and organize information differently about a prospective partner if they expect to interact with a new acquaintance in a laboratory setting only once or a few times as opposed to seeing someone on a number of occasions in a real-life setting (cf. Devine, Sedikides, & Fuhrman, 1989). There may be unique demand characteristics influencing research participants' reactions to instructions in a laboratory setting that reduce the generalizability of the results of an acquaintance exercise in understanding relationship phenomena in comparison to a field study of actual relationship partners such as new dormitory roommates. But the acquaintance exercise, using self-disclosure to "prime" closeness, allows researchers to test in a laboratory situation the impact of theoretically important predictor variables (e.g., the impact of anticipated future interaction and/or interaction goals, expectations of acceptance and rejection, and individual differences in shyness and loneliness) and possible mediators (e.g., descriptive versus evaluative disclosures, and perceptions of partner's responsiveness) that are likely to affect the start of a relationship (cf. Snapp & Leary, 2001).

SUMMARY

This chapter has covered a range of topics illustrating the importance of self-disclosure at the start of a relationship. People will incorporate self-disclosure in conversations (including disclosing about superficial and maybe more personal content) to assess one another's interest, suitability, and trustworthiness for starting a close relationship. Decisions about self-disclosure (either face-to-face or online) will affect how new relationships develop or cycle over time. But, most importantly, the disclosure recipient's and the discloser's reactions to self-disclosure input, including expressions of concern, understanding, and acceptance, will influence perceptions of intimacy and whether or not they see themselves as partners in a new relationship. In turn, the perception of intimacy and relationship closeness will affect subsequent decisions about self-disclosure between the new relationship partners.

DIRECTIONS FOR FUTURE RESEARCH AND CONCLUSIONS

The following issues might be examined in future research on self-disclosure and starting a close relationship: First, the literature reviewed in this chapter focuses on "voluntary relationships," where the self-disclosure transaction contributes to making decisions about a partner's suitability for a relationship. This research may not be generalizable to relationships that start "involuntarily." In some conservative traditions (e.g., Muslim and Hindu cultures), partners may expect to meet for the first time either shortly before or at the time of an "arranged" marriage, or individuals (in a supervised setting) may have only a brief opportunity to assess one another's suitability as a spouse

(MacFarquhar, 2006). Research is necessary on the relevance of self-disclosure for starting and developing closeness in these "arranged" relationships.

Second, persons who incorporate values associated with their culture of origin (e.g., individualistic in the United States versus collectivistic in China and Japan) may have different expectations about whether or not, what, and how much to disclose to a relationship partner (Gudykunst & Nishida, 1983; Seki, Matsumoto, & Imahori, 2002; Ting-Toomey, 1991; Wang & Mallinckrodt, 2006). If collectivistic societies favor emotional restraint and individualistic societies favor self-expression, then it would be worthwhile to study the impact of culture on how prospective partners acquire information about one another and the status of their relationship.

Third, the research on self-disclosure and beginning a friendship or romantic relationship focuses mostly on heterosexual individuals as research participants. It would be useful to examine the role of self-disclosure in starting a relationship among gay men and lesbians—for whom stereotypical expectations about gender roles and masculinity–femininity affecting self-disclosure may be less important than among heterosexual men and women (Klinkenberg & Rose, 1994; Rose, 2000; Rose & Frieze, 1993; Rose & Zand, 2000).

Fourth, more research is necessary on the "ebb and flow" of self-disclosure on an everyday basis as partners begin their relationship. The construction of diary methods for collecting data about daily experiences and advances in statistical techniques to analyze developmental trajectories (Bolger, Davis, & Rafaeli, 2003; Jones, Nagin, & Roeder, 2001; Kashy, Campbell, & Harris, 2006; Singer & Willett, 2003) will allow researchers to document changes and cycling in self-disclosure (and its association with responsiveness, intimacy, and relationship closeness) over repeated social interactions for new relationship partners.

Fifth, experimental and laboratory-based research on self-disclosure at the start of a relationship should be expanded. The acquaintance procedure incorporating self-disclosure and relationship building (Aron et al., 1997) could be combined with social-cognitive manipulations of "transference" (i.e., priming mental representations of significant others; Andersen & Adil Saribay, 2005) to examine how mental models and experiences with self-disclosure jointly affect interactions and feelings of closeness between new partners.

Sixth, this chapter has focused on the self-disclosure transaction between prospective partners (in the roles of discloser and disclosure recipient) and how it influences the start of their relationship. But the development of the relationship also depends on the support and reactions that the partners receive from members of their social networks (including friends, family, and coworkers). Leslie Baxter and her colleagues (Baxter & Erbert, 1999; Baxter & Widenmann, 1993) have examined when and how someone reveals information about a new romantic relationship to network members. It would be appropriate to examine how self-disclosure input to members of the social network about new relationships (including network members' reactions) also impacts on a relationship's progress.

Rick Archer (1987) wrote a commentary two decades ago arguing that self-disclosure is a "useful behavior," particularly for studying the development of close relationships. We agree! Self-disclosure, including reactions by the disclosure recipient, is useful for prospective partners to learn about one another, to assess their interest in starting a relationship, and to infer how they feel about each other and their relationship. It is useful in intensifying or limiting social interactions and/or the development of closeness and intimacy. It is also at the crux of a major dilemma in starting a new relationship: how to balance the risks of openness (e.g., being rejected, exploited, hurt, or shunned) against its potential benefits (e.g., being authentic, accepted, and loved by a friend or an intimate partner).

AUTHOR NOTE

Thanks are expressed to the editors (Susan Sprecher, Amy Wenzel, and John Harvey) and to an anonymous reviewer for their helpful comments. Appreciation is also extended to Dawn Braithwaite, James Bliss, and Matt Henson for their input.

REFERENCES

Afifi, W. A., & Guerrero, L. K. (2000). Motivations underlying topic avoidance in close relationships. In S. Petronio (Ed.), *Balancing the secrets of private disclosures* (pp. 165–179). Mahwah, NJ: Lawrence Erlbaum.

Altman, I. (1973). Reciprocity of interpersonal exchange. *Journal for the Theory of Social Behavior, 3*, 249–261.

Altman, I. (1975). *The environment and social behavior: Privacy, personal space, territory, crowding.* Monterey, CA: Brooks/Cole.

Altman, I. (1977). Privacy regulation: Culturally universal or culturally specific? *Journal of Social Issues, 33*(3), 66–84.

Altman, I., & Taylor, D. A. (1973). *Social penetration: The development of interpersonal relationships.* New York: Holt, Rinehart & Winston.

Altman, I., Vinsel, A., & Brown, B. H. (1981). Dialectic conceptions in social psychology: An application to social penetration and privacy regulation. In L. Berkowitz (Ed.), *Advances in experimental social psychology* (Vol. 14, pp. 107–160). New York: Academic Press.

Andersen, S. M., & Adil Saribay, S. (2005). The relational self and transference: Evoking motives, self-regulation, and emotions through activation of mental representations of significant others. In M. W. Baldwin (Ed.), *Interpersonal cognition* (pp. 1–32). New York: Guilford.

Archer, R. L. (1980). Self-disclosure. In D. M. Wegner & R. R. Vallacher (Eds.), *The self in social psychology* (pp. 183–205). New York: Oxford University Press.

Archer, R. L. (1987). Commentary: Self-disclosure, a very useful behavior. In V. J. Derlega & J. H. Berg (Eds.), *Self-disclosure: Theory, research, and therapy* (pp. 329–342). New York: Plenum.

Aron, A., Aron, E. N., & Smollan, D. (1992). Inclusion of Other in the Self Scale and the structure of interpersonal closeness. *Journal of Personality and Social Psychology, 63*, 596–612.

Aron, A., Melinat, E., Aron, E. N., Vallone, R. D., & Bator, R. J. (1997). The experimental generation of interpersonal closeness: A procedure and some preliminary findings. *Personality and Social Psychology Bulletin, 23*, 363–377.

Bargh, J. A., McKenna, K. Y. A., & Fitzsimons, G. M. (2002). Can you see the real me? Activation and expression of the "true self" on the Internet. *Journal of Social Issues, 58*, 33–48.

Bartholomew, K., & Horowitz, L. M. (1991). Attachment styles among young adults: A test of a four-category model. *Journal of Personality and Social Psychology, 61*, 226–244.

Bavelas, J. B., Coates, L., & Johnson, T. (2000). Listeners as co-narrators. *Journal of Personality and Social Psychology, 79*, 941–952.

Baxter, L. A. (1987). Self-disclosure and relationship disengagement. In V. J. Derlega & J. H. Berg (Eds.), *Self-disclosure: Theory, research, and therapy* (pp. 155–174). New York: Plenum.

Baxter, L. A. (1990). Dialectical contradictions in relationship development. *Journal of Social and Personal Relationships, 7*, 69–88.

Baxter, L. A. (2004). Relationships as dialogues. *Personal Relationships, 11*, 1–22.

Baxter, L. A., Dun, T., & Sahlstein, E. (2001). Rules for relating communicated among social network members. *Journal of Social and Personal Relationships, 18*, 173–199.

Baxter, L. A., & Erbert, L. A. (1999). Perceptions of dialectical contradictions in turning points of development in heterosexual romantic relationships. *Journal of Social and Personal Relationships, 16*, 547–569.

Baxter, L. A., & Widenmann, S. (1993). Revealing and not revealing the status of romantic relationships to social networks. *Journal of Social and Personal Relationships, 10*, 321–337.

Baxter, L. A., & Wilmot, W. W. (1984). "Secret tests": Social strategies for acquiring information about the state of the relationship. *Human Communication Research, 11*, 171–201.

Baxter, L. A., & Wilmot, W. W. (1985). Taboo topics in close relationships. *Journal of Social and Personal Relationships, 2*, 253–269.

Berg, J. H. (1984). The development of friendships between roommates. *Journal of Personality and Social Psychology, 46*, 346–356.

Berg, J. H. (1987). Responsiveness and self-disclosure. In V. J. Derlega & J. H. Berg (Eds.), *Self-disclosure: Theory, research, and therapy* (pp. 101–130). New York: Plenum.

Berg, J. H., & Archer, R. L. (1980). Disclosure or concern: A second look at liking for the norm-breaker. *Journal of Personality, 48*, 245–257.

Berg, J. H., & Archer, R. L. (1982). Responses to self-disclosure and interaction goals. *Journal of Experimental Social Psychology, 18*, 501–512.

Berg, J. H., & Clark, M. S. (1986). Differences in social exchange between intimate and other relationships: Gradually evolving or quickly apparent? In V. J. Derlega & B. A. Winstead (Eds.), *Friendship and social interaction* (pp. 1101–1128). New York: Springer-Verlag.

Berg, J. H., & McQuinn, R. D. (1986). Attraction and exchange in continuing and noncontinuing dating relationships. *Journal of Personality and Social Psychology, 50*, 942–952.

Berger, C. R., & Bradac, J. J. (1982). *Language and social knowledge.* London: Edward Arnold.

Berger, C. R., & Calabrese, R. J. (1975). Some explorations in initial interaction and beyond: Toward a developmental theory of interpersonal communication. *Human Communication Research, 1*, 99–112.

Berscheid, E., Snyder, M., & Omoto, A. M. (1989). The Relationship Closeness Inventory: Assessing the closeness of interpersonal relationships. *Journal of Personality and Social Psychology, 576*, 792–807.

Bolger, N., Davis, A., & Rafaeli, E. (2003). Diary methods: Capturing life as it is lived. *Annual Review of Psychology, 54*, 579–616.

Boon, S. D., & Pasveer, K. A. (1999). Charting the topography of risky relationship experiences. *Personal Relationships, 6*, 317–336.

Caughlin, J. P., & Afifi, T. D. (2004). When is topic avoidance unsatisfying? Examining moderators of the association between avoidance and dissatisfaction. *Human Communication Research, 30*, 479–513.

Chaikin, A. L., & Derlega, V. J. (1974). Liking for the norm-breaker in self-disclosure. *Journal of Personality, 42*, 117–129.

Chan, D. K-S., & Cheng, G. H-L. (2004). A comparison of offline and online friendship qualities at different stages of relationship development. *Journal of Social and Personal Relationships, 21*, 305–320.

Chelune, G. J. (1976). Reactions to male and female disclosure at two levels. *Journal of Personality and Social Psychology, 5*, 1000–1003.

Clark, M. S., & Mills, J. (1979). Interpersonal attraction in exchange and communal relationships. *Journal of Personality and Social Psychology, 37*, 12–24.

Cross, S. E., Bacon, P. L., & Morris, M. L. (2000). The relational-interdependent self-construal and relationships. *Journal of Personality and Social Psychology, 78*, 791–808.

Davis, D. (1982). Determinants of responsiveness in dyadic interactions. In W. Ickes & E. G. Knowles (Eds.), *Personality, roles and social behavior* (pp. 85–140). New York: Springer-Verlag.

Davis, D., & Perkowitz, W. T. (1979). Consequences of responsiveness in dyadic interaction: Effects of probability of response and proportion of content-related responses on interpersonal attraction. *Journal of Personality and Social Psychology, 37*, 534–550.

Davis, J. D. (1978). When boy meets girl: Sex roles and the negotiation of intimacy in an acquaintance exercise. *Journal of Personality and Social Psychology, 36*, 684–692.

Derlega, V. J., & Chaikin, A. L. (1976). Norms affecting self-disclosure in men and women. *Journal of Consulting and Clinical Psychology, 44*, 376–380.

Derlega, V. J., & Chaikin, A. L. (1977). Privacy and self-disclosure in social relationships. *Journal of Social Issues, 33*(3), 102–115.

Derlega, V. J., & Grzelak, J. (1979). Appropriateness of self-disclosure. In G. J. Chelune (Ed.), *Self-disclosure: Origins, patterns, and implications of openness in interpersonal relationships* (pp. 151–176). San Francisco: Jossey-Bass.

Derlega, V. J., Wilson, J., & Chaikin, A. L. (1976). Friendship and disclosure reciprocity. *Journal of Personality and Social Psychology, 34*, 578–582.

Derlega, V. J., & Winstead, B. A. (2001). HIV-infected persons' attributions for the disclosure and nondisclosure of the seropositive diagnosis to significant others. In V. Manusov & J. H. Harvey (Eds.), *Attribution, communication behavior, and close relationships* (pp. 266–284). Cambridge: Cambridge University Press.

Derlega, V. J., Winstead, B. A., Wong, P. T. P., & Hunter, S. (1985). Gender effects in an initial encounter: A case where men exceed women in disclosure. *Journal of Social and Personal Relationships, 2*, 25–44.

Devine, P. G., Sedikides, C., & Fuhrman, R. W. (1989). Goals in social information processing: The case of anticipated interaction. *Journal of Personality and Social Psychology, 56*, 680–690.

Dindia, K. (1998). "Going into and coming out of the closet": The dialectics of stigma disclosure. In B. M. Montgomery & L. A. Baxter (Eds.), *Dialectical approaches to studying personal relationships* (pp. 83–108). Mahwah, NJ: Lawrence Erlbaum.

Dindia, K. (2002). Self-disclosure research: Knowledge through meta-analysis. In M. Allen, R. W. Preiss, B. M. Gayle, & N. A. Burrell (Eds.), *Interpersonal communication research: Advances through meta-analysis* (pp. 169–185). Mahwah, NJ: Lawrence Erlbaum.

Dindia, K., & Allen, M. (1992). Sex differences in self-disclosure: A meta-analysis. *Psychological Bulletin, 112*, 106–124.

Duck, S. (1988). Introduction. In S. Duck (Ed.), *Handbook of personal relationships: Theory, research and intervention* (pp. xiii–xvii). Chichester, UK: John Wiley.

Edelstein, R. S., & Shaver, P. R. (2004). Avoidant attachment: Exploration of an oxymoron. In D. J. Mashek & A. Aron (Eds.), *Handbook of closeness and intimacy* (pp. 397–412). Mahwah, NJ: Lawrence Erlbaum.

Fehr, B. (2004a). Intimacy expectations in same-sex friendships: A prototype interaction pattern model. *Journal of Personality and Social Psychology, 86*, 265–284.

Fehr, B. (2004b). A prototype model of intimacy interactions in same-sex friendships. In D. J. Mashek & A. Aron (Eds.), *Handbook of closeness and intimacy* (pp. 9–26). Mahwah, NJ: Lawrence Erlbaum.

Finkenauer, C., & Hazam, H. (2000). Disclosure and secrecy in marriage: Do both contribute to marital satisfaction? *Journal of Social and Personal Relationships, 17*, 245–263.

Garcia, S., Stinson, L., Ickes, W., Bissonnette, V., & Briggs, S. R. (1991). Shyness and physical attractiveness in mixed-sex dyads. *Journal of Personality and Social Psychology, 61*, 35–49.

Giordano, P. C., Longmore, M. A., & Manning, W. D. (2006). Gender and the meanings of adolescent romantic relationships: A focus on boys. *American Sociological Review, 71*, 260–287.

Goffman, E. (1963). *Stigma: Notes on the management of spoiled identity.* Englewood Cliffs, NJ: Prentice Hall.

Goffman, E. (1969). *Strategic interaction.* New York: Ballantine.

Gore, J. S., Cross, S. E., & Morris, M. L. (2006). Let's be friends: Relational self-construal and the development of intimacy. *Personal Relationships, 13*, 83–102.

Greene, K., Derlega, V. J., & Mathews, A. (2006). Self-disclosure in personal relationships. In A. L. Vangelisti & D. Perlman (Eds.), *The Cambridge handbook of personal relationships* (pp. 409–427). Cambridge: Cambridge University Press.

Greene, K., Derlega, V. J., Yep, G. A., & Petronio, S. (2003). *Privacy and disclosure of HIV in interpersonal relationships: A sourcebook for researchers and practitioners.* Mahwah, NJ: Lawrence Erlbaum.

Gudykunst, W. B., & Nishida, T. (1983). Social penetration in Japanese and American close friendships. In R. N. Bostrom (Ed.), *Communication yearbook 7* (pp. 592–610). Beverly Hills, CA: Sage.

Hassebrauck, M., & Fehr, B. (2002). Dimensions of relationship quality. *Personal Relationships, 9*, 253–270.

Hays, R. B. (1984). The development and maintenance of friendship. *Journal of Social and Personal Relationships, 1*, 75–98.

Hays, R. B. (1985). A longitudinal study of friendship development. *Journal of Personality and Social Psychology, 48*, 909–924.

Irvine, M. (2006, October 7). Where is the face-to-face in cyberspace? *Virginian Pilot*, pp. A1, A13.

Jones, B. L., Nagin, D. S., & Roeder, K. (2001). A SAS procedure based on mixture models for estimating developmental trajectories. *Sociological Methods & Research, 29*, 374–393.

Jones, E. E., & Archer, R. L. (1976). Are there special effects of personalistic self-disclosure? *Journal of Experimental Social Psychology, 12*, 180–193.

Jones, E. E., & Gordon, E. M. (1972). Timing of self-disclosure and its effects on personal attraction. *Journal of Personality and Social Psychology, 24*, 358–365.

Jones, S. (2002). *The Internet goes to college: How students are living in the future with today's technology.* Washington, DC: Pew Internet & American Life Project. Retrieved October 4, 2006, from http://www.pewinternet.org

Kashy, D. A., Campbell, L., & Harris, D. W. (2006). Advances in data analytic approaches for relationships research: The broad utility of hierarchical linear modeling. In A. L. Vangelisti & D. Perlman (Eds.), *The Cambridge handbook of personal relationships* (pp. 73–89). Cambridge: Cambridge University Press.

Kleinke, C. L., & Kahn, M. L. (1980). Perceptions of self-disclosers: Effects of sex and physical attractiveness. *Journal of Personality, 48*, 190–205.

Klineberg, D., & Rose, S. (1994). Dating scripts of gay men and lesbians. *Journal of Homosexuality, 66*, 502–512.

Knobloch, L. K., & Carpenter-Theune, K. E. (2004). Topic avoidance in developing romantic relationships. *Communication Research, 31*, 173–205.

Laurenceau, J-P., Barrett, L. F., & Pietromonaco, P. R. (1998). Intimacy as an interpersonal process: The importance of self-disclosure, partner disclosure, and perceived partner responsiveness in interpersonal exchanges. *Journal of Personality and Social Psychology, 74*, 1238–1251.

Laurenceau, J-P., Barrett, L. F., & Rovine, M. J. (2005). The interpersonal process model of intimacy in marriage: A daily-diary and multilevel modeling approach. *Journal of Family Psychology, 19*, 314–323.

Levinger, G., & Snoek, J. D. (1972). *Attraction in relationship: A new look at interpersonal attraction.* Morristown, NJ: General Learning Press.

MacFarquhar, N. (2006, September 19). It's Muslim boy meets girl, but don't call it dating. *New York Times*. Retrieved October 4, 2006, from http://www.nytimes.com/2006/09/19/us/19dating.html?ex=116010720 0&en=cf761bfe15a9f7c58&ei=5070

Margulis, S. T. (2003). On the status and contribution of Westin's and Altman's theories of privacy. *Journal of Social Issues, 59*, 411–429.

McKenna, K. Y. A., Green, A. S., & Gleason, M. E. J. (2002). Relationship formation on the Internet: What's the big attraction? *Journal of Social Issues, 58*, 9–31.

McPherson, M., Smith-Lovin, L., & Brashears, M. E. (2006). Social isolation in America: Changes in core discussion networks over two decades. *American Sociological Review, 71*, 353–375.

Miell, D., & Duck, S. (1986). Strategies in developing friendships. In V. J. Derlega & B. A. Winstead (Eds.), *Friendship and social interaction* (pp. 129–143). New York: Springer-Verlag.

Mikulincer, M. (1998). Attachment working models and the sense of trust: An exploration of interaction goals and affect regulation. *Journal of Personality and Social Psychology, 74*, 1209–1224.

Mikulincer, M., & Erev, I. (1991). Attachment style and the structure of romantic love. *British Journal of Social Psychology, 30*, 273–291.

Mikulincer, M., & Nachshon, O. (1991). Attachment styles and patterns of self-disclosure. *Journal of Personality and Social Psychology, 61*, 321–331.

Miller, L. C., & Berg, J. H. (1984). Selectivity and urgency in interpersonal exchange. In V. J. Deriega (Ed.), *Communication, intimacy, and close relationships* (pp. 161–205). Orlando, FL: Academic Press.

Miller, L. C., Berg, J. H., & Archer, R. L. (1983). Openers: Individuals who elicit intimate self-disclosure. *Journal of Personality and Social Psychology, 44*, 1234–1244.

Montgomery, B. M., & Baxter, L. A. (Eds.). (1998). *Dialectical approaches to studying personal relationships.* Mahwah, NJ: Lawrence Erlbaum.

Morton, T. L. (1976). *Two-dimensional intimacy scoring system: Training manual.* Unpublished manuscript, University of Utah, Salt Lake City.

Morton, T. L. (1978). Intimacy and reciprocity of exchange: A comparison of spouses and strangers. *Journal of Personality and Social Psychology, 36*, 72–71.

Muthén, B., & Muthén, L. (2000). Integrating person-centered and variable-centered analyses: Growth mixture modeling with latent trajectory classes. *Alcoholism: Clinical and Experimental Research, 24*, 882–891.

Nakanishi, M. (1986). Perceptions of self-disclosure in initial interaction: A Japanese sample. *Human Communication Research, 13*, 167–190.

Parks, M. R., & Floyd, K. (1996). Making friends in cyberspace. *Journal of Communication, 46*, 80–97.

Parks, M. R., & Roberts, L. D. (1998). "Making MOOsic": The development of personal relationships on line and a comparison to their off-line counterparts. *Journal of Social and Personal Relationships, 15*, 517–537.

Pearce, W. B., & Sharp, S. M. (1973). Self-disclosing communication. *Journal of Communication, 23*, 409–425.

Petronio, S. (1991). Communication boundary management: A theoretical model of managing disclosure of private information between marital couples. *Communication Theory, 1*, 311–335.

Petronio, S. (2002). *Boundaries of privacy: Dialectics of disclosure.* Albany: State University of New York Press.

Prager, K. J. (1995). *The psychology of intimacy.* New York: Guilford.

Prager, K. J., & Roberts, L. J. (2004). Deep intimate connection: Self and intimacy in couple relationships. In D. J. Mashek & A. Aron (Eds.), *Handbook of closeness and intimacy* (pp. 43–60). Mahwah, NJ: Lawrence Erlbaum.

Purvis, J. A., Dabbs, J. M., Jr., & Hopper, C. H. (1984). The "opener": Skilled user of facial expression and speech pattern. *Personality and Social Psychology Bulletin, 10*, 61–66.

Reis, H. T. (1998). Gender differences in intimacy and related behaviors: Context and process. In D. J. Canary & K. Dindia (Eds.), *Sex differences and similarities in communication* (pp. 203–231). Mahwah, NJ: Lawrence Erlbaum.

Reis, H. T., Clark, M. S., & Holmes, J. G. (2004). Perceived partner responsiveness as an organizing construct in the study of intimacy and closeness. In D. J. Mashek & A. Aron (Eds.), *Handbook of closeness and intimacy* (pp. 201–225). Mahwah, NJ: Lawrence Erlbaum.

Reis, H. T., & Patrick, B. C. (1996). Attachment and intimacy: Component processes. In E. T. Higgins & A. W. Kruglanski (Eds.), *Social psychology: Handbook of basic principles* (pp. 523–563). New York: Guilford.

Reis, H. T., & Shaver, P. (1988). Intimacy as an interpersonal process. In S. W. Duck (Ed.), *Handbook of personal relationships: Theory, research and intervention* (pp. 376–389). Chichester, UK: John Wiley.

Rose, S. (2000). Heterosexism and the study of women's romantic and friend relationships. *Journal of Social Issues, 56*, 315–328.

Rose, S., & Frieze, I. H. (1993). Young singles' contemporary dating scripts. *Sex Roles, 28, 499–509.*

Rose, S., & Zand, D. (2000). Lesbian dating and courtship from young adulthood to midlife. *Journal of Gay & Lesbian Social Services, 11*, 77–104.

Rosenfeld, L. B. (1979). Self-disclosure avoidance: Why I am afraid to tell you who I am. *Communication Monographs, 46*, 63–74.

Rubin, Z., Hill, C. T., Peplau, L. A., & Dunkel-Schetter, C. (1980). Self-disclosure in dating couples: Sex roles and the ethic of openness. *Journal of Marriage and the Family, 42*, 305–317.

Seki, K., Matsumoto, D., & Imahori, T. T. (2002). The conceptualization and expression of intimacy in Japan and the United States. *Journal of Cross-Cultural Psychology, 33*, 303–319.

Shaffer, D. R., & Ogden, J. K. (1986). On sex differences in self-disclosure during the acquaintance process: The role of anticipated future interaction. *Journal of Personality and Social Psychology, 51*, 92–101.

Shaffer, D. R., Pegalis, L. J., & Bazzini, D. G. (1996). When boy meets girl (revisited): Gender, gender-role orientation, and prospect of future interaction as determinants of self-disclosure among same- and opposite-sex acquaintances. *Personality and Social Psychology Bulletin, 22*, 495–506.

Singer, J. D., & Willett, J. B. (2003). *Applied longitudinal data analysis: Modeling change and event occurrence.* New York: Oxford.

Snapp, C. M., & Leary, M. R. (2001). Hurt feelings among new acquaintances: Moderating effects of interpersonal familiarity. *Journal of Social and Personal Relationships, 18*, 315–326.

Sunnafrank, M. (1986). Predicted outcome value during initial interactions: A reformulation of uncertainty reduction theory. *Human Communication Research, 13*, 3–33.

Sunnafrank, M. (1988). Predicted outcome value in initial interactions. *Communication Research Reports, 5*, 169–172.

Sunnafrank, M., & Ramirez, A., Jr. (2004). At first sight: Persistent relational effects of get-acquainted conversations. *Journal of Social and Personal Relationships, 21*, 361–379.

Taylor, D. A. (1968). Some aspects of the development of interpersonal relationships: Social penetration processes. *Journal of Social Psychology, 75*, 79–90.

Taylor, D. A., Gould, R., & Brounstein, P. (1981). Effects of personalistic self-disclosure. *Personality and Social Psychology Bulletin, 7*, 487–492.

Taylor, D. A., Wheeler, L., & Altman, I. (1973). Self-disclosure in isolate groups. *Journal of Personality and Social Psychology, 26*, 39–47.

Ting-Toomey, S. (1991). Intimacy expressions in three cultures: France, Japan, and the United States. *International Journal of Intercultural Relations, 15*, 29–46.

Tolhuizen, J. H. (1989). Communication strategies for intensifying dating relationships: Identification, use and structure. *Journal of Social and Personal Relationships, 6*, 413–434.

Vanlear, C. A. (1991). Testing a cyclinical model of communicative openness in relationship development: Two longitudinal studies. *Communication Monographs, 58*, 337–361.

Vanlear, C. A. (1998). Dialectic empiricism: Science and relationship metaphors. In B. M. Montgomery & L. A. Baxter (Eds.), *Dialectical approaches to studying personal relationships* (pp. 109–136). Mahwah, NJ: Lawrence Erlbaum.

Wang, C-C. D. C, & Mallinckrodt, B. S. (2006). Differences in Taiwanese and U.S. cultural beliefs about ideal adult attachment. *Journal of Counseling Psychology, 53*, 192–204.

Ward, C. C., & Tracey, T. J. G. (2004). Relation of shyness with aspects of online relationship involvement. *Journal of Social and Personal Relationships, 21*, 611–623.

Waring, E. M. (1987). Self-disclosure in cognitive marital therapy. In V. J. Derlega & J. H. Berg (Eds.), *Self-disclosure: Theory, research, and therapy* (pp. 282–301). New York: Plenum.

Wei, M., Russell, D. W., & Zakalik, R. A. (2005). Adult attachment, social self-efficacy, self-disclosure, loneliness, and subsequent depression for freshman college students: A longitudinal study. *Journal of Counseling Psychology, 52*, 602–614.

Winstead, B. A., Derlega, V. J., Barbee, A. P., Sachdev, M., Antle, B., & Greene, K. (2002). Close relationships as sources of strength or obstacles for mothers coping with HIV. *Journal of Loss and Trauma, 7*, 157–184.

Won-Doornink, M. J. (1979). On getting to know you: The association between the stage of a relationship and reciprocity of self-disclosure. *Journal of Experimental Social Psychology, 15*, 229–241.

Won-Doornink, M. J. (1985). Self-disclosure and reciprocity in conversation: A cross national study. *Social Psychology Quarterly, 48*, 97–107.

Yum, Y-O., & Hara, K. (2005). Computer-mediated relationship development: A cross-cultural comparison. *Journal of Computer-Mediated Communication, 11*(1): art. 7. Retrieved January 9, 2007, from http://jcmc.indiana.edu/vol11/issue1/yum.html

9

On Becoming "More Than Friends"
The Transition from Friendship to Romantic Relationship

LAURA K. GUERRERO and PAUL A. MONGEAU

Romantic relationships can develop in countless ways. Sometimes people meet, feel an instant attraction, and quickly develop a committed romantic relationship. Other times romantic relationships unfold more gradually as two people who are physically attracted to one another become increasingly committed over time. This chapter focuses on another trajectory that relationships sometimes take—the transition from an established friendship to romance in heterosexual relationships. Even within this narrow focus, the transition can follow various paths. For example, long-term platonic friends may suddenly experience romantic or sexual feelings for one another, friends may become free to pursue a romantic relationship when they are no longer dating other people, or "friends with benefits" (i.e., friends who have sex but do not consider themselves to be in a romantic relationship; Mongeau, Ramirez, & Vorell, 2003) may decide to become a romantic couple. As Afifi and Lucas (this volume) suggest, the process of relationship initiation reemerges during these types of transitions.

Although most people recognize that a considerable proportion of romances start out as friendships, there has been little research on the transition from friendship to romance. Part of the difficulty may be conceptual. Our title of "more than friends" suggests that romantic relationships have some element(s) that other relationships (e.g., friendships) lack, but identifying those characteristics is more difficult than it seems at first blush. Mongeau, Serewicz, Henningsen, and Davis (2006) argued that, in some cases at least, friendships and romantic relationships do not differ in emotional intensity or sexual behavior. In the end, one of the important characteristics that differentiates a friendship and a romantic relationship is the partners' mutual definition for their particular entanglement. A romantic relationship, given this view, is a relationship labeled as such by partners.

The understudied topic of transitions to romance deserves scholarly attention for at least two reasons. First, research has demonstrated that friendship is an important component within, or foundation for, many romantic relationships (Hendrick & Hendrick, 2000). People tend to be especially satisfied with their romantic relationships when they consider their partner to be a close friend (Metts, Sprecher & Regan, 1998). This suggests that friendships provide a good starting point for many romantic relationships. Second, as we demonstrate in this chapter, the transition from friendship to romance challenges traditional explanations of relationship development and extends theories related to uncertainty and expectancies.

To understand this understudied yet important topic more completely, this chapter begins by reviewing four theoretical perspectives relevant to the friendship-to-romance transition. Next, we look at the roles that topic avoidance, secret tests, and maintenance behavior play in the process of turning a friendship romantic. People sometimes use topic avoidance and secret tests to cope with the ambiguity and uncertainty that characterize cross-sex friendships that have the potential to turn romantic (Afifi & Burgoon, 1998; Baxter & Wilmot, 1984). Maintenance behaviors are important for keeping cross-sex friendships satisfying during this period of uncertainty, as well as helping those friendships transition successfully into romantic relationships (Guerrero & Chavez, 2005).

Before we begin, it is important to note that our review follows the extant literature and, as a consequence, focuses exclusively on heterosexual relationships. Although transitions to heterosexual romantic relationships are understudied, research on transitions to romantic same-sex relationships is virtually nonexistent. Therefore, our review is limited because we do not know the extent to which the claims we make generalize to gay male and lesbian relationships.

THEORETICAL PERSPECTIVES ON THE FRIENDSHIP-TO-ROMANCE TRANSITION

As is the case with many understudied topics, there is no single unified theoretical framework for examining the transition from friendship to romance. However, stage theories of relationship development, such as social penetration theory, are relevant to the transition from friendship to romance. Ideas from three other theories—the turning point approach, uncertainty reduction theory, and expectancy violations theory—have also been applied to study this transition point. We also review research showing how relationship history and the social network influence the transition from friendship to a romantic relationship.

Stage Theories of Relationship Development

The traditional trajectory of heterosexual romantic relationships goes something like this: Girl and Boy meet. Boy is physically attracted to Girl, so he asks her out (Laner & Ventrone, 2000). Boy and Girl go on a few dates. Their physical attraction deepens as they get to know and like one another. As their relationship becomes more emotionally close and committed, they engage in increasingly intimate sexual activities (Christopher & Cate, 1985). If their relationship continues to progress over time, eventually they marry. Of course, this scenario represents only one way that romantic relationships evolve. In this section, we discuss how stage theories explain (or fail to explain) three trajectories: (a) acquaintanceship to romantic relationship, (b) platonic friendship to romantic relationship, and (c) "friends with benefits" to romantic relationship (see Cate & Lloyd, 1992, for a more detailed survey of stage models).

The Traditional Trajectory: Acquaintanceship to Romantic Relationship   The traditional romantic development trajectory is marked by a gradual increase in intimate self-disclosure, emotional closeness, and sexual intimacy that is preceded by physical attraction. Such linear trajectories are common in stage theories of relational development. For example, Altman and Taylor's (1973) seminal work on social penetration theory suggested that relationships often (but not always) follow a gradual linear path, with people in a typical relationship moving through four stages that represent increasing intimacy—orientation, exploratory affective exchange, affective exchange, and stable exchange. Small talk marks the initial stages of relationship development as partners get to know and feel comfortable with one another. If the relationship progresses, self-disclosure becomes more personal until partners feel free to exchange all types of intimate information with one another.

Knapp developed a similar stage theory. He argued that couples typically go through five stages of relationship development (Knapp & Vangelisti, 2005). The initiating stage involves greetings and superficial information exchange. The experimenting stage is similar to the exploratory affective exchange stage in social penetration theory; partners engage in small talk to discover commonalities and reduce uncertainty. The intensifying stage occurs when partners become emotionally connected and decide to move their relationship to the next level. Romantic couples often first say, "I love you," during this stage. The next stage, integrating, is marked by a fusion of the individuals so that they share a relational identity. When couples reach this stage, not only do they see themselves as a couple, but other members of their social network also regard them as a pair. Finally, the last stage, bonding, occurs when couples institutionalize their relationship by making a formal commitment such as marriage.

It is important to note that these models are less linear than they might appear. The stages within both social penetration theory (Altman & Taylor, 1973) and Knapp's model (Knapp & Vangelisti, 2005) are designed to be flexible enough to cover a wide variety of trajectories. Altman and Taylor, for example, claimed that there is no set number of relationship stages. Knapp and Vangelisti, along similar lines, presumed that all directions of movement are possible from each stage. However, these stage models provide only a detailed account of how relationships develop linearly; they provide less concrete information about how alternative trajectories might unfold.

The Trajectory from Platonic Friendship to Romantic Relationship   Although the
stage theories reviewed above fit the trajectory of some romantic relationships fairly well, they are less well suited to explain relationships that transition from friendship to romance. This is because stage theories of relationship development depict the various types of intimacy as developing simultaneously. Yet scholars have argued that intimacy is located in different types of interactions, ranging from sexual activity and physical contact to warm, cozy interactions that can occur between friends, family members, and lovers (Andersen, Guerrero, & Jones, 2006; Prager, 1995). Lewis (1973), for example, posited that relationships progress through a series of processes that reflect these various forms of intimacy. The initial stages in this model (i.e., perceiving similarities, achieving rapport, and inducing self-disclosure) likely reflect building communicative intimacies. The latter stages in the model (i.e., role taking, achieving interpersonal role fit, and achieving dyadic crystallization) likely include more cognitive forms of intimacy.

It is also important to distinguish between *friendship-based intimacy*, which arises out of emotional connection, warmth, and understanding; and *passion-based intimacy*, which is based on romantic and sexual feelings. Scholars have made similar distinctions between companionate and passionate love (Hatfield & Rapson, 1987; Sternberg, 1987), as well as between physical and social attraction (McCroskey & McCain, 1974). In her work on cross-sex friendships, Reeder (2000, 2003) distinguished between three types of attraction: *friendship attraction*, *physical-sexual attraction*, and *romantic attraction* (i.e., the desire to form a romantic relationship with the friend). The majority of cross-sex friends that Reeder studied reported experiencing only friendship attraction; romantic attraction was reported the most rarely. Men were more likely to report physical-sexual attraction than women (see also Bleske-Rechek & Buss, 2001; Rose, 1985). These findings suggest that many friendships that transition into romantic relationships are initially developed based only on friendship attraction, especially for women.

Yet within the traditional romantic relationship trajectory, passion-based intimacy and physical-sexual attraction are viewed as preceding, or at least accompanying, the development of friendship-based intimacy. Indeed, stage theories suggest that developing a romantic relationship involves exchanging self-disclosure and nonverbal communication that simultaneously reflect both these types of intimacy. Murstein's (1970) idea of an "open field" also suggests that physical attraction is often what draws people together. In an open field, strangers or nodding acquaintances have the ability to communicate for the first time (e.g., at a party). These conditions facilitate the choice of a partner based on physical attractiveness, a context ripe for the early development of passion-based intimacy.

There are many cases, however, in which partners who are transitioning from friendship to romance have already developed high levels of friendship-based intimacy. Murstein (1970), for example, asserted that in "closed field" encounters, partners are forced to interact "by reason of the environmental setting in which they find themselves" (p. 466). In short, partners have a chance to interact (e.g., at work), get to know one another, and develop friendship-based intimacy. In these cases, friendship-based intimacy might exist long (e.g., many months or even years) before passion-based intimacy. When considered from a linear trajectory, these partners may need to retrace their steps (so to speak) to develop the newly passionate part of their relationship. For these couples, the transition from friendship to romance likely represents a new relationship stage. In this case, couples sustain high levels of friendship-based intimacy while adding passion-based intimacy. In a sense, these couples have already laid part of the groundwork for building a close romantic relationship.

The Trajectory from "Friends with Benefits" to Romantic Relationship

Another alternative to the traditional trajectory is a move from being "friends with benefits" (FWB) to becoming a romantic couple. People define themselves as FWB when they have sex with one another on more than one occasion, but do not label their relationship as romantic (Mongeau et al., 2003). An FWB relationship is different than a hookup. Hookups are sexual encounters (usually one-night stands) that occur between strangers or mere acquaintances without the expectation of developing any type of relationship (Paul & Hayes, 2002; see also Paul, Wenzel, & Harvey, this volume). FWB relationships, in contrast, typically occur between people who hope to maintain a friendship. Recent research suggests that the FWB relationship is not uncommon. Mongeau et al. (2003) found that around 55% of the students they surveyed on two college campuses reported that they had had (or currently had) at least one FWB relationship. The rules for maintaining this type of friendship often include staying emotionally detached, promising not to get jealous, and agreeing not to fall in love (Hughes, Morrison, & Asada, 2005). Of course, in some cases people in FWB relationships cannot help getting jealous or falling in love. Hughes et al. (2005) found that although some people were able to maintain the status quo and stay "friends" despite being lovers, others stopped having sex or ended their friendship altogether, whereas still others ended up becoming a romantic couple despite their initial intentions not to.

For those who transition from an FWB to a romantic relationship, passion-based intimacy has already developed, at least in terms of sexual intimacy. In fact, these couples may face special challenges because the passion that often characterizes new romantic relationships may have already waned somewhat. As Berscheid (1983) lamented, passion is often swift and intense, but also fleeting and fragile. Depending on how close their friendship is, these couples may or may not need to increase their level of emotional and communicative closeness when they become a romantic couple.

Couples who move from being friends with benefits to being a romantic couple challenge traditional perspectives about how romantic relationships develop. They also challenge both scholarly and lay notions of what it means to be "friends" versus a "romantic couple." For example, Davis and Todd (1982) suggested that passion, mutual love, and exclusivity distinguish romantic relationships from friendships. FWB relationships defy the passion part of this distinction, leaving mutual love and exclusivity as the defining features of a romantic relationship. Thus, communicating mutual love and negotiating exclusivity may be critical components of the process involved in changing an FWB relationship into a romantic relationship.

The Influence of Relationship History

As our discussion of stage theories suggests, people who transition from friendship to a romantic relationship differ in terms of the kinds of intimacy they have developed. Thus, it follows that relationship history would play a substantial role in determining the relationship trajectory. Specifically, how the transition to a romantic relationship works depends, in part at least, on the type of relationship (if any) two people shared prior to the transition.

Mongeau and Teubner (2002) investigated, among other issues, how relationship history influenced romantic relationship transitions. They reported that how well partners knew each other exerted an important influence on the transition to a romantic relationship. Partners who knew each other well tended to engage in relatively slow transitions and dated before the friendship was redefined as a romantic relationship. Dating served as a testing ground rather than as a clear marker that the relationship had turned romantic. In these cases, partners tended to ease into a new relationship definition while at the same time making sure that they did not harm the existing friendship. By using dating as a testing ground, friends could try the new relationship "on for size" before fully committing to it. Partners wanted the ability to move back to a friendship if the transition did not work out well. Although research suggests that cross-sex friends often avoid talking about the state of their relationship (Afifi & Burgoon, 1998; Baxter & Wilmot, 1984), a surprisingly large proportion of participants broke the taboo and talked about the relationship and the transition, although exactly when this talk took place was not perfectly clear. At some point during the dating process, cross-sex friends may begin to feel comfortable talking about their romantic feelings. Thus, dating before the transition may serve the important function of allowing cross-sex friends to gauge one another's feelings and reduce uncertainty—a point that is discussed in more detail later in this chapter.

Partners who did not know each other well before the transition tended to have very quick transitions, often facilitated by alcohol (Mongeau & Teubner, 2002). A typical scenario indicated that partners met initially at a bar or party, drank and danced together, and engaged in some mild sexual intimacy before the end of the evening. Within the space of a few days or a week, the couple found themselves in a romantic relationship. Partners in these relationships reported dating following the transition, in large part, because there was so little time to date before the transition.

Mongeau et al. (2006) reported that relationship history also influences behavior during the transition to a romantic relationship. Moreover, in terms of first dates, first sexual interaction, and first significant disclosure, they argued that the nature of the relationship tends to exert a stronger impact on women's behavior when compared with men's behavior. For example, Baumeister (2000) posited that women's sexual responses would be more strongly influenced by relationship status and history than would be true for men. Men tend to have much more positive views of casual sex than do women; however, men and women are much more similar in their views of sex in the context of a close personal relationship (Hyde & Oliver, 2000). Along similar lines, Morr and Mongeau (2004) reported relationship history effects on first-date communication expectations such that close friends were expected to communicate much more intimately than acquaintances. This relationship history effect, however, was significantly stronger for women when compared with men. In other words, just as was true with sexual interaction, relationship history played a more important role in women's (when compared with men's) communicative expectations for first dates.

The Influence of the Social Network   Romantic relationships do not occur in a vacuum. Instead, they occur in the context (and many times in the presence) of family, friends, and coworkers. A romantic couple does not spend all their time together alone. Instead, they spend considerable time with their social network. The social network may affect the trajectory of a relationship that moves from friendship to romance. Mongeau, Shaw, and Bacue (2000) discussed the concept of "group dating," or the process of "hanging out" in mixed-sex groups on repeated occasions. These social contexts allow people to interact and reduce uncertainty without the anxiety and pressure of an "on-record" first date. The social network can be useful in facilitating (or inhibiting) interaction between potential partners. When partners discover mutual attraction, they can split off from the group and develop a dyadic identity while alone. This pattern differs quite a bit from the traditional trajectory of romantic relationships wherein couples get to know each other first and then introduce one another to their social networks. Instead, dating partners in many cases come from the same social network. The Mongeau et al. (2000) research indicated that group dating is now a fairly common phenomenon among U.S. college students. In addition to challenging traditional ways of viewing the dating process, this finding also suggests that a considerable portion of romantic relationships among college students emerge out of the friendships that are first forged from group interaction, making the move from friendship to romantic relationship commonplace.

The social network can influence romantic relationships at more developed stages as well. In Knapp and Vangelisti's (2005) integrating stage, the social network considers the romantic dyad as a single unit rather than two individuals. Thus, many stage theories imply that the social network is integral to the process of relationship development. As people become closer and more committed to each other, there is more overlap between their social networks (Milardo, 1982; Sprecher & Felmlee, 1992), and increased communication with one another's family and friends (Parks & Adelman, 1983). The results from a study by Guerrero and Chavez (2005) imply that people may be aware that integration into one's social network is an important part of relationship development. In their study on cross-sex friendships, Guerrero and Chavez found that women tended to report relatively low levels of social networking (i.e., hanging out with each other's friends and family, and having common friends) when they wanted to keep the friendship platonic but perceived their friend wanted the relationship to turn romantic.

Interestingly, O'Meara (1989) claimed that many cross-sex friends face a public presentation challenge. In other words, cross-sex friends have to cope with how people outside of their relationship, including their social network, perceive their friendship. Cross-sex friends are sometimes asked to explain the state of their relationship to others who question whether they are really "just friends." This may help explain why women report using less social networking with male friends who they are rejecting as romantic partners. Women may not want to lead the man on or to send the wrong signal to their social networks. For those transitioning from friendship to a romantic relationship, similar questions regarding the nature of the relationship are likely to surface, with the newly emerging couple needing to explain the change in their relationship to the social network. If friends and family approve of the change in relationship status, the transition from friendship to romantic relationship is likely to go more smoothly than if the social network disapproves. Generally speaking, others' positive evaluations of one's potential partner likely facilitate romantic intentions (e.g., Fishbein & Ajzen, 1975). If one's family and close friends like a potential partner, it likely makes it easier to form a romantic relationship with him or her. Indeed, studies have shown that romantic relationships are more satisfying and enduring when they are supported by family and friends (Parks & Adelman, 1983; Sprecher & Felmlee, 1992). On the other hand, disapproval from important network members likely inhibits the ability to form romantic entanglements.

The Turning Point Approach

In contrast to stage theories, the turning point approach emphasizes that relationships often develop in a nonlinear fashion. Baxter and Bullis (1986) defined a turning point as "any event or occurrence that is associated with change in a relationship" (p. 469). Specifically, turning points are often related to changes in commitment or relational satisfaction. When turning points are mapped out based on people's recollections, they often show a pattern of highs and lows rather than a gradual increase or decrease in intimacy. Indeed, studies suggest that the linear trajectory of gradually increasing or decreasing intimacy only fits about 40 to 50% of friendships (Johnson et al., 2004; Johnson, Wittenberg, Villagran, Mazur, & Villagran, 2003). Chang and Chan (2007) found a similar pattern for newlyweds. Relationships transitioning from friendship to romance may be particularly unlikely to unfold in a linear fashion for two reasons. First, the transition itself may be a period of turbulence, and, second, they may experience turning points in the context of both their friendship and their newly forming romantic relationship.

This leads to the question: What are the common turning points in romantic relationships and friendships? In romantic relationships, common turning points include get-to-know time, conflict, disengagement, special occasions (e.g., taking a trip together and meeting someone's family), passionate events (e.g., first kiss, first sex, and saying, "I love you"), signs of commitment (e.g., dropping rivals, moving in together, and getting married), physical separation, and reunion (Baxter & Bullis, 1986). In friendships, engaging in special activities together and helping each other in times of crisis are common turning points related to increased closeness (Johnson et al., 2003, 2004). Johnson and her colleagues also found that turning points such as physical distance and moving out after being roommates were common turning points related to decreased closeness in friendships. Baxter and Bullis' (1986) study suggests that exclusivity, serious commitment, and external competition (such as feeling jealous) are turning points that distinguish romantic relationships from friendships. Interestingly, "friends with benefits" appear to understand the importance of these turning points because they often try to stay emotionally detached, uncommitted, and nonjealous (Hughes et al., 2005). These turning points may also mark the transition to romance. For example, when people feel jealous they might realize they have romantic feelings for their friend.

This type of realization is just one of many microlevel turning points that might occur during the friendship-to-romance transition. Mongeau et al. (2006) defined the *romantic relationship transition* (RRT) as a macrolevel turning point that captures "that point or period in time when a relationship changes from being either platonic or nonexistent to being romantic" (p. 338). All romantic relationships contain at least one RRT, whether they evolved from friendships, acquaintanceships, or "friends with benefits," or occurred when the couple "fell in love at first sight" (p. 338). Turning points within RRTs can include, but are not limited to, disclosure of romantic feelings, a first kiss, a first date, or first sex. Mongeau et al. (2006) contended that "RRTs do not represent a single turning point; they are multifaceted processes that involve a number of affective, behavioral, and cognitive changes that can represent" smaller turning points that occur during the process of developing or changing a relationship (p. 340).

Dates, especially those that occur early in the transition (like the first date), are likely to constitute a major turning point and to provide a context for many microlevel turning points such as the first disclosure of romantic feelings or the first romantic kiss. Dates provide a context where partners can express their own interest and gauge their partner's interest in a romantic relationship. The ability to express and gauge romantic interest on a first date is complicated, as we noted previously, by the fact that the state of the relationship is often a taboo topic (Baxter & Wilmot, 1984). Abbey (1987) asserted that asking someone for a date is a fairly direct way of expressing sexual interest, so such expressions on the date itself are likely to be relatively subtle. Thus, although the discovery of feelings of romantic and sexual interest can be regarded as important turning points in all romantic relationships, they may be especially critical in relationships that transition from friendships to romance (Aron, Dutton, Aron, & Iverson, 1989).

Uncertainty Reduction Theory

Discovering a friend's romantic and/or sexual interest may also constitute an important turning point. Sometimes such a discovery helps reduce uncertainty about the nature of the relationship two people share. Paradoxically, however, such a discovery can also increase uncertainty about one's own feelings and/or the direction the relationships might take. Uncertainty reduction theory helps explain the process of seeking information to be able to better understand other people and our relationships with them (Afifi & Lucas, this volume; Baxter & Wilmot, 1985; Berger, 1979; Knobloch & Miller, this volume). The theory was originally advanced to explain how people seek information to reduce uncertainty during initial encounters (Berger & Calabrese, 1975). According to the theory, people are uncomfortable when they perceive that they cannot predict and explain the behavior of others. Therefore, in initial interactions people seek information to reduce this uncertainty.

People also experience uncertainty in established relationships. In fact, Planalp and Honeycutt (1985) found that around 90% of the college students they surveyed could recall a time when something caused them to experience uncertainty in a close relationship. Common events leading to uncertainty included *competing relationships* (e.g., a friend suddenly starts dating someone), *unexplained loss of contact or closeness* (e.g., a friend stops calling for no particular reason), *sexual behavior* (e.g., a friend reveals something surprising about her or his sexual history), *deception* (e.g., a friend is caught lying or concealing important information), *change in personality or values* (e.g., a friend starts acting more flirtatious than usual), and *betraying confidence* (e.g., a friend shares private information with a third party).

All six of these events could occur within cross-sex friendships that are transitioning to romance, but some of these events might be more relevant to the friendship-to-romance transition than others. For instance, competing relationships could make a person realize how much he or she cares for a friend. Changes in personality or values could also trigger a transition. Acting more affectionate and flirtatious might signal romantic interest, and friends who formerly thought they would be incompatible as a romantic couple might change their minds if they perceive themselves to be more similar in values. As these possibilities suggest, more research needs to be conducted to determine how uncertainty-increasing events affect the transition from friendship to romance.

In addition to identifying events that cause uncertainty in established relationships, researchers have described various types of uncertainty, including uncertainty about one's self, one's partner, and one's relationship (see Knobloch & Miller, this volume). Knobloch and Solomon (1999) identified four types of relational uncertainty. *Behavioral norms uncertainty* refers to uncertainty about what constitutes acceptable versus unacceptable behavior in a relationship. *Mutuality uncertainty* comprises uncertainty about whether or not one's feelings are reciprocated. *Definitional uncertainty* occurs when people experience uncertainty about the nature or state of the relationship. Finally, *future uncertainty* taps into uncertainty about commitment and the direction the relationship will take in the future. All four types of relational uncertainty can surface in cross-sex friendships that are in the process of transitioning into a romantic relationship. For example, imagine that Carrie starts to fall in love with her good friend, Brandon. Carrie might be confused regarding the acceptability of kissing or touching Brandon (behavioral norm uncertainty). She might also wonder if Brandon feels the same level of attraction that she feels (mutuality uncertainty), if their recent activities together mark the beginning of a dating relationship or just a continuation of their friendship (definitional uncertainty), and if they would be better off staying friends or becoming a couple in the long run (future uncertainty).

As the example of Carrie and Brandon illustrates, cross-sex friends are likely to experience some degree of relational uncertainty as they transition into a romantic relationship. In fact, some theory and research suggest that transition points are more likely to be marked by uncertainty than are the beginning stages of a relationship. Solomon and Knobloch developed a model of relational turbulence that is based on this premise (Knobloch & Solomon, 2002; Solomon & Knobloch, 2001, 2004). According to their model, people are especially likely to experience uncertainty during the transition from a casual to a committed relationship. The increased uncertainty that marks this transitional stage is theorized to stem from having to renegotiate levels of interdependence and adjust relationship expectations. In contrast to stage models that predict that uncertainty decreases linearly as relationships develop, the turbulence model specifies that uncertainty peaks during the middle stages of relationship development. Of course, some types of uncertainty (such as uncertainty about a friend's values or personality) may decline linearly as a relationship develops, whereas relational uncertainty may peak as partners renegotiate their relationships. Although Solomon and her colleagues have examined their model of relational turbulence only in dating relationships, the model seems especially applicable to cross-sex friends who are transitioning into a romantic relationship because they are likely in the process of renegotiating the nature of their relationship as well as the commitment level.

In fact, theory and research suggest that cross-sex friendships are generally characterized by more relational uncertainty than dating relationships (Afifi & Burgoon, 1998; Rawlins, 1982) because people have a tendency to classify relationships between men and women as romantic or sexual rather than platonic (Baxter & Wilmot, 1985). Furthermore, the characteristics associated with romantic relationships and friendships overlap; both types of relationships typically include openness, caring, and comfort, which often make for "fuzzy distinctions" between friendship and romance that produce relational uncertainty (Baxter & Wilmot, 1985, p. 175; see also Baxter & Wilmot, 1984). Baxter and Wilmot (1985) also argued that cross-sex friendships that have romantic potential are fraught with more ambiguity than either romantic relationships or platonic cross-sex friendships. As they put it,

> Unlike the more stable platonic and romantic types, in which both parties have agreed on the definition of the relationship, the romantic potential relationship is in transition. One or both of the relationship parties desires a romantic relationship, but such a transformation has not been explicitly negotiated by both parties. Thus, relational uncertainty is high because of the absence of recognized consensus on the relationship definition. (p. 177)

O'Meara's (1989) classic work on tensions in cross-sex friendships also helps explain why uncertainty is a feature of some friendships between men and women. Of the four tensions originally proposed by O'Meara, two seem particularly relevant to uncertainty in cross-sex friendships that have the potential to transition into romantic relationships. First, the *emotional bond challenge* refers to the tension cross-sex friends sometimes feel regarding the potential romantic nature of their relationship. Because men and women are socialized to see one another as potential romantic partners rather than friends, cross-sex friends may be confused by their feelings of intimacy and closeness. Thought of in a different way, people may feel uncertainty over where the line between friendship- and passion-based intimacy is drawn in cross-sex friendships.

Second, the *sexual challenge* involves coping with the potential sexual attraction that can occur in cross-sex friendships among heterosexuals. Although many cross-sex friends consider their relationships to be completely platonic (Guerrero & Chavez, 2005; Messman, Canary, & Hause, 2000), others must deal with the issue of sexual attraction. Indeed, Afifi and Faulkner (2000) found that almost half of the college students they surveyed reported having sex with a friend at least once. This finding, along with the research on FWB, suggests that sexual tension does exist in many cross-sex friendships. Many of the students in Afifi and Faulkner's study reported experiencing aversive uncertainty after having sex with a cross-sex friend. Sexual activity can lead to uncertainty about the state of the relationship at the present time as well as in the future.

Interestingly, cross-sex friends may be especially likely to experience uncertainty when they perceive that their goals for the relationship differ from their friend's goals. Guerrero and Chavez (2005) found that cross-sex friends reported relatively high relational uncertainty when they wanted their friendship to turn romantic but suspected that their friend wanted to keep the relationship platonic. Importantly, however, uncertainty levels were not very high in this study or in Afifi and Burgoon's (1998) study of cross-sex friends and daters. Thus, the results can be best described as showing that people in cross-sex friendships tend to experience moderate levels of uncertainty, especially if they have romantic feelings and are unsure if their friend feels the same way. Still, even moderate levels of uncertainty can prompt people to engage in information-seeking behaviors or in topic avoidance, as will be discussed later in this chapter.

Attempts to seek information, as well as partner disclosures, may also influence the transition from friendship to romance. For example, uncertainty might be reduced when partners disclose previously hidden feelings from one another, discuss the future of their relationship, or begin introducing one another as *boyfriend* or *girlfriend* rather than *friend*. If these types of events reduce rather than increase uncertainty, they might mark a transition to a more stable and less turbulent relationship stage.

Expectancy Violations Theory

People usually have general expectancies of how friends and romantic partners will and should act. These expectations can change dramatically throughout the course of a relationship, as would likely be the case if friends transitioned into a romantic relationship. Part of the turbulence inherent in romantic relationship transitions comes from changing expectancies (Solomon & Knobloch, 2001). Given the differences in expectancies between relationship types and given the centrality of expectancy change to relationship turbulence, Burgoon and Hale's (1988) expectancy violation theory (EVT) can help explain the process of transition from friendship to a romantic relationship.

According to EVT, expectancies come from three sources: what we know about the other person (i.e., communicator characteristics), what we know about the situation (i.e., context characteristics), and what we know about the relationship (i.e., relational characteristics). In short, we might expect one set of behaviors when going to a movie with a friend as opposed to going to a movie with a romantic partner. Suppose that Carrie and Brandon are at the beginning of a romantic relationship transition. Brandon asks Carrie out to a movie—something that they have done before, but now with the potentially changing relational landscape, this may or may not be a date. The different sets of expectations may set up a conundrum for cross-sex friends who are uncertain about the nature of their relationship. Specifically, who should drive? Should they each pay for their own ticket and refreshments, or should one friend offer to pay for the other? Is a kiss goodnight acceptable, or would such behavior be inappropriate? Part of navigating the waters between friendship and romance likely involves renegotiating expectancies such as these. If the state of the relationship is a primary taboo topic, it is unlikely that these expectations will be a direct topic of conversation.

Sometimes expectancy violations are unambiguous. Showing up an hour late normally constitutes a negative violation of expectancies, whereas giving a good friend an extra-nice gift normally constitutes a positive violation. In other cases, however, unexpected behavior has no inherent evaluation. According to EVT, ambiguous and unexpected behaviors (e.g., Carrie reaches over and puts her hand on top of Brandon's during a movie) generate arousal, uncertainty, and an attempt to explain the unexpected behavior (Burgoon & Hale, 1988). Brandon's attribution search likely focuses on possible causes related to the context and Carrie's personality or mood (e.g., is the movie sad or scary, is Carrie stressed out and in need of comfort, etc.).

Carrie's level of attractiveness is also likely to influence Brandon's evaluation of the expectancy violation. In EVT, the term *reward value* or *rewardingness* captures the overall degree of liking and regard a person has for someone. Reward value is associated with characteristics such as physical attractiveness, social attractiveness, and status (Burgoon, Stern, & Dillman, 1995). Someone who is highly rewarding can violate expectancies without as much penalty as someone who is unrewarding. In fact, highly rewarding communicators are usually perceived more positively after violating behavioral expectations (Burgoon et al., 1995). For example, people are much more likely to respond positively to a display of affection by a rewarding than nonrewarding person. Furthermore, when a rewarding person engages in a negative behavior, such as acting unusually crabby and surly, people are likely to compensate by asking the rewarding person, "What's wrong? Is there anything I can do for you?" rather than reciprocating the negative behavior as they would for a less rewarding person. Guerrero, Jones, and Burgoon (2000) found just this—people in romantic relationships were likely to verbally compensate for a partner's negative behavior even if they ended up reciprocating negative affect nonverbally.

The predictions for reactions to expectancy violations are undoubtedly complicated for cross-sex friends who are considering a transition to a romantic relationship. For example, if Carrie reaches over and puts her hand on top of Brandon's during a movie, will Brandon's high regard for Carrie cause him to evaluate her behavior positively and reciprocate by closing his hand around hers? Perhaps, but it may be more likely that Brandon's interpretation of their relationship (as "friends only" or as "potentially romantic") would be the determining factor in how Brandon reacts. Of course, if Brandon is unsure about the nature of his friendship with Carrie, the reward value he associates with her may end up influencing how he reacts as well as if he considers pursuing a romantic relationship. Thus, in the context of a possible transition from friendship to romantic relationship, the reward value of a partner likely is placed within the context of the broader relationship.

As this example illustrates, expectancy violations provide an interesting explanatory mechanism for studying the friendship to romantic relationship transition because they focus, in part, on how the nature of the relationship influences expectations for one's partner's behavior. As the relationship definition shifts, the behavioral expectancies for the partner should shift as well. Therefore, what might have been an expectancy violation (e.g., a prolonged goodnight kiss at the end of a mutual outing) is likely what is merely expected once the relational transition takes place.

Expectancy violations may also mark important turning points in cross-sex friendships that evolve into romantic relationships. Afifi and Metts (1998) asked people to describe something a friend or romantic partner recently said or did that was unexpected. They uncovered a number of common expectancy violations, many of which can be evaluated either positively or negatively depending on the circumstances. Some of the expectancy violations they identified seem especially relevant to the transition from friendship to romance. For example, *relationship escalation* includes behaviors that intensify commitment, such as saying, "I love you," or giving an especially personal gift. *Acts of devotion* include behaviors that show that someone is important and special, such as helping someone during a crisis or doing a favor for someone. *Uncharacteristic relational behavior* refers to actions that are inconsistent with how a person defines the relationship, such as wanting to have sex with a friend or asking a friend out on a formal date. Finally, *gestures of inclusion* refer to behaviors that show a person's desire to include someone in her or his social network by actions such as asking the person to meet one's parents or spend the holidays together.

In and of themselves, these acts do not constitute positive or negative expectancy violations; rather, the valence of these violations is dependent upon how they are interpreted. Thus, the positive interpretation of these types of events may be a key predictor of whether a friendship evolves into a romantic relationship. When such events are interpreted negatively, the transition may be much less likely to occur. In some cases, negative interpretations of expectancy violations may even lead to the breakdown of the friendship. In Afifi and Metts' (1998) study, many of the expectancy violations they identified (including events that are more commonly associated with negativity, such as acts of disregard, transgressions, and relational de-escalation) were associated with uncertainty. If uncertainty persists, it could eventually damage the friendship.

As Afifi and Metts' (1998) work showed, the act of initiating a first date is an expectancy violation in some cross-sex friendships. Dates differ from going out with a friend in that the former have romantic overtones that the latter lacks. Therefore, what people do on a date (e.g., go to a movie or concert) might look very similar to what friends do when they go out together, but expectations and goals differ strongly across these events (e.g., Mongeau, Jacobsen, & Donnerstein, 2007).

Research has also examined expectancies related to *who* initiates a date. Throughout most of the past century, the prerogative to initiate dates has been within the male's domain. Therefore, until recently at least, female date initiation was unexpected behavior (Mongeau, Hale, Johnson, & Hillis, 1993). It should come as no surprise, then, that female date initiation influences males' perceptions of their date partner and expectations for the date. Women who initiate dates are perceived as more active, extroverted, liberal, and open than women who wait to be asked out by a man, but they are also perceived as less attractive (Mongeau & Carey, 1996; Mongeau et al., 1993). Men also have higher sexual expectations when the woman initiates the date (e.g., Bostwick & DeLucia, 1992; Mongeau & Carey, 1996). When actual male- and female-initiated first dates are compared, however, there is evidence of less intimacy, both in terms of communication (Mongeau, Yeazell, & Hale, 1994) and sexual activity (Mongeau & Johnson, 1995) on female-initiated first dates when compared with male-initiated ones. This pattern of results has typically been interpreted in terms of expectancy violations. Men have unrealistically high sexual expectations that are violated on the date itself. These violations, however, do not appear to damage the budding romantic relationship. Specifically, Mongeau et al. (1993) reported that female-initiated first dates generated nearly the same number of subsequent dates as did male-initiated first dates (see also, however, Kelley, Pilchowicz, & Byrne, 1981).

In addition to examining female date initiation as an expectancy violation, Mongeau, Serewicz, and Therrien (2004) have investigated how relationship history influences goals and expectations on first dates. Specifically, they have demonstrated that partners who have already established a friendship have different goals and expectations for first dates than those who were previously strangers or acquaintances. Common first-date goals include having fun, reducing uncertainty about the partner, investigating romantic potential, developing a friendship, and engaging in sexual activity (Mongeau et al., 2004). In general, having fun and reducing uncertainty about the partner are the most common goals for first dates, whereas engaging in sexual activity is the least common of these five goals. However, partners who are friends prior to the date are more likely to pursue goals related to investigating romantic potential and engaging in sexual activity than those who were strangers or acquaintances prior to the date (Mongeau et al., 2004). Furthermore, friends are likely to expect higher levels of intimacy and affection on first dates (Morr & Mongeau, 2004), which comports with our earlier argument regarding stage theories of relationship development: New dating partners who were previously friends have already developed friendship- and communication-based intimacy, so therefore they may focus on developing the more passionate, romantic aspects of their relationship during the transition from friendship to romantic relationship. This line of thinking led Morr and Mongeau to suggest that friends may be disappointed if their first "real date" does not contain higher levels of intimacy than a typical date between acquaintances.

COMMUNICATION IN CROSS-SEX FRIENDSHIPS
WITH ROMANTIC POTENTIAL

Ultimately, the transition from friendship to romantic relationship is accomplished via communication. Research suggests that, prior to the transition, friends may have some trepidation about disclosing romantic feelings (Baxter & Wilmot, 1984). It is somewhat ironic, then, that at a very important point in romantic relationship development, the topic that partners are sometimes least likely to discuss is the state of the relationship. This may lead them to avoid talking about certain topics, such as their feelings of attraction or liking, with their friend. They may also use a number of secret tests (i.e., indirect strategies used to try to determine how one's partner feels) before disclosing their feelings. In some cases, secret tests may help friends reduce uncertainty by determining whether their feelings are mutual or not. Research has also demonstrated that friends report using different maintenance behaviors on the basis of romantic intent and perceived mutuality. Specifically, when people perceive that the desire to move the friendship toward romance is mutual, they report engaging in especially high levels of relational maintenance. Accordingly, we turn to a discussion of three communication issues next: topic avoidance, secret tests, and maintenance behavior.

Topic Avoidance

Whereas theories such as social penetration theory (Altman & Taylor, 1973) emphasize the role that self-disclosure plays in the process of developing and intensifying relationships, other scholars have examined topic avoidance in regard to relationship development. Topic avoidance occurs when a person deliberately decides to avoid disclosing information on a particular subject (Guerrero, Andersen, & Afifi, 2007). In one of the first studies related to topic avoidance, Baxter and Wilmot (1984) examined taboo topics in friendships and dating relationships. About 95% of the college students they surveyed named at least one topic they considered taboo in the relationship they referenced.

According to Guerrero and Afifi's (1995) summary of the literature on topic avoidance, commonly reported taboo topics in friendships and dating relationships include *relationship issues* (e.g., talking about the "state" of the relationship, or sharing feelings for one another), *negative experiences and failures* (e.g., rejection, embarrassing situations, or being abused), *romantic relationship experiences* (e.g., past dating or marital partners), *sexual experiences* (e.g., sexual preferences or sexual history), and *outside friendships* (e.g., feelings for other friends or activities engaged in with other friends). Cross-sex friends are more likely to avoid talking about certain topics, such as romantic relationship experiences and sexual experiences, than same-sex friends (Afifi & Guerrero, 1998).

Several studies suggest that cross-sex friends are also especially likely to mention relationship issues as a taboo topic, presumably because there could be uncertainty regarding the friend's possible romantic feelings or intentions. Baxter and Wilmot (1984) found the "state of the relationship" to be a fairly common taboo topic in cross-sex friendships. Similarly, Afifi and Burgoon (1998) found that cross-sex friends were more likely to report avoiding sensitive topics such as the "state of the relationship" than were dating partners. They reasoned that cross-sex friends sometimes worry that discussing their feelings could have negative relational consequences, such as scaring away the partner or ruining the friendship. Messman et al.'s (2000) study supported this reasoning: Cross-sex friends in platonic relationships reported avoiding certain topics as a way of safeguarding their friendship. Other studies have shown that the desire to protect one's relationship is the strongest predictor of topic avoidance across various types of close relationships (e.g., Afifi & Guerrero, 1998; Baxter & Wilmot, 1985; Guerrero & Afifi, 1995).

Uncertainty is also associated with topic avoidance in cross-sex friendships. In Afifi and Burgoon's (1998) study, individuals who reported experiencing uncertainty in their cross-sex friendships also tended to report engaging in less relationship talk with their friends. Afifi and Burgoon noted that the causal path underlying this finding is unclear. On the one hand, cross-sex friends might avoid talking about their relationship because they are uncertain about their friend's reaction and they fear that revealing their feelings could harm the friendship. On the other hand, cross-sex friends may experience relational uncertainty precisely because they have not talked with their friend about their feelings. At some point, cross-sex friends who transition from friendship to romance probably talk about their feelings—an event that could mark a significant turning point in the relationship (Mongeau et al., 2006).

To our knowledge, no studies have examined how topic avoidance changes as cross-sex friendships transition into romantic relationships. However, Knobloch and Carpenter-Theune's (2004) study on dating relationships provides insight into how topic avoidance is associated with relational development in general. They found that topic avoidance occurs most frequently at moderate levels of intimacy, when dating partners are in the process of escalating their relationship from casual to serious. At this point, dating partners may be especially careful not to discuss topics that could damage the relationship or lead to negative judgments. Instead, they may focus on managing positive impressions and engaging in prosocial behavior that promotes relationship growth. The same may be true for cross-sex friends who are in the process of becoming romantic partners, but this hypothesis has yet to be tested.

Cross-sex friends may be especially likely to avoid discussing the state of their relationship when they worry that their romantic interest is not reciprocated. Guerrero and Chavez (2005) found that people reported the least relationship talk when they perceived that they wanted the friendship to evolve into a romantic relationship but their cross-sex friend did not. By contrast, the most relationship talk was reported by cross-sex friends who perceived that both friends either wanted the friendship to stay platonic or wanted the friendship to turn romantic. These findings suggest that the transition from friendship to romance may be marked by the most topic avoidance in situations where one or both friends are uncertain about the other friend's feelings. If uncertainty is reduced and friends feel more confident that their romantic feelings will be reciprocated, they are likely to feel less of a need to avoid discussing the state of the relationship.

This reasoning is consonant with Afifi and Weiner's (2004) theory of motivated information management. According to this theory, people's strategies for reducing uncertainty are based on two judgments: how positive or negative they expect the information they receive will be, and how effective they expect to be in gathering and coping with the information. Thus, this theory helps explain why cross-sex friends would be most likely to avoid relationship talk when they fear their romantic advances will be rejected. In cases where cross-sex friends believe that their partner reciprocates their romantic interest, direct strategies for reducing uncertainty, such as disclosing one's feelings or questioning the partner, may be much less threatening. Moreover, cross-sex friends may be most likely to discuss the state of the relationship when they believe they can cope with rejection and their friendship can survive the turbulence that could accompany such a disclosure. In some cases, people may maintain uncertainty rather than risk the potential rejection and negative consequences that could follow a disclosure of unreciprocated feelings of romantic attraction. Thus, friendships characterized by only one person wanting to turn the relationship romantic may exemplify a situation where uncertainty does not necessarily lead to increased information seeking (see also Afifi & Lucas, this volume; Knobloch & Miller, this volume).

Secret Tests

In cases where cross-sex friends fear rejection and/or worry about negative consequences of disclosing their feelings, they may decide to use secret tests to reduce their uncertainty about the nature of the friendship. Secret tests are indirect strategies that help people determine their partner's feelings without directly asking them for information (Baxter & Wilmot, 1985; see also Afifi & Lucas, this volume). Such strategies, if undetected, allow people to save face if the information they receive is not what they wanted or expected.

In a classic study, Baxter and Wilmot (1985) interviewed people in three types of relationships—cross-sex friendships with romantic potential, cross-sex platonic friendships, and romantic relationships—and asked them how they obtained information to reduce their uncertainty. Participants in cross-sex friendships with romantic potential typically described their relationship as "more than friends," even though the relationship was "not yet mutually recognized and defined as romantic. Typically, these relationships were in transition … at least one of the parties wanted to become romantically involved but the mutual consensus on redefinition had not yet been achieved" (Baxter & Wilmot, 1985, p. 179).

Baxter and Wilmot (1985) described six types of secret tests: *third-party tests* (e.g., asking a mutual friend to find out if your cross-sex friend is romantically interested in you), *triangle tests* (e.g., seeing if your cross-sex friend gets jealous when you flirt with someone else), *separation tests* (e.g., taking a break from each other to see if your friend misses you), *endurance tests* (e.g., decreasing rewards to see if your friend will still stick by you), *public presentation tests* (e.g., introducing a friend as your "boyfriend" or "girlfriend" to see how he or she reacts), and *indirect suggestion tests* (e.g., joking or hinting about becoming a "couple" to see how your friend reacts). They also discussed directness, which involves self-disclosure and direct questioning.

As the examples we have given illustrate, all of these secret tests are applicable to friendships in transition to romantic relationships. Indeed, Baxter and Wilmot (1985) found that people in friendships with romantic potential were, in general, more likely to report using secret tests than people in platonic friendships or romantic relationships. In particular, people in friendships with romantic potential were more likely to report using indirect suggestion tests and separation tests than were people in the other two relationships. These two secret tests appear to be fairly common in friendships characterized by romantic potential, with 52% of participants in this type of friendship reporting indirect suggestion tests and 44% reporting separation tests. Although triangle tests were used most often in romantic relationships (i.e., 34% of participants in romantic relationships reported this type of test), they were also reported by 28% of the participants who referenced a friendship with romantic potential.

Only about 16% of participants reported using direct communication to reduce uncertainty in friendships with romantic potential. Apparently, people feel more comfortable using indirect rather than direct strategies for acquiring information when the relationship is in transition from friendship to romance. As relationships develop past this transition point, research suggests that partners will use less secret tests in general (Baxter & Wilmot, 1984) and more direct communication to reduce uncertainty (Bell & Buerkel-Rothfuss, 1990).

Finally, people in friendships with romantic potential seldom reported using secret tests that involve the social network, with only 8% and 4% of the participants in Baxter and Wilmot's (1985) study reporting use of public presentation and third-party tests, respectively. If Carrie does not want to go "on the record" with her feelings toward Brandon, she probably does not want to go public with her friends either.

Relational Maintenance Behavior

So far we have discussed the difficulty that cross-sex friends sometimes have in talking about the state of their relationship and using direct communication to reduce uncertainty, especially when romantic feelings surface for one of the partners. Obviously, however, some cross-sex friends talk about their feelings and eventually make the transition to a romantic relationship. One way to accomplish such a transition is through the use of relational maintenance behavior.

Researchers have identified a host of maintenance behaviors that are associated with relationship satisfaction, trust, and commitment across a variety of relationships, including those between romantic partners and friends (Dainton, Zelley, & Langan, 2003; Stafford, 2003; Stafford & Canary, 1991). Although some scholars regard relational maintenance as behavior that keeps a relationship at a particular level or stage, Dindia (2003) argued that the term *relational maintenance* "need not imply that a relationship is static and unchanging" (p. 3). Indeed, relationships are dynamic entities. Adapting to the changing needs and goals that characterize a relationship is a critical ingredient in maintaining satisfying relationships (Guerrero & Chavez, 2005). Friendships that are transitioning from a friendship to a romantic relationship exemplify how change can be integral to maintaining relationships. If one or both friends become interested in starting a romantic relationship, the friendship could stagnate or become dissatisfying (or even distressing) if those goals are not pursued.

Guerrero and Chavez (2005) compared self-reported maintenance behavior in four types of cross-sex friendships: *strictly platonic*, *mutual romance*, *desires romance*, and *rejects romance*. Participants in the strictly platonic situation perceived that neither they nor their partner wanted the friendship to turn romantic. Those in the mutual romance situation perceived that both they and their partner wanted the friendship to evolve into a romantic relationship. People in the desires romance situation reported that they wanted a romantic relationship but thought that their friend did not. Conversely, those in the rejects romance situation reported that they did not want the friendship to turn romantic, but thought their friend did.

Their results demonstrated that cross-sex friends were especially likely to report using prosocial maintenance behaviors if they perceived themselves to be in the mutual romance situation. Specifically, those in the mutual romance situation reported relatively high levels of routine contact and activity (e.g., calling or visiting each other and doing things together), emotional support and positivity (e.g., providing comfort and acting optimistic and cheerful), relationship talk (e.g., talking about the state of their friendship and the feelings they have for one another), instrumental support (e.g., sharing tasks and giving advice), and flirtation. The finding for flirting parallels that of Messman et al. (2000), who found that cross-sex friends in platonic relationships avoid flirtation as a way of keeping the friendship from turning romantic.

The finding that those in the mutual romance situation showed the most consistent pattern of high maintenance behavior also complements results from a study by Guerrero, Eloy, and Wabnik (1993). In that study, dating partners completed measures related to maintenance and relationship commitment at the beginning and end of an 8-week period. Participants who reported especially high levels of relational maintenance at Time 1 were more likely to report that their relationships had become more serious and committed at Time 2. Taken together, these studies suggest that increases in prosocial maintenance behavior may mark transition points in various types of relationships. For dating partners, high levels of maintenance may promote and/or reflect increased closeness and commitment. High levels of maintenance behavior may also help cross-sex friends transition into a romantic relationship.

Guerrero and Chavez's (2005) findings also highlight how important mutuality is for a successful romantic relationship transition. In order to have a functional romantic relationship, both partners have to agree that the relationship is, in fact, romantic in nature. For example, Aron et al. (1989) found that the two predominant factors evident in "falling in love" narratives were mutual liking and the other having desirable characteristics. "Indeed, reading the actual narratives leads to the impression that people are just waiting for an attractive person to do something they can interpret as liking them" (Aron et al., p. 251). In many cases, however, there is not sufficient mutual liking to facilitate a romantic relationship. For example, mutuality likely differentiates a romantic relationship from a FWB relationship. In some FWB relationships, one partner might desire a romantic relationship much more than the other. This person might maintain the FWB relationship with the hope that the partner will eventually develop romantic feelings and desires. Indeed, Reeder (2000, 2003) found that cross-sex friends often have different goals related to sex and romance.

Let's assume that Carrie likes Brandon and wants to transform their friendship into a romantic relationship. Brandon, in turn, likes Carrie, but has no desire for a romantic relationship with her. If Carrie suspects that her feelings are not reciprocated, she can either divulge her feelings or keep quiet. Of course, neither option is optimal. Keeping quiet might cause her to lose an opportunity for romantic interactions, whereas communicating them ineffectively might create the loss of a friendship (Baumeister, Worman, & Stillwell, 1993).

If Carrie communicates her feelings and Brandon rejects the idea of a romantic relationship, a difficult situation is created for both partners. Based on repeated media portrayals of unrequited love, Baumeister et al. (1993) argued that in this case Carrie (the rejected) has a fairly clear cultural script. Simply put, she is expected to doggedly pursue Brandon in hopes that he will change his feelings or give in. Many cases of obsessive relational intrusion or stalking occur as a function of just this sort of situation, where one partner doesn't want to take "no" for a relational answer (Cupach & Spitzberg, 2004.) Cupach and Spitzberg (this volume) argue that some would-be lovers continue to see the goal of eventually establishing a romantic relationship as realistic despite evidence to the contrary, leading them to continue engaging in obsessive relational intrusion behavior.

Although Carrie has a clear script on how to pursue her would-be lover, Brandon (as the rejector) has no such cultural-level script to rely upon. There simply are not as many media portrayals of how the rejector is supposed to act (Baumeister et al., 1993). Brandon, in this case, is caught between a desire not to enter into a romantic relationship with Carrie and, at the same time, not wanting to hurt her feelings. In answer to this conundrum, research indicates that Brandon would be indirect; he would try to help Carrie save face by not communicating his real reasons for rejection (e.g., Baumeister et al., 1993; Folkes 1982). The problem with indirect refusals, though, is that these responses may not be taken seriously (see Cupach & Spitzberg, this volume). In response to his carefully worded rejection (e.g., "I'm just too busy to date anyone right now"), Carrie might see considerable room for a positive interpretation (e.g., "If I do a lot of favors for him, he'll have the time to date me").

Guerrero and Chavez's (2005) study sheds further light on how cross-sex friends in the rejector versus would-be lover positions communicate. They found that women in the desires romance position tended to report using relatively high levels of antisocial behavior, such as arguing, complaining, and expressing frustration. Women in the desires romance position likely experience negative affect when their cross-sex friend rejects their romantic overtures, leading them to report more antisocial behavior. Interestingly, men did not report higher than usual levels of antisocial behavior when they were in the would-be lover position. One explanation for this sex difference is that women are less accustomed than men to having their romantic advances rejected (Motley & Reeder, 1995), which causes them to experience more negative affect.

Several other differences also emerged in the self-reported maintenance behaviors of those who were in the rejecting position versus the would-be lover position (Guerrero & Chavez, 2005). Specifically, would-be lovers were more likely than rejectors to report using routine contact and activity, as well as flirtation. Rejectors, on the other hand, were more likely than would-be lovers to report talking about the state of the relationship and their romantic relationships with other people. Notice that this finding introduces a potential caveat to the finding that cross-sex friends tend to treat talk about the relationship as a taboo topic. In some cases, people in the rejecting position may feel that it is necessary to talk about the relationship in order to thwart the would-be lovers' attempts to turn a friendship romantic.

CONCLUSION

The transition from a friendship to a romantic relationship is fairly commonplace, yet little scholarly research has investigated this issue directly. Nonetheless, a few tentative conclusions emerge from the literature. First, traditional stage theories may not adequately describe the developmental path that typically characterizes romantic relationships that began as friendships. Therefore, researchers should examine how various types of intimacy develop within these relationships. Researchers should also identify common turning points that mark significant changes in the nature of the relationship.

Second, theories of uncertainty reduction and expectancy violations can inform scholarly knowledge regarding the friendship-to-romance transition. There is much to learn in this area. For example, which secret tests are most effective in reducing uncertainty for friends with romantic potential? Does uncertainty increase right before or during the transition, as Solomon and Knobloch's (2004) relational turbulence model suggests? The reduction of uncertainty may serve as a pathway for confirming one another's romantic feelings and redefining the relationship. There may also be times when cross-sex friends prefer uncertainty to possible rejection or the potential destruction of their relationships. The principles underlying Afifi and Weiner's (2004) theory of motivated information management may help explain if and how cross-sex friends attempt to reduce uncertainty when one (or both) of the partners is interested in turning the friendship romantic. Considerable work also needs to be conducted on how expectations and goals impact the transition from friendship to romance, including how positive and negative expectancy violations might impede or enhance the probability that a friendship will evolve into a romantic relationship. Mongeau's work (reviewed throughout this chapter) illustrates that goals and expectations for first dates differ on the basis of relationship history, but little is known about how goals and expectations operate beyond the first date in transitioned relationships.

Third, research on topic avoidance, secret tests, and relational maintenance suggests that the transition between friendship and romance can be marked by both decreases and increases in communication. Although the state of the relationship may be a taboo topic in some cross-sex friendships, people may be most likely to avoid relationship talk when they are interested in moving a friendship toward romance but fear that their friend is not. By contrast, people may talk about the state of the relationship and engage in increased maintenance behavior when they perceive romantic interest to be mutual. Topic avoidance and secret tests may dominate up until the point when partners perceive mutuality, then increased maintenance and openness about the state of the relationship may flourish.

Finally, research on the transition from friendships to romantic relationships should diversify its contextual base above and beyond the readily available sample of undergraduate college students (Sears, 1986). As we noted earlier, we know very little about, and desperately need research on, how friendships transition from platonic to romantic in gay male or lesbian relationships. As another example, research generally should focus on a greater variety of age groups. A greater concern for long-term entanglements among middle-aged adults (Mongeau et al., 2007) may influence how partners approach friendships and their transitions to romantic relationships. Extending the age limit even further by focusing on senior citizens would provide an interesting perspective on these transitions. This is an age group that is growing rapidly in size yet is nearly absent from research on relationship development. Investigating transitions in older populations might also allow us to consider how relationships interlay with health and caregiving issues. Examining how research generalizes across gay and straight relationships, as well as different age groups, will help scholars further understand the complexities involved in the transition from a friendship to a romantic relationship.

REFERENCES

Abbey, A. (1987). Misperceptions of friendly behavior as sexual interest: A survey of naturally occurring incidents. *Psychology of Women Quarterly, 11*, 173–194.

Afifi, W. A., & Burgoon, J. K. (1998). "We never talk about that": A comparison of cross-sex friendships and dating relationships on uncertainty and topic avoidance. *Personal Relationships, 5*, 255–272.

Afifi, W. A., & Faulkner, S. L. (2000). On being "just friends": The frequency and impact of sexual activity in cross-sex friendships. *Journal of Social and Personal Relationships, 17*, 205–222.

Afifi, W. A., & Guerrero, L. K. (1998). Some things are better left unsaid II: Topic avoidance in friendships. *Communication Quarterly, 46*, 231–249.

Afifi, W. A., & Metts, S. (1998). Characteristics and consequences of expectation violations in close relationships. *Journal of Social and Personal Relationships, 15*, 365–392.

Afifi, W. A., & Weiner, J. L. (2004). Toward a theory of motivated information management. *Communication Theory, 14*, 167–190.

Altman, I., & Taylor, D. A. (1973). *Social penetration: The development of interpersonal relationships.* New York: Holt, Rinehart & Winston.

Andersen, P. A., Guerrero, L. K., & Jones, S. M. (2006). Nonverbal behavior in intimate interactions and intimate relationships. In V. Manusov & M. Patterson (Eds.), *Handbook of nonverbal communication* (pp. 259–277). Thousand Oaks, CA: Sage.

Aron, A., Dutton, D. G., Aron, E. A., & Iverson, A. (1989). Experiences of falling in love. *Journal of Social and Personal Relationships, 6*, 243–157.

Baumeister, R. F. (2000). Gender differences in erotic plasticity: The female sex drive as socially flexible and responsive. *Psychological Bulletin, 126*, 347–374.

Baumeister, R. F., Worman, S. R., & Stillwell, A. M. (1993). Unrequited love: On heartbreak, anger, guilt, scriptlessness and humiliation. *Journal of Personality and Social Psychology*, 64, 377–394.

Baxter, L. A., & Bullis, C. (1986). Turning points in developing romantic relationships. *Human Communication Research*, 12, 469–493.

Baxter, L. A., & Wilmot, W. W. (1984). "Secret tests": Social strategies for acquiring information about the state of the relationship. *Human Communication Research*, 2, 171–201.

Baxter, L. A., & Wilmot, W. W. (1985). Taboo topics in close relationships. *Journal of Social and Personal Relationships*, 2, 253–269.

Bell, R. A., & Buerkel-Rothfuss, N. L. (1990). S(he) loves me, s(he) loves me not: Predictors of relational information-seeking in courtship and beyond. *Communication Quarterly*, 38, 64–82.

Berger, C. R. (1979). Beyond initial interaction: Uncertainty, understanding, and the development of interpersonal relationships. In H. Giles & R. N. St. Clair (Eds.), *Language and social psychology* (pp. 122–144). Oxford: Basil Blackwell.

Berger, C. R., & Calabrese, R. J. (1975). Some explorations in initial interactions and beyond: Toward a developmental theory of interpersonal communication. *Human Communication Research*, 1, 99–112.

Berscheid, E. (1983). Emotion. In H. H. Kelly, E. Berscheid, A. Christensen, J. H. Harvey, T. L. Huston, G. Levinger, E. McClintock, L. A. Peplau, & D. R. Peterson (Eds.), *Close relationships* (pp. 110–168). San Francisco: Freeman.

Bleske-Rechek, A. L., & Buss, D. M. (2001). Opposite-sex friendship: Sex differences and similarities in initiation, selection, and dissolution. *Personality and Social Psychology Bulletin*, 27, 1310–1323.

Bostwick, T. D., & DeLucia, J. L. (1992). Effects of gender and specific dating behaviors on perceptions of sex willingness and date rape. *Journal of Social and Clinical Psychology*, 11, 14–25.

Burgoon, J. K., & Hale, J. L. (1988). Nonverbal expectancy violations: Model elaboration and application to immediacy behaviors. *Communication Monographs*, 55, 58–79.

Burgoon, J. K., Stern, L. A., & Dillman, L. (1995). *Interpersonal adaptation: Dyadic interaction patterns*. New York: Cambridge University Press.

Cate, R. M., & Lloyd, S. A. (1992). *Courtship*. Newbury Park, CA: Sage.

Chang, S-C., & Chan, C-N. (2007). Perceptions of commitment change during mate selection: The case of Taiwanese newlyweds. *Journal of Social and Personal Relationships*, 24, 55–68.

Christopher, F. S., & Cate, R, M. (1985). Premarital sexual pathways and relationship development. *Journal of Social and Personal Relationships*, 2, 271–288.

Cupach, W. R, & Spitzberg, B. H. (2004). *The dark side of relationship pursuit: From attraction to obsession and stalking*. Mahwah, NJ: Lawrence Erlbaum.

Dainton, M., Zelley, E., & Langan, E. (2003). Maintaining friendships throughout the lifespan. In D. J. Canary & M. Dainton (Eds.), *Maintaining relationships through communication: Relational, contextual, and cultural variations* (pp. 79–102). Mahwah, NJ: Lawrence Erlbaum.

Davis, K. E., & Todd, M. J. (1982). Friendship and love relationships. In E. E. Davis (Ed.), *Advances in descriptive psychology* (Vol. 2, pp. 79–122). Greenwich, CT: JAI.

Dindia, K. (2003). Definitions and perspectives on relational maintenance communication. In D. J. Canary & M. Dainton (Eds.), *Maintaining relationships through communication: Relational, contextual, and cultural variations* (pp. 1–28). Mahwah, NJ: Lawrence Erlbaum.

Fishbein, M., & Ajzen, I. (1975). *Belief, attitude, intention, and behavior*. Reading, MA: Addison-Wesley.

Folkes, V. S. (1982). Communicating the causes of social rejection. *Journal of Experimental Social Psychology*, 18, 235–252.

Guerrero, L. K., & Afifi, W. A. (1995). Some things are better left unsaid: Topic avoidance in family relationships. *Communication Quarterly*, 43, 276–296.

Guerrero, L. K., Andersen, P. A., & Afifi, W. A. (2007). *Close encounters: Communicating in relationships* (2nd ed.). Thousand Oaks, CA: Sage.

Guerrero, L. K., & Chavez, A. M. (2005). Relational maintenance in cross-sex friendships characterized by different types of romantic intent: An exploratory study. *Western Journal of Communication*, 69, 341–360.

Guerrero, L. K., Eloy, S. V., & Wabnik, A. I. (1993). Linking maintenance strategies to relationship development and disengagement: A reconceptualization. *Journal of Social and Personal Relationships*, 10, 273–283.

Guerrero, L. K., Jones, S. M., & Burgoon, J. K. (2000). Responses to nonverbal intimacy change in romantic dyads: Effects of behavioral valence and expectancy violation. *Communication Monographs*, 67, 325–346.

Hatfield, E., & Rapson, R. L. (1987). Passionate love: New directions in research. In W. H. Jones & D. Perlman (Eds.), *Advances in personal relationships* (Vol. 1, pp. 109–139). Greenwich, CT: JAI.

Hendrick, S. S., & Hendrick, C. (2000). Romantic love. In C. Hendrick & S. S. Hendrick (Eds.). *Close relationships: A sourcebook* (pp. 203–215). Thousand Oaks, CA: Sage.

Hughes, M., Morrison, K., & Asada, J. K. (2005). What's love got to do with it? Exploring the impact of maintenance rules, love attitudes, and network support on friends with benefits relationships. *Western Journal of Communication, 69,* 49–66.

Hyde, J. S., & Oliver, M. B. (2000). Gender differences in sexuality: Results from meta-analysis. In C. B. Travis & J. W. White (Eds.), *Sexuality, society, and feminism* (pp. 59–77). Washington, DC: American Psychological Association.

Johnson, A. J., Wittenberg, E., Haigh, M., Wigley, S., Becker, J., Brown, K., et al. (2004). The process of relationship development and deterioration: Turning points in friendships that have terminated. *Communication Quarterly, 52,* 54–68.

Johnson, A. J., Wittenberg, E., Villagran, M., Mazure, M., & Villagran, P. (2003). Relational progression as a dialectic: Examining turning points in communication among friends. *Communication Monographs, 70,* 230–249.

Kelley, K., Pilchowicz, E., & Byrne, D. (1981). Responses of males to female-initiated dates. *Bulletin of the Psychonomic Society, 17,* 195–196.

Knapp, M. L., & Vangelisti, A. L. (2005). *Interpersonal communication and human relationships* (5th ed.). Boston: Allyn & Bacon.

Knobloch, L. K., & Carpenter-Theune, K. E. (2004). Topic avoidance in developing romantic relationships: Associations with intimacy and relational uncertainty. *Communication Research, 31,* 173–205.

Knobloch, L. K., & Solomon, D. H. (1999). Measuring the sources and content of relational uncertainty. *Communication Studies, 50,* 261–278.

Knobloch, L. K., & Solomon, D. H. (2002). Intimacy and the magnitude and experience of episodic uncertainty within romantic relationships. *Personal Relationships, 9,* 457–478.

Laner, M. R., & Ventrone, N. A. (2000). Dating scripts revisited. *Journal of Family Issues, 21,* 488–500.

Lewis, R. A. (1973). A longitudinal test of a developmental framework for premarital dyadic formation. Journal of Marriage and the Family, 35, 16–25.

McCroskey, J. C., & McCain, T. A. (1974). The measurement of interpersonal attraction. *Speech Monographs, 41,* 261–266.

Messman, S. J., Canary, D. J., & Hause, K. S. (2000). Motives to remain platonic, equity, and the use of maintenance strategies in opposite-sex friendships. *Journal of Social and Personal Relationships, 17,* 67–94.

Metts, S., Sprecher, S., & Regan, P. C. (1998). Communication and sexual desire. In P. A. Andersen & L. K. Guerrero (Eds.). *Handbook of communication and emotion: Research, theory, applications, and contexts* (pp. 353–377). San Diego, CA: Academic Press.

Milardo, R. M. (1982). Friendship networks in developing relationships: Converging and diverging social environments. *Social Psychology Quarterly, 45,* 162–172.

Mongeau, P. A., & Carey, C. M. (1996). Who's wooing whom II: An experimental investigation of date-initiation and expectancy violation. *Western Journal of Communication, 60,* 195–213.

Mongeau, P. A., Hale, J. L., Johnson, K. L., & Hillis, J. D. (1993). Who's wooing whom? An investigation of female-initiated dating. In P. J. Kalbfleisch (Ed.), *Interpersonal communication: Evolving interpersonal relationships* (pp. 51–68). Hillsdale, NJ: Lawrence Erlbaum.

Mongeau, P. A., Jacobsen, J., & Donnerstein, C. (2007). Defining dates and first date goals: Generalizing from undergraduates to single adults. *Communication Research, 34*(5), 526–547.

Mongeau, P. A., & Johnson, K. L. (1995). Predicting cross-sex first-date sexual expectations and involvement: Contextual and individual difference factors. *Personal Relationships, 2,* 301–312.

Mongeau, P. A., Ramirez, A., & Vorell, M. (2003, February). *Friends with benefits: Initial exploration of sexual, non-romantic relationships.* Paper presented at the annual meeting of the Western States Communication Association, Salt Lake City, UT.

Mongeau, P. A., Serewicz, M. C. M., Henningsen, M. L. M., & Davis, K. L. (2006). Sex differences in the transition to a heterosexual romantic relationship. In K. Dindia & D. J. Canary (Eds.), *Sex differences and similarities in communication* (2nd ed., pp. 337–358). Mahwah, NJ: Lawrence Erlbaum.

Mongeau, P. A., Serewicz, M. C. M., & Therrien, L. F. (2004). Goals for cross-sex first dates: Identification, measurement, and the influence of contextual factors. *Communication Monographs, 71,* 121–147.

Mongeau, P. A., Shaw, C., & Bacue, A. (2000, February). *Dating norms on one college campus.* Paper presented to the Western States Communication Association, Sacramento, CA.

Mongeau, P. A., & Teubner, G. (2002, November). *Romantic relationship transitions.* Paper presented to the National Communication Association, New Orleans, LA.

Mongeau, P. A., Yeazell, M., & Hale, J. L. (1994). Sex differences in relational message interpretations on male- and female-initiated first dates: A research note. *Journal of Social Behavior and Personality, 9,* 731–742.

Morr, M. C., & Mongeau, P. A. (2004). First date expectations: The impact of sex of initiator, alcohol consumption, and relationship type. *Communication Research, 31,* 3–35.

Motley, M. T., & Reeder, H. M. (1995). Unwanted escalation of sexual intimacy: Male and female perceptions of connotations and relational consequences of resistance messages. *Communication Monographs, 62,* 355–382.

Murstein, B. I. (1970). Stimulus-value-role: A theory of marital choice. *Journal of Marriage and the Family, 32,* 465–481.

O'Meara, D. (1989). Cross-sex friendship: Four basic challenges of an ignored relationship. *Sex Roles, 21,* 525–543.

Parks, M. R., & Adelman, M. B. (1983). Communication networks and the development of romantic relationships: An expansion of uncertainty reduction theory. *Human Communication Research, 10,* 55–79.

Paul, E. L., & Hayes, K. A. (2002). The casualties of "casual" sex: A qualitative exploration of the phenomenology of college students' hookups. *Journal of Social and Personal Relationships, 19,* 639–661.

Planalp, S., & Honeycutt, J. M. (1985). Events that increase uncertainty in personal relationships. *Human Communication Research, 11,* 593–604.

Prager, K. J. (1995). *The psychology of intimacy.* New York: Guilford.

Rawlins, W. (1982). Cross-sex friendship and the communicative management of sex-role expectations. *Communication Quarterly, 30,* 343–352.

Reeder, H. M. (2000). "I like you … as a friend": The role of attraction in cross-sex friendship. *Journal of Social and Personal Relationships, 17,* 329–348.

Reeder, H. M. (2003). *"I like you … as a friend": Attraction in cross-sex friendship.* Los Angeles: Roxbury.

Rose, S. M. (1985). Same- and cross-sex friendships and the psychology of homosociality. *Sex Roles, 12,* 63–74.

Sears, D. O. (1986). College sophomores in the laboratory: Influences of a narrow data base on social psychology's view of human nature. *Journal of Personality and Social Psychology, 51,* 515–530.

Solomon, D. H., & Knobloch, L. K. (2001). Relationship uncertainty, partner interference, and intimacy within dating relationships. *Journal of Social and Personal Relationships, 18,* 804–820.

Solomon, D. H., & Knobloch, L. K. (2004). A model of relational turbulence: The role of intimacy, relational uncertainty, and inference from partners in appraisals of irritations. *Journal of Social and Personal Relationships, 21,* 795–816.

Stafford, L. (2003). Maintaining romantic relationships: A summary and analysis of one research program. In D. J. Canary & M. Dainton (Eds.), *Maintaining relationships through communication: Relational, contextual, and cultural variations* (pp. 51–77). Mahwah, NJ: Lawrence Erlbaum.

Stafford, L., & Canary, D. J. (1991). Maintenance strategies and romantic relationship type, gender and relational characteristics. *Journal of Social and Personal Relationships, 8,* 217–242.

Sternberg, R. J. (1987). *The triangle of love: Intimacy, passion, commitment.* New York: Basic Books.

Section *III*

Diverse Contexts of Relationship Initiation

10

The Social and Physical Environment of Relationship Initiation
An Interdependence Analysis

XIMENA B. ARRIAGA, CHRISTOPHER R. AGNEW,
NICOLE M. CAPEZZA, and JUSTIN J. LEHMILLER

*T*here are a myriad of factors that might influence the onset of a romantic relationship. Various factors may influence whether two people are more or less likely to meet (e.g., whether they have overlapping social circles), likely to interact (e.g., whether they tend to visit similar establishments), and likely to continue on a course toward a relationship (e.g., whether they enjoy doing the same things). In this chapter we examine a specific set of factors, namely, the social and physical environments in which relationships are situated, that play a significant role in guiding the onset and course of close relationships. One of our goals is to discuss extant research on social and physical factors that influence relationship initiation. However, a second, more central goal is to elucidate how such factors are considered in explaining relationship initiation from an interdependence theory framework (Holmes, 2004; Kelley et al., 2003). As such, we limit our review of social and physical factors insofar as they are relevant to an interdependence analysis (see Parks, 2007, as well as Fehr, this volume, for a review of additional social and physical factors).

In this chapter we use concepts from interdependence theory to describe social and physical factors that influence when, how, and in what form relationships begin. We begin by defining social and physical environments, and thereafter discuss how influences from others and from the physical setting can be understood in terms of four major interdependence concepts: (a) expectations about interactions; (b) the immediate situation in which interaction partners find themselves; (c) the motives they bring to the interaction as determined by their respective histories, individual characteristics, relationship goals, and adherence to broader social norms; and (d) the role of inferences they each draw about their interaction in directing future behavior.

OVERVIEW OF SOCIAL AND PHYSICAL ENVIRONMENTS

We have previously used the term *social environment* to refer to the network of important individuals with whom couple members feel close bonds (Arriaga, Goodfriend, & Lohmann, 2004). Milardo (1982) has similarly conceptualized social environments as comprising the interrelations linking couples to their respective networks of kin relations and friends. Here, we broaden *social environment* to include all persons who potentially affect relationship processes, even persons who are mere acquaintances but nonetheless exert an influence. This can include, among others, family members, friends, past partners, religious groups, and work groups.

We define the *physical environment* in relationship settings as the physical properties of a situation that affect interpersonal behavior. Roger Barker (1978) suggested that people organize their environment based on their immediate activities and that their environment may influence activities. Similarly, we suggest that people seek relationships in particular physical environments and that some environments allow for relationship initiation more than others. For example, those interested in meeting others are more likely to go to an informal restaurant with a bar area than a formal restaurant, circular chair arrangements for group meetings are more conducive to interacting with others than line arrangements in which everyone faces the front of a room, and a lecture to the same group of students may differ if it is to be delivered in a pizza parlor versus a classroom. Throughout this chapter we identify instances in which the physical environment influences relationship initiation behavior.

Social and physical environments share the characteristics of influencing a couple's behavior and yet existing independent of the couple members themselves. A substantial body of research documents the ways in which social environments exert direct and indirect influences on couples' behaviors. Indeed, being embedded in social networks can create opportunities to meet others and initiate relationships. Parks (2007) described "social proximity effects" on relationship initiation, namely, that two people are more likely to initiate a relationship with each other if they are embedded in social networks that have linkages (i.e., chances of meeting increase as the number of social "links" separating any two people decreases). For example, Parks and Eggert (1991) revealed that two people who initiate same-sex friendships and premarital romantic relationships often knew one or more persons in common prior to meeting each other.

Less research has been devoted to studying the manner in which physical environments influence relationships. That said, groundbreaking research on this topic has shown how people become friendlier when their physical proximity provides more opportunities to meet, although physical proximity may no longer be a necessary condition for relationship initiation given the proliferation of computer-mediated interaction (Festinger, Schachter, & Back, 1950; Parks, 2007). Even factors as subtle as the ambient temperature, ambient music, and concentration of ions in the air (atmospheric electricity) can influence whether two individuals become attracted to one another (Baron, 1987; Griffiitt, 1970; Houston, Wright, Ellis, Holloway, & Hudson, 2005). Other research has focused on how physical locations and objects are meaningful to individuals and cultural groups (Valsiner, 2000). Despite this groundbreaking work, there has not been a systematic theoretical analysis (one that can generalize from one set of relationship-promoting physical factors to another) as to how physical characteristics of a given situation direct expectations, interaction motives and behavior, or attribution of partner motives.

EXPECTATIONS AND THE ONSET OF RELATIONSHIPS

Expectations about Anticipated Interactions

In many anticipated interactions, people have expectations, or hunches, about aspects of interactions—for example, expectations about what each person will say or do, how rewarding the interaction will be, or whether there will be future interactions. Visits with friends, the home environment, the workplace, and other settings in which people spend significant amounts of time typically are saturated with opportunities to interact with others in predictable ways, so much so that people often give little thought to their expectations about the interaction (e.g., automatically greeting someone at work by saying, "Hey, how's it going?" and anticipating a reply such as "Fine, and you?" rather than a genuine analysis of how it really is going). In contrast, some anticipated interactions generate a fair amount of uncertainty, often because they are with unfamiliar others, they are interactions that are not well rehearsed (e.g., meeting an extremely powerful or celebrated person), or the appropriate level of intimacy has yet to be established (cf. Solomon & Knobloch, 2001).

Either within or beyond awareness, people perpetually evaluate situations for their desirability or value, that is, for the outcomes they afford. New situations are evaluated by comparing the new experiences with one's generalized expectations based on previous experiences. Interdependence theory describes expectations in terms of a comparison level, or CL (Thibaut & Kelley, 1959). A CL is the standard against which individuals evaluate the "goodness versus badness" of specific interaction outcomes. Outcomes that exceed one's CL are experienced as positive and satisfying, and outcomes that are below one's CL are experienced as negative and dissatisfying. In short, the discrepancy between one's current outcomes and one's expectations directly affects one's current level of satisfaction. Research has shown that people are happier with their close partners to the extent that the partner matches or exceeds their internal standards (Sternberg & Barnes, 1985; Wetzel & Insko, 1982).

An individual's CL is shaped by his or her own prior and current experiences, by observing interactions and relationships of comparable friends and kin, and by noting norms for relationships that are conveyed in popular media and other sources of information. Expectation-relevant information (from one's own or others' experiences) that is most memorable or salient has greater weight in shaping an individual's CL than less salient information. New experiences and information, because of their recency, may be weighed heavily in setting expectations; first impressions and early interactions with a potential partner will "set the tone" for what to expect with that person in the immediate future. In sum, expectations provide a heuristic for what to anticipate in each new interaction and play a significant role in determining how satisfying particular interactions are experienced to be.

Expectations about Interactions Not Experienced

In addition to expectations about a current interaction, interdependence theory describes expectations regarding alternative interactions in terms of a comparison level for alternatives, or CL_{alt} (Thibaut & Kelley, 1959). CL_{alt} describes the quality of the best alternative to the current relationship. What might be the best available alternative? The current involvement may be judged against other involvements or situations that would seem to be attainable, such as initiating another relationship, going back to a previous relationship, having multiple relationships, or having none at all. Most individuals have expectations about what their alternate situation(s) to the current one might be.

In contrast to CL and its influence on satisfaction, expectations about the best alternate situation influence one's level of dependence, or the extent to which an individual relies uniquely on the current situation for attaining good outcomes. When current outcomes exceed CL_{alt}, an individual is increasingly dependent or reliant on the current situation for good outcomes; when current outcomes remain below CL_{alt}, an individual becomes increasingly less dependent on the current situation and thus more likely to abandon the current situation for the very best one. Existing research reveals that dependence on a relationship is lower—and the likelihood of voluntarily ending a relationship is greater—among individuals who experience poor outcomes in the current relationship and regard their alternatives as attractive (Agnew, Arriaga, & Wilson, in press; Bui, Peplau, & Hill, 1996; Drigotas & Rusbult, 1992; Felmlee, Sprecher, & Bassin, 1990; Le & Agnew, 2003; Rusbult, 1983; Simpson, 1987).

Physical and Social Influences on Expectations

Characteristics of the physical environment influence generalized expectations for the type of interaction that might occur. Physical settings are saturated with expectations that have been learned as a result of being raised in a particular culture (Valsiner, 2000); for example, people anticipate somber interactions rather than joyous ones in funeral homes (even when a funeral is not taking place), lively interactions at a wedding reception, low-key interactions in a library, and respectful interactions in a doctor's office.

Physical settings can influence a person's generalized expectations in ongoing relationships, as is the case in long-distance relationships (i.e., those in which couple members see each other less than they would otherwise because they are separated by a large physical distance) The general shared expectation about long-distance relationships is that they are doomed to failure. One study reported that 66% of individuals in a long-distance relationship believed that the average long-distance relationship would end within a year (Helgeson, 1994). Why continue in a relationship that is expected to fail? Trust, which is an expectation about whether a partner will be caring, responsive, and faithful (see Holmes & Rempel, 1989), is a key factor in any relationship, but it is particularly important in long-distance relationships. Some individuals may be less likely to venture into a long-distance relationship because they are insecure and unable to trust others, or because they had negative past experiences in similar situations, making the prospect of a long-distance relationship much less likely. Other individuals are more secure and trusting of others and have strong desires to make a relationship work.

Physical settings and objects may also influence a person's more specific expectations when initiating a relationship. For example, a "first date" at a country club social function is likely to elicit a different set of anticipated interactions than one at a bikini mud-wrestling match. Whether or not these interactions are satisfying will by affected by past experiences and other factors that weigh into one's CL; a person who has had bad (or perhaps boring) experiences at country clubs may feel more satisfied when the partner departs from the formal club traditions, and a woman who has come to see bikini mud wrestling as a new form of free feminine expression may take pleasure in knowing her partner likes the sport.

Social influences on interaction expectations abound. Research has shown peers can directly affect one's standard for appropriate behavior in relationships (i.e., one's CL) and one's standard for remaining in a relationship (i.e., one's CL_{alt}). For example, friends have opinions about others' relationships (Agnew, Loving, & Drigotas, 2001), and these opinions may influence whether a relationship continues or ends (Etcheverry & Agnew, 2004; Felmlee, 2001; Lehmiller & Agnew, 2006). At a broader social level, fraternities and sororities set norms for what is considered appropriate versus inappropriate behavior for those who just joined the group ("pledges") and thus are in the early stages of establishing relationships; norms for them differ from norms for established members (Keltner, Young, Heerey, Oemig, & Monarch, 1998). Merely being a member of certain social groups may influence generalized expectations about the types of interactions one has. For example, merely being a member of a sorority or fraternity has been shown to increase the likelihood of dating, as compared with nonmembers (Whitbeck & Hoyt, 1991). Similarly, being affiliated with religious groups that set restrictions on their members can influence expectations about appropriate behaviors and even appropriate partners, namely, those with the appropriate values. We speculate that the vast number of Internet chat groups that have emerged in the last decade may influence what chat members seek in a partner and what expectations they have about interactions.

In summary, expectations figure prominently in the mental state a person has upon entering a situation. In the next section, we consider the situational and personal underpinnings that explain interaction behaviors. Interdependence theory provides an account of the process by which some behaviors make their way into an interaction but others do not.

INTERACTION: THE ROLE OF SITUATIONS AND PERSONAL MOTIVES

"Interaction is a function of the Situation, Person A, and Person B" (Kelley et al., 2003). This seemingly straightforward statement is a major premise of interdependence theory, so we elaborate on its meaning with respect to relationship initiation.

The Given Situation

Theoretical Background   What is meant by "the Situation" in the statement above? The situation (also referred to as the "given matrix" by Kelley and Thibaut, 1978, and the "geo-behavioral environment" by Kelley, 1991) has been defined as having two components.

One component is the environment in which two interaction partners find themselves (the "geographic environment"; Kelley, 1991). The *environment* refers to the physical setting (i.e., the immediate space within which an interaction takes place, the objects within immediate reach that may be of use to the interaction partners, and primes or objects that bring to mind specific ideas, such as posters, music, bookshelves, guns, and other symbols) as well as the social setting (e.g., the type of social event, knowledge of the typical social behaviors for that social event, and the actual or implied presence of known or unknown others).

The second component of the given situation concerns what one can refer to as the *generic qualities* of interaction partners: their generalized characteristics at the time of interaction (i.e., their current mental and physical states, broadly speaking), how most people of a particular social group would approach the given interaction in light of their physical abilities (e.g., being able to move around freely, and being capable of given physical tasks), and generally shared assumptions that have been acquired through basic learning processes (e.g., carrying more things is more onerous than carrying fewer things, being around happy people is more pleasant than being around sad people, and a $10 bill is better to have than a $1 bill). Although people vary in their basic physical abilities and generally shared assumptions, the important distinction to be made is that these personal characteristics are ones that a person brings to any interpersonal interaction, not ones that are unique or tailored to the given interaction.

To illustrate the given situation and other interdependence concepts, we will refer to a hypothetical example of relationship initiation. This example involves Mike and Mona, two college students in a typical midsize college town in the United States. They do not know each other, but they separately show up at a bar that is populated by other college students, and they happen to sit next to each other. They are each there with friends; Mike's friends brought Mike with the hope that he could forget about his recent breakup by "hooking up" with someone (see Paul, Wenzel, & Harvey, this volume); that is, they anticipated he would have a single-occurrence sexual encounter in which there would be no expectations of emotional intimacy. Mona's friends were having their weekly "girls' night out," in which they go to a social setting with the purpose of enjoying each other's company. In the course of an hour, Mike and Mona each had several drinks, the lights dimmed, and the bar became extremely crowded. At one point while making his way through the crowded bar, Mike accidentally bumped into Mona and spilled his bloody Mary on her white shirt.

This given situation can be described in terms of the environment defined above. From an interdependence standpoint, some of the relevant aspects of the physical and social setting include the following: Mike and Mona are in a bar populated by other college students in a social setting, where a typical behavior is to meet others; the music is not too loud, making it possible to talk; they are drinking alcohol, which may have the effect of lowering their inhibitions; Mike causes an accident that forces the issue of whether they will make contact with one another; and the presence of their friends makes it ambiguous whether they are at the bar to meet others or to enjoy a bar environment with their friends, without the goal of meeting others.

A more formal interdependence analysis would involve representing this (or any) given situation in terms of possible responses by Mike and Mona, as well as the outcomes attached to different behavior options in the given situation. One attaches specific outcomes to Mike and Mona's potential responses by assuming they each have no concern for the other, and without considering their unique hopes, concerns, or considerations that might ensue in the interaction. As such, when Mike spills his drink on Mona, the outcomes represented in the given situation are those that a reasonable, typical, peer college student would make, ignoring potential interaction hopes or considerations. Mike's choices at this juncture may be to pretend the spill did not happen and ignore Mona, acknowledge the spill but make no overtures to amend the situation, take responsibility for the spill and make some amends, or a variation of these options. Ignoring any social or interaction considerations (e.g., "She's attractive, and I hate to do this to her," "If I ignore her, she may spill her drink on me to get me back," and "The 'right' thing to do is to apologize"), the most rational behavior for a person who has no concern for the other (i.e., the behavior with the highest outcome) is to ignore the situation and not be hassled by the accident; making amends may be the most costly behavior.

So far, we have provided a simplified description of a hypothetical situation by describing some (but not all) of the factors relevant to the given situation. Interdependence theory provides a sophisticated set of ideas for analyzing given situations, which we only briefly mention here (see Kelley et al., 2003, or Rusbult and Van Lange, 2003, for a more detailed description). It suggests that there are a few key characteristics or properties that are most relevant for understanding and predicting the interactions that are likely to take place in a given situation.

One set of properties concerns the pattern of outcomes for different response options and the ways in which partners affect each other's outcomes (namely, whether they strongly versus weakly affect each other, whether they share preferences for certain behavior or instead differ in their preferences, whether a person's outcomes are a function of his or her own behavior versus the partner's behavior versus their coordinated behavior, and whether each affects the other to a similar degree or instead one affects the other more; see Kelley et al., 2003, Sections 2.3 to 2.5). A second set of properties concerns whether both persons are aware of, and can communicate about, the outcome patterns at hand (see "information conditions" in Kelley et al., 2003). A third set of properties concerns the temporal and sequential order of two persons' actions (whether the situation is such that either could respond at any time, both could or must respond simultaneously, or they must take turns responding; see "response conditions" in Kelley et al., 2003). These are particular features that differentiate situations in ways that matter for interactions.

On their own and without knowledge of interdependence concepts, laypeople frequently (albeit not always) differentiate situations on the basis of some of these features. Even people unlikely to use the interdependence term *unilateral dependence* are familiar with situations in which one person "has the upper hand"; without formal knowledge of "response conditions," many people can recognize the meaning of failing to get a return phone call from a potential suitor; partners can recognize when they both tend to enjoy doing the same kinds of things, without labeling it *correspondence of outcomes*; and people intrinsically know which relationships affect them a lot and which affect them very little, without making references to specific "levels of dependence" in different relationships. Failing to detect key characteristics of situations—for example, that one is more affected by the partner's behavior than the partner is affected by one's behavior—is likely to be maladaptive, as partners will not be aware of the positives that are afforded in a given situation and may fall prey to costly interactions (Kelley et al., 2003, p. 8).

What is the nature of relationship initiation situations? Initiating intimate relationships frequently poses a dilemma between wanting to seek greater closeness yet having to take the risk inherent in revealing relatively personal information (Murray, 2005). Getting too close too fast may raise the desire to maintain autonomy. As such, "at early stages of relationship development, partners may alternate between selecting situations characterized by closeness and interdependence versus selecting situations characterized by autonomy and independence" (Kelley et al., 2003, p. 442). Situations in which partners seek more closeness reflect a shift in the properties of a situation, from one characterized by affecting each other's outcomes very little (i.e., more independent) to one characterized by being affected more (i.e., more interdependent). Partners may avoid situations that elicit differences in what they prefer to do (i.e., noncorrespondent outcomes) rather than highlight similarities (i.e., correspondent outcomes). Moreover, recently initiated relationships are likely to face issues of each partner having incomplete information about each other or about the future prospects of their relationship. Indeed, partners face substantial uncertainty in the early stages of intimacy (Solomon & Knobloch, 2001).

The Given Situation as Defined by Social Network Members and Physical Features   It seems obvious that many situations are created, and others avoided, at the behest of social network members. Family members, peers, and other members of one's network repeatedly define the interaction situations one might face. As one example, parents of young children may put effort into arranging "play dates" with children whom they can coach toward positive interactions (Pettit, Brown, Mize, & Lindsey, 1998). Later in life, parents may attempt to disrupt the romantic involvements of their teenaged children when they do not like or approve of the partner (Dowdy & Kliewer,

1998); their teenagers may conceal information regarding a romantic partner from their parents that they believe may lead to negative impressions (Baxter & Widenmann, 1993). Even the mere suggestion of repercussions from one's network may be enough to direct the new situations one seeks with a relationship partner. For example, the mere possibility that a couple's friendships may be disrupted may be enough to keep the couple's relationship intact (Milardo, 1986).

More specific to relationship initiation, arranging a child's marriage is still practiced in a number of cultures (Malhotra, 1991; Netting, 2006; Quinn, 1993). Typically parents select mates for their children with little or no input from the children themselves. In this way, parents directly influence with whom one will marry and thus have spousal interactions. At a broader level, religious institutions frequently influence the specific type of relationship initiation situation one faces, organizing highly structured social functions that encourage meeting potential dating partners. In light of attitudes opposing interfaith dating (Marshall & Markstrom-Adams, 1995), many recent "speed-dating" programs are sponsored by religious institutions so as to spark relationships among same-faith partners (visit, for example, http://www.offlinespeeddating.com). As another example, fundamentalist Christian groups in the United States that oppose homosexuality will frequently have programs for gay men to "reprogram" them so that they become heterosexual (Harvey, 1987), although there is little to no evidence that such "reparative" therapies work (see Haldeman, 1994). As such, these programs attempt to directly influence which relationships will *not* be initiated as well as which will.

What may be less obvious are the physical features of given situations that direct subsequent behavior (cf. Roger Barker's concept of a "behavior setting"; Barker, 1978). In general, people give little thought to how a physical setting might influence social interaction; if any influence is acknowledged, the physical setting is considered the mere background in which interactions take their own course. However, on occasion, the physical setting strongly imposes itself on social interaction. To illustrate this point, Kelley used the example of strangers who find themselves sitting next to each other on an airplane and must share the armrest (Kelley et al., 2003, pp. 338–342). They immediately become interdependent insofar as they each may affect the other's experience (e.g., each might make the other physically uncomfortable, each can interrupt the other's reading, and one may have to get up and thus must ask the other to move). This presents a physical constraint that directly influences the given situation.

Past research confirms that the physical setting can heavily influence the immediate situation in which initial interactions occur. There are even physical objects that infuse a situation with particular meaning and direct behavior uniformly across individuals. For example, early research by Berkowitz (1968) demonstrated how guns may bring to mind (or *prime*) an aggressive context; in one study, participants who interacted in a lab experiment in the presence (versus absence) of a handgun became more aggressive. Another study found that prior exposure to a business-related object (such as a briefcase) led participants to behave more competitively (Kay, Wheeler, Bargh, & Ross, 2004). What is particularly interesting about these research examples is that physical characteristics (in this case, a handgun and a briefcase) elicited a response to the given situation, and yet their heavy-handed effect was beyond the awareness of the participants. The general finding that objects and situations can act as cognitive and behavioral primes has become a hallmark of modern social psychological theory and research (Bargh & Chartrand, 2000).

The physical properties of a given situation may direct the course of close relationships. New college roommates must share a small dorm room and thus face immediate decisions about how to manage their physical space. They must also contend with differences in their individual personalities and propensities to get along with others (e.g., their respective levels of agreeableness may contribute to initial and sustained liking; Graziano & Eisenberg, 1997). However, research on naval recruits suggests (Altman, Taylor, & Wheeler, 1971) that, beyond these physical and personal constraints, what may be most likely to influence whether they have an amicable or contentious relationship is what they make of the situation, as we discuss in the next section. The physical constraints test their ability to set rules for use of the space and for their interactions, issues that involve taking into account the broader relationship (e.g., they must be around each other for many months, and cooperative roommate relationships are easier to manage than conflictive ones). Although such broader considerations may ultimately direct the course of the relationship (as we discuss in the next section), the given situation also exerts a direct influence in that it creates circumstances that make possible broader considerations; were new roommates living in individual rooms connected by a shared suite, their interaction considerations, resultant rules, and actions from that point forward might take a very different course. Couples who move into the same household face similar constraints; newlywed husbands in particular are more distressed shortly after moving in together than later (Kurdek, 1991).

Having described the concept of a given situation, we now turn to analyzing behavioral responses to the given situation. The interdependence concept relevant to analyzing the process leading up to actual behavior is that of *transforming a situation* (Kelley et al., 2003; also referred to as "transformation of motivation" in Kelley, 1979, 1991; Kelley & Thibaut, 1978).

Transforming a Given Situation and Resulting Behavior

Theoretical Background   How do the interaction partners respond to the given situation? For example, what does Mike do immediately after he spills his drink on Mona? His response may remain in the realm of the given situation. Specifically, he may not have noticed he spilled his drink and do nothing, thus demonstrating a lack of awareness of the given situation. Alternatively, he may have noticed he spilled the drink but choose not to be responsive to the broader social or interpersonal situation, and instead act on the basis of the given situation; as such, he may walk away, acting on the immediate urge of a person who does not consider Mona's circumstances or what he may want to achieve in the given situation.

Mike's response moves beyond the given situation once he considers Mona and how he will coordinate his behavior with her to achieve his interaction goals. He may recognize the immediate urge to walk away but instead take a moment to reflect on the broader normative and interpersonal considerations surrounding his blunder. If he considers social norms, he might be inclined to apologize; doing nothing becomes an aversive (low-outcome) option because social norms would lead him to perceive himself (and for others to perceive him) as a louse. If he is generally selfish in social interactions with strangers and he brings this generalized tendency to bear here, he may consider whether he is likely to see Mona again. If he is, the most attractive option may be to do the minimum so that she will not treat him badly in the future; if he is not likely to see her again, he may walk away. If Mike derives satisfaction from knowing he is a particularly selfless person—that is, he has a motive to be selfless—he may apologize, help Mona clean up, give her money to pay for the shirt, and offer to pay for a cab so that she may go home and change her clothes. If Mike considers his friends' efforts to make him forget his recent breakup by having a one-night stand—that is, he is motivated to heed his friends' expectations, directly falling prey to peer influence—he may not only apologize but also seize the opportunity to get to know her better with the hope of hooking up with her. The main point is that the given situation provides an immediate context or backdrop for an interaction. The actual response (vis-à-vis the situation) is the forefront of interaction. Either a person acts in the realm of the given situation (Mike walks away) or comes to see the situation in a new way that allows one to invoke broader social considerations and interaction goals.[1]

Whereas the given situation is defined in terms of behavioral choices and outcomes that are determined by factors external to the specific relationship itself, actual behavior frequently reflects what persons make of the given situation in light of their social and interpersonal considerations (Kelley et al., 2003; Kelley & Thibaut, 1978, pp. 16–17). Importantly, these considerations are highly individualized, more so than the given situation reactions of a generic person void of any concerns for the interaction partner (as reflected in reactions based on the given situation). As Kelley (1991) reflected on why he and John Thibaut developed the concept of transforming the situation, he wrote, "Thibaut and I were led to introduce this transformation step by the growing evidence (and obvious fact) that different subclasses of people act in consistently different ways in the same given [situation]" (p. 223).[2] People act in different ways because they typically do take into account where they stand with another person and have individualized motives, attitudes, and behavioral tendencies that they bring to bear in situations.

We have suggested that the situation as well as personal interaction motives or social considerations are crucial causal factors directing interpersonal behavior. The key elements to the analysis of behavior are the given situation, the interactants' actual behavior, and the intermediary psychological process that involves transforming the situation by reflecting on broader social and interpersonal considerations. Which element is most important? In most cases, all are necessary considerations in predicting behavior, but none can sufficiently account for behavior in the absence of the others. The situation plays a causal role in what interaction partners do; if the situation were different, the interaction that ensues would likely be different (or possibly not occur at all). However, behavior is only partly attributable to the given situation, and largely attributable to what a specific person makes of the given situation. As Kelley (Kelley et al., 2003) suggested, "[T]he behavior cannot be explained simply by the 'psychophysical' or given situation, but requires an attribution to a 'social person'" (p. 75; cf. Parks, 2007, p. 59). The social person reinterprets the current situation in light of his or her interaction goals, assessing which behavioral option would be most consistent with those goals.

In this way, behaviors based on transforming the given situation reflect the social aspects or "social personality" of a person (Kelley et al., 2003, p. 75). The more a specific behavior departs from given situation choices, the more the behavior reflects unique aspects of a particular individual (Kelley, 1991). For example, if Mike apologizes so as to conform to social norms, he would have transformed the given situation in ways that many people would have, and this would not say much about him as a person; a cad might use the situation to "help" Mona clean her shirt and seize the opportunity to touch her breast, an even bigger departure from an expected response but not among a subset of people seeking sexual contact; and if Mike is instantly attracted to Mona in ways that other men have never been, he might apologize profusely in an effort to see her again, a response that would convey a lot about Mike as a person. Thus, immediate responses to the spill vary in how much they communicate things about Mike individually. The same holds for what transpires after the spill. There is a possibility that Mike and Mona interact further, and Mona asks Mike if he would like to come with her to her apartment but he declines, stating he would like to take her out on a formal date another night. His decline of her invitation and request to see her again would reflect a sharp departure from expected behavior in the given situation; as such, his behavior would reveal much about his personal goal in this specific relationship and very little about the situation at hand, his general approach to relationships, or generalized norms and values. The more a behavior departs from what might be expected given the situation, the social norms, the general type of interaction, or even what generally occurs in a particular relationship, the more that behavior provides rich information about specialized motives driving a person. (Of course, some norms are specific to certain groups rather than generally shared, such as perceiving that certain types of partner violence are acceptable; see Capezza & Arriaga, in press.)

Influence of Social Network Members on Interaction Motives   Just as network members influence how a given situation is defined, they also influence the motives one invokes in an interaction. For example, although parents deter their children's risky and deviant behaviors by monitoring them, they also teach their children how to respond to such situations by invoking considerations of what is "right," thereby preempting deviant behavior (e.g., Dishion & Kavanagh, 2003). People may also be directed toward the "right" relationships. In one study, individuals in relationships experienced less uncertainty about their romantic partners and were less likely to break up when they communicated more often with their partners' family and friends, and received greater support for their romantic relationship from their own family and friends (Parks & Adelman, 1983).

Research on the influence of a "third party"—a common friend or acquaintance—also exemplifies how interactions may follow the influence of social network members. A third party may bring together two individuals and jump-start their relationship using various direct and indirect strategies (Parks, 2007). The two individuals are usually aware of the third party's efforts to join them. Thus, one of their interaction goals may be to please (or at least appease) the third party. Research suggests that two individuals are more likely to pursue a dating relationship when third parties bring them together than without third-party intervention (Parks, 2007).

Often the influence of others on one's interaction motives is implied, rather than direct. For example, members of high-status sororities and fraternities on average spend less money on dates than members of low-status ones (Whitbeck & Hoyt, 1991); it stands to reason that high-status members are not all acting on the basis of the given situation, but rather on the basis of directly or indirectly communicated norms defined by their peers that low-status others should have to pay to be on a date with them. Harris and Kalbfleisch (2000) demonstrated that the primary deterrent reported to beginning an interracial relationship was the perception that others would disapprove of the union. In this study, participants' fear of disapproval not only was limited to social network members (i.e., family and friends) but also extended to fear of disapproval in the workplace as well as by strangers. This finding suggests that when interracial interactions occur with a potential partner, as they often might on college campuses and other settings that bring together people from different backgrounds, some students may respond based merely on the anticipated or even implied reactions of others.

Influence of a Situation's Physical Properties on Interaction Motives   Earlier we provided several examples of how given situations may be strongly influenced by physical properties. For example, one may have to share an armrest on an airplane. The key question is, What do people make of the physical properties in the given situation? One or both may act solely on the basis of the given situation and attempt to hoard the armrest for the entire flight. More typically (but not always), the two people will assess the situation. As Kelley noted (Kelley et al., 2003), each quickly takes into account the other person and thus begins to consider likely interaction motives. Each would likely develop expectations about the other's "dispositions" based on the other's appearance, nonverbal behavior, and general stereotypes, and each would anticipate how the other will respond based on expectations.

Past research confirms that people consider, and act on, the broader interaction implications of a given situation with salient physical properties. Early research by Altman (Altman & Haythorn, 1967; Altman, Taylor, & Wheeler, 1971) revealed how effective (versus ineffective) use of space directed the quality of an ongoing interaction. Altman et al. (1971) studied naval recruits. They created a given situation highly infused with physical constraints by simulating an isolation mission in which pairs of men spent 8 days in confined quarters that were described as austere (bunks, a table, two chairs, a file cabinet, task equipment, a lamp, a refrigerator, a chemical toilet, and basic living supplies); the men lived on a survival-ration diet. The data suggested that men differed in what they made of the situation. Compared to those who could not complete the mission, those who did were more proactive in establishing rules about their social interactions and physical setting; more specifically, they were more likely to establish daily routines, which directly affected the extent and nature of their interactions, and they were more likely to designate use of a particular bed, chair, side of the table, and other physical objects.

There may be very subtle physical properties of a situation that trigger thoughts about the relationship at hand. In the context of relationship initiation, Dutton and Aron (1974) induced varying physiological states in male participants to examine what a person makes of an arousing versus nonarousing situation. Following an arousal manipulation, participants interacted with a female research assistant. When aroused by having to stand on a high, rickety bridge (versus a nonfrightening bridge), participants transformed a nonromantic interaction into one affording romantic interests.

People actively use physical settings to reflect their personality and thus channel how others might interact with them. Individuals who reside in a particular setting organize decorations and personalize the setting in ways that convey their individual dispositions to others (Gosling, Ko, Mannarelli, & Morris, 2002). Posters or color schemes frequently are used to decorate a bedroom, and they also convey personal likes and dislikes as well as how a person wants to be perceived by others. Indeed, others may form impressions of that person based on the physical setting. One study revealed that the cleanliness of a person's apartment led to various impressions of that individual's personality such that poor housekeepers received lower ratings of agreeableness, conscientiousness, and intelligence (Harris & Sachau, 2005).

Couple members similarly organize their physical settings to convey aspects of their "couple-hood." Altman (Altman, Brown, Staples, & Werner, 1992) used the term *placemaking* to capture ways that a couple's home communicates to others something about the couple. For example, couple members may display photographs of them together, rather than photographs of them apart, to convey they are a unit. In addition to communicating to others, home objects may remind the couple members themselves of a special occasion or moment in their lives together (Arriaga et al., 2004). These objects may have no meaning to others, but they hold special meaning for the couple and act as behavioral cues. Even a token gift at the early stages of a relationship can take on special meaning if the partners anticipate a committed, long-lasting relationship.

Are there relationship dispositions that guide couple members' interaction behaviors and that may be reflected in physical objects? By *relationship dispositions*, we are referring to those stable tendencies that develop over the course of interaction that are dyadic in nature, such as trust and commitment (Agnew, Van Lange, Rusbult, & Langston, 1998; Arriaga & Agnew, 2001; Holmes & Rempel, 1989). Recent research by Lohmann, Arriaga, and Goodfriend (2003) revealed that couples' physical settings map onto their relationship-specific dispositions (as would be suggested by an interdependence analysis). In their study, couple members living together (married or cohabitating) were visited in their home; once in separate rooms, one completed a questionnaire tapping various relationship characteristics, and the other went to the room in their home where they entertain others and answered questions regarding their favorite objects in the room and the objects they wanted visitors to notice. Controlling for relationship duration, couple members with a greater percentage of favorite and other-oriented objects that were acquired together (as opposed to acquired individually) reported feeling closer to their partner, having better relationship functioning, and having higher levels of commitment. Thus, holding constant relationship duration, couple members who were more motivated to keep the relationship intact resided in physical settings that were more "couple focused" (as compared with "individual focused").

Long-distance relationships provide another example in which the physical setting imposes itself on interaction behaviors. For couple members in long-distance relationships, communication often takes place either over the telephone or on a computer. As such, the immediate physical space for these interactions is not a shared space. In this situation, the objects within each couple member's space may take on more meaning because they are used as reminders of the partner and the relationship. For example, photographs from a special occasion or gifts from one's partner are likely to serve an important function in helping to maintain the sense of closeness despite the physical distance between two partners.

Distinguishing a Given Situation versus Transformed Responses

How can those observing an interaction tell the difference between a given situation response versus a response that occurred after transforming the given situation? Indeed, Mike generally may be a selfish person, and as such, he might take into account broader considerations and still walk away, a response that would be indistinguishable from acting on the basis of the given situation.

There are several ways to differentiate given situations versus transformed responses. One is to assess the extent to which a response deviated from normative patterns of behavior. As stated above, significant deviation from what one might expect another to do may be seen as a telltale sign of a response that is tailored to an individual's specific goals or concerns (e.g., Mike declining Mona's invitation to her apartment and asking her out for another night).

A second, related way is to assess whether a response differs from immediate self-interest; many do. In committed relationships, partners frequently transform a situation in which their and their partner's preferences are at odds by forgoing self-interest and responding in ways that further promote a strong commitment (Rusbult, Olsen, Davis, & Hannon, 2001). Committed partners also tend to think and reveal their thinking about their relationship to others in increasingly pluralistic ways (e.g., in terms of *we* and *us* as opposed to *me* and *she or he*; Agnew & Etcheverry, 2006; Agnew et al., 1998). In competitive relationships or others that reward self-interest, partners frequently transform a given competitive situation in ways that not only benefit themselves (a self-interested response) but also are costly to the partner (for example, by maximizing the difference in one's outcomes).

However, there may still be cases where two responses "look" the same (e.g., Mike walking away), but one is based on the given situation (e.g., it was in Mike's immediate self-interest to ignore broader considerations), whereas another is based on transforming the given situation (e.g., Mike considered what "makes sense" in the situation; he inferred it unlikely that he would see Mona again; and as a selfish person, he dreaded having to make amends, so he walked away). When given situation responses and transformed responses are indistinguishable, one way to differentiate them is based on their timing: Responses based on the given situation are faster than those that take into account broader considerations, presumably because consideration of broader aspects of a situation requires additional cognitive processing time (Yovetich & Rusbult, 1994). Although different reaction times may be difficult to detect in everyday interaction, Yovetich and Rusbult demonstrated how lab settings provide a controlled context in which measuring reaction times is not only feasible but also telling of given versus transformed responses.

Continuing Interactions

As individuals (Person A and Person B) respond to a given situation, the interaction does not stop there. Each person's response creates a new given situation for the other, and subsequent responses form the basis of an ongoing interaction. For example, if Mona suggests to Mike that they go to her apartment and Mike invokes his specific interaction goal by declining her invitation and suggesting they go out on a formal date, this poses a new given situation for Mona in which she can invoke her own goals for the interaction. In weighing whether to accept versus decline Mike's date invitation, the immediate choice that involves little consideration beyond the given situation is to accept; she can change her mind later, she can accept his offer so as to obtain an evening of entertainment at no cost, she can avoid the possible cost of rejecting someone, and so on. However, if, for example, she suffers from low self-esteem, she may imagine that Mike will regret asking her out on a date and deem her to be an unworthy relationship partner; she may decline in anticipation of his rejection of her. Alternatively, she may be interested in Mike and motivated to see him again, and her past experiences in relationships may have led her to develop a relatively secure attachment style (see Creasey & Jarvis, this volume); she may be inclined to explore this opportunity with Mike and graciously accept his offer.

Over time, individuals who repeatedly interact with each other invoke the same interaction goals. They face many situations that are similar to each other, and transform them in typical ways. As such, they develop expectations about interactions with a specific partner, expectations that differ from the ones we described earlier. Our initial analysis of expectations involved generalized expectations about interacting with others; they are less fine-tuned than expectations that emerge from repeated interactions with a specific partner in a specific relationship. As a couple with established expectations and interaction patterns comes across new situations (as all inevitably do), they use their established expectations to guide their behavior in the new situation. For example, Mona and Mike may establish a steady romantic relationship based on each wanting to be a caring, loving partner to the other. When a new situation arises with the potential for conflict—perhaps Mike's friends make surprise plans to take him out on the same night he had planned a date with Mona—Mike may be initially tempted to go with his friends but then explain to them that he is not available, and Mona might even expect (albeit appreciate) this response from Mike as she applies her expectations based on his past relationship-focused acts to this new situation.

We have described how interaction is a function of the Situation, Person A, and Person B (Kelley et al., 2003), in which Persons A and B exert their effects by bringing to bear their individual perspectives and motives. (If they fail to do this and act on the given situation, then interaction becomes largely a function of the situation.)[3] We now describe how each person makes attributions about his or her interaction partner.

INTERACTION AND INFERRING PARTNER MOTIVES

Behaviors convey information about the interaction partners' personal motives for the interaction and/or relationship. In inferring motives of people one does not know well, it is common to rely on expectations or stereotypes for a given situation. For example, when Mona asked Mike whether he would like to go to her apartment, the common expectation for college students in that particular setting would be that he would agree to go with her (see Paul et al., this volume). If Mike declines her request and instead suggests they make date plans for another night, he provides a response from which she can begin to infer Mike's personal motives; clearly, he is not interested in a short-term sexual relationship. In short, personal motives can more readily be inferred when a person's behavior stands in contrast to what would have been expected in a situation.

The process of inferring a partner's motives is not without its pitfalls. One potential pitfall occurs frequently in the onset of new relationships: It becomes impossible to infer partner motives on the basis of a single interaction (Kelley et al., 2003, p. 74). Mona simply has not observed Mike in enough situations to ascertain his exact motives; she can rule out his interest in an immediate, short-term, sexual interaction, but she cannot establish his exact motive beyond that, such as whether he is interested in a long-term relationship with her, whether he is morally opposed to sexual relationships, whether he is strategically positioning himself as a "nice guy" but really has ulterior motives inconsistent with such a label, whether he prefers sexual relationships with men rather than women, and so on. The attribution analysis suggested here—conditions under which one can identify a specific motive—has been described more formally in several attribution theories (see Reeder, this volume). Situations pertaining to relationship initiation are saturated with instances in which partners lack information about each other and thus are limited in the motives they can accurately infer about each other. The "speed-dating" situation described by Eastwick and Finkel (this volume) is one particularly vivid example. Only over time can partners attain a level of certainty about each others' motives that serves to sustain their relationship (Arriaga, Reed, Goodfriend, & Agnew, 2006).

Another pitfall in inferring partner motives is that not all given situations are good vehicles for this (Kelley, 1979, pp. 142–145; Kelley & Thibaut, 1978, pp. 222–223). Some situations call for behaviors that reflect clear social norms. For example, in U.S. culture, it is common (albeit paternalistic) for the men to pay for expenses incurred on a date, particularly at the onset of a relationship. It is also normative (though increasingly less common) for the men to hold open doors for the women. These situations do not provide an opportunity to infer specific motives held by a person. In contract, situations in which there is a direct conflict of interest between two people may be particularly telling (see "diagnostic situations" in Holmes & Rempel, 1989)—what benefits one person hurts the other, and vice versa. When a person responds to these situations by acting on self-interest, it remains ambiguous whether the person was doing what many people would do or was revealing a unique tendency to be a self-interested person. However, when a person forgoes the urge to act on self-interest and instead acts in favor of the partner's interest, this suggests the selfless person specifically wants to be good to the partner.

Although there are pitfalls in attempting to draw inferences when a relationship is just being established, these pitfalls decline as the couple moves beyond the initiation stage. Over repeated interactions, as one learns more about a partner's behavior, it becomes easier to detect instances in which the behavior is out of character for that situation or is perfectly consistent with his or her character for that situation. As such, acts of uncharacteristic kindness or malice jump out from the backdrop of ideographic knowledge about a partner's behavioral tendencies (see Kelley, 1979, p. 228) and suggest specific situations that strongly influence the partner's behavior (that is, they influence the partner enough that the partner suspends his or her more generalized motives).

COMPARISONS TO OTHER THEORETICAL PERSPECTIVES

What can be gained from applying an interdependence analysis to understanding relationship initiation, versus applying other theoretical frameworks? Interdependence theory provides a comprehensive account of many relationship processes, which is also the case with other theoretical orientations (e.g., attachment theory; see Creasey & Jarvis, this volume). Here, we examined expectations, interaction situations and behavior, and inferences relevant to relationship initiation, but there other aspects of interpersonal processes that might also be explained with interdependence theory (e.g., relationship maintenance behaviors, or ongoing conflicts).

Interdependence theory has been considered a theory of personality formation (see Kelley, 1983). Where do personality traits, or "dispositions," come from? Interdependence theory suggests that the origins of personality dispositions lie in how people react to interpersonal situations over time (Kelley, 1983). As Reis, Capobianco, and Tsai (2002) have noted, an interdependence approach stands in contrast to personality approaches that emphasize the static dispositions of interaction partners that change little over the course of personal interactions. What is gained from an interdependence approach is greater precision in predicting how people react to specific interaction partners at specific junctures in their relationships with their partner.

Interdependence theory and attachment theory both advance explanations of how each interaction partner's interpersonal history comes into play in determining his or her respective behavior. Attachment theory (see Hazan & Shaver, 1994) emphasizes past instances of the support versus failed responsiveness of another on which one depends. However, other factors independent of attachment processes may also define expectations, such as various individual differences (in addition to attachment style), relationship-specific goals, and more generalized social norms for a given situation. Interdependence theory takes into account a history of being with others who are responsive (or not) if this figures prominently in a person's expectations about a current interaction, and it also allows for other factors. Just as attachment theory accounts for how novel reassuring versus distressing interactions may affect one's attachment style, interdependence theory accounts for how novel situations may affect one's expectations in subsequent interactions.

In addition, like attachment theory, interdependence theory places emphasis on past experiences in shaping expectations about anticipated or future interactions. The attachment theory concept of a mental model and the interdependence theory concept of a comparison level both have expectations at their core (Hazan & Shaver, 1994). Attachment theory tends to emphasize the general effect of early childhood mental models on *all* adult caring relationships—including relationships with family members, peers, and romantic partners. In contrast, interdependence theory suggests that expectations exert specific effects on specific interactions and relationships. For example, a person may have one comparison level for initial dates with romantic partners and yet another for spending time with a long-term partner. What is gained is greater precision in explaining variations in behaviors across relationships—not all expectations are relevant.

We know of few theoretical perspectives that suggest how physical properties of a situation might matter in predicting behavior. Evolutionary perspectives take into account the physical environment in that people are presumed to have adapted to immediate environmental conditions (e.g., many natives of western African regions are immune to malaria-infected mosquito bites as a result of adapting to the physical environment). However, most evolutionary perspectives on romantic relationships seem to downplay the importance of the social context when it comes to initiating romantic involvements. For instance, one of the main ideas behind sexual strategies theory (SST; Buss & Schmitt, 1993) is that men and women have evolved different strategies when it comes to initiating both short- and long-term sexual involvements. This explains general sex differences in behaviors relevant to mating, but does not easily account for specific behaviors within a specific situation between two partners, including initiation processes.

Interdependence theory can also be compared with other theoretical frameworks that describe how perceived rewards and costs associated with interaction might influence behavior. Social exchange theory (see Agnew & Lehmiller, in press; Homans, 1961) emphasizes the general role that perceived cost–benefit ratios play in people's social interactions and advances the hypothesis that more favorable ratios lead to more satisfying and stable involvements. Social penetration theory (Altman & Taylor, 1973) states that mutual self-disclosure is the key to developing intimate and satisfying relationships. Drawing heavily on social exchange principles, however, this theory posits that the amount and type of personal information that one discloses depend upon the perceived rewards and costs associated with revealing such information. Similarly, interdependence theory takes into account the rewards and costs associated with a given social interaction. However, when it comes to romantic relationships, people do not always act in self-centered ways (i.e., maximizing rewards and minimizing costs). Rather, people may act altruistically or communally, knowing that their actions may be costly to themselves but will ultimately be to the benefit of their partner and/or relationship. Unlike most social exchange–based perspectives, interdependence theory can account for situations in which partners do and do not act out of self-interest.

Finally, as is the case with many attribution theories that shed light on relationship initiation processes (see Reeder, this volume), interdependence theory moves beyond an analysis focused on interaction per se and also emphasizes the inferences that each interaction partner draws about the other over the course of the interaction. As such, this perspective fits squarely with those that emphasize attribution processes in addition to behavior itself (e.g., Bradbury & Fincham, 1990). These inferences shape expectations about the partner's motives, expectations that influence whether future interactions occur and what one anticipates getting from future interactions.

FUTURE DIRECTIONS

Interdependence theory stands to make unique contributions to theories of interpersonal behavior in future research. Here, we highlight two ways in which future research may enrich a theoretical understanding of relationship initiation. One concerns the outcomes associated with difficult given situations. Situations vary in the extent to which partners want to do the same things or want to do different things, and thus the extent to which one person has to give up what he or she wants for the sake of the other person. Two couples in the relationship initiation stage may display similar behaviors, but they may differ in what preceded their behaviors. For one couple, those behaviors may have been preferred by both partners and thus come easily to them; they enjoy having similar preferences and experience few conflicts. For the other, the behaviors may reflect a compromise, where one person had to give up his or her own preferences for the sake of the other. How well off will these two couples be? One might expect that the conflict-free couple will be more likely to survive and the one with conflicting preferences would have "baggage" of past conflict. However, the two couples will likely differ in the attributions they have made about their partners. The couple members who had similar preferences may not give much thought to each other's behavior; for the other couple, the person who was able to do what he or she wanted will recognize the partner's sacrifice and make positive attributions about the partner (e.g., "He must really care for me because he did what I wanted instead of what he wanted"). An important direction for future research is to examine whether couples who successfully overcame differences at earlier moments, and thus had more opportunities for positive partner attributions, are more likely to establish long-lasting, caring relationships than couples who did not contend with such challenges (and thus, in theory, had fewer opportunities for positive attributions). Although one might assume that couple members who have less conflicting given preferences early in their relationship would have an easier path toward establishing a lasting relationship, it could be argued that the absence of the positive attributions that flow from the recognition of a partner's sacrifice might actually jeopardize the relationship over time. Exploring such provocative possibilities awaits future research.

The other direction for future research concerns examining whether a person's behavior is primarily directed by the physical and social properties of a given situation, or instead by one's personal motives. When situations are heavily defined by physical properties—such as being a naval recruit in a confined space—there are normative pressures to react in specific ways. Although some people may react in unexpected or highly individualized ways, many naval recruits would set up informal rules governing each person's territory, as noted above. Similarly, when situations are heavily defined by social pressures from others beyond the relationship—such as not being interested in dating but going on a blind date to appease a third-party friend—a person may limit interaction to small talk rather than disclose more personal information. In short, heavily constrained situations limit the likelihood of highly personalized interactions and may stifle movement toward greater intimacy. Comparing the situations that individuals face in the early stages of their relationship—the extent to which they are highly constrained versus open to new directions and increased self-disclosure—may predict whether, and the speed at which, a relationship moves to greater stages of intimacy (Reis & Shaver, 1988). Such predictions rely on theoretically differentiating (and empirically partitioning) the influence of a situation versus a person's interaction motives.

FINAL THOUGHTS

Through the lens of interdependence theory, we have described the social and physical environments in which relationships are initiated and sustained. Aspects of the social and physical environment have clear, measurable, and strong impacts on the expectations partners have about interactions. Moreover, these environmental factors influence not only the immediate situation in which interaction partners find themselves but also the motives partners bring to the interaction as determined by their respective backgrounds, goals, and adherence to broader social norms. It is our hope that researchers interested in understanding the initiation of interpersonal relationships will recognize both the complexities and the challenges inherent in the task. Grasping the true interdependencies of social life is far from simple, yet it is crucial to forming a comprehensive understanding of the onset and subsequent course of close relationships.

AUTHOR NOTE

We would like to thank John Holmes, Harry Reis, Caryl Rusbult, and Paul Van Lange, as well as the editors and an anonymous reviewer, for their helpful comments on an earlier version of this chapter. Their reactions and insights were invaluable.

NOTES

1. Readers familiar with Kurt Lewin's seminal work on the life space might recognize that the idea of transforming a given situation is similar to Lewin's concept of "cognitively restructuring the field" (see Kelley, 1991, p. 223).
2. The idea that groups of people or individuals may vary in their interpretation of, and response to, a given situation may seem obvious to social psychologists and others today. When it was proposed by Kelley and Thibaut in 1978, however, it stood in sharp contrast to prevailing ideas borrowed from economic theories, namely, that individuals are rational beings who typically act in self-interested ways and thus act in uniform ways to the same situation.
3. Readers may note that characteristics of a person enter the production of behavior at two different points. There are person factors that influence how the given situation is defined; they are generic "preset" characteristics that exist independently of interactions with others (such as one's physical abilities and state). These are distinct from person factors (Person A and Person B) defined as the unique interaction goals (e.g., social norms, attachment style, trust, and commitment). See Kelley et al. (2003, sections 3.5 and 3.6) for a more complete discussion of this distinction.

REFERENCES

Agnew, C. R., Arriaga, X. B., & Wilson, J. E. (2008). Committed to what? Using the Bases of Relational Commitment Model to understand continuity and changes in social relationships. In J. P. Forgas & J. Fitness (Eds.), *Social relationships: Cognitive, affective and motivational processes* (pp. 147–164). New York: Psychology Press.

Agnew, C. R., & Etcheverry, P. E. (2006). Cognitive interdependence: Considering self-in-relationship. In K. D. Vohs & E. J. Finkel (Eds.), *Self and relationships: Connecting intrapersonal and interpersonal processes* (pp. 274–293). New York: Guilford.

Agnew, C. R., Loving, T. J., & Drigotas, S. M. (2001). Substituting the forest for the trees: Social networks and the prediction of romantic relationship state and fate. *Journal of Personality and Social Psychology, 81,* 1042–1057.

Agnew, C. R., & Lehmiller, J. J. (2007). Social exchange theory. In R. Baumeister & K. D. Vohs (Eds.), *Encyclopedia of social psychology* (Vol. 2), pp 895–896. Thousand Oaks, CA: Sage.

Agnew, C. R., Van Lange, P. A. M., Rusbult, C. E., & Langston, C. A. (1998). Cognitive interdependence: Commitment and the mental representation of close relationships. *Journal of Personality and Social Psychology, 74,* 939–954.

Altman, I., Brown, B. B., Staples, B., & Werner, C. M. (1992). A transactional approach to close relationships: Courtship, weddings and placemaking. In B. Walsh, K. Craik, & R. Price (Eds.), *Person-environment psychology* (pp. 193–241). Hillsdale, NJ: Lawrence Erlbaum.

Altman, I., & Haythorn, W. W. (1967). The ecology of isolated groups. *Behavioral Science, 12,* 169–182.

Altman, I., & Taylor, D. (1973). *Social penetration: The development of interpersonal relationships.* New York: Holt, Rinehart & Winston.

Altman, I., Taylor, D. A., & Wheeler, L. (1971). Ecological aspects of group behavior in social isolation. *Journal of Applied Social Psychology, 1,* 76–100.

Arriaga, X. B., & Agnew, C. R. (2001). Being committed: The affective, cognitive, and conative components of relationship commitment. *Personality and Social Psychology Bulletin, 27,* 1190–1203.

Arriaga, X. B., Goodfriend, W., & Lohmann, A. (2004). Beyond the individual: Concomitants of closeness in the social and physical environment. In D. Mashek & A. Aron (Eds.), *Handbook of closeness and intimacy* (pp. 287–303). Mahwah, NJ: Lawrence Erlbaum.

Arriaga, X. B., Reed, J., Goodfriend, W., & Agnew, C. R. (2006). Relationship perceptions and persistence: Do fluctuations in perceived partner commitment undermine dating relationships? *Journal of Personality and Social Psychology, 91,* 1045–1065.

Bargh, J. A., & Chartrand, T. L (2000). The mind in the middle: A practical guide to priming and automaticity research. In H. T. Reis & C. M. Judd (Eds.), *Handbook of research methods in social and personality psychology* (pp. 253–285). New York: Cambridge University Press.

Barker, R. G. (1978). Theory of behavior settings. In R. G. Barker (Ed.), *Habitats, environments, and human behavior: Studies in eco-behavioral science from the Midwest Psychological Field Station* (pp. 213–228). Stanford, CA: Stanford University Press.

Baron, R. A. Effects of negative ions on interpersonal attraction: Evidence for intensification. *Journal of Personality and Social Psychology, 52,* 547–553.

Baxter, L. A., & Widenmann, S. (1993). Revealing and not revealing the status of romantic relationships to social networks. *Journal of Social and Personal Relationships, 10,* 321–337.

Berkowitz, L. (1968). Impulse, aggression and the gun. *Psychology Today, 2,* 19–22.

Bradbury, T. N., & Fincham, F. D. (1990). Attributions in marriage: Review and critique. *Psychological Bulletin, 107,* 3–23.

Bui, K. T., Peplau, L. A., & Hill, C. T. (1996). Testing the Rusbult model of relationship commitment and stability in a 15-year study of heterosexual couples. *Personality and Social Psychology Bulletin, 22,* 1244–1257.

Capezza, N. M., & Arriaga, X. B. (in press). Factors associated with acceptance of psychological aggression against women. *Violence Against Women.*

Dishion, T. J., & Kavanagh, K. (2003). *Intervening in adolescent problem behavior: A family-centered approach.* New York: Guilford Press.

Dowdy, B. B., & Kliewer, W. (1998). Dating, parent-adolescent conflict, and behavioral autonomy. *Journal of Youth and Adolescence, 27,* 473–192.

Drigotas, S. M., & Rusbult, C. E. (1992). Should I stay or should I go? A dependence model of breakups. *Journal of Personality and Social Psychology, 62,* 62–87.

Dutton, D. G., & Aron, A. P. (1974). Some evidence for heightened sexual attraction under conditions of high anxiety. *Journal of Personality and Social Psychology, 30,* 510–517.

Etcheverry, P. E., & Agnew, C. R. (2004). Subjective norms and the prediction of romantic relationship state and fate. *Personal Relationships, 11,* 409–428.

Felmlee, D. H. (2001). No couple is an island: A social network perspective on dyadic stability. *Social Forces, 79,* 1259–1287.

Felmlee, D., Sprecher, S., & Bassin, E. (1990). The dissolution of intimate relationships: A hazard model. *Social Psychology Quarterly, 53,* 13–30.

Festinger, L., Schachter, S., & Back, K. (1950). *Social pressures in informal groups: A study of human factors in housing.* Oxford: Harper.

Gosling, S. D., Ko, S. J., Mannarelli, T., & Morris, M. E. (2002). A room with a cue: Judgments of personality based on offices and bedrooms. *Journal of Personality and Social Psychology, 82,* 379–398.

Graziano, W. G., & Eisenberg, N. (1997). Agreeableness: A dimension of personality. In R. Hogan, J. Johnson, & S. Briggs (Eds.), *Handbook of personality psychology* (pp. 795–824). San Diego, CA: Academic Press.

Griffitt, W. (1970). Environmental effects on interpersonal affective behavior: Ambient effective temperature and attraction. *Journal of Personality and Social Psychology, 15,* 240–244.

Haldeman, D. (1994). The practice and ethics of sexual orientation conversion therapy. *Journal of Consulting and Clinical Psychology, 62,* 221–227.

Harris, P. B., & Sachau, D. (2005). Is cleanliness next to godliness? The role of housekeeping in impression formation. *Environment & Behavior, 37,* 81–101.

Harris, T. M., & Kalbfleisch, P. J. (2000). Interracial dating: The implications of race for initiating a romantic relationship. *Howard Journal of Communication, 11,* 49–64.

Harvey, J. (1987). *The homosexual person: New thinking in pastoral care.* San Francisco: Ignatius.

Hazan, C., & Shaver, P. R. (1994). Attachment as an organizational framework for research on close relationships. *Psychological Inquiry, 5,* 1–22.

Helgeson, V. S. (1994). The effects of self-beliefs and relationship beliefs on adjustment to a relationship stressor. *Personal Relationships, 1,* 241–258.

Holmes, J. G. (2004). The benefits of abstract functional analysis in theory construction: The case of interdependence theory. *Personality and Social Psychology Review, 8,* 146–155.

Holmes, J. G., & Rempel, J. K. (1989). Trust in close relationships. In C. Hendrick (Ed.), *Close relationships: Review of personality and social psychology* (Vol. 10, pp. 187–220). Thousand Oaks, CA: Sage.

Homans, G. C. (1961). *Social behavior and its elementary forms.* New York: Harcourt, Brace, and World.

Kay, A. C., Wheeler, S. C., Bargh, J. A., & Ross, L. (2004). Material priming: The influence of mundane physical objects on situational construal and competitive behavioral choice. *Organizational Behavior and Human Decision Processes, 95,* 83–96.

Kelley, H. H. (1979). *Personal relationships: Their structures and properties.* Hillsdale, NJ: Lawrence Erlbaum.

Kelley, H. H. (1983). The situational origins of human tendencies: A further reason for the formal analysis of structures. *Personality and Social Psychology Bulletin, 9,* 8–36.

Kelley, H. H. (1991). Lewin, situations, and interdependence. *Journal of Social Issues, 47,* 211–233.

Kelley, H. H., Holmes, J. G., Kerr, N. L., Reis, H. T., Rusbult, C. E., & Van Lange, P. A. M. (2003). *An atlas of interpersonal situations.* New York: Cambridge University Press.

Kelley, H. H., & Thibaut, J. W. (1978). *Interpersonal relations: A theory of interdependence.* New York: Wiley.

Keltner, D., Young, R. C., Heerey, E. A., Oemig, C., & Monarch, N. D. (1998). Teasing in hierarchical and intimate relations. *Journal of Personality and Social Psychology, 75,* 1231–1247.

Kurdek, L. A. (1991). Predictors of increases in marital distress in newlywed couples: A 3-year prospective longitudinal study. *Developmental Psychology, 27,* 627–636.

Le, B., & Agnew, C. R. (2003). Commitment and its theorized determinants: A meta-analysis of the investment model. *Personal Relationships, 10,* 37–57.

Lehmiller, J. J., & Agnew, C. R. (2006). Marginalized relationships: The impact of social disapproval on relationship commitment. *Personality and Social Psychology Bulletin, 32,* 40–51.

Lohmann, A., Arriaga, X. B., & Goodfriend, W. (2003). Close relationships and placemaking: Do objects in a couple's home reflect couplehood? *Personal Relationships, 10,* 439–451.

Malhotra, A. (1991). Gender and changing generational relations: Spouse choice in Indonesia. *Demography, 28,* 549–570.

Marshall, S. K., & Markstrom-Adams, C. (1995). Attitudes on interfaith dating among Jewish adolescents: Contextual and developmental considerations. *Journal of Family Issues, 16,* 787–811.

May, J. L., & Hamilton, P. A. (1980). Effects of musically evoked affect on women's interpersonal attraction toward and perceptual judgments of physical attractiveness of men. *Motivation and Emotion, 4,* 217–228.

Milardo, R. M. (1982). Friendship networks in developing relationships: Converging and diverging social environments. *Social Psychology Quarterly, 45,* 162–172.

Milardo, R. M. (1986). Personal choice and social constraint in close relationships: Applications of network analysis. In V. J. Derlega & B. A. Winstead (Eds.), *Friendship and social interaction* (pp. 145–166). New York: Springer-Verlag.

Murray, S. (2005). Regulating the risks of closeness: A relationship-specific sense of felt security. *Current Directions in Psychological Sciences, 14*, 74–78.

Netting, N. S. (2006). Two-lives, one partner: Indo-Canadian youth between love and arranged marriages. *Journal of Comparative Family Studies, 37*, 129.

Parks, M. R. (2007). *Personal relationships and personal networks*. Mahwah, NJ: Lawrence Erlbaum.

Parks, M. R., & Adelman, M. B. (1983). Communication networks and the development of romantic relationships: An expansion of uncertainty reduction theory. *Human Communication Research, 10*, 55–79.

Parks, M. R., & Eggert, L. L. (1991). The role of social context in the dynamics of personal relationships. In W. H. Jones & D. Perlman (Eds.), *Advances in personal relationships* (Vol. 2, pp. 1–34). London: Jessica Kingsley.

Pettit, G. S., Brown, E. G., Mize, J., & Lindsey, E. (1998). Mothers' and fathers' socializing behaviors in three contexts: Links with children's peer competence. *Merrill-Palmer Quarterly, 44*, 173–193.

Quinn, D. M. (1993). Plural marriage and modern fundamentalism. In M. E. Marty & R. S. Appleby (Eds.), *Fundamentalisms and society: Reclaiming the sciences, the family, and education* (pp. 240–293). Chicago: University of Chicago Press.

Reis, H. T., Capobianco, A., & Tsai, F. (2002). Finding the person in personal relationships. *Journal of Personality, 70*, 813–850.

Reis, H. T., & Shaver, P. (1988). Intimacy as an interpersonal process. In S. Duck, D. F. Hale, S. Hobfoll, W. Ickes, & B. Montgomery (Eds.), *Handbook of personal relationships: Theory, research and interventions* (pp. 367–389). Oxford: John Wiley.

Rusbult, C. E. (1983). A longitudinal test of the investment model: The development (and deterioration) of satisfaction and commitment in heterosexual involvements. *Journal of Personality and Social Psychology, 45*, 101–117.

Rusbult, C. E., Olsen, N., Davis, J. L., & Hannon, P. A. (2001). Commitment and relationship maintenance mechanisms. In J. Harvey & A. Wenzel (Eds.), *Close romantic relationships: Maintenance and enhancement* (pp. 87–113). Mahwah, NJ: Lawrence Erlbaum.

Rusbult, C. E., & Van Lange, P. A. M. (2003). Interdependence, interaction and relationships. *Annual Review of Psychology, 54*, 351–375.

Simpson, J. A. (1987). The dissolution of romantic relationships: Factors involved in relationship stability and emotional distress. *Journal of Personality and Social Psychology, 53*, 683–692.

Solomon, D. H., & Knobloch, L. K. (2001). Relationship uncertainty, partner interference, and intimacy within dating relationships. *Journal of Social and Personal Relationships, 18*, 804–820.

Sternberg, R. J., & Barnes, M. L. (1985). Real and ideal others in romantic relationships: Is four a crowd? *Journal of Personality and Social Psychology, 49*, 1586–1608.

Valsiner, J. (2000). *Culture and human development*. Thousand Oaks, CA: Sage.

Wetzel, C. G., & Insko, C. A. (1982). The similarity-attraction relationship: Is there an ideal one? *Journal of Experimental Social Psychology, 18*, 253–276.

Whitbeck, L. B., & Hoyt, D. R. (1991). Campus prestige and dating behaviors. *College Student Journal, 25*, 457–469.

Yovetich, N. A., & Rusbult, C. E. (1994). Accommodative behavior in close relationships: Exploring transformation of motivation. *Journal of Experimental Social Psychology, 30*, 138–164.

11

Speed-Dating
A Powerful and Flexible Paradigm for Studying Romantic Relationship Initiation

PAUL W. EASTWICK and ELI J. FINKEL

*I*n all areas of scientific inquiry, the ideas that researchers pursue are constrained by the methods available to them. Thankfully, new and generative methodological paradigms are frequently born, often directly as a result of scientists' own ingenuity. Two prominent examples in psychology include Thurstone's (1928) insight that attitudes can be measured, a revelation that served as the foundation for the myriad self-report measures in use today, and Byrne's (1961) "bogus stranger" experiment, which became one of the most enduring paradigms in the study of attraction. In other cases, scientists have capitalized on the emergence of a new technology or some other product of our evolving culture. For instance, as millions of people currently have access to the Internet, a massive participant pool is available for studies that choose to harness this resource (Fraley, 2004). We have become increasingly enthusiastic about a promising methodological advance for researchers interested in attraction and relationship initiation: a providential gift from popular singles' culture known as *speed-dating*.

Speed-dating was conceived by Rabbi Yaacov Deyo in the late 1990s as an efficient means for Jewish singles in Los Angeles to meet one another. Since that time, it has rapidly become a fixture of pop culture, spreading throughout metropolitan areas in the United States, Great Britain, and Australia and recently emerging in nations as diverse as Japan and South Africa. In speed-dating, individuals who are interested in meeting potential romantic partners pay to attend events (a typical price in Chicago in 2008 was US$35) where they have a series of brief "dates" with other attendees. Each date lasts a set number of minutes, though the duration will vary from event to event (typically in the 3 to 8-minute range), as will the total number of dates. At the end of the evening, speed-daters indicate (on either a short questionnaire or a website) whom they would ("yes") or would not ("no") be interested in meeting again. The host of the speed-dating event then provides a means for mutually interested parties to contact one another.

A speed-date bears little resemblance to a traditional, presumably longer date; instead, speed-dating events are roughly analogous to parties, bars, or other social settings where single individuals might hope to connect with other singles. Speed-dating possesses several unique advantages over these alternatives, including (a) the assurance that the people one meets are (to some extent) romantically available, (b) the fact that great confidence is not a prerequisite to approach the more desirable preferred-sex individuals present, and (c) the knowledge that any unpleasant dates will have a mercifully quick end. Speed-dating is also a flexible concept; it has even been adapted for populations who generally disapprove of dating by allowing participants' parents to chaperone the events

(MacFarquhar, 2006). For these reasons, thousands of people have turned to speed-dating as an efficient and promising means of meeting new potential romantic partners.

Recently, researchers have begun to recognize the potential for speed-dating to reveal insights about relationship initiation processes (e.g., Eastwick, Finkel, Mochon, & Ariely, 2007; Finkel, Eastwick, & Matthews, 2007; Fisman, Iyengar, Kamenica, & Simonson, 2006; Kurzban & Weeden, 2005). Of course, when attraction research grew to prominence in the 1960s and 1970s, several ambitious researchers indeed recognized the scientific value of studying participants' impressions of real-life dating partners. In these live dating studies, researchers set participants on an actual date, collected impressions immediately after the date, and in some cases contacted participants later to see if any subsequent dating had taken place. Most famous of these was the "computer dance" study conducted by Elaine Hatfield (formerly Walster) and colleagues (Walster, Aronson, Abrahams, & Rottmann, 1966), which is especially well cited for unearthing the large association between physical attractiveness and romantic desirability. Even as recently as the 1990s, relationship scientists were generating new and creative ways to study men and women on actual dates (e.g., Sprecher & Duck, 1994). Speed-dating continues this tradition of live dating research, but also draws from the literature on "thin slices" of behavior (Ambady & Rosenthal, 1992), which has demonstrated that individuals can make accurate inferences about a target person after a very short observation of that target. For many research questions, therefore, it would not be necessary to send participants on full, evening-length dates; there is good reason to believe that participants can make accurate judgments about a potential romantic partner rather quickly. In this way, speed-dating satisfies scholars' desire to understand romantic relationship initiation as it happens in real life while simultaneously maximizing data collection efficiency.

Elsewhere, we have provided a "rough-and-ready" manual that includes discussions of recruitment, payment, possible institutional review board (IRB) concerns, and various methodological issues for researchers who might wish to conduct their own speed-dating studies (Finkel et al., 2007). In this chapter, we discuss in detail the myriad benefits that speed-dating can offer attraction and relationship initiation research. We note how speed-dating takes advantage of several tried-and-true procedural features already familiar to those who study attraction and close relationships; as a result, speed-dating imports the strengths of these literatures and essentially provides a "greatest hits" compilation of methods to researchers who study relationship initiation. To further illustrate why we have become excited about the potential of speed-dating to lead attraction research in new and generative directions, we then present findings on a variety of topics—from ideal partner preferences to interracial romantic desire—from the Northwestern Speed-Dating Study. Finally, we explore some potential limitations of speed-dating methods and propose how they might be rectified in future research.

WHAT WOULD AN IDEAL PARADIGM FOR THE STUDY OF RELATIONSHIP INITIATION LOOK LIKE?

Initial romantic attraction and early relationship development are complex processes that can be understood only through diverse empirical investigations. Nevertheless, it is interesting to muse about a comprehensive or ideal paradigm for the study of romantic relationship initiation. Given the lessons of previous findings and the generative paradigms of past and present, what features would attraction scholars *in principle* desire in an ideal empirical method? We describe eight features that would be included in such an ideal method; later, we argue that speed-dating procedures (and straightforward extensions thereof) can in principle incorporate all these ideal features, allowing investigators to address a wide array of research questions relevant to initial attraction and early relationship development.

Eight Features of the Ideal Paradigm

1. Study Real Relationships with a Potential Future   Relationships characterized by a potential future (i.e., those that individuals hope or expect to persist) are qualitatively different from

those with no possible future. One compelling illustration is provided by research comparing participants' behavior during one-trial and iterated-trial prisoner's dilemma games, research tools designed to instill in participants conflicting motives to cooperate or compete. Although competitive behavior dominates most single-trial games, complex interpersonal phenomena, including cooperation and reciprocity, emerge during iterated games in which participants expect to interact with the same partner repeatedly (Axelrod, 1984; Kelley & Thibaut, 1978; Luce & Raiffa, 1957).

For logical reasons, close relationships researchers almost uniformly study relationships with a future, and several important phenomena would likely have gone undetected if scholars had studied only relationships that were hypothetical or limited to the duration of a single experimental session. One compelling example is research on the interpersonal nature of trust (e.g., Holmes & Rempel, 1989; for a review, see Simpson, 2007). Although trust had previously been conceptualized primarily as an individual difference, Holmes and Rempel argued that trust is best understood as a product of an evolving relationship. Another construct that is central to relationships researchers and is typically assessed within the context of an ongoing relationship is commitment (for a review, see Rusbult, Olsen, Davis, & Hannon, 2001), which explicitly includes beliefs about the future of the relationship (e.g., long-term orientation and an intent to persist). Intimacy (Laurenceau, Barrett, & Pietromonaco, 1998; Reis & Shaver, 1988) is yet another key construct that grew to prominence as researchers started to explore the relationships that genuinely held meaning and significance for participants. Indeed, most contemporary research on romantic relationships takes place within the context of ongoing relationships that participants hope or expect to persist.

Should attraction researchers similarly prioritize the study of relationships that have a potential future? Although attraction research can certainly be generative and informative without assessing participants' responses to real-life potential romantic partners, there are several reasons to consider such assessments to be a feature of the ideal attraction paradigm. Even at the most basic level, participants pay much closer attention to strangers with whom they have a likely future than to strangers with whom no such future is likely (Berscheid, Graziano, Monson, & Dermer, 1976). Furthermore, participants show unique biases when they expect future interaction with someone. For example, a recent study (Goodwin, Fiske, Rosen, & Rosenthal, 2002) found that participants successfully distinguished between the competent and incompetent work of an opposite-sex other with whom they did not expect to interact. However, when participants anticipated that they would date the person later in the week, they judged the work to be competent and coherent, regardless of its actual quality. In addition, if participants are interacting with and reporting on individuals with whom they could potentially form a relationship, it would likely increase the likelihood that participants will take the experiment seriously and thereby provide valid and meaningful data. Attraction researchers can therefore create a compelling paradigm by studying how participants evaluate real-life potential partners, whether such fledgling couples meet in or out of a laboratory setting. In fact, the computer dance study (Walster et al., 1966) is a paragon of social psychological research because, like other classics such as the Robber's Cave study (Sherif, Harvey, White, Hood, & Sherif, 1954/1961) and the Stanford prison experiment (Haney, Banks, & Zimbardo, 1973), it exquisitely blurs the lines between research study and real life, and thus manages to capture the best features of both. By providing or allowing for a potential future in the relationships that attraction researchers study, it imbues them with additional power and meaning in the moment for participants.

2. Study Both Interactants   The ideal paradigm for studying initial romantic attraction would also allow scholars to examine attraction as it emerges between two individuals. Because attraction is fundamentally a social process whereby two individuals simultaneously perceive and are perceived by one another, researchers may not detect important attraction phenomena unless they have the ability to consider the dyad as the unit of analysis. In fact, several inherently dyadic phenomena have been identified using the social relations model (SRM; Kenny, 1994) and the actor–partner interdependence model (APIM; Kashy & Kenny, 2000), two powerful techniques that are especially well suited to the study of attraction. For instance, these methods have revealed that strangers tend to reciprocate nonromantic liking for one another after only a brief initial encounter (Chapdelaine,

Kenny, & LaFontana, 1994) and that people tend to be happier in their relationships when they measure up to their partner's ideals (Campbell, Simpson, Kashy, & Fletcher, 2001). Later in this chapter,
we will advocate the use of the social relations model in conjunction with speed-dating; for now, it is
sufficient to note that the ideal attraction paradigm has much to gain by analyzing romantic dynamics in situations where both individuals may be interested in one another (Kenny, 1994). Although
research employing experimental confederates or other well-controlled stimuli will always remain
important for discerning the processes underlying romantic attraction, there is a deep and desirable
richness to be found in the data of naïve interacting dyads.

3. Maintain Experimental Control

Initial romantic attraction is enormously complex. The
ideal attraction paradigm would allow investigators to exert substantial methodological control
over the romantic context in which potential partners meet one another. Although the dynamics
of romantic attraction will surely remain complex even in a well-controlled environment, researchers will typically want to hold constant a large array of confounding factors such as location, light-
ing, food, music, and time of day. Of course, researchers can learn a great deal about relationship
initiation by simply asking participants about their naturally occurring dating experiences, but the
lack of control provided by such procedures could prove problematic. For example, if men's wealth
correlated with their reported number of sexual partners, a researcher might want to argue that
wealthy men are naturally romantically desirable (e.g., Perusse, 1993). However, if wealthy men
experience less pressure to "punch in" at exactly 8:30 each morning, they might simply have more
sexual opportunities as a consequence of this extra freedom to stay out late. A paradigm that allowed
researchers to control for such factors would help rule out various alternative explanations for any
results revealed by the study.

4. Give Participants Multiple Romantic Options

Imagine two different high-quality stud-
ies of initial romantic attraction, each of which lasts 2 hours. In one, participants go on a date with
one person for the allotted time (e.g., Walster et al., 1966). In the other, participants go on 12 brief
dates during the allotted time (e.g., Finkel et al., 2007). Although a single-date study has many excellent features (e.g., the ability to observe romantic phenomena that might emerge only over the course
of an evening), here we emphasize two especially exciting advantages of the multiple-date study.
First, investigators can learn unique information about romantic attraction dynamics by examining
the choices individuals make when they select among several potential partners as opposed to when
they report their attraction to a single partner. For example, a study that sets participants on a single
date can indeed inform scholars about participants' decisions to go out with their assigned partner
again. A multiple-date study provides this information and additionally sheds light on why some
partners *and not others* are more desirable to a particular individual. Of course, studies that have
examined real-life dating dyads are some of the most impressive examples of attraction research
(e.g., Byrne, Ervin, & Lamberth, 1970; Sprecher & Duck, 1994; Walster et al., 1966); what is exciting
is that a multiple-date study can provide a new kind of insight into romantic choice processes while
maintaining the identical time commitment for participants.

A second advantage of the multiple-date study (for both researchers and participants alike) is that
it may be more successful at introducing participants to at least one person who is a good romantic
fit for them. This point has not yet been addressed empirically, however, and it is certainly possible
that the shorter dates necessitated by the multiple-date study are wildly ineffective at inspiring
second dates among participants. Therefore, to get a cursory sense of speed-dating's efficacy, we
conducted the following analysis using data from the 163 participants who took part in the Northwestern Speed-Dating Study (NSDS). As part of the NSDS, we conducted a one-month longitudinal
follow-up that required participants to answer questions every 3 days about each of their matches.
Using these follow-up data, we determined that 33% of our speed-dating participants spent at least
some time "hanging out" with a match whom they did not know well prior to the speed-dating event,
and 21% of this subsample did so for at least two of their speed-dating matches. One could compare
the 33% value with that obtained, for example, in a relatively recent study that set men and women

on single dates (Sprecher & Duck, 1994). Sprecher and Duck also included a follow-up component in their study and found that 14% of participants answered in the affirmative to the question "Did you ever go on a second date or get together again as friends?" Although such a cross-study comparison is certainly imprecise, it provides reason to suspect that researchers may be more successful at generating fledgling relationships if they introduce participants to a larger number of romantic eligibles, even if this requires making the interactions very short. (Intriguingly, this implication does not mean that investigators should try to force as many dates into an evening as possible, as Iyengar, Simonson, Fisman, and Mogilner, 2005, have reported that participants who had roughly 10 speed-dates in an evening garnered *more* matches than participants who had roughly 20 dates.)

5. Get Background Characteristics before Participants Meet

The ideal methodological paradigm would assess a diverse range of background information on both members of the dyad before they ever meet one another. Many research questions necessitate such information, and most researchers are familiar with self-report techniques that assess background demographics, personality characteristics, ideal partner preferences, or self-evaluations. Although such measurements could certainly be assessed once potential romantic partners have already met one another, this approach could sacrifice explanatory clarity. One vivid illustration of this point is provided by Fletcher, Simpson, and Thomas (2000): Participants who held positive perceptions of their relationships were more likely to change their ideal partner preferences over a 1 to 2-month period to become more congruent with their current partner. This finding inspires caution against concluding, for example, that selecting a romantic partner who closely matches one's ideal will result in greater relationship satisfaction unless those ideals were assessed before the partners met. In fact, relationship partners are known to change the self in myriad ways (Aron, Paris, & Aron, 1995; Drigotas, Rusbult, Wieselquist, & Whitton, 1999; Murray, Holmes, & Griffin, 1996); if these changes can take place over time spans as short as one month (Fletcher et al., 2000), attraction researchers need to be aware of such possibilities. Therefore, the ideal attraction paradigm would enable researchers to collect background data on potential romantic partners before they ever have a chance to influence each other and create explanatory confounds.

6. Implement Experimental Manipulations

Depending on the researcher's goals, he or she might choose to extend experimental control by incorporating experimental manipulations into the speed-dating event. For example, one might wish to manipulate how long individuals meet one another, how closely they sit next to one another, or whether they are listening to Black Sabbath or the Bee Gees. In fact, one classic live dating study (Byrne et al., 1970) manipulated whether participants went on a "Coke date" with either a similar or dissimilar opposite-sex participant. Moreover, one could in principle employ trained research confederates to enact different behavioral strategies while meeting naïve participants in a romantic context (assuming the associated ethical concerns associated with this deception could be addressed). Such procedures could allow for causal conclusions about which strategies are most effective at making good impressions on potential romantic partners. Of course, many researchers will initially be satisfied to observe the processes of romantic attraction without including experimental manipulations, but the option is likely to be useful to researchers as they hone in on the mechanism underlying an effect of interest.

7. Collect "Objective" Ratings of Participants

A major difficulty of studying initial romantic attraction is that the degree to which scholars can trust individuals' self-reports on the topic remains unknown. Although self-reports are certainly a useful way to gather data on individuals' subjective experiences, they can frequently be inaccurate due to diverse self-report biases, including the tendency to deceive oneself (e.g., by believing that one is more desired by a partner than is actually the case; Paulhus, 1984), the desire to present oneself positively (Paulhus, 1984), and the failure to have accurate introspection regarding the motives underlying one's own behaviors (Nisbett & Wilson, 1977). The ideal paradigm for studying romantic attraction would provide scholars with the ability to collect "objective" ratings of independent or dependent variables of interest. The paradigm could borrow procedures from the clinical psychology literature investigating couple conflict, in which scholars record the interaction and later code it according to objective criteria (for a review, see Heyman, 2001). In the initial romantic attraction domain, scholars could use similar procedures to record participants' interactions and train raters who were not at the session to code the participants for physical attractiveness, sense of humor, charisma, use of flattery or other romantic strategies, and so forth. Of course, investigators may not possess the resources for such a procedure (e.g., insufficient funds to collect video and audio data) or may be concerned that employing such assessments would undesirably alter the dynamics of romantic attraction. Even so, researchers could still collect "objective" ratings of physical attractiveness by simply taking a photograph of each participant either before or after the session and having raters code the attractiveness of the photos. Finally, a paradigm allowing ratings from both objective coders and the participants themselves has the additional advantage of comparing these two sets of ratings to one another, a comparison that could lead to novel insights into how involvement in a romantic interaction alters perceptions of it (see Loving, 2006).

One additional type of data that is not solely based on one participant's self-report is consensus data, which emerge when researchers (a) collect data on both interactants (see feature 2, above), and (b) have participants meet and rate multiple potential partners on various dimensions (see feature 4, above). Such ratings retain an objective quality because they are not subject to the biases of a single individual, yet they still provide an "inside view" of the romantic attraction process that nicely complements standard self-reports and the objective ratings provided by independent coders. In addition, the consensus ratings are an essential ingredient in the social relations model (Kenny, 1994), which is a powerful analytic tool in its own right.

8. Follow Potential Relationships into the Future   Previously, we discussed the importance of studying real relationships with a potential future (see feature 1, above). An ideal paradigm for studying initial romantic attraction would also allow investigators to follow relationships into that future, examining the processes taking place in the days, weeks, months, and even years following the initial meeting. There exist countless fascinating questions about the development of romantic relationships. For example, what factors distinguish relationships that evolve into long-term close relationships from those that never make it to that stage? Under what circumstances do individuals who had initially experienced little sexual desire toward a given partner develop increased desire over time (or vice versa)? Such questions parallel those asked by close relationships researchers who have used longitudinal designs for several decades to examine breakup (e.g., Bui, Peplau, & Hill, 1996; Gottman, 1994; Karney & Bradbury, 1995) and relationship growth and maintenance mechanisms (e.g., Drigotas et al., 1999). Because it is often difficult to recruit romantic partners for a study until they are officially a "couple," the span of time between the initial romantic encounter and relationship formation is one of the great untouched canvases of social scientific research. Furthermore, there exists very little empirical overlap at the present time between research in the attraction tradition and in the close relationships tradition (see Finkel et al., 2007). The ideal attraction paradigm would allow researchers to (a) extend attraction principles into the domain of close relationships, and (b) use the theoretical orientations (e.g., attachment theory and interdependence theory) and relationship-specific constructs (e.g., trust, commitment, and intimacy) of close relationships research to connect these two disciplines. In this way, a longitudinal component provides a potent tool for scholars to examine a large array of important and largely unexplored questions regarding early relationship development.

Speed-Dating Can Incorporate All Eight Features

Speed-dating is a single method that can include all eight of these desirable features. By definition, a speed-dating event entails that participants meet real-life potential romantic partners (feature 1), that these meetings happen in dyads (feature 2) in a well-controlled setting (feature 3), and that participants are given multiple romantic options (feature 4). In addition, optional yet straightforward extensions of the basic paradigm allow researchers to obtain background information before the event (feature 5), incorporate an experimental manipulation (feature 6), collect objective data by recording the speed-dates (feature 7), and/or administer longitudinal follow-up questionnaires after the event (feature 8). In addition, speed-dating procedures could be adapted to incorporate other features that we have not thoroughly considered (e.g., recoding biomarkers such as blood pressure or cortisol levels) or that the field itself has yet to provide. As new theory and new methods for the study of attraction are continuously updated and innovated, speed-dating may remain a valuable method that readily incorporates these developments.

To illustrate how speed-dating makes use of the eight ideal features of an attraction paradigm that we have described, we present a hypothetical example. Imagine a researcher who is broadly interested in the predictors and consequences of passionate love (e.g., Hatfield & Sprecher, 1986): Would speed-dating be an effective tool to explore such a research agenda? We suggest that the answer is "Absolutely."

First, speed-dating naturally introduces participants to real-life potential romantic partners and encourages them to obtain matches, thereby explicitly opening up the possibility of a future for each dyad (feature 1). Such a context is ideal for exploring passionate love; in fact, it is difficult to imagine that passionate love could emerge if feature 1 were not present. Although there are probably circumstances in which some individuals experience passionate love with no possibility of spending time with the love object (e.g., a movie star crush), it is probably exceedingly rare that passion would be aroused by anything other than an actual real-life person (as opposed to a hypothetical ideal or a character in a vignette). Second, researchers are sure to uncover wonderful insights about passionate love when it is studied as a dyadic process (feature 2). For example, Tennov (1979) described how limerence, a state roughly synonymous with passionate love, is spawned by a delicate balance of hope and uncertainty with regard to the love object's feelings for the self. Surely, Participant A's overtures of romantic interest (or lack of interest) toward Participant B will impact B's uncertainty, who may in turn engage in behaviors that impact A's level of uncertainty, and so forth. The dance of hope and uncertainty that characterizes fledgling relationships is exquisitely dyadic at its core. Third, the ability to control for confounding factors could aid researchers who desire an extra degree of confidence about the source of their effects (feature 3). The example provided above remains apropos: Wealthy individuals could hypothetically inspire more passionate love, or they could simply have more free time to frequent locations where people are eager for a passionate encounter. Fourth, if subsequent dating is more likely to occur when participants are provided with multiple romantic options (feature 4; see our previous analysis of this issue, above), it is plausible that such a feature would increase the odds that researchers will detect passionate love among their participants. Furthermore, if participants are meeting multiple possible targets for their romantic desire, it allows researchers to better explore why passionate love emerged in one particular case but not in another.

The optional speed-dating features could also be useful to scholars who wish to study passionate love. As a fifth example, using background information collected prior to the event (feature 5), researchers could examine which individuals are more likely to experience passionate love, which individuals are more likely to inspire passionate love in others, and what combination of characteristics makes two individuals more likely to feel passionate love for one another. Sixth, a researcher might try to inspire more passionate love by experimentally altering the nature of the speed-dates themselves (feature 6). For example, one could convince participants to disclose more self-relevant information on some dates than on others; it is possible, if such elevated disclosure is experienced by the partner as an increase in intimacy, that this manipulation could inspire passionate feelings (see Baumeister & Bratslavsky, 1999). Seventh, a researcher could employ audiotaping or videotaping procedures, objectively code participants' behavior, and then examine what romantic strategies (e.g., humor or flattery) successfully inspire passionate love in participants' dates (feature 7). Of course, a researcher could simply ask participants to self-report on their strategies, but it is likely that most people are only partially aware of the strategies they employ to elicit romantic interest from the opposite sex. Eighth, and finally, passionate love is probably most likely to reach its full intensity as two participants start spending more time with one another in the wake of the speed-dating event.

Therefore, researchers could conduct a longitudinal follow-up to learn how passionate love develops (feature 8): Under what circumstances does it either increase or decline in the wake of the speed-dating event? Though scholars may choose to include or not include these four optional features (5–8), they are sure to provide additional valuable insights for many research endeavors.

A SAMPLER PLATTER FROM THE NORTHWESTERN SPEED-DATING STUDY

We have argued that speed-dating possesses many features that make it an ideal method for studying relationship initiation and that it is broadly relevant to an array of research questions. When we conducted the Northwestern Speed-Dating Study, we had several programs of research that we hoped could be informed by speed-dating. We were not disappointed. Below, we describe four different sets of findings from the NSDS that are especially exciting for us. We hope that they illustrate some of speed-dating's ideal features as well as the breadth of questions that can be addressed by such a method.

Before proceeding, we provide a few details on the general structure of the NSDS that pertain to the results discussed below (for greater detail, see Finkel et al., 2007). We recruited 163 undergraduate students (81 female and 82 males) to participate in one of seven speed-dating events held in the spring of 2005. First, upon signing up for the event, each participant completed a 30-minute *pre-event questionnaire* online. Next, at the event itself, participants had between 9 and 13 speed-dates with opposite-sex participants (depending on event attendance); each speed-date lasted for 4 minutes. At the end of each date, participants completed a brief 2-minute *interaction record questionnaire*. Later in the evening, participants recorded whom they would ("yes") or would not ("no") be interested in meeting again, and matches (mutual yesses) were given the ability to e-mail one another through a secure messaging website. Finally, every third day for a month following the event, participants completed a *follow-up questionnaire* that asked questions about their life in general, about each speed-dating match, and about any other romantic interests in their life whom they had met outside of speed-dating ("write-ins").

Sex Differences in Ideal Partner Preferences

Sex differences readily emerge when men and women report on the importance they place on two particular characteristics in a romantic partner: physical attractiveness and good earning prospects (see Buss, 1989). Typically, men place more importance than women on physical attractiveness, and women place more importance than men on earning prospects. Support for these two sex differences has been robust in paradigms where participants state their preferences (Buss; Feingold, 1990, 1992; Sprecher, Sullivan, & Hatfield, 1994) or examine vignettes, photographs, or personal ads (e.g., Harrison & Saeed, 1977; Stroebe, Insko, Thompson, & Layton, 1971; Townsend & Wasserman, 1998). Curiously, evidence for these sex differences has proven equivocal in paradigms where participants actually meet and date one another. For example, physical attractiveness and earning prospects seem to be equally important determinants of popularity for men and women (e.g., Speed & Gangestad, 1997). In addition, across the studies that set men and women on actual dates (e.g., Walster et al., 1966), the meta-analyzed sex difference in the effect of physical attractiveness on desirability was very small and nonsignificant (Feingold, 1990). Noting this inconsistency in the literature, the NSDS had several features that were specifically designed to examine the nature of sex differences in the importance of physical attractiveness and earning prospects (Eastwick & Finkel, 2008a).

We asked our participants on the pre-event questionnaire to report the importance of physical attractiveness (assessed by the items *physically attractive* and *sexy/hot*) and earning prospects (*good career prospects* and *ambitious/driven*) in an ideal romantic partner (*ideal partner preferences*). This questionnaire also asked participants to estimate how much these same characteristics would matter in their decision to respond "yes" to someone after a speed-date (*speed-date preferences*). As expected, both the ideal partner and speed-date preferences showed the expected sex differences, with men giving higher ratings to physical attractiveness than women did and women giving higher ratings to earning prospects than men did.

Given that these expected sex differences emerged among our sample of speed-daters, one would anticipate finding these same sex differences in the characteristics that inspired men's and women's romantic interest at and after the speed-dating event. In other words, men (more than women) should demonstrate romantic interest in physically attractive individuals, and women (more than men) should demonstrate romantic interest in individuals with good earning prospects. We culled 17 different dependent variables from the NSDS data set to assess participants' romantic interest. Some of these dependent variables were assessed on the *interaction record*, including *romantic desire* (e.g., "I was sexually attracted to my interaction partner") and *chemistry* (e.g., "My interaction partner and I had a real connection"), whereas others were assessed on the follow-up questionnaires, such as *passion* (e.g., "[Name][1] always seems to be on my mind") and *date enjoyment* ("Corresponding / hanging out with [name] has been enjoyable"). Also on these same questionnaires, we asked participants to rate each speed-date or match using the items mentioned above that assessed physical attractiveness and earning prospects. Finally, we calculated the overall association between romantic interest and these two characteristics separately for men and women.

The results were striking. We did indeed find a strong association between participants' reports of romantic interest in a speed-date or match and physical attractiveness judgments of that speed-date or match, $r = .43$ for men's reports and $r = .46$ for women's. However, these two correlations did not differ significantly and are, if anything, trending in a direction opposite of that predicted by the ideal partner and speed-date preferences. In addition, no sex differences emerged in the association between romantic interest and earning prospects judgments, $r = .19$ for men and $r = .16$ for women. As we dug further into the data, we found no evidence of sex differences in the association between romantic interest and physical attractiveness or earning prospects when using (a) consensus ratings of these two characteristics (which showed considerable intersubject agreement, even for earning prospects) or (b) objective ratings of physical attractiveness assessed from participants' photographs. Finally, we similarly failed to find these sex differences when we examined participants' write-in reports, which suggests that these results did not appear to be a strange artifact of the speed-dating process.[2]

Though these results may seem odd at first, there is actually a compelling theoretical rationale for why sex differences would emerge in one context (i.e., stated reports) but not another (i.e., live dating). Nisbett and Wilson (1977) provided evidence that participants do not employ true introspection when asked the "why" question about their judgments or behavior; that is, participants judge only what elements of a stimulus might *plausibly* lead them to behave in a certain way. It is therefore possible that ideal partner preferences reflect participants' inaccurate a priori theories about what kind of person would inspire their romantic interest in the moment or why they would choose one partner over another (see also Sprecher, 1989).

To test this idea, we examined correlations between participants' stated preferences (for an ideal partner or a speed-date) and the ratings they made of their 9 to 13 speed-dating partners. For example, some participants (male and female) were especially likely to romantically desire the speed-dates they found physically attractive, whereas other participants were less romantically inspired by attractiveness; we refer to this individual difference as an *in vivo preference* (a preference revealed by one's live judgments at the speed-dating event). Both stated and in vivo preferences exhibited strong reliability. Nevertheless, as the Nisbett and Wilson (1977) framework predicts, stated and in vivo preferences did not correlate (average $r = .05$) for either the physical attractiveness or earning prospects characteristics (nor did they correlate for the characteristic *personable*, which was assessed by items such as *fun/exciting* and *friendly*). These findings suggest that people may have little insight into the characteristics that they truly desire in a romantic partner. Currently, we are collecting new data that explore *where* in the process of meeting and getting to know a potential romantic partner participants falter in comparing that partner with their stated ideals.

Not All Reciprocity Is Created Equal

Reciprocal liking, or the tendency for individuals to like those who like them, has long been considered one of the great principles of attraction (Berscheid & Reis, 1998; Berscheid & Walster, 1978; Kenny, 1994). In fact, reciprocity of liking is even found among strangers who are meeting for the first time (Chapdelaine et al., 1994). However, the volume of research examining reciprocity specifically within a romantic setting is somewhat meager. One oft-cited study indeed found that participants, when asked to recall a falling-in-love experience, reported that learning of another's affection inspired their own passionate feelings in return (Aron, Dutton, Aron, & Iverson, 1989). However, there is another possibility that in principle could be a more common occurrence: romantic partners becoming more desirable if they play "hard to get" by not making their romantic interest immediately apparent (for discussion, see Walster, Walster, Piliavin, & Schmidt, 1973). Therefore, we took the opportunity provided by the NSDS to examine reciprocity of liking in an explicitly romantic setting (Eastwick et al., 2007).

In the NSDS, each participant rated many speed-dating partners and was in turn rated by those partners; this enabled us to make use of the SRM (Kenny & La Voie, 1984), a statistical model that has provided some of the best evidence for reciprocity in nonromantic settings (see Kenny, 1994). SRM distinguishes between two types of reciprocity that are statistically and conceptually independent. The first is *dyadic reciprocity*, which is liking that is shared uniquely between two individuals, and the second is *generalized reciprocity*, which is the tendency for people who generally like others to be liked themselves. Both of these correlations tend to be positive in nonromantic settings. This is especially true for dyadic reciprocity (which ranges from $r = .26$ to $r = .61$, depending on the context), but even the generalized correlations are strong among individuals meeting for the first time (on average, $r = .43$; see Kenny). We hypothesized that dyadic reciprocity would remain positive in the romantic context provided by speed-dating but that the generalized reciprocity correlation would be robustly negative. Platonic "likers" may indeed be likable themselves (Folkes & Sears, 1977), but romantic likers, we predicted, are likely to radiate unselectivity and desperation.

This is in fact what our SRM analyses revealed. If Laura experienced unique romantic desire for Brett, Brett was likely to reciprocate that unique desire for Laura (dyadic reciprocity; $r = .14$). However, Laura was *anti*desired to the extent that she generally desired all her speed-dates (generalized reciprocity; $r = -.41$). Furthermore, we found that the negative generalized correlation was partially mediated by the date's *perceived unselectivity* as measured by the interaction record item "To what percentage of the other people here today will this person say 'yes'?" In other words, participants who desired everyone were perceived as likely to say yes to a large percentage of their speed-dates, and this in turn negatively predicted their desirability.

These findings add a level of nuance to the principle of reciprocity as it occurs in fledgling romantic relationships: Whether one expresses romantic desire with either a selective or unselective "flavor" will have a big impact on whether that desire is reciprocated. In fact, the negative generalized correlation is quite distinctive, in comparison both to previous nonromantic studies (Kenny, 1994) and to laboratory-based studies that have specifically examined selective liking (Walster et al., 1973, Study 6). We have speculated that these findings reflect a need to feel special or unique in relationships, a need that is crucial even in the very opening moments of a romantic encounter.

Predicting "Breakoff" from Perceived Regard and Partner-Specific Attachment Anxiety

Close relationships researchers have revealed numerous predictors of relationship maintenance and well-being. One important predictor is *perceived regard*, or the belief that one's romantic partner values, accepts, and feels positively toward the self (for a review, see Murray, Holmes, & Collins, 2006). For example, individuals who do not feel positively regarded by their partners are more likely to feel threatened by their partner's negative behavior and devalue their relationship as a result (Murray, Bellavia, Rose, & Griffin, 2003). Although perceived regard has been almost exclusively examined within ongoing romantic relationships, this construct is likely to encourage the development of fledgling relationships as well. In other words, participants should be more likely to pursue a romantic relationship with a potential partner if they believe that partner also regards them highly, a prediction that is reminiscent of a simple reciprocity hypothesis.

However, we hypothesized that fledging romantic relationships would show an interesting twist on this perceived regard effect. Recall that, according to Tennov (1979), romantic passion best flourishes when there is a combination of both hope (e.g., beliefs that the love interest desires the self) and uncertainty (e.g., doubt that the love interest desires the self). Perceived regard, assessed by items such as "I think that [name] is romantically interested in me" in the NSDS follow-up, is very similar to Tennov's conception of "hope"[3] and should positively predict one's romantic interest in a potential partner. But what about Tennov's "uncertainty"—the yin to hope's yang? We suggest that Tennov's uncertainty is essentially the construct we call *partner-specific attachment anxiety*, measured in the NSDS by items such as "I need a lot of reassurance that [name] cares about me" and "I worry that [name] doesn't care about me as much as I care about him/her" (see Eastwick & Finkel, in press). Perhaps not surprisingly, perceived regard and partner-specific attachment anxiety correlated negatively ($r = -.14$) in the NSDS, indicating that it was perhaps difficult for both to remain simultaneously entrenched in one individual's psyche. Nevertheless, we follow Tennov in suggesting that the two are independent and critical ingredients that inspire the pursuit of a potential romantic relationship—the fact that perceived regard and partner-specific attachment anxiety tend to repel one another exemplifies the delicate balance that fledgling relationships must negotiate.

To explore these predictions, we examined participants' reports of perceived regard and partner-specific attachment anxiety from the 10-wave NSDS follow-up (Eastwick & Finkel, 2008b). We conducted a hazard model (Singer & Willett, 2003) to predict "breakoff": the point at which a participant stops reporting that a speed-dating match or write-in has "romantic potential" (i.e., the prerelationship equivalent of a breakup). When both perceived regard and partner-specific attachment anxiety were simultaneously (or independently) added to the hazard model predicting breakoff, both constructs were highly significant negative predictors. In other words, participants were more likely to stay romantically interested in a potential partner to the extent that they (a) thought the partner was interested in them and (b) were uncertain whether or not the partner was interested in them.

Figure 11.1 displays three examples of perceived regard and partner-specific attachment anxiety trajectories that nicely demonstrate the precarious balance of these two constructs. Panel A reveals that participant 317 broke off the pursuit of a romantic relationship with partner 130 at wave 5. This breakoff may have happened because participant 317 felt insufficiently positively regarded by partner 130; his or her perceived regard dropped steadily from wave 3 to wave 5, possibly reflecting a sense of hopelessness about the future of this potential relationship. Contrast this breakoff with that shown in Panel B, in which participant 572 broke off a potential relationship with partner 244 at wave 9. Here, perceived regard was not the problem—rather, partner-specific attachment anxiety had been declining from wave 6 to wave 9. This probably indicates that participant 572 was insufficiently inspired to continue pursuing the relationship, perhaps because he or she no longer experienced any uncertainty about partner 244's feelings (see Eastwick & Finkel, in press, for a theoretical discussion of why partner-specific attachment anxiety would encourage early relationship pursuit). Finally, Panel C presents participant 263's reports of partner 41; these data are censored, which means that breakoff did not occur during the course of the study (in fact, these two participants were "dating casually" from wave 3 on). This panel nicely exemplifies the balance of hope and uncertainty as envisioned by Tennov (1979): Perceived regard and partner-specific attachment anxiety ebb and flow and are visibly negatively correlated, but both are always present, and the relationship continues as a result. To be sure, these three examples are hand-picked and represent ideal cases, yet in conjunction with the hazard model results reported above, they illustrate how perceived regard and partner-specific attachment anxiety are jointly critical in inspiring the pursuit of a potential romantic relationship.

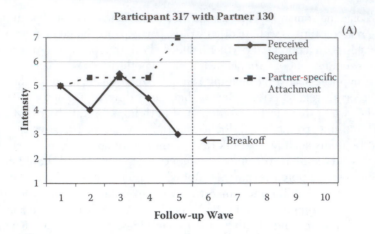

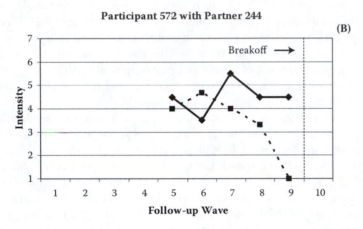

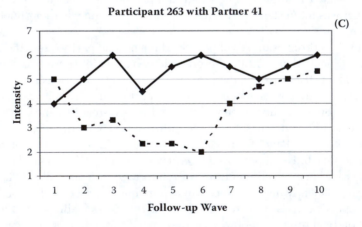

Figure 11.1   Three example trajectories of perceived regard and partner-specific attachment anxiety. *Note*: In Panel A, participant 317 broke off a potential relationship with partner 130 at wave 5. In Panel B, participant 572 broke off a potential relationship with partner 244 at wave 9 (participant 572 did not report that partner 244 had "romantic potential" until wave 5, hence the missing data). In Panel C, participant 263 did not break off a potential relationship with partner 41 during the 10 waves (i.e., these data are censored). *Source*: From Eastwick and Finkel (2008b).

Race and Political Ideology

Given the large volume of social psychological research on race and on romantic relationships, the meager crosstalk between these two topics is somewhat surprising. Existing research indeed reveals that individuals involved in interracial relationships experience stigma and disapproval (e.g., Miller, Olson, & Fazio, 2004), but it remains largely a mystery how such relationships coalesce in the first place. We hypothesized that political orientation could prove a powerful predictor of participants' interest in initiating an interracial romantic relationship (Eastwick, Richeson, & Finkel, 2008). On the *pre-event questionnaire*, we asked participants to report their race or ethnicity as well as their political orientation (e.g., "I endorse many aspects of conservative political ideology"). At the event itself, we examined White participants' interaction record reports of romantic desire as a function of their own political orientation and the race of their speed-dating partner (White versus racial minority).

The results of this analysis are plotted in Figure 11.2. The data revealed a crossover interaction: White conservative participants experienced more romantic desire for White speed-daters compared to racial minority speed-daters, whereas White liberal participants (i.e., those low in conservatism) experienced more romantic desire for other-race speed-daters compared to White speed-daters. The finding for conservatives is similar to those obtained by survey methods, which have revealed that political conservatism is correlated with unfavorable attitudes toward interracial marriage (e.g., Johnson & Jacobson, 2005). However, the finding that White liberals actually prefer *other*-race individuals is unique and somewhat unexpected; perhaps liberals are interested in dating individuals from a variety of backgrounds as a consequence of their greater openness. Alternatively, some evidence suggests that liberals are *more* likely than conservatives to experience heightened arousal during interracial interactions (Nail, Harton, & Decker, 2003), and it is possible that in the romantic context of speed-dating, this arousal was misattributed as romantic desire (e.g., Dutton & Aron, 1974). Future work will be needed to tease apart differing explanations for this effect; for now, it indeed appears that political orientation may be an important factor that determines who is willing to initiate an interracial romantic relationship, despite their rarity and stigma.

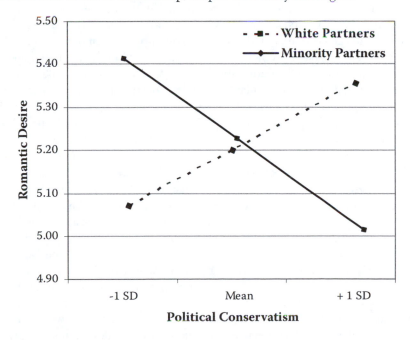

Figure 11.2   White participants' romantic desire toward an opposite-sex speed-dating partner as a function of their own political conservatism and the partner's race. *Source*: From Eastwick, Richeson, and Finkel (2007).

LIMITATIONS AND FUTURE DIRECTIONS FOR SPEED-DATING RESEARCH

As speed-dating is a relatively new addition to the methodological repertoire of social scientists, much about it still remains a mystery. Though we have been unabashedly sanguine about the potential of speed-dating to shed light on romantic relationship initiation, it is also appropriate to exercise some measure of caution at the present time. In principle, this caution can come in one of two forms: concern about the generalizability of speed-dating *processes* and concern about the representativeness of speed-dating *participants*. Regarding the former, one could argue that speed-dating is an unusual and artificial way to meet potential romantic partners. Speed-dating does indeed have several unique features, as mentioned above (e.g., bad dates end mercifully quickly); however, we do not think it likely that speed-dating differs so starkly from the myriad other ways that people meet potential romantic partners. Keep in mind that romantic partners meet at neighborhood cookouts, bars, classrooms, churches, dating websites (see Sprecher, Schwartz, Harvey, & Hatfield, this volume), and countless other settings that may or may not differ in systematic ways. Very little research has considered how romantic processes differ between settings, so to saddle speed-dating alone with such a criticism is premature. In fact, researchers have often studied attraction in the laboratory using the get-acquainted paradigm (e.g., Insko & Wilson, 1977). When individuals meet in such a context, the processes at play are surely not the same as if the people were introduced by a friend, for example, but such a concern has not dampened the usefulness of such a paradigm (nor should it).

The second concern is that an individual who volunteers for a speed-dating study might not be representative of the broader population of single individuals. Again, this is not a concern unique to speed-dating per se, but unfortunately applies broadly to most psychological studies that employ volunteer participants. Even still, this concern could be particularly acute if both (a) speed-dating appealed only to a small subset of that population of willing volunteers, and (b) that small subset was unusual in its approach to dating and romantic relationships. At the present time, scholars simply do not have the data to know if both (a) and (b) are true. There is at least one reason to doubt point (a): Given that speed-dating is probably more appealing for participants than a typical psychological experiment, it may attract a different, and perhaps broader, population of volunteers. Perhaps individuals who are unlikely to take a psychology class or participate for monetary compensation alone would eagerly volunteer for a speed-dating study. It is not clear a priori which sample, those who would consider speed-dating or the standard psychology participant pool, is more unusual or less representative of the population as a whole. Finally, though point (b) is certainly plausible, a priori hypotheses about how exactly speed-daters might be unique are often inconsistent. For example, a speed-dater could be someone who enjoys spontaneously interacting with strangers (i.e., extroverts) or, alternatively, someone who needs help initiating a conversation with strangers (i.e., introverts).

Thankfully, these potential concerns can ultimately be addressed with data, and this marks one important future direction for speed-dating research. It would be valuable to know whether there is anything strange about meeting a potential romantic partner at a speed-dating event and whether speed-dating participants differ systematically from other research samples. In fact, the NSDS enabled us to partially address the former question using the follow-up questionnaire reports on write-ins (romantic interests met outside of speed-dating). In many of our analyses, we have examined whether the psychological processes at play characterize both speed-dating matches and write-ins, and we have yet to find systematic differences as we have explored our particular research questions. One simple way that researchers could address the latter concern (participant sample) is by using surveys to identify important differences between individuals who would or would not volunteer for a speed-dating study. An especially constructive way to address this concern would entail recruiting community (or, better yet, representative) samples for speed-dating research; this would present a difficult challenge in terms of recruitment but would ultimately provide a sample more diverse than the standard university student pool.

Of course, there are many other future avenues for speed-dating research that go beyond addressing and resolving potential shortcomings. As mentioned earlier, a great wealth of data would be generated by videotaping and/or audiotaping each speed-date. These interactions could be coded for countless features—from body language to conversational topics to romantic strategies—and researchers could explore what features positively or negatively predict dating success. Such a study would bring an unprecedented level of insight to the processes underlying romantic relationship initiation. Researchers might also want to consider the use of innovative measurement techniques: biological measures such as testosterone, oxytocin, or fluctuating asymmetry; implicit measures such as implicit racial beliefs or implicit attitudes toward members of the preferred sex; or even brain-imaging techniques such as functional magnetic resonance imaging (fMRI) could be used to collect data before, during, or after the speed-dating event. For example, it would be fascinating to explore whether certain biomarkers, such as fluctuating asymmetry or testosterone, predict participants' romantic success and use of certain strategies at the speed-dating event. Finally, if researchers wanted to manipulate these processes experimentally, they could employ trained confederates to attend the speed-dating sessions. Employing a confederate does present a unique ethical challenge, but there could potentially be ways to implement such a procedure without compromising the speed-dating experience for the participants. In truth, we have faith that the IRB at most institutions would be receptive to one or another variant on all of these procedures, especially if researchers initiate dialogue with the IRB early in the process of planning a speed-dating study (for discussion, see Finkel et al., 2007).

Ultimately, the future of speed-dating research will be shaped by scholars' own ingenuity as they adapt their specific research questions to the flexible and comprehensive speed-dating paradigm. Although conducting a speed-dating study may be somewhat labor intensive, we have argued herein that the myriad strengths of this method should persuade scholars to consider whether speed-dating could make a valuable addition to their current research programs (for how-to guidance on conducting speed-dating studies, see Finkel et al., 2007). Indeed, speed-dating essentially capitalizes on paradigms, such as dyadic and longitudinal data collection, that are already familiar to many attraction and relationships researchers. We are therefore hopeful that researchers will increasingly embrace speed-dating as an important methodological innovation, and that new and exciting insights into the dynamics of initial romantic attraction will follow accordingly.

NOTES

1. "[Name]" indicates that the website inserted the target person's first name.
2. Some evolutionary models would predict that sex differences in the importance of physical attractiveness and earning prospects are diminished to the extent that men and women are interested in a short-term (versus a long-term) relationship (e.g., Buss & Schmitt, 1993). However, we could not find any evidence that this short-term/long-term distinction moderated any of our effects, despite the fact that we assessed this construct in several different ways.
3. Our perceived regard item is akin to the construct "hope" given that "[name]" refers to an individual toward whom one experiences romantic interest.

REFERENCES

Ambady, N., & Rosenthal, R. (1992). Thin slices of expressive behavior as predictors of interpersonal consequences: A meta-analysis. *Psychological Bulletin, 111*, 256–274.

Aron, A., Dutton, D. G., Aron, E. N., & Iverson, A. (1989). Experiences of falling in love. *Journal of Social and Personal Relationships, 6*, 243–257.

Aron, A., Paris, M., & Aron, E. N. (1995). Falling in love: Prospective studies of self-concept change. *Journal of Personality and Social Psychology, 69*, 1102–1112.

Axelrod, R. (1984). *The evolution of cooperation*. New York: Basic Books.

Baumeister, R. F., & Bratslavsky, E. (1999). Passion, intimacy, and time: Passionate love as a function of change in intimacy. *Personality and Social Psychology Review, 3*, 49–67.

Berscheid, E., Graziano, W., Monson, T., & Dermer, M. (1976). Outcome dependency: Attention, attribution, and attraction. *Journal of Personality and Social Psychology, 34*, 978–989.

Berscheid, E., & Reis, H. T. (1998). Attraction and close relationships. In D. T. Gilbert, S. T. Fiske, & G. Lindzey (Eds.), *The handbook of social psychology* (4th ed., Vol. 2, pp. 193–281). New York: McGraw-Hill.

Berscheid, E., & Walster, E. H. (1978). *Interpersonal attraction* (2nd ed.). Reading, MA: Addison-Wesley.

Bui, K-V. T., Peplau, L. A., & Hill, C. T. (1996). Testing the Rusbult model of relationship commitment and stability in a 15-year study of heterosexual couples. *Personality and Social Psychology Bulletin, 22*, 1244–1257.

Buss, D. M. (1989). Sex differences in human mate preferences: Evolutionary hypotheses tested in 37 cultures. *Behavioral and Brain Sciences, 12*, 1–49.

Buss, D. M., & Schmitt, D. P. (1993). Sexual strategies theory: An evolutionary perspective on human mating. *Psychological Review, 100*, 204–232.

Byrne, D. (1961). Interpersonal attraction and attitude similarity. *Journal of Abnormal and Social Psychology, 62*, 713–715.

Byrne, D., Ervin, C. R., & Lamberth, J. (1970). Continuity between the experimental study of attraction and real-life computer dating. *Journal of Personality and Social Psychology, 16*, 157–165.

Campbell, L., Simpson, J. A., Kashy, D. A., & Fletcher, G. J. O. (2001). Ideal standards, the self, and flexibility of ideals in close relationships. *Personality and Social Psychology Bulletin, 27*, 447–462.

Chapdelaine, A., Kenny, D. A., & LaFontana, K. M. (1994). Matchmaker, matchmaker, can you make me a match? Predicting liking between two unacquainted persons. *Journal of Personality and Social Psychology, 67*, 83–91.

Drigotas, S. M., Rusbult, C. E., Wieselquist, J., & Whitton, S. W. (1999). Close partner as sculptor of the ideal self: Behavioral affirmation and the Michelangelo phenomenon. *Journal of Personality and Social Psychology, 77*, 293–323.

Dutton, D. G., & Aron, A. P. (1974). Some evidence for heightened sexual attraction under conditions of high anxiety. *Journal of Personality and Social Psychology, 30*, 510–517.

Eastwick, P. W., & Finkel, E. J. (in press). The attachment system in fledgling relationships: An activating role for attachment anxiety. *Journal of Personality and Social Psychology.*

Eastwick, P. W., & Finkel, E. J. (2008a). Sex differences in mate preferences revisited: Do people know what they initially desire in a romantic partner? *Journal of Personality and Social Psychology, 94*, 245–264.

Eastwick, P. W., & Finkel, E. J. (2008b). *The tenuous balance of perceived regard and attachment anxiety in developing relationships.* Unpublished manuscript, Northwestern University.

Eastwick, P. W., Finkel, E. J., Mochon, D., & Ariely, D. (2007). Selective versus unselective romantic desire: Not all reciprocity is created equal. *Psychological Science, 18*, 317–319.

Eastwick, P. W., Richeson, J. A., & Finkel, E. J. (2008). *Is love colorblind? Political orientation moderates interracial romantic desire.* Unpublished manuscript, Northwestern University.

Feingold, A. (1990). Gender differences in effects of physical attractiveness on romantic attraction: A comparison across five research paradigms. *Journal of Personality and Social Psychology, 59*, 981–993.

Feingold, A. (1992). Gender differences in mate selection preferences: A test of the parental investment model. *Psychological Bulletin, 112*, 125–139.

Finkel, E. J., Eastwick, P. W., & Matthews, J. (2007). Speed-dating as an invaluable tool for studying initial romantic attraction: A conceptual and methodological primer. *Personal Relationships, 14*, 149–166.

Fisman, R., Iyengar, S. S., Kamenica, E., & Simonson, I. (2006). Gender differences in mate selection: Evidence from a speed-dating experiment. *Quarterly Journal of Economics, 121*, 673–697.

Fletcher, G. J. O., Simpson, J. A., & Thomas, G. (2000). Ideals, perceptions, and evaluations in early relationship development. *Journal of Personality and Social Psychology, 79*, 933–940.

Folkes, V. S., & Sears, D. O. (1977). Does everybody like a liker? *Journal of Experimental Social Psychology, 13*, 505–519.

Fraley, R. C. (2004). *How to conduct behavioral research over the Internet: A beginner's guide to HTML and CGI/Perl.* New York: Guilford Press.

Goodwin, S. A., Fiske, S. T., Rosen, L. D., & Rosenthal, A. M. (2002). The eye of the beholder: Romantic goals and impression biases. *Journal of Experimental Social Psychology, 38*, 232–241.

Gottman, J. M. (1994). *What predicts divorce? The relationship between marital processes and marital outcomes.* Hillsdale, NJ: Lawrence Erlbaum.

Haney, C., Banks, W. C., & Zimbardo, P. G. (1973). Interpersonal dynamics in a simulated prison. *International Journal of Criminology and Penology, 1*, 69–97.

Harrison, A. A., & Saeed, L. (1977). Let's make a deal: An analysis of revelations and stipulations in lonely hearts advertisements. *Journal of Personality and Social Psychology, 35*, 257–264.

Hatfield, E., & Sprecher, S. (1986). Measuring passionate love in intimate relationships. *Journal of Adolescence, 9*, 383–410.

Heyman, R. E. (2001). Observation of couple conflicts: Clinical assessment applications, stubborn truths, and shaky foundations. *Psychological Assessment, 13*, 5–35.

Holmes, J. G., & Rempel, J. K. (1989). Trust in close relationships. In C. Hendrick (Ed.), *Close relationships: Review of personality and social psychology* (Vol. 10, pp. 187–220). Thousand Oaks, CA: Sage.

Insko, C. A., & Wilson, M. (1977). Interpersonal attraction as a function of social interaction. *Journal of Personality and Social Psychology, 35*, 903–911.

Iyengar, S. S., Simonson, I., Fisman, R., & Mogilner, C. (2005, January). *I know what I want but can I find it? Examining the dynamic relationship between stated and revealed preferences.* Paper presented at the Society for Personality and Social Psychology annual meeting, New Orleans, LA.

Johnson, B. R., & Jacobson, C. K. (2005). Contact in context: An examination of social settings on whites' attitudes toward interracial marriage. *Social Psychology, 68*, 387–399.

Karney, B. R., & Bradbury, T. N. (1995). The longitudinal course of marital quality and stability: A review of theory, methods, and research. *Psychological Bulletin, 118*, 3–34.

Kashy, D. A., & Kenny, D. A. (2000). The analysis of data from dyads and groups. In H. T. Reis & C. M. Judd (Eds.), *Handbook of research methods in social psychology* (pp. 451–477). New York: Cambridge University Press.

Kelley, H. H., & Thibaut, J. W. (1978). *Interpersonal relations: A theory of interdependence.* New York: Wiley.

Kenny, D. A. (1994). *Interpersonal perception: A social relations analysis.* New York: Guilford.

Kenny, D. A., & La Voie, L. (1984). The social relations model. In L. Berkowitz (Ed.), *Advances in experimental social psychology* (Vol. 18, pp. 141–182). New York: Academic Press.

Kurzban, R., & Weeden, J. (2005). Hurrydate: Mate preferences in action. *Evolution and Human Behavior, 26*, 227–244.

Laurenceau, J. P., Barrett, L. F., & Pietromonaco, P. R. (1998). Intimacy as an interpersonal process: The importance of self-disclosure, partner disclosure, and perceived partner responsiveness in interpersonal exchanges. *Journal of Personality and Social Psychology, 74*, 1238–1251.

Loving, T. J. (2006). Predicting dating relationship fate with insiders' and outsiders' perspectives: Who and what is asked matters. *Personal Relationships, 13*, 349–362.

Luce, R. D., & Raiffa, H. (1957). *Games and decisions.* New York: Wiley.

MacFarquhar, N. (2006, September 19). It's Muslim boy meets girl, but don't call it dating. *New York Times*, p. A1.

Miller, S. C., Olson, M. A., & Fazio, R. H. (2004). Perceived reactions to interracial romantic relationships: When race is used as a cue to status. *Group Processes and Intergroup Relations, 7*, 354–369.

Murray, S. L., Bellavia, G. M., Rose, P., & Griffin, D. W. (2003). Once hurt, twice hurtful: How perceived regard regulates daily marital interactions. *Journal of Personality and Social Psychology, 84*, 126–147.

Murray, S. L., Holmes, J. G., & Collins, N. L. (2006). Optimizing assurance: The risk regulation system in relationships. *Psychological Bulletin, 132*, 641–666.

Murray, S. L., Holmes, J. G., & Griffin, D. W. (1996). The self-fulfilling nature of positive illusions in romantic relationships: Love is not blind, but prescient. *Journal of Personality and Social Psychology, 71*, 1155–1180.

Nail, P. R., Harton, H. C., & Decker, B. P. (2003). Political orientation and modern versus aversive racism: Tests of Dovidio and Gaertner's (1998) integrated model. *Journal of Personality and Social Psychology, 84*, 754–770.

Nisbett, R. E., & Wilson, T. D. (1977). Telling more than we can know: Verbal reports on mental processes. *Psychological Review, 84*, 231–259.

Paulhus, D. L. (1984). Two-component models of socially desirable responding. *Journal of Personality and Social Psychology, 46*, 598–609.

Perusse, D. (1993). Cultural and reproductive success in industrial societies: Testing the relationship at the proximate and ultimate levels. *Behavioral and Brain Sciences, 16*, 267–322.

Reis, H. T., & Shaver, P. (1988). Intimacy as an interpersonal process. In S. Duck (Ed.), *Handbook of personal relationships* (pp. 367–389). Chichester, UK: Wiley.

Rusbult, C. E., Olsen, N., Davis, J. L., & Hannon, P. A. (2001). Commitment and relationship maintenance mechanisms. In J. H. Harvey & A. Wenzel (Eds.), *Close romantic relationships: Maintenance and enhancement* (pp. 87–113). Mahwah, NJ: Lawrence Erlbaum.

Sherif, M., Harvey, O. J., White, B. J., Hood, W. R., & Sherif, C. W. (1961). *The robber's cave experiment: Intergroup conflict and cooperation*. Middletown, CT: Wesleyan University Press. (Original work published 1954)

Simpson, J. A. (2007). Foundations of interpersonal trust. In A. W. Kruglanski & E. T. Higgins (Eds.), *Social psychology: A handbook of basic principles* (2nd ed., pp. 587–607). New York: Guilford.

Singer, J. D., & Willett, J. B. (2003). *Applied longitudinal data analysis*. New York: Oxford University Press.

Speed, A., & Gangestad, S. W. (1997). Romantic popularity and mate preferences: A peer-nomination study. *Personality and Social Psychology Bulletin, 23*, 928–936.

Sprecher, S. (1989). The importance to males and females of physical attractiveness, earning potential, and expressiveness in initial attraction. *Sex Roles, 21*, 591–607.

Sprecher, S., & Duck, S. (1994). Sweet talk: The importance of perceived communication for romantic and friendship attraction experienced during a get-acquainted date. *Personality and Social Psychology Bulletin, 20*, 391–400.

Sprecher, S., Sullivan, Q., & Hatfield, E. (1994). Mate selection preferences: Gender differences examined in a national sample. *Journal of Personality and Social Psychology, 66*, 1074–1080.

Stroebe, W., Insko, C. A., Thompson, V. D., & Layton, B. D. (1971). Effects of physical attractiveness, attitude similarity, and sex on various aspects of interpersonal attraction. *Journal of Personality and Social Psychology, 18*, 79–91.

Tennov, D. (1979). *Love and limerence*. New York: Stein and Day.

Thurstone, L. L. (1928). Attitudes can be measured. *American Journal of Sociology, 33*, 529–554.

Townsend, J. M., & Wasserman, T. (1998). Sexual attractiveness: Sex differences in assessment and criteria. *Evolution and Human Behavior, 19*, 171–191.

Walster, E., Aronson, V., Abrahams, D., & Rottmann, L. (1966). Importance of physical attractiveness in dating behavior. *Journal of Personality and Social Psychology, 4*, 508–516.

Walster, E., Walster, G. W., Piliavin, J., & Schmidt, L. (1973). "Playing hard to get": Understanding an elusive phenomenon. *Journal of Personality and Social Psychology, 26*, 113–121.

12

MySpace or Your Place
Relationship Initiation and Development in the Wired and Wireless World

KATELYN Y. A. MCKENNA (YAEL KAYNAN)

N ot long ago my mother called to ask me for advice. It seems that after several months of participating as a commenter on a politically oriented blog, a fellow commenter with whom she had had many debates and discussions decided that he had fallen in love with her. Indeed, he was proclaiming his love and admiration publicly on the commenting forum and pleading with her to make contact with him in person. She was, to say the least, surprised at this turn of events.

Sight unseen, he had fallen in love with her through the power of her words: through the ideas and thoughts she had expressed, and the way she had approached difficult issues and differences of opinion. Because they were participating in a text-based forum, he had no way of knowing that the woman who was expressing these ideas, and whose personality he found so attractive, was old enough to be his mother.

The words we use and the way we use them, whether in written or in spoken form, are a primary means through which others get to know us, to form impressions of us, and to decide what kind of a person we are and what personality characteristics we possess. Yet, other factors have been shown to be far more influential in the impression formation process. Indeed, physical appearance has been found to be perhaps the most influential factor in what attracts us to others, certainly in relationships that develop through traditional, face-to-face means but also through many, but not all, online meeting places (e.g., Hatfield & Sprecher, 1986).

Certainly, the dynamics of new relationship initiation and development can unfold somewhat differently on the Internet than when individuals meet in more traditional, face-to-face settings, or there would be no need for this chapter. In addition to the presence versus the absence of physical appearance, there are a number of other differences that can profoundly and differentially affect the course of a relationship that develops online as opposed to one that develops in person. In this chapter, these principle differences between online and traditional interactions are discussed along with the factors influencing how, when, and why relationships that are initiated online blossom into relationships that continue and thrive in person. Particular attention is paid to three different kinds of relationships that occur online: naturally forming, targeted, and networked relationships.

Social mores dictate that conversational topics generally begin at the superficial level when we meet others in person and then gradually become more intimate, should we choose to pursue the relationship further. In contrast, introductory conversations online often leapfrog over the "getting to know you" icebreakers and into the meaty discussions that only rarely take place so early among fresh acquaintances in person (McKenna, Buffardi, & Seidman, 2005). Indeed, individuals often discuss intimate issues with their relatively new online acquaintances that they have never discussed with their nearest and dearest (e.g., Joinson, 2001; Joinson & Paine, 2007; McKenna & Bargh, 1998). By following online group discussions or by reading through someone's personal blog prior to interacting, a reader can initiate a discussion with a new online acquaintance already armed with a great deal of knowledge about that person's opinions, values, background, and behavior. It is rare, indeed, to be privy to this depth of information prior to making the acquaintance of another through traditional means and venues. And, although such conversation starters as "I've been following your life for the past year now and just want to say …" are neither uncommon nor unwelcome in the weblog sphere, imagine the reaction that such a statement would receive if it came from a stranger on the street or in a café.

Yet, interaction venues on the Internet also differ from one another, as do the motivations and personality characteristics of the users. The dynamics of attraction, relationship initiation, and development between users of online matchmaking services (see Whitty & Carr, 2006) are often quite different from those that take place in an online discussion forum devoted to a specific interest, and are different again from the dynamics between bloggers and their readers.

FIVE INFLUENTIAL FACTORS FOR ONLINE RELATIONSHIP FACILITATION

Absence of Gating Features

Physical appearance and mannerisms play an essential role in impression formation. Together they create the primary initial "gate" that determines whom we will approach when in a crowded room of strangers, whom we will befriend, and with whom we will develop romantic relationships (e.g., Hatfield & Sprecher, 1986). Without being aware that we are doing so, we habitually and automatically use physically available features to immediately categorize others (e.g., by their ethnicity, attractiveness, or age; Bargh, 1989; Brewer, 1988). For example, research on impressions at the zero-acquaintance level (that is, having only been shown a photograph of a stranger's face with no additional information provided) has shown that there is extremely high consensus about the judgments people tend to make about a given person, across a wide variety of personality measurements, based only on physical appearance (e.g., Allbright, Kenny, & Malloy, 1988; Kenny, 1994). In other words, based solely on our facial features others may tend to assume that we are smart, kind, witty, honest, and outgoing—or they may form less flattering impressions—before we have ever exchanged a single word and before they have had a chance to learn a single thing about us beyond the physical characteristics our parents bestowed upon us.

Research has shown that first impressions tend to be lasting impressions. That is, it is rather difficult to get past our first impressions (e.g., Fiske & Taylor, 1991) because people tend to selectively focus on information that confirms rather than disconfirms their initial judgment when they interact with these same people again (e.g., Higgins & Bargh, 1987). Furthermore, the expectations others form based on their first impression may actually elicit confirmatory behavior from the target (Snyder, Tanke, & Berscheid, 1977).

Features that are readily perceived, such as physical appearance (attractiveness), an apparent stigma (e.g., obesity), or apparent shyness or social anxiety, often serve as gates in our face-to-face interactions (e.g., Dion, Berscheid, & Walster [now Hatfield], 1972; Hatfield & Sprecher, 1986). These gates often open to admit those who are physically attractive and outgoing, but also often close when we encounter the less socially skilled or physically attractive, keeping these individuals out of our social circles and our romantic lives.

When interactions take place with new online acquaintances in common interest groups, instant messages, chat rooms, the comment sections of blogs, and so forth online, such gating features are not usually immediately apparent. They do not become a barrier to potential relationships. Whitty (2004) found that the emphasis on physical aspects of self and other is much less when individuals engage in romantic cyberflirting in chat rooms than when flirting in person. Instead, different criteria form the basis of initial impressions. The opinions expressed, and the information about the self that is revealed, form the basis of first impressions in such online venues (Bargh et al., 2002; McKenna, Green, & Gleason, 2002), rather than more superficial features, such as attractiveness, which drive impression formation in face-to-face interactions.

However, when such gating features *are* in evidence initially (e.g., online dating services provide member profiles with an accompanying picture), then the same biases that operate in our face-to-face lives will come into play. We are thus likely to bypass, or reject from the outset, potentially satisfactory and mutually profitable relationships, or perhaps to form relationships that we will maintain at a less deep level, relegating these individuals to the periphery of our social circles.

This is not to say, of course, that with online interactions, when physical appearance and mannerisms, along with the accompanying information such as age or ethnicity, do eventually come into play, their gating role is negated. These potentially biasing factors do still play quite a strong role. However, research has shown that the gates tend to open a little wider than they otherwise might if a person's physical characteristics were visible from the start (e.g., Bargh, McKenna, & Fitzsimons, 2002; McKenna et al., 2002). In some cases an online-initiated romantic relationship or a friendship may continue to flourish after the partners meet "eye-to-eye" but otherwise would not have begun had they met in person initially. In some cases the deviation from an individual's "acceptable limits" may prove too great, and the relationship may end. In still others the relationship may continue but in altered form. Thus, although the romantic hopes of the young man were dashed when my mother gently rebuffed him and revealed her age, a friendship has remained, and he now fondly refers to her as "Mother Lynne" in the discussions.

Identifiability

Anonymous communication on the Internet is one difference between online and offline interaction that has been made much of in the past. In our face-to-face lives we frequently, and often repeatedly, interact with others (e.g., the man who runs the nearby gas station, or the woman who maintains a similar workout schedule at the gym) to whom we do not reveal personal information. However, despite the relative anonymity we have with these people, they may still be able to easily recognize us in a different setting.

On occasion, we may engage in what Rubin (1975) called the "strangers on a train" phenomenon. That is, we may share deeply intimate details of our lives, details our partners, parents, and closest friends may not know, with the perfect stranger in the seat next to us. We generally feel safe making such disclosures to complete strangers whom we expect to never see again because of the very fact that we do not think we will ever see them again—they do not know us or our social contacts, and so we are assured that our disclosures remain "safe" and do not reach the ears of the family and friends with whom we may not have shared these details (e.g., Derlega & Chaiken, 1977).

Whereas we may make "hit-and-run" intimate disclosures to complete strangers, when meeting someone in a face-to-face situation it is very rare to develop lasting intimacy with that person while still retaining anonymity. However, on the Internet, feelings of closeness and intimacy can emerge between individuals who are completely anonymous to one another and, over time, can ultimately lead to the development of close relationships (e.g., McKenna et al., 2002; Parks & Floyd, 1995; Walther, 1996).

Times, however, are changing. Today, seeking a romantic partner online and getting together for coffee with an online friend are common activities, but, not so many years ago, getting together with an online acquaintance in person was seen as being a dangerous venture, and there was a strong public perception that there must be something slightly wrong with someone who forged a romantic partnership online (see Sprecher, Schwartz, Harvey, & Hatfield, this volume). Similarly, people used to guard their personal information quite carefully in their online interactions, sharing their names, pictures, and locatable information only with those with whom they had developed a trusting relationship, if at all. Increasingly, however, people are choosing to interact online, to maintain personal blogs, and to sign up with matchmaking sites with a great deal of identifying information about themselves available for all to see. They may post pictures of themselves, list their real names, and publicly provide information about their general or specific location and career. Users of matchmaking sites often rush home from a first date with someone they met through the site and, now armed with the person's full name, "Google" their date to see what else they can turn up about the person and, if possible, to verify information given to them during the date.

Yet, even when people interact openly (i.e., using their true names, and providing pictures and information about their profession) on the Internet, they often still feel relatively anonymous or, rather, nonidentifiable (McKenna & Bargh, 2000; McKenna et al., 2005). One "anonymous" blogger expressed it this way: "I've got my picture up and blog under my first name. I'm sure I've left enough clues that someone could find me if they really wanted to, but I never think about it when I'm posting."

Due to this sense of anonymity, online users often engage in a "strangers on the Internet" phenomenon. Unlike disclosures made to strangers on a train, they disclose personal, intimate information to others whom they may well encounter online again. These disclosures can thus form the groundwork for a continuing and close relationship. As has been noted elsewhere, the ability to interact anonymously also allows people to join groups and explore aspects of self on the Internet that they might otherwise keep hidden in their existing relationships, and to form relationships with others who share this aspect of identity or interest (e.g., McKenna & Bargh, 1998; McKenna et al., 2002).

Control

Online interactions also allow individuals to control their side of interactions in a way that is not possible in face-to-face or telephone communication. In spoken interactions one is expected to respond immediately and "off the cuff." However, an immediate response is not always expected in online communication. People realize that typing a reply can take time and that people tend to multitask while chatting online (and often to engage in multiple chat conversations simultaneously), and thus their attention may be momentarily devoted to something else on the computer screen. Pauses that may seem unnaturally long in speech or that may be filled with many statements like *uhhhh* and *well, you know* as the person searches for the right response can go unnoticed in an online instant message. Further, those verbal indicators (e.g., *uhmmmm*) that may suggest that the individual is nervous or unsure how to respond also go unnoticed online when, after a brief delay, a polished text response pops into your chat box. Instantaneous replies to e-mails are not expected because we know that it often takes time for people to check their e-mail and write a response. The opportunity to delay response provides individuals with the chance to edit their message before sending it. It gives them more time to think about and formulate what they are going to say. This removes the pressure to respond instantaneously and allows for a more thoughtful response if the sender so chooses (see Ben-Ze'ev, 2005; McKenna & Bargh, 2000).

Further, spoken conversational norms require people to communicate in short reciprocal bursts, rather than long speeches. However, talking in "sound bites" can inhibit the degree to which people can express and explain themselves. Online, long e-mails and quite detailed comments and replies on blogs or forums are perfectly acceptable and quite common.

Interaction partners online, therefore, have more time to plan what they will say and how much they want to say in a single reply. They can edit responses before sending them. Bloggers can be as long and rambling as they wish in their posts. Indeed, it is not uncommon for bloggers to write about their experiences over multiple posts, much like the old weekly serials that used to run in newspapers and magazines—"Stay tuned: Part 3 appearing tomorrow." All of these factors give individuals greater control over how they present themselves and their ideas and opinions to others than generally occurs in face-to-face or telephone exchanges.

Discovering Similar Others

Another relationship-facilitative aspect of the Internet is the ease with which people can discover and connect with similar others. In our busy daily lives, even if we are aware of groups in our physically based community that share our interests, we may not have the time or means to attend those get-togethers. Online, people can participate in interest groups at times that are most convenient for them. There is no need for the other members to necessarily be online at the same time. These features allow interpersonal and group connections to be made day or night and with those who live just down the street or in another country. The Internet can be particularly useful for locating others who share very specialized interests (such as hand dying one's own wool), who are experiencing similar health or emotional difficulties, or who share aspects of identity that are socially sanctioned and thus are often not readily identifiable in one's physical community (Bargh & McKenna, 2004; Boase & Wellman, 2005; Davison, Pennebaker, & Dickerson, 2000).

Knowing the Other before "Knowing the Other"

A final unique aspect has emerged in recent years, and it is being put to use by many, ranging from potential employers to those unseen strangers who follow the daily musings of a blogger. This aspect is, of course, the ability to obtain a great deal of information about another person prior to initiating an interaction with him or her. This is especially the case when it comes to those who maintain personal blogs, but it is also true of those who take part in online dating sites and online discussion forums, as well as those who leave a "Google-able" trail online.

When we are introduced to a potential friend or love interest through family or friends, we may be told some information about him or her beforehand. Thus, before meeting we may know basic details such as the age, career path, and religious affiliation of the other. We may even have gotten brief glimpses into the other's personality or interests by having heard accounts of the camping trip he or she and the mutual friend made or by having been assured that he or she is "really smart." The information we learn beforehand is generally somewhat limited, however, and it comes second- or thirdhand. Things can be quite different online. Following a person's personal blog or reading through his or her archives, for instance, may tell us more about the person than his or her own mother knows before we ever initiate contact. Rather than secondhand, this information comes right from the "horse's mouth," so to speak. By reading online discussion groups, we can observe how other individuals formulate arguments and opinions, note how they behave during debates within the group, and glean other personality and behavioral characteristics through what they say and how they seem to conduct themselves within the group. Further, we may also gain an idea of how these people are perceived by others, at least within the online environment, as we observe the kinds of reactions their words elicit from other contributors and the value those others seem to place on these people's opinions or claims.

RELATIONSHIP FORMATION

It is old news now that relationships can and do form over the Internet and that these relationships can become intimate and close, potentially leading to lasting friendship or marriage (e.g., McKenna et al., 2002; Parks & Floyd, 1995). It is not for nothing that millions of people have turned to online dating. However, there are important differences in the ways in which relationships are initiated and unfold in different kinds of online venues. Different processes are at work when relationships develop in common interest groups than when they develop between participants in online dating sites, although they may lead to a similar result: The perfect match is found, or a good friend is made.

One important and influential factor is the motivation for participation by the users in the particular venues. In dating sites, for example, the primary motivation is straightforwardly to find a mate or sexual partner, whereas in common interest groups the motivation is generally to discuss and share with others the interest in question. Relationships that form in the latter groups are by-products. Other differences include the manner in which a partner is selected and contacted, the length of time participants generally interact online prior to moving to the telephone or meeting in person, and the issues discussed.

Below, relationship formation will be discussed first in terms of findings that relate to *natu-rally forming relationships*—relationships that develop out of the interaction as opposed to those in which the interaction is specifically for the purpose of potential relationship formation. The latter can be thought of as *targeted relationships* and will be discussed here mainly in terms of the inter-actions and relationships that take place in online dating sites. Next, we will examine *networked relationships*—those connections made through a friend of a friend, for instance.

Naturally Forming Relationships

The extent to which individuals feel better able to express their true or inner self online than in traditional interaction settings has been shown to be an important factor in whether or not close relationships will form online between participants in electronic groups. McKenna et al. (2002) tested this prediction through survey responses provided by hundreds of randomly selected Internet newsgroup members who were taking part in group discussions related to topics such as history, computer science, fashion, and health. "Personals" groups, the precursors of online matchmaking sites and similar to the personal ad sections of newspapers ("SWF seeks …"), were not included in the study.

The participants in these groups were not actively seeking a romantic partner or close friend-ship from among the other members of their particular group, yet a significant percentage of the survey respondents reported having done just that. The majority of respondents reported having formed friendships with other group members, but approximately 20% of the participants had found a romantic partner through their online interactions.

Through structural equation modeling of the responses, a critical mediator emerged that appears to determine whether an individual will form close Internet relationships. This mediating factor was his or her responses to a "Real Me" scale (for a copy of the scale, see Bargh, Fitzsimons, & McKenna, 2002). This scale measured whether or not the participant felt better able to express aspects of self and personality in Internet interactions than in his or her offline social life. Respondents who felt they expressed more of the "real me" on the Internet were significantly more likely to have formed close, intimate online relationships. They were also more likely to have taken steps to integrate those online friends and romantic partners into their face-to-face life, as compared to those who reported feeling more like their true, inner self in traditional social settings. These close Internet relationships also turned out to be remarkably durable, as a 2-year follow-up study demonstrated (see McKenna et al., 2002).

One of the important ingredients for the formation of close relationships over the Internet is the tendency to engage in greater self-disclosure there (see Derlega, Winstead, & Greene, this volume). Anonymity, shared interests, and interacting in the physical absence of one's communication partner can produce this heightened tendency to disclose. The fact that people tend to more readily engage in acts of self-disclosure on the Internet has been well documented (e.g., Joinson, 2001; Levine, 2000; Walther, 1996). As is argued by a number of theorists (e.g., Derlega, Metts, Petronio, & Mar-gulis, 1993; Derlega et al., this volume; Laurenceau, Barrett, & Pietromonaco, 1998), self-disclosure is important to the development of intimacy, as it entails being able to express and having accepted one's true personality and inner feelings. Situation-appropriate self-disclosure fosters feelings of lik-ing between people: We tend to like those to whom we self-disclose, to like those who disclose to us, and to disclose more to those we like (e.g., Collins & Miller, 1994). Early mutual self-disclosure should lead to greater liking for the other (see Aron, Melinat, Aron, Vallone, & Bator, 1997) and, in turn, to the relationship developing more quickly.

A number of experimental studies suggest that this is the case. McKenna and colleagues (McK-enna et al., 2002) examined first encounters and short-term encounters in a laboratory setting. In one study (Study 3), undergraduates were randomly assigned (in cross-sex pairs) to meet one another for the first time in an Internet chat room or to meet face-to-face for a period of 20 minutes. Those who interacted with a partner online liked one another more than did those who interacted face-to-face. Furthermore, this effect held when participants met one another twice. For those who initially met over the Internet, there was a significant correlation between the degree of liking for the partner and how well the participant felt he or she had gotten to know the other person. However, there was no such correlation in the face-to-face condition. Nor did meeting for a second time in person significantly change the original assessments of liking for the partner in the face-to-face-only condition (see also Hian, Chuan, Trevor, & Detenber, 2004).

In a study by Bargh et al. (2002), undergraduates were randomly assigned (in cross-sex pairs) to meet one another for the first time in an Internet chat room or to meet face-to-face for a period of 45 minutes. In line with predictions, those who met online both liked each other more and felt that they had gotten to know one another better than did those who interacted face-to-face.

Hian et al. (2004) found that greater intimacy develops, *over time*, among online partners than those who meet and interact in person. Undergraduates in their study were randomly assigned to work with a partner in a laboratory setting over a period of 3 consecutive days. At the end of the first meeting, feelings of intimacy and liking were comparable for those who interacted online and those who interacted in person. The degree of liking and intimacy between partners who met face-to-face did not change between the first and the final meeting, remaining at the same moderate level. In contrast, intimacy significantly increased for those who met online.

Along similar lines, Walther (1996, 1997) found that new acquaintances can achieve greater intimacy through online communication than they do in parallel face-to-face interactions, particularly when the interactions take place over time. Walther (1997) examined intimacy development between members who took part in short-term group interactions and those who took part in long-term group interactions. Those who interacted over an extended period of time online developed greater affection and closeness for their partners than did those who interacted over a shorter period of time (online or face-to-face) and those who interacted in long-term face-to-face interactions.

Once intimacy has been established and the online relationship becomes an integral part of a person's life, he or she is generally reluctant to leave the relationship solely in the virtual realm. People tend to be motivated to make their important online relationships into a social reality (see Wicklund & Gollwitzer, 1986) by integrating them into their everyday, face-to-face lives if possible. As McKenna and colleagues (2002) found in their survey of newsgroup users, people tend to do this in a series of stages, moving first from online communication to telephone conversations and then to meeting in person.

Targeted Relationships

The findings discussed above, however, do not appear to apply when it comes to interactions between participants in online dating sites (see Sprecher et al., this volume). There are important differences between interactions that take place in forums where participants meet to discuss common interests and those that take place in online dating sites. For instance, users of dating sites routinely select potential interaction partners to contact based on the pictures in their profiles: If the picture passes muster, they then look at the other attributes listed in the profile (e.g., Hitsch, Hortaçsu, & Ariely, 2006; Whitty & Carr, 2006). That is, physical attractiveness is the first and most important factor in their selection of potential partners. In other words, we use the same criteria as when we select potential partners and friends in our traditional interactions. As noted previously, dating site participants will thus form a priori assumptions about the person, based on his or her evident physical characteristics, and will tend to filter any further information they receive through these (often inaccurate) judgments (e.g., Fiske & Taylor, 1991).

Once a potential partner has made it beyond the physical appearance "gate," the user then begins to narrow the contact options based on self-provided information about income and occupation, hobbies, previous marital status, and so forth (Hitsch et al., 2006). If all of these factors seem to be desirable, the participant will send an introductory e-mail and wait to see if he or she, in turn, passes the other person's criteria and is contacted in return.

Unlike in interactions that typically take place within common interest groups or even within the laboratory conditions described above (see also McKenna, 2007), Whitty and Carr (2006) found that users in the online dating sites are extremely conscious of the self that they are presenting through their profile and are very strategic about that self-presentation. Furthermore, they are highly aware of the fact that others, that is, their potential dating partners, are also engaging in strategic self-presentation.

Interestingly, whether on dating sites, in common interest groups, or via e-mail or their blogs, people in general seem to be intent on, and concerned with, presenting "authentic" versions of self. Although many anecdotes can be heard and several high-profile cases of deception have been covered in the media, in general it appears that people are not using the relative anonymity and lack of co-presence provided by the Internet to engage in more deception than they do in their face-to-face lives. DePaulo, Kashy, Kirkendol, Wyer, and Epstein (1996) found that the average person, over the course of an average day, will tell 1 to 2 lies, including lies in the workplace or at home between family and friends. Research by Hancock (2007) found that people lied most frequently to others via the telephone (in 37% of social interactions), followed by deceptions in face-to-face situations (27%). They told the fewest lies within the online environment, where deceptions took place in 21% of instant message interactions and in 14% of e-mail exchanges.

DePaulo and colleagues (1996) found that the lies that people generally tell are minor rather than major deceptions along the lines of fudging one's true political beliefs when conversing with someone whose beliefs differ, claiming to have been held up in traffic when late for work rather than admitting that the alarm clock did not do the trick, or giving a compliment one does not mean. Hancock (2007) also found this to be the case, whether the deception takes place in verbal venues or in text-based ones. Whitty and Carr (2006) found that users of dating sites are so concerned about presenting an "accurate" description of self and personality that many have their family members and friends assist with creating their dating profiles. That said, they are also concerned about quickly "validating" the claims made by their online dating partners.

In line with this concern, once reciprocal contact is established between two members on the dating sites, the next step—establishing a face-to-face meeting—generally happens quite quickly. Whitty and Carr (2006) found that participants in dating sites do not engage in a great deal of self-disclosure with one another prior to arranging an in-person meeting. Nor do they spend much time communicating with one another online before meeting. In their survey of online dating site users, Whitty and Carr discovered that participants typically meet in person within one week of reciprocal contact being established. This is in marked contrast to those who meet through common interest forums online: Participants in these groups communicated regularly online for an average of 3 to 4 months prior to picking up the telephone (McKenna et al., 2002).

Networked Relationships

There is an intermediary kind of relationship formation process online that lies somewhere between naturally forming relationships and targeted relationships: the networked relationship. These relationships come about in a similar manner to one of the main ways in which we have traditionally expanded our social circles: introduction to a new acquaintance through a mutual friend, family member, or coworker. In the face-to-face world, these introductions can run the gamut from being introduced to your best friend's other closest chums to being set up on a blind date through the winding connection where it turns out that he is the brother of the cousin's wife of a neighbor of a friend of your friend.

On the Internet, web spaces such as Facebook, Friendster, and MySpace provide the opportunity to capitalize on just such networking online. Within these web spaces, when someone links his or her profile or personal page to those of friends using the same web service, they then have access to the profiles and personal web pages of all the friends' friends and acquaintances whom they have also linked. Similarly, through the links others provide on their weblogs, a fellow blogger or simply a reader, a close in-person friend of the linker, or an online acquaintance can discover and connect with still others.

As in the face-to-face world, such connections tend to be perceived and coded somewhat differently than meetings with rank strangers. Although the new person in question is indeed a stranger, he or she is a stranger with a recommendation attached. This recommendation may be positive or negative. There may be a sense of ready acceptance because of the shared connection with the friend or relative if one values the friend or relative and has found in the past that other friends of theirs are "my kind of people." Equally, there may be a healthy skepticism about the new prospect if one does not hold the mutual relationship in high regard or has found through experience that his or her taste in friends does not always dovetail with one's own.

The primary difference between the networked connection online and that which occurs offline is that in the offline world one must wait until a friend decides to make the connection between two unacquainted friends by introducing them to one another. By the click on a link online, however, one can take the reins oneself and explore the extended network of various friends and acquaintances that one's friends have been squirreling away in other parts of their life.

Interestingly, this ability to actively connect with the friends of a friend or to voyeuristically explore them may well have an influence on one's relationship with the friend-connector him or herself. Just as one can more readily "get the goods" on new acquaintances online even before being formally acquainted, one can learn quite a bit about existing acquaintances through exploring their available social networks online.

CONCLUSIONS AND FUTURE AVENUES FOR RESEARCH

Little research has, as yet, examined social networking from the perspective described above. Although research has consistently found that people do use the online world to extend and expand their social networks through the many ways that one can meet others online (e.g., Kraut et al., 2002; Wellman et al., 2001), the "networked" relationship itself has not yet been examined and is a subject ripe for future research. What, for instance, is the quality of relationships formed in this way—do they tend to remain at the level of acquaintance, or do they tend to become integrated into one's more intimate social circle?

As Sprecher et al. (this volume) note, romantic relationships quite frequently come about through introductions made via one's offline social network. And, indeed, one's circle of family and friends can strongly influence the success or failure of relationships that form in this way. Are people using the expanded access they have to "friends of friends" online in order to connect with potential romantic partners, as well as expanding their friendship circle? What influence, if any, does the "connecting" network have on relationships that do form in this way?

Does online networking not only make one's social circle larger but also lend to the stability of the relationships we maintain? Consider, for instance, that when a close friendship or romantic partnership ends, often the social network(s) most closely attached to that relationship fracture(s) as well. Friends and acquaintances "choose sides," maintaining contact and closeness with only one partner of the pair—often the initial, or "primary," friend. When access to one's social networks was more readily controlled by oneself—that is, you selected which of your friends to introduce to which of your other friends and under what circumstances—things may have been simpler. The nonprimary partner of the failed relationship may have been introduced to only a few others in your social network, and, most likely, the interactions they had with those others were in the context of "the couple" ("I'd like you to meet my friend Betty, and this is her husband, Joe"). Thus, if your friend Betty and her husband separated, it may have been a simple matter to drop Joe from your life, with few repercussions for your own wider social circle. If, however, through online networking, that nonprimary friend is able to penetrate deeper into your social circle(s), independently forming relationships with friends from a variety of your social spheres (e.g., Joe has befriended your old college roommate, your favorite golfing partner, and your "other" best friend's close friend), then "choosing sides" and discarding the relationship may become much more difficult and much less desirable. The net result may well be that our wider social networks become more stable and less vulnerable to blows from the loss of a single relationship.

Similarly, it is possible that acquaintanceships—those relationships most vulnerable to falling by the wayside with shifting circumstances (e.g., a change of job or location that removes you from direct and frequent contact)—will be more likely to be maintained long term if there is also an online component to the relationship. Further, should ties be developed with friends of the acquaintance through online networking, it is possible that not only will the acquaintanceship continue but also those additional ties will draw the acquaintance from the periphery of one's social circle into one of the inner rings. Or perhaps not. There is much we do not know about how our changing means of connecting with others will affect the stability and coherence of our social networks.

Nor do we yet know how one's existing relationships are affected by the rich access into the lives, thoughts, and social networks of those we, perhaps, only thought we knew—information that was previously unavailable to us or carefully screened and partitioned by these others. How do our perceptions and feelings about them change, and how do our perceptions and feelings about ourselves, in turn, alter? Does the deeper knowledge of, and insight into, the other that may be gained through these more indirect means lead to a deeper and more meaningful relationship with that person? Or, is it the case that the critical factor for bringing about greater closeness is the act of self-disclosure itself—the fact that the other has chosen to make you a confidant to his or her inner feelings, dreams, and thoughts—and that this same information, if learned another way, matters not?

Research into nonconscious processes that occur during, and as a result of, online interaction is just beginning. What are the effects of nonconscious processes on the relationships that are carried out, in whole or in part, in the virtual domain? We know, for instance, that text-based online interaction appears to activate, nonconsciously, aspects of self that are frequently suppressed in one's face-to-face interactions and with one's existing (face-to-face-originated) relationship partners, and that these self-aspects are then effectively expressed and perceived by one's online acquaintances (see McKenna, 2007). Further, the expression and validation one receives for these self-aspects have important implications for the self and one's relationships. Undoubtedly, other processes unfold online outside of our awareness and affect our first impressions, judgments, goals, relationships, and sense of self in a myriad of ways as yet undiscovered. This, indeed, is one of the most exciting areas for future research.

The unique aspects of online communications can, but not necessarily will, prompt online relationships to unfold quite differently from those formed in traditional spheres. Relationship formation within different kinds of online meeting places also does not conform to a single model. Impression and relationship formation in common interest forums and in dating sites often unfold quite differently. The networked relationship may deviate even more in its evolution.

The initial motivations for contact often differ markedly in the various venues. In online dating sites, contact is made for the express purpose of potential romantic involvement; in common interest groups, the motive is to engage in a discussion of an interest that is important or enjoyable to both. In social networking the motivation may be either—or a little of both. Connections made based on common interests may give these potential relationships a better chance of developing into a lasting and close relationship. Research on traditional relationships has shown that sharing similar interests and values is an important factor for successful relationship formation and, importantly, for the longevity of the relationship (e.g., Byrne, 1971; Hatfield & Sprecher, 1986).

The presence or absence of one's own and the other's physical appearance also has a strong influence on the initial impressions made and the subsequent course of the relationship. Critically, having those visual cues present or not is a primary determinant of whether a potential relationship will be initiated in the first place. In many of the available common interest forums, interactions take place without having any visual information about the other prior to contact initiation. Thus, initial impressions are formed on the basis of the opinions, values, and behavior the "person of interest" expresses, and initial contacts are made without knowing the physical details. Romantic relationships or friendships, such as the one my mother formed with her admirer, may thus come to fruition that would otherwise never had occurred simply because the two would never have approached one another in the first place in order to discover one another's interests or opinions. In dating sites, physical attractiveness is what drives the contact, with opinions, values, and interests coming in much lower on the scale. Indeed, the opinions, values, and interests of those who fail the physical appearance test are never explored at all. In this respect, dating sites are not at all dissimilar to traditional face-to-face meeting places for singles, such as bars, parties, and cafés.

Higher levels of self-disclosure compared to that which occurs in typical face-to-face interactions can occur in common interest, networking, and dating venues online. Not only do people often disclose more online, but they also disclose sooner. Yet here too there are differences. Interactions that take place in common interest groups often are initiated, and early disclosures made, with participants never intending to meet one another in person. It is on the very basis of the closeness that does develop through such mutual self-disclosure that many of these participants do eventually get together in person. Conversely, contacts are made through dating sites with the very intent of meeting the other in person from the outset. Under these conditions, participants may be more reticent about making intimate disclosures. More reticent still may be those who use the social-networking sites—disclosures made to the people met in this fashion may well end up being disclosures they in turn make to the mutual friend who connects them. In other words, there may be fear that the dyadic boundary not only can but also will be broken, thus hindering one's willingness to disclose information that is not already known to those in one's social circle.

The content of one's disclosures may also differ widely depending on where one is interacting. In dating sites, participants make their disclosures through answers to relatively short questionnaires about their likes and dislikes, marital status, hobbies, and so forth. In common interest forums, such as on a Yahoo! group, individuals may disclose more (or less) information to the group, and the information that is disclosed is generally qualitatively different from the kind of information listed in a dating site profile. The amount of "upfront" information is certainly significantly less, and disclosures generally occur over time and in small chunks. Those who blog about their daily personal lives tend to disclose even more still but, again, not in a single, large chunk of information upfront. The "back-channel" private disclosures that take place between dating site participants, specific comrades in common interest groups, and bloggers and their readers, through e-mail or instant messaging, also differ. Although numerous such "conversations" may take place between the latter participants, in which further and more private disclosures may be made—those that one prefers not to announce to the world—the backchannel disclosures of two dating site participants generally include little more than a statement of interest and an exchange of phone numbers.

The moving of a potential dating site relationship from online to offline is generally a high-speed version of what occurs between participants in other kinds of online venues. Because little contact generally occurs prior to meeting, these relationships are unlikely to have the same depth and importance for the participants, and this may be a critical missing step for getting beyond a first in-person meeting. When time and effort have been invested in a relationship (and also perhaps quite intimate disclosures exchanged), people may be more motivated to maintain a positive opinion of the other and to wish to continue that relationship even if, upon meeting, the other's physical and personality attributes are less than expected or optimally desired.

On a positive note, however, dating sites allow people to connect with many more potential partners than they will encounter in everyday life. Dating sites give access to more potential partners than will be encountered through a typical common interest group on the Internet, as well. Simply having a wider pool of potential partners may increase the chance that one of those potentials will turn out to be a match made in heaven.

Clearly, many factors influence relationship formation online. In some cases, these factors will mirror those that influence relationships in the face-to-face world, and in others, they will differ. The Internet offers no instant solutions for those seeking a life partner. What it does do is widen the opportunities and options for connecting with possible partners. Some online meeting venues are more likely to bring together two compatible partners than others, just as in the face-to-face world. In the nonvirtual world, relationships are, generally speaking, more successfully initiated and developed through common interest or goal settings (e.g., through churches, hobby groups, or places of work) than through "date-seeking" venues such as bars. Friendships and romantic relationships often come about through the contacts we make through our existing family members and friends—both online and offline. The online world and its many interaction possibilities and venues seem to be, increasingly, mirroring those of our "in-person" world.

REFERENCES

Allbright, L., Kenny, D. A., & Malloy, T. E. (1988). Consensus in personality judgments at zero acquaintance. *Journal of Personality and Social Psychology*, 55, 387–395.

Aron, A., Melinat, E., Aron, E. N., Vallone, R. D., & Bator, R. J. (1997). The experimental generation of interpersonal closeness: A procedure and some preliminary findings. *Personality and Social Psychology Bulletin*, 23, 363–377.

Bargh, J. A. (1989). Conditional automaticity: Varieties of automatic influence in social perception and cognition. In J. S. Uleman & J. A. Bargh (Eds.). *Unintended thought* (pp. 3–51). New York: Guilford Press.

Bargh, J. A., Fitzsimons, G. J., & McKenna, K. Y. A. (2002). The self, online. In S. Spencer & S. Fein (Eds.), *Motivated social perception: The 9th Ontario Symposium on Social Cognition* (pp. 195–214). Mahwah, NJ: Lawrence Erlbaum.

Bargh, J. A., & McKenna, K. Y. A. (2004). The Internet and social life. *Annual Review of Psychology*, 55, 573–590.

Bargh, J. A., McKenna, K. Y. A., & Fitzsimons, G. M. (2002). Can you see the real me? Activation and expression of the "true self" on the Internet. *Journal of Social Issues*, 58, 33–48.

Ben-Ze'ev, A. (2005). Detattachment: The unique nature of online romantic relationships. In Y. Amichai-Hamburger (Ed.), The social net: The social psychology of the Internet (pp. 115–138). Oxford: Oxford University Press.

Boase, J., & Wellman, B. (2005). Personal relationships: On and off the Internet. In D. Perlman & A. L. Vangelisti (Eds.), *Handbook of personal relationships* (pp. 709–723). Oxford: Blackwell.

Brewer, M. B. (1988). A dual process model of impression formation. In R. S. Wyer & T. K. Srull (Eds.), *Advances in social cognition* (Vol. 1, pp. 1–36). Hillsdale, NJ: Lawrence Erlbaum.

Byrne, D. (1971). *The attraction paradigm*. New York: Academic Press.

Collins, N. L., & Miller, L. C. (1994). Self-disclosure and liking: A meta-analytic review. *Psychological Bulletin*, 116, 457–475.

Davison, K. P., Pennebaker, J. W., & Dickerson, S. S. (2000). Who talks? The social psychology of illness support groups. *American Psychologist*, 55, 205–217.

DePaulo, B. M., Kashy, D. A., Kirkendol, S. E., Wyer, M. M., & Epstein, J. A. (1996). Lying in everyday life. *Journal of Personality and Social Psychology*, 70, 979–995.

Derlega, V. J., & Chaikin, A. L. (1977). Privacy and self-disclosure in social relationships. *Journal of Social Issues*, 33, 102–115.

Derlega, V. L., Metts, S., Petronio, S., & Margulis, S. T. (1993). *Self-disclosure*. London: Sage.

Dion, K. K., Berscheid, E., & Walster, E. (1972). What is beautiful is good. *Journal of Personality and Social Psychology*, 24, 285–290.

Douglas, K. M., & McGarty, C. (2001). Identifiability and self-presentation: Computer-mediated communication and intergroup interaction. *British Journal of Social Psychology*, 40, 399–416.

Fiske, S. T., & Taylor, S. E. (1991). *Social cognition* (2nd ed.). New York: Scott, Foresman.

Gollwitzer, P. M. (1986). Striving for specific identities: The social reality of self-symbolizing. In R. Baumeister (Ed.), *Public self and private self* (pp. 143–159). New York: Springer.

Hancock, J. T. (2007). Digital deception: Why, when and how people lie online. In A. N. Joinson, K. Y. A. McKenna, T. Postmes, & U-D. Reips (Eds.), *The Oxford handbook of Internet psychology* (pp. 289–302). Oxford: Oxford University Press.

Hatfield, E., & Sprecher, S. (1986). *Mirror, mirror: The importance of looks in everyday life*. Albany: State University of New York Press.

Hian, L. B., Chuan, S. L., Trevor, T. M. K., & Detenber, B. H. (2004). Getting to know you: Exploring the development of relational intimacy in computer-mediated communication. *Journal of Computer Mediated Communication*, 9, 1–24.

Higgins, E. T., & Bargh, J. A. (1987). Social cognition and social perception. *Annual Review of Psychology*, 38, 369–425.

Hitsch, G., Hortaçsu, A., & Ariely, D. (2006). *What makes you click? Mate preferences and matching outcomes in online dating*. University of Chicago. Retrieved November 28, 2007, from http://home.uchicago.edu/ghitsch-Hitsch-Research/Guenter%20Hitsch_files/Online-Dating.pdf

Joinson, A. N. (2001). Knowing me, knowing you: Reciprocal self-disclosure in Internet-based surveys. *CyberPsychology and Behaviour, 4*, 587–591.

Joinson, A. N., & Paine, C. B. (2007). Self-disclosure, privacy, and the Internet. In A. N. Joinson, K. Y. A. McKenna, T. Postmes, & U-D. Reips (Eds), *The Oxford handbook of Internet psychology* (pp. 237–251). Oxford: Oxford University Press.

Kenny, D. (1994). *Interpersonal perception: A social relations analysis*. New York: Guilford.

Kraut, R., Kiesler, S., Boneva, B., Cummings, J., Helgeson, V., & Crawford, A. (2002). Internet paradox revisited. *Journal of Social Issues, 58*, 49–74.

Laurenceau, J., Barrett, L. F., & Pietromonaco, P. R. (1998). Intimacy as a process: The importance of self-disclosure and responsiveness in interpersonal exchanges. *Journal of Personality and Social Psychology, 74*, 1238–1251.

McKenna, K. Y. A. (2007). Through the Internet looking glass: Expressing and validating the true self. In A. N. Joinson, K. Y. A. McKenna, T. Postmes, & U-D. Reips (Eds), *The Oxford handbook of Internet psychology* (pp. 205–222). Oxford: Oxford University Press.

McKenna, K. Y. A., & Bargh, J. A. (1998). Coming out in the age of the Internet: Identity 'de-marginalization' from virtual group participation. *Journal of Personality and Social Psychology, 75*, 681–694.

McKenna, K. Y. A., & Bargh, J. A. (2000). Plan 9 from Cyberspace: The implications of the Internet for personality and social psychology. *Personality and Social Psychology Review, 4*, 57–75.

McKenna, K. Y. A., Buffardi, L., & Seidman, G. (2005). Self presentation to friends and strangers online. In K-H. Renner, A Schutz, & F. Machilek (Eds.), *Internet and personality* (pp. 176–189). Ashland, OH: Hogrefe & Huber.

McKenna, K. Y. A., Green, A. S., & Gleason, M. E. J. (2002). Relationship formation on the Internet: What's the big attraction? *Journal of Social Issues, 58*, 9–31.

Parks, M. R., & Floyd, K. (1995). Making friends in cyberspace. *Journal of Communication, 46*, 80–97.

Rubin, Z. (1975). Disclosing oneself to a stranger: Reciprocity and its limits. *Journal of Experimental Social Psychology, 11*, 233–260.

Snyder, M., Tanke, E., & Berscheid, E. (1977). Social perception and interpersonal behavior: On the self-fulfilling nature of social stereotypes. *Journal of Personality and Social Psychology, 35*, 656–666.

Walther, J. B. (1996). Computer-mediated communication: impersonal, interpersonal, and hyperpersonal interaction. *Communication Research, 23*, 3–43.

Walther, J. B. (1997). Group and interpersonal effects in international computer-mediated collaboration. *Human Communication Research, 23*(3). 342–369.

Wellman, B., Haase, A. Q., Whitte, J., & Hampton, K. (2001). Does the Internet increase, decrease, or supplement social capital? *American Behavioral Scientist, 45*, 436–455.

Whitty, M. T. (2004). Cyber-flirting: An examination of men's and women's flirting behaviour both offline and on the Internet. *Behaviour Change, 21*, 115–126.

Whitty, M. T., & Carr, A. N. (2006). *Cyberspace romance: The psychology of online relationships*. Basingstoke, UK: Palgrave Macmillan.

13

TheBusinessofLove.com
Relationship Initiation at Internet Matchmaking Services

SUSAN SPRECHER, PEPPER SCHWARTZ, JOHN
HARVEY, and ELAINE HATFIELD

INTRODUCTION

Anytime a new form of communication is invented—the penny newspaper, Morse code and the telegraph, the ham radio, TV, or computers—men and women find ways to use that technology to find love (Joinson, 2003). The definitive history of commercial computer matching has yet to be written, but it is known that in the 1950s, almost as soon as computers appeared, commercial matchmaking services sprang up (CBC Archives, 1957). Recognized as the first widespread computer matching service was Operation Match, which was created in the mid-1960s by Harvard students after a discussion of the evils of blind dates and mixers. They distributed thousands of questionnaires to college students at several universities and asked them to rate themselves on looks, intelligence, and other dimensions and also to indicate what they would desire in a partner on these same dimensions. In return for the completed questionnaire and a fee of $3.00, they were promised a list of compatible matches. Data were entered on punch cards and analyzed with an Avco 1790 computer (which was probably the size of a small room). According to media reports, it took the computer 6 weeks to generate the lists. Not surprisingly, the business failed (for a description of this experiment, see Leonhardt, 2006).

"Computer dates" were also conducted on university campuses in the 1960s and 1970s for academic research purposes. This was the heyday period for the study of interpersonal attraction in social psychology, and the focus was specifically on attraction that occurs between strangers. The bogus stranger experimental study (e.g., Byrne, 1971) was a common method used at the time to study attraction. In this method, people indicated how attracted they were to a stranger (a "bogus" person, unbeknownst to them) after receiving information about him or her. However, social psychologists also occasionally matched previously unacquainted students and sent them on "dates" in order to determine what factors predicted attraction after initial interaction (e.g., Byrne, Ervin, & Lamberth, 1970). One of the authors of this chapter (Hatfield, formerly Walster) conducted the best known of these studies (i.e., Walster, Aronson, Abrahams, & Rottman, 1966), a dance study with incoming freshmen at the University of Minnesota. Some such studies used a computer to assist with the matching, although the help was rudimentary and on the order of generating random numbers for the matching of questionnaires. Computers at the time were still not powerful enough to do sophisticated matching based on multiple variables.

Over time, as computers became faster and more powerful, people would eventually sit in front of computers, and the high-speed Internet was created. It was not long after these technological advances that the new generation of computer matchmaking businesses was created. Match.com was the first, launched in 1995. Match.com as well as Yahoo! Personals, two of the largest dating sites, began primarily as online personal advertisements, and "personal ads" continue today to be the primary service offered at these dating websites and many others. People post self-profiles, which include demographic information, personality descriptions, interests, and a photograph. They hope that potential eligibles will spot their posted information and want to communicate; they also browse the profiles of other members looking for possible dating prospects. Dating sites that offer this service have added many additional features over time, including keyword searches to narrow the pool, the ability to send preprogrammed icebreaker messages, voice and video greetings, anonymous instant messaging and e-mails, relationship advice, and personality testing. Whereas some sites, such as Match.com, are for the general population of singles, other sites target special niches of the population. There are those designed to appeal to various age groups (e.g., HookUp.com and SilverSingles.com), political groups (ConservativeMatch.com and LiberalHearts.com), religious groups (CatholicSingles.com, Jdate.com, ChristianCafe.com, and HappyBuddhist.com), and sexual orientation (GayWired.com and superEva.com). Dating sites also exist for people who possess mental and physical disabilities, unusual sexual preferences, and so forth. Even people who wish to find dates for themselves and their favorite pets can sign on to a site (DateMyPet.com). At the time this chapter was written, there may be almost 1,000 dating websites servicing the United States (e.g., Thompson, Zimbardo, & Hutchinson, 2005), and the technology available to create another one in an afternoon.

Whereas most dating websites are essentially an electronic version of personal advertisements, eHarmony.com (and founder, Dr. Neil Clark Warren) was the first to launch, in 2000, an alternative commercial matching website, followed by Perfectmatch.com in 2002. These sites distinguish themselves from the others by using a "scientific approach" to matching. Members complete a lengthy questionnaire, presumably based on scientific principles, and their questionnaire data are subjected to "matching algorithms" also developed based on scientific studies. For this effort and a monthly fee, members are promised a list of people who would make "perfect" or "compatible" matches. These sites have changed the online dating industry, with other major websites following suit. In 2005, Match.com launched Chemistry.com (which focuses on matching with "chemistry" in mind), and Yahoo! Personals now includes Yahoo! Premier, an in-depth matching service based on a relationship test. Independent research and development firms also market products and systems for multiple dating websites. Most notably, weAttract.com has developed personality-testing systems for both Match.com and Yahoo.com, and now has a scientific advisory board that includes American Psychological Association Past President Philip Zimbardo. Other social scientists who are involved as scientific advisors at some of the major dating sites include sociologist Pepper Schwartz (an author of this chapter) at Perfectmatch.com and anthropologist Helen Fisher (also an author in this volume) at Chemistry.com.

What scientific principles are being used to match people at the major relationship websites, such as eHarmony.com and Perfectmatch.com? How does relationship initiation through online dating websites differ from relationship initiation that occurs through more traditional ways of meeting, such as introductions from friends? Is it possible that commercial websites could help the scientific community of relationship scholars advance scientific knowledge about relationship initiation and development? These are some of the questions that our chapter will address. We will begin, however, by examining public attitudes toward online relationship initiation and a description of who is using the services and why.

Because online matching is relatively new, not much published, peer-reviewed research on the topic exists. Clearly, dating websites have developed faster than research agendas to investigate them. In order to write this chapter and review the process of relationship initiation at online matching services, it was necessary to draw upon other sources of information, including Internet reports, media accounts, and information provided on the matchmaking websites.

ATTITUDES ABOUT RELATIONSHIP INITIATION AT INTERNET MATCHING SERVICES

Only anecdotal evidence exists as to the public's attitudes toward Internet dating and Internet matching services when such online services first burst upon the scene in the mid- to late 1990s. The general public impression, reflected and perpetuated in newspaper accounts at the time, was negative. The people who used the services were assumed to be "lonely" and "desperate," and attention focused on those who lied about their marital status or gender and on cases of sexual predators who used the Internet to prey on innocent victims. Such negative media reports have continued to appear (e.g., Kleinfeld, 2003, as reported in Albright, 2007), although the media have also extolled the virtues of Internet dating.

More recently, research has been conducted on attitudes toward online dating, primarily with small convenience samples of young adults. Even though men and women in such samples are generally Internet experienced, their attitudes about online dating have been found to be more unfavorable than favorable. For example, Donn and Sherman (2002) conducted two studies examining college students' attitudes about online relationship formation. In Study 1, participants responded to several attitude statements about relationships formed over the Internet (e.g., "I would trust that the information people gave me about themselves over the Internet was true"). The sample overall was negative about online dating. For example, the participants indicated that they would worry that people on the Internet would not tell the truth, they were concerned about their safety when meeting someone online, and they generally thought it would take longer to get to know someone online than in person. In Study 2, the authors manipulated the level of information participants received about matching services (brief written description versus exposure by reviewing two matching websites) and found that greater exposure was associated with more positive (or less negative) attitudes. They also found that students with more frequent Internet usage had more favorable attitudes toward online dating.

Similar findings emerged in another survey study conducted with college students. Anderson (2005) asked the participants the degree to which it was right versus wrong, positive versus negative, and acceptable versus unacceptable for someone to enter into an online romantic relationship. Once again, the respondents had somewhat negative attitudes toward such "dating." However, greater Internet affinity, more time on the Internet, and being *less* romantic (as assessed on the Sprecher and Metts [1989] Romanticism scale) were associated with more positive attitudes.

In the research described above, the participants were relatively young and in college, and therefore likely to be surrounded by potential mates. Most had no prior exposure to matching services. A recent large-scale, national study assessed the attitudes of individuals across several ages, and included a subgroup of online daters. The Pew Internet and American Life project, a nonprofit research center that monitors the social effects of the Internet on Americans, conducted telephone interviews with a national representative sample of 3,215 adults, from age 18 to over 65 (reported in Madden & Lenhart, 2006). Of these, 2,252 (70%) were Internet users who were asked several questions about their attitudes about online dating.

Madden and Lenhart (2006) reported that their national sample of Internet users were divided in their views about whether online dating is a good way to meet people (44% agreed, and 44% disagreed). However, a greater percent (47%) agreed than disagreed (38%) with the statement "Online dating allows people to find a better match for themselves because they get to know a lot more people." Online dating was not viewed as easier and more efficient than other ways of meeting people (only 33% agreed that it was easier). Although people no longer believe that those who engage in online dating are desperate (61% disagreed), they do still worry that online dating can be dangerous (66% agreed with this statement). The subsample of respondents in the Pew Internet project who were classified as online daters (those who had gone to an online dating website or other sites where they could meet people) were more positive about online dating overall than were nonusers. For example, 79% of the online daters believed that using a dating website is a good way to meet people, and 64% agreed that online dating helps people find a better match. In addition, those who were classified as single and looking had a more positive attitude toward dating services than did the others.

The Pew data (Madden & Lenhart, 2006) suggest that Americans have a more positive attitude about online dating than is indicated by the earlier studies conducted with college students (Anderson, 2005; Donn & Sherman, 2002). Why the difference? It could be that postcollege singles are more positive than college students (perhaps because they have fewer opportunities than college students to meet others), but it could also be that attitudes about online dating have become more favorable in just a few years. The years from 2000 to 2005 experienced exponential growth in the number of visitors to dating websites (e.g., Madden & Lenhart, 2006; Thompson et al., 2005). Thus, relationship formation through dating websites has become increasingly mainstream, and correspondingly, attitudes have likely become more positive.

Although the general public may be more accepting of online dating than they were several years ago, it has also been speculated that many consumers are becoming disillusioned, perhaps after experiencing several failed attempts at matching. In a 2005 report entitled "Consumers Are Having Second Thoughts About Online Dating," produced at weAttract.com and authored by Thompson and his colleagues (2005), one conclusion was that customer satisfaction with online dating has dropped. However, the evidence for that conclusion was indirect and based primarily on the leveling of revenue in the matching industry and on anecdotal evidence. Computer matching sites are probably here for the long haul. There will always be new groups of single adults who turn to the Internet after becoming disillusioned with other ways of meeting potential partners. A particular customer's attitudes toward online dating websites, however, are likely to depend on his or her personal success in finding a mate in cyberspace.

PROFILE OF USERS

Obviously not all single adults are turning to the Internet to find a partner. It is difficult to know how many singles have subscribed to an Internet matching service in search of a partner and how they might be described demographically because the answer depends on *who* is doing the counting and *what* they are counting. The Pew Internet and American Life project survey referred to earlier (Madden & Lenhart, 2006) examined respondents' experiences with online dating. Most of the sample who were married or in a serious dating relationship had met their partners in more traditional ways (e.g., through friends, at work, or at school). Only 3% of the sample reported meeting through the Internet. However, about 15% of the total sample knew of someone who has been in a long-term relationship with or has married someone who he or she met online. Even more (31%) knew someone who had at least tried online dating sites. Of the total Internet users, 11% said they had gone to a dating website to meet people at least once (16 million people nationally). Within the smaller sample of online adults who were currently seeking romantic partners, 37% had tried a dating website (4 million nationally). Among these online daters, 43% (7 million nationally) reported going on a date with people whom they had met through dating websites.

The data from the Pew Internet project survey are not consistent with the numbers obtained from the web pages of the dating sites. In 2007, Match.com by itself indicates 15 million members, Yahoo.com has stated about 8 million, eHarmony.com over 5 million, and Perfectmatch.com about 3 million. However, as noted by Thompson et al. (2005), when dating sites refer to "millions," they are generally referring to their cumulated subscriptions. In addition, non-Americans can be included in these totals, as can people who have joined more than one website. On the other hand, the 3% of respondents from the Pew Internet project who said that they were in Internet-initiated relationships also include those relationships initiated in Internet venues other than matchmaking services, such as newsgroups and online support groups (Parks & Floyd, 1996; Parks & Robert, 1998).

Is there a demographic profile that distinguishes those who visit dating websites from their peers? According to the Pew national study (Madden & Lenhart, 2006), a greater percentage of men (12%)

than of women (9%) visit dating websites. The proportion of Hispanics (14%) and Blacks (13%) who are Internet daters is higher than the proportion of Whites (10%). A higher proportion of urbanites (13%) as compared to suburbanites (10%) and those from rural areas (9%) visit dating websites. Most importantly, the age group of Internet daters in the sample seems to be heavily weighted to people ages 18 to 29 (18%), followed by those ages 30 to 49 (11%), then ages 50 to 64 (6%) and over 65 (3%). In addition, the Pew study found that the online daters were more liberal on most social attitudes than the general American public and, often, also other Internet users. More specifically, they found Internet daters to be less likely to define themselves as religious, less likely to believe in traditional gender roles, and more likely to try new things. Of course, the profile of users will be skewed in particular ways at the specialty sites. For example, religiosity will be higher at Christiansingles.com, and education will be more salient at TheRightStuff.com, a dating service for people at elite and Ivy League colleges and universities.

REASONS FOR USING MATCHING SERVICES

Although there is a large number of singles in the United States and worldwide, only a proportion of even the most computer savvy and love hungry of the singles turn to commercial dating sites in order to find a serious relationship, as noted in the previous section. Many factors may go into the decision to seek matchmaking assistance from an Internet commercial site, as well as into the decision about how long to remain a member of a site when a successful match does not occur. Most likely, individuals will weigh the attractions and advantages to online matching (or, conversely, the barriers to traditional ways of meeting others) against the financial costs and possible stigma of being an "online dater."

Attraction to Online Matching

Commercial matchmaking services are not a recent phenomenon and not limited to the Internet. Before online matching services existed, there were matchmakers as well as printed personal advertisements, video-dating services, singles clubs, "lonely hearts clubs," singles travel clubs, and mail-order brides. Many of these alternative methods of meeting partners still exist, although they seem to have received less attention in recent years because of the increasing popularity of Internet matching services.

Several years ago, in a discussion of alternatives to traditional methods of relationship initiation, Woll and Cozby (1987) identified several barriers to traditional ways of meeting others that would motivate people to seek commercial alternatives, such as video-dating services, personal advertisements, and computer dating services. One factor that they mentioned was *lack of access* to available partners. They noted that as people become older (over 30), they have an increasingly difficult time meeting potential partners because they are usually removed from school settings and other locations with a large number of singles. A second barrier was *lack of time*. They wrote that "busy professionals who have many work and civic responsibilities simply do not have time to seek out others through 'normal channels'" (Woll & Cozby, 1987, p. 72). Woll and Cozby also referred to the limited time experienced by the single head of a household who is raising children. People with *special needs or interests* may also turn to alternative ways of meeting others because of the difficulty of finding a partner in the more traditional ways. For example, people whose work mandates brief stays in many different countries may need online help in locating potential dates because they will not have well-established friendship or work networks. *Shyness* may also lead some people to choose an alternative method over a traditional method of meeting others, although Woll and Cozby commented that, surprisingly, shyness appears to play a less motivating role than one might expect.

Although Woll and Cozby (1987) based their analysis of attraction to alternative methods for meeting others primarily on studies conducted with individuals who use personal advertisements and video-dating services, the same considerations likely apply also to users of online matching services.

People are likely motivated to seek online matchmaking services because such services provide them with access to many eligible and available others and the process can be efficient and even begin in the convenience and privacy of one's home, day or night. As Merkle and Richardson (2000) noted in a commentary about Internet dating, a person could sample scores of other potential partners via Internet matching services. The potential exists for connecting with large numbers of people, who may be spread across a large geographical region, in a relatively short period of time. Furthermore, presumably, the people with whom one connects at matching services are "available," "eligible," and interested in making a connection—assumptions that often are less tenable for in-person meetings in diverse public settings. Given the millions of people using matching services in the early 21st century, the potential for contacts at this stage of relationship development is enormous. Another advantage is that people who have atypical interests or possess certain stigmata (such as being HIV positive) may be likely to find a partner or at least someone to chat with online by casting a wide net.

The degree to which people are attracted to the Internet is also related to the qualities (or lack thereof) of the "singles scene" in which they are currently searching. Some people live in geographical locations or work at jobs that make it difficult to find partners, particularly those who share their values and interests. Among the singles who were actively looking for a partner in the Pew sample, 55% said it was difficult to meet new people, and 47% said that there were very few single people nearby who they would be interested in dating (Madden & Lenhart, 2006). People in urban areas had an easier time finding potential dates and mates than did those in suburban or rural areas.

As another special attraction, Internet services provide considerable help in matching people according to age, occupation, wealth, physical looks, psychological qualities including values and attitudes, lifestyle preferences, and many other factors. The Internet increases one's chances of connecting with like-minded (or "like-bodied") people due to the computer's ability to rapidly sort along many dimensions. In fact, the biggest attraction to matching services may be the hope that one can obtain a soul mate, "the love of one's life," a special partner who would unlikely be found through normal channels. Many matching services promote this hope. Finding a compatible mate through an Internet matching service may be possible, although it may take time and investment. In a 2003 *New York Times* article, "Online Dating Sheds Its Stigma as Losers.com," Amy Harmon describes a 33-year-old woman (name replaced by *X* below):

> Of the 120 men she traded messages with online in her first four months of Internet dating X talked to 20 on the telephone at least once and met 11 in person. Of those X dated four several times before realizing she had not found "the one." It is one of the first lessons learned by many in the swelling ranks of subscribers to Internet dating sites: soul mates are harder to come by than dinner and a movie. But like a growing number of single adults X remains convinced that the chances of finding her life partner are better online than off.

Barriers

With all the potential advantages to commercial services for matching, why would not all singles who are looking for a partner choose to use the Internet to find love? Some practical barriers to finding partners in this way for at least some people are the costs involved, illiteracy in the use of computers and online services, and time investment. Costs to belonging to an online dating service can be as high as $60 (in 2007) per month, plus the costs of owning a computer ($500 and beyond) and subscribing to an Internet service ($25 and up, depending on the speed of the Internet connection desired). These costs, however, may not be overwhelming for most, especially as compared to the costs of going to nightclubs and bars to meet others, taking cruises and trips with singles groups, and engaging in other elaborate ways of meeting people in person.

There is, however, a set of more imposing social psychological barriers to the use of the Internet for connecting. In particular, there still is a stigma associated with Internet matchmaking. Some people do not want the stigma and negative stereotypes that they believe might become associated with them if they use such services (e.g., Donn & Sherman, 2002). Although the stigma is dissipating with millions of Internet users and the popularity of the Internet in television and movie portrayals (e.g., the movies *You've Got Mail* and *Log in for Love*), it still nonetheless affects some (29% of the Pew respondents agreed that people who engage in online dating are desperate, as reported by Madden & Lenhart, 2006).

Another barrier is that occasionally online searchers need to settle for matches who are at a geographical distance, which can introduce costs to the relationship. Although most online daters request that matches be within a nearby radius, those who do not live in geographical areas with high-density populations may need to expand the radius in order to have any matches. In contrast, traditionally people fell in love with the person next door (e.g., Bossard, 1932). Although it was unlikely that the person next door would have a similar score on the type of compatibility test completed at a popular Internet matching service today, neither person had to travel very far to see the other, and neither had to be uprooted in order to move in together. Now, people may be connected through Internet sites with people from other states or cities (or even countries), which creates all kinds of logistic and financial challenges. The fact that these kinds of relationships require commuting to see one another can exacerbate a related barrier: A pair formed over the Internet does not have the opportunity to possess support from family and friends. Often, family and friends do not know about the developing online relationship, and when they first learn about the Internet-initiated romance, they may not always be supportive (Wildermuth, 2004).

In addition, some singles may be reluctant to try online dating because they do not trust what online members post and say about themselves. Merkle and Richardson (2000) pointed to the anonymity of the Internet as a key issue for all parties in using this medium for communication. In particular, an abiding concern is that potential partners listing their wares on dating sites are not being honest about their marital status, their current romantic involvements, the age of photos posted, their financial status, their personal health, and the like. Singles have reason to be suspicious. Hortacsu, Hitsch, and Ariely (as reported in Levitt & Dubner, 2005) analyzed the profiles provided by 30,000 users at a dating website and compared their data with national averages. Men and women were an inch taller than the national average, and women reported weighing 20 pounds less than the national average. Most people reported themselves to be above average in looks; only 30% of users reported themselves as average in looks, and a mere 1% said they were "less than average." Of course, lying to get a date also occurs in face-to-face interactions (Boon & McCloud, 2001; Rowatt, Cunningham, & Druen, 1999), although in face-to-face situations it is difficult to be deceptive about such personal attributes as appearance and age.

There is also a more sinister side to the Internet that may serve as a formidable barrier to the most cautious of singles. Although they may be fewer in number now that the online dating industry has become mainstream and background checks exist at some sites, Internet predators still exist. Similar to what can occur in face-to-face interaction, some men may initiate a first date in order to isolate a woman and sexually assault her (Shotland, 1989). For further discussion of Internet stalking, see Spitzberg and Cupach (2007).

RELATIONSHIP INITIATION AT COMPUTER MATCHING SERVICES

This section discusses the process by which relationships begin through online matching services. We first discuss the formal role of computer matching services as a commercial market intermediary in relationship initiation. Second, we discuss more specifically how members search for compatible mates at the leading relationship-oriented Internet matching sites. Third, we discuss how relationship initiation that occurs through online matching sites is different from relationship initiation that occurs face-to-face, including through other commercial means.

Matching Services as a Formal Marriage Market Intermediary

Rarely have people formed intimate relationships completely unassisted by others. In some cultures, especially in past times, marriages were arranged by families. Even within societies that offer freedom in mate selection (e.g., those in North America), mating choices are influenced by family and friends. Friends, in particular, are helpful in providing social opportunities for people to meet others for romantic liaisons (e.g., Sprecher, Felmlee, Orbuch, & Willetts, 2002). To the degree that family and social networks help people initiate relationships, they serve as "informal marriage market intermediaries (MMIs)" (Ahuvia & Adelman, 1992).

The same social opportunities provided informally by social networks to facilitate potential pairings are also offered more formally and for a cost by commercial (formal) MMIs, such as Internet matching services. As we noted earlier, there has always been a commercial aspect to mate selection. However, a recent explosion has occurred in market functions that commercial niches offer to assist in relationship formation, especially for busy professionals (Ahuvia & Adelman, 1992; Bernard & Adelman, 1990).

Ahuvia and Adelman (1992) introduced a framework referred to as the "Searching-Matching-Interaction" (SMI) model to describe the marriage market functions served by these MMIs. The *searching* function refers to acquiring information on who is available. The *matching* stage refers to actual decision making for creating compatible matches. The third stage of the SMI framework refers to the "transaction," or *interaction*, which can lead to the development of a romantic relationship. MMIs can provide one, two, or all three marriage functions. Although informal MMIs (e.g., social networks) also serve these functions, they do so less efficiently (Ahuvia & Adelman, 1992).

Ahuvia and Adelman (1992) described computer dating services as potentially assisting in both searching and matching. We note that some online matching sites (e.g., Match.com) focus primarily on the searching function, others (e.g., eHarmony.com) focus primarily on the matching function, and still others (e.g., Perfectmatch.com) offer both. In the early 1990s, when Ahuvia and Adelman's review was written, computer dating services were limited to those developed by college researchers interested in studying interpersonal attraction processes (e.g., Coombs & Kenkel, 1966; Walster et al., 1966). The purpose of these computer dating studies was to match people based on certain criteria and then to see how much they were attracted to each other (as we noted earlier, the assistance of computers was minimal in these studies). Ahuvia and Adelman (1992, p. 459) summarized the findings of these studies in the following way: "physical attractiveness has shown to be highly correlated with attraction …. Attempts to predict attraction based on personality variables and attitudes, however, have met with only limited success." At the time they wrote their review, Ahuvia and Adelman could find only two studies more specifically on commercial dating services. One was a conference paper by Woll (1987), who during the 1980s had conducted several studies on matching through video-dating services. As summarized in Ahuvia and Adelman, Woll (1987) presented "a compelling argument that a properly programmed computer would be better than a human matchmaker at predicting a couple's compatibility" (p. 459). In the other computer dating study available at the time, Sindberg, Roberts, and McClain (1972) compared a group of couples that had married after being matched by a computer matching agency with a control group of couples that met but did not marry. Generally, the couples in both groups were homogeneous on many traits, with homogamy on a few traits (e.g., degree of optimism versus pessimism) particularly associated with the likelihood of marrying.

Much has changed since Ahuvia and Adelman's (1992) theoretical review of market intermediaries was published. Computer services have advanced to the forefront of the market of formal intermediaries in matchmaking. The more general result of the popularity of matchmaking services is the increased social legitimacy of the marketing of the *searching* and *matching* functions of relationship formation. In addition, we predict that there soon will be a large number of scientific studies conducted with commercial dating services and the relationships that are formed from them, although currently there is a limited amount of published literature. In addition, future matching sites may also go beyond the searching and matching functions to offer more online interactions to facilitate singles finding an appropriate match (see work on "virtual dates" by Frost, as discussed in Evans, 2006).

From First Submission of Profile to the Development of the Relationship

How do people engage in relationship initiation through online relationship sites? In this section, we describe the process based on what we have gleaned from dating websites and popular articles (e.g.,

Gottlieb, 2006) and through the lens of a theoretical model from the relationship field, Levinger's (1974; see also Levinger & Snoek, 1972) model of pair relatedness. The model presents relationship development as progressing through the following stages: zero contact, unilateral awareness, surface contact, and a continuum of mutuality. We will refer to the two people who are meeting as *P* (person) and *O* (other).

Level 0 (*zero contact*) serves primarily as a benchmark, but the first stage (Level 1) in which relationship initiation occurs is *unilateral awareness*. At this stage, P becomes aware of O. O may become aware of P at nearly the same time, at a later time, or not at all. At Level 2, *surface contact*, P and O have initial contact. If positive impressions are formed between P and O at surface contact, the relationship may progress to Level 3, a stage representing increasing degrees of *mutuality*, during which more mutual disclosure, discovery, and investment occur (Levinger, 1974). Of course, the relationship could end at any time, and often does end after brief surface contact occurring through Internet interactions.

Below we discuss how P and O move through the stages of awareness, surface contact, and mutuality in the online world of matching services. We distinguish between relationship initiation on those sites that rely on members to make their own matches versus relationship initiation on sites that offer assistance in the matching process.

Relationship Sites with Member-Initiated Matches   Most websites facilitate searching by allowing people to post profile information as well as search the profiles of others. The profile information includes vital demographic information (e.g., age and gender), education, likes and dislikes, and usually a photograph. Online profile information is generally lengthier and more detailed than printed versions of personal advertisements (e.g., in the newspaper) because, in contrast to the printed version, there is no cost based on length. Some websites also allow video profiles.

If a P visiting one of the dating websites has the time and motivation, she could search many profiles, and therefore experience unilateral awareness with many Os. To narrow the field to those who are geographically accessible for offline relationships, she would likely search based on zip code, city, or state. To assist members in finding the most compatible matches, some sites (e.g., Match. com) offer keyword searches, in which members narrow their searches to those who mention in their profile a particular word or phrase (e.g., *dancer* or *like to travel*). Even so, a frustration that has been expressed by some members of large dating websites is that there are too many profiles to review. As noted by Thompson and his colleagues (2005), it can sometimes feel like "trying to find a needle in a bigger and bigger haystack" (p. 26).

From the pool of Os that P becomes aware of after searching through online profiles, she can decide with whom she would like to advance to surface contact. To our knowledge, research has not been conducted on the decision-making process that occurs during profile searches at online matching sites. However, an early study on decision strategies used in video dating is relevant. Woll (1986) instructed members of a video-dating service to read the profile sheets of other members of the video-dating service and describe into a tape recorder the exact factors they were considering in the decisions about whether to view their videotapes. He found that the members were most likely to refer to the age and physical attractiveness of the other members as affecting their choices.

Websites encourage their members to post a photo because the chances of being selected without a photo are small. Levitt and Dubner (2005) cited research by Hortacsu and his colleagues, who found men who included their photo in their profile receive three times the responses of men who did not; for women, the increase is sixfold. The photos allow "chemistry" to begin (or not), and the assumption among people who post their own photos is that the omission of a photo means that the person is unattractive. This may not be true (many of the profiles without photos insist that these members are quite good-looking), but in the absence of data to the contrary, searchers assume that photoless profiles hide less physically compelling candidates. Whitty's in-depth interviews with users of online dating also revealed the importance of posting a photograph (Whitty & Carr, 2006).

Surface contact on matching websites involves first engaging in a form of anonymous contact, which is usually controlled by the particular website. For example, at some sites, the first surface contact that members can have with others is to send a wink, "icebreaker," happy face, "spark," or another type of sign of interest. This represents a request from P to O to return the awareness, and serves as an invitation to move the relationship to surface contact. O may completely ignore the request or may read P's profile information and decide whether he or she wants to respond. O may not respond if he or she (a) is flooded with messages of interest from many others (has "alternatives"), (b) does not think the other would make a good match after reviewing P's profile information, or (c) is not a paid member of the relationship site (some sites allow "visitors" to post profiles for free but not respond to messages from others until they pay).

If O responds to P, the surface contact stage of relationship initiation continues. Next, the two are likely to move to two-way online communication, which is usually in a structured anonymous format offered through the relationship site. For example, electronic messages can be exchanged between P and O without names or other identifying information. An interview study conducted with couples who met online (Baker, 1998) suggests that people's early attraction is influenced not only by what they learn about the other's attributes, but also by O's writing style and speed of responding to messages. Attraction and the likelihood of continuing the initiation process may also be influenced by how the social network is responding to the developing relationship—assuming they know about it (Wildermuth, 2004).

Similar to the surface contact stage that occurs in face-to-face interaction, two people who communicate for the first time online often begin with superficial information and then progress to sharing more personal information and disclosures. Research indicates that it is fairly easy to disclose online (Merkle & Richardson, 2000; Wysocki, 1996, 1998; also see McKenna, this volume), and thus minor intersections of mutuality and interdependence can develop fairly easily even before there is a face-to-face meeting (e.g., Parks & Floyd, 1996; Parks & Robert, 1998). Experts on interaction in cyberspace have noted that individuals are often strategic in the presentation of the "self" that they choose to emphasize in initial online interactions (Albright, 2007; Whitty, 2007; Whitty & Carr, 2006).

The P who has the time and motivation to have surface contact with many Os is likely to move to a stage of mutuality with at least one person but possibly several others. Initial stages of mutuality may begin online, but are likely to advance to phone calls; the exchange of cards, letters, and photographs through mail; and possibly a face-to-face meeting. When people decide to approach another person after an initial Internet screening, they are moving to another stage of cues and information. Each stage can involve different cues (e.g., voice cues in telephone contacts). Some sites now offer a way to make anonymous phone calls so that the recipient cannot have access to the caller's phone number. If P and O meet in person, they are encouraged to do so in a public location. When P and O do meet offline, the relationship is likely to either move to deeper levels of mutuality or end if they discover the chemistry they had online does not transfer to face-to-face interaction. Merkle and Richardson (2000) noted that many online relationships fade away well before personal contact occurs, and many others are likely to end after a first meeting. Not only does lack of chemistry in face-to-face interaction cool what might have been a spark of romance occurring in online communication, but also so does any disappointment experienced if it is realized that the other misrepresented him or herself in the profile (e.g., Whitty, 2004).

Relationship Sites with Matching Assistance

As noted earlier, eHarmony.com, Perfectmatch.com, Chemistry.com, and an increasing number of other sites offer "matching assistance." These sites require members to complete lengthy questionnaires, and based on the information provided in these questionnaires, the site sends members "compatibility matches" and a procedure to begin communicating if they wish. To match members based on their questionnaire data, matching sites are using what have been referred to in the business as "love or matching algorithms" (e.g., Orenstein, 2003), matching formulas based supposedly on scientific principles and translated into computer programs that can sift through the volumes of data collected from the members. Dating websites generally do not publish their matching formulas or subject them to peer review, but information on their websites and in the media (e.g., Gottlieb, 2006) suggests that the focus is on compatibility (mostly similarities, although occasionally differences too) in personality characteristics.

The sites that offer scientific matching have been able to charge more, and as a result, other dating sites such as Match.com that have traditionally offered only the searching function are beginning to incorporate objective science into the matching process (e.g., Orenstein, 2003).

Some of the dating sites also offer a multiple-stage process for initiating contact, which is described to help two people learn more about each other in a nonthreatening way. For example, at eHarmony.com, this involves responding to multiple-choice items, sharing "must haves" and "can't stands," and writing and exchanging questions. The other sites recommend similar steps for initial interaction.

Regardless of the specific type of online dating world in which P and O maneuver through awareness, through surface contact, and on to minor intersections of mutuality, the pair may or may not migrate offline. Some friendships form online and remain online. Most people who become members of matching services, though, are interested in forming a romantic relationship, and therefore success is measured by a relationship that moves to face-to-face contact and on to a long-term commitment.

RELATIONSHIP FORMATION AT INTERNET SERVICES COMPARED TO OTHER WAYS OF FORMING RELATIONSHIPS

Above we discussed the specific steps of relationship initiation at online dating sites. In this section, we speculate how initiation steps and basic attraction processes may differ online versus offline.

Predictors of Attraction Online versus Offline

Some of the factors that have been found to affect attraction and the formation of relationships include similarity in attitudes and values, physical proximity, the physical attractiveness of potential partners, self-disclosure in the process of getting to know another person, and support from friends and family for the relationship (Berscheid & Reis, 1998; Hatfield & Rapson, 2005). Each of these factors may affect relationship formation, and each may work via the medium of the Internet (or e-mail) or via in-person interaction. However, these factors play out in different ways and points in time in the different means of meeting.

According to Merkle and Richardson (2000), the process of attraction in a face-to-face romantic relationship is likely to involve first the influence of spatial and physical attractiveness, and then the discovery of similarity and the role of self-disclosure. They stated that in contrast, Internet-initiated romantic relationships involve "an inverted developmental sequence," which first involves a high level of mutual and sometimes intense self-disclosure and an initial minimal role for physical attractiveness and proximity (see also Cooper & Sportolari, 1997). Physical attractiveness will still play a role once two people meet in person, as noted by Cooper and Sportolari (p. 9), but its impact may be less because it follows learning other information about each other. Cooper and Sportolari speculated that by the time two people meet, "the felt intensity and meaning of any unappealing physical traits are then more likely to be mitigated by the overall attraction that exists" (p. 9).

An interesting finding from early work on face-to-face versus online initiation is that Internet users may come to personally know one another better and share intimate knowledge more quickly than do persons who meet in person (Wysocki, 1998). In a survey of persons using the Internet for matchmaking, Wysocki found that people often spend a great amount of time writing about themselves and asking questions of others. Such activity may constitute a type of social penetration (Altman & Taylor, 1973). Presumably, the safety of anonymity and the alacrity of writing on the computer versus talking face-to-face may mediate such findings. Walther and Parks (2002) argued that not only does the intensity of self-disclosure lead to the development of closeness, but also closeness is enhanced by the ability to present oneself carefully by editing messages and by the tendency to make idealistic attributes of the (initially distant) other. Although closeness based on intense self-disclosure may develop more quickly in the Internet-developed relationships, the relationships may also more easily and quickly *dissolve* if there is not an adequate reward–cost ratio. That is, there may be fewer barriers to breaking up, which includes the influence of having many additional alternatives (Merkle & Richardson, 2000).

What do couples themselves say attracted them to the other when they first became acquainted online? In a small study of 18 couples who met online and then migrated offline, Baker (1998) reported that couples mentioned sense of humor, response time, interests, qualities described online, and writing style. Whitty and Gavin (2001) interviewed people who had developed online relationships and found that they valued many of the same relationship characteristics that people valued in face-to-face relationships, including trust, honesty, and commitment. In addition, people are attracted to those who were honest in how they presented themselves in their profile.

Getting Help from Friends versus an Internet Service

One common traditional way of meeting another is through friends. Friends assist in the mating process in a variety of ways, including by presenting social opportunities for others to meet and by actually making introductions (e.g., Sprecher et al., 2002). It is useful to compare relationship initiation that occurs through the assistance of computer matching services (and their scientific advisors) and relationship initiation that occurs through the assistance of friends.

Although in both cases there is assistance by a third party, there are differences between formal MMIs (e.g., computer matchmaking services) and informal MMIs (e.g., social networks) in addition to formality and cost. First, formal MMIs are typically more *efficient* (Ahuvia & Adelman, 1992). The online services often are always available and can be accessed as needed. Conversely, there is a limit to the degree that people can ask friends to host social events or introduce them to their friends. Furthermore, an almost unlimited number of people can be serviced by online matching services (millions are now members of some online dating services), whereas there is a limit in how many single friends are available through the network of one's friends.

A second difference between formal and informal MMIs is that the formal MMIs can be anonymous. One can remain anonymous to potential matches during the early stages of contact, revealing one's identity to the other only after trust has developed. In addition, in a way that might not be possible when one is searching for a partner in face-to-face interactions, people can search for a partner online without family and friends being aware.

The third difference is that the formal MMIs emphasize to a greater degree than the informal MMIs that mating is a transaction in which assets are exchanged and people possess market value (for a review of exchange and equity principles, see Hatfield, Rapson, & Aumer-Ryan, in press; Sprecher & Schwartz, 1994). As noted by Ahuvia and Adelman (1992), "[S]ocial scientists have long seen mate selection as occurring in a marriage market where both economic and interpersonal assets are exchanged. Commercial dating services, by making these assets explicit, further emphasize the relevance of market theory" (p. 454). The explicitness of the market value of individuals may be particularly evidenced in online personal advertisements, in which participants must emphasize their assets in a few sentences in order to appeal to potential seekers. To have others become interested enough to want to pursue them, members need to emphasize and even augment their professional status, appearance, and any other personal assets that they can offer. This is in contrast to relationships formed face-to-face, in which spatial and social proximity may naturally bring people together who have similar exchange assets and/or information about "exchange value" can be indirectly acquired through observations and information from the social network. On the other hand, some experts have argued that just the opposite occurs once there is online interaction. As noted by Cooper and Sportolari (1997, p. 9), "Electronic relating offers a different basis for interaction than that of the 'meat market' of the singles scene." People can get to know each other before there is an opportunity to exhaustively evaluate each other's appearance.

Online Relationships versus Other Commercial Means for Meeting Others

We can also compare relationship initiation that occurs through online dating services with that which occurs in other commercial ways of meeting. Other commercial means include the now old-fashioned newspaper advertisements, as well as singles groups meetings, parties, dinners, dances, and so-called speed dating. Most of these other commercial means for meeting people focus on the "interaction" aspect of the SMI framework presented above; less assistance is provided in matching decision making. Most of these other alternative ways also focus on finding matches within one particular geographic location. These activities may provide the advantages of information gained through in-person meetings. However, those attending these events also are dependent on who shows up and the ease of singling out any one individual for chatting. At singles functions, including dances, one may have to wade through a host of people to get to the one for whom there is attraction. Those who are shy or socially awkward, however, may have a difficult time in these settings (Sprecher & McKinney, 1987).

There is a plethora of variables associated with each type of in-person meeting, from random encounters to hookups at bars, meetings at singles' events, and setups by friends. These variables include the availability and density of singles, their interests in meeting others, and the amount of time and special interaction circumstances required for meeting (e.g., a man may want to ask one woman in a group of women to spend time with him, but be deterred by the size and nature of the group). These variables also speak to the delicate tactical and self-presentation considerations that frequently go into these in-person meetings (Goffman, 1959).

Speed dating is an interesting activity that has flourished in recent years. It is a commercially brokered service that involves advertising an event and then regulating the time each possible person has to talk to an "assigned date" (see chapter 11 in this book by Eastwick & Finkel). It usually is done in large meeting rooms in hotels or bars, and also involves a concluding questionnaire that asks persons to indicate which of the possible partners they might like to interact with further. Speed dating appears to be successful only to the degree that a host of well-qualified partners show up for the event. If advertising, practical matters such as the time and place of the event, geography in terms of density of the local singles population, or word-of-mouth commentaries are not favorable, then the event will not be successful, especially over the long run. Such events require capital and lots of organization. A sponsor may put on a few such events, not make enough money to continue, and thus leave at the doorstep users who began to rely on this means of meaning possible partners. On the other hand, speed dating has its admirers. It is ideal for people who feel that they know almost immediately whether they are interested in someone (see Eastwick & Finkel, this volume).

CONCLUSIONS AND FUTURE RESEARCH DIRECTIONS

Although relationships are still far more likely to be initiated offline than online, an increasing number of men and women are seeking the assistance of Internet matchmaking services (e.g., Madden & Lenhart, 2006). An interesting development that has occurred as a result of the popularity of matching services is the greater awareness by the media and lay public of the scientific study of relationships, particularly that of mate selection and attraction. Several dating websites (e.g., eHarmony.com and Perfectmatch.com) claim to be utilizing the existing scientific literature on relationship initiation, mate choice, and factors leading to relationship success in crafting their compatibility questionnaires and in devising matching algorithms for pairing members. Some dating websites also seem genuinely interested in contributing to the scientific base of relationships. For example, eHarmony.com has created a research laboratory and hired a team of scientists. Among other projects, they are conducting longitudinal research with couples who met through eHarmony.com matching (Gottlieb, 2006). Therefore, a mutually beneficial merger is being developed between the scientific field of relationships and the commercial matchmaking services. The sites have benefited from the scientific knowledge created in academe about personal relationships, but the scientific field also has the opportunity to benefit from the commercial websites' desire to make matchmaking a science. Nonetheless, whether the profit-making motive of the commercial enterprises will be compatible with the openness and objectivity required in scientific analysis is yet to be determined (e.g., Houran, Lange, Rentfrow, & Bruckner, 2004).

We would like to comment on three types of research that may be conducted in the future that will enhance our understanding of relationship initiation. First, the matchmaking sites are likely to (or likely to continue to, in some cases) conduct proprietary research that tests aspects of their matching algorithms or examines customer satisfaction and relationship success in response to matching innovations or online get-acquainted strategies. Although such findings may never be published in scientific journals, the findings may become available through the websites and in other reports and therefore have indirect implications for the scientific study of relationships.

Second, the scientific advisors and others who gain access to the matching services may be allowed to test theories about relationship initiation and development with a sample obtained from the website. The sample of online daters is not representative of singles who are at early stages of relationship development, but the generalizability of a sample of online daters may not be any more problematic, and may even be less problematic in some cases, than relying on college samples (Buchanan, 2000). In addition, the unique advantage of samples from matching websites is the ability to collect data from individuals in the midst of initial acquaintance-ship, or even before they have noticed each other, something that is difficult to do even with convenient human subject pools in psychology. Furthermore, because members of websites often interact with many others before finding a successful relationship, within-subject comparisons can be conducted to examine the types of initial pairings and interactions that are most successful for the development of relationships, controlling for individual factors. Various innovative methods can be used, including interaction records (Wheeler & Reis, 1991), in which the members complete a brief record after each significant get-acquainted interaction. This approach has already been used in the Northwestern Speed-Dating Study (see Eastwick & Finkel, this volume).

A third type of research can compare later stages of successful relationships that had their origins in online matching with later stages of relationships that were initiated offline. If Dr. Warren, founder of eHarmony, is correct, relationships that are formed based on "the deep com-patibility" that is claimed to be possible with compatibility matching at dating websites should have greater happiness and lower divorce rates than relationships that begin in more traditional ways, controlling for such critical variables as length of relationship, divorce status, and the pres-ence of children. However, another viewpoint discussed in this chapter is that such cyberspace-initiated relationships will not benefit from the support that comes from being in a relationship that emerges through social networks and will have costs involved if at least one of the partners has to relocate in order for the pair to be in the same geographical region. Such comparison research has been conducted by eHarmony.com (Carter & Snow, 2004), but would be better conducted by independent research organizations or teams. One possible project could be to examine how the relationships that are formed online differ from relationships that are formed offline on a number of dimensions, including whether they are less homogeneous than relation-ships formed in more traditional dating practices, and also whether they differ on relationship satisfaction, longevity, and other indicators of quality. We speculate that once relationships that have begun through online dating services migrate offline, they may not be that different from relationships that form in other ways. The dissolution and divorce rates are likely to be the same, and probably the same factors will influence success versus dissolution. However, whether or not this is so is an empirical question that can be examined in future research.

In sum, commercial matching services are still in their infancy. In time—given the resources and money that are bound to be lavished on improving such commercial enterprises—it is reason-able to hope that matching sites will provide increased opportunities for men and women to find dating and marital relationships that are fulfilling. It is also hoped that in the future, the Busines-sofLove.com sites will use more complex versions of relationship science to inform their question-naire construction, website construction, and matching algorithms; and that, in turn, Internet matching services will allow scholars to conduct the research needed to enrich understanding of attraction and love relationships.

REFERENCES

Ahuvia, A. C., & Adelman, M. B. (1992). Formal intermediaries in the marriage market: A typology and review. *Journal of Marriage and the Family, 54,* 452–463.

Albright, J. M. (2007). How do I love thee and thee and thee: Self-presentation, deception, and multiple relationships online. In M. T. Whitty, A. J. Baker, & J. A. Inman (Eds.), *Online matching* (pp. 81–93). Hampshire, UK: Palgrave Macmillan.

Altman, I., & Taylor, D. (1973). *Social penetration: The development of interpersonal relationships.* New York: Holt, Rinehart & Winston.

Anderson, T. L. (2005). Relationships among Internet attitudes, Internet use, romantic beliefs, and perceptions of online romantic relationships. *CyberPsychology & Behavior, 8,* 521–531.

Baker, A. (1998, July). Cyberspace couples finding romance online then meeting for the first time in real life. *CMC Magazine.* Retrieved November 29, 2007, from http://www.december.com/cmc/mag/1998/jul/baker.html

Bernard, A. C., & Adelman, M. B. (1990). Market metaphors for meeting mates. In M. E. Goldberg, G. Gorn, & R. W. Pollay (Eds.), *Advances in consumer research* (Vol. 17, p. 78). Provo, UT: Association for Consumer Research.

Berscheid, E., & Reis, H. T. (1998). Attraction and close relationships. In D. Gilbert, S. Fiske, & G. Lindzey (Eds.), *The handbook of social psychology* (4th ed., Vol. 2, pp. 193–281). New York: McGraw-Hill.

Boon, S., & McCloud, B. (2001). Deception in romantic relationships: Subjective estimates at success at deceiving and attitudes toward deception. *Journal of Social and Personal Relationships, 18,* 463–476.

Bossard, J. H. S. (1932). Residential propinquity in marriage selection. *American Journal of Sociology, 38,* 219–224.

Buchanan, T. (2000). Potential of the Internet for personality research. In M. H. Burnham (Ed.), *Psychological experiments on the Internet* (pp. 121–140). San Diego, CA: Academic Press.

Byrne, D. (1971). *The attraction paradigm.* New York: Academic Press.

Byrne, D., Ervin, C. R., & Lamberth, J. (1970). Continuity between the experimental study of attraction and real-life computer dating. *Journal of Personality and Social Psychology, 16,* 157–165.

Carter, S., & Snow, C. (2004, May). *Helping singles enter better marriages using predictive models of marital success.* Paper presented at the 16th annual convention of the American Psychological Society, Chicago.

CBC Archives. (1957, July 17). *Clip: Computer matchmaker.* Retrieved November 29, 2007, from http://archives.cbc.ca/400i.asp?IDCat=75&IDDos=710&IDCli=4199&IDLan=1&NoCli=3&type=clip

Coombs, R. H., & Kenkel, W. F. (1966). Sex differences in dating aspirations and satisfaction with computer-arranged partners. *Journal of Marriage and the Family, 28,* 62–66.

Cooper, A., & Sportolari, L. (1997). Romance in cyberspace: Understanding online attraction. *Journal of Sex Education and Therapy, 22,* 7–14.

Donn, J. E., & Sherman, R. C. (2002). Attitudes and practices regarding the formation of romantic relationships on the Internet. *CyberPsychology & Behavior, 5,* 107–123.

Evans, D. (2006, September 6). Online matchmaking with virtual dates. *Online Dating.* Retrieved November 29, 2007, from http://dating.corante.com/archives2006/09/06/online_matchmaking

Goffman, E. (1959). *The presentation of self in everyday life.* Garden City, NY: Doubleday.

Gottlieb, L. (2006, March). How do I love thee? *Atlantic Monthly,* 58–70.

Harmon, A. (2003, June 29). Online dating sheds its stigma as Losers.com. *New York Times.* Retrieved November 29, 2007, from http://www.nytimes.com/2003/06/29/national/29DATE.html?ex=1372219200&en=116d836a4d43845c&ei=5007&partner=USERLAND

Hatfield, E., & Rapson, R. L. (2005). *Love and sex: Cross-cultural perspectives.* Lanham, MD: University Press of America.

Hatfield, E., Rapson, R. L., & Aumer-Ryan, K. (in press). Social justice in love relationships: Recent developments. *Social Justice Research.*

Houran, J., Lange, R., Rentfrow, J. P., & Bruckner, K. H. (2004). Do online matchmaking tests work? An assessment of preliminary evidence for a publicized "predictive model of marital success." *North American Journal of Psychology, 6,* 507–526.

Joinson, A. N. (2003). *Understanding the psychology of internet behaviour: Virtual worlds, real lives.* New York: Palgrave Macmillan.

Kleinfeld, N. (2003, June 11). An officer and a gentleman? 50 women would disagree. *New York Times,* p. A1.

Leonhardt, D. (2006, March 28). The famous founder of Operation Match. *New York Times.* Retrieved December 22, 2007, from http://www.nytimes.com/2006/03/28/business/29leonside.html

Levinger, G. (1974). A three-level approach to attraction: Toward an understanding of pair relatedness. In T. L. Huston (Ed.), *Foundations of interpersonal attraction* (pp. 99–120). New York: Academic Press.

Levinger, G., & Snoek, J. D. (1972). *Attraction in relationships: A new look at interpersonal attraction*. Morristown, NJ: General Learning Press.

Levitt, S. D., & Dubner, S. J. (2005). *Freakonomics: A rogue economist explores the hidden side of everything*. New York: William Morrow.

Madden, M., & Lenhart, A. (2006, March 5). *Online dating* (Report for the Pew Internet & American Life Project). Retrieved December 22, 2007, from http://www.pewinternet.org/pdfs/PIP_Online_Dating.pdf

Merkle, E. R., & Richardson, R. A. (2000). Digital dating and virtual relating: Conceptualizing computer mediated romantic relationships. *Family Relations, 490,* 187–192.

Orenstein, S. (2003, August 1). The love algorithm Match.com thinks it has found a formula for ruling the online dating business: A scientific way to find Mr. or Ms. Right. *Business 2.0 Magazine.* Retrieved November 29, 2007, from http://money.cnn.com/magazines/business2/business2_archive/2003/08

Parks, M. R., & Floyd, K. (1996). Making friends in cyberspace. *Journal of Communication, 46,* 80–97.

Parks, M. R., & Roberts, L. D. (1998). "Making MOOsic": The development of personal relationships online and a comparison to their off-line counterparts. *Journal of Social and Personal Relationships, 15,* 517–537.

Rowatt, W. C., Cunningham, M. R., & Druen, P. B. (1999). Lying to get a date: The effect of facial physical attractiveness on the willingness to deceive prospective dating partners. *Journal of Social and Personal Relationships, 16,* 209–223.

Shotland, R. L. (1989). A model of the causes of date rape in developing and close relationships. In C. Hendrick (Ed.), *Close relationships* (pp. 247–270). Newbury Park, CA: Sage.

Sindberg, R. M., Roberts, A. F., & McClain, D. (1972). Mate selection factors in computer matched marriages. *Journal of Marriage and the Family, 34,* 611–614.

Spitzberg, B. H., & Cupach, W. R. (2007). Cyber-stalking as (mis)matchmaking. In M. Whitty, A. Baker, & J. A. Inman (Eds.), *Online matchmaking* (pp. 127–146). Hampshire, UK: Palgrave Macmillan.

Sprecher, S., Felmlee, D., Orbuch, T. L., & Willetts, M. C. (2002). Social networks and change in personal relationships. In A. Vangelisti, H. Reis, & M. A. Fitzpatrick (Eds.), *Stability and change in relationships* (pp. 257–284). New York: Cambridge.

Sprecher, S., & Metts, S. (1989). Development of the "Romantic Beliefs Scale" and examination of the effects of gender and gender-role orientation. *Journal of Social and Personal Relationships, 6,* 387–411.

Sprecher, S., & McKinney, K. (1987). Barriers in the initiation of intimate heterosexual relationships. *Journal of Social Work and Human Sexuality, 5,* 97–110.

Sprecher, S., & Schwartz, P. (1994). Equity and balance in the exchange of contributions in close relationships. In M. J. Lerner & G. Mikula (Eds.), *Entitlement and the affectional bond* (pp. 11–42). New York: Plenum.

Thompson, M., Zimbardo, P., & Hutchinson, G. (2005, April 29). *Consumers are having second thoughts about online dating.* Unpublished report. Retrieved November 29, 2007, from http://weAttract.com

Walster, E., Aronson, V., Abrahams, D., & Rottman, L. (1966). Importance of physical attractiveness in dating behavior. *Journal of Personality and Social Psychology, 4,* 508–516.

Walther, J. B., & Parks, M. R. (2002). Cues filtered out, cues filtered in: Computer-mediated communication and relationships. In M. L. Knapp & J. A. Daly (Eds.), *Handbook of interpersonal communication* (3rd ed., pp. 529–563). Thousand Oaks, CA: Sage.

Wheeler, L., & Reis, H. T. (1991). Self-recording of everyday life events: Origins, types, and uses. *Journal of Personality, 59,* 339–354.

Whitty, M. T. (2004, May). *Shopping for love on the Internet: Men and women's experiences of using an Australian Internet dating site.* Paper presented at the Communication Research in the Public Interest ICA meeting, New Orleans, LA.

Whitty, M. T. (2007). The art of selling one's "self" on an online dating site: The BAR approach. In M. T. Whitty, A. J. Baker, & J. A. Inman (Eds.), *Online matching* (pp. 57–69). Hampshire, UK: Palgrave Macmillan.

Whitty, M. T., & Carr, A. N. (2006). *Cyberspace romance: The psychology of online relationships.* Basingstoke, UK: Palgrave Macmillan.

Whitty, M., & Gavin, J. (2001). Age/sex/location: Uncovering the social cues in the development of online relationships. *CyberPsychology and Behavior, 4,* 623–630.

Wildermuth, S. M. (2004). The effects of stigmatizing discourse on the quality of on-line relationships. *CyberPsychology & Behavior, 7,* 73–84.

Woll, S. (1986, June). So many to choose from: Decision strategies in videodating. *Journal of Social and Personal Relationships, 3,* 43–53.

Woll, S. B. (1987). *Improper linear models of matchmaking.* Paper presented at the Iowa Conference on Personal Relationships, Iowa City.

Woll, S., & Cozby, P. (1987). Videodating and other alternatives to traditional methods of relationship initiation. In W. Jones & D. Perlman (Eds.), *Advances in personal relationships* (Vol. 1, pp. 69–109). Greenwich, CT: JAI.

Wysocki, D. K. (1996). *Somewhere over the modem: Relationships over computer bulletin boards.* Unpublished doctoral dissertation, University of California, Santa Barbara.

Wysocki, D. K. (1998). Let your fingers do the talking. Sex on an adult chat-line. *Sexualities, 1,* 425–452.

Section *IV*

Attraction and Other Emotions in Relationship Initiation

14

Attraction and the Initiation of Relationships
A Review of the Empirical Literature

WILLIAM G. GRAZIANO and JENNIFER WEISHO BRUCE

This chapter reviews selectively the empirical research literature addressing the processes that lead people to begin (or to avoid) a relationship with another individual person. Because the potential literature is large,[1] it was necessary to restrict topical coverage. "Relationships" here will be restricted to romance and sexual attraction, and will exclude friendships, alliances, business partnerships, and kin relations. Due to this focus, the review will be attentive to sex differences in attraction processes. The spotlight will be on programs of empirical, experimental research examining factors that lead to attraction such as similarity, physical attractiveness, kindness, warmth, and dominance. In experimental research participants are randomly assigned to two or more conditions, which are manipulated using environmental or situational variables. The primary strength of experimental research is that, within defined limits, it allows direct assessment of causation (Shadish, Cook, & Campbell, 2002). Observational and correlational methods lack this capacity. Experimental work describes what *could* happen in certain specific contexts, not necessarily what will happen. (The reverse is also true, of course: Correlation studies describe what is happening here and now, not what could happen.) The primary weakness in experimental research on initiation of relationships involves reliance on brief encounters of unacquainted college students as research participants, potentially limiting generality to other kinds of persons, settings, and times (Shadish et al., 2002). This set of weaknesses involves tendencies in implementation, not in the methods per se. In this volume, Sprecher and Felmlee (2000) focus on the retrospective method. Eastwick and Finkel (this volume) consider the speed-dating methodology. They are reviewed separately because each method has relative strengths and weaknesses, and they may be regarded as supplements to each other rather than rival alternatives. This review does not include potentially important lines of work due to limitations in space. For example, the issue of mutuality and reciprocity in attraction is not reviewed, despite its potential relevance to relationship initiation, in part because the recent literature focuses on the maintenance phase of relationships (e.g., Shackelford, Schmitt, & Buss, 2005; Sprecher, 1998).

Unless stated otherwise, this review focused on work published between 1985 and June 2007. To identify studies for the review, we searched for all empirical studies dealing with the initiation of romantic relationships between adults published in English in refereed journals from 1985 to June 2007. The research studies reviewed here were identified by searching citations in earlier reviews and subsequent citation of earlier comprehensive reviews (e.g., Berscheid, 1985). We also used computerized searches of PsycINFO (1985 to 2007), including title, abstract, heading word, table of contents, and key concepts. Keywords used in the searches included *initiation*, *initiation of relationships*, *initial attraction*, and *interpersonal attraction*. The review is limited to articles that (a) offer data and are primarily empirical contributions, (b) appear in peer-reviewed journals or their equivalent, (c) are written in English, (d) focus on populations living in North America (i.e., Canada and the United States of America), and (e) focus on nonclinical samples[2] (as opposed to deficit-based groups). These studies were categorized based on their preponderant focus on the target of evaluation, on the perceiver who is evaluating, or on the perceiver X target interaction. Research studies can sometimes fit into more than one category, so all differences in categorization were resolved by discussion between the two authors.

SETTING THE STAGE

The Starting Point: Why Select 1985?

The year 1985 represents a convenient starting point. In that year, Ellen Berscheid's (1985) comprehensive review of the area called *interpersonal attraction* appeared in the *Handbook of Social Psychology*. A bit more than 10 years earlier, Berscheid and Walster (now Hatfield) (1974) published an influential paper titled simply "Physical Attractiveness" in the *Advances in Experimental Social Psychology* series. Shortly thereafter, Berscheid and Walster (1978) published the second edition of their book titled *Interpersonal Attraction*, as well as an attraction-related book titled *Equity: Theory and Research*. Berscheid's 1985 review was the work of a seasoned experimental social psychology researcher and theorist, who had a firsthand perspective on the field. Inspection of the structure and content of her 1985 review is instructive for how a first-line expert conceptualized this area. Even the title is informative because it focused attention on processes occurring between two or more people, not on intrapsychic activity in one individual. Conceptually, Berscheid opened with a distinction among the antecedents, consequences, and correlates of interpersonal attraction. Next, she discussed the measurement of attraction, which was defined as an attitude, and then considered theoretical approaches that guided past research. Berscheid noted that attraction is integrally related to a larger, separate field dealing with affiliation with others. It was telling that the chapter included only one reference to the work of Phillip Shaver and his colleagues, and one to Harry Reis and his colleagues. They were cited just once, each for one empirical paper on loneliness. David Buss' name, prominent in 2007 for his work on evolution and relationship processes, does not appear in the review. As of June 2007, Buss, Reis, and Shaver are now among the most cited researchers in the field.

Patterns and trajectories for the field were appearing. Berscheid (1985) anticipated the emerging separation of social cognition research from work on relationships: "[T]his chapter will not consider in detail the impression formation process ... since these topics are treated elsewhere in this *Handbook*" (p. 415). A second trend may be related to the first. Prior to 1985, the bulk of the influential research (as defined by what is cited frequently by others) was done by experimental social psychologists who focused almost exclusively on initiation. Berscheid discussed "emerging theory and evidence relevant to attraction and relationship development, maintenance, and dissolution" (p. 462). Finally, we see that as Berscheid anticipated, that experimental social psychology hegemony over research on relationship initiation was breaking. In 2007 experimental social psychology is far from gone, but there are many more and different kinds of players on the initiation and relationships playing field, including researchers in sociology, communications, family social sciences, evolutionary biology, and clinical psychology.

Was Research Prior to 1985 Ungrounded?

Some writers characterized the attraction area prior to 1985 as being predominantly variable centered and atheoretical. Even Berscheid (1985) said that it just "'grew,' proceeding without the advantage of a master plan provide[d] by God or Omniscient Jones or more importantly, without the advantage of the hindsight of a reviewer, critic or student of attraction research" (p. 417).

With the wisdom of hindsight, we can see considerably more order beneath the apparent disorganization than there seemed to be at the time. First, the vast majority of research focused on the earliest period in relationships, later labeled the *initiation phase* (e.g., Berscheid & Graziano, 1979; Finkel, Eastwick, & Matthews, 2007), using college students in laboratory settings. Reliable patterns were reported in the literature (e.g., not only was attitudinal similarity correlated with liking for strangers but also, when it was manipulated, similarity could cause attraction). Second, there was near consensus that attraction was an attitude (see in particular Berscheid & Walster, 1978, pp. 1–20; Griffith, 1974; Zajonc, 1968). Traditionally, attitudes were conceived as having three aspects, namely, cognitive, affective, and behavioral components (Petty & Cacioppo, 2006). The affective component of attitudes came to be regarded as central to attitudes in general, and to attraction in particular (Zajonc, 1968, 1980). Furthermore, the tripartite perspective provided a big tent, covering virtually all forms of attraction research. Just as there were cognitive, affective, and behavioral components to attitudes, attraction had its corresponding thought, feeling, and behavior dimensions. Just as attitudes described a predisposition to respond, which might or might not translate directly into overt behavior, attraction also predisposed without necessarily predicting behavior directly across all situations. Just as in attitudes, attraction-related thoughts, feelings, and behavior may not be in perfect concert, creating dissonance. Thoughts about people may not match behavior or feelings, and this would bring about an unpleasant tension (e.g., Cooper, Zanna, & Goethals, 1974). On the positive side of the ledger, the identification of attraction with attitudes helped attraction researchers make use of sophisticated self-report measurement techniques developed for attitudes, and it also helped attraction remain near one of the most central constructs of the parent discipline of social psychology.

Contrary to what some writers imply, there were indeed theories steering most of the early attraction research. Berscheid (1985) noted three broad classes of theories that applied to interpersonal attraction. These can be conceptualized in terms of level of focus. First, at the highest level of focus were general social psychological theories that have predictive implications for social behavior, including attraction. Examples are cognitive consistency theories, Heider's (1958) balance theory, social exchange (Kelley & Thibaut, 1978), and equity theories (Walster et al., 1978). Down one level of focus were midlevel theories dedicated specifically to interpersonal attraction (e.g., gain–loss theory; Aronson, 1969; Berscheid, Brothen, & Graziano, 1976). At the tightest level of focus were narrow theories, largely untested, centered on various separate attraction phenomena like romantic love (e.g., Reik, 1944).

Making Sense of the Pre-1985 Theories

Looking at the pre-1985 theories in a somewhat different way, we can see that they are part of three larger metatheoretical approaches, which influenced not only social psychology but also superordinate disciplines that employed social scientists at the time. The first of these three, the dominant metatheory, was the reinforcement approach (e.g., Homans' [1974] social exchange theory, equity theories, and interdependence theory [Kelley & Thibaut, 1978]). A person's attraction to another was a function of the frequency with which the latter rewarded (or expected to be rewarded by) the former. If we assume that rewardingness becomes mutual over time, then it is a short inference that attitudinal similarity is rewarding and leads to mutual attraction (Byrne, 1971; Newcomb, 1956). The second is the cognitive consistency approach, which assumes that people are motivated to keep their cognitions (attitudes?) in psychologically congruent relations with each other. The third metatheory, just emerging at the time, was the attribution approach, pioneered by Heider's (1958) *Psychology of Interpersonal Relations*, and expanded by Jones and Davis (1965) and by Kelley (1967; Kelley et al., 1983) into close relationships. The second and third metatheories are related, as both are primarily cognitive, share theorists, and originated from within social psychology.

The two dimensions in the level-of-focus X metatheoretical approach framework are admittedly not independent, but the framework allows us to classify the theories, research, and variables in use in the interpersonal attraction literature of the time. If we take 1985 as a starting point, we see a literature that designs studies that can be completed in one hour in a social psychology laboratory. It concentrates on variables that could be manipulated, and could be linked to interaction in dyads or small groups of strangers, or persons in the very earliest, initiation phase of relationships. (Some researchers later labeled it *zero acquaintance*.) Within this framework, it made sense to use strangers for experiments, because any pre-experimental history participants had with each other could confound an experiment and undermine its internal validity, making research largely uninterpretable (Aronson & Carlsmith, 1968). The research participants of choice were college sophomores. In one way or another, much scientifically oriented interpersonal attraction research up to 1985 was behavioral and tied loosely to a liberalized reinforcement approach dealing with the rewards and punishments in interaction (e.g., Berscheid & Walster, 1978, Chap. 2; Clark & Pataki, 1995, pp. 286–289; Clore & Byrne, 1974; Burgess & Huston, 1979). The densest cells in the matrix were for a generalized reinforcement approach. These cells provide exemplars of the era.

What Happened to Interpersonal Attraction after 1985?

In the period immediately preceding 1985, an outside observer (Berscheid's "Omniscient Jones") would see rapid increases in the cognitive and attribution approaches to attraction (Kelley et al., 1983; Reis, 2007). Because they were still new, studies based on this approach were concentrated in general psychological theory, albeit social psychological theory (Kelley et al., 2003, pp. 6–7). These newer studies did not ignore the rewards of social interaction, but they focused more on the cognitive processes in attraction, often as it extends over time (e.g., Agnew, Arriaga, & Wilson, in press; Clark, Mills & Powell, 1986; Kelley et al., 1983; but see Kelley, 1991, pp. 220–221, especially the last paragraph on p. 220).

Changes were on the horizon. What happened to interpersonal attraction after 1985? Let us paint with broad brushstrokes major events and milestones, as seen from the perspective of mid-2007. First, both researchers and theorists began to question the merits of a purely experimental and laboratory-based approach to interpersonal interaction (see Reis, 2007, for an especially thoughtful analysis). Even the label *interpersonal attraction* seems limiting, given the larger goal of understanding the psychological and interpersonal processes in close relationships (Kelley et al., 1983, 2003). In a prescient concluding sentence, Berscheid (1985) noted that her review did not adequately "telegraph the degree to which the attraction area is in the process of transition and change" (p. 415).

The field of interpersonal attraction, as an organized literature, largely faded into the background, supplanted but not replaced by a field called "close relationships" (Clark & Pataki, 1995; Kelley et al., 1983; Reis, 2007). Increased attention was directed to processes within naturally occurring couples, and with this came increased attention to the maintenance phase of relationships. No one denied that relationship initiation was important, but maintenance, decline, and repair captured the attention of relationship researchers (e.g., Rusbult & Buunk, 1993; Rusbult & Martz, 1995). This was not merely a matter of differences between short-term and long-term relationships. Even the *expectation* that a relationship could become long term affected the initiation (e.g., Buss & Schmitt, 1993; Clark & Mills, 1991; Crawford, Skowronski, & Stiff, 2007; Kenrick, 1994). Second, the cognitive revolution in psychology began to bear fruit, and with it came the decline in learning and reinforcement approaches to human social behavior. The Skinnerian aversion for cognitive explanations lost considerable ground in psychology. Again, no one denied that rewards and punishments affected social interaction, but the new focus was on cognitive mediation of rewards and expected rewards (e.g., the transformation of the given matrix into an effective matrix, in Kelley et al., 2003; Kenrick).

New Methodological Tools for Understanding Interpersonal Processes

Adding to the post-1985 zeitgeist, methodological advances gave researchers tools for studying mediation and moderation in interpersonal interaction (Baron & Kenny, 1986; see comments by Finkel et al., 2007). For example, people may be more likely to initiate a relationship (IR) with physically attractive persons because physical attractiveness (PA) activates stereotypes about certain personality traits (SPT) that are linked to physical attractiveness. If people assume that physically attractive persons are more sociable and outgoing than less attractive persons, they may initiate interaction because they seek the (assumed) traits, not the physical qualities per se. In this case, the sequence is PA–SPT–IR, and SPT is a mediator because it stands between PA and IR. If the moderator SPT were reduced to zero (e.g., convincing perceivers that desirable traits were not associated with PA), then the link between PA and IR would disappear. Continuing the example, if PA is related to IR in a different way in men than in women (MW), then in this case WM is a moderator of the PA-IR link. The mediator–moderator distinction is important because mediators are tied more closely to causal mechanisms than are moderators. Moderators are valuable because they suggest mediators. (For a more detailed description and analysis, see Edwards & Lambert, 2007.)

Moving from theory to actual research, David Kenny and his colleagues (e.g., Kashy & Kenny, 2000; Kenny, 1994; Kenny & La Voie, 1984) developed and made available practical tools for unwrapping dyadic dependency. When persons P and T interact as a dyad, effects could now be partitioned into those due to the perceiver (P), to the target (T) that the perceiver observed, and to the emergent effects due to the unique P × T interaction of perceiver and target. Researchers and theorists tacitly knew that some part of attraction was due to processes within perceivers (e.g., motivation, comparison levels, and personality), whereas other parts were due to properties of the target (e.g., physical attractiveness). These tools allowed researchers to reexamine and ask more penetrating questions about initiation. For example, exactly what processes are at work with people's very first encounter with each other at "zero acquaintance" (Ambady, Hallahan, & Rosenthal, 1995; Kenny, Horner, Kashy, & Chu, 1992)?

Yet again, no attraction researcher or theorist denied that some part of attractiveness was in the eye of the beholder, and some other part was in the target. Even the earliest work in interpersonal attraction recognized that beyond these main effects, emergent forms of attraction-related behavior came from the unique interaction of certain perceiver qualities and aspects of the target. For example, even if people agree on the physical attractiveness of a target, not all people hold the same expectancies or react the same way to that person (e.g., Dermer & Thiel, 1975; Hatfield, Utne, & Traupmann, 1979; Moore, Graziano, & Millar, 1987; Walster, Walster, & Traupmann, 1978).

New Theoretical Approaches: Attachment and Evolution   Arguably more important than the past milestones outlined previously, two new theoretical approaches appeared on the scene and quickly gained ascendancy among interpersonal process researchers. These were adult attachment theory (Hazan & Shaver, 1987; Shaver, Belsky, & Brennan, 2000) and evolutionary psychology (Berry, 2000; Buss, 1989, 1995, 1999; Buss & Schmitt, 1993; Kendrick, 1994). Technically, neither of these two approaches was new in the sense of introducing radically new concepts not seen previously. They certainly were new in reorganizing and refocusing the social psychology of interpersonal processes on different sets of relationship variables (e.g., waist-to-hip ratio and the internal working model) or different ways of conceptualizing traditional variables like similarity. More importantly, these two approaches offered ways to conceptualize the basic construct of selective affiliation that were different from the traditional attitude. Attraction might be conceptualized better as a modularized, distinctively specialized emotion and motivation than as one of many attitudes.

Even when the consensus among experts was that attraction was an attitude, there was debate about the measurement of attraction. In practice, most researchers treated attraction as a one-dimensional construct, ranging from extreme attraction on one pole to extreme repulsion at the other pole (see Byrne, 1971, pp. 44–47; cf. Huston, 1974, pp. 14–15). Berscheid and Walster (1978) were clear: "Interpersonal attraction (or interpersonal hostility), then, can be defined as an individual's tendency or predisposition to evaluate another person or the symbol of the person in a positive or negative way" (pp. 3–4). This conception could be operationalized in many different ways, but the most common methods involved self-report ratings on questionnaires, yielding a single attraction score.

A one-dimensional view of attraction brings many problems. First, this definition places many seemingly different phenomena under the same umbrella. For example, the unidimensional conceptualization gives prejudice the same definition as attraction. Both are commonly defined as evaluative attitudes (e.g., Nelson, 2002, pp. 7–11). Is prejudice merely a low level of attraction, or is it a qualitatively different phenomenon (Devine, 1995; Gardner, 1994; Rubin, 1974)? Is a person who dislikes most people prejudiced, low in attraction (to humankind), or just misanthropic (Graziano, Bruce, Sheese, & Tobin, 2007)? Is love merely a quantitatively higher level of attraction than, say, affection or selective affiliation (Hazan & Shaver, 1987)? Even if we grant that attraction can be measured as a unidimensional construct, does it follow that underlying attraction processes are the same or similar at all levels of attraction? Is the "active ingredient" in initiation selectivity due primarily to unidimensional approach tendencies (at the high end of attraction) that diminish to zero at the low end, to unidimensional avoidance and/or repulsion tendencies (at the low end) that diminish to zero at the high end, or to both; or does it depend heavily on context (Chen & Kenrick, 2002; Higgins, 2006; Rosenbaum, 1986; Stone, Shackelford, & Buss, 2007)?

In sum, the unidimensional conceptualizations of attraction raised fundamental questions about discriminant validity and, ultimately, the construct validity of attraction itself (e.g., Griffin & Langlois, 2006; Rosenbaum, 1986). Second, the one-dimensional approach leaves no room for multiple conflicting evaluations (e.g., high respect coupled with low affection, or vice versa) that seem to characterize ambivalence. Perhaps this was due in part to the fact that attitude researchers had not yet come to grips with ambivalence (e.g., Petty, Tormala, Brinol, & Jarvis, 2006; Priester & Petty, 1996, 2001). After all, attraction was an attitude. This becomes especially problematic when we move from attraction to love, the latter state being characterized by feelings of ambivalence (Berscheid & Walster, 1974; Reik, 1944). It could be argued, of course, that love is not a phenomenon of the initiation stage of attraction, and could be qualitatively different from attraction. The unidimensional, evaluative attitude definition of attraction may not be rich enough to cover a full range of initiation phenomena, much less all of attraction or selective affiliation. In the end, any definition can become an obstacle if it is not regarded as one disposable tool among many that serves a purpose within a theory or program of research (Shadish et al., 2002).

What Have We Learned?

This lengthy prolegomenon provides the context for the selective review that follows. First, a simple, linear, historical review of the literature relevant to the initiation of relationships is not possible. The last two decades have seen tectonic changes in theory and research on the phenomenon of the initiation of relationships. It will be necessary to discuss specific variables within the context of different theories, not just the theory that initiated the research. Research on variables like similarity or physical attractiveness may be interpreted by reinforcement theory (e.g., Griffith, 1974), interdependence theory (Rusbult & Buunk, 1993), or self-expansion theory (Aron, Steele, Kashdan, & Perez, 2006) in ways very different from evolutionary psychology (Buss, 1999; Cunningham, Druen, & Barbee, 1997; Kenrick & Simpson, 1997; Meston & Buss, 2007).

EMPIRICAL LITERATURE (1985 TO JUNE 2007)

Overview

For purposes of exposition, we organized the literature under three headings. First, we review research investigating properties of the target-person being evaluated that lead to initiation and liking. For want of a better name, we call this *classical realist research* because it seems to assume that objective qualities inherent in the target can be measured and can elicit attraction from perceivers. Despite differences among perceivers, for both conceptual and methodological reasons, some convergence could be reached on the evaluation (Hofstee, 1994, esp. pp. 153–154; Wiggins, Conger, & Conger, 1968). Included here is research on variables such as large prominent eyes, age, height and weight (e.g., Crandall, 1994; Hatfield & Sprecher, 1986, pp. 194–237; Kenrick, 1994) and waist-to-hip ratios (e.g., Singh, 1993), and nonverbal cues like vocal attractiveness (e.g., Zuckerman, Miyake, & Hodgins, 1991) and gait (e.g., Berry, 1992). Second, we review research investigating properties and states of perceivers that influence their tendencies to initiate interaction. We call this *constructivist research* because it emphasizes the active production process generated from within the perceiver that influences attraction (e.g., Lemay, Clark, & Feeney, 2007). Third, we review studies suggesting that attractiveness is a quasi-catalytic, interactive process between an object-person and the perceiver. We call this *emergent research.*

Three variables provide good barometers of the changing climate in research on the initiation of relationships. These are PA, similarity, and dominance. Researchers at various times located these three variables as residing preponderantly in the target of evaluation, in the perceiver, or in the interaction between target and perceiver. In the early research, an implicit assumption seemed to be that those three variables were objective attributes of targets, in the sense that observers would reach consensus in evaluating others on PA (e.g., Berry, 2000, pp. 275–276; Langlois et al., 2000), similarity, and dominance (e.g., Buss, 1986). These three variables also highlight the general trend in research to embed the variables more within complex interpersonal and relationship contexts (e.g., Aron et al., 2006; Watson et al., 2004). They also show the importance of sex differences in the initiation of relationships. We shall highlight research dedicated to them as we move through the review.

REALISM: PROPERTIES OF TARGETS MAKING THEM ATTRACTIVE

Main Effects of Targets

If we restrict our review to empirical studies of relationship initiation for sexual and romantic purposes published between 1986 and June 2007, we find a minimum of 34 papers on properties of targets that are immediately relevant to this review. This number could be expanded considerably if we included social-cognitive processes like stereotyping and prejudice (e.g., Eagly, Ashmore, Makhijani, & Longo, 1991), but we shall not do that here. If we accept this restricted view, then we observe that approximately twice as many papers were devoted to characteristics of targets as were devoted to characteristics of perceivers ($N = 19$, minimum). This apparent differential interest in targets may reflect an Aristotelian bias (Lewin, 1943) or researchers' efforts to explore the naïve phenomenology of beauty (Heider, 1958), or reflect that attributes of targets may be easier to study than processes in perceivers.

Beauty: In the Eyes of the Beholder or the Beheld?   In 1986, Michael Cunningham and his colleagues began publishing a series of studies on physical properties of people that made them attractive. This work was a harbinger of what was to come in subsequent research. Cunningham (1986) began by focusing on facial characteristics in women that would make them attractive to men. He asked male college students to evaluate photographs of women (half of whom were college seniors; the other half were international beauty contestants). The beauty contestants were include to insure a wider range of attractiveness than one might find using college seniors alone. The men were unaware of the status of the women as contestants or not, but the contestants received higher overall attractiveness ratings than did the seniors. He then correlated these evaluations with carefully measured facial characteristics associated with neonatal features (e.g., large eyes, and large mouth relative to facial area), mature features (e.g., chin width), and expressive features (e.g., smile width). Building on ethological theory, he tested the hypothesis that neonatal cues would serve as "innate cuteness releasers," eliciting positive evaluations and caregiving responses from men. He found that rated attractiveness correlated positively with female facial characteristics. Because the characteristics were not independent of each other, Cunningham ran regression analyses, treating attractiveness ratings as the criterion and cues as predictors. The optimal multiple regression analysis used the neonatal features of eye height and nose area, the mature feature of narrow cheek width, and the expressive feature of smile width. This regression as the full set was statistically significant and accounted for 53% of the variance in mean attractiveness ratings. Cunningham emphasized that sexual maturity features were a separate dimension of attractiveness, but from an empirical perspective uncovering quasi-neonatal female facial cues that predict male attraction ratings was no small

discovery. This is especially true because the cues had been out in the open, looking at researchers, and had been as clear as the eyes on their faces, so to speak.

In a second study pursuing the innate releaser idea further, Cunningham (1986) then correlated the cues associated with attractiveness ratings with the men's personality attributions and preferences. For example, among the cues, eye height (EH) has the single largest correlation with attractiveness ($r = .62$), but smile width (SW) came in a close second. In turn, EH was significantly and positively correlated with evaluations of the women as being bright, sociable, and assertive, but negatively correlated with being modest. EH was correlated positively with health-related issues like having few medical problems, being fertile, but being more likely to have affairs. In terms of altruistic and reproductive behaviors, EH was correlated significantly and positively with men's willingness to self-sacrifice on her behalf, to take physical risks, to invest money in her, to hire her for a job, to prefer to date her, to prefer her for sex, and even to prefer her for raising children ($r = .49$). Smile width showed a nearly identical pattern in the first set of attribution variables, but not for altruistic and reproductive behaviors.

In his discussion, Cunningham (1986) noted,

> The fact that facial features predicted the perception of fertility and health independently of rated attractiveness adds some support to the hypothesis that rated attractiveness may be caused, in part, by the tendency of facial features to stimulate directly the impression of certain personal characteristics. (p. 933)

He also noted,

> The consistent relations obtained in these studies between attractiveness and neonate, mature, and expressive features demonstrated that beauty is not an inexplicable quality which lies only in the eye of the beholder. Yet such results do not preclude some variability in judgments of attractiveness. Women may use slightly different standards than males. (p. 934)

Later research by Cunningham and his colleagues demonstrated and extended this last point well (e.g., Cunningham, Barbee, & Pike, 1990; Cunningham, Druen, & Barbee, 1997; Lundy, Tan, & Cunningham, 1998). College-age women had more ways for categorizing men than college-age men had for categorizing women. For a related discussion, see Bogg and Ray (2006) on women's attraction to "Byronic heroes."

One characteristic of targets that deserves attention is "averageness," or typicality of the face. Research by Judith Langlois and her colleagues (e.g., Langlois & Roggman, 1990) found that average faces are more attractive than individual faces. Langlois and Roggman suggested that aversion for faces different from the norm informs the perceiver of the presence of mutations, congenital defects, other abnormalities, and general health. At least two studies explored this hypothesis and found mixed support (at best) for it (Kalick, Zebrowitz, Langlois, & Johnson, 1998; Shackelford & Larsen, 1997; and see Alley & Cunningham, 1991). Whatever its merits as an "honest advertisement for health," facial symmetry is related to judged attractiveness in both adults and infants, and the latter presumably have not had time to learn stereotypes or cultural norms (Langlois et al., 2000; Langlois, Roggman, & Musselman, 1994; Rhodes, Sumich, & Byatt, 1999).

At a minimum, this research illustrates several points. First, when college men evaluate women of approximately their own age, facial cues in the targets are reliably related to male observers' personality attributions, expectations for health, willingness to behave altruistically, and preferences for sexual and reproductive behavior. This is among the first programs of social psychology studies to integrate data in support of an evolutionary approach to relationship initiation and the previous attraction literature. It would not be the last. The Langlois research suggests that facial cues are activating something more basic than trait attribution. Second, adult men and women appear to respond to different aspects of persons of the other sex, and may even be differentially sensitive to those aspects. Third, evolutionary approaches were making their presence felt in the nearly empty space left by the older interpersonal attraction research (Berry, 2000; Kenrick & Simpson, 1997).

As in many pioneering studies, research by Cunningham and by Langlois raised questions that had not been considered systematically, at least in print. First, what do men seek, and what do they think they will obtain, from women with large eyes? Is it primarily a cue for locating good personality traits, as in "what is beautiful is good" attitudinal stereotypes (e.g., Eagly et al., 1991)? How much awareness, if any, do people have of their responsiveness to physical cues like symmetry? Do they think about this at all? Perhaps physical cues in women signify for men something deeper than cuteness, or even attitudinal stereotypes.

The second question is related to the first: Are attraction and relationship initiation primarily driven by facial cues? From an evolutionary perspective the body below the neck should be at least as interesting as that above it. Earlier research explored this idea (e.g., Wiggins et al., 1968; see also Hatfield & Sprecher, 1986, chap. 7), but not within the framework of evolutionary theory. Third, if we accept for the moment the evolutionary approach to relationship initiation, and if men's and women's psychology have different reproductive agendas (Buss, 2004), then the principles described previously may not generalize to women. This qualification could be framed as a minor matter of external validity ("It wouldn't work with Eskimos"), or it could be cast as an issue of the construct validity of attraction as part of relationship initiation. We will return to this matter again in the section on perceiver characteristics (e.g., Cunningham et al., 1995, 1997; Schmitt, this volume; Schmitt et al., 2004a, 2004b).

EVOLUTIONARY APPROACHES: SEARCHING FOR HONEST ADVERTISERS BELOW THE NECK

Several of the questions outlined previously were addressed by Devendra Singh (1993; see also 2004). Singh noted that evolutionary approaches to human mate selection claim that both men and women select mating partners not for their expressiveness or cuteness per se, but for qualities that enable them to enhance reproductive success. A fundamental assumption of all evolution-based theories of human mate selection is that men's responsiveness to physical attractiveness is largely a reflection of reliable cues to a woman's reproductive success (Buss, 1989, 1999; Kenrick, 1994; but see Marcus & Cunningham, 2003). In general, a woman can increase her reproductive success by choosing a man who can provide resources to raise her children securely. A man increases his reproductive success by picking a woman who is fertile and receptive, and has qualities indicating she is a good prospect for successful motherhood. The reproductive value of a woman, however, cannot be as easily assessed. Because direct signs of fertility are concealed, the man must use indirect cues such as physical attractiveness as a proxy for the reproductive value of the woman. (Parenthetically, it could be argued that the opposite would be plausible, namely, that modern men in industrialized societies would be interested in cues showing that a woman was *not* fertile. For now, we follow the evolutionary logic.)

What aspects of physical attractiveness are the best reliable predictors of reproductive value? Rather than large eyes, high cheekbones, and a big smile, it would be indicators of health and freedom from parasites and infections (e.g., Gangestad & Thornhill, 1997). Distribution of body fat is a good indicator because it is regulated by sex hormones and shows a striking gender difference, particularly in the abdominal and gluteofemoral (buttocks and thighs) regions. Singh noted that testosterone stimulates fat deposits in the abdominal region and inhibits fat deposits in the gluteofemoral region. Estrogen, by contrast, inhibits fat deposits in the abdomen and stimulates fat deposits in the gluteofemoral region more than in any other region of the body. This results in gynoid (female) or android (male) body fat distribution (Singh, 1993).

The fat distribution can be measured using waist (the narrowest portion between the ribs and iliac crest) and hip (the level of the greatest protrusion of the buttocks) circumferences and computing a waist-to-hip ratio (WHR). The WHR reflects both the distribution of fat between upper and lower body and the relative amount of intra- versus extra-abdominal fat. The WHR is a stable measure with high within-person reliability and correlates with direct measures of the intra-abdominal–subcutaneous fat ratio, and deep abdominal fat.

Before puberty, both sexes have similar WHRs. After puberty, however, women deposit more fat on the hips, and, therefore, the WHR becomes significantly lower in women than in men. The WHR has a bimodal distribution with relatively little overlap between genders. The typical range of a WHR for healthy premenopausal women has been shown to be .67 to .80, whereas healthy men have WHRs in the range of .85 to .95. Women usually maintain a lower WHR than men except during menopause, when the female WHR becomes similar to the male WHR.

If the attributes of good health and reproductive capability are critical in mate selection as posited by evolutionarily based theories, then men should possess mechanisms (conscious or unconscious) to detect these features in women and assign them greater importance than other bodily features in assessing female attractiveness. Singh (1993) presented a set of studies showing that the WHR is correlated with youthfulness, reproductive endocrine status, and long-term health risk in women. College-age men find female figures with a low WHR more attractive, healthier, and of greater reproductive value than figures with a higher WHR. Adult men aged 25 to 85 years preferred female figures with a lower WHR and assigned them higher ratings of attractiveness and reproductive potential. Singh and Bronstad (1997) explored the hypothesis that men and women would focus on different body zones in efforts to enhance beauty (e.g., tattoos) and amplify the best WHR for their sex. Support for this hypothesis was mixed, but women were more likely to tattoo their abdomen than were men (but see Singh, 1995).

Tassinary and Hansen (1998) noted that Singh portrayed WHRs with line drawings. Singh's stimulus material had a built-in bias in that WHRs were confounded with perceived weight. That is, differences in attraction that Singh attributed to WHRs could be as plausibly attributed to the well-established negative evaluation of overweight women (e.g., Crandall, 1994; Graziano et al., 2007). Tassinary and Hansen constructed stimuli that systematically and independently varied weight, waist size, and hip size (WHR). College students individually ranked drawings of women, once for attractiveness and once for capability of bearing children. Results show that judgments of attractiveness and fecundity can be either unrelated or related, positively or negatively, to the WHR depending on waist size, hip size, and weight. Tassinary and Hansen concluded that WHRs are inconsistent with the evolutionary argument that human physical attractiveness is fundamentally a sign of mate value. Subsequent research by Singh and his colleagues (e.g., Schmitt et al., 2004b; Singh & Luis, 1995) showed that bias against overweight women appears across ethnicity and diverse cultures.

The overall evidence suggests that WHRs are related to evaluations of attractiveness, but the mechanism is not yet clear. Overweight women are rated as less attractive than typical-weight women, but there are several reasons to be reserved about the WHR, or at least its presumed link to evolution (e.g., Swami & Tovee, 2005). Further research should clarify the matter.

A conceptually related line of research comes from Randy Thornhill and Steven Gangestad in their work on systematic physical correlates of sexual selection (e.g., Gangestad, Thornhill, & Yeo, 1994). To make functional mate choices, women must distinguish traits possessed by preferred men relative to other men. Certain traits must "honestly advertise" good genes or a good provider. Building on the idea of "honest advertisement of mate quality," Gangestad and Thornhill (1997) noted that in bilaterally symmetric organisms, the same genes control the development of both sides of the body. If asymmetry occurs, these deviations are due in part to developmental instability. That is, during development, all organisms are subjected to many environmental assaults like parasites, toxins, or infections. Organisms that do not effectively fight off these assaults show less symmetry. Deviations from symmetry serve as markers of developmental instability.

Gangestad and Thornhill (1997) noted that in a range of species, measures of deviations from symmetry called fluctuating asymmetry (FA) correlate with fecundity, rate of growth, and survival. From this line of thinking, they made the prediction that men who show greater symmetry (i.e., have low FA) will experience greater mating success. To test this hypothesis, Thornhill and Gangestad (1994) measured seven bilateral features, such as foot width, hand width, and ear length, in 59 college men. They created a summed composite index of absolute difference between the left and right measurements, and correlated these with the men's self-reported number of sexual partners. FA was correlated negatively with number of partners, with $r = -.32$. In a sample of 200 college women, there was no evidence that FA was related to number of sexual partners. One complication is that Gangestad and Thornhill (1997) noted that the skeletal FA they measured "probably does not function as an observable cue that people assess in others" (p. 179). Either FA is a proxy for an individual difference manifested in observable behaviors, which serve as the selection cue, or women are not aware of the attributes that affect their choices.

Do Behaviors Make People Seem More or Less Attractive?

Douglas Kenrick (Kenrick, 1994) and his colleagues initiated several different lines of research within the evolutionary approach. Like Gangestad and Thornhill, Kendrick's team also turned the table around from women to men as objects of heterosexual and romantic interest. It could be argued that Kenrick and colleagues raised the bar several notches by examining behaviors of targets not tied to specific physical attributes (but see Cunningham, 1989). Their research program covered a range of variables relevant to evolutionary theories like relative age and status (e.g., Kenrick, Keffe, Bryan, Barr, & Brown, 1995), but we concentrate first on research concerned with dominance as an attribute of men that makes them attractive to women. As noted previously, from an evolutionary psychology perspective, men gain their attractiveness to women through their social status and resources, and dominance is a contributor to both. Dominance is expressed behaviorally, and such behavior presumably reflects an underlying disposition.

The pioneering empirical, experimental research with humans on dominance and heterosexual attraction was done by Sadalla, Kenrick, and Vershure (1987). In a set of four studies, Sadalla et al. (1987) examined the relation among expressions of dominance and the heterosexual attractiveness of men and women. Dominance was manipulated experimentally by having a confederate engage in specific dominant or nondominant behaviors (e.g., direct eye gaze, or relaxed seating postures). All four experiments showed an interaction between dominance and sex of target. Dominance behavior increased the attractiveness of men, but had no effect on the attractiveness of women. The effect did not depend on the sex of the rater or on the sex of those with whom the dominant target interacted. The effect was specific to dominance as an independent variable and did not occur for related constructs (aggressive or domineering). This study also found that manipulated dominance enhanced only a male's sexual attractiveness and not his general likeability. Sadalla et al. (1987) noted that there is nothing explicit in sociocultural or social learning theories that would predict this result, whereas evolutionary theories would (cf. Howard, Blumstein, & Schwartz, 1987). Sadalla et al. asserted that "male dominance is an attribute whose genetic mechanism spread because it conferred a reproductive advantage to its carriers" (1987, p. 737). That is, male dominance is a pervasive aspect of human behavior because its underlying genetic mechanism allowed dominant men to produce more children.

Lauri Jensen-Campbell and her colleagues suggested that there are multiple routes to status and resources, one of which goes through cooperation and altruism (Jensen-Campbell, Graziano, & West, 1995; but see Graziano, Jensen-Campbell, & Hair, 1996). This represents an alternative to the Sadalla et al. (1987) approach, but it is not necessarily incompatible with evolutionary accounts (Howard et al., 1987). Cooperation and altruism can be understood as social resources or, in Trivers' (1972) terms, "investments." Men who are predisposed to cooperate with their partners, or who show nurturance and altruism, may be selectively preferred over other men. This preference may reflect not only the woman's attribution that such men would be rewarding to her personally but also that such men would be disposed to invest more heavily in their offspring. Furthermore, such men may be able to draw on a larger pool of community resources due to their contributions to that community. The problem with this alternative is that it does not reconcile well with the Sadalla et al. conclusion that sexual attraction may be qualitatively different from generalized attraction, or that women may derogate a cooperative, altruistic man for being a nonmasculine weakling. Jensen-Campbell et al. noted that dominance is not necessarily the bipolar opposite of altruism, or that these two aspects of male behavior are incompatible, either conceptually or empirically.

Jensen-Campbell et al. (1995) experimentally manipulated behavioral expressions of both male dominance and prosocial orientation. Conceptually, the design was a 2 × 2 matrix of male behavior, crossing factorially dominance (high versus low) with prosocial tendencies and agreeableness (high versus low). Female college students evaluated the men for overall attractiveness, subjective physical attractiveness, sexual attractiveness, and dating desirability. The researchers also manipulated male physical attractiveness and the target of dominance—another man or a woman. Results showed that in each case, low-agreeable men were not attractive sexually, physically, or as dating partners. Adding or subtracting dominance did not alter that outcome. For men who were high in agreeableness, however, dominance enhanced their attractiveness significantly. Of the four male personae generated by the 2 × 2 design, the high-agreeable, high-dominant man was the most attractive to women. This pattern held whether the man interacted with another man or a woman. In another paper, Graziano, Jensen-Campbell, Todd, and Finch (1997) replicated and extended Jensen-Campbell et al.'s work. They explored the phenomenology of both men's and women's attraction to persons of the other sex using 372 college men and women. Both men and women reported that high-agreeable targets of the other sex were more physically attractive. When considered as a direct effect on attraction, agreeableness had almost six times the impact of dominance in predicting women's attraction to men. Mediation analyses showed that dominance had less direct (and indirect) impact on women's attraction to men when they expected a long-term relationship than when they expected a short-term relationship (see also Miller, Niehuis, & Huston, 2006).

Extended Nonverbal Cues to Attraction

If we move past faces and bodies, we find research on nonverbal variables extending over time that are related to attraction and relationship initiation. Human voices seem to differ in their attractiveness, and people with attractive voices are judged more positively than their peers (Berry, 1992; Zuckerman et al., 1991). Zuckerman et al. reported that vocal attractiveness can be as strong a predictor of overall attractiveness as facial attractiveness. Another extended variable is movement: Some patterns of movement in gait are related to judgments of age, sex, and even mental health (e.g., McArthur & Baron, 1983). For example, women walk in a pattern recognizably different from that of men due to their lower centers of gravity (i.e., women have proportionally more weight in the hips than men.) As plausible as it seems, this hypothesis linking movement to attraction has not been tested systematically with empirical studies (but see Sakaguci, Jonsson, & Hasegawa, 2005; for review of suggestive studies, see Berry, 2000).

In summary, there may be divergences in particulars, but overall there is solid empirical evidence that attributes of individual persons can make them more or less attractive to others. These include (but are not restricted to) physical attributes like facial attractiveness, eye size, and body symmetry. Perhaps more surprising, an individual's less concrete agentic and prosocial behavior, qualities in their voice and their gate, can also make them more or less attractive.

Constructivism: Processes in Perceivers Making Others Attractive

In restricting this review to empirical studies of relationship initiation for sexual and romantic purposes published between 1985 and June 2007, we find a minimum of 20 papers on properties of perceivers that are immediately relevant to this review. We call this *constructivism* because it emphasized the active generating process from within the perceiver that influences attraction to other persons. It would be possible to consider many more studies if we expanded coverage into related work on attachment processes (e.g., Clark, Shaver, & Abrahams, 1999), but arguably most of these studies are concerned primarily with relationship maintenance, not initiation (e.g., Klohnen & Luo, 2003; Knee, 1998; Miller et al., 2006; Zayas & Shoda, 2007), so they will not be discussed here unless they are immediately relevant.

In 1985, relationship researchers knew that some part of attraction came from the perceivers (e.g., Berscheid, Graziano, Monson, & Dermer, 1976; Kelley et al., 2003, pp. 256–260; Pennebaker et al., 1979; Tjosvold, Johnson, & Johnson, 1984). Implicit within much of this research is the idea that need states in the perceiver affected perception, and that reactions to others were filtered through existing psychological structures. Here we discuss need-related variables like perceivers' personality characteristics, states of perceivers, and interpersonal situations including conformity pressures that affect the perceivers' initiation of interaction with others. See Witt, Proffitt, and Epstein (2005) for a related discussion of how intended use can influence perception of even basic dimensions like distance.

Several conceptual issues confront us at this point. First, implicit in the exposition of initiation earlier in this chapter was the implication of selectivity. The key idea is that a perceiver P will initiate interaction with target A but not B or C. It is possible, however, that P might initiate or avoid interaction with A, B, and C at higher rates, frequencies, or intensities than would perceiver R. If P systematically approaches or avoids all (or many) people but R does not, this points toward state or dispositional processes within the perceiver. If researchers do not take into account selectivity differences within chronic levels of approach or avoidance, they may be missing many important aspects of relationship initiation. This selectivity of choices need not be conscious (e.g., Dijksterhuis & van Olden, 2006).

In the period prior to the one under consideration for this review, Pennebaker et al. (1979) published a field study on the effects of motivation and changing goal structures on attraction. This team found that as closing time in a Texas bar approached, patrons' evaluation of potential romantic partners shifted: The remaining prospects increased in attractiveness. The authors summarized the study's outcomes using the lyrics from a country and western song, to the effect that "girls get prettier at closing time." In a follow-up, Madey et al. (1996) explored perceiver state variables in initiation. They interviewed 237 university students patronizing a popular college town nightclub. They found that persons of the other sex got prettier at closing time, but only for people not currently in a relationship. Significant differences in the perceived attractiveness of opposite-sex patrons were found at each of three time periods (10 p.m., midnight, and 1:30 a.m.) for persons not in a relationship, whereas persons in a relationship did not differ in their perceived attractiveness of opposite-sex patrons at each time period. This shows some evidence of a state-induced lack of selectivity in persons not in relationships. Presumably, initiation processes are different in persons not in relationships relative to their partnered peers. Perceivers are not necessarily aware of the processes that influence their choices.

Perceiver dispositions are also related to selectivity in attraction and initiation. Graziano et al. (2007) found that the big five personality dimension of agreeableness was related to chronic differences in attraction and liking for all or most people. Persons high in agreeableness say that they like more people, including traditional targets of prejudice, than do their peers. Persons low in agreeableness (particularly men) show lower levels of attraction and actively discriminate against out-group women (in this case, overweight women) at the initiation phase of a relationship.

One tool useful for understanding this effect is the Kenny, Kashy, and Cook (2006, pp. 188–190) "round robin technique," in which each person in a group can rate, and be rated by, every other member of the group. This procedure allows researchers to separate quasi-objective properties of targets from the projective effects in perceivers. That is, if most people in a group rate Mary as likeable and Martha as not likable, then it is plausible that likeableness is located in the targets of Mary and Martha. On the other hand, if Peter rates all group members as likeable, but Paul rates them as not likeable, then it is plausible that likeableness is projected by perceivers onto others. Graziano and Tobin (2002) found that agreeableness was more in the perceiver than in the target. That is, persons high in agreeableness saw others as being more likable than did persons low in agreeableness. Apparently, the former project positivity onto strangers at minimal acquaintance, whereas the latter project negativity (see also Lemay et al., 2007). In this study, there was no evidence that extroversion had a systematic link to attraction or liking.

Another dispositional variable related to selectivity at the initiation phase is self-monitoring, an individual difference related to impression management (Gangestad & Snyder, 1985; Graziano & Bryant, 1998; Leone & Hawkins, 2006; Rowatt, Cunningham, & Druen, 1998). Snyder, Berscheid, and Glick (1985) found that when low- and high-self monitoring men chose a woman for a date, low-self-monitoring men paid more attention and assigned great weight to information about interior personal attributes, whereas high-self-monitoring men paid more attention to exterior physical appearance. Snyder, Simpson, and Gangestad (1986) found that high self-monitors tended to establish unrestricted sexual relations, such as having sex with others to whom they were not psychologically close, whereas low self-monitors tended to have restricted sexual orientations. At the behavioral level, high-self-monitoring persons reported having more different sexual partners than did low-self-monitoring persons. At the attitude level, low self-monitors said that they would be more reluctant to have sex with someone to whom they were not committed than were the high self-monitors. Jamieson, Lydon, and Zanna (1987) conducted an experiment in which they manipulated the kind of similarity (attitude versus activity preferences) of a partner during initial interaction. For low self-monitors, attitude similarity affected initial attraction more than did activity preference similarity. For high self-monitors, the exact opposite pattern emerged. This study used partners of the same gender, however, so its generality to opposite-sex romantic relationships is suggestive, not definitive. Leck and Simpson (1999) found that when instructed to feign interest, high-self-monitoring men and women were more successful in conveying greater interest to an opposite-sex partner, at least through the verbal channel. For a comprehensive review of self-monitoring and other kinds of relationships, see Leone and Hawkins (2006).

Sex Differences in Attraction and Initiation Processes

This chapter is attentive to sex differences because several major theories relevant to relationship initiation, as well as numerous empirical studies, focus on them (Stone et al., 2007). Sex differences in the recalled importance of relationships for identity development are well documented (McLean & Thorne, 2003; Thorne & Michaelieu, 1996). Clark, Shaver, and Abrahams (1999) found that when students were asked to write narratives about their own relationship initiation experiences, sex differences emerged. Men reported being more direct and active in the beginning stage of the relationship, and are more interested in sexual intimacy, than were women. Both reported the larger goals of gaining love, intimacy, and emotional disclosure. Recent work suggests that the strength of an individual's intimacy goals affects relationship initiation strategies. Intimacy needs may act as a kind of filter for initiating certain kinds of dating relationships, but the pattern is different in men and women (Sanderson, Keiter, Miles, & Yopyk, 2007, Study 1; but see Meston & Buss, 2007). On the other hand, Graziano, Jensen-Campbell, Shebilske, and Lundgren (1993) found relationship-related sex differences, but no evidence that college men differed from college women in self-rated expertise in relationship initiation or relationship maintenance. Whatever the pattern might have been in the past, there is evidence that computer-based dating might alter basic sex differences in the initiation of relationships. This suggests that safety and anonymity helped women in particular to break free from traditional sex role norms for initiating dating (e.g., Scharlott & Christ, 1995).

From the perspective of evolutionary theory, women's preferences for men reflect a concern for the resources that the male could bring to her and her offspring. Gangestad, Garver-Apgar, and Simpson (2007) tested the hypothesis that women's preferences for men would change across the ovulatory cycle. In particular, women should prefer men with "good genes" when they are fertile and more interested in short-term relationships. Gangestad et al. found that when women were fertile and rating men for their potential as short-term mates, they were particularly attracted to traits like physical attractiveness, muscularity, and a confrontative style. They found no shifts in preferences associated with long-term mates, like being a good father, warm, faithful, intelligent, and financially successful. Some of these (e.g., intelligence) could also be regarded as an indicator of good genes (e.g., Gangestad, 1993).

A perceiver characteristic like sexual orientation would influence attraction and initiation, but beyond this vague assertion, many other questions arise. Based on the evolutionary logic discussed previously, men and women seek different qualities when they initiate relationships. Men should seek women who are healthy and fertile and probably younger than themselves. Women should seek men who have good genes (Gangestad et al., 2007) and are old enough to have secured resources, but not so old that they might die during the child's infancy. It is not clear, however, how natural selection would operate on homosexual preferences. Kenrick et al. (1995) found that the age preferences of homosexual men were very similar to those of heterosexual men. Homosexual women showed an age preference "somewhat between" those of heterosexual women and men. Kenrick et al. noted that their results suggest that homosexual preferences are not merely a reversal of heterosexual roles. This issue is one deserving more empirical research.

In summary, outcomes of recent research support the claim that an important part of attraction and relationship initiation is centered in the perceiver. Motivational states within persons affect their attraction to others. Changes in need states (e.g., ovulatory cycles) covary with attraction. The girls (and boys) get prettier at closing time for a reason. Long-term motivation states and goals (e.g., sexual orientation) also affect attraction and relationship initiation. This literature is consistent with a long line of social psychological research on motivated social cognition (e.g., Jost, Glaser, Kruglanski, & Sulloway, 2003). Sex differences point to a similar conclusion about motivational differences underlying corresponding sex differences in relationship processes.

Emergent Processes Arising in Target X Perceiver Interaction

Several studies described in the previous section on perceiver processes might have been classified as emergent processes because perceiver processes appeared to be activated selectively by certain targets (e.g., Cunningham, Shamblen, Ault, & Barbee, 2005). In most of those studies, the critical processes were described as occurring in the perceiver. Here we describe quasi-synergistic processes that, at a minimum, require at least two persons. Few studies on relationship initiation (and maintenance) have been more influential than the work by Margaret Clark and Judson Mills on the qualitative difference between communal versus exchange relationships. Their first exposition was published prior to 1985, but interest in this distinction increased in subsequent years (e.g., Clark, Mills, & Powell, 1986; Clark & Pataki, 1995; Lemay et al., 2007). The Clark and Mills team proposed that distinctly different norms apply to communal relationships, which are concerned with feelings of responsibility for another's well-being. Here benefits are provided to others in return for benefits received (e.g., Walster, Walster, & Berscheid, 1978). Exchange relationships are more common among strangers and among persons anticipating short-term relationships. This is just the kind of situation one finds in a typical laboratory study of attraction and relationship initiation.

This distinction has several implications. One is that the bulk of the pre-1985 laboratory-based research on attraction was biased toward the study of exchange relationships. Such research probably does not generalize in a simple or direct way to existing, nonlaboratory relationships. Another is that relationship initiation itself may be more of an exchange process than a communal one because one always begins a new relationship with a relative stranger. Initiation processes are propaedeutic—necessary but not sufficient exchange conditions for the development of longer term communal relationships. Rather than abandoning experimental laboratory research, however, Clark and Mills (1991) embraced it by manipulating the prospects for communal relationships in the laboratory (Clark & Pataki, 1995). In the prototypical study, the prospect of a communal relationship is manipulated by having a male college student interact with an attractive female confederate who was friendly, new to college, and interested in meeting new friends. For exchange relations, men interacted with the same confederate, but she provided information that she was married and already established in the community, and expressed no particular interest in meeting new people. Clark, Mills, and colleagues found that in the exchange condition, the men liked the woman more when she repaid him for helping her. In the communal condition, the men liked the confederate more when she did not repay him.

The bulk of communal and exchange research focuses on relationship maintenance, not initiation, but this work puts a different cast on classic attraction and initiation phase variables like similarity. If persons have or desire a communal relationship with a partner, the partner can better understand

and meet needs if the two share similar attitudes, beliefs, and backgrounds. One implication is that some forms of similarity may be more important than others, namely, those most closely connected to understanding and meeting the other partner's needs in communal relationships (Miller et al., 2006). For example, in their Iowa Newlywed Study, Watson et al. (2004) found that in newlyweds, similarity in religiosity and political attitude was considerably greater than was similarity in abilities or even personality.

Another important line of work related to similarity emerged after 1986 in the theory of self-expansion (Aron & Aron, 1986; Aron, Aron, Tudor, & Nelson, 1991). This theory presents the idea that people are motivated to expand their self, and this can be accomplished in part by forming relationships. It is similar in several respects to Theodore Reik's (1944) theorizing about completion processes when falling in love. Approximately 62 years after Reik's book, these ideas were explored more systematically and empirically. Aron et al. (2006) observed that people should be attracted to others perceived to offer the greatest possibilities for expanding the self in a positive direction.

On its face, self-expansion theory seems to imply that people should be more attracted to dissimilar mates than similar ones because similar others would add less to the self. Aron and Aron (1986) noted that similarity is related to attraction in the typical case because it serves as an indicator that a future relationship is possible. If people could be confident that they would not be rejected or excluded, then they would find dissimilar others more attractive than similar others, assuming the dissimilar attribute was positively valued. If the other was dissimilar on a negatively valued attribute, then a relationship would not promote expanding the self in a positive direction. (See Witt et al., 2005, regarding perceptual changes based on anticipated use.)

In the Aron et al. (2006) study, college students (57 women and 27 men) were randomly assigned to a *relationship likely condition* or a *relationship uncertain condition*. A random half of the participants were given a list of interests, supposedly from their partner, showing interests similar or dissimilar to their own. Then students completed a 2-item liking measure. Results showed that when a relationship was unlikely, the similar partner was consistently liked more than the dissimilar partner, the usual finding in the classic attraction literature (e.g., Byrne, 1971). When a relationship was likely, however, men (but not women) reported greater liking for the dissimilar partner than for the similar partner. This outcome is provocative in showing an effect opposite to one of the best-established relations in the attraction literature. Many uncertainties remain, however, about generalizability in that the predicted outcomes appeared only in men, and just 27 of them participated in the study.

Graziano et al. (1993) explored the hypothesis that women's judgment of men's attractiveness can be influenced by conformity pressure to be similar in evaluating attractiveness. College women evaluated physical attractiveness ratings supposedly made by same-sex peers. Women were influenced by other women's ratings, especially negative ratings. In another study, women were influenced by female peers in rating both male and female stimulus pictures. In the final study in this set, college students evaluated physical attractiveness in persons of the other sex after reading a detailed behavioral description, supposedly written by persons of the other sex who knew the person well. Women's ratings of attractiveness were more influenced by peers' verbal descriptions than were men's. Overall, women were more responsive to additional social information about other persons beyond the physical image than were men. There may indeed be convergence among observers in rating physical attractiveness (Berry, 2000), but some part of that convergence comes from social influence making raters (especially women) more similar.

Perhaps the most unusual similarity-attraction study within the emergent category between 1985 and 2007 is a study by David Lykken and Auke Tellegen (1993). Because identical twins are very similar in cognitive abilities, personality, attitudes, and values, it is possible that they are also similar in the characteristics they find attractive in romantic partners. If this is true, then the romantic partners of identical twins may be more similar than the spouses of nonidentical twins. Furthermore, twins may be attracted to their co-twin's romantic partner. Pairs of middle-age twins and their spouses (738 couples) independently rated their initial attraction to their co-twin's mate, or to their spouse's twin. Pairs of individuals who were selected as spouses of identical twins were no more similar than those of nonidentical twins, and hardly more than random pairs of same-sex adults. Identical twins approved of their co-twin's spousal choice no more than did nonidentical twins. Nearly twice as many husbands of identical twins were favorable rather than unfavorable about their wives' co-twin, but only 13% endorsed that they "could have fallen for her myself." The wives of identical twins were equally divided between a favorable and unfavorable rating of their spouse's co-twin. Overall, twins make similar choices in many areas of living, but their specific choices of romantic partners are no more alike than choices made by unrelated random pairs. From these data, Lykken and Tellegen concluded that romantic infatuation, and associated choices of spouses, is "inherently random, in the same sense as is imprinting in precocial birds" (p. 56).

Missing in Action?

Several lines of initiation research are conspicuous in their absence. Some are virtually missing from the empirical research literature. Well prior to 1985, relationship researchers noted the need for treating relationships in developmental terms (e.g., Duck & Allison, 1978). If relationships are developmental processes extending past the sophomore year of college, then where is the empirical research on relationship initiation among persons younger and older than college sophomores? Research on adolescent relationships and romance is now underway, and shows promise for expanding understanding of relationships in general (Furman & Simon, 2006; Jensen-Campbell, & Graziano, 2000; McLean & Thorne, 2003; Thorne & Michaelieu, 1996). On the other side of the sophomore divide, as adults live longer and healthier lives, their relationships can include more initiation events than they received in the past. Redirecting attention toward persons of younger and older ages is not merely a matter of external validity, but of construct validity (Moorman, Booth, & Fingerman, 2006). We may learn a great deal about initiation per se by studying persons of various ages. For one example, how critical is the prospect of rejection for initiation (Hatfield & Sprecher, 1986, p. 308)? It is conceivable that older persons may appear to move faster through initiation phases than do younger persons because (a) they have more experience with relationships, (b) they have more experience with rejection, and (c) they spend more time in reconnaissance from a distance to estimate the prospects for rejection. Paul at age 35 spends more time observing Martha from a distance before initiating a relationship with her than does Paul at age 17 with his 17-year-old Martha. The former has more experience with relationships, can anticipate the prospects for rejection, and yet may be more willing to risk rejection than would his younger persona. For another example, what is the impact of drugs like sildenafil (Viagra) on relationships among older couples? How might its use enhance or undermine established relationships or initiate new ones (Tomlinson & Wright, 2004)?

Turning to another point in the life cycle, adolescent romance may be more traumatic and volatile than corresponding romances in young adults because adolescents have not yet developed skills in coping with rejection (e.g., Furman & Simon, 2006; Schulman & Scharf, 2000). In turn, the development of adequate coping skills may influence not only the frequency and pattern of relationship initiation but also the way relationships are conceptualized. As of June 2007, research shows that rejection (and presumably its anticipation) is nearly universally a reflex, which is not moderated by any individual difference or contextual moderators (e.g., rejection by despised groups is still painful). For a review, see Williams (2007). It is possible, however, that the link between anticipation of rejection and relationship initiation is moderated by processes connected to the age and developmental level of the participants.

Other topics are missing here due to limitations in space. This review does not include potentially important lines of work on the issue of mutuality and reciprocity in attraction, despite its potential relevance to relationship initiation. In part it was omitted because the recent literature focuses on the maintenance phase of relationships (e.g., Shackelford et al., 2005). Apparently, persons married for 3 years place more importance on having an agreeable partner than do newlyweds. This review does not include work on age preferences, the role of parental influence, or arranged versus self-selected relationships.

CONCLUSIONS AND FUTURE DIRECTIONS: FOOTPRINTS IN THE SANDS OF TIME

Research and theory on relationships changed focus dramatically in the period from 1985 to 2007, and this affected the literature on relationship initiation. Two major theories—namely, attachment theory and evolutionary psychology—changed the relationship landscape. The unidimensional attitude approach seemed too narrow to encompass the range of initiation phenomena supposedly within its theater of operation. New theories refocused not only on variables like waist-to-hip ratios but also on alternative interpretations of classic variables like physical attractiveness, similarity, and dominance. Methodological advances by David Kenny and his colleagues helped researchers to study interdependency in new ways, and this opened the door to scientifically sound work outside the laboratory on existing relationships.

With the wisdom of hindsight, we see that the post-1985 changes were part of more general changes in the superordinate fields that employed attraction and relationship researchers. It was supplanted but not replaced by a field called *close relationships*. With this shift came a corresponding redirection of attention toward the maintenance phase of relationships and away from initiation. Once attention was shifted toward maintenance, variables concerning the quality of existing relationships (e.g., satisfaction, ambivalence, and feeling overjoyed) came to the fore. An affirmative assessment is that theory and research on relationship initiation are more integrative, sophisticated, and mature now than they were a mere 25 years ago.

Despite the major changes, initiation continued to be an active area for relationship researchers. Patterns of empirical publications suggest important continuities with the pre-1985 literature on interpersonal attraction and relationship initiation. Variables like physical attractiveness and similarity continue to be topics of high-quality experimental research (e.g., Chen & Kenrick, 2002; Sprecher, 1998). Current researchers find that some variables uncovered in the past still cannot be ignored.

In sheer numbers of papers, correlational and observation studies dominate the post-1985 literature. Given the putative decline in interest in laboratory experiments on unacquainted college-age strangers using attitude-based approaches, these kinds of studies should be as rare as dodo birds in current issues of top journals. That appears not to be the case, however. In the *Journal of Experimental Social Psychology*, a rigorous social-cognition-oriented journal not noted historically for its commitment to relationship research, empirical studies on classic issues in initiation continue to appear (e.g., Greitemeyer, 2007). In 2006, the most recent year with full data, 77 articles were published in that journal, and a minimum of 8 studies clearly involved relationship initiation in one form or another (e.g., Kiefer, Sekaquaptewa, & Barczyk, 2006). The number would be considerably larger if studies of social-cognitive and interpersonal processes relevant to relationship initiation were added (e.g., Dijksterhuis & van Olden, 2006). These quasi-impressionistic numbers are open to many different interpretations, of course. It would require systematic tallies to reach firm conclusions. At the least, we can infer that when used with appropriate scientific sobriety and creativity, laboratory experiments and the attitude approach have more merits for relationship research, especially its initiation phase, than was recognized by critics in 1985.

There is much to recommend an experimental approach in relationships research, but some phenomena associated with the dark side of relationships (e.g., stalking; Spitzberg & Cupach, 2007) probably will remain forever out of reach of randomized experiments due to ethical considerations. Even for phenomena within bounds, researchers need to show greater imagination in their implementation, thinking beyond small-scale laboratory experiments of unacquainted college sophomores. Future initiation research must move past antiquated paper-and-pencil surveys, and come to grips with the computer and technology revolution. Some of the most obvious areas for initiation research are computer-based matching services like eHarmony (Carter & Snow, 2004; Gonzaga, Campos, & Bradbury, 2007), and speed dating (Finkel et al., 2007). Technological advances offer other new phenomena as well as opportunities for theory development. In the past 10 years, computers promoted relationship initiation with a wider range of persons, with less threat of overt rejection, than in the past. Both of these variables (availability of alternative options, and rejection potential) are important in relationship initiation. Do technology-based approaches to initiation alter outcomes only quantitatively (more options = less commitment), or do they create qualitative differences even in things as basic as sex roles and shyness (e.g., Scharlott & Christ, 1995)?

Forecasting future patterns is hazardous. Nevertheless, some predictions seem safe. New research will continue the 1985 to 2007 trends away from narrow theories and toward increasingly broad, process-oriented theories that provide more integration. Research on initiation should be integrated increasingly into related processes at the maintenance, decline, and repair stages. Within this pattern, more attention will be paid to the matter of processes underlying *transition* from the initiation phase to the maintenance phase. We already have clues as to why some relationships die on the vine, and others endure for long periods (e.g., Sprecher & Felmlee, 2000). Clues are foundational first steps, however; they are not explanations. The next steps will involve identifying the specific processes that are generating these clues.

Here the forecast becomes speculative. The current research literature has matured to the point where it should move past the intuitive to the theoretical level. In the early development of a research area, it is valuable to have studies demonstrating nearly intuitive ideas like, say, agreeable people are well liked, or persons with anxious attachment initiate relationships in different ways, and have less satisfactory relationships, compared with persons who are securely attached. These studies show that at least some part of everyday phenomenology matches a scientific regularity. The literature is mature enough now, however, to venture more boldly into the unknown. For one example, at this point in a chapter a reader might expect to see the usual call for more research on relationships as they extend over time. This call has been long-standing in the area (e.g., Berscheid, 1985; Berscheid & Graziano, 1979; Duck & Allison, 1978), but is one that has been acknowledged more than actually implemented (Reis, 2007). Implicitly, the initiation of a process must precede in time the maintenance of that same process. How would we study the important processes of transition without some prior state? Processes do unfold over time, and it is intuitive that prior events condition subsequent ones. Causes must precede effects (except for superheroes). However, a prior event is not necessarily a causal event, even if the prior regularly precedes the posterior. This caveat is especially important in correlational research. Some (but not all) girls coming from father-absent homes are more likely to develop relaxed attitudes toward casual sex, but to assert that father absence causes later relaxed sexual attitudes in girls is imprudent in the absence of other evidence. Some (but not all) boys exposed to "harsh punishment" as children are more likely to use coercive conflict tactics in later relationships, but to assert that harsh punishment causes later use of coercive tactics requires more than an antecedent–consequent correlation.

It is certainly valuable to study some relationship processes over time, but implicit assumptions may blind us to other possibilities (e.g., McGuire, 1997). Virtually all of our theorizing about relationship initiation assumes that time variables are critical. Perhaps the temporal sequence view and its assumption that initiation and maintenance are part of the "same process" or even related processes are incorrect. What is less intuitive is that in taking a process approach to relationships, researchers build time into the formula implicitly. Processes need time to unfold. It is the process, not the time per se, that is important. The temporal sequence might be unimportant as long as the critical process is triggered (Lewin, 1943). Now researchers have an opportunity to examine these and other implicit assumptions. For example, motivational accounts assume that some prior need state activates, directs, and maintains subsequent goal seeking. Commitment is a motivational variable that appears to require time to unfold. It is commonly absent at the initiation phase. Exactly what time-dependent processes initiate, support, or undermine the development of commitment to a relationship? Is it merely that time permits dawning recognition of "sunken costs," or are psychological and social processes critical (Agnew et al., in press; Watson et al., 2004)? How much time does it take to begin thinking about sunken costs? Even then, what is the necessary time interval to expect an effect after a putative cause in a relationship?

Consistent with Kelley et al. (2003), Cunningham (personal communication, 2007) hypothesized that relationships involved learning, and some of the most important learning processes needed repetition across time to consolidate. Taking this perspective, relationships are similar to large "habit complexes." It is not so much that people stay in relationships because of sunken costs, but because habits are difficult to break ("I've grown accustomed to your face"). Cairns (1966) offered a related approach for the development of most animate and inanimate attachments. The larger point here is that there is an opportunity to move past the intuitive, implicit approach and toward more refined theoretical analyses of initiation processes.

One strategy is to use research heuristics (McGuire, 1997) as a tool for theory development. For example, one heuristic is to take an established proposition, and examine when (if ever) its opposite might be true. In effect, this forced researchers to make implicit assumptions explicit. When will persons who are anxiously attached have *better* relationships than their peers? When will positive prior states be associated with *negative* outcomes, and vice versa? What theoretical process will explain the pattern of effects? This is the situation in which experimental studies are most valuable. The challenge then is to explain how the established proposition and its opposite are both true. Work of this sort advances a literature more quickly than does confirmation of intuitive propositions.

All this being said, the literature of the future will contain studies of relationship initiation processes extended over time. Some of these will test causal hypotheses with experimental studies. If we learned anything from the past research, it is that small laboratory studies by themselves do not provide a complete picture; researchers need to maintain a broad scope. To do so, the studies will probably look increasingly like interventions or full-scale randomized clinical trials used in epidemiology and public health. To gain support for such expensive research, sources of funding will need to be identified. One possibility is that relationship processes in general could be connected explicitly to important health outcomes. For example, is success in making a transition from the initiation phase to the maintenance phase associated uniquely with health-preserving outcomes, such as reductions in health-threatening levels of cortisol, cholesterol, or other hormones? The field is seeing only the tip of an iceberg on this issue.

It is hard not to be excited about the prospects facing researchers in relationship initiation. Conceptual and methodological changes provide opportunities for new lines of work. Conceptual and methodological advances allowed researchers to examine relationships, including their initiation, in new ways. These new perspectives will allow us to develop more sophisticated, comprehensive explanations for relationship phenomena so critically important to human life. The future looks brighter than even Berscheid (1985) anticipated.

AUTHOR NOTE

We thank Christopher R. Agnew, Eli J. Finkel, Lauri A. Jensen-Campbell, C. Raymond (Chip) Knee, and Rowland Spence (Rody) Miller for their thoughtful comments on earlier versions of this chapter. They do not necessarily endorse material discussed in this chapter.

NOTES

1. Using PsycINFO and keyword search, the number of entries for *initial attraction* for 1986 to 2007, restricting to English language and human participants, was 34,770. The corresponding number for *interpersonal attraction* was 503.
2. According to the *DSM-IV*, one of the distinctive characteristics of Axis II personality disorders is their common symptom of relationship difficulties, often at the initiation phase (American Psychiatric Association, 1994). Whether such disorders are primarily a cause or an effect of relationship initiation difficulties remains unclear, but in either case, they underline the importance of basic relationship processes in adjustment.

REFERENCES

Agnew, C. R., Arriaga, X. B., & Wilson, J. E. (In press). Committed to what? Using the bases of relational commitment model to understand continuity and changes in social relationships. In J. P. Forgas & J. Fitness (Eds.), *Social relationships: Cognitive, affective and motivational processes*. New York: Psychology Press.

Alley, T. R., & Cunningham, M. R. (1991). Averaged faces are attractive, but very attractive faces are not average. *Psychological Science, 2*, 123–125.

Ambady, N., Hallahan, M., & Rosenthal, R. (1995). On judging and being judged accurately in zero-acquaintance situations. *Journal of Personality and Social Psychology, 69*, 518–529.

American Psychiatric Association. (1994). *Diagnostic and statistical manual of mental disorders* (4th ed.). Washington, DC: Author.

Aron, A., & Aron, E. N. (1986). *Love and the expansion of self: Understanding attraction and satisfaction.* New York: Hemisphere/Harper & Row.

Aron, A., Aron, E. N., Tudor, M., & Nelson, G. (1991). Close relationships as including others in the self. *Journal of Personality and Social Psychology, 60*, 241–253.

Aron, A., Steele, J., Kashdan, T. B., & Perez, M. (2006). When similars do not attract: Test of a prediction from the self-expansion model. *Personal Relationships, 13*, 387–396.

Aronson, E. (1969). Some antecedents of interpersonal attraction. In W. J. Arnold & D. Levine (Eds.), *Nebraska symposium on motivation* (Vol. 17, pp. 143–177). Lincoln: University of Nebraska Press.

Aronson, E., & Carlsmith, J. M. (1968). Experimentation in social psychology. In G. Lindzey & E. Aronson (Eds.), *Handbook of social psychology* (2nd ed., Vol. 2, pp. 1–79). Reading, MA: Addison Wesley.

Baron, R. M., & Kenny, D. A. (1986). The moderator-mediator variable distinction in social psychological research: Conceptual, strategic, and statistical considerations. *Journal of Personality and Social Psychology, 51*, 1173–1182.

Berry, D. (1992). Vocal types and stereotypes: Joint effects of vocal attractiveness and vocal maturity on person perception. *Journal of Nonverbal Behavior, 16*, 41–54.

Berry, D. S. (2000). Attractiveness, attraction and sexual selection: Evolutionary perspectives on the form and function of physical attractiveness. In M. P. Zanna (Ed.), *Advances in experimental social psychology* (Vol. 32, pp. 273–343). San Diego, CA: Academic Press.

Berscheid, E. S. (1985). Interpersonal attraction. In G. Lindzey & E. Aronson (Eds.), *Handbook of social psychology* (3rd ed., Vol. 2, pp. 413–483). New York: Random House.

Berscheid, E., Brothen, T., & Graziano, W. G. (1976). Gain/loss theory and the "law of infidelity": Mr. Doting vs. the admiring stranger. *Journal of Personality and Social Psychology, 33*, 709–718.

Berscheid, E. S., & Graziano, W. G. (1979). The initiation of social relations and social attraction. In R. L. Burgess & T. L. Huston (Eds.), *Social exchange in developing relationships.* (pp. 31–60). New York: Academic Press.

Berscheid, E., Graziano, W. G., Monson, T., & Dermer, M. (1976). Outcome dependency: Attention, attraction, and attribution. *Journal of Personality and Social Psychology, 34*, 978–989.

Berscheid, E. S., & Walster, E. (1974). A little bit about love. In T. L Huston (Ed.), *Foundations of interpersonal attraction* (pp. 355–381). New York: Academic Press.

Berscheid, E. S., & Walster, E. (1978). *Interpersonal attraction* (2nd ed.). Reading, MA: Addison Wesley.

Bogg, R. A., & Ray, J. M. (2006). The heterosexual appeal of socially marginal men. *Deviant Behavior, 27*, 457–477.

Burgess, R. L., & Huston, T. L. (Eds.). (1979). *Social exchange in developing relationships*. New York: Academic Press.

Buss, A. (1986). Dominance. In A. Buss (Ed.), *Social behavior and personality.* (pp. 51–74). Hillsdale, NJ: Lawrence Erlbaum.

Buss, D. (1989). Sex differences in human mate selection: Evolutionary hypotheses tested in 37 cultures. *Behavioral and Brain Sciences, 12*, 1–49.

Buss, D. (1995). Evolutionary psychology: A new paradigm for psychological science. *Psychological Inquiry, 6*, 1–30.

Buss, D. (1999). *Evolutionary psychology: The new science of the mind.* Needham Heights, MA: Allyn & Bacon.

Buss, D. (2004). Sex differences in human mate preferences: Evolutionary hypotheses tested in 37 cultures. In H. Reis & C. Rusbult (Eds.), *Close relationships: Key readings* (pp. 135–151). Philadelphia: Taylor & Francis.

Buss, D. M., & Schmitt, D. P. (1993). Sexual strategies theory. *Psychological Review, 100*, 204–232.

Byrne, D. (1971). *The attraction paradigm*. New York: Academic Press.

Byrne, D. (1997). An overview (and underview) of research and theory within the attraction paradigm. *Journal of Social and Personal Relationships, 14*, 417–431.

Cairns, R. B. (1966). Attachment behavior of mammals. *Psychological Review, 72,* 409–426.

Carter, S., & Snow, C. (2004, May). *Helping singles enter better marriages using predictive models of marital success.* Paper presented the 16th annual meeting of the American Psychological Society.

Chen, F. F., & Kenrick, D. T. (2002). Repulsion or attraction? Group membership and assumed attitudinal similarity. *Journal of Personality and Social Psychology, 83,* 111–125.

Clark, C. L., Shaver, P. R., & Abrahams, M. F. (1999). Strategic behaviors in romantic relationship initiation. *Personality and Social Psychology Bulletin, 25,* 707–720.

Clark, M. S., & Mills, J. (1991). Reactions to and willingness to express emotion in communal and exchange relationships. *Journal of Experimental Social Psychology, 27,* 324–336.

Clark, M. S., Mills, J., & Powell, M. C. (1986). Keeping track of needs in communal and exchange relationships. *Journal of Personality and Social Psychology, 51,* 333–338.

Clark, M. S., & Pataki, S. P. (1995). Interpersonal processes influencing attraction and relationships. In A. Tesser (Ed.), *Advanced social psychology* (pp. 283–332). New York: McGraw-Hill.

Clore, G. L., & Byrne, D. (1974). A reinforcement-affect model of attraction. In T. L Huston (Ed.), *Foundations of interpersonal attraction* (pp. 143–170). New York: Academic Press.

Cooper, J., Zanna, M. P., & Goethals, G. R. (1974). Mistreatment of an esteemed other as a consequence affecting dissonance reduction. *Journal of Experimental Social Psychology, 10,* 224–233.

Crandall, C. S. (1994). Prejudice against fat people: Ideology and self-interest. *Journal of Personality and Social Psychology, 66,* 882–894.

Crawford, M., Skowronski, J. J., & Stiff, C. (2007). Limiting the spread of spontaneous trait inference. *Journal of Experimental Social Psychology, 43,* 466–472.

Cunningham, M. R. (1986). Measuring the physical in physical attractiveness: Quasi-experiments on the sociobiology of female facial beauty. *Journal of Personality and Social Psychology, 50,* 925–935.

Cunningham, M. R. (1989). Reactions to heterosexual opening gambits: Female selectivity and male responsiveness. *Personality and Social Psychology Bulletin, 15,* 27–41.

Cunningham, M. R., Barbee, A. P., & Pike, C. L. (1990). What do women want? Faciometric assessment of multiple motives in the perception of male physical attractiveness. *Journal of Personality and Social Psychology, 59,* 61–72.

Cunningham, M. R., Druen, P. B., & Barbee, A. P. (1997). Angels, mentors, and friends: Trade-offs among evolutionary, social and individual variables in physical appearance. In J. A. Simpson & D. T. Kenrick (Eds.), *Evolutionary social psychology* (pp. 109–140). Mahwah, NJ: Lawrence Erlbaum.

Cunningham, M. R., Roberts, A. R., Wu, C-H., Barbee, A. P., & Druen, P. B. (1995). "Their ideas of beauty are, on the whole, the same as ours": Consistency and variability in the cross-cultural perception of female physical attractiveness. *Journal of Personality and Social Psychology, 68,* 261–279.

Cunningham, M. R., Shamblen, S. R., Ault, L. K., & Barbee, A. P. (2005). Social allergies in romantic relationships: Behavioral repetition, emotional sensitization, and dissatisfaction in dating couples. *Personal Relationships, 12,* 273–296.

Dermer, M., & Thiel, R. (1975). When beauty may fail. *Journal of Personality and Social Psychology, 31,* 1168–1176.

Devine, P. (1995). Prejudice and out-group perception. In A. Tesser (Ed.), *Advanced social psychology* (pp. 467–524). New York: McGraw-Hill.

Dijksterhuis, A., & van Olden, Z. (2006). On the benefits of thinking unconsciously: Unconscious thought can increase post-choice satisfaction. *Journal of Experimental Social Psychology, 42,* 627–631.

Duck, S., & Allison, D. (1978). I liked you but I can't live with you: A study of lapsed friendships. *Social Behavior and Personality, 6,* 43–47.

Eagly, A., Ashmore, R. D., Makhijani, M., & Longo, L. C. (1991). What is beautiful is good, but … : A meta-analytic review of research on the physical attractiveness stereotype. *Psychological Bulletin, 110,* 109–128.

Edwards, J. R., & Lambert, L. S. (2007). Methods for integrating moderation and mediation: A general analytical framework using moderated path analysis. *Psychological Methods, 12,* 1–22.

Finkel, E., Eastwick, P. W., & Matthews, J. (2007). Speed-dating as an invaluable tool for studying romantic attraction: A methodological primer. *Personal Relationships, 14,* 149–166.

Furman, W., & Simon, V. A. (2006). Actor and partner effects of adolescents' romantic working models and styles on interactions with romantic partners. *Child Development, 77,* 588–604.

Gangestad, S. W. (1993). Sexual selection and physical attractiveness: Implications for mating dynamics. *Human Nature, 4,* 205–235.

Gangestad, S. W., Garver-Apgar, C. E., & Simpson, J. A. (2007). Changes in women's mate preferences across the ovulatory cycle. *Journal of Personality and Social Psychology, 92,* 151–163.

Gangestad, S., & Snyder, M. (1985). To carve nature at its joints: On the existence of distinct classes in personality. *Psychological Review, 92*, 317–349.

Gangestad, S. W., Thornhill, R., & Yeo, R. A. (1994). Facial attractiveness, developmental stability, and fluctuating asymmetry. *Ethology and Sociobiology, 15*, 73–85.

Gangestad, S. W., & Thornhill, R. (1997). Human sexual selection and developmental stability. In J. A. Simpson & D. T. Kenrick (Eds.), *Evolutionary social psychology* (pp. 169–198). Mahwah, NJ: Lawrence Erlbaum.

Gardner, R. C. (1994). Stereotypes as consensual beliefs. In M. P. Zanna & J. M. Olson (Eds.), *The psychology of prejudice: The Ontario Symposium* (Vol. 7, pp. 1–31). Hillsdale, NJ: Lawrence Erlbaum.

Gonzaga, G. C., Campos, B., & Bradbury, T. (2007). Similarity, convergence, and relationship satisfaction in dating and married couples. *Journal of Personality and Social Psychology, 93*, 34–48.

Graziano, W. G., Bruce, J. W., Sheese, B., & Tobin, R. M. (2007). Attraction, personality, and prejudice: Liking none of the people most of the time. *Journal of Personality and Social Psychology, 93*(4), 565–581.

Graziano, W. G., & Bryant, W. H. (1998). Self-monitoring and the self-attribution of positive emotions. *Journal of Personality and Social Psychology, 74*, 250–261.

Graziano, W. G., Jensen-Campbell, L. A., & Hair, E. C. (1996). Perceiving interpersonal conflict and reacting to it: The case for agreeableness. *Journal of Personality and Social Psychology, 70*, 820–835.

Graziano, W. G., Jensen-Campbell, L., Shebilske, L., & Lundgren, S. (1993). Social influence, sex differences, and judgments of beauty: Putting the "interpersonal" back in interpersonal attraction. *Journal of Personality and Social Psychology, 65*, 522–531.

Graziano, W. G., Jensen-Campbell, L. A., Todd, M., & Finch, J. F. (1997). Interpersonal attraction from an evolutionary perspective: Women's reactions to dominant and prosocial men. In J. A. Simpson & D. T. Kenrick (Eds.), *Evolutionary social psychology* (pp. 141–168). Mahwah, NJ: Lawrence Erlbaum.

Graziano, W. G., & Tobin, R. M. (2002). Agreeableness: Dimension of personality or social desirability artifact? *Journal of Personality, 70*, 695–727.

Graziano, W. G., & Waschull, S. B. (1995). Social development and self-monitoring. In N. Eisenberg (Ed), *Social development* (pp. 233–260). Thousand Oaks, CA: Sage

Greitemeyer, T. (2007). What do men and women want in a partner? Are educated partners always more desirable? *Journal of Experimental Social Psychology, 43*, 180–194.

Griffin, A. M., & Langlois, J. H. (2006). Stereotype directionality and attractiveness stereotyping: Is beauty good or is ugly bad? *Social Cognition, 24*, 187–206.

Griffith, W. (1974). Attitude similarity and attraction. In T. L. Huston (Ed.), *Foundations of interpersonal attraction* (pp. 285–308). New York: Academic Press.

Hatfield, E., & Sprecher, S. (1986). *Mirror, mirror … the importance of looks in everyday life*. Albany: State University of New York Press.

Hatfield, E., Utne, M., & Traupmann, J. (1979). Equity theory and intimate relationships. In R. L. Burgess & T. L. Huston (Eds.), *Social exchange in developing relationships* (pp. 99–133). New York: Academic Press.

Hazan, C., & Shaver, P. (1987). Romantic love conceptualized as an attachment process. *Journal of Personality and Social Psychology, 52*, 511–524.

Heider, F. (1958). *The psychology of interpersonal relations*. New York: Wiley.

Higgins, E. T. (2006). Value from hedonic experience and engagement. *Psychological Review, 113*, 439–460.

Hofstee, W. K. B. (1994). Who should own the definition of personality? *European Journal of Personality, 8*, 149–162.

Homans, G. C. (1974). *Social behavior: Its elementary forms* (Rev. ed.). New York: Harcourt, Brace, & Jovanovich.

Howard, J., Blumstein, P., & Schwartz, P. (1987). Social or evolutionary theories? Some observations on preferences in human mate selection. *Journal of Personality and Social Psychology, 53*, 194–200.

Huston, T. L. (Ed.). (1974). *Foundations of interpersonal attraction*. New York: Academic Press.

Jamieson, D. W., Lydon, J. E., & Zanna, M. P. (1987). Attitude and activity preference similarity: Differential bases of interpersonal attraction for low and high self-monitors. *Journal of Personality and Social Psychology, 53*, 1052–1060.

Jensen-Campbell, L. A., & Graziano, W. G. (2000). Beyond the schoolyard: Relationships as moderators of daily interpersonal conflict. *Personality and Social Psychology Bulletin, 26*, 923–935.

Jensen-Campbell, L. A., Graziano, W. G., & West, S. G. (1995). Dominance, prosocial orientation, and female preferences: Do nice guys really finish last? *Journal of Personality and Social Psychology, 68*, 427–440.

Jones, E. E., & Davis, K. E. (1965). From acts to dispositions: The attribution process in person perception. In L. Berkowitz (Ed.), *Advances in experimental social psychology* (Vol. 2, pp. 141–182). New York: Academic Press.

Jost, J. T., Glaser, J., Kruglanski, A. W., & Sulloway, F. J. (2003). Exceptions that prove the rule—using a theory of motivated social cognition to account for ideological incongruities and political anomalies: Reply to Greenberg and Jonas (2003). *Psychological Bulletin, 129,* 383–393.

Kalick, S. M., Zebrowitz, L. A., Langlois, J. H., & Johnson, R. M. (1998). Does human facial attractiveness honestly advertise health? Longitudinal data on an evolutionary question. *Psychological Science, 9,* 8–13.

Kashy, D. A., & Kenny, D. A. (2000). The analysis of data from dyads and groups. In Harry T. Reis & Charles M. Judd (Eds.), *Handbook of research methods in social and personality psychology* (pp. 451–477). New York: Cambridge University Press.

Kelley, H. H. (1967). Attribution theory in social psychology. In D. Levine (Ed.), *Nebraska symposium on motivation* (Vol. 15, pp. 192–238). Lincoln: University of Nebraska Press.

Kelley, H. H. (1991). Lewin, situations, and interdependence. *Journal of Social Issues, 47,* 211–233.

Kelley, H. H., Berscheid, E. S., Christiansen, A., Harvey, J., Huston, T., Levinger, G., et al. (1983). *Close relationships.* New York: Freeman.

Kelley, H. H., Holmes, J. G., Kerr, N., Reis, H. T., Rusbult, C. E., & Van Lange, P. A. M. (2003). *An atlas of interpersonal situations.* Cambridge: Cambridge University Press.

Kelley, H. H., & Thibaut, J. (1978). *Interpersonal relations: A theory of interdependence.* New York: Wiley.

Kenny, D. A. (1994). Using the social relations model to understand relationships. In R. Erber & R. Gilmour (Eds.), *Theoretical frameworks for personal relationships* (pp. 111–127). Hillsdale, NJ: Lawrence Erlbaum.

Kenny, D. A., Horner, C., Kashy, D. A., & Chu, L. C. (1992). Consensus at zero acquaintance: Replication, behavioral cues, and stability. *Journal of Personality and Social Psychology, 62,* 88–97.

Kenny, D. A., Kashy, D. A., & Cook, W. L. (2006). *Dyadic data analysis.* New York: Guilford.

Kenny, D. A., & La Voie, L. (1984). The social relations model. In L. Berkowitz (Ed.), *Advances in experimental social psychology* (Vol. 18, pp. 141–182). Orlando, FL: Academic Press.

Kenrick, D. (1994). Evolutionary social psychology: From sexual selection to social cognition. In M. P. Zanna (Ed.), *Advances in experimental social psychology* (Vol. 26, pp. 75–118). San Diego, CA: Academic Press.

Kenrick, D., Keffe, R. C., Bryan, A., Barr, A., & Brown, C. (1995). Age preferences and mate choices among homosexuals and heterosexuals: A case for modular psychological mechanisms. *Journal of Personality and Social Psychology, 69,* 1166–1172.

Kenrick, D. T., & Simpson, J. A. (1997). Why social psychology and evolutionary psychology need one another. In J. A. Simpson & D. T. Kenrick (Eds.), *Evolutionary social psychology* (pp. 1–20). Mahwah, NJ: Lawrence Erlbaum.

Kiefer, A., Sekaquaptewa, D., & Barczyk, A. (2006). When appearance concerns make women look bad: Solo status and body image concerns diminish women's academic performance. *Journal of Experimental Social Psychology, 42,* 78–86.

Klohnen, E., & Luo, S. (2003). Interpersonal attraction and personality: What is attractive—self-similarity, ideal similarity, complementarity or attachment security? *Journal of Personality and Social Psychology, 85,* 709–722.

Knee, C. (1998). Implicit theories of relationships: Assessment and prediction of romantic relationship initiation, coping, and longevity. *Journal of Personality and Social Psychology, 74,* 360–370.

Langlois, J. H., Kalakanis, L., Rubenstein, A. J., Larson, A., Hallam, M., & Smoot, M. (2000). Maxims or myths of beauty? A meta-analytic and theoretical review. *Psychological Bulletin, 126,* 390–423.

Langlois, J., & Roggman, L. (1990). Attractive faces are only average. *Psychological Science, 1,* 115–121.

Langlois, J. H., Roggman, L., & Musselman, L. (1994). What is average and what is not average about attractive faces? *Psychological Science, 5,* 214–220.

Leck, K., & Simpson, J. (1999). Feigning romantic interest: The role of self-monitoring. *Journal of Research in Personality, 33,* 69–91.

Lemay, E. P., Clark, M. S., & Feeney, B. C. (2007). Projection of responsiveness to needs and the construction of satisfying communal relationships. *Journal of Personality and Social Psychology, 92,* 834–853.

Leone, C., & Hawkins, L. B. (2006). Self-monitoring and close relationships. *Journal of Personality, 74,* 739–778.

Lewin, K. (1943). Defining the field at a given time. *Psychological Review, 50,* 292–310.

Lundy, D. E., Tan, J., & Cunningham, M. R. (1998). Heterosexual romantic preferences: The importance of humor and physical attractiveness for different types of relationships. *Journal of Social and Personal Relationships, 5,* 311–325.

Lykken, D. T., & Tellegen, A. (1993). Is human mating adventitious or the result of lawful choice? A twin study of mate selection. *Journal of Personality and Social Psychology, 65,* 56–68.

Madey, S. F., Simo, M., Dillworth, D., Kemper, D., Toczynski, S., & Perella, A. (1996). They do get more attractive at closing time, but only when you are not in a relationship. *Basic and Applied Social Psychology, 18*, 387–393.

Marcus, D. K., & Cunningham, M. R. (2003). Do child molesters have aberrant perceptions of adult female facial attractiveness? *Journal of Applied Social Psychology, 33*, 99–512.

McArthur, L., & Baron, R. S. (1983). Toward an ecological theory of social perception. *Psychological Bulletin, 90*, 215–238.

McGuire, W. (1997). Creative hypothesis generating in psychology: Some useful heuristics. *Annual Review of Psychology, 48*, 1–30.

McLean, K. C., & Thorne, A. (2003). Adolescents' self-defining memories about relationships. *Developmental Psychology, 39*, 635–645.

Meston, C., & Buss, D. M. (2007). Why humans have sex. *Archives of Sexual Behavior, 36*, 477–507.

Miller, P. J. E., Niehuis, S., & Huston, T. L. (2006). Positive illusions in marital relationships: A 13-year longitudinal study. *Personality and Social Psychology Bulletin, 32*, 1579–1594.

Moore, J. S., Graziano, W. G., & Millar, M. G. (1987). Physical attractiveness, sex role orientation, and the evaluation of adults and children. *Personality and Social Psychology Bulletin, 13*, 95–102.

Moorman, S. M., Booth, A., & Fingerman, K. L. (2006). Women's romantic relationships after widowhood. *Journal of Family Issues, 27*, 1281–1304.

Muscarella, F., & Cunningham, M. R. (1996). The evolutionary significance and social perception of male pattern baldness and facial hair. *Ethology and Sociobiology, 17*, 99–117.

Nelson, T. D. (2002). *The psychology of prejudice.* Boston: Allyn & Bacon.

Newcomb, T. (1956). The prediction of interpersonal attraction. *American Psychologist, 11*, 575–586.

Pennebaker, J. W., Dyer, M. A., Caulkins, R. S., Litowitz, D. L., Ackerman, P. L., Anderson, D. B., et al. (1979). Don't the girls get prettier at closing time: Country and Western application to social psychology. *Personality and Social Psychology Bulletin, 5*, 122–125.

Petty, R. E.., & Cacioppo, J. T. (2006). *Attitudes and persuasion: Classic and contemporary approaches* (2nd ed.). Dubuque, IA: Brown.

Petty, R. E., Tormala, Z. L., Brinol, P. & Jarvis, W. B. G. (2006). Implicit ambivalence from attitude change: An exploration of the PAST model. *Journal of Personality and Social Psychology, 90*, 21–41.

Priester, J. M., & Petty, R. E. (1996). The gradual threshold model of ambivalence: Relating the positive and negative bases of attitudes to subjective ambivalence. *Journal of Personality and Social Psychology, 71*, 431–449.

Priester, J. M., & Petty, R. E. (2001). The gradual threshold model of ambivalence: Relating the positive and negative. Extending the bases of attitudes to subjective attitudinal ambivalence: Interpersonal and intrapersonal antecedents of evaluative tension. *Journal of Personality and Social Psychology, 80*, 19–34.

Reik, T. (1944). *A psychologist looks at love.* New York: Lancer.

Reis, H. T. (2007). Steps toward the ripening of relationship science. *Personal Relationships, 14*, 1–23.

Rhodes, G., Sumich, A., & Byatt, G. (1999). Are average facial configurations attractive only because of their symmetry? *Psychological Science, 10*, 53–59.

Rosenbaum, M. (1986). The repulsion hypothesis: On the nondevelopment of relationships. *Journal of Personality and Social Psychology, 51*, 1156–1166.

Rowatt, W. C., Cunningham, M. R., & Druen, P. B. (1998). Deceptions to get a date: Self-monitoring and strategically modified self-presentation during dating relationship initiation. *Personality and Social Psychology Bulletin, 16*, 209–223.

Rubin, Z. (1974). From liking to loving: Patterns of attraction in dating relationships. In T. L. Huston (Ed.), *Foundations of interpersonal attraction* (pp. 383–402). New York: Academic Press.

Rusbult, C., & Buunk, B. (1993). Commitment processes in close relationships: An interdependence analysis. *Journal of Personal and Social Relationships, 10*, 175–204.

Rusbult, C., & Martz, J. M. (1995). Remaining in an abusive relationship: An investment model analysis of nonvoluntary commitment. *Personality and Social Psychology Bulletin, 21*, 558–571.

Sadalla, E. K., Kenrick, D. T., & Vershure, B. (1987). Dominance and heterosexual attraction. *Journal of Personality and Social Psychology, 52*, 730–738.

Sakaguci, K., Jonsson, G. K., & Hasegawa, T. (2005). Initial interpersonal attraction among mixed-sex dyads and movement synchrony. In L. Anolli, S. Duncan, M. S. Magnusson, & G. Riva (Eds.), *The hidden structure of interaction: From neurons to culture* (pp. 107–121). Amsterdam: AOS Press.

Sanderson, C. A., Keiter, E. J., Miles, M. G., & Yopyk, D. J. (2007). The association between intimacy goals and plans for initiating dating relationships. *Personal Relationships, 14*, 225–244.

Scharlott, B. W., & Christ, W. G. (1995). Overcoming relationship-initiation barriers: The impact of a computer-dating system on sex role, shyness, and appearance inhibitions. *Computers in Human Behavior*, *11*, 191–204.

Schmitt, D. P., Alcalay, L., Allensworth, M., Allik, J., Ault, L., Austers, I., et al. (2004a). Patterns and universals of adult romantic attachment across 62 cultural regions: Are models of self and of other pancultural constructs? *Journal of Cross-Cultural Psychology*, *35*, 367–402.

Schmitt, D. P., Alcalay, L., Allensworth, M., Allik, J., Ault, L., Austers, I., et al. (2004b). Patterns and universals of mate poaching across 53 nations: The effects of sex, culture, and personality on romantically attracting another person's partner. *Journal of Personality and Social Psychology*, *86*, 560–584.

Schulman, S., & Scharf, M. (2000). Adolescent romantic behaviors and perceptions: Age- and gender-related differences, and links with family and peer relationships. *Journal of Research on Adolescence*, *10*, 99–118.

Shackelford, T. K., & Larsen, R. J. (1997). Facial asymmetry as an indicator of psychological, emotional, and physiological distress. *Journal of Personality and Social Psychology*, *72*, 456–466.

Shackelford, T. K., Schmitt, D. P., & Buss, D. M. (2005). Mate preferences of married persons in the newlywed year and three years later. *Cognition and Emotion*, *19*, 1262–1270.

Shadish, W. R., Cook, T. D., & Campbell, D. T. (2002). *Experimental and quasi-experimental designs for generalized causal inference*. Boston: Houghton Mifflin.

Shaver, P., Belsky, J., & Brennan, K. (2000). The adult attachment interview and self-report of romantic attachment: Associations across domains and methods. *Personal Relationships*, *7*, 25–43.

Singh, D. (1993). Adaptive significance of female physical attractiveness: Role of waist-to-hip ratio. *Journal of Personality and Social Psychology*, *65*, 293–307.

Singh, D. (1995). Female judgment of male attractiveness and desirability for relationships: Role of waist-to-hip ratio and financial status. *Journal of Personality and Social Psychology*, *69*, 1089–1101.

Singh, D. (2004). Mating strategies of young women: Role of physical attractiveness. *Journal of Sex Research*, *41*, 43–54.

Singh, D., & Bronstad, P. M. (1997). Sex differences in the anatomical locations of human body scarification and tattooing as a function of pathogen prevalence. *Evolution and Human Behavior*, *18*, 403–416.

Singh, D., & Luis, S. (1995). Ethnic and gender consensus for the effect of waist-to-hip ratio on judgment of women's attractiveness. *Human Nature*, *6*, 51–65.

Snyder, M., Berscheid, E., & Glick, P. (1985). Focusing on the exterior and interior: Two investigations of the initiation of personal relationships. *Journal of Personality and Social Psychology*, *48*, 1427–1439.

Snyder, M., Simpson, J. A., & Gangestad, S. (1986). Personality and sexual relations. *Journal of Personality and Social Psychology*, *51*, 181–190.

Spitzburg, B. H., & Cupach, W. R. (2007). The state of the art of stalking: Taking stock of the emerging literature. *Aggression and Violent Behavior*, *12*, 64–86

Sprecher, S. (1998). Insiders' perspectives on reasons for attraction to a close other. *Social Psychology Quarterly*, *61*, 287–300.

Sprecher, S., & Felmlee, D. (2000). Romantic partners' perceptions of social network attributes with the passage of time and relationship transitions. *Personal Relationships*, *7*, 325–340.

Stone, E. A., Shackelford, T. K., & Buss, D. M. (2007). Sex ratio and mate preferences: A cross-cultural investigation. *European Journal of Social Psychology*, *37*, 288–296.

Swami, V., & Tovee, M. J. (2005). Does hunger influence judgments of female physical attractiveness? *British Journal of Psychology*, *10*, 1348.

Tassinary, L. G., & Hansen, K. A. (1998). A critical test of the waist-to-hip ratio hypothesis of female physical attractiveness. *Psychological Science*, *9*, 150–155.

Thorne, A., & Michaelieu, Q. (1996). Situating adolescent gender and self-esteem with personal memories. *Child Development*, *67*, 1362–1378.

Thornhill, R., & Gangestad, S. (1994). Fluctuating asymmetry and human sexual behavior. *Psychological Science*, *5*, 297–302.

Tjosvold, D., Johnson, D. W., & Johnson, R. (1984). Influence strategy, perspective taking, and relationships between high- and low-power individuals in cooperative and competitive contexts. *Journal of Psychology*, *116*, 187–202.

Tomlinson, J. M., & Wright, D. (2004). Impact of erectile dysfunction and its subsequent treatment with sildenafil: Qualitative study. *BMJ: British Medical Journal*, *328*. Retrieved December 22, 2007, from http://www.bmj.com/cgi/content/full/328/7447/1037

Trivers, R. L. (1972). Parental investment and sexual selection. In B. Campbell (Ed.), *Sexual selection and the decent of man* (pp. 136–179). Chicago: Aldine-Atherton.

Walster, E., Walster, G. W., & Traupmann, J. (1978). Equity and premarital sex. *Journal of Personality and Social Psychology, 36,* 82–92.

Walster, E., Walster, W., & Berscheid, E. (1978). *Equity: Theory and research.* Rockleigh, NJ: Allyn & Bacon.

Watson, D., Klohnen, E. C., Casillias, A., Simms, E. N., Haig, J., & Berry, D. S. (2004). Match makers and deal breakers: Analyses of assortative mating in newlywed couples. *Journal of Personality, 72,* 1029–1068.

Wiggins, J., Conger, J., & Conger, J. C. (1968). Correlates of heterosexual somatic preference. *Journal of Personality and Social Psychology, 10,* 82–90.

Williams, K. D. (2007). Ostracism. *Annual Review of Psychology, 58,* 425–452.

Witt, J. K., Proffitt, D. R., & Epstein, W. (2005). Tool use affects perceived distance but only when you intend to use it. *Journal of Experimental Psychology: Human Perception and Performance, 31,* 880–888.

Zajonc, R. (1968). The attitudinal effect of mere exposure. *Journal of Personality and Social Psychology* (Monograph Supplement 2), 9(Pt. 2), 1–27.

Zajonc, R. (1980). Feeling and thinking: Preferences need no inferences. *American Psychologist, 35,* 151–175.

Zayas, V., & Shoda, Y. (2007). Predicting preferences for dating partners from past experiences of psychological abuse: Identifying the psychological ingredients of situations. *Personality and Social Psychology Bulletin, 33,* 123–138.

Zuckerman, M., Miyake, K., & Hodgins, H. S. (1991). Cross-channel effects of vocal and physical attractiveness and their implications for interpersonal perception. *Journal of Personality and Social Psychology, 60,* 545–554.

15

Insider Perspectives on Attraction

SUSAN SPRECHER and DIANE FELMLEE

INTRODUCTION

Attraction is the essential motive underlying many attempts at relationship initiation. People become attracted to another often based on minimal, visible information and then want to initiate a relationship. Attraction can then escalate if the early interactions involved in relationship initiation are rewarding (e.g., Altman & Taylor, 1973). Attraction is most often conceptualized as an attitude toward another consisting of feelings, cognitions, and behaviors (Berscheid, 1985), and may be experienced in an intense form (romantic, sexual attraction) or a mild form (friendship attraction or liking). This chapter is on the topic of attraction that occurs in the stage of relationship initiation. Attraction to a partner continues at more committed stages, although often it is then referred to as love; see the Aron et al. chapter in this volume on the topic of falling in love.

The study of attraction, at least within social psychology, initially focused on attraction that develops between strangers or between psychology participants and a "bogus other," based on minimal information. When interpersonal attraction was first recognized as a subarea within social psychology in the 1960s and 1970s, the focus was on experiments in which information about an "Other," or the situation, was manipulated. This was referred to as the bogus stranger paradigm (Byrne, 1971). This tradition of research, which continues today, is summarized in Graziano and Bruce (this volume).

This current chapter focuses on some of the same variables manipulated in experimental research, but here we examine people's *beliefs* about how these factors affect attraction. Although people may under- or overestimate the effects of certain factors on their attraction for someone, their accounts or explanations are important to examine because, as explained by Aron, Dutton, Aron, and Iverson (1989), they "probably represent to a significant degree the psychological reality at the time of the event, and this reality often underlies what people do" (p. 254).

In the first section of the chapter, we provide an overview of the various types of determinants of attraction that have been considered in past research from the insider perspective. These include qualities of the Other to whom attraction is experienced, as well as factors such as similarity, proximity, and social network support. Second, we provide methodological detail on how the self-report method can be used to identify determinants of attraction, including a discussion of the advantages and disadvantages of this method relative to others (e.g., the experiment). In the third section, illustrative findings from research on predictors of attraction, using the insider perspective, are presented. We focus more specifically on what insiders *say* are the most important factors that lead to their attraction, and the degree to which there is variation based on relationship type (e.g., friendship versus romantic relationship) and individual characteristics (e.g., gender). In the fourth section, we examine how insiders' reasons for their attraction to someone are associated with their reports on other aspects of the relationship, including trajectories and outcomes in the relationship. In this section, we focus particularly on *fatal attraction*, which refers to the phenomenon in which the qualities that people believe lead to their attraction are related to the reasons that the relationship later has conflict and even results in dissolution. We end the chapter with general conclusions and suggestions for future research.

DETERMINANTS OF ATTRACTION

Various literatures, including the social psychology of general attraction and research on mate selection, include reference to several predictors or determinants of attraction or mate choice. As summarized by Aron et al. (1989), these literatures highlight similarity, propinquity, desirable characteristics of the other, reciprocal liking, social influences (e.g., approval from the social network), and meeting one's needs as determinants of attraction. Aron et al. also identified additional predictors of an intense attraction (falling in love), including arousing situations, specific cues (related to the other), readiness to enter a relationship, isolation from others, and mystery. A psychological phenomenon as complex as attraction will likely be affected by many diverse factors.

Predictors of attraction can be organized according to their primary locus, for example in a person or a situation. Acknowledging different causal sources for attraction, some scholars (e.g., Simpson & Harris, 1994; Sprecher, 1989) have organized the predictors of attraction according to a model developed by a team of prominent scholars of personal relationships (e.g., Kelley et al., 1983), who have argued that the quality of interaction between two people is influenced by four causal factors: P (*person*), O (*other*), P × O, and E (*environmental*) factors.

P factors consist of qualities of the person who potentially experiences attraction for the other. For example, readiness to enter a relationship, strong affiliation needs, and social deficiencies (e.g., shyness) may affect the process of becoming attracted to another (e.g., Simpson & Harris, 1994). O factors, frequently examined in attraction research, are qualities of the other. Some O characteristics are stable internal characteristics of the other (personality characteristics, attitudes, and beliefs). Other O variables are extrinsic characteristics, such as physical attractiveness, wealth, and possessions. Fletcher (e.g., 2002) further divided the ideal characteristics of a partner into three categories: warmth and loyalty (e.g., the partner is understanding, considerate, and sensitive), vitality and attractiveness (e.g., he or she is attractive and outgoing), and status and resources (e.g., the partner has a good job and is successful). Although the focus has primarily been on desirable characteristics of the other (e.g., Aron et al., 1989), Cunningham and his colleagues (e.g., Cunningham, Barbee, & Druen, 1996) have argued that it is important to also examine repulsion to O's negative traits (e.g., annoying habits and traits), which they refer to as social allergens.

P × O variables, unique to the association between P and O, are the third category of causal variables. This causal source, however, can be further divided into two types. One type refers to the intersection between P and O attributes, such as similarity or complementarity. In order to determine whether P and O are similar, the attributes of both P and O must be considered. The other type of P × O causal factor refers to the properties that emerge through their joint interaction, such as quality of communication.

E variables are the final set of causal factors and refer to the environment of P, O, or P and O together. There are two types of environmental variables that can affect attraction. The social environment consists of family and friends surrounding P and O. Family and friends can try to facilitate experiences that lead to attraction, or conversely, they can attempt to hinder attraction from developing between P and O. The second type of E variable is the physical environment, which includes conditions that could contribute to people's good mood (e.g., temperature, sunshine, and/ or pleasant smells) or provide interaction accessibility to each other (e.g., spacing of residence hall rooms). It could also include negative environmental conditions such as bad weather.

Principles from several social psychological theories can explain why P, O, P × O, and E factors lead to attraction (e.g., Berscheid & Reis, 1998; Perlman & Fehr, 1987). According to *reinforcement theories* of interpersonal attraction (e.g., Byrne & Clore, 1970; Lott & Lott, 1974), people will like those who provide rewards, as well as those who are present when the individual experiences rewards. For instance, someone who has desirable qualities is intrinsically rewarding. As another example, meeting someone in an unusual and pleasant situation can be reinforcing and associated with positive affect, which then can become associated with the person who was met in that situation. The emphasis of this theory is on positive affect that is experienced as a result of reinforcement, direct rewards, or association with rewards (e.g., Byrne & Clore, 1970).

Rewards are also central to a *social exchange perspective* (e.g., Thibaut & Kelley, 1959), although they are considered in conjunction with other exchange elements. First, from this perspective, the overall benefit is important, which is rewards minus costs. In addition, the overall benefit is considered relative to a comparison level (CL, or what one expects to receive) and a comparison level for alternatives (CL_{alt}, or what one can expect to receive from alternative others). For example, individuals may become attracted to a person with certain attributes to the degree that they believe that the reward value offered by that person is greater than what they expected to receive and more desirable than any alternatives. According to *equity theory* (e.g., Hatfield, Traupmann, Sprecher, Utne, & Hay, 1984), which shares certain assumptions with traditional exchange theory, certain factors will lead to attraction if they increase the likelihood that the relationship between the two individuals can be equitable. An equitable relationship exists when the ratio between inputs and outcomes for one individual is approximately equal to the ratio between inputs and outcomes for his or her partner. Whereas equity theory has been applied more frequently to ongoing relationships than to the very early stages of relationships, the theory in a basic form predicts that people will become attracted to those others who offer the opportunity of creating a well-matched pair, equal in social worth. This has been referred to as the *matching hypothesis* (Walster [now Hatfield], Aronson, Abrahams, & Rottman, 1966).

Another set of theories of interpersonal attraction focuses on issues of *cognitive consistency and balance*. For example, Newcomb's (1961, 1971) balance theory has been used to explain why both similarity between P and O and positive social support from network members for the couple's relationship can lead to attraction. In both cases, the two people come to like each other because they have a similar relationship or attitude toward an outside object or person. A very different set of theories focuses on *arousal* leading to attraction. People can experience physical arousal due to extraneous sources (e.g., exercise) and label it as attraction to the other (e.g., Berscheid & Walster, 1974; Dutton & Aron, 1974; Schachter, 1964).

More recently, *evolutionary principles* have become popular to explain the association found between some predictors (e.g., physical attractiveness, or wealth) and attraction. According to this perspective, humans become attracted to those whom they believe (subconsciously or consciously) will maximize their opportunities for conception, birth, and survival of their offspring (e.g., Buss, 1989; Fletcher, 2002). The theory argues that people's attraction strategies have evolved through natural selection; that is, the attraction strategies that allowed our ancestors to reproduce and have offspring who survived have been naturally selected (e.g., Buss & Schmitt, 1993). This theory also emphasizes gender differences in predictors of attraction, which arise based on the different reproduction issues faced in humans' ancestral past (for more detail on this theory, see Schmitt, this volume).

Another theory applied to the study of attraction is Aron and Aron's (1986) self-expansion theory. This theory argues that people have a desire to expand themselves, which includes the acquisition of resources, perspectives, and identities. One way to achieve self-expansion is through relationships with others. According to the theory, people become attracted to those who have attributes or resources that are perceived to present opportunities to increase self-expansion. However, in choosing who to approach for a relationship, people consider not only the other's desirability but also the probability that the relationship could develop and therefore offer self-expansion opportunities.

In sum, multiple theories have been used to explain why certain P, O, P × O, and E variables lead to attraction. However, when people are asked to provide an insider perspective to attraction, they are likely to be aware only that they are attracted to a particular set of attributes. They are unlikely to be cognizant of the causes behind their attraction, particularly those in remote or abstract sources (e.g., the evolutionary past).

METHODOLOGICAL ISSUES

There are many methodological approaches that have been used to study attraction. We opened the chapter by referring to the experimental method that was used frequently in the 1960s and 1970s, when the interpersonal attraction subfield in social psychology was in its heyday (Byrne, 1971). The experimental method continues to be used to study issues related to interpersonal attraction (e.g., Lundy, Tan, & Cunningham, 1998). Another approach involved assessments obtained in naturally occurring interactions (e.g., Festinger, Schachter, & Back, 1950; Newcomb, 1961). Alternatively, researchers arranged interaction settings in which pairs of strangers were matched for a date or interaction, and the researchers measured variables (e.g., physical attractiveness) in advance that might predict their attraction for each other (e.g., Byrne, Ervin, & Lamberth, 1970; Sprecher & Duck, 1994; Walster et al., 1966). In both the experiment and the get-acquainted date study, the researcher measures or operationalizes both the independent variable (the predictor variable, such as similarity between P and O) and the dependent variable (P's attraction to O), and examines the association through a statistical test to determine whether the predictor variable affects attraction. We refer to this approach as the *researcher*, or *outsider, perspective on attraction predictors*.

Conversely, this chapter focuses on the *insider perspective on attraction predictors*, assessed through the self-report method. This approach involves asking participants about the association between the independent variable (e.g., the physical attractiveness of the partner) and the dependent variable (e.g., attraction). That is, this method assesses what people say are the reasons they became attracted to another or what factors they believe are associated with their attraction. This approach has sometimes been called the *phenomenology of attraction*. The more specific method described in this chapter also has been called the *retrospective account*, or *report*, *on attraction*. However, we prefer the terminology *self-reports of attraction predictors* because, as we discuss later, the data could be either retrospective or concurrent. Other methods also, to varying degrees, take an insider perspective to predictors of attraction, including mate selection lists (e.g., Sprecher, Sullivan, & Hatfield, 1994) and content analysis of personal want ads (e.g., Koestner & Wheeler, 1988). We focus this chapter, however, specifically on the predictors of attraction in ongoing relationships, which can feasibly be examined only through self-reports provided from insiders.

We do not claim that the insider perspective is inherently better than the researcher (or outsider) perspective for studying determinants of attraction. The two general approaches address distinct issues, and each has its own advantages and disadvantages. We will next highlight what is unique about the self-report method in understanding predictors of attraction, while also acknowledging the disadvantages of this approach.

The Scientific Potential of Self-Reports of Attraction Predictors

Although interpersonal attraction research began in the 1960s with a study of strangers in the laboratory setting, which probably legitimized it as an area of study within social psychology (e.g., Miller, Perlman, & Brehm, 2007), the approach also was quickly criticized for being removed from real relationships. By the 1980s, relationship researchers had shifted from the study of initial interpersonal attraction to the study of ongoing intimate relationships, with all of their complexity. Over the years, the field of initial attraction has remained somewhat separate and overshadowed by the study of close relationships. One advantage of the self-report method to assess attraction predictors within ongoing relationships is that it facilitates a bridge between these two areas of research, initial attraction and close relationships.

Although experiments and get-acquainted interaction studies, with their more objective and outsider approaches to the study of predictors of attraction, are very useful, such methods focus on relationships that do not generally have a future beyond a limited initial interaction or, in some cases, beyond a reaction to a bogus profile. Therefore, the predictors of attraction that are found to be important in such situations may not generalize to predictors of attraction in relationships that have a potential future. Relationships arranged by an experimenter that last one brief interaction may be very different from those that develop naturally and extend into long-term dating relationships, friendships, and even marital unions. Yet, the intimate relationship is what scientists most want to understand.

Relationship scientists have focused on causal factors that influence the relationship at more developed stages, such as why some relationships last and others do not (for a review of this extensive area, see Berscheid & Reis, 1998), but it is also important to examine the causal factors that occur at its very beginning. As noted by Berscheid and Regan (2005),

> [T]o understand why others currently are in the relationships they are—and to understand why we ourselves developed the relationships we did—it is usually necessary to retrace the history of the relationship back to its very beginning and to identify the causal conditions that were in force at that time. (p. 159)

There is generally only one way to retrace the history of the relationship, and that is to ask the members of the relationship how they perceive its history (e.g., Metts, Sprecher, & Cupach, 1991). Why did they initially become attracted to the other? (See also a discussion of retrospective accounts of relationship initiation in Custer, Holmberg, Blair, & Orbuch, this volume.)

Another advantage of examining members' own perspectives of the causes of early attraction in ongoing relationships is that these reports can be linked to later trajectories and outcomes of the relationship. This is an issue that is not possible to examine in experiments and get-acquainted date studies conducted with strangers meeting for the first time, except possibly with the limited subsample of participants who might go on to form a relationship beyond that artificial, initial interaction. Research, however, indicates that only a very small proportion of the participants ever meet again after the researcher-arranged interaction (e.g., Sprecher & Duck, 1994).

The self-report method also has the advantage that a variety of predictors of attraction can be assessed, including from multiple sources (e.g., O factors, P x O factors, and E factors). The experimental study is limited by the number of variables that can be manipulated, which is usually three or fewer. In addition, it is unethical, impractical, or impossible to manipulate some factors, such as the chemistry between the two people or the degree of support from parents for the relationship. These same variables may be difficult to measure or are nonrelevant to the interaction that occurs in the brief encounters of the get-acquainted interaction study. As noted by Berscheid and Regan (2005), however, "It is especially important to identify the environmental conditions under which the relationship was established, because their influence is likely to be overlooked" (p. 159).

The Major Disadvantage of the Self-Report Method in the Study of Predictors of Attraction

Despite the advantages noted above of the insider perspective (i.e., self-report) for studying predictors of attraction, the method is limited by the ability of participants to accurately *remember* and be *aware* of why they experience attraction toward someone. Concerning the issue of awareness, Nisbett and Wilson (1977), in a classic paper on social cognition, noted that people often report on cognitive processes without true introspection. In a series of studies, they found that research participants often cannot accurately explain the causes of their behaviors, although they offer explanations, if asked, often based on common causal theories. These are reasons that are easy to verbalize and that sound plausible. Nisbett and Wilson referred to this phenomenon as "telling more than we can know." In addition, Wilson (2002) described research that found that being asked to analyze the reasons for an affective response can result in the analysis not being predictive of a future outcome.

Second, even if people had insight into the reasons they became attracted to someone at the time they became attracted, they may not be able to accurately recall these reasons when they are asked weeks, months, or years later. Furthermore, research indicates that the current state of the relationship can affect the recall of prior events and feelings (Ross, 1989). More specifically, a person who is currently happy in the relationship may be more likely to recall reasons referring to positive traits of the partner than a person who is currently unhappy in the relationship.

Although participants' retrospective reports of reasons for attraction may not be completely congruent with the factors that actually influence attraction (if there could be an omniscient way of knowing), the insiders' perspective is important to examine. As noted above, because such reports are perceived to represent reality at the time, they can have lasting effects on what people do (Aron et al., 1989). When people tell the story of their relationship, including their get-acquainted initial stage, they may include in the story the reasons they first became attracted to the other. The initiation story, including the reasons, may then affect what they do later in the relationship and the meaning they give to events that occur. For example, in a study of married couples from Michigan (Orbuch, Veroff, & Holmberg, 1993), it was found that talking about the initiation stages of their relationship in a positive tone without romanticism significantly predicted subsequent marital well-being in the third year.

A Primer on the Method

Although the self-report method focuses on the insider perspective to attraction, specific formats of this method vary in the degree to which the insider "voice" is obtained (e.g., Adams, Berggren, Docherty, Ruffin, & Wright, 2006). At one end, the researcher has little control over what responses are obtained from the participants because the questions are asked in an open-ended format. Participants write their account in their own voice, emphasizing what they view to be the reasons for their attraction without any prompts from the researcher. Their reports also could be retained in the data (e.g., original quotes), although more likely the responses are content-analyzed for categories of predictors.

At the other end, the researcher provides a list of predictors (perhaps generated from initial, qualitative, pilot studies), and the participants indicate how important each predictor was in increasing their attraction. Although researcher control is greater in this format, nonetheless the participants are providing an insider perspective of the causal role of predictors of their attraction; thus, it still represents an assessment of attraction predictors from an insider perspective.

Various options also exist for what to include in the directions to the participants. At a minimum, the directions should identify the particular relationship to which they should respond (e.g., current romantic relationship, past romantic relationship, or close friendship), the emotional experience of focus (e.g., attraction, upsurge of attraction, falling in love, or becoming committed), and the time frame (e.g., initial stage, first few weeks of becoming acquainted, or currently). The directions also could provide additional guidance in how to recall relevant information, which may be particularly important for the open-ended format (e.g., Aron et al., 1989).

Although the self-report method is *not* an experimental design, manipulations can be included in the directions. For example, type of relationship could be manipulated if one research goal is to examine whether predictors of attraction vary by type of relationship. Some participants could be asked to report the reasons for attraction in a friendship, and others could be asked about the reasons for attraction in a romantic relationship (Sprecher, 1998a). Such a manipulation makes it possible to examine whether predictors of attraction in the two types of relationships differ, controlling for other factors. The time frame also could be manipulated. For example, participants could be asked to indicate what factors affect either their current attraction or their attraction at an earlier stage (i.e., the initial stage of the relationship). Other manipulations are also possible, including whether the focus is on one's own attraction or what are believed to be the causal factors for the partner's attraction (e.g., Seligman, Fazio, & Zanna, 1980).

Another methodological issue is the type of sample. A researcher may not have access to samples other than college students in a classroom setting or those in a psychology human subject pool. Although samples of college students can be criticized for a number of reasons, young adults can be ideal for research on predictors of initial attraction because they, compared to older adults, are apt to be in a state of initial attraction more frequently. Some research questions, however, may require more diverse samples. For example, if the goal is to examine the insider perspective on factors that contribute to the initiation of attraction in a relationship that ultimately results in marriage, a married sample is needed. Furthermore, if the researcher wants to study predictors of initial attraction but avoid problems of memory bias, a sample could be obtained of individuals who are in an initial stage of becoming acquainted.

There are various ways of obtaining select samples, including contacting a probability sample of a population and then using screening questions, or advertising on a college campus for volunteers who meet certain criteria. Other approaches include distributing a questionnaire to large university classes but using the data only from those who meet the criteria, and obtaining a network or snowball sample based on enlisting the assistance of students as research assistants who then obtain participants from their networks.

If the investigator uses a researcher-generated list of predictors, decisions also need to be made about the final list of items, the order in which the items are presented (including whether the order should be randomized), and the response options. Whereas most existing research focuses only on predictors that are considered to have positive influences on attraction, it also would be possible to include predictors that potentially lead to repulsion or negative attraction, such as annoying habits (see Cunningham et al., 1996).

SAMPLE FINDINGS FROM THE LITERATURE

Research on Predictors of Intense Attraction

Aron et al. (1989) conducted three studies to examine people's accounts of intense attraction or falling in love. They began by reviewing various literatures to identify the major variables that could be classified as predictors of falling in love or an intense attraction. Eleven variables were identified from three types of literature. From the social psychology research on interpersonal attraction, they identified (a) similarity, (b) propinquity, (c) desirable characteristics of the other, and (d) reciprocal liking. They noted that the mate selection literature focuses on similarity and desirable characteristics, and two other variables: (e) social influence, and (f) filling needs. Finally, five other predictors of initial attraction were identified from the smaller literature on falling in love: (g) arousal and/or unusualness, (h) specific cues (about the other), (i) readiness for entry into a relationship, (j) isolation from others, and (k) mystery. The purpose of their research was to examine the relative importance of the various predictors of intense attraction or falling in love (from the insiders' perspective) and to determine whether the predictors of falling in love are different from the predictors of "falling in friendship."

Aron et al.'s (1989) Study 1 consisted of 50 undergraduate students who responded to an advertisement that requested participants who had fallen in love or became strongly attracted to someone within the last 6 to 8 months. The participants were asked to write an account of the experience in as much detail as possible, including explaining what happened just before they felt strong attraction and indicating what they perceived to be the causes of their attraction. References were made in the participants' accounts to all 11 attraction predictors, although there was variation in the number of times each was mentioned. Almost all respondents reported predictors that were coded as reciprocal liking (e.g., "other likes me," "other self-discloses," and "other easy to relate to"; Aron et al., 1989, p. 247) and desirable characteristics (e.g., good looks, or attractive personality traits). Mentioned in one third to two thirds of the accounts were arousal and/or unusualness, readiness, and special cues. The least frequently mentioned factors were mystery, filling needs, propinquity, and similarity.

Aron et al.'s (1989) Study 2 was based on 200 accounts randomly selected from 1,013 accounts written by adults who participated in educational seminars in several U.S. cities. The participants (their average age was about 30) were asked to write a brief account of "falling in love" or "falling in friendship." The same coding scheme used in Study 1 was used to content-analyze the accounts. Similar to Study 1, reciprocal liking and desirable characteristics were mentioned most frequently. However, unlike Sample 1, similarity and propinquity were the third and fourth most frequently mentioned factors. A comparison between those who wrote an account about falling in love and those who wrote about friendship indicated that those who wrote about falling in love were more likely to mention reciprocal liking and desirable characteristics and less likely to refer to propinquity.

In Study 3, Aron et al. (1989) created a list of items based on the categories that had been created in the content analysis of Study 1 responses. The questionnaire was distributed to two samples; one sample was asked to think about a falling in love experience, and a separate sample was asked to respond in regard to a friend. Once again, reciprocal liking and desirable characteristics were rated as most important; a majority of the respondents rated these items as either 8 or 9 on a 1 to 9 scale, indicating that they believed these factors had a *very positive* or *extremely positive* impact. Desirable characteristics (e.g., good looks, and attractive personality), isolation from others, mystery, and fulfilling needs were found to be more important for those writing about falling in love (intense attraction) than those writing about friendship.

Aron et al.'s (1989) research highlights the importance of desired characteristics and reciprocal liking (feeling liked by the other) as predictors of (intense) attraction. Interestingly, although the literature on interpersonal attraction and mate selection emphasizes the important role of similarity, similarity was not rated as one of the most important factors leading to attraction in the accounts of the participants in Aron et al.'s study.

In separate research (Sprecher, Aron, et al., 1994) that extended Aron et al.'s (1989) research, a list of predictors of intense attraction or falling in love was developed and included in a large survey that was distributed to young adults in three countries: the United States, Japan, and Russia. Sprecher, Aron, et al. included three items to measure desirable characteristics of the other: personality, physical attractiveness, and social standing (note that these three variables have congruence with the three types of "O" variables identified by Fletcher, 2002, referenced earlier). After dropping three items (e.g., "arousal/unusualness of situation") that either were difficult to translate or were confusing to a U.S. pilot sample, a list of 11 factors was provided to the participants. Table 15.1 provides a list of these items, and the mean for the U.S. sample and for men and women separately.

The factors that were rated as the most important influences on intense attraction within the U.S. sample were personality, being liked by the other (reciprocal liking), physical attractiveness, something very specific about the other, similarity, and familiarity. These results are generally consistent with those of Aron et al. (1989) and further clarify which O characteristics are particularly desirable (personality and physical attractiveness to a greater degree than social standing). Aron et al. did not

TABLE 15.1   Mean Importance of Predictors of Intense Attraction

	Total U.S. Sample (Mean)	Men (Mean)	Women (Mean)
Personality	5.07 (1)	4.83	5.21°
Other's liking and affection for you	4.69 (2)	4.55	4.77°
Physical attractiveness	4.66 (3)	4.91	4.51°
Something very specific (his or her eyes, voice, or similarity to a person who has been important to you)	4.20 (4)	4.06	4.28
Similarity to you (in attitudes, experiences, background, etc.)	4.06 (5)	4.05	4.06
Familiarity (having spent a lot of time together)	4.03 (6)	3.85	4.14°
Isolation that the two of you had from others	3.83 (7)	3.75	3.87
Some "mystery" about the other person	3.69 (8)	3.50	3.80°
Your readiness to enter a relationship	3.64 (9)	3.62	3.65
Family's and/or friends' approval	3.29 (10)	3.08	3.41°
Social standing (career success or potential career success, social status, and/or family standing)	3.15 (11)	2.97	3.26°

° = *Significant difference between the genders.*
Source: Sprecher, Aron, et al. (1994, U.S. sample).

focus on gender differences in their research, although Sprecher, Felmlee, Metts, Fehr, and Vanni (1998) noted that unpublished data from Aron et al. (1989) indicated that physical attractiveness was more important for men than for women. In the Sprecher, Aron, et al. (1994) U.S. sample, men rated physical attractiveness as more important than did women, whereas women rated reciprocal liking, personality, social standing, and family and friend approval as more important than did men. Cross-cultural analyses indicated that the U.S. sample rated many of the predictors as being more important than did respondents in Russia and Japan. However, in all three societies, personality, reciprocal liking (affection from the other), and physical appearance were rated as relatively important. Relatively unimportant in all three societies were social standing and approval from family and friends.

Research on Predictors of Attraction

Extending Aron et al.'s (1989) and Sprecher, Aron, et al.'s (1994) work on predictors of intense attraction was another set of studies examining people's reports of predictors of attraction (Sprecher, 1998a, 1998b). Sprecher (1998a) examined insiders' view of the importance of various factors as reasons for their attraction to a close other, who could be a romantic partner or a friend. The list of predictors had some overlap with that used in the prior research described above, but included six specific desirable characteristics of the O, four types of similarity, and also complementarity (or being opposites). Table 15.2 presents the items that were assessed, grouped in the P × O, P, and E

TABLE 15.2   Results of Importance of Predictors of Attraction

			Study 3		
	Study 1	Study 2	Romantic Relationships	Same-Gender Friendships	Opposite-Gender Relationships
Types of Similarity and Other P × O Factors					
Similarity on attitudes and values	3.25 (4)	3.26 (5)	2.96 (5)	3.10 (4)	2.88 (8–9)
Similarity on interests and leisure activities	3.15 (6)	3.14 (6)	2.79 (8)	3.29 (2)	3.02 (6)
Similarity on social skills	2.84 (10)	3.08 (7)	2.87 (7)	3.01 (6)	3.07 (5)
Similarity on background characteristics	2.86 (9)	2.85 (10)	2.74 (11)	2.89 (9)	2.82 (10)
Complementarity on personality	2.76 (11)	2.69 (12)	2.49 (14)	2.46 (11)	2.57 (12)
Reciprocal liking (P's liking for O)	3.20 (5)	3.58 (2)	3.17 (3)	2.99 (7)	3.11 (3–4)
Familiarity of the other	2.91 (8)	2.96 (8)	2.77 (9)	2.73 (10)	2.79 (7)
Characteristics of Other (O)					
O's warmth and kindness	3.57 (1)	3.64 (1)	3.43 (2)	3.08 (5)	3.40 (1)
O's (desirable) personality	3.50 (2)	3.57 (3)	3.50 (1)	3.33 (1)	3.37 (2)
Something specific about O	3.28 (3)	3.41 (4)	3.14 (4)	2.91 (8)	3.11 (3–4)
O's intelligence and/or competence	3.00 (7)	2.94 (9)	2.94 (6)	2.40 (13)	2.75 (11)
O's ambition	2.60 (13)	2.66 (13)	2.61 (13)	2.42 (12)	2.22 (13)
O's physical attractiveness	2.55 (15)	2.49 (15)	2.65 (12)	1.35 (16)	1.95 (16)
O's money and/or earning potential	1.39 (17)	1.45 (17)	1.43 (17)	1.11 (17)	1.25 (17)
Environmental Factors					
Proximity	2.74 (12)	2.71 (11)	2.76 (10)	3.11 (3)	2.88 (8–9)
Support from significant others	2.59 (14)	2.51 (14)	2.46 (15)	2.23 (14)	2.09 (14)
Special setting	2.14 (16)	2.40 (16)	2.21 (16)	2.21 (15)	1.96 (15)

Note: The means above were on a scale that ranged from 1 (*not a reason*) to 4 (*the major reason*). The number in parentheses represents the rank order of the means in the column.
Source: Sprecher (1998a).

categories of variables. The table includes the mean responses to the items from across relevant samples or subsamples from the three studies presented in Sprecher (1998a).

Almost all of the factors measured were judged by the participants to be at least somewhat important reasons for their attraction to the other, across the studies. The major exception was O's money or earning potential, which was rated as relatively unimportant. Intrinsic O characteristics (warmth and kindness, and desirable personality) were rated among the most important reasons for attraction in all three studies. The P × O variable, reciprocal liking, was also rated as an important reason for attraction. The different types of similarity were rated as somewhat important reasons for attraction. The one complementarity item (opposites in personality) was rated to be less important than similarity.

Study 3 of Sprecher (1998a) yielded a few differences in the importance ratings of the factors as a function of the type of relationship. In this study, participants were randomly assigned to complete the list of predictors of their initial attraction for one of three types of relationships: same-gender friendship, opposite-gender friendship, or romantic relationship. O's physical attractiveness, intelligence and/or competence, and money and/or earning potential were rated as more important in a romantic relationship than in a friendship (particularly a same-gender friendship). Similarity in interests and leisure activities was found to be a more important reason for attraction in same-gender friendships than in romantic relationships. A few gender differences were found in reports of predictors of attraction in these studies. The two most robust gender differences were that men reported, to a greater degree than women, that O's physical attractiveness was a predictor of attraction, whereas women rated O's personality to be a more important reason for attraction than did men. Similar results were found in a study in which married individuals were asked to recall what initially attracted them to their marriage partner early in the relationship (Sprecher, 1998b).

Other Research on Reasons for Entering Relationships

We highlight a few other studies that have examined predictors of attraction from an insider perspective. Felmlee (1995, 1998a) used a qualitative approach to assess the characteristics of partners that draw one person to another in an intimate relationship. In one study (Felmlee, 1995), young adults were asked to describe in an open-ended format the specific qualities that first attracted them to their romantic partner. Coders then grouped the reported partner traits into distinct categories of similar qualities. Nine unique categories were identified. In order of relative frequency, these categories of attractive partner qualities were (a) physical (e.g., physically attractive), (b) fun (e.g., good sense of humor), (c) caring (e.g., nice), (d) competent (e.g., intelligent), (e) similar (e.g., common interests), (f) exciting (e.g., spontaneous), (g) open (e.g., self-discloses), (h) dependable (e.g., honest), and (i) easygoing (e.g., laid-back). Women were more likely to report being attracted to qualities in the caring, dependable, and fun categories than were men. Men, on the other hand, were more likely to be attracted initially to the physical aspects of their partners.

Another study focused on self-reported attraction among middle-aged adults (mean age = 37), most of whom were married and/or in long-term, committed relationships (Felmlee, Flynn, & Bahr, 2006). This study utilized a more quantitative form of data collection; that is, individuals responded on Likert-type scales to indicate the degree to which a range of personality qualities, taken from traditional personality scales, attracted them to their spouse or partner. Seven factors of partner traits emerged from the data: physical attractiveness (e.g., attractive), motivation (e.g., ambitious), and factors from each of the "big five" dimensions of personality (that is, extroversion, agreeableness, conscientiousness, emotional stability, and openness).

Taken together, findings from these multiple studies of falling in love and attraction demonstrate that an insider's perspective generates a wide range of partner characteristics reported as sources of attraction in both romantic and marital unions. See Table 15.3 for a summary of the most frequent types of romantic attractors from each of the studies discussed above. Next, we review studies that address the association between individuals' beliefs about the initial stages of their relationship and later relationship outcomes.

TABLE 15.3   Most Frequent Types of Self-Reported Romantic Attractors

Factors	Study
Reciprocal liking, and desirable characteristics	Aron, Dutton, Aron, and Iverson (1989)
Personality, reciprocal liking, and physical appearance	Sprecher, Aron, et al. (1994)
Personality, warmth and kindness, and reciprocal liking	Sprecher (1998a)
Physically attractive, fun, and caring	Felmlee (1995)
Motivated, extraverted, and physically attractive	Felmlee, Flynn, and Bahr (2006)

LINKS BETWEEN PREDICTORS OF ATTRACTION AND LATER RELATIONSHIP OUTCOMES

As we noted earlier, one advantage to obtaining insider reports of the reasons people become attracted to another or want to escalate a relationship is that the data can also be used to determine whether the reasons for initial attraction are related to later relationship outcomes. In this section, we consider examples of recent research on this topic.

Reasons for Commitment and Relationship Outcomes

Surra and colleagues (Surra & Hughes, 1997; Surra, Hughes, & Jacquet, 1999) have studied the development of premarital relationships from an insider perspective. In particular, they examine individuals' reasons for deciding whether or not to marry a partner, studying the subjective processes by which partners become more or less committed to each other. The primary focus of this body of work is not directly on attraction per se, but on the process of relationship commitment, which is examined from the insider's perspective. Although reasons for attraction to a partner are not synonymous with those for commitment, they are closely related. Similar interests, for instance, is one explanation that individuals give both for their intent to marry a partner (Surra & Hughes, 1997) and for their initial attraction to a partner (Felmlee, 1995). Therefore, research on the topic of reasons for early commitment has direct implications for that on attraction.

Typically, in phenomenological studies on commitment, relationship partners or newlyweds are asked in interviews to report on the status of the likelihood of marriage at various points in time and on the status of their relationship (e.g., Surra & Hughes, 1997). Participants graph how their estimates of their chances of marriage to their partners changed over time, either retrospectively or concurrently. The estimate is plotted on a time graph, in which the chance of marriage ranges from 0 to 100%. When respondents report a change in the likelihood of marriage, they explain why it occurred in their own words. The researchers code the explanations into categories that represent the insider's views regarding the causes of their degree of commitment to their partner.

There are two types of subjective commitment processes in premarital relationships, according to this body of research (e.g., Surra & Hughes, 1997; Surra et al., 1999): relationship driven and event driven. Relationship-driven commitments refer to those where the perceived reasons for changes in the perceptions of the chances of marriage are based on behavioral interdependence (e.g., activities and time spent together) and positive and negative dyadic attributions (e.g., degree of comfort with one another). Relationship-driven commitments reflect compatibility-testing theories of mate selection (e.g., Huston, Surra, Fitzgerald, & Cate, 1981), which suggest that partners regularly evaluate the degree to which they are well matched on the basis of their interactions. Event-driven commitments, on the other hand, are those in which the reasons cited for commitment focus on external events, such as separate interactions with the couple's social network (e.g., one partner's meeting with a parent) or making attributions about network members (e.g., getting along well with friends).

The type of subjective commitment process that individuals report is closely tied to their relationship outcomes and experiences. In particular, men and women are more satisfied with their relationships, and report greater increases in satisfaction over time from their perspective, when they describe a commitment to their partner that is relationship driven (Surra & Hughes, 1997). The developmental pattern of commitment in relationship-driven dyads changes positively over time, exhibits relatively few reversals, and changes at a relatively slow rate, as compared to those that are more event driven. Individuals explain these changes based on activities and time spent together, and they are more positive in their attitudes toward their networks. Partners who report event-driven commitments experience more turmoil, more downturns, and more extreme negative and positive changes in commitment. Individuals in such relationships report more negative attributions and more instances of conflict when accounting for these ups and downs. Yet, event-driven and relationship-driven partners do not differ significantly in terms of love, relationship length, or stability.

In sum, this research contributes to our phenomenological knowledge concerning subjective explanations for commitment to a partner. Individuals themselves report very different types of reasons for their intent to increase, or decrease, their relationship commitment. These dissimilar processes are powerful predictors of distinct paths of relationship development over time. It is likely that these results have implications specifically for attraction, as well. In particular, the type of subjective explanation for attraction, whether it is relationship or event driven, may influence change in couples in a similar manner to that for commitment.

Fatal Attraction

We saw above that reasons for relationship commitment influence relationship outcomes. Additional research finds that the process by which individuals become attracted to each other early in a relationship also is not independent of later relationship outcomes. In particular, the qualities that initially attract one person to another may be directly related to those partner qualities that later cause conflict in a relationship, and may even play a role in its demise. The qualities that individuals come to dislike in their partners can be an exaggerated version, or a negative interpretation, of those that first drew them to their partner in the first place. A confident partner, for instance, may eventually be seen as "too confident," or arrogant. This process is referred to as "fatal attraction" (Felmlee, 1995). Contrary to the public's perception of fatal attraction as portending death, social psychologists define fatal attraction as "fatal" in the foretelling of an inevitable sequence that can result in conflict and sometimes disillusionment.

Illustrations of fatal attractions (Felmlee, 1998b) include a woman who was drawn to her partner because of his "I don't care, I'll have fun anyway" attitude, but then reported that she did not like his "immaturity." In this case, the lack of maturity that she disliked in her boyfriend is a potential drawback to the carefree attitude that first attracted her. Another example is a man who said he initially liked his wife because of her "strong character and beliefs." He later was irritated that she was "pushy, loud, domineering, and always took the initiative." Thus, pushiness or domineering behavior appears to be the vice associated with the virtue of character strength.

There are several explanations for this pattern of enchantment to disenchantment. First, fatal attractions may reflect the presence of opposing relationship tensions that occur in intimate relationships. Dialectical theory maintains that couples encounter contradictory forces, such as autonomy and connection, novelty and predictability, and closeness and openness (e.g., Baxter & Montgomery, 1996). Fatal attractions may occur because individuals seek a partner on the basis of one pole of a dialectical force (e.g., novelty), but then find that their relationship is deficient in terms of the opposing pole (e.g., predictability).

Second, an individual's strengths and weaknesses are apt to be entwined. This notion is a theme in both the popular and clinical psychology literature (e.g., Jung, 1973). What are virtues in the first place? Virtues are likely to be positive traits displayed in the extreme. Yet extreme qualities may be particularly prone to exhibiting a downside, and this downside may be inextricably linked to the upside. A person who is unusually nice, for instance, may be too passive or even a pushover. Thus, when people pursue a partner because of that person's virtues, they simultaneously encounter that person's "shadow side," and therefore they may come to reject aspects of the very quality that first interested them. This type of disenchantment is particularly likely to set in when initial infatuation recedes (Felmlee, 1998b).

Fatal attractions occur with some regularity in largely heterosexual relationships among young college students (Felmlee, 1995, 1998a), in married and long-term couples (Felmlee et al., 2006; Pines, 1999), as well as among lesbian and gay partners (Fortes, 2005). This type of disenchantment is found when these attractions are identified either via an open-ended, qualitative method of identification (e.g., Felmlee, 1995; Pines, 1999) or when employing a more quantitative approach based on Likert-type scales (Felmlee et al., 2006). Fatal attractions have occurred in approximately 30% (Felmlee, 1995) to 67% (Felmlee et al., 2006) of respondents, depending upon the method of data collection and the particular sample.

Findings suggest that attractions to extreme qualities in an individual, or to dissimilarity, are particularly vulnerable to subsequent disenchantment. That is, fatal attractions are significantly more frequent when individuals are attracted to extreme partner qualities (Felmlee, 2001; Felmlee et al., 2006), or those described in an exaggerated manner (e.g., *unusually confident*). They also occur more often when individuals report being drawn to partner qualities that are dissimilar or different from their own (e.g., *unique*; Felmlee, 1998a, 2001) and are less frequent when similarities, or common interests, are the source of attraction (Felmlee, 1998a; Felmlee et al., 2006). These findings underscore the argument that although dissimilarity between partners may be initially alluring, it also is liable to serve as a source of subsequent relationship discontent.

SUMMARY AND FUTURE RESEARCH DIRECTIONS

In our literature, we see that there are numerous factors that individuals say attracted them to another in a romantic relationship and friendship. Yet there are patterns in these attractors, as can be seen in Table 15.3. First, individuals frequently report being attracted to the desirable, or positive, personality characteristics of O (Aron et al., 1989; Sprecher, Aron et al., 1994) such as being fun (Felmlee, 1995) or warm and kind (Sprecher, 1998a, 1998b). A second factor that appears in virtually all insider studies of attraction is the physical attractiveness of O, with men typically rating it as a significantly more salient factor than women (e.g., Felmlee, 1995; Sprecher, Aron et al., 1994). Note that the term *desirable characteristics* (Aron et al.) includes both physical appearance and personality qualities. Reciprocal liking (a P × O interaction) is an additional factor that is rated highly as a reason for attraction (e.g., Aron et al.; Sprecher, 1998a). These three factors—desirable personality, physical appearance, and reciprocal liking—appear in cross-cultural self-report studies across several different societies (Sprecher, Aron et al., 1994).

Types of attractors also vary by the relationship being studied. Several factors are more important in romantic relationships as compared to friendships, including reciprocal liking, desirable characteristics, physical attractiveness, and other specific O variables (Aron et al., 1989; Sprecher, 1998a). Factors such as similarity of interests (P × O) and propinquity (E) were found to a greater degree among friendships (Aron et al.; Sprecher, 1998a). The attraction process also differs somewhat in marriages and long-term partnerships, when compared to that of short-term, romantic relationships. For example, individuals in married or committed relationships (Felmlee et al., 2006) frequently report being attracted to their spouse or partner's high level of motivation and ambition (Felmlee et al.), characteristics that are less commonly mentioned in dating relationships. Perhaps ambition is particularly relevant for a long-term committed partnership because it is viewed as an indicator of future work potential.

There seems to be a heightened salience of intrinsic O factors in romantic attraction, both in the short and long term. When individuals are asked to report on the factors that initially interested them in their partner or mate, they invariably point to a variety of positive personality and physical characteristics of that individual. They also mention a relationship-specific factor (P × O), the fact that their partner is also interested in them. Seldom do individuals report that characteristics of themselves (P factors), such as their own gregariousness or neediness, drew them romantically to another. Nor do they often point to the role of external (E) factors, such as geographical proximity. More generally, individuals' explanations for their attraction are primarily "relationship driven" (or "partner driven") as opposed to "event driven," to borrow terminology from Surra et al.'s (1999) studies of subjective commitment processes.

This heightened focus on internal relationship and partner characteristics in individuals' own accounts of intimate relationship initiation is not surprising. Inherent to a cultural notion of romantic love is the idea of a unique and special partner (Swidler, 2001), and this is apt to be particularly true in an individualist society such as the United States. Moreover, research on the fundamental attribution error and explanations for it (e.g., Storms, 1973) suggest that a focus on another person can lead to overlooking explanations in other sources, such as the environment. Another cultural assumption about romantic love is that a choice of a loved one is voluntary or unforced (e.g., Kemper & Reid, 1997) rather than externally determined, and it may even unfold in defiance of societal constraints. Therefore, when individuals specify internal partner and relationship attractors in their self-reports, they are reinforcing the belief that their relationship was not a result of accidental, social forces. They are emphasizing instead the personal and voluntary nature of their choice, and that of their loved one. This pattern of internal relationship attribution is likely to reinforce, rather than lessen, perceptions of love toward their partner.

We see here, too, that an insider's perception of attraction is important because it has implications for subsequent relationship quality and relationship developmental over time. First, as discussed earlier, individuals who focus on the relationship, rather than external events, as reasons for commitment experience higher levels of relationship quality, and less turmoil, over time (e.g., Surra & Hughes, 1997). Beliefs about commitment can therefore become associated with relationship outcomes. Second, there is often a connection between the characteristics that attract one person to another initially and those that are later disliked in a partner and become a source of relationship conflict, that is, a "fatal attraction" (Felmlee, 1995). What enchants one in another can be closely related to what leads to later disenchantment, in particular in cases in which individuals are drawn to extreme and dissimilar qualities in a partner. Thus, we see that relationship beginnings and relationship outcomes may be linked in multiple ways. Furthermore, additional research suggests that attraction is associated with relationship perceptions following a breakup. In particular, Sprecher et al. (1998) found that a greater number of reported reasons for becoming attracted, assessed retrospectively, was associated with greater distress after the relationship ended.

There are a number of important paths for future research. First, an insider perspective could be used to examine various theories of interpersonal attraction. Individuals themselves could be asked to report the degree to which critical elements of classic theories were salient in the initiation of their relationship. For example, participants could rate the degree to which various factors were involved, such as the reward level of attractors (Byrne & Clore, 1970), comparison level and comparison level for alternatives (Thibaut & Kelley, 1959), or the degree to which attractors present opportunities to enhance self-expansion (e.g., Aron & Aron, 1986). Findings from such a study could be helpful in determining whether a particular theory, such as reinforcement theory, exchange theory, or a self-expansion perspective, is useful in accounting for relationship initiation, at least according to individuals' own beliefs.

Second, there are methodological innovations that would serve as promising avenues for further investigations. Gathering information on attraction at multiple time points over the course of a relationship would be useful for comparing the ways in which attractors change over time. This may be facilitated by Internet or Web-based surveys (Buchanan, 2000). Certain factors may be more salient initially, such as physical attractiveness, whereas others may grow in importance in the long term, such as commitment and stability. Other ways of assessing self-reports are promising, too, such as the use of repeated assessments using a diary format in the early stages of a relationship. More subtle methods of looking at self-accounts could be used in addition, such as thought listening studies to assess how much time is spent on thinking about various types of attraction. Finally, a multimethod design to the investigation of attraction, in which both "insider" and "outsider" approaches are taken within the same study, is particularly promising. For example, Sprecher (1989) included self-report questions about reasons for attraction within an experimental study using the bogus stranger paradigm. As another illustration, it would be possible to do observational investigations of people in naturalistic settings in which attraction can be experienced (e.g., a singles bar) and then conduct interviews with the patrons in the setting about to whom they are attracted and why. Similarly, perhaps self-reports of reasons for attraction could be conducted with users of Internet matching services in combination with data collected from the sites on the eventual success of the matches (see Sprecher, Schwartz, Harvey, & Hatfield, this volume). Such multimethod studies could be used to compare directly the advantages and disadvantages of various methods.

It also would be useful to broaden the base of self-report studies of attraction. For example, we need to gather data from more ethnically diverse populations, as well as from lesbians, gays, and transgendered individuals (e.g., see the chapter by Custer et al., this volume). There are likely to be certain unique factors involved in romantic attraction among those from culturally diverse and disadvantaged societal groups, and more attention to these distinctions is warranted. Cross-cultural studies, in addition to the one discussed earlier (Sprecher, Aron, et al., 1994), also would further expand our knowledge of the robustness of relationship initiation processes. Furthermore, there is a paucity of work addressing the relationships of older populations (Harvey & Hansen, 2000). However, certain findings with regard to attraction are likely to differ by age. For example, attraction to ambition in a partner may be less salient among those who are retired. Finally, it is important to obtain information about attraction predictors from both partners of a couple. Do both individuals agree regarding the initial relationship predictors? If one partner experiences relationship disenchantment, or a fatal attraction, is the other partner likely to do so as well? Gathering data from both couple members is essential to the development of a truly dyadic perspective on attraction.

Finally, it will be important to further explore the ways in which factors involved in initial attraction relate to later relationship development and outcomes. Are there particular types of attractors that predict couple decay and breakup, whereas others portend more promising outcomes? Are partner- or relationship-based, as opposed to event-based, attributions for attraction more closely related to subsequent relationship satisfaction and love? How promising are initial encounters that develop because partners want to expand their sense of self? More generally, it will be noteworthy to further investigate the degree to which eventual relationship development can be traced back to the very beginning stages of a couple's involvement.

In conclusion, attraction is an intriguing relationship process that has been studied in a number of ways, most commonly among strangers or hypothetical persons. Here we see what can be gained when researchers take the perspective toward the attraction of individuals who are involved in actual intimate relationships. Although this approach has its downsides, it has several distinct advantages, including the fact that people's perceptions of reality are likely to shape much of their behavior. We see evidence of that process, too, in that individuals' beliefs regarding attraction have ramifications for later relationship outcomes. Thus, this unique approach to the study of attraction has a good deal of potential for future research on this important relationship topic, including to help link the study of attraction with the study of close relationships.

REFERENCES

Adams, R. G., Berggren, J., Docherty, L., Ruffin, K., & Wright, C. P. (2006). Gender-of-author differences in study design of older adult friendship surveys. *Personal Relationships, 13,* 503–520.

Altman, I., & Taylor, D. (1973). *Social penetration: The development of interpersonal relationships.* New York: Holt, Rinehart & Winston.

Aron, A., & Aron, E. (1986). *Love and the expansion of self: Understanding attraction and satisfaction.* New York: Hemisphere.

Aron, A., Dutton, D. G., Aron, E. N., & Iverson, A. (1989). Experiences of falling in love. *Journal of Social and Personal Relationships, 6,* 243–257.

Baxter, L. A., & Montgomery, B. M. (1996). *Relating: Dialogues and dialectics.* New York: Guilford Press.

Berscheid, E. (1985). Interpersonal attraction. In G. Lindzey & E. Aronson (Eds.), *The handbook of social psychology* (pp. 413–484). New York: Random House.

Berscheid, E., & Regan, P. (2005). *The psychology of interpersonal relationships*. Upper Saddle River, NJ: Pearson Education.

Berscheid, E., & Reis, H. (1998). Attraction and close relationships. In D. T. Gilbert, S. T. Fiske, & G. Lindzey (Eds.), *The handbook of social psychology* (4th ed., pp. 193–281). New York: McGraw-Hill.

Berscheid, E., & Walster, E. (1974). A little bit about love. In T. L. Huston (Ed.), *Foundations of interpersonal attraction* (pp. 355–391). New York: Academic Press.

Buchanan, T. (2000). Potential of the Internet for personality research. In M. H. Burnham (Ed.), *Psychological experiments on the Internet* (pp. 121–140). San Diego, CA: Academic Press.

Buss, D. M. (1989). Sex differences in human mate preferences: Evolutionary hypotheses tested in 37 cultures. *Behavioral and Brain Sciences, 12*, 1–49.

Buss, D. M., & Schmitt, D. P. (1993). Sexual strategies theory: An evolutionary perspective on human mating. *Psychological Review, 100*, 204–232.

Byrne, D. (1971). *The attraction paradigm*. New York: Academic Press.

Byrne, D., & Clore, G. L. (1970). A reinforcement model of evaluative processes. *Personality: An International Journal, 1*, 103–128.

Byrne, D., Ervin, C. R., & Lamberth, J. (1970). Continuity between the experimental study of attraction and real-life computer dating. *Journal of Personality and Social Psychology, 16*, 157–165.

Cunningham, M. R., Barbee, A. P., & Druen, P. B. (1996). Social allergens and the reactions that they produce: Escalation of annoyance and disgust in love and work. In R. M. Kowalski (Ed.), *Aversive interpersonal behaviors* (pp. 189–214). New York: Plenum.

Dutton, D. G., & Aron, A. (1974). Some evidence for heightened sexual attraction under conditions of high anxiety. *Journal of Personality and Social Psychology, 30*, 510–517.

Felmlee, D. H. (1995). Fatal attractions: Affection and disaffection in intimate relationships. *Journal of Social and Personal Relationships, 12*, 295–311.

Felmlee, D. H. (1998a). "Be careful what you wish for … ": A quantitative and qualitative investigation of fatal attractions. *Personal Relationships, 5*, 235–253.

Felmlee, D. H. (1998b). Loss and contradictions in intimate relationships. In J. Harvey (Ed.), *Perspectives on loss: A sourcebook* (pp. 113–124). Philadelphia: Taylor and Francis.

Felmlee, D. H. (2001). From appealing to appalling: Disenchantment with a romantic partner. *Sociological Perspectives, 44*, 263–280.

Felmlee, D. H., Flynn, H., & Bahr, P. (2006, August). *Too much of a good thing: Disenchantment in marriages and intimate relationships*. Paper presented at the annual meetings of the American Sociological Association, San Francisco.

Festinger, L., Schachter, S., & Back, K. (1950). *Social pressure in informal groups: A study of human factors in housing*. New York: Harper.

Fletcher, G. (2002). *The new science of intimate relationships*. Cambridge, MA: Blackwell.

Fortes, C. (2005). Myths and enchantment tales: Attraction and disillusionment in same-sex romantic relationships. *McNair Research Journal*.

Harvey, J. H., & Hansen, A. (2000). Loss and bereavement in close romantic relationships. In C. Hendrick & S. Hendrick (Eds.), *Sourcebook on close relationships* (pp. 359–370). Thousand Oaks, CA: Sage.

Hatfield, E., Traupmann, J., Sprecher, S., Utne, M., & Hay, J. (1984). Equity and intimate relations: Recent research. In W. Ickes (Ed.), *Compatible and incompatible relationships* (pp. 91–117). New York: Springer-Verlag.

Huston, T. L., Surra, C. A., Fitzgerald, N. M., & Cate, R. M. (1981). From courtship to marriage: Mate selection as an interpersonal process. In S. Duck & R. Gilmour (Eds.), *Personal relationships 2: Developing personal relationships* (pp. 53–88). London: Academic Press.

Jung, C. (1973). *Memories, dreams, reflections* (A. Jaffe, Ed., & R. Winston & C. Winston, Trans.). New York: Pantheon.

Kelley, H. H., Berscheid, E., Christensen, A., Harvey, J. H., Huston, T. L., Levinger, G., et al. (1983). Analyzing close relationships. In H. H. Kelley (Ed.), *Close relationships* (pp. 20–67). New York: W. H. Freeman.

Kemper, T. D., & Reid, M. T. (1997). Love and liking in the attraction and maintenance phases of long-term relationships. *Social Perspectives on Emotions, 4*, 37–69.

Koestner, R., & Wheeler, L. (1988). Self-presentation in personal advertisements: The influence of implicit notions of attraction and role expectations. *Journal of Social and Personal Relationships, 5*, 149–160.

Lott, A. J., & Lott, B. E. (1974). The role of reward in the formulation of positive interpersonal attitudes. In T. L. Huston (Ed.), *Foundations of interpersonal attraction* (pp. 171–189). New York: Academic Press.

Lundy, D. E., Tan, J., & Cunningham, M. R. (1998). Heterosexual romantic preferences: The importance of humor and physical attractiveness for different types of relationships. *Personal Relationships, 5,* 311–325.

Metts, S., Sprecher, S., & Cupach, W. (1991). Retrospective self-reports. In B. Montgomery & S. Duck (Eds.), *Studying interpersonal interaction* (pp. 162–178). New York: Guilford.

Miller, R. S., Perlman, D., & Brehm, S. S. (2007). *Intimate relationships.* Boston: McGraw-Hill.

Newcomb, T. M. (1961). *The acquaintance process.* New York: Holt, Rinehart & Winston.

Newcomb, T. M. (1971). Dyadic balance as a source of clues about interpersonal attraction. In B. I. Murstein (Ed.), *Theories of attraction and love* (pp. 31–45). New York: Springer.

Nisbett, R. E., & Wilson, T. D. (1977). Telling more than we can know: Verbal reports on mental processes. *Psychological Review, 84,* 231–259.

Orbuch, T. L., Veroff, J., & Holmberg, D. (1993). Becoming a married couple: The emergence of meaning in the first years of marriage. *Journal of Marriage and Family, 55,* 815–826.

Perlman, D., & Fehr, B. (1987). The development of intimate relationships. In D. Perlman & S. Duck (Eds.), *Intimate relationships: Development, dynamics and deterioration* (pp. 13–42). Beverly Hills, CA: Sage.

Pines, A. (1999). *Falling in love: Why we choose the lovers we choose.* New York: Routledge.

Ross, M. A. (1989). The relation of implicit theories to the construction of personal histories. *Psychological Review, 96,* 341–357.

Schachter, S. (1964). The interaction of cognitive and physiological determinants of emotional state. In L. Berkowitz (Ed.), *Advances in experimental social psychology* (Vol. 1, pp. 49–80). New York: Academic Press.

Seligman, C., Fazio, R. H., & Zanna, M. P. (1980). Effects of salience of extrinsic rewards on liking and loving. *Journal of Personality and Social Psychology, 38,* 453–460.

Simpson, J. A., & Harris, B. A. (1994). Interpersonal attraction. In A. L. Weber & J. H. Harvey (Eds.), *Perspectives on close relationships* (pp. 45–66). Boston: Allyn & Bacon.

Sprecher, S. (1989). Influences on choice of a partner and on sexual decision-making in the relationship. In K. McKinney & S. Sprecher (Eds.), *Human sexuality: The societal and interpersonal context* (pp. 115–138). Norwood, NJ: Ablex.

Sprecher, S. (1998a). Insiders' perspectives on reasons for attraction to a close other. *Social Psychology Quarterly, 61,* 287–300.

Sprecher, S. (1998b). What keeps married partners attracted to each other? *Free Inquiry in Creative Sociology, 26,* 193–200.

Sprecher, S., Aron, A., Hatfield, E., Cortese, A., Potapova, E., & Levitskaya, A. (1994). Love: American style, Russian style, and Japanese style. *Personal Relationships, 1,* 349–369.

Sprecher, S., & Duck, S. (1994). Sweet talk: The importance of perceived communication for romantic and friendship attraction experienced during a get-acquainted date. *Personality and Social Psychology Bulletin, 20,* 391–400.

Sprecher, S., Felmlee, D., Metts, S., Fehr, B., & Vanni, D. (1998). Factors associated with distress following the breakup of a close relationship. *Journal of Social and Personal Relationships, 15,* 791–809.

Sprecher, S., Sullivan, Q., & Hatfield, E. (1994). Mate selection preferences: Gender differences examined in a national sample. *Journal of Personality and Social Psychology, 66,* 1074–1080.

Storms, M. D. (1973). Videotape and the attribution process: Reversing actors' and observers' points of view. *Journal of Personality and Social Psychology, 27,* 165–175.

Surra, C. A., & Hughes, D. K. (1997). Commitment processes in accounts of the development of premarital relationships. *Journal of Marriage and the Family, 59,* 5–21.

Surra, C. A., Hughes, D. K., & Jacquet, S. (1999). The development of commitment to marriage: A phenomenological approach. In W. H. Jones & J. Adams (Eds.), *The handbook of interpersonal commitment and relationship stability* (pp. 125–148). New York: Kluwer/Plenum.

Swidler, A. (2001). *Talk of love: How culture matters.* Chicago: University of Chicago.

Thibaut, J. W., & Kelley, H. H. (1959). *The social psychology of groups.* New York: Wiley.

Walster, E., Aronson, V., Abrahams, D., & Rottman, L. (1966). The importance of physical attractiveness in dating behavior. *Journal of Personality and Social Psychology, 4,* 508–516.

Wilson, T. D. (2002). *Strangers to ourselves: Discovering the adaptive unconscious.* Cambridge, MA: Belknap Press.

16

Falling in Love

ARTHUR ARON, HELEN E. FISHER, GREG STRONG, BIANCA
ACEVEDO, SUZANNE RIELA, and IRENE TSAPELAS

Romantic love is a universal or nearly universal phenomenon, appearing in every culture for which data are available (Jankowiak & Fischer, 1992), in every historical era (Hatfield & Rapson, 2002), and in every age group (Tennov, 1979). Analogs to romantic love are found in a wide variety of higher animal species, and romantic love may well have played a central role in the evolution of our primary human reproductive strategies (Fisher, 1998, 2004). Romantic love seems to be a key factor in quality of life generally. It can be a source of some of the greatest joys, including connectedness, ecstasy, and fulfillment (e.g., Aron & Aron, 1986; Hatfield & Rapson, 1987), and some of the greatest problems, including depression, rage, stalking, suicide, and homicide (e.g., Cupach & Spitzberg, 2004; Meloy & Fisher, 2005).

If romantic love is universal, then falling in love, the transition from not being in love to being in love, is also universal. Similarly, if romantic love plays a significant role in people's lives, then the transition to romantic love presumably also plays such a role. Indeed, because change is so salient, particularly in emotional contexts (e.g., Berscheid, 1983), falling in love—and above all, rapidly falling in love—is likely to be highly salient and thus to have especially strong impacts on experience and behavior. As with the weather, it can be ignored when all is calm; but it becomes a topic of intense interest when we are tossed about by a great storm or laid flat by a nearly unbearable heat wave.

Given the prevalence and importance of falling in love, it is not surprising that it has been the subject of both artistic and scholarly attention from the earliest times. Among the most significant early scholarly treatments of love, including falling in love, in Western culture is Plato's *Symposium*, a systematic analysis of love that continues to be influential today (e.g., Aron & Aron, 1991). There has been a continuous stream of interest in falling in love since the classical Greeks (and perhaps from even earlier in both Western and other cultural contexts), with landmarks that continue to be influential on contemporary thought, including Stendhal's (1822/1927) book-length essay *de L'Amour* and Freud's extensive discussions of the topic (e.g., Freud, 1927). The 19th and early 20th centuries also saw interest in the onset of romantic love, including anthropologists (e.g., Mead, 1928) and clinical writers outside the Freudian tradition (e.g., Grant, 1957).

Scholarly work on falling in love in the last few decades has been mainly centered in social psychology, largely starting with the experiments on attitude similarity and attraction of Donn Byrne (1971) and other studies of romantic attraction (e.g., Walster [now Hatfield], Aronson, Abrahams, & Rottman, 1966), and Berscheid and Hatfield's (1969) significant distinction between companionate and passionate love. This work was quickly followed by contributions of Rubin (1970, 1974) on loving and liking, those of Dutton and Aron (1974) on the arousal–attraction effect, and an edited book on attraction (Huston, 1974). The 1980s set the stage for much current thinking on romantic love, including work on falling in love, such as the extension of attachment theory to adult love (Hazan & Shaver, 1987), Sternberg's (1986) triangular theory of love, Tennov's (1979) descriptive work on intense passionate love, the development of lay understandings of love (Fehr, 1988), Aron and Aron's (1986) self-expansion model of love, evolutionary psychology (e.g., Buss, 1989; Fisher, 1992, 2004), and Hendrick and Hendrick's (1986) adaptation of Lee's (1977) love typology into a psychometrically strong, widely used, multidimensional scale.

These trends from the 1960s through the 1980s have all continued and expanded into the present, with the early 1990s bringing some new strands, such as work on unreciprocated love (Aron, Aron, & Allen, 1998; Baumeister, Wotman, & Stillwell, 1993) and love ideals (e.g., Fletcher, Simpson, Thomas, & Giles, 1999; Rusbult, Onizuka, & Lipkus, 1993). The major developments in the late 1990s and early 21st century have included an upsurge of interest in romantic love in adolescence (e.g., Collins, 2003) and in old age (e.g., Le & Levenson, 2005), ethnic and cultural differences (e.g., Hatfield & Rapson, 2002), love as an emotion (e.g., Gonzaga, Keltner, Londahl, & Smith, 2001), and the biology of love (e.g., Fisher, 1998), notably including work on oxytocin and vasopressin in monogamous prairie voles (e.g., Carter et al., 1997; Lim, Murphy, & Young, 2004; Young, Wang, & Insel, 1998), the related work it has inspired in humans (e.g., Gonzaga, 2002), and recent neuroimaging studies of romantic love (e.g., Aron et al., 2005; Bartels & Zeki, 2000; Fisher et al., 2005; Xu, Aron, et al., 2008).

Nevertheless, the great majority of the relevant work to date is about either initial romantic attraction (not necessarily of the intensity or duration one would associate with "falling in love") or romantic love that has been somewhat established ("being in love" versus the transition). Thus, in many places we will be forced to extrapolate toward the middle from what is known from these two poles—initial attraction and being in love. In addition, we will consider the trajectory of falling in love, in that it may not always be experienced as "falling." Furthermore, although the focus of this review is on "falling in love," other facets of love (e.g., friendship and companionate love) also play major roles in relationship initiation and stability (Hendrick & Hendrick, 1993; Hendrick, Hendrick, & Adler, 1988). For ease of presentation, we refer to *falling in love* as the transition from not being in love to being in love. However, it is important to highlight that there are numerous trajectories and rates (e.g., this may occur very suddenly or gradually over time), and that the experience does not necessarily occur in isolation of other relationship processes (e.g., commitment, intimacy, and investment) and styles of love in the context of requited love. Rather, it often occurs concurrently with friendship and companionate love among young adults' romantic relationships (Hendrick & Hendrick, 1993) and those of older individuals (Hatfield, Traupmann, & Sprecher, 1984). We will also rely heavily on work on "early-stage" romantic love, a period that as operationally defined in many studies seems to overlap with, or even encompass, falling in love (as in the case of "love at first sight").

WHAT IS FALLING IN LOVE?

Aron, Paris, and Aron (1995) defined "falling in love" as "the onset of a strong desire for a close, romantic relationship with a particular person … the transition from not being in love to being in love" (p. 1102). The metaphor of "falling" suggests a particularly rapid transition, as emphasized by Aron, Dutton, Aron, and Iverson (1989). However, many individuals when asked to describe an "experience of falling in love" in fact report on a gradual transition, sometimes over years, as from an acquaintanceship or friendship to an intense passion (Riela, Acevedo, Aron, & Rodriguez, 2007; Riela, Aron, & Acevedo, 2006; Sangrador & Yela, 2000). Thus, we will not limit our discussion of falling in love to rapid transitions. Nevertheless, it is clear from both how respondents interpret the term and how it seems to be used in ordinary discourse that *falling in love* refers to a transition from something not at all intense to something quite intense. It involves a major redirection of one's attention and energy. It is more than just a passing or ephemeral attraction to or valuing of an individual; it corresponds to the early stages of intense passionate love. In broader terms, falling in love also corresponds to Fisher et al.'s (2002) "selective attraction" seen in mammalian and avian species.

It is also a common phenomenon. It has long been described as a transforming experience by poets and troubadours, philosophers and psychologists (James, 1890/1948; Jung, 1925/1959), and it happens at least once to most North Americans at some point in their lives (Aron et al., 1989; Dion & Dion, 1993; Hendrick & Hendrick, 1986). Nor is it exclusive to Western societies, although rates may differ somewhat across cultures (Regan, Durvasula, Howell, Ureño, & Rea, 2004; Riela et al., 2006, 2007; Sprecher et al., 1994).

Perhaps the key definitional issue regarding falling in love is about what is being fallen into—the age-old question of "What is love?" Thus, we first consider the major approaches to answering this question about love in general and how each relates to falling in love in particular.

Scientific and Scholarly Delineations: Types of Love

Work on the nature of love has mainly emphasized identifying and differentiating varieties of love, notably in the present context, and the distinction between romantic and more general kinds of love, such as familial love, compassionate love for strangers, love of God, or love of country. Romantic love is love in the context of romantic relationships—that is, relationships of the kind that typically have an explicit actual or potential sexual component, such as dating and marital relationships. Aron and Aron (1991) defined *love* as "the constellation of behaviors, cognitions, and emotions associated with a desire to enter or maintain a close relationship with a specific other person" (p. 26). With regard to the relation of romantic love to other relationship constructs, Rubin (1970) explicitly distinguished loving from liking and developed a measure that included separate scales for each. His 13-item Love Scale emphasizes dependence, caring, and exclusiveness, and was validated in part by showing that college dating couples who scored higher on the scale gazed longer into their partner's eyes. His parallel liking scale, on the other hand, emphasizes similarity, respect, and positive evaluation. Importantly, the two scales were only moderately correlated. Indeed, Wong (1989) found that higher levels of reported intensity of an unrequited love experience were associated with higher love scores on Rubin's scale, but *lower* liking scores. Rubin's scale has been widely used, and other researchers have found the conceptual distinction between liking and loving to be very useful (e.g., Davis & Todd, 1985; Sternberg, 1987). Indeed, when we have explicitly asked subjects about precursors of "falling in friendship" (Aron et al., 1989), their answers revealed predictable commonalities and differences from those of subjects who were asked about "falling in love." For example, the love narratives placed greater emphasis on reciprocal liking (believing the other likes or is attracted to the self), desirable characteristics of the other, filling one's needs, isolation as a couple, and mysteriousness. In contrast, the friendship narratives were more likely to mention familiarity (having known the person for some time).

Turning specifically to romantic love, a key distinction has been made between passionate and companionate love. Berscheid and Hatfield (1978) defined passionate love as "a state of intense longing for union with another" (p. 9); they defined companionate love as "the affection we feel for those with whom our lives are deeply entwined" (p. 9). Based on their definition of passionate love, Hatfield and Sprecher (1986) developed a Passionate Love Scale (PLS) with items such as "I would rather be with ___ than with anyone else" and "I melt when looking deeply into ____'s eyes." The PLS has been used successfully in many studies, including studies that distinguish what it measures from companionate love (e.g., Sprecher & Regan, 1998). Most recently, it was used in an functional magnetic resonance imaging (fMRI) study in which PLS scores correlated with activation in the antero-medial body of the caudate nucleus, a region associated with reward, motivation, and goal-oriented behaviors (Aron et al., 2005). The distinction between companionate and passionate love also parallels the related distinction between those whom one "loves" and the subset of these with whom one is "in love," for whom people also typically report sexual desire (Meyers & Berscheid, 1997). "Falling in love" appears to be specifically about the transition into passionate love, or from not "being in love" to "being in love."

Another influential categorization focuses on "love styles," originally a circumplex model based on historical conceptions and systematic analysis of interview reports (Lee, 1977). However, most research applications have employed the Hendrick and Hendrick (1986, 2003) measure, which treats Lee's styles as six relatively independent dimensions: eros (romantic, passionate love), ludus (game-playing love), storge (friendship love), pragma (logical, "shopping-list" love), mania (possessive, dependent love), and agape (selfless love). Falling in love would seem to correspond best to a transition from no love to eros- or mania-type love. Eros is characterized by an intense desire for union, sexual intimacy, and self-disclosure with the beloved, without obsession. Mania shows some similarities to eros (e.g., self-disclosure and idealization), but it is characterized by greater turbulence, obsession, and lower self-esteem. Further, other work found that individuals in love were more agapic and erotic and less game playing in their love attitudes, and less permissive in their sexual attitudes, compared to individuals not in love. Participants in love were also lower in self-monitoring and sensation seeking than those not in love (Hendrick & Hendrick, 1988).

Yet another influential categorization of romantic love was developed by Sternberg (1986), based on his attempt to integrate the existing psychology models at the time and related literatures. Sternberg's triangular theory conceptualizes love in terms of intimacy, commitment and decision, and passion, treating these three components as ingredients that in various combinations define types of love. Attempts to develop measures of the ingredients (Sternberg, 1997) have run into difficulty, with discriminant validity among them (e.g., Whitley, 1993). However, the three components do seem to correspond reasonably well with the latent dimensions of lay conceptions of love (Aron & Westbay, 1996).

How Ordinary People Construe Love

Fehr (1988, 2001) suggested that the long-standing philosophical controversies over the meaning of love, and the corresponding diversity of conceptual and operational definitions in the scientific literature, are due to the possibility that ordinary people recognize instances of love not by their conforming to some formal definition but rather by their family resemblance to a prototypical exemplar (just as people seem to recognize something as a fruit by its similarity to an apple). Specifically, in one series of studies, Fehr (1988) first had a sample simply list words they considered features of love. Then, she took the features listed by more than one person and had another sample rate them for centrality to love. There was striking agreement across persons, such that some features were consistently rated as central (e.g., caring and intimacy) and others, although clearly part of the concept, as more peripheral (e.g., butterflies in the stomach and euphoria). Additional studies found that people used the various prototypical features (particularly central ones) to recognize instances of love, and that these features structured processing and memory for love-related information. Sets of features of love with clear prototype structures, and in most cases even the particular features and relative centrality of those features, have been found to be reasonably common across age groups and cultures (reviewed in Fehr, 2001). What is the nature of those features? Across seven studies, Aron and Westbay (1996) identified and cross-validated three latent dimensions of these features: intimacy (which included mainly features with the highest centrality ratings), commitment (mainly the next most central items), and passion (mainly the least central items). Falling in love, as used in participants' narratives of falling in love (e.g., Aron et al., 1989), seems to be about the transition to high levels of all three, but especially the passion aspect.

Other approaches to how ordinary people understand love have included Shaver, Schwartz, Kirson, and O'Connor's (1987) prototype work in which they found that love and joy are related or similar, but love is more personalized toward the object of affection, whereas joy is more general in nature. They also noted that people describe love as a form of social contact that is highly specific and focused on the love object, such as a desire to be near, touch, or kiss the loved one. Yet another approach has been to focus not on prototypical features but on prototypical kinds of love. Taking this approach, Fehr and Russell (1991) found that maternal and friendship types of love were prototypical of love in general, but romantic love was less prototypical and sexual types of love (e.g., lust, and sexual love) were even less prototypical. Consistent with these findings, categories related to "falling in love," such as infatuation and love at first sight, were listed but were viewed as not being prototypical of love in general.

Thus, based on both the centrality structure of Fehr's (2001) features and the work by Shaver et al. (1987) and Fehr and Russell (1991), "falling in love," and passionate love in general, are very specific instances of love in people's minds. In this light, research and theory based on people's experiences of "love" in general may be misleading if applied to falling in love.

Falling in Love versus the Onset of Sexual Desire

Ellen Berscheid (1988) made the influential comment that passionate love is "about 90% sexual desire as yet not sated" (p. 373). Clearly, sexual desire is linked with passionate love. For example, in the lay prototype of love developed by Fehr (1988), many of the features identified by Aron and Westbay (1996) as part of the passion factor were sexual in nature, including sexual passion and sex appeal. Similarly, the PLS, the most widely used measure of passionate love, includes items that emphasize sexual desire, including "I sense my body responding when ____ touches me"; "In the presence of ____, I yearn to touch and be touched"; and "Sometimes my body trembles with excitement at the sight of ____"—all items that correlate highly with the other scale items.

Nevertheless, it does seem possible to distinguish passionate love from sexual desire (Aron & Aron, 1991). In terms of evolutionary foundations, as will be discussed in more detail below, Fisher (1998) argued that romantic attraction and the sex drive are associated with distinct brain systems, and each evolved to facilitate a different aspect of courtship, mating, and reproduction. Specifically, whereas sexual desire is not focused on a specific individual, romantic attraction (or falling in love) is typically so focused. Several studies also support there being such a distinction. Gonzaga et al. (2001) found positive correlations between love and sexual desire, but also found that the two states were associated with different nonverbal cues and behavioral responses. For example, head nodding and smiling were significant predictors of love but not sexual desire.

Also relevant is Diamond's (2003) argument that sexual orientation does not completely predict the gender of the objects of passionate love; thus, individuals sometimes appear to fall in love with partners of the "wrong" gender with whom they may have no initial desire to have sexual contact, even though they show all the other symptoms of passionate love. Yet another relevant finding is that 4- and 5-year-old children, who presumably do not have the same kind of sexual response as adolescents, report levels of passionate love as high as those of 14 to 18 year olds (Hatfield & Rapson, 1987). Finally, fMRI studies of romantic love (Aron et al., 2005; Bartels & Zeki, 2000; Xu, Aron, et al., 2008) have consistently found patterns of brain activity that only minimally overlap with activation patterns found in studies of sexual arousal (e.g., Arnow et al., 2002; Karama et al., 2002). In sum, sexuality almost surely plays an important role in falling in love, but it is also conceptually and empirically distinguishable from it and cannot fully explain its functioning.

VARIATIONS IN FALLING IN LOVE

As noted, almost everyone falls in love. But the frequency and intensity differ in systematic ways. There are, for example, various differences with regard to issues discussed in the later section on attraction, such as who is likely to be an object of falling in love and under what circumstances falling in love is most likely to occur. There are yet additional variations that have received little study, such as the difference between falling in love when one is versus is not able or desiring to pursue the beloved. Here we focus on five important sources of variation that have been subjected to systematic research: personality, gender, cultural context, rate of falling in love, and whether the love is reciprocated.

Personality

There appear to be consistent effects on love and falling in love for individual differences in attachment style. Those who fall in love most often and most intensely are people with preoccupied (also called *anxious-ambivalent*) attachment styles (Hazan & Shaver, 1987). Individuals with preoccupied attachment styles are generally characterized as being hungry for love and needy, and thus tend to seek love more avidly and to be more engaged in concern about the partner's response. Further, because their relationships tend not to last as long as compared to those of people with secure attachment styles (Hazan & Shaver, 1987), perhaps individuals with a preoccupied attachment style are more often open and ready to fall in love. In earlier research, Dion and Dion (1975) reported a similar pattern for those low in self-esteem.

Gender

Patterns of falling in love seem to differ somewhat for women and men. Hendrick and Hendrick (1986, 1995), in samples of U.S. college students, found that men reported being in love more times than women. However, women were more likely to report being currently in love, that they were more deeply in love, and that love was more important to them. When asked about the number of times they have been in love, men were also more extreme in their responses, indicating they had either never been in love or been in love three or more times. This is consistent with earlier research in U.S. college students (Kephart, 1967) in which men scored higher than women on whether they considered love to be a necessary basis for marriage. Similarly, men report greater degrees of passionate love (Dion & Dion, 1993; Traupmann & Hatfield, 1981). Indeed, Kim and Hatfield (2004) found larger correlations between passionate love and positive or negative affect for men than women in both U.S. and Korean samples. Consistent with this general trend, Sprecher et al. (1994) found more women than men currently in love across Japanese, Russian, and U.S. college student samples; however, they did not find gender differences in number of times in love. The overall pattern appears to be one in which, on the average, men are more variable and are more romantic and passionate than women. (In this light, the apparent paradox—assuming most love relationships are heterosexual—of gender differences in likelihood of current love status may be due to what women and men count as being in love; women may discount instances that are less passionate. Another logical possibility is that women are more likely to be in unrequited love; however, such gender differences have not been found in studies of unrequited love [e.g., Aron et al., 1998].)

A similar gender difference is seen with regard to love styles. Men typically score higher than women on ludus or game-playing love (Hendrick & Hendrick, 1986, 1988; Sprecher & Toro-Morn, 2002) and agape or selfless love (Neto et al., 2000; Sprecher & Toro-Morn, 2002), which might be taken as indicators of both the greater variability and extremes that seem more typical of men than women. Some work has found women endorsing the eros or romantic love style more than men (Sprecher & Toro-Morn, 2002). Eros is, more or less, passionate love without the obsessive components. Thus, this result is generally consistent with women being more deeply and in a sense more reliably in love. On the other hand, because eros does have a passionate component, this result is somewhat contradictory to other findings. It is notable, however, that this particular result has mainly been found in North American samples and not replicated in other cultures.

It is important to emphasize, however, that nearly all of the above gender difference findings represent small effect sizes and that there are very substantial overlapping distributions. Indeed, fMRI studies on intense passionate love have found little in the way of gender differences. The importance of gender as a social group membership variable may be overrated, and factors such as culture and social class may exert a greater influence on falling in love (Hyde, 2005; Sprecher & Toro-Morn, 2002). Similarly, Hatfield (1982) noted that among North Americans, gender similarities in attitudes toward romantic love seem to be far greater than gender differences. As will be seen more fully in the next section, when gender differences are found, they often vary by culture; differences consistently found in North American and Western European samples are not always found in other cultural contexts.

Cultural Context

Many studies have compared romantic love, including falling in love, across cultural contexts. With regard to frequency, Fisher, Tsapelas, and Aron (2008), in a large-sample study, found that many more college-age U.S. (70.8%) than college-age Japanese (52.6%) respondents reported being currently in love. However, slightly more Japanese than American (99.5% versus 89.3%) respondents reported having been in love in the past. Sprecher et al. (1994) also reported a greater proportion of Japanese than Americans currently in love; however, in their study, Japanese were somewhat *less* likely to have ever been in love. Still, those Japanese who had ever been in love reported more love experiences than Americans.

With regard to precursors to falling in love, it has been found that European Americans mention filling needs (of the self and partner) most often in their narrative accounts of the experience when compared with Mexican Americans and Asian Americans (Riela et al., 2006, 2007). The same type of effect was found for readiness. Overall, however, there were more similarities than differences across these ethnic groups. Similarly, a questionnaire study of precursors (Sprecher et al., 1994) among Russian, Japanese, and U.S. college students found that across all three cultural contexts, reciprocal liking and desirable personality and physical appearance were the most important rated precursors for falling in love. However, compared to Japanese and Russian respondents, physical appearance and similarity were especially important for Americans.

With regard to types of love, several studies have compared cultures on Lee's (1977) six styles. Neto et al. (2000) examined these love styles in a large number of countries in Africa, Asia, South America, and Europe. However, although the structure of the different styles was relatively consistent across cultures, the relative importance of those styles showed several notable differences. Styles involving strong personal feelings, such as eros, mania, and agape, were found to have very modest cross-cultural differences. In fact, the only significant difference involved the eros love style, in which respondents from Macao used fewer eros-type statements than did Portuguese respondents. Love styles involving strict social rules and low levels of affect, such as pragma and storge, were found to have greater cross-cultural differences. Specifically, Africans were more pragmatic and storgic in their responses than French and Swiss participants.

However, another study found some cultural differences in the actual structure of the love styles. Cho and Cross (1995) reported that Taiwanese students living in the United States demonstrated love styles generally similar to those of Americans, but with distinct Chinese features. Factor analysis of the Love Attitudes Scale (Hendrick & Hendrick, 1986) in the Taiwanese students yielded dimensions similar to storge, ludus, and mania, but a new dimension of love composed of some of the eros and agape items appeared, which they labeled *romantic/considerate love*. Also, two separate factors appeared that corresponded to the single pragma factor in Western samples. These two factors were *calculated love* that was individualistically oriented and *obligatory love* that involved self-sacrifice and choosing an acceptable partner for the family's sake.

Regarding the original six Hendrick and Hendrick (1986) love styles, in their comparison of American, Japanese, and Russian college students, Sprecher et al. (1994), on the one hand, found considerable agreement across cultures, with the eros love style the most highly rated across cultural groups. However, compared to Japanese and Russian respondents, Americans scored high on eros and storge, and Russian respondents differed from the other two groups by scoring higher on the ludus and agape love styles. Additional relevant results of that study found that most of the college students surveyed in all three cultures believed that love should be the basis of marriage. However, compared to Japanese and Russian respondents, Americans scored high on secure attachment, and Russian respondents differed from the other two groups by scoring higher on avoidant attachment and being most willing to marry someone they did not love romantically.

With regard to other aspects, Hatfield and Rapson (1987) found that intensity of passionate love was similar among Americans of European, Filipino, and Japanese ancestry. However, Simmons, vom Kolke, and Shimizu (1986) found romantic love to be less positively valued by Japanese than by Americans and Germans. Further, the Japanese sample had a complex pattern of responses, endorsing both traditional romantic ideas and the attitude that romantic love should be controlled. They viewed love as a dazed state and considered jealousy to be integral to the experience of love; they also most strongly endorsed the idea that true love lasts forever.

Finally, Xu, Aron, et al. (2008) recently conducted a replication of the Aron et al. (2005) fMRI study of early-stage passionate love in China. The replication was conducted with a sample of college students in Beijing of the same age, gender distribution, length of time in love, and reported love intensity as in the Aron et al. American sample. Preliminary analyses indicate that the primary pattern of neural activation for the Chinese participants was nearly identical to that found for the American sample, although this pattern was strongest in those who had the lowest scores on a standard questionnaire measure of Chinese traditionality.

Overall, these examples and other studies of cultural (and ethnic or subcultural) differences and similarities (e.g., Contreras, Hendrick, & Hendrick, 1996; Doherty, Hatfield, Thompson, & Choo, 1994; Kim & Hatfield, 2004; Levine, Sato, Hashimoto, & Verma, 1995; Simmons et al., 1986) suggest that there is a core element of passionate love found in every culture (that may even have an evolutionary foundation and a common basic neural substrate), but how it is enacted may depend heavily on the cultural context. Indeed, the differences may be greater for falling in love than for what is fallen into. That is, just what precursors lead to falling in love, different styles of expressing and experiencing love, and its incidence across the life cycle may well be exactly the kinds of factors that are most influenced by the different values, traditions, and other aspects of cultural context. With regard to differences, Dion and Dion (1988, 1996) suggested that much of the cultural variation in romantic love generally might be explained by individualism and collectivism, with couples in collectivistic cultures having a difficult time separating from the family and community context to become intimate with each other. However, the diverse findings to date specifically on falling in love do not all seem easily explained by this single cultural context variable.

Rate of Falling in Love

Riela and colleagues (2006, 2007) conducted a systematic content analysis of free-response narratives of falling in love experiences in U.S. samples. Participants were asked to briefly describe their most recent falling in love experience, including what led up to it (e.g., specific events) and how they were feeling. Judges coded the narratives, from a list of 30 items, for precursors to falling in love such as reciprocal liking and desirable characteristics (as outlined by Aron et al., 1989). In addition, experiences were coded for rate of falling in love. Fast experiences were defined as those occurring over a short period of time, or as a result of a strong upsurge in attraction. Slow experiences were defined as those occurring gradually over time, or without a strong upsurge of attraction. (This is not to say that the experiences were less intense; rather, the experience was not rapid.)

Across the studies, for those narratives that could be coded for rate of falling in love, the majority (approximately 58%) were classified as fast. As might be expected, the narratives of those who fell in love slowly were more likely to have mentioned having been already familiar with the person before falling in love. Among individuals falling in love quickly, some emphasis was placed on readiness for entering a relationship, as well as specific characteristics of the other person (e.g., eyes and smile). Another study, using a Spanish sample, found that physical attractiveness was more important for love at first sight compared with gradual or reciprocally developed love (Sangrador & Yela, 2000).

Whether or Not the Love Is Reciprocated

Most U.S. college students have had at least one experience of loving someone who did not love them (Aron et al., 1998). Baumeister et al. (1993) compared autobiographical accounts of being rejected and of being the undesired object of someone's attraction. They found that rejection can lead to strong organization as well as strong disorganization of thoughts, behaviors, and emotions; both the rejector's and rejectee's behaviors are mostly passive; both wish (but do not necessarily act) for different behaviors and outcomes from the other; and both usually end up disappointed.

Aron et al. (1998) found that intensity of unrequited love was predicted by three factors. The most important was perceived desirability of the partner and the relationship (e.g., high ratings for "How perfect is this person in your eyes?"); the second most important was perceived desirability of the state of being in love, whether reciprocated or not (e.g., "How fulfilling is it to love this person even though it is unrequited?"); and the least important (but still significant) was mistakenly believing at the outset that the other would reciprocate the love (e.g., "Even though you don't feel this person loves you as much as you would like, to what extent has this person done things that would make most people think he or she loves you?").

Aron and colleagues (1998) also found differences by self-reported attachment style. Secure individuals were least likely to experience unrequited love; when they did, they were the group with the strongest association with mistaken expectation of reciprocation. Avoidant individuals were somewhat more likely than secures to experience unrequited love; when they did, they were the group with a strong positive association with desirability of the state of being in love. (Aron et al. suggested that for them, unrequited love is a chance to experience the culturally valued state of intense love without having to deal with a relationship. Indeed, this was the only group for whom desirability of the state of being in unrequited love was positively associated with intensity of the experience.) Finally, anxious-ambivalent individuals were most likely to experience unrequited love and were the group with the strongest association with desirability of the partner. Desirability of the partner was very highly correlated with intensity for them; however, desirability of the state of being in love was clearly *negatively* correlated for them with intensity of the love.

ROMANTIC ATTRACTION

Interpersonal attraction is a long-standing major topic of social psychology, which has been reviewed extensively elsewhere (e.g., Berschied & Reis, 1998; Bruce & Graziano, this volume). Much of the research has focused on attraction in nonromantic contexts, such as liking for potential friends or work partners. Even work on "romantic attraction" or "romantic liking" has usually been conducted in the context of the very initial response to a potential romantic partner. Nevertheless, there would seem to be a clear element of general liking in falling in love, and initial romantic attraction is presumably a common first step in developing a full-fledged falling in love experience. Research over the years has identified several factors that lead to general liking, which also have been found to play a role in romantic attraction. These include reciprocal liking (discovering that the other likes the self; e.g., Walster & Walster, 1963); desirability of the other (kindness, intelligence, humor, good looks, social status, etc.; e.g., Buss, 1989); similarity, especially of attitudes, values, and demographic characteristics (e.g., Byrne, 1971; Laumann, Gagnon, Michael, & Michaels, 1994; Rushton, 1989); mere exposure (e.g., Zajonc, 1968); filling needs (e.g., Aron et al., 1989; Dion & Dion, 1993; Tennov, 1979); and social appropriateness and social network support and/or encouragement (e.g., Sprecher et al., 1994).

In the specific context of falling in love, reciprocal liking and partner's desirability appear to be most influential (Aron et al., 1989), even across cultures (Buss, 1989; Riela et al., 2006, 2007; Sprecher et al., 1994). For example, in a sample of Canadian college students who very recently fell in love, 90% of accounts mentioned some indicator of perceiving the other as attracted to self (with eye contact being a particularly common cue), and 78% mentioned desirable characteristics (Aron et al., 1989). Other studies have found similar results (Riela et al., 2006, 2007). Aron et al. (1989) commented that the data suggest that "people are just waiting for an attractive person to do something they can interpret as liking them" (p. 251).

Among desirable characteristics, across many cultures, kindness and intelligence (Buss, 1989) are especially important for both women and men. However, men, somewhat more than women, are attracted to partners who shows visual signs of youth, health, and beauty; women more than men are attracted to partners who exhibit signs of status and resources (e.g., Buss; Ingoldsby, Schvaneveldt, & Uribe, 2003; Li, Bailey, & Kenrick, 2002; Pines, 2001). Also, women are slightly more affected than men by desirable personality traits (Sprecher et al., 1994).

Regarding similarity, perceived shared attitudes is the most thoroughly studied and has shown a highly consistent positive effect on attraction across many experiments (Byrne, 1971). However, in most of these studies all other factors that might affect attraction are experimentally controlled. In more naturalistic contexts, where other variables are not held constant, the effect sizes for the role of attitude similarity in predicting attraction are often relatively small (e.g., Newcomb, 1956). Further, much of the attitude similarity effects may be due to reduced attraction to perceived dissimilars (Rosenbaum, 1986). It is also clear that perceived similarity is much more important than actual similarity (Berscheid & Reis, 1998). Also, personality similarity plays a much smaller role than attitude similarity (Botwin, Buss, & Shackelford, 1997; Caspi & Herbener, 1993). In general, dissimilarity ("opposites attract") seems to play little positive role in attraction, although there is some evidence that when one believes a relationship with an appropriate other is likely, similarity effects are reduced and one may even prefer those with dissimilar interests (Aron, Steele, Kashdan, & Perez, 2006). Thus, similarity may not be as major a factor as has been thought in influencing attraction and falling in love.

In contrast, exposure or "propinquity" may strongly influence the falling in love process, mainly by providing an opportunity. Specifically, recent work (Riela et al., 2006, 2007) suggests that propinquity may have more of a direct impact than was thought previously (Aron et al., 1989; Sprecher et al., 1994), given that it was mentioned in 65% of the narrative accounts of falling in love. This may arise because platonic friendships are a common beginning for romance via the romantic attractions they often include (Kaplan & Keys, 1997).

The partner filling one's needs also appears to be instrumental to falling in love. *Filling needs* refers to satisfying the needs of another individual, such as happiness, and alludes to personality traits of the other person (e.g., compassion and honesty) that are highly valued. The incidence of filling needs coded in narrative accounts is not as high as that of other precursors (Aron et al., 1989; Riela et al., 2006, 2007). However, Riela et al. found that women mention filling needs more often than men, which may be consistent with research suggesting that men are more autonomous and women more relational (e.g., Dion & Dion, 1993).

There are few studies of the role of social appropriateness and social networks in falling in love. Sprecher et al. (1994) found social networks were more important in Japanese than American culture, perhaps due to the former being more collectivist. There is also some evidence in American culture for a "Romeo and Juliet effect" in which romantic love is inversely correlated with parental approval (Driscoll, Davis, & Lipetz, 1972); but most studies find parental approval to be a positive factor (Sprecher, Felmlee, Orbuch, & Willetts, 2002).

Aron et al. (1989) argued that, in addition to these general attraction variables, there are at least three variables that may be specific to falling in love: arousal at time of meeting the partner (the "arousal–attraction effect"), readiness for falling in love, and "specific cues." Among the first demonstrations of the arousal–attraction effect was the Dutton and Aron (1974) "shaky bridge" study, in which men were more attracted to a good-looking confederate who met her on an anxiety-provoking suspension bridge than were men who met her on a solid, low bridge. A number of subsequent studies (see Foster, Witcher, Campbell, & Green, 1998) have demonstrated the generalizability of the effect across a great variety of positive and negative sources of arousal, as well as supporting at least two mechanisms (e.g., reattribution of arousal and elicitation of a dominant response). Recent research shows the effect generalizes across women and men and holds when the partner is not a confederate (Lewandowski & Aron, 2004).

The main direct support for a readiness effect comes from the Aron et al. (1989) study in which it was moderately mentioned in falling in love narratives and the Sprecher et al. (1994) cross-cultural study in which Russian, Japanese, and U.S. participants all rated it as being moderately important for falling in love. Indeed, it seems reasonable that people are less likely to fall in love with Person A when they have just fallen in love with Person B, and may be more likely to fall in love when they have just broken up with someone. Tennov (1979) also reported that a striking difference between those "in love" and not in love (e.g., including those who reported never having been in love) was that the "in love" group reported having had a strong readiness. They expressed a strong desire for being in love illustrated by statements such as "wanted it badly," "needing someone to love," and "couldn't imagine being happy without it" (p. 107). Similarly, Riela and colleagues (2006, 2007) found that those who reported more readiness to fall in love were more likely to have fallen in love quickly. One should keep in mind, though, that readiness could change over the life span, being most important in early adulthood.

The role of specific cues was first suggested by Binet (1887), who noted that people are often strongly attracted to others with some very specific characteristic (smile, color of hair, shape of face, way of walking, etc.), a theme extended by Grant (1957). Aron et al. (1989) found a number of falling in love narratives that seemed especially well explained by specific cues, perhaps consistent with studies suggesting that people select romantic partners similar to their parents (e.g., Aron et al., 1974; Little, Penton-Voak, & Burt, 2003). Money (1997) hypothesized that between the ages of 5 and 8, children develop an unconscious "love map" of traits they will seek in adult mates.

EFFECTS OF FALLING IN LOVE

Taking a largely qualitative approach, Tennov (1979) studied individuals who reported intense romantic love. Such individuals commonly reported focused attention, strong motivation, goal-oriented behaviors, heightened energy, sleeplessness, loss of appetite, feelings of euphoria, obsessive thinking about the beloved, and heightened attraction during adversity in the relationship, all characteristics corresponding well with those emphasized in Hatfield and Sprecher's (1986) widely used PLS questionnaire (described earlier).

Is falling in love a good thing? Aron et al. (1995) predicted that falling in love, when reciprocated, would lead to an enhancement of the self-concept, including increased identity domain, greater sense of self-efficacy, and greater self-esteem. They studied two large samples of mainly first- and second-year U.S. college students, collecting data every 2 weeks over the first 10 weeks of the fall term. In both studies, at each testing, participants completed a series of items about what had happened in the last 2 weeks, among which were items about whether they had fallen in love. In addition, in the first study, at each testing, they also answered an open-ended question: "Who are you today?" In the second study, at each testing they instead completed standard self-efficacy and self-esteem scales. About a fourth of the participants fell in love at some point over the 10 weeks. The key results were that participants who fell in love showed significant increases in diversity of the self-concept and increased self-efficacy and self-esteem from the testing session before to the testing session after they fell in love. These changes were significantly greater than the changes across other testing-to-testing periods for the participants who fell in love, and also significantly greater than the average testing-to-testing changes for the participants who did not fall in love. Further, all of these results remained significant even after statistically controlling for mood changes associated with falling in love.

On the other hand, there are certainly contexts in which falling in love may be much less than a good thing. The most obvious is unreciprocated love, as noted earlier. Similarly, if one is already in a relationship, falling in love with someone else could be quite disruptive. Indeed, even when it is reciprocated, the effect on one's social network can be negative (Goode, 1959; Nyrop, 1985; Skolnick, 1996). The way love is interpreted can also be less than completely positive. Acevedo, Aron, Xu, and Gross (2008), in samples of U.S. college students, Mexican-Americans recruited from English as a second language courses in the U.S., and Chinese college students from a Beijing University, all reported a significantly greater number of opposite-valence emotion words (e.g., *anxiety, frustration,* and *suffering*) when asked about a love experience than when asked about basic emotions (such as joy, anger, fear, or sadness).

Whether falling in love is a good or bad thing also may differ by cultures. For example, Wu and Shaver (1992; see also Shaver, Wu, & Schwartz, 1991) compared people's conceptions of love in the United States and China. For Chinese participants, love tended to be associated with sadness, heartbreak, and darkness, including terms such as *infatuation, unrequited love, attachment, nostalgia, pity,* and *sorrow.* For Americans, love tended to be associated with positive features, such as adoration, attraction, and desire. In another study, Wu and Shaver (1993) found that Chinese participants spontaneously listed more negative items for love compared to Americans.

Is falling in love, especially falling in love intensely, a good thing in terms of its effect on the relationship over time? Huston, Caughlin, Houts, Smith, and George (2001) followed 156 couples for 13 years starting from their wedding day. Couples who divorced within 2 years were significantly less in love as newlyweds compared to all the other couples in the study. Also, among couples still married at the 13-year testing, those who were more deeply in love as newlyweds were considerably happier than those who were less deeply in love as newlyweds. In related work, Miller, Niehuis, and Huston (2006) also found that couples who idealized one another as newlyweds were less likely to suffer declines in love over time. In another study, Hendrick et al. (1988) found that of 30 couples, those who stayed together after 2 months were initially significantly more in love.

THE BIOLOGICAL BASIS OF FALLING IN LOVE

Based on a review of the relevant biological literature, Fisher (1998) hypothesized that avian and mammalian species have evolved three distinct brain systems for courtship, mating, reproduction, and parenting: (a) the sex drive, characterized by a craving for sexual gratification; (b) attraction ("favoritism," "sexual preference," or "mate choice"), characterized by focused attention on a preferred partner, heightened energy, motivation, and goal-oriented courtship behaviors; and (c) attachment, characterized by the maintenance of proximity, and affiliative gestures and expressions of calm when in social contact with a mating partner and separation anxiety when apart (as well as parental behaviors such as territory defense, nest building, mutual feeding, grooming, and other parental chores). Each emotion–motivation system is associated with a different constellation of brain circuits, different behavior patterns, and different affective states. Each emotion–motivation system varies according to the reproductive strategy of each species, and evolved to play a different role in courtship, mating, reproduction, and parenting. The sex drive evolved principally to motivate individuals to seek sexual union with a range of partners. Attraction evolved to motivate individuals to prefer particular mating partners and focus their courtship attention on these mates, thereby making a mate choice. The system for adult male–female attachment evolved primarily to motivate individuals to sustain affiliative connections long enough to complete species-specific parental duties. From the perspective of the present chapter, we can equate Fisher's "attraction" with falling in love.

It is well established that many creatures have mate preferences and make mate choices. The phenomenon of mate choice is so common that the ethological literature regularly uses several terms to describe it, including *mate choice, female choice, mate preference, individual preference, favoritism, sexual choice, selective proceptivity,* and *courtship attraction.* Fisher (1998; Fisher et al., 2002) argued that this brain system for courtship attraction has a specific and distinct constellation of neural correlates; that this system operates in tandem with other neural systems, including the sex drive and specific sensory circuits for mate discrimination; that it is expressed at different times and to different degrees according to each species' specific reproductive strategy; and that this brain system evolved to enable the chooser to discriminate between courtship displays and prefer those who advertise superior genes, better resources, and/or more parental investment, and motivate the chooser to focus his or her courtship attention on and pursue specific mating partners.

In most species of mammals and birds, this excitatory state of attraction is brief. Feelings of attraction last only minutes, hours, days, or weeks. In humans, Fisher (1998) argued, the neural mechanism for courtship attraction is more developed, forming the physiological basis of what is commonly known as passionate love, obsessive love, or romantic love.

Ethologists generally lump this system, attraction, with the sex drive and call this behavioral-physiological state *proceptivity.* There are exceptions. Beach (1976) made a distinction between the sex drive and attraction, writing, "The occurrence or non-occurrence of copulation depends as much on individual affinities and aversions as upon the presence or absence of sex hormones in the female" (p. 131). Moreover, "[P]roceptive and receptive behavior may depend upon different anatomical and neurochemical systems in the brain" (Beach, p. 131). Goodall (1986) wrote that "partner preferences, independent of hormonal influences, are clearly of major significance for chimpanzees" (p. 446).

Few scientists have considered the anatomical and neurochemical mechanisms that produce mate preference (see Fisher et al., 2002). However, Beach (1976) and Liebowitz (1983) proposed that the neurotransmitters associated with arousal, dopamine and/or norepinephrine, may be involved. Fisher (1998) hypothesized that attraction (romantic love) may be associated with *elevated* activity of the brain's pathways for dopamine and/or norepinephrine and *decreased* activity of the brain's serotonin system. These hypotheses are consistent with considerable correlational evidence. As noted earlier, characteristics of intense passionate love include focused attention, strong motivation, goal-oriented behaviors, heightened energy, sleeplessness, loss of appetite, feelings of euphoria, obsessive thinking about the beloved, and heightened attraction during adversity in the relationship (e.g., Tennov, 1979). Each of these characteristics is associated with elevated activities of central dopamine and norepinephrine and/or decreased activity of central serotonin in the corresponding brain regions (Flament, Rapoport, & Bert, 1985; Hollander et al., 1988; Schultz, 2000; Thoren, Asberg, & Bertilsson, 1980; Wise, 1989; and see Fisher, 1998). Passionate attraction takes a variety of graded forms, however, ranging from romantic love that is returned to unrequited love. So it is expected that these gradations of attraction are associated with different combinations of dopamine, norepinephrine, and serotonin, in conjunction with the activities of many other neural systems (Fisher, 1998).

Data from animal studies also support the hypothesis that elevated activities of central dopamine play a primary role in attraction in mammalian species. In rats, blocking the activities of dopamine diminishes specific proceptive behaviors, including hopping and darting (Herbert, 1996). Further, when a female lab-raised prairie vole is mated with a male, she forms a distinct preference for this partner. This preference is associated with a 50% increase of dopamine in the nucleus accumbens (Gingrich, Liu, Cascio, Wang, & Insel, 2000). In fact, when a dopamine antagonist is injected directly into the nucleus accumbens, females no longer prefer this partner; and when a female is injected with a dopamine agonist, she begins to prefer a conspecific who is present at the time of infusion, even if the female has not mated with this male (Aragona, Yan, Curtis, Stephan, & Wang, 2003; Wang et al., 1999).

Recent studies using fMRI lend relatively direct support to the dopamine hypothesis in humans. fMRI technology scans the brain to register blood flow changes in any or all brain regions that are either increasing or decreasing their metabolic activities. Bartels and Zeki (2000) scanned a group of participants who reported being "truly, deeply, and madly in love" (p. 3829), and compared brain activation when looking at the beloved partner versus when looking at familiar friends. They found a specific constellation of brain activity associated with looking at the beloved, including activity in the caudate nucleus. The caudate nucleus is largely associated with motivation and goal-oriented behaviors; 80% of receptor sites for dopamine reside here, and the caudate is a central part of the brain's "reward system," the system associated with the identification of, focus on, and motivation to win rewards. These data suggest that passionate romantic love is primarily a motivation system associated with dopamine pathways in the reward system of the brain.

Aron et al. (2005) conducted a similar study, but their participants were more recently and even more intensely in love than those in the Bartels and Zeki (2000) study. (In the Aron et al. sample, mean length of time in love was 7 months and mean PLS score was 8.54 on a 9-point scale; in the Bartels & Zeki sample, the corresponding means were 2.5 years and 7.55.) In the Aron et al. study, comparison of activations when looking at and thinking about the beloved (versus looking at and thinking about the familiar neutral individual) again yielded significant activation in the caudate. Indeed, in this study, the caudate activation was especially strong. Further, as noted earlier, Aron et al. found that this caudate activation was significantly correlated ($r = .60$) with scores on the PLS (Bartels & Zeki did not test this correlation). Most importantly, Aron et al. also found significant activity in a region of the right ventral tegmental area, which is primarily associated with the production and distribution of dopamine to several other brain regions. As noted earlier, preliminary analyses of an exact replication of the Aron et al. study in China have found nearly identical results (Xu, Aron, et al., 2008). These data further suggest that dopamine plays a central role in the focused attention, motivation, and goal-oriented behaviors associated with romantic love.

In sum, the considerable data on mate preference in mammalian (and avian) species, and the association of this mate preference with subcortical dopaminergic pathways in human and animal studies, suggest that attraction in mammals (and its human counterpart, falling in love) is a specific but dynamic biobehavioral brain system; that it is associated with at least one specific neurotransmitter, dopamine; and that this brain system evolved to facilitate a specific reproductive function: mate preference and pursuit of this preferred mating partner.

HOW DOES FALLING IN LOVE WORK?

Below, we briefly review five particularly influential approaches for understanding the dynamics of romantic love, each of which bears directly on the present topic of falling in love. Other important theoretical approaches in the relationship area, such as interdependence theory (Kelley & Thibaut, 1979), have rarely been applied to falling in love.

Love as Emotion

Many emotion theorists have treated love as an emotion (e.g., Gonzaga et al., 2001; Shaver et al., 1987; Shaver, Morgan, & Wu, 1996). Shaver and colleagues, for example, noted that it is typically the first response given when participants are asked for an example of an emotion. Similarly, when one focuses on "moments of love," love shows many of the features of emotions. On the other hand, although love is highly emotional, it may be better characterized as a goal-oriented motivational state and not as a specific emotion in its own right (Aron & Aron, 1991). As Fisher (2004) noted, it tends to be hard to control, is not associated with any specific facial expression, is focused on a specific reward, and, like basic drives (Pfaff, 1999), is associated with subcortical dopaminergic pathways in the brain. To date this latter view is supported by three lines of research. First, in various experiments (Acevedo & Aron, 2004, Studies 1–6; Rousar, 1990), participants check many more emotions when asked about the emotions one feels or has felt when experiencing "love" (or "romantic love," "passionate love," or a "moment of passionate love") than when asked about fear, anger, sadness, or happiness; in each case, there were also more opposite-valence emotions checked when rating experiences of love than of fear and so forth. These findings have held up using diverse procedures (e.g., Acevedo, Aron, & Xu, 2007). The results were predicted based on the idea that like other goal-oriented states, love generates a variety of specific emotions according to the extent to which it is satisfied or frustrated.

The second line of work supporting the view of falling in love as a motivational state deals with the extent to which individuals report being able to successfully up-regulate (or increase) and down-regulate (or decrease) feelings of love compared to emotions. Results from two studies (Acevedo, Aron, & Gross, 2006) suggest that people can down-regulate feelings of passionate love with about the same level of difficulty as for down-regulating emotions such as anger, fear, pride, and happiness. However, they find it is much more difficult than it is for those emotions to up-regulate (increase) feelings of passionate love. In addition, a majority of participants that were interviewed reported that forcing themselves to fall in love with someone for whom they did not initially feel "a spark" was impossible. The third line of work is the recent fMRI studies of romantic love (Aron et al., 2005; Bartels & Zeki, 2000; Xu, Aron, et al., 2008), which, as noted earlier, found consistent activation across participants primarily in reward-related brain regions, with greater diversity of response in emotion-related regions.

At this point, it seems clear that falling in love has a strong motivational component. Nevertheless, it remains possible that falling in love may also be a specific, intense emotion or represent a specific motivational experience. Of course, both a constellation of emotions and several motivations are clearly involved, and definitions of what are called *emotions* versus *motivations* are somewhat overlapping.

Love as Attachment

Attachment theory (Bowlby, 1969) has been among the influential approaches to understanding romantic love, and the primary approach that emphasizes individual differences. The theory posits that love develops out of three behavioral systems that evolved to promote the development and survival of infants in humans and perhaps other primates or even other, nonprimate species (Shaver, Hazan, & Bradshaw, 1988). These systems include attachment, caregiving, and sexuality. In human adults, according to this model, passionate love is a combination of the desires for attachment and sexuality. Further, this model emphasizes that early experience with caregivers strongly shapes individual differences in adult love experiences. Thus, for example, those who have had inconsistent caregiving (e.g., those high on the anxious-attachment or preoccupied dimension) are much more likely to experience intense passionate love and more likely to experience intense unrequited love given their propensity to easily fall in love, but not find true love; in contrast, those who experienced a consistent lack of security (e.g., those high on the avoidance dimension) are especially unlikely to experience passionate love in adulthood given their tendency to reject passionate love as real (Aron et al., 1998; Hazan & Shaver, 1987; Hendrick & Hendrick, 1989). Some preliminary evidence even suggests that the brain systems engaged by passionate love may be moderated by individual differences in attachment style (Aron, Fisher, Mashek, Strong, Shaver, et al., 2004).

Love as a Story

Sternberg (1998) suggested that loving relationships can be described accurately by the people involved through narrative autobiographies, often suggesting culturally prototypical "stories." For example, the story of a couple locked in constant struggle is common, as is the story of couples growing to love each other over time. In their recent work, Sternberg, Hojjat, and Barnes (2001) described other central aspects of these stories. Each type of story has a characteristic mode of thought and behavior that often corresponds to other views of love (e.g., someone with a game-based love story will behave in ways consistent with the ludus love style). Having a particular love story can also impact one's expectations of what a romantic relationship should be like. People tend to seek romantic partners with similar love stories and complementary roles within these stories. Finally, these stories are inextricably linked with the rest of one's life: Particular stories can influence behavior in a relationship, and stories can also be shaped and modified by one's experiences.

This approach seems promising given the general tendency for people to organize their world in narrative form, and there has been some preliminary research support for the model (Sternberg et al., 2001). Preferences for particular love stories were measured in couples, and relationship satisfaction was found to be strongly related to story similarity between partners.

Evolutionary Approaches

Because courtship and mate choice are central aspects of reproduction in avian and mammalian species, it seems plausible that the experiences, behaviors, and neural underpinnings of falling in love might be strongly shaped by evolution. Thus, as noted in the section on the biology of romantic love, Fisher (1998) proposed that the brain system for romantic attraction evolved to motivate individuals to select among potential mating partners, prefer particular conspecifics, and focus their courtship attention on these favored individuals, thereby conserving precious courtship and mating time and energy. Miller (2000) proposed that many human traits, including language and many artistic talents, evolved as display devices to trigger attraction.

As also noted earlier, another important line of evolutionary thinking, largely based on parental investment theory (Trivers, 1972), has emphasized gender differences in what features are desirable in a mate and in the basis for jealousy (e.g., Buss & Schmitt, 1993). There have also been some approaches to the evolutionary basis of experience and behavior in romantic love arguing that the mating system exploits an evolved bonding module between infants and parents (Hazan & Dia-mond, 2000; Miller & Fishkin, 1997).

Self-Expansion Model

Aron and Aron's (1986) self-expansion model posits (a) a primary human motivation to expand one's self in terms of potential to attain desired goals, and (b) that a main way people seek to expand the self is in terms of "including others in the self" through close relationships so that the other's resources, perspectives, and identities are treated to some extent as one's own. Both principles have received considerable research support (for reviews, see Aron, Aron, & Norman, 2001; Aron, Mashek, & Aron, 2004). In terms of romantic love, Aron, Norman, Aron, McKenna, and Heyman (2000) argued that the exhilaration and intense, focused attention of passionate love arise from the rapid rate of including the other in the self often associated with forming a new romantic relationship. We have cited several relevant studies throughout this chapter. Falling in love, according to this model, arises when one perceives the opportunity for substantial self-expansion by including a particular other person in the self (Aron et al., 1995, 1998).

CONCLUSIONS AND FUTURE DIRECTIONS

Falling in love is much less a mystery than it once was. At least as scientists, we are no longer just watching the storms and heat waves with at best only a poetic sense of what is going on. As we have seen in this review, we have learned a great deal. We can identify fairly precisely what we (and laypeople) mean by falling in love, including that it is not just sexual desire. We know many of the systematic similarities and differences across personality, gender, culture, rate, and whether or not the love is reciprocated. Especially by extension of the work on general interpersonal attraction, we know a lot about the variables that predict falling in love. We have a growing basis for understanding its biological correlates and cross-species similarities. And as we have just seen, several theoretical approaches offer substantial insights into underlying mechanisms.

Yet, mystery remains. Most of what we know, as noted throughout, is extrapolation from work on initial attraction or on romantic love, the states on either side of falling in love, each of which have been much more thoroughly studied. Why has falling in love specifically been less well studied? We do not think it is because it is a trivial phenomenon. It does not happen often in any one person's life, but it seems to happen at some point at least once to almost everyone in almost every culture. When it does happen, especially when it is rapid, it seems to be extremely important both as a significant life event in its own right and often as the entry to a lifelong relationship.

It part, the relative lack of work specifically on falling in love may be due to it being particu-larly difficult to study. There has been great progress in applying scientific methods to seemingly equally difficult topics, including *being in* romantic love (Aron et al., 2006), which until recent years seems to have been considered inaccessible to science. But a special difficulty for studying *falling in* love is that it is typically a very short-term process (e.g., as compared to being in love), and one that is too intense to create easily in a laboratory setting (e.g., as compared to initial inter-personal attraction). To study falling in love as it happens naturally requires being at just the right place at the right time. The Aron et al. (1995) studies suggest one practical approach to catching such transitions as they happen: If one follows North American college students over their first semester, the incidence of falling in love is 25% or more. Another successful approach has been to actively recruit individuals who are in the transition (e.g., Aron et al., 2005). And of course, a very great deal has been learned (indeed, most of what is in this review) from asking people about falling in love experiences retrospectively, especially when the experience was recent—straight-forward methods that directly tap subjective life and that will undoubtedly continue to make the greatest contributions.

However, we look forward not only to continued important work using existing approaches but also to exciting findings from entirely new approaches or new adaptations of successful paradigms from other research domains. The application of fMRI and other neuroscience methods is certainly one significant contemporary development. (For a discussion of the potentials and limitations of "relationship neuroscience," see Aron, 2006.) Another important development is increased focus on observing the behavior of people who are in love (e.g., Gonzaga et al., 2001). Especially important, however, may be finding ways to apply various methods to the study of falling in love *as it happens*.

Given the sophistication and innovation that have characterized research in this area to date (Berscheid, 1999), our prediction is that it will not be long before falling in love is as well understood as being in love has become. Indeed, we look forward in the not too distant future to both being and falling in love becoming as well understood and predictable as the next storm or heat wave.

REFERENCES

Acevedo, B., & Aron, A. (2004, July). *On the emotional categorization of love and beyond*. Paper presented at the International Association for Relationship Research Conference, Madison, WI.

Acevedo, B., Aron, A., & Gross, J. (2006). *Up-regulation and down-regulation of emotions and passionate love*. Paper presented at the seventh annual meeting of the Society for Personality and Social Psychology, Palm Springs, CA.

Acevedo, B., Aron, A., Xu, X., & Gross, J. (2008). Romantic love: Basic emotion or motivation? Manuscript under review.

Aragona, B. J., Yan, L., Curtis, J. T., Stephan, F. K., & Wang, Z. (2003). A critical role for nucleus accumbens dopamine in partner-preference formation in male prairie voles. *Journal of Neuroscience, 23*, 3483–3490.

Arnow, B. A., Desmond, J. E., Banner, L. L., Glover, G. H., Solomon, A., Polan, M. L., et al. (2002). Brain activation and sexual arousal in healthy, heterosexual males. *Brain, 125*(pt. 5), 1014–1023.

Aron, A. (2006). Relationship neuroscience: Advancing the social psychology of close relationships using functional neuroimaging. In P. A. M. VanLange (Ed.), *Bridging social psychology: Benefits of transdisciplinary approaches* (pp. 261–266). Mahwah, NJ: Lawrence Erlbaum.

Aron, A., Ain, R., Anderson, J. A., Burd, H., Filman, G., & McCallum, R. (1974). Relationships with opposite-sexed parents and mate choice. *Human Relations, 27*, 17–24.

Aron, A., & Aron, E. N. (1986). *Love and the expansion of self: Understanding attraction and satisfaction*. New York: Hemisphere.

Aron, A., & Aron, E. N. (1991). Love and sexuality. In K. McKinney & S. Sprecher (Eds.), *Sexuality in close relationships* (pp. 25–48). Hillsdale, NJ: Lawrence Erlbaum.

Aron, A., Aron, E. N., & Allen, J. (1998). Motivations for unreciprocated love. *Personality and Social Psychology Bulletin, 24*, 787–796.

Aron, A., Aron, E. N., & Norman, C. (2001). The self expansion model of motivation and cognition in close relationships and beyond. In G. Fletcher & M. Clark (Eds.), *Blackwell handbook in social psychology: Vol. 2. Interpersonal processes* (pp. 478–501). Oxford: Blackwell.

Aron, A., Dutton, D. G., Aron, E. N., & Iverson, A. (1989). Experiences of falling in love. *Journal of Social and Personal Relationships, 6*, 243–257.

Aron, A., Fisher, H., Mashek, D., Strong, G., Li, H., & Brown, L. (2005) Reward, motivation, and emotion systems associated with early-stage romantic love. *Journal of Neurophysiology, 93*, 327–337. .

Aron, A., Fisher, H. E., Mashek, D., Strong, G., Shaver, P., Mikulincer, M., et al. (2004, August). *Individual differences in attachment anxiety and attachment avoidance: An fMRI study*. Paper presented at the Conference on Biological Basis of Personality and Individual Differences, Stony Brook, NY.

Aron, A., Mashek, D., & Aron, E. N. (2004). Closeness, intimacy, and including other in the self. In D. Mashek & A. Aron (Eds.), *Handbook of closeness and intimacy* (pp. 27–41). Mahwah, NJ: Lawrence Erlbaum.

Aron, A., Norman, C. C., Aron, E. N., McKenna, C., & Heyman, R. (2000). Couples' shared participation in novel and arousing activities and experienced relationship quality. *Journal of Personality and Social Psychology, 78*, 273–283.

Aron, A., Paris, M., & Aron, E. N. (1995). Falling in love: Prospective studies of self-concept change. *Journal of Personality and Social Psychology, 69*, 1102–1112.

Aron, A., Steele, J. L., Kashdan, T., & Perez, M. (2006). When similars do not attract: Tests of a prediction from the self-expansion model. *Personal Relationships, 13*, 387–396.

Aron, A., & Westbay, L. (1996). Dimensions of the prototype of love. *Journal of Personality and Social Psychology, 70*, 535–551.

Bartels, A., & Zeki, S. (2000). The neural basis of romantic love. *NeuroReport, 11*, 3829–3834.

Baumeister, R. F., Wotman, S. R., & Stillwell, A. M. (1993). Unrequited love: On heartbreak, anger, guilt, scriptlessness, and humiliation. *Journal of Personality and Social Psychology, 64*, 377–394.

Beach, F. A. (1976). Sexual attractivity, proceptivity, and receptivity in female mammals. *Hormones and Behavior, 7*, 105–138.

Berscheid, E. (1983). Emotion. In H. H. Kelley, E. Berscheid, A. Christensen, J. H. Harvey, T. L. Huston, G. Levinger, et al. (Eds.), *Close relationships* (pp. 110–168). New York: Freeman.

Berscheid, E. (1988). Some comments on love's anatomy: Or, whatever happened to old-fashioned lust? In R. J. Sternberg & M. L. Barnes (Eds.), *The psychology of love* (pp. 359–371). New Haven, CT: Yale University Press.

Berscheid, E. (1999). The greening of relationship science. *American Psychologist, 54*, 260–266.

Berscheid, E., & Hatfield, E. H. (1969). *Interpersonal attraction.* New York: Addison-Wesley.

Berscheid, E., & Hatfield, E. H. (1978). *Interpersonal attraction* (2nd ed.). Reading, MA: Addison-Wesley.

Berscheid, E., & Reis, H. T. (1998). Attraction and close relationships. In S. Fiske, D. Gilbert, & G. Lindzey (Eds.), *Handbook of social psychology* (4th ed., pp. 193–281). Boston: McGraw-Hill.

Binet, A. (1887). Le fetischisme dans l'amour. *Revue philosophique, 24*, 260.

Botwin, M. D., Buss, D. M., & Shackelford, T. K. (1997). Personality and mate preferences: Five factors in mate selection and satisfaction. *Journal of Personality, 65*, 107–136.

Bowlby, J. (1969). *Attachment and loss: Vol. 1. Attachment.* London: Hogarth Press and the Institute of Psycho-Analysis.

Buss, D. M. (1989). Sex differences in human mate preferences: Evolutionary hypotheses tested in 37 cultures. *Behavioral and Brain Sciences, 12*, 1–49.

Buss, D. M., & Schmitt, D. P. (1993). Sexual strategies theory: An evolutionary perspective on human mating. *Psychological Review, 100*, 204–232.

Byrne, D. (1971). *The attraction paradigm.* New York: Academic Press.

Carter, C. S., DeVries, A. C., Taymans, S. E., Roberts, R. L., Williams, J. R., & Getz, L. L. (1997). Peptides, steroids, and pair bonding. In C. S. Carter, I. I. Lederhendler, & B. Kirkpatrick (Eds.), *The integrative neurobiology of affiliation* (Vol. 807, pp. 260–272). New York: Annals of the New York Academy of Sciences.

Caspi, A., & Herbener, E. S. (1993). Phenotypic convergence and marital assortment: Longitudinal evidence. *Social Biology, 40*, 48–59.

Cho, W., & Cross, S. E. (1995). Taiwanese love styles and their association with self-esteem and relationship quality. *Genetic, Social and General Psychology Monographs, 121*, 281–309.

Collins, W. A. (2003). More than myth. The developmental significance of romantic relationships during adolescence. *Journal of Research on Adolescence, 13*, 1–24.

Contreras, R., Hendrick, S. S., & Hendrick, C. (1996). Perspectives on marital love and satisfaction in Mexican American and Anglo couples. *Journal of Counseling and Development, 74*, 408–415.

Cupach, W., & Spitzberg, B. H. (2004). *The dark side of relationship pursuit: From attraction to obsession and stalking.* Mahwah, NJ: Lawrence Erlbaum.

Davis, K. E., & Todd, M. J. (1985). Assessing friendship: Prototypes, paradigm cases and relationship description. In S. Duck & D. Perlman (Eds.), *Understanding personal relationships: An interdisciplinary approach* (pp. 17–38). Thousand Oaks, CA: Sage.

Diamond, L. M. (2003). What does sexual orientation orient? A biobehavioral model distinguishing romantic love and sexual desire. *Psychological Review, 110*, 173–192.

Dion, K. K., & Dion, K. (1993). Individualistic and collectivistic perspectives on gender and the cultural concept of intimacy. *Journal of Social Issues, 49*, 53–69.

Dion, K. K., & Dion, K. L. (1996). Cultural perspectives on romantic love. *Personal Relationships, 3*, 5–18.

Dion, K. L., & Dion, K. K. (1975). Self-esteem and romantic love. *Journal of Personality, 43*, 39–57.

Dion, K. L., & Dion, K. K. (1988). Romantic love: Individual and cultural perspectives. In R. J. Sternberg & M. L. Barnes (Eds.), *The psychology of love* (pp. 264–289). New Haven, CT: Yale University Press.

Doherty, R. W., Hatfield, E., Thompson, K., & Choo, P. (1994). Cultural and ethnic influences on love and attachment. *Personal Relationships, 1*, 391–398.

Driscoll, R., Davis, K. E., & Lipetz, M. E. (1972). Parental interference and romantic love: The Romeo and Juliet effect. *Journal of Personality and Social Psychology, 24*, 1–10.

Dutton, D. G., & Aron, A. (1974). Some evidence for heightened sexual attraction under conditions of high anxiety. *Journal of Personality and Social Psychology, 30,* 510–517.

Fehr, B. (1988). Prototype analysis of the concepts of love and commitment. *Journal of Personality and Social Psychology, 55,* 557–579.

Fehr, B. (2001). The status of theory and research on love and commitment. In G. Fletcher & M. Clark (Eds.), *Blackwell handbook in social psychology: Vol. 2. Interpersonal processes* (pp. 331–336). Oxford: Blackwell.

Fehr, B., & Russell, J. A. (1991). The concept of love viewed from a prototypical perspective. *Journal of Personality and Social Psychology, 60,* 425–438.

Fisher, H. E. (1992). *Anatomy of love: The natural history of monogamy, adultery and divorce.* New York: W. W. Norton.

Fisher, H. E. (1998). Lust, attraction and attachment in mammalian reproduction. *Human Nature, 9*(1), 23–52.

Fisher, H. E. (2004). *Why we love: The nature and chemistry of romantic love.* New York: Henry Holt.

Fisher, H. E., Aron, A., Mashek, D., Li, H., Strong, G., & Brown, L. L. (2002). The neural mechanisms of mate choice. *Neuroendocrinology Letters, 23*(Special issue, Suppl. 4), 92–97.

Fisher, H. E., Aron, A., Strong, G., Mashek, D. J., Li, H., & Brown, L. L. (2005). Motivation and emotion systems associated with romantic love following rejection: An fMRI study (Program No. 660.7). In Society for Neuroscience, *2005 abstract viewer/itinerary planner.* Washington, DC: Society for Neuroscience.

Fisher, H. E., Tsapelas, I., & Aron, A. (2008). *Romantic love in the United States and Japan.* Manuscript in preparation.

Flament, M. F., Rapoport, J. L., & Bert, C. L. (1985). Clomipramine treatment of childhood obsessive-compulsive disorder: A double-blind controlled study. *Archives of General Psychiatry, 42,* 977–986.

Fletcher, G. J. O., Simpson, J. A., Thomas, G., & Giles, L. (1999). Ideals in intimate relationships. *Journal of Personality and Social Psychology, 76,* 72–89.

Foster, C. A., Witcher, B. S., Campbell, W. K., & Green, J. D. (1998). Arousal and attraction: Evidence for automatic and controlled processes. *Journal of Personality and Social Psychology, 74,* 86–101.

Freud, S. (1927). Some psychological consequences of anatomical distinction between the sexes. *International Journal of Psycho-Analysis, 8,* 133–142.

Gingrich, B., Liu, Y., Cascio, C., Wang, Z., & Insel, T. R. (2000). D2 receptors in the nucleus accumbens are important for social attachment in female prairie voles (*Microtus ochrogaster*). *Behavioral Neuroscience, 114,* 173–183.

Gonzaga, G. C. (2002). Distinctions between sexual desire and love in narrative report, nonverbal expression and physiology. *Dissertation Abstracts International: Section B: The Sciences & Engineering, 63*(2-B), 1087.

Gonzaga, G. C., Keltner, D., Londahl, E. A., & Smith, M. D. (2001). Love and the commitment problem in romantic relations and friendship. *Journal of Personality and Social Psychology, 81,* 247–262.

Goodall, J. (1986). *The chimpanzees of Gombe: Patterns of behavior.* Cambridge, MA: Belknap Press of Harvard University Press.

Goode, W. J. (1959). The theoretical importance of love. *American Sociological Review, 24,* 38–47.

Grant, V. W. (1957). *The psychology of sexual emotions: The basis of selective attraction.* New York: Longmans, Green.

Hatfield, E. (1982). What do women and men want from love and sex? In E. R. Allgeier & N. B. McCormick (Eds.), *Changing boundaries: Gender roles and sexual behavior* (pp. 106–134). Palo Alto, CA: Mayfield.

Hatfield, E., & Rapson, R. L. (1987). Passionate love: New directions in research. In W. H. Jones & D. Perlman (Eds.), *Advances in personal relationships* (Vol. 1, pp. 109–139). Greenwich, CT: JAI.

Hatfield, E., & Rapson, R. L. (2002). Passionate love and sexual desire. In H. T. Reis, M. A. Fitzpatrick, & A. L. Vangelisti (Eds.), *Stability and change in relationships* (pp. 306–324). Cambridge: Cambridge University Press.

Hatfield, E., & Sprecher, S. (1986). Measuring passionate love in intimate relations. *Journal of Adolescence, 9,* 383–410.

Hatfield, E., Traupmann, J., & Sprecher, S. (1984). Older women's perceptions of their intimate relationships. *Journal of Social and Clinical Psychology, 2,* 108–124.

Hazan, C., & Diamond, L. M. (2000). The place of attachment in human mating. *Review of General Psychology, 4*(2), 186–204.

Hazan, C., & Shaver, P. (1987). Romantic love conceptualized as an attachment process. *Journal of Personality and Social Psychology, 52,* 511–524.

Hendrick, C., & Hendrick, S. S. (1986). A theory and method of love. *Journal of Personality and Social Psychology, 50,* 392–402.

Hendrick, C., & Hendrick, S. S. (1988). Lovers wear rose colored glasses. *Journal of Social and Personal Relationships, 5*, 161–183.

Hendrick, C., & Hendrick, S. S. (1989). Research on love: Does it measure up? *Journal of Personality and Social Psychology, 56*, 784–794.

Hendrick, C., & Hendrick, S. S. (2003). Romantic love: Measuring cupid's arrow. In S. J. Lopez & C. R. Snyder (Eds.), *Positive psychological assessment: A handbook of models and measures* (pp. 235–249). Washington, DC: American Psychological Association.

Hendrick, S., & Hendrick, C. (1995). Gender differences and similarities in sex and love. *Personal Relationships, 2*, 55–65.

Hendrick, S., Hendrick, C., & Adler, N. L. (1988). Romantic relationships: Love, satisfaction, and staying together. *Journal of Personality and Social Psychology, 54*, 980–988.

Hendrick, S. S., & Hendrick, C. (1993). Lovers as friends. *Journal of Social and Personal Relationships, 10*, 459–466.

Herbert, J. (1996). Sexuality, stress and the chemical architecture of the brain. *Annual Review of Sex Research, 7*, 1–44.

Hollander, E., Fay, M., Cohen, B., Campeas, R., Gorman, J. M., & Liebowitz, M. R. (1988). Serotonergic and noradrenergic sensitivity in obsessive-compulsive disorder: Behavioral findings. *American Journal of Psychiatry, 145*, 1015–1017.

Huston, T. (Ed.). (1974). *Foundations of interpersonal attraction*. New York: Academic Press.

Huston, T. L., Caughlin, J. P., Houts, R. M., Smith, S. E., & George, L. J. (2001). The connubial crucible: Newlywed years as predictors of marital delight, distress, and divorce. *Journal of Personality and Social Psychology, 80*, 237–252.

Hyde, J. S. (2005). The gender similarities hypothesis. *American Psychologist, 60*, 581–592.

Ingoldsby, B., Schvaneveldt, P., & Uribe, C. (2003). Perceptions of acceptable mate attributes in Ecuador. *Journal of Comparative Family Studies, 34*, 171–185.

James, W. (1948). *Psychology*. Cleveland: Fine Editions Press. (Original work published 1890)

Jankowiak, W. R., & Fischer, E. F. (1992). A cross-cultural perspective on romantic love. *Ethnology, 31*(2), 149.

Jung, C. G. (1959). Marriage as a psychological relationship. In V. S. DeLaszlo (Ed.), *The basic writings of C. G. Jung* (R. F. C. Hull, Trans., pp. 531–544). New York: Modern Library. (Original work published 1925)

Kaplan, D. L., & Keys, C. B. (1997). Sex and relationship variables as predictors of sexual attraction in cross-sex platonic friendships between young heterosexual adults. *Journal of Social and Personal Relationships, 14*, 191–206.

Karama, S., Lecours, A. R., Leroux, J. M., Bourgouin, P., Beaudoin, G., Joubert, S., et al. (2002). Areas of brain activation in males and females during viewing of erotic film excerpts. *Human Brain Mapping, 16*, 1–13.

Kelley, H. H., & Thibaut, J. W. (1979). *Interpersonal relations: A theory of interdependence*. New York: Wiley-Interscience.

Kephart, W. M. (1967). Some correlates of romantic love. *Journal of Marriage and the Family, 29*, 470–474.

Kim, J., & Hatfield, E. (2004). Love types and subjective well-being: A cross cultural study. *Social Behavior and Personality, 32*, 173–182.

Laumann, E. O., Gagnon, J. H., Michael, R. T., & Michaels, S. (1994). *The social organization of sexuality: Sexual practices in the United States*. Chicago: University of Chicago Press.

Le, T. N., & Levenson, M. R. (2005). Wisdom as self-transcendence: What's love (& individualism) got to do with it? *Journal of Research in Personality, 39*, 443–457.

Lee, J. A. (1977). A typology of styles of loving. *Personality and Social Psychology Bulletin, 3*, 173–182.

Levine, R., Sato, S., Hashimoto, T., & Verma, J. (1995). Love and marriage in eleven cultures. *Journal of Cross-Cultural Psychology, 26*, 554–571.

Lewandowski, G. W., & Aron, A. P. (2004). Distinguishing arousal from novelty and challenge in initial romantic attraction. *Social Behavior and Personality, 32*, 361–372.

Li, N. P., Bailey, J. M., & Kenrick, D. T. (2002). The necessities and luxuries of mate preferences: Testing the tradeoffs. *Journal of Personality and Social Psychology, 82*, 947–955.

Liebowitz, M. R. (1983). *The chemistry of love*. Boston: Little, Brown.

Lim, M. M., Murphy, A. Z., & Young, L. J. (2004). Ventral striatopallidal oxytocin and vasopressin V1a receptors in the monogamous prairie vole (*Microtus ochrogaster*). *Journal of Comparative Neurology, 468*, 555–570.

Little, A. C., Penton-Voak, I. S., & Burt, D. M. (2003). Investigating an imprinting-like phenomenon in humans: Partners and opposite-sex parents have similar hair and eye colour. *Evolution and Human Behavior, 24,* 43–51.

Mead, M. (1928). *Coming of age in Samoa: A psychological study of primitive youth for Western civilization.* New York: William Morrow.

Meloy, J. R., & Fisher, H. E. (2005). Some thoughts on the neurobiology of stalking. *Journal of Forensic Sciences, 50,* 1472–1480.

Meyers, S. A., & Berscheid, E. (1997). The language of love: The difference a preposition makes. *Personality and Social Psychology Bulletin, 23,* 347–362.

Miller, G. F. (2000). *The mating mind: How sexual choice shaped the evolution of human nature.* New York: Doubleday.

Miller, L. C., & Fishkin, S. A. (1997). On the dynamics of human bonding and reproductive success: Seeking windows on the adapted-for human environmental interface. In J. Simpson & D. T. Kenrick (Eds.), *Evolutionary social psychology* (pp. 197–235). Hillsdale, NJ: Lawrence Erlbaum.

Miller, P. J. E., Niehuis, S., & Huston, T. L. (2006). Positive illusions in marital relationships: A 13-year longitudinal study. *Personality and Social Psychology Bulletin, 32,* 1579–1594.

Money, J. (1977). Peking: The sexual revolution. In J. Money & H. Musaph (Eds.), *Handbook of sexology* (pp. 543–550). Amsterdam: Excerpta Medica.

Neto, F., Mullet, E., Deschamps, J., Barros, J., Benvindo, R., Camino, L., et al. (2000). Cross-cultural variations in attitudes toward love. *Journal of Cross-Cultural Psychology, 31,* 626–635.

Newcomb, T. M. (1956). The prediction of interpersonal attraction. *American Psychologist, 11,* 575–586.

Nyrop, R. E. (1985). *India: A country study.* Washington, DC: Government Printing Office.

Pfaff, D. W. 1999. *DRIVE: Neurobiological and molecular mechanisms of sexual motivation.* Cambridge, MA: MIT Press.

Pines, A. M. (2001). The role of gender and culture in romantic attraction. *European Psychologist, 6*(2), 96–102.

Regan, P., Durvasula, R., Howell, L., Ureño, O., & Rea, M. (2004). Gender, ethnicity, and the developmental timing of first sexual and romantic experiences. *Social Behavior and Personality, 37,* 667–676.

Riela, S., Acevedo, B., Aron, A., & Rodriguez, N. (2007, January). *Precursors of falling in love: Gender, ethnic, and rate differences.* Poster presented at the annual meeting of the Society of Personality and Social Psychology, Memphis, TN.

Riela, S., Aron, A., & Acevedo, B. (2006, July). *Precursors of falling in love: Category, rate, and ethnic differences.* Paper presented at the biannual meeting of the International Association for Relationship Research, Rethymnon, Crete, Greece.

Rosenbaum, M. E. (1986). The repulsion hypothesis: On the nondevelopment of relationships. *Journal of Personality and Social Psychology, 51,* 1156–1166.

Rousar, E. E. (1990). *Valuing's role in romantic love.* Unpublished doctoral dissertation, California Graduate School of Family Psychology.

Rubin, Z. (1970). Measurement of romantic love. *Journal of Personality and Social Psychology, 16,* 265–273.

Rubin, Z. (1974). From liking to loving: Patterns of attraction in dating relationships. In T. L. Huston (Ed.), *Foundations of interpersonal attraction* (pp. 383–402). New York: Academic Press.

Rusbult, C. E., Onizuka, R. K., & Lipkus, I. (1993). What do we really want? Mental models of ideal romantic involvement explored through multidimensional scaling. *Journal of Experimental Social Psychology, 29,* 493–527.

Rushton, J. P. (1989). Epigenesis and social preference. *Behavioral and Brain Sciences, 12,* 31–32.

Sangrador, J. L., & Yela, C. (2000). "What is beautiful is loved": Physical attractiveness in love relationships in a representative sample. *Social Behavior and Personality, 28,* 207–218.

Schultz, W. (2000). Multiple reward signals in the brain. *Nature Reviews. Neuroscience, 1,* 199–207.

Shaver, P., Schwartz, J., Kirson, D., & O'Connor, C. (1987). Emotion knowledge: Further exploration of a prototype approach. *Journal of Personality and Social Psychology, 52,* 1061–1086.

Shaver, P. R., Hazan, C., & Bradshaw, D. (1988). Love as attachment: The integration of three behavioral systems. In R. J. Sternberg & M. L. Barnes (Eds.), *The psychology of love* (pp. 68–99). New Haven, CT: Yale University Press.

Shaver, P. R., Morgan, H. J., & Wu, S. (1996). Is love a "basic" emotion? *Personal Relationships, 3,* 81–96.

Shaver, P. R., Wu, S., & Schwartz, J. C. (1991). Cross-cultural similarities and differences in emotion and its representation: A prototype approach. In M. S. Clark (Ed.), *Review of personality and social psychology* (Vol. 13, pp. 175–212). Beverly Hills, CA: Sage.

Simmons, C. H., vom Kolke, A., & Shimizu, H. (1986). Attitudes toward romantic love among American, German, and Japanese students. *Journal of Social Psychology, 126,* 327–336.

Skolnick, A. S. (1996). *The intimate environment: Exploring marriage and the family.* Boston: Little, Brown.

Sprecher, S., Aron, A., Hatfield, E., Cortese, A., Potapova, E., & Levitskaya, A. (1994). Love: American style, Russian style and Japanese style. *Personal Relationships, 1,* 349–369.

Sprecher, S., Felmlee, D., Orbuch, T. L., & Willetts, M. C. (2002). Social networks and change in personal relationships. In A. L. Vangelisti, H. T. Reis, & M. A. Fitzpatrick (Eds.), *Stability and change in relationships* (pp. 257–284). New York: Cambridge University Press.

Sprecher, S., & Regan, P. C. (1998). Passionate and companionate love in courting and young married couples. *Sociological Inquiry, 68*(2), 163–185.

Sprecher, S., & Toro-Morn, M. (2002). A study of men and women from different sides of the Earth to determine if men are from Mars and women are from Venus in their beliefs about love and romantic relationships. *Sex Roles, 46,* 131–147.

Stendhal (Marie-Henri Beyle) (1927). *On love* (Trans. J. Marshall). New York: International Universities Press. (Original work published 1822)

Sternberg, R. J. (1986). A triangular theory of love. *Psychological Review, 93,* 119–135.

Sternberg, R. J. (1987). Liking versus loving: A comparative evaluation of theories. *Psychological Bulletin, 102,* 331–345.

Sternberg, R. J. (1997). Construct validation of a triangular love scale. *European Journal of Social Psychology, 27,* 313–335.

Sternberg, R. J. (1998). *Love is a story: A new theory of relationships.* London: Oxford University Press.

Sternberg, R. J., Hojjat, M., & Barnes, M. L. (2001). Empirical tests of aspects of a theory of love as a story. *European Journal of Personality, 15,* 199–218.Tennov, D. (1979). *Love and limerence: The experience of being in love.* New York: Stein & Day.

Thoren, P., Asberg, M., & Bertilsson, L. (1980). Clomipramine treatment of obsessive disorder: Biochemical and clinical aspects. *Archives of General Psychiatry, 37,* 1289–1294.

Traupmann, J., & Hatfield, E. (1981). Love and its effect on mental and physical health. In J. March, S. Kiesler, R. Fogel, E. Hatfield, & E. Shanas (Eds.), *Aging: Stability and change in the family* (pp. 253–274). New York: Academic Press.

Trivers, R. L. (1972). Parental investment and sexual selection. In B. Campbell (Ed.), *Sexual selection and the descent of man* (pp. 1871–1971). Chicago: Aldine.

Walster, E., Aronson, V., Abrahams, D., & Rottman, L. (1966). The importance of physical attractiveness in dating behavior. *Journal of Personality and Social Psychology, 4,* 508–516.

Walster, E., & Walster, G. W. (1963). Effect of expecting to be liked on choice of associates. *Journal of Personality and Social Psychology, 67,* 402–404.

Wang, Z., Yu, G., Cascio, C., Liu, Y., Gingrich, B., & Insel, T. R. (1999). Dopamine D2 receptor-mediated regulation of partner preferences in female prairie voles (*Microtus ochrogaster*): A mechanism for pair bonding? *Behavioral Neuroscience, 113,* 602–611.

Whitley, B. E. (1993). Reliability and aspects of the construct validity of Sternberg's Triangular Love Scale. *Journal of Social and Personal Relationships, 10,* 475–480.

Wise, R. A. (1989). Brain dopamine and reward. *Annual Review of Psychology, 40,* 191–225.

Wong, P. T. P. (1989, May). *Theory and measurement of unrequited love.* Paper presented at the Iowa Conference on Personal Relationships, Iowa City.

Wu, S., & Shaver, P. R. (1992, July). *Conceptions of love in the United States and the People's Republic of China.* Paper presented at the Sixth Conference of the International Society for the Study of Personal Relationships, Orono, ME.

Wu, S., & Shaver, P. R. (1993, August). *American and Chinese love conceptions: Variations on a theme.* Poster session presented at the American Psychological Association Convention, Toronto.

Xu, X., Aron, A., Cao, G., Feng, T., Fisher, H., Brown, L., & Weng, W. (2008, February). *Is love universal? An fMRI study of early-stage intense romantic love in China.* Presented at the Society for Personality and Social Psychology, Albuquerque, NM.

Young, L. J., Wang, Z., & Insel, T. R. (1998). Neuroendocrine bases of monogamy. *Trends in Neuroscience, 21*(2), 71–75.

Zajonc, R. B. (1968). Attitudinal effects of mere exposure. *Journal of Personality and Social Psychology Monograph Supplement, 9,* 1–27.

17

Satisfaction, Love, and Respect in the Initiation of Romantic Relationships

SUSAN S. HENDRICK and CLYDE HENDRICK

INTRODUCTION

Have you ever planted a flower garden? If you have, did you think about what you wanted your garden to look like, visualizing it in green, growing glory, fresh with dew in the early morning and fragrant with blossoms in the warmth of a summer afternoon? Did you plan your flowers by variety and color and growth pattern, so that something would always be blooming and so that colors would "pop"? Or perhaps you are a less planning-oriented gardener, picking what catches your eye at the nursery or in the garden section of a discount store, thinking about price or hardiness or simply what is easiest to plant and care for?

Whether you are a thoughtful, systematic gardener or a more casual, spontaneous one, however, you are still a gardener! Whether you begin a relationship carefully, thinking about what you seek in your romantic partner and envisioning what you want your relationship to look like down the road, or you simply meet someone to whom you are attracted and begin a relationship spontaneously, you are a relationship initiator!

Both gardens and relationships can be meticulously manicured or be free-form displays of flowers. Both may either be cared for or be neglected and go to seed. The current volume is one of a landscape design of romantic relationships, presenting options for the borders, perennials, and annuals that may comprise a relationship. It is concerned with how relationships are "planted." This chapter offers what might be considered a mix of annuals and perennials. Annuals last only a season and must then be replanted, whereas perennials, once soundly rooted, may appear dormant for a time but then faithfully reappear in due course.

Relationship satisfaction is a bit like an annual. It may burst with color but then die out, requiring replanting periodically. Love—or, as we envision it, types of love—is both an annual and a perennial, with passionate love sometimes coming and going like an annual, and abiding companionate friendship love much more a relational constant, a perennial. Finally, respect, a frequently mentioned but little studied quality in relationships, must be a hardy perennial in a thriving relational garden.

This chapter will consider the roles of relationship satisfaction, love styles, and respect in relationship initiation. These emotions and attitudes are ones we have studied over the years, and here we focus more specifically on their role in the early stage of relationship formation. First, however, we will consider briefly some basic questions about relationship formation.

What is relationship initiation, and why does it occur? For our purposes in this chapter, relationship initiation is the formative process that occurs as two people begin forging a romantic relationship, though we realize that initiation occurs also with friendships, relationships with newly acquired in-laws, and the like. For romantic relationships, we view initiation as not the first sighting, the first introduction, or the first hookup. Rather, we view it as the period during the first few months of the life of the relationship. For example, Campbell, Lackenbauer, and Muise (2006) required couples to have been in a relationship for at least 3 months to be considered for a study of short-term and long-term relationships.

There are many theories of relationship formation, and two rather broad theories are presented briefly because they deepen our understanding of the "why" question of relationship initiation and formation.

Evolutionary Theory

The evolutionary psychology approach emphasizes reproduction and the fact that humans are among the species requiring two mating parents. In order to ensure reproduction and survival of the species, mating must accommodate women's and men's somewhat different mating strategies. For example, Trivers (1972) proposed the parental investment model. This model purports that women, who must invest heavily in each pregnancy, must be more selective about mating (and possible conception) than are men, who can afford to be less selective about any given sexual encounter. Relationship formation must somehow meet these somewhat different goals, while maximizing the potential for pair bonding of sufficient strength to provide for women during pregnancy and lactation and for offspring for a considerable period after birth. Relationship formation is thus a key element in the ultimate survival of the species (e.g., Buss, 1999). This major theoretical approach is concerned with "why" humans might form intimate relationships and is thus related to the other approach we consider (see also Schmitt, this volume, chap. 3).

The Need to Belong

One compelling way to consider the "why" question is that relationships are initiated and formed because there is a *fundamental* need for humans to bond with one another and to belong (Baumeister & Leary, 1995). This perspective takes account of evolutionary theory while offering a more textured conceptual framework for considering human relating.

Baumeister and Leary (1995) proposed that, in general, "human beings have a pervasive drive to form and maintain at least a minimum quantity of lasting, positive, and significant interpersonal relationships" (p. 497). There are several elements of Baumeister and Leary's theoretical approach, including the propositions that (a) people need both frequent and emotionally positive interactions with some number of close others, and (b) these interactions and presumably the relationships they constitute should be stable over time. This approach is consistent with attachment theory (e.g., Bowlby, 1969) and more general evolutionary science. On a straightforward commonsense level, however, Baumeister and Leary's perspective supports what seems to have been known intuitively: People need others.

This intuitive truth, that people need other people, guides our thinking in the current chapter as we move beyond the "why" of relationship formation to the "how" of formation. For example, if people need frequent, positive, and stable interactions with close others, as noted by Baumeister and Leary (1995), then surely intimate romantic partners are among those with whom such interactions should be most significant. Virtually all positive relational qualities could be considered as important in the process of relationship formation. The current chapter considers three such relational qualities that we believe play a substantial part in relationship formation. These are relationship satisfaction, romantic love, and partner respect.

Satisfaction

Satisfaction is a very important and complex aspect of a romantic relationship (e.g., Sternberg & Hojjat, 1997). It is typically considered to be a person's subjective emotional and cognitive evaluation of his or her romantic relationship. Although defining satisfaction thus would seem to be a rather simple first step in considering its importance in relationship initiation, this step is not simple at all.

Defining Satisfaction   The term relationship *satisfaction* (especially marital satisfaction) has been used interchangeably with words such as *adjustment*, *happiness*, and *quality*, although controversy exists about the terms' meanings and measurement (Berscheid & Regan, 2005; Fincham & Beach, 2006; Hendrick, 1995). In the current chapter, we will use the term *relationship satisfaction* to refer to someone's overall pleasure in and contentment with their close, romantic relationship.

Most of the research discussed in this chapter and elsewhere in the relationship literature is cross-sectional rather than longitudinal, and for a thorough discussion of the methodological (including measurement) issues surrounding cross-sectional research on relationship satisfaction, see Berscheid and Regan (2005). Yet there also are a considerable number of studies exploring satisfaction from a longitudinal perspective (e.g., Karney & Bradbury, 1995). Although we agree with Berscheid and Regan that longitudinal research offers a number of analytic advantages over cross-sectional work, the latter seems appropriate when considering relationship initiation. In the case of relationship initiation, we are interested in a snapshot view of satisfaction as a relationship is begun.

The wording "as a relationship is begun" is very intentional on our parts, although it is more customary to say that "a relationship begins." The latter phrasing can give the impression of a relationship "rising from the dust" of its own accord. Rather, we wish to emphasize an individual's intentionality and responsibility in choosing to initiate a relationship. Unlike wildflowers that may grow without human intervention, a sustainable relational garden requires volition—though not necessarily meticulous planning.

Satisfaction in Context   Although our introduction referred to satisfaction as a person's subjective evaluation of his or her overall contentment in a relationship, Fletcher, Simpson, and Thomas (2000) proposed a more contextually complex conceptual framework for satisfaction's role in the relationship landscape. They viewed satisfaction as one of six basic components comprising "relationship quality." The other components are commitment, intimacy, love, passion, and trust. Fletcher and his colleagues (2000) compared statistical models using measures available in the literature to measure these components, and they developed a scale to "maximize the face validity and internal reliability of each relationship construct while avoiding item overlap as much as possible" (p. 344). They found their scale compared very favorably with the multiple measures, in that it was much shorter yet performed similarly in confirmatory factor analyses. For these scholars, satisfaction is only one among several important constructs that predict relationship quality.

Another perspective on satisfaction, that of Karney and Bradbury (1995), viewed satisfaction as only one aspect of relationship quality and stability, and they proposed that overall quality is predicted by three sets of characteristics: (a) enduring vulnerabilities (e.g., the temperaments and personalities that partners bring into the relationship), (b) stressful events (e.g., illness, addiction, and/or job loss), and (c) adaptive skills (e.g., the abilities to problem-solve and cope successfully). Early in a relationship, during the initiation period, it seems that enduring vulnerabilities might be most important to satisfaction, in that what partners bring to the relationship is "front and center." Although partners' abilities to adjust and cope (i.e., adaptive skills) are important, there is often little to cope with in the first flush of a romantic relationship. Later, when life stresses inevitably occur, abilities to adapt and adjust are crucially important.

Arriaga (2001) examined relationship satisfaction for couples in newly formed relationships and found that it was less the sheer level than the *variability* of the level of satisfaction that was related to eventual continuation or breakup of the relationship: "Individuals who exhibited greater fluctuation in their repeated satisfaction ratings were more likely to be in relationships that eventually ended" (p. 754). So keeping satisfaction in a positive range and keeping it consistent are both important for relationship stability.

Satisfaction in Different Relationship Stages   Although in this chapter we are interested primarily in relationship satisfaction during the course of relationship initiation, the level of satisfaction at one relationship stage is most clearly understood when it is contrasted with satisfaction at another relationship stage. In summarizing research on marital relationship satisfaction in both cross-sectional and longitudinal studies, Berscheid and Regan (2005) noted that newlywed couples are typically very satisfied with their relationship. This satisfaction decreases during the first year of marriage but is still solid. Satisfaction continues to decline, albeit more gradually, for another couple of years and then levels out for a few years, at which time it may begin declining more. Yet absolute levels of satisfaction remain in the "satisfied" range. Wives and husbands seem to have similar satisfaction trajectories. Finally, satisfaction levels decrease more rapidly for people who are less satisfied at the beginning of their marriage (see Berscheid & Regan, 2005, for a review).

A number of interpersonal factors contribute to relationship satisfaction early (and indeed later) in a relationship. For example, self-disclosure to the partner as well as commitment to the relationship have been correlated with satisfaction for dating partners (Hendrick, Hendrick, & Adler, 1988). In other research, the ability of someone to take his or her partner's perspective or "stand in the partner's shoes," along with conflict strategies that avoided aggression and hostility (Meeks, Hendrick, & Hendrick, 1998), also was related to greater satisfaction. Traupmann and Hatfield (1981) viewed satisfaction as composed of passionate and companionate love and sexual satisfaction. They found that passionate and companionate love both declined slightly over time for couples but concluded that "the prospects of love's lasting do seem to be reasonably good" (Traupmann & Hatfield, 1981, p. 263). Tucker and Aron (1993) found similar results in a cross-sectional study of couples at major relational turning points (i.e., marriage, parenthood, and empty nest), finding only slight declines in passionate love and relative stability for marital satisfaction.

What seems clear is that most relationship partners are relatively high in satisfaction at the beginning of a relationship, with this satisfaction influenced by a number of different characteristics. Less clear is satisfaction as a relationship continues. The question of how satisfaction and its correlates may differ from the initiation stage to later relationship stages remains. Some of our own research speaks to that question.

Recent Research on Satisfaction   Research with 257 female and male college students, all of whom reported themselves to be *in a relationship*, focused on a number of relationship themes, including satisfaction (C. Hendrick & Hendrick, 2006; S. Hendrick & Hendrick, 2006a). Sixty-nine people had been in a romantic relationship for 3 months or less, and another 69 had been in a relationship for 3 months to one year. The remaining 119 persons had been in a relationship for over one year.

In reporting on their relationship satisfaction, all groups seemed quite satisfied (i.e., scoring well over the average or midpoint on the measure of satisfaction), but there were some differences between the groups. The respondents who had been in a relationship for 3 months or less rated themselves as significantly less satisfied in their relationship than did those in a relationship 3 months to one year or those in a relationship over one year. However, those in a relationship for 3 months to one year did not differ in satisfaction from those in a relationship for over a year. Thus, the differences among the groups were subtle. It is difficult to say with absolute certainty whether the group in a relationship for 3 months or less was in the process of relationship initiation, whether the group in a relationship for 3 months to one year was in the process of relationship initiation, or whether both groups were in fact in "initiation mode."

We also examined relationship satisfaction for a group of employed adults (C. Hendrick & Hendrick, 2006; S. Hendrick & Hendrick, 2006b) who were either in married relationships ($n = 185$) or in dating or committed relationships ($n = 42$). Approximately one third of the respondents were aged 22 to 35, with the other two thirds aged 36 to 64. We assessed levels of reported satisfaction, as well as other relational variables. Interestingly, the groups did not differ in satisfaction, though presumably the married persons, on average, would have been in their relationships longer than would those in dating relationships. One explanation for this finding of "no difference" is perhaps that it is a result of some of the problems with sampling and analysis that occur in cross-sectional research. Or it might be that older couples, if followed longitudinally, would show decreases in satisfaction, simply because satisfaction does seem to ebb slightly over time. However, research by Vaillant and Vaillant (1993) showed considerable stability in satisfaction over time for long-term married couples.

Another possible explanation is that older adults may be more intentional in conducting their romantic relationships, both seeking and valuing relational qualities that are relatively consistent over time. Partners may also sustain more consistent levels of satisfaction, whether the relationship consists of dating, dating with commitment, or marriage, and whether the relationship is new or has endured for some years.

What all these findings suggest to us is that although there are some definite differences among people in terms of their satisfaction with aspects of their romantic relationship, people who declare themselves to be in a relationship tend to report rather high satisfaction. It may not be so much that satisfaction is a harbinger of people staying in stable close relationships, but rather that *dissatisfaction* is a harbinger of current problems and breakups as well as future problems and breakups (Berscheid & Regan, 2005; see also Huston, Caughlin, Houts, Smith, & George, 2001). Having lovely flowers in a garden does not guarantee the garden's health, but the presence of a crop of weeds is a sure sign that the garden needs attention.

It is also important to remember the selection biases in long-term studies. One such serious bias is breakups and divorce. For any given age cohort, when satisfaction drops into the dissatisfaction range, at some point the couple may divorce. Because such couples are then lost from the sample, it follows that for each age cohort, the "divorce pruning" will leave the remaining sample with a relatively stable average level of satisfaction. It is thus quite important in such research to account for couples who were lost from the sample in order to track their (presumed) decline in satisfaction at measurement points prior to the breakup.

Conclusions   Relationship satisfaction may be defined as someone's subjective evaluation of his or her relationship. It is also considered by some scholars to be just one aspect of overall relationship quality. Marital satisfaction has been studied in depth, and it appears that it is typically high at the beginning of marriage and decreases over the course of the marriage, though still remaining in the "satisfied" range. Qualities such as self-disclosure, love, perspective taking, and many others influence satisfaction positively. Some research has shown virtually no differences in satisfaction between persons in the relationship initiation period and persons in long-term relationships, and it appears that satisfaction can remain strong throughout the years. Ultimately, satisfaction will ebb and flow to some degree, but it can remain high in a relationship if the partners concentrate on maintaining the positive aspects of their interaction. Like any annual flower, it requires periodic replanting.

Love

One of the most profound influences on how relationships are initiated and maintained is love—the love that romantic partners have for each other. A number of conceptions exist concerning what constitutes "love" (for a discussion of "falling in love," see Aron et al., chap. 16). Irving Singer (1984), a philosopher, conceptualized love as based either on someone's essence as a human being, called "bestowal," or on someone's positive and negative attributes, called "appraisal." Another approach, developed by Berscheid and Walster (now Hatfield) (1978), is that romantic love is primarily of two types. One type is passionate love, which is love that is intense, emotional, and like a hot flame. Companionate love, on the other hand, is almost like a magnified form of liking in that it is quiet and steady-state. It is more like a glowing ember than a roaring flame. In a gardener's terms, "Whereas passionate love is the exotic hothouse variety, companionate love is more like the garden variety of love" (Hendrick & Hendrick, 1992, p. 48).

Yet another way of viewing love was developed by Sternberg (e.g., 1986), who viewed love as a triangle, with intimacy, passion, and commitment at the vertices. These three qualities can be combined in differing amounts to form eight types of love: consummate love, companionate love, empty love, fatuous love, infatuated love, liking, romantic love, and nonlove. Still other love approaches include the prototype approach (e.g., Fehr, 1988; Fehr & Russell, 1991) and the extensive literature on attachment (e.g., Feeney, Noller, & Roberts, 2000; Hazan & Shaver, 1987).

The Love Styles   The overarching conceptualization of love that we employ in this chapter is drawn from the love styles theory of Lee (1973). We have worked within this approach for three principal reasons. First, it offers several types of romantic love rather than just a few, so it begins to encompass people's lived experiences of love as a multifaceted emotion. Second, it resonates personally for most of the people who hear about it—the love styles "make sense" to people in terms of their own lives. Third, this approach has been empirically solid, with measurement and results relatively consistent across many different samples.

Within Lee's (1973) love styles conceptualization, there are multiple types or styles of love, with six styles predominating and then mixing to form additional styles. The six styles are *eros* (passionate love), *ludus* (game-playing love), *storge* (friendship love), *pragma* (practical love), *mania* (possessive, dependent love), and *agape* (altruistic or "gift" love). Lee considered these styles to be different but all equally appropriate ways of approaching love with a romantic partner. In other words, no style is inherently "better or worse" than another style. It is interesting to consider how someone strongly oriented to each of these love styles might go about initiating a romantic relationship.

Within Lee's (1973) conceptualization, *eros* is a passionate love style that may respond to a partner with intense attraction, sometimes called "love at first sight." Thus the eros lover would initiate quickly, seeking to know the partner mentally, emotionally, and physically. Marathon dates with heavy self-disclosure and warm physical contact would characterize the eros initiator. It would not be unusual for eros initiators to meet, see sparks, and then be virtually inseparable from that time forward. Passionate love is viewed by some scholars (e.g., Hatfield & Rapson, 1993) as the classic type of romantic love that takes place not only during a relationship's initiation stage but also throughout the life span and across virtually all cultures (Hatfield & Rapson, 2002).

Ludus is a playful and much less serious love style, and the ludus lover would likely initiate a relationship with attention to appropriate distance that would contrast with eros's attention to closeness. The ludus lover undertakes the "game" of love, taking care that both partners in a relationship enjoy the relationship experience, yet avoiding commitment. A ludus lover would likely maintain several (certainly more than one) romantic relationships at one time, with relationship initiation characterized by activity-oriented and "fun" dates that would occur frequently enough to keep the relationship alive yet infrequently enough to keep the new partner from getting too serious. Although there can be a darker, manipulative aspect to ludic behavior, in Lee's conception of ludus in its truest form, it is playful rather than manipulative.

Storge is a love style based on solid friendship, shared values, and steady commitment to "growing" a relationship. It might be difficult to pinpoint how a storge lover would initiate a relationship because the process would indeed be a *process*. People inclined toward storgic love would become companionable with a partner, sharing more and more time and experiences in an everyday way, and gradually easing into a deeper connection. Early on, the storge lover would not necessarily have formal dates with the partner but might rather be part of a group that includes the partner, slowly but surely spending more and more time with the partner both as part of the group and eventually as a twosome. This gradual evolution of a relationship contrasts with the intense involvement of eros as well as with the studied distance of ludus. Over the long term, storge love might assume the depth that an eros lover would attempt to achieve more quickly. A seasoned observer of love might even give storge higher odds of relationship success than some of the other love styles.

Pragma is a practical love style, but differs from ludus in that serious commitment is actually a pragma lover's goal. Such a lover has some of the calculating qualities of the ludus lover but employs practical calculation in the service of finding an appropriate and compatible long-term romantic partner. A pragma lover would do her or his homework in trying to wisely select a partner and would likely initiate a relationship slowly, firmly, and strategically, attempting to secure the best possible relational outcome. For example, early dates would be well planned and might include dinner and a movie, or tickets to a play or concert, depending on the age and preferences of the partners. Practical efforts to get to know each other, rather than heavy self-disclosure (as in eros) or avoidance of disclosure (as in ludus), would likely prevail.

Mania, as the name implies, is a somewhat emotionally volatile love style. The mania lover may be possessive and dependent, fervently wishing for rapid involvement and intensity in the relationship while at the same time staying alert for any signal that the partner may be losing interest. The manic lover hopes for more than the best and fears more than the worst, which makes for a rather tumultuous courtship. Relationship initiation may be exciting and intense, almost resembling the early connection that characterizes an eros-based relationship. At some point, however, the mania lover becomes possessive of the partner's time, not so much out of a sense of "wanting" the partner but more out of a sense of "needing" the partner. Relationship initiation is thus likely to be "bumpy," including lovers' quarrels, dramatic reunions, and the like.

Finally, *agape* love is "all about the partner." As agape is centrally altruistic, sometimes more concerned about the partner's well-being than one's own well-being, an agape lover is likely to initiate a relationship carefully and with great consideration for the partner's needs, wants, and preferences. It is not necessarily an exaggeration to imagine two agapic partners discussing what to do on a date and having a very difficult time deciding: "What do you want to do? I want to do what *you* want to do." "No, I want to do what *you* want to do!" Eventually, of course, the partners decide on a course of action, and the date—and the larger relationship—proceed. In choosing a single word to describe how each of the love styles might handle relationship initiation, we might suggest the following: Eros is intense, ludus is playful, storge is slow, pragma is practical, mania is volatile, and agape is gentle.

Of course, most people are not characterized by just one love style but rather have some combination of the six styles, and a scale was specifically designed to allow respondents a score on each of the six styles (Hendrick & Hendrick, 1986; Hendrick, Hendrick, & Dicke, 1998). Using this scale, considerable research has looked at love styles in different types of relationships. For example, Hahn and Blass (1997) were interested in whether people would choose hypothetical partners based on descriptions of that partner's love styles. The authors proposed that people would choose partners similar to themselves, thus displaying homogamy. This was largely the case, and respondents preferred partners with relatively similar love styles. In addition, the authors examined whether particular love styles appeal to most people, and indeed, agape and storge were most preferred, whereas ludus was dispreferred. Other research (Hendrick et al., 1988) has shown that dating couples—couples typically initiating their relationships—are endorsing of passionate, friendship, and altruistic love and distinctly nonendorsing of game-playing love. And still other research (Hendrick & Hendrick, 1993) underlines the importance of the friendship component of love.

Love, Matching, and Satisfaction
Based on the research discussed previously, it appears that certain love styles are more conducive to relationship initiation and maintenance than others. It is also possible that partners who are similar in one or more of the love styles (i.e., have "matching" love styles) might be more likely to initiate and maintain a relationship successfully. A vast amount of research demonstrates that similarity leads to attraction (e.g., Byrne, 1971), and indeed, romantic partners have shown relative similarity in several love styles, such as eros, agape, storge, and mania (Hendrick et al., 1988) and agape, eros, storge, and ludus (Davis & Latty-Mann, 1987). In addition, we know that passionate, companionate, and altruistic love are important positive relational qualities (e.g., Hendrick & Hendrick, 1993; Hendrick et al., 1988). Thus a "prescription" for relational maintenance and continuation might well include valuing love styles of passion, friendship, and altruism; avoiding a game-playing love style; and seeking a partner similar to oneself in these love styles.

Love across Ages and Stages
Although it is easy to conflate issues of age, type of relationship, length of relationship, and relationship stage, they are different but related concepts. At times we may use age of respondent or type of relationship (e.g., dating versus married) as

a proxy for the relationship stage (e.g., initiating or early versus developed or later). In fact, considerable research has explored the question of how younger and older persons might differ in their love styles, implicitly assuming that younger persons are more likely to be in the process of relationship initiation, whereas older persons are more likely in confirmed relationships. Contreras and her colleagues (Contreras, Hendrick, & Hendrick, 1996) assessed love and other relational variables in a married Mexican American and White sample that ranged in age from 20 to 60 years. Eros, or passionate love, was the strongest and most consistent predictor of relational satisfaction across the age groups. Another study (Inman-Amos, Hendrick, & Hendrick, 1994) compared college students and their parents on relational variables and found virtually no similarity in love attitudes between students and their own parents. However, when the students as a group were compared with parents as a group, students and parents did not differ on passionate love. College men did not differ from parents on friendship love, whereas daughters were significantly less endorsing of friendship love than were parents. Although we might expect that people in relationship initiation stages might well be more passionate and less friendship oriented than people in longer term married relationships, that was generally not the case in the Inman et al. (1994) study.

Recent Research on Love

Some research has explored whether couples beginning their relationships would differ in their love styles from couples who have been together for a long time. Referring to research discussed earlier (C. Hendrick & Hendrick, 2006; S. Hendrick & Hendrick, 2006a), we compared persons in a romantic relationship for 3 months or less, 3 months to one year, and over one year (n = 69, 69, and 119, respectively) on their reported love styles. The groups differed on passionate love (eros), altruistic love (agape), and friendship love (storge). Respondents who had been in a relationship for 3 months or less rated themselves as significantly less passionate in their love styles than did those in a relationship for 3 months to one year or over one year, with those two groups not differing from each other. Friendship love showed a somewhat different pattern. Those persons in a relationship for over one year were the most friendship oriented, differing significantly from those in a relationship for 3 months to one year. Persons in a relationship less than 3 months did not differ significantly in friendship love from either of the other two groups, thus falling in between.

We also assessed love styles for the group of employed individuals mentioned earlier in our discussion of relationship satisfaction (n = 185 married and 42 dating; C. Hendrick & Hendrick, 2006; S. Hendrick & Hendrick, 2006b). Only the love styles of passionate, friendship, altruistic, and pragmatic love were examined, and the two groups did not differ on any of these love styles. As with the findings for satisfaction, the lack of differences displayed may have been due to methodological issues or perhaps to the increased intentionality and maturity that could characterize the intimate romantic relationships of adults older than the average college-age students.

Conclusions

Love is an intense emotion, and the intensity is particularly notable in the early stages of romantic relationships. There are many theories of what love is (e.g., passionate or companionate) and how it influences the course that a relationship takes. The love styles approach includes six styles (eros, ludus, storge, pragma, mania, and agape) that are all considered to be viable, though the passionate, friendship, and altruistic styles are particularly positive markers in romantic relationships. Passionate love may lessen over time in a relationship; however, a variety of research has shown that this lessening is not inevitable. Passion is not essential for a solid relationship, but people for whom passion is important can feel relatively confident that it can be maintained over the years. Although companionate love may be a perennial flower, passionate love, an annual, will need more than occasional replanting.

Love is clearly important to relationships, yet it is interesting to puzzle out some of the other characteristics particular to relationship initiation. One construct that has been explored very little by relationship researchers but that shows promise in increasing our understanding of romantic relationships is *respect*.

Respect

Importance of Respect

Feeling respected is an important part of being human. "People require standing, respect, a feeling of worthiness, [and] individual and collective identity" (Markus, 2004, p. 3). Although there has been considerable research on *dis*respect (see review by Miller, 2001), respect has been relatively understudied. Yet, it keeps surfacing in various venues, particularly those involving intimate relationships. For example, Hirsch (2003) provided a detailed ethnographic account of Mexican transnational couples who move back and forth between Mexico and the United States. *Respeto* (formal respect) has been an integral part of traditional Mexican marriages, but more recently this *respeto* has broadened to include *confianza* (trust) in these marriage relationships. Thus, spousal role-related respect now more often is accompanied by the relationship-related trust.

Clinicians have long been aware of the significance of respect in intimate, particularly marital, relationships. Gottman (1994), a noted couples scholar, stated that couples largely want "just two things from their marriage—love and respect" (p. 18). Gottman proposed four conflictual behaviors that he called warning signs of impending marital disaster, or the "Four Horsemen of the Apocalypse." In fact, these qualities of contempt, criticism, defensiveness, and (especially) stonewalling seem to us to typify the very essence of *dis*respect. Other clinicians, Markman, Stanley, and Blumberg (2001) suggested that honoring and respecting one's partner are necessary in building a strong relationship, noting that the best way to handle the inevitable partner differences is to "handle the differences with respect" (p. 263).

Respect was also found by Fehr and Russell (1991) to be one of the characteristics people viewed as part of many types of love, and Feeney, Noller, and Ward (1997) discovered, somewhat unexpectedly, that respect was a key factor in a model of marital quality. They noted that their scaling and model-building work suggested "that Respect is a very important and robust dimension of marital interaction" (p. 181).

More recently, Frei and Shaver (2002) explored respect in romantic relationships across three studies, using a prototype methodology initially, and subsequently developing a 45-item measure of respect. Their respondents in all three studies were college students, roughly half of whom were in romantic relationships. Their relationships averaged approximately a year in duration, and many of the partners could be construed as being involved in the initiation stage of the relationship. The Frei and Shaver measure seemed to tap into a respondent's assessment of the positive qualities of his or her partner, and indeed it emphasized "features of a respectworthy relationship partner" (p. 125). At the same time that Frei and Shaver were developing their measure, we undertook research on the construct of respect, looking at romantic partners, including those in the initiation stage of relationships.

Recent Research on Respect

Additional research on respect was inspired by the work of sociologist Sara Lawrence-Lightfoot (2000), who wove together strands of the intrapersonal, interpersonal, and social worlds to present six biographical portraits of persons whom she viewed as exemplifying the six dimensions inherent in respect: attention, curiosity, dialogue, empowerment, healing, and self-respect. Her exemplars included a midwife, a pediatrician, a high school teacher, a photographer, a law professor, and a chaplain to persons who were dying. Each one of these people embodied one or more of Lawrence-Lightfoot's six central characteristics of respect.

We developed a 6-item scale (S. Hendrick & Hendrick, 2006a) to measure these dimensions, and although the final scale version did not completely map onto Lawrence-Lightfoot's (2000) concepts, the meaning our scale ascribes to respect is either similar to or compatible with her meaning(s). In our scaling work, we completed three studies, two with college students and one with working adults; two of those studies were referred to earlier and are referred to again below. We completed one study with college men and women in dating relationships (C. Hendrick & Hendrick, 2006; S. Hendrick & Hendrick, 2006a). We compared persons in a romantic relationship for 3 months or less, 3 months to one year, and over one year (n = 69, 69, and 119, respectively). One measure on which we compared them was the 6-item Respect Toward Partner Scale, shown in the Appendix at the end of this chapter. Items in this scale are general respect for the partner (an anchor item), interest in the partner, being a source of healing for the partner, honoring the partner, approving of the partner, and communicating well with the partner. When the groups were compared, the group in a relationship for 3 months or less reported significantly less respect toward the romantic partner than did the groups in a relationship for 3 months to one year and for over one year. These findings were similar to those reported earlier for satisfaction as well as for passionate and altruistic love.

We also assessed respect for the group of older, employed persons in relationships, which was also discussed earlier ($n = 185$ married and 42 dating; C. Hendrick & Hendrick, 2006; S. Hendrick & Hendrick, 2006b). The groups did not differ in respect toward the partner, just as they had not differed in satisfaction or on the four love styles assessed. Once again, we may puzzle about the lack of differences between groups who have been in relationships for different periods of time, some presumably in the initiation stage.

Conclusions

Respect has been much talked about but little researched until relatively recently. It appears to be an important quality to have in a romantic relationship because it is a key factor in overall relational quality and satisfaction. One approach views respect as focused on a partner's respectworthiness. Another approach conceptualizes respect as being composed of giving attention to the partner, showing curiosity about the partner, communicating with the partner, empowering the partner, and being a source of healing for the partner. Some research indicates that people in the initiation stage of relationships do not differ from people in long-term relationships in terms of how much they respect their relationship partner. It is important to maintain mutual respect in any type of relationship, particularly a romantic one. Respect may be a hardy perennial flower, but it still requires regular tending.

Overall, we have found both similarities and differences between groups in different relationship stages on the various constructs that we have discussed. We cannot with certainty explain these findings, though ideally future research may be able to do so. In the meantime, we will consider some ways in which satisfaction, love, and respect might be related for couples in early relationship stages.

Satisfaction, Love, and Respect

Love and satisfaction have been linked in a number of studies (e.g., Hendrick et al., 1988). Love may be necessary for most love relationships but is certainly not sufficient in and of itself. Relational gardens need more than just one type of flower. Many other relational qualities are also important to relationship health and prosperity. For example, Meeks and her colleagues (1998) were concerned not just with love but also with conflict in relationships and with partners' ability to take the perspective of their partner. This ability to see the world through one's partner's eyes can be called *perspective taking*, *empathy*, or *role taking*. In a study with 140 dating couples, Meeks et al. found that not only were love styles related to satisfaction but so also were communication (one component of respect) and conflict approaches. The best predictors of relationship satisfaction were ultimately positive love (a combination of passionate, altruistic, and friendship love) felt for the partner, the absence of game-playing love, the perception that one did not use aggressive conflict tactics in the relationship, and the perception that the partner was able to take one's perspective.

White, Hendrick, and Hendrick (2004) were concerned with personality characteristics and how these might interact both with love styles and with relationship satisfaction. Participants in dating relationships answered questions about personality (Costa & McCrae, 1992), love, and satisfaction. The personality quality of neuroticism was negatively associated with satisfaction, but this relationship was completely mediated by mania (possessive, dependent love) for women. Agreeableness and extraversion were positively associated with satisfaction, particularly for men.

Finally, satisfaction, love, and respect were all studied together (S. Hendrick & Hendrick, 2006a) and were assessed across three studies, with the first two studies assessing college students in dating relationships, and the third study assessing working individuals, most of whom were married (see earlier discussion). The six love styles as well as respect toward the partner were used as predictors of relationship satisfaction, and three predictors were significant. Eros was a strong positive predictor of satisfaction for college students and for those in the older sample, and respect for partner was almost as strong a positive predictor in both samples. For the college students only, possessive, dependent love was a negative predictor of satisfaction. So although it is useful to look at the relational constructs considered in this chapter—satisfaction, love, and respect—individually, to understand their role in relationship initiation, it is also useful to look at them conjointly.

Ultimately, the utility of any consideration of relationships and their components depends on the ability of research to contribute to our understanding of "reality," in this case the reality of intimate romantic relationships. Thus, it seems worthwhile to consider how information about satisfaction, love, and respect might be useful to partners as they traverse the process of relationship initiation.

Applications to Couples

It would be rather unusual for a couple in the process of truly initiating their relationship to seek external help in the form of couple counseling, but it is not impossible to imagine. Take the example of Katie and Rick, college seniors who have just started dating. They were introduced by mutual friends on a blind date and have been seeing each other for about a month. Both have had several unsuccessful romantic relationships during their college years, and each was rather reluctant to even go out on the blind date in the first place. But both Rick and Katie want to eventually find a long-term romantic partner and "settle down," so they agreed to the date. Much to their surprise, they were quite attracted to each other, got along well, and really enjoyed each other's company. Thus, although they have been dating for only a month or so, they have seen each other several times a week. Their dating experiences have ranged in formality, and much of the time they have just hung out together.

Because the relationship seems to be moving rather quickly, and because they do not want this relationship to end like their previous ones, they have talked about seeing a therapist at their university's counseling center. The pace of the relationship is not the only reason why Katie and Rick are considering seeing a therapist. They have already noticed behaviors in themselves and each other that they feel sabotaged their previous relationships. For example, Katie has found herself becoming somewhat possessive about Rick's time, and she has even begun to depend on him for help with her car—something she was managing to take care of herself before she met Rick. In turn, Rick is beginning to be annoyed by some of Katie's behaviors, though not the possessiveness or the dependence. Rather, he gets frustrated by her being late for dates and by being what he considers "a perfectionist" about how she looks, no matter where they are going. "So what if she doesn't have makeup on—can't she just go out for coffee?" he frequently asks himself.

Whereas in earlier relationships Rick would have just let these annoyances build to breakup level, with Katie he has handled things differently and has talked with her about some of his reactions. For her part, Katie has admitted that she is feeling more possessive and dependent than she wants to feel. Together, they decided to schedule a session with a therapist at the counseling center.

Their first session involved filling out paperwork and then having an intake session with Monica, one of the center's staff therapists. She asked them about their backgrounds, including their family relationships, their previous romantic relationships, and the process thus far of their current relationship. At the end of the session, she offered several suggestions. First, she suggested that they meet for a few sessions; she thought that would probably give them enough time to get a clear view about what was going on in the relationship and what they might want to change or maintain. Second, she said they should continue to enjoy the relationship and not worry about "diagnosing" what might be going on. She said that they could do that with her in counseling sessions rather than getting "bogged down" by talking about things endlessly. Finally, she mentioned that although there were a number of topics and issues they could consider addressing, she had three that she thought were particularly relevant to their situation. She wanted to discuss relationship satisfaction, love styles, and partner respect. Katie and Rick agreed.

Session 2 focused on satisfaction. A relationship satisfaction scale had been part of the paperwork Katie and Rick had filled out in the first session, and Monica told them that their scores were high, as is appropriate for most people early in their relationship. She told them that satisfaction is usually highest in early relationship stages and then likely settles down a bit as partners have been together longer. She pointed out that satisfaction is "in the eye of the beholder," and that it was not important that they measure up to some external standard of being satisfied 24/7 or that they have a relationship that other people regarded as a satisfying one. The measure of satisfaction that is important is their own feelings of being content in the relationship. She told them to be aware of what they liked about each other, knowing that some things are more consistent over time than others. Rick talked about his small irritations at Katie's lateness and at her perfectionism about her appearance, though as Monica probed a bit, he admitted that he thought Katie was beautiful, and he really appreciated her efforts to look good. Katie then revealed that she felt some pressure to look her best for Rick nearly all the time. Monica talked about the mixed messages that Rick might be giving Katie about appearance, and he told Katie that he sometimes thought she was most beautiful when she wasn't wearing any makeup and had her hair in a ponytail. So she expressed relief that she could "dress down" a little. Both Rick and Katie seemed satisfied with this conclusion, and Monica congratulated them on being able to talk openly with each other, noting that open communication was very important in a relationship and was even related to satisfaction. At the end of the session, Monica gave each of them a questionnaire about their love styles, saying she would discuss their results at the next session.

Session 3 centered on love. Monica had scored their love questionnaires, and she was quick to tell them about their love styles. She explained the six different love styles (i.e., eros, ludus, storge, pragma, mania, and agape) and told them that she liked to counsel couples using each partner's top three scores as a kind of "profile" of that person's preferred orientation toward love. She said that both Rick and Katie had eros, storge, and agape as their three preferred love styles, and so there was considerable similarity between them. She also noticed that neither one was a game player, that they both were a bit pragmatic, and that Katie scored fairly high on mania (possessive, dependent love). For the most part, they were not surprised by the information and were pleased that they saw things the same way—especially love. But Katie's mania score was a subject of mild concern to her more than to Rick. In the first session with Monica, Katie had talked about a particularly painful and almost disastrous love affair that she had had the previous year. Monica linked that experience to Katie's tendencies to be possessive of and dependent on Rick, pointing out that when we have traumatic experiences, they can influence our emotions, thoughts, and behaviors for a long time. She also pointed out a couple of positives in Katie and Rick's relationship, noting that (a) they could talk about the issue, (b) Katie wanted to put the brakes on her behavior, and (c) Rick's high score on friendship love indicated that he would be both supportive and consistent in his relationship with Katie. Consistency is something that can go a long way to blunt the emotionality of mania. All three of them were pleased about this third counseling session, and Monica told them that respect would be next on the agenda.

In the beginning of session 4, Monica gave Rick and Katie a brief respect scale, asking them to fill it out so she could score it and give them the results. As she told them about their scores, she seemed pleased and unsurprised that they each had considerable respect for the other. She said that she was pleased about their responses because respect has been shown to be highly related to relationship satisfaction, and she said that she was unsurprised because they exhibited a great deal of respect for each other in the sessions. They looked at each other when they spoke, they did not interrupt, they were sympathetic to each other, and they seemed to really appreciate each other's qualities. She pointed out how various aspects of respect—communicating well with the partner, being interested in the partner as a person, and trying to be a healing force in the partner's life—all can be powerful ways of communicating profound regard and respect for the partner. She urged them to stay aware of these qualities in their relationship and, rather than let them ebb as the relationship continued, make sure they flowed more and more each day.

Monica, Katie, and Rick talked about the sessions they had shared. Rick and Katie said that they were pleased with how understanding Monica had been and said that they were starting to apply things they had learned in counseling to their own interaction. Both they and Monica expressed a great deal of hope for the relationship. Monica concluded the session by suggesting that Katie and Rick schedule a follow-up session in 2 months to see how things were going.

Conclusions

Initiating a relationship is an exciting, delicate, and often intense process. As the current volume demonstrates, there is a world of issues to consider as one initiates a relationship with a new romantic partner. A small corner of this world has been explored in the current chapter. Satisfaction, love styles, and respect are all important factors as a relationship is initiated and, perhaps even more important, as a relationship continues. These factors are interrelated, and it will be useful for future research to see how these, and other relationship characteristics, might predict ongoing relational stability. The obvious need is for additional research with larger samples, research with people of diverse ethnic and racial backgrounds, and the elusive but necessary longitudinal work. For example, much of our own work and that of others has been conducted with college students. Imagine scholars conducting longitudinal research with sizable samples of married and unmarried couples from different ethnic, racial, and socioeconomic groups. We might find influences on relationship processes and outcomes that are completely unexpected. Or we might not. Whatever we might find, we could perhaps be a bit more confident that we are capturing people's real-life experiences in our scientific studies.

It will also become increasingly important to study love, respect, and satisfaction in the context of relationship initiation in older couples. People are living longer, and this trend is likely to continue. Due to death, divorce, or some other relationship disruptor, people in and beyond middle age are beginning relationships again (and again). Is matching of love styles more or less important for older couples? Is respect as important, or even more important, when partners are in their sixth, seventh, or eighth decade of life? Such questions are important and deserve answers.

We have studied relationship satisfaction and love styles for several decades and continue to believe that additional, creative research is possible. We have also seen how both these factors manifest themselves in clinical work with couples, whether these are couples in early, relationship initiation stages or in much later stages. More recently, we have begun to study respect, an understudied but to us fascinating window on relationship "quality." For us professionally, respect is where the relational "rubber meets the road" in one partner's behavior toward the other; and it is the nexus of gender and relationships, particularly for heterosexual couples, for whom traditional gender roles may challenge the egalitarianism that we find essential to respect. For us personally, respect is the subtext of our own relationship.

To circle back to the garden metaphor with which we began this chapter, both annuals and perennials have their place in the relational garden. Different parts of the growing season foster different flowers, and to have a garden that is continuously beautiful, a variety of flowers must thrive. Thus research on the many aspects of relationships and the application of this research to actual couples leading actual lives should have the brightest of futures.

APPENDIX: RESPECT TOWARD PARTNER SCALE

1. I respect my partner.
2. I am interested in my partner as a person.
3. I am a source of healing for my partner.
4. I honor my partner.
5. I approve of the person my partner is.
6. I communicate well with my partner.

For purposes of analyses, the items are scored on a 1 (*strongly agree*) to 5 (*strongly disagree*) basis. The set of items is averaged to produce a scale score.

REFERENCES

Arriaga, X. B. (2001). The ups and downs of dating: Fluctuations in satisfaction in newly formed romantic relationships. *Journal of Personality and Social Psychology, 80,* 754–765.

Baumeister, R. F., & Leary, M. R. (1995). The need to belong: Desire for interpersonal attachments as a fundamental human motivation. *Psychological Bulletin, 117,* 497–529.

Berscheid, E., & Regan, P. (2005). *The psychology of interpersonal relationships.* Upper Saddle River, NJ: Prentice Hall.

Berscheid, E., & Walster, E. (1978). *Interpersonal attraction* (2nd ed.). Reading, MA: Addison-Wesley.

Bowlby, J. (1969). *Attachment and loss: Vol. 1. Attachment.* New York: Basic Books.

Buss, D. M. (1999). *Evolutionary psychology: The new science of the mind.* Boston: Allyn & Bacon.

Byrne, D. (1971). *The attraction paradigm.* New York: Academic Press.

Campbell, L., Lackenbauer, S. D., & Muise, A. (2006). When is being known or adored by romantic partners most beneficial? Self-perceptions, relationship length, and responses to partner's verifying and enhancing appraisals. *Personality and Social Psychology Bulletin, 32,* 1283–1294.

Contreras, R., Hendrick, S. S., & Hendrick, C. (1996). Perspectives on marital love and satisfaction in Mexican American and Anglo couples. *Journal of Counseling and Development, 74,* 408–415.

Costa, P. T., Jr., & McCrae, R. R. (1992). *Revised NEO Personality Inventory (NEO PI-R) and NEO Five-Factor Inventory (NEO-FFI) professional manual.* Odessa, FL: Psychological Assessment Resources.

Davis, K. E., & Latty-Mann, H. (1987). Love styles and relationship quality: A contribution to validation. *Journal of Social and Personal Relationships, 4,* 409–428.

Feeney, J. A., Noller, P., & Roberts, N. (2000). Attachment and close relationships: In C. Hendrick & S. S. Hendrick (Eds.), *Close relationships : A sourcebook* (pp. 185–201). Thousand Oaks, CA: Sage.

Feeney, J. A., Noller, P., & Ward, C. (1997). Marital satisfaction and spousal interaction. In R. J. Sternberg & M. Hojjat (Eds.), *Satisfaction in close relationships* (pp. 160–189). New York: Guilford Press.

Fehr, B. (1988). Prototype analysis of the concepts of love and commitment. *Journal of Personality and Social Psychology, 54,* 557–579.

Fehr, B., & Russell, J. A. (1991). The concept of love viewed from a prototype perspective. *Journal of Personality and Social Psychology, 60,* 425–438.

Fincham, F. D., & Beach, S. R. H. (2006). Relationship satisfaction. In A. L. Vangelisti & D. Perlman (Eds.), *The Cambridge handbook of personal relationships* (pp. 579–594). New York: Cambridge University Press.

Fletcher, G. J. O., Simpson, J. A., & Thomas, G. (2000). The measurement of perceived relationship quality components: A confirmatory factor analytic approach. *Personality and Social Psychology Bulletin, 26,* 340–354.

Frei, J. R., & Shaver, P. R. (2002). Respect in close relationships: Prototype definition, self-report assessment, and initial correlates. *Personal Relationships, 9,* 121–139.

Gottman, J. M. (1994). *Why marriages succeed or fail.* New York: Simon & Schuster.

Hahn, J., & Blass, T. (1997). Dating partner preferences: A function of similarity of love styles. *Journal of Social Behavior and Personality, 12,* 595–610.

Hatfield, E., & Rapson, R. L. (1993). *Love, sex, and intimacy.* New York: HarperCollins.

Hatfield, E., & Rapson, R. L. (2002). Passionate love and sexual desire: Cultural and historical perspectives. In A. L. Vangelisti, H. T. Reis, & M. A. Fitzpatrick (Eds.), *Stability and change in relationships* (pp. 306–324). New York: Cambridge University Press.

Hazan, C., & Shaver, P. (1987). Romantic love conceptualized as an attachment process. *Journal of Personality and Social Psychology, 50,* 392–402.

Hendrick, C., & Hendrick, S. S. (1986). A theory and method of love. *Journal of Personality and Social Psychology, 50,* 392–402.

Hendrick, C., & Hendrick, S. S. (2006). [Satisfaction, love, and respect across age groups]. Unpublished raw data.

Hendrick, C., Hendrick, S. S., & Dicke, A. (1998). The Love Attitudes Scale: Short Form. *Journal of Social and Personal Relationships, 15,* 147–159.

Hendrick, S. S. (1995). *Close relationships: What couple therapists can learn.* Pacific Grove, CA: Brooks/Cole.

Hendrick, S. S., & Hendrick, C. (1992). *Romantic love.* Thousand Oaks, CA: Sage.

Hendrick, S. S., & Hendrick, C. (1993). Lovers as friends. *Journal of Social and Personal Relationships, 10,* 459–466.

Hendrick, S. S., & Hendrick, C. (2006a). Measuring respect in close relationships. *Journal of Social and Personal Relationships, 23*, 881–899.

Hendrick, S. S., & Hendrick, C. (2006b, November). *Respect: An important predictor of relationship satisfaction.* Paper presented at the annual conference of the National Council on Family Relations, Minneapolis, MN.

Hendrick, S. S., Hendrick, C., & Adler, N. L. (1988). Romantic relationships: Love, satisfaction, and staying together. *Journal of Personality and Social Psychology, 54*, 980–988.

Hirsch, J. S. (2003). *A courtship after marriage: Sexuality and love in Mexican transnational families.* Berkeley: University of California Press.

Huston, T. L., Caughlin, J. P., Houts, R. M., Smith, S. E., & George, L. J. (2001). The connubial crucible: Newlywed years as predictors of marital delight, distress, and divorce. *Journal of Personality and Social Psychology, 80*, 237–252.

Inman-Amos, J., Hendrick, S. S., & Hendrick, C. (1994). Love attitudes: Similarities between parents and between parents and children. *Family Relations, 43*, 456–461.

Karney, B. R., & Bradbury, T. N. (1995). The longitudinal course of marital satisfaction and stability: A review of theory, method, and research. *Psychological Bulletin, 118*, 3–34.

Lawrence-Lightfoot, S. (2000). *Respect.* Cambridge, MA: Perseus.

Lee, J. A. (1973). *The colors of love: An exploration of the ways of loving.* Don Mills, ON: New Press.

Markman, H. J., Stanley, S. M., & Blumberg, S. L. (2001). *Fighting for your marriage.* San Francisco: Jossey-Bass.

Markus, H. R. (2004). A social psychological model of behavior. *Dialogue, 19*(1, Suppl.), 1–4.

Meeks, B. S., Hendrick, S. S., & Hendrick, C. (1998). Communication, love, and relationship satisfaction. *Journal of Social and Personal Relationships, 15*, 755–773.

Miller, D. T. (2001). Disrespect and the experience of injustice. *Annual Review of Psychology, 52*, 527–553.

Singer, I. (1984). *The nature of love: Vol.1. Plato to Luther* (2nd ed.). Chicago: University of Chicago Press.

Sternberg, R. J. (1986). A triangular theory of love. *Psychological Review, 93*, 119–135.

Sternberg, R. J., & Hojjat, M. (Eds.). (1997). *Satisfaction in close relationships.* New York: Guilford.

Traupmann, J., & Hatfield, E. (1981). Love and its effect on mental and physical health. In R. Fogel, E. Hatfield, S. Kiesler, & E. Shanas (Eds.), *Aging: Stability and change in the family* (pp. 253–274). New York: Academic Press.

Trivers, R. L. (1972). Parental investment and sexual selection. In B. Campbell (Ed.), *Sexual selection and the descent of man* (pp. 136–179). Chicago: Aldine de Gruyter.

Tucker, P., & Aron, A. (1993). Passionate love and marital satisfaction at key transition points in the family life cycle. *Journal of Social and Clinical Psychology, 12*, 135–147.

Vaillant, C. O., & Vaillant, G. E. (1993). Is the U-curve of marital satisfaction an illusion? A 40-year study of marriage. *Journal of Marriage and the Family, 55*, 230–239.

White, J. K., Hendrick, S. S., & Hendrick, C. (2004). Big five personality variables and relationship constructs. *Personality and Individual Differences, 37*, 1519–1530.

18

The Emotional Landscape of Romantic Relationship Initiation

SANDRA METTS and SYLVIA L. MIKUCKI

Hello, I love you, won't you tell me your name?

Despite the appeal of messages celebrated in contemporary song lyrics such as those above by the Doors, the emotional transition from a first sighting to the expression of love is neither instantaneous nor automatic. Indeed, a more realistic lyrical verse might be something like the following: "Hello, you seem to be emitting positive affect, which leads me to feel some type of arousal as I look at you, and as I appraise these sensations I believe they suggest some degree of attraction, although I am not sure if it is merely physical attraction or something deeper. Could we begin communicating so I can assess our degree of compatibility and your self-perceived level of arousal so I can better characterize what these sensations are that I am feeling?" Of course, this is a not a very catchy opening line for a song, and few listeners would find much romantic appeal in it. However, it more accurately reflects the emotional processes between first sightings and declarations of love.

This chapter will elaborate the role of emotion in romantic relationship initiation. As the landscape metaphor of the title implies, the early stages of relationship formation are characterized by emotional uncertainty—scenes of beauty and awe (excitement and hope) as well as scenes of potential danger and threat (fear of failure and disappointment). However, it also contains elements commonly recognized by cultural members as pathways frequently traveled, as settings where certain events are likely to transpire, and where paths are likely to cross. In sum, emotional experience and expression during relationship initiation are emergent and complex, but they are also more organized and systematic than popular mythology might lead us to believe.

Our goal in this chapter is to synthesize emotion theory and research in order to illustrate the patterned—indeed, the scripted—interface between emotion and relationship initiation. This goal is more challenging than might be immediately apparent. Not only is the initiation phase itself varied in origin and duration, but the range of possible emotions experienced during the process is varied as well. Most people in Western societies would assume that love is the prototypical emotion associated with the formative phases of a relationship (see Aron et al., this volume; Hendrick & Hendrick, this volume). However, as Guerrero and Andersen (2000) noted, relationship initiation is characterized by not only bright emotions (e.g., passion, infatuation, warmth, anticipation, and joy) but also dark emotions (e.g., anxiety, uncertainty, fear, envy, and embarrassment) (p. 175). Guerrero and Andersen attributed this emotional complexity during initial encounters to three general principles: (a) Initial encounters are novel and unpredictable, which evoke both positive and negative arousal; (b) personality dispositions such as social anxiety and shyness serve as filters that shape attitudes, behaviors, attributions, and ultimately emotional experience; and (c) a positivity bias encourages people to expect and express positive emotions and hide negative emotions.

Although no coherent line of research focuses on the experience and expression of specific emotions during relationship initiation, other than love and perhaps liking, indirect support for Guerrero and Andersen's (2000) recognition of the importance of context during initial encounters is evident in a study of relationship development by Flora and Segrin (2000). In order to measure the trajectory of relationship development, Flora and Segrin created a list of cognitive, behavioral, and affective indicators. Some affective indicators suggest positive emotions, for example, "Felt like you were 'on cloud nine' or 'walking one foot off the ground' during or after being with this person" and "Felt an emotional connection to this person that you never imagined you would feel in any relationship." Other affective indicators suggest negative emotions that arise, ironically, from the very fact that another is highly valued, for example, "Felt like it would be extremely difficult to carry on with your life if something tragic ever happened to this person" and "Became very distressed following an argument or disagreement with this person." Not surprisingly, the euphoric state of walking on cloud nine was experienced by 91% of the respondents after only 2.76 months, whereas the distress following an argument was experienced by 79% of respondents after 4.25 months. The actual behavioral statement of "I love you" seems to occur somewhere between these affective states, with 84% stating it on average 3.63 months after the first meeting.

What we hope to make clear as this chapter unfolds is the "logic" behind patterns of emotional experience such as that in the Flora and Segrin (2000) study as well as behind patterns of emotional expression as referenced in Guerrero and Andersen's (2000) essay. We draw on emotion theory, particularly the sociofunctional approach, to provide a framework for integrating both the experience and expression of emotion more centrally into the relationship initiation process.

We begin with a summary of the key elements within the sociofunctional approach in order to establish its relevance to the relationship initiation processes. We then review the research on relationship initiation schemas and scripts, particularly in the early phases of relationship formation (i.e., the first meeting and first date). In the third section of the chapter, we integrate emotion theory with script theory to illustrate how emotion functions as both motivation and communicative moves during the early initiation process before couples have developed their own idiosyncratic relational interaction patterns. In the fourth section, we focus on two personality dispositions associated with emotion and communication in the enactment of initiation routines: shyness and self-monitoring. We conclude the chapter with suggestions for further research.

THE SOCIOFUNCTIONAL APPROACH TO EMOTIONS

Emotions are a primary mode of interaction between an individual and his or her environment. From a biological and evolutionary perspective, states of arousal and the corresponding behavioral response tendencies of the so-called basic emotions function to facilitate the survival of groups or individuals within a physical environment (e.g., fear activates a response tendency to "freeze" or to move quickly away from danger). However, from a sociological perspective, the functional nature of emotions in modern societies is more broadly construed because both the definition of emotion and the concept of environment are more complex (Parkinson, 2005).

For scholars in the sociofunctional tradition of emotion research, physiological arousal is part of the emotion process, but it does not necessarily bear a uniform relationship to a particular emotion, or to a predictable manifestation through facial or bodily display. An environmental or psychological stimulus activates the arousal, which is then interpreted and labeled through an appraisal process that is typically very rapid and often below the level of conscious awareness. This interpretative process is guided by cultural knowledge structures activated by cues available in the relational, situational, and social contexts (Lazarus, 2006; Smith & Lazarus, 1993; Smith & Pope, 1992). For example, we might feel a sort of nervous arousal when meeting strangers but quickly appraise that arousal as the emotion of happiness or joy when our smiles are returned; alternatively, we might appraise nervous arousal as the emotion of disappointment or even sadness if we find no cues of positive response in that environment (Roseman & Smith, 2001). Of course, given the fluid nature of contextual cues, we might even experience several emotions sequentially as our interpretation of the situation changes and we reappraise the nature and intensity of our arousal.

Thus, the environment in which emotions are aroused and displayed is socially constructed and interactive (Kemper, 1984; Miller, 2004). In essence, our understanding of the norms and rules embedded within the social context guides both the experience of emotions and the form and function of their expression. For example, the experience of embarrassment arises from loss of poise (or face) during an interaction, and its display through blushing or remedial actions such as apologies indicates awareness of the need to restore social (interactional) order (Cupach & Metts, 1994; Miller & Leary, 1992). The experience of guilt arises from the violation of social or relational rules and motivates restoration behaviors through acts of contrition and remorse (Frijda & Mesquita, 1994). When emotions are expressed, they elicit both behavioral and attributional responses (Ekman & Davidson, 1994; Frijda, 1994; Manstead & Fischer, 2001). For example, displays of sadness elicit sympathy and empathy from others (Izard & Ackerman, 2000) as well as caretaking behaviors (Murray, 1979) and emotional support (Burleson, 2003). Of course, excessive or prolonged displays, or those that are perceived as insincere, may fail to elicit the intended response from others because they violate cultural or situational norms of appropriate (expected) expression.

Indeed, the form and function of emotional expression have generated considerable scholarly research. Although books in the popular press tell us how to "read" what people are thinking by observing their emotional cues, the link between emotion experience and expression is seldom so simple. As Buck, Losow, Murphy, and Costanzo (1992) argued, emotional expression is both *spontaneous* and *symbolic*. Spontaneous displays of the basic emotions such as fear, disgust, anger, sadness, and joy are hard-wired or innate physical displays that evolved among early humans to signal environmental threats or safety. Over time, however, the need to maintain social order and harmony led to the expansion of basic emotions into more abstract social emotions such as embarrassment, jealousy, guilt, shame, and envy. This more complex emotional configuration necessitated, or perhaps emerged from, the ability to represent emotional states in abstract linguistic symbols. Thus, the symbolic expression of emotion that prevails in modern cultures is "learned, culturally patterned, linguistically structured, and exquisitely tuned to the social situation" (Buck et al., 1992, p. 967).

The strategic and communicative nature of emotion expression is perhaps most clearly evident in the work on *display rules* initially formulated by Ekman and Friesen (1975). The term *display rules* refers to the "socially learned, often culturally different, rules about the management of expression, about who can show which emotion to whom and when they can do so" (Ekman, 2003, p. 4). The five techniques that comprise the set of display rules are *simulation* (displaying emotion that is not felt), *inhibition* (expressing no emotion when one is in fact feeling an emotion), *intensification* (creating the appearance that emotions are felt more strongly than they are), *deintensification* (creating the impression that emotions are felt less strongly than they are), and *masking* (displaying an emotion that is different from the emotion actually being experienced) (Ekman & Friesen, 1975).

In a parallel line of research, Hochschild (1979) introduced the concepts of feeling rules and expression rules. She defined *feeling rules* as "social guidelines" (p. 565) for what one should feel in a social situation and *expression rules* as prescriptions for the appropriate expression of emotions in social contexts. Both feeling and expression rules echo the sentiments of Ekman's (Ekman & Friesen, 1975) display rules. Hochschild (1979) found that participants described their *emotion work* when following these rules, for example, "I *psyched* myself up" and "I *tried* hard not to feel disappointed" (p. 561).

Emotion expression can also be used as a strategy to achieve self-presentational goals. A series of studies reported by Clark, Pataki, and Carver (1996) indicated that emotional displays are associated with impression management goals in predictable ways. For example, anger is used to elicit attributions of dominance and power, facilitating the goal of intimidation. Conversely, signals of happiness and suppression of sadness or anger elicit attributions of likeability and friendliness, facilitating the goal of ingratiation. Similarly, Knutson (1996) found that a combination of sad and fearful expression elicits attributions of vulnerability and facilitates the goal of supplication.

In sum, emotions are processed responses to situational cues, and their expression is communicative. More specifically, like other types of messages, emotional messages are adapted to situational constraints, interactional rules, and normative conventions (Parrott & Harré, 1996; Planalp & Fitness, 1999); they are other directed, providing and soliciting information (Buck, 1989; Metts & Planalp, 2002); and they serve pragmatic functions that facilitate or hinder interactional and relational goals (Gibbs & Van Orden, 2003; Parkinson, 2005; Vorauer & Ross, 1996; Zaalberg, Manstead, & Fischer, 2004). Emotions might be expressed verbally or nonverbally, with or without conscious thought, and like any message, their expression exists on a continuum of veracity. We smile during a greeting exchange whether we feel happy or not; we show sadness when hearing of another's distress even when we would prefer to say, "I told you so." And, of course, we respond to "I love you" with a comparable expression, "I love you too," whether we are experiencing some level of passionate arousal or not.

Although little research to date has attempted to formalize the role of specific emotions in relationship initiation scripts, the scholarship on emotion more broadly suggests that emotions and emotion displays are normative and pragmatic elements in the script enactment process. In Western culture, we tend to view emotions as highly subjective experiences, as illogical, irrational, and uncontrollable. Cultural metaphors such as "falling in love" and "falling out of love" suggest we exert little control over the processes once we step off the precipice. In actual practice, emotional experience and expression are logical and rational responses to the social and relational environment. As Knapp and Vangelisti (2005) remarked, "[E]motional responses are an important part of intimate relationships, but sometimes these relationships develop through an orderly, dispassionate, and sober process" in contrast to the "emotional drunkenness that so often characterizes romantic intimacy" (p. 235). We turn now to a brief review of initiation schemas and scripts to serve as a foundation for a better understanding of how emotion functions within these cultural structures and routines.

RELATIONSHIP SCHEMAS AND SCRIPTS

Relationship initiation is a goal-directed enterprise (Vorauer & Ross, 1996). Initiation goals vary in their scope, focus, and hierarchical configuration. That is, some goals are vague and unfocused (e.g., to have a fun evening), whereas some are more specific and self-focused (e.g., to appear attractive to a target of interest) or other focused (e.g., to learn more about a particular other person). Some goals are short term (e.g., to have a one-night stand), and some are long-term (e.g., to find a person I want to date). Finally, some goals are preexisting (e.g., If Mary comes to the party without a date, I hope I can spend time with her), and some are contextual and emergent (e.g., I am enjoying this conversation; I need to keep it going). Whatever the goals and their configuration may be, people draw on the resources available to them in order to reach their goals (Dillard, 1990). Among the resources people use more commonly to initiate relationships, particularly romantic relationships, are mental schemas and interaction scripts.

Schemas

Although there is some variation across disciplines concerning the specific definition of the term *schema*, a synthesis at the conceptual level suggests that the term *schema* generally refers to knowledge structures or prototypes that aid in the organization and evaluation of information relevant to domains of social roles and social activity. For example, cultural expectations for "appropriate" qualities, attitudes, and behaviors associated with men and women are gender role schemas that are shaped by cultural and co-cultural norms (Bem, 1981). Individuals do not necessarily endorse all cultural expectations to the same degree, but these expectations do influence socialization of children and media portrayals of "typical" men and women (West & Zimmerman, 2002).

Schemas also exist for personal relationships. In cultures where arranged marriages are normative, parental influences in mate selection are expected and appropriate. In societies where dating is the accepted process by which individuals select their own mates, individuals have implicit schemas for how relationships should be expected to develop over time (Honeycutt, Cantrill, & Greene, 1989). They recognize and categorize events typical of "good" or "normal" development and events typical of stagnation and deterioration (Holmberg & MacKenzie, 2002; Holmberg & Veroff, 1996). For example, casual dating among college students tends to include certain activities (e.g., dinner and a movie) but exclude others (e.g., spending the evening with parents). Indeed, when meeting parents is part of a date, the definition of the relationship has likely moved from casual dating to more committed dating (Metts, 2006).

Not only do cultural-level schemas guide early relationship development, but they are also adapted by couples over time to fit their needs (Fehr & Harasymchuk, 2005). Such relationship-specific schemas emerge from the coordinated intersection of each person's self-schema and his or her schema for the partner (Baldwin, 1992). Moreover, romantic partners eventually develop event- or episode-level *scripts*. Such scripts are composed of "expectations about what behaviors tend to be followed by what responses" (Baldwin, p. 468).

Scripts

As indicated in Baldwin's (1992) description of developed relationships, when knowledge structures guide specific interactional patterns, they are referred to as *scripts*. Scripts are a particular type of schema that organizes interaction sequences and moves: who says and does what to whom, when, and (presumably) why. Some scripts are fairly standardized rituals widely shared within a culture (e.g., wedding and funeral rituals), and some are more idiosyncratic and localized (e.g., a family's unique dinner script). Most social scripts are found between these extremes. They are culturally derived from relevant schemas, but are loosely structured sequences that allow for some degree of innovation and adaptation in accord with preexisting and emergent goals in a given context. For example, the simple normative script known as a *greeting ritual* may consist of nothing more than acknowledging another's greeting and returning a similar greeting matched in level of formality and detail. However, in certain contexts, a greeting ritual might also function as the first step in a more sustained interaction episode in which the goals of reducing uncertainty and assessing the other's interest in possible future interactions emerge from and then guide subsequent talk. We illustrate this point with a brief review of two such scripts in the early stages of dating: the first meeting and the first date.

First Meeting Scripts   Early studies of verbal and nonverbal signals of interest during a first meeting identified sequences of "moves" exhibited by potential partners. For example, Scheflen's (1965) quasi-courtship behavior sequence contains four steps: courtship readiness, preening behavior, positional cues, and resolution (actions of appeal or invitation). Lockard and Adams' (1980) typology of courtship moves includes attention, recognition, interaction, sexual arousal, and resolution. These moves have been observed during first meetings in bars (Perper, 1985). In addition, it appears that these co-orientation moves, particularly those that precede interaction, are initiated by women using nonverbal signals of interest directed toward specific men. Moore's (1985) observations of women in settings conducive to first meetings (e.g., singles' bars) revealed that women have a repertoire of 52 nonverbal behaviors (e.g., eye gaze of various durations, smiling, primping, lip licking, and head tossing) that preceded and functioned as invitations for the approach of a selected man. The man then offered an opening line expressing his interest in initiating a conversation.

First Date Scripts   Assuming that an initial meeting leads to a first date, potential partners then move through a series of episodes in which more specific goals become salient. Although many of these interaction goals are similar for men and women (e.g., getting acquainted and judging compatibility), and some behaviors are common to both (e.g., groom for the date and engage in small talk), gender-role expectations distinguish certain goals for men and women and prescribe appropriate behaviors to meet those goals (Laner & Ventrone, 2000; Morr & Mongeau, 2004; Winstead, Derlega, & Rose, 1997). For example, men are expected to initiate, plan, and orchestrate the date; display their resources (usually by paying for the date); and test for female sexual availability. Women are expected to wait for and then accept the date request, display their physical attractiveness, and respond with restraint to tests of sexual availability. Rose and Friese (1989) characterized these as a focus on men's control in the public sphere and women's control in the private sphere.

Despite what we might assume to be a lessening of rigid sex-role scripts in romantic relationships, the expectations noted above for men and women on a first date appear to be relatively unchanging. For example, the male role as initiator and the female role as recipient and sexual gatekeeper reported in 2000 were similar to those reported in 1993 (Laner & Ventrone, 2000), and those reported in 1993 were similar to those reported in the 1950s (Rose & Frieze, 1993). In fact, these scripts are apparently so prescriptive that men and women find it difficult to deviate from them even when instructed to do so. Gilbert, Walker, McKinney, and Snell (1999) instructed college student (stranger) dyads to enact the initiation of a first date and then suggest a move to greater sexual intimacy. In those dyads where assigned gender roles were reversed, 31% of the men initiated the date even when his female partner was assigned the initiator role. Likewise, only about half of the women were able to initiate moves toward sexual intimacy.

In these descriptions of initial meetings and first dates, it is easy to see how verbal messages and behavioral actions function to organize the sequence of events that propel potential partners through the initial phases of dating. Although not so immediately apparent, emotions experienced, displayed, and evoked from others are also strategic devices that function in much the same way. We begin with a discussion of the role of emotion in facilitating relationship initiation enactment. During these first encounters, emotions are especially important in the pursuit of three broad goals: (a) entering the scene with poise and emotional availability, (b) attracting others through displays of affiliation and evoking affiliative responses, and (c) facilitating uncertainty reduction. Each of these goals in the initiation enactment process will be discussed in the following section.

EMOTIONS AND RELATIONSHIP INITIATION ENACTMENT

Romantic relationships originate in a variety of social environments: classrooms, work settings, social events, network contacts, bars, parties, dances, and online. In order for these settings to include courtship initiation "scenes," potential partners must be open to the possibility of forming a relationship. Some individuals do not enter the scene—that is, enact the initiation script or respond to the moves of others—because they are simply not interested or are already in a committed relationship. However, other individuals do not enter the scene or do so unsuccessfully because they are apprehensive about their social performance or because lingering hurt or anger from a previous relationship has left them emotionally unavailable for romantic involvement (Collins, 1997). We turn now to a discussion of the role of emotional states that prospective partners bring with them as they enter the initiation scene.

Entering the Scene: Poise and Emotional Availability

Inherent in courtship moves such as displaying courtship readiness, sending attention cues, and gaining recognition is an underlying affective subtext. Negative affect restricts potential success in these moves, whereas positive affect enhances potential success.

Negative Affective States   Negative affect, particularly fear, is traditionally associated with responses to environmental threats. However, in the context of relationship initiation scenes, fear is more aptly seen as responses to prospective social evaluation. As Gasper and Robinson (2004) argued, fear may have allowed early humans to survive danger, but in modern times how often do we see a bear? More likely we experience fear arising from projected social failure or anxiety about public performance. The initiation of a relationship is very much a public performance, one in which efforts to present oneself as charming, desirable, and attractive entail vulnerability to loss of face and associated emotional responses. According to Goffman (1967),

> A person tends to experience an immediate emotional response to the face which a contact with others allows him … his "feelings" become attached to it … . If events establish a face for him that is better than he might have expected, he is likely to "feel good"; if his ordinary expectations are not fulfilled, one expects that he will "feel bad" or "feel hurt." (p. 6)

This same principle holds true during relationship initiation phases. As Kunkel, Wilson, Olufo-wote, and Robson (2003) found in a comparison of perceived face threats during phases of initiating, intensifying, and terminating relationships, threats to face were salient in all three contexts. More specifically, during initiation, respondents reported that they would feel such affective states as nervous, anxious, uneasy, uncomfortable, awkward, afraid, and scared, presumably because they are opening themselves to loss of face. Similar affective states were reported by young adults (college students) in focus group discussions of "how people feel" in the initiating stage of a relationship—nervous, cautious, curious, scared, and hesitant (Avtgis, West, & Anderson, 1998). Whether these affective states are labeled as particular emotions depends, in large measure, on the feedback from others during the unfolding episode.

Self-presentational concerns prove to be particularly problematic for those who have experienced failure in the past (Vorauer & Ratner, 1996). Such individuals are more likely to fear rejection than those who are feeling confident when entering an initiation scene. Fear of rejection is a localized negative affect that prompts individuals to assume a "self-protective" interaction demeanor, much like the response to fear in a nonsocial context. As a coping mechanism, those who are fearful tend to use affinity-seeking strategies that are self-deprecating, assuming that others will provide reassurances and show positive feelings toward them (Vorauer, Cameron, Holmes, & Pearce, 2003). Unfortunately, such self-deprecating messages during a first meeting are less likely to evoke positive regard from others than are self-positive or other-positive strategies.

Fearful individuals also assume they communicate signals of interest and attraction to a much greater degree than they actually do, a phenomenon known as *signal amplification* (Vorauer et al., 2003). Ironically, their own inhibitions foster restraint in the level of expression of affect and interest cues, a tendency that increases as levels of attraction to a target other increase. When potential partners do not respond to what the fearful person believes to be obvious signals of interest, his or her expectation of rejection is confirmed.

Interestingly, research motivated by the goal of understanding patterns of responsiveness in attachment-related anxiety suggests a judgment bias in perceiving the emotion cues of others that is complementary to the fearful individual's display bias. That is, much like the individual who fears rejection assuming he or she is effectively sending emotion signals of interest to others, the individual who is high in attachment-related anxiety assumes that he or she is correctly interpreting the emotion cues of others. However, hypervigilant attention to the emotion cues of others may actually impair interpretive accuracy. Using a morph movie technique displaying changes in facial displays of emotion from neutral to anger, sadness, or happiness, Fraley, Niedenthal, Marks, Brumbaugh, and Vicary (2006) found that anxious individuals tended to perceive emotion cues more quickly than less anxious individuals, but to make more errors in judging the emotion being displayed. As Fraley et al. (2006) noted, "If anxious individuals are more sensitive to interpersonal cues that indicate changes in other people's emotional states, they may respond to those changes before having the opportunity to evaluate the situation properly" (p. 1184). In the early phase of initiating a relationship, such rapid and error-prone assessments of others' signals may encourage inappropriate optimism or pessimism about a potential partner based on his or her emotional displays.

Positive Affective States   Entering a scene where dating potential is present in a state of positive affect is highly functional. Unlike negative emotions, which tend to narrow response tendencies, positive emotions, particularly contentment and joy, tend to broaden the range of response tendencies. Positive emotions promote openness; facilitate approach behaviors; activate interest levels, optimism, and creativity; and open individuals to the pleasure of play (Fredrickson, 1998, 2001; Izard & Ackerman, 2000). Positive emotions also enhance "broad-minded" coping, or the ability to assess situations objectively and generate a range of possible options for responding (Fredrickson & Joiner, 2002). In two experiments using film clips to activate positive and negative emotions, Fredrickson and Branigan (2005) found that whereas the experience of negative emotional states narrowed the scope of attention, cognition, and action tendencies among participants, the experience of positive emotions broadened these same perceptual and behavioral domains.

Thus, the person whose emotional state is positive when he or she enters a scene where dating potential is present is more likely than those whose emotional state is negative to be adaptable, poised, and emotionally available for interaction. And in contrast to the narrowed and self-protective orientation of the fearful person, the broadened attention orientation of the happy and contented person encourages display of affiliation cues and attention to signs of approachability from others. The result is a smoother transition from the entrance phase to the possibility of engagement in social interaction.

An interesting paradox may emerge, however, for the person who enters a dating scene in a positive state of mind. Because happy individuals perceive the social environment as benign (not threatening), they may feel no particular need to engage in "effortful processing" of messages and other social cues even though they are cognitively capable of doing so (Handley & Lassiter, 2002). In a meta-analysis of 14 mood and persuasion studies, Hullett (2005) concluded that people in positive moods seek to maintain these states by "avoiding dissonance arousing information" (p. 437) and messages that have "negative hedonic consequences" (p. 436). To the extent that findings from persuasion studies can be generalized to the relational contexts of first meetings, we might speculate that people in happy mood states are relatively inattentive to signals of incompatibility in the messages of others to whom they are attracted. They may be prone to forming favorable first impressions of others—impressions that on later reflection should not have been so favorable.

Of course, preexisting affective states, whether positive or negative, are generally transient motivational states. Assuming that individuals remain in the scene and begin interaction, the successful coordination of emotional displays and responses is necessary to move potential partners through the steps of approach and interaction noted by Lockard and Adams (1980). We move now to the preliminary step of attracting others by displaying and evoking affiliation.

Attracting Others: Displaying Affiliation and Evoking Affiliative Responses

The incredible proliferation of "emoticons" in the public media and Internet messages may bring groans from some people. However, their utility as communicative mechanisms is indirectly evident in scholarly research. Empirical and theoretical scholarship suggests that emotional expressivity contributes to interpersonal attraction. For example, Sabatelli and Rubin (1986) found that emotional expressivity is positively related to judgments of interpersonal liking. Interestingly, this effect is independent of physical attractiveness (of targets), but both are equally predictive of liking. Boone and Buck (2003) attributed this effect to a latent evolutionary function, suggesting that a sender's emotional expressivity may imply openness or transparency that signals to observers a state of cooperative intent or personal trustworthiness. Receivers are thereby encouraged to interact with the expressive person.

However, the premise that emotional expressivity leads to both liking and affiliative responses from others is qualified by two important considerations. First, moderate expressivity functions more effectively than extremely high or extremely low expressivity. The former suggests apathy, and the latter suggests mania. The attractiveness of the emotionally expressive person that Boone and Buck (2003) identified arises from a moderate or socially appropriate level of expressivity, in terms of both frequency and intensity.

Second, and more importantly, expression of positive emotions is far more likely to evoke affiliative responses than is the expression of negative emotions. Metts and Bowers (1994) concluded from a review of the expressivity literature that "social harmony/cohesion mandates positive and affiliative emotions and sanctions negative and conflictual emotions" (p. 533). Implicit in this cultural preference for positive emotional displays is the assumption that when people experience negative emotions, they ought to hide them, or perhaps even mask them by covering them with the expression of positive emotions (Zaalberg et al., 2004). Indeed, Reysen (2006) found in both videotapes and photographs of individuals displaying genuine laughter, faked laughter, or no laughter (reading a paragraph) that individuals were rated higher on likeability when they were laughing. Remarkably, this effect emerged for both genuine and fake laughter, even though participants were able to distinguish the false laughter from the genuine laughter.

Research also indicates that the cultural preference for expression of positive emotion is especially binding during initial interactions. In much the same way that the verbal moves constituting initiation scripts are predictive and to some degree prescriptive (e.g., the man asks for the date), so too is the expectation that initial greetings will manifest positive emotion. Interestingly, this expectation is so compelling that when cues signaling dislike are displayed, they occur only after the initial, ritualistic cues of positive affect have been displayed. In a study of nonverbal expressions of affect during initial interactions, Ray and Floyd (2006) instructed participants to act as though they liked or did not like the person with whom they had been paired. In both dyad conditions, participants used basic nonverbal indicators of liking such as smiling and leaning forward during conversation initiation. However, the use of a particular constellation of nonverbal cues associated with affiliation (e.g., hand gesturing, facial expressions and postural matching, proximity, and variation in vocal pitch) increased over time in the liking condition but decreased over time in the disliking condition. This pattern suggests that the broad cultural mandate to signal positive affect is subtly adapted to emergent goals of signaling interest in extending or, alternatively, curtailing future interaction. In short, to form relationships people must be able to exhibit and be willing to reciprocate expressions of positive emotion.

Presumably, in interactions where initial exchanges of positive affect and verbal messages arouse interest in pursuing further conversation and a potential relationship, the goals of revealing self and learning about the other become salient. We turn now to a discussion of the role of emotion in the uncertainty reduction process.

Reducing Uncertainty

Relationship initiation is often marked by both cognitive and emotional uncertainty. Although the dating scripts described previously are useful devices for coordinating initiation moves, the lack of person-specific knowledge is an uncomfortable state that individuals attempt to reduce (Berger, 1987; Berger & Bell, 1988). Berger outlined three strategies that individuals employ in an attempt to gain information about the target: passive (observing the target, preferably in an unstructured situation), active (seeking information from others about the target), and interactive (employing self-disclosure, questions, and relaxation techniques to encourage the target's participation) (see also Knobloch & Miller, this volume).

During interaction, potential partners manipulate their emotion expression and evocation to create an emotionally open and secure environment that facilitates the self-disclosure and relaxation noted by Berger (1987). In a study of the male "seductive" voice, Anolli and Ciceri (2002) found that men who were successful in arranging a second meeting with a woman randomly assigned to them displayed the *seductive voice* to a much greater degree than the men who were not successful.

Of interest for our purposes here is Anolli and Ciceri's (2002) interpretation of the vocal variations during the course of the seductive sequence. The beginning of the sequence is marked by higher pitch, elevated intensity, and faster rate of articulation. The middle phase shifts gradually to a lower, weaker, and warmer voice, which the authors referred to as the "self-disclosure voice." The third phase moves back to a higher pitch, higher intensity, and accelerated rate when actually making the request for the woman to meet him again. Anolli and Ciceri (2002) concluded that men use the initial resonant voice to raise the interest of the woman and impress her with his "strength, vitality, enthusiasm, sociability, virility, and confidence" (p. 167). However, the shift to a lower pitch and softer volume is not designed to impress, but to suggest warmth, tenderness, and affability, which facilitate conversational openness, relaxation, and self-disclosure. These findings underscore the pragmatic nature of emotion expression. Vocally displayed cues of warmth, tenderness, and affability evoke positive emotional responses from women listeners and create the affective preconditions for trust, openness, and thus uncertainty reduction.

In one of the few investigations of relationship initiation goals and strategies that tests for and confirms the role of emotion, Clark, Shaver, and Abrahams (1999) conducted two studies. In the first, a sample of college undergraduates was given the following instructions: "Imagine you are romantically attracted to an available person who might also be attracted to you" (Clark et al., 1999, p. 711). Respondents then rated how likely they would be to do certain behaviors (e.g., manipulate the setting) and experience certain feelings (e.g., nervous or confident). They were also asked to rate a list of strategies such as becoming emotionally involved (revealing personal information), directly initiating the relationship, and signaling relational intent indirectly. In the second study, a sample of college undergraduates was asked to describe in as much detail as possible "their two most recent successful romantic relationship initiation episodes" (p. 715). These descriptions were then coded for initiation goals and strategies. Findings across both studies confirm the importance of self-disclosure generally, and emotional disclosure more specifically. The authors concluded that "the most frequently used behaviors in romantic relationship initiation are those that promote emotional intimacy (emotional disclosure in Study 1 and seeking love, talking, and spending time together in Study 2)" (p. 719).

The verbal expression of love is typically studied as a relationship intensification strategy rather than a relationship initiation strategy (e.g., Tolhuizen, 1989). However, it can also be employed as an indirect strategy to reduce uncertainty about a potential partner. For example, Booth-Butterfield and Trotta (1994) analyzed dating couples' written descriptions of the circumstances surrounding the first expression of love. Consistent with the gender profile in the dating script described previously, 70% of the sample reported that men said, "I love you," first. Approximately half of the sample linked the expression of love to true feelings, and about 20% to situational influences (e.g., had a delightful evening or "made love" for the first time). However, about 13% attributed the expression to a specific motive such as gaining sexual compliance or testing how the other person would respond. Whether or not the statement of love functions as intended (i.e., sexual compliance is granted or expression of love is returned), the speaker nonetheless learns relevant information about his or her partner.

Managing Hope and Disappointment

The implications of the initial phases of uncertainty reduction practices are important, not simply because they facilitate mutual interest and stimulate attraction but also because they are largely scripted exchanges. This fact often leads to one of the most challenging dilemmas in establishing and maintaining a long-term relationship. At the heart of this dilemma is the tension between the cultural preference for and the functional utility of experiencing and expressing positive emotion while at the same time the need to reveal aspects of identity that may be inconsistent with the positivity bias in the initiation script.

Over time, if not resolved, this challenge becomes the dialectic referred to by Murray and Holmes (1996) as the dialectic of hope and doubt. The emotion of hope that this will be the "right person" is fostered during the early phases of relationship initiation, when partners are conscious of self-presentation goals and their interactions tend to be restricted to environments in which arousal is experienced within the traditional relationship schema and easily appraised as attraction and liking. Murray and Holmes argued, "Intimates' models of ideal relationships may also help them 'fill in the gaps' in their limited knowledge about their partners, a process of wish fulfillment where realities become reflections of desires" (p. 92). However, as interdependence increases and partners interact in a wider variety of environments, the potential for partners to reveal negative behaviors increases. "As time passes, negative behaviors that intimates once explained away as anomalies may show patterns of consistency that undercut such situational attributions" (Murray & Holmes, p. 92). At this point, doubt about one's original confidence in the rightness of the relationship may surface. Although doubt is a cognitive assessment, its origin is in the emotional blend of fear, disappointment, and perhaps regret, depending upon the appraisal process.

In those relationships that continue to be satisfying, partners will integrate anomalies into coherent schemas of each other's worthiness known as *positive illusions* (Murray & Holmes, 1996) and will accommodate divergent behaviors through benign attributions (Rusbult, Yovetich, & Verette, 1996). Indeed, over time, satisfied couples will even converge in their emotional similarity. Because emotions are socially and relationally embedded responses, partners tend to validate and perpetuate emotional responses that confirm their shared appraisals of situations and reflect their similarity in response modes. This type of matching tends to enhance the ease of communication even when personality differences do not converge (Anderson, Keltner, & John, 2003).

To this point, our focus has been on the role of emotions during initial interactions and early relationship development. As evidenced throughout this discussion, the ability to successfully display expected patterns of emotion and to elicit positive emotional responses from others is critical in performing the cultural-level scripts for relationship initiation. In addition, the ability to successfully manage the transition between strong positive emotions such as joy, excitement, and hope (which stem naturally from the positive bias of the initiation script) and strong negative emotions such as disappointment, fear, and regret (which sometimes emerge later) is critical in sustaining a relationship.

Although most people, most of the time, are able to enact initiation scripts and to manage relational dialectics, research suggests that individuals do differ in the extent to which they are able and willing to do so. These differences stem, in part, from preexisting (and in some cases persistent) affective states such as loneliness and depression. Although not considered emotions per se, both loneliness and depression have distinctive emotional dimensions. For example, loneliness is not simply a cognitive assessment of being isolated from or unfulfilled by social connections but also an affective response to this cognition that includes feelings of disappointment, confusion, sadness, and perhaps even hurt (Chipuer, 2004; Segrin, 1998). Depression is a mood state, of various degrees of intensity and duration, accompanied by a complex negative affective system with a strong sadness component (Sedikides, 1992; Watson, Clark, & Carey, 1988). Both of these affective dispositions impair the communicative skills necessary for enacting the sequences in the initiation process (Segrin). As detailed by Wenzel and Kashdan (this volume), these affective states are also associated with other affective states such as social anxiety (Bradshaw, 2006), which further perpetuate and complicate their inhibiting effect on successful relationship initiation.

In addition to these preexisting affective states, individual differences in personality dispositions also influence the initiation process and the stability of the relationship during its early phases. We focus on two such personality traits: shyness and self-monitoring. Although psychological components of personality such as extroversion, introversion, and neuroticism no doubt influence the initiation process through their link to emotional experience (Watson & Clark, 1992), their communicative manifestations are less fully established than those of shyness and self-monitoring. We turn now to a discussion of the role of these personality dispositions in the initiation process with particular attention to how they interface with initial interactions, emotion experience, and emotion expression.

INDIVIDUAL DIFFERENCES: SHYNESS AND SELF-MONITORING

As mentioned previously, the fear of rejection is a localized inhibitor for relationship initiation. However, it is transient to the extent that if this fear is alleviated by successful enactments, the individual is generally comfortable revealing aspects of his or her personality during the dating stages. Thus, once the first meeting terrain is crossed, the relationship trajectory is much like any other. By contrast, for the dispositionally shy person, not only is the first meeting a daunting challenge to relationship initiation, but also subsequent social events during which a relationship partner might be able to learn more about him or her may also be constrained by the debilitating effects of shyness (Bradshaw, 2006). Ironically, for the high self-monitor, although the initiation script is enacted with skill and finesse, subsequent social events are also likely to be carefully controlled, which may limit the information that a relationship partner might be able to learn. The consequence in both cases for relationship partners may be a more pronounced hope–disappointment dilemma if the relationship continues to progress.

Shyness

Shyness is a dispositional tendency characterized by high levels of social anxiety and social fear (Caprara, Steca, Cervone, & Artistico, 2003). Shy individuals have less success in face-to-face interactions and derive less enjoyment from such interactions compared to nonshy individuals (Ward & Tracey, 2004). In addition, shy individuals are self-conscious and self-deprecating, have lower opinions of themselves (Cheek & Melchior, 1990), and have lower self-esteem compared to nonshy individuals (Bradshaw, 2006). They also evaluate their social skills negatively and believe that they do not have the skills necessary for successful social interaction (Bradshaw, 2006).

Such negative self-evaluations are particularly problematic during initial encounters. When shy individuals do engage in interaction, they have low expectancies for the outcomes of interaction (Cheek & Melchior, 1990). These appraisals foster negative affect such as fear, disgust, and anticipated embarrassment (Schmidt, 1999)—emotions that are manifested physically as protective withdrawal, tension, anxiety, and interactional awkwardness (Cheek & Melchior, 1990). These displays may be particularly problematic during a first meeting or first date. Not only are positive emotional displays normative and expected, but also withdrawal and displays of tension, anxiety, and awkwardness are more difficult to "read" than displays of specific negative emotions. Thus, although displays of sadness, for example, are not usually expected in the formative encounters of a relationship, at least they prompt a characteristic response from others such as sympathy or support. However, ambiguous displays of negative affect may confuse or frustrate others. When uncharacteristic or "unscripted" emotional displays are exhibited, others may become "out of face" (Metts, 2000) and uncertain as to how to continue the interaction. If uncertainty becomes too extreme, others may choose to prematurely terminate the encounter. Therefore, not only are nonnormative and unexpected emotional displays of shy individuals more difficult for others to interpret, but they also are more difficult to negotiate during initial encounters.

In addition, whereas most people attempt to gain social approval through positive self-presentation, shy individuals are more concerned with *avoiding disapproval* rather than *gaining approval* (Sheppard & Arkin, 1990). In fact, shy individuals are so fearful of being negatively evaluated (e.g., not doing the right thing or not enacting a script properly) that they engage in systematic *avoidant behaviors*. Contrary to popular beliefs, shy individuals do not necessarily avoid interaction (Ward & Tracey, 2004), but they do avoid assertive communication behaviors. For example, they do not initiate conversations, tend to speak less, allow for longer and more frequent silences in conversation, and avoid interruptions (Asendorpf, 1990). They avoid prolonged eye contact, speak softly, and refrain from demonstrating assertiveness by avoiding requests or criticism, and remaining neutral in opinion (Van Der Molen, 1990). By not expressing strong opinions, a shy person avoids disapproval and negative emotional arousal (Garcia, Stinson, Ickes, Bisonnette, & Briggs, 1991). As functional as these adaptations may be for the shy person to avoid increased emotional distress, they simultaneously limit what a potential partner can learn about the shy person during face-to-face interactions and by observing him or her in conversations with others.

Finally, shyness in men appears to be more problematic during initial interactions than is shyness in women (Crozier, 2001). This differential effect is no doubt linked to the nature of the initiation script, which prescribes more assertive moves for men and more reactive moves for women. Garcia et al. (1991) examined the effects of shyness and attraction on thoughts, behaviors, and feelings of male–female strangers in initial, unstructured interactions. Those men who reported greater shyness also reported experiencing more negative thoughts and feelings about themselves during interactions and tended to inhibit their verbal and nonverbal communication with a female partner compared to men reporting less shyness. The behaviors exhibited (or not exhibited) by the shy men not only influenced their partners' negative evaluation of the interaction but also caused the women to become more self-conscious and anxious, and inhibited their efforts to sustain mutual gaze. By contrast, women's shyness did not induce feelings of discomfort or inhibit nonverbal or verbal behaviors in their male partners. Indeed, shyness in women is sometimes seen as a positive quality, indicating modesty (Crozier, 2001). In general, then, shyness is problematic, but particularly during initial interactions, and particularly so for men due to the inhibitory effect of shyness on the enactment of male gender roles.

Self-Monitoring

Self-monitoring refers to the use of social cues during interaction to guide judgments about the appropriateness of self-presentation strategies and/or expressive behaviors (see Snyder, 1974). High self-monitors are keenly attuned to their changing social environment and use cues embedded within these contexts (e.g., others' emotions, social scripts, and status hierarchies) to guide their expressive behavior as well as self-presentation (i.e., presenting a desirable image) (Snyder). Furthermore, Friedman and Herringer (1991) suggested that high self-monitors respond better to the situational demands of emotion expression compared to low self-monitors, who use their internal affective states or psychological motivations, such as attitudes and values (Leone & Hawkins, 2006), as a guide for expressive behavior and self-presentation.

Given the highly scripted nature of relationship initiation and the normative expectations regarding positive and negative emotion displays, it is not surprising that high self-monitors are skilled initiators. In a study examining the relationship between self-presentational goals (ingratiation and self-promotion) and the expression of emotions during social interactions for individuals high and low in self-monitoring needs, Levine and Feldman (1997) found that across goal type, high self-monitors displayed less negative emotion (i.e., fear, anger, and disgust) and more happiness than low self-monitors and were rated by judges as more competent and likeable.

In an interesting extension of Snyder's (1974) characterization of high self-monitors as skillful in the art of posing emotions, Leck and Simpson (1999) studied the phenomenon of "feigning romantic interest" in a potential romantic partner, defined as the ability to "send more convincing and believable messages expressing their 'intentions,' even when their intentions do not reflect their underlying attitudes and feelings" (p. 72). Results indicated that high self-monitors successfully conveyed their feigned interest through verbal and nonverbal channels significantly more than did low self-monitors. In addition, high self-monitors believed they would be better at, and derive more enjoyment from, feigning romantic interest than low self-monitors. This may explain their ability to initiate romantic relationships more readily than low self-monitors. Thus, the difference between high and low self-monitors' ability to regulate emotional expression by attending to appropriate social and emotional scripts may account for their success or failure at initiating relationships.

As is sometimes the case, however, with a finely tuned skill associated with impression management, the very appeal that it holds for a potential partner during the initiation phase of relationship development may prove to be the "fatal attraction" that later turns a partner away (Felmlee, 1998). The high self-monitor's emotion management skill may be one such example. Although high self-monitors are charming when charm is required, and date almost double the amount of low self-monitors, their relationships lack the trust and intimacy seen in those of low self-monitors (Snyder & Simpson, 1984). They have an uncommitted orientation toward relationships (Snyder, Berscheid, & Glick, 1985) and have a higher desire than low self-monitors to "trade in" their current partner in favor of another (Snyder & Simpson, 1984). Due to their ability to adapt to different situations, high self-monitors prefer "segmented" and "non-exclusive" social networks, including romantic partners (Leone & Hawkins, 2006, p. 741). This allows self-monitors to choose partners who are appropriate for a given situation. Often, this choice is dependent on situational or extrinsic factors such as physical appearance (Snyder et al., 1985), social status, and approval from others (Jones, 1993).

By contrast, when selecting a romantic partner, low self-monitors tend to place greater importance on internal attributes, such as personality or attitude. Low self-monitors are more likely and willing to select a physically unattractive partner with stellar internal qualities over a physically attractive partner with less than desirable internal qualities (Snyder et al., 1985). In addition, low self-monitors have a committed orientation toward romantic relationships, prefer to date exclusively, and demonstrate substantial growth of intimacy as a relationships continues (Snyder & Simpson, 1984). Unlike high self-monitors, who tend to view "love as a game" (Leone & Hawkins, 2006, p. 750), low self-monitors prefer quality over quantity. Thus, it is not surprising that high self-monitors may be able to initiate relationships with ease, but are less successful than the low self-monitor at maintaining them (Leck & Simpson, 1999).

CONCLUSION

Emotions are an integral aspect of the relationship initiation process. Their range, valence, intensity, transformations, reappraisals, and communicative consequences cannot be bracketed from the experience of relationship initiation. Considerable scholarly attention has been given to emotion broadly construed and to particular emotion prototypes such as jealousy (Guerrero & Andersen, 1998) and love in dating relationships (Aron et al., this volume; Hendrick & Hendrick, this volume) and in marriage (Fitness, 1996). Considerable scholarly attention has also been given to the initiation of romantic relationships and the factors that influence the process. Unfortunately, systematic application of emotion theory to the nuances of relationship initiation is lacking.

We believe that several directions for research in this important area hold promise. First, the current emphasis in psychological studies of emotion on experimental designs in which emotions are induced with film clips or music could be augmented by more naturalistic designs. For example, diary studies of individuals who are seeking partners could be used to obtain information about the emotions experienced and expressed during first meetings, first dates, and early phases of relationship formation. We recently conducted such a study using college students who were in relationships at the time to assess the degree to which several positive and negative emotions were experienced and expressed. If emotions were experienced but not expressed, respondents were asked why expression was withheld. With remarkable insights reflecting both the normative and relational constraints of emotion expression, respondents recorded such statements as "I couldn't say I love you yet because it is too soon," or "I didn't express my hurt (anger, disappointment, sadness, etc.) because he/she just wouldn't care so why bother" (Metts, Mikucki, & Smith, 2007). We think this design could be a useful approach for research on relationship initiation.

Second, we encourage study of emotional states that may be unique motivational systems in the domain of relationship initiation. For example, scholars have investigated both the fear of failure and the fear of rejection during the initiation phase. However, a different type of fear may also be worth conceptualizing and measuring: the fear of "aloneness"—a fear evoked by thoughts of the possibility that one may grow old alone, not have children, or not be part of someone else's life in an enduring and intimate relationship. Presumably, a person would be motivated to engage in relationship initiation attempts in an effort to allay this fear and feel the more positive emotion of hope. Future research might explore the extent to which initiation attempts motivated by this fear are successful and the extent to which they are similar to or different from the scripts previously described.

Our third suggestion is to move beyond the college student sample. The emotional landscape of relationship initiation might be configured differently for persons who are not the typical young, socially enmeshed college student. For example, the fear of aloneness might be more common among divorced or never-married older people. For the single parent with children in the home, every phase of the initiation process outlined in this chapter might be complicated by the fact that increasing emotional investment necessarily brings with it consideration of the children's emotional responses as well.

In closing, we acknowledge that continued research is needed to further our knowledge about the dynamic emotional processes and functions that occur during relationship initiation. Although our spin on the Doors' classic lyrics is neither catchy nor romantic, it is at least an initial articulation of the patterned complexity of emotion during relationship initiation.

REFERENCES

Anderson, C., Keltner, D., & John, O. P. (2003). Emotional convergence between people over time. *Journal of Personality and Social Psychology, 84,* 1054–1068.

Anolli, L., & Ciceri, R. (2002). Analysis of the vocal profiles of male seduction: From exhibition to self-disclosure. *Journal of General Psychology, 129,* 149–169.

Asendorpf, J. (1990). The expression of shyness and embarrassment. In W. R. Crozier (Ed.), *Shyness and embarrassment: Perspectives from social psychology* (pp. 87–118). New York: Cambridge University Press.

Avtgis, T. A., West, D. V., & Anderson, T. L. (1998). Relationship stages: An inductive analysis identifying cognitive, affective, and behavioral dimensions of Knapp's relational stages model. *Communication Research Reports, 15,* 280–287.

Baldwin, M. W. (1992). Relational schemas and the processing of social information. *Psychological Bulletin, 112,* 461–484.

Bem, S. L. (1981). Gender schema theory: A cognitive account of sex typing. *Psychological Review, 88,* 354–364.

Berger, C. R. (1987). Planning and scheming: Strategies for initiating relationships. In R. Burnett, P. McGhee, & D. Clarke (Eds.), *Communication, social cognition, and affect* (pp. 93–116). Hillside, NJ: Lawrence Erlbaum.

Berger, C. R., & Bell, R. A. (1988). Plans and the initiation of social relationships. *Human Communication Research, 15,* 217–235.

Boone, R. T., & Buck, R. (2003). Emotional expressivity and trustworthiness: The role of nonverbal behavior in the evolution of cooperation. *Journal of Nonverbal Behavior, 27,* 163–182.

Booth-Butterfield, M., & Trotta, M. R. (1994). Attributional patterns for expressions of love. *Communication Reports, 7,* 119–129.

Bradshaw, S. D. (2006). Shyness and difficult relationships: Formation is just the beginning. In D. C. Kirkpatrick, S. Duck, & M. K. Foley (Eds.), *Relating difficulty: The process of constructing and managing difficult interaction* (pp. 15–41). Mahwah, NJ: Lawrence Erlbaum.

Buck, R. (1989). Emotional communication in personal relationships: A developmental-interactionist view. In C. Hendrick (Ed.), *Close relationships* (pp. 144–163). Newbury Park, CA: Sage.

Buck, R., Losow, J. I., Murphy, M. M., & Costanzo, P. (1992). Social facilitation and inhibition of emotional expression and communication. *Journal of Personality and Social Psychology, 63,* 962–968.

Burleson, B. R. (2003). The experience and effects of emotional support: What the study of cultural and gender differences can tell us about close relationships, emotion, and interpersonal communication. *Personal Relationships, 10,* 1–23.

Caprara, G. V., Steca, P., Cervone, D., & Artistico, D. (2003). The contribution of self-efficacy beliefs to dispositional shyness: On social-cognition systems and the development of personality dispositions. *Journal of Personality, 71,* 943–970.

Cheek, J. M., & Melchior, L. A. (1990). Shyness, self-esteem, and self-consciousness. In H. Leitenberg (Ed.), *Handbook of social and evaluation anxiety* (pp. 47–82). New York: Plenum Press.

Chipuer, H. M. (2004). Australian children's understanding of loneliness. *Australian Journal of Psychology, 56,* 147–153.

Clark, C. L., Shaver, P. R., & Abrahams, M. F. (1999). Strategic behaviors in romantic relationship initiation. *Personality and Social Psychology Bulletin, 25,* 709–722.

Clark, M. S., Pataki, S. P., & Carver, V. H. (1996). Some thoughts and findings on self-presentation of emotions in relationships. In G. J. O. Fletcher & J. Fitness (Eds.), *Knowledge structures in close relationships: A social psychological approach* (pp. 247–274). Mahwah, NJ: Lawrence Erlbaum.

Collins, B. C. (1997). *Emotional unavailability: Recognizing it, understanding it and avoiding its trap.* Chicago: Contemporary Publishing.

Crozier, W. R. (2001). *Understanding shyness: Psychological perspectives.* New York: Palgrave.

Cupach, W. W., & Metts, S. (1994). *Facework.* Thousand Oaks, CA: Sage.

Dillard, J. P. (1990). A goal-driven model of interpersonal influence. In J. P. Dillard (Ed.), *Seeking compliance: The production of interpersonal influence messages* (pp. 41–56). Scottsdale, AZ: Gorsuch-Scarisbrick.

Ekman, P. (2003). *Emotions revealed*. New York: Henry Holt.

Ekman, P., & Davidson, R. J. (1994). Afterword. In *The nature of emotion: Fundamental questions* (pp. 137–139). New York: Oxford University Press.

Ekman, P., & Friesen, W. V. (1975). *Unmasking the face*. Englewood Cliffs, NJ: Prentice-Hall.

Fehr, B., & Harasymchuk, C. (2005). The experience of emotion in close relationships: Toward an integration of the emotion-in-relationships and interpersonal script models. *Personal Relationships, 12*, 181–196.

Felmlee, D. H. (1998). Fatal attraction. In B. H. Spitzberg & W. R. Cupach (Eds.), *The dark side of close relationships* (pp. 3–31). Mahwah, NJ: Lawrence Erlbaum.

Fitness, J. (1996). Emotion knowledge structures in close relationships. In G. J. O. Fletcher & J. Fitness (Eds.), *Knowledge structures in close relationships: A social psychological approach* (pp. 195–217). Mahwah, NJ: Lawrence Erlbaum.

Flora, J., & Segrin, C. (2000). Relationship development in dating couples: Implications for relational satisfaction and loneliness. *Journal of Social and Personal Relationships, 17*, 811–825.

Fraley, R. C., Niedenthal, P. M., Marks, M., Brumbaugh, C., & Vicary, A. (2006). Adult attachment and the perception of emotional expressions: Probing the hyperactivating strategies underlying anxious attachment. *Journal of Personality, 74*, 1163–1190.

Fredrickson, B. L. (1998). What good are positive emotions? *Review of General Psychology, 2*, 300–319.

Fredrickson, B. L. (2001). Positive emotions. In T. J. Mayne & G. A. Bonanno (Eds.), *Emotions: Current issues and future directions* (pp. 123–151). New York: Guilford.

Fredrickson, B. L., & Branigan, C. (2005). Positive emotions broaden the scope of attention and thought-action repertoires. *Cognition and Emotion, 19*, 313–332.

Fredrickson, B. L., & Joiner, T. (2002). Positive emotions trigger upward spirals toward emotional well-being. *Psychological Science, 13*, 172–176.

Friedman, H. S., & Herringer, T. M. (1991). Nonverbal display of emotion in public and private: Self-monitoring, personality, and expressive cues. *Journal of Personality and Social Psychology, 61*, 766–775.

Frijda, N. H. (1994). Emotions are functional, most of the time. In P. Ekman & R. J. Davidson (Eds.), *The nature of emotion: Fundamental questions* (pp. 113–122). New York: Oxford University Press.

Frijda, N. H., & Mesquita, B. (1994). The social roles and functions of emotions. In S. Kitayama & H. R. Markus (Eds.), *Emotion and culture: Empirical studies of mutual influence* (pp. 51–87). Washington, DC: American Psychological Association.

Garcia, S., Stinson, L., Ickes, W., Bisonnette, V., & Briggs, S. R. (1991). Shyness and physical attractiveness in mixed-sex dyads. *Journal of Personality and Social Psychology, 61*, 35–49.

Gasper, K., & Robinson, M. D. (2004). Locating the self in the stream of emotion: Promises and problems. *Psychological Inquiry, 15*, 145–149.

Gibbs, R. W., Jr., & Van Orden, G. C. (2003). Are emotional expressions intentional? A self-organizational approach. *Consciousness & Emotion, 4*, 1–16.

Gilbert, L. A., Walker, S. J., McKinney, S., & Snell, J. L. (1999). Challenging discourse themes reproducing gender in heterosexual dating: An analog study. *Sex Roles, 41*, 753–774.

Goffman, E. (1967). *Interaction ritual*. New York: Pantheon.

Guerrero, L. K., & Andersen, P. A. (1998). Jealousy experience and expression in romantic relationships. In P. A. Andersen & L. K. Guerrero (Eds.), *Handbook of communication and emotion: Research, theory, applications, and contexts* (pp. 155–188). San Diego, CA: Academic Press.

Guerrero, L., & Andersen, P. A. (2000). Emotion in close relationships. In C. Hendrick & S. S. Hendrick (Eds.), *Close relationships: A sourcebook* (pp. 171–183). Thousand Oaks, CA: Sage.

Handley, I. M., & Lassiter, G. D. (2002). Mood and information processing: When happy and sad look the same. *Motivation and Emotion, 26*, 223–255.

Hochschild, A. R. (1979). Emotion work, feeling rules, and social structure. *American Journal of Sociology, 85*, 551–575.

Holmberg, D., & MacKenzie, S. (2002). So far, so good: Scripts for romantic relationship development as predictors of relational well-being. *Journal of Social and Personal Relationships, 19*, 777–796.

Holmberg, D., & Veroff, J. (1996). Rewriting relationship memories: The effects of courtship and wedding scripts. In G. J. O. Fletcher & J. Fitness (Eds.), *Knowledge structures in close relationships: A social psychological approach* (pp. 345–368). Mahwah, NJ: Lawrence Erlbaum.

Honeycutt, J. M., Cantrill, J. G., & Greene, R. W. (1989). Memory structures for relational escalation: A cognitive test of the sequencing of relational actions and stages. *Human Communication Research, 16*, 62–90.

Hullett, C. R. (2005). The impact of mood on persuasion: A meta-analysis. *Communication Research, 32*, 423–442.

Izard, C. E., & Ackerman, B. P. (2000). Motivational, organizational, and regulatory functions of discrete emotions. In M. Lewis & J. M. Haviland-Jones (Eds.), *Handbook of emotions* (2nd ed., pp. 253–264). New York: Guilford Press.

Jones, M. (1993). Influence of self-monitoring on dating motivations. *Journal of Research in Personality, 27,* 197–206.

Kemper, T. D. (1984). Power, status, and emotions: A sociological contribution to a psychological domain. In K. R. Scherer & P. Ekman (Eds.), *Approaches to emotion* (pp. 369–383). Hillsdale, NJ: Lawrence Erlbaum.

Knapp, M. L., & Vangelisti, A. L. (2005). *Interpersonal communication and human relationships* (5th ed.). Boston: Allyn & Bacon.

Knutson, B. (1996). Facial expressions of emotion influence interpersonal trait inferences. *Journal of Nonverbal Behavior, 20,* 165–182.

Kunkel, A. D., Wilson, S. R., Olufowote, J., & Robson, S. (2003). Identity implications of influence goals: Initiating, intensifying, and ending romantic relationships. *Western Journal of Communication, 67,* 382–412.

Laner, M. R., & Ventrone, N. A. (2000). Dating scripts revisited. *Journal of Family Issues, 21,* 488–500.

Lazarus, R. S. (2006). Emotions and interpersonal relationships: Toward a person-centered conceptualization of emotions and coping. *Journal of Personality, 74,* 9–46.

Leck, K., & Simpson, J. A. (1999). Feigning romantic interest: The role of self-monitoring. *Journal of Research in Personality, 33,* 69–91.

Leone, C., & Hawkins, L. B. (2006). Self-monitoring and close relationships. *Journal of Personality, 74,* 740–778.

Levine, S. P., & Feldman, R. S. (1997). Self-presentational goals, self-monitoring, and non-verbal behavior. *Basic and Applied Social Psychology, 19,* 505–518.

Lockard, J. S., & Adams, R. M. (1980). Courtship behaviors in public: Different age/sex roles. *Ethology and Sociobiology, 1,* 245–253.

Manstead, A. S. R., & Fischer, A. H. (2001). Social appraisal: The social world as object of and influence on appraisal processes. In K. R. Scherer, A. Schorr, & T. Johnstone (Eds.), *Appraisal processes in emotion: Theory, method, research* (pp. 221–232). New York: Oxford University Press.

Metts, S. (2000). Face and facework: Implications for the study of personal relationship. In K. Dindia & S. Duck (Eds.), *Communication in personal relationships* (pp. 77–94). New York: Wiley & Sons.

Metts, S. (2006). Gendered communication in dating relationships. In B. J. Dow & J. T. Wood (Eds.), *The Sage handbook of gender and communication* (pp. 25–40). Thousand Oaks, CA: Sage.

Metts, S., & Bowers, J. W. (1994). Emotion in interpersonal communication. In M. L. Knapp & G. R. Miller (Eds.), *Handbook of interpersonal communication* (pp. 508–541). Thousand Oaks, CA: Sage.

Metts, S., Mikucki, S. L., & Smith, A. C. (2007, April). *The challenges and consequences of emotion expression in close relationships.* Paper presented at the annual meeting of the Central States Communication Association Convention, Minneapolis, MN.

Metts, S., & Planalp, S. (2002). Emotional communication. In M. L. Knapp & J. A. Daly (Eds.), *Handbook of interpersonal communication* (3rd ed., pp. 339–373). Thousand Oaks, CA: Sage.

Miller, R. S. (2004). Emotion as adaptive interpersonal communication: The case of embarrassment. In L. Z. Tiedens & C. W. Leach (Eds.), *The social life of emotions* (pp. 87–104). Cambridge: Cambridge University Press.

Miller, R. S., & Leary, M. R. (1992). Social sources and interactive functions of emotion: The case of embarrassment. In M. S. Clark (Ed.), *Emotion and social behavior* (pp. 202–221). Newbury Park, CA: Sage.

Moore, M. M. (1985). Nonverbal courtship patterns in women: Context and consequences. *Ethology and Sociobiology, 6,* 237–247.

Morr, M. C., & Mongeau, P. A. (2004). First date expectations: The impact of sex initiator, alcohol consumption, and relationship type. *Communication Research, 31,* 3–35.

Murray, A. D. (1979). Infant crying as an elicitor of parental behavior: An examination of two models. *Psychological Bulletin, 86,* 191–215.

Murray, S. L., & Holmes, J. G. (1996). The construction of relationship realities. In G. J. O. Fletcher & J. Fitness (Eds.), *Knowledge structures in close relationships: A social psychological approach* (pp. 91–120). Mahwah, NJ: Lawrence Erlbaum.

Parkinson, B. (2005). Do facial movements express emotions or communicate motives? *Personality and Social Psychology Review, 9,* 278–311.

Parrott, W. G., & Harré, R. (1996). Introduction: Some complexities in the study of emotions. In R. Harré & W. G. Parrott (Eds.), *The emotions: Social, cultural and biological dimensions* (pp. 1–29). Thousand Oaks, CA: Sage.

Perper, T. (1985). *Sex signals: The biology of love*. Philadelphia: ISI Press.

Planalp, S., & Fitness, J. (1999). Thinking/feeling about social and personal relationships. *Journal of Social and Personal Relationships, 16,* 731–750.

Ray, G. B., & Floyd, K. (2006). Nonverbal expressions of liking and disliking in initial interaction: Encoding and decoding perspectives. *Southern Communication Journal, 71,* 45–65.

Reysen, S. (2006). A new predictor of likeability: Laughter. *Northern American Journal of Psychology, 8,* 373–382.

Rose, S., & Friese, I. H. (1989). Young singles' scripts for a first date. *Gender & Society, 3,* 258–268.

Rose, S., & Friese, I. H. (1993). Young singles' contemporary dating scripts. *Sex Roles, 28,* 499–509.

Roseman, I. J., & Smith, C. A. (2001). Appraisal theory: Overview, assumptions, varieties, controversies. In K. R. Scherer, A. Schorr, & T. Johnstone (Eds.), *Appraisal processes in emotion: Theory, method, research* (pp. 3–19). New York: Oxford University Press.

Rusbult, C. E., Yovetich, N. A., & Verette, J. (1996). An interdependence analysis of accommodation processes. In G. J. O. Fletcher & J. Fitness (Eds.), *Knowledge structures in close relationships: A social psychological approach* (pp. 63–90). Mahwah, NJ: Lawrence Erlbaum.

Sabatelli, R. M., & Rubin, M. (1986). Nonverbal expressiveness and physical attractiveness as mediators of interpersonal perceptions. *Journal of Nonverbal Behavior, 10,* 120–133.

Scheflen, A. E. (1965). Quasi-courtship behavior in psychotherapy. *Psychiatry, 28,* 245–257.

Schmidt, L. A. (1999). Frontal brain electrical activity in shyness and sociability. *Psychological Science, 10,* 316–320.

Sedikides, C. (1992). Changes in the valence of the self as a function of mood. In M. S. Clark (Ed.), *Emotion and social behavior* (pp. 271–311). Newbury Park, CA: Sage.

Segrin, C. (1998). Interpersonal communication problems associated with depression and loneliness. In P. A. Andersen & L. K. Guerrero (Eds.), *Handbook of communication and emotion: Research, theory, applications, and contexts* (pp. 215–242). San Diego, CA: Academic Press.

Sheppard, J. A., & Arkin, R. M. (1990). Shyness and self-presentation. In W. R. Crozier (Ed.), *Shyness and embarrassment: Perspectives from social psychology* (pp. 286–314). New York: Cambridge University Press.

Smith, C. A., & Lazarus, R. S. (1993). Appraisal components, core relational themes, and the emotions. *Cognition and Emotion, 7,* 233–269.

Smith, C. A., & Pope, L. K. (1992). Appraisal and emotion: The interactional contributions of dispositional and situational factors. In M. S. Clark (Ed.), *Emotion and social behavior* (pp. 32–62). Newbury Park, CA: Sage.

Snyder, M. (1974). Self-monitoring of expressive behavior. *Journal of Personality and Social Psychology, 30,* 526–537.

Snyder, M., Berscheid, E., & Glick, P. (1985). Focusing on the exterior and the interior: Two investigations of the initiation of personal relationships. *Journal of Personality and Social Psychology, 48,* 1427–1439.

Snyder, M., & Simpson, J. A. (1984). Self-monitoring and dating relationships. *Journal of Personality and Social Psychology, 47,* 1281–1291.

Tolhuizen, J. H. (1989). Communication strategies for intensifying dating relationships: Identification, use and structure. *Journal of Social and Personal Relationships, 6,* 413–434.

Van Der Molen, H. T. (1990). A definition of shyness and its implications for clinical practice. In W. R. Crozier (Ed.), *Shyness and embarrassment: Perspectives from social psychology* (pp. 255–285). New York: Cambridge University Press.

Vorauer, J. D., Cameron, J. J., Holmes, J. G., & Pearce, D. G. (2003). Invisible overtures: Fears of rejection and the signal amplification bias. *Journal of Personality and Social Psychology, 84,* 793–812.

Vorauer, J. D., & Ratner, R. K. (1996). Who's going to make the first move? Pluralistic ignorance as an impediment to relationship formation. *Journal of Social and Personal Relationships, 13,* 483–506.

Vorauer, J. D., & Ross, M. (1996). The pursuit of knowledge in close relationships: An informational goals analysis. In G. J. O. Fletcher & J. Fitness (Eds.), *Knowledge structures in close relationships: A social psychological approach* (pp. 369–396). Mahwah, NJ: Lawrence Erlbaum.

Ward, C. C., & Tracey, T. J. G. (2004). Relation of shyness with aspects of on-line relationship involvement. *Journal of Social and Personal Relationships, 21,* 611–623.

Watson, D., & Clark, L. A. (1992). On traits and temperament: General and specific factors of emotional experience and their relation to the five factor model. *Journal of Personality, 60,* 441–476.

Watson, D., Clark, L. A., & Carey, G. (1988). Positive and negative affectivity and their relation to anxiety and depressive disorders. *Journal of Abnormal Psychology, 97,* 346–353.

West, C., & Zimmerman, D. H. (2002). Doing gender. In S. Fenstermaker & C. West (Eds.), *Doing gender, doing difference: Inequality, power, and institutional change* (pp. 3–24). New York: Routledge.

Winstead, B. A., Derlega, V. J., & Rose, S. (1997). *Gender and close relationships*. Thousand Oaks, CA: Sage.

Zaalberg, R., Manstead, A. S. R., & Fischer, A. H. (2004). Relations between emotions, display rules, social motives, and facial behaviour. *Cognition and Emotion, 18,* 183–207.

Section V

Challenges and Problematic Relationship Initiation

Hookups

A Facilitator or a Barrier to Relationship Initiation and Intimacy Development?

ELIZABETH L. PAUL, AMY WENZEL, and JOHN HARVEY

I lost my virginity when I was 15 years old. Since then, I have hooked up with many people, girls and guys. I am not currently in a relationship since I am not very big on commitment. My longest relationship was one year, and that was the only time I've ever been in love. I haven't dated since that relationship ended, but I have been with quite a few guys since then. I don't have sex because I'm in love with the person. As a matter of fact that has only happened once. I have sex because at the moment I think I need it or I am under the influence of alcohol. I've never considered it anything special, and maybe I'm missing out on something, or maybe I'm just 19, and haven't experienced love or sex to the greatest potential yet. Right now, I don't want a relationship. I'm too young, and I'm having too much fun to be tied down to just one person. I've cheated on a few of my ex-boyfriends, and I always feel awful about it, so now, I don't want to put myself in a situation where I would cheat on someone again, especially because they don't deserve it. I joke around with my friends all the time, saying I'll probably be divorced at least three times before I find the right guy. But truthfully, I really hope that I will find the perfect husband and I won't want to cheat on him and I won't want to spend time with other people and I'll be totally and completely happy with him and stay with him for the rest of my life. I don't want to be remarried a million times, always searching for someone better. I just haven't found that yet, and I don't really know how, and so sometimes it scares me that I'll continue on this path and never settle down.

Female, age 19

The above narrative exemplifies the complex challenge of initiating relationships for contemporary youth. Intense intrapersonal questioning is prompted by diverse and seemingly haphazard forays into sexual exploration and a search for meaningful interpersonal connection—whatever that is. Many youth express confusion about what meaningful connection is all about, whether they are capable or worthy of such connection, and how they can move toward satisfying and fulfilling connection. Meanwhile, their social lives often include *hookups*—short-lived and intense sexual exploration apart from emotional connection that rarely builds beyond one or two "steamy" meetings. Although such casual sexual interactions may occur throughout the life course, experiences with these quick and intense sexual interactions are particularly interesting to consider in the context of late adolescence and young adulthood as youth develop their capacity for intimacy and skill in initiating close relationships.

In this chapter, we explore associations between hooking up and relationship initiation among heterosexual late adolescents and young adults attending college. We assert that the potential function of youth's hookup experiences is both immediate (i.e., for building a specific relationship) and long term (i.e., for developing the capacity for intimacy). Thus, we will review relevant literature and some exploratory data to examine the following questions:

1. What is the potential of hookups as a stage in initiating a committed romantic relationship? What typically happens after a hookup ends? How often do committed relationships result from hookups?
2. What is the emotional experience of hookups? What sense do young people make from their hookup experiences? What lessons and insights, fears and worries, and hopes and expectations do youth take forward to future relationships?

Our analysis is informed by (a) social psychological theory and research on relationship initiation, (b) developmental theory and research on the formative significance of adolescent romantic relationships and the importance of intimacy development for well-being, and (c) current insights into contemporary youth culture. Data include quantitative evidence of hookup prevalence, characteristics, and sequelae, and narrative pieces from college students from a midsized northeastern college on the subjective experience of hookups and the meaning youth make of their experiences. This analysis has important clinical and societal implications for relationship development during the transition to adulthood.

We begin by setting a context for our analysis that includes discussion of the significance of adolescence and young adulthood for intimacy development and description of patterns of youth sexual and relationship experience, including casual sexual hookup experience. We then analyze literature and data that pertain to the effectiveness of hookups in initiating relationships and theorize about features of hookup experiences that appear to potentate relationship initiation. Next, we speculate about the effectiveness of hookup experiences in advancing intimacy development, including analysis of excerpted narratives from youth about their perceptions of future consequences. Finally, we discuss limitations for our understanding of hookups as relationship initiators and make suggestions for future directions in research in this important area of study.

THE DEVELOPMENTAL SIGNIFICANCE OF ADOLESCENCE AND YOUNG ADULTHOOD

Meaningful connection with others is a critical element of humans' health and well-being. Interpersonal connection can expand our mind, deepen our emotions, and sustain our health. Seeking meaningful connection is a lifelong pursuit. Whereas childhood is an important "playground" for attachment building and early relationship exploration, arguably the most intense time for relationship exploration is adolescence, when the full array of human needs emerges, and youth take on increasing personal volition in working social interactions to satisfy needs. Advancing cognitive and emotional development deepens awareness of self and others, social development prompts greater complexity of social interaction and opportunity, and the onset of puberty stimulates sexual interests and impulses. Together, this confluence brings on heightened preoccupation with interpersonal connection in pursuit of self and satisfaction.

Also shifting in adolescence is the relational locus of the pursuit of self and satisfaction. Early definition of the self occurs as children learn to separate from their parents, supplemented by social mirroring with peers. In adolescence, peer relationships intensify, becoming a focal context for self-exploration and satisfaction. Romantic relating becomes more predominant as young people advance from preadolescence through adolescence (Richards, Crowe, Larsen, & Swarr, 1998).

Adult love relationships have their roots in adolescent and young adult sexual and emotional intimacy exploration (Erikson, 1968; Orlofsky, 1993). A critical focus of adolescence and young adulthood is on the development of aptitude for intimate relationships. Erikson (1963, 1968) theorized that individuals develop across the life span by facing and resolving a series of crises, or times of heightened preoccupation. Failure to resolve a crisis negatively impacts future development. Youth are preoccupied with developing an ability to love and feel satisfying closeness in committed relationships; failure to resolve this crisis leads to isolation and an inability to form close relationships. Thus, successfully resolving this *intimacy versus isolation* crisis enables young adults to establish and maintain enduring intimate relationships (Orlofsky, 1993). Indeed, research demonstrates that positive romantic relationship experiences during adolescence can promote well-being (Collins, 2003), advance identity development and parent–child individuation (Furman & Shaffer, 2003), lower stress and loneliness (Moore & Leung, 2002), and contribute to subsequent relationship functioning (Furman & Flanagan, 1997). However, negative romantic relationship experiences increase risk of early and frequent romantic involvement (Zimmer-Gembeck, Siebenbruner, & Collins, 2001), difficult breakups (Monroe, Rhode, Seeley, & Lewinsohn, 1999), and abuse (Silverman, Raj, Mucci, & Hathaway, 2001).

YOUTH SEXUAL AND RELATIONSHIP EXPERIENCE

Exploration and experimentation with sex and relationships are challenging to young people as they struggle to develop their capacity for intimacy. Social customs have helped to structure youth's evolving relationship interests and patterns. Traditionally, dating had served the function of getting to know someone before entering into a committed relationship with him or her. In traditional notions of dating and social customs such as "going steady," commitment and felt emotion or love for one's partner were important precursors to sexual interaction. Sexual interaction, defined narrowly as sexual intercourse, was conditionally connected to marriage. However, Cate and Lloyd (1992) identified three major ways in which dating changed in the later years of the 20th century, such that there was (a) more frequent informal opportunity for interacting with available peers, (b) less formality in dating, and (c) a disbanding of formal stages of progression from meeting to marriage. The trend in the late 20th century and into the 21st century has been toward earlier ages of sexual initiation, sexual interaction at earlier stages of relationship development (or even disconnected from relationship development), and a greater time span between sexual initiation and marriage or other long-term relationship commitment (e.g., Santelli, Lindberg, Abma, McNeely, & Resnick, 2000; Sieving, Oliphant, & Blum, 2002).

Recent national studies provide data to illustrate the sexual experiences among contemporary youth. These studies suggest a highly sexualized youth culture. Most youth become sexually active (i.e., engage in sexual intercourse) in adolescence, with some entering into a repeated behavior pattern with different partners. At the turn of the 21st century, nearly half of high-school-aged students report having ever had sexual intercourse (Grunbaum et al., 2002). Eighty percent of young adults ranging in age from 18 to 24 reported having had sexual intercourse (Hoff, Greene, & Davis, 2003). Noncoital sexual behavior is also prevalent; 36% of late adolescents (ages 15 to 17) and 66% of young adults (ages 18 to 24) reported having had oral sex (Hoff et al., 2003). In fact, many youth appear to distinguish oral sex as less risky and less of a "big deal" than sexual intercourse (Henry Kaiser Family Foundation and *Seventeen*, 2000).

Research has often assessed youth sexual experience apart from the relationship context within which it occurs. Although some youth abstain from sexual interaction or confine sexual involvement to a special committed relationship, recent evidence suggests that many youth engage in sexual interaction that is more itinerant. Research on sexual initiation has revealed that for the majority of adolescents, first sexual interactions occur in the context of dating relationships (Cooksey, Mott, & Neubauer, 2003; Manning, Longmore, & Giordano, 2000). However, this leaves about a quarter of adolescents whose first sexual encounter is with someone who is a new or brief acquaintance (Manning et al., 2000). Recent research suggests that over 60% of sexually active adolescents have engaged in sexual intercourse with partners they are not dating (Bearman, 1997; Manning, Longmore, &

Giordino, 2005). Moreover, frequently unaddressed in this research are other types of physically intimate sexual interactions (e.g., oral sex) that may or may not be accompanied by sexual intercourse.

It is debatable whether casual sexual interaction is more prevalent for contemporary youth than in past cohorts; unfortunately, there is a dearth of research on such cross-cohort comparisons. Nonetheless, it appears that contemporary youth are in a situation where they must negotiate an environment in which it is common to engage in very physically intimate behavior, often outside of a committed relationship. Furthermore, it seems that there is at least a subset of youth who are experiencing quick *hookups* and *not* gaining experience with initiating and maintaining committed relationships. Below, we describe in detail characteristics of youth's hookup interactions, focusing on college students, on whom most research has focused to date.

CHARACTERISTICS OF CASUAL SEXUAL HOOKUPS

Hookups, presumed to be noncommittal and emotionally inconsequential sexual interactions, are regarded as casual sexual encounters and have sometimes been referred to as "one-night stands." Recent research suggests that more than three quarters of college students have experienced at least one hookup (but typically numerous hookups; Paul & Hayes, 2002; Paul, McManus, & Hayes, 2000). Nearly one half of young men's and one third of young women's hookup experiences involved sexual intercourse, although hookups often involved other sexual behavior such as kissing, petting, and oral sex (Paul et al., 2000; Weaver & Herold, 2000).

Paul and Hayes (2002) queried 187 college students about their perceptions of typical hookup experiences. A series of questions with associated behavioral checklists prompted students to describe different aspects of typical hookup interactions (including questions about the relationship between hookup partners, where hookups typically occur, and what sexual behaviors occur). The results provide a sketch of youth's typical hookup experiences. Hookups tend to involve two never-before-acquainted partners. Flirting, drinking alcohol, hanging out, and partying are the most common factors leading up to a hookup. Often, youth (both men and women) "plan" to hook up, although the plan may not specify a particular hookup partner but rather a general intention to hook up. Hookups most often occur at parties or in a dorm or fraternity house, but any available place will do. Alcohol is typically involved; in fact, Paul et al. (2000) found that the severity of alcohol intoxication predicted both the likelihood of hooking up and the likelihood that hookups included sexual intercourse. Precautions to prevent STD transmission and/or pregnancy are infrequently taken. Verbal communication about personal or sexual matters during hookups is uncommon; only 4% of youth reported that hookup partners talk about what is happening, 2% reported that partners talk about future interaction, and only 1% reported that hookup partners talk about sexual history, preferences, or precautions (Paul & Hayes, 2002). Hookups typically end when one person leaves or passes out, or when one or both partners reach orgasm. The emotional experience during a hookup often includes feeling good, aroused, or excited, as well as anxious and confused. After hookups, common emotions were regret or disappointment (see also Kilmann, Boland, West, Jonet, & Ramsey, 1993) as well as happiness and satisfaction.

What is the function of such experiences in relationship formation and intimacy development? In what ways and how effectively do hookups contribute to building romantic relationships and developing youth's capacity for future intimate relating? We consider these issues in the next sections.

THE EFFECTIVENESS OF HOOKUPS IN INITIATING RELATIONSHIPS

Only a few studies have examined the extent to which casual sexual interactions have persisted into repeat interaction and/or developed into relationships (i.e., intimate interaction over time rather than a onetime interaction). Paul et al. (2000), in a study of 550 college students, found that 50% of respondents with a hookup experience that included sexual intercourse reported that after hooking up they did not interact with their hookup partner again. In contrast, hookups that do *not* involve sexual intercourse appear to be more likely to result in future interactions; 75% of individuals who hooked up but did not engage in sexual intercourse during hookups reported interacting with the hookup partner at another time (Paul et al., 2000). Some youth have a "hookup buddy" with whom they hook up multiple times and only interact during hookups. Other youth hook up with a friend, known as "friends with benefits" (Hughes, Morrison, & Asada, 2005; see also Guerrero & Mongeau, this volume).

Few hookups appear to evolve into a committed romantic relationship. In Paul et al.'s (2000) study, only 12% of youth reported a hookup experience that evolved into a romantic relationship, and the average duration of these romantic relationships was only 4 months. Not surprisingly, the likelihood of hookups evolving into romantic relationships appears to be related to the valence of the hookup experience (i.e., perceived as good or bad experiences). Paul and Hayes (2002) found that 38% of hookup experiences perceived as "best" evolved into relationships, whereas only 3% of hookups reported as "worst" persisted.

What might explain the fact that hookups only rarely lead to longer term relationships? It may be that relationship partners who met during a hookup later define the relationship by what it evolved into rather than how it started. Thus, Paul and colleagues (2000) may have underestimated the frequency of hookup interactions that evolved into romantic relationships. Another explanation for the apparent paucity of relationships that develop from hookups is that there is no well-developed script for these youth to follow. Relationship scripts are cognitive roadmaps specifying the key events in romantic relationships and the typical order in which they occur (Baldwin, 1992). Scripts can pertain to specific relationship events (e.g., a first date, or a relationship breakup) or can be broad construals of how relationships develop. In other words, scripts are shared, culturally specific internalized norms, and relationship scripts help individuals process information about relationship events and help guide their script-relevant behavior. Scripts also help individuals evaluate their behavior and experience vis-à-vis the perceived norms; this comparison may help individuals adjust their behavior (Fletcher & Simpson, 2000) and feel comfort and confidence in conforming to perceived norms, and may contribute to individual and relationship well-being (Holmberg & MacKenzie, 2002). Although contemporary youth appear to have a relatively uniform set of expectations or an internalized script for the typical progression of a hookup (as evidenced by Paul and Hayes, 2002, who found uniformity in college students' perceptions of what constituted a *typical* hookup), a script for romantic relationship development that emerges from a hookup seems to be more elusive. Rather, individuals perceive *many* normative paths of relationship progression (Cate & Lloyd, 1992). In addition, relationship partners may be following *different* internalized guides for developing relationships. In fact, partner differences in relationship scripts may cause conflict as partners differentially try to negotiate their relationship on their own terms (Holmberg & MacKenzie, 2000).

Another factor that prevents the development of relationships from hookups is the fact that many hookups take place while on vacation, such as spring break (e.g., Herold, Maticka-Tyndale, & Mewhinney, 1998; Maticka-Tyndale, Herold, & Mewhinney, 1998; Maticka-Tyndale, Herold, & Oppermann, 2003; Mewhinney, Herold, & Maticka-Tyndale, 1995). Results from these studies indicate that between 15 and 30% of advanced high school and college students who go on spring break have sexual intercourse with a person they had just met while on vacation, and a much higher percentage of these students "fool around," broadly defined, with a person they had met while on vacation. Students in Mewhinney et al.'s (1995) focus groups indicated that there is a sense of anonymity on spring break, where students can engage in behaviors that would otherwise be unacceptable at home. Youth believe that vacations are also times to relax one's inhibitions and focus on having a good time, with less regard for consequences (Herold & Van Kerkwijk, 1992). Although Paul's (Paul & Hayes, 2002; Paul, McManus, & Hayes, 2000) studies certainly indicate that a sizable percentage of hookups occur on or around college campuses (and thus, with partners with whom there is potential for future interaction), results from these studies raise the possibility that, at times, relationships with hookup partners are not pursued because students would likely never again have the opportunity to have contact with their hookup partner.

There may be particular characteristics of hookup experiences that increase or decrease the likelihood of relationship initiation in instances where both partners live in the same location and could feasibly enter into a relationship. Three aspects of hookup experiences may foretell the differential potential of hookups for initiating a romantic relationship, including (a) motivations for hooking up, (b) the subjective experience of the hookup, and (c) the emotional realities of hooking up. Each aspect will be discussed in the following sections, drawing from relevant research evidence and applying social psychological theory to explore implications for relationship initiation.

Motivations for Hooking Up

Youth hook up for different reasons—reasons that may foretell what happens after hookups. Some youth hook up solely for sexual experimentation, exploration, and gratification. In fact, Greiling and Buss (2000) indicated that sexual gratification is the most common reason for both men and women to engage in casual sexual encounters. Many of these individuals express little interest in romantic relating and may even be skeptical of the "emotional baggage" they perceive as part of longer time love relationships. Still others are concurrently involved in a "committed" romantic relationship and are "cheating" on their romantic partner by hooking up with someone else. Thus, the low likelihood of hookups as effective relationship initiators may, in part, be because many youth engage in hookups for reasons other than relationship initiation. Nevertheless, other youth indeed report that they hook up with the hope that their hookup will turn into a longer term relationship (Regan & Dreyer, 1999), and Greiling and Buss's data suggested that some individuals engage in casual sexual encounters for the purpose of finding a desirable mate, or a more desirable mate than they currently have. The variability in motivations for hooking up highlights the high likelihood that partners' motivations and interests will be mismatched (Paul, 2006a; Paul & Hayes, 2002; Regan & Dreyer, 1999). Hookups may sometimes go awry because the partners have different motivations and expectations, leaving one or both partners with expectations or intentions that are unrequited.

The most common presumption is that young women and men hook up for different and contrasting reasons, consistent with evolutionary theory that explains men's greater interest in casual sex as a function of their pursuit of reproductive success, and women's greater interest in selective interpersonal connection as a mechanism for ensuring commitment and support in raising offspring (Buss, 1995). There is some empirical evidence to support this presumption; for example, women are more likely to prioritize interpersonal motivations, and men more often emphasize sexual desire and the pursuit of social status, when asked to provide a reason for why they engaged in a hookup (Regan & Dreyer, 1999). However, it is important to note that many women also feel motivated by sexual desire to engage in casual sex; Regan and Dreyer found that sexual desire was the third strongest motivation for women to engage in casual sex. Moreover, female participants in Weaver and Herold's (2000) study indicated that they engage in casual sex to "live it up," because they enjoy the novelty of new partners, and because they feel like they are doing something "forbidden." Indeed, Schmitt's (2005b) analysis of short- and long-term mating strategies in individuals from 48 nations suggests that, although men generally are more oriented to short-term sexual encounters than are women, in many circumstances women also engage in short-term sexual encounters (e.g., when they have greater access to political power and resources). Thus, it would not be accurate to conclude that women enter into hookup interactions solely because they are hoping to secure a longer term relationship, and modern evolutionary theory suggests that women, as well as men, have developed adaptive strategies for achieving substantial benefits from short-term mating (Gangestad & Simpson, 2000).

Paul and Hayes (2002) also suggested that motivations may differ across specific hookups; sometimes men and women reported they "just" wanted to hook up to have a sexual thrill or to "fit in" with their peers (see also Denizet-Lewis, 2004). In other instances, some men and women reported that they were looking for interpersonal comfort and had some hope that the connection would continue. Some youth "talked themselves out" of expecting any further connection with a hookup partner, given how infrequently this actually happens. Some admitted that they were so intoxicated that they did not know why they had hooked up, let alone remember what actually happened. Moreover, some young people spoke of confusion regarding their hookup behavior; they either were unsure of what they were looking for in a hookup or admitted that they were hooking up with lots of different expectations and hopes, some of which might even be contradictory.

It appears, then, that achieving clarity in one's motivations for hooking up is important for making clear behavioral decisions, although it is acknowledged that, at least from an evolutionary perspective, these motivations may or may not be conscious (cf. Schmitt, 2005b). However, the research described in this section also suggests that going into a hookup with the sole expectation that it will lead to a romantic relationship has the potential to set up a person for hurt and disappointment. Thus, detecting early and thereby avoiding clashing expectations with a potential hookup partner, and being intentional and deliberate when one's interest is building a romantic relationship, have the potential to reduce negative emotional experiences in the aftermath of the hookup.

The Subjective Experience of Hookups: Youth's Perceptions of Their Best and Worst Hookups

Paul and Hayes (2002) examined the characteristics of and perceived reasons for 130 college students' self-described best and worst hookup experiences, many of which provide clues about why relationships do or do not follow from hookups. When asked why the selected hookups were considered to be best or worst, both men and women agreed that hookups were best when (a) there was interest and attraction, and the partner was good-looking; (b) sexual behavior was enjoyable; and (c) they felt wanted and cared about. About one quarter of the women (27%) and 16% of the men thought the hookup was best because a relationship evolved afterwards. Ten percent of both women and men thought the hookup was best because there was no attachment or emotional involvement. Significantly more men (26%) than women (4%) reported that the hookup was best because it helped them achieve a social goal (i.e., to feel socially accepted), which is consistent with studies conducted from an evolutionary framework suggesting that greater orientation toward casual sexual encounters (i.e., higher levels of sociosexuality) was associated with higher levels of self-esteem (Greiling & Buss, 2000; Schmitt 2005a).

In contrast, worst hookup experiences were often described as quite distressing for youth. Alcohol played a large role in the worst hookups, although it also played a role in young men's best hookups. The worst hookups occurred more often in a car or in a club or bar. At times, they ended when one partner stopped the hookup because it was going too far. Partners in the worst hookups were unlikely to see each other again. During worst hookups, youth reported feeling a combination of good, aroused, excited, confused, unsure, regretful, embarrassed, nervous, and scared; women more than men felt uncomfortable and anxious for the end. After the worst hookups, youth felt confused, unsure, used, anxious to leave, and glad it was over. Some women felt regretful, whereas some men reported feeling disappointed. Such complex emotional reactions leave youth with uncertainty about the meaning and continuation of the dyad. Initial interactions that fail to reduce uncertainty are unlikely to develop into further romantic relating (Mongeau, Serewicz, & Therrien, 2004). Communicating these emotions to others might help youth reflect on productive strategies for achieving satisfaction and for avoiding discomfort and disappointment. Yet, few youth discussed their worst hookup experiences with anyone, thereby limiting the processing of their complicated emotions and probably suppressing them without resolution. Perhaps these youth feared peers' negative reaction or negative impression formation—threats to their friendship that were too great to risk (Goldsmith & Parks, 1990).

The profile of the best hookups, especially when contrasted with the worst hookups, helps define the positive potential of hookups for initiating a relationship. The key contributors include (a) communication, (b) enjoyment (albeit a little anxiety) and posthookup feelings of comfort and security, (c) interest in and care about the partner, (d) peer support, and (e) conscious involvement (i.e., lack of intoxication). The larger theoretical and empirical literature on relationship initiation can help us to understand how these conditions are conducive for advancing the hookup into a relationship. First, critical in many classic theories of relationship development is *communication and self-disclosure* (e.g., Altman & Taylor, 1973; Levinger, 1980). One could argue that initiating a relationship through a hookup might involve too much sharing too fast (i.e., Altman and Taylor's warning of a "tyranny of openness"); indeed, perhaps this is one reason why hookups are generally unlikely to develop into romantic or platonic relationships. Yet, the sharing that takes place in hookups is rarely verbal disclosure about the *self*. Descriptions of best hookups include verbal communication that includes "small talk" and some discussion of future interaction. This level of verbal communication appears to be effective in advancing some of these interactions into relationships, perhaps because it serves as a mechanism for the two partners to get to know one another and forge the beginnings of a "connection."

Second, *enjoyment and satisfaction* of interactions have also been theorized to promote relationship development (Altman & Taylor, 1973). Positive feeling and response increase the likelihood of further contact. Optimism about the future of the relationship is also helpful in advancing an interaction beyond a hookup (Carnelley & Janoff-Bulman, 1992). An important function of enjoyment in early encounters is uncertainty reduction (Mongeau et al., 2004). Particularly important for pursuing further interaction are detecting and liking partner characteristics as well as perceiving a possibility for continued romantic interaction with the partner.

Third, having some *interest in and affection for* a partner at the time of sexual initiation increases the likelihood of relationship formation (Peplau, Rubin, & Hill, 1977). Feeling satisfaction with the sexual interaction also prompts interest in furthering interaction and expanding communication (Pinney, Gerrard, & Denney, 1987).

Fourth, *social networks* can play an important role in promoting relationship development (Parks & Adelman, 1983). Youth's tendency to talk with friends about their positive hookup experiences stimulates social support. Just as peer endorsement of casual sex can promote casual sexual behavior (Herold et al., 1998), it is likely that peers' positive reactions to friends' reports of posthookup satisfaction and intrigue would promote pursuit of further interaction (Goldsmith & Parks, 1990).

Fifth, conscious and chosen involvement in sexual interaction is important for relationship formation. Consensual entrance to sexual interaction is critical for potentiating relationship development; feeling pressured into sexual interaction is likely to trigger feelings of guilt that diminish any likelihood of relationship initiation (Cate, Long, Angera, & Draper, 1993). It is also significant that the best hookups are less likely to include alcohol use. Alcohol reduces self-awareness, clouds rational decision making, and blurs short-term memory (Cooper, Frone, Russell, & Mudar, 1995; Hull, 1987). Youth who hook up without the influence of alcohol are more likely to make conscious decisions about engaging in sexual behavior. Arguably, heavy alcohol use is also likely to co-occur with other potential psychological and behavioral risks, further detracting from relationship initiation and development success.

In summary, conditions that are conducive for hookups to lead to a longer term relationship are those that promote positive emotional experiences. That is, these hookup experiences have the potential to enhance self-worth and promote optimism for the future. Extrapolating from Paul and Hayes' (2002) qualitative data, it seems that hookups are more likely to develop into relationships when neither partner feels pressure to engage in sexual activity and neither partner experiences a sense of regret about the hookup in its aftermath. Hookups seem to lead to relationships when there is a sense of connection with the hookup partner, such that the interaction spontaneously unfolds, and both partners have similar emotional experiences and expectations for the future. The aftermath of the hookup also contributes to the likelihood that a relationship will develop based on the degree to which hookup partners receive positive reinforcement from others in their support network.

The Emotional Realities of Hookups

Casual sex has been a popular topic of investigation given the risky *physical* consequences of such sexual behaviors (Levinson, Jaccard, & Beamer, 1995; Weaver & Herold, 2000). Despite the presumption of emotional detachment prototypical of casual sexual interactions, as mentioned earlier, recent research has revealed the *emotional* complexities of hookups (Paul, 2006a). Although college students anticipate positive emotions and easy detachment following casual sex (Levinson et al., 1995), the prevalence of negative emotional responses following hookups makes this perceived norm seem distorted (Paul & Hayes, 2002). The degree of emotional involvement unexpectedly turns hookups into a complex experience that is often anything but "casual" (Paul & Hayes; Paul, 2006a).

Paul (2006a) argued that difficult hookup experiences result from contradictions between the perceived personal and social benefits of hooking up and the unexpected painful emotional and social reality of many hookup experiences. Youth pursue hookups with desires that include being a *self* they want to be—attractive, socially accepted, sexually competent, and not alone. But the unexpected complex reality of many hookup experiences leaves many youth with dashed hopes, self-doubt, shame, and loneliness. The seeming elusiveness of the wanted self and the pain of the unwanted self catapult some youth into a *serial* pattern of hooking up, wherein they desperately seek self-salvation.

Arguably, this pattern is highly unlikely to contribute to relationship initiation and is symptomatic of pathology in the struggle to achieve intimacy. Furthermore, there appears to be confusion and doubt about options for more self-protective mechanisms for relationship initiation and development. The potential longer term implications of this emotional complexity will be explored in greater depth in the next section.

Summary

Only a minority of hookups turns into longer term relationships, and even then there is evidence that those relationships last, on average, only a few months (Paul et al., 2000). Hookups are most likely to evolve into longer term relationships when (a) both partners had positive emotional experiences during and after the hookup, (b) there was communication during the hookup, and (c) both partners had similar motivations for the hookup. However, there are many characteristics of hookups that decrease the likelihood that they will facilitate the initiation of a new relationship. The vast majority of college hookups occur when one or both partners are under the influence of alcohol, which increases the likelihood that they will "go farther" sexually than they would if they were sober (Paul & Hayes, 2002) or that they end up regretting their choice of relationship partners (Mewhinney et al., 1995). Moreover, many youth who engage in hookups are not particularly interested in initiating a romantic relationship; instead, they seek opportunities for sexual exploration, gratification of their sexual desires, or even an increase in their social status (Greiling & Buss, 2000; Regan & Dreyer, 1999). Thus, a central part of the "hookup script" may very well be the notion that relationships do *not* evolve from hookups. In the next section, we consider the implications of these contemporary youth relationships for intimacy development and relationship functioning in the long term.

THE EFFECTIVENESS OF HOOKUPS IN ADVANCING INTIMACY DEVELOPMENT

Construing casual sexual interactions as emotionally complex experiences opens inquiry into the meaning youth make of their challenging experiences. Moreover, this view challenges dominant notions of casual sex as "trivial" or irrelevant to the important developmental challenge for adolescents and young adults of learning how to be intimate and develop fulfilling close relationships (Erikson, 1968; Paul & White, 1990). What is the formative function of adolescent and young adult romantic experiences in developing the capacity for intimacy? This question cannot be answered with empirical data at this time, as there are no longitudinal studies that have been designed to measure the consequences of hookups. Moreover, early theories describing intimacy development during the transition to adulthood were construed before the advent of the "hookup culture." Nevertheless, we can speculate about the manner in which hookups facilitate or detract from intimacy development by applying relevant theories to insights from youth who engage in hookups. These qualitative data come from an unpublished study by Paul (2006b) that explores college students' perceptions of the impact of their hookup experience for their development and future experience as a committed relationship partner.

One's first romantic relationships serve various social and emotional functions. Furman and Wehner (1994) suggested that romantic relationships contribute to experience in four behavioral systems, including (a) affiliation, (b) sex reproduction, (c) attachment, and (d) caregiving. Early romantic relationships contribute primarily to affiliation and sexual exploration; as individuals invest in longer term relationships, attachment and caretaking become salient (Shulman & Kipnis, 2001). Mature romantic relationships integrate these four behavioral systems.

Another developmental perspective is that of Brown (1999), who proposed that romantic relationship development progresses through a four-phase sequence. In the *initiation* phase, young adolescents expand their self-concept to include being a romantic partner. The *status* phase follows, in which adolescents feel pressure for social acceptability; choosing the "right" romantic partners can improve one's social standing. In the third phase, the *affection* phase, adolescents turn their attention to the romantic partner, deepening care and commitment and expanding sexual activity. The *bonding* phase follows, in which romanticism is combined with pragmatism (the reality of maintaining a relationship for the long term), and connection is balanced with individuality.

From these two theoretical frameworks, it appears that youth whose social lives focus on hookups are functioning primarily in the affiliation and sexual exploration behavioral systems and are still grappling with the challenges posed in the initiation and status phases of romantic relationship development. Some youth can even be considered avoidant of moving toward the affection phase, not yet exercising the attachment and caretaking systems. One 19-year-old woman from Paul's unpublished study (2006b) expressed the pull of the status phase:

> Commitment isn't cool. Hookups are what it's about. My friends are into it. We talk about how fun hookups are, well, how they're supposed to be. We have hookup weekends where we have goals for how many different people we hook up with—it makes you get with people you maybe wouldn't otherwise. Long-term relationships have a more negative aspect—like it is more of a job. No, I'm about hanging with my friends, having fun. Long-term relationships are a drag.

Other youth show awareness of the affection phase but are grappling with whether and how to move there. Consider the following reflection of a 19-year-old woman, who described both interest in and concern about seeking affection:

> I have learned that I have a strong desire to be intimate with people, which is why I do not seem to try to stop sexual encounters from happening. I think it would be healthier for me if I could find a long-term partner, but I just can't seem to meet one. I have some "relationships" with others that are strictly on a need-for-sex basis. The more hookups that I experience are increasing my desire for a long-term partner. I do not think others would appreciate knowing about my sexual history, and I think my increasing number of sexual partners is steadily hindering my chances of finding someone who really cares about me.

Some youth who hook up also have experience with longer term romantic relationships and thus may have experimented with the more advanced behavioral systems of affection and bonding. In fact, some are engaging concurrently in hookup *and* "committed" romantic relationships. Some of these youth express angst and self-doubt about their ability to succeed in the affection and bonding phases. One 20-year-old woman explained,

> I had a boyfriend for a while, but sometimes I just need the freedom of hooking up. There's no baggage like there is with my boyfriend. Hookups are disposable relationships. But because I'm so used to hooking up so much, I fear that in the future I will feel like escaping or finding someone new in the face of any difficulty in the relationship. I don't know if I can trust myself—or anyone else actually.

Many youth discussed experiences with infidelity in hookups, leaving them skeptical of trust and commitment, and hesitant to invest themselves in care for and commitment to a romantic partner. Consider the following concern, echoed by many youth, expressed by a 20-year-old young man:

> My hookups have made me concerned about future long-term love relationships and whether I can trust anyone. Several girls that I've hooked up with, even had sex with, have had boyfriends. Knowing this will most likely make me very jealous throughout a long-term relationship. I also think that I might never want to settle down with just one partner.

The learning potential of hookups may also be mediated by the manner in which youth cope with the complex emotions often triggered by hookups. Paul and Hayes (2002) found that youth rarely talk to their friends about a hookup if the experience was primarily negative. It appears that, in the face of a "rosy" social norm that is dissonant with their complicated reality, youth suppress their experience rather than seek rational meaning construction through peer support, thereby limiting positive growth and subsequent behavior change (Connolly, Furman, & Konarski, 2000).

In an empirical test of the developmental progressions proposed by Brown (1999) and Furman and Wehner (1994), Seiffge-Krenke (2003) found individual differences in the "developmental speed" with which adolescents progress through the romantic developmental progression. She found that accelerated speed among adolescents who had been continuously involved romantically (whether in one longer term relationship or in several different relationships) promoted faster advancement in romantic development. She suggested that "the sheer quantity of exposure and involvement provides the individual with learning experiences that ensure a positive romantic outcome" (p. 529). It could be argued that hookups are too fleeting to be considered as romantic experiences with potential for relationship learning. On the other hand, the emotional depth of many hookup experiences (described earlier in this chapter) contradicts this notion. Instead, it is more likely that the emotional suppression of complicated responses to hookups is what is limiting the learning potential.

But some youth with more modest hookup experience did realize learning from hookups that gave them more hope for future romantic relating. Consider, for example, the reflections of this 21-year-old man:

> I've learned that relationships are made of both the emotional and the sexual. I've learned that to be in a relationship with someone else, I would have to get past all the sexual stuff and really connect with that person or else the relationship will fail. I know now, at the least, that people are physically attracted to me, so I have some hope of attracting a partner. But I also know that it's better to have the emotional aspect of a relationship, just as much as the sexual aspect.

Seiffge-Krenke (2003) also found that the strongest predictor of the quality of bonded long-term love is the quality of early romantic experience, particularly during the affection phase. This may explain why youth who report involvement in a committed romantic relationship are less likely to be experienced in hooking up, particularly in hookups that involve sexual intercourse (Paul et al., 2000). Furthermore, the longer the involvement in the current romantic relationship, the less likely they were to have hooked up (despite the fact that 25% of romantically involved youth concurrently hook up with other partners). It is plausible that this romantic relationship experience advanced these youth beyond the lure of hookups.

On the other hand, there is other evidence that casual sexual experience begets more—and riskier—casual sexual experience. For example, Lindblade, Foxman, and Koopman (1994) found that successive sexual partnerships were more likely to occur in an informal setting with an unknown partner, had a briefer presexual phase, and were less likely to involve condom use. Thus, once embedded in a repeat pattern of hookups, it may be difficult for youth to extract themselves and move toward more emotionally intimate relating. Moreover, Grello, Welsh, Harper, and Dixon (2003), in a study of the mental health correlates of sexual and relationship trajectories of non-dating-experienced virgin adolescents, found that transition to casual sex (quite pervasive in their sample) was associated with greater depressive symptoms and problem behaviors. Transition to dating or sexual intercourse in the context of a romantic relationship was not associated with negative psychological or behavioral outcomes.

Previous interpersonal experience also affects one's attitude or orientation to future relating. Paul (2006b) revealed that many hookup experiences leave one or both partners with self-doubt and relationship doubt that prompt pessimism about future relating. Similarly, Carnelley and Janoff-Bulman (1992) found that past romantic relationship experience is the most significant predictor of judgments of the success of future love relationships. They theorized that individuals' experiences in relationships, as well as the culture's definitions and expectations for relationships, affect their judgments and expectations for the success of future relationships. These relationship experience–informed judgments and expectations may function as self-fulfilling prophecies, such that one's optimistic or pessimistic beliefs about the success of future relationships influence how one behaves toward and interprets the behavior of and interaction with relationship partners.

Individual differences in attachment style may also filter youth's reflections on their hookup experiences and attitudes toward future relating. According to attachment theory, people develop beliefs about themselves and others that shape their thoughts and behaviors in social interactions and relationships with others (Bowlby, 1973). Securely attached individuals are better able to manage their emotions, resulting in better ability to cope with stress and pressure (Tolmacz, 2004). It is likely that those individuals will learn most from both good and bad hookups and will be able to apply rational thought to their experiences.

In contrast, individuals with an avoidant attachment style tend to hook up more than secure and anxious people (Paul et al., 2000). Those individuals also tend to have less restrictive casual sex beliefs and are likely to have unwanted but consensual sexual experiences (Gentzler & Kerns, 2004). Avoidant people are also characterized by using denial to deal with stress, a strategy that inhibits learning from difficult experiences. Thus, avoidant people are likely to experience sex as aversive (Birnbaum, Reis, Mikulincer, Gillath, & Orpaz, 2006) and engage in less meaning making and more dissociation following difficult hookups. Anxiously attached individuals have been found to be less accepting of casual sex (Gentzler & Kerns). In general, they have difficulties being in romantic relationships because they lack self-confidence (Tolmacz, 2004). If such people engage in a casual sexual relationship with another person, rational meaning making is not likely to occur.

Young men's and women's reflections about how their hookup experiences have affected them as future relationship partners are likely to be influenced by the continued prevalence of a sexual "double standard" (continuing despite change in women's sexual behavior patterns such that they are more and more similar to men's). Men are expected in Western society to display higher levels of sexual interest and are celebrated for their virility (Oliver & Hyde, 1993). Men are more accepting of casual sex than women (Oliver & Hyde, 1993; Regan & Dreyer, 1999). In contrast, engaging in casual sexual activities and having a large number of sexual partners are discouraged for women (Oliver & Hyde, 1993). Women who are sexually promiscuous are more quickly than promiscuous men to be condemned as immoral, unrespectable, and less desirable as a long-term relationship partner (Oliver & Hyde, 1993). These societal value judgments, if internalized, can have long-term impact on one's self-concept as a desirable and competent relationship partner.

In sum, youth who engage in hookups often are not gaining experience with advanced levels of relationship functioning, such as affection and bonding. Many youth would like to move into these phases, but they are unsure how to do so, or they are fearful that they will get hurt. Because many youth perceive that much infidelity pervades the hookup culture, they are hesitant to trust others, or even themselves. Nevertheless, some learning about relationships does indeed occur through hookups. It is likely that individual differences underlie the degree to which a youth will reflect upon and gain meaning from hookups, such as one's attachment style. Moreover, it is possible that individuals contemplate the meaning of their hookup experiences through the lens of the dominant views in their society.

LIMITATIONS AND FUTURE DIRECTIONS FOR OUR UNDERSTANDING OF HOOKUPS AS RELATIONSHIP INITIATORS

The research that informs our analysis has largely focused on late adolescents and young adults who are attending college. Although research is emerging on more diverse early and midadolescent sexual and relationship patterns and experiences, little is known about late adolescents who are not matriculated in higher education. Clydesdale's (2007) ethnographic work following a cohort of high school students post graduation is a promising exception. Research is also needed comparing different higher education institutional characteristics and cultures. Are there geographic regional differences in hookup phenomena? Does the size of the school influence the social experience of hooking up? How does the campus culture or environment affect the prevalence and nature of hooking up; for example, is hooking up more prevalent in closely knit, campus-oriented schools versus large urban commuter schools? Moreover, the literature on casual sex and hookups is focused almost exclusively on the behavior of young adults, so little is known about the characteristics of adults' hookups or about associations between older adults' casual sexual interaction and their relationship initiation success.

Consideration of *culture* as an important analytic variable is also lacking in research on youth sexual and relational experiences. Paul's college student samples, for example, include predominantly Caucasian students and smaller segments of Hispanic and African American students. An unpublished study (Paul, 2002) of a more ethnically diverse sample of college students' meaning making of hookup experiences (e.g., definitions, experiences, expectations, motivations, and judgments) suggests similarity of behavior patterns but some cultural variability in expectations and judgments. Not only is research including more ethnically diverse samples needed, but also viewing existing research on predominantly Caucasian samples through a cultural lens may reveal important elements of dominant Caucasian culture and influences on youth's experiences. Further, how do youth's experiences vary depending on whether they are in a minority or majority ethnic group at their college or university?

Our analysis focused explicitly on heterosexual youth's experiences. Research is needed on the casual-sexual and relationship–exploration experiences of homosexual, bisexual, and transgendered people. It is also important to study the implications of casual sexual behavior for sexual orientation exploration. Narrative data from college students suggest active sexual orientation exploration, and sexual orientation does not necessarily delimit the gender of hookup partners. Analysis must also explore the effect of continuing societal biases and discrimination on these experiences.

Moreover, this chapter focused on the implications of hookups for intimacy development and the capacity to have healthy romantic relationships in adulthood. However, there are other domains of implications that are worthy of consideration. For example, what, if any, effects do particularly hookup experiences have on one's sense of self-worth? It is not difficult to imagine, if a person is hoping to develop a romantic relationship, that repeated negative hookup experiences characterized by shame and regret would contribute to a sense that one is not an attractive relationship prospect and anxiety about future social interactions. In contrast, there is evidence that short-term mating enhances self-esteem (e.g., Greiling & Buss, 2000; Schmitt, 2005a), and an extension of this research would be to identify the effects of enhanced self-esteem due to hookups on other areas of life functioning.

This exploratory analysis suggests that there are complex implications of youth's hookup experiences for relationship initiation and intimacy development. Research has only begun to explore these potent phenomena. Although there is an extensive body of literature from the late 20th century on the incidence of casual sexual interaction, there has been little attention to the subjective or emotional aspects of these interpersonal interactions. Moreover, there has been scant exploration of the implications of casual sexual interaction for relationship initiation and intimacy development. Even if a particular casual sexual interaction is discrete and does not develop into a close relationship, it is likely that casual sexual experiences contribute to youth's learning about interpersonal relating and to their hopes, fears, and expectations about themselves as future relationship partners.

Several areas of study are now emerging that promise to contribute to a more comprehensive and therefore effective understanding of youth sexual and relationship development, including (a) public health research on demographic and environmental predictors of youth's sexual behavior patterns, (b) social psychological research on youth peer culture, (c) communications research on the quickly changing dominant modes of youth interpersonal communication, (d) developmental psychological research exploring the roles of adolescent romantic relationships in self and relational development, (e) personal relationships and family studies research on precursors of adult relationship dysfunction and dissolution, and (f) clinical case studies revealing the emotional complexities and complications of youth self-, sexual, and relational development.

We suggest three important directions for advancing this work: (a) interdisciplinary investigations that draw together these disparate perspectives, areas of study, and potential applications; (b) longitudinal research that helps to elucidate the implications of early and late adolescent sexual and relational experiences for adult interpersonal functioning; and (c) qualitative methodologies (e.g., narrative analysis and diary studies) that help to explicate the complicated emotional realities of youths' experience and development. Advancing this research holds promise for educational and therapeutic implications necessary for helping youth navigate a path to fulfilling adult sexuality and intimate relating.

REFERENCES

Altman, I., & Taylor, D. A. (1973). *Social penetration: The development of interpersonal relationships.* New York: Holt, Rinehart & Winston.

Baldwin, M. W. (1992). Relational schemas and the processing of social information. *Psychological Bulletin, 112,* 461–484.

Bearman, P. (1997). *Reducing the risk: Connections that make a difference in the lives of youth.* Bethesda, MD: Add Health.

Birnbaum, G. E., Reis, H. T., Mikulincer, M., Gillath, O., & Orpaz, A. (2006). When sex is more than just sex: Attachment orientations, sexual experience, and relationship quality. *Journal of Personality and Social Psychology, 91,* 929–943.

Bowlby, J. (1973). *Attachment and loss: Vol. 2. Separation: Anxiety and anger.* London: Hogarth.

Brown, B. B. (1999). "You're going out with who?": Peer group influences on adolescent romantic relationships. In W. Furman, B. B. Brown, & C. Feiring (Eds.), *The development of romantic relationships in adolescence* (pp. 291–329). Cambridge: Cambridge University Press.

Buss, D. M. (1995). Psychological sex differences: Origins through sexual selection. *American Psychologist, 50,* 164–168.

Carnelley, K. B., & Janoff-Bulman, R. (1992). Optimism about love relationships: General vs. specific lessons from one's personal experiences. *Journal of Social and Personal Relationships, 9,* 5–20.

Cate, R. M., & Lloyd, S. A. (1992). *Courtship.* Thousand Oaks, CA: Sage.

Cate, R. M., Long, E., Angera, J. J., & Draper, K. K. (1993). Sexual intercourse and relationship development. *Family Relations, 42,* 158–164.

Clydesdale, T. (2007). *The first year out: Understanding American teens after high school.* Chicago: University of Chicago Press.

Collins, W. A. (2003). More than myth: The developmental significance of romantic relationships during adolescence. *Journal of Research on Adolescence, 13,* 1–24.

Connolly, J. A., Furman, W., & Konarski, R. (2000). The role of peers in the emergence of heterosexual relationships in adolescence. *Child Development, 71,* 1395–1408.

Cooksey, E. C., Mott, F. L., & Neubauer, S. A. (2003). Friendships and early relationships: Links to sexual initiation among American adolescents born to young mothers. *Perspectives on Sexual and Reproductive Health, 34,* 118–126.

Cooper, M. L., Frone, M. R., Russell, M., & Mudar, P. (1995). Drinking to regulate positive and negative emotions: A motivational model of alcohol use. *Journal of Personality and Social Psychology, 69,* 990–1005.

Denizet-Lewis, B. (2004, May 30). Friends, friends with benefits and the benefits of the local mall. *New York Times Magazine.* Retrieved December 26, 2007, from http://www.nytimes.com/2004/05/30/magazine/30NONDATING.html?ei=5007&en=b8ab7c02ae2d206b&ex=1401249600

Erikson, E. H. (1963). *Childhood and society* (2nd ed.). New York: Norton.

Erikson, E. H. (1968). *Identity: Youth and crisis.* New York: Norton.

Fletcher, G. J. O., & Simpson, J. A. (2000). Ideal standards in close relationships: Their structure and functions. *Current Directions in Psychological Science, 9,* 102–105.

Furman, W., & Flanagan, A. (1997). The influence of earlier relationships on marriage: An attachment perspective. In W. Halford & H. Markman (Eds.), *Clinical handbook of marriage and couples interventions* (pp. 179–202). New York: John Wiley.

Furman, W., & Shaffer, L. (2003). The role of romantic relationships in adolescent development. In P. Florsheim (Ed.), *Adolescent romantic relations and sexual behavior: Theory, research, and practical implications* (pp. 3–22). Mahwah, NJ: Lawrence Erlbaum.

Furman, W., & Wehner, E. A. (1994). Romantic views: Toward a theory of adolescent romantic relationships. In R. Montemayor, G. R. Adams, & G. P. Gulotta (Eds.), *Advances in adolescent development: Vol. 6. Relationships during adolescence* (pp. 168–175). Thousand Oaks, CA: Sage.

Gangestad, S. W., & Simpson, J. A. (2000). The evolution of human mating: Trade-offs and strategic pluralism. *Behavioral and Brain Sciences, 23,* 573–644.

Gentzler, A. L., & Kerns, K. A. (2004). Associations between insecure attachment and sexual experiences. *Personal Relationships, 11,* 294–265.

Goldsmith, D., & Parks, M. (1990). Communicative strategies for managing the risks of seeking social support. In S. W. Duck with R. C. Silver (Eds.), *Personal relationships and social support* (pp. 104–121). Newbury Park, CA: Sage.

Greiling, H., & Buss, D. M. (2000). Women's sexual strategies: The hidden dimension of extra-pair mating. *Personality and Individual Differences, 28,* 929–963.

Grello, C. M., Welsh, D. P., Harper, M. S., & Dickson, J. W. (2003). Dating and sexual relationship trajectories and adolescent functioning. *Adolescent and Family Health, 3,* 103–112.

Grunbaum, J., Kann, L., Kinchen, S. A., Williams, B., Ross, R. J., Lowry, R., et al. (2002). Youth Risk Behavior Surveillance (YRBS)—United States, 2001. *Morbidity and Mortality Weekly Report, 51,* 1–64.

Henry Kaiser Family Foundation and *Seventeen.* (2000). *SexSmarts: Decision making.* Menlo Park, CA: Authors.

Herold, E. S., Maticka-Tyndale, E., & Mewhinney, D. (1998). Predicting intentions to engage in casual sex. *Journal of Social and Personal Relationships, 15,* 502–516.

Herold, E. S., & Van Kerkwijk, C. (1992). AIDS and sex tourism. *AIDS and Society, 4,* 1–8.

Hoff, T., Greene, L., & Davis, J. (2003). *National survey of adolescents and young adults: Sexual health knowledge, attitudes, and experiences.* Menlo Park, CA: Henry J. Kaiser Family Foundation.

Holmberg, D., & MacKenzie, S. (2002). So far so good: Scripts for romantic relationship development as predictors of relational well-being. *Journal of Social and Personal Relationships, 19,* 777–796.

Hughes, M., Morrison, K., & Asada, K. J. K. (2005). What's love got to do with it? Exploring the impact of maintenance rules, love attitudes, and network support on friends with benefits relationships. *Western Journal of Communication, 69,* 49–66.

Hull, J. G. (1987). Self-awareness model. In H. T. Blane & K. E. Leonard (Eds.), *Psychological theories of drinking and alcoholism* (pp. 272–301). New York: Guilford.

Kilmann, P. R., Boland, J. P., West, M. O., Jonet, C. J., & Ramsey, R. E. (1993). Sexual arousal of college students in relation to sexual experiences. *Journal of Sex Education and Therapy, 19,* 157–164.

Levinger, G. (1980). Toward the analysis of close relationships. *Journal of Experimental and Social Psychology, 16,* 510–544.

Levinson, R. A., Jaccard, J., & Beamer, L. (1995). Older adolescents' engagement in casual sex: Impact of risk perception and psychosocial motivations. *Journal of Youth and Adolescence, 24,* 349–364.

Lindblade, K., Foxman, B., & Koopman, J. S. (1994). Heterosexual partnership characteristics of university women. *International Journal of STD and AIDS, 5,* 37–40.

Manning, W. D., Longmore, M. A., & Giordano, P. C. (2000). The relationship context of contraceptive use at first intercourse. *Family Planning Perspectives, 32,* 104–110.

Manning, W. D., Longmore, M. A., & Giordano, P. C. (2005). Adolescents' involvement in non-romantic sexual activity. *Social Science Research, 34,* 384–407.

Maticka-Tyndale, E., Herold, E. S., & Mewhinney, D. (1998). Casual sex on spring break: Intentions and behaviors of Canadian students. *Journal of Sex Research, 35,* 254–264.

Maticka-Tyndale, E., Herold, E. S., & Oppermann, M. (2003). Casual sex among Australian schoolies. *Journal of Sex Research, 40,* 158–169.

Mewhinney, D. M., Herold, E. S., & Maticka-Tyndale, E. (1995). Sexual scripts and risk-taking of Canadian university students on spring break in Daytona Beach, Florida. *Canadian Journal of Human Sexuality, 4,* 273–288.

Mongeau, P. A., Serewicz, M. C. M., & Therrien, L. F. (2004). Goals for cross-sex first dates: Identification, measurement, and the influence of contextual factors. *Communication Monographs, 71,* 121–147.

Monroe, S. M., Rhode, P., Seeley, J. R., & Lewinsohn, P. M. (1999). Life events and depression in adolescence: Relationship loss as a prospective risk factor for first onset of major depressive disorder. *Journal of Abnormal Psychology, 108,* 606–614.

Moore, S., & Leung, C. (2002). Young people's romantic attachment styles and their associations with well-being. *Journal of Adolescence, 25,* 243–255.

Oliver, M. B., & Hyde, J. S. (1993). Gender differences in sexuality: A meta-analysis. *Psychological Bulletin, 114,* 29–51.

Orlofsky, J. L. (1993). Intimacy status: Theory and research. In J. E. Marcia, A. S. Waterman, D. R. Mateson, S. L. Archer, & J. L. Orlofsky (Eds.), *Ego identity: A handbook for psychosocial research* (pp. 111–133). New York: Springer-Verlag.

Parks, M. R., & Adelman, M. (1983). Communication networks and the development of romantic relationships: An expansion of uncertainty reduction theory. *Human Communication Research, 10,* 55–79.

Paul, E. L. (2002). *Ethnic variability in college students' meaning making about casual sexual interaction.* Unpublished manuscript.

Paul, E. L. (2006a). Beer goggles, catching feelings, and the walk of shame: The myths and realities of the hookup experience. In S. Duck, D. C. Kirkpatrick, & M. Foley (Eds.), *Difficult relationships* (LEA Personal Relationships Series, pp. 141–160). Mahwah, NJ: Lawrence Erlbaum.

Paul, E. L. (2006b). *College students' reflections on lessons learned from hookups.* Unpublished manuscript.

Paul, E. L., & Hayes, A. (2002). The casualties of "casual" sex: A qualitative exploration of the phenomenology of college students' hookups. *Journal of Social and Personal Relationships, 19,* 639–661.

Paul, E. L., McManus, B., & Hayes, A. (2000). "Hookups": Characteristics and correlates of college students' spontaneous and anonymous sexual experiences. *Journal of Sex Research, 37,* 76–88.

Paul, E. L., & White, K. M. (1990). The development of intimate relationships in late adolescence. *Adolescence, 25,* 375–400.

Peplau, L. A., Rubin, Z., & Hill, C. T. (1977). Sexual intimacy in dating relationships. *Journal of Social Issues, 33,* 86–109.

Pinney, E. M., Gerrard, M., & Denney, N. W. (1987). The Pinney Sexual Satisfaction Inventory. *Journal of Sex Research, 23,* 233–251.

Regan, P. C., & Dreyer, C. S. (1999). Lust? Love? Status? Young adults' motives for engaging in casual sex. *Journal of Psychological and Human Sexuality, 11,* 1–24.

Richards, M. H., Crowe, P. A., Larson, R., & Swarr, A. (1998). Developmental patterns and gender differences in the experience of peer companionship during adolescence. *Child Development, 69,* 154–163.

Santelli, J. S., Lindberg, L. D., Abma, J., McNeely, C. S., & Resnick, M. (2000). Adolescent sexual behavior: Estimates and trends from four nationally representative surveys. *Family Planning Perspectives, 32,* 156–165.

Schmitt, D. P. (2005a). Is short-term mating the maladaptive result of insecure attachment? A test of competing evolutionary perspectives. *Personality and Social Psychology Bulletin, 31,* 747–768.

Schmitt, D. P. (2005b). Sociosexuality from Argentina to Zimbabwe: A 48-nation study of sex, culture, and strategies of human mating. *Behavioral and Brain Sciences, 28,* 247–275.

Seiffge-Krenke, I. (2003). Testing theories of romantic development from adolescence to young adulthood: Evidence of a developmental sequence. *International Journal of Behavioral Development, 27,* 519–531.

Shulman, S., & Kipnis, O. (2001). Adolescent romantic relationships: A look from the future. *Journal of Adolescence, 24,* 337–351.

Sieving, R. E., Oliphant, J. A., & Blum, R. W. (2002). Adolescent sexual behavior and sexual health. *Pediatrics in Review, 23,* 407–416.

Silverman, J. G., Raj, A., Mucci, I. A., & Hathaway, J. E. (2001). Dating violence against adolescent girls and associated substance use, unhealthy weight control, sexual risk behavior, pregnancy, and suicidality. *Journal of the American Medical Association, 286,* 572–579.

Tolmacz, R. (2004). Attachment style and willingness to compromise when choosing a mate. *Journal of Social and Personal Relationships, 21,* 267–272.

Weaver, S. J., & Herold, E. S. (2000). Casual sex and women: Measurement and motivational issues. *Journal of Psychology and Human Sexuality, 12,* 23–41.

Zimmer-Gembeck, M. J., Siebenbruner, J., & Collins, W. A. (2001). Diverse aspects of dating: Associations with psychosocial functioning from early to middle adolescence. *Journal of Adolescence, 24,* 313–336.

20

Romantic Relationship Initiation Following Relationship Dissolution

MARK A. FINE, TINA A. COFFELT, and LOREEN N. OLSON

Besides the fact that love has many different meanings (Berscheid, 2006) and comes in various forms (Hendrick & Hendrick, 2006), many individuals find themselves in romantic relationships that are defined, in part, by the love between the partners. Unfortunately, many relationships end. Yet, following the termination of a romantic relationship, the odds are overwhelming that each partner will enter fairly quickly into another romantic relationship. Some researchers even note that we are compelled to (re)partner because of our "drive to love" (Fisher, 2006). Guided by tenets of the life course perspective, and three other compatible theoretical foundations, this chapter focuses on the initiation of new romantic relationships following divorce or relationship dissolution.

Why should we attempt to understand how new romantic relationships are initiated? This topic is important not only because virtually all ex-partners enter into another romantic relationship but also because there is a wealth of evidence that there are both emotional and physical health benefits for those who are in romantic relationships (Kiecolt-Glaser & Newton, 2001), although there are some noteworthy caveats and exceptions that will be discussed later. In addition, there are compelling reasons to suggest that initiation following the termination of a committed romantic relationship might be quite different than the initiation of first or early romantic relationships, because of such factors as finances, advancing age, the presence of children, different personal and relationship histories, and differing goals and objectives for later relationships.

We restrict our focus in this chapter in several ways. First, we focus on divorce or dissolution rather than partner death because this is the most common manner in which romantic relationships end (Teachman, Tedrow, & Hall, 2006) and because the experiences of establishing a new romantic relationship are likely to be different for those whose previous partner died. Second, we primarily consider relationship initiation following divorce, because there is considerably more information available on postdivorce relationships (see Harvey & Fine, 2006). However, we suspect that some of the findings from divorced individuals may generalize to individuals whose relationships ended in another manner. Third, our primary concentration is on the initiation and establishment of committed romantic relationships (i.e., the partners want and expect their relationship to continue into the future) and not romantic relationships in which the partners have not committed themselves to each other and to the relationship. Finally, we focus primarily on relationship *initiation*, but also occasionally draw from related research on postinitiation stages (particularly in stepfamilies) because (a) there is a limited amount of literature on the initiation stage, and (b) information from these later periods may shed light on some of the issues and challenges that relationship-initiating parties may later experience.

To organize this chapter, we first briefly review four theories that we think can be helpful in this area of study, ending with a presentation of the key tenets of the life course perspective. We then use the life course perspective to ground our review of the literature related to the initiation of new romantic relationships following divorce or dissolution. Finally, we conclude with directions for future research.

THEORETICAL PERSPECTIVES AND RELATIONSHIP INITIATION POST DISSOLUTION

A number of different theoretical perspectives have been used or could be used to further our understanding of how relationships are initiated following relationship dissolution. Although any number of theoretical perspectives could have been highlighted in this chapter, we have chosen those that we think shed the most light on some of the key issues and findings in the field. The first three—the investment model, the feminist perspective, and communication privacy management theory—help make sense of some of the issues and findings presented later in the chapter. They also complement the fourth and primary framework for this chapter: the life course perspective.

The *investment model*, a variant of social exchange theories, suggests that relationship stability is most strongly determined by the levels of commitment that the relationship partners have to the relationship (Rusbult, 1983). Further, each partner's level of commitment is determined by his or her level of relationship satisfaction, the quality of perceived alternatives, and the level of investments made in the relationship. Finally, relationship satisfaction is based on the balance of rewards to costs experienced in the relationship relative to the reward–cost ratio one expects to have (i.e., comparison level).

The investment model directs our attention in this chapter both backward into the relationship past and forward into the future. With respect to the past, the most typical scenario is likely to be that the individual had an unfavorable reward–cost ratio in the previous relationship and may, therefore, be somewhat hesitant to enter into another relationship for fear that the same disappointment and frustration may arise. Another possibility, however, is that the previous relationship ended even though one or both parties may have been relationally satisfied and even though the partners may have made substantial investments in the relationship, especially if there were high-quality alternative relationships available for one or both partners. As a result, it is quite possible, for example, that individuals who are looking to enter a committed romantic relationship were not necessarily unhappy in the previous relationship and, consequently, may not be overly optimistic that a new relationship will be more satisfying than the previous one, which may pose challenges for any new relationship.

In addition, the investment model directs us to consider one's comparison level and one's beliefs regarding how successful one could be in finding an attractive partner to replace the current one (i.e., comparison level for alternatives). Each of these expectations, derived from past experiences in relationships, will strongly influence the course of any newly developing relationship.

With respect to the relationship future, the investment model suggests that individuals consistently identify, whether at an unconscious or conscious level, the rewards and costs of being in a particular new romantic relationship. Further, the new relationship is likely to be compared to the previous relationship—a comparison that may either be easy to "win" or be exceedingly difficult if the previous relationship was very satisfying. Finally, the investment model posits that the extent to which one is willing to commit to a new romantic relationship will be based on not only how satisfied one is with it but also the quality of perceived alternative relationships and the magnitude of investments made in the new relationship. Another way of interpreting this tenet of the investment model is that, unlike what many people believe about relationship development, many rewards and few costs are not the only or even primary determinant of one's willingness to commit to a new relationship—a variety of contextual factors influence one's evaluation of rewards and costs, as well as perceived alternatives and investments.

The *feminist perspective* is important because it directs us to attend to how power and authority are distributed in new relationships. As noted below, there is reason to believe that power is distributed more equitably in subsequent committed romantic relationships than it is in earlier ones. Most typically, in early romantic relationships, men assume more power than women. Women, even those with full-time careers, are expected to perform the majority of household and childrearing labor (Hochschild, 2003). Partly because such an arrangement is oppressive to women and is experienced as restrictive and unjust, many women expect and demand to have more power and equity in subsequent relationships, which will, of course, influence the way that new relationships unfold.

The feminist perspective is very compatible with the investment model, as, in the investment model, one could argue that having an egalitarian relationship is considered to be a relationship reward and that being expected to perform (and actually performing) the majority of household and childcare tasks is a cost. In addition, the investment model might suggest that women whose relationships have ended in divorce or dissolution have a different comparison level than do women in their first committed romantic relationships—a comparison level that expects more equity and more authority.

According to Petronio's (2002) *communication privacy management* (CPM) *theory*, individuals continually face a dialectical dilemma between revealing and concealing personal information. The theory delineates the factors that individuals consider in making these decisions, and places communication at the center of the process because the theory "focuses on the interplay of granting or denying access to information that is defined as private" (Petronio, 2002, p. 3). Although CPM theory has not been explicitly used to ground empirical studies of relationship initiation following dissolution, it sheds light on the critical issues, decisions, and dilemmas revolving around what individuals choose to reveal to potential new romantic partners. For example, individuals with children from a previous relationship must decide when and how to reveal this information to new romantic partners. Further, the disclosure dialectic is not reserved solely for dilemmas regarding disclosure to romantic partners; parents, for example, must decide whether or not to tell their children of their new romantic involvements. Individuals who have had a primary relationship dissolve would seem to have a wide range of previous experiences (e.g., they may have children, their previous relationships may have ended tumultuously, or they may have considerable debt that affects their financial well-being) that may be delicate to share with new partners. Thus, by explaining some of the dynamics involved in disclosure processes during relationship initiation, CPM theory is a useful complement to other theories.

According to Bengston and Allen (1993) and Elder (1998), there are seven key tenets of the *life course perspective*: time, context, agency, linked lives, process, meaning, and diversity. First, *time* refers to several interacting dimensions of change that influence how new relationships are initiated, including ontogenetic time (i.e., each individual's particular stage of development), generational time (i.e., each individual's and couple's generational stage, such as "baby boomers" or "Generation Xers"), and historical time (i.e., the particular cultural ethos and Zeitgeist of the era). Second, *context* examines how individuals' and couples' development is directly influenced by the environment and circumstances in which they live their lives. *Agency*, a third construct, acknowledges that individuals and couples are not passive in their responses to environmental circumstances and changes over time, but are active in creating their own contexts (including their close relationships) and in creatively adapting to changes in their environments.

Fourth, *linked lives* is a concept that suggests that individuals' development does not occur in isolation and that, in particular, individuals' development is intertwined with that of others with whom they are close. In terms of relationship initiation, this notion suggests that two partners' developing relationship will be affected by linkages in their own personal development, as well as links between their development and that of others in their social networks. Next, *process* refers to the nature of interactions as the new relationship unfolds, including communication processes involved in beginning new relationships, how and when to disclose information about previous relationships, how finances are managed, the benefits and hindrances of social support and social networks, and possible differences in values. *Meaning* is the term used to describe how individuals' interpretations and thoughts assigned to different life events influence their developmental trajectories. Also included in this aspect of the life course perspective are social cognitions that individuals have regarding their relationships in particular and relationships in general. Finally, *diversity* refers to the notion that individuals' and couples' developmental paths are likely to differ depending on such dimensions as race and ethnicity, sexual orientation, gender, socioeconomic status, nationality, and age (Bengston & Allen, 1993).

We believe that the life course perspective has particular advantages in furthering our understanding of the development of new relationships following relationship dissolution. In particular, understanding how new relationships are initiated following dissolution necessarily involves an examination of how individuals and relationships change over time and how these changes are embedded in a particular cultural context. Further, the life course perspective directs our attention to the ways in which individuals proactively navigate through their lives and the interpersonal processes that they engage in as they do so. As a caveat, we note that the life course perspective does not provide an *explanation* of how people initiate new relationships, nor does it lead to clear predictions about how people will behave in the future. Rather, it provides a framework that will hopefully bring greater clarity and organization to this area of research.

A REVIEW OF RELEVANT FINDINGS THROUGH THE LIFE COURSE LENS

In this section, organized by the seven key tenets of the life course perspective, we review the literature on the initiation of new relationships following divorce or dissolution.

Time

The initiation of new relationships following relationship dissolution is influenced by several interacting time-related dimensions. First, as discussed above, *ontogenetic time* refers to each partner's particular individual stage of development. For example, a 25-year-old woman who is focused on establishing her career is likely to have different relationship initiation experiences than is a 45-year-old woman with two children whose career and financial health are already established. Second, *generational time* refers to the particular cohort (e.g., baby boomers, Generation X, and Generation Y) into which individual partners were born. Baby boomers, for example, are thought to work very hard, sometimes placing much greater value on work than on other aspects of life (Lancaster & Stillman, 2002; Zemke, Raines, & Filipczak, 2000). By contrast, "Xers" have been characterized as more casual about work and more concerned with finding work–family balance (Lancaster & Stillman, 2002). Such generational differences, to the extent that they characterize potential relationship partners, are likely to have a great impact on relationship initiation (and development). Finally, *historical time* refers to the particular cultural ethos that provides the context in which new relationships are formed. For example, relationship formation, particularly sexual initiation, has been greatly affected by the emergence of AIDS and HIV in the 1980s (Wood, 2004).

Context

The life course perspective also accounts for the context in which events or relational processes occur. The physical, social, historical, psychological, and cultural contexts frame the setting for relationship initiation and development after dissolution. Each dimension of context will be discussed separately, highlighting the contextual factors that are unique to postdissolution relationship initiation and development. Of course, the contextual factors are not mutually exclusive because they interact in myriad ways for individuals.

The *physical context* is shaped by a person's tangible surroundings. Geographic location, community setting, and the structure of the home are common elements under the physical context umbrella. But, perhaps the most salient physical aspect of relationship initiation after divorce or dissolution is the presence or absence of children. Of course, some dissolved relationships end without children, and these partners can proceed into new relationships without having to deal with issues pertaining to children. However, divorced partners with children from the previous relationship discuss the children more than any other topic when contemplating commitment or remarriage (Ganong & Coleman, 1989), suggesting that partners with children place considerable emphasis on how the new relationship will impact their children. As a result, our focus here now turns to the impact that children have on their parents' ability to develop new, intimate relationships.

In what ways do children affect their parents' initiation and development of new relationships? First, children impact the availability of time that divorced parents have to socialize and meet potential partners. Because of his or her greater childrearing responsibilities, the parent who retains physical custody—usually the mother—experiences more challenges in finding time to pursue and develop new relationships than does the nonresidential parent. This disparity in available time to meet new partners may be a factor in the rate of remarriage after a divorce; divorced fathers with children remarry more frequently and more quickly after the divorce than do mothers with children (Wilson & Clarke, 1992).

Second, after the divorced parent meets a person of potential interest, children affect the nature and timing of dating activities. Montgomery, Anderson, Hetherington, and Clingempeel (1992) reported that 56% of the mothers in their study indicated that their children had contact with the new dating partner at least once a week during the courtship period, whereas only 17% indicated that contact occurred less than once per month. Thus, dating activities may expand beyond the cultural norm of dinner and a movie to include activities that include the children. When both partners have children, dating becomes even more complex because coordination of schedules and activities creates even more challenges due to more people being involved.

Third, the ages of the children appear to affect their parents' dating activities (Lampard & Peggs, 1999). In general, parents of adult children would have the most time to initiate and pursue new committed romantic relationships, whereas parents of minor children face greater restrictions. Infants and toddlers need constant supervision, whereas middle school– or high school–aged children need less supervision from a parent. Further, adolescents transition into adulthood by engaging in school or social activities in which supervision is provided by a teacher or another adult, rather than the parent. Thus, parents of adolescents may have more time available to pursue relationship initiation than parents of toddlers and infants. However, as noted further below, adolescents present their own unique challenges as relationships become more committed.

The age disparity between each partner's children and whether the children are minors or adults themselves also can affect relationship initiation and development. In complex ways that are affected by multiple contextual factors, children's age affects their postdivorce adjustment as well as stepparent–stepchild relations (Hetherington & Clingempeel, 1992). Therefore, absent relevant research, it is reasonable to assume that the age of children would also influence parents' dating interactions during relationship initiation after dissolution. For example, if one partner has teenagers and the other has preschool-aged children, the different cognitive and physical abilities of the children may limit activities or require further coordination and compromise.

Fourth, children's reactions to the divorce or dissolution (see Barber & Demo, 2006, for an extensive review of the literature on how children respond to divorce) affect their responses to parents' potential new romantic partners. For example, children who are adjusting reasonably well to the dissolution of their parents' relationship may be more open to the possibility of their parent entering a new romantic union. By contrast, children who resent a loss of attention from the parent and who harbor hopes or fantasies that their parents may reunite may attempt to sabotage new relationships.

Finally, not only do children affect the initiation of new relationships, but they also affect the course that these new relationships take. For example, in a study conducted by Knox and Zusman (2001), stepmothers who reported having problems with stepchildren reported less marital happiness and more frequent thoughts of divorce. This link between (re)marital functioning and problems with stepchildren suggests that women who are considering initiating and establishing new relationships with men with children from a previous relationship should proceed with caution. In fact, Knox and Zusman recommended delaying remarriage because most of the stepmothers in their sample married a man within 2 years of his divorce.

In terms of relationship initiation following divorce and/or dissolution, the *social context* refers to the *relationship or marriage market*, which includes the number of available partners, the characteristics of the available partners, and the places to meet the available partners. If approximately 50% of marriages end in divorce (Teachman et al., 2006), then there is a sizeable proportion of the population that is available for new romantic relationships. Further, the vast majority of divorced individuals eventually remarry (Bumpass, Sweet, & Castro-Martin, 1990; Kreider & Fields, 2002), and 54% and 75% of divorced women remarry within 5 and 10 years of their divorce, respectively (Montgomery et al., 1992).

Where do individuals go to meet new partners following divorce and/or dissolution? The social context also includes (as mentioned above) where to meet available partners. Divorced individuals may seek "unconventional" venues such as online or telephone dating services in which to socialize and meet potential new partners (Anderson & Clandos, 2003). As age increases, individuals' preferences for where to socialize often change. Bars and social clubs are appealing to many young, single individuals but are usually less attractive to divorced or separated individuals. Hence, when a divorce or dissolution occurs in middle age (or even older), the opportunity to meet other singles diminishes due to a lack of social activities catering to an older singles market. Single individuals who are divorced or have had their relationships dissolved may reenter the "bar scene" but quickly realize the age gap between themselves and younger singles. Further, the (possible) maturity experienced through marriage and parenting diminishes the attractiveness of bars and their regular clientele. Therefore, finding other singles (never married or divorced), particularly *compatible* ones, at an older age presents a challenge for individuals ready to socialize and explore new, intimate relationships.

Because of the challenges involved in finding compatible partners, many divorcees turn to online dating to meet people. In a poll of 2,006 subscribers to Match.com conducted in April 2002, 49% of singles said they look online and do not "waste their time" at bars (Match.com, 2002). For more detailed treatments of online dating, see the chapters by McKenna and Sprecher, Schwartz, Harvey, and Hatfield in this volume. Here, we focus on online dating as it pertains to new relationships following relationship dissolution.

Unfortunately, the small body of empirical research on online dating (Lea & Spears, 1995) has typically failed to distinguish between never-married and divorced respondents. A study that did make this distinction was conducted by Gibbs, Ellison, and Heino (2006), who examined self-presentation in the online dating environment in a sample of subscribers to Match.com (2002). In Gibbs et al.'s (2006) sample, 62% were divorced or separated, suggesting that online dating has become a viable option for meeting partners following divorce or dissolution.

There are a number of potential advantages that the online social context offers to single individuals following the termination of earlier romantic relationships. First, the confidentiality and anonymity of computer-mediated communication (CMC) may allow interactants to be more expressive or to feel less inhibited, real, open, or honest (Wysocki, 1998). Communication privacy management theory (Petronio, 2002) offers an explanation for this by positing that an individual may be more willing to disclose personal information when his or her identity is protected. In the context of new relationships following the dissolution of a previous one, individuals whose previous relationships have terminated may feel that they have more "baggage" (e.g., children from a previous marriage and a conflictual relationship with an ex-spouse) from their past relationship histories than do individuals initiating their first committed romantic relationship. Nevertheless, as Wysocki suggested, disclosure of this baggage may occur more rapidly in the online environment than in traditional face-to-face dating environments.

Second, online interactions are private; there is no chance that there is a community of friends or acquaintances who may be observing one's romantic interactions, as is the case in traditional dating situations. This may be a particularly attractive feature for older established individuals whose relationships have terminated.

Third, when one interacts with someone online, some of one's personal characteristics, such as appearance, socioeconomic status, and speech style, are hidden (McKenna, this volume). Thus, for example, high-profile or wealthy individuals in a particular community may prefer the online environment, where there is less fear of being pursued for status or money.

Finally, individuals with children from previous relationships can remain at home while caring for their children and still explore new relationships. In the Match.com (2002) poll mentioned earlier, 80% of subscribers logged in at home, suggesting that the convenience that comes from online dating is an attractive feature for many individuals, including those with children and other caretaking commitments.

Despite the plethora of advantages, there are also several disadvantages to online dating. First, although this is dissipating, perhaps rapidly, over time, there is still a stigma attached to online dating (Sprecher et al., this volume). Some consider individuals who utilize such services to be desperate to find a partner, which may negatively affect potential online daters in a number of ways (e.g., many potential partners may not use such services because of the perceived stigma).

Second, face-to-face interactions allow partners to see the other. CMC relies on demographic variables (and sometimes personality characteristics derived from an online "test") for search criteria, and personal attractiveness can only be determined by a photograph, if provided. The photograph is extremely important in the online environment; 54.7% of the Match.com subscribers in the April 2002 poll reported that the photograph was the first thing they looked at before viewing a profile. However, photographs are not as good as live interactions as depictions of a person's physical appearance because of variations in photograph quality, the recency of the photo, and the extent to which the person's physical characteristics are represented in the photo.

Third, CMC is facilitated by written communication. As such, behaviors are challenging to depict through written communication, some people are uncomfortable with writing, and some are even unable to write. Emoticons—symbols used to depict emotions—provide some level of inflecting emotion into the written dialogue, but the written nature of communication and lack of nonverbal cues permit greater opportunities for miscommunication than face-to-face encounters. Future research needs to determine whether the extent of online miscommunication differs for individuals in first romantic relationships as opposed to those in subsequent ones. Because individuals in subsequent relationships may have more life experience, may have more to lose should miscommunication occur, and are perhaps better known in their communities, the costs of online miscommunication may be greater for these individuals.

Finally, written communication can be used in a socially desirable fashion to place the person in the most positive light possible, and is more easily altered than the combination of verbal and nonverbal communication that takes place in face-to-face interactions (Sprecher et al., this volume; Yurchisin, Watchravesringkan, & McCabe, 2005). Nevertheless, Gibbs and colleagues (2006) found that individuals using the online social milieu who anticipate future interaction are more honest and have a higher amount of self-disclosure than users who do not anticipate future interactions, and are not necessarily more positive in their disclosures. Again, it is conceivable, although not yet empirically studied, that the initiation of new romantic relationships may be especially vulnerable to the possibility of socially desirable communication.

The *psychological context* includes individuals' personality traits, thoughts, and feelings. One general psychological factor relevant to relationship initiation after divorce is level of personal adjustment, which changes to some extent over time. Amato's (2000) divorce–stress adjustment model offers one way to conceptualize postdivorce adjustment and preparedness for new relationships. The model emphasizes processes instead of linear stages. The extent to which individuals have "worked through" the processes of grieving, coping, and healing after a divorce (Harvey & Fine, 2006) affects their readiness for new relationships. There is an ebb and flow to one's passage through these processes, with adjustment being quite positive at some points, but, when triggered by stressful events, periods of less positive adjustment occur at other times. Signs of positive adjustment include personal growth and autonomy, whereas indices of maladjustment may be depression, poor physical health, and poor self-concept, among others (Amato, 2000).

In addition, Amato's (2000) model considers psychological characteristics that the individual brings to the process of initiating new relationships. Some individuals are thought to be "poor marriage material," which has been shown to be a risk factor for later divorce. For example, a key personality characteristic that may influence subsequent relationships is the extent to which the individual is high in "neuroticism" (Amato, 1996), which is a generalized predisposition to experience negative emotions, such as fear, sadness, anxiety, guilt, and anger (Rodrigues, Hall, & Fincham, 2006). In addition, other personality characteristics that contribute to an individual being poor marriage material include drug and alcohol abuse, engaging in risky behavior, and low levels of conscientiousness and agreeableness (Rodrigues et al., 2006). To the extent that one brings some level of neuroticism and these other undesirable characteristics to new potential relationships, the course of initiating and then maintaining new romances is likely to be more tumultuous.

With specific reference to initiating new relationships following dissolution, several other psychological characteristics affect how new relationships are initiated and maintained. First, it is important to understand the extent to which the individual still harbors hostility, anger, and resentment regarding the ending of the previous relationship. When individuals carry this "baggage" with them into new relationships, it is likely that they will have a difficult time fully devoting themselves to potential new relationship partners. By being "stuck" in the past relationship, it is difficult to attend to new potential partners.

Second, another psychological characteristic that individuals bring to subsequent relationships pertains to who initiated the divorce. Because the initiator is more likely to have a quicker and/or healthier adjustment than the noninitiator (Braver, Shapiro, & Goodman, 2006), new relationship development is likewise predicted to be more rapid for the initiator than the noninitiator (Sweeney, 2002). However, it is important to realize that determining who initiated the divorce is extremely difficult for several reasons, including that (a) it is seldom the case that one and only one individual was interested in and pursued ending a relationship; (b) filing for divorce, which women do more frequently than men, is not necessarily synonymous with who actually wanted and "pushed for" the divorce; and (c) individuals often reconstruct accounts of who initiated the divorce in ways that place them in a favorable light (Hopper, 2001).

Ganong and Coleman (2004) acknowledged a lack of research in this area, but presented six possible explanations for the more rapid relationship development for those who initiated the divorce:

1. The previous relationship may have been dissatisfying, and there is the hope that entering a new relationship will return one to the desired state of happiness.
2. The initiator may be more adjusted to the ending of a relationship than the noninitiator because he or she spent more time preparing for the dissolution.
3. The initiator may be more capable of attracting new partners.
4. The initiator may have a personality that is more open to change.
5. A new partner may have been present before the previous relationship ended.
6. Initiators may have idealistic views about and high expectations for marriage that, even though they may have led to dissatisfaction in the prior relationship, still persist and lead the initiator to want to try again soon.

The *cultural context* includes beliefs, values, and meaning shared among a group of people. The dominant cultural norm in the United States favors heterosexual unions and first-time marriages. Partly as a result of this dominant ideology, there is a stigma attached to divorce, albeit a reduced one relative to earlier time periods (for a historical review of U.S. divorce trends, see Amato & Irving, 2006). Consequently, relationships initiated and developed following divorce are often viewed differently than are relationships that could lead to a first marriage for both partners. In some instances, such relationships may be more heavily scrutinized and viewed more cautiously, whereas, in other cases, they may be viewed as a welcomed new chance for happiness (Kitson, 2006). Within a dominant culture such as the United States, different cultural groups may have varying views of and reactions toward postdivorce romantic pairings (see, for example, Orbuch & Brown, 2006; Umana-Taylor

& Alfaro, 2006). These views, both those of the dominant culture and those of various co-cultural groups, affect how new relationships are initiated and formed.

Agency

The life course perspective maintains that individuals exercise agency when making decisions about their lives. Agency directs attention to the level of independence and initiative that individuals possess. Individuals with high levels of agency take initiative and pursue personal goals. Applied to those who want to repartner, *agency* refers to the choices and behaviors they initiate to forge new relationships. After relationship dissolution, partners need time to grieve, reflect, adjust, and make sense of the now-ended relationship (Harvey & Fine, 2006). Adjustment to previous levels of functioning typically occurs within 2 to 3 years after the divorce provided that no other major life stressors occur (Hetherington & Kelly, 2002). As ex-partners emerge from dissolved relationships, they often proactively make decisions about whether or not to seek out new relationships by utilizing their skills and resources (Demo, Aquilino, & Fine, 2005).

Hetherington (2003) and Hetherington and Kelly (2002) derived six types of postdivorce adjustment "personalities"—enhancers, goodenoughs, seekers, swingers, competent loners, and the defeated—which characterize the agency and variability involved in repartnering. *Enhancers* become more competent and well-adjusted after a divorce, and have much higher self-efficacy than those in the other types of adjustment. This group of mostly women eventually moves on into new marriages that are more successful than the first marriage. *Goodenoughs* are described as the average person trying to cope with life and the changes associated with divorce. Goodenoughs exhibit qualities very similar to those of enhancers but are less well adjusted. The agency of the Goodenoughs is lower than that of the Enhancers. As a result, Goodenoughs' remarriages are often quite similar to their first marriage. *Seekers* quickly and actively seek new partners. Seekers, who are predominantly men, depend upon women for support and encouragement. They utilize agency in the short term as they seek new partners, but their agency becomes limited in the long term because they are independent and autonomous only until they secure another relationship. *Swingers* enjoy the freedom of divorce and engage in serial, uncommitted relationships of varying durations. They possess agency, but use it for their own personal expression of emancipation from the previous marriage, rather than for establishing committed intimate relationships. *Competent loners* also exhibit high levels of agency, but choose to continue life without a partner. Their quality of life is high, and they utilize friend and social networks to alleviate potential loneliness. Finally, the *defeated* have low levels of self-efficacy, possess poor social skills, and often partake in unhealthy behaviors such as alcohol or drug abuse.

Guided, of course, by their postdivorce personality, as relationships begin to develop, individuals have a number of choices that reflect their agency. Here, we present three examples of such choices. First, individuals have decisions regarding how much to disclose from previous relationships and experiences. Although self-disclosure is generally considered to lead to positive outcomes, including reciprocity and intimacy (Altman & Taylor, 1973), there are also forces restricting self-disclosure (Petronio, 2002). For postdivorce and postdissolution individuals, disclosure of certain details from the past relationship may be unappealing to potential new romantic partners. In fact, prior relationships have been labeled as a "taboo topic" by Baxter and Wilmot (1985). The family history may be marked by shameful or embarrassing behaviors such as infidelity, physical abuse, unsupportiveness, poor financial skills, or a poor employment record, which could potentially deter prospective partners. Disclosing private secrets can also be face threatening and increase vulnerability. Thus, a dialectical tension between privacy and disclosure results during relationship initiation and development (Baxter & Montgomery, 1996).

Second, another relational display of agency between partners in newly developing relationships is the decision regarding living arrangements. Typically, in first-time relationships and marriages, the intimacy of living arrangements often coincides with advancing commitment levels. For example, dating partners typically progress from having separate households, to "living apart together" (i.e., each partner maintains his or her own household, while sharing living space with each other at alternating intervals), to cohabiting, and, finally, to residing in the same household as a married couple. However, the agency involved in decisions surrounding the living arrangements of divorced partners is often much more complex and restrictive, especially when minor children are in the picture. For instance, committed individuals may maintain separate households *indefinitely*. Or, another scenario may involve one or both partners having shared custody of children from the previous relationships of one or both partners. This situation may lead to the partners living together only when the children are not in the home. Finally, if one partner transitions from being a nonresidential parent to a residential one, the couple may decide to live apart despite maintaining a committed relationship. As these examples illustrate, there is wide variability in the agency that divorced individuals can enact as they make decisions regarding their domiciles.

The variability in living arrangements that characterizes new romantic partnerships also depends on the ages of the partners. For example, the "living apart together" option may be particularly common among older adults (Gierveld, 2004). In Gierveld's Dutch sample of repartnered individuals over age 55, 24% had this form of living arrangement.

Third, in newly formed relationships following divorce or dissolution, there is a decision regarding whether or not to have additional children—a decision that often seems to be more deliberate and thoughtful than is the comparable decision in first marriages. Factors involved in this decision include such issues as whether or not one or both of the partners have children from a previous relationship, if they want to have (additional) children, the partners' biological ages at the time of remarriage and related fertility considerations, the age gap between present and potential new children, and how old the parents would be when new children would leave the home.

In a study conducted by Lampard and Peggs (1999), divorced women under the age of 35 reported having relatively little desire to have additional children, and women between the ages of 35 and 44 reported even less desire to have additional children in a new partnership. The fact that these women already had children may have played a role in their not wanting to have additional children. Also, partners may have differing desires, preferences, and inclinations regarding whether to bear children together. For example, one partner may desire additional children, whereas the other one may not. For these and other reasons, childbearing is a salient and complex issue for discussion during relationship initiation after divorce or dissolution. Further, the decision regarding whether or not to have a child affects the subsequent course of one's romantic relationship. For example, for White but not African American partners, having children following divorce increases the likelihood that one will remarry, as single women who give birth to children after divorce are almost twice as likely to remarry as are divorced women who bear no children (Suchindran, Koo, & Griffith, 1985).

Linked Lives

Repartnering after dissolution impacts more than the individuals in the new dyad. Each partner may bring children, grandchildren, former partners and/or in-laws, or other social support members into the new relationship, creating a web of new relationships and interdependencies. The introduction of new family members necessitates the redefinition of roles and boundaries for everyone affected. The new couple quickly realizes that their relationship to each other links them to other new relationships, some voluntary and others nonvoluntary. The notion of linked lives within the life course perspective explicates the effects of new relationships on the kin and family network, particularly on children.

For example, early work on the effects of remarriage on children led Rodgers and Conrad (1986) to postulate that divorced parents who allow time to reestablish new roles and boundaries with their children before entering new, committed relationships were thought to have better adjusted children than divorced parents who quickly reenter new relationships. However, by contrast, more recent work has suggested that the *longer* the period of time between the divorce and the mother's new union, the lower the child's social competence (Montgomery et al., 1992). Apparently, when mothers and their children establish new roles and routines after the divorce and the altered relationships have become comfortable over time, the transition to living with a stepparent in a stepfamily is even more stressful for children and at least temporarily leads to lower levels of social competence. Although there must be other factors—besides length of time between the divorce and the remarriage—that affect children's social competence, it is clear that parents' behaviors are linked in complex ways with their children's plight.

As yet another example of the linked lives notion, Montgomery et al. (1992) found that the number of mothers' dating partners has implications for children's adjustment. Remarried women reported dating a median of 3 to 5 partners before remarrying, and there was an inverse relation between the number of mothers' dating partners and the social competence of their children during the first year after remarriage.

Linkages among parents, new partners, and adolescents require special attention because adolescents have more difficulty adjusting to divorce and remarriage than younger children (Skaggs & Jodl, 1999), even when the divorce and/or remarriage occurred before adolescence. Several studies have shed light on some specific and unique aspects of adolescents' reactions to their parents' new relationship initiation and development. Koerner, Rankin, Kenyon, and Korn (2004), for example, examined mothers' and their adolescents' accounts regarding the mother initiating a new relationship. Interestingly, there were important differences in the mothers' and the adolescents' accounts. Some mothers indicated that the child and stepparent get along quite well, or the mothers described an unchanged relationship with their adolescents, but the child's narrative indicated hostility or dislike for the new partner, or a very different relationship with the mother (Koerner et al., 2004). Most notable in the discrepancies was that the adolescents reported spending less time with their mother when the mother believed that no change had occurred in the time spent together. These findings suggest, on the one hand, that parents may be psychologically motivated to minimize the possibility that new relationships have potentially negative outcomes on their children. On the other hand, children may be motivated to exaggerate negative outcomes because they resent the loss of attention and authority that they have experienced. Regardless of the source of the discrepancies, these results suggest that parents and children need to openly communicate regarding changes resulting from new romantic relationships.

The linkages to other kin have received far less attention in the extant literature than have linkages to children. Although divorced partners exhibit agency to pursue new relationships, children, former spouses, former in-laws, and other family or friends have very little or no control over the new relationship. For example, nonresidential parents have little or no say regarding their ex-spouses' choices in new partners, resulting in nonvoluntary and possibly tension-filled and unpleasant interactions between nonresidential parents and stepparents (Ganong, Coleman, & Hans, 2006). Children's grandparents, aunts, uncles, and cousins also must renegotiate relationships when ex-relatives remarry if they hope to remain a continuing presence in the children's lives.

Process

The life course perspective emphasizes the processes that occur as individuals navigate through their life experiences. Rather than describing these processes as transpiring in a linear, stagelike manner, the life course perspective suggests that there is an ebb and flow to these processes as they unfold in differing contexts at different times over the life course. Nevertheless, at the risk of sounding as if we are adopting a stage model, we argue that the initiation and development of new romantic relationships following divorce or dissolution can be thought of as transpiring over roughly three sets of experiences: (a) before the new relationship begins (prerelationship period), (b) at the beginning of the new relationship before either party becomes committed to it (beginning period), and (c) in the middle of the new relationship after the parties become committed to it (committed period). Many of the issues and factors discussed earlier with respect to initiating new relationships can be categorized into one of these periods.

Examples of relevant issues in the prerelationship period include where and how to meet new partners, the individual histories and personality characteristics that each partner brings to the new relationship, and the relationship cognitions that the individuals bring to the new relationship. In the beginning period, relevant issues include how much private information to disclose to each other, the nature of the communicative interactions, and how partners integrate their new relationship with other aspects of their lives, such as their children and their careers. In the committed period, pertinent issues include the extent to which the couple will equitably share decision making, allow each other to establish a sense of independence, and retain control of their personal finances. Underlying the processes throughout these three periods is each individual's overall level of functioning, as well as the level of adjustment to the dissolution of the previous relationship.

Meaning

The life course perspective also draws attention to the meaning that individuals assign to their experiences. In the context of forming new relationships, we conceptualize meaning in terms of the social cognitions that individuals bring to their new relationships. Below, we share several ways that the social cognitions of individuals who have divorced or had their relationships dissolve may differ from those that partners possess in first relationships. First, perhaps because of their previous relationship experiences and the realities of childrearing responsibilities, newly remarried spouses may view their relationships in less romantic and more practical ways than do spouses in first marriages (Hetherington & Stanley-Hagan, 2000). For partners with children from a previous relationship, the characteristics that they desire in a committed romantic partner are likely to have changed from being narrowly defined in terms of meeting one's romantic needs to being defined in terms of meeting a broader array of one's needs for instrumental support, such as help in rearing children and assistance in meeting one's financial obligations. Further, even the very meaning assigned to *romance* may change over the life course. For example, later life widows or widowers may search for a partner who can provide much needed companionship, which may be conceptualized as romantic even if it does not involve sexuality and passion.

Second, spouses in remarriages tend to hold more egalitarian relationship values and are more willing to confront their partners in comparison to individuals in first marriages (Giles-Sims, 1987). Further, the existence of these beliefs has been verified by observational studies that have shown that spouses in stepfamilies are freer in expressing criticism and anger (Hetherington, 1993; Hetherington & Stanley-Hagan, 2000). Another reflection of this greater belief in egalitarianism is that repartnered individuals are more likely to believe in shared decision making that is sensitive to both partners' needs (Ganong et al., 2006).

Third, remarried spouses tend to hold stronger beliefs that each partner should maintain some degree of independence and autonomy even when they are in a committed romantic relationship. Reflecting this value placed on independence, remarried individuals are more likely than are spouses in first marriages to place at least some of their economic resources under their personal control (Burgoyne & Morison, 1997). In addition, because of their belief that each partner should retain some autonomy, it is plausible that remarried spouses also may be more accepting of their partners maintaining separate hobbies and interests. This possibility, however, has yet to be empirically tested.

Diversity

A final component to the life span perspective is diversity. Although there are an infinite number of possible dimensions of diversity, we focus on several that have been examined in the literature: race, biological sex, age, and socioeconomic status.

Race   A limited body of research has examined how race relates to relationship initiation and development, and the existing research has been based primarily on European Americans, African Americans, and to some extent Hispanics. Evidence suggests that African Americans are less likely to remarry than European Americans and Hispanics (Bumpass, Sweet, & Martin, 1990; Orbuch &

Brown, 2006; Wilson & Clarke, 1992). However, when considering that many couples cohabit without marrying, the gap closes between White men and African American men (Bumpass et al., 1990). African Americans who remarry are older than Whites at the time of remarriage, and the length of time between divorce and remarriage is greater for African Americans than Whites (Wilson & Clarke). In addition, African American and Hispanic couples have the highest rate of long-term separation. At least 15% of African American (and Hispanic) marriages involve permanently separated spouses who have no intention to ever divorce (National Center for Health Statistics, 2002). The fact that many separated African Americans are still legally married may partially explain why African Americans have the lowest remarriage rate of any ethnic or racial group.

Biological Sex Men are more likely to repartner than women (Lampard & Peggs, 1999). As women age, their chances of remarriage decrease, but this is not the case for men (Sweeney, 2002). Women with more education are more likely to remarry than are women with less education (Sweeney). Men's education level has no association with their likelihood of remarriage. However, when considering cohabitation in addition to remarriage, women's educational level is no longer significantly related to the likelihood of repartnering (cohabiting or remarrying; Sweeney).

Age Another diversity marker relevant to the prevalence and timing of repartnering is age. The mean age at the time of remarriage is 38.6 years for men and 35.0 years for women (Wilson & Clarke, 1992). The older one is at the time of divorce, the less likely the individual is to remarry, but, as noted above, this trend is more pronounced for women than for men (Lampard & Peggs, 1999; Wilson & Clarke). Women under the age of 25 at the time of divorce have an 84% probability of remarriage within 10 years. The probability decreases to 68% for women over age 30 (National Center for Health Statistics, 2002). Further, age differences between husbands and wives are greater in remarriages than in first marriages (Gelissen, 2004).

Socioeconomic Status Socioeconomic status (SES) is also associated with the frequency of remarriage. Those with higher SES are more likely to remarry than those with lower SES (Lampard & Peggs, 1999). The size and location of one's residence are also related to the likelihood of remarriage. When comparing central cities, suburbs, and nonmetropolitan areas, women from nonmetropolitan areas have a 48% higher probability of remarriage than women in central cities (National Center for Health Statistics, 2002).

A FUTURE RESEARCH AGENDA

Our review indicates that, despite the importance of understanding how individuals initiate new relationships after the termination of their previous relationship, there are major gaps in our understanding of this growing phenomenon.

In terms of *content*, there is a need to study the communication processes involved in the initiation of new romantic relationships post divorce. For example, we need information on how people who are seeking new relationships communicate their romantic interest in and pursue a relationship with another person, with a possible focus on how such communicative processes may differ from those involved when seeking a first committed relationship. Further, we also need to learn more about how individuals communicate with others about their new relationships, including addressing such questions as the following: When and how do they tell their children, friends, and/or family that they are going to begin dating again? When and how do they tell their children, family, and/or friends that they have a new romantic partner? Petronio's (2002) communication privacy management theory is a useful resource to identify factors that influence these disclosure decisions. As a final example, further work is needed that examines interaction patterns, such as conflict management and decision making, for couples in later relationships and how these patterns may differ from when they were in their first relationship.

We encourage future researchers to take a more fluid and long-term view of the relationship careers that individuals experience. In a sense, we have fed into the false dichotomy established in the literature between first and subsequent relationships in our discussion of how relationship initiation may be different in new relationships after dissolution. More accurately, virtually all individuals experience the initiation and termination of at least several romantic relationships over their lifetimes, and we need more information on how these relationships are interrelated, how different relationship careers have potentially differential effects on the individuals involved, and both the positive and negative consequences that earlier relationships have on later ones. The life course perspective employed in this chapter is ideal for this purpose because it encourages researchers to examine not only a single relationship at a time but also the ebb and flow that inevitably characterize individuals' relationship careers.

In terms of *methodology*, the bulk of the research reviewed for this chapter has relied on quantitative research methods and the use of secondary data. Although this work has begun to build a body of literature on postdivorce relationship initiation and development, more methodological diversity is necessary. In particular, we call for more qualitative research to explore the meaning-making processes involved in initiating new relationships following divorce. How do potential partners think about later relationships when an earlier one has ended in dissolution? How eagerly does one pursue such relationships? To what extent are individuals more cautious in subsequent relationships than in earlier ones? Qualitative methods, such as grounded theory, narrative, ethnography, autoethnography, interpretive interviews, and/or phenomenology, among others, would be particularly useful for studying such meaning-related questions regarding relationship initiation after divorce or dissolution. As a group, these methods give voice to the participants and their lived experiences (Creswell, 2006).

In addition, the elements of the life course perspective lend themselves well to qualitative research methods. *Context*, for instance, refers to the specific cultural milieus in which relationships occur. As such, because an understanding of context would seem to require an in-depth examination of how individuals interpret and assign meaning to the nuances of their cultural milieu, ethnography seems an appropriate choice to understand postdivorce relationship initiation in a variety of contexts. For example, ethnographies could be developed that explore individuals' experiences of the online dating culture.

From a *sampling and generalization* standpoint, we need much more research on how non-White, gay and lesbian, and lower socioeconomic status individuals and couples experience the beginnings of new relationships following relationship dissolution. Although there are clearly significant gaps in the literature on new relationship initiation, the research base that does exist is based on an overrepresentation of White, heterosexual, and middle– to upper–socioeconomic status individuals. Although it is routine for researchers to provide this recommendation to study more diverse samples, we believe that the most critical need is to study the *intersections* among these dimensions in terms of how they influence the relationship initiation process (Marks & Leslie, 2000). In other words, rather than studying each of these dimensions of diversity in isolation from one another, which may provide misleading conclusions, we believe that we need thoughtful investigations of how these dimensions interact with each other. We recognize how difficult it is to acquire sufficiently large sample sizes to conduct quantitative statistical analyses of the various moderating effects of these dimensions of diversity, but nevertheless still encourage researchers to take on this challenge because of how important it is to address the interactions among these diversity dimensions. Large national secondary data sets may be helpful in achieving sufficiently large sample sizes.

Also with respect to generalization, more focused inquiry is necessary into nonmarital subsequent relationships. As cohabitation following divorce or dissolution becomes even more common, we need to direct attention to these relationships that are not defined by the legal status of being married. In this regard, we also note that, although we have chosen in this chapter not to focus on nonromantic relationships because of space limitations, there are a host of nonmarital relationships that provide romantic-like companionship. For example, some elderly individuals may seek companionate relationships following the death of their spouse. These quasi-romantic relationships may provide companionship and some of the other provisions of romantic relationships (e.g., emotional support and instrumental aid; Heinemann & Evans, 1990).

Finally, theory development is in order. As is clear from the literature reviewed in this chapter, there are few theories specifically developed to understand romantic relationship initiation in general, and relationship initiation following dissolution in particular. To address this deficiency, we need midrange theories that are constructed specifically to address the initiation of new romantic relationships following dissolution. Such theories can help provide a foundation for integrating existing research findings, as well as providing direction for future research endeavors. For example, a midrange theory may consider how such factors as the manner in which the previous relationship ended (e.g., death of the partner, conflictual divorce or dissolution, or cooperative separation), individuals' beliefs regarding relationship formation following dissolution (e.g., the length of time one should wait before beginning to date, and whether it is appropriate to use online dating services), and life course factors (e.g., whether one has grown children from a previous relationship) influence behaviors carried out to initiate new relationships.

CONCLUSIONS

Ironically, in the course of writing this chapter, we have found that theoretical and empirical efforts do not always follow social trends and practices. Although thousands of individuals in the United States repartner every year after a previous romantic relationship has ended, social scientists have failed to provide much theoretical or empirical insight into this practice. As such, we have pulled from various, related literature bases, such as research on remarriage and stepfamilies, to present a preliminary life course framework through which to help conceptualize new relationships post dissolution. Although the life course perspective provides us with a mechanism to bring attention to certain aspects of these understudied relationships, we have also failed to capture their true diversity—namely, nonmarital relationships; nonsexual romantic relationships; gay, lesbian, and transgendered relationships; nonromantic relationships; and family relationships. So, in many ways, in this chapter as well as in the literature itself, we believe that more questions have been unearthed than answered. The good news is that for those individuals interested in studying the life course of relationships, there are many fields to hoe.

REFERENCES

Altman, I., & Taylor, D. A. (1973). *Social penetration: The development of interpersonal relationships.* New York: Holt, Rinehart & Winston.

Amato, P. R. (1996). Explaining the intergenerational transmission of divorce. *Journal of Marriage and the Family, 58,* 628–640.

Amato, P. R. (2000). The consequences of divorce for adults and children. *Journal of Marriage and the Family, 62,* 1269–1287.

Amato, P. R., & Irving, S. (2006). Historical trends in divorce in the United States. In M. A. Fine & J. H. Harvey (Eds.), *Handbook of divorce and relationship dissolution* (pp. 41–57). Mahwah, NJ: Lawrence Erlbaum.

Anderson, D., & Clandos, R. (2003, January/February). Dating after divorce. *Psychology Today,* 46–56.

Barber, B. L., & Demo, D. H. (2006). The kids are alright (at least, most of them): Links between divorce and dissolution and child well-being. In M. A. Fine & J. H. Harvey (Eds.), *Handbook of divorce and relationship dissolution* (pp. 289–311). Mahwah, NJ: Lawrence Erlbaum.

Baxter, L. A., & Montgomery, B. M. (1996). *Relating: Dialogues and dialectics.* New York: Guilford.

Baxter, L. A., & Wilmot, W. W. (1985). Taboo topics in close relationships. *Journal of Social and Personal Relationships, 2,* 253–269.

Bengston, V., & Allen, K. R. (1993). The life course perspective applied to families over time. In P. Boss, W. J. Doherty, R. LaRossa, W. R. Schumm, & S. K. Steinmetz (Eds.), *Sourcebook of family theory and methods: A contextual approach* (pp. 469–499). New York: Plenum Press.

Berscheid, E. (2006). Searching for the meaning of "love." In R. J. Sternberg & K. Weis (Eds.), *The new psychology of* love (pp. 171–183). New Haven, CT: Yale University Press.

Braver, S. L., Shapiro, J. R., & Goodman, M. R. (2006). Consequences of divorce for parents. In M. A. Fine & J. H. Harvey (Eds.), *Handbook of divorce and relationship dissolution* (pp. 313–337). Mahwah, NJ: Lawrence Erlbaum.

Bumpass, L. L., Sweet, J., & Castro-Martin, T. (1990). Changing patterns of remarriage in the U.S. *Journal of Marriage and the Family, 52,* 747–756.

Bumpass, L. L., Sweet, J., & Cherlin, A. (1991). The role of cohabitation in declining rates of marriage. *Journal of Marriage and the Family, 53,* 913–927.

Burgoyne, C. B., & Morison, V. (1997). Money in remarriage: Keeping things simple and separate. *Sociological Review, 45,* 363–395.

Creswell, J. W. (2006). *Qualitative inquiry and research design: Choosing among five traditions* (2nd ed.). Thousand Oaks, CA: Sage.

Demo, D. H., Aquilino, W. S., & Fine, M. A. (2005). Family composition and family traditions. In V. L. Bengtson, A. C. Acock, K. R. Allen, P. Dilworth-Anderson, & D. M. Klein (Eds.), *Sourcebook of family theory and research* (pp. 119–142). Thousand Oaks, CA: Sage.

Elder, G. H., Jr. (1998). The life course as developmental theory. *Child Development, 69,* 1–12.

Fine, M. A., & Harvey, J. H. (Eds.) (2006). *Handbook of divorce and relationship dissolution.* Mahwah, NJ: Lawrence Erlbaum.

Ganong, L. H., & Coleman, M. (1989). Preparing for remarriage: Anticipating the issues, seeking solutions. *Family Relations, 38,* 28–33.

Ganong, L. H., & Coleman, M. (2004). *Stepfamily relationships.* New York: Kluwer/Plenum.

Ganong, L. H., Coleman, M., & Hans, J. (2006). Divorce as prelude to stepfamily living and the consequences of redivorce. In M. A. Fine & J. H. Harvey (Eds.), *Handbook of divorce and relationship dissolution* (pp. 409–434). Mahwah, NJ: Lawrence Erlbaum.

Gelissen, J. (2004). Assortative mating after divorce: A test of two competing hypotheses using marginal models. *Social Science Research, 33,* 361–384.

Gibbs, J. L., Ellison, N. B., & Heino, R. D. (2006). Self-presentation in online personals: The role of anticipated future interaction, self-disclosure, and perceived success in Internet dating. *Communication Research, 33,* 152–177.

Gierveld, J. D. J. (2004). Remarriage, unmarried cohabitation, living apart together: Partner relationships following bereavement or divorce. *Journal of Marriage and Family, 66,* 236–243.

Giles-Sims, J. (1987). Social exchange in remarried families. In K. Pasley & M. Ihinger-Tallman (Eds.), *Remarriage and stepparenting today: Current research and theory* (pp. 141–163). New York: Guilford Press.

Harvey, J. H., & Fine, M. A. (2006). Social construction of accounts in the process of relationship termination. In M. A. Fine & J. H. Harvey (Eds.), *Handbook of divorce and relationship dissolution* (pp. 189–199). Mahwah, NJ: Lawrence Erlbaum.

Heinemann, G. D., & Evans, P. L. (1990). Widowhood: Loss, change, and adaptation. In T. H. Brubaker (Ed.), *Family relationships in later life* (2nd ed., pp. 142–168). Thousand Oaks, CA: Sage.

Hendrick, C., & Hendrick, S. (2006). Styles of romantic love. In R. J. Sternberg & K. Weis (Eds.), *The new psychology of love* (pp. 149–170). New Haven, CT: Yale University Press.

Hetherington, E. M. (1993). An overview of the Virginia longitudinal study of divorce and remarriage with a focus on early adolescence. *Journal of Family Psychology, 7,* 1–18.

Hetherington, E. M. (2003). Intimate pathways: Changing patterns in close personal relationships across time. *Family Relations, 52,* 318–331.

Hetherington, E. M., & Clingempeel, W. G. (1992). Coping with marital transitions: A family systems perspective. *Monographs of the Society for Research in Child Development, 57*(2/3, Serial No. 227), 1–14.

Hetherington, E. M., & Kelly, J. (2002). *For better or for worse: Divorce reconsidered.* New York: Norton.

Hetherington, E. M., & Stanley-Hagan, M. (2000). Diversity among stepfamilies. In D. H. Demo, K. R. Allen, & M. A. Fine (Eds.), *Handbook of family diversity* (pp. 173–196). New York: Oxford University Press.

Hochschild, A., with Machung, A. (2003). *The second shift* (Rev. ed.). New York: Viking/Penguin.

Hopper, J. (2001). The symbolic origins of conflict in divorce. *Journal of Marriage and Family, 63,* 430–445.

Kiecolt-Glaser, J. K., & Newton, T. L. (2001). Marriage and health: His and hers. *Psychological Bulletin, 127,* 472–503.

Kitson, G. C. (2006). Divorce and relationship dissolution research: Then and now. In M. A. Fine & J. H. Harvey (Eds.), *Handbook of divorce and relationship dissolution* (pp. 15–40). Mahwah, NJ: Lawrence Erlbaum.

Knox, D., & Zusman, M. E. (2001). Marrying a man with "baggage": Implications for second wives. *Journal of Divorce and Remarriage, 35,* 67–79.

Koerner, S. S., Rankin, L. A., Kenyon, D. Y. B., & Korn, M. (2004). Mothers re-partnering after divorce: Diverging perceptions of mothers and adolescents. *Journal of Divorce and Remarriage, 41*, 25–38.

Kreider, R. M., & Fields, J. M. (2002). *Number, timing, and duration of marriage and divorce: 1996* (Current Population Reports, Series P70-80). Washington, DC: Government Printing Office.

Lampard, R., & Peggs, K. (1999). Repartnering: The relevance of parenthood and gender to cohabitation and remarriage among the formerly married. *British Journal of Sociology, 50*, 443–465.

Lancaster, L. C., & Stillman, D. (2002). *When generations collide.* New York: HarperCollins.

Lea, M., & Spears, R. (1995). Love at first byte? Building personal relationships over computer networks. In J. T. Wood & S. Duck (Eds.), *Under-studied relationships: Off the beaten track* (pp. 197–233). Thousand Oaks, CA: Sage.

Marks, S. R., & Leslie, L. A. (2000). Family diversity and intersecting categories: Toward a richer approach to multiple roles. In D. H. Demo, K. R. Allen, & M. A. Fine (Eds.), *Handbook of family diversity* (pp. 402–423). New York: Oxford University Press.

Match.com. (2002). *Online dating usage.* Retrieved July 31, 2006, from http://www.corp.match.com

Montgomery, M. J., Anderson, E. R., Hetherington, E. M., & Clingempeel, W. G. (1992). Patterns of courtship for remarriage: Implications for child adjustment and parent-child relationships. *Journal of Marriage and the Family, 54*, 686–698.

National Center for Health Statistics. (2002). *Cohabitation, marriage, divorce, and remarriage in the United States* (Publication No. PHS 98-1998). Hyattsville, MD: Author.

Orbuch, T. L., & Brown, E. (2006). Divorce in the context of being African American. In M. A. Fine & J. H. Harvey (Eds.), *Handbook of divorce and relationship dissolution* (pp. 481–498). Mahwah, NJ: Lawrence Erlbaum.

Petronio, S. (2002). *Boundaries of privacy: Dialectics of disclosure.* Albany: State University of New York Press.

Rodgers, R. H., & Conrad, L. M. (1986). Courtship for remarriage: Influences on family reorganization after divorce. *Journal of Marriage and the Family, 48*, 767–775.

Rodrigues, A. E., Hall, J. H., & Fincham, F. D. (2006). What predicts divorce and relationship dissolution? In M. A. Fine & J. H. Harvey (Eds.), *Handbook of divorce and relationship dissolution* (pp. 85–112). Mahwah, NJ: Lawrence Erlbaum.

Rusbult, C. E. (1983). A longitudinal test of the investment model: The development (and deterioration) of satisfaction and commitment in heterosexual involvements. *Journal of Personality and Social Psychology, 45*, 101–117.

Skaggs, M. J., & Jodl, K. M. (1999). Adolescent adjustment in nonstepfamilies and stepfamilies. *Monographs of the Society for Research in Child Development, 64*, 1–25.

Suchindran, C. M., Koo, H. P., & Griffith, J. D. (1985). The effects of post-marital childbearing on divorce and remarriage: An application of hazards models with time-dependent covariates. *Population Studies, 39*, 471–486.

Sweeney, M. M. (2002). Remarriage and the nature of divorce: Does it matter which spouse chose to leave? *Journal of Family Issues, 23*, 410–440.

Teachman, J., Tedrow, L., & Hall, M. (2006). The demographic future of divorce and dissolution. In M. A. Fine & J. H. Harvey (Eds.), *Handbook of divorce and relationship dissolution* (pp. 59–82). Mahwah, NJ: Lawrence Erlbaum.

Umana-Taylor, A. J., & Alfaro, E. C. (2006). Divorce and relationship dissolution among Latino populations in the United States. In M. A. Fine & J. H. Harvey (Eds.), *Handbook of divorce and relationship dissolution* (pp. 515–530). Mahwah, NJ: Lawrence Erlbaum.

Wilson, B. F., & Clarke, S. C. (1992). Remarriages: A demographic profile. *Journal of Family Issues, 13*, 123–141.

Wood, J. T. (2004). *Interpersonal communication: Everyday encounters.* Belmont, CA: Wadsworth.

Wysocki, D. K. (1998). Let your fingers do the talking: Sex on an adult chatline. *Sexualities, 1*, 425–452.

Yurchisin, J., Watchravesringkan, K., & McCabe, D. B. (2005). An exploration of identity re-creation in the context of Internet dating. *Advances in Consumer Research, 32*, 193–194.

Zemke, R., Raines, C., & Filipczak, B. (2000). *Generations at work.* New York: American Management Association.

21

"Thanks, but No Thanks ..."
The Occurrence and Management of Unwanted Relationship Pursuit

WILLIAM R. CUPACH and BRIAN H. SPITZBERG

S ome relationships grow out of spontaneous interactions between people; others are strategically sought. In either case, relationships are normally thought of as conjunctive affairs. Their emergence and development suggest that the parties, at least to some degree, possess compatible goals, experience forms of mutuality, and coordinate their actions. Unfortunately, some relationships are *disjunctive* in nature, reflecting nonmutuality and a mismatching of goals and expectations. One prototypical form of disjunctive relationship occurs when two people desire different levels of connection with one another. Although relationship initiations can represent conjunctive efforts, they exhibit disjunction when one person resists and eschews the efforts of another person to (a) begin a new relationship, (b) initiate a new kind of relationship (e.g., escalate intimacy in an existing relationship), or (c) rekindle a terminated relationship. These forms of incompatibility sometimes lead to unwanted relationship pursuit, with the person who desires more connection persistently trying to get closer to the person who wants less connection (Cupach & Spitzberg, 2004a; Spitzberg & Cupach, 2001, 2002). Unwanted relationship pursuit can produce feelings of embarrassment, anger, or rejection for the pursuer. For the rejecting person, unwanted pursuit can be associated with feelings of guilt, awkwardness, annoyance, and in some cases fear. In the present chapter we explicate the phenomenon of unwanted relationship pursuit. In addition to describing its various forms, we consider the factors that motivate its persistence, and we review the manifestations and consequences of various responses to unwanted pursuit. We conclude with suggestions for advancing a research agenda on this phenomenon.

THE ORIGINS OF UNWANTED RELATIONSHIP PURSUIT

Unwanted relationship pursuit occurs when two individuals possess and pursue incompatible goals regarding the type of relationship (if any) they desire to have with one another. The incompatibility may simply reflect the fact that one person wants to interact and the other person does not. Or it can reveal itself when two people do not want to share the same *kind* of relationship, such as when one person desires friendship and the other pursues romance (e.g., Bleske-Rechek & Buss, 2001; Reeder, 2000; Schneider & Kenny, 2000). It should not be surprising that unwanted relationship initiations are commonplace. Attractions are not always mutual, and most people can recall experiences of unreciprocated lust and/or unrequited love (Aron, Aron, & Allen, 1998; Baumeister, Wotman, & Stillwell, 1993; Bratslavsky, Baumeister, & Sommer, 1998; Cupach & Spitzberg, 2004b; Hill,

Blakemore, & Drumm, 1997; Sinclair & Frieze, 2000; Tennov, 1970, 1998) Often when romantic relationships terminate, one of the partners would prefer the relationship to continue (Hill, Rubin, & Peplau, 1976; Sprecher, Felmlee, Metts, Fehr, & Vanni, 1998).

The circumstances of unwanted relationship pursuit are varied, ranging from the simple and mundane to the complex and exotic. These include being entrapped in an unwanted conversation (Kellermann, Reynolds, & Chen, 1991; Kellermann & Park, 2001; Reynolds, 1991), receiving undesired dating requests (Folkes, 1982; Paulson & Roloff, 1997), repelling flirtatious overtures (Metts & Spitzberg, 1996; Snow, Robinson, & McCall, 1991), resisting unwanted sexual advances (Afifi & Lee, 2000; Motley & Reeder, 1995; Murnen, Perot, & Byrne, 1989), rejecting those who want to be included in a relationship or group (Leary, 2005), rejecting bids for escalating relational closeness, and refusing to reconcile with a former relational partner (Bevan, Cameron, & Dillow, 2003). Some unwanted relationship pursuit is innocuous and tolerated. Unwanted expressions of interest can be fleeting and sometimes extinguished by ignoring them or by politely but strategically retreating from the interaction (e.g., Kellermann et al., 1991). Unwanted pursuit is problematic to the extent it becomes persistent. A common denominator of these forms of unwanted pursuit is the disjunctive goal structure underlying the interaction (Cupach & Spitzberg, 2004a), and an interaction structure involving reciprocal compliance-seeking and compliance-resisting attempts (Dillard, Anderson, & Knobloch, 2002; Wilson, 2002).

PERSISTENCE OF UNWANTED RELATIONSHIP PURSUIT

Persistence characterizes relationship initiations that are expressly rejected by the pursued party but nevertheless repeated by the pursuer (Cupach & Spitzberg, 1998, 2004a). Thus, when a pursued individual explicitly conveys that the initiation behaviors are unwelcome, continued or escalated initiation attempts represent excessive and sometimes obsessive behavior. Persistent unwanted initiations have been studied under various rubrics, including forcible interaction (Dunn, 1999, 2002), obsessive relational intrusion (Asada, Lee, Levine, & Ferrara, 2004; Cupach & Spitzberg, 1998, 2000; Spitzberg, Nicastro, & Cousins, 1998), unwanted pursuit behavior (Dutton & Winstead, 2006; Langhinrichsen-Rohling, Palarea, Cohen, & Rohling, 2000), intrusive contact (Haugaard & Seri, 2003, 2004), postbreakup harassment (Davis, Ace, & Andra, 2000; Jason, Reichler, Easton, Neal, & Wilson, 1984), courtship persistence (Williams & Frieze, 2005), reconciliation persistence (Cupach, Spitzberg, Younghans, & Gibbons, 2006), disengagement resistance (Buchanan, O'Hair, & Becker, 2006), obsessional following (Meloy, 1996a, 1996b), and stalking (Logan, Cole, Shannon, & Walker, 2006; Morewitz, 2003; Mullen, Pathé, & Purcell, 2000).

For various reasons, the boundary between normal relationship pursuit and excessively persistent pursuit can be fuzzy (Cupach & Spitzberg, 2004a). First, individuals differ from each other in how much unwanted pursuit they expect to receive and are willing to tolerate. Second, a person can experience ambivalence regarding whether a pursuer's efforts are wanted or unwanted. Third, a person's persistence threshold can differ across relationship pursuers, such that more persistent pursuit is accepted from one pursuer whereas less persistence is tolerated from another pursuer. Fourth, there are likely to be cultural differences in how much pursuit is considered normal, thus exacerbating threshold differences in intercultural interactions.

Relationship pursuit behaviors initially may not be recognized as such. Relationship initiation and escalation strategies are mostly indirect and prosocial. Similarly, flirtation behaviors are intentionally ambiguous, in part to allow deniability of intent (Egland, Spitzberg, & Zormeier, 1996; Metts & Spitzberg, 1996; Sabini & Silver, 1982). Relationship pursuers seek affinity, test affinity, reduce uncertainty, and escalate intimacy through such behaviors as acting pleasant, giving compliments, displaying similarity, asking questions, self-disclosing, presenting a positive image, being attentive, and showing nonverbal immediacy (Baxter & Philpott, 1982; Baxter & Wilmot, 1984; Bell & Daly, 1984; Berger, 1979, 1987; Clark, Shaver, & Abrahams, 1999; Daly & Kreiser, 1994; Muehlenhard, Koralewski, Andrews, & Burdick, 1986; Tolhuizen, 1989). These behaviors are subtle and ingratiating, inviting different interpretations. They can simply represent friendly, cordial, and polite forms of social interaction. Alternatively, they may reflect an intention to develop an ongoing relationship or escalate the intimacy of an existing relationship. Thus, one may be the object of (unwanted) relationship pursuit without realizing it. The friendly behaviors and pleasant interaction are not necessarily unwanted; rather, it is the unknown relational intention that is undesired. Indeed, some research indicates that victims of unwanted relationship pursuit often view the experience with considerable ambivalence, perceiving it as simultaneously threatening and romantic, aversive and positive, and frustrating and flattering (e.g., Dunn, 1999, 2002; Haugaard & Seri, 2003, 2004).

Even if the unreciprocated relational intention is surmised, it can take several episodes of interaction for persistence of undesired relational pursuit to become salient. Behaviors that initially seem normal and innocuous become more disturbing when they are repeated and intensified over time. As Cupach and Spitzberg (2004a) indicated, "[T]he obsessive nature of persistent pursuit can emerge subtly and incrementally as ordinary bids for intimacy gradually appear more desperate and unregulated" (p. 27; see also Spitzberg & Cupach, 2002). Indeed, it is the cumulative impact of ongoing pursuit behaviors that evidences their persistence. As Emerson and colleagues (Emerson, Ferris, & Gardner, 1998) suggested,

> The core activities of "pre-stalking," activities such as writing, calling, following, visiting, and gathering information about the other, also mark familiar, everyday courtship and uncoupling practices. Those who become the focus of such attention may initially frame these activities as romantic pursuit or friendship-building, only later reinterpreting them as stalking. (p. 292)

Persistence of unwanted pursuit occurs in varying degrees (Cupach & Spitzberg, 1998). Frequent contacts and overt relational bids (e.g., date requests) are annoying, but not particularly bothersome. *Mild persistence* involves typical affinity-seeking and flirtation behavior, as well as maneuvers to be in proximity to the object of pursuit. This includes pursuit behaviors such as unexpectedly "showing up" or approaching the object of pursuit in public places, giving gifts and other tokens, using third parties to obtain information or access to the object, and contacting the object by telephone, e-mail, letters, and the like (Cupach & Spitzberg, 2004a; Spitzberg & Cupach, 2007).

As pursuit becomes more pestering and invasive of the pursued person's privacy, it is *moderately persistent* and more aggravating and inconvenient. Moderately persistent pursuit behaviors include surveillance of the object of pursuit (i.e., observing, following, and driving by), trespassing, stealing information, stealing property, badgering the object's network members, damaging the object's reputation, and other forms of harassment and intimidation (Cupach & Spitzberg, 2004a; Spitzberg & Cupach, 2007).

When pursuers behave desperately and are unrelenting in their pursuit activities, persistence seems "creepy" and is considered *severe*. Severe pursuit can induce fear in the pursued individual (or at least the average person would be frightened), in which case the unwanted pursuit constitutes *stalking* (Cupach & Spitzberg, 2004a; Tjaden & Thoennes, 1998). Although stalking can reflect various motives, it most commonly represents a campaign to establish or reestablish relational connection (Cupach & Spitzberg, 2004a). Ironically, the obsessive relationship pursuer can demonstrate coercive, threatening, abusive, and violent behavior—actions that seem contrary to the goal of pursuing a relationship. A descriptive meta-analysis of dozens of studies of stalking indicates that about 54% of stalking cases involve some use of threat, 32% involve physical violence, and 12% involve sexual violence (Spitzberg & Cupach, 2007).

When rejection leads an obsessive pursuer to abandon pursuit of intimacy, the desire for revenge can perpetuate stalking activity. Cupach and Spitzberg (2004a) explained,

> In these cases, the underlying motivation for stalking transforms from seeking a relationship to salving the wounds of humiliation. Such transformations may be gradual or sudden, and it is not uncommon for desperate relationship pursuers to intersperse messages of both affinity and vengefulness as manifestations of their own dialectical struggle with the competing motives of rage and romance. (p. ix)

As much as the frequency and type of pursuit behaviors, the *duration* of unwanted pursuit reflects persistence. Jason and colleagues (1984) studied a group of 50 women who terminated or refused a romantic relationship and subsequently were harassed for at least one month by their pursuer. They found that the harassment lasted an average of 13 months, and in one case it lasted 10 years. In a descriptive meta-analysis of 28 studies of stalking, we found that the average duration of stalking behavior was 22 months (Spitzberg & Cupach, 2007). A nationally representative sample of stalking victims revealed that 25% of victims were stalked for 2 to 5 years, and 10% were stalked for more than 5 years (Tjaden & Thoennes, 1998). Purcell, Pathé, and Mullen (2004) identified a 2-week threshold: Those who experienced unwanted intrusions for less than 2 weeks experienced an average of 5 such intrusions, most often by strangers (75.5%), and those who were harassed for over 2 weeks experienced an average of 20 intrusions, most often by previously acquainted persons (82.5%). Those experiencing the more "protracted" types of intrusion also reported significantly greater levels of threat, physical assault, and property damage. The duration of unwanted pursuit undoubtedly contributes to its aversiveness and distress for the pursued individual.

FACTORS THAT CONTRIBUTE TO THE PERSISTENCE OF UNWANTED RELATIONSHIP INITIATION

Numerous factors have been proposed to account for unwanted relationship pursuit (for review, see Cupach & Spitzberg, 2004a). Three common causal explanations for stalking, for example, include psychopathology, interpersonal skill deficits, and attachment losses. It is commonly assumed that individual pathologies such as borderline personality disorder, antisocial personality disorder, and schizophrenia might be root causes of stalking. Indeed, in the population of stalkers who come to the attention of law enforcement and forensic counseling, such presenting diagnoses are not rare. In a large database of clinical stalking cases, 46% had some "clear or probable DSM-IV-TR diagnosis at the time of the stalking" (Mohandie, Meloy, McGowan, & Williams, 2006, p. 149), although there is relatively little evidence that these domains of pathology are common among the general population of persistent and unwanted relationship pursuers (for review, see Cupach & Spitzberg, 2004a). Furthermore, despite their assumed relevance, diagnosed psychiatric disorders tend to reduce the likelihood of violence in stalking cases, rather than increase the likelihood (Rosenfeld & Lewis, 2005). Another common assumption, apparently more directly encountered in clinical experience than in large-scale samples, is that unwanted pursuers tend to lack social skills and interpersonal competence (Meloy, 1996b; Mullen et al., 2000). Clinical samples of persistent pursuers also tend to reveal a history of one or more significant attachment losses (Meloy, 1996b), consistent with research demonstrating associations between insecure attachment styles and the perpetration of unwanted pursuit (e.g., Dutton & Winstead, 2006; Langhinrichsen-Rohling & Rohling, 2000). Consistent with all three associations, stalkers are far more likely to be single, divorced, or separated than married or in a relationship (Mohandie et al., 2006). Despite the promise of such "disorder" approaches, here we concentrate on two additional sets of more proximal variables that might better explain how ordinary relationship initiation can turn into unwanted persistence. First, we summarize some cultural and contextual factors that catalyze persistence of relationship pursuit. These influences emerge out of life experiences as well as portrayals in popular media. Then we review relational goal pursuit theory, which explains why some individuals become disinhibited in their pursuit of a relationship that is rejected by the pursued party.

Cultural and Contextual Catalysts of Unwanted Relationship Pursuit

Relationships are initiated and constructed in tacit ways. Because "the details of relationship definition are neither explicitly negotiated nor precisely codified in verifiable text," there is ample opportunity for misunderstanding (Cupach & Spitzberg, 2004a, p. 21). Ordinarily people do not explicitly discuss the relational implications of their utterances and gestures (Baxter & Wilmot, 1985). Rather, they enact "a web of ambiguity" by which they signal their relationship goals and intentions (Baxter, 1987). Consequently, the relational meanings that two individuals respectively ascribe to their shared interactions can diverge in significant ways. One person's casual conversation can be another person's bid for a more serious relationship. Flirtation can mean playful teasing to one person, whereas it conveys serious sexual invitation to another (Abbey, 1987; Metts & Spitzberg, 1996). Polite evasion of relationship escalation cues can be taken as acceptance or encouragement. One can be the object of relationship pursuit and not even realize it. It is difficult to reject the intentions of another when it is not clear what the intentions are. In the absence of overt rejection, relationship pursuit tends to persist.

Further contributing to the persistence of relationship pursuit is the occurrence of token resistance. Although studied originally in the context of feigning lack of interest in sex (Muehlenhard & Hollabaugh, 1988; Sprecher, Hatfield, Cortese, Potapova, & Levitskaya, 1994), token resistance extends to romantic relationship formation in the form of "playing hard to get." Potential relationship partners do not want to reciprocate romantic interest prematurely lest they be perceived as desperate or undiscerning. Moreover, if a pursued object of affection initially rebuffs bids for a relationship, then the pursuer presumably will value the relationship even more when it is attained. Thus, a pursuer may have difficulty determining if an initial rejection is token or real. Optimism tilts the interpretation toward *token*.

Just as relationship initiations exhibit elements of ambiguity, so do relationship breakups and reinitiations. Because breakups often are not mutually desired (e.g., Clark & Labeff, 1986; Hill et al., 1976), it is not uncommon for a former partner to seek reconciliation (Bevan et al., 2003; Patterson & O'Hair, 1992; Wineberg, 1994). Even the partner who initiated termination can have a "change of heart" and seek to reestablish the relationship (Vaughan, 1986). In a study of terminated romantic relationships, Langhinrichsen-Rohling et al. (2000, p. 77) found that 40% of the participants "had broken up at least once previous to the breakup they were describing." Indeed, some couples break up and get back together again several times before their relationship stabilizes or dissolves permanently. In Dunn's (2002) investigation of stalking victims, 30% "had left their partners repeatedly prior to prosecution for stalking, and 7.6 percent of victims resumed a relationship with the defendant during prosecution" (p. 77). A history of success in seeking reconciliation reinforces the persistence of future reconciliation attempts. One study found that the number of prior breakups with a particular partner was positively associated with the persistence of pursuit behaviors following the most recent breakup with that partner (Davis et al., 2000). In another study, the frequency of prior reconciliations reported by the pursued partner was positively associated with the current frequency of the pursuing partner's reconciliation attempts and the perceived degree of reconciliation pursuit persistence (Cupach & Metts, 2002).

Whether pursuing an initial relationship or attempting to reconcile a terminated one, persistence is fueled by the cultural script that success is a function of effort. In virtually all facets of life we are taught, "If at first you don't succeed, try, try again"; "No pain, no gain"; "Quitters never win, and winners never quit"; "Persistence pays off"; "If you fall off the horse, get right back up in the saddle"; and "Nice guys finish last." Persistence is self-reinforcing precisely because it pays off so frequently, and this appears to apply to the pursuit of relationships as much as it does to other important goals. Indeed, some degree of relationship pursuit persistence is normally expected and thereby tolerated by those who are pursued.

Another complicating factor that promotes persistent relationship pursuit is that rejection is typically conveyed in an ambiguous fashion (Emerson et al., 1998; Folkes, 1982; Metts & Spitzberg, 1996). It is assumed that relationship initiations are well intentioned, so refusals tend to be indirect and conform to norms of politeness. This accomplishes rejection in a face-preserving way (e.g., Cupach & Metts, 1994; Metts, Cupach, & Imahori, 1992), and expiates some of the guilt experienced by rejecters (Bratslavsky et al., 1998). The mixed cues conveyed by polite rejection also derive from the ambivalent feelings that pursued individuals experience. Because they are recipients of messages communicating liking and attraction, pursued individuals can experience flattery at the same time they are feeling annoyance or even fear. Dunn (1999, 2002) demonstrated that the trappings of romance and courtship, such as flowers and gifts, contribute to mixed responses to unwanted relationship pursuit. These potent symbols serve to undermine a "sense of invasion by triggering ambivalence and confusion and thus masking the intrusive, instrumental character of interaction that follows the expressed desire that such interaction cease" (Dunn, 1999, p. 455).

The collective suggestion of these tacit moves and countermoves has led some to liken the process of courtship to a delicately choreographed game (e.g., Cunningham, 1989; McCormick & Jesser, 1983; Rosenthal & Peart, 1996). Games and their rules can be negotiated with lesser or greater clarity, but one of the obvious complicating factors is that each individual in the game also is engaged in a constant process of sense making, and sometimes that sense making goes wrong. We propose a theory to account for the development of such disordered perceptions that provide an individual the engine for disordered play.

Relational Goal Pursuit Theory

Relational goal pursuit theory (Cupach & Spitzberg, 2004a; Cupach, Spitzberg, & Carson, 2000; Spitzberg & Cupach, 2001, 2002) is predicated on the assumption that individuals pursue relationships because they are desired end states. As with all goals, the effort exerted to pursue a particular relational goal is commensurate with the extent to which it is perceived to be desirable and attainable (DiPaula & Campbell, 2002; Locke & Latham, 1990). When goal achievement is blocked, goal pursuit is intensified. Goal striving continues as long as the goal is seen as attainable and worth the effort. When the costs of pursuing a goal exceed the value of its attainment, or when goal achievement is deemed impossible, then the goal is abandoned in favor of pursuing an alternative goal. According to relational goal pursuit theory, individuals who persistently pursue a relationship with another person who expressly rejects the relationship tend to exaggerate the importance and feasibility of their relational goal. This leads the pursuer to experience a constellation of thoughts and emotions that drive escalated goal striving—that is, intensified relationship goal pursuit.

An individual's goals are organized hierarchically (Martin & Tesser, 1989). Goals lower in the hierarchy often serve to facilitate the attainment of higher order goals. For instance, the lower order goal of getting good grades in school can be a pathway to achieving the higher order goal of obtaining a prestigious and well-paying job. Goals lower in one's hierarchy are generally easier to discard or replace compared to those higher in the hierarchy. The student who fails to get the desired grades in school might decide that the alternative lower order goal of cultivating family business connections is a good pathway to the prestigious, well-paying job.

Some individuals exhibit the propensity to link lower order goals to higher order goals (McIntosh, 1996; McIntosh, Harlow, & Martin, 1995). *Linking* occurs when an individual views the attainment of higher order goals to be contingent upon the attainment of specific lower order goals. In other words, certain lower order goals must be fulfilled in the service of higher order goals, rendering the lower order goals less substitutable and less likely to be abandoned in the face of obstacles. Relational goal pursuit theory proposes that persistent relationship pursuers link the lower order goal of having a relationship with a particular person with higher order goals such as life happiness and self-worth (Carson & Cupach, 2000; Cupach et al., 2000). The pursuer believes that attaining life happiness and self-worth is contingent upon having the desired relationship. This greatly exaggerates the importance of the relational goal because there can be no substitute for the desired relationship. The inflated desirability of the relational goal, in turn, fosters persistent and intensified relational goal striving, even in the face of obstacles and rejection (Cupach et al., 2006; Kam & Spitzberg, 2005).

Linking, coupled with the nonattainment of the relational goal, fosters rumination (McIntosh et al., 1995; McIntosh & Martin, 1992). Failing to meet an important goal produces repeated, intrusive, persistent, and unpleasant thoughts (Martin & Tesser, 1989, 1996). The pursuer anticipates the emotional consequences of failing to achieve the relational goal, imagining sadness, distress, and anguish (Bagozzi, Baumgartner, & Pieters, 1998). By this time, many pursuers may give up because their cognitions are too aversive or they believe they lack the efficacy to achieve their intimacy goals with a given person; this may explain why 45% of the unwanted intruders in Purcell et al.'s (2004) study stopped their intrusions within 2 weeks of initiation. Among those for whom the relational goal is highly important to their sense of self-worth, however, persistent pursuers are likely to make "dire predictions about the emotional impact of such failure" (Pomerantz, Saxon, & Oishi, 2000, p. 618). Ruminative thoughts intensify over time and tend to be self-perpetuating. Attempts to suppress these thoughts usually backfire as rebound effects exacerbate subsequent rumination (Wegner, Schneider, Carter, & White, 1987). Because rumination is aversive, the perceived pathway to relief is relational goal attainment. Thus, rumination fosters persistence in goal striving (e.g., Carson & Cupach, 2000; Dennison & Stewart, 2006).

Unmet relational goals can lead to a vicious cycle of escalating negative thoughts and feelings that reinforce one another. Thwarted goals stimulate negative emotions (Berscheid, 1983; Lazarus, 1991) and rumination (Martin & Tesser, 1989, 1996). Rumination fosters more negative affect (McIntosh & Martin, 1992), and negative affect leads to further rumination as the aversive feelings are a constant reminder of the unmet goal (Martin & Tesser, 1996). Persistent pursuers experience emotional flooding—that is, an overwhelming and unpleasant physiological arousal (Cupach et al., 2006; Dutton-Greene, 2004). In addition to diffuse emotional flooding, certain discrete emotions—particularly the combination of anger and jealousy—predict persistent unwanted relationship pursuit (Davis et al., 2000; Dutton-Greene, 2004). Many of the ways that people respond to feeling jealous mirror obsessive pursuit behaviors (e.g., surveillance, sending flowers, being especially nice, arguing, and so forth; Carson & Cupach, 2000; Guerrero, Andersen, Jorgensen, Spitzberg, & Eloy, 1995).

Finally, persistent pursuers rationalize their excessive pursuit behaviors in a number of ways. They idealize the sought-after partner and downplay the potential partner's faults, they justify persistence in the name of a noble cause (e.g., love), they overlook the adverse consequences of their actions for the pursued partner, and they misconstrue responses of avoidance and rejection as signs of affection and encouragement (Cupach et al., 2000; Spitzberg & Cupach, 2001, 2002). Moreover, persistent pursuers possess exaggerated self-efficacy with regard to pursuing the difficult relational goal (Bagozzi, 1992; Cupach et al., 2006). They rationalize that relational goal achievement is attainable with persistent effort. Normal relational pursuers would abandon a relational goal, even a highly desirable one, once the goal is seen as illusory. Persistent pursuers, however, continue to believe that goal achievement is possible, even with apparent evidence to the contrary. Their intense and exaggerated thoughts and feelings reinforce the desirability and feasibility of the relational goal and inflate their conception of what constitutes an appropriate level of effort for obtaining the desired goal, thereby enabling relational pursuit that is obsessive and excessive.

RESPONSES TO UNWANTED RELATIONSHIP PURSUIT

Much research and theory have examined the initiation, progressive development, deescalation, and eventual ending of relationships. Far less examined are the processes involving "failure to launch" in relationships: those relationships in which an attempt is made to initiate or escalate a relationship, but the pursuer's initiation is stalled by the response of the person pursued. There are, however, various relatively isolated literatures investigating peripherally related types of episodes.

Although it is not generally discussed in relation to avoiding unwanted relationship initiation, several lines of research have examined various ways in which people create unpleasant, unlikable, or unattractive impressions. The study of obnoxious (Davis & Schmidt, 1977), boring (Leary, Rogers, Canfield, & Coe, 1986), troublesome (Levitt, Silver, & Franco, 1996), hurtful (Leary, Springer, Negel, Ansell, & Evans, 1998; Vangelisti, 2007), guilt-inducing (Miceli, 1992; Vangelisti, Daly, & Rudnick, 1991), embarrassing (Bradford & Petronio, 1998; Sharkey, 1992), and egotistical (Leary, Bednarski, Hammon, & Duncan, 1997) persons reveals quite an arsenal of interactional weapons through which people deter or sour relations with others. Indeed, research by Kellermann and Lee (2001) found that respondents reported a mean of two times every 3 months intentionally trying to make someone *not* like them, and they also report a similar rate (.79 per month) of others attempting to get the respondent to dislike the other person. They identified five types of disaffinity-seeking tactics: objectionable acts (e.g., be spiteful, be mean, or be physical), subtle opposition (e.g., act uncomfortable, bring in an ally, or be uncooperative), perspective taking (e.g., differentiate: "You aren't seeing things from my point of view"; or tell stories: describe a personal experience, real or fictional, that illustrates why the person should stay away), personal attack (e.g., verbally abuse other, or directly reject other), and refusals (e.g., turn away). Only 4% of their sample considered their efforts as completely ineffective. It appears that when motivated, and unconcerned with their own portrayed image, individuals have a rich set of tactical options for diminishing the average pursuer's interests. However, some pursuers have particular relational goals that may be more challenging to deter.

Other literatures have addressed the ways in which individuals respond to undesired relationships. These include investigations regarding how individuals respond to sexual harassment (e.g., Clair, McGoun, & Spirek, 1993; Firestone & Harris, 2003), resist unwanted sexual advances and flirtatious overtures (e.g., Afifi & Lee, 2000; Cochran, Frazier, & Olson, 1997; Snow et al., 1991), and manage unpleasant or undesired relationships in the workplace (e.g., Fritz, 1997; Sias & Perry, 2004). It is beyond the scope of the present chapter to review these extensive literatures. However, they tend to show similar functional categories of response. People can be passive, avoidant, aggressive, or integrative, or seek external assistance. That these five categories may represent a relatively exhaustive typology of potential responses to unwanted pursuit is evidenced by an extensive inductive coding of almost 500 tactics reported by stalking victims across 58 studies (Cupach & Spitzberg, 2004a).

Assisted initially by Horney's (1945) distinctions, Cupach and Spitzberg (2004a; see also Cupach & Spitzberg, 2004b; Spitzberg, 2002; Spitzberg & Cupach, 2007) identified five clusters of responses to stalking that reflect functional or directional strategies: moving inward, moving outward, moving away, moving with, and moving against. *Moving inward* represents efforts at denial, distraction, or redefinition, which would include activities such as becoming more socially isolated, practicing meditation, seeking release through drugs or exercise, or pursuing deeper faith. *Moving outward* tactics include efforts to seek contact or assistance from police, counselors, institutional authorities, friends, family, Samaritans, or religious authorities. *Moving away* tactics are those behaviors that function to help one avoid contact with the pursuer, including walking away, treating the pursuer as a nonentity, changing routines, increasing societal invisibility (e.g., delisting one's phone number, obtaining a P.O. box, and removing information from publicly accessible sources such as the Internet), and enhancing security at home, work, school, or other destinations. *Moving with* tactics represent attempts to negotiate a workable, more conjunctive relationship with the pursuer. The "relationship talk" about the need to "just be friends" is a prototypical example, but this strategy would include various sorts of reasoning and civil tactics of persuasion. Finally, *moving against* tactics attempt to deter through fear, coercion, aggression, and/or punishment of the pursuer. These tactics may involve not only direct aggression against the pursuer by the pursued, but also threats or actions that invoke legal or third-party aggression against the pursuer.

One of the most formal responses, which involves a form of moving against in the hope of moving away, is to seek a protective order against the pursuer. Protective orders are legal orders, issued by a judge, that specify conditions of access and proximity between the persons. In many jurisdictions, protective orders can be either civil or criminal, and violation of such orders can increase the penalties from misdemeanor to felony status. Research across 40 studies of protective orders, mostly among domestic violence victims, indicates that such orders are violated about 40% of the time and are perceived to make matters worse about a fifth of the time (Cupach & Spitzberg, 2004a; Spitzberg, 2002; Spitzberg & Cupach, 2007). However, Johnson, Luna, and Stein (2003) found that even when domestic violence victims indicated that the orders were violated, 48% of the women perceived the orders to have been effective, even when the violation involved violence. Indeed, only 17% of the women whose orders were *not* violated considered the orders ineffective. It appears that protective orders provide the plaintiff a measure of satisfaction merely by virtue of their official recognition of the seriousness of the situation.

There is surprisingly little research directly addressing the effectiveness of tactics in reducing or ending unwanted pursuit. Several studies have asked whether direct communication with the pursuer, or direct requests to stop, have been successful. The results suggest that such tactics are not very effective: 6% (Blackburn, 1999), 12% (Bjerregaard, 2000), 37.5% (Dutton-Greene & Winstead, 2001), and 10% (Tjaden & Thoennes, 1998). Direct communication or requests to stop were not even mentioned by Sheridan, Davies, and Boon's (2001) sample of British victims as attributed reasons why the stalking stopped. In one of the few studies to ask pursuers why they stopped their pursuit, Dutton-Greene and Winstead (2001) found that pursuers were more likely than victims to claim that they ended their pursuit due to direct communication from the object of pursuit, with a comparable 11.5% due to indirect communication, 11.5% due to victim avoidance, 8% due to a third party intervening, and 8% due to the elapse of time. Ironically, 4% of the pursuers and 12.5% of the victims indicated that the reason the pursuit ended was because they renewed their relationship with each other.

When victims are asked to attribute the cause of stalking ending, a variety of reasons are provided that do not appear particularly rooted in purely interactional strategies. Victims in Sheridan et al.'s (2001) sample attributed the cessation to the victim moving (25%), the arrest of the pursuer (14%), the victim's new partner (11%), and the pursuer moving (11%). Similarly, Walby and Allen's (2004) sample attributed the end to changing a phone number or address (16% of the men, and 24% of the women), the threat of legal intervention (19% men, 19% women), the involvement of informal third parties (5% men, 12% women), and moving away (6% men, 9% women). In the large-scale representative study by Tjaden and Thoennes (1998), victims were most likely to attribute the reason for the stalking ending to the victim moving (19%), the stalker getting a new love interest (18%), the stalker being warned by the police (15%), the victim having a talk with the pursuer (10%), the stalker being arrested (9%), the stalker moving (7%), the stalker obtaining assistance or counseling (6%), the victim getting a new love interest (4%), the death of the stalker (4%), the stalker being convicted (1%), or the stalking simply stopping (3%).

Blackburn (1999) observed that different forms of unwanted pursuit were perceived to stop for different reasons. Unwanted telephone calls, for example, were thought to stop because the number was changed (23%), the pursuer was told to stop (19%), someone was told about the harassment (12%), or the pursuer became interested in another target (8%). Unwanted following behavior, in contrast, was thought to stop because of a restraining order (18%), the victim moved (18%), police intervention (16%), someone was told about the pursuit (10%), the pursuer became interested in someone else (8%), the victim's routine pattern of behavior changed (7%), or the pursuer was told to stop (7%).

Such diverse findings suggest glimmers of hope for victims, but studies investigating the extent to which *any* tactics are perceived to improve their situation are not particularly optimistic. Jason et al. (1984) interviewed women who had been harassed after breaking up, and found that the more assertive the women were in attempting to end the relationship, the longer the harassment lasted, the more frequent the harassment was, and the more threatening and disruptive it was. In her interviews, Brewster (1998) reported, "Of the 408 reported types of discouragement, victims reported behavior improvements following only 37 (9.1%) of these attempts" (p. 47). All of the extralegal attempts had no effect or a negative effect according to the majority of the victims interviewed. Indeed, even though 80.2% of the victims claimed to have also sought various legal sources of assistance to discourage the stalker, 77% indicated that "police involvement either had no effect or made the stalkers' behavior worse" (p. 48). Sheridan (2001) found in a small British sample that although 41% of stalking victims thought that various actions helped to reduce their stalking (e.g., legal interventions, ignoring the stalker, and threatening the stalker), an equal proportion (41%) thought that certain actions worsened the situation (e.g., legal interventions, victim getting involved with someone new, and going into hiding).

Spitzberg and Cupach (in press) asked college students who had experienced someone seeking more intimacy with them than they were comfortable having or returning to rate 40 coping tactics derived from the five functional strategies (e.g., moving inward and moving against) in terms of their appropriateness and effectiveness. They found that the vast majority of tactics were rated below the theoretical scale midpoints, suggesting that such tactics are generally not viewed as particularly competent. Despite the distinct implications of concerns for appropriateness versus effectiveness, there were few differences in ratings of tactics across these two dimensions, suggesting that rejection and resistance per se are difficult to achieve successfully. Finally, women tended to perceive more of the tactics as appropriate and effective than men did, supporting the cultural script that women tend to be more specialized in the role of rejecting advances, and men tend to be more specialized in the role of pursuing (Cate & Lloyd, 1992).

Collectively, the varied research indicates that no strategy is effective a majority of the time in ending unwanted pursuit. Furthermore, given that the average case of stalking lasts almost 2 years (Cupach & Spitzberg, 2004a; Spitzberg & Cupach, 2007), and given that the victim-reported tactic totals add up to more than 100%, it is obvious that over the course of such unwanted relationship pursuits, victims try multiple tactics to deter their pursuer, and these tactics characteristically and repeatedly fail.

As pessimistic as this conclusion seems, there are some glimmers of hope. First, although moving with the pursuer through reasoning or direct requests to stop infrequently works, it does work occasionally (5 to 40% of the time). Furthermore, any attempt to put off persistent unwanted relationship initiation is likely to require at least one episode of clear, direct, assertive expression of a desire by the victim that the pursuer cease and desist. Second, although those pursued in unwanted ways may seldom prefer to escalate what is often perceived as an informal issue into the courts, when legal remedies are sought, they are generally viewed as effective. Third, much of the research on stalking resistance involves parties who already had ongoing relationships with their pursuer. Approximately 75 to 85% of stalking emerges from preexisting relationships, and about half of stalking victims were romantically involved with their stalker (Cupach & Spitzberg, 2004a; Spitzberg & Cupach, 2007). It seems reasonable to conclude that resisting *initial relationship initiation* will generally be significantly more successful than resisting pursuit by someone who already has a relational history and emotional investment in the relationship (i.e., reinitiation, or initiation of a different type of relationship). This reinforces the importance, however, of articulating "definite" messages of disinterest or obvious messages of disaffinity, and these are tactics that interactants often shy away from because of the cultural imperatives of politeness (Brown & Levinson, 1987). Fourth, there is no dearth of tactical resistance options from which to choose. Cupach and Spitzberg (2004a) identified over 70 distinct tactics by which victims may seek to cope with unwanted pursuit across the five functional categories. If employed early and often in the trajectory of unwanted pursuit, it seems likely that they can have a cumulative impact and a reasonable chance for success, especially if the target explicitly articulates disinterest, avoids further opportunities for interaction, and maintains a willingness to seek more formal remedies should the occasion require.

FUTURE RESEARCH ON UNWANTED RELATIONSHIP PURSUIT

As this *Handbook* attests, much is known about the processes surrounding the initiation of relationships. Less is known, however, about the processes by which unwanted relationship initiations are anticipated and thwarted. We recommend three lines of inquiry that would yield beneficial knowledge. First, research should address how individuals can better detect signals that unwanted relationship pursuit is becoming persistent. What specific patterns of early pursuit behaviors predict the likelihood that the pursuer's future actions will be excessive and obsessive? Many stalking victims see the obsessive pattern of pursuit only in retrospect (Emerson et al., 1998). It is important to discover if there are common *early warning signs* that would forecast eventual stalking, thereby facilitating the early termination of contact with the unwanted pursuer before pursuit activity reaches a tipping point.

Second, more detailed and precise information is needed about the efficacy of various coping responses—particularly those designed to cease unwanted relationship pursuit. Although the numerous coping behaviors have been documented, little is known about the effects of various *combinations and patterns of responses*. A more complete picture of response efficacy needs to take into account both the timing and the sequencing of coping responses. Moreover, it would be valuable to explore pursuit cessation from the perspective of the persistent pursuer. To date, most research has focused on what pursued individuals perceive was effective in halting the unwanted pursuit. Asking persistent pursuers what caused them to finally abandon their relational goal would offer a more complete understanding of how to cease unwanted pursuit (e.g., Dutton-Greene & Winstead, 2001). Hopefully, this additional knowledge will help diminish protracted and persistent forms of unwanted relationship initiations.

Third, given the particularly relational nature of most stalking, future research will need to find avenues for studying the phenomenon dyadically. To date, we know of no studies in which both victim and pursuer perceptions in stalking "dyads" have been studied. It is commonly assumed that the pursuer's perceptions will be more self-serving and distorted than the victim's, but there is relatively little evidence beyond the more pathological and clinical samples to support this view. At some point, studying the ways in which stalkers and unwanted pursuers interpret the victim's coping responses in the context of their particular relational history will be an important key to unlocking the disjunctive nature of the relationship, and identifying better recommendations for victim management of such experiences.

In conclusion, unreciprocated relationship pursuit is usefully viewed as an inherent component of the broader domain of relationship initiations. Research verifies that a substantial number of relationship initiations are unwanted, yet inappropriately persistent. The past decade has yielded a wealth of information regarding the descriptive topography of unwanted relationship pursuit, the motives of persistent pursuers, and the debilitating consequences for those who are obsessively pursued (Cupach & Spitzberg, 2004a). Less understood at this point are the mechanisms that can diminish the occurrence and adverse consequences of persistent unwanted relationship initiation. Further inquiry into this phenomenon will provide better guidance regarding the competent enactment of relationship initiations in general, as well as the productive management of failed relationship initiations.

AUTHOR NOTE

We gratefully acknowledge the helpful feedback on this chapter provided by Laura Guerrero, John Harvey, Susan Sprecher, and Amy Wenzel.

REFERENCES

Abbey, A. (1987). Misperceptions of friendly behavior as sexual interest: A survey of naturally occurring incidents. *Psychology of Women Quarterly, 11*, 173–194.

Afifi, W. A., & Lee, J. W. (2000). Balancing instrumental and identity goals in relationships: The role of request directness and request persistence in the selection of sexual resistance strategies. *Communication Monographs, 67*, 284–305.

Aron, A., Aron, E. N., & Allen, J. (1998). Motivations for unreciprocated love. *Personality and Social Psychology Bulletin, 24*, 787–796.

Asada, K. J. K., Lee, E., Levine, T. R., & Ferrara, M. H. (2004). Narcissism and empathy as predictors of obsessive relational intrusion. *Communication Research Reports, 21*, 379–390.

Bagozzi, R. P. (1992). The self-regulation of attitudes, intentions, and behavior. *Social Psychology Quarterly, 55*, 178–204.

Bagozzi, R. P., Baumgartner, H., & Pieters, R. (1998). Goal-directed emotions. *Cognition and Emotion, 12*, 1–26.

Baumeister, R. F., Wotman, S. R., & Stillwell, A. M. (1993). Unrequited love: On heartbreak, anger, guilt, scriptlessness, and humiliation. *Journal of Personality and Social Psychology, 64*, 377–394.

Baxter, L. A. (1987). Cognition and communication in the relationship process. In R. Burnett, P. McGhee, & D. D. Clarke (Eds.), *Accounting for relationships* (pp. 192–212). London: Methuen.

Baxter, L. A., & Philpott, J. (1982). Attribution-based strategies for initiating and terminating relationships. *Communication Quarterly, 30*, 217–224.

Baxter, L. A., & Wilmot, W. W. (1984). "Secret tests": Strategies for acquiring information about the state of the relationship. *Human Communication Research*, *11*, 171–201.

Baxter, L. A., & Wilmot, W. W. (1985). Taboo topics in close relationships. *Journal of Social and Personal Relationships*, *2*, 253–269.

Bell, R. A., & Daly, J. A. (1984). The affinity-seeking function of communication. *Communication Monographs*, *51*, 91–115.

Berger, C. R. (1979). Beyond initial interaction: Uncertainty, understanding, and the development of interpersonal relationships. In H. Giles & R. St. Clair (Eds.), *Language and social psychology* (pp. 122–144). Oxford: Blackwell.

Berger, C. R. (1987). Communicating under uncertainty. In M. E. Roloff & G. R. Miller (Eds.), *Interpersonal processes: New directions in communication research* (pp. 39–62). Newbury Park, CA: Sage.

Berscheid, E. (1983). Emotion. In H. H. Kelley, E. Berscheid, A. Christensen, J. H. Harvey, T. L. Huston, G. Levinger, E. McClintock, L. A. Peplau, & D. R. Peterson (Eds.), *Close relationships* (pp. 110–168). San Francisco: Freeman.

Bevan, J. L., Cameron, K. A., & Dillow, M. R. (2003). One more try: Compliance-gaining strategies associated with romantic reconciliation attempts. *Southern Communication Journal*, *68*, 121–135.

Bjerregaard, B. (2000). An empirical study of stalking victimization. *Violence and Victims*, *15*, 389–406.

Blackburn, E. J. (1999). *"Forever yours": Rates of stalking victimization, risk factors and traumatic responses among college women*. Unpublished doctoral dissertation, University of Massachusetts, Boston.

Bleske-Rechek, A. L., & Buss, D. M. (2001). Opposite-sex friendship: Sex differences and similarities in initiation, selection, and dissolution. *Personality and Social Psychology Bulletin*, *27*, 1310–1323.

Bradford, L., & Petronio, S. (1998). Strategic embarrassment: The culprit of emotion. In P. A. Andersen & L. K. Guerrero (Eds.), *The handbook of communication and emotion: Theory, application, and contexts* (pp. 99–121). San Diego, CA: Academic.

Bratslavsky, E., Baumeister, R. F., & Sommer, K. L. (1998). To love or be loved in vain: The trials and tribulations of unrequited love. In B. H. Spitzberg & W. R. Cupach (Eds.), *The dark side of close relationships* (pp. 307–326). Mahwah, NJ: Lawrence Erlbaum.

Brewster, M. P. (1998). An exploration of the experiences and needs of former intimate stalking victims (Final report submitted to the National Institute of Justice, NCJ 175475). Washington, DC: National Institute of Justice.

Brown, P., & Levinson, S. (1987). *Politeness: Some universals in language usage*. Cambridge: Cambridge University Press.

Buchanan, M. C., O'Hair, H. D., & Becker, J. A. H. (2006). Strategic communication during marital relationship dissolution: Disengagement resistance strategies. *Communication Research Reports*, *23*, 139–147.

Carson, C. L., & Cupach, W. R. (2000). Fueling the flames of the green-eyed monster: The role of ruminative thought in reaction to romantic jealousy. *Western Journal of Communication*, *64*, 308–329.

Cate, R. M., & Lloyd, S. A. (1992). *Courtship*. Thousand Oaks, CA: Sage.

Clair, R. P., McGoun, M. J., & Spirek, M. M. (1993). Sexual harassment responses of working women: An assessment of communication-oriented typologies and perceived effectiveness of the response. In G. L. Kreps (Ed.), *Sexual harassment: Communication implications* (pp. 209–233). Cresskill, NJ: Hampton Press.

Clark, C. L., Shaver, P. R., & Abrahams, M. F. (1999). Strategic behaviors in romantic relationship initiation. *Personality and Social Psychology Bulletin*, *25*, 707–720.

Clark, R. E., & Labeff, E. E. (1986). Ending intimate relationships: Strategies of breaking off. *Sociological Spectrum*, *6*, 245–267.

Cochran, C. C., Frazier, P. A., & Olson, A. M. (1997). Predictors of responses to unwanted sexual attention. *Psychology of Women Quarterly*, *21*, 207–226.

Cunningham, M. R. (1989). Reactions to heterosexual opening gambits: Female selectivity and male responsiveness. *Personality and Social Psychology Bulletin*, *15*, 27–41.

Cupach, W. R., & Metts, S. (1994). *Facework*. Thousand Oaks, CA: Sage.

Cupach, W. R., & Metts, S. (2002, July). *Face management in romantic uncoupling: Precursors and consequences of relationship disengagement messages*. Paper presented at the 11th International Conference on Personal Relationships, Halifax, NS, Canada.

Cupach, W. R., & Spitzberg, B. H. (1998). Obsessive relational intrusion and stalking. In B. H. Spitzberg & W. R. Cupach (Eds.), *The dark side of close relationships* (pp. 233–263). Mahwah, NJ: Lawrence Erlbaum.

Cupach, W. R., & Spitzberg, B. H. (2000). Obsessive relational intrusion: Incidence, perceived severity, and coping. *Violence and Victims*, *15*, 357–372.

Cupach, W. R., & Spitzberg, B. H. (2004a). *The dark side of relationship pursuit: From attraction to obsession and stalking*. Mahwah, NJ: Lawrence Erlbaum.

Cupach, W. R., & Spitzberg, B. H. (2004b). Unrequited lust. In J. Harvey, A. Wenzel, & S. Sprecher (Eds.), *Handbook of sexuality in close relationships* (pp. 259–286). Mahwah, NJ: Lawrence Erlbaum.

Cupach, W. R., Spitzberg, B. H., & Carson, C. L. (2000). Toward a theory of obsessive relational intrusion and stalking. In K. Dindia & S. Duck (Eds.), *Communication and personal relationships* (pp. 131–146). New York: Wiley.

Cupach, W. R., Spitzberg, B. H., Younghans, C. M., & Gibbons, B. S. (2006, February). *Persistence of attempts to reconcile a terminated romantic relationship: An application and partial test of relational goal pursuit theory.* Paper presented at the Western States Communication Association convention, Palm Springs, CA.

Daly, J. A., & Kreiser, P. O. (1994). Affinity seeking. In J. A. Daly & J. M. Wiemann (Eds.), *Strategic interpersonal communication* (pp. 109–134). Hillsdale, NJ: Lawrence Erlbaum.

Davis, K. E., Ace, A., & Andra, A. (2000). Stalking perpetrators and psychological maltreatment of partners: Anger-jealousy, attachment insecurity, need for control, and break-up context. *Violence and Victims, 15,* 407–425.

Davis, M. S., & Schmidt, C. J. (1977). The obnoxious and the nice: Some sociological consequences of two psychological types. *Sociometry, 40,* 201–213.

Dennison, S. M., & Stewart, A. (2006). Facing rejection: New relationships, broken relationships, shame, and stalking. *International Journal of Offender Therapy and Comparative Criminology, 50,* 324–337.

Dillard, J. P., Anderson, J. W., & Knobloch, L. K. (2002). Interpersonal influence. In M. L. Knapp & J. Daly (Eds.), *Handbook of interpersonal communication* (3rd ed., pp. 425–474). Newbury Park, CA: Sage.

DiPaula, A., & Campbell, J. D. (2002). Self-esteem and persistence in the face of failure. *Journal of Personality and Social Psychology, 83,* 711–724.

Dunn, J. L. (1999). What love has to do with it: The cultural construction of emotion and sorority women's responses to forcible interaction. *Social Problems, 46,* 440–459.

Dunn, J. L. (2002). *Courting disaster: Intimate stalking, culture, and criminal justice.* New York: Aldine de Gruyter.

Dutton, L. B., & Winstead, B. A. (2006). Predicting unwanted pursuit: Attachment, relationship satisfaction, relationship alternatives, and break-up distress. *Journal of Social and Personal Relationships, 23,* 565–586.

Dutton-Greene, L. B. (2004). *Testing a model of unwanted pursuit and stalking.* Unpublished doctoral dissertation, University of Rhode Island.

Dutton-Greene, L. B., & Winstead, B. A. (2001, July). *Factors associated with the occurrence and cessation of obsessive relational intrusion.* Paper presented at the joint conference of the International Network on Personal Relationships and the International Society for the Study of Personal Relationships, Prescott, AZ.

Egland, K. L., Spitzberg, B. H., & Zormeier, M. M. (1996). Flirtation and conversational competence in cross-sex platonic and romantic relationships. *Communication Reports, 9,* 105–118.

Emerson, R. E., Ferris, K. O., & Gardner, C. B. (1998). On being stalked. *Social Problems, 45,* 289–314.

Firestone, J. M., & Harris, R. J. (2003). Perceptions of effectiveness of responses to sexual harassment in the US military, 1988 and 1995. *Gender, Work and Organization, 10,* 42–64.

Folkes, V. S. (1982). Communicating the reasons for social rejection. *Journal of Experimental Social Psychology, 18,* 235–252.

Fritz, J. M. H. (1997). Responses to unpleasant work relationships. *Communication Research Reports, 14,* 302–311.

Guerrero, L. K., Andersen, P. A., Jorgensen, P. F., Spitzberg, B. H., & Eloy, S. V. (1995). Coping with the green-eyed monster: Conceptualizing and measuring communicative responses to romantic jealousy. *Western Journal of Communication, 59,* 270–304.

Haugaard, J. J., & Seri, L. G. (2003). Stalking and other forms of intrusive contact after the dissolution of adolescent dating or romantic relationships. *Violence and Victims, 18,* 279–297.

Haugaard, J. J., & Seri, L. G. (2004). Stalking and other forms of intrusive contact among adolescents and young adults from the perspective of the person initiating the intrusive contact. *Criminal Justice and Behavior, 31,* 37–54.

Hill, C. A., Blakemore, J. E. O., & Drumm, P. (1997). Mutual and unrequited love in adolescence and young adulthood. *Personal Relationships, 4,* 15–23.

Hill, C. T., Rubin, Z., & Peplau, L. A. (1976). Breakups before marriage: The end of 103 affairs. *Journal of Social Issues, 32,* 147–168.

Horney, K. (1945). *Our inner conflicts: A constructive theory of neurosis.* New York: Norton.

Jason, L. A., Reichler, A., Easton, J., Neal, A., & Wilson, M. (1984). Female harassment after ending a relationship: A preliminary study. *Alternative Lifestyles, 6,* 259–269.

Johnson, J. M., Luna, Y., & Stein, J. (2003). Victim protection orders and the stake in conformity thesis. *Journal of Family Violence, 18*, 317–323.

Kam, J. A., & Spitzberg, B. H. (2005, February). *A test of a relational goal pursuit theory of unwanted relationship pursuit.* Paper presented at the Western States Communication Association Convention, San Francisco.

Kellermann, K., & Lee, C. M. (2001, November). *Seeking disaffinity: Making others dislike and feel negative about you.* Paper presented at the National Communication Association Conference, Atlanta, GA.

Kellermann, K., & Park, H. S. (2001). Situational urgency and conversational retreat: When politeness and efficiency matter. *Communication Research, 28*, 3–47.

Kellermann, K., Reynolds, R., & Chen, J. B-S. (1991). Strategies of conversational retreat: When parting is not sweet sorrow. *Communication Monographs, 58*, 362–383.

Langhinrichsen-Rohling, J., Palarea, R. E., Cohen, J., & Rohling, M. L. (2000). Breaking up is hard to do: Unwanted pursuit behaviors following the dissolution of a romantic relationship. *Violence and Victims, 15*, 73–90.

Langhinrichsen-Rohling, J., & Rohling, M. (2000). Negative family-of-origin experiences: Are they associated with perpetrating unwanted pursuit behaviors? *Violence and Victims, 15*, 459–471.

Lazarus, R. S. (1991). *Emotion and adaptation.* New York: Oxford University Press.

Leary, M. (2005). Varieties of interpersonal rejection. In K. D. Williams, J. P. Forgas, & W. von Hippel (Eds.), *The social outcast: Ostracism, social exclusion, rejection, and bullying* (pp. 35–51). New York: Psychology Press.

Leary, M. R., Bednarski, R., Hammon, D., & Duncan, T. (1997). Blowhards, snobs, and narcissists: Interpersonal reactions to excessive egotism. In R. M. Kowalski (Ed.), *Aversive interpersonal behaviors* (pp. 111–131). New York: Plenum.

Leary, M. R., Rogers, P. A., Canfield, R. W., & Coe, C. (1986). Boredom in interpersonal encounters: Antecedents and social implications. *Journal of Personality and Social Psychology, 51*, 968–975.

Leary, M. R., Springer, C., Negel, L., Ansell, E., & Evans, K. (1998). The causes, phenomenology, and consequences of hurt feelings. *Journal of Personality and Social Psychology, 74*, 1225–1237.

Levitt, M. J., Silver, M. E., & Franco, N. (1996). Troublesome relationships: A part of human experience. *Journal of Social and Personal Relationships, 13*, 523–536.

Locke, E. A., & Latham, G. P. (1990). *A theory of goal setting and task performance.* Englewood Cliffs, NJ: Prentice-Hall.

Logan, T., Cole, J., Shannon, L., & Walker, R. (2006). *Partner stalking: How women respond, cope, and survive.* New York: Springer.

Martin, L. L., & Tesser, A. (1989). Toward a motivational and structural theory of ruminative thought. In J. S. Uleman & J. A. Bargh (Eds.), *Unintended thought* (pp. 306–326). New York: Guilford.

Martin, L. L., & Tesser, A. (1996). Some ruminative thoughts. In R. S. Wyer (Ed.), *Ruminative thoughts* (pp. 1–47). Mahwah, NJ: Lawrence Erlbaum.

McCormick, N. B., & Jesser, C. J. (1983). The courtship game: Power in the sexual encounter. In E. R. Allgeier & N. B. McCormick (Eds.), *Changing boundaries: Gender roles and sexual behavior* (pp. 64–86). Palo Alto, CA: Mayfield.

McIntosh, W. D. (1996). When does goal nonattainment lead to negative emotional reactions, and when doesn't it? The role of linking and rumination. In L. L. Martin & A. Tesser (Eds.), *Striving and feeling: Interactions among goals, affect, and self-regulation* (pp. 53–77). Mahwah, NJ: Lawrence Erlbaum.

McIntosh, W. D., Harlow, T. F., & Martin, L. L. (1995). Linkers and nonlinkers: Goal beliefs as a moderator of the effects of everyday hassles on rumination, depression, and physical complaints. *Journal of Applied Social Psychology, 25*(14), 1231–1244.

McIntosh, W. D., & Martin, L. L. (1992). The cybernetics of happiness: The relation of goal attainment, rumination, and affect. In M. S. Clark (Ed.), *Emotion and social behavior* (pp. 222–246). Newbury Park, CA: Sage.

Meloy, J. R. (1996a). A clinical investigation of the obsessional follower: "She loves me, she loves me not…" In L. Schlesinger (Ed.), *Explorations in criminal psychopathology* (pp. 9–32) Springfield, IL: Charles C. Thomas.

Meloy, J. R. (1996b). Stalking (obsessional following): A review of some preliminary studies. *Aggression and Violent Behavior, 1*, 147–162.

Metts, S., Cupach, W. R., & Imahori, T. T. (1992). Perceptions of sexual compliance-resisting messages in three types of cross-sex relationships. *Western Journal of Speech Communication, 56*, 1–17.

Metts, S., & Spitzberg, B. H. (1996). Sexual communication in interpersonal contexts: A script-based approach. In B. R. Burleson (Ed.), *Communication yearbook 19* (pp. 49–91). Thousand Oaks, CA: Sage.

Miceli, M. (1992). How to make someone feel guilty: Strategies of guilt inducement and their goals. *Journal for the Theory of Social Behaviour, 22*, 81–104.

Mohandie, K., Meloy, R., McGowan, M. G., & Williams, J. (2006). The RECON typology of stalking: Reliability and validity based upon a large sample of North American stalkers. *Journal of Forensic Sciences*, *51*, 147–155.

Morewitz, S. J. (2003). *Stalking and violence: New patterns of trauma and obsession*. New York: Kluwer/Plenum.

Motley, M. T., & Reeder, H. M. (1995). Unwanted escalation of sexual intimacy: Male and female perceptions of connotations and relational consequences of resistance messages. *Communication Monographs*, *62*, 355–382.

Muehlenhard, C. L., & Hollabaugh, L. C. (1988). Do women sometimes say no when they mean yes? The prevalence and correlates of women's token resistance to sex. *Journal of Personality and Social Psychology*, *54*, 872–879.

Muehlenhard, C. L., Koralewski, M. A., Andrews, S. L., & Burdick, C. A. (1986). Verbal and nonverbal cues that convey interest in dating: Two studies. *Behavior Therapy*, *17*, 404–419.

Mullen, P. E., Pathé, M., & Purcell, R. (2000). *Stalkers and their victims*. Cambridge: Cambridge University Press.

Murnen, S. K., Perot, A., & Byrne, D. (1989). Coping with unwanted sexual activity: Normative responses, situational determinants, and individual differences. *Journal of Sex Research*, *26*, 85–106.

Patterson, B., & O'Hair, D. (1992). Relational reconciliation: Toward a more comprehensive model of relational development. *Communication Research Reports*, *9*, 119–129.

Paulson, G. D., & Roloff, M. E. (1997). The effect of request form and content on constructing obstacles to compliance. *Communication Research*, *24*, 261–290.

Pomerantz, E. M., Saxon, J. L., & Oishi, S. (2000). The psychological trade-offs of goal investment. *Journal of Personality and Social Psychology*, *79*, 617–630.

Purcell, R., Pathé, M., & Mullen, P. E. (2004). When do repeated intrusions become stalking? *Journal of Forensic Psychiatry & Psychology*, *15*, 571–583.

Reeder, H. M. (2000). "I like you … as a friend": The role of attraction in cross-sex friendship. *Journal of Social and Personal Relationships*, *17*, 329–348.

Reynolds, R. A. (1991). Beliefs about conversation abandonment: I do; you don't; but we will. *Journal of Language and Social Psychology*, *10*, 61–69.

Rosenfeld, B., & Lewis, C. (2005). Assessing violence risk in stalking cases: A regression tree approach. *Law and Human Behavior*, *29*, 343–357.

Rosenthal, D., & Peart, R. (1996). The rules of the game: Teenagers communicating about sex. *Journal of Adolescence*, *19*, 321–332.

Sabini, J., & Silver, M. (1982). *Moralities of everyday life*. Oxford: Oxford University Press.

Schneider, C. S., & Kenny, D. A. (2000). Cross-sex friends who were once romantic partners: Are they platonic friends now? *Journal of Social and Personal Relationships*, *17*, 451–466.

Sharkey, W. F. (1992). Use and responses to intentional embarrassment. *Communication Studies*, *43*, 257–275.

Sheridan, L. (2001). The course and nature of stalking: An in-depth victim survey. *Journal of Threat Assessment*, *1*, 61–79.

Sheridan, L., Davies, G. M., & Boon, J. C. (2001). The course and nature of stalking: A victim perspective. *Howard Journal of Criminal Justice*, *40*, 215–234.

Sias, P. M., & Perry, T. (2004). Disengaging from workplace relationships: A research note. *Human Communication Research*, *30*, 589–602.

Sinclair, H. C., & Frieze, I. H. (2000). Initial courtship behavior and stalking: How should we draw the line? *Violence and Victims*, *15*, 23–40.

Snow, D. A., Robinson, C., & McCall, P. L. (1991). "Cooling out" men in singles bars and nightclubs: Observations on the interpersonal survival strategies of women in public places. *Journal of Contemporary Ethnography*, *19*, 423–449.

Spitzberg, B. H. (2002). The tactical topography of stalking victimization and management. *Trauma, Violence, & Abuse*, *3*, 261–288.

Spitzberg, B. H., & Cupach, W. R. (2001). Paradoxes of pursuit: Toward a relational model of stalking-related phenomena. In J. A. Davis (Ed.), *Stalking crimes and victim protection: Prevention, intervention, threat assessment, and case management* (pp. 97–136). Boca Raton, FL: CRC Press.

Spitzberg, B. H., & Cupach, W. R. (2002). The inappropriateness of relational intrusion. In R. Goodwin & D. Cramer (Eds.), *Inappropriate relationships: The unconventional, the disapproved, and the forbidden* (pp. 191–219). Mahwah, NJ: Lawrence Erlbaum.

Spitzberg, B. H., & Cupach, W. R. (2007). The state of the art of stalking: Taking stock of the emerging literature. *Aggression and Violent Behavior*, *12*, 64–86.

Spitzberg, B. H., & Cupach, W. R. (in press). Managing unwanted pursuit. In M. T. Motley (Ed.), *Studies in applied interpersonal communication*. Thousand Oaks, CA: Sage.

Spitzberg, B. H., Nicastro, A. M., & Cousins, A. V. (1998). Exploring the interactional phenomenon of stalking and obsessive relational intrusion. *Communication Reports, 11*, 33–48.

Sprecher, S., Felmlee, D., Metts, S., Fehr, B., & Vanni, D. (1998). Factors associated with distress following the breakup of a close relationship. *Journal of Social and Personal Relationships, 15*, 791–809.

Sprecher, S., Hatfield, E., Cortese, A., Potapova, E., & Levitskaya, A. (1994). Token resistance to sexual intercourse and consent to unwanted sexual intercourse: College students' dating experiences in three countries. *Journal of Sex Research, 31*, 125–132.

Tennov, D. (1979). *Love and limerance*. New York: Stein and Day.

Tennov, D. (1998). Love madness. In V. C. de Munck (Ed.), *Romantic love and sexual behavior: Perspectives from the social sciences* (pp. 77–88). Westport, CT: Praeger.

Tjaden, P., & Thoennes, N. (1998). *Stalking in America: Findings from the National Violence Against Women Survey*. Washington, DC: National Institute of Justice and Centers for Disease Control and Prevention.

Tolhuizen, J. H. (1989). Communication strategies for intensifying dating relationships: Identification, use and structure. *Journal of Social and Personal Relationships, 6*, 413–434.

Vangelisti, A. L. (2007). Communicating hurt. In B. H. Spitzberg & W. R. Cupach (Eds.), *The dark side of interpersonal communication* (2nd ed., pp. 121–142). Mahwah, NJ: Lawrence Erlbaum.

Vangelisti, A. L., Daly, J. A., & Rudnick, J. R. (1991). Making people feel guilty in conversations: Techniques and correlates. *Human Communication Research, 18*, 3–39.

Vaughan, D. (1986). *Uncoupling: How relationships come apart*. New York: Vintage.

Walby, S., & Allen, J. (2004, March). *Domestic violence, sexual assault and stalking: Findings from the British Crime Survey* (Home Office Research Study 276). London: Home Office Research, Development and Statistics Directorate.

Wegner, D. M., Schneider, D. J., Carter, S. R., III, & White, T. L. (1987). Paradoxical effects of thought suppression. *Journal of Personality and Social Psychology, 53*, 5–13.

Williams, S. L., & Frieze, I. H. (2005). Courtship behaviors, relationship violence, and breakup persistence in college men and women. *Psychology of Women Quarterly, 29*, 248–257.

Wilson, S. R. (2002). *Seeking and resisting compliance: Why people say what they do when trying to influence others*. Thousand Oaks, CA: Sage.

Wineberg, H. (1994). Marital reconciliation in the United States: Which couples are successful? *Journal of Marriage and the Family, 56*, 80–88.

22

Emotional Disturbances and the Initial Stages of Relationship Development
Processes and Consequences of Social Anxiety and Depression

AMY WENZEL and TODD B. KASHDAN

A s is explained in the other chapters in this volume, the process of cultivating new relationships requires the delicate negotiation of different communication styles and relationship beliefs, as well as the participation in shared experiences. There is an inherent ambiguity in the relationship initiation process as two people get to know each other and consider whether they would like to pursue a deeper, more meaningful relationship (see Knobloch & Miller, this volume). Although the successful initiation of a new relationship undoubtedly is life enhancing, there are many points throughout the process where some discomfort, awkwardness, and miscommunication are expected. Imagine, then, how daunting the process of relationship initiation would be for individuals who are struggling with emotional disturbances that are associated with impaired social skills, distorted views of the self and others, and difficulties connecting with others during social interaction. Consider the following cases:

"James" is a 20-year-old part-time community college student who lives at home with his parents. Other than attending two classes per week, he stays in the house, mainly in his room playing video games and listening to music. He admits that he is lonely and would like to make friends, and perhaps even have a girlfriend someday. However, whenever he attempts to talk with others he does not know, he begins to stutter, avoids eye contact, and leaves the conversation with the impression that others think he is a "loser." James has struggled with these difficulties since he was a young child, and his discomfort around others has been so severe that his parents decided to have him home-schooled. Thus, he has had very few opportunities throughout his life to build relationships with people other than his parents and sister.

"Gina" is a 28-year-old associate in a prestigious legal firm. Recently, she was turned down for a promotion to senior associate, and the position was instead given to an individual whom she views as her "rival." Gina now avoids talking with her friends and family, claiming that she is too embarrassed to tell them she did not get the promotion. For the past 4 weeks, she has not engaged in activities that were once part of her normal routine, including going to the gym after work, going to "happy hour" with her coworkers, and attending her book club with her girlfriends. She has difficulty falling asleep, she has lost her appetite, and she is having difficulty concentrating on her work. The one person she turned to for support is the man she has been dating for about 8 weeks. Although she believes he has done his best to "be there" for her, he admits that his patience is wearing thin. After all, she calls him crying multiple times per day, is too tired or upset to have sex, and does not want to go out and do the fun things they used to do when they were first getting to know each other.

The case of James illustrates the manner in which social anxiety interferes with relationship initiation. Social anxiety is defined as a fear of being negatively evaluated, embarrassed, or judged by others (cf. Schlenker & Leary, 1982). Social anxiety can be regarded in two ways—as a personality trait (Schlenker & Leary, 1982) or as a clinical syndrome (*Diagnostic and Statistical Manual of Mental Disorders* [*DSM*]; American Psychiatric Association, 2000). When it is viewed as a personality trait, it is assumed to be a dimensional construct that is normally distributed in the general population and correlates positively with discomfort in social and evaluative situations. In contrast with the trait view of social anxiety, diagnoses of social anxiety disorder (or social phobia, as listed in the *DSM*) are categorical, such that people either do or do not meet criteria for a diagnosis. Diagnoses of social anxiety disorder are made when a person's social anxiety exceeds a threshold, such that it causes significant life interference and/or distress. James, then, clearly meets criteria for social anxiety disorder, as his social anxiety has prevented him from forming meaningful friendships and romantic relationships and pursuing conventional educational opportunities.

According to the most recent version of the *DSM*, the criteria for social anxiety disorder are (a) a marked or persistent fear of one or more social or performance situations in which the person is exposed to unfamiliar people or possible scrutiny by others, for fear that he or she will act in a way that is humiliating or embarrassing; (b) exposure to the feared social situation almost invariably provokes anxiety; (c) the person recognizes that the fear is excessive or unreasonable; (d) the feared social or performance situations are avoided or else are endured with intense anxiety and distress; and (e) the avoidance, anxious anticipation, or distress in the feared social or performance situation(s) significantly interferes with the person's normal routine, occupational or academic functioning, or social activities and relationships, or there is marked distress about having the disorder. Given that social anxiety, by definition, involves intense anxiety in and avoidance of the presence of others, it is logical to assume that social anxiety would interfere with close relationships, particularly the development of new relationships when people are first getting to know each other.

Gina, in contrast, does not struggle with social anxiety—she is normally outgoing, she enjoys social gatherings, she has many friends, and she actively dates. However, she has recently had a major setback in her life, which has had a profound effect on her mood and behavior that in turn has affected her relatively new romantic relationship. Gina is currently experiencing a major depressive episode. According to the *DSM*, major depression is characterized by at least five of the following symptoms that occur within at least a 2-week period: (a) depressed mood; (b) markedly diminished interest and pleasure in all, or almost all, activities; (c) significant weight loss or weight gain, or a decrease or increase in appetite; (d) insomnia or hypersomnia; (e) psychomotor agitation or retardation; (f) fatigue or loss of energy; (g) feelings of worthlessness or inappropriate guilt; (h) diminished ability to think or concentrate, or indecisiveness; and (i) recurrent thoughts of death, suicide ideation without a specific plan, a specific plan for committing suicide, or a suicide attempt. Although social functioning is not mentioned specifically in the *DSM* criteria for a major depressive episode, it is clear that many depressive symptoms would interfere with relationship initiation. Depression is more often conceptualized from a clinical, or categorical, standpoint rather than a dispositional, or dimensional, standpoint; nevertheless, as will be illustrated in this chapter, research with participants who report depressive symptoms but are not necessarily diagnosed with major depressive disorder reveals that they often exhibit functional impairment, particularly in their close relationships.

The systematic study of emotional disturbance and relationship functioning reflects the rise and modification of dominant theoretical traditions that have driven psychological research over the past 30 years. For example, much empirical research was conducted in the 1970s from a behavioral perspective, in which researchers identified specific behavioral skills deficits associated with emotional disturbance that had implications for interpersonal functioning. The "cognitive revolution" of the 1980s introduced the idea that thoughts, beliefs, and expectations have significant influences upon our emotions and behaviors. Although there is a paucity of studies examining thoughts, beliefs, and expectations in the context of initiating relationships, people with emotional disturbances certainly express distorted ideas about their ability to negotiate interactions with others (e.g., Glass, Merluzzi, Biever, & Larsen, 1982). Over time, research conducted within behavioral and cognitive frameworks made important discoveries about *individual* functioning, but it did not necessarily capture the dynamic processes at work in *relationship* functioning. Because close relationships involve (at least) two people, it is important to understand cognitions and behavior in the context of and from the perspective of both relationship partners and the dyad as a unit (cf. Walters & Hope, 1998). Thus, recent work has attempted to capture these subtleties from an interpersonal perspective by assessing both the emotionally impaired individual and the person with whom he or she is interacting (e.g., Alden & Wallace, 1995), or by adopting interpersonally oriented theoretical frameworks, such as attachment theory (e.g., Roberts, Gotlib, & Kassel, 1996).

This chapter will consider the manner in which emotional disturbances affect relationship initiation, from various theoretical frameworks and empirical findings, with an eye toward intervention. In the next section, we will describe three theoretical frameworks—behavioral, cognitive, and interpersonal—and consider the manner in which they facilitate the understanding of relationship initiation in emotionally impaired individuals. The subsequent section will focus on two domains of emotional disturbance—social anxiety and depression—and describe empirical research that suggests ways in which they disrupt relationship initiation. In addition, we will briefly highlight therapeutic interventions that stem from these theories and findings, and we will discuss data, when available, that support their efficacy in improving interpersonal functioning. We will conclude with the beginnings of a relational-cognitive-behavioral model of interpersonal impairment in emotional disturbances (with a specific focus on relationship initiation), and generate directions for future research.

THEORETICAL FRAMEWORKS

Behavioral Tradition

The behavioral assessment of relationship functioning emphasizes the precise measurement of observable behaviors, which are assumed to represent important relationship processes. Although no close relationships scholars would suggest that subjective, internal processes are irrelevant in understanding the development of close relationships, behavioral researchers believe that these processes cannot be measured in a reliable and valid manner. For example, Bellack, Hersen, and Turner (1979) found little agreement between people's estimates of their social competence and actual behavior observed, suggesting that people's judgments of their own behavior have little bearing on reality. James is a classic example of a person characterized by behaviors that make it difficult to initiate relationships, such as stuttering and lack of eye contact. It is likely that his awkward behavior in turn makes others uncomfortable, which would reduce the probability that they would want to interact with him in the future.

Much of the empirical behavioral literature focuses on participants' *social skills* exhibited in simulated or actual situations where they are meeting another person for the first time. According to Meier and Hope (1998), social skills comprise

> a group of behaviors that enable an individual to effectively engage in, maintain, and succeed in social interactions. These behaviors include the expression of both positive and negative emotions, facial expressions, the tone, volume, and speed of verbal expression, posture, and appropriate content. (p. 235)

A socially skilled person will accurately perceive social cues, evaluate their relevance to current motivations and goals, and generate responses to advance these motivations and goals (Norton & Hope, 2001). Scholars who conduct research on social skills consider behaviors along two broad dimensions. *Molar* ratings are global indices of overall skill, appropriateness, or effectiveness. In contrast, *molecular* ratings quantify behaviors such as head nods, gestures, and smiles (McNeil, Ries, & Turk, 1995; Meier & Hope, 1998), and it is assumed that these behaviors are important in forming a positive impression, engaging the other individual, and creating a context for a relationship to emerge.

Cognitive Tradition

The major assumption in the cognitive framework is that thoughts, beliefs, and expectations have a significant impact on emotions and subsequent behavioral responses (e.g., Beck, 1967; see Beck, 1988, for an application of the cognitive framework to relationship distress). From this perspective, although people's judgments of their own behavior might not accurately reflect reality, these perceptions are important in their own right because of their potential to influence emotional distress and, in turn, behavior. For example, when Gina is feeling like herself and receives an invitation to a social gathering, she might think to herself, "Great! I'm looking forward to meeting some new people." However, when she is depressed and receives the same invitation, she might think to herself, "What's the use? Nothing's going to make me feel better." The subsequent emotional reactions associated with the former cognition might include excitement and anticipation, whereas the subsequent emotional reactions associated with the latter cognition might include dejection and hopelessness. Not surprisingly, Gina is much more likely to attend the social gathering in the first scenario.

The thoughts that jump to mind in these particular situations are called *automatic thoughts*, a term that reflects how these thoughts often arise so quickly that people are not aware of them. An examination of automatic thoughts elicited over time usually reveals that there is some coherent theme or pattern. Such themes represent an individual's *core belief* about the self, others, and/or world. Thus, according to this model (cf. J. S. Beck, 1995), emotionally impaired individuals are characterized by maladaptive core beliefs that color the automatic thoughts and interpretations made in specific situations and form the basis of rigid rules and assumptions by which they live their lives. It is plausible, for example, that James' early experiences (e.g., difficulty making friends) shaped a fundamental belief that he is unlikable. As he grew up, he developed rules and assumptions such as "Isolating myself is the only way to ensure that I don't get hurt" and "If I make one social blunder, others will reject me." When he is confronted with a situation in which he must interact with a person he does not know, he has the ideas "I will make a fool out of myself" or "This person will think I'm inept," which in turn prompt elevated somatic anxiety and social withdrawal. As a result, he has the expectation that others will reject him, and when he engages in social interactions, he is biased toward evaluating his performance in an unfavorable manner.

So far, we have focused on what might actually run through the minds of emotionally impaired individuals when they are in situations ripe for relationship initiation; this is called their cognitive *content*. Equally important, however, is the manner in which emotionally impaired individuals *process* information about social cues in these situations (cf. Ingram & Kendall, 1986). For example, many emotionally impaired individuals are characterized by self-focused attention, defined as "an awareness of self-referent, internally generated information that stands in contrast to an awareness of externally generated information derived through sensory receptors" (Ingram, 1990, p. 156). This self-preoccupation prevents emotionally impaired individuals from attending to their social performance, which often results in real social errors (Clark & Wells, 1995) and an inability to solve problems as they arise (Lyubomirsky & Nolen-Hoeksema, 1995). In addition, some emotionally impaired individuals are characterized by the tendency to detect negative social cues at the expense of other social cues (e.g., Mogg, Philippot, & Bradley, 2004), or the tendency to fixate on negative social cues once they are detected (Mogg & Bradley, 2005). This sort of bias makes it likely that emotionally impaired individuals will easily notice indications of threat to new relationships, ignore indications of success or progress, and have difficulty disengaging from those cues. The end result of these cognitive processing biases is that information signaling rejection and negative judgment is given prominence, which reinforces core beliefs of unlikeability and failure.

Interpersonal Tradition

For the most part, empirical research conducted from behavioral and cognitive traditions focused on assessments of *individuals*, such as by coding their behavior in interactions with a confederate, eliciting self-reports of their experiences within relationships, or measuring how quickly they detect (or avoid) standardized stimuli with interpersonal relevance. Research conducted from an interpersonal perspective often retains a focus on observable behavior and cognition (e.g., Alden & Wallace, 1995), but it does so in the context of the *dyad*. Variables relevant to both people are subjected to analyses that yield important information about the manner in which particular behaviors enhance or disrupt the development of a relationship. Such an approach might be particularly useful in understanding the processes at work in Gina's relationship with her boyfriend, as her reassurance-seeking efforts are becoming increasingly aversive for her partner. Thus, one way of understanding the interpersonal perspective is the primacy of particular methodological and data analytic approaches.

In addition to the focus on collecting data from both members of the dyad, researchers who study relationships in emotionally impaired individuals have reached beyond behavioral and cognitive traditions to incorporate aspects of other, more interpersonally oriented theoretical frameworks into their work. Interpersonal theories of emotional disturbances posit that supportive relationships are essential for our emotional well-being and conversely, that disruptions in relationships and social interaction are central to understanding pathology (Alden & Taylor, 2004; Leary & Kowalski, 1995). Unlike the behavioral and cognitive traditions, the interpersonal framework is less organized into one coherent paradigm (Segrin, 2000, 2001), and there are several specific theories that would be regarded as interpersonal. In this chapter, we will focus on adult attachment approaches.

The basic premises of attachment theory have been described in many other chapters in this *Handbook* (e.g., Creasey & Jarvis) and will not be reiterated in detail here. For our purposes, we view adult attachment style as a habitual set of cognitive, emotional, and behavioral responses in close relationships that stems from interactions in significant childhood relationships, most notably the caregiver–infant relationship (Hazan & Shaver, 1987). Adult attachment styles reliably predict closeness, intimacy, openness, and sexual behavior in relationships (e.g., Feeney, 1999; Feeney & Noller, 1990; Feeney, Noller, & Patty, 1993). Attachment scholars currently conceptualize adult attachment along two broad dimensions: (a) anxiety about not being able to obtain or sustain satisfying relationships, and (b) discomfort with closeness (Brennan, Clark, & Shaver, 1998; Fraley & Waller, 1998). However, earlier work on adult attachment utilizes a three-category scheme of secure, avoidant, and anxious-ambivalent styles (Hazan & Shaver, 1987) or a four-category scheme of secure (i.e., positive feelings about self and others), dismissing (i.e., positive feelings about self and negative feelings about others), preoccupied (i.e., negative feelings about self and positive feelings about others), and fearful (i.e., negative feelings about self and others) styles (Bartholomew & Horowitz, 1991).

Attachment theory has the potential to explain the mechanisms by which certain behaviors are exhibited and certain cognitions are experienced as relationships develop (Harvey & Wenzel, 2006). Moreover, it can account for the core beliefs that people have about relationships and the ease with which they are activated during specific relational events. James, for example, would be characterized by an excessive amount of anxiety about relationships with others. Because of this orientation toward relationships, it is logical that he would have negative views of his ability to form relationships and be judged favorably by others, which would in turn affect his skill in negotiating relationship initiation.

Summary

Although the behavioral, cognitive, and interpersonal explanations for deficits in interpersonal interaction arise from distinct theoretical traditions, it is evident even from these brief descriptions that they are not mutually exclusive. Maladaptive cognition is one mechanism by which people fail to engage in effective behavior when they are interacting with others. Attachment theory provides a clue as to why certain individuals develop and maintain maladaptive cognition despite repeated negative consequences. In the next sections, we summarize and critique empirical research designed to validate aspects of these theoretical approaches to understanding disrupted interpersonal interaction.

SOCIAL ANXIETY AND RELATIONSHIP INITIATION

The core features of social anxiety are avoidance of and distress in social and performance situations in which a person believes there is a possibility of embarrassment, humiliation, or judgment. Socially anxious people would like to make a positive impression on others, but doubt their ability to do so (Leary & Kowalski, 1995). In a case of severe social anxiety, like James, such fears prevent the person from making attempts to form relationships with others. However, most socially anxious people do not suffer from such extreme disturbance (Segrin, 2001). A more typical presentation is someone who perhaps has a romantic partner and a few close friends, but who avoids large social gatherings with strangers (Faravelli et al., 2000), has a limited history of dating and sexual activity (Leary & Dobbins, 1983), and has difficulty communicating effectively about relationship issues (Wenzel, Graff-Dolezal, Macho, & Brendle, 2005). Many of these people report a great deal of loneliness (Solano & Koester, 1989) and rarely take the lead in initiating relationships with others (Twentyman & McFall, 1975). Thus, socially anxious people may not necessarily avoid all social interactions, but their distorted perceptions about themselves and others and their avoidance behavior have negative implications for the quality of their relationships (cf. Eng, Coles, Heimberg, & Safran, 2005). Next, we turn to a review of empirical research, conducted from behavioral, cognitive, and interpersonal frameworks that pertain to social anxiety and disruptions in relationship initiation.

Behavioral Tradition

Empirical research conducted from a behavioral framework tests the hypothesis that socially anxious people are characterized by impaired social skills relative to less anxious peers. Using molar ratings of social skill, objective raters often judge that socially anxious people are less skilled in interactions that simulate meeting another person, frequently someone of the opposite gender, for the first time (e.g., Beidel, Turner, & Dancu, 1985; Twentyman & McFall, 1975; see Curran, 1977, for a review). These results are even more compelling when one takes into consideration that socially anxious people often are not judged as less skilled in other social and evaluative situations, such as job interviews with attractive opposite-sex interviewers (Strahan & Conger, 1998) and speeches (Beidel et al., 1985). Thus, molar ratings of social skill suggest that social interaction during the beginning stages of relationships is particularly difficult for socially anxious people.

In contrast, there is less consistent evidence that socially anxious people are characterized by deficits in molecular social skills when meeting someone for the first time (cf. Norton & Hope, 2001). Some studies have found that, relative to nonanxious individuals, socially anxious individuals make less eye contact (e.g., Beidel et al., 1985), talk less (e.g., Fydrich, Chambless, Perry, Buergener, & Beazley, 1998), fail to engage in effective conversational turn taking (Cappella, 1985), make more excuses and apologies (Schlenker, 1987), and engage in fewer behaviors classified as dominant and cooperative (Walters & Hope, 1998). However, oftentimes studies find deficits in one particular molecular social skill but not another (e.g., Beidel et al., 1985), and it is unclear which particular skill is most central to dysfunction in social interaction (cf. Segrin, 1990). In addition, molecular skill deficits found in one study often are not replicated in others (see Stravynski & Amado, 2001, for a review). Moreover, Strahan and Conger (1999) pointed out that even when socially anxious people are judged as less skilled than less anxious peers, the absolute ratings of skill still suggest that socially anxious people are performing adequately.

Thus, socially anxious people may demonstrate particular social skills deficits in some situations, but these deficits are far from pervasive (cf. Alden & Taylor, 2004; Stravynski & Amado, 2001).

Meier and Hope (1998) called attention to the distinction between skills and performance deficits to explain these discrepancies. In the former instance, socially anxious people simply do not have the repertoire of skills necessary to function adequately in social or evaluative situations. In the latter instance, socially anxious people possess adequate skill level, but they are unable to apply their skills in social or evaluative situations. It is likely that this latter conceptualization is more accurate in characterizing the behavioral problems observed in social anxiety (Curran, 1977), as interpersonal dysfunction is most evident when situations are ambiguous or when there is possible scrutiny by others (Pilkonis, 1977). It is incumbent upon scholars who conduct research in this area, then, to identify the factors that prevent socially anxious people from responding appropriately in certain types of social situations. As will be discussed in the next section, one leading candidate to explain this inability is maladaptive cognition, or the negative ideas, thoughts, and expectations about one's own performance and others' likely reactions that are associated with behavioral inhibition.

Cognitive Tradition

The evidence is abundant that, relative to less anxious people, socially anxious people indeed report fewer positive thoughts and more negative thoughts while conversing with confederates in experimental social interactions (Beidel et al., 1985; Dodge, Hope, Heimberg, & Becker, 1988; Glass et al., 1982). Socially anxious people estimate they have functioned poorly in particular social situations even when objective raters do not concur, and these estimates often are associated with negative emotional experiences (e.g., Clark & Arkowitz, 1975; Segrin & Kinney, 1995; Wallace & Alden, 1997). Thus, one hypothesis is that socially anxious people are characterized by overall performance deficits because they are inhibited by, and/or distracted by, negative cognitions. When these cognitions are activated, performance suffers (and conversely, when these cognitions are not activated, performance does not suffer).

Contemporary research has identified a number of specific expectations, judgments, and attributions about social interaction that are associated with social anxiety and have the potential to disrupt interpersonal performance in relationship initiation. Relative to less anxious people, socially anxious people believe that they are less desirable romantic and sexual partners and admit that they would be more likely to engage in a relationship with others who are viewed as very unattractive (Wenzel & Emerson, 2006). During "getting acquainted" interactions with attractive people of the opposite sex, they are less likely than less anxious people to attribute the outcome to factors that are controllable (Bruch & Pearl, 1995). Rather than feeling relieved when a "getting acquainted" interaction goes well, socially anxious people endorse just as much negative affect as before the interaction and worry that others will create higher expectations for them (Wallace & Alden, 1997). Even when presented with vignettes of hypothetical scenarios, which should be less threatening than actual situations, socially anxious people are more likely than less anxious people to interpret ambiguous information in a negative manner and expect negative social outcomes to be particularly costly (Amir, Foa, & Coles, 1998; Foa, Franklin, Perry, & Herbert, 1996).

As stated previously, *cognition* is a broad term that encompasses not only *what* people are thinking but also *how* people are thinking. Many studies have found that socially anxious individuals detect indicators of social threat, such as anxiety-relevant words (e.g., *criticized* or *embarrassed*; see Heinrichs & Hofmann, 2001) and angry faces (Mogg et al., 2004), more quickly than cues signaling neutrality or safety. When socially anxious people are instructed to identify a neutral face among an array of angry faces, their performance is slowed, which suggests that they are distracted by indicators of social threat because their attention is drawn to and subsequently fixated on them (Gilboa-Schechtman, Foa, & Amir, 1999). During actual interactions with others, the attention of socially anxious individuals is focused inward, causing them to miss important social cues that would facilitate further interaction (Clark & Wells, 1995; Schlenker & Leary, 1982; see Spurr & Stopa, 2002, for a review). Specifically, self-focused attention draws their focus to anxiety-related sensations and behaviors, which further increases anxiety (Kashdan & Roberts, 2004; Woody, 1996) and leads them to judge that observable indicators of anxiety are more pronounced than they really are (Mansell &

Clark, 1999; Woody & Rodriguez, 2000). Moreover, self-focused attention is associated with distinct interpersonal consequences, such as lower levels of recall of partner-related information (Mellings & Alden, 2000) and increases in partners' level of self-focus (Stephenson & Wickland, 1984).

Thus, two domains of cognition are associated with interpersonal problems in social anxiety. Socially anxious people experience negative thoughts about their performance, their desirability, and the cost of making social errors, which likely inhibit their capacity for spontaneous and open social interaction. Depending on the particular circumstances, they are either hypervigilant for external signals of social threat, or they turn their attention inward to carefully monitor their performance, creating a situation where they are ignoring what is happening in their social environment. Either way, this biased deployment of attention has deleterious consequences for forming accurate perceptions of how well the interaction went, as well as for registering important social cues that would enhance the interaction. How does this cognitive-behavioral style impact relationships? How might we account for the development of this cognitive-behavioral style? Research conducted from an interpersonal framework can provide some insights into these questions.

Interpersonal Tradition

Equally important as the degree to which socially anxious individuals demonstrate appropriate social skills is the manner in which others respond to them as a consequence of their behavior in social situations. Alden and her colleagues (e.g., Alden & Mellings, 2004; Alden & Wallace, 1995; Papsdorf & Alden, 1998; see Alden & Taylor, 2004, for a review) have conducted a number of "getting acquainted" studies, such that socially anxious and less anxious people are observed in the context of a discussion with an interaction partner in a similar manner as in many of the studies designed to identify social skills deficits. The key feature of these studies is that the consequences of participants' performance is also considered, as interaction partners rate the degree to which they would like to have future contact with them. Results from these studies indicate that socially anxious people exhibit fewer positive behaviors than less anxious peers, and in turn, interaction partners report little desire to have interactions with them in the future. The presence of anxiety-related social skills deficits (e.g., little eye contact) is modestly associated with less desire for future interaction, suggesting that social skills deficits have a small but tangible influence upon others' judgments (e.g., Papsdorf & Alden, 1998). However, the most salient predictor of the lack of desire for future interaction is a failure to reciprocate others' self-disclosures, which leads interaction partners to view socially anxious people as dissimilar and disinterested (Alden & Taylor, 2004). Thus, results from Alden's studies indicate that it is not always socially anxious individuals' lack of social skill that is off-putting toward others, but more importantly, it is their inability to form a meaningful connection with interaction partners by failing to self-disclose in a manner that facilitates closeness.

One limitation of Alden's studies is that socially anxious and less anxious participants interacted with a trained confederate, making it questionable the degree to which these interactions simulated naturalistic social interaction. Kashdan and Wenzel (2005) overcame this limitation by randomly assigning undergraduate participants who did not know each other to one of two 45-minute conditions: a "small talk" condition where they conversed about superficial topics (e.g., what they did that summer), or a "personal disclosure" condition where they conversed about intimate topics (e.g., their most treasured memory). Social anxiety was measured by the Social Interaction Anxiety Scale (SIAS; Mattick & Clarke, 1998), a standard self-report inventory used to identify socially anxious research participants. Results indicated that socially anxious participants who interacted with other socially anxious participants reported a great deal of closeness, particularly in the personal disclosure condition, and the lowest levels of closeness were reported by dyads composed of one socially anxious and one less anxious participant. Kashdan and Wenzel concluded that socially anxious people can indeed foster meaningful interactions in certain contexts, particularly when they are interacting with other socially anxious people. They proposed several potential explanations for the particularly high level of closeness endorsed by pairs of socially anxious interaction partners, including that they were (a) able to overcome initial anticipatory anxiety when they discovered similarities in their partners and enjoyed the rare positive social interaction; (b) sensitive to social anxiety in their partners, which reduced their anxiety level and allowed them to fully engage in the interaction task; and (c) pleasantly surprised by the ease of the task, relative to presumed low expectations for their performance. In contrast, it is possible that a meaningful connection does not emerge when socially anxious and less anxious people interact because socially anxious people perceive less anxious people as hostile or dominant, and they respond with meek, submissive behavior (cf. Trower & Gilbert, 1989).

Very few studies have examined patterns of adult attachment in socially anxious people, but those that have done so have found remarkably consistent results. For example, Duggan and Brennan (1994) reported that individuals classified as preoccupied and fearful scored higher on a self-reported measure of shyness than individuals classified as secure or dismissing. Wenzel (2002) administered Bartholomew and Horowitz's (1991) Relationship Questionnaire to a small sample of patients with social anxiety disorder and nonanxious individuals and found that relative to nonanxious individuals, socially anxious patients estimated that the description of the secure attachment style was less characteristic of them and that the descriptions of the fearful and preoccupied attachment styles were more characteristic of them. Darcy, Davila, and Beck (2005) obtained similar results using this measure, although they instructed participants to endorse attachment descriptions of individuals with whom they already had developed close relationships (e.g., parents or a romantic partner). Eng, Heimberg, Hart, Schneier, and Liebowitz (2001) used cluster analysis to determine the predominant attachment style of patients with social anxiety disorder. Although they identified one cluster of patients who were characterized by a secure attachment style, they identified another cluster of patients who were characterized by an anxious-ambivalent attachment style, and it was this latter subgroup of patients who reported elevated levels of depression and impairment and lower levels of life satisfaction.

Thus, all four empirical studies found results suggesting that socially anxious people are characterized by a preoccupied or anxious-ambivalent attachment style. That is, socially anxious people described themselves as being uncomfortable without close relationships and as perceiving that others are reluctant to get as close to them as they would like. Three of the four empirical studies found that socially anxious people were characterized by a fearful or avoidant attachment style, which indicates that they describe themselves as being uncomfortable in close relationships and as worrying that others will hurt them. It appears that many socially anxious individuals find themselves in a dilemma—they are uncomfortable in close relationships, and they are uncomfortable without them, and regardless of whether or not they have close relationships, they worry about rejection.

Summary

When interacting with socially anxious people, one often gets the general sense that they lack the social skills to behave appropriately in the interaction, and as a result, it seems difficult to connect with them. However, it might not necessarily appear that way because socially anxious people do not know what to do. Instead, it is more likely that negative beliefs about their ability to make a good impression, their own desirability, and the probability that others will be interested in them are detrimental to their performance. Socially anxious people are likely to detect even minute indicators that they are being rejected or are somehow failing, and once detected, they exaggerate the importance of them. When actively conversing with others, they tend to focus their attention inward on their own thoughts, emotions, and physiological sensations in order to monitor their performance and detect signs of failure. Unfortunately, this self-focus leads them to evaluate their social performance in an excessively negative manner, as they equate signs of anxiety with poor performance, and in some instances their performance objectively suffers because they miss important social cues that would inform their behavior (cf. Clark & Wells, 1995). Even if their performance does not suffer from a global standpoint, it is likely that distorted cognitive content and biased information processing prevent them from truly engaging and connecting with individuals with whom they are interacting.

As evidenced by results from empirical studies investigating attachment styles associated with social anxiety, socially anxious individuals would like to have close relationships, but these relationships create a great deal of discomfort, and they worry about others rejecting and hurting them. The beginning stages of close relationships are likely to be painful for socially anxious people, as their self-doubt leads them to ruminate over perceptions of mistakes in social interaction (Kashdan & Roberts, 2007; Mellings & Alden, 2000). Unfortunately, this vicious cycle likely thwarts the development of many relationships that otherwise would have been satisfying for them—research shows that socially anxious individuals indeed have fewer friends, dating relationships, and sexual relationships, and are less likely to marry, than individuals in the general population (e.g., Schneier et al., 1994; Turner, Beidel, Dancu, & Keys, 1986; Wittchen, Fuetsch, Sonntag, Müller, & Liebowitz, 2000), and, at times, they are dissatisfied with their social support network (Ham, Hayes, & Hope, 2005). On the other hand, many socially anxious people report satisfying relationships with their partners (Wenzel, 2002), raising the possibility that some of these negative expectations and worries abate as their relationship moves from the initiation stage to the maintenance stage. Moreover, our clinical experience suggests that some socially anxious individuals are satisfied with a small support network and that they view a relatively solitary existence as fulfilling.

DEPRESSION AND RELATIONSHIP INITIATION

Like social anxiety, depression is associated with problems in social functioning (Fredman, Weissman, Leaf, & Bruce, 1988; Hammen & Brennan, 2002; Leader & Klein, 1996). Gina's case exemplifies a number of common symptoms of depression that interfere with social interaction and relationship initiation. She is lethargic and apathetic, so she rarely feels like leaving the house to socialize with others. Even if her boyfriend is able to convince her to go out, she does not enjoy herself in the same manner as she does when she is not depressed. She has trouble concentrating, which disrupts her ability to track conversations. The end result of this amalgam of symptoms is that, over time, others find it aversive to be in Gina's presence. In fact, people with whom she is in existing relationships might begin to feel depressed themselves, a phenomenon called *emotional contagion* (Coyne, 1976a; see Joiner & Katz, 1999, for a review). Gina might not initiate relationships with people with whom she might otherwise because her symptoms prevent her from being in social situations in the first place. If she does attempt to initiate new relationships while she is depressed, there is an increased probability that others will not find her desirable. Next, we turn to a review of empirical research, conducted from behavioral, cognitive, and interpersonal frameworks, that pertains to disruption in relationship initiation in depressed individuals.

Behavioral Tradition

Lewinsohn's (1974, 1975a) classic behavioral theory of depression specifies that depressed individuals have deficits in social skills that reduce the probability of obtaining positive reinforcement from their social interactions and that increase the probability of negative social consequences. In fact, Lewinsohn suggested that poor social skills are a precursor to depression, such that depressive symptoms emerge over time with repeated failures to obtain positive reinforcement from interactions with others. Although most studies conducted to validate the causal pathway between poor social skills and depression have failed to find supporting evidence (e.g., Segrin, 1999; but see Wierzbicki, 1984, for an exception), recent work suggests that poor social skills make people vulnerable to experience depression in times of stress, when they would most need to make effective use of their social support system (e.g., Segrin & Flora, 2000).

As we saw with socially anxious people, depressed individuals are often rated as having poorer levels of overall social skill than nondepressed individuals when rated by objective raters (e.g., Lewinsohn, Mischel, Chaplin, & Barton, 1980) as well as when rated by individuals with whom they are interacting (Strack & Coyne, 1983). Also as we saw with socially anxious people, there is mixed evidence that depressed individuals are characterized by deficits in particular molecular social skills (for reviews, see Segrin, 1990, 2000, 2001). Unlike the state of the literature examining social skills deficits associated with social anxiety, meta-analytic approaches have been adopted to quantify the precise magnitude of relations between depression and social skills deficits. Segrin (1990), for example, conducted a meta-analysis of molar and molecular social skills deficits in depressed individuals by combining results from studies that compared depressed and nondepressed participants in social skills as assessed by self-reports, peer or observer ratings, and behavioral assessments. The majority of the studies included in the meta-analysis used nonclinical participants, meaning that their depressive symptoms were not necessarily severe enough to warrant a *DSM-IV* diagnosis of major depression.

According to Segrin (1990), the effect size, corrected for measurement error, reflecting observers' ratings of *molar* skill in depressed and nondepressed individuals across 13 studies is $r_c = .26$. Corrected effect sizes (r_c) reflecting differences between depressed and nondepressed individuals in *molecular* social skills, in descending order, as follows: (a) pitch variation = .71 (2 studies), (b) gaze = .31 (12 studies), (c) gestures = .37 (2 studies), (d) talk time = .22 (7 studies), (e) activity level = .19 (4 studies), and (f) silences during simulated interaction = .12 (3 studies). That is, results from his meta-analysis suggested that, relative to nondepressed individuals, depressed individuals are more likely to (a) carry on conversations in a monotone voice, (b) make less eye contact with people with whom they are interacting, (c) make fewer gestures that complement their verbal content, (d) talk for a lesser total amount of time, (e) emit fewer actions, and (f) have more silences in their conversations. However, Segrin (1990) noted that the studies examining pitch variation did not incorporate an actual interaction in their designs. He suggested that gaze and talk time might be the two most salient molecular indicators of social skills deficits in depression because their effect sizes are substantial and homogeneous in distribution, and because previous research has demonstrated that there are robust correlations between these variables and global ratings of skill (e.g., Dillard & Spitzberg, 1984).

Other studies have examined the specific topics that depressed individuals introduce during "getting acquainted" interactions. These studies demonstrate that, relative to nondepressed individuals, depressed individuals emit fewer positive appraisals of their interaction partner (Gotlib & Robinson, 1982) and more negative statements, including those reflecting sadness, self-devaluation, and even anger and hostility toward others (Blumberg & Hokanson, 1983; Hokanson, Sacco, Blumberg, & Landrum, 1980; Jacobson & Anderson, 1982). Jacobson and Anderson found that depressed individuals self-disclosed more information than nondepressed individuals and did so at inopportune times during conversations with interaction partners. Moreover, Kuiper and McCabe (1985) reported that depressed individuals rated negative topics (i.e., those that were judged as topics that make people uncomfortable or lead to negative social interaction) as more appropriate than nondepressed individuals.

Thus, objective raters judge that depressed individuals give the general impression that they lack social skills, and depressed individuals engage in particular behaviors that impair social interaction, such as avoiding eye contact and making inappropriate statements. Is it the case that depressed individuals, like socially anxious people, know what to do in social interactions but are inhibited by one or more parameters of the particular situation? As will be seen in the next section, depressed individuals are indeed characterized by distorted cognitive content and biased information processing that have the potential to disrupt behaviors that are necessary for successful social interaction. We will consider the degree to which maladaptive cognition has the potential to mediate the relation between depression and interpersonal behavior and contribute to a performance deficit associated with depressed individuals' social performance.

Cognitive Tradition

Segrin's (1990) meta-analysis revealed that the largest effect sizes characterizing differences in social skill between depressed and nondepressed individuals come from participants' self-report of their own social skills $(r = .41)$. Because this effect size is substantially larger than the effect size for global observer ratings of social skills $(r_c = .26)$, it can be reasoned that depressed individuals have distorted perceptions of their social performance. There is much research confirming that depressed individuals are excessively self-critical (see Coyne & Gotlib, 1983, for a review); depressed individuals estimate that their social performance will be poor (Ducharme & Bachelor, 1993), attribute negative social outcomes to personal shortcomings (Anderson, Horowitz, & French, 1983), and predict that people will not be interested in interacting with them in the future (Borden & Baum, 1987). Dykman, Horowitz, Abramson, and Usher (1991) recruited depressed and nonde-pressed undergraduate participants to engage in a 30-minute group discussion, during which time they received bogus ambiguous feedback about their performance. A regression analysis indicated that *both* negative views of their social competence and actual performance deficits, as measured by others' ratings of their performance, contributed to depressed participants' negative interpretation of their performance. Moreover, we would be remiss not to acknowledge Lewinsohn et al.'s (1980) classic study, which found that depressed individuals' negative evaluation of their social performance was largely in line with observers' ratings, whereas nondepressed individuals' evaluation of their social performance was much higher than that of observers. That is, this study provided evidence that depressed individuals are characterized by *depressive realism*, such that they lack the positivity bias that characterizes nondepressed individuals' self-appraisals in the absence of significant threat or stress. Not all studies find evidence for depressive realism (Ducharme & Bachelor; Dykman et al., 1991; see Dobson & Franche, 1989, for a review). Nevertheless, the body of literature as a whole suggests that depressed individuals judge their social performance in a more negative manner than nondepressed individuals, but this assessment is at least to some degree accurate.

Depressed individuals are also characterized by negative information-processing biases, albeit in a different manner than socially anxious people. For example, there is much less evidence that depressed individuals are characterized by an attentional bias toward negative information (see Mogg & Bradley, 2005, for a review). That is, they are less likely to detect subtle indicators of unsuc-cessful interaction, perhaps because of their cognitive sluggishness. Unfortunately, it may be this inability to detect negative information that contributes to instances in which they demonstrate poor social skills, as others' cues that they are engaging in inappropriate conversation topics might be missed. Moreover, depressed individuals exhibit a unique information-processing bias in their memory functioning, such that they retrieve excessive amounts of negative information (cf. Blaney, 1986) and have great difficulty in retrieving specific positive memories (cf. Williams, 1996). This sort of memory bias would make it likely that depressed individuals would recall previous instances of failure with social interaction and unlikely that they would recall previous instances of success with social interaction. Such a retrieval bias undoubtedly would have great influence on depressed individuals' estimates that they would be successful in future social interaction.

Like socially anxious people, depressed individuals are also characterized by self-focused atten-tion (cf. Ingram, 1990). One type of self-focus that is particularly relevant to depression is rumina-tion, defined as "behaviors and thoughts that focus one's attention on one's depressive symptoms and on the implications of those symptoms" (Nolen-Hoeksema, 1991, p. 569). Depressed individuals with a ruminative coping style focus excessively on the causes, meaning, and consequences of their emo-tional state at the expense of taking some sort of action to change their mood, such as by engaging in a pleasurable activity. Depressed individuals who ruminate are particularly likely to interpret their current situation in a negative light (Lyubomirsky, Caldwell, & Nolen-Hoeksema, 1998), predict negative outcomes for the future (Lyubomirsky & Nolen-Hoeksema, 1995), and exhibit cognitive inflexibility (Davis & Nolen-Hoeksema, 2000). Moreover, there is evidence that a ruminative coping style has specific interpersonal consequences, as these individuals exhibit poor interpersonal prob-lem solving (Lyubomirsky & Nolen-Hoeksema, 1995) and, relative to nonruminators, estimate that they receive less social support (Nolen-Hoeksema & Davis, 1999). A ruminative style could adversely affect relationship initiation in depressed individuals in three ways: (a) by making it particularly aversive to be in the presence of the depressed person, as he or she constantly talks about his or her problems; (b) by taking cognitive resources away from important relationship processes, such as interpersonal problem solving or support seeking and receiving; or (c) by focusing the rumina-tion specifically on perceived problems in the new relationship (e.g., "Why isn't he calling me?" and "What's wrong with me?"), which would in turn lead to an overly pessimistic appraisal.

Thus, as with socially anxious people, several domains of cognition have the potential to affect depressed individuals' relationships. Depressed individuals are characterized by negative cognitive content; although they correctly perceive that aspects of their social performance are subpar, they are excessively critical of themselves and lack the self-serving bias that might in fact protect healthy individuals from emotional distress. Unlike socially anxious people, they fail to detect negative information in their environment, which has the potential to be problematic because others with whom they are interacting might very well be giving them subtle cues that their behavior is inappropriate. They easily remember negative experiences and have difficulty remembering specific positive experiences, which increases the likelihood that they will remember only failed attempts at relationship initiation and will, therefore, view their competence to initiate relationships as very poor. Moreover, their self-focus often reaches a level of rumination, which is unpleasant for others and impairs their ability to engage in normal relationship behaviors. In the next section, we turn to the interpersonal consequences of depression, highlighting a coherent interpersonal theory of depression and demonstrating the manner in which attachment style is linked specifically to cognitions that depressed individuals experience in interpersonal interaction.

Interpersonal Tradition

Unlike the case with social anxiety, interpersonal approaches to understanding depression have been considered for several decades. Coyne's (1976b) interpersonal theory of depression suggests that people who are vulnerable to depression continually seek reassurance and validation from others. When they receive that reassurance, oftentimes they doubt its sincerity, which leads them to solicit additional feedback and support. Over time, the people from whom they seek reassurance and validation become irritated, increasing the probability that they will reject the vulnerable individual. When rejection occurs, the vulnerable individual experiences depressive symptoms, and his or her support system is disrupted. Of course, a disrupted social support system simply exacerbates depressive symptoms.

Joiner and his colleagues (Joiner, Metalsky, Katz, & Beach, 1999) regarded *excessive reassurance seeking* as the central feature of this interpersonal model of depression, defining it as "the relatively stable tendency to excessively and persistently seek assurances from others that one is loveable and worthy, regardless of whether such assurance has already been provided" (p. 270). Although some empirical studies designed to test this hypothesis gather data from the standpoint of only one individual, rather than an interaction or relationship partner (e.g., Potthoff, Holahan, & Joiner, 1995), we nevertheless view this line of research as being conducted in light of the interpersonal tradition because it is grounded so heavily in Coyne's (1976b) interpersonal theory of depression. Results from studies examining the association between excessive reassurance seeking and depression indicate that excessive reassurance seeking (a) is unique to depression rather than other types of psychopathology, including anxiety (Joiner & Metalsky, 2001); (b) predicts future depressive symptoms in individuals who are initially symptom free (Joiner & Metalsky, 2001; Joiner & Schmidt, 1998); and (c) when paired with symptoms of distress, is associated with rejection by others (Joiner & Metalsky, 1995). Thus, the construct of excessive reassurance seeking has the potential to unify the three theoretical traditions, as it is a behavioral (verbal) phenomenon, is associated with negative interpersonal interpretations (e.g., that others are insincere), and instigates a cycle that clearly has adverse effects on others, thereby disrupting relationships.

Attachment theory has also been used to capture the interpersonal processes at work in depression. As we saw in the section on social anxiety, higher levels of depression are associated with higher levels of avoidant-fearful and anxious-preoccupied attachment insecurity (e.g., Carnelley, Pietromonaco, & Jaffe, 1994; Hankin, Kassel, & Abela, 2005; Reinecke & Rogers, 2001; Roberts et al., 1996). However, unlike the literature on the association between social anxiety and adult attachment, scholars who examine attachment in depressed individuals have taken steps to identify the specific mechanism by which these constructs are related. For example, Roberts et al. found that the relation between depression and attachment insecurity was mediated by dysfunctional attitudes and low self-esteem, such that insecurely attached individuals were characterized by dysfunctional attitudes, which in turn prompted lower levels of self-esteem, which in turn made them vulnerable to experience depression (see replications by Hankin et al., 2005; Reinecke & Rogers, 2001). Other researchers have identified low self-efficacy (Strodl & Noller, 2003) and interpersonal stress (Hankin et al., 2005) as additional mediators between insecure attachment and depressive symptoms. In a sophisticated longitudinal design using a large sample of college freshmen, Wei, Russell, and Zakalik (2005) found that lack of social self-efficacy partially mediated the relation between attachment anxiety and subsequent loneliness and depression, whereas discomfort with self-disclosure mediated the relation between attachment avoidance and subsequent loneliness and depression. Not only do these studies demonstrate that adult attachment styles are associated with depressive symptoms, but they also illustrate that symptoms are exacerbated through maladaptive cognitions, such as dysfunctional attitudes or low self-efficacy. In other words, certain adult attachment styles provide the context for maladaptive cognitions to emerge, which have tangible effects on emotional well-being. The next step in this program of research is to identify the mechanism by which attachment style, maladaptive cognition, and depressive symptoms work in conjunction to affect specific interpersonal interactions, including those associated with relationship initiation.

Summary

Like socially anxious people, depressed individuals often behave in ways that impair their interpersonal interactions, and as a result, others find it aversive to spend time with them. Although at times depressed individuals are accurate in their ratings of the quality of their performance, they are excessively self-critical, they ruminate over their emotional experiences, and they seek additional reassurance from others—all of which likely disrupt personal relationships to a much greater degree than the lack of skill by itself. In other words, cognitive distortions exacerbate the behavioral problems that interfere with depressed individuals' personal relationships. Is it the case, as we suggested in the section on social anxiety, that depressed individuals have the knowledge of how to behave in interpersonal interaction but fail to act on this knowledge because they are inhibited by one or more aspects of the specific situation? We speculate that depressed individuals are indeed characterized by performance deficits, rather than skills deficits, although the mechanism underlying performance deficits is likely to be much different than in socially anxious individuals. Socially anxious people are hypervigilant for cues, either internal or external, that signal failure and negative judgment from others. When they detect these cues, their cognitive resources are consumed by the implication of these cues and monitoring for additional cues, which in turn disrupt performance. Depressed individuals, in contrast, are absorbed by their emotional distress (Nolen-Hoeksema, 1991) and perceptions of failure (Beck, 1967), leaving few cognitive resources to register others' reactions toward them. Moreover, depressed individuals are characterized by motivational deficits (e.g., fatigue) that further inhibit the execution of interpersonal skills (Segrin, 1992). Thus, it is likely that concern about the judgment of others impairs socially anxious individuals' social performance, and self-absorption with their current problems and motivational deficits impairs depressed individuals' social performance (see Alden, Bieling, & Meleshko, 1995, for a similar conceptualization).

Unfortunately, interpersonal problems often do not abate after the remission of the depressive episode (e.g., Hammen & Brennan, 2002; Rohde, Lewinsohn, & Seeley, 1994), suggesting that cognitive distortions activated by depression and motivational deficits are not the sole reasons for depressed individuals' impaired social performance. Perhaps interpersonal problems persist because these individuals continue to be characterized by an insecure attachment style that makes them vulnerable to future mood disturbance, negative cognitions (e.g., low self-efficacy), and interpersonal impairment. It is incumbent, then, upon researchers to identify the degree to which standard interventions for emotional disturbance affect interpersonal functioning and, if necessary, consider ways in which these interventions can be modified to promote lasting changes in emotionally impaired individuals' close relationships.

INTERVENTION

Although there are many empirically supported psychosocial interventions for emotional disturbances, rarely do these protocols focus on relationship initiation per se. However, a large segment of quality of life comprises interpersonal relationships and social interaction (e.g., Eng et al., 2005); thus, many patients seeking treatment for emotional disturbances target improvements in these areas as major goals for treatment. A few clinical trials designed to evaluate the efficacy of psychosocial treatments for emotional disturbances include some sort of assessment of interpersonal functioning, which provides preliminary data to evaluate whether and how aspects of personal relationships improve following treatment. In the following section, we briefly describe behavioral, cognitive, and interpersonal psychosocial interventions for emotional disturbance and reference data that speak to the efficacy of these interventions in improving interpersonal functioning.

Behavioral Intervention

Treatment from a behavioral perspective often focuses on the development of appropriate social skills with the goal of improving patients' ability to interact appropriately and effectively, which is in turn assumed to improve happiness and life satisfaction (Curran, 1977; Segrin & Givertz, 2003). There is no one approach to social skills training, and in fact, it can be argued that even within one social skills protocol, each individual course of treatment will be unique because it should be tailored to target the specific deficits of each patient (Segrin & Givertz, 2003). Social skills intervention packages have included training in assertiveness (e.g., Zeiss, Lewinsohn, & Munoz, 1979); asking people out on dates (Curran, 1977); other communication skills such as making apologies, expressing affection, and giving compliments (e.g., Curran, 1977; Hersen, Bellack, & Himmelhoch, 1980; van Dam-Baggen & Kraaimaat, 2000); listening (e.g., van Dam-Baggen & Kraaimaat, 2000); and making eye contact (e.g., Curran; Hersen et al., 1980). Typically, there are three methods by which patients develop skills (cf. Segrin & Givertz, 2003). *Modeling* is a strategy by which patients learn social skills by observing others, which provides them with a guide for their own behavior and increases their confidence that success can be achieved. *Role playing* is a strategy in which patients practice particular communication and social skills strategies in session, which allows the clinician to provide specific feedback to optimize patients' performance. Finally, *homework assignments* provide the opportunity for patients to practice their newly acquired skills in a naturalistic environment.

Results from studies designed to evaluate the efficacy of social skills training for emotionally impaired individuals suggest that these interventions significantly reduce symptoms of emotional disturbance and increase the level of social skill demonstrated by patients at the end of treatment (for reviews, see Curran, 1977; Segrin & Givertz, 2003). Although social skills trainings are implemented with the rationale that they will improve interpersonal functioning to a greater degree than psychosocial interventions that do not focus on this domain, results from many studies suggest that patients receiving social skills interventions report similar levels of reduced psychiatric symptoms and improved interpersonal functioning as people receiving other treatments (e.g., Fedoroff & Taylor, 2001; Mersch, Emmelkamp, Bögels, & van der Sleen, 1989; Zeiss et al., 1979). This pattern of results occurs even when emotionally impaired patients who are judged as having particularly poor social skills receive social skills training, which would presumably target their greatest deficit (Mersch et al., 1989). Stravynski, Grey, and Elie (1987) raised the possibility that emotionally impaired patients' improvement following a trial of social skills training has more to do with anxiety reduction and exposure to feared situations than the acquisition of new skills. Thus, social skills training appears to be an efficacious treatment in reducing symptoms of emotional distress, improving social skills that are rated by objective judges, and reducing discomfort when interacting with others, although it is unclear whether these changes occur through skill acquisition or through other mechanisms.

We focused on social skills training in this section on behavioral intervention as a logical outgrowth of our discussion of social skills deficits associated with social anxiety and depression. However, it is important to acknowledge that there are other empirically supported behavioral treatments for social anxiety and depression. For example, socially anxious patients sometimes undergo *exposure* therapy, which involves systematic and sustained contact with a graded hierarchy of feared situations (e.g., interacting one-on-one with a stranger, then interacting with a group of strangers; Feske & Chambless, 1995). As will be seen in the subsequent section, exposure is often combined with cognitive strategies in a combined cognitive-behavioral approach to the treatment of social anxiety. An alternative behavioral treatment for depression focuses on increasing patients' involvement in and enjoyment of pleasurable activities, with the rationale that they will obtain increased levels of positive reinforcement from their environment (e.g., Lewinsohn, 1975b; Zeiss et al., 1979). A contemporary outgrowth of this approach, *behavioral activation*, is often included in cognitive-behavioral approaches to the treatment of depression.

Cognitive Intervention

Cognitive interventions for emotional disturbances center on identifying and modifying situational automatic thoughts, underlying core beliefs, and pessimistic expectations, a process called *cognitive restructuring* (Beck, 1995). Patients develop specific strategies to evaluate problematic situations in a more balanced manner (e.g., "What's the worst that can happen?" and "Does ____'s opinion really reflect everyone else's opinion?"). Additionally, clinicians help emotionally impaired patients to construct creative "experiments" to test out their maladaptive beliefs and expectations in their everyday lives. In reality, most cognitive interventions do not focus solely on cognitive strategies; in fact, as mentioned previously, behavioral strategies often are given prominent focus (hence the term that often refers to cognitive interventions, *cognitive-behavioral therapy* [CBT]). Even when treatments are labeled cognitive therapy rather than cognitive-behavioral therapy, behavioral strategies are included in the protocol with the rationale that they will bring about significant cognitive change (cf. Foa & Rauch, 2004). For example, exposure strategies provide evidence to patients that nothing catastrophic will occur when they are engaging in a feared situation, such as interactions with strangers.

There is an abundance of research demonstrating that cognitive interventions are efficacious in treating emotional disturbances. Dobson's (1989) meta-analysis demonstrated that the typical depressed patient receiving cognitive therapy has a better outcome (i.e., reduction in self-reported depressive symptoms) than 67% of depressed patients receiving behavior therapy and 70% of depressed patients receiving pharmacotherapy. Depressed patients successfully treated with cognitive therapy are half as likely to relapse relative to people treated successfully with antidepressant medication (Hollon, Stewart, & Strunk, 2006). One of the most promising cognitive-behavioral treatments for social anxiety is cognitive-behavioral group therapy (CBGT; Heimberg & Becker, 2002). CBGT is a short-term, time-limited treatment that includes training in cognitive restructuring, exposures to simulated feared situations during group sessions, and homework assignments designed to facilitate exposure to feared situations in patients' everyday lives. Socially anxious patients are encouraged to use their cognitive restructuring skills to manage their anxiety before and during interactions, as well as to arrive at an accurate judgment of their performance.

Although research clearly suggests that CBGT is an efficacious treatment for social anxiety, approximately one third of patients, primarily those with generalized or pervasive social anxiety, do not achieve high end-state functioning (Rodebaugh, Holaway, & Heimberg, 2004). Thus, many researchers have attempted to identify ways to modify CBGT to increase its value. For example, there is some evidence that individual cognitive therapy focusing on modifying the problematic cognitive and behavioral patterns identified in Clark and Wells' (1995) model (e.g., decreasing reliance on safety behaviors, and shifting self-focused attention) is more effective than group treatment (Stangier, Heidenreich, Peitz, Lauterbach, & Clark, 2003) and strictly behavioral treatments, such as exposure and relaxation (Clark et al., 2006). Herbert et al. (2005) incorporated social skills training into CBGT, with the rationale that it would be especially useful for patients with generalized social anxiety disorder who are characterized by impaired social functioning, and found that it significantly improved outcome.

The majority of outcome studies examining outcomes of CBT for emotional disturbance focus on reductions in symptoms of depression and anxiety. It is much rarer to encounter analyses that focus on improvements in interpersonal functioning. In notable exceptions, Eng et al. (2005) and Scott et al. (2000) reported that socially anxious patients completing a trial of CBGT and depressed patients completing a trial of cognitive therapy reported significant improvements in social functioning, although their average level of social functioning post treatment was still in the low range. Vittengl, Clark, and Jarrett (2004) found that cognitive therapy improved depressed patients' social functioning in interpersonal roles; reduced dysfunctional thoughts, feelings, and behaviors relevant to interpersonal functioning; and decreased marital distress. Regression analyses suggested that these changes were accounted for by improvements in depressive symptoms. Thus, there is promising evidence that CBT is effective in reducing interpersonal distress, although it is likely that improvements in this domain arise as a function of symptom reduction, as opposed to the acquisition of cognitive and behavioral strategies that are specific in addressing interpersonal functioning. However, there is a paucity of evidence that speaks to whether CBT improves relationship *initiation* in emotionally impaired individuals, rather than enhancing their existing close relationships. Although it is logical that improved social skills and adaptive cognitions would be beneficial as emotionally impaired individuals develop new relationships post treatment, we await future empirical research to confirm this notion.

Interpersonal Intervention

Interpersonal interventions, not surprisingly, focus on disruptions in close relationships and their association to psychiatric symptoms. Bowlby (1977), for example, described strategies for identifying patterns in past relationships and relating them to current relationship problems, including problems in the therapeutic relationship. In this section, we focus on a contemporary empirically supported interpersonal intervention, interpersonal psychotherapy (IPT). Patients in IPT address conflicts and transitions in their current relationships and develop strategies for utilizing their social support network in times of stress (Parker, Parker, Brotchie, & Stuart, 2006; Weissman, Markowitz, & Klerman, 2000). Insecure adult attachment styles are not directly targeted in IPT, although attachment theory is implicated in helping the interpersonal psychotherapist to conceptualize his or her patient's symptoms and concomitant dysfunction (Parker et al., 2006). Maladaptive cognitions (e.g., unreasonable expectations for relationships) and behavioral deficits (e.g., communication skills deficits) might be considered during the course of treatment, but they are not done so systematically, as in cognitive and behavioral interventions. Instead, they are targeted as needed in sessions, as discussion of interpersonal dysfunction spontaneously unfolds (Weissman et al., 2000). Interpersonal psychotherapists typically focus on one or two of four major problem areas—grief, role transitions, role disputes, and interpersonal deficits.

As we saw in the sections on behavioral and cognitive interventions, empirical research indicates that IPT is efficacious in treating patients with emotional disturbances. For depressed patients, IPT reduces depressive symptoms to a greater degree than placebo treatment and to a similar degree as antidepressant medication (see de Mello, de Jesus Mari, Bacaltchuk, Verdeli, & Neugebauer, 2005). In addition, IPT for depression is associated with improvements in marital satisfaction and relationships with immediate family members, children, and friends (O'Hara, Stuart, Gorman, & Wenzel, 2000), although there is a surprising paucity of IPT outcome studies that include other indices of interpersonal functioning as dependent measures. In contrast, far fewer studies have examined the efficacy of IPT for social anxiety. Weissman et al. (2000) indicated that IPT for social anxiety is conducted in much the same manner as IPT for depression, but that "the boundary between the disorder and the interpersonal anxiety is often less distinct" (pp. 331–332). Role insecurity is an additional problem area often targeted in IPT for socially anxious patients, which involves problems with assertiveness, conflict avoidance, difficulty expressing anger, and sensitivity to rejection (Lipsitz, Markowitz, Cherry, & Fyer, 1999). In the context of this problem area, sessions often focus on hypersensitivity to the comments of others, precipitants of social avoidance, and indicators of successful social interaction (Weissman et al., 2000). In one open trial designed to evaluate the efficacy of 14 weeks of IPT for social anxiety, seven of nine patients improved significantly on self-reported and clinician-rated measures of social anxiety, and a self-report measure of quality of life (Lipsitz et al., 1999).

Thus, like behavioral and cognitive approaches to psychotherapy, IPT is clearly efficacious in reducing symptoms of depression and social anxiety, and there is preliminary evidence that it improves patients' interpersonal functioning. Evidence is lacking, however, in the degree to which IPT improves emotionally impaired people's ability to successfully initiate new relationships. In theory, we would expect that IPT would improve patients' abilities to develop new relationships in that maladaptive grief associated with the loss of previous relationships would be reduced and specific strategies for handling role transitions, role disputes, and interpersonal deficits would be strengthened. We encourage clinical scientists to examine these mechanisms and outcomes in future research.

Summary

Results from outcome studies clearly indicate that behavioral interventions, cognitive interventions, and IPT are efficacious in reducing social anxiety and depressive symptoms. Although there is a small body of evidence that these interventions improve interpersonal functioning, this conclusion must be tempered by the fact that, in most instances, interpersonal functioning is measured by a self-report inventory assessing broad functioning in already established relationships, such as the Social Adjustment Scale (Weissman & Bothwell, 1976). Outcome studies evaluating the efficacy of social skills training constitute one exception, as often patients' social skills in the context of an interaction with a confederate are evaluated by objective raters pre- and post treatment. However, the ecological validity of these assessments is questionable. Thus, it remains to be seen whether these interventions make tangible differences in the everyday lives of emotionally impaired individuals, as well as in their ability to initiate, engage in, and sustain new relationships. We suspect that the ability to negotiate new relationships improves to some degree simply because of the reduction in acute symptoms (cf. Vittengl et al., 2004) but that patients with remitted emotional disturbances could benefit from additional intervention that would target interpersonal skills (cf. Hammen & Brennan, 2002; Rodhe et al., 1994).

Particularly alarming is the fact that a substantial minority of patients who undergo these interventions do not report significant improvements in their symptoms (Rodebaugh et al., 2004). To address this concern, many scholars have devised combined treatments, such as social skills training combined with CBGT (Herbert et al., 2005), social skills training combined with psychoeducation and exposure (Turner, Beidel, Cooley, Woody, & Messer, 1994), and CBT combined with attachment-focused family therapy (Siqueland, Rynn, & Diamond, 2005). We applaud the creativity of scholars who devise these interventions but pose the question of whether there are so many active ingredients of these that no one specific strategy is able to have a potent impact on reducing symptomatology and improving functioning, particularly when these treatments comprise only 12 to 16 sessions. We propose two possibilities for future intervention research. First, it might be beneficial for people who demonstrate significant behavioral skills deficits, cognitive dysfunction specifically about relationships, and/or insecure attachment orientation to participate in a separate intervention focused exclusively on initiating, negotiating, and maintaining interpersonal relationships, much in the same way that patients with pervasive emotional disturbance and behavioral dysfunction participate in skills training in addition to intensive individual psychotherapy (Linehan, 1993). Second, people who successfully complete a trial of one of these interventions could complete a course of maintenance treatment (cf. Spanier & Frank, 1998) that would focus on maintaining the reduction in symptoms gained during the acute course of treatment and addressing functioning, particularly in close relationships, in everyday life.

CONCLUSION

Although behavioral, cognitive, and attachment models specify the manner in which emotional disturbances disrupt personal relationships *in general*, we must extrapolate from the available literature to form a conceptualization of the manner in which they disrupt relationship *initiation*. In a very general sense, we propose that insecure attachment styles predispose emotionally impaired individuals to experience negative cognitions, and to process interpersonal information in a biased manner, when they are in a situation where a new relationship is developing. These cognitive distortions and biases, in turn, disrupt the execution of adaptive behavior. However, there are many subtleties of this relational-cognitive-behavioral style, all of which vary depending on the particular person (e.g., history of success versus failure with relationship initiation), the parameters of the particular situation (e.g., large group versus one-on-one), and the characteristics of the person with whom the emotionally impaired person is forming a relationship (e.g., attractiveness, social status, and similarity in level of social anxiety).

There are many avenues for future research that can advance a model of relationship initiation and emotional disturbances that accounts for individual and situational variables, and the interaction between them. The common denominator of the specific directions that we propose is that the richest source of data will come from designs in which ratings are collected from both the target individual and the person with whom he or she is interacting. Such designs will elucidate the dynamics of relationship initiation, or the reciprocal nature of cognitions experienced and behaviors exhibited in interpersonal interaction by both members of the dyad. Moreover, these designs will identify the specific cognitions and behaviors that are incorrectly *perceived* by the emotionally impaired individual as being detrimental to the relationship as well as those that *actually* have the effect of making the partner less eager to interact with him or her in the future.

As described previously in the chapter, depressed individuals exhibit a great deal of aversive behavior in interpersonal interactions, such as excessive reassurance seeking, negative statements toward themselves and others, and inappropriate self-disclosure. Much less research has identified specific verbal behaviors that are detrimental to socially anxious individuals' interactions, although Walters and Hope's (1998) study raised the possibility that verbal behavior (or the lack thereof) is more important than nonverbal behavior in characterizing the social skills deficits associated with social anxiety. We encourage future researchers to code instances of appropriate and inappropriate verbal and nonverbal behaviors during getting acquainted interactions and identify the relative weight that each of these skill domains carries in explaining partners' willingness to interact with socially anxious individuals in the future. A direct comparison of socially anxious with depressed participants would be useful to develop a taxonomy of shared and unique behavioral deficits. We suspect that many behavioral deficits (e.g., lack of eye contact) will be nonspecific or indicative of general emotional disturbances. However, some will be unique to a particular domain of emotional disturbance (e.g., excessive reassurance seeking with depression; see Joiner & Metalsky, 2001), which will be central as researchers outline the specific mechanisms by which emotional disturbances beget interpersonal problems. Moreover, we would be remiss not to acknowledge that there is substantial comorbidity between social anxiety and depression (Wenzel & Holt, 2001), suggesting that many emotionally impaired individuals exhibit interpersonal deficits reflective of both domains.

In addition to behaviors that disrupt relationship initiation, we have evidence that emotionally impaired individuals experience negative thoughts during interpersonal interaction, expect that these interactions will go poorly, and exhibit biased processing of social cues. How exactly does this cognitive pattern disrupt social performance? Researchers can sample the automatic thoughts, both self and other oriented, that are experienced at various points in getting acquainted interactions to identify emotionally impaired participants' thoughts that precede specific performance deficits and reactions of interaction partners to specific performance deficits. After interactions, they can assess participants' recall and interpretation of central and peripheral events that occurred in the interaction (see Hope, Heimberg, & Klein, 1990) and identify associations between these negative cognitive biases, performance deficits, and partners' willingness to interact with them in the future.

Moreover, researchers can identify cognitive distortions and biases that arise as a function of particular characteristics of the interaction partner, such as perceived attractiveness, or the situation, such as the presence of other observers, in order to paint a clearer picture of the parameters that work in concert to disrupt interpersonal functioning. We would anticipate, for example, that socially anxious people would endorse particularly distorted cognitions and demonstrate particularly submissive behavior when interacting with attractive, high-status partners.

We also encourage researchers to elucidate the precise nature and role of adult attachment styles in disrupting emotionally impaired individuals' interpersonal functioning. Are attachment styles, from an interpersonal perspective, synonymous with core beliefs about the self and others, from a cognitive perspective? Does an insecure attachment style predict problems with relationship initiation above and beyond symptoms of emotional disturbance and a negative cognitive style? If it does, what is the specific mechanism by which it affects behavior? It is possible that attachment style has greater explanatory power in accounting for interpersonal dysfunction in people with chronic emotional disturbances, like James, rather than people who have a single episode of emotional difficulties, like Gina. These questions can best be answered by longitudinal research that assesses vulnerability factors for relationship disturbance, specific cognitions activated and behaviors exhibited in interpersonal interactions, and cognitive, emotional, and behavioral characteristics of the aftermath of interpersonal interactions.

At the end of the section on social anxiety, we indicated that many socially anxious people have a few close, satisfying relationships and that disruptions to relationship development might lessen as the relationship moves from initiation to maintenance stages. We encourage researchers to track the course of new relationships over time in emotionally impaired individuals to identify the factors that make these relationships successful. It is possible that very different sets of behavioral and cognitive styles contribute to success or failure at different relationship stages. In addition, although Wenzel's (2002) data suggested that socially anxious people reported satisfaction with their close relationships, we should not necessarily conclude that these relationships are healthy. For example, it is possible that emotionally impaired individuals exhibit excessive dependency on close others (cf. Davila & Beck, 2002), which has the potential to (a) cause severe distress if there are threats to the relationship; (b) be off-putting to the partner, much in the same way as excessive reassurance seeking is; and (c) prevent them from pursuing relationships with others because they perceive that their needs are being met by their partner. In the latter instance, emotionally impaired individuals who report satisfying relationships with a few close others might be overly reliant on these relationships and miss the opportunity to form new relationships that would otherwise be satisfying and meaningful.

Finally, we must acknowledge some major limitations of the literature reviewed in this chapter. The vast majority of studies designed to evaluate emotionally impaired individuals' interpersonal functioning used college student samples with elevated scores on self-report symptom measures. Thus, the degree to which results from these studies generalize to adult patients with emotional disturbances, like James or Gina, is unclear. In addition, nearly all of the getting acquainted studies are designed to simulate heterosocial interaction, so little is known about the manner in which emotional disturbances affect the initiation of same-sex friendships or homosexual romantic relationships. Moreover, no known studies have been designed to examine emotional disturbances and relationship initiation in dyads of mixed cultural, ethnic, and religious backgrounds, so it remains to be seen whether emotional disturbances contribute to partners' perceptions of dissimilarity to a greater degree than demographic variables.

In sum, research clearly demonstrates that socially anxious and depressed individuals are characterized by behavioral deficits, cognitive distortions about their performance and others' reactions to them, and biased processing of social cues in the context of interpersonal interactions. It is possible that an insecure adult attachment style forms the basis for many of these behaviors and cognitions to emerge. Fortunately, there are many well-established psychosocial interventions that have lasting effects on symptoms of social anxiety and depression, which are in turn associated with improvements in social functioning and quality of life. Moreover, researchers are actively designing additional components for these interventions to target emotionally impaired individuals who do not respond fully to these standard treatments. We are optimistic that, over time, specific factors associated with disrupted relationship initiation will be identified, which will in turn lead to even more refined interventions to promote interpersonal fulfillment in emotionally impaired individuals.

REFERENCES

Alden, L. A., Bieling, P. J., & Meleshko, K. G. A. (1995). An interpersonal comparison of depression and social anxiety. In K. D. Craig & K. S. Dobson (Eds.), *Anxiety and depression in adults and children* (pp. 57–81). Thousand Oaks, CA: Sage.

Alden, L. E., & Mellings, T. M. B. (2004). Generalized social phobia and social judgments: The salience of self- and partner-information. *Journal of Anxiety Disorders, 18*, 143–157.

Alden, L. E., & Taylor, C. T. (2004). Interpersonal processes in social phobia. *Clinical Psychology Review, 24*, 857–882.

Alden, L. E., & Wallace, S. T. (1995). Social phobia and social appraisal in successful and unsuccessful interactions. *Behaviour Research and Therapy, 33*, 497–506.

American Psychiatric Association. (2000). *Diagnostic and statistical manual of mental disorders* (*DSM-IV-TR*; 4th ed., text rev.). Washington, DC: American Psychiatric Association.

Amir, N., Foa, E. B., & Coles, M. E. (1998). Automatic activation and strategic avoidance of threat-relevant information in social phobia. *Journal of Abnormal Psychology, 107*, 285–290.

Anderson, C. A., Horowitz, L. M., & French, R. D. (1983). Attributional style of lonely and depressed people. *Journal of Personality and Social Psychology, 45*, 127–136.

Bartholomew, K., & Horowitz, L. M. (1991). Attachment styles among young adults: A test of a four-category model. *Journal of Personality and Social Psychology, 61*, 226–244.

Beck, A. T. (1967). *Depression: Causes and treatment.* Philadelphia: University of Pennsylvania Press.

Beck, A. T. (1988). *Love is never enough.* New York: Harper & Row.

Beck, J. S. (1995). *Cognitive therapy: Basics and beyond.* New York: Guilford.

Beidel, D. C., Turner, S. M., & Dancu, C. V. (1985). Physiological, cognitive, and behavioral aspects of social anxiety. *Behaviour Research and Therapy, 23*, 109–117.

Bellack, A. S., Hersen, M., & Turner, S. M. (1979). The relationship of role playing and knowledge of appropriate behavior to assertion in the natural environment. *Journal of Consulting and Clinical Psychology, 47*, 670–678.

Blaney, P. H. (1986). Affect and memory: A review. *Psychological Bulletin, 99*, 229–246.

Blumberg, S. R., & Hokanson, J. E. (1983). The effects of another person's response style on interpersonal behavior in depression. *Journal of Abnormal Psychology, 92*, 196–209.

Borden, J. W., & Baum, C. G. (1987). Investigation of a social-interactional model of depression with mildly depressed males and females. *Sex Roles, 17*, 449–465.

Bowlby, J. (1977). The making and breaking of affectional bonds II: Some principles of psychotherapy. *British Journal of Psychiatry, 130*, 421–431.

Brennan, K. A., Clark, C. L., & Shaver, P. R. (1998). Self-report measurement of adult attachment: An integrated overview. In J. A. Simpson & W. S. Rhodes (Eds.), *Attachment theory and close relationships* (pp. 46–76). New York: Guilford.

Bruch, M. A., & Pearl, L. (1995). Attributional style and symptoms of shyness in a heterosexual interaction. *Cognitive Therapy and Research, 19*, 91–107.

Cappella, J. N. (1985). Production principles for turn-taking in social interaction: Socially anxious vs. socially secure persons. *Journal of Language and Social Psychology, 4*, 193–212.

Carnelley, K. B., Pietromonaco, P. R., & Jaffe, K. (1994). Depression, working models of others, and relationship functioning. *Journal of Personality and Social Psychology, 66*, 127–140.

Clark, D. M., Ehlers, A., Hackmann, A., McManus, F., Fennell, M., Grey, N., et al. (2006). Cognitive therapy versus exposure and applied relaxation in social phobia: A randomized controlled trial. *Journal of Consulting and Clinical Psychology, 74*, 568–578.

Clark, D. M., & Wells, A. (1995). A cognitive model of social phobia. In R. G. Heimberg, M. R. Liebowitz, D. A. Hope, & F. R. Schneier (Eds.), *Social phobia: Diagnosis, assessment, and treatment* (pp. 69–93). New York: Guilford.

Clark, J. V., & Arkowitz, H. (1975). Social anxiety and self-evaluation of interpersonal performance. *Psychological Reports, 36*, 211–221.

Coyne, J. C. (1976a). Depression and the response of others. *Journal of Abnormal Psychology, 85*, 186–193.

Coyne, J. C. (1976b). Toward and interactional description of depression. *Psychiatry, 39*, 28–40.

Coyne, J. C., & Gotlib, I. A. (1983). The role of cognition in depression: A critical appraisal. *Psychological Bulletin, 94*, 472–505.

Curran, J. P. (1977). Skills training as an approach to the treatment of heterosexual-social anxiety: A review. *Psychological Bulletin, 84*, 140–157.

Darcy, K., Davila, J., & Beck, J. G. (2005). Is social anxiety associated with both interpersonal avoidance and interpersonal dependence? *Cognitive Therapy and Research, 29*, 171–186.

Davila, J., & Beck, J. G. (2002). Is social anxiety associated with impairment in close relationships? *Behavior Therapy, 33*, 427–446.

Davis, R. N., & Nolen-Hoeksema, S. (2000). Cognitive inflexibility among ruminators and nonruminators. *Cognitive Therapy and Research, 24*, 699–711.

De Mello, M. F., de Jesus Mari, J., Bacaltchuk, J., Verdeli, H., & Neugebauer, R. (2005). A systematic review of research findings on the efficacy of interpersonal therapy for depressive disorders. *European Archives of Psychiatry and Clinical Neuroscience, 255*, 75–82.

Dillard, J. P., & Spitzberg, B. H. (1984). Global impressions of social skills: Behavioral predictors. In R. N. Bostrom (Ed.), *Communication yearbook 8* (pp. 446–463). Beverly Hills, CA: Sage.

Dobson, K., & Franche, R-L. (1989). A conceptual and empirical review of the depressive realism hypothesis. *Canadian Journal of Behavioral Science, 21*, 419–433.

Dobson, K. S. (1989). A meta-analysis of the efficacy of cognitive therapy for depression. *Journal of Consulting and Clinical Psychology, 57*, 414–419.

Dodge, C. S., Hope, D. A., Heimberg, R. G., & Becker, R. E. (1988). Evaluation of the Social Interaction Self-Statement Test with a social phobic population. *Cognitive Therapy and Research, 12*, 211–222.

Ducharme, J., & Bachelor, A. (1993). Perceptions of social functioning in dysphoria. *Cognitive Therapy and Research, 17*, 53–70.

Duggan, E. S., & Brennan, K. A. (1994). Social avoidance and its relation to Bartholomew's adult attachment typology. *Journal of Social and Personal Relationships, 62*, 457–468.

Dykman, B. M., Horowitz, L. M., Abramson, L. Y., & Usher, M. (1991). Schematic and situation determinants of depressed and nondepressed students' interpretation of feedback. *Journal of Abnormal Psychology, 100*, 45–55.

Eng, W., Coles, M. E., Heimberg, R. G., & Safran. S. A. (2005). Domains of life satisfaction in social anxiety disorder: Relation to symptoms and response to cognitive-behavioral therapy. *Journal of Anxiety Disorders, 19*, 143–156.

Eng, W., Heimberg, R. G., Hart, T. A., Schneier, F. R., & Liebowitz, M. R. (2001). Attachment in individuals with social anxiety disorder: The relationship among adult attachment styles, social anxiety, and depression. *Emotion, 1*, 365–380.

Faravelli, C., Zucchi, T., Viviani, B., Salmoria, R., Perone, A., Paionni, A., et al. (2000). Epidemiology of social phobia: A clinical approach. *European Psychiatry, 15*, 17–24.

Fedoroff, I. C., & Taylor, S. T. (2001). Psychological and pharmacological treatments of social phobia: A meta-analysis. *Behavior Therapy, 26*, 695–720.

Feeney, J. A. (1999). Issues of closeness and distance in dating relationships: Effects of sex and attachment style. *Journal of Social and Personal Relationships, 16*, 571–590.

Feeney, J. A., & Noller, P. (1990). Attachment style as a predictor of adult romantic relationships. *Journal of Personality and Social Psychology, 58*, 281–291.

Feeney, J. A., Noller, P., & Patty, J. (1993). Adolescents' interactions with the opposite sex: Influence of attachment style and gender. *Journal of Adolescence, 16*, 169–183.

Feske, U., & Chambless, D. L. (1995). Cognitive behavioral vs. exposure only treatment for social phobia: A meta-analysis. *Behaviour Research and Therapy, 26*, 695–720.

Foa, E. B., Franklin, M. E., Perry, K. J., & Herbert, J. D. (1996). Cognitive biases in generalized social phobia. *Journal of Abnormal Psychology, 105*, 433–439.

Foa, E. B., & Rauch, S. A. M. (2004). Cognitive changes during prolonged exposure versus prolonged exposure plus cognitive restructuring in female assault survivors with posttraumatic stress disorder. *Journal of Consulting and Clinical Psychology, 72*, 879–884.

Fraley, W. C., & Waller, N. G. (1998). Adult attachment patterns: A test of the typological model. In J. A. Simpson & W. S. Rhodes (Eds.), *Attachment theory and close relationships* (pp. 77–144). New York: Guilford.

Fredman, L., Weissman, M. W., Leaf, P. J., & Bruce, M. L. (1988). Social functioning in community residents with depression and other psychiatric disorders: Results of the New Haven epidemiologic catchment area study. *Journal of Affective Disorders, 15*, 103–112.

Fydrich, T., Chambless, D. L., Perry, K. J., Buergener, F., & Beazley, M. B. (1998). Behavioural assessment of social performance: A rating system for social phobia. *Behaviour Research and Therapy*, *36*, 995–1010.

Gilboa-Schechtman, E., Foa, E. B., & Amir, N. (1999). Attentional biases for facial expressions in social phobia: The face-in-the-crowd paradigm. *Cognition and Emotion*, *13*, 305–318.

Glass, C. R., Merluzzi, T. V., Biever, J. L., & Larsen, K. H. (1982). Cognitive assessment of social anxiety: Development and validation of a self–statement questionnaire. *Cognitive Therapy and Research*, *6*, 37–55.

Gotlib, I. H., & Robinson, L. A. (1982). Responses to depressed individuals: Discrepancies between self-report and observer-rated behavior. *Journal of Abnormal Psychology*, *91*, 231–240.

Ham, L., Hayes, S. A., & Hope, D. A. (2005). Gender differences in social support for socially anxious individuals. *Cognitive Behaviour Therapy*, *34*, 201–206.

Hammen, C., & Brennan, P. A. (2002). Interpersonal dysfunction in depressed women: Impairments independent of depressive symptoms. *Journal of Affective Disorders*, *72*, 145–156.

Hankin, B. L., Kassel, J. D., & Abela, J. R. Z. (2005). Adult attachment dimensions and specificity of emotional distress symptoms: Prospective investigations of cognitive risk and interpersonal stress generation as mediating mechanisms. *Personality and Social Psychology Bulletin*, *31*, 136–151.

Harvey, J. H., & Wenzel, A. (2006). Theoretical perspectives in the study of close relationships. In D. Perlman & A. L. Vangelisti (Eds.), *Handbook of personal relationships* (pp. 35–49). London: Cambridge University Press.

Hazan, C., & Shaver, P. R. (1987). Romantic love conceptualized as an attachment process. *Journal of Personality and Social Psychology*, *52*, 511–524.

Heimberg, R. G., & Becker, R. E. (2002). *Cognitive-behavioral group therapy for social phobia: Basic mechanisms and clinical strategies*. New York: Guilford.

Heinrichs, N., & Hofmann, S. G. (2001). Information processing in social phobia. *Clinical Psychology Review*, *21*, 751–770.

Herbert, J. D., Gaudiano, B. A., Rheingold, A. A., Myers, V. H., Dalrymple, K., & Nolan, E. M. (2005). Social skills training augments the effectiveness of cognitive behavioral group therapy for social anxiety disorder. *Behavior Therapy*, *36*, 125–138.

Hersen, M., Bellack, A. S., & Himmelhoch, J. M. (1980). Treatment of unipolar depression with social skills training. *Behavior Modification*, *4*, 547–556.

Hokanson, I. E., Sacco, W. P., Blumberg, S. R., & Landrum, G. C. (1980). Interpersonal behavior of depressed individuals in a mixed motive game. *Journal of Abnormal Psychology*, *89*, 320–332.

Hollon, S. D., Stewart, M. O., & Strunk, D. (2006). Enduring effects for cognitive behavior therapy in the treatment of depression and anxiety. *Annual Review of Psychology*, *57*, 285–315.

Hope, D. A., Heimberg, R. G., & Klein, J. F. (1990). Social anxiety and the recall of interpersonal information. *Journal of Cognitive Psychotherapy*, *4*, 185–195.

Ingram, R. E. (1990). Self-focused attention in clinical disorders: A review and conceptual model. *Psychological Bulletin*, *107*, 156–176.

Ingram, R. E., & Kendall, P. C. (1986). Cognitive clinical psychology: Implications of an information processing perspective. In R. E. Ingram (Ed.), *Information processing approaches to clinical psychology* (pp. 3–21). San Diego, CA: Academic Press.

Jacobson, N. S., & Anderson, E. A. (1982). Interpersonal skill and depression in college students: An analysis of the timing of self-disclosures. *Behavior Therapy*, *13*, 271–282.

Joiner, T. E., & Katz, J. (1999). Contagious depression: Meta-analytic review and explanations from cognitive, behavioral, and interpersonal viewpoints. *Clinical Psychology: Science and Practice*, *6*, 149–164.

Joiner, T. E., & Metalsky, G. I. (1995). A prospective test of an integrative interpersonal theory of depression: A naturalistic study of college roommates. *Journal of Personality and Social Psychology*, *69*, 778–788.

Joiner, T. E., & Metalsky, G. I. (2001). Excessive reassurance seeking: Delineating a risk factor involved in the development of depressive symptoms. *Psychological Science*, *12*, 371–378.

Joiner, T. E., Metalsky, G. I., Katz, J., & Beach, S. R. H. (1999). Depression and excessive reassurance seeking. *Psychological Inquiry*, *10*, 269–278.

Joiner, T. E., & Schmidt, N. B. (1998). Excessive reassurance-seeking predicts depressive but not anxious reactions to acute stress. *Journal of Abnormal Psychology*, *107*, 533–537.

Kashdan, T. B., & Roberts, J. E. (2004). Social anxiety's impact on affect, curiosity, and social self-efficacy during a high self-focus social threat situation. *Cognitive Therapy and Research*, *28*, 119–141.

Kashdan, T. B., & Roberts, J. E. (2007). Social anxiety, depressive symptoms, and post-event rumination: Affective consequences and social contextual influences. *Journal of Anxiety Disorders*, *21*, 284–301.

Kashdan, T. B., & Wenzel, A. (2005). A transactional approach to social anxiety and the genesis of interpersonal closeness: Social anxiety, status of the self and partner, and social context. *Behavior Therapy*, *36*, 335–346.

Kuiper, N. A., & McCabe, S. B. (1985). The appropriateness of social topics: Effects of depression and cognitive vulnerability and self and other judgments. *Cognitive Therapy and Research, 9*, 371–379.

Leader, J. B., & Klein, D. N. (1996). Social adjustment in dysthymia, double depression and episodic major depression. *Journal of Affective Disorders, 37*, 91–101.

Leary, M. R., & Dobbins, S. E. (1983). Social anxiety, sexual behavior, and contraceptive use. *Journal of Personality and Social Psychology, 45*, 1347–1354.

Leary, M. R., & Kowalski, R. M. (1995). The self-presentation model of social phobia. In R. G. Heimberg, M. R. Liebowitz, D. A. Hope, & F. R. Schneier (Eds.), *Social phobia: Diagnosis, assessment, and treatment* (pp. 94–112). New York: Guilford Press.

Lewinsohn, P. M. (1974). A behavioral approach to depression. In R. J. Friedman & M. M. Katz (Eds.), *The psychology of depression: Contemporary theory and research* (pp. 157–185). Washington, DC: Winston-Wiley.

Lewinsohn, P. M. (1975a). The behavioral study and treatment of depression. In M. Hersen, R. M. Eisler, & P. M. Miller (Eds.), *Progress in behavior modification* (Vol. 1, pp. 19–64). New York: Academic Press.

Lewinsohn, P. M. (1975b). The use of activity schedules in the treatment of depressed individuals. In C. E. Thoreson & J. D. Krumboltz (Eds.), *Counseling methods* (pp. 74–83). New York: Holt, Rinehart & Winston.

Lewinsohn, P. M., Mischel, W., Chaplin, W., & Barton, R. (1980). Social competence and depression: The role of illusory self-perceptions. *Journal of Abnormal Psychology, 89*, 203–212.

Linehan, M. M. (1993). *Cognitive behavioral treatment of borderline personality disorder.* New York: Guilford.

Lipsitz, J. D., Markowitz, J. C., Cherry, S., & Fyer, A. J. (1999). Open trial of interpersonal psychotherapy for the treatment of social phobia. *American Journal of Psychiatry, 156*, 1814–1816.

Lyubomirsky, S., Caldwell, N. D., & Nolen-Hoeksema, S. (1998). Effects of ruminative and distracting responses to depressed mood on the retrieval of autobiographical memories. *Journal of Personality and Social Psychology, 75*, 166–177.

Lyubomirsky, S., & Nolen-Hoeksema, S. (1995). Effects of self-focused rumination on negative thinking and interpersonal problem solving. *Journal of Personality and Social Psychology, 69*, 176–190.

Mansell, W., & Clark, D. M. (1999). How do I appear to others? Social anxiety and processing the observable self. *Behaviour Research and Therapy, 37*, 419–434.

Mattick, R. P., & Clarke, J. C. (1998). Development and validation of measures of social phobia scrutiny fear and social interaction anxiety. *Behaviour Research and Therapy, 36*, 455–470.

McNeil, D. W., Ries, B. J., & Turk, C. L. (1995). Behavioral assessment: Self-report, physiology, and overt behavior. In R. G. Heimberg, M. R. Liebowitz, D. A. Hope, & F. R. Schneier (Eds.), *Social phobia: Diagnosis, assessment, and treatment* (pp. 202–231). New York: Guilford.

Meier, V. J., & Hope, D. A. (1998). Assessment of social skills. In A. S. Bellack & M. Hersen (Eds.), *Behavioral assessment: A practical handbook* (4th ed., pp. 232–255). Needham Heights, MA: Allyn & Bacon.

Mellings, T. M. B., & Alden, L. E. (2000). Cognitive processes in social anxiety: The effects of self-focus, rumination, and anticipatory processing. *Behaviour Research and Therapy, 38*, 243–257.

Mersch, P. P., Emmelkamp, P. M., Bögels, S. M., & van der Sleen, J. (1989). Social phobia: Individual response patterns and the effects of behavioral and cognitive interventions. *Behaviour Research and Therapy, 27*, 421–434.

Mogg, K., & Bradley, B. P. (2005). Attentional bias in generalized anxiety disorder versus depressive disorder. *Cognitive Therapy and Research, 29*, 29–45.

Mogg, K., Philippot, P., & Bradley, B. P. (2004). Selective attention to angry faces in clinical social phobia. *Journal of Abnormal Psychology, 113*, 160–165.

Nolen-Hoeksema, S. (1991). Responses to depression and their effects on the duration of depressive episodes. *Journal of Abnormal Psychology, 100*, 569–582.

Nolen-Hoeksema, S., & Davis, C. G. (1999). "Thanks for sharing that": Ruminators and their social support networks. *Journal of Personality and Social Psychology, 77*, 801–814.

Norton, P. J., & Hope, D. A. (2001). Analogue observational methods in the assessment of social functioning in adults. *Psychological Assessment, 13*, 59–72.

O'Hara, M. W., Stuart, S., Gorman, L. L., & Wenzel, A. (2000). Efficacy of interpersonal psychotherapy for postpartum depression. *Archives of General Psychiatry, 57*, 1039–1045.

Papsdorf, M. P., & Alden, L. E. (1998). Mediators of social rejection in socially anxious individuals. *Journal of Research in Personality, 32*, 351–369.

Parker, G., Parker, I., Brotchie, H., & Stuart, S. (2006). Interpersonal psychotherapy for depression? The need to define its ecological niche. *Journal of Affective Disorders, 95*, 1–11.

Pilkonis, P. A. (1977). The behavioral consequences of shyness. *Journal of Personality, 45*, 596–611.

Potthoff, J. G., Holahan, C. J., & Joiner, T. E. (1995). Reassurance seeking, stress generation, and depressive symptoms. *Journal of Personality and Social Psychology, 68*, 664–670.

Reinecke, M. A., & Rogers, G. M. (2001). Dysfunctional attitudes and attachment style among clinically depressed adults. *Behavioural and Cognitive Psychotherapy, 29*, 129–141.

Roberts, J. E., Gotlib, I. H., & Kassel, J. D. (1996). Adult attachment security and symptoms of depression: The mediating roles of dysfunctional attitudes and low self-esteem. *Journal of Personality and Social Psychology, 70*, 310–320.

Rodebaugh, T. L., Holaway, R. M., & Heimberg, R. G. (2004). The treatment of social anxiety disorder. *Clinical Psychology Review, 24*, 883–908.

Rohde, P., Lewinsohn, P. M., & Seeley, J. R. (1994). Are adolescents changed by episodes of major depression? *Journal of the American Academy of Child and Adolescent Psychiatry, 33*, 1289–1298.

Schlenker, B. R. (1987). Threats to identity: Self–identification and social stress. In C. R. Snyder & C. Ford (Eds.), *Coping with negative life events: Clinical and social psychology perspectives* (pp. 273–321). New York: Plenum .

Schlenker, B. R., & Leary, M. R. (1982). Social anxiety and self-presentation: A conceptualization and model. *Psychological Bulletin, 92*, 641–669.

Schneier, F. R., Heckelman, L. R., Garfinkel, R., Campeas, R., Fallon, B. A., Gitow, A., et al. (1994). Functional impairment in social phobia. *Journal of Clinical Psychiatry, 55*, 322–331.

Scott, J., Teasdale, J. D., Paykel, E. S., Johnson, A. L., Abbott, R., Hayhurst, H., et al. (2000). Effects of cognitive therapy on psychological symptoms and social functioning in residual depression. *British Journal of Psychiatry, 177*, 440–446.

Segrin, C. (1990). A meta-analytic review of social skills deficits in depression. *Communication Monographs, 57*, 292–308.

Segrin, C. (1992). Specifying the nature of social skill deficits associated with depression. *Human Communication Research, 19*, 89–123.

Segrin, C. (1999). Social skills, stressful life events, and the development of psychosocial problems. *Journal of Social and Clinical Psychology, 18*, 14–34.

Segrin, C. (2000). Social skills deficits associated with depression. *Clinical Psychology Review, 20*, 379–403.

Segrin, C. (2001). *Interpersonal processes in psychological problems.* New York: Guilford.

Segrin, C., & Flora, J. (2000). Poor social skills are a vulnerability factor in the development of psychosocial problems. *Human Communication Research, 26*, 489–514.

Segrin, C., & Givertz, M. (2003). Methods of social skills training and development. In J. O. Greene & B. R. Burleson (Eds.), *Handbook of communication and social skills* (pp. 135–176). Mahwah, NJ: Lawrence Erlbaum.

Segrin, C., & Kinney, T. (1995). Social skills deficits among the socially anxious: Rejection from others and loneliness. *Motivation and Emotion, 19*, 1–24.

Siqueland, L., Rynn, M., & Diamond, G. S. (2005). Cognitive behavioral and attachment based family therapy for anxious adolescents: Phase I and II studies. *Journal of Anxiety Disorders, 19*, 361–381.

Solano, C. H., & Koester, N. H. (1989). Loneliness and communication problems: Subjective anxiety or objective skills. *Personality and Social Psychology Bulletin, 15*, 126–133.

Spanier, C., & Frank, E. C. (1998). Maintenance interpersonal psychotherapy: A preventive treatment for depression. In J. C. Markowitz (Ed.), *Interpersonal psychotherapy* (pp. 67–97). Washington, DC: American Psychiatric Association.

Spurr, J. M., & Stopa, L. (2002). Self-focused attention in social phobia and social anxiety. *Clinical Psychology Review, 22*, 947–975.

Strodl, E., & Noller, P. (2003). The relationship of adult attachment dimensions of depression and agoraphobia. *Personal Relationships, 10*, 171–185.

Stangier, U., Heidenreich, T., Peitz, M., Lauterbach, W., & Clark, D. M. (2003). Cognitive therapy for social phobia: Individual versus group treatment. *Behaviour Research and Therapy, 41*, 991–1007.

Stephenson, B., & Wickland, R. A. (1984). The contagion of self-focus within a dyad. *Journal of Social and Personality Psychology, 46*, 163–168.

Strack, S., & Coyne, J. C. (1983). Social confirmation of dysphoria: Shared and private reactions to depressives. *Journal of Personality and Social Psychology, 44*, 798–806.

Strahan, E., & Conger, A. J. (1998). Social anxiety and its effects on performance and perception. *Journal of Anxiety Disorders, 12*, 293–305.

Strahan, E. Y., & Conger, A. J. (1999). Social anxiety and social performance: Why don't we see more catastrophes? *Journal of Anxiety Disorders, 13*, 399–416.

Stravynski, A., & Amado, D. (2001). Social phobia as a deficit in social skills. In S. G. Hofmann & P. M. DiBartolo (Eds.), *From social anxiety to social phobia: Multiple perspectives* (pp. 107–129). Boston: Allyn & Bacon.

Stravynski, A., Grey, S., & Elie, R. (1987). Outline of the therapeutic process in social skills training with socially dysfunctional patients. *Journal of Consulting and Clinical Psychology, 55*, 224–228.

Trower, P., & Gilbert, P. (1989). New theoretical conceptions of social anxiety and social phobia. *Clinical Psychology Review, 9*, 19–35.

Turner, S. M., Beidel, D. C., Cooley, M. R., Woody, S. R., & Messer, S. C. (1994). A multicomponent behavioral treatment for social phobia: Social effectiveness therapy. *Behaviour Research and Therapy, 32*, 381–390.

Turner, S. M., Beidel, D. C., Dancu, C. V., & Keys, D. J. (1986). Psychopathology of social phobia and comparison to avoidant personality disorder. *Journal of Abnormal Psychology, 95*, 389–394.

Twentyman, C. T., & McFall, R. M. (1975). Behavioral training of social skills in shy males. *Journal of Consulting and Clinical Psychology, 43*, 384–395.

Van Dam-Baggen, R., & Kraaimaat, F. (2000). Group social skills training or cognitive group therapy as the clinical treatment of choice for generalized social phobia? *Journal of Anxiety Disorders, 14*, 437–451.

Vittengl, J. R., Clark, L. A., & Jarrett, R. B. (2004). Improvement in social-interpersonal functioning after cognitive therapy for recurrent depression. *Psychological Medicine, 34*, 643–658.

Wallace, S. T., & Alden, L. E. (1997). Social phobia and positive social events: The price of success. *Journal of Abnormal Psychology, 106*, 416–424.

Walters, K. S., & Hope, D. A. (1998). Analysis of social behavior in individuals with social phobia and nonanxious participants using a psychobiological model. *Behavior Therapy, 29*, 387–407.

Wei, M., Russell, D. W., & Zakalik, R. A. (2005). Adult attachment, social self-efficacy, self-disclosure, loneliness, and subsequent depression for freshmen college students: A longitudinal study. *Journal of Counseling Psychology, 52*, 602–614.

Weissman, M. M., & Bothwell, S. (1976). Assessment of social adjustment by patient self-report. *Archives of General Psychiatry, 33*, 1111–1115.

Weissman, M. M., Merkowitz, J. C., & Klerman, G. L. (2000). *Comprehensive guide to interpersonal psychotherapy*. New York: Basic Books.

Wenzel, A. (2002). Characteristics of close relationships in individuals with social phobia: A preliminary comparison with nonanxious individuals. In J. H. Harvey & A. Wenzel (Eds.), *A clinician's guide to maintaining and enhancing close relationships* (pp. 199–213). Mahwah, NJ: Lawrence Erlbaum.

Wenzel, A., & Emerson, T. (2006). *Partner selection and sexuality in socially anxious and nonanxious individuals*. Manuscript submitted for publication.

Wenzel, A., Graff-Dolezal, J., Macho, M., & Brendle, J. R. (2005). Communication and social skills in the context of close relationships in socially anxious and nonanxious individuals. *Behaviour Research and Therapy, 43*, 505–519.

Wenzel, A., & Holt, C. S. (2001). Social phobia and its relationship to clinical syndromes in adulthood. In S. G. Hofmann & P. M. DiBartolo (Eds.), *From social anxiety to social phobia: Multiple perspectives* (pp. 130–147). New York: Allyn & Bacon.

Wierzbicki, M. (1984). Social skills deficits and subsequent depressed mood in students. *Personality and Social Psychology Bulletin, 10*, 605–610.

Williams, J. M. G. (1996). Depression and the specificity of autobiographical memory. In D. C. Rubin (Ed.), *Remembering our past: Studies in autobiographical memory* (pp. 244–267). New York: Cambridge University Press.

Wittchen, H. U., Fuetsch, M., Sonntag, H., Müller, N., & Liebowitz, M. (2000). Disability and quality of life in pure and comorbid social phobia: Findings from a controlled study. *European Psychiatry, 15*, 46–58.

Woody, S. R. (1996). Effects of focus of attention on social phobics' anxiety and social performance. *Journal of Abnormal Psychology, 105*, 61–69.

Woody, S. R., & Rodriguez, B. J. (2000). Self-focused attention and social anxiety in social phobics and normal controls. *Cognitive Therapy and Research, 24*, 473–488.

Zeiss, A. M., Lewinsohn, P. M., & Munoz, R. F. (1979). Nonspecific improvement effects in depression using interpersonal skills training, pleasant activity schedules, or cognitive training. *Journal of Consulting and Clinical Psychology, 47*, 427–439.

Section VI

Cognitions, Beliefs, and Memories about Relationship Initiation

23

"So How Did You Two Meet?"
Narratives of Relationship Initiation

LINDSAY CUSTER, DIANE HOLMBERG, KAREN
BLAIR, and TERRI L. ORBUCH

Almost anyone in a serious relationship has probably been asked, at some point, to tell the story of how that relationship began. Friends eager for gossip about the latest prospect, parents probing as to where their offspring met a potential suitor, children at an anniversary party curious as to where their parents' relationship began: All are intrigued by the stories individuals and couples tell about the origins of their relationship. In this chapter, we propose that such stories, or narratives, of relationship initiation also can provide valuable information to relationship researchers. Researchers are seldom able to observe the initiation of relationships directly; furthermore, when they are able to do so (e.g., "getting-to-know-you" conversations arranged in the laboratory), such scenarios are unlikely to be very representative of real-world relationship beginnings. Therefore, relationship initiation research is largely forced to rely on self-report, usually through standardized questionnaires. We propose that collecting open-ended narratives of relationship initiation may reveal additional information to complement that obtained in more standardized measures. Investigating how people choose to talk about their relationship beginnings may be even more revealing than examining the bare "facts" of the situation.

Our investigation of relationship initiation narratives is divided into three main sections. First, we begin with a brief general overview of the narrative approach. Second, we describe three key aspects of relationship initiation narratives: (a) narrative style, or how the stories are told, in terms of joint storytelling, drama, and coherence; (b) narrative content, or what the stories are told about, including strategies, goals, and initiators or facilitators; and (c) narrative consistency, including consistency over time, across individuals, and between social contexts. Third, we look at how relationship initiation narratives might vary according to gender, race and ethnicity, and sexual orientation. Throughout, we pay special attention to which aspects of relationship initiation narratives are most predictive of relational well-being. As many questions still remain regarding relationship initiation narratives, we highlight future research directions throughout this chapter.

OVERVIEW OF NARRATIVES AND NARRATIVE APPROACH

Narratives are the stories that people present to others, usually orally and to a public audience (Gergen & Gergen, 1983). They represent the ways in which people try to make sense or meaning of the realities of their lives, their experiences, and the social world around them. Many narratives contain rich and detailed information about people's views of self, experiences, and relationships. Bruner

(1990) argued that people are driven to search for meaning in all that they do and that this meaning-making process is fundamental to human nature. He emphasized that people do not just live their experiences in an unexamined way; they also actively seek to understand and make sense of those experiences. They shape and reshape the stories they tell, to themselves and to others, in an effort to achieve a coherent whole. In the process of sharing these stories, individuals (both storytellers and audience) are afforded many rewards. The meaning-making process helps individuals gain control and understanding of their social world, cope with stressful events, and create order and coherence in their lives (Orbuch, 1997). Evidence also suggests that both the process of searching for meaning and the interaction process of confiding that meaning to others can have substantial mental and physical health benefits (Lichtman & Taylor, 1986; Orbuch, Harvey, Davis, & Merbach, 1994; Pennebaker & Harber, 1993).

The objective reality of an event may or may not be the same as it is put forth in the narratives that are presented to others. Thus, the observer cannot be separated from what is being observed. Stories might well change and evolve over time and across situations. In addition, stories evolve in the context of cultural and social factors. Thus, the goal of the narrative approach is not a quest for historical truth, but an exploration for a satisfying "narrative truth" (Orbuch, 1997; Spence, 1982). Stories may not be 100% "accurate," but Gergen and Gergen (1987) claimed that by allowing individuals to narrate their own experiences, "the investigator is left to consider the form and function of person description in its own right—independent of its truth value" (p. 270). A narrative approach to the study of relationships follows a major trend in the social sciences, which encourages researchers to collect and interpret stories that people tell about their lives (Bochner, Ellis, & Tillmann-Healy, 2000; Orbuch; Orbuch, Veroff, & Holmberg, 1993). This approach has theoretical and conceptual links to several other bodies of work (Orbuch, 1997), including attribution theory (Heider, 1958), accounts as explanations or justifications for behaviors that are unanticipated or deviant (Scott & Lyman, 1968), and symbolic interactionism (Blumer, 1969; Mead, 1934).

Orbuch (1997) argued that by applying the narrative approach to the study of relationships, we move away from describing language as a means to discover or mirror reality to the view that language and meaning are ongoing and constitutive parts of reality. Indeed, recent work provides strong evidence that a narrative approach to the study of relationships can reveal important information to researchers (Clark, Shaver, & Abrahams, 1999; Holmberg, Orbuch, & Veroff, 2004; Killian, 2002; Wamboldt, 1999). Narratives give insight into the more subjective reality of how individuals and couples make sense of their relationships and their experiences in those relationships. According to Holmberg et al. (2004), one important aspect about relationships that is revealed in couples' narratives is their overall level of well-being or satisfaction. They found that the stories told by happy couples differed in many ways from those told by unhappy couples. By examining the overall narrative themes, feelings or needs discussed in the context of the narrative, and the way the story was built up in a collaborative or conflictful fashion, they gleaned information about couples' current level of relationship well-being. Many have argued that the narrative approach to relationships gives us a fuller and more accurate understanding of the day-to-day realities of individuals than standardized survey instruments (Veroff, Chadiha, Leber, & Sutherland, 1993; Weber, 1992). Weber stated that "stories and the story-telling process are real. If we wish to learn about the realities of personal relationships, we would do well to pay attention to such natural forms these realities take on" (p. 181).

Despite the fact that the narrative approach has been quite valuable for gaining insights into the meanings of relationships, theory and systematic research have been slower to catch on, particularly with respect to relationship beginnings. Berger and Kellner (1964) were some of the first to specifically focus on the role of narrative processes in the early years of marriage. They emphasized that a key task for long-term couples is the co-construction of reality. They argued that through communication and exchange, the couple takes their individual styles and perspectives, and together forges a new way of being together as a couple. The merging of individual realities results in a new joint "reality," or a new meaning that defines for the couple the nature of the world around them and their place or role in that new reality. This emergence of meaning is then incorporated into the couple's norms and becomes important for the future of the relationship.

In the rest of the chapter, we discuss work by a number of scholars who have utilized storytelling methods in their research on relationship beginnings. We argue throughout the chapter that looking at *how* people choose to tell the stories of their relationship beginnings (how they work together with their partner to tell the story, what aspects they emphasize, and what aspects they downplay) may be very revealing and critical for understanding the meaning and sense of relationships in people's lives.

KEY ASPECTS OF RELATIONSHIP INITIATION NARRATIVES

In this section, we examine what is already known about relationship initiation narratives among heterosexual couples (same-sex couples are discussed in a later section). There are relatively few published works that examine such narratives; therefore, most of the results in this section come from three programs of research. First, Clark and colleagues (1999) collected written narratives of participants' two most recent successful romantic relationship initiation episodes from 177 male and 153 female undergraduates. These narratives were content-analyzed for initiation strategies and goals.

Second, in 1986, the Early Years of Marriage (EYM) program at the University of Michigan recruited 373 newly married couples (half White, half African American) to take part in a longitudinal study of the marital experience. The spouses completed individual structured interviews; in addition, they jointly provided a narrative describing the progression of their relationship. The first part of this narrative, the courtship story, is of particular interest here. In it, couples described how they met, how they became interested in each other, and how they became a couple. Thus, these narratives move beyond the very earliest stages of relationship initiation; however, they do provide information as to how married couples began their lives together. These oral narratives were first recorded several months after the couples married; they were collected again in the third and seventh years of their marriage. These narratives were analyzed on a wide variety of dimensions (see Holmberg et al., 2004, for full details on sample, procedure, and coding schemes). The primary measure of marital well-being in this program of research was a 6-item self-report measure of marital happiness, assessing aspects of relationship satisfaction and stability. Data from this program of research appear in several publications, by the current authors and by others (e.g., Holmberg & Holmes, 1994; Holmberg & Orbuch, 2004; Holmberg et al., 2004; Orbuch et al., 1993; Veroff, Sutherland, Chadiha, & Ortega, 1993).

Finally, Wamboldt (1999) recruited 63 premarital couples who considered themselves to be "seriously attached." They participated as a couple in a videotaped, semistructured interview about their relationship for approximately 60 minutes. Although these narratives also asked about other issues, a portion focused on a description of how the couples met. These narratives were coded for coherence and interaction style, using rating scales developed by the Family Narrative Consortium. In this section, we look at what these three studies can tell us about the style, content, and consistency of relationship initiation narratives.

Style

First, examining the style of storytelling, *how* the couple tells their story, independent of the content of what they say, may be informative. For example, here is one relationship initiation narrative from the EYM study, told solely by the husband, in a very straightforward, "just-the-facts" manner:

> We met at a friend's house, basically over pizza and soft drinks, and just had a sociable and enjoyable evening. And, we basically agreed to see each other, exchanged phone numbers, and made plans for a future date, which we then, of course, kept.

In contrast, here is another narrative, told by a husband and wife working together, in a much more dramatic and engaging style:

Wife: This girl that was working for me, we were just standing around looking out the window, and Chris walked by. And the girl said, "Oh, my God!!" and she ran in the back and says, "I used to go out with him!" And she ran in the back and started combing her hair and everything. And then I go, "Sure you did, sure," you know. I thought she was just goofing around. But then she goes, "His name is Chris." So, I opened the door, and yelled out, "Is your name Chris?" And he turned around, all confused because he didn't know who I was. "Yeah." "Okay." So then I shut the door, and he just kept on walking down the street. But then he kept coming into my store and buying cookies (*giggling*) … .

Husband: Buying anything I could just to get a chance to talk to her (*chuckling*).

Wife: Right, it was quite a while, and then he finally asked me out after a long, long time. I was getting impatient!

Husband: Yeah, I didn't know whether to ask her out or not. I had gone in there, I bought candy bars, bread … .

Wife: Cookies and everything.

Husband: … Lots of cookies! Anything just to talk to her. I've always been shy, so finally I asked her out.

Wife: And that's how we met.

This second excerpt could have been relayed in a much more prosaic manner, similar to the first: "We met when he came into the store where I was working to buy cookies." Does the fact that the story was told in a more dramatic style, by the couple working together as a team, tell us anything about their relational well-being?

Joint Storytelling

When couples tell their relationship initiation story together, one important issue is how smoothly they are able to coordinate that joint task. Do they work together seamlessly to tell a truly joint story together? Or do they contest the issues, disagreeing over the details, each vying to have his or her own vision hold?

First, most relationship initiation stories are jointly told. Holmberg et al. (2004) reported that 74% of their newly married couples told joint stories, rather than stories dominated by only one partner. If one partner did dominate, it was slightly more likely to be the wife than the husband.

Furthermore, research suggests that those couples who are able to smoothly coordinate their stories show better relationship well-being. Wamboldt (1999) scored premarital couples' degree of coordination in telling their story on a 5-point scale (see Fiese & Sameroff, 1999, for coding details). Couples who scored higher on coordination of their joint narrative also scored higher on relational satisfaction, using the Dyadic Adjustment Scale (DAS). In addition, Wamboldt gave each partner a 5-point score for confirmation or disconfirmation, ranging from *overtly disconfirming* to *actively confirming*. Women who disconfirmed their partner's view of events during the joint narrative showed lower DAS scores, and both men and women who disconfirmed their partner's views scored higher on a 45-item measure of perceived relational instability. Similarly, Orbuch et al. (1993) found that newly married couples who were coded as displaying some conflict while telling their courtship story had lower marital happiness 2 years later (controlling for Time 1 marital happiness), compared to those who were coded as telling their courtship story without conflict. Thus, smoothly and effortlessly negotiating a joint storytelling task seems to be associated with better relational well-being, whereas disagreeing over a relationship story bodes poorly for a couple.

An important issue that remains to be explored is the extent to which these findings simply reflect a more conflictful style in general. Are couples who disagree about the story of their relationship simply the same couples who disagree almost any issue? In other words, the *unique* predictive effect of the relationship storytelling situation should be demonstrated, over and above any more general measures of couple conflict.

Coherence

In theory, narrative researchers often emphasize the value of constructing a clear, coherent, integrated story, one that can help shape one's view of events and provide meaning and structure to experiences in retrospect (Gergen & Gergen, 1983). For example, research on narratives about traumatic events showed that increased use of insight-oriented words (e.g. *realize* and *understand*) and causal words (e.g. *because* and *reason*) in narratives over the course of the study was associated with improved health (Pennebaker & Francis, 1996). A coherent and well-integrated story is assumed to display more insight into the processes and issues underlying a narrative than a simple recounting of events without any storylike structure. Narrative researchers thus tend to assume that a more coherent narrative will be associated with higher well-being on the part of the storyteller.

Accordingly, Wamboldt (1999) scored premarital couples' narratives on four 5-point measures of narrative coherence (internal consistency, organization, flexibility, and congruence of affect and content; see Fiese & Sameroff, 1999). Orbuch and colleagues (1993) coded overall narrative coherence on one 5-point scale, ranging from *mere answering of questions in question–answer format* through *a story or set of stories told intermittently* to *an integrated overall story, with plot elaboration and coherence*. Contrary to expectations, however, neither Wamboldt nor Orbuch et al. found any connection between measures of the coherence or integration of couples' relationship narratives and their relational well-being. One possibility is that these couples' stories were still works in progress, and had not yet achieved their final, more coherent form. For example, Cowan (1999) noted that Wamboldt's premarital couples had considerably lower narrative coherence scores, and fewer connections between coherence scores and outcome measures, than other samples of more established married couples. However, Holmberg et al. (2004), using the same data set as Orbuch et al. (1993), actually found that the integration of couples' courtship stories dropped considerably over their first 7 years of marriage, suggesting that couples were not necessarily working toward a cleaner, more integrated story with time and experience.

A likely explanation for the lack of relevance of coherence and integration measures is that the relatively positive events of relationship beginnings do not spur the same deep search for meaning as traumatic or difficult events do, just as positive actions do not inspire the same amount of cognitive effort and attributions as negative actions (Weiner, 1985). Any cognitive reshaping of the relationship initiation story might therefore be relatively short-lived. Work by Wilkinson (1987) examining cognitive activity during friendship formation demonstrated that individuals devoted a great deal of cognitive effort in the first meeting or two to understanding the other person, and how the other person may or may not fit with the self. However, a transition point was reached quite rapidly. If a relationship was identified as not being a promising one, people were less inclined to think about it deeply; on the other hand, if the relationship "took off" and developed its own momentum, people seemed to forget to monitor their interactions closely, and simply enjoyed each other's company. Either way, the period of intense cognitive focus did not last long. Similarly, it is possible that those in romantic relationships may think about and work through their relationship initiation story intensely for a rather brief period of time; at this point, coherence might be important, in that those who are able to develop a more satisfying story of a promising relationship will be more inclined to pursue it than those who cannot make good sense of the early stages. After this brief period, however, the relationship is defined, and there is little motivation to continue to rework the relationship initiation story into a more and more polished form over time.

Drama and Emotion   Some people are excellent storytellers, able to construct an exciting, emotion-filled, engaging, and dramatic tale; others prefer a more prosaic, "just-the-facts" approach. Does either style bode better for overall relational well-being? Holmberg et al. (2004) found that most of their couples were not particularly dramatic in their storytelling style. Furthermore, the overall drama of storytellers' style (i.e., amount of vivacity, articulation, elaboration, and enthusiasm) was not associated with relational well-being.

However, other variables suggested that a blander, more pragmatic story might actually be better for well-being than a more emotional or dramatic one. Holmberg et al. (2004) found that newlywed women who told particularly emotion-packed courtship stories were *less* satisfied with their marriage than those who told less emotional stories. Similarly, Orbuch et al. (1993) found that those who told quietly positive but nonromantic courtship stories as newlyweds (e.g., the relationship gradually developed out of a friendship) tended to be happier with their relationship 2 years later. In contrast, those who told dramatic stories of overcoming obstacles to be together (e.g., the resistance of others) were less happy 2 years later. The most romantic stories (e.g., love at first sight) were the least common, and did not predict well-being at all. These findings held even when a variety of background measures (e.g., parental status, socioeconomic status, length of relationship, and first-year marital well-being) were controlled for, hinting that the differences might lie more in the way the stories were told than in demographic differences between groups.

A "Hollywood romance" full of emotion, tension, ups and downs, whirlwind romance, and obstacles to overcome may make for a good story. However, it probably makes for an uncomfortable and uncertain relationship. The most satisfying relationships in the long term may be quiet, comfortable, and nondramatic; the stories of those relationships are likely to share those features.

Couple Orientation   A final issue regarding the style of couples' narratives is the extent to which the couple tells the story with an emphasis on *us*, as opposed to *you and I*. Aron (e.g., Aron & Fraley, 1999) suggested that partners in close relationships tend to include the other in the self over time. Acitelli (1992) has shown that a focus on the relationship is important to relational well-being, especially for women. Thus, we might expect that couples who develop a *we* orientation toward their storytelling might be more satisfied than those who maintain a more individual perspective. Veroff, Sutherland, et al. (1993) found exactly that. They counted the number of relational affects (i.e., feelings or needs with *we* as the source of the affect, and with a focus on the relationship) mentioned in newlyweds' relationship stories. Those who mentioned more relational affects in their story displayed enhanced well-being 2 years later, even when controlling for demographics, Year 1 happiness, and survey measures of affective quality and relational tensions. Here, the narrative seemed to provide a relatively implicit measure of the extent to which the couple viewed themselves as a unit. Those who developed this joint perspective in the early stages of the relationship seemed to be happier later on, even when taking into account their more conscious reports of the quality of their relationship.

Summary   To summarize, in previous research, higher relational well-being has been associated with relationship initiation stories that (a) were agreed on readily by both partners; (b) were not particularly romantic, emotional, or dramatic in tone; and (c) reflected a *we* orientation. Coherence of the story and skill of the storytellers, on the other hand, did vary across participants, but were not particularly important in predicting relational well-being. These findings seem somewhat reminiscent of the distinction between romantic, passionate love versus companionate, friendship-based love (Sternberg, 1986; Walster [now Hatfield] & Walster, 1978). The former is exciting, engaging, and fun to hear about, and forms the basis of many inquiries into the topic of love, whether from researchers, poets, or the popular media. The latter is calmer, more sedate, and perhaps less inherently interesting, but is nonetheless a much better predictor of overall relationship well-being (Grote & Frieze, 1994), especially over the long term. Likewise, one might intuitively believe that a romantic, dramatic, engaging, coherent relationship initiation story relayed by a master storyteller would be indicative of strong relational well-being; instead, a better predictor seems to be a very calm, content, matter-of-fact, couple-based account. Drama is fun to hear about but less fun to live; our "best" relationship stories, as stories, are probably told about some of our worst relationships.

Content

A second aspect of narratives that provides information about relationship initiation is the content of the stories that couples tell. In particular, researchers have used narrative techniques to examine how, why, and by whom relationships are typically initiated.

Strategies and Goals   How and why do individuals typically initiate romantic relationships? Clark et al. (1999) found the most frequently mentioned strategies were direct ones, such as talking in person (or over the phone), touching, and asking the person directly. Indirect methods, such as acting interested, joking, game playing, and dressing up, were used much less often. However, these researchers only asked participants about the strategies used in their last two *successful* romantic relationship initiation episodes. It is possible that direct strategies are more successful than indirect ones; thus, direct strategies might have been overrepresented in this study. Future research could include both successful and unsuccessful relationship initiation episodes to address this issue.

The strategies used to initiate romantic relationships may depend on the goals of the initiator. Clark et al. (1999) showed that the majority of both men and women emphasized emotional intimacy rather than sexual intimacy as the goal of relationship initiation. Moreover, participants seeking love as a goal were more likely to report using direct relationship initiation strategies, whereas participants seeking sexual intimacy were more likely to describe indirect strategies, such as flirting, manipulating the setting, and self-presentation. These results are consistent with other findings suggesting that indirect, manipulative strategies are used when individuals are pursuing sexual intimacy (Greer & Buss, 1994).

Initiators and Facilitators

Despite changes in gender roles over the past several decades, courtship stories still follow a traditional script among heterosexual couples, with men most commonly cast as the initiator of the relationship. It is less common for courtship stories to indicate that both partners mutually initiated the relationship. Holmberg and Orbuch (2004) found that the least frequent scenario of all was female-initiated courtship.

Though men are still the initiators in most stories, Clark et al. (1999) discovered that social networks were described as playing a much more prominent role in facilitating new relationships when initiation was assessed using narrative techniques, compared to more direct, closed-ended questionnaire methodologies. This discrepancy between techniques suggests that couples may underestimate the influence that family and friends have over the formation of their relationships. Future research could compare narratives of American couples to narratives of couples from more collectivistic cultures, where third parties typically play a more prominent role in facilitating relationship initiation. One might expect that among couples in collectivistic cultures, courtship stories would put more emphasis on outside forces.

Content and Well-Being

Holmberg and Orbuch (2004) identified four themes from courtship stories that were associated with lower marital well-being over time: pregnancy, cohabitation, lack of commitment, and female initiation of the relationship. Although these four themes were not linked to lower well-being in the first year of marriage (with the exception of pregnancy), couples who continued to emphasize these themes in later years of marriage were at risk for lower marital well-being. These authors were careful to point out that it is not necessarily the presence of these conditions themselves that puts the couple at risk for lower well-being, as many of the couples they studied experienced the same issues. Rather, it may be the couple's continued emphasis on these themes beyond the first year of marriage that is problematic. Couples who continued to emphasize these themes over time may not have fully resolved these issues.

Summary

In sum, research to date indicates that (a) direct strategies were reported more frequently than indirect strategies in relationship initiation, especially when emotional intimacy was the goal; (b) most men and women reported that they were seeking emotional, rather than sexual, intimacy when initiating new relationships; (c) narratives typically cast the men as the relationship initiator; and (d) continued emphasis on counternormative themes (e.g., female initiation) during the courtship story was linked to lower well-being over the course of the relationship. These findings indicate that by and large, the content of courtship stories is consistent with social norms regarding relationship initiation. Narratives that go against these norms have been linked to lower relationship well-being. Thus, adhering to social norms during the relationship initiation process, or at least presenting a narrative consistent with social norms, seems important to subsequent relationship well-being. If norms are in fact so important, how do couples whose very relationship challenges social norms (e.g., interracial couples and same-sex couples) construct socially acceptable narratives? We will explore this question in more detail in a later section.

Consistency

In this section, we examine narrative consistency. Because narratives frequently reflect the needs of the storytellers to achieve understanding and construct meaning out of their experiences rather than reflecting historical truths, one might expect that stories of the same event will vary over time, between individuals, and across contexts.

Consistency over Time   As we have mentioned, most couples demonstrated a high degree of collaboration and relatively low levels of conflict in the joint storytelling of their courtship narrative. Holmberg et al. (2004) found that these high levels of collaboration remained consistent over the course of the relationship. However, these researchers also demonstrated that the quality of courtship stories declined over time. They found that narratives got shorter, less dramatic, and less integrated as the relationship progressed. The narratives also generally became more ambiguous and vague over time; for instance, in many cases it became unclear who exactly had initiated the relationship. Additionally, couples talked about earlier parts of their lives together as simply being generally positive (or negative), rather than providing specific details. Dramatic tensions, which had been emphasized in earlier interviews, seemed to dissipate over time. Overall, the stories of relationship initiation became briefer, blander, and more unclear. These researchers found that all sections of the relationship narrative showed these changes, not just the courtship story.

Although there may be other possible interpretations of this finding, the authors argue that the most likely interpretation is that the longer couples were together, the less likely they were to feel a need to use narratives as a tool for meaning making, because they had already worked through many important issues in their relationship. On the other hand, it is possible that the narratives became poorer because couples simply forgot the details of their courtship, or grew tired of producing detailed stories for the researchers on multiple occasions.

In addition to changes in narrative quality, Holmberg et al. (2004) also found that the affective tone of relationship initiation narratives changed over time. Courtship stories became less affect laden in general and slightly less positive. These researchers also found that in the courtship narratives, affects that focused on self-expression declined over time, whereas relational affects increased. In contrast, those parts of the narrative that focused on the present relationship showed more of a tension between self-expression and connection, and those parts of the narrative that focused on the future remained highly focused on self-expression. This pattern suggests that once couples have shared an experience and worked through the meaning of it together, it becomes "theirs."

Changes in affective tone over time also seem to predict changes in relationship well-being. Holmberg and Holmes (1994) compared couples that began their marriages very happily and remained happy through the third year of marriage to couples who also began their marriages very happily, but experienced a significant decline in happiness by the third year of marriage. The latter group was more likely to tell courtship stories that included more statements expressing negative affect and ambivalence in Year 3 than in Year 1. This research supports the notion that current tensions and feelings about the relationship color past memories of earlier parts of the relationship (Ross, 1989).

Although research from EYM has provided a great deal of information regarding narrative consistency over the first 7 years of marriage, there are still some areas that need further exploration. First, we know very little about the consistency of narratives over the very early part of the relationship. How much do courtship stories change over the first few tellings? Second, EYM continues to collect narratives only from couples who stay together. We wonder how relationship initiation stories may change among couples whose relationships dissolve. Future studies should collect relationship narratives and well-being measures at multiple points in time, amongst both individuals who have stayed together and those whose relationship has ended. Such a design would allow us to compare courtship stories over time in both successful and unsuccessful relationships, and would therefore provide greater insight into the role that forming consistent courtship stories plays in promoting relationship well-being.

Consistency between Individuals   Narratives can vary not only over time but also between individuals. For instance, research indicates that the narratives of men and women do differ somewhat, as will be discussed in the next section of this chapter. A more complicated issue, though, is how individual and joint narratives might differ from one another. For instance, do husbands and wives tell distinctly different stories separately than they do together? When couples tell their story together, whose version of events is more likely to guide the joint narrative? There is some evidence to indicate that women are more likely than men to take control of the joint narrative. As we mentioned earlier, in EYM narratives where one spouse dominated, the wife was more likely to be the dominant spouse. Further, women were more likely than men to interrupt their spouse during the telling of the joint narrative. Because wives are frequently viewed by both spouses as the "relationship watchers" (Holmberg et al., 2004), it would make sense that their version of events would be more likely to guide the joint narrative. It remains to be seen how consistency between individual and joint narratives relates to relationship well-being, though.

Consistency across Contexts   Narratives may also vary across situations. There is little research examining the degree to which couples are consistent in telling the story of their courtship to different audiences. Do characteristics of the audience influence which aspects of the story are emphasized or left undisclosed? How does altering a courtship narrative to fit the audience relate to well-being? It is possible that certain types of couples, particularly those whose relationships are not positively sanctioned by the larger society, are more prone to adapting their courtship stories according to the audience.

Summary   Much work remains in the area of relationship initiation narrative consistency. Currently, study results indicate that (a) the process of joint storytelling did not change much over time; (b) however, other aspects of the narrative did change—narratives generally became shorter, less dramatic, less affective, less positive, more ambiguous, more general, and more relational; and (c) current relationship well-being colored the narrative of the relationship's beginnings. Little is known about how individuals change their narrative in the presence of their spouse or how narratives might be adapted for different audiences, but it seems quite plausible to us that narratives might be altered in different settings. These findings underscore the subjective and contextual nature of relationship initiation narratives. The story that one tells about a relationship's beginnings is not necessarily an objective retelling of events, but rather it is a highly personal account that may change over time and across contexts.

VARIATIONS ON A THEME

In this section, we explore how various social statuses, such as gender and race and ethnicity, shape courtship stories. We also examine the initiation narratives of couples whose relationships may be viewed as nontraditional. As we have emphasized throughout this chapter, narratives allow individuals to understand and construct meaning out of life experiences. However, the meaning given to experience frequently varies according to one's position in society.

Gender

Relationship Initiation   Do men and women differ in their reported reasons for initiating new romantic relationships? Clark et al. (1999) found that although the sexes did not differ in the likelihood of reporting emotional intimacy as a goal of relationship initiation, men were more likely than women to report pursuing sexual intimacy. Possibly, men really do hold sexual intimacy as a more prominent goal than women. However, social desirability must also be considered. It is still socially unacceptable for women to acknowledge their sexual desires, at least publicly; thus, they may not emphasize sexual intimacy as a primary goal in their narratives. Conversely, men may overemphasize the extent to which they desire sexual intimacy, due to societal messages encouraging them to exhibit strong sexual appetites and to pursue women as sexual conquests (see Reeder, this volume).

Clark et al. (1999) showed that men and women reported using different strategies in relationship initiation episodes. They examined the use of eight different strategies: becoming emotionally involved (e.g., revealing personal information), directly initiating a relationship (e.g., asking the person out, or making physical contact), signaling indirectly (e.g., hinting or talking about romance generally), manipulating the situation (e.g., creating a romantic setting), joking, demonstrating resources (e.g., gift giving and showing off possessions), using third parties to initiate the relationship, and acting passively (waiting for the other to initiate the relationship). These researchers found that men were more likely than women to demonstrate resources through gift giving and to directly initiate a relationship through asking or touching. In contrast, women were more likely to report acting passively. These findings are similar to the results of a study conducted by Rose and Frieze (1993), who found that dating scripts typically reflected a proactive male role and a reactive female role. They also resonate with the findings reported earlier in this chapter, wherein female initiation of the courtship was rarely reported, and was predictive of lower relationship well-being when it did occur. Thus, consistent with societal norms, men discuss being more active, and women more passive, when describing the relationship initiation process.

Why is it that men seem to emphasize taking a more active role in initiating romantic relationships? According to evolutionary psychologists (Buss, 1994; Schmitt, this volume), differences in relationship initiation strategies and goals are due to sex differences in evolutionary opportunities and constraints for reproductive success. Males use direct tactics (e.g., gift giving and showing off possessions) to attract females, who are constrained by their access to resources. In contrast, females use more indirect approaches like trying to appear healthy and young to attract males, who are constrained by their access to fertile females. Of course, an alternative explanation for sex differences in relationship strategies and goals is gender socialization. In other words, men and women may learn through their interactions with others how to act in ways that are consistent with societal expectations.

In an attempt to disentangle the effects of biological and societal influences, Clark et al. (1999) examined the relative power of biological sex and sex role orientation in predicting self-reported relationship initiation strategies. These researchers found that although a masculine sex role orientation accounted for some variance in relationship initiation strategies, it did not account for as much variance as biological sex did. Femininity seemed to play a less important role in determining relationship initiation strategies, although it was linked to touch. Clark and colleagues concluded, "Because biological sex was a much stronger predictor than sex-role orientation, it appears that … the strategies used in relationship initiation are more strongly linked to being male or female than to psychological masculinity or femininity" (p. 720). The authors acknowledged that this discrepancy may be because biological sex itself is a direct cause of relational strategies, or because it is strongly associated with effects of socialization not adequately captured by the measures of masculinity and femininity used in their study.

It is important to keep in mind that courtship narratives casting men as active initiators and women as passive participants do not necessarily reflect reality. Research conducted in naturalistic settings has suggested that although men were frequently the initiators of relationships, they tended to approach only after women had indicated their interest in being approached (Perper, 1985). Thus, women may take a more active role in initiating the relationship than narratives have suggested. Additionally, research has demonstrated that men and women tend to reinterpret the past in ways that are consistent with gender role expectations (Veroff, Sutherland, et al., 1993). Thus, some couples may reconstruct their courtship stories to be consistent with societal norms. Research in more naturalistic settings would allow researchers to determine to what extent gendered courtship narratives reflect reality, and to what extent individuals alter the story of their courtship to be more consistent with societal expectations. Moreover, such research would allow us to further investigate the link between narrative consistency (over time) and relationship well-being. It may be the case that this link is contingent on whether narratives become more or less consistent with societal expectations over retellings.

Gender Differences in Associations between Narratives and Well-Being   As one might expect, relationship initiation narratives are linked to well-being in different ways for men and women. Holmberg et al. (2004) found that women who were unhappy in the first year of marriage told courtship stories that emphasized the theme of pregnancy. By the third year of marriage, unhappily married women told courtship stories that brought up concerns about the husband's lack of commitment. These findings did not apply to men. One interpretation of these results is that experiencing a pregnancy during the courtship phase may create doubts about the basis of the husband's commitment to the relationship later on. A feeling that one's partner is committed to the relationship for emotional reasons, rather than a sense of duty, may be important to women's well-being.

In contrast, Holmberg et al. (2004) found that for men, themes of agency and freedom were linked to well-being. Men who were happy in their seventh year of marriage were more likely to reconstruct courtship stories that put increasing emphasis on agency, and less on communion, compared to less happy men. Additionally, men who were especially unhappy in Year 3 were more likely to emphasize living together before marriage. According to Holmberg et al., cohabitation may be perceived as the "mark of someone who is tied down even before the marriage" (p. 134) for some men. These authors argued that men who cohabit prior to marriage may experience a lower sense of agency than men who do not cohabit before marriage. Additionally, Holmberg et al. showed that courtship stories emphasizing female initiation of the relationship were more common among unhappily married men than among happily married men in Year 7. They argued that taken together, these findings suggest that men are happiest when they are able to maintain a sense of control and freedom in the relationship.

Summary   Narrative research provides a great deal of insight into the different experiences of men and women during the relationship process. To date, this research indicates that (a) men were more likely than women to report sexual intimacy as a goal of relationship initiation, (b) men were more likely than women to report using direct strategies to initiate a relationship, and (c) women who emphasized pregnancy and subsequent commitment issues in their courtship narratives experience lower marital well-being; conversely, men who emphasized agency, freedom, and control in their courtship narratives experienced higher marital well-being. These findings further support the idea that constructing relationship initiation stories consistent with societal expectations, particularly regarding gender roles, is important to later relationship well-being.

Race and Ethnicity

As is the case in most areas of relationship research, studies employing narrative techniques have concentrated primarily on White couples. EYM is the only study we know of that examines racial differences in relationship initiation using a narrative technique. In this section, we will summarize some of the findings from that project and suggest directions for future research in this area.

Racial Differences in Narrative Style and Content   In the EYM sample, Black and White couples differed in their narrative styles. Black couples told longer stories, used a more dramatic style, and demonstrated more conflict during the storytelling process than White couples (Orbuch et al., 1993). Other research has shown that a conflictful style of communication is more acceptable among African Americans (Kochman, 1981), so it may be that conflict is simply viewed as a normal aspect of marital communication for Black couples.

Black and White couples also emphasized different themes in their courtship narratives. Black couples were more likely than White couples to mention living together and being pregnant before marriage (Holmberg et al., 2004). Additionally, Blacks mentioned religious issues, emphasized themes of romance, and discussed overcoming obstacles in their courtship narratives to a greater degree than Whites (Orbuch et al., 1993). Although themes of achievement, family, and couple relations were prominent for both Black and White couples, one study found Blacks were less likely than

Whites to mention achievement and more likely to focus on couple relations. One possible explanation for this difference is that in the face of externally imposed structural and economic barriers, African American couples may rely more heavily on the couple relationship to maintain a sense of personal well-being (Chadiha, Veroff, & Leber, 1998).

Racial Differences in Associations between Narratives and Well-Being   Narrative style and marital well-being were related in different ways for Blacks and Whites. As was reviewed in the style section, couple conflict during the storytelling process generally has been linked to lower well-being. However, Orbuch et al. (1993) found this connection did not hold true for Black husbands. As mentioned above, a conflictful style of communication may be more acceptable among Black couples. Similarly, although collaboration during the storytelling process has been linked to higher marital happiness among White couples, Orbuch et al. (1993) found it was linked to lower marital happiness among Black couples, especially Black wives. In fact, for Black spouses, being the dominant storyteller was linked to the greatest marital well-being (Orbuch et al., 1993). Black couples may be happier with their married lives when they are able to maintain a strong individual perspective about how their relationship developed.

The content of the courtship narrative also was linked to marital well-being in distinct ways for Blacks and Whites. Work from the EYM project demonstrated that for Black women, narratives that dealt with themes of religion were linked to higher marital well-being; and for Black men, narratives dealing with themes of children or finances were linked to lower well-being (Veroff, Sutherland, et al., 1993). Moreover, courtship narratives containing the theme of female initiation were more strongly linked to lower marital happiness among Black couples than among White couples (Holmberg et al., 2004). Additionally, Orbuch et al. (1993) found that whereas plots suggesting that the couple had to overcome some obstacles were linked to lower marital well-being for Whites, the same was not true for Black couples (Orbuch et al., 1993). For Black couples, obstacles may be viewed as a normative part of the courtship process. Finally, Orbuch et al. (1993) found that Black husbands and wives who told courtship stories attributing tension to external, rather than internal, sources experienced lower marital well-being. This could be due to the fact that Black couples are more likely than White couples to face externally imposed structural and economic constraints, which are unlikely to be easily overcome. These constraints may carry over and affect the well-being of the marriage.

Research from the EYM project has proved to be fertile ground for exploring racial differences in the relationship initiation process. However, future studies must begin to include other groups within North America. It also would be valuable to extend such research to other cultures globally, particularly to collectivistic cultures, where the courtship process is typically influenced by family members to a greater extent. By expanding our focus to include different racial and ethnic groups, we may be able to identify new sociocultural factors that influence the relationship initiation process.

Summary   Findings from the EYM project indicate that (a) Blacks told longer, more dramatic, more conflictful narratives than Whites; (b) Blacks were more likely than Whites to mention themes of premarital cohabitation and pregnancy, religion, romance, and overcoming obstacles, whereas Whites were more likely than Blacks to mention achievement as a theme; and (c) the content of relationship initiation narratives was linked to relationship well-being in different ways for Blacks and Whites. These findings point to important cultural factors (e.g., communication styles) as well as structural factors (e.g., economic constraints) that may shape the relationship initiation process (and the eventual stories that are told about that process) differently for Blacks and Whites.

Less Traditional Couples

Couples whose relationship represents a violation of societal norms (e.g., interracial, interethnic, same-sex, or highly age-discrepant couples) are likely to encounter resistance from external sources in the process of relationship initiation. One might expect that such couples' courtship stories would emphasize themes of overcoming obstacles, and perhaps isolation from friends and family. Although we argue that all couples use narratives as a means of constructing a new reality together, narratives may be an especially important tool for less traditional couples, who typically cannot rely on culturally established relationship norms and meanings. These couples also might rely heavily on narratives as a means of legitimizing their relationship to others, such as family, friends, and other members of society, who might disapprove of their relationship. They also may be called upon to engage in public retellings of their courtship more frequently than other types of couples, because outsiders may be curious about their attraction to one another. In this section, we examine narrative research regarding two types of less traditional romantic relationships: intercultural couples and same-sex couples.

Intercultural Couples

Intercultural couples is a broad term that includes relationships in which partners have different racial, ethnic, religious, or cultural backgrounds (Gaines, Gurung, Lin, & Pouli, 2006). Narrative studies of intercultural couples typically focus on interracial and interethnic marriages. These studies concentrate primarily on trying to understand why individuals decided to marry outside their own racial and/or ethnic groups. Two dominant themes emerge from this literature: similarity and difference, and overcoming obstacles.

Some individuals may initiate romantic relationships outside their ethnic or racial group because they perceive their own culture to be lacking something that they desire. For instance, in a study of interracial marriages, Fong and Yung (1995 to 1996) found that many Asian Americans chose to intermarry with Whites because they wanted to escape traditional Asian views of marriage, particularly the patriarchal family structure. Similarly, in a study of 20 interethnically married women, Khatib-Chahidi, Hill, and Paton (1998) found that about a third of the women stated that they were initially attracted to their spouse because he was "different."

Although some individuals initiate intercultural relationships based on an attraction to perceived differences, evidence suggests many individuals emphasize their similarities, rather than their differences, in their courtship stories (Killian, 2002; Rosenblatt, Karis, & Powell, 1995). For instance, one interracial couple stated, "Our courtship wasn't a long one, for right from [the] beginning we felt that we wanted to be together. Our ideas, values, and opinions seemed to click and I guess we could say it was love at first sight" (Johnson & Warren, 1994, p. 117). Though most intercultural couples are cognizant of their differences, these differences play a relatively unimportant role in their decision to initiate the relationship. Regarding his initial attraction to his Black wife, one White husband said, "From the beginning I was surprised less by how important race was than how important it wasn't" (Johnson & Warren, 1994, p. 148).

There are at least two possible explanations for the pervasive theme of perceived similarities in the courtship narratives of intercultural couples. One is that "like follows like"; differences such as race or religion may simply be viewed as less important than other characteristics when couples assess their similarities. Another explanation, however, is that intercultural couples use their courtship narratives to forge similarity in the face of societal messages that they are too different for their marriage to succeed. These couples are obviously aware of society's skepticism regarding their relationship; by emphasizing their similarities, they may use their narratives as a mechanism to bolster their relationship, as well as prove to potentially hostile outsiders that they are "made for each other."

Intercultural couples must frequently overcome tremendous obstacles in order to initiate a relationship. For instance, interracial marriage was not legalized in the United States until 1967. Even today, interracial couples may encounter opposition when they initiate relationships. Although interracial couples may not view their differences as important, the surrounding culture often does. Thus, the early stages of the relationship are often conducted in secret. When couples decide to make their relationship public, they may find their view of themselves challenged by the outside community (Rosenblatt et al., 1995).

Intercultural couples often view the obstacles that they must overcome during the courtship stage as strengthening their relationship or as evidence for the power of their love for one another. For instance, a Black American man married to a Namibian woman stated, "We first had initial difficulties in that Elizabeth belonged to a liberation movement ... which actively discouraged marriage of their womenfolk to male non-Namibians … . Many obstacles were thus placed in our way, but that probably strengthened our relationship" (Johnson & Warren, 1994, p. 227). The degree to which intercultural couples experience opposition during the courtship stage is likely to depend on the context in which they interact. Clearly, some environments are more supportive of these relationships than others.

Relationship initiation among intercultural couples is an area ripe for further study using the narrative technique. There are many issues that have yet to be explored. For instance, we do not know whether intercultural couples continue to emphasize themes of similarity and overcoming obstacles during the courtship as their relationship progresses. Nor do we know how these themes may be related to the couple's well-being. Another area that should be considered is the extent to which the courtship narratives of these couples change across such contexts. For instance, do couples emphasize their similarities more when they are telling their courtship stories to potentially hostile audiences, as compared to audiences that are more supportive? Finally, it seems especially important to consider the congruency of spouses' narratives among intercultural couples. Future research should examine whether spouses who belong to a minority group view their courtship differently than spouses who belong to the majority group. Such comparisons would help us to further understand how social status and power shape relationship views.

Same-Sex Couples

Though research on same-sex couples has been growing at a considerable pace over the past few years, it still lags far behind research on other-sex couples (Kurdek, 2004). Narratives of same-sex relationship initiation do not seem to be present within the existing literature. Therefore, this section of the chapter will focus on the results of one study, conducted by the authors, in which same-sex and other-sex couples were compared in their narratives of relationship initiation (Blair & Holmberg, 2006).

Participants from a large online study of relationships and health were asked to participate in a brief secondary study. Participants ($n = 324$; 242 females and 80 males; 172 heterosexual and 152 nonheterosexual; mean age = 30) answered three open-ended questions describing how they met their partner, how they became attracted to their partner, and, finally, how they became a couple. Responses to the question "How did you and your partner meet?" were coded for the location of meeting, as well as for whether or not the couple was introduced by mutual friends or a family member. Two significant differences were found between same-sex and other-sex couples.

First, other-sex couples were more likely than same-sex couples to have been introduced by a third party, such as a family member or friend (30% versus 20%, $\chi2(2) = 7.2$, $p = .027$). It should be noted that previous research has indicated that social network support is an important predictor of relationship quality and stability (Sprecher & Felmlee, 1992). To be introduced by a member of a social network provides a sense of support for the match from the very beginning. As one participant described it, "My mother offered to send me to the ball as a fun thing to do, and as an aside because she wanted to set me up with her friend's son … . When I first saw him, I thought, 'This is who my mum thinks I should be with.'" In addition to signaling the social network's approval, being introduced by a social network member may also reduce the number of stressful stages a relationship must go through, such as meeting the friends and family.

In the current study, those in heterosexual relationships were more likely to experience this comforting "preapproval" process than those in same-sex relationships. Even parents who are relatively supportive of their sexual minority children may not take an active role in the relationship initiation process by setting up potential same-sex matches; likely more common is the scenario of attempting to set up their child with some "nice young man (or woman)" in the hope that the "problem" is simply not having met the *right* opposite-sex other. Future research should continue to examine the role of social networks in relationship initiation, including examining whether the differences noted are primarily due to a lack of parental introduction, or whether friends and siblings are also less likely to aid nonheterosexuals in their relationship initiation attempts.

The second significant difference between the narratives of same-sex and other-sex couples was that same-sex couples were much more likely to report having met through the use of the Internet (30% versus 7%, $\chi2(2) = 33.04$, $p < .001$). As one participant describes the process:

> I was living in a small town and spent a lot of time on the computer, as this was my only connection to other GLBT people. I was scanning a Canadian lesbian website … which allowed people to post on a bulletin board. I read a posting by someone who had similar interests as I had, was tired of being a third wheel to her friend's relationship, and wanted to meet other single people to socialize with.

Those in same-sex and other-sex relationships also differed in the tone of their stories of Internet initiation. Gay and lesbian participants tended to be very matter-of-fact about looking for partners in online forums. Heterosexuals, in contrast, tended to be apologetic, frequently providing excuses or justifications, such as a busy lifestyle, to explain why they were participating in online dating rather than more mainstream forms of dating. For heterosexuals, online dating still appears to be a "taboo" subject that raises questions or concerns: "Why can't you meet someone offline? What if they are not who they pretend to be? What if they're a predator?" Thus, for heterosexuals, the potential risks of online dating may still outnumber the potential benefits.

Although the same risks are possible for nonheterosexuals, a greater number of benefits also are available, making the Internet an attractive alternative to more mainstream forms of dating. Dating online provides nonheterosexuals with the ability to control the extent to which they are "out" in their day-to-day lives, in fact, offering them the option to remain completely "in the closet" if they so choose. It thus allows a relatively safe way to explore sexual identity issues (e.g., "I was finally starting to explore my confusion over my sexual orientation, and so I joined a lot of online gay profile sites. I met a few people off the sites in person and had online relationships with others"). Even for those comfortable with their sexuality, the Internet provides an alternative to meeting potential partners at gay and lesbian bars, which may not appeal to all nonheterosexuals, and which may not be available venues in rural areas and even some major city centers. Online dating also is a simple numbers game for nonheterosexuals, especially for those living away from major urban centers. If less than 10% of the population shares your sexual orientation, your possible matches are limited; expanding your search to neighboring communities may be very attractive.

However, perhaps the biggest benefit offered to nonheterosexuals using the Internet as a means of meeting potential dating partners is the relative assurance they have of the sexuality of those potential partners. Although heterosexuals may occasionally wrongly assume the sexual orientation of a potential partner, there are unlikely to be many negative repercussions of such an error, beyond some minor embarrassment. In contrast, gays and lesbians who wrongly assume the sexual identity of a potential partner could be opening themselves up to a variety of risks, including causing personal offense, eliciting a violent reaction, or revealing their sexual identity, which in turn could carry risks of losing their job, friends, or family. For nonheterosexuals, correctly identifying the sexual identity of a potential partner can be one of the largest stressors in the relationship initiation process. Meeting online removes this stressor for sexual minorities, allowing them to go back to worrying about the little things ("Will we hit it off? Is she a cat person or a dog person?").

The differences between same-sex and other-sex couples highlighted by this study are not likely due to any inherent differences in the individuals, but are more likely symptomatic of the current societal context in which these relationships function. Future research should examine how relationship initiation narratives vary by situation or audience. For example, those who met online (in both same-sex and other-sex relationships) sometimes mentioned that they adjusted their story depending on what audience they are sharing it with, due to societal views about online dating. For example, one participant, who got to know a schoolmate better through chat room conversations, reported, "Depending on who asks, we say that we met through friends, at school, or online. All are technically true." Whether or not stories change based upon other variables should also be a topic of further investigation. In addition, many other questions remain in the area of same-sex relationship initiation stories. As a start, stories provided in this study will be analyzed further and coded for content, style, consistency, and couple orientation to examine other potential similarities or differences between the stories of same-sex and other-sex relationship initiation.

Summary   We know much less about the relationship initiation narratives of nontraditional couples than we do about those of more "mainstream" couples. The scant research that exists indicates that (a) intercultural couples emphasized their similarities, rather than their differences, in their relationship initiation narratives; (b) these couples also mentioned the obstacles that they had to overcome in order to initiate their relationship; and (c) same-sex couples were more likely to meet through the Internet, whereas other-sex couples were more likely to meet through a third party. Though at first glance intercultural couples and same-sex couples might not seem to have that much in common, the courtship narratives of these two groups reflect the challenges that less traditional couples face in even initiating a relationship. It would seem that relationship initiation narratives might be a particularly important tool for these couples. Being able to construct a positive relationship narrative even in the face of adversity and being able to adapt one's narrative to appropriate audiences may be skills that are essential for all couples, but particularly for couples whose relationship is most likely to be met with adversity.

SEVERAL THEMES FOR FUTURE RESEARCH

Although there has been a growth of research in the last decade examining relationship beginnings from a narrative approach, there is still so much to learn and explore. Throughout the entire chapter, we have provided specific suggestions or themes for future research. Here, we continue to encourage researchers to expand their work in the area of relationship beginnings using the narrative approach. We offer several additional themes for future research.

First, we know very little about where and when people choose to tell their initiation stories. Examining the context within which stories are told, and how these stories are generally elicited, would clarify the functions and consequences of initiation stories for individuals and their developing relationships. Further, does the content of an initiation story vary depending on whether it was spontaneously offered by a couple or individual or requested by someone who is interested in hearing the story? This issue might be especially critical to understand because many narrative researchers ask couples or individuals to tell their initiation story, rather than waiting to see how the narrative is spontaneously created. Requests for stories can indicate interest on the part of the social network or researchers, but also may alter the vision of the relationship that is presented. In addition, it also would be interesting to examine the different functions of recounting a relationship initiation story privately with your partner versus publicly telling the story to a member of your social network. Requests for public retelling by others may signal ongoing approval of the relationship, or provide an opportunity to publicly cement the role as a couple. Private retelling within the couple in theory cements bonds, but in practice frequent retelling might prove detrimental; it may be diagnostic that the story is not fully satisfying to one partner or the other, and so it must be worked through. Private retelling of the story also might be a sign of longing for glory days of the past.

Further, as suggested earlier in the chapter, there is little research on the ways initiation narratives may change across situations, audiences, and the presence or absence of the partner. We need to explore whether characteristics of the audience influence which aspects of the initiation story are emphasized or left undisclosed, and in turn whether this altering is related to relationship well-being. According to symbolic interactionists, reality is constructed subjectively through interaction and meaning-making processes within groups. It may be possible, then, to shape individuals' relationships (and their relationship satisfaction) by altering the audience and context within which they tell their stories. Existing work on initiation stories also has begun to account for the influences of race and ethnicity and gender, but there are other qualities of the individual (e.g., age and religion) or relationship (e.g., friendship, dating, or married) that may influence the stories and process of relationship beginnings. How do relationship initiation stories of young adolescents, young adults, and older adults differ? What themes are prominent and diagnostic of well-being in new relationship initiations of divorced or widowed individuals? In addition, do initiation narratives reveal important information about nonromantic relationships as well? If we change from romantic relationships to friendships or work relationships, are relationship initiation narratives developed or prompted for in these settings? What about for very casual relationships or one-night stands? How do those narratives differ from narratives for long-term relationship initiation? Do the differences reflect larger cultural beliefs and messages that shape how individuals think about these relationships?

Next, we need to understand more about whether the way narratives are collected (written versus oral, and individual versus dyadic) affects the stories that are told and the predictive power of those stories. A very important question that researchers also need to address is whether narratives about the beginning of a relationship are more or less important to the functioning and well-being of the relationship than stories about the middle or later stages of the relationship. Finally, additional research is definitely needed to address whether narratives predict outcomes over and above more quantitative measures (Veroff, Chadiha, et al., 1993). Such in-depth research will help us to clarify and expand our thoughts on how initiation narratives shape relationships and individuals' experiences in them. Clearly, we have only begun to "scratch the surface" of these intriguing issues.

REFERENCES

Acitelli, L. K. (1992). Gender differences in relationship awareness and marital satisfaction among young married couples. *Personality and Social Psychology Bulletin, 18,* 102–110.

Aron, A., & Fraley, B. (1999). Relationship closeness as including other in the self: Cognitive underpinnings and measures. *Social Cognition, 17*(2), 140–160.

Berger, P., & Kellner, H. (1964). Marriage and the construction of reality. *Diogenes, 46,* 1–24.

Blair, K., & Holmberg, D. (2006, May). *How did you two meet? Narratives of relationship initiation.* Paper presented at the Third International Narrative Matters Conference, Wolfville, NS, Canada.

Blumer, H. (1969). *Symbolic interactionism.* Englewood Cliffs, NJ: Prentice Hall.

Bochner, A. P., Ellis, C., & Tillmann-Healy, L. M. (2000). Relationships as stories: Accounts, storied lives, evocative narratives. In K. Dindia & S. Duck (Eds.), *Communication and personal relationships* (pp. 12–29). Chichester, UK: John Wiley.

Bruner, J. (1990). *Acts of meaning.* Cambridge, MA: Harvard University Press.

Buss, D. M. (1994). *Evolution of desire: Strategies for human mating.* New York: Basic Books.

Chadiha, L. A., Veroff, J., & Leber, D. (1998). Newlywed's narrative themes: Meaning in the first year of marriage for African American and White couples. *Journal of Comparative Family Studies, 29,* 115–130.

Clark, C. L., Shaver, P. R., & Abrahams, M. F. (1999). Strategic behaviors in romantic relationship initiation. *Personality and Social Psychology Bulletin, 25*(6), 709–722.

Cowan, P. A. (1999). What we talk about when we talk about families. *Monographs of the Society for Research in Child Development, 64*(2), 163–176.

Fiese, B. H., & Sameroff, A. J. (1999). The Family Narrative Consortium: A multidimensional approach to narratives. *Monographs of the Society for Research in Child Development, 64*(2), 1–36.

Fong, C., & Yung, J. (1995–1996). In search of the right spouse: Interracial marriage among Chinese and Japanese Americans. *Amerasia Journal, 21*(3), 77–98.

Gaines, S. O., Gurung, R. A. R., Lin, Y., & Pouli, N. (2006). Interethnic relationships. In J. Feeney & P. Noller (Eds.), *Close relationships: Functions, forms, and processes* (pp. 171–187). New York: Psychology Press.

Gergen, K. J., & Gergen, M. N. (1983). Narratives of the self. In T. R. Sarbin & K. E. Scheibe (Eds.), *Studies of social identity* (pp. 254–272). New York: Praeger.

Gergen, K. J., & Gergen, M. M. (1987). Narratives of relationships. In R. Burnett, P. McGhee, & D. Clark (Eds.), *Accounting for relationships* (pp. 269–288). New York: Methuen.

Greer, A. E., & Buss, D. M. (1994). Tactics for promoting sexual encounters. *Journal of Sex Research, 31,* 185–201.

Grote, N. K., & Frieze, I. H. (1994). The measurement of friendship-based love in intimate relationships. **Personal Relationships,** 1, 275–300.

Heider, F. (1958). *The psychology of interpersonal relations.* New York: John Wiley.

Holmberg, D., & Holmes, J. G. (1994). Reconstruction of relationship memories: A mental models approach. In N. Schwarz & S. Sudman (Eds.), *Autobiographical memory and the validity of retrospective reports* (pp. 267–288). New York: Springer-Verlag.

Holmberg, D., & Orbuch, T. L. (2004). How ideal is ideal? Style and content of marriage narratives as predictors of marital well-being over time. In W. L. Randall, D. Furlong, & T. Poitras (Eds.), *Narrative Matters 2004 conference proceedings* (pp. 454–466). Fredericton, NB, Canada: Narrative Matters Conference Planning Committee.

Holmberg, D., Orbuch, T. L., & Veroff, J. (2004). *Thrice-told tales: Married couples tell their stories*. Mahwah, NJ: Lawrence Erlbaum.

Johnson, W. R., & Warren, D. M. (1994). *Inside the mixed marriage: Accounts of changing attitudes, patterns, and perceptions of cross-cultural and interracial marriages*. New York: University Press of America.

Khatib-Chahidi, J., Hill, R., & Paton, R. (1998). Chance, choice and circumstance: A study of women in cross-cultural marriages. In R. Breger & R. Hill (Eds.), *Cross-cultural marriage: Identity and choice* (pp. 49–66). New York: Berg.

Killian, K. D. (2002). Dominant and marginalized discourses in interracial couples' narratives: Implications for family therapists. *Family Process, 41*, 603–618.

Kochman, T. (1981). *Black and white styles in conflict*. Chicago: University of Chicago Press.

Kurdek, L. A. (2004). Are gay and lesbian cohabiting couples *really* different from heterosexual married couples? *Journal of Marriage and the Family, 66*, 880–900.

Lichtman, R. R., & Taylor, S. E. (1986). Close relationships of female cancer patients. In B. L. Andersen (Ed.), *Women with cancer* (pp. 233–256). New York: Springer.

Mead, G. H. (1934). *Mind, self, and society*. Chicago: University of Chicago Press.

Orbuch, T., Veroff, J., & Holmberg, D. (1993). Becoming a married couple: The emergence of meaning. *Journal of Marriage and the Family, 55*, 815–826.

Orbuch, T. L. (1997). People's accounts count: The sociology of accounts. *Annual Review of Sociology, 23*, 455–478.

Orbuch, T. L., Harvey, J., Davis, S., & Merbach, N. (1994). Account-making and confiding as acts of meaning in response to sexual assault. *Journal of Family Violence, 9*(3), 249–264.

Pennebaker, J., & Harber, K. (1993). A social stage model of collective coping: The Loma Prieta Earthquake and the Persian Gulf War. *Journal of Social Issues, 49*, 125–145.

Pennebaker, J. W., & Francis, M. E. (1996). Cognitive, emotional, and language processes in disclosure. *Cognition and Emotion, 10*(6), 601–626.

Perper, T. (1985). *Sexual signals: The biology of love*. Philadelphia: ISI Press.

Rose, S., & Frieze, I. H. (1993). Young singles' contemporary dating scripts. *Sex Roles, 28*, 499–509.

Rosenblatt, P. C., Karis, T., & Powell, R. R. (1995). *Multi-racial couples: Black and white voices*. Thousand Oaks, CA: Sage.

Ross, M. (1989). Relation of implicit theories to the construction of personal histories. *Psychological Review, 96*, 341–357.

Scott, M. B., & Lyman, S. (1968). Accounts. *American Sociological Review, 33*, 46–62.

Spence, D. (1982). *Narrative truth and historical truth: Meaning and interpretation in psychoanalysis*. New York: Norton.

Sprecher, S., & Felmlee, D. (1992). The influence of parents and friends on the quality and stability of romantic relationships: A three-wave longitudinal investigation. *Journal of Marriage and the Family, 54*(4), 888–900.

Sternberg, R. J. (1986). A triangular theory of love. **Psychological Review**, *93*, 119–135.

Veroff, J., Chadiha, L., Leber, D., & Sutherland, L. (1993). Affects and interactions in newlywed narratives: Black and white couples compared. *Journal of Narrative Life History, 3*(4), 361–390.

Veroff, J., Sutherland, L., Chadiha, L. A., & Ortega, R. M. (1993). Predicting marital quality with narrative assessments of marital experience. *Journal of Marriage and the Family, 55*(2), 326–337.

Walster, E., & Walster, G. W. (1978). *A new look at love*. Reading, MA: Addison-Wesley.

Wamboldt, F. S. (1999). Co-constructing a marriage: Analyses of young couples' relationship narratives. *Monographs of the Society for Research in Child Development, 64*(2), 37–51.

Weber, A. L. (1992). The account-making process: A phenomenological approach. In T. L. Orbuch (Ed.), *Close relationship loss* (pp. 174–191). New York: Springer.

Weiner, B. (1985). "Spontaneous" causal thinking. *Psychological Bulletin, 97*, 74–84.

Wilkinson, S. (1987). Explorations of self and other in a developing relationship. In R. Burnett, P. McGhee, & D. Clark (Eds.), *Accounting for relationships* (pp. 40–59). London: Methuen.

24

Relationship Beliefs and Their Role in Romantic Relationship Initiation

C. RAYMOND KNEE and AMBER L. BUSH

J ack and Jill met on a hill. They immediately hit it off and felt a strong sense of rapport and connection with each other. The initiation of this potential relationship could be interpreted in multiple ways. If Jack believes that people either "hit it off or they don't," then he will assign considerable positive meaning to that initial rapport, and doing so will probably make him feel more interested in pursuing a relationship with Jill. If Jill believes that people cannot forecast a relationship's potential from only a brief encounter, then she might interpret the immediate rapport as irrelevant and unstable—as something that might be a fluke and that does not have great significance for the future of Jack and Jill.

What people believe about the nature of romantic relationships can determine, in part, how they initiate and maintain close relationships. Much of the research on relationship beliefs has tended to examine long-term established relationships, ironically overlooking their potential role in setting up and guiding how events take on meaning in newer relationships. One thing that most of the beliefs reviewed here seem to share is their potential role in moderating the way in which early relationship events can take on different meanings depending on the mental filter that such beliefs provide. For example, attachment theorists describe how one's working models, derived in large part from prior relationship experiences, guide felt security and interpretations of initiating events (Collins & Read, 1994; Mikulincer, Florian, & Tolmacz, 1990; Simpson, 1990). Fletcher and Simpson's (Fletcher, Simpson, Thomas, & Giles, 1999; Simpson, Fletcher, & Campbell, 2001) ideals model argues that the ideals one brings to a new relationship play a key role in one's evaluation of the relationship, depending on how one perceives one's partner stacking up to that ideal. Romantic beliefs (Sprecher & Metts, 1989, 1999) contain an overriding optimistic interpretation on how events are viewed early in the relationship. Dysfunctional beliefs (Eidelson & Epstein, 1982; Epstein & Eidelson, 1981) can lead one to interpret relationship experiences in detrimental ways. Finally, implicit theories of relationships (Knee, 1998; Knee, Patrick, & Lonsbary, 2003) center on ways in which individuals' beliefs about the stability of impressions and the stability of problems guide the way in which meaning gets assigned to new relationship experiences.

These belief frameworks have a lot to say about how the same events, in relatively new relationships, come to be interpreted and acted upon rather differently. We briefly mention the initial impressions literature, which provided the basis for studying the schemas and beliefs that people bring with them to their romantic relationships. We then provide a general conceptual model for how relationship beliefs may moderate the way that initiating events come to affect relationship attributions, evaluations, and outcomes. Finally, we review how a variety of relationship beliefs, including internal working models, romantic beliefs, dysfunctional beliefs, relationship and partner ideals, and implicit theories of relationships, may play a role in the way that relatively new relationships unfold. Throughout, we attend to how the beliefs can fit into the general conceptual model provided.

INITIAL IMPRESSIONS

Initial impressions and expectations guide how individuals perceive a partner's interaction behaviors such that they are viewed as consistent with those expectations (e.g., Berscheid, Graziano, Monson, & Dermer, 1976; Snyder, Tanke, & Berscheid, 1977; Zadny & Gerard, 1974; see Berscheid & Reis, 1998, for review). Out of these relatively early studies emerged the notion that expectancies can exert an active role in how people notice, interpret, and remember relational events (e.g., Brewer & Treyens, 1981; Trafimow & Wyer, 1993). Early impressions and expectations, in turn, form the basis of relationship schemas, which are thought to guide the categorization and interpretation of new information about relationship partners, and to influence relationship behaviors (Baldwin, 1992; Planalp, 1987). For close relationships, such knowledge structures tend to be relatively complex because we have a continuing stream of relationship experiences, and we are bombarded by observations of others' relationship experiences (Berscheid, 1994; Fletcher & Thomas, 1996). For our purposes, we will think of relationship beliefs as a diverse collection of knowledge structures that contain assumptions about what is beneficial, typical, and relevant in developing close relationships.

OUR GENERAL CONCEPTUAL MODEL

Relationship beliefs encompass ideas about what is important or key to relationship success. In this way, events occurring in the early phases of relationship development are filtered through the beliefs and schemas that one brings to the potential relationship. One can think of relationship beliefs and schemas as glasses that color and filter one's perception of events as they occur, and as they are assigned meaning early in a potential relationship. Events can take on an entirely different meaning depending on the cognitive structures through which they are filtered. Figure 24.1 provides a general conceptual model for how a variety of relationship beliefs may filter and guide perception of early events in developing relationships. The model begins with initiating events that may or may not lead to continued interest and relationship development. We think of initiating events broadly as those experiences that may or may not actually impact a new relationship, but that potentially provoke inferences about the relationship. Initiating events include, but are not limited to, a romantic gesture such as a first date or kiss, and felt rapport upon meeting and interacting with a potential partner, and realizing that a potential partner possesses similar (and/or desirable) traits, beliefs, interests, and goals—or perceiving differences on such dimensions. Further, as the potential relationship develops, initiating events could include a disagreement or conflict between partners, and feedback or information about how well the relationship is going or how well one is "achieving" a successful relationship. Some events may also be relational turning points that reflect changes in the relationship (Baxter & Bullis, 1986). Initiating events also include events from the social context such as comments about the potential relationship from friends or family (Agnew, Loving, & Drigotas, 2001), or even events that may make salient potential alternative partners, as well as one's own feelings of discontent (Vangelisti & Alexander, 2002). These experiences may or may not co-occur or be followed by later satisfaction, closeness, felt risk, and relationship evaluation. It is posited that the particular reaction one has to such initiating events depends on the beliefs that one brings to the potential relationship, and the meaning that is assigned to the event (i.e., the filter through which the event is interpreted) as a function of those relationship beliefs.

Relationship beliefs moderate the implications that relationship events have on the relationship because of the way that meaning is assigned to those early events on several dimensions. For example, feeling immediate rapport with a potential partner may be interpreted as something beneficial or as something detrimental, depending on the beliefs one holds. Some beliefs, by their nature, impart beneficial meaning to immediate rapport and chemistry. Such beliefs might include those that emphasize the importance of "hitting it off" from the start, and romantic beliefs more generally. Other beliefs impart no meaning or even detrimental meaning to immediate rapport and "synchrony." Such beliefs might involve the assumption that immediate passion and rapport are irrelevant, or even antithetical to developing successful long-term relationships. These beliefs could be the opposite of romantic beliefs, or they could contain an emphasis on gradual, long-term building of relationships. Another dimension of meaning that is potentially assigned to initiating events concerns whether the event (and potential relationship) is perceived as unique versus typical. Some beliefs (e.g., the romantic belief in one true love) may engender a tendency to view an initiating event, such as immediate rapport, as reflecting something unique and special as opposed to something rather mundane and typical. These beliefs would then imbue the nascent relationship with a special uniqueness that is not believed to be common to other potential relationships. In a different vein, if the initiating event is the recognition of differences between a potential partner and oneself, then beliefs that impart uniqueness to those differences rather than seeing them as typical and expected could lead to unfavorable evaluations and assessments of the relationship's potential.

Relationship beliefs also carry assumptions about what one considers relevant versus irrelevant to relationship success. For example, if one believes that passion is essential for a successful relationship, then one will come to judge and evaluate one's relationship on that basis. The ideal standards one holds for potential partners and successful relationships, in part, determine the relevance placed on particular initiating events and perceptions (Fletcher et al., 1999). In this way, discovering differences between a potential partner and one's ideal potential partner will carry stronger meaning for some attributes than others, and thus will result in different evaluations of the relationship's value and potential depending on those ideals.

Finally, some beliefs help define what it means to feel safe and secure in moving forward with a new relationship. For example, working models of anxiety and avoidance may filter the way in which early relationship events and experiences are interpreted along the dimension of feeling that the potential relationship is safe and comfortable versus unsafe and insecure. The potential moderating role of relationship beliefs in determining how initiating events take on meaning and guide later evaluations, decisions, and behaviors is the primary focus of this review. That is not to say that relationship beliefs cannot also predict the initiating events that transpire, but rather that potential moderation is emphasized here. In the next sections, we review a number of relationship beliefs and discuss ways in which these beliefs fit into the generic conceptual model in Figure 24.1. It should be noted that the dimensions of meaning mentioned here are neither entirely independent nor exhaustive. They are not meant to necessarily follow from particular relationship beliefs, and are meant to be general enough to account for the assumptions of more than one particular belief at a time. Further, the beliefs vary in extant empirical support as moderators of how initiating events predict later judgments, evaluations, and outcomes. Some beliefs were specifically identified and studied with those research goals in mind (e.g., implicit theories of relationships) and have substantial empirical support for such a moderating role, whereas others have been examined primarily with other goals in mind, such as direct associations with relationship outcomes (e.g., romantic beliefs, and dysfunctional beliefs).

INTERNAL WORKING MODELS

Originally conceptualized by Bowlby (1969, 1973) and later empirically tested by Ainsworth, Blehar, Walters, and Wall (1978), attachment theory suggests that there are individual differences in how individuals approach and respond to the world. Further, these different styles of dealing with the world are presumed to be based on past experiences of relating to and interacting with important others, most notably the primary caretaker. For example, whereas infants with secure working attachments had caretakers who were responsive to the infants' needs, those with avoidant attachments had caretakers who were dismissive and neglectful. Further, those with anxious-ambivalent attachments had caretakers who were generally inconsistent in responding to the infants' needs. Hazan and Shaver (1987, 1990) were among the first to perceive a parallel between infant attachment and adult romantic attachment. They posited that how adults think, feel, and behave in close relationships is contingent on attachment histories. Effects of childhood attachment relationships are thought to carry over into adulthood via working models, where these models become applied to one's romantic relationships. Romantic love is essentially an attachment process itself, where deep bonds are formed (Hazan & Shaver, 1987).

Working models can be conceptualized as mental representations of the self and others that stem from experiences with attachment figures (Bowlby, 1973). Typically, early working models are based on infant–caregiver relationships and are fairly specific to that particular relationship. However, these working models become more general representations of what to expect from relationships in adult life. Internal working models of attachment include expectations about one's own worth and the perceived availability of the attachment figure. Individual differences in attachment are thought to remain relatively stable over time because of working models (e.g., Rothbard & Shaver, 1994; Scharfe & Bartholomew, 1994).

It is generally thought that working models reflect two underlying dimensions, although there is still some disagreement over how those dimensions should be labeled. For example, Bartholomew and Horowitz (1991) confirmed Bowlby's (1973) original claim that internal working models consisted of a model of self and a model of others. One's model of self referred to one's sense of self-worth versus anxiety and uncertainty over one's lovability. One's model of others concerned one's expectations about the degree to which others are available, supportive, and trustworthy. Additionally, Bartholomew and Horowitz posited that these two continuous dimensions could be combined to reveal four prototypical primary attachment styles in adults. Specifically, a positive view of both self and others was considered secure attachment, reflecting internalized self-worth and comfort with intimacy with others. A negative view of self and others was considered fearful-avoidant attachment, reflecting negative expectations about one's lovability and a tendency to avoid others as a way to avoid pain and loss. A positive view of self and negative view of others were considered dismissive avoidant, reflecting an avoidance of closeness because of the expectations that others will not be available, and dismissing the value of close relationships. Finally, a negative view of self and positive view of others were considered preoccupied, reflecting a trust that others will provide intimacy but also feeling that one does not deserve that intimacy. It is now generally accepted that attachment is not best reflected by types or categories but rather as locations on continuous dimensions (Brennan, Clark, & Shaver, 1998; Fraley & Waller, 1998). For example, Brennan et al. (1998) argued for two primary dimensions of avoidance and anxiety, which are reflected in the 36-item Experiences in Close Relationships Scale. This measure was derived from multiple self-report adult romantic attachment measures. The avoidance dimension captures the working model of others (from positive to negative) and the anxiety dimension reflects the working model of self (from positive to negative).

Working models are presumed to operate as part of a broader system of cognitive, affective, and behavioral processes that respond to relational experiences in learned ways that promote or protect felt security (Collins & Read, 1994; Feeney, 2006). Although working models are sensitive to relational experiences, and can be modified by prior experience (e.g., Davila, Burge, & Hammen, 1997), they can also exert a "top-down" influence. In other words, people are not merely passive recipients of environmental stimuli. Instead, working models can function like other beliefs by guiding and shaping the way that events are interpreted. For example, working models are likely to influence the interpretation of significant others (and potential significant others), such that people tend to interpret behaviors consistent with their expectations (Collins & Feeney, 2004). Collins and Feeney found that chronic working models of attachment are linked to systematic differences in perceptions of social support, especially when supportive events are relatively ambiguous and more open to subjective construal. Generally, those with secure working models, relative to those with more insecure working models, appear predisposed to interpret their social interactions in more generous ways. Working models may also guide how and whether romantic relationships are initiated. For example, highly avoidant individuals are less likely to fall in love and are less interested in being involved in long-term committed relationships (Hatfield, Brinton, & Cornelius, 1989; Shaver & Brennan, 1992). On the other hand, highly anxious individuals may be more likely to fall in love and seek out romance obsessively (Hatfield et al., 1989; Hazan & Shaver, 1987).

One particularly significant study on adult attachment in romantic relationships revealed basic associations between attachment style and both one's own and one's partner's perceptions of a variety of relationship evaluations and emotional experiences within the relationship (Simpson, 1990). Specifically, men and women who scored higher on secure attachment reported more interdependent relationships, higher relationship quality, less negative emotions, and more positive emotions within the relationship. Men and women who were highly avoidant reported less interdependence and lower relationship quality, whereas men who were higher in attachment anxiety reported less trust and satisfaction and anxiously attached women reported less trust and commitment. More recently, working models have been associated with an array of different social cognitive processes and outcomes such as attributions, openness to incongruent information, and cognitive flexibility (e.g., Baldwin, Keelan, Fehr, Enns, & Koh-Rangarajoo, 1996; Collins, 1996; Mikulincer & Arad, 1999).

Attachment models carry, among other things, assumptions about what is safe and secure in developing romantic relationships. In Figure 24.1, then, depending upon one's attachment model, an initiating event such as immediate rapport could be interpreted as a safe and secure (even necessary) experience that would then promote satisfaction, closeness, commitment, and less perception of risk. So, if Jill holds an anxious attachment model, she might interpret her feelings of immediate rapport with Jack as a necessary condition for her to feel safe and secure with him. Alternatively, if Jill holds an avoidant attachment model, experiencing rapport quickly with Jack could be interpreted as unsafe and insecure, which could then promote dissatisfaction, less closeness, less commitment, and greater perception of the relationship being intrusive. Perceived differences can carry different meanings as well, depending on the nature of the working model one brings to the scenario. Judgment of how risky it is to continue to pursue a potential relationship seems fundamentally like an issue of felt security (or even anticipated security), which would be colored by the attachment model one brings to that situation. Thus, attachment models, like other relationship beliefs, provide a filter through which relationship events are viewed and assigned meaning, and different models carry different assumptions about what produces felt security.

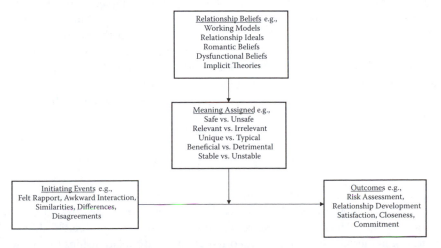

Figure 24.1

RELATIONSHIP IDEALS

General beliefs about what produces good, successful relationships are not necessarily the same qualities that one seeks in an ideal partner or relationship. Relationship ideals are considered chronically activated knowledge structures that contain images of self, ideal partner, and ideal relationship (Campbell, Simpson, Kashy, & Fletcher, 2001). Relationship ideals regarding what qualities are personally important in a romantic partner or relationship tend to be more specific than relationship beliefs, which are broad views about what attributes lead to successful relationships (Fletcher et al., 1999). A series of studies on the content and structure of ideals showed that ratings of one's "ideal partner" fell into three primary dimensions: *Warmth and trustworthiness* contained characteristics relevant to the development of intimacy and loyalty, *vitality and attractiveness* contained characteristics related to attractiveness and health, and *status and resources* contained qualities such as dressing well and having a good job and a nice house. For both men and women, warmth and trustworthiness were rated as most important in an ideal partner, followed by vitality and attractiveness, and then status and resources. Relationship ideals were somewhat different in that two primary dimensions emerged: *Intimacy and loyalty* refer to the importance of intimacy and stability; *passion* refers to the importance of excitement and passion in the relationship.

The beliefs people have about what produces successful relationships are strongly related to the kinds of relationship and partner ideals one possesses (Fletcher & Kininmonth, 1992; Fletcher et al., 1999, Study 4). When one believes that a certain factor is important for relationship success, he or she is more likely to rate that factor as important in an ideal relationship or partner (e.g., honesty). What is perhaps more interesting is the way in which one's partner and relationship ideals, when compared against one's current perceptions of those qualities in one's partner or relationship, predict one's level of satisfaction with the relationship (Fletcher et al., 1999). In fact, Fletcher, Simpson, and Thomas (2000) stated that the consistency between ideal standards and perceptions of one's current partner and relationship can serve several functions, including providing a basis for relationship evaluation. Relationship evaluations are assessed and used to make decisions about whether to continue the relationship. Greater consistency between ideals and current perceptions leads one to more positively evaluate an established relationship (Campbell et al., 2001; Fletcher et al., 1999), as well as newly developed relationships (Fletcher et al., 2000). Evaluations of potential and current partners may also be more relevant and salient (compared to evaluations of the relationship) during the early relationship stages (Tran, Simpson, & Fletcher, this volume).

Like more general relationship beliefs, ideals are knowledge structures that affect how meaning is assigned to initiating events and perceptions in developing relationships. Ideals determine which perceptions are considered relevant versus irrelevant, and the degree of meaning that is assigned to various perceptions of a potential partner and relationship. For example, returning to Figure 24.1, if Jack learned that Jill had lied and/or cheated in a previous relationship, it may or may not influence his view of her as a romantic partner. It would seem to depend on the degree to which Jack held trustworthiness as a strong ideal (among other things, of course). If Jack were ideally seeking passion rather than honesty, then learning about Jill's sordid past may not alter his evaluation of the potential relationship as much. In this way, ideals can guide the extent to which perceptions of a current or potential partner are given importance when evaluating one's satisfaction with or assessment of a future potential relationship.

ROMANTIC BELIEFS

Relationship schemas are composed of multiple general beliefs or orientations about relationships; some may promote relationship development, and others may hinder healthy relationship growth. Some relationship beliefs facilitate a positive, optimistic perspective on relationship initiation and development. Romanticism, for example, is an orientation toward relationships that views love as the basis for mate selection (Weaver & Ganong, 2004), and constitutes one set of general relationship beliefs that serve to guide perceptions and interpretations of one's own and others' behaviors. The Romantic Beliefs Scale, developed by Sprecher and Metts (1989), was designed to measure individual differences in endorsement of romantic love. Items were originally created to measure the five romantic beliefs specified in the romantic love ideal typology (Lantz, Britton, Schmitt, & Snyder, 1968). The five beliefs contained within the romantic love ideal are that (a) true love is possible without prior interaction (*love at first sight*), (b) we can truly love only one person (*one and only*), (c) true love can overcome any obstacle (*true love conquers all*), (d) our true love will be perfect in every way (*idealization*), and (e) partner selection should be based on true love rather than on more rational considerations (*follow the heart*). Although five romantic beliefs were expected, factor analyses of the 15 final items assessing the romantic love ideal revealed only four separate factors of romanticism. Those high in romanticism believe that love is possible at first sight (*love at first sight*), each of us has only one true love (*one and only*), true love will find a way to overcome any obstacle (*love finds a way*), and true loves are perfect (*idealization*).

Returning to Figure 24.1, romantic beliefs generally filter one's perception and interpretation of initiating events through an optimistic, rose-colored lens in which events that might otherwise carry negative implications instead become interpreted as less detrimental or even beneficial. Certain romantic beliefs (e.g., in the "one and only") also imbue relationship events with uniqueness and special meaning in a way that may facilitate positive relationship evaluations and outcomes. Additionally, believing that "love finds a way" could filter perceived differences and disagreements in a way that makes them seem typical and expected rather than unique and surprising, or makes such differences seem less detrimental and even possibly beneficial.

Turning to empirical data, for those in established relationships, higher romanticism scores, both in general and for specific facets (except love at first sight), were concurrently related to greater reports of love, satisfaction, and commitment for both men and women (Sprecher & Metts, 1999). The relationship between beliefs in love at first sight and relationship processes is thought to be particularly potent in the early stages of relationship development (Metts, 2004; Sprecher & Metts, 1989). In fact, belief in love at first sight allows one to interpret and respond to sexual involvement differently. Specifically, for women, belief in love at first sight was a predictor of commitment to one's partner following first sexual involvement (Metts, 2004). Additionally, with regard to early relationship development, those higher in general romanticism tended to recall fewer dates before experiencing true love (Sprecher & Metts, 1989). However, romanticism scores were not found to predict relationship stability across a 4-year time span (Sprecher & Metts, 1999).

DYSFUNCTIONAL BELIEFS

Whereas endorsement of romantic beliefs appears to be generally associated with positive relationship outcomes, a particular set of beliefs has been described as maladaptive, tainting one's perceptions and interpretations of one's own and others' behavior. Such beliefs have been associated with relationship distress in ongoing committed relationships, and may play a moderating role in newly forming relationships as well. The Relationship Belief Inventory (RBI; Eidelson & Epstein, 1982; Epstein & Eidelson, 1981) was developed to measure five key "dysfunctional" relationship beliefs: that disagreements indicate a lack of love (Disagreement Is Destructive), that couples who really know and love each other should be able to know what the other is thinking without overt communication (Mind-Reading Is Expected), that one cannot change oneself or the quality of the relationship (Partners Cannot Change), that sexual experiences should be perfect each and every time (Sexual Perfectionism), and that the personality and relational needs of men and women are drastically different (Sexes Are Different). Each 8-item subscale can be examined individually or in combination.

The notion that all of the beliefs assessed by the RBI are "dysfunctional" has not always been supported by data. For example, more dysfunctional beliefs were reported by nondissatisfied couples than those actively seeking marital therapy (Emmelkamp, Krol, Sanderman, & Ruphan, 1987). Further, Bradbury and Fincham (1993) raised questions about the construct validity of the Mind-Reading

Is Expected and Sexual Performance subscales of the RBI, because neither was related to marital satisfaction, and the construct validity increased when these subscales were dropped. Their further examination of partial correlations between RBI scores and conflict resolution behavior, controlling for marital satisfaction, revealed different associations for men and women, and not all of these associations were in the direction expected of "dysfunctional" beliefs (Bradbury & Fincham, 1993).

That said, these five beliefs clearly may impart meaning to events in the initiating stages of a relationship. Although much of the research has been conducted on established relationships, these beliefs may still guide processing in newly forming relationships. For example, if one believes that disagreement is destructive, then when differences are perceived or when disagreements arise, one would interpret these experiences as detrimental to the potential relationship, and may accordingly perceive the relationship as more risky, less secure, and less satisfying to pursue. Alternatively, believing that disagreement is destructive could lead one to view perceived similarities as particularly beneficial and even typical, and thus feel that the relationship is less risky, more safe, and more satisfying. As another example, if one believes that mind-reading is expected, then having an awkward interaction may take on greater negative meaning because it is viewed as more detrimental and unique, and may promote more negative relationship evaluations. On the other hand, believing that mind-reading is expected may assign particular positive meaning to smooth interactions and felt rapport because this synchrony is considered highly relevant and typical.

As a final example, consider the belief that partners cannot change, which invokes the stable versus unstable dimension in interpreting things that one does not like about a potential partner or developing relationship. Noticing a few less than perfect qualities about a potential partner or developing relationship would probably not lead one to immediately abandon the effort if one believed that these qualities would change over time and perhaps become more appealing. It is the assumption that those qualities or differences cannot and will not change—that they are stable and fixed for all eternity—that would make such differences seem insurmountable and detrimental, and possibly make the relationship seem too risky to pursue.

IMPLICIT THEORIES OF RELATIONSHIPS

Implicit theories of relationships refer to naïve assumptions about the nature of relationships that help guide how people perceive and interpret relationship events. The notion of implicit theories, more generally, is grounded in Heider's (1958) field theory of social perception and Kelly's (1955) theory of personality. Ross (1989) defined implicit theories as schematic knowledge structures that involve specific beliefs about the stability of an attribute and the conditions that promote change, such as the belief that intelligence is fixed and immutable (see Dweck, Chiu, & Hong, 1995, for review). With regard to the domain of romantic relationships, research on implicit theories of relationships suggests that what people believe about relationships guides their goals and motivations in developing relationships. Knee (1998) identified two such beliefs: destiny and growth. Franiuk and her colleagues (Franiuk, Cohen, & Pomerantz, 2002; Franiuk, Pomerantz, & Cohen, 2004) independently identified similar beliefs called soul mate and work-it-out theories. Destiny belief concerns the stability of one's impressions about relationships. Growth belief concerns the stability of problems in relationships. Together, these beliefs guide how people orient toward and interpret events as the relationship develops. Another relationship belief that centers on the stability dimension of potential relationships is belief in the Chinese notion of *yuan* (Goodwin & Findlay, 1997). *Yuan* concerns the belief that relationships are predestined and that they will either succeed or fail regardless of effort.

Research suggests that the assumptions people hold about the stability of their perceptions of both partner compatibility and the stability of problems in romantic relationships guide how meaning is assigned to particular relationship events and situations (Franiuk et al., 2002, 2004; Knee, 1998; Knee & Canevello, 2006; Knee, Nanayakkara, Vietor, Neighbors, & Patrick, 2001; Knee et al., 2003; Knee, Patrick, Vietor, & Neighbors, 2004). Destiny belief concerns the stability of one's impressions about relationships. Destiny belief, the conviction that one's impressions of relationships are generally fixed and stable, sets up an emphasis on determining the compatibility of a potential romantic partner and the future success of the relationship from whatever information is immediately available. Independently, growth belief concerns the stability of problems in relationships. Growth belief is characterized by an emphasis on relationship development and the belief that relationships grow not despite obstacles, but in part because of the opportunities those obstacles provide for further relationship development.

A central aspect of the assumptions that people have about themselves and others is that such assumptions guide the way people assign meaning to events and situations, and act as a lens or filter through which people come away with different appraisals of the same objective event. Destiny belief involves assuming that either relationships are meant to be or they are not. This dimension concerns the stability of one's impressions about relationships. When one believes strongly (compared to weakly) in destiny belief, one assumes that one's impression of the match between partners is relatively accurate and can be used to forecast the future potential of the relationship. Growth belief involves assuming that relationships can be maintained and problems can be overcome. When one believes strongly (relative to weakly) in relationship growth, one assumes that problems and disagreements are unstable, can be managed as they occur, and fluctuate throughout the course of the relationship. These relationship beliefs function as fundamental assumptions about the nature of romantic relationships, and guide inferences and attributions about relationships. For example, those who more strongly (compared to weakly) endorse destiny belief tend to be especially sensitive to their initial impressions of the relationship and cues that might suggest that the relationship does or does not have potential (Knee, 1998).

Because destiny and growth beliefs, in part, determine how meaning will be ascribed to relationship-relevant events and partner qualities, the same events or qualities can take on different meaning with different relationship implications. For example, considerable research has shown that idealistic views of one's partner are associated with increased relationship satisfaction (Murray, Holmes, & Griffin, 1996). However, this tendency to feel more satisfied when one views one's partner more favorably than one's partner views him or herself has been shown to depend on one's implicit theories of relationships. Knee et al. (2001) found that implicit theories of relationships moderate the association between wanting more in one's partner and feeling satisfied with the relationship. Study 1 defined "wanting more" in terms of perceiving a discrepancy between what one wants in an ideal partner and what one believes one has in a current partner. Across several indices of discrepancy from an ideal, wanting more in one's partner was consistently related to feeling less happy with the relationship. However, this relation was moderated by destiny and growth beliefs such that "wanting more" was less strongly linked to one's satisfaction when one was both higher in growth and lower in destiny beliefs. With higher growth and lower destiny beliefs, people were able to acknowledge their partner's less positive attributes while still remaining relatively satisfied. In this way, these individuals did not view their partner's imperfections as flaws in the relationship that were permanent.

Study 2 of Knee et al. (2001) tested whether implicit theories of relationships moderate the projected illusions hypothesis (Murray et al., 1996). It was found that viewing one's partner more favorably than one's partner views him or herself was generally linked to feeling more satisfied with the relationship. This relation was moderated by implicit theories of relationships such that the link between viewing one's partner favorably and feeling satisfied was weaker among those who believed more strongly in growth, without regard to destiny belief. Indeed, using a slightly different method of measuring implicit theories of relationships, Franiuk et al. (2004) found that feeling that one's specific partner was ideal predicted relationship satisfaction and longevity to a greater extent for those with stronger soul mate (destiny) beliefs.

When one holds a belief that conflict is a healthy part of relationships and can bring partners closer by resolving it, then differences and disagreements can take on different meaning than when one believes that conflict is a sign of insurmountable problems in the relationship. A series of studies tested this hypothesis (Knee et al., 2004). In Study 1, individuals in romantic relationships kept event-contingent diaries, recording every disagreement they and their partner had over a 10-day period. *Disagreement* was broadly defined as "anytime it becomes evident to you that you and your partner disagree on an opinion, perspective, idea, goal, etc." Relationship quality was assessed after each disagreement as well. Multilevel analyses showed that, consistent with the hypothesis, the association between having longer conflicts and reporting reduced relationship quality afterward was generally strong, except among those who were both higher in growth and lower in destiny. Among these individuals, there was virtually no relation between the amount or length of disagreements and reduced relationship quality on a daily basis.

In Study 2, dating couples discussed problems in their relationship, with commitment measured before and after the discussion. Multilevel analyses examined changes in commitment. As hypothesized, higher scores on growth belief combined with lower scores on destiny belief were associated with less decrease in commitment after discussing problems with one's partner. Further, because those with stronger growth beliefs are particularly motivated to improve the relationship when it is lacking, the relation between growth belief and commitment was stronger when one had a less favorable view of one's partner. Taken together, being higher in growth beliefs and lower in destiny beliefs can filter the negative impact of arguments, discrepancies, and differences of opinion, which are events that would generally be associated with a decline in satisfaction and commitment.

Returning to the general model in Figure 24.1, empirical evidence has supported the basic notion that implicit theories of relationships moderate the way that early events and perceptions predict evaluations of the relationship and even eventual longevity (Franiuk et al., 2002; Knee, 1998; Knee et al., 2001). As mentioned earlier, a key aspect of this inferential process is the meaning that is assigned to the event as a function of one's relationship beliefs. Once an initiating event occurs, or several such events occur over time, they may lead to changes (both momentary and long-term changes) in relationship outcomes including satisfaction with and commitment to the relationship. However, the key point of the model is that the assumptions one brings to the relationship, in part, determine the extent to which momentary and long-term changes in such outcomes emerge as a function of those initiating events. Thus, the path between initiating events and relationship outcomes is intersected by the meaning that gets assigned to those events because of the relationship beliefs that one brings to the relationship. As we mentioned earlier, implicit theories have been found to moderate how initiating events predict relationship outcomes. However, the intervening variable in this moderation is thought to be the meaning ascribed to these events or the degree to which the initiating event is interpreted as something that is stable versus unstable, unique versus special, and beneficial or detrimental to the potential of the relationship. These interpretations, in turn, rest largely on one's underlying assumptions about how relationships operate. For example, when one believes in destiny, one tends to interpret negative relationship events as relatively fixed, stable, and unchanging, and thus as threatening to the potential of the relationship. Interpreting relationship events in this way will in turn make one's feelings about the relationship more strongly affected by those initiating events.

Independently, when one believes in growth, one tends to assume and expect that problems can be resolved and that relationships can improve. This assumption leads to an interpretation of immediate relationship events (both positive and negative) as relatively unimportant or irrelevant in what they may imply about the quality of the relationship or its future course. Negative events are not viewed as a threat because such events are viewed as typical and changeable (and perhaps even beneficial) given that it is assumed that relationships require maintenance and coping with issues as they arise. This interpretation of initiating events as relatively expected and irrelevant to the success of the relationship makes one's feelings about the relationship relatively unaffected by those events. This moderation is largely based on the assumption that problems and differences in relationships can be resolved as they arise.

CONCLUSION

Much of the research on how relationship beliefs operate has been conducted on already established relationships. We find it ironic that relatively little empirical research has been conducted on the role that relationship beliefs play in beginning relationships. It is probably within those initial stages of seeking and identifying potential relationship partners, and evaluating those early events as they occur, where the beliefs that one brings to the relationship can have the strongest impact on later outcomes. Beliefs generally help guide the manner in which information is processed and interpreted. We have reviewed a variety of relationship beliefs including internal working models, relationship ideals, romantic beliefs, dysfunctional beliefs, and implicit theories of relationships. One thing that most of these beliefs seem to share is their potential role in moderating the way in which early relationship events can take on different meanings depending on the interpretive filter that such beliefs provide. With this in mind, we proposed a general conceptual model for how relationship beliefs, through their assignment of meaning along several dimensions, may filter one's interpretation of experiences in newly forming relationships. This is not to say that the only role that relationship beliefs play is one of moderation. To the contrary, many relationship beliefs have been directly associated with relationship quality and other outcomes. We suspect, however, that many of these beliefs also exhibit moderating roles in how early relationship events are linked to later evaluations and outcomes. Clearly, further research is needed to test the uniqueness of beliefs and the dimensions of meaning that may be assigned, when interpreting early relationship experiences.

Much knowledge also remains to be gained on the ways in which beliefs about relationships function. As mentioned earlier, beliefs serve as knowledge structures that help guide the manner in which information is processed and interpreted (e.g., Fiske & Linville, 1980). With regard to relationship initiation, early events are interpreted in the context of the beliefs that one brings into the relationship. What determines which belief, among many, will filter the meaning of a particular relationship event? The social cognition literature has had much to say about the conditions under which beliefs are activated, and this work is only beginning to uncover specific processes and mechanisms with regard to romantic relationships. A better understanding of the conditions under which relationship beliefs play a moderating role would be useful.

First, the social cognition literature has shown that when the meaning of an event is ambiguous, one's interpretation of the event is more likely to be influenced by one's beliefs (e.g., Locksley, Borgida, Brekke, & Hepburn, 1980; Tuckey & Brewer, 2003). For example, after a few dates, a couple may come to learn that although they are similar in many ways, they also have somewhat different tastes, opinions, and life perspectives. The meaning of this observation is ambiguous without a better understanding of the beliefs that one holds. If one holds a growth belief, then such differences could be interpreted as positive features that hold potential for further relationship development. If one's relationship or partner ideal portrays similarity of life perspectives as central and relevant, then one will interpret the event as significant and negative. Conversely, when an event is highly diagnostic and relatively clear (e.g., after a first date, your date articulates that he or she is not and will not be interested in seeing you again), there is little need for reliance on one's beliefs to interpret the information, other than to protect a damaged ego.

Second, research suggests that interpretation of events is particularly likely to be dictated by beliefs when one's mental resources are taxed (Moskowitz, 2005). When one is distracted, fatigued, or otherwise "cognitively busy," beliefs may be particularly likely to come into play. When one is preoccupied and unable to devote full attention to the meaning and implications of a relationship event, one's beliefs may guide a preexisting interpretation and filter the meaning of the event, rather than allowing full understanding of the event and the conditions that surrounded it. For example, when one's mental resources are taxed, and one holds an anxious attachment model, one may be more likely to interpret a delayed phone call as a sign of rejection.

Third, individuals can potentially hold multiple relationship beliefs simultaneously (i.e., attachment models, romantic beliefs, dysfunctional beliefs, ideals, and implicit theories), all of which may guide how one interprets events that transpire as relationships develop. Research on social cognition suggests that the belief that is most salient and accessible at any given time is most likely to guide thoughts and behavior at that time (Moskowitz, 2005). Each belief an individual possesses varies along a continuum from highly active and salient to highly inactive and dormant. In fact, Higgins, Bargh, and Lombardi (1985) compared beliefs to batteries, such that we all hold many batteries, each being a chargeable unit with a given amount of power. Those with the most power have the greatest ability to guide our interpretation of events.

A number of studies have shown that relationship representations can be primed momentarily, even automatically (e.g., Andersen & Cole, 1990; Fitzsimmons, & Bargh, 2003; Fletcher, Rosanowski, & Fitness, 1994). For example, in several studies, Fitzsimmons and Bargh showed that priming relationship representations produced goal-directed behavior such as achievement, helping, and understanding, in line with the goal content of those representations. With regard to which particular belief might be most influential at a given time, further research is needed that assesses the centrality or relative strength of simultaneously held beliefs. For example, one may hold a destiny belief and have an avoidant attachment model simultaneously. How one interprets a strong sense of rapport and emotional connection on a first date may depend on which belief is most salient or accessible. If one's belief in destiny is relatively more "charged" and active, then the strong rapport may be interpreted as a stable positive event that reflects compatibility and forecasts wonderful long-term potential. However, if one's avoidant attachment style is relatively more salient, then the same strong rapport might be interpreted as threatening and unsafe, leading to feelings of wanting to withdraw. Further research is needed on belief centrality, as well as how temporarily and chronically activated beliefs can potentially have unique interpretive effects beyond other less central, or less activated, beliefs.

The social cognition literature has also suggested that those beliefs that were activated most frequently and recently are generally likely to be most accessible (Moskowitz, 2005). However, there may be times in which one belief is activated because it was recently triggered, and another belief is activated because it has been frequently triggered. For example, in a recently formed relationship, one may be consistently and routinely exposed to friends who are working hard to overcome obstacles in their relationships, which may activate a growth belief. One also may have just encountered an old romantic letter from an ex-boyfriend, thereby activating romantic beliefs. If one then has an awkward dating experience, which relationship belief will guide the interpretation? According to Higgins et al. (1985), whereas recently activated beliefs have a strong but brief influence on perception, frequently activated beliefs can have a weaker but longer lasting influence. Therefore, if one encounters a relationship event immediately after a belief has been activated, that belief may guide the interpretation. However, if the relationship event occurs at a later time, the recently activated belief is likely to fade, allowing the frequently activated belief to prevail. It is also important to note that beliefs that are very frequently and consistently activated may eventually have a chronic influence rendering them most likely to play a role in the interpretation of many relationship events. However, research suggests that one's social environment can do more than just activate relationship beliefs. Relationship beliefs may also be modified through experiences. For example, research on ideals suggests that one's ideals become more flexible following repeated rejections (Tran et al., this volume). Working models are also sensitive to ongoing relational experiences (e.g., Davila et al., 1997).

Finally, an emerging issue concerns the difference between general beliefs (one's beliefs about relationships in general) and relationship-specific beliefs (one's beliefs about one's current relationship). The literature on working models, for example, has merely begun to explore how these different levels guide social cognition and social interaction in unique ways (e.g., Baldwin et al., 1996; Collins & Allard, 2001). The degree to which general beliefs and specific beliefs impart unique interpretive filters as relationships develop may tell us something about the importance of current versus past significant relationship events. Indeed, further research on the extent to which both general and specific beliefs guide the interpretation of ongoing events may also aid our understanding of the underlying processes by which relationship beliefs exert an interpretive influence in novel relationship situations.

AUTHOR NOTE

We thank the Interpersonal Relations and Motivation Research Group at the University of Houston for help in commenting on previous drafts.

REFERENCES

Agnew, C. R., Loving, T. J., & Drigotas, S. M. (2001). Substituting the forest for the trees: Social networks and the prediction of romantic relationship state and fate. *Journal of Personality and Social Psychology, 81,* 1042–1057.

Ainsworth, M. S., Blehar, M. C., Walters, E., & Wall, S. (1978). *Patterns of attachment: A psychological study of the strange situation.* Hillsdale, NJ: Lawrence Erlbaum.

Andersen, S. M., & Cole, S. W. (1990). "Do I know you?" The role of significant others in general social perception. *Journal of Personality and Social Psychology, 59,* 384–399.

Baldwin, M. W. (1992). Relational schemas and the processing of social information. *Psychological Bulletin, 112*(3), 461–484.

Baldwin, M. W., Keelan, J. P. R., Fehr, B., Enns, V., & Koh-Rangarajoo, E. (1996). Social cognitive conceptualization of attachment working models: Availability and accessibility effects. *Journal of Personality and Social Psychology, 71,* 94–109.

Bartholomew, K., & Horowitz, L. M. (1991). Attachment styles among young adults: A test of a four-category model. *Journal of Personality and Social Psychology, 61,* 226–244.

Baxter, L. A., & Bullis, C. (1986). Turning points in developing romantic relationships. *Human Communication Research, 12,* 469–493.

Berscheid, E. (1994). Interpersonal relationships. *Annual Review of Psychology, 45,* 79–129.

Berscheid, E., Graziano, W., Monson, T., & Dermer, M. (1976). Outcome dependency: Attention, attribution, and attraction. *Journal of Personality and Social Psychology, 34*(5), 978–989.

Berscheid, E., & Reis, H. T. (1998). Attraction and close relationships. In D. T. Gilbert, S. T. Fiske, & G. Lindzey (Eds.), *The handbook of social psychology* (Vol. 2, pp. 193–281). New York: McGraw-Hill.

Bowlby, J. (1969). Disruption of affectional bonds and its effects on behavior. *Canada's Mental Health Supplement, 59,* 12.

Bowlby, J. (1973). *Attachment and loss: Vol. 2. Separation: Anxiety and anger.* New York: Basic Books.

Bradbury, T. N., & Fincham, F. D. (1993). Assessing dysfunctional cognition in marriage: A reconsideration of the relationship belief inventory. *Psychological Assessment, 5*(1), 92–101.

Brennan, K. A., Clark, C. L., & Shaver, P. R. (1998). Self-report measurement of adult attachment: An integrative overview. In J. A. Simpson & W. S. Rholes (Eds.), *Attachment theory and close relationships* (pp. 46–76). New York: Guilford Press.

Brewer, W. F., & Treyens, J. C. (1981). Role of schemata in memory for places. *Cognitive Psychology, 13*(2), 207–230.

Campbell, L., Simpson, J. A., Kashy, D. A., & Fletcher, G. J. O. (2001). Ideal standards, the self, and flexibility of ideals in close relationships. *Personality and Social Psychology Bulletin, 27*(4), 447–462.

Collins, N. L. (1996). Working models of attachment: Implications for explanation, emotion, and behavior. *Journal of Personality and Social Psychology, 71,* 810–832.

Collins, N. L., & Allard, L. M. (2001). Cognitive representations of attachment: The content and function of working models. In G. J. O. Fletcher & M. S. Clark (Eds.), *Blackwell handbook of social psychology: Vol. 2. Interpersonal processes* (pp. 60–85). Oxford: Blackwell.

Collins, N. L., & Feeney, B. C. (2004). Working models of attachment shape perceptions of social support: Evidence from experimental and observational studies. *Journal of Personality and Social Psychology, 87*(3), 363–383.

Collins, N. L., & Read, S. J. (1994). Cognitive representations of attachment: The structure and function of working models. In K. Bartholomew & D. Perlman (Eds.), *Advances in personal relationships* (Vol. 5, pp. 53–90). London: Jessica Kingsley.

Davila, J., Burge, D., & Hammen, C. (1997). Why does attachment style change? *Journal of Personality and Social Psychology, 73*(4), 826–838.

Dweck, C. S., Chiu, C., & Hong, Y. (1995). Implicit theories and their role in judgments and reactions: A world from two perspectives. *Psychological Inquiry, 6*(4), 267–285.

Eidelson, R. J., & Epstein, N. (1982). Cognition and relationship maladjustment: Development of a measure of dysfunctional relationship beliefs. *Journal of Consulting and Clinical Psychology, 50*(5), 715–720.

Emmelkamp, P. M., Krol, B., Sanderman, R., & Ruphan, M. (1987). The assessment of relationship beliefs in a marital context. *Personality and Individual Differences, 8*(6), 775–780.

Epstein, N., & Eidelson, R. J. (1981). Unrealistic beliefs of clinical couples: Their relationship to expectations, goals, and satisfaction. *American Journal of Family Therapy, 9*(4), 13–22.

Feeney, B. C. (2006). An attachment theory perspective on the interplay between intrapersonal and interpersonal processes. In K. D. Vohs & E. J. Finkel (Eds.), *Self and relationships: Connecting intrapersonal and interpersonal processes* (pp. 133–159). New York: Guilford Press.

Fiske, S. T., & Linville, P. W. (1980). What does the schema concept buy us? *Personality and Social Psychology Bulletin, 6,* 543–557.

Fitzsimmons, G. M., & Bargh, J. A. (2003). Thinking of you: Nonconscious pursuit of interpersonal goals associated with relationship partners. *Journal of Personality and Social Psychology, 84,* 148–164.

Fletcher, G. J. O., & Kininmonth, L. A. (1992). Measuring relationship beliefs: An individual differences scale. *Journal of Research in Personality, 26,* 371–397.

Fletcher, G. J. O., Rosanowski, J., & Fitness, J. (1994). Automatic processing in intimate contexts: The role of relationship beliefs. *Journal of Personality and Social Psychology, 67,* 888–897.

Fletcher, G. J. O., Simpson, J. A., & Thomas, G. (2000). Ideals, perceptions, and evaluations in early relationship development. *Journal of Personality and Social Psychology, 79*(6), 933–940.

Fletcher, G. J. O., Simpson, J. A., Thomas, G., & Giles, L. (1999). Ideals in intimate relationships. *Journal of Personality and Social Psychology, 76*(1), 72–89.

Fletcher, G. J. O., & Thomas, G. (1996). Close relationship lay theories: Their structure and function. In G. J. O. Fletcher & J. Fitness (Eds.), *Knowledge structures and interaction in close relationships: A social psychological approach* (pp. 3–24). Hillsdale, NJ: Lawrence Erlbaum.

Fraley, R. C., & Waller, N. G. (1998). Adult attachment patterns: A test of the typological model. In J. A. Simpson & W. S. Rholes (Eds.), *Attachment theory and close relationships* (pp. 77–114). New York: Guilford Press.

Franiuk, R., Cohen, D., & Pomerantz, E. M. (2002). Implicit theories of relationships: Implications for relationship satisfaction and longevity. *Personal Relationships, 9*(4), 345–367.

Franiuk, R., Pomerantz, E. M., & Cohen, D. (2004). The causal role of theories of relationships: Consequences for satisfaction and cognitive strategies. *Personality and Social Psychology Bulletin, 30*(11), 1494–1507.

Goodwin, R., & Findlay, C. (1997). "We were just fated together" … Chinese love and the concept of yuan in England and Hong Kong. *Personal Relationships, 4,* 85–92.

Hatfield, E., Brinton, C., & Cornelius, J. (1989). Passionate love and anxiety in young adolescents. *Motivation and Emotion, 13,* 271–289.

Hazan, C., & Shaver, P. (1987). Romantic love conceptualized as an attachment process. *Journal of Personality and Social Psychology, 52,* 511–524.

Hazan, C., & Shaver, P. R. (1990). Love and work: An attachment-theoretical perspective. *Journal of Personality and Social Psychology, 59,* 270–280.

Heider, F. (1958). *The psychology of interpersonal relations.* New York: Wiley.

Higgins, E. T., Bargh, J. A., & Lombardi, W. (1985). Nature of priming effects on categorization. *Journal of Experimental Psychology: Learning, Memory, and Cognition, 11,* 59–69.

Kelly, E. L. (1955). Consistency of the adult personality. *American Psychologist, 10,* 659–681.

Knee, C. R. (1998). Implicit theories of relationships: Assessment and prediction of romantic relationship initiation, coping, and longevity. *Journal of Personality and Social Psychology, 74,* 360–370.

Knee, C. R., & Canevello, A. (2006). Implicit theories of relationships and coping in romantic relationships. In K. D. Vohs & E. J. Finkel (Eds.), *Self and relationships: Connecting intrapersonal and interpersonal processes* (pp. 160–176). New York: Guilford Press.

Knee, C. R., Nanayakkara, A., Vietor, N., Neighbors, C., & Patrick, H. (2001). Implicit theories of relationships: Who cares if romantic partners are less than ideal? *Personality and Social Psychology Bulletin, 27,* 808–819.

Knee, C. R., Patrick, H., & Lonsbary, C. (2003). Implicit theories of relationships: Orientations toward evaluation and cultivation. *Personality and Social Psychology Review, 7*(1), 41–55.

Knee, C. R., Patrick, H., Vietor, N., & Neighbors, C. (2004). Implicit theories of relationships: Moderators of the link between conflict and commitment. *Personality and Social Psychology Bulletin, 30*(5), 617–628.

Lantz, H. R., Britton, M., Schmitt, R. L., & Snyder, E. C. (1968). Pre-industrial patterns in colonial family in America: A content analysis of colonial magazines. *American Sociological Review, 33,* 413–427.

Locksley, A., Borgida, E., Brekke, N., & Hepburn, C. (1980). Sex stereotypes and social judgment. *Journal of Personality and Social Psychology, 39,* 821–831.

Metts, S. (2004). First sexual involvement in romantic relationships: An empirical investigation of communicative framing, romantic beliefs, and attachment orientation in the passion turning point. In J. H. Harvey, A. Wenzel, & S. Sprecher (Eds.), *The handbook of sexuality in close relationships* (pp. 135–158). Mahwah, NJ: Lawrence Erlbaum.

Mikulincer, M., & Arad, D. (1999). Attachment working models and cognitive openness in close relationships: A test of chronic and temporary accessibility effects. *Journal of Personality and Social Psychology, 77,* 710–725.

Mikulincer, M., Florian, V., & Tolmacz, R. (1990). Attachment styles and fear of personal death: A case study of affect regulation. *Journal of Personality and Social Psychology, 58*(2), 273–280.

Moskowitz, G. B. (2005). *Social cognition: Understanding self and others.* New York: Guilford Press.

Murray, S. L., Holmes, J. G., & Griffin, D. W. (1996). The benefits of positive illusions: Idealization and the construction of satisfaction in close relationships. *Journal of Personality and Social Psychology, 70,* 79–98.

Planalp, S. (1987). Interplay between relational knowledge and events. In R. Burnett, P. McGhee, & D. Clarke (Eds.), *Accounting for relationships: Explanation, representation and knowledge* (pp. 175–191). New York: Methuen.

Ross, M. (1989). Relation of implicit theories to the construct of personal histories. *Psychological Review, 96,* 341–357.

Rothbard, J. C., & Shaver, P. R. (1994). Continuity of attachment across the life span. In M. B. Sperling & W. H. Barman (Eds.), *Attachment in adults: Clinical and developmental perspectives* (pp. 31–71). New York: Guilford Press.

Scharfe, E., & Bartholomew, K. (1994). Reliability and stability of adult attachment patterns. *Personal Relationships, 1,* 23–43.

Simpson, J. A. (1990). Influence of attachment styles on romantic relationships. *Journal of Personality and Social Psychology, 59*(5), 971–980.

Simpson, J. A., Fletcher, G. J. O., & Campbell, L. (2001). The structure and function of ideal standards in close relationships. In G. J. O. Fletcher & M. Clark (Eds.), *Blackwell handbook of social psychology: Interpersonal processes* (pp. 86–106). Oxford: Blackwell.

Snyder, M., Tanke, E. D., & Berscheid, E. (1977). Social perception and interpersonal behavior: On the self-fulfilling nature of social stereotypes. *Journal of Personality and Social Psychology, 35*(9), 656–666.

Sprecher, S., & Metts, S. (1989). Development of the "romantic beliefs scale" and examination of the effects of gender and gender-role orientation. *Journal of Social and Personal Relationships, 6,* 387–411.

Sprecher, S., & Metts, S. (1999). Romantic beliefs: Their influence on relationships and patterns of change over time. *Journal of Social and Personal Relationships, 16*(6), 834–851.

Trafimow, D., & Wyer, R. S. (1993). Cognitive representation of mundane events. *Journal of Personality and Social Psychology, 64,* 365–376.

Tuckey, M. R., & Brewer, N. (2003). The influence of schemas, stimulus ambiguity, and interview schedule on eyewitness memory over time. *Journal of Experimental Psychology: Applied, 9*(2), 101–118.

Vangelisti, A. L., & Alexander, A. L. (2002). Coping with disappointment in marriage: When partner's standards are unmet. In P. Noller & B. Feeney (Eds.), *Understanding marriage* (pp. 201–227). Cambridge: Cambridge University Press.

Weaver, S. E., & Ganong, L. H. (2004). The factor structure of the romantic beliefs scale for African Americans and European Americans. *Journal of Social and Personal Relationships, 21*(2), 171–185.

Zadny, J., & Gerard, H. B. (1974). Attributed intentions and informational selectivity. *Journal of Experimental Social Psychology, 10,* 43–52.

25

The Role of Ideal Standards in Relationship Initiation Processes

SISI TRAN, JEFFRY A. SIMPSON, and GARTH J. O. FLETCHER

Many scholars consider the beginning of relationships one of the most critical and influential stages of relationship development (see Berscheid & Graziano, 1979). The reasons for this special emphasis are numerous. For example, the grounds on which individuals initially seek and select partners, decide whether or not to commit and invest in the new partner and relationship, and think, feel, and behave during the relationship's opening days and weeks can shape its course and trajectory. Without some understanding of when, how, and why a relationship is launched, it is difficult to forecast and comprehend what happens when individuals and their partners experience myriad events during later stages of relationship development. Relationship beginnings, therefore, often "orient" the general developmental course of many—and perhaps most—close relationships.

Though many factors can impact relationship beginnings, the core relationship-relevant values and standards that people bring to new relationships should play particularly consequential roles. For the past several years, we have been investigating the effects that "hidden others" in relationships—especially conceptions of ideal partners—have on the initiation and early formation of romantic relationships. This research has led us to address a series of questions that lie at the center of relationship initiation processes: How do people decide whether to become involved with a new partner? How do they know when a partner meets their standards for living together, getting married, or breaking up? What guidelines do people use to evaluate their relationships? In our work, we have used the ideal standards model (ISM; Fletcher, Simpson, Thomas, & Giles, 1999; Simpson, Fletcher, & Campbell, 2001) to clarify and extend our understanding of when, how, and why close relationships develop.

In this chapter, we review what has been learned so far about how ideal standards may affect relationship initiation processes. In the first section of the chapter, we review the major tenets of the ISM. Given that the ISM was developed to examine the evaluation, explanation, and regulation of romantic partners and relationships, the chapter will focus principally on romantic relationships. In the second section, we review and summarize empirical tests of the model, focusing on findings most germane to relationship beginnings. In the final section, we highlight several important unanswered questions and suggest promising directions for future research.

THE IDEAL STANDARDS MODEL

Relationship and partner ideals are key components of the social mind that people use to guide their interpersonal and motivational strategies. An ideal is a mental image of someone or something that serves as a standard of excellence and is highly desirable. According to the ISM (Fletcher et al., 1999; Simpson et al., 2001), partner and relationship ideals operate as chronically accessible knowledge

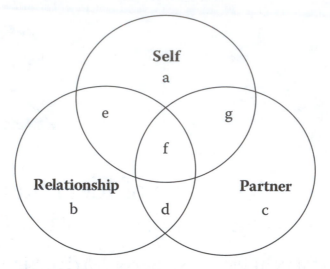

Examples of Cognition
(a) I am intelligent
(b) Relationships fail without good communication
(c) Men are aggressive
(d) Relationships work well when one partner is dominant
(e) I want an exciting relationship
(f) I want an honest relationship with a partner I can trust
(g) I am suited to someone who is sporty and athletic

Figure 25.1   General model of relationship cognition. *Source*: Taken from Fletcher, Simpson, Thomas, and Giles (1999).

structures that predate specific relationships. As we shall argue later, the nature of such ideal standards is not arbitrary or infinitely plastic, but is rooted in human nature as it has been shaped through evolutionary history. However, ideal standards also develop as a function of socialization from parents, family, friends, surrounding communities, and images portrayed in the media. Such sources provide information about socially desired ideal standards for both partners and relationships. Individuals form their own ideal standards by adopting these general social preferences and adjusting them to match their personal values and strengths. The level of consistency between ideal standards and accompanying perceptions (i.e., ideal–perception consistency) is believed to drive evaluative judgments of both potential mates and current partners in existing relationships.

Relationship-based knowledge structures involve three interlocking components: (a) the self, (b) the partner, and (c) the relationship (Fletcher & Thomas, 1996). Goals, expectations, and beliefs about ideals should exist where the self, the partner, and the relationship intersect. Ideal standards, therefore, combine elements of the actual self, the ideal partner, and the ideal relationship. As shown in Figure 25.1, ideal partner and ideal relationship standards should be stored and represented cognitively as separate, semi-independent constructs (see Simpson et al., 2001). However, ideal partner and ideal relationship categories are likely to overlap because people should prefer ideal partners who can help them achieve their ideal relationships. Individuals who believe that laughter and humor are important features of an ideal relationship, for example, should value a sense of humor in their ideal mates, who in turn should be more capable of creating a relationship filled with laughter and humor.

Evaluative Dimensions

Informed by evolutionary principles (especially the strategic pluralism model; Gangestad & Simpson, 2000), the ISM postulates that individuals evaluate prospective or current partners on three dimensions: (a) warmth and trustworthiness, (b) attractiveness and vitality, and (c) status and resources (see Fletcher et al., 1999). Each dimension may reflect a different route—focusing on good investment or on "good genes"—to obtain a mate and, ultimately, to promote one's reproductive fitness (cf. Buss & Schmitt, 1993). Greater warmth and trustworthiness in a partner, for instance, may signal his or her greater capacity to be a good, emotionally investing mate and parent. Greater status and resources may signal a partner's superior ability to provide high-quality material investment in oneself and/or one's children. And greater attractiveness and vitality may convey that a partner has "good genes" (e.g., better health and other positive qualities that might be passed on genetically to children).

Why don't people pursue the perfect mates, in terms of their ideals, searching for partners who are incredibly warm, rich, *and* attractive? To begin with, there are very few people who fit such a description. Second, most individuals would not be able to attract such a person even if he or she were available. Third, even if an individual succeeded in attracting such a paragon of virtue, it probably would be quite difficult to retain him or her as an investing mate over time. In short, people are often forced to form realistic standards and make trade-offs among these three mate dimensions when evaluating and choosing romantic partners (Regan, 1998).

According to the ISM, individuals also evaluate relationships on two dimensions: (a) the importance of intimacy and stability (labeled *relationship intimacy and loyalty*), and (b) how passionate and exciting the relationship is expected to be (labeled *relationship passion*). Both partner ideals and relationship ideals should play a role in determining relationship quality and longevity, as we discuss in a later section. Evaluations of potential and current partners, however, may be more relevant and salient during the initial stages of relationship development. For this reason, we will focus primarily on partner ideals rather than relationship ideals in this chapter.

Functions of Ideal Standards

The ISM proposes that partner and relationship ideals serve three core functions: (a) *evaluation*: estimating and evaluating the quality of partners and relationships (e.g., to assess the appropriateness of potential or current partners and relationships); (b) *explanation*: explaining and understanding what is currently happening in relationships (e.g., the generation of plausible causal accounts that explain current relationship satisfaction, problems, or conflicts); and (c) *regulation*: regulating and making adjustments in relationships (e.g., to predict and possibly control or change current partners and relationships). According to the ISM, relationship evaluations include mental components that people access and use automatically to make important decisions and judgments (e.g., whether to remain in or leave a current partner and relationship). Thus, the evaluation function of ideals should play a pivotal role in guiding the early stages of relationship development.

The flexibility of ideal standards (i.e., the degree to which partners can fall below an ideal standard and still be considered acceptable) should also affect relationship decisions. The level at which individuals set their ideal standards and their ideal flexibility ought to be influenced, at least in part, by their self-assessments on the same dimensions. Individuals who perceive themselves as highly physically attractive, for example, should set higher ideal partner standards on the attractiveness and vitality dimension, and they ought to have a less flexible "range of acceptance" on that dimension. If a person is very fit and highly attractive, she or he should be in a relatively better position to obtain a partner who also is highly attractive. Moreover, if the chosen partner becomes less attractive over time (e.g., she or he gains excessive weight), the individual should be in a better position to attract a new partner who meets his or her exacting standards on attractiveness and vitality. Given that individuals' ideal standards are, in fact, moderately positively correlated with their self-perceptions on corresponding dimensions, flexibility beliefs are likely to be relatively stable (Campbell, Simpson, Kashy, & Fletcher, 2001).

The flexibility of ideal standards, however, can also be labile and sensitive to situational feedback (Campbell et al., 2001). For example, individuals who have just been rebuffed by a series of prospective romantic partners may increase the range of "acceptability" lying below their ideal standards (i.e., temporarily "settling for less" to improve their chances of finding a new partner). If rejections are experienced repeatedly, an individual's ideal standards should gradually decline as flexibility increases. Conversely, if potential partners eagerly accept an individual's romantic overtures, ideal standards should gradually rise over time, and flexibility should decline. Shifts in flexibility, therefore, might act as a barometer of an individual's recent romantic experiences.

Enhancement and Accuracy Motives

Flexibility and adjustments in ideal standards may depend in part on the type of motive that is salient at any given point in time. Simpson et al. (2001) suggested that two basic motives should guide how individuals evaluate, explain, and regulate their relationships: (a) partner and relationship *enhancement motives*, and (b) partner and relationship *accuracy motives*. The negative consequences of large discrepancies between ideal partner and relationship standards and current partner and relationship perceptions (i.e., ideal–perception discrepancies) may depend on which motivational set is predominant in a given situation.

According to research on the self (see Baumeister, 1998, for a review), the self-enhancement motive typically leads people to view the social world through "rose-colored glasses" to exaggerate their own positive attributes and the control they wield over social outcomes, and to be unduly optimistic about future events. When practiced in moderation and not carried to extremes, these enhancement tendencies are associated with greater personal happiness, better relationships, higher motivation and persistence, better psychological adjustment, and superior mental health (see Taylor & Brown, 1988, for a review). Relationship theorists have proposed that people are also motivated to idealize and enhance their romantic partners and relationships (see Murray, 2001). Indeed, there is abundant evidence that individuals often do perceive their partners and relationships in an excessively positive light, and that the tendency to idealize one's partner is associated with greater relationship satisfaction and lower rates of relationship dissolution (Murray, Holmes, & Collins, 2006; Murray, Holmes, & Griffin, 1996).

Unfortunately, people frequently encounter relationship-relevant challenges or difficulties that make maintaining an overly optimistic view of their partner or relationship difficult, especially when such perceptions cannot be supported or sustained in light of clearly disconfirming information or feedback. In these situations, striving to accurately understand and attribute motives and beliefs to partners ought to be adaptive. Such situations are likely to exist, for example, when individuals must decide whether or not to start or remain in a relationship, or when they need to determine how to best predict, control, or change undesirable partner behaviors.

In certain contexts, partner and relationship idealization processes may conflict with accuracy aims. Both the enhancement and accuracy motives serve distinct and valuable functions, but they may work best under different circumstances (Gagne & Lydon, 2004; Gollwitzer & Kinney, 1989). For example, when the need to make accurate, unbiased judgments becomes critical in relationships (e.g., when individuals must decide whether or not to date someone, to get married, or to have a child), the accuracy motive should assume precedence. However, once a couple settles into a comfortable relationship maintenance phase, the enhancement motive should become more important.

Consequences of Discrepancies between Ideals and Partner Perceptions

According to the ISM, the consequences of large discrepancies between ideals and perceptions of the current partner and relationship should vary depending on the accessibility and relative strength of relationship enhancement versus accuracy motives. Enhanced perceptions of the partner should narrow the gap between ideal standards and perceptions of the current partner, whereas more accurate perceptions of the partner may widen the gap. Larger ideal–perception partner perception gaps should create instability in relationships. Nevertheless, during critical decision points in relationships, the heightened motivation for accuracy (i.e., making good and well-informed decisions) may be necessary and even adaptive. In all likelihood, evolutionary pressures should have selected humans to seek out and face the truth in situations where it would have been dangerous or extremely costly to do otherwise (see Gangestad & Simpson, 2000).

As already noted, relationship enhancement and partner and relationship idealization should be dominant when a relationship is stable, when it has reached a high level of commitment, or after major decisions have already been made. When enhancement motives are active, individuals should handle ideal partner–current partner perception discrepancies using cognitive strategies that (a) change perceptions of the current partner and/or relationship, (b) change one's ideal standards so they more closely match one's perceptions of the current partner and relationship, or (c) discount the importance of ideal standards that one's partner is not likely to meet. We suspect that these cognitive dissonance reduction processes occur automatically and largely outside of conscious awareness.

In situations that demand greater accuracy (e.g., when deciding whether or not to start or remain in a relationship), moderate-to-large discrepancies should motivate individuals to engage in more in-depth analysis and information processing about the partner or the relationship. One consequence of engaging in more systematic, in-depth processing might be that individuals will use ideal partner–current partner discrepancies to explain their relationship problems (e.g., "My ideal partner is very warm and you are cold and aloof, which explains why I am unhappy"). In-depth processing may also motivate individuals to try to alter their own behavior, their partner's behavior, or both. If in-depth processing leads individuals to the conclusion that ideal partner–current partner discrepancies are important and cannot be reduced, individuals may decide to leave the relationship, look for alternate partners, or seek solace in other activities (e.g., hobbies and work).

EMPIRICAL EVIDENCE FOR THE ISM

Although research testing of the ISM is less than a decade old, several lines of work have provided support for various hypotheses derived from the model. We review each of these lines in this section.

Structure and Content of Partner and Relationship Ideals

In a series of studies reported by Fletcher et al. (1999), college men and women were asked to "build a mental picture of your ideal partner in a dating or marital relationship and describe the important characteristics" (p. 75). The lists of characteristics were sorted into categories, which were then rated by a large sample of undergraduate students in terms of their importance for each participant's own ideal partner and ideal relationship. Several waves of confirmatory factor analyses on different samples documented that the qualities of ideal partners are represented by three factors (i.e., partner warmth and trustworthiness, partner vitality and attractiveness, and partner status and resources), and the qualities of ideal relationships are represented by two factors (i.e., relationship intimacy and loyalty, and relationship passion). These results support and extend previous research and theorizing from an evolutionary perspective. Each factor represents a different mating criterion for promoting one's own reproductive fitness by attempting to secure "good genes" and/or good investment for potential mates (Gangestad & Simpson, 2000). The good genes component is associated with certain characteristics (e.g., attractiveness and vitality) that may signal genetic advantages that can be inherited by offspring. The good investment component reflects characteristics (e.g., warmth and trustworthiness, and status and resources) that convey that a partner has the potential to be a supportive and helpful mate and parent, thus ensuring that offspring survive to adulthood.

Recently, Fletcher, Tither, O'Loughlin, Friesen, and Overall (2004) documented that women tend to place greater importance on warmth and trustworthiness and on status and resources in potential mates than men do, but relatively less importance on attractiveness and vitality, and this is true across both long-term and short-term mating contexts. These results replicate a large body of prior research (e.g., Buss, 1989; Regan, 1998; Shackelford, Schmitt, & Buss, 2005). Interestingly, Fletcher and colleagues' (2004) research revealed that the size and nature of these gender differences were moderated by both the relationship context and the nature of the traits being traded off. First, gender differences became more marked when relationships were described in terms that denoted a long-term, more committed relationship. Second, when warmth and trust-worthiness were pitted against status and resources, gender differences virtually disappeared, with most men and women preferring partners who were poor and warm to those who were cold and rich. This was true regardless of the specific relationship goal (i.e., wanting a "fling," a short-term relationship, or a long-term relationship). In contrast, when warmth and trustworthi-ness were pitted against attractiveness and vitality, partner preferences were strongly affected by long-term versus short-term relationship goals. For instance, when selecting a partner for a "per-manent" relationship, nearly everyone chose a warm and homely person over a cold and attractive person. When choosing a partner for a short-term fling, however, virtually everyone chose a cold and attractive person over a warm and homely one. This pattern of within-gender and between-gender differences is consistent with Gangestad and Simpson's (2000) strategic pluralism model of mating, which suggests that both genders ought to shift their mating preferences depending on the relationship context (i.e., short- versus long-term mating goals) and as a function of criteria associated with "good investment" and "good genes."

Flexibility of Partner and Relationship Ideals

In a study conducted by Campbell and his colleagues (2001), individuals rated themselves and their ideal romantic partners on three dimensions: (a) warmth and trustworthiness, (b) vitality and attractiveness, and (c) status and resources. They then reported how flexible their ideals were on each dimension and how closely their current partner matched their ideal standards. This research revealed that individuals who rate themselves higher on a given dimension (e.g., attractiveness and vitality) tend to have higher and less flexible ideal standards on that dimension. Furthermore, indi-viduals who report having less flexible ideal standards typically report the highest relationship qual-ity when their partners match their ideals. Relationship quality is lowest, on the other hand, when individuals are less flexible and partner discrepancies are large. Thus, less flexible ideal standards can either enhance or diminish perceptions of relationship quality, depending on ideal partner–cur-rent partner discrepancies.

Campbell et al. (2001) also found that the connection between positive self-ratings on the three ideal standard dimensions and higher perceived relationship quality was mediated by smaller part-ner discrepancies. In other words, more positive self-ratings predicted smaller partner discrepan-cies, and smaller partner discrepancies, in turn, predicted higher relationship quality.

Ideal Partner–Current Partner Comparisons

Research has also confirmed that the more closely an individual's ideal standards match his or her perceptions of the current partner and relationship, the more positively she or he evaluates the current relationship (Fletcher et al., 1999; Murray et al., 1996), and the less likely the relation-ship is to disband over time (Fletcher, Simpson, & Thomas, 2000). The finding that higher ideal partner–current partner consistency tends to be associated with better relationship quality sup-ports the premise that individuals make cognitive comparisons between their current partners and their ideal standards when evaluating their relationships (Fletcher & Simpson, 2001; Simpson et al., 2001).

It has also been hypothesized that people not only make cognitive comparisons between their current partners and their ideal standards, but also make comparisons between potentially avail-able alternative partners and ideal standards (cf. Simpson, 1987). People tend to be more satisfied with their relationships when they either assimilate their relationship outcomes to a high standard or contrast them against a low standard (Broemer & Diehl, 2003). Consistent with this framework, satisfaction tends to increase when alternative relationships are contrasted against a high standard of comparison or when they are assimilated to a low standard (Broemer & Diehl, 2003). The type of comparison focus, therefore, moderates the link between ideal–perception consistency and relationship satisfaction.

Moderating Effects of Growth and Destiny Beliefs

Examining ideal standards and current partner comparisons, Knee and his colleagues have corroborated that perceptions of ideal partner–current partner discrepancies are associated with lower satisfaction (Knee, Nanayakkara, Vietor, Neighbors, & Patrick, 2001; see also Knee & Bush, this volume). However, they have also found that the discrepancy–satisfaction association is moderated by destiny and growth beliefs. According to Knee et al. (2001), a belief in destiny holds that relationships are dictated by fate—partners are either meant for each other or not—whereas a belief in growth holds that relationships are cultivated and developed with time and persistence. In particular, individuals who perceive discrepancies between their ideal standards and their partner's qualities suffer less from diminished relationship satisfaction if they possess a "cultivation" orientation (higher growth beliefs *and* lower destiny beliefs). Individuals who have a cultivation orientation believe that relationships evolve and grow through development, constructive confrontations, and continued efforts to maintain and improve the relationship. Cultivation-oriented individuals are also less interested in evaluating and diagnosing relationships. As a result, they rely somewhat less heavily on ideal partner–current partner comparisons to gauge their overall level of relationship satisfaction.

Knee et al. (2001) also documented that possessing a stronger "cultivation" orientation (i.e., high growth and low destiny) predicts more positive reactions when individuals discuss discrepant opinions with their romantic partners, whereas possessing a stronger "evaluation" orientation (i.e., high destiny and low growth) predicts elevated hostility. In general, cultivation-oriented people can openly acknowledge their partners' shortcomings while remaining relatively satisfied with their relationships, using their partners' limitations and weaknesses as opportunities for developing more closeness and deeper understanding of their partners. Evaluation-oriented people, in contrast, tend to rely more on ideal partner–current partner comparisons as "diagnostic" information regarding the status of the relationship, exaggerating the difficulties of perceived discrepancies and sometimes seeing them as insurmountable (see also Knee & Bush, this volume).

Regulation Functions of Ideal Standards

Overall, Fletcher, and Simpson (2006) recently tested the regulation functions of the ISM. This research confirmed that larger ideal partner–current partner discrepancies usually motivate individuals to try to alter their partners' undesirable behaviors. Furthermore, more strenuous attempts at partner regulation (e.g., trying to change a displeasing behavior or characteristic of the partner) were also associated with larger ideal partner–current partner discrepancies. Analyses of the dyadic links in a sample of couples (Study 2) suggested that vigorous and sustained attempts to change the partner's behavior conveyed a lack of acceptance and a failure to meet important expectations, which amplified the psychological significance of partner shortcomings as perceived by *both* members of the dyad.

As predicted, Overall et al. (2006) reported that the link between partner regulation and relationship quality was mediated through ideal partner–current partner consistency, both cross-sectionally and longitudinally. Specifically, more strenuous partner regulation attempts predicted lower perceptions of ideal partner–current partner consistency, which in turn forecasted more negative relationship evaluations. Importantly, these results held up when controlling for either partner perceptions or ideal standards. Taken together, these results provide compelling evidence for a fundamental tenet of the ISM, namely, that the discrepancy between standards and perceptions forms natural social cognitive units that drive subsequent pivotal relationship evaluations and strategies.

Despite the influence that ideal–perception comparisons tend to have on relationship evaluations, relationship quality, and relationship stability, the degree to which ideal standards and ideal partner–current partner discrepancies are accessible may depend on the developmental stage of relationships. Ideal–partner consistency judgments, for example, should be most important during critical decision points (e.g., when deciding whether to date someone, to get married, or to have a child; see Simpson et al., 2001). During such turning points in relationships, individuals must make good, well-informed decisions that call for accurate and unbiased judgments. Love and commitment should be less influential as biasing forces during such decision-making periods, because it is (in large part) the levels of love and commitment that are essentially being decided. The frequency and importance of such ideal–perception comparisons should decline when relationships become more stable and couples primarily rely on relationship maintenance strategies.

Ideal Standards in Early Relationship Development

Studying the development of dating relationships longitudinally from the first to the 12th month of their inception, Fletcher et al. (2000) documented that holding more positive perceptions of one's partner or relationship at earlier points in relationship development predicted greater importance being placed on corresponding ideals across time, but not vice versa. More specifically, early perceptions of one's romantic partner appeared to influence which ideal standards became more important over time, whereas the reverse pattern (prior ideal standards causing current partner perceptions) did not hold. This finding is consistent with other research indicating that romantic partners who idealize each other more initially report greater increases in satisfaction and decreases in conflict and doubts over time (see Murray et al., 1996). Changing one's ideal standards to match perceptions of the current partner, therefore, may be one means by which relationships are stabilized and maintained.

Summary of Empirical Evidence

In sum, empirical evidence has documented that (a) there are three ideal partner dimensions and two ideal relationship dimensions (Fletcher et al., 1999), (b) there are gender differences in the importance placed on the various ideal dimensions (Fletcher et al., 2004), and (c) there are moderating influences of relationship context and the nature of the traits being traded off by women and men (Fletcher et al., 2004). Research has also confirmed that (d) higher self-ratings on ideal dimensions tend to be associated with higher ideal standards and less flexibility on those dimensions (Campbell et al., 2001). Despite having higher expectations and firm ideal standards, (e) these individuals tend to experience the greatest relationship quality when their partners match their ideal standards. In general, regardless of the level of ideal standards or their degree of flexibility, (f) the more closely individuals' ideal standards match their perceptions of the current partner and relationship, the more positively they evaluate the current relationship (Fletcher et al., 1999; see also Murray et al., 1996).

Knee et al. (2001) have also found that (g) the discrepancy–satisfaction association is moderated by destiny and growth beliefs, such that people who have stronger cultivation orientations have more positive reactions when discussing discrepant opinions, whereas those who have stronger evaluation orientations display elevated hostility. More recent research conducted by Overall et al. (2006) has revealed that (h) more strenuous partner regulation attempts predict larger ideal partner–current partner perceived discrepancies, which in turn forecast more negative relationship evaluations. Finally, Fletcher et al. (2000) have documented that (i) harboring more positive perceptions of one's partner or relationship at earlier points in relationship development predicts greater importance being placed on corresponding ideals over time, but not vice versa.

In conclusion, the representations that one holds for a standard of excellence in romantic partners and relationships are shaped by several variables (i.e., gender, self-perceptions, and relationship goals). The cognitive comparisons between ideal partner standards and current partner qualities can alter evaluations of the current partner and relationship, subsequently influencing regulation strategies and even future ideal standards.

UNANSWERED QUESTIONS AND FUTURE DIRECTIONS

Several questions and promising avenues for research relevant to the ISM and relationship "beginnings" remain unaddressed. In this final section, we broach some of these issues, which can be divided into processes that are likely to occur before a relationship is initiated and those that are likely to occur early in relationship development.

Processes Prior to Relationship Initiation

One major unanswered question asks how ideal standards develop. As stated earlier, these standards are rooted in biological adaptations, but are also shaped by early experiences and socialization processes with parents, family, friends, local communities, and the media. We suspect that these early sources of information may guide individuals' personal mate preferences. Over time, however, people may adapt their ideal standards to match their own personal strengths and limitations (i.e., their self-perceived mate value). Not every person can attain a partner who is simultaneously warm, rich, healthy, and good-looking. Difficulties associated with attracting and retaining such paragons of virtue should motivate most individuals to calibrate their ideals to a more realistic level based on their own self-perceived mate value, the quality and number of available alternative partners, and so forth.

Another related set of unanswered questions asks how an individual's self-perceived mate value (i.e., the degree to which individuals believe they are desirable mates, relative to their same-age peers) is associated with the level and flexibility of ideal standards. According to the ISM, individuals who have lower self-perceived mate values should set lower ideal standards that are also more flexible (that is, have lower thresholds of minimal acceptance). In contrast, individuals who have higher self-perceived mate values should set higher ideal standards that are less flexible. Regan (1998), for example, has found that women's self-perceived mate value correlates positively with their ideal preferences. We suspect, however, that this process may vary across different dimensions of ideal standards. For example, if individuals have elevated standards on a specific dimension (e.g., status and resources), they may hold higher and less flexible standards on that dimension relative to other ones, even if they harbor doubts about their general value as a mate.

A third major unresolved issue is whether ideal dimensions follow a "screening pattern" when individuals first meet a prospective mate. People might, for instance, have a basic "threshold of acceptance" for certain ideal dimensions that potential partners must surpass before they are even considered as possible mates. Individuals who, overall, perceive themselves as having low mate value may conceivably just go for the best deal they can get, and forget about their own standards, at least until a relationship is up and running. In contrast, those with high standards may apply more fine-grained comparisons between their standards and perceptions of relationship partners from the start.

A fourth set of unanswered questions revolves around how the perceived importance of specific ideal standards might affect initial judgments of prospective mates. According to the ISM, the adoption of short-term versus long-term mating strategies influences both the level and the flexibility of specific ideal standards. Individuals who are interested in short-term mating, for example, should place more weight on attractiveness and vitality, whereas those who value long-term mating might put more weight on the other ideal dimensions, especially warmth and trustworthiness (see Buss & Schmitt, 1993; Gangestad & Simpson, 2000). Individuals should also place greater emphasis on those ideal dimensions that they value the most, which again may be influenced by whether they are pursuing short-term or long-term mating strategies.

A fifth set of unresolved issues involves how individuals produce "trade-offs" between different ideal dimensions (e.g., sacrificing some status and resources for more attractiveness and vitality in a given partner). Trade-offs presumably only go so far, with all deals being called off if any of the three critical dimensions dip below a barely acceptable level. In an episode of *Sex in the City*, the four main protagonists (i.e., attractive professional women in their 30s) sit in a bar in New York bemoaning the lack of available men in New York. In fact, the establishment is stacked with young, reasonably attractive men—busboys, doormen, barmen, water waiters, and so forth. These men, however, are not mateworthy (and are almost invisible to the four women) because they fall well below the minimum criteria of status and resources that such women will normally possess.

Finally, what happens when individuals hold unrealistically high ideal standards or standards that are too inflexible? In such cases, individuals are likely to bypass many potentially good and compatible partners, or they may never get past dating individuals more than a few times because they never measure up. According to the ISM, however, most individuals should gradually adjust their ideal standards based on "corrective" feedback over time, given the harsh consequences of maintaining unrealistically high standards. This fact may explain why partner matching is such a robust phenomenon (see Ellis & Kelley, 1999).

Processes Following Relationship Initiation

Several intriguing questions also exist regarding the role that ideal standards play in the very early stages of relationship development, say over the first 3 months. For example, what happens when a current partner exceeds an individual's ideal standards, or is perceived as offering far more than the individual has to offer? One possibility is that this will motivate trade-off processing (e.g., "He is more attractive than me, but I have more ambition and drive"). However, if the partner is perceived as possessing higher mate value on all three dimensions, then we suspect that this will set the scene for an anxious and unhappy relationship that may be marked by power differentials and uneven levels of commitment (although this may crucially depend on the level of agreement across partners on these matters). Additionally, research on fatal attractions (Felmlee, 1995; see also Sprecher & Felmlee, this volume) may explain how qualities that initially attract a potential mate may be the same characteristics that produce subsequent disaffection, particularly if the quality or dimension is different from the individual's own qualities.

Another unresolved issue is what happens to ideal standards and evaluations of partners when relationships and partners change over time. Partners are bound to change during the course of most relationships. If negative changes occur on a dimension that an individual views as central to his or her ideal standards, the perception of larger discrepancies could result in more negative evaluations of the partner and, ultimately, may have negative implications for the relationship. Conversely, if positive changes occur on a dimension that an individual considers central to his or her ideal standards, the perception of smaller discrepancies should enhance evaluations of the partner or the relationship. If, however, an individual is highly committed to the relationship and the partner changes on an ideal dimension that is less important, the individual might gradually change the less important ideal standard to match the direction of the partner's change.

Finally, we do not know what happens when an individual perceives larger ideal partner–current partner discrepancies than his or her partner. It is possible that this instigates inferences that one of the individuals is "underbenefited" in the relationship, which, in turn, is likely to launch what Attridge, Berscheid, and Simpson (1995) termed the "weak link" effect that makes the less committed person even less committed and more likely to leave the relationship. All of these questions merit future research.

CONCLUSION

Fruitful and lengthy research traditions in both social psychology and evolutionary psychology have revealed a great deal concerning the mental and emotional working models, schemas, and theories that people bring with them into relationships (see Knee & Bush, this volume). Clinicians and social psychologists know a good deal about the developmental course of relationships once they are up and running, but there is a yawning gap in knowledge about the development of relationships across the first few days, weeks, and months. One major reason for this state of affairs is, almost certainly, the difficulties in conducting research on such samples given the narrow window of time involved.

We would argue that although such research is hard to do, it is worth the effort involved. The gains in knowledge and understanding of a pivotal developmental stage in intimate relationships would be invaluable in moving the field forward. The ISM is one model that has clear applications to this field, and may help to answer intriguing and difficult questions, some of which we have mentioned. One reason why the ISM has promise in this domain is that it is one of the few models that applies both to mate selection contexts (that are in operation before the parties even meet) and to relationship processes over long periods of time (once the relationship has been initiated). Given that individuals can deselect their mates at any time throughout the course of a relationship, mate selection in *Homo sapiens* can, and should, be construed as a continual process.

REFERENCES

Attridge, M., Berscheid, E., & Simpson, J. A. (1995). Predicting relationship stability from both partners versus one. *Journal of Personality and Social Psychology, 69,* 254–268.

Baumeister, R. F. (1998). The self. In D. T. Gilbert, S. T. Fiske, & G. Lindzey (Eds.), *The handbook of social psychology* (4th ed., pp. 680–740). New York: McGraw-Hill.

Berscheid, E., & Graziano, W. (1979). The initiation of social relationships and interpersonal attraction. In R. L. Burgess & T. L. Huston (Eds.), *Social exchange in developing relationships* (pp. 31–60). New York: Academic Press.

Broemer, P., & Diehl, M. (2003). What you think is what you get: Comparative evaluations of close relationships. *Personality and Social Psychology Bulletin, 29,* 1560–1569.

Buss, D. M. (1989). Sex differences in human mate preferences: Evolutionary hypotheses testing in 37 cultures. *Behavioral and Brain Sciences, 12,* 1–49.

Buss, D. M., & Schmitt, D. P. (1993). Sexual strategies theory: A contextual evolutionary analysis of human mating. *Psychological Review, 100,* 204–232.

Campbell, L., Simpson, J. A., Kashy, D., & Fletcher, G. J. O. (2001). Ideal standards, the self, and flexibility of ideals in close relationships. *Personality and Social Psychology Bulletin, 27,* 447–462.

Ellis, B. J., & Kelley, H. H. (1999). The pairing game: A classroom demonstration of the matching phenomenon. *Teaching of Psychology, 26,* 118–121.

Felmlee, D. H. (1995). Fatal attractions: Affection and disaffection in intimate relationships. *Journal of Social and Personal Relationships, 12,* 295–311.

Fletcher, G. J. O., & Simpson, J. A. (2001). Ideal standards in close relationships. In J. P. Forgas, K. P. Williams, & L. Wheeler (Eds.), *The social mind: Cognitive and motivational aspects of interpersonal behavior* (pp. 257–273). New York: Cambridge University Press.

Fletcher, G. J. O., Simpson, J. A., & Thomas, G. (2000). Ideals, perceptions, and evaluations in early relationship development. *Journal of Personality and Social Psychology, 79,* 933–940.

Fletcher, G. J. O., Simpson, J. A., Thomas, G., & Giles, L. (1999). Ideals in intimate relationships. *Journal of Personality and Social Psychology, 76,* 72–89.

Fletcher, G. J. O., & Thomas, G. (1996). Lay theories in close relationships: Their structure and function. In G. J. O. Fletcher & J. Fitness (Eds.), *Knowledge structures in close relationships: A social psychological approach* (pp. 3–24). Mahwah, NJ: Lawrence Erlbaum.

Fletcher. G. J. O., Tither, J. M., O'Loughlin, C., Friesen, M., & Overall, N. (2004). Warm and homely or cold and beautiful? Sex differences in trading off traits in mate selection. *Personality and Social Psychology Bulletin, 30,* 659–672.

Gagne, F. M., & Lydon, J. E. (2004). Bias and accuracy in close relationships: An integrative review. *Personality and Social Psychology Review, 8,* 322–338.

Gangestad, S. W., & Simpson, J. A. (2000). The evolution of human mating: Trade-offs and strategic pluralism. *Behavioral and Brain Sciences, 23,* 573–587.

Gollwitzer, P. M., & Kinney, R. F. (1989). Effects of deliberative and implemental mind-sets on illusion of control. *Journal of Personality and Social Psychology, 56,* 531–542.

Knee, C. R., Nanayakkara, A., Vietor, N. A., Neighbors, C., & Patrick, H. (2001). Implicit theories of relationships: Who cares if romantic partners are less than ideal? *Personality and Social Psychology Bulletin, 27,* 808–819.

Murray, S. L. (2001). Seeking a sense of conviction: Motivated cognition in close relationships. In G. J. O. Fletcher & M. S. Clark (Eds.), *Blackwell handbook of social psychology* (pp. 107–126). Oxford: Blackwell.

Murray, S. L., Holmes, J. G., & Collins, N. L. (2006). Optimizing assurance: The risk regulation system in relationships. *Psychological Bulletin, 132,* 641–666.

Murray, S. L., Holmes, J. G., & Griffin, D. W. (1996). The self-fulfilling nature of positive illusions in romantic relationships: Love is not blind but prescient. *Journal of Personality and Social Psychology, 71,* 1155–1180.

Overall, N., Fletcher, G. J. O., & Simpson, J. A. (2006). Regulation processes in intimate relationships: The role of ideal standards. *Journal of Personality and Social Psychology, 91,* 662–685.

Regan, P. C. (1998). What if you can't get what you want? Willingness to compromise ideal mate selection standards as a function of sex, mate value, and relationship context. *Personality and Social Psychology Bulletin, 24,* 1288–1297.

Shackelford, T. K., Schmitt, D. P., & Buss, D. M. (2005). The universal dimensions of human mate preferences. *Personality and Individual Differences, 39,* 447–458.

Simpson, J. A. (1987). The dissolution of romantic relationships: Factors involved in relationship stability and emotional distress. *Journal of Personality and Social Psychology, 53,* 683–692.

Simpson, J. A., Fletcher, G. J. O., & Campbell, L. (2001). The structure and function of ideal standards in close relationships. In G. J. O. Fletcher & M. S. Clark (Eds.), *Blackwell handbook of social psychology* (pp. 86–106). Oxford: Blackwell.

Taylor, S. E., & Brown, J. D. (1988). *Positive illusions: Creative self-deception and the healthy mind.* New York: Basic Books.

26

Perceptions of Goals and Motives in Romantic Relationships

GLENN D. REEDER

In a chart of the top five women's and men's basic needs, the curriculum lists "sexual fulfillment" and "physical attractiveness" as two of the top five "needs" in the men's section. "Affection", "Conversation", "Honesty and Openness" and "Family Commitment" are listed only as women's needs.

***The Content of Federally Funded Abstinence-Only Educational Programs*, report prepared by the Committee on Government Reform for U.S. Representative Henry A. Waxman (D-CA; Committee on Government Reform, 2004)**

The problem was that she was just inviting me (to her birthday party) because she thought I was a nice guy and not because she was interested in me. She actually spent the whole night (and I mean the whole night) with this guy who looked like John Secada.

Website Blog

The quotes above deal with perceptions of goals and motives within close relationships. This chapter will address two important questions regarding such perceptions. At the most general level, what goals do people attribute to men and women for entering into romantic relationships? At a more specific level, how do people go about attributing motives to men and women who act in particular ways and say particular things in relationships (Malle, 2004; Reeder & Trafimow, 2005)? Most of the time—regardless of whether or not we make our living researching close relationships—we think we know the answers to these questions. For example, the first quote above represents a set of assumptions made by the designers of "abstinence-only" programs. The designers assume that there are clear differences in the goals that men and women have for beginning a romantic encounter. In a nutshell, men are assumed to be guided by sexual needs, whereas women are assumed to be more concerned with communication and long-term commitment. Assumptions about gender differences concerning relationship goals are merely stereotypes, of course, but they are not trivial. Not only do such stereotypes guide the formation of government programs but also it is likely that they guide the actual behavior of men and women as they begin to form romantic attachments (Karney, McNulty, & Bradbury, 2003).

In contrast to the first quote involving general stereotypes about goals, the second quote above represents a more specific kind of motive attribution. A male college student is offering an account of a disappointing evening in which his plans for beginning a new relationship failed to materialize. At such times, perceivers often rely on some of the same stereotypes made by the designers of the abstinence-only program (e.g., a woman's interest in a man may merely reflect a "friendship" motive). But when attempting to explain the specific actions of their relationship partners, perceivers often move beyond the use of simple stereotypes. They may actively strive to enter into the minds of their partners in order to understand their motives (e.g., "What was she thinking?" or "Was she trying to make me jealous?"). This chapter aims to shed light on both of these phenomena. That is, we will explore both the general stereotypes about relationship goals that people hold and the psychological processes that govern the more specific motive attributions we make about our relationship partners.

The first section of this chapter examines the reasons why people care about the goals and motives of their relationship partners. The second section presents a brief review of past literature related to perceptions of goals and motives relevant to relationship initiation. Because no previous studies have directly examined people's expectations about the different goals men and women have for entering into romantic relationships, the third section of this chapter describes an empirical investigation of this topic. The fourth section examines the processes that people rely on to infer the specific motives of their relationship partners. Finally, the last section outlines future research directions.

WHY PEOPLE CARE ABOUT A PROSPECTIVE PARTNER'S GOALS AND MOTIVES

There is a great deal of overlap in the way people talk about goals and motives. Yet, we often think of goals as being more general and conscious, and as involving more long-term planning. In contrast, we often think in terms of motives when we are trying to figure out the reasons for specific actions, such as why our partner broke our lunch date ("Does she need to catch up on work?" "Is she paying me back for not remembering her birthday?" or "Is she interested in another guy?"). In this chapter, then, I will use the term *goals* to refer to the broad, general aims and plans of others. I will use the word *motives*, on the other hand, to refer to the reasons that are thought to underlie specific actions.

Let us turn to our main concern in this section: Why do people care about the goals and motives of prospective romantic partners? Imagine a social world in which you never thought about other people's goals and motives. For instance, suppose you are sitting in an airport bar when an attractive stranger sidles up next to you and offers to buy you a drink. If you lacked a "theory of mind" that prevented you from understanding other people's desires and expectations (Malle & Hodges, 2005), you would respond solely on the basis of your own inclination for another drink (and perhaps your flight schedule). Such a narrow interpretation of your new acquaintance's behavior is characteristic of certain forms of autism (Baron-Cohen & Belmonte, 2005). Most adults would read quite a bit more into the stranger's offer. They might infer that the stranger is lonely and wants a conversation partner or perhaps even that the stranger finds them attractive and is seeking a sexual partner. In general, if you fail to engage in mind-reading—including making inferences about others' goals—you will have no chance of understanding the real meaning behind other people's actions.

In an early demonstration of goal perception, Heider and Simmel (1944) produced a film in which black geometric figures (such as a circle and a triangle) were shown moving against a white background. When a large triangle moved toward a circle, viewers tended to see the triangle as a "bully" that was chasing the circle. Thus, people look for motivational patterns in even the most minimal interactions. Not surprisingly, therefore, we tend to attribute motives to the characters in the books we read and in the films we see. In the movie *Titanic* (Cameron, 1997), for instance, Kate Winslet's character (Rose) rejects advice from her mother, starts arguments with her fiancée, and is strangely attracted to a young stranger named Jack (played by Leonardo DiCaprio). The pattern in her actions becomes apparent to the viewer once it is recognized that, in a very modern sense, she is seeking independence. In summary, then, inferences about goals and motives allow us to better understand and remember human interactions (Berger, 1993; Read & Miller, 1993, 2005; Schank & Abelson, 1977; Wilensky, 1983; Zwaan & Radvansky, 1998).

Along with furthering your understanding of prospective partners, an appreciation of goals and motives may allow you to better predict and control your interactions with them (Dennet, 1993). For example, if you are happily married or otherwise committed to another person, it may be important to steer clear of persons who desire more intimacy than you do. The consequences of not doing so could include awkward interchanges, hurt feelings, and possibly aggressive confrontations (Abbey, 1987). Some evolutionary psychologists believe that we are "hard-wired" to read motives into other people's actions. Early humans who understood the motives and desires of friends and enemies could better anticipate their actions and thereby gained a survival advantage. Thus, early humans who understood that a stranger might feign friendship in order to later exploit them (i.e., a "wolf in sheep's clothing") were better prepared to deal with treachery. Observations of this sort suggest that domain-specific "cheater detector" mechanisms may have evolved (Cosmides, 1989). If we are looking for a long-term romantic partner, such mechanisms might protect us from the schemes of others whose only agenda is a one-night stand. For instance, we may be skeptical of a prospective partner who says, "I love you," on a first date.

At least two themes emerge from the above discussion. First, it is often important to hold accurate perceptions about the goals of a prospective or current relationship partner (Ickes, Simpson, & Oriña, 2005; Laner, 1977). Second, it is important that your partner's goals mesh well with your own goals. Partners with similar goals (e.g., "climbing the corporate ladder") may initially experience greater attraction or "hit it off" (Berger, 1993), compared to couples with dissimilar goals. But *compatibility* of goals may matter even more in the long run. For instance, if both partners view the relationship primarily as a means of furthering their own occupational success, conflicts may emerge over the sharing of child-rearing tasks and housework. Indeed, research indicates that when partners meet each other's ideals (or goals) for the relationship, the relationship is evaluated more positively (Fletcher, Simpson, Thomas, & Giles, 1999). The next section of this chapter examines several lines of research that are closely related to the perception of relationship goals.

A BRIEF REVIEW OF CONSTRUCTS RELATED TO PERCEIVED GOALS: GENDER STEREOTYPES, MATE PREFERENCES, AND RELATIONSHIP IDEALS

Although I could identify no research that directly examined perceptions of why men and women enter relationships, there are large bodies of data on related constructs. For example, research on gender stereotypes, mating preferences, and relationship ideals are potentially relevant. In summarizing each of these areas of research, I will focus on implications that are relevant to inferring relationship goals.

Gender Stereotypes

People commonly believe that men and women possess different personality traits. A now classic study asked college students to rate the typical adult man and typical adult woman on a large number of personality dimensions (Rosenkrantz, Vogel, Bee, Broverman, & Broverman, 1968). A reasonable consensus emerged that men are higher on instrumental attributes (such as independence, assertiveness, and decisiveness), which prepare a person to function well outside the family in occupational roles. In contrast, women were perceived as higher on expressive attributes (such as kindness, sensitivity to others, and need for affiliation). Traits of this kind should facilitate the formation and maintenance of close relationships, particularly those within the family. Although general sex role attitudes (including those regarding women's appropriate occupational roles) have undergone a sea change in the last 40 years (Bolzendahl & Myers, 2004), gender stereotypes about personality traits are still with us today (Falk & Kenski, 2006).

Given that men are still seen as more instrumental and less expressive than women, are there any implications for perceiving relationship goals? A straightforward prediction is that men and women, in general, will be seen as looking for intimacy (expressiveness) and status (instrumentality) from close relationships. But will men and women be seen as seeking these to different degrees? The answer may not be as straightforward as it seems. There are at least two alternative sets of hypotheses that can be offered. On the one hand, each gender might be perceived as holding goals that reflect their personality. According to this "similarity hypothesis," women's expressive orientation would be seen as leading them to seek intimacy in a romantic relationship. Likewise, men's instrumental orientation might be thought to lead them to seek status from the relationship. In other words, each gender might be expected to seek things in a relationship that are most important to them. On the other hand, perceivers might think that partners are seeking complementarity (Winch, 1963). For example, given the stereotype of women as more expressive, they may be seen as looking for status in a romantic relationship as a way to "complete themselves." Similarly, men might be seen as seeking intimacy from the relationship as a way to complement their own orientation. Given the conflicting hypotheses outlined above, it is difficult to predict how gender stereotypes will influence beliefs about relationship goals.

Mating Preferences

Evolutionary explanations have sparked a great deal of interest in gender differences concerning mate selection (Buss & Kenrick, 1998; Gangestad & Simpson, 2000; Schmitt, this volume). According to this perspective, men and women seek partners who can best enhance their chances of reproductive success. By this logic, men should prefer women who signal their reproductive potential with youth and good looks. On the other hand, women should prefer men who signal their ability to provide resources or status to the family unit (by being wealthy or ambitious). Gender differences of this sort can also be explained on the basis of sociocultural factors (Sprecher, Sullivan, & Hatfield, 1994). Accordingly, men's preference for youth and beauty in a partner and women's relatively greater preference for resources and social status are due to traditional sex role socialization and the restricted economic opportunities that are available to women.

In general, research supports these predictions about gender differences. Questionnaire studies indicate that men rate the physical attractiveness of their partners as more important than women do, whereas women tend to rate the earning potential or social status of their partner as more important. In fact, a survey conducted with a national probability sample in the United States indicated that these tendencies are present to some extent across different age samples and across Black and White populations (Sprecher et al., 1994). Such gender differences are also reflected in personal want ads, where men often seek beauty in a partner and women seek financial stability. Note, however, that such gender differences may be weaker if the relationship is conceived of as short term (Kenrick, Sadalla, Groth, & Trost, 1990).

Of course, the existence of these gender differences in mating strategies does not guarantee that naïve perceivers are aware of these differences. Nevertheless, if we assume such awareness, what are the implications for perceiving relationship goals? First, given that men desire youth and beauty, perceivers may expect that men will be more likely than women to hold the goal of finding sexual pleasure and excitement. Second, given women's preference for partners with economic resources, women should be perceived as more likely to hold the goal of obtaining status from the relationship.

Research by Haselton and Buss (2000) is consistent with the above predictions. Although their research was designed with other purposes in mind, their data strongly suggest that sexual intentions are perceived to be greater in men than in women. For example, when men go out to a bar, they are thought more likely than women to be interested in finding someone to have sex with that night. Haselton and Buss' research also suggests that commitment intentions are perceived to be greater in women than in men. For example, women are thought more likely to need to know that their partner is committed to the relationship before they feel comfortable having sex. These tendencies held for both male and female perceivers. That is, both male and female perceivers thought that men were more motivated by sex and that women were more concerned about their partner's commitment.

Of greater interest, however, the evidence indicates that male and female perceivers differ in certain respects. In particular, relative to female perceivers, male perceivers tend to see greater sexual intent in women (Abbey, 1982; Haselton & Buss, 2000). For example, after watching a man and woman having a casual conversation, male perceivers were more likely to think the woman was sexually attracted to the man (Abbey, 1982). As discussed in a later section of this chapter, a variety of factors may contribute to this interpretational bias. In addition to replicating this sexual intent bias, Haselton and Buss reported a commitment intent bias: Female perceivers were *less* likely than male perceivers to think that a man's behavior reflected his commitment to the relationship. Thus, women tend to be skeptical of a man's commitment intentions. In summary, although there are general tendencies to think that men and women initiate relationships with different goals in mind, male and female perceivers tend to have their own biases as well.

Dimensions of Importance for Ideal Partners and Ideal Relationships

A number of researchers have explored the underlying dimensions that are considered important for judging an ideal partner or an ideal relationship. Fletcher and his colleagues (Fletcher et al., 1999; Tran, Simpson, & Fletcher, this volume) have investigated both of these topics. They found that people primarily seek three things from their ideal partners and relationships: (a) intimacy, trust, and loyalty; (b) passion and excitement; and (c) social status and resources. Related research points to two additional goals. Partners may be concerned about maintaining their (d) freedom and independence (Sabatelli, 1984), and may see a romantic relationship as a way to (e) increase their own self-esteem (Sedikides, Oliver, & Campbell, 1994). For example, Sedikides et al. (1994) asked participants to rate a variety of different benefits that close relationships might offer. Overall, they found that companionship and feeling loved were rated most important. They also reported some sex differences: Women regarded intimacy, self-esteem, and self-growth as more important than men did. Men, in contrast, tended to put a high value on sexual gratification. It is important to note that these five factors emerged when research participants expressed their *own* concerns about relationships. The research reported in the next section explored the possibility that similar factors may emerge when people predict why others initiate romantic attachments.

DO PEOPLE EXPECT MEN AND WOMEN TO ENTER RELATIONSHIPS WITH DIFFERENT GOALS? AN EMPIRICAL INVESTIGATION

As the previous section revealed, there are extensive literatures on gender stereotypes, mate preferences, and related concepts. The research to date has focused on perceptions of a few narrow goals for entering relationships, but there is a need to focus on a wider range of goals. Consequently, Susan Sprecher and I designed a study to investigate this topic more systematically (Reeder & Sprecher, 2007). As described below, we surveyed 128 college students (46 men and 82 women) at Illinois State University about the relationship goals they attributed to other college students.

In essence, this survey assessed stereotypes about why college men and women form romantic relationships. Based on our review of the literature in the previous section and numerous conversations with colleagues and students, we developed a list of 32 goals that men and women may seek when forming a romantic relationship. The goals covered a wide variety of issues such as intimacy, commitment and loyalty, status, excitement and passion, freedom and independence, self-esteem, mentoring, spirituality, personal growth, and seeking a larger social network. Each research participant was asked to rate the importance of these goals for developing a new romantic relationship as they applied to either college men or college women. In other words, each questionnaire dealt with just one gender as the impression target. In order to provide a more reliable set of ratings, we presented these 32 goals in two question formats. Questions in the first format appeared in one particular order, randomly determined, and read as follows: "To what degree do they want to form a relationship that will allow them to (obtain goal)?" Each goal was rated on a 9-point scale with end-points labeled 1 (*not at all important*) and 9 (*extremely important*). In the second question format, the goals were listed in a different, fixed random order and were rated on the same 9-point scale of importance. Except for two items, average ratings of the goals were similar across the two types of question formats, $r = .78$. Consequently, a decision was made to delete those two items and combine the two ratings given to each of the remaining 30 goals.

Specific Research Questions and Predictions

The research addressed three related questions focusing on (a) the relative importance of different relationship goals, (b) the gender of the impression target ("Are women perceived to have different goals than men?"), and (c) the gender of the perceiver ("Do female perceivers stress different goals than male perceivers do?"). We will consider each of these questions in turn. First, overall, what relationship goals are seen as most important in college students? In the previous section, we reviewed the literature that bears most directly on the actual goals that people might have for entering relationships. This analysis highlighted a variety of factors that relate to goals for entering relationships: (a) intimacy, trust, and commitment; (b) passion and excitement; (c) social status; (d) freedom and independence; and (e) raising self-esteem. We expected that similar dimensions would emerge when male and female perceivers rated the importance of a wide range of goals people have for entering relationships.

In addition to expecting the emergence of the five factors listed above, we suspected that some of these factors might be rated as more important than others. Sedikides and his colleagues (1994) found that the major benefits of close relationships were companionship and "feeling loved." Indeed, relationships without intimacy or trust may be perceived as "hollow" or meaningless (Harvey & Omarzu, 1999). On this basis, we expected that intimacy would be seen as one of the strongest goals for starting a relationship. In addition, because of the age and relative immaturity of our college student participants, we also expected the goal of excitement to be rated as important. Of course, differences of this sort may be moderated by the gender of the impression target. We turn to this issue next.

Our second set of research questions focused on the gender of the impression target. Will our respondents think that college men and women have different goals for entering into romantic relationships? If such gender stereotypes exist, they may be based on *actual* differences between what men and women look for in relationships. As previously noted, studies on mating preferences indicate that men are relatively more interested in the physical attractiveness of their partners, whereas women are relatively more concerned with the resources or social status of their partner (Buss & Kenrick, 1998; Sprecher et al., 1994). On this basis, we expected that men would be perceived as having stronger goals to seek excitement and passion in the relationship. In contrast, we expected that women would be seen as seeking a relationship in order to increase their status.

Research on gender stereotypes indicates that women are perceived as caring about intimacy and interpersonal relationships to a greater extent than men (Rosenkrantz et al., 1968). Such differences may represent more than stereotypes: Sedikides et al. (1994) reported that, relative to men, women saw intimacy as a more important benefit of close relationships. It also follows that if women are more concerned with relationships, their self-esteem may be seen as more contingent on romantic relationships. In sum, we expected that goals related to finding intimacy and using the relationship to bolster one's own self-esteem would be seen as stronger when women were the impression targets than when men were the impression targets.

Our third and final set of research questions concerned the gender of the perceiver. Will male and female college students perceive different relationship goals in others? Before considering such differences, we point to two basic psychological processes that guide inferences about the goals and motives of others (Reeder & Trafimow, 2005). First, perceivers may project their own goals onto others (Ames, 2004; Goldman, 2001). For example, if female perceivers think that intimacy is especially important in their own relationships, female perceivers may think that other people (regardless of gender) will also stress intimacy goals. Second, as discussed earlier, perceivers may rely on gender stereotypes when judging the goals of others (e.g., "Men are only concerned about sex"). But what determines whether projection or stereotyping predominates? Research suggests that stereotyping is less likely when perceivers feel empathy or have a general feeling of similarity with the impression target (Ames, 2004).

Most people probably feel less similar to the opposite sex than to their own sex. If so, the discussion above suggests that people should be especially likely to stereotype the *opposite* sex. In particular, compared to male perceivers, female perceivers should be especially likely to stereotype men as lacking intimacy goals and as possessing strong goals related to excitement and freedom. Likewise, compared to female perceivers, male perceivers should stereotype women as being especially concerned with intimacy goals and as being unconcerned with goals related to excitement and freedom.

Major Findings

What Relationship Goals Are Seen as Most Important in College Students?   In an effort to uncover the dimensions among the 30 goals that were rated, we subjected these ratings to an exploratory factor analysis (principal components analysis with varimax rotation). The first five factors to emerge accounted for 74% of the total variance, and all five appeared to be meaningfully related to constructs discussed earlier in this chapter. The first factor, which appears to represent intimacy, accounted for 32% of the variance. Twelve items—including goals related to companionship, loyalty, trust, and finding a marriage partner—had high loadings on this factor. The second factor represented seeking status (accounting for 18% of the variance) and included items such as wanting to impress people and find a larger social network. The third factor (accounting for 7% of the variance) related to excitement, fun, and having an available sex partner. The fourth factor (accounting for 5% of the variance) related to freedom and independence. The fifth factor (accounting for 3% of the variance) pertained to raising one's own self-esteem and feeling good about one's self. We took the mean of the items loading at .60 or above on each factor, resulting in five scales with at least adequate reliability (coefficient alphas ranged between .66 and .95).

The ratings on the five goal scales were subjected to a 5 (type of goal) × 2 (gender of perceiver) × 2 (gender of impression target) analysis of variance, with type of goal treated as a repeated measures factor. The results revealed a large number of significant findings, including a significant main effect of goals; significant interactions between goals and gender of impression target, and goals and gender of perceiver; and a three-way interaction involving goals, gender of target, and gender of perceiver. The major conclusions to be derived from this analysis are summarized below.

As described earlier, we predicted that intimacy and excitement would be rated as the two most important reasons for relationship initiation. This expectation received mixed support. As shown in Table 26.1, the overall order of importance of the five goals is as follows: excitement ($M = 7.56$), raising one's own self-esteem ($M = 7.44$), maintaining freedom ($M = 7.08$), intimacy ($M = 6.32$), and status ($M = 6.28$). In general, these ratings are quite high. Nevertheless, the relatively higher ratings of excitement are in line with our predictions, but the relatively lower ratings given to intimacy are unexpected. It is also worth emphasizing that the goal of raising one's own self-esteem was seen as more important than we had anticipated. As described below, however, it is important to keep in mind that these overall trends were qualified by the gender of the impression target and the gender of the perceiver.

Are men and women perceived as having different goals?   The short answer to this question is "yes." As shown in Table 26.1, compared to men as impression targets, women were perceived as placing relatively more importance on intimacy goals. In contrast, men were perceived as placing relatively more importance on excitement. Although there are other trends in

TABLE 26.1   Perceiving the Importance of Relationship Goals

Relationship Goal	Male Perceiver		Female Perceiver	
	Male Target	Female Target	Male Target	Female Target
Intimacy				
M	5.95	6.93	5.42	7.16
SD	1.09	.96	1.24	.89
Status				
M	6.48	6.58	6.65	5.60
SD	.90	1.11	1.30	1.63
Excitement				
M	7.50	7.20	8.06	7.27
SD	.91	.73	.57	.70
Freedom				
M	6.98	6.69	7.35	7.08
SD	1.12	1.37	1.29	.99
Self-Esteem				
M	7.22	7.63	7.31	7.61
SD	.95	1.31	1.02	.96

Note: Each relationship goal was rated on a 9-point scale with endpoints labeled 1 (*not at all important*) and 9 (*extremely important*).

Table 26.1—men were perceived to be slightly more concerned with status and freedom, whereas women were perceived as slightly more concerned with self-esteem—these tendencies fell short of statistical significance.

It is worth noting, however, that the (nonsignificant) trend for men to be more concerned with status is in the opposite direction of what we predicted. Based on our review of mating preferences (Buss & Kenrick, 1998; Sprecher et al., 1994), we expected that women would be perceived as more likely than men to enter romantic relationships with the goal of increasing their status. I will return to this finding later in this chapter.

Do Male and Female College Students Perceive Different Relationship Goals in Others?   To some extent, stereotypes about the differences between men and women depend on the gender of the perceiver. For instance, compared to male perceivers, female perceivers were especially likely to see men as guided by excitement goals: Note that the highest importance ratings in Table 26.1 ($M = 8.06$) were given by female perceivers who were rating the importance that men placed on excitement. In what is perhaps a complementary pattern, female perceivers were also somewhat more likely ($p > .06$) to think that women place greater importance on intimacy than men do. Finally, although male perceivers saw men and women as about equally concerned with status, female perceivers thought that status was more important to men than women.

The alert reader may detect a pattern in these ratings: Female perceivers seem to rely more on stereotypes that differentiate men and women. For example, although both male and female perceivers tended to see men as relatively more concerned with excitement than intimacy, this pattern was exaggerated among female perceivers. The *very* alert reader may recall, however, that we expected a somewhat different pattern of results. Our prediction was that perceivers should be more likely to rely on stereotypes when judging the relationship goals of the *opposite* gender. Female perceivers did indeed show a pattern of stereotyping men's intimacy and excitement goals. But there is no evidence that male perceivers stereotyped women in a complementary fashion. For example, male perceivers thought that men placed more importance on excitement (M = 7.50) than intimacy (M = 5.95), but they saw little difference in the importance women placed on excitement (M = 7.20) and intimacy (M = 6.93). This latter comparison of means is inconsistent with the notion that male perceivers were especially prone to stereotype women. Overall, then, the data do not support our expectation that people would be especially prone to stereotype the opposite gender.

In summary, our survey respondents believed that relationship goals concerning excitement and self-esteem were more important than those concerned with intimacy and status (goals related to freedom fell in between these extremes). The findings also supported certain stereotypes: Compared to women, men were perceived as less concerned with finding intimacy in new relationships and as more concerned with excitement. Finally, these stereotypes were especially prevalent in the minds of female perceivers.

For a number of reasons, however, these findings should be regarded with some caution. First, our results may partially reflect the kinds of items we included in our survey. For instance, although we expected that women (compared to men) would be perceived as more concerned with the status of their partners, we did not find this pattern. Our status items dealt mainly with social status, rather than economic status. If we had included items tapping interest in a partner who is financially successful, we might have found different results. Second, the abstract nature of our survey items may have affected the results. Unlike previous studies (Abbey, 1982; Haselton & Buss, 2000), we found little evidence that men were predisposed to perceive sexual (or excitement) motivation in women. If our methods had focused on more specific encounters between men and women, different results might have emerged. Finally, our findings represent the perceptions of college students at a single university. It is possible that older populations or students at other universities would predict different relationship goals. The next section examines the processes people use to infer motives for the specific actions of their partners.

ATTRIBUTING MOTIVES FOR THE SPECIFIC ACTIONS OF RELATIONSHIP PARTNERS

Imagine that you recently became romantically involved with Chris, who is an attractive, unmarried lawyer. Over the past two weekends, you have been inseparable. But this Friday, your new partner does not answer the phone in the afternoon and does not call you until after 8 p.m. As an explanation for keeping you waiting, Chris points to a heavy workload at the office. How will you interpret your partner's actions? Most likely, you will wonder about your partner's motives. Is Chris merely coping with heavy work demands? Or is Chris interested in someone else?

Perceivers make inferences about motives in order to explain a person's voluntary or intentional behavior (Malle, 2004; Reeder & Trafimow, 2005). In the remainder of this chapter, I hope to shed light on how this occurs in the context of close relationships. I will suggest that there are two basic processes at work. First, people may engage in a process of simulation whereby they mentally place themselves in their partner's shoes. This simulation process may be effortless and relatively automatic, as when we merely project our own motives onto our partner ("I am sure Chris is as motivated to succeed at work as I am"). Alternatively, the process of simulation may involve a more effortful and controlled attempt at perspective taking ("Right now Chris is probably thinking about an upcoming performance evaluation, and that's why Chris works so hard"). In addition to relying on simulation, people can use abstract, implicit knowledge when inferring their partner's motives. For example, people may employ the logic of covariation (Kelley, 1973), attempting to isolate a particular motive that covaries over time in a unique way with a partner's behavior ("I think Chris is selfish because Chris is sweet only when there is something Chris wants from me"). People also employ broader principles of explanatory coherence to integrate a variety of types of information into a coherent impression (Read & Miller, 2005; Reeder, Vonk, Ronk, Ham, & Lawrence, 2004). As described below, these various processes are not mutually exclusive and may overlap to some extent.

Simulation: Putting Ourselves in Our Partner's Shoes

People often use themselves as a departure point for making judgments about others. In reaction to a partner who works late, we may wonder, "What would motivate me to work late on Friday night?" In other words, we look to our own imagination to recreate the situation as we believe our partner might see it (Goldman, 2001). When conducting this mental simulation, we implicitly assume that our own (imagined) reaction to that situation will resemble the (actual) reaction of our partner. In fact, work on the false consensus bias (Ross, Greene, & House, 1977) suggests that there is a widespread egocentric tendency to assume that others will see the world and respond to it as we do. Kelley and Stahelski (1970), for instance, asked participants who were playing a prisoner's dilemma game to predict whether their partner was motivated to cooperate or to compete with them. They found that participants projected their own motives onto others: Competitive players were especially likely to expect a competitive partner. In the context of close relationships, individuals with intimacy goals tend to perceive their partners as also having intimacy goals, even when there is no correlation between own and partner's goals (Sanderson & Evans, 2001).

Work by Daniel Ames (2004) suggests that we tend to engage in this type of social projection when we judge that a person is similar to us. In one of his studies, Ames asked research participants to read a story about a fraternity man who met a woman at a social gathering and then asked her to leave with him. The participants were asked to judge whether the man was motivated to get to know the woman on a personal basis or whether the man was motivated to have casual sex with her. The results indicated that participants were more likely to project their own motives on the man if they felt similar to him (e.g., participants who were motivated to have casual sex tended to attribute the same motive to the character in the story). Another study by Ames (2004) indicated that participants were more likely to project their own motivation toward competition on another person if that person shared their taste in artwork (e.g., preferring Paul Klee over Wassily Kandinsky). The implication, then, is that to the extent we believe our romantic partners share our own interests and attitudes, we are likely to project our own motives onto them.

But what specific mental operations are involved when we engage in mental simulation to infer our partner's motives? There may be two routes to mental simulation that differ in their degree of cognitive effort. The first is represented by simple projection, which occurs when we make a snap judgment without expending much effort. For example, we may infer that because we look forward to watching the football playoffs on TV, our partner will have a similar level of interest. Simple projection occurs when the perceiver relies only on his or her own perspective, wants, and needs, simply assuming that the other person will see things the same way. Such assumptions are frequently misguided, of course. For this reason, simple projection often represents a failure of what we ordinarily mean by *perspective taking*.

In contrast to simple projection, the other form of mental simulation involves effortful perspective taking (Reeder & Trafimow, 2005). In this form of simulation we actively imagine our partner's situation, placing ourselves in his or her shoes in an effort to understand what he or she is thinking and feeling. The mental operations here go beyond simply projecting our own imagined reactions onto our partner. Instead, we may ponder similarities and differences between our self and our partner. If we believe our partner would have a different perspective on the situation, we are likely to adjust our inferences about his or her motivations ("Considering that Chris doesn't like beer, doesn't know the rules of football, and hates violence, I guess Chris is not looking forward to the big game").

Although I have portrayed simple projection and effortful perspective taking as separate routes to mental simulation, the two may occur in sequence (Epley, Keysar, Van Boven, & Gilovich, 2004). Thus, our first thoughts may tend toward simple projection ("Chris will love watching the game with me!"), followed by more effortful (and possibly sober) perspective taking. Indeed, current theories of perspective taking suggest that simple, egocentric interpretations often dominate people's first reactions to new information. But if given sufficient time and motivation, people can make an adjustment toward adopting the perspective of other persons (Epley et al., 2004). I will conclude this discussion by observing that mental simulation represents a highly intuitive strategy for inferring motives. But there is an alternative approach to which I turn in the next section.

Relying on Implicit Theory to Infer Motives

The study of how people infer motives can be viewed as part of a larger field concerned with questions of theory of mind (Malle & Hodges, 2005). Such questions have intrigued researchers across a variety of academic fields, including philosophy, neuroscience, and developmental psychology. Although there is widespread agreement in these fields that a theory of mind exists and that it plays an important role in social adjustment, there is less attention devoted to clarifying concrete assumptions or delineating the specific processes that are at work. Drawing on the social psychology literature, I will suggest two general processes by which we may use implicit knowledge to infer the motives of our relationship partners. The first process concerns causal analysis in terms of covariational logic, as depicted by the early attribution theorists (Jones & Davis, 1965; Kelley, 1973). The second process, which involves the search for explanatory coherence and constraint satisfaction, is represented by recent theories of dispositional inference (Read & Miller, 2005; Reeder et al., 2004). As described below, constraint satisfaction offers a plausible account of how perceivers integrate many different types of information to infer motives. For instance, it may help to explain how people integrate general stereotypes about relationship goals, partner-specific expectations, and particular behaviors in the analysis of motives.

Inferring Motives by the Logic of Covariation   Expanding on Heider's (1958) analysis, Harold Kelley (1973) suggested that people determine the causes of behavior by utilizing the logic of covariation. According to the covariation principle, perceivers are looking for a motive that seems to covary with the presence of a given behavior (Sutton & McClure, 2001). Specifically, a motive will be identified as underlying a given type of behavior to the extent that (a) the motive is present when the behavior occurs, and (b) the motive is absent when the behavior is absent. For instance, if Harry actively courts wealthy women, but habitually rejects any woman who works behind a counter, we are likely to infer that Harry is motivated to find a wealthy spouse. In this example, Harry's courting behavior covaries with the wealth of his prospective partners. In order to apply such covariational logic, however, we need to know quite a bit about Harry, observing his behavior in different situations over time.

Oftentimes we know less about a person, perhaps only knowing that a man is attracted to a particular woman (without knowing the history of the man's romantic interests). In this simplified case, Kelley's (1973) discounting principle may be invoked to infer his motivations. According to the discounting principle, we will be confident in a given motive to the extent that there are no other plausible motives. But if there is more than one plausible motive, our confidence in a given motive will decrease. For example, if Harry asks Simone to marry him, despite the fact that Simone is penniless and all his relatives are against the union, we may be confident in assuming that he loves her. But if Harry is deep in debt and Simone is heir to the Hewlett fortune, Harry's motives will be in doubt.

Using Constraint Satisfaction to Infer Motives   Recall the earlier example in which your new partner, Chris, stood you up on Friday night. Suppose further that Chris has been working closely with an attractive assistant and sometimes calls the assistant in your presence. You were hoping to patch things up with Chris over the New Year until Chris started fretting over your ailing mother, suggesting that you should spend some "quality time" alone with your mother over the holidays. There appears to be a pattern in these events, suggesting that your partner has another lover. This search for a coherent story or pattern in the evidence represents the essence of constraint satisfaction (Read & Miller, 2005; Thagard, 1996). In line with the process of constraint satisfaction, Heider (1958, p. 51) suggested that people look for a motive that reconciles apparent contradictions in a person's behavior. For instance, Chris' sudden interest in your mother "makes sense" if it paves the way for you to leave town.

Perhaps the main advantage of a constraint satisfaction model is its explanatory breadth. As shown in Figure 26.1, the influence of many different types of information can be included within the same general framework. Consistent with dual-process accounts of social information processing

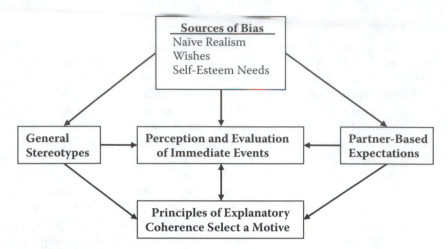

Figure 26.1   Constraint–satisfaction model of motive attribution

(Gawronski & Bodenhausen, 2006; Pryor, Reeder, Yeadon, & Hesson-McInnis, 2004; Smith & DeCoster, 2000; Strack & Deutsch, 2004), the model assumes that there is a time course to inferences about motives. The initial stage of processing is dominated by relatively automatic, associative thinking. In an earlier section of this chapter, I described the nature of general stereotypes about relationship goals (Abbey, 1982; Haselton & Buss, 2000). Such general stereotypes (e.g., the belief that women are seeking sex) may shape the perceived meaning of an observed behavior, leading a man to interpret a woman's friendly touch as signifying sexual interest. In addition to general stereotypes (which are treated as if they apply to all members of a given gender), perceivers may gradually acquire unique expectations about their individual partner (Jones & McGillis, 1976). These "partner-based" expectancies reflect the specific motives that we attribute to our partner when he or she behaves in a particular way in particular situations (e.g., "When Chris touches my arm at a party, I know Chris wants to go home").

The initial meaning that is assigned to a behavior will also be influenced by a variety of other factors, including naïve realism, wishes and desires, and self-esteem needs, as shown in the top-middle portion of Figure 26.1. *Naïve realism* refers to an egocentric tendency whereby we fail to recognize that others may have a different perspective on events (Reeder, Pryor, Wohl, & Griswell, 2005; Ross & Ward, 1996). For example, if a man is thinking about sex when a woman says, "It's late—I think I'll go back to my place," he may interpret the remark as an invitation to accompany her home, whereas she may intend it as a graceful exit from the interaction (Abbey, 1982). The influence of naïve realism has a cognitive flavor, but biases of a more motivational nature may also be at work. For example, a person's wishes and desires may contribute to the tendency to misread motives. Heider (1958, p. 172) implied that when we interpret another person's motives, we will gravitate toward a motive that (a) fits our own wishes and (b) fits the data. Thus, if a man *wants* sex, he may be predisposed to pick up on or misinterpret cues that point in that direction. Finally, our self-esteem needs are relevant here as well (Crocker & Park, 2004). To fulfill his need for self-esteem, a man who is invested in seeing himself as "god's gift to women" may interpret even the most ambiguous behavior as a sign that a woman is interested in him.

The evaluation of behavior plays an important role in this model. As part of identifying another person's behavior, we tend to react to it in a positive or negative manner (Srull & Wyer, 1989; Zajonc, 1980). This evaluation may occur even before we have time to consciously reflect on what we are seeing or hearing (Gawronski & Bodenhausen, 2006; Zajonc, 1980). As shown in Figure 26.1, general stereotypes and partner-based expectations can play a role here (Srull & Wyer, 1989). For example, people who hold positive expectancies about their relationship partners will be predisposed to interpret their partner's actions in a positive light. In contrast, people with negative expectancies of their partners may see the same behavior in a darker light (Bradbury & Fincham, 1990).

In summary, a variety of factors shape the perception and evaluation of immediate events related to our partner's behavior (see also Knee & Bush, this volume). In Figure 26.1, these initial reactions then contribute to inferences about motives. Are inferences about motives automatic, or is deliberative processing required? The answer will depend on the circumstances. When there is not a lot of information to be integrated, inferences of motives may occur quickly and relatively automatically (Kawada, Oettingen, Gollwitzer, & Bargh, 2004). In contrast, when a person actively considers how the various behaviors of his or her partner fit together to explain a particular action that occurred in a particular social context, there is more conscious deliberation.

When different sources of information are integrated to arrive at a coherent inference of motives, the model assumes that principles of explanatory coherence play a role (Read & Miller, 2005; Thagard, 1996). For example, perceivers are likely to search for a motive with *breadth* and *simplicity* (i.e., a single motive that explains multiple behaviors). The model assumes that evaluative consistency is of overriding importance in this search (Srull & Wyer, 1989). As suggested earlier, a person who holds a negative view of a prospective partner is likely to interpret that person's ambiguous behaviors as motivated by selfishness or other negative motives. In this light, even apparently positive behaviors may be seen as serving a darker motive. For example, if a woman's girlfriends have told her that a man is a "player," she is likely to interpret his offer to buy her a drink as a thinly veiled act of seduction. Sometimes perceivers see multiple motives at work in a prospective partner's behavior. In such cases, there is a tendency for these motives to share a common evaluative tone (Reeder et al., 2004). For instance, a man at a bar who offers to buy drinks for all of a woman's friends may be perceived as motivated to show off his wealth *and* to seduce, both of which may be perceived negatively.

In concluding this description of how specific motives are inferred, I want to emphasize that the various processes discussed here are not mutually exclusive. To begin with, it can be quite difficult to distinguish between psychological processes of simulation versus processes that involve implicit knowledge (Perner & Kühberger, 2005). For example, before you ask your partner to play tennis with you, you might employ abstract knowledge (such as a partner-based expectation about your partner's enjoyment of sports) to simulate in your mind how your partner will react to your request. In addition, although I have discussed covariation logic separately from the process of constraint satisfaction, a constraint satisfaction model is capable of incorporating covariation principles such as discounting (Read & Miller, 1993). Given such overlap at the level of process, it is apparent that a wide variety of factors contribute to inferences of motive.

CONCLUSION

The conventional wisdom in the social perception literature is that perceivers are primarily concerned with abstract causal attribution and trait inferences (Gilbert, 1998). Accordingly, numerous theories have been offered to explain how perceivers make attributions to abstract situational versus personal causes. Not surprisingly, a variety of attempts have been made to apply this literature on causal attribution to the domain of close relationships (Bradbury & Fincham, 1990; Miller & Rempel, 2004). In contrast to a focus on abstract causal reasoning, the present chapter is unique in focusing exclusively on how people infer specific goals and motives within a relationship.

There are a variety of reasons why people are interested in each others' goals and motives at the beginning of a relationship, including wanting to better understand, predict, remember, and control their partner's behavior. Surprisingly, little research has directly examined the perception of goals and motives in this context (although there are extensive literatures on gender stereotypes, mating strategies, and partner ideals). This chapter presented some of the first empirical data to systematically explore the perception of relationship goals. The results suggest that college students expect that others are primarily seeking excitement and higher levels of self-esteem from their relationships. Certain stereotypes were also supported (e.g., compared to women, men are seen as caring more about excitement than intimacy).

The major theoretical contribution of this chapter concerns the perception of specific motives in a relationship context. Two basic processes are relevant here: simulation and reliance on implicit knowledge. The process of simulation may involve a simple, relatively effortless attempt at projecting our own motives onto others, or it may involve a more intensive process of imagining the world from the standpoint of our partner. As an alternative to simulation (or in addition to it), people can use their abstract knowledge to infer motives. In doing so, people employ principles of covariation logic and explanatory coherence. Principles of explanatory coherence may be of particular interest to close relationship researchers. The theoretical model presented in this chapter represents a step toward explaining how diverse sources of perceiver bias (such as naïve realism, wishes, and self-esteem needs), stereotypes, and expectations about particular partners are combined when we infer motives.

Despite the theoretical progress noted above, much remains to be learned about how people infer goals and motives in beginning relationships. One promising research approach is to ask questions about the process as it typically unfolds over time. For example, at what point in the relationship do partners typically shift from simple inference strategies that rely on projection and general stereotypes to more complex strategies that rely on effortful perspective taking and unique partner-based expectations? In other words, when do people really try to get "inside their partner's head"? Another promising research approach is to identify the situational variables (e.g., stressful circumstances or sexual excitement) that are related to the use of different inference strategies. Finally, research might investigate individual difference variables (e.g., attachment styles) that predict various patterns of motive attribution. By shedding light on how romantic partners infer goals and motives, these research approaches hold the promise of explaining how partners come to understand each other at a very basic level.

REFERENCES

Abbey, A. (1982). Sex differences in attributions for friendly behavior: Do males misperceive females friendliness? *Journal of Personality and Social Psychology, 42,* 830–838.

Abbey, A. (1987). Misperceptions of friendly behavior as sexual interest: A survey of naturally occurring incidents. *Psychology of Women Quarterly, 11,* 173–194.

Ames, D. R. (2004). Inside the mind reader's tool kit: Projection and stereotyping in mental state inference. *Journal of Personality and Social Psychology, 87,* 340–353.

Baron-Cohen, S., & Belmonte, M. K. (2005). Autism: A window onto the development of the social and analytic brain. *Annual Review of Neuroscience, 28,* 109–126.

Berger, C. R. (1993). Goals, plans, and mutual understanding in relationships. In S. Duck (Ed.), *Individuals in relationships* (pp. 30–59). Newbury Park, CA: Sage.

Bolzendahl, C. I., & Myers, D. J. (2004). Feminist attitudes and support for gender equality: Opinion change in women and men. *Social Forces, 83,* 759–789.

Bradbury, T. N., & Fincham, F. D. (1990). Attributions in marriage: Review and critique. *Psychological Bulletin, 107,* 3–33.

Buss, D. M., & Kenrick, D. T. (1998). Evolutionary social psychology. In D. T. Gilbert, S. T. Fiske, & G. Lindzey (Eds.), *The handbook of social psychology* (4th ed., Vol. 2, pp. 982–1026). Boston: McGraw-Hill.

Cameron, J. (Director). (1997). *Titanic* [Motion picture]. United States: Twentieth-Century Fox.

Committee on Government Reform. (2004). *The content of federally funded abstinence-only educational programs* (Report prepared for U.S. Representative Henry A. Waxman, D-CA). Retrieved December 27, 2007, from http://oversight.house.gov/documents/20041201102153-50247.pdf

Cosmides, L. (1989). The logic of social exchange: Has natural selection shaped how humans reason? Studies with the Watson selection task. *Cognition, 31,* 187–276.

Crocker, J., & Park, L. E. (2004). The costly pursuit of self-esteem. *Psychological Bulletin, 130,* 392–414.

Dennet, D. C. (1993). Three kinds of intentional psychology. In S. M. Christensen & D. R. Turner (Eds.), *Folk psychology and the philosophy of mind* (pp. 121–143). Hillsdale, NJ: Lawrence Erlbaum.

Epley, N., Keysar, B., Van Boven, L., & Gilovich, T. (2004). Perspective taking as egocentric anchoring and adjustment. *Journal of Personality and Social Psychology, 87,* 327–339.

Falk, E., & Kenski, K. (2006). Issue saliency and gender stereotypes: Support for women as presidents in times of war and terrorism. *Social Science Quarterly, 87,* 1–18.

Fletcher, G. J. O., Simpson, J. A., Thomas, G., & Giles, L. (1999). Ideals in intimate relationships. *Journal of Personality and Social Psychology, 76*, 72–89.

Gangestad, S. W., & Simpson, J. A. (2000). The evolution of human mating: Trade-offs and strategic pluralism. *Behavioral and Brain Sciences, 23*, 573–587.

Gawronski, B., & Bodenhausen, G. V. (2006). Associative and propositional processes in evaluation: An integrative review of implicit and explicit attitude change. *Psychological Bulletin, 132*, 692–731.

Gilbert, D. T. (1998). Ordinary personology. In D. T. Gilbert, S. T. Fiske, & G. Lindzey (Eds.), *The handbook of social psychology* (4th ed., Vol. 2, pp. 89–150). Boston: McGraw-Hill.

Goldman, A. I. (2001). Desire, intention, and the simulation theory. In B. F. Malle, L. J. Moses, & D. A. Baldwin (Eds.), *Intentions and intentionality: Foundations of social cognition* (pp. 207–224). Cambridge, MA: MIT Press.

Harvey, J. H., & Omarzu, J. (1999). *Minding the close relationship: A theory of relationship enhancement.* New York: Cambridge University Press.

Haselton, M. G., & Buss, D. M. (2000). Error management theory: A new perspective on biases in cross-sex mind reading. *Journal of Personality and Social Psychology, 78*, 81–91.

Heider, F. (1958). *The psychology of interpersonal relations.* New York: Wiley.

Heider, F., & Simmel, M. (1944). An experimental study of apparent behavior. *American Journal of Psychology, 57*, 243–259.

Ickes, W., Simpson, J. A., & Oriña, M. (2005). Empathic accuracy and inaccuracy in close relationships. In B. F. Malle & S. D. Hodges (Eds.), *Other minds: How humans bridge the divide between self and others* (pp. 310–322). New York: Guilford Press.

Jones, E. E., & Davis, K. E. (1965). From acts to dispositions: The attribution process in person perception. In L. Berkowitz (Ed.), *Advances in experimental social psychology* (Vol. 2, pp. 219–266). New York: Academic Press.

Jones, E. E., & McGillis, D. (1976). Correspondent inferences and the attribution cube: A comparative appraisal. In J. H. Harvey, W. J. Ickes, & R. F. Kidd (Eds.), *New directions in attribution research* (Vol. 1, pp. 389–420). Hillsdale, NJ: Lawrence Erlbaum.

Karney, B. R., McNulty, J. K., & Bradbury, T. N. (2003). Cognition and development of close relationships. In G. J. O. Fletcher & M. Clash (Eds.), *Interpersonal processes* (pp. 32–59). Malden, MA: Blackwell.

Kawada, C. L. K., Oettingen, G., Gollwitzer, P. M., & Bargh, J. A. (2004). The projection of implicit and explicit goals. *Journal of Personality and Social Psychology, 86*, 545–559.

Kelley, H. H. (1973). The process of causal attribution. *American Psychologist, 28*, 107–128.

Kelley, H. H., & Stahelski, A. J. (1970). The inference of intention from moves in the prisoner's dilemma game. *Journal of Experimental Social Psychology, 6*, 401–419.

Kenrick, D. T., Sadalla, E. K., Groth, G., & Trost, M. R. (1990). Evolution, traits, and stages of human courtship: Qualifying the parental investment model. *Journal of Personality, 58*, 97–116.

Laner, M. R. (1977). Permanent partner priorities: Gay and straight. *Journal of Homosexuality, 3*, 21–39.

Malle, B. F. (2004). *How the mind explains behavior: Folk explanations, meaning, and social interaction.* Cambridge, MA: MIT Press.

Malle, B. F., & Hodges, S. D. (2005). *Other minds: How humans bridge the divide between self and others.* New York: Guilford Press.

Miller, P. J. E., & Rempel, J. K. (2004). Trust and partner-enhancing attributions in close relationships. *Personality and Social Psychology Bulletin, 30*, 695–705.

Perner, J., & Kühberger, A. (2005). Mental simulation: Royal road to other minds? In B. F. Malle & S. D. Hodges (Eds.), *Other minds: How humans bridge the divide between self and others* (pp. 174–189). New York: Guilford Press.

Pryor, J. B., Reeder, G. D., Yeadon, C., & Hesson-McInnis, M. (2004). A dual-process model of reactions to perceived stigma. *Journal of Personality and Social Psychology, 87*, 436–452.

Read, S. J., & Miller, L. C. (1993). Rapist or "regular guy": Explanatory coherence in the construction of mental models about others. *Personality and Social Psychology Bulletin, 19*, 526–541.

Read, S. J., & Miller, L. C. (2005). Explanatory coherence and goal-based knowledge structures in making dispositional inferences. In B. F. Malle & S. D. Hodges (Eds.), *Other minds: How humans bridge the divide between self and others* (pp. 124–157). New York: Guilford Press.

Reeder, G. D., Pryor, J. B., Wohl, M. J. A., & Griswell, M. L. (2005). On attributing negative motives to others who disagree with our opinions. *Personality and Social Psychology Bulletin, 31*, 1498–1510.

Reeder, G. D., & Sprecher, S. (2007). Stereotypes about the importance of relationship goals held by male and female college students. Unpublished data.

Reeder, G. D., & Trafimow, D. (2005). Attributing motives to other people. In B. F. Malle & S. D. Hodges (Eds.), *Other minds: How humans bridge the divide between self and others* (pp. 106–123). New York: Guilford Press.

Reeder, G. D., Vonk, R., Ronk, M. J., Ham, J., & Lawrence, M. (2004). Dispositional attribution: Multiple inferences about motive-related traits. *Journal of Personality and Social Psychology, 86*, 530–544.

Rosenkrantz, P. S., Vogel, D. M., Bee, H., Broverman, F. E., & Broverman, D. M. (1968). Sex-role stereotypes and self-concepts in college students. *Journal of Consulting and Clinical Psychology, 32*, 287–295.

Ross, L., Greene, D., & House, P. (1977). The false consensus phenomenon: An attributional bias in self-perception and social perception processes. *Journal of Experimental Social Psychology, 13*, 279–301.

Ross, L., & Ward, A. (1996). Naïve realism in everyday life: Implications for social conflict and misunderstanding. In E. S. Reed, E. Turiel, & T. Brown (Eds.), *Values and knowledge* (pp. 103–135). Mahwah, NJ: Lawrence Erlbaum.

Sabatelli, R. M. (1984). The marital comparison level index: A measure for assessing outcomes relative to expectations. *Journal of Marriage and the Family, 46*, 651–662.

Sanderson, C. A., & Evans, S. M. (2001). Seeing one's partner through intimacy-colored glasses: An examination of the processes underlying the intimacy goals–relationship satisfaction link. *Personality and Social Psychology Bulletin, 27*, 463–473.

Schank, R. C., & Abelson, R. P. (1977). *Scripts, plans, goals, and understanding: An inquiry into human knowledge structures*. Hillsdale, NJ: Lawrence Erlbaum.

Sedikides, C., Oliver, M. B., & Campbell, W. (1994). Perceived benefits and costs of romantic relationships for women and men: Implications for exchange theory. *Personal Relationships, 1*, 5–21.

Smith, E. R., & DeCoster, J. (2000). Dual-process models in social and cognitive psychology: Conceptual integration and links to underlying memory systems. *Personality and Social Psychology Review, 4*, 108–131.

Sprecher, S., Sullivan, Q., & Hatfield, E. (1994). Mate selection preferences: Gender differences examined in a national sample. *Journal of Personality and Social Psychology, 66*, 1074–1080.

Srull, T. K., & Wyer, R. S. (1989). Person memory and judgment. *Psychological Review, 96*, 58–83.

Strack, F., & Deutsch, R. (2004). Reflective and impulsive determinants of social behavior. *Personality and Social Psychology Review, 8*, 220–247.

Sutton, R. M., & McClure, J. (2001). Covariational influences on goal-based explanation: An integrative model. *Journal of Personality and Social Psychology, 80*, 222–236.

Thagard, P. (1996). *Mind: Introduction to cognitive science*. Cambridge, MA: MIT Press.

Wilensky, R. (1983). *Planning and understanding*. Reading, MA: Addison-Wesley.

Winch, R. F. (1963). *The modern family*. New York: Holt, Rinehart & Winston.

Zajonc, R. B. (1980). Feeling and thinking: Preferences need no inferences. *American Psychologist, 35*, 151–175.

Zwaan, R. A., & Radvansky, G. A. (1998). Situation models in language comprehension and memory. *Psychological Bulletin, 123*, 163–185.

Section *VII*

Commentary

27

Ending the Beginning of Relationships

DANIEL PERLMAN

Friendship improves happiness and abates misery, by the doubling of our joy and the dividing of our grief.

Cicero

As a considerable body of evidence indicates, romantic and other forms of relationships (e.g., family ties and friendships) generally enhance our lives (Perlman, 2007). Yet to get these benefits, we have to initiate relationships. This book is about relationships' beginning. My task is to bring the book to an end. I will do so by taking the chapters in the volume as a foundation for a commentary. My overall goal is to offer my perspective on what the contributors to the volume have accomplished. In part I will be commenting on the chapters in the book, and in part I will be commenting on relationship initiation as an area of research. I will highlight recurrent themes in the volume itself; describe where current relationship initiation research fits in the broader panorama of relationship scholarship; discuss how recent endeavors advance knowledge; and note a few things the prior chapters do not. My reflections are organized into the following major parts: describing the phenomenon of relationship initiation, placing research on relationship initiation into a historical context, summarizing key knowledge gained, and considering the future directions of work on relationship initiation.

DESCRIBING THE PHENOMENA

What Exactly Do We Mean by Relationship Initiation?

Often in books on specific aspects of relationships, many of the contributors offer their definitions of the focal phenomenon. For example, in this volume, the Hendricks give the following definition: "For our purposes in this chapter, relationship initiation is the formative process that occurs as two people begin forging a romantic relationship, though we realize that initiation occurs also with friendships, relationships with newly acquired in-laws, and the like" (see Chapter 17). Other terms do get defined or discussed (e.g., Aron et al. define *falling in love*; Paul, Wenzel, & Harvey define *hookups*; and Graziano & Bruce discuss deficiencies in earlier conceptualizations of interpersonal attraction).* The Hendricks, however, are unusual among contributors to this collection; relatively few other authors explicitly define the concept of relationship initiation.

One can, however, infer what authors mean by the beginning of relationships from the phenomena they cover in their chapters. In a generic sense, the authors are concerned with the start of

---

* Throughout this chapter, all citations without dates refer to chapters in this volume.

relationships. Nonetheless, they differ in what aspects of the beginning of relationships are prominent in their writing. For example, what authors are discussing as the beginning of relationships can be placed along a time line. For some authors (e.g., Cunningham & Barbee), key concerns are the extent to which people attend to one another, how they initially engage in nonverbal behavior, and the opening lines they use to initiate conversations. Eastwick and Finkel examine speed-dating situations involving 3 to 8-minute interactions. Many attraction scholars (e.g., Aron, Melinat, Aron, Vallone, & Bator, 1997) have had participants engage in get-acquainted exercises lasting perhaps 45 minutes or an hour. Moving slightly further along on the time dimensions, Paul et al. describe hook-ups as "short-lived and intense sexual exploration apart from emotional connection that rarely builds beyond one or two 'steamy' meetings" (see Chapter 19). The Hendricks view relationship initiation as "the first few months of the life of the relationship" (see Chapter 17). Attachment theorists (e.g., Hazan & Zeifman, 1994) have argued that it takes 2 years for all the attachment functions to become associated with a new partner. Others might consider the premarital courtship period (lasting 2.33 years on average in Huston's (1982) study mentioned by Bredow, Cate, & Huston) as the beginning of marital relationships. Extending the duration possibly even longer are authors (Creasey & Jarvis; Guerrero & Mongeau) who equate beginnings with the transitions of existing relationships of infinite duration to new states.

Although some might consider it splitting hairs, I would distinguish between initial interactions and initiating relationships. Traditional definitions of relationships (Hinde, 1979) stress that relationships involve a series of interactions over time rather than just single contacts. Thus, initial interactions are preludes to relationships but often fail to lead to relationships. Nonetheless, as they have the possibility of resulting in relationships they are important to understanding the beginning of relationships. A key question is which initial interactions lead further and which are terminal.

Beginnings in Various Relationships

Chapters in this volume deal with the beginnings of a reasonably wide range of relationships, including for example friendships, dating relations, sexual or mating relations, marriages, intergenerational family relationships (i.e., grandparents, parents, and children and grandchildren), caregivers, coworkers, mentors, relationships after loss, and therapeutic relationships. The authors in this volume, however, are most concerned with the beginnings of sexual and romantic relationships and friendships. Along with family relations, these are among our most central and important relationships. Nonetheless, there are many other forms of relationships whose beginnings are worth understanding (see VanLear, Koerner, & Allen, 2006, for an indication of the numerous ways relationships can be categorized). There may be commonalities across relationships in how they start, but there are also clearly differences. For example, Fine, Coffelt, and Olson underscore the unique role that children play in the formation of postmarital (as opposed to other types of) romances. Similarly, for gays and lesbians, it is crucial to establish the sexual orientation of potential partners (Custer, Holmberg, Blair, & Orbuch).

Beginnings as a Phase or Stage

The beginnings of a relationship imply there is something after that. Maintenance and deterioration are two frequently mentioned aspects of relationships that follow beginnings. At their most generic level, one could think of beginnings as simply something demarked by their time of occurrence without implying much else. Some authors appear to do this.

The Hendricks talk of relationship initiation as a process. Other contributors (e.g., Afifi & Lucas; Bredow et al.; Guerrero & Mongeau) use the notion of stages. The beginning of a relationship could be considered a stage in itself, although it is also possible to think about smaller stages within a larger phase of beginning a relationship, as do Cunningham and Barbee. This same approach is also apparent, albeit less prominently, in Guerrero and Mongeau's summary of Knapp and Vangelisti's

(2005) model, and Sprecher, Schwartz, Harvey, and Hatfield's presentation of Levinger's (1974; see also Levinger & Snoek, 1972) three-level model. When considering stages, I think of discrete phases, each with interrelated, unique qualities; having boundaries between them; and typically sequentially ordered, with each successive stage being not simply a shift along a dimension but also a change between one set of properties and another. A couple of questions for stage theorists are "When does a stage end?" and "How do people go from one stage to the next?"

Verifying the assumption of invariant sequences of progression has been a challenge to classical stage theories. Instead, as Guerrero and Mongeau note, the early portions of a relationship can often be characterized by a pattern of highs and lows more typical of turning point models. Some of the specific stage models identified by authors do have reasonably clear ending points, although given the range of phenomena considered under the rubric of beginnings, there does not appear to be a commonly agreed-on point at which relationship beginnings end.

The Prevalence of Relationship Initiation

In opening their chapter, Afifi and Lucas make an incidental remark on which I wish to embellish: "[W]e typically start with very little information about the thousands of people with whom we interact over a lifetime. Ultimately, we make decisions to pursue close relationships with a tiny percentage of those people." One wonders, "What exactly is the prevalence of forming new relationships?" and "What can be said about the rates of this phenomenon?" Aron et al. cite a 10-week longitudinal study in which a quarter of first- and second-year university students entered new romantic relationships, but none of the authors in this volume fully address the topic of prevalence.

At least four parameters influence estimations of the number of new relationships people form: the number of relationships we have, the length those relationships last, the amount of turnover in our networks, and the segment of our network being discussed. Some evidence is available on each of those parameters. Apropos of the size of our networks, average North American adults have perhaps 400 individuals with whom they interact superficially but only roughly 20 people with whom they engage in helpful exchanges (e.g., discussing personal matters, giving advice, lending money, and watching the house), and even fewer close network members (e.g., approximately a half dozen) (Milardo, 1992). In terms of sexually intimate relationships, an ABC poll of 1,501 American adults (Langer, Arnedt, & Sussman, 2004) found the number of their lifetime partners to be small (5.5 partners averaged across men and women).

Once we form relationships, they frequently endure. For example, using representative samples of northern Californians and older residents from the Netherlands, de Jong Gierveld and Perlman (2006) found that northern Californians had known their key network members for an average of 9 years. Adults 55 and older had substantially longer lasting relationships on average (18 years in California, and 28.5 in the Netherlands). Marriages uninterrupted by divorce now last nearly 50 years on average (Phillips, 1988).

A few longitudinal surveys have investigated the extent of stability in social networks (see Suitor, Wellman, & Morgan, 1997). Such studies suggest that even in samples selected in light of their undergoing life transitions, about two thirds of network members are named again at the end of one year. In a longer study of a general cross-section of Toronto residents, Wellman, Wong, Tindall, and Nazer (1997) found, "On the average, three or four of their network members had ceased being intimates over 10 years, a change of only one intimate every 2 or 3 years" (p. 32). Furthermore, the longitudinal studies consistently show that so-called strong ties persist longer than weak ones (Suitor et al., 1997). Thus, kin ties persist longer than friendships, which in turn generally persist longer than neighborly relations.

To sum up on prevalence, I resonate to Afifi and Lucas' comment. The number of intimate relationships we initiate is probably small, although there is likely more initiation in the peripheral sectors of our networks and at times of transition (e.g., beginning university). Furthermore, we have many initial interactions that do not result in relationship initiations. In any case, more elaborate mapping of the incidence of relationship initiation would be useful.

HISTORICAL ROOTS OF CONTEMPORARY
RESEARCH ON RELATIONSHIP INITIATION

One useful way of putting recent work on relationship initiation in perspective is via historical comparison. Several chapter authors reference historical changes in their area of work. Graziano and Bruce have an especially nice treatment. My remarks will overlap some with points made by others, but I wish to take a slightly different starting point than some authors and look at the area as a whole rather than at specific streams of research within it. Two challenges in doing this are that the study of close relationships has roots in several disciplines and the tale of the area's development undoubtedly reflects the intellectual background from which one views it. Two seminal roots of contemporary research on relationship initiation are the work on dating and courtship and the interest in interpersonal attraction.

The Study of Relationship Development

Surra, Gray, Boettcher, Cottle, and West (2006) provided a 50-year retrospective on the courtship literature. Analysis of the citations in a review of the courtship literature during the 1960s shows that work on courtship during that era was primarily associated with the field of family studies, followed by sociology and psychology (Moss, Apolonio, & Jensen, 1971). Some of the most noted researchers in this tradition recruited samples of already engaged or seriously involved couples, and followed them over time. A main emphasis in early research was relationship development and change especially with an emphasis on progress toward marriage. Steady dating was seen as a significant step along the way. Love and empathy were identified as two major forces in relationship development. Early researchers were concerned with such topics as descriptive information about dating (e.g., at what age do youth begin dating), Waller's (1937) rating and dating complex (students' criteria for the ideal characteristics of a dating partner), residential propinquity, the role of similarity (e.g., both homogamy and the hypothesis that opposites or complementary partners attract), marriage markets (e.g., effects of sex ratios and economic opportunities on marriages rates and timing), and the reactions of parents to their children's dating and dating partners.

In the period from the late 1950s until the mid-1970s, some noteworthy illustrative contributions included Winch's (1958) theory of complementary needs, Reiss' (1960) wheel theory of love, Murstein's (1976) stimulus–value–role theory, and Lewis' (1972) model for the development of dyadic relations. In very abbreviated form, Winch believed that individuals with complementary needs (e.g., dominance and submission) attract. Reiss conceptualized love as a cyclical process of rapport, revelation, mutual dependency, and need fulfillment. Murstein believed that progress toward intimacy is determined first by stimulus factors (e.g., appearance), then the values of the partners, and finally how well their behavioral patterns fit together. Robert Lewis' developmental framework for the analysis of premarital dyadic formation consisted of the time-ordered interrelating of six dyadic processes: the achieving of perceptions of similarity, dyadic rapport, self-disclosure, role taking, role fit, and dyadic crystallization.

The Study of Interpersonal Attraction

Turning to interpersonal attraction, it was an important focus of social psychological research in the 1960s and 1970s. In earlier publications (Duck & Perlman, 1985; Perlman & Duck, 2006), Steve Duck and I have characterized this epoch in the history of research on close relationships. Donn Byrne was one of the preeminent scholars of that time. He was concerned with attitude similarity and liking. In his first of many publications on this topic, which I will use as a prototypical example of the era, he began by obtaining data from 64 University of Texas students on their attitudes toward issues of the day (Byrne, 1961). Two weeks later he falsely informed them that the attitude scales had been given as part of a study in interpersonal prediction. He then asked the students to look at another person's answers in order to determine how much they could learn about that person from this information alone. The questionnaires students received at this time were actually made up by Byrne so that half the students received attitude scales filled out "exactly" the same as theirs, and the other half received scales exactly opposite to theirs. The dependent variable was a measure of how much the students liked the hypothetical stranger. Students in the attitude-similar condition gave more favorable ratings of the target person than did students in the attitude-dissimilar condition. Using Donn Byrne's work on attitude similarity and attraction as an exemplar (e.g., Byrne, 1961), we identified several characteristics of work during this era.

- Byrne was a North American scholar, publishing his work primarily for an audience of social psychologists.
- His article was three pages long, reported just one study (with a total of four conditions rather than just the two we have described), and contained 11 references.
- His scientific goal was causal inference.
- Byrne performed an experiment in which he manipulated his independent variable, attitude similarity, and randomly assigned subjects to experimental conditions. Thus, he was able to have greater confidence in his causal inferences.
- The experiment involved a fallacious cover story.
- His subjects were introductory psychology students who were presumably middle-class Whites.
- The study involved strangers who never actually interacted.
- Interpersonal attraction was the dependent variable.
- Byrne was concerned with one person's, the subject's, attraction.
- Byrne used between-group t tests to perform his statistical analyses.
- Byrne was concerned only with the outcome of how well subjects liked the stranger, not with the processes involved in their becoming friendly.
- Byrne offered a reinforcement explanation for why attitude similarity was associated with liking (in opposition to cognitive consistency views that were also in vogue at the time).
- Byrne was not concerned with such variables as the subjects' other relationships or the subjects' stage in the life cycle. He did not consider stages of relationships. He neither examined sex differences nor discussed practical implications of his findings, although in his later work (e.g., Byrne, 1971) he did both.

As manifest in the current volume and elsewhere, in the 45+ years since the publication of Byrne's (1961) article, the study of close relationships has changed substantially. I will first address these changes in terms of the changing place of relationship research in various fields of study, and then look at a key aspect of how the courtship and relationship development literature has evolved (i.e., toward universal principles). Finally, I will rely heavily on research in the interpersonal attraction tradition as a comparison point for describing what I see the chapters in this volume suggesting as changes in research methods, theories, and findings.

THE CHANGING PLACE OF RELATIONSHIP INITIATION RESEARCH IN FIELDS OF STUDY

One of the first points of difference is that rather than researching close relationships within various disciplines (e.g., psychology, sociology, and family studies), researchers on the topic now have their own journals (*Personal Relationships* and the *Journal of Social and Personal Relationships*) and organization (the International Association for Relationship Research). As these organizational structures have emerged, communication scholars have become important contributors to the understanding of close relationships. Several chapters in the present volume nicely testify to this trend (e.g., Afifi & Lucas; Cupach & Spitzberg; Guerrero & Mongeau; Knobloch & Miller; Metts & Mikucki).

In the late 1960s and early 1970s, what can be considered the first psychological text on close relationships (Berscheid & Walster [now Hatfield], 1969) and a key annual review article (Byrne & Griffitt, 1973) on the psychological study of relationships both selected "Interpersonal Attraction" as their title. Although there were other topics of importance in the 1960s, interpersonal attraction was the central question of the era. In proposing the present volume, the editors argued that there was no other recent comprehensive collection on the beginnings of relationships. Although the questions of attraction and relationship initiation are important today, they do not have the centrality in research that interpersonal attraction had earlier.

SHIFT OF COURTSHIP RESEARCH TOWARD UNIVERSAL TOPICS

Surra et al. (2006) saw sustained interest in several topics specific to dating and courtship, but they depicted a major shift in focus "away from the study of specific types of relationships and toward dimensions of relationships that apply to close relationships generally" (p. 115). In other words, there has been a growing emphasis on basic processes (e.g., trust, accommodation, commitment, power, and forgiveness) that apply to various types of relationships. In the most recent years for which they had data (1999 to 2000), Surra et al. (2006) found this process approach manifest in just over half of all articles. They believed this serves to bring researchers from different disciplines together (e.g., with psychologists benefiting from a stronger sociocultural perspective and sociologists gaining from a better appreciation of relationships not defined by roles). Surra et al. (2006) contended that the emphasis on courtship as a continuum leading to marriage has declined in recent years.

From Surra et al.'s (2006) perspective, one should find three trends in the present volume: (a) concern with general processes, (b) evidence of scholars from different disciplines being influenced by one another, and (c) less concern about courtship leading to marriage. Some evidence for all three is present:

A. Within this volume, there are concerns with specific forms of relationships, yet several illustrations of the trend toward universal processes can be seen (e.g., Metts & Mikucki's concern with emotions). This is especially true in theoretical approaches. Creasey and Jarvis demonstrate how attachment processes including generalized attachment representations apply to a range of relationships. Interdependency (Arriaga, Agnew, Capezza, & Lehmiller), uncertainty (Afifi & Lucas; Knobloch & Miller), and attribution (Reeder) are all general processes that can be applied to the development of intimate relationships but have wider applications.

B. That the editors brought together scholars from multiple disciplines itself signifies a form of interdisciplinary influence. Undoubtedly authors still draw more heavily on their own disciplinary training in their work, yet clear examples of how authors combine intellectual traditions are manifest at several points in the volume (for example, the POV [point of view] uncertainty analysis draws heavily on social exchange ideas, discussed in Knobloch & Miller; in discussing the role of emotion in the initiation of romantic relationships, Metts & Mikucki draw heavily on both the communication and psychological literatures; and the Hendricks' work on love styles has its roots in the insights of a sociologist, John Lee, 1973).

C. As Surra et al. (2006) would have expected, there is relatively little focus on courtship as a step toward marriage. Evolutionary theorists in this volume (Schmitt) are concerned with mating for reproductive purposes rather than marriage per se. Several authors limit their examination of initiation of relationships to earlier phases of coupling (Cunningham & Barbee; Eastwick & Finkel; McKenna) or are vague regarding the final form intimate relationships will take.

In reflecting on 50 years of research on courtship, Surra et al. (2006, p. 114) observed that the theme of courtship development itself "has faded" in the scholarly literature. Perhaps scholars' reduced concern with courtship leading to marriage, their increased emphasis on universal processes, and demographic trends toward more cohabitation as opposed to marriage are all shaping the focus and framing of current research. In any case, the fact that even a volume on relationship initiation has no chapter specifically devoted to dating or courtship per se is consistent with Surra et al.'s (2006, p. 114) view of the declining prominence of courtship development.

SHIFTING METHODOLOGIES

A prominent feature of the early research on interpersonal attraction was its reliance on experimental methods involving student "subjects" participating in laboratory tasks. Although some experiments are still conducted, the grip of the experimental approach has clearly been broken. Research designs, sampling, means of data collection, and statistical procedures all keep changing. Of 484 studies of dating and mating coded by Surra, Gray, Boettcher, Cottle, and Jarvis (2002), only 4 involved experiments. Perhaps other areas of relationship initiation research have more than 1% of studies that are experiments, but clearly the percentage does not reach the level of social psychology in the 1960s, when experiments dominated. Contemporary relationship researchers use roughly equal percentages of student and nonstudent samples (de Jong Gierveld, 1995), rely heavily on self-reports (questionnaires, interviews, and/or diaries; de Jong Gierveld; Surra et al., 2002), and usually collect data from individuals but also collect information from dyads moderately often (Kashy, Campbell, & Harris, 2006; Surra et al., 2002). Longitudinal and observational methods are also reasonably common.

Since the 1980s, substantial statistical advances (see Kashy et al., 2006) have taken place in dealing with dyadic (yoked) data; partitioning variance into group, dyad, and individual effects (the social relations model used by Eastwick & Finkel); and using multivariate techniques (e.g., structural equation modeling). Meta-analyses (statistical procedures for combining the results of multiple studies) have become common (as reported in several chapters: Arriaga et al.; Creasey & Jarvis; Cupach & Spitzberg; Derlega, Winstead, & Greene; Eastwick & Finkel; Guerrero & Mongeau; McKenna; Metts & Mikucki; Paul et al.; Wenzel & Kashdan). As Graziano and Bruce note, statistical advances also allow researchers to be concerned with both mediation (intervening processes between antecedents and outcomes) and moderation (third variables whose levels alter associations between variables a and b).

In place of experiments and the analysis of variance techniques used in the 1960s and 1970s, contemporary relationship researchers use causal modeling techniques to hopefully make stronger causal inferences from correlational data. Overall, today's research has the advantage that much of it pertains to people in their everyday lives.

In as much as they provide syntheses rather than primary reports of research, for the most part the authors in this volume do not get into methodological details. Nonetheless three methodological aspects do stand out. First, Aron et al. report on physiological and fMRI studies. This is part of the larger trend within social psychology and the study of relationships to be concerned with health and better understanding of the biological mechanisms that underlie social processes. Second, the Early Years of Marriage Study (Custer et al.) made creative use within a larger survey study of having couples provide a narrative on multiple occasions describing the progression of their relationships. This provides a rich data source. Although self-report is common in relationship research, narratives get at the participants' own views. This methodology complements Sprecher and Felmlee's concern with insiders' descriptions of attraction, as well as prototype and story views of love (Aron et al.), in placing emphasis on laypeople's perceptions.

Third, Eastwick and Finkel identify eight desirable features of designs for studying relationship initiation. Eastwick and Finkel advocate that participants meet real-life potential partners with whom they have dyadic interaction in a well-controlled setting and are given multiple romantic options. For researchers, such settings must include the opportunity to collect background information in advance of the event, have experimental interventions, collect objective data, and gather follow-up information after the event. Eastwick and Finkel's speed-dating paradigm permits all of these features.

SHIFTING THEORETICAL PERSPECTIVES

In the 1970s, reinforcement (or reward), cognitive consistency, and social exchange theories helped frame scholars' understanding of interpersonal attraction. In this volume, the reward and cognitive consistency approaches are largely in the background. The social exchange camp has been the most resilient of these traditions (in this volume especially represented in Arriaga et al.'s chapter as well as elsewhere, including Bredow et al.; Fine et al.; Knobloch & Miller; Sprecher & Felmlee). As Graziano and Bruce note, two new theoretical approaches emerged in the 1980s and 1990s: adult attachment theory (Creasey & Jarvis) and evolutionary psychology (Schmitt).

Although I consider attachment theory, evolutionary views, and social exchange the dominant theoretical traditions of contemporary relationship research, this volume testifies to the vitality and diversity of theoretical views. Uncertainty reduction models dating back to Berger and Calabrese (1975) are well represented in the chapters by communication scholars (Afifi & Lucas; Guerrero & Mongeau; Knobloch & Miller). At least four authors have advanced smaller range theories to guide their work on specific topics: Afifi's theory of motivated information management, Aron's self-expansion view of love, Cupach and Spitzberg's relational goal pursuit theory, and Simpson and Fletcher's ideal standards model. There are also references to such frameworks as social penetration (Derlega et al.), dialectical approaches (Derlega et al.; Sprecher & Felmlee), scripts (Metts & Mikucki), the life course perspective (Fine et al.), and feminist views (Fine et al.) in various chapters.

Arriaga et al. offer nice reflections on how interdependence theory compares with several other perspectives including attachment theory, evolutionary psychology, social penetration, and attribution theory. For example, interdependence and attachment theories are similar in that both address a range of close relationship issues and both take into consideration individuals' histories. Elsewhere I have discussed comparisons and criteria for evaluating theories used in the close relationships field (Perlman & Campbell, 2004).

What can be said about the directions in which conceptual frameworks used to understand relationship initiation are heading? Graziano and Bruce spot a shift away from anchoring conceptualizations of attraction in the attitude tradition to viewing it more in terms of emotion and motivation.

In the 1980s and 1990s, there was a cognitive emphasis in social psychology. I am impressed with its impact on the close relationship area generally and its place in conceptualizing relationship initiation more specifically. Such concepts as schemas, prototypes, and scripts all are essentially cognitive structures. In attachment theory, the cognitive notion of mental models has been emphasized. To the extent that the self is a cognitive representation, Aron's self-expansion theory as well as his view on closeness as self–other overlap have a crucial cognitive aspect. Arriaga et al.'s focus on expectations brings cognitions into interdependence theory. Finally, the cognitive tradition can be seen in Tran, Simpson, and Fletcher's notion of ideals as well as Knee and Bush's concept of relationships beliefs.

A second thrust I detect in theoretical frameworks is what I would call a *strategic emphasis*. Here I would include concepts such as goals, plans, strategies, and tests. Bredow et al. assume that attraction is rooted in people's relational goals and that they use strategic self-presentation to achieve those objectives. Evolutionary theorists are concerned with short- versus long-term mating strategies. Cunningham and Barbee discuss strategies used by players and parasites; steps in their flirtation and courtship stages (attract attention, and extrapersonal displays) have an active, striving component to them. In the uncertainty reduction literature, uncertainty can be viewed as a driving force behind people's communication behavior that motivates individuals to try to maximize the rewards of social interaction. Uncertainty theorists (Knobloch & Miller) have delineated various strategies people use to reduce uncertainty (e.g., seeking information, planning, and hedging). Secrets tests are the strategies people use to gain knowledge about the state of their relationships (Afifi & Lucas; Guerrero & Mongeau). Turning to love styles, the Hendricks describe the calculating nature of ludic and pragmatic lovers. Metts and Mikucki describe relationship initiation as "a goal-directed enterprise" and see emotions as signaling one's own intentions and eliciting desired responses from others. Fine et al. illuminate the role that personal agency plays in seeking out new relationships after divorce. Those with high agency are more likely to take initiative and pursue personal goals. Cupach and Spitzberg use a relational goal pursuit model to explain why individuals sometimes engage in unwanted relational pursuit. They see pursuit as a function of the desirability and attainability of the goal. Reeder examines people's perceptions of the goals of their partners, that is, their partners' general aims and plans.

Despite the prominence of strategic aspects of relationship initiation in current research, not all aspects of starting relationships are planned or directed by the partners involved. A fundamental tenet of social psychology is that behavior is a function of the person and the environment. Thus, presumably there are external and chance elements in virtually all our behaviors. As Fehr's review testifies, contextual factors (e.g., proximity) do matter in relationship formation. In terms of chance, consider the romantic beliefs Knee and Bush describe. Among them is the belief that love can occur at first sight without partners interacting. In this vision of Cupid's arrow striking, there is little room for partners planning or acting strategically. Thus, the forging of new relationships is undoubtedly something both within and *beyond* the partners' strategic planning and goals. Complementing this position, even in Fine et al.'s analysis emphasizing agency in relationship development, they see agency as a personal attribute with some varying in how much of it they have. Not everyone is efficacious in achieving their relational goals; other forces batter some of us around.

SHIFTING SUBSTANTIVE FOCI

In the 1960s and 1970s there was social psychological work on interpersonal attraction, self-disclosure, physical attractiveness, the impact of environmental factors on attraction, investigator-organized dances at which students were told they were being matched via computer, love, romantic beliefs, and the like (Perlman & Duck, 2006). The social exchange perspective was reasonably influential. Investigators tested whether personality traits moderated the strength of the attitude similarity–attraction relationship, and in the later 1970s, Zimbardo (1977) published his popular yet influential book on shyness. Although its importance was not immediately recognized by psychologically oriented attraction researchers, Berger and Calabrese (1975) wrote on uncertainty reduction during this period. As previously noted, sociological work on attributes of an ideal date had a longer history. So one can see historical roots to many of the chapters and topics covered in the present volume.

Dropped Topics

Overall, however, it feels to me that there have been substantial changes in substantive foci over the years. This is represented in at least three ways: topics dropped, new and generally more sophisticated ways of examining old topics, and new foci. Examples of social psychological topics whose prominence has waned since the 1970s include first impressions, the mere exposure effect, and affiliation. In the dating literature, the topic of going steady has become a historical anachronism.

Shifting Treatment of Topics

As an example in changing views of a similar topic, compare Waller's (1937) early rating and dating analysis mentioned above with Tran et al.'s treatment of dating ideals. Both Waller and Tran et al. believe people have criteria for evaluating potential partners. Both see competition for desirable mates, and both see gender differences. There are, however, significant differences in their formulations. Waller wrote without embedding his ideas in past literature (he has only two references, each in a footnote), and he did not describe his methodology (presumably he relied on informal observations of and discussions with students). Waller was concerned with dating, which he viewed from a functional perspective, its function being to move people along a continuum of steps leading to marriage. He lamented a moral decay that was making possible the "emergence of thrill seeking and exploitive relationships" (p. 728). He described the most desirable dates as follows:

> In order to have a Class A rating they [men] must belong to one of the better fraternities, be prominent in activities, have a copious supply of spending money, be well-dressed, "smooth" in manners and appearance, have a "good line," dance well, and have access to an automobile … .
> The factors which appear to be important for girls are good clothes, a smooth line, ability to dance well, and popularity as a date. (p. 730)

Waller indicated that the criteria for a desirable date vary in importance, but he treated them all together in a lump.

Compared with Waller, the work of Fletcher, Simpson, and their associates (Tran et al.) is much more explicitly grounded in past literature, specifically in the evolutionary tradition. Rather than being exclusively concerned with dating, Tran et al. discuss ideals vis-à-vis dating, marital relationships, and mating relationships. In addition to partner ideals, they are concerned with relationship ideals. They use factor analytic techniques to identify three domains of partner ideals: (a) warmth and trustworthiness, (b) attractiveness and vitality, and (c) status and resources. Beyond seeing how ideal standards influence the evaluation of potential partners, Simpson and Fletcher believe that ideal standards also help explain important aspects of our relationships (e.g., satisfaction and conflicts) and affect the extent to which we try to influence or change our partners. Fletcher and Simpson have a model including additional constructs that has been used in formulating several propositions that have guided a successful program of research.

New Topics Stemming from Societal Change

New topics within the social sciences come from a variety of sources such as societal changes, new methodologies, and the life of ideas (including the evolution of lines of research). In this volume, four prominent examples of social change leading to research are the work on hookups (Paul et al.), speed dating (Eastwick & Finkel), the use of electronically mediated communication (e-mail, chat rooms, etc.; McKenna; and cf. Bredow et al.; Cunningham & Barbee; Derlega et al.; Fehr), and web-based dating services (Sprecher et al.). Certainly casual sex has existed for a long time, but popular culture's designating a label for these activities has focused attention on them. It is good to see a series of studies describing the emotional complexities of best and worst hookups and illuminating their relatively low probability of serving to initiate ongoing relationships (Paul et al.). As I discuss elsewhere in this chapter, Eastwick and Finkel's studies of speed dating are valuable both in giving a model research paradigm and in noteworthy findings.

With the Pew Internet and American Life project estimating that 70% of Americans use the Internet (circa December 2006; see Sprecher et al.), it is fair to say that the World Wide Web and electronic communication have become part of North Americans' everyday life. As Boase and Wellman (2006) described, in early discussions of the Internet there were those who praised its potential for fostering relationships and others who felt it would undermine community, creating loneliness rather than connections. As research has accumulated, we have developed a more complex and nuanced picture of the role that computer-mediated communication plays in our social lives. McKenna's chapter does a good job of illuminating ways that relationships unfold somewhat differently on the Internet than when individuals meet in person. In terms of relationship initiation via the Internet, I like her discussion of the differences between different Internet venues (e.g., matchmaking services versus discussion forums devoted to a specific interest). Rather than painting the Internet as either a panacea or death knoll, she nicely identifies factors influencing how, when, and why online relationships will or will not blossom.

Sprecher et al. provide insights into the attitudes people have toward matching services, what brings and prevents people from using matching services, and the process of relationship initiation via these services. One of the features of some matchmaking sites is their use of scientific principles to help clients identify suitable partners. Presumably, underlying matching business' use of these principles is the allure that they will help people in finding a suitable partner. In a society where separation is common, this is undoubtedly attractive to many individuals seeking intimate relationships. Sprecher et al. make important points on how business and scientific values differ (e.g., businesses but not science are characterized by the profit motive, a lack of objectivity, and a lack of openness). Nonetheless, the use of scientific information for practical purposes is one of the key reasons society supports science and is in keeping with the applied social science traditions such as the philosophy of Kurt Lewin. Lewin (1951) felt that conceptual perspectives have practical value and that if you want to understand something, try changing it. Thus, I would echo Sprecher et al.'s sentiment, at least under optimal conditions, that the merger of relationship science with matchmaking businesses can benefit the businesses, the people using them, and science.

Topics Filling Gaps

In looking at the literature on interpersonal attraction in the 1960s and early 1970s, researchers primarily investigated attraction between North American college students. It largely ignored life span issues, how people transition between forms of relationships, how students' peers and network of relationships impact on friendship choices, or what individuals do to discourage the establishment of friendships. The interpersonal attraction literature also largely ignored cultural and demographic variation, although these types of variation did get attention in studies of dating and courtship. Other ways I see topics being added to the literature are in response to what critics have felt was missing and in the expansion of lines of research from one question to the next. As illustrations of these sorts of changes, I will reflect on life span issues, social networks, and rejection.

In this volume, Creasey and Jarvis look at attachment as it occurs in relationships associated with different points in life (parent–child relations, grandparent–grandchild relations, romantic bonds, mentors, caregiving, and relations following bereavement). Paul et al. relate hookups to adolescent development, and Fine at al. consider relationship formation after a major life transition, divorce. Thus, there is reasonable attention to the life span, although specific niches such as how children form friendships, which was nicely addressed by Gottman and Graziano (1983), are overlooked.

An Evolving Topic: Peers and Networks

The place of networks and peers in relationship beginnings is a topic that has evolved over time. By the 1990s, it had taken a moderate place in the courtship literature (2.3% of recent articles; Surra et al., 2006). The early dating literature examined parent–child conflict over dating (Moss et al., 1971), and a classic study by Driscoll, Davis, and Lipetz (1972) looked at how parental interference was related to the intensification of romantic feelings. In the early friendship literature, Newcomb (1956) reported that we tend to like the friends of our friends. Networks, however, were not part of the classic interpersonal attraction paradigm.

Several contributors to this volume discuss the seminal work of Parks and his associates in the 1980s (e.g., Parks & Adelman, 1983) showing that we often form new relationships with the friends of our friends and that these friends may play a role in the initiation of those relationships (Afifi & Lucas; Arriaga et al.; Bredow et al.; Fehr; Guerrero & Mongeau; Knobloch & Miller; Paul et al.). As Afifi and Lucas underscore, friends play as important a role in uncertainty reduction as the partner him or herself. During the 1980s we also learned that people's network patterns change as relationships evolve: For example, the size of friendship networks declines, overlap between partners' networks increases as relationships progress, and network overlap is a useful predictor of relationship progression versus deterioration (Johnson & Leslie, 1982; Milardo, 1982). During the later part of the 1980s, Aron and his associates, followed by Sprecher and her associates, were doing research on what laypeople consider to be important factors in falling in love. Although not at the top of the list, family and friends' approval was among the key factors (see Sprecher & Felmlee). Speaking with network members to assess how much partners like us was identified as an affinity test (Afifi & Lucas). In the 1990s, Graziano and his associates (see Graziano & Bruce as well as Cunningham & Barbee) found that ratings of a potential partner's physical attractiveness were influenced by peer judgments. More recently the role of peer disapproval as a deterrent to interracial dating has been illuminated (see Arriaga et al.), the process of dyads splitting off from group dating has been noted (Guerrero

& Mongeau), and Paul et al. have found that hookups' best and worst experiences were intertwined with communication to friends: Individuals experience peer support for their best hookups but avoid discussing their worst experiences. McKenna notes that on the Internet, web spaces such Facebook now have the capacity for intermediaries to establish links among their friends to one another.

Rejection

Rejection is another topic that fell largely outside the purview of interpersonal attraction research in the 1960s and 1970s. If one thinks of friendship formation as a zero-sum phenomenon, perhaps liking one person implies disliking others, but social psychologists of the 1960s and 1970s were not highlighting this point. Nonetheless, there were some allusions to rejection in early research. In the 1950s, motivational theorists conceptualized need for affiliation as concern about establishing, maintaining, or restoring positive affective relationships but included in their need for affiliation scoring system both the positive aspects of relationships and unpleasant thoughts of rejection (Atkinson, Heyns, & Veroff, 1954). By the mid-1970s separate measures of affiliative tendencies and fear of rejection had been developed (Mehrabian, 1976). Between the 1950s and the mid-1970s, Berscheid, Dion, Walster, and Walster (1971) demonstrated that the tendency to select partners of relatively comparable physical attractiveness depended upon realizing one might be rejected by potential partners; otherwise, most people seek highly attractive partners. In the 1980s, Rodin (1982) conceptualized relationship initiation as starting with excluding people and then deciding with whom one did want to form relationships (see Fehr). Shortly thereafter, Rosenbaum (1986) reinterpreted the similarity–liking relationship, arguing that the key reason individuals form friendships with similar others is that early in the friendship formation process they reject dissimilar others.

Turning to the more contemporary era, Vorauer and her associates (Vorauer & Ratner, 1996) did research cited in the present volume on pluralistic ignorance, showing that partners each refrain from initiating a relationship because they both incorrectly fear that the other will reject them (see Afifi & Lucas; Bredow et al.; Metts). Both Bredow et al. and Afifi and Lucas mention the notion of rejection sensitivity, the tendency to anxiously expect, readily perceive, and overreact to social rejection. Graziano and Bruce speculate on whether the detrimental effects of rejection on relationship initiation may be less for older adults than adolescents. Wenzel and Kashdan note how the negative cognitive-processing biases of socially anxious individuals signaling rejection and negative judgment reinforce their core beliefs of unlikeability. Tran et al.'s research suggests that one's ideals become more flexible following repeated rejections. Derlega et al. identify restricting scripts (e.g., infrequent contact, superficial disclosure, and acting disinterested) that partners employ to end budding relationships. Unrequited or nonreciprocated love has become a legitimate topic (Aron et al.). Drawing on Guerrero's work, Guerrero and Mongeau examine the rejectors' communication behaviors such as talking about the state of the relationship in unrequited love. Cupach and Spitzberg thoroughly discuss the numerous strategies people use to end unwanted pursuit by others (e.g., telling the pursuer to stop, avoiding the person, seeking external assistance, and being aggressive). None work perfectly, but Cupach and Spitzberg hold out hope that, if used early and often, they can have cumulative impact.

In concluding this discussion on historical change, I am reminded that Isaac Newton said, "If I've seen far, it's because I've stood on tall shoulders." Contemporary social science is a process of building on what has come before. Over time, however, the foci, methods, and theories of science shift noticeably. The study of the initiation of relationships is mature enough so that these changing trends can be readily seen.

WHAT DO WE KNOW?

Tran et al. write, "Without some understanding of when, how, and why a relationship is launched, it is difficult to forecast and comprehend what happens when individuals and their partners experience myriad events during later stages of relationship development" (see Chapter 25). With this simple sentence, they point to core questions about relationship initiation. When do people form new relationships? What is involved in doing so? Although not identified explicitly in their sentence, to whom are we attracted? Are there individual differences or other factors that shape the relationship initiation experiences people have? What are the consequences of how relationships begin? After considering the current state of knowledge on relationship initiation, what conclusions can we draw? The contributors to this volume have elaborated on these questions in detail. Although I cannot hope to answer them as fully, I will highlight some key findings and reflect on the state of our knowledge.

When Do Relationships Begin?

A first question is "When are we likely to start relationships in terms of seeking to meet or interact with others?" This has not been a central question, but a few glimpses of answers can be noted. Fehr writes, "[I]f we already have a full store of friendships or have other time-consuming commitments (e.g., family, work, or studies), we will be less available for new friendships" (see Chapter 2). Consistent with Fehr's point regarding time, Fine et al. note that the time taken by children decreases the likelihood of divorced mothers establishing new romantic relationships. Bredow et al. don't believe time by itself is enough. Instead, they postulate that making an opening overture is a product of the attractiveness of the other person and the perceived likelihood that the person will reciprocate (i.e., accept the overture). For evolutionary theorists, factors such as high levels of testosterone in men, ovulation in women, and low sex ratios (more women than men) should make mating more likely. Paul et al. see partying involving alcohol as fertile ground for hookups. In both Cunningham and Barbee and Levinger's (1974; see also Levinger & Snoek, 1972; Sprecher et al.) stage models, there is a crucial step where people go from awareness of one another to interacting. Cunningham and Barbee see engaging in interaction as triggered by nonverbal behaviors such as solicitation (e.g., smile and eye contact) and moving closer. For Metts and Mikucki, entering a situation with a positive emotional state increases the likelihood of being available for interaction. Levinger and Snoek identified a person's time and opportunity, as well as the attractiveness of the other person and perception they will reciprocate, as factors making interaction likely as facilitating the initiation of contact. For Arriaga et al., a person should be more likely to initiate a relationship when he or she has positive expectations about the outcomes of that relationship with reference to his or her CL and CL_{alt}. Turning to falling in love, Aron et al. argue it is more likely to happen when a person is ready for it, there is arousal at the time of the meeting, and appropriate cues are present.

Why Do We Form Relationships?

The Hendricks offer two reasons why we initiate relationships: (a) to insure mating and the survival of the species, and (b) because we have a need to belong. Akin to the Hendricks' first point, evolutionary theorists see the goal of mating as being the perpetuation of one's genes, and attachment theorists (see Creasey & Jarvis) see attachment bonds as fostering survival. Attachment figures serve proximity-seeking, safe haven, and secure base functions: that is, they are there for people in their times of need to provide comfort and support, and also allow children or adults a safe environment from which to explore and pursue nonattachment goals. Turning to a social exchange perspective, the basic motivation for forming relationships (or selecting one potential partner over another) rests in our motivation to garner more rewards than costs in life (see Bredow et al.).

In addition to answering the fundamental question of why humans form relationships, contributors to this volume answer the questions of how our motives for initiating relationships have changed over time, how motives play into our being attracted to some potential partners as opposed to others (Bredow et al.), and why we seek specific types of relationships. For example, Bredow et al. contend that the primary reason for initiating romantic relationships in the early 20th century was to find a spouse, but toward the end of the century, the motives behind relationship initiation had become more varied (e.g., to include companionship, recreation, intimacy, or economic partnership). Sprecher et al. identify several reasons why people might be motivated to seek online matchmaking services: access to many eligible, available others; efficiency and convenience; access to people living outside one's own geographical region; access to potential partners with atypical interests; and so on.

Determinants of Attraction

After over 50 years of relevant research, we have a relatively clear picture of who likes whom. Fehr summarizes these factors for friendship; Graziano and Bruce treat sexual and romantic attraction (cf. Aron et al.; Sprecher & Felmlee). It is common to consider how P (the person), O (the other person), their interaction, and the environmental context influence attraction to potential partners. Such factors as proximity, similarity, self-disclosure, responsiveness, expecting to have future interactions, physical attractiveness, and being liked by the other person (cf. Eastwick & Finkel) have been extensively investigated and generally show their importance in attraction. Fehr adds humor and fun as previously neglected antecedents of friendship that recent research suggests are likely noteworthy contributors.

In contrasting Fehr's review of the determinants of friendship with Graziano and Bruce's review of sexual and romantic attraction, a major difference between the two is the greater influence of evolutionary theory on the investigation of sex and romance. This can be seen in two lines of work that Graziano and Bruce feature. First, the evolutionary perspective has led to careful examination of facial symmetry and averageness, waist-to-hip ratios, and other presumed indicators of reproductive fitness and health. Overall, these factors promote attraction. As a side benefit of this work, we now know much more about what makes a person attractive (i.e., the components of attractiveness) than we did when physical attractiveness research began. Second, the evolutionary perspective has led to research on dominance, which can confer a reproductive advantage. Here the results are more complex but indicate that agreeable, dominant males are attractive.

Although similarity is one of the most frequently mentioned predictors of attraction, some challenges to this proposition have been made. Contemporary social trends in many communities suggest increasing rates of relationships between members of different groups. In the United States, for example, interracial marriages accounted for less than 1% of marriages in 1970 but grew to over 5% by 2000 (Batson, Qian, & Lichter, 2006). In the current volume, Eastwick and Finkel found that White liberals preferred speed dates with other-race partners to speed dates with White partners. At a theoretical level, Aron's self-expansion theory postulates that those who expand our self-concept should be attractive to us, and Winch's (1958) theory of complementary needs likewise predicts the viability of relationships between partners whose needs mesh even if they are opposites.

We are beginning, in my judgment, to be able to make greater sense of the similarity evidence. First, Fehr indicates that similarity of partners depends to some extent on the domain being considered. Along with this, Tesser (1993) has demonstrated that the more heritable an attitude, the more consequential attitude similarity is for attraction. Second, based on fatal attraction research, Sprecher and Felmlee speculate that dissimilarity between partners may initially be alluring but become a source of discontent later. Third, Eastwick and Finkel's results suggest that the importance of similarity may vary as a function of people's political orientation, with it being more important for conservatives. Fourth, it may be that partners from different racial or ethnic backgrounds are nonetheless highly similar in other ways (Rushton, 1989). Finally, Aron, Steele, Kashdan, and Perez (2006) suggested that differences are most likely to lead to greater attraction when partners believe a relationship is likely to develop. So we are beginning to have a map of when and for whom similarity matters most.

There Are Core Processes in Initiating Relationships

One section of this volume is devoted to what the editors classify as the processes of initiating relationships. These especially include self-disclosure and uncertainty reduction. Elsewhere in the volume, contributors discuss emotions and cognitions, which can also be considered processes. In a very general sense, these processes play a key role in how relationship events are interpreted, in the actions people take, and in how they evaluate their relationships.

There Are Stages or Phases in Relationship Initiation

I have already noted that authors offer their own (Bredow et al.; Cunningham & Barbee) or use others' (Guerrero & Mongeau; Sprecher et al.) stages of relationship initiation. These models differ in the number of stages they specify and whether they are concerned with initial interactions or deeper aspects of relationship development. Collectively they suggest relationship initiation involves awareness of the other person, a decision to interact, interaction leading to points of contact or rapport, and eventually some investment in or integration (i.e., sharing a relational identity) with the other person.

There Are Systematic Differences in Initiating Relationships

One of the recurrent themes cutting across this volume is that there are systematic differences between people in how they initiate relationships. These can be illustrated by discussing styles, personality-type factors, and gender. Regarding styles, Cunningham and Barbee identify four mating styles: partner (caring and responsive), player (warm but not interested in commitment), parasite (egocentric individuals seeking relationships to address personal needs and deficiencies), and predator (exploitive and abandoning). The Hendricks depict six love styles: eros (intense, passionate love), ludus (game-playing love), storge (slow, friendship love), pragma (practical love), mania (possessive, dependent love), and agape (gentle, altruistic love).

Consider the following remarks pertaining to personality-type factors:

> Secure people of all ages are curious, socially competent, persistent, open to experience, and autonomous, and possess good social information–processing skills … . These are qualities that theoretically could spur relationship initiation and, as importantly, might mark just the type of individuals with whom one would like to initiate a close relationship … . A predominant finding is that secure people negotiate new and transformed attachment relationships better than insecure adults. (Creasey & Jarvis, Chapter 4)
>
> Persons high in agreeableness say that they like more people, including traditional targets of prejudice, than do their peers. Persons low in agreeableness (particularly males) show lower levels of attraction and actively discriminate against out-group women (in this case, overweight females) at the initiation phase of a relationship. (Graziano & Bruce, Chapter 14)
>
> [I]ndividuals high in global uncertainty are more apprehensive when meeting strangers, communicate less effectively during initial interaction, and develop less satisfying long-term relationships. (Knobloch & Miller, Chapter 6)
>
> [S]ocial anxiety interferes with relationship initiation … . [I]t is clear that many depressive symptoms would interfere with relationship initiation. (Wenzel & Kashdan, Chapter 22; cf. Metts & Mikucki for a similar view of shyness)
>
> Given the highly scripted nature of relationship initiation, it is not surprising that high self-monitors are skilled initiators. (Metts & Mikucki, Chapter 18)

In short, based on individual difference factors, some people seem to be more likely and more effective in initiating relationships than others. Exactly how much these personal attributes foster (or inhibit) initiating relationships is unclear, but the magnitude of any given variable's effect in the social sciences is often modest. One could argue whether the above mentioned differences are due to genetics or social influences, but several of them have a trait-like, persistent quality. Thus, the differences are presumably resistant to change. Nonetheless Wenzel and Kashdan review behavioral, cognitive, and interpersonal approaches that can assist clients in dealing with social anxiety and depression.

With regard to gender, Canary and Dindia (1998) divided researchers into two camps: those with what they called "alpha biases," and those with "beta biases." Those with an alpha bias observe that gender differences are pervasive. Those with a beta bias note that the magnitude of any difference is small and may be due to other factors than gender per se.

Alpha versus beta biases are linked to theoretical orientations. Evolutionary theorists (e.g., Schmitt) generally fall into the alpha camp; they assume that men veer toward short-term mating strategies, whereas women are generally oriented toward longer term mating strategies. From their perspective, there are substantial gender differences in mating behavior. Schmitt cites studies showing that men are more concerned with potential partners' physical attractiveness, whereas women are more concerned with men's wealth and status. Similarly, he reports data showing that (a) women possess less desire than men do for a variety of sexual partners, (b) women require more time to elapse than men do before consenting to sexual intercourse, and (c) women tend to less actively seek short-term mateships than men do. Compared with evolutionary psychologists, proponents of the interdependence (Arriaga et al.) and uncertainty reduction positions (Afifi & Lucas; Knobloch & Miller) pay relatively little attention to gender. Arriaga et al., for example, discuss how the operation of gender norms may make it more difficult to infer a partner's motives, but otherwise do not stress gender differences in their analysis.

Most authors in this volume mention gender at least in passing. For example, Afifi and Lucas note that men are more likely than women to see behavior as signaling sexual interest. Cunningham and Barbee describe women's nonverbal solicitation behaviors that they believe subtly give women considerable control over the early stages of courting. Roughly a quarter of the authors have sections devoted to the topic of gender (Aron et al.; Graziano & Bruce; Custer et al.; Derlega et al.; Eastwick & Finkel; Fine et al.; Reeder). Representative findings reported in these chapters are as follows:

- Women are stereotypically seen as more expressive and interested in seeking intimacy in romantic relationships. Reeder reviews research showing that college students expect men and women to enter relationships with different goals: Men were perceived as placing more weight on excitement, and women on intimacy goals.
- Although women generally disclose more than men, studies of the initiation of relationships provide exceptions to this in which men disclose more (Derlega et al.).
- In speed dating, men state a preference for physically attractive partners, whereas women state a preference for men with a high earning capacity. There are no gender differences, however, in how strongly the physical attractiveness (or the earning capacity) of a potential partner is associated with how well the partner is actually liked (Eastwick & Finkel).
- In narratives about their relationship initiation, men report being more active and direct, and women more passive (Graziano & Bruce; Custer et al.).
- Men report more passionate love, but women are more likely to report currently being in love, being more deeply in love, and that love is more important to them (Aron et al.).
- Men are more likely to repartner after divorce than women, especially in the later stages of the life cycle (Fine et al.).

Many of the findings on gender differences fit with either an evolutionary perspective or the cultural norm that men should be the initiators in relationships. In looking for differences, one should not overlook similarities. For example, Aron et al. argue that "gender similarities in attitudes toward romantic love seem to be far greater than gender differences" (see Chapter 16). Similarly, despite numerous studies showing gender differences in ideals, both men and women give the same rank order to the importance of three ideal characteristics of partners: warmth and trustworthiness were rated as most important in an ideal partner, followed by vitality and attractiveness, and then status and resources (see Knee & Bush).

The Sequelae of Relationship Initiation

Initiating relations has sequelae for our lives generally as well as for later stages of our relationships. The exact sequelae may be a function of the way relationship initiation occurs. For example, as noted above, relationship initiation alters our networks. Aron (see Aron et al.) has shown that falling in love leads to greater diversity in one's self-concept, higher self-esteem, and a greater sense of self-efficacy. Custer et al. describe how features of courtship narratives are associated with well-being at various points in marriage (e.g., women who reported lower life satisfaction as newlyweds emphasized the theme of pregnancy in their courtship narratives). Paul et al. speculate on how, depending largely on personality factors, hookup experiences can facilitate or detract from the subsequent development of intimate relationships.

Turning to the relationship domain, one of the ways that studying relationship initiation and development can be useful is in predicting the longevity and longer term properties of those relationships (see Huston, 1994; Huston, Niehuis, & Smith, 2001). For instance, a couple's love before marriage is associated with their love and satisfaction after marriage (Huston, 1994). Although this topic is not a major focus of the present volume, the contributors do present some glimpses of how relationship initiation and later outcomes are associated. For example, evolutionary psychologists stress differences between relationships that are short-term versus those that are longer lasting. In the initial stages of short-term relationships, men would search for sexually available partners unconcerned about commitment, but in seeking longer term mates, they would seek partners likely to be high in fidelity with good parenting skills (Schmitt; see Table 3.1). Paul et al. note that hookups with the most potential to lead to subsequent relationships are characterized by "(a) communication, (b) enjoyment (albeit a little anxiety) and posthookup feelings of comfort and security, (c) interest in and care about the partner, (d) peer support, and (e) conscious involvement (i.e., lack of intoxication)" (see Chapter 19). In speed dating, Eastwick and Finkel found that the perception of the other's romantic interest twinged with a touch of uncertainty predicted the persistence of one's own romantic interest over time. Sprecher and Felmlee describe how dating partners who see the reasons for their courtship progress as due to aspects of the relationship itself (as opposed to external events) were more satisfied with their relationships, and reported greater increases in satisfaction over a one-year time period. They also note that in cases of fatal attraction, what start out as positive attributes of a potential partner may become irritating over time.

Overall, we know a considerable amount about the basic issues of when, why, how, and with whom we initiate relationships. We have depicted the steps and processes involved in initiation and how initiation is associated with various consequences. We have a good catalog of information as well as frameworks for understanding it. But the contributors to this volume are not resting on their laurels. A common element of the chapters in this volume is that authors have a section on future directions for research or offer relevant reflections in their concluding remarks. I have clustered reflections on future directions around 10 themes.

FUTURE DIRECTIONS OF WORK ON RELATIONSHIP INITIATION

Focus on Relationship Initiation

One of the first noteworthy points about needed future research is to focus on relationship initiation per se (Afifi & Lucas; Aron et al.; Knee & Bush; Knobloch & Miller; Wenzel & Kashdan). Some authors found they could address relationship initiation, but to do so they had to rely on more general studies of relationships. As Aron et al. and others note, getting people at the moment they are initiating a relationship is a matter that requires good timing on the investigators' part. Two solutions are to use longitudinal designs with populations where relationship initiation is more likely or to rely on retrospective reports such as narratives.

Expand Already Existing Lines of Research

Several authors identify ways in which lines of research on their topic could be expanded. For example, Custer et al. want to know when and to whom people tell their initiation stories, and how initiation stories vary as a function of the person(s) to whom they are being told. Cupach and Spitzberg would like research on how individuals detect signals that unwanted relational pursuit is becoming persistent and on the efficacy of coping responses. Tran et al. list several questions, including how an individual's perception of his or her own desirability as a mate is associated with his or her level and flexibility of ideal standards, and how individuals "trade off" between different ideal dimensions (e.g., sacrificing some status and resources for more attractiveness and vitality in a given partner).

More Varied Sampling

Although contemporary relationship research employs more varied samples than did classic investigations of interpersonal attraction, a recurrent suggestion that several authors explicitly or implicitly make is to expand the samples used in relationship initiation research (Creasey & Jarvis; Derlega et al.; Fine et al.; Guerrero & Mongeau; Hendrick & Hendrick; Metts & Mikucki; Sprecher & Felmlee; Wenzel & Kashdan; cf. Eastwick & Finkel). Guerrero and Mongeau voice this as follows:

> Finally, research on the transition from friendship to romantic relationships should diversify its contextual base above and beyond the readily available sample of undergraduate college students (Sears, 1986). As we noted earlier, we know very little about, and desperately need research on, how friendships transition from platonic to romantic in gay male or lesbian relationships. As another example, research generally should focus on a greater variety of age groups. (see Chapter 9)

Fine et al. call for samples representing ethnically diverse and lower socioeconomic status (SES) populations. Wenzel and Kashdan map out suggestions for research with emotionally impaired individuals. To this list, I would add people with various disabilities (including physical impairment, sensory impairment, cognitive impairment, intellectual impairment, or mental health issues) and social stigmas.

Methodological Directions

Contributors also make several suggestions about the methodologies that will help advance relationship initiation research. In addition to Eastwick and Finkel (see above) articulating eight exemplary design features of speed dating, these include doing experiments (Derlega et al.), using naturalistic designs (Metts & Mikucki), coding interactions (Eastwick & Finkel), using insider (Sprecher & Felmlee) and qualitative (Fine et al.; Paul et al.) methods, collecting data from or about both partners (Sprecher & Felmlee; Wenzel & Kashdan), expanding the range of measures (e.g., to get biological indicators, implicit attitude measures, or fMRI data; Eastwick & Finkel), and using longitudinal designs (Paul et al.). Obviously there is diversity in what authors would like, but it is likely that the convergence of multiple methods is leading to a stronger knowledge base.

Consider More Kinds of Relationships

Types of relationships must be considered in future research. Derlega et al. underscore that most of the research on relationship initiation deals with voluntary or participant selected relationships. They advocate doing more research on the relationships we enter that are arranged by others. Knobloch and Miller call for expanding the range of relationships to include friendships and patient–doctor and coworker relationships. In the postmarital domain, Fine et al. call for more attention to the initiation of subsequent nonmarital relationships. Creasy and Jarvis briefly treat attachment processes in client–therapist relationships. Given the crucial role of client–therapist relationships for treatment outcomes (Martin, Garske, & Davis, 2000), it seems especially useful to me to have a broad, more detailed view of how client–therapist relationships are initiated.

Considering the initiation of various types of relationships raises comparative considerations. Presumably authors want a wider variety of relationships to be investigated because they believe that each has unique properties. Juxtaposed against this assumption, as noted above, Surra et al. (2006) noted that there is a trend toward universal principles of courtship. Thus, there are still questions of the extent to which the processes noted in one form of relationship generalize to others (Custer et al.; Eastwick & Finkel).

Consider Both Internal and External Causes

One way of classifying many of the causes of our behavior is in terms of internal versus external factors. Scattered throughout the recommendations are suggestions to examine specific internal factors (e.g., attachment styles; Reeder; Wenzel & Kashdan) and situational variables such as stressors (Reeder). Arriaga et al. advocate "for future research … examining whether a person's behavior is primarily directed by the physical and social properties of a given situation, or instead by one's personal motives" (see Chapter 10). Clearly external factors have been considered in the research on relationship initiation, yet overall I perceive the current momentum as toward internal factors. I feel researchers should not lose interest in the external or seemingly chance factors that promote the beginning of relationships.

Continue Considering Developmental Aspects of Relationship Initiation

Several contributors point to developmental aspects of relationship initiation that warrant further investigation. For example, Derlega et al. would like more information about the ebb and flow of self-disclosure over time and how revelations about the relationship to network members influence relationship progress. Guerrero and Mongeau want to identify common turning points in relationships and to get data on when, in relation to transition points, relational turbulence is high. Tran et al. would like more information on what happens to ideal standards and evaluations of partners when relationships and partners change over time. Sprecher and Felmlee see the importance of further exploring the ways in which factors involved in initial attraction relate to later relationship development and outcomes. For me, one of the crucial questions here is why do some initial interactions lead to relationships but others terminate before repeated interaction occurs. Arriaga et al. would like to know whether partners who initially face challenges (e.g., differences) are more likely than those who did not to establish long-lasting relationships. Sprecher et al. would like to compare couples who began their relationships online versus offline once they have reached the later stages of their relationships.

Derlega et al. note both gradual and "clicking" (more immediate rapport) models of development. There is evidence in support of both processes. Several other authors touch on the pace of relationship initiation in various ways (e.g., Schmitt's short- versus long-term mating strategies, Knee and Bush's destiny versus growth beliefs, and differences among the Hendricks' love styles). Aron et al. report data that among people reflecting on the speed of their relationship's development, 61% perceived it as fast, and 39% as slow. One wonders what possible causal factors distinguish relationships that start rapidly from those that begin gradually. Are there different emotions associated with different rates of relationship development? How is the pace of relationship development associated with the subsequent success of the relationships formed?

Use and Elaborate Theory

Theory or at least some explicit or implicit conceptualization underpins virtually all research. As discussed already, several theoretical perspectives have been used to guide our understanding of relationship initiation, although in most cases these are more general theories that have been adapted to focus on relationship initiation rather than theories developed especially to explain relationship initiation. Fine et al. call for construction of a midrange theory that specifically addresses the initiation of new romantic relationships following dissolution. Sprecher et al. hope that the proprietors of matching services will allow researchers to use web services for testing theoretical models. One emerging theoretical perspective that I believe holds promise for guiding research on relationship initiation is Shelly Gable's (2006) perspective on social motivation. Although accepting the view that humans have a need to belong, Gable saw two relatively independent motivational systems: approach motives to reach desired end states and avoidance motives to avoid undesired end states. Intuitively one might expect people high in approach motivation and low in avoidance to seek new relationships and approach them in a more positive manner. Individuals high in both approach and avoidance motivation present an interesting group not identified in most past research. Exploration of the unique ways they might initiate relationships seems fruitful.

Consider Nonconscious Aspects of Relationship Initiation

McKenna urges more research into the nonconscious aspects of online dating. Much of the research on relationship initiation has been done via verbal report, which privileges the factors of which research participants are aware. Yet, as Sprecher and Felmlee remind readers, "[R]esearch participants often cannot accurately explain the causes of their behaviors" (see Chapter 16). Thus I feel McKenna's call for more research on processes outside of awareness is valuable general advice for relationship initiation researchers.

Engage in Knowledge Utilization

A final direction I hope the work on relationship initiation takes is toward knowledge translation. Given our knowledge, can we formulate guidelines for people wanting advice on how to initiate relationships? Can we engage in environmental design, social policy formulation, and psychoeducational or therapeutic interventions to assist such individuals? In an era of evidence-based practice, can we show the efficacy of these interventions?

SUMMARY AND CONCLUSIONS

In this set of concluding reflections, I have described relationship initiation, indicating that authors in this volume vary in the aspects of the beginning of relationships on which they focus. I contended that the initiation of intimate relationships is not actually too frequent. I identified two seminal historical precursors of contemporary research: (a) research on dating and relationship development and (b) research on interpersonal attraction. I described significant ways contemporary research differs from past research (e.g., a shift toward universal principles, a shift away from a very heavy reliance on experimental methods, and the replacement of cognitive consistency and reinforcement theories with evolutionary and attachment views). I traced the treatment of peer relations and rejection as illustrations of substantive changes since the 1950s. I highlighted the answers we now have to key questions about relationships initiation: For example, when, why, and with whom do we initiate relationships? What are the processes and steps involved? How do relationship outcomes vary as a function of relationship initiation? Finally, I identified 10 directions for future research.

Research on interpersonal attraction dates back to the end of the 19th century (Monroe, 1898). In the approximately 110 years since then, we have come a long way in our understanding of how relationships begin. The last 25 or so years have seen a paradigm shift in our knowledge. Today, we have a richer, more nuanced vision that draws on insights of scholars from multiple disciplines. This volume succeeds marvelously in bringing that work together and provides an update that has been overdue in coming. Providing a concluding commentary on the chapters of this book has been a pleasure for me. In ending, however, I realize that science, like our relationships in life, is a constantly changing pool: Old information is fading in salience, and new knowledge is being added. Thus, in addition to providing a wonderful synthesis, this book provides for another era of scholarship a springboard to further beginnings.

REFERENCES

Aron, A., Melinat, E., Aron, E. N., Vallone, R. D., & Bator, R. J. (1997). The experimental generation of inter-personal closeness: A procedure and some preliminary findings. *Personality and Social Psychology Bulletin, 23,* 363–377.

Aron, A., Steele, J. L., Kashdan, T. B., & Perez, M. (2006). When similars do not attract: Tests of a prediction from the self-expansion model. *Personal Relationships, 13,* 387–396.

Atkinson, J. W., Heyns, R. W., & Veroff, J. (1954). The effect of experimental arousal of the affiliation motive on thematic apperception . *Journal of Abnormal and Social Psychology, 49,* 405–410.

Batson, C. D., Qian, Z., & Lichter, D. T. (2006). Interracial and intraracial patterns of mate selection among America's diverse Black populations. *Journal of Marriage and Family, 68,* 658–672.

Berger, C. R., & Calabrese, R. J. (1975). Some explorations in initial interactions and beyond: Toward a developmental theory of interpersonal communication. *Human Communication Research, 1,* 99–112.

Berscheid, E., Dion, K., Walster, E., & Walster, G. W. (1971). Physical attractiveness and dating choice: A test of the matching hypothesis. *Journal of Experimental Social Psychology, 7,* 173–189.

Berscheid, E., & Walster, E. H. (1969). *Interpersonal attraction.* Reading, MA: Addison-Wesley.

Boase, J., & Wellman, B. (2006). Personal relationships: On and off the Internet. In A. Vangelisti & D. Perlman (Eds.), *Cambridge handbook of personal relationships* (pp. 709–723). New York: Cambridge University Press.

Byrne, D. (1961). Interpersonal attraction and attitude similarity. *Journal of Abnormal and Social Psychology, 62,* 713–715.

Byrne, D. (1971). *The attraction paradigm.* New York: Academic Press.

Byrne, D., & Griffitt, W. (1973). Interpersonal attraction. *Annual Review of Psychology, 24,* 317–336.

Canary, D. J., & Dindia, K. (Eds.). (1998). Prologue: Recurring issues in sex differences and similarities in communication. In D. J. Canary & K. Dindia (Eds.), *Sex differences and similarities in communication: Critical essays and empirical investigations of sex and gender in interaction* (pp. 1–17). Mahwah, NJ: Lawrence Erlbaum.

De Jong Gierveld, J. (1995). Research into relationship research designs: Personal relationships under the microscope. *Journal of Social and Personal Relationships, 12,* 583–588.

De Jong Gierveld, J., & Perlman, D. (2006). Longstanding non-kin relationships of older adults in the Netherlands and the U.S.A. *Research on Aging, 28,* 730–748.

Driscoll, R., Davis, K. E., & Lipetz, M. E. (1972). Parental interference and romantic love: The Romeo and Juliet effect. *Journal of Personality and Social Psychology, 24,* 1–10.

Duck, S., & Perlman, D. (1985). The thousand islands of personal relationships: A prescriptive analysis for future explorations. In S. Duck & D. Perlman (Eds.), *Understanding personal relationships* (pp. 1–15). London: Sage.

Fehr, B. (1996). *Friendship processes.* Thousand Oaks, CA: Sage.

Gable, S. L. (2006). Approach and avoidance social motives and goals. *Journal of Personality, 71,* 175–222.

Gottman, J. M., & Graziano, W. G. (1983). How children become friends. *Monographs of the Society for Research in Child Development, 48*(3, Serial No. 201), 1–86.

Hazan, C., & Zeifman, D. (1994). Sex and the psychological tether. In K. Bartholomew & D. Perlman (Eds.), *Attachment processes in adulthood* (pp. 151–178). London: Jessica Kingsley.

Hinde, R. A. (1979). *Toward understanding relationships.* London: Academic Press.

Huston, T. L. (1982, January). *The Penn State PAIR Project Newsletter, 1,* 1–4.

Huston, T. L. (1994). Courtship antecedents of marital love and satisfaction. In R. Erber & R. Gilmour (Eds.), *Theoretical perspectives on personal relationships* (pp. 43–65). Hillsdale, NJ: Lawrence Erlbaum.

Huston, T. L., Niehuis, S., & Smith, S. E. (2001). The early marital roots of conjugal distress and divorce. *Current Directions in Psychological Science, 10,* 116–119.

Johnson, M. P., & Leslie, L. (1982). Couple involvement and network structure: A test of the dyadic withdrawal hypothesis. *Social Psychology Quarterly, 45,* 34–43.

Kashy, D. A., Campbell, L., & Harris, D. W. (2006). Advances in data analytic approaches from relationship research: The broad utility of hierarchical linear modeling. In A. Vangelisti & D. Perlman (Eds.), *Cambridge handbook of personal relationships* (pp. 73–89). New York: Cambridge University Press.

Knapp, M. L., & Vangelisti, A. L. (2005). *Interpersonal communication and human relationships* (5th ed.). Boston: Allyn & Bacon.

Langer, G., Arnedt, C., & Sussman, D. (2004, October 21). *Primetime Live poll: American sex survey: A peek beneath the sheets.* Retrieved May 15, 2007, from http://abcnews.go.com/Primetime/PollVault/story?id=156921&page=1

Lee, J. A. (1973). *The colors of love: An exploration of the ways of loving.* Don Mills, ON: New Press.

Levinger, G. (1974). A three-level approach to attraction: Toward an understanding of pair relatedness. In T. L. Huston (Ed.), *Foundations of interpersonal attraction* (pp. 99–120). New York: Academic Press.

Levinger, G., & Snoek, J. (1972). *Attraction in relationship: A new look at interpersonal attraction*. New York: General Learning Press.

Lewin, K. (1951). Problems of research in social psychology. In D. Cartwright (Ed.), *Field theory in social science: Selected theoretical papers* (pp. 155–169). New York: Harper & Brothers Publishers.

Lewis, R. A. (1972). A developmental framework for the analysis of premarital dyadic formation. *Family Process, 11*, 17–48.

Martin, D. J., Garske, J. P., & Davis, M. K. (2000). Relation of the therapeutic alliance with outcome and other variables: A meta-analytic review. *Journal of Consulting and Clinical Psychology, 68*, 438–450.

Mehrabian, A. (1976). Questionnaire measures of affiliative tendency and sensitivity to rejection. *Psychological Reports, 38*, 199–209.

Milardo, R. M. (1982). Friendship networks in developing relationships: Converging and diverging social environments. *Social Psychology Quarterly, 45*, 162–172.

Milardo, R. M. (1992). Comparative methods for delineating social networks. *Journal of Social and Personal Relationships, 9*, 447–461.

Monroe, W. S. (1898). Discussion and reports: Social consciousness in children. *Psychological Review, 5*, 68–70.

Moss, J. J., Apolonio, F., & Jensen, M. (1971). The premarital dyad during the sixties. *Journal of Marriage and the Family, 33*, 50–69.

Murstein, B. I. (1976). The stimulus-value-role theory of marital choice. In H. Grunebaum & J. Christ (Eds.), *Contemporary marriage: Structures, dynamics, and therapy* (pp. 165–168). Boston: Little, Brown.

Newcomb, T. M. (1956). The prediction of interpersonal attraction. *American Psychologist, 11*, 575–586.

Parks, M. R., & Adelman, M. B. (1983). Communication networks and the development of romantic relationships: An expansion of uncertainty reduction theory. *Human Communication Research, 10*, 55–80.

Perlman, D. (2007). The best of times, the worst of times: The place of close relationships in psychology and our daily lives. *Canadian Psychology, 48*, 7–18.

Perlman, D., & Campbell, S. (2004). Sexuality in close relationships: Concluding commentary. In J. Harvey, A. Wenzel, & S. Sprecher (Eds.), *Handbook of sexuality in close relationships* (pp. 613–635). Mahwah, NJ: Lawrence Erlbaum.

Perlman, D., & Duck, S. (2006). The seven seas of the study of personal relationships: From "the thousand islands" to interconnected waterways. In A. Vangelisti & D. Perlman (Eds.), *Cambridge handbook of personal relationships* (pp. 11–34). New York: Cambridge University Press.

Phillips, R. (1988). *Putting asunder: A history of divorce in Western society*. Cambridge: Cambridge University Press.

Reiss, I. L. (1960). Toward a sociology of the heterosexual love relationship. *Marriage and Family Living, 22*, 139–145.

Rodin, M. (1982). Non-engagement, failure to engage, and disengagement. In S. Duck (Ed.), *Personal relationships 4: Dissolving relationships* (pp. 31–49). New York: Academic Press.

Rosenbaum, M. E. (1986). The repulsion hypothesis: On the nondevelopment of relationships. *Journal of Personality and Social Psychology, 51*, 1156–1166.

Rushton, J. P. (1989). Genetic similarity, human altruism, and group selection. *Behavioral and Brain Sciences, 12*, 503–559.

Sears, D. O. (1986). College sophomores in the laboratory: Influences of a narrow data base on social psychology's view of human nature. *Journal of Personality and Social Psychology, 51*, 515–530.

Suitor, J. J., Wellman, B., & Morgan, D. L. (1997). It's about time: How, why, and when networks change. *Social Networks, 19*, 1–7.

Surra, C. A., Gray, C. R., Boettcher, T. M. J., Cottle, N. R., & Jarvis, M. O. (2002, November). *Research on dating and mate selection: Where does it stand?* Paper presented at 32nd Theory Construction and Research Methodology Workshop, National Council on Family Relations, Houston, TX.

Surra, C. A., Gray, C. R., Boettcher, T. M. J., Cottle, N. R., & West, A. R. (2006). From courtship to universal properties: Research on dating and mate selection, 1950 to 2003. In A. Vangelisti & D. Perlman (Eds.), *Cambridge handbook of personal relationships* (pp. 113–130). New York: Cambridge University Press.

Tesser, A. (1993). The importance of heritability in psychological research: The case of attitudes. *Psychological Review, 100*, 129–142.

VanLear, C. A., Koerner, A., & Allen, D. M. (2006). Relationship typologies. In A. Vangelisti & D. Perlman (Eds.), *Cambridge handbook of personal relationships* (pp. 11–34). New York: Cambridge University Press.

Vorauer, J. D., & Ratner, R. K. (1996). Who's going to make the first move? Pluralistic ignorance as an impediment to relationship formation. *Journal of Social and Personal Relationships, 13,* 483–506.

Waller, W. (1937). The rating and dating complex. *American Sociological Review, 2,* 727–734.

Wellman, B., Wong, R. Y., Tindall, D., & Nazer, N. (1997). A decade of network change: Turnover, persistence and stability in personal communities. *Social Networks, 19,* 27–50.

Winch, R. F. (1958). *Mate selection: A theory of complementary needs.* New York: Harper & Brothers.

Zimbardo, P. G. (1977). *Shyness.* Reading, MA: Addison-Wesley.

Author Index

A

Abakoumkin, G., 88, 94
Abbey, A., 105, 106, 115, 138, 139, 149, 181, 191, 413, 419, 501, 503, 507, 510, 512
Abbott, R., 441, 449
Abeernathy, T., 113, 115
Abela, J. R. Z., 437, 438, 447
Abelson, R. P., 500, 514
Abma, J., 377, 390
Aboud, F. E., 45, 49
Abrahams, D., 113, 120, 218, 219, 220, 224, 249, 256, 264, 299, 300, 313, 315, 336
Abrahams, M., 79, 91
Abrahams, M. F., 280, 282, 290, 362, 367, 410, 420, 454, 455, 458, 459, 461, 462, 469
Abrahams, M. R., 7, 17, 24
Abramson, L. Y., 436, 446
Ace, A., 410, 413, 415, 421
Acevedo, B., 315, 316, 317, 321, 322, 323, 324, 325, 328, 331, 335
Acitelli, L. K., 458, 469
Ackerman, B. P., 355, 360, 369
Ackerman, P. L., 280, 281, 293
Adams, R. G., 34, 49, 302, 311
Adams, R. M., 357, 360, 369
Adelman, M. B., 123, 125, 133, 140, 151, 179, 180, 194, 205, 215, 256, 260, 263, 382, 390, 527, 538
Adesman, P., 41, 54
Adil Saribay, S., 159, 169, 170
Adler, N. L., 316, 326, 334, 340, 343, 351
Afifi, T. D., 122, 130, 131, 158, 171
Afifi, W. A., 13, 106, 110, 115, 119, 121, 122, 127, 129, 130, 131, 135, 138, 141, 142, 143, 144, 147, 149, 157, 170, 175, 176, 179, 181, 182, 183, 184, 185, 186, 187, 190, 191, 192, 410, 416, 419, 518, 519, 521, 522, 524, 527, 528, 532, 533
Agnew, C. R., 15, 197, 199, 200, 207, 209, 210, 212, 213, 214, 272, 287, 288, 289, 472, 483, 522
Agostinelli, G., 58, 73
Agyei, Y., 58, 67
Ahuvia, A. C., 256, 260, 263
Ain, R., 325, 331
Ainsworth, M. S., 76, 77, 82, 91, 473, 483
Ajzen, I., 180, 192
Albright, J. M., 251, 258, 263
Albus, K., 90, 92
Alcalay, L., 55, 56, 59, 60, 66, 72, 277, 278, 294
Alcock, J., 57, 67
Alden, L. A., 438, 445
Alden, L. E., 427, 429, 430, 431, 432, 434, 445, 448, 450
Alexander, A. L., 472, 485
Alexander, G. M., 63, 67
Alexander, K., 18, 27, 45, 53
Alexander, R. D., 55, 57, 67

Alexandrov, E., 82, 91
Alfaro, E. C., 398, 407
Allan, G., 29, 32, 35, 37, 49
Allard, L. M., 482, 483
Allbright, L., 236, 246
Allen, D. M., 518, 538
Allen, J., 78, 80, 85, 90, 91, 316, 317, 320, 322, 323, 329, 330, 331, 409, 417, 419, 424
Allen, K. R., 393, 394, 405
Allen, M., 164, 171
Allensworth, M., 66, 72, 277, 278, 294
Alley, T. R., 276, 289
Allik, J., 55, 56, 59, 60, 66, 72, 277, 278, 294
Allison, D., 285, 286, 290
Altman, I., 19, 24, 30, 40, 41, 49, 122, 126, 131, 154, 155, 156, 157, 158, 162, 170, 174, 176, 177, 186, 191, 203, 206, 207, 210, 213, 259, 263, 297, 311, 382, 388, 399, 405
Amado, D., 430, 449
Amato, P. R., 397, 398, 405
Ambady, N., 218, 231, 273, 289
Ames, D. R., 505, 508, 512
Amir, N., 431, 445, 447
Anafarta, M., 76, 77, 94
Andersen, P. A., 177, 186, 191, 192, 353, 354, 366, 368, 415, 421
Andersen, S. M., 159, 169, 170, 482, 483
Anderson, C. A., 363, 367, 436, 445
Anderson, D. B., 280, 281, 293, 396, 405
Anderson, E. A., 435, 447
Anderson, E. R., 395, 396, 400, 401, 407
Anderson, J. A., 325, 331
Anderson, J. W., 410, 421
Anderson, T. L., 251, 252, 263, 359, 367
Andra, A., 410, 413, 415, 421
Andrews, S. L., 410, 423
Angera, J. J., 382, 388
Angleiter, A., 55, 72
Anolli, L., 361, 362, 367
Ansel, E., 415, 422
Antle, B., 161, 174
Apolonia, F., 520, 527, 538
Aquilino, W. C., 399, 406
Arad, D., 471, 475, 485
Aragona, B. J., 327, 331
Archer, J., 55, 57, 67
Archer, R. L., 39, 41, 49, 53, 153, 154, 159, 161, 162, 165, 169, 170, 172, 173
Argyle, M., 39, 49
Ariely, D., 129, 133, 218, 226, 241, 246, 255
Arkin, R. M., 364, 370
Arkowitz, H., 431, 445
Arlinghaus, K., 84, 93
Arnedt, C., 519, 537
Arnow, B. A., 319, 331

Aron, A. P., 12, 18, 24, 25, 40, 42, 46, 47, 49, 51, 108, 117, 167, 168, 169, 170, 181, 189, 191, 206, 213, 221, 226, 229, 231, 232, 240, 246, 274, 275, 284, 289, 297, 298, 299, 302, 303, 304, 305, 307, 309, 310, 311, 312, 313, 315, 316, 317, 318, 319, 320, 321, 322, 323, 324, 325, 326, 327, 328, 329, 330, 331, 332, 333, 334, 335, 336, 340, 341, 351, 353, 366, 409, 419, 458, 469, 517, 518, 519, 523, 524, 527, 528, 529, 530, 532, 533, 535, 537

Aron, D. G., 181, 189, 191

Aron, E. N., 40, 46, 49, 167, 168, 169, 170, 221, 226, 231, 240, 246, 284, 289, 297, 298, 299, 302, 303, 304, 305, 307, 309, 310, 311, 315, 316, 317, 318, 319, 320, 322, 323, 324, 325, 327, 328, 329, 330, 331, 409, 419, 518, 537

Aronson, E., 33, 39, 106, 118, 271, 272, 289

Aronson, V., 113, 120, 218, 219, 220, 224, 249, 256, 264, 299, 300, 313, 315, 336

Arriaga, X. B., 15, 19, 197, 199, 205, 207, 209, 212, 213, 214, 272, 287, 289, 339, 350, 522, 523, 527, 529, 532, 535

Arrington, M., 148, 149

Artistico, D., 364, 367

Asada, J. K., 178, 180, 183, 379, 389, 410, 419

Asberg, M., 327, 336

Asch, S. E., 103, 115

Asendorpf, J., 364, 367

Asher, S. R., 39, 49

Ashmore, R. D., 38, 51, 275, 277, 290

Aspelmeier, J., 80, 89, 91

Atkinson, J. W., 528, 537

Attridge, M., 496, 497

Atwood, K. A., 143, 151

Ault, L. K., 55, 56, 59, 60, 66, 72, 277, 278, 283, 290, 294

Aumeer-Ryan, K., 260, 263

Austers, I., 55, 56, 59, 60, 66, 72, 277, 278, 294

Avtgis, T. A., 359, 367

Axelrod, R., 219, 231

Axinn, W. G., 8, 24

Ayduk, O., 148, 149

Ayers, J., 126, 131

B

Babrow, A. S., 127, 130, 131

Bacaltchuk, J., 441, 446

Bachelor, A., 436, 446

Back, K., 31, 51, 198, 214, 300, 312

Backman, C. W., 40, 49

Bacon, P. L., 163, 171

Bacue, A., 179, 193

Bagozzi, R. P., 414, 415, 419

Bahr, P., 306, 307, 309, 312

Bailey, B. L., 5, 24

Bailey, J. M., 58, 61, 63, 64, 67, 71, 99, 118, 323, 334

Bailey, M. J., 11, 26, 59, 71

Baker, A., 258, 260, 263

Baker, M., 59, 73

Baker, R. R., 55, 67

Bakermans-Kranenburg, M., 90, 94

Baldassare, M., 32, 51

Baldwin, M. W., 14, 24, 146, 149, 357, 367, 379, 388, 472, 475, 482, 483

Balka, E. B., 113, 115

Bandura, A., 147, 149

Banfield, S., 60, 67

Banks, W. C., 219, 232

Banner, L. L., 319, 331

Barash, D. P., 56, 68

Barbee, A. P., 14, 16, 17, 21, 59, 69, 97, 100, 101, 102, 104, 109, 116, 161, 174, 274, 276, 277, 283, 290, 298, 303, 312, 518, 522, 524, 526, 527, 529, 531, 532

Barber, B. L., 395, 405

Barber, N., 65, 66, 68, 98, 103, 115

Barczyk, A., 286, 292

Bargh, J. A., 21, 23, 24, 33, 34, 53, 165, 166, 167, 170, 203, 213, 214, 236, 237, 238, 239, 240, 241, 246, 247, 481, 482, 484, 511, 513

Barhman, R., 143, 150

Barker, R. G., 198, 203, 213

Barnes, M. L., 11, 21, 24, 199, 215, 329, 336

Barnett, L., 87, 92

Baron-Cohen, S., 500, 512

Baron, R. A., 198, 213

Baron, R. M., 113, 115, 272, 289

Baron, R. S., 280, 293

Barr, A., 279, 283, 292

Barr, E., 84, 93

Barrett, E. S., 63, 70

Barrett, L. F., 19, 26, 154, 163, 172, 219, 233, 240, 247

Barros, J., 320, 321, 335

Bartels, A., 316, 319, 327, 328, 332

Bartholomew, K., 14, 22, 24, 25, 77, 78, 91, 101, 115, 168, 170, 429, 433, 445, 474, 483, 485

Barton, R., 434, 436, 448

Bassin, E., 199, 214

Bates, J. E., 98, 116

Bateson, P., 57, 68

Bator, R. H., 518, 537

Bator, R. J., 40, 49, 167, 168, 169, 170, 240, 246

Batson, C. D., 530, 537

Batson, E., 122, 132

Baum, C. G., 436, 445

Baumeister, R. F., 14, 16, 24, 61, 66, 68, 139, 149, 179, 189, 190, 191, 192, 223, 232, 316, 322, 332, 338, 350, 409, 413, 419, 420, 490, 497

Baumgartner, H., 414, 415, 419

Bavelas, J. B., 154, 170

Baxter, L. A., 129, 130, 131, 132, 139, 140, 143, 149, 154, 155, 157, 158, 160, 165, 169, 170, 173, 176, 179, 180, 181, 182, 186, 187, 188, 192, 203, 213, 308, 311, 399, 405, 410, 413, 419, 420, 472, 483

Bazzini, D. G., 165, 174

Beach, F. A., 326, 327, 332

Beach, S. R. H., 16, 26, 339, 350, 437, 447

Beamer, L., 382, 383, 389

Bearman, P., 377, 388

Beaudoin, G., 319, 334

Beazley, M. B., 430, 447

Beck, A. T., 428, 438, 445

Beck, J. G., 433, 444, 446

Beck, J. S., 428, 440, 445

Becker, D. V., 101, 118

Becker, J., 180, 193

Becker, J. A. H., 410, 420

Becker, R. E., 336, 431, 440, 446, 447

Bednarski, R., 415, 422

Bee, H., 501, 504, 514

Beggan, J. K., 103, 115
Beidel, D. C., 430, 431, 434, 442, 445, 450
Beilin, Y., 12, 24
Bell, R. A., 124, 126, 132, 140, 149, 188, 192, 361, 367,
          410, 420
Bellack, A. S., 427, 439, 445, 447
Bellavia, G. M., 226, 233
Bellis, M. A., 55, 67
Belmonte, M. K., 500, 512
Belsky, J., 56, 64, 65, 66, 68, 71, 83, 92, 270, 273, 294
Bem, S. L., 356, 367
Bengston, V., 393, 394, 405
Bennett, K. L., 56, 59, 60, 72
Benoit, D., 84, 91
Benson, A., 41, 53
Bento, S., 82, 93
Benvindo, R., 320, 321, 335
Ben-Ze'ev, A., 238, 246
Berg, J. H., 36, 39, 41, 46, 49, 53, 154, 156, 158, 159, 161,
          162, 163, 165, 167, 170, 171, 173
Berger, C. R., 19, 24, 121, 122, 123, 124, 128, 129, 130,
          132, 136, 137, 138, 143, 149, 150, 159, 160, 171,
          181, 192, 361, 367, 410, 420, 500, 501, 512, 524,
          525, 537
Berger, P., 454, 469
Berggren, J., 302, 311
Berkowitz, L., 203, 213
Berman, W., 84, 92
Bernard, A. C., 256, 263
Bernier, A., 86, 93
Berry, D. S., 102, 113, 115, 273, 274, 275, 276, 280, 284,
          287, 289
Berscheid, E., 12, 25, 27, 35, 36, 38, 40, 45, 50, 51, 59, 72,
          79, 94, 167, 171, 178, 192, 219, 226, 232, 236,
          246, 247, 259, 263, 269, 270, 271, 272, 273, 274,
          280, 281, 283, 287, 288, 289, 292, 294, 295, 297,
          298, 299, 301, 312, 315, 317, 319, 323, 324, 331,
          332, 335, 339, 340, 341, 350, 365, 366, 370, 391,
          406, 415, 420, 472, 483, 485, 487, 496, 497, 522,
          528, 537
Bert, C. L., 327, 333
Bertilsson, L., 327, 336
Betzig, L., 56, 59, 61, 68, 73
Bevan, J. L., 122, 132, 410, 413, 420
Bhatia, A., 112, 120
Biek, M., 100, 119, 138, 151
Bieling, P. J., 438, 445
Biever, J. L., 427, 431, 447
Binet, A., 325
Birch, J. D., 44, 50
Birnbaum, G. E., 386
Bissonnette, V., 165, 166, 172, 364, 368
Bjerregaard, B., 417, 420
Blackburn, E. J., 417, 420
Blair, K., 3, 301, 453, 466, 469, 518
Blakemore, J. E. O., 409, 421
Blaney, P. H., 436, 445
Blass, T., 343, 350
Blau, P., 15, 18, 19, 24
Blehar, M. C., 76, 77, 82, 91, 473, 483
Bleske, A. L., 59, 68
Bleske-Rechek, A. L., 59, 68, 177, 192, 409, 420
Blieszner, R., 38, 42, 47, 50
Bliss, J., 169
Blum, R. W., 377, 390

Blumberg, S. L., 345, 351
Blumberg, S. R., 435, 445, 447
Blumer, H., 453, 454, 469
Blumstein, P., 279, 291
Blurton Jones, N., 57, 68
Blustein, D., 86, 91
Boase, J., 239, 246, 526, 537
Bochner, A. P., 454, 469
Bodenhausen, G. V., 510, 513
Boettcher, T. M. J., 520, 522, 523, 527, 535, 538
Bögels, S. M., 439, 448
Bogerhoff Mulder, M., 61, 68
Bogg, R. A., 276, 289
Bojan, D., 100, 118
Boland, J. P., 378, 389
Bolger, N., 169, 171
Bolzendahl, C. I., 501, 512
Bonanno, G., 87, 91
Bond, B. J., 122, 129, 133
Boneva, B., 243, 247
Bons, T. A., 45, 54
Boon, J. C., 417, 423
Boon, S. D., 160, 171, 255, 263
Boone, R. T., 360, 367
Booth, A., 63, 71, 285, 293
Booth-Butterfield, M., 362, 367
Borden, J. W., 436, 445
Borden, R. J., 112, 115
Borgida, E., 481, 484
Bornstein, R. F., 36, 50
Bossard, J. H. S., 255, 263
Bostwick, T. D., 185, 192
Bothwell, S., 442, 450
Botwin, M. D., 324, 332
Bourgouin, P., 319, 334
Bowers, J. W., 361, 369
Bowlby, J., 65, 68, 75, 76, 77, 84, 87, 88, 89, 90, 91, 329,
          332, 338, 350, 386, 388, 441, 445, 473, 474, 483
Boyd, D. M., 148, 150
Bradac, J. J., 121, 124, 128, 129, 132, 143, 149, 159, 171
Bradbury, T. N., 81, 82, 92, 211, 213, 222, 233, 286, 291,
          339, 351, 477, 478, 483, 499, 510, 511, 512, 513
Bradford, L., 415, 420
Bradley, B. P., 428, 431, 436, 448
Bradney, N., 29, 52
Bradshaw, D., 22, 27, 329, 335
Bradshaw, S. D., 363, 364, 367
Braithwaite, D., 169
Branierd, E. G., 130, 132
Branigan, C., 360, 368
Brashears, M. E., 75, 93, 159, 173
Brashers, D. E., 127, 130, 131, 132
Bratslavsky, E., 223, 232, 409, 413, 420
Braver, S. L., 398, 406
Bredow, C. A., 3, 518, 524, 526, 527, 528, 529, 531
Brehm, S. S., 42, 48, 50, 300, 313
Brekke, N., 481, 484
Brendle, J. R., 430, 450
Brennan, K. A., 22, 24, 270, 273, 294, 429, 433, 445, 446,
          474, 483
Brennan, P. A., 434, 438, 442, 447
Brenton, M., 37, 50
Bretherton, I., 76, 90, 91
Brewer, M. B., 236, 246
Brewer, N., 481, 485

Brewer, W. F., 472, 483
Brewster, M. P., 417, 420
Bridgeman, D., 33, 39
Briggs, M. A., 35, 53
Briggs, S. R., 165, 166, 172, 364, 368
Brinol, P., 274, 293
Brinton, C., 475, 484
Brislin, T. R., 113, 115
Britton, M., 477, 484
Bröder, A., 64, 68
Brodie, M., 113, 120
Broemer, P., 492, 497
Broesen van Groeou, M., 88, 93
Bronstad, P. M., 278, 294
Brook, J. S., 113, 115
Brooks, J. L., 106, 119
Brotchie, H., 441, 448
Brothen, T., 271, 289
Broude, G. J., 55, 56, 68
Broverman, D. M., 501, 504, 514
Broverman, F. E., 501, 504, 514
Brown, B. B., 207, 213, 384, 385, 388
Brown, B. H., 154, 156, 157, 170
Brown, C., 279, 283, 292
Brown, D. E., 55, 61, 68
Brown, E., 398, 402, 407
Brown, E. G., 202, 215
Brown, J. D., 490, 498
Brown, K., 180, 193
Brown, L. L., 316, 317, 319, 322, 326, 327, 328, 330, 331, 336
Brown, M., 79, 92
Brown, P., 418, 420
Brownell, C. A., 32, 33, 36, 39, 42, 51
Bruce, J. W., 12, 136, 269, 274, 278, 291, 297, 323, 517, 520, 523, 524, 527, 530, 531, 532
Bruce, M. L., 434, 446
Bruch, M. A., 431, 445
Bruckner, K. H., 261, 263
Brumbaugh, C., 78, 92, 359, 368
Bryan, A., 279, 283, 292
Bryant, W. H., 281, 291
Buchanan, G. M., 63, 69
Buchanan, M. C., 410, 420
Buchanan, T., 262, 263, 310, 312
Bucholz, K. K., 64, 69
Buck, P. O., 106, 115
Buck, R., 355, 356, 360, 367
Buergener, F., 430, 447
Buerkel-Rothfuss, N. L., 126, 132, 140, 149, 188, 192
Buffardi, L., 235, 238, 247
Buhr, K., 127, 132
Buhrmester, D., 39, 50, 54
Bui, K-V. T., 199, 213, 222, 232
Buller, D., 110, 115
Bullis, C., 180, 192, 472, 483
Bullo, K., 122, 132
Bumpass, L. L., 396, 402, 403, 406
Burch, R. L., 55, 69
Burchinal, M., 80, 83, 93
Burd, H., 325, 331
Burdick, C. A., 410, 423
Burge, D., 474, 482, 483
Burgess, R. L., 14, 18, 26, 272, 289
Burgoon, J. K., 110, 115, 121, 122, 130, 131, 138, 150, 176, 179, 182, 183, 184, 186, 191, 192

Burgoyne, C. B., 402, 406
Burleson, B. R., 44, 45, 50, 355, 367
Burleson, J. A., 41, 49
Burnam, M. A., 31, 52
Burnham, T. C., 63, 68, 71
Burns, K. C., 147, 150
Burr, R., 112, 118
Burrows, L., 23, 24
Burt, D. M., 56, 63, 72, 102, 118, 325, 335
Burt, M., 12, 26
Bush, A. L., 471, 493, 496, 511, 524, 525, 532, 533, 535
Buslig, A. L. S., 110, 115
Buss, A., 270, 272, 273, 274, 275, 277, 289
Buss, D. M., 11, 20, 21, 24, 27, 55, 56, 58, 59, 60, 61, 63, 64, 66, 68, 69, 70, 72, 73, 99, 102, 103, 109, 115, 177, 192, 210, 224, 231, 232, 269, 274, 282, 285, 293, 294, 299, 312, 316, 323, 324, 329, 332, 338, 350, 380, 381, 383, 387, 388, 389, 409, 420, 459, 462, 469, 489, 491, 495, 497, 498, 502, 503, 504, 506, 507, 510, 512, 513
Butler, D. L., 104, 119
Buunk, A. P., 58, 68
Buunk, B., 272, 274, 293
Byatt, G., 276, 293
Byer, A., 79, 92
Byrne, D., 42, 43, 45, 50, 185, 193, 217, 220, 221, 232, 244, 246, 249, 263, 271, 272, 273, 284, 289, 290, 297, 299, 300, 310, 312, 315, 323, 332, 343, 350, 410, 423, 520, 521, 522, 537

C

Cacioppo, J. T., 271, 293
Cadiz Menne, J. M., 31, 50
Cairns, R. B., 288, 290
Calabrese, R. J., 121, 122, 123, 129, 130, 132, 136, 149, 160, 171, 181, 192, 524, 525, 537
Caldwell, N. D., 436, 448
Cameron, J., 500, 512
Cameron, J. J., 18, 28, 359, 370
Cameron, K. A., 410, 413, 420
Camino, L., 320, 321, 335
Camire, L., 58, 59, 73, 109, 120
Campbell, B. C., 63, 73
Campbell, D. T., 269, 274, 294
Campbell, J. D., 414, 421
Campbell, L., 16, 24, 82, 83, 94, 169, 172, 220, 232, 338, 350, 471, 476, 483, 485, 487, 488, 489, 490, 492, 494, 497, 498, 523, 537
Campbell, S., 524, 538
Campbell, W., 503, 504, 514
Campbell, W. K., 324, 333
Campeas, R., 327, 334, 434, 449
Campos, B., 286, 291
Canary, D. J., 183, 186, 188, 189, 193, 194, 531, 537
Canevello, A., 478, 484
Canfield, R. W., 415, 422
Cantrill, J. G., 357, 368
Cao, G., 316, 319, 322, 327, 328, 336
Capezza, N. M., 15, 197, 205, 213, 522
Caplan, S. E., 34, 50
Caplow, T., 31, 50
Capobianco, A., 210, 215

Cappella, J. N., 430, 445
Caprara, G. V., 364, 367
Cardillo, L. W., 127, 132
Carey, C. M., 6, 27, 185, 193
Carey, G., 363, 370
Carlsmith, J. M., 272, 289
Carlson, E., 78, 80, 94
Carnegie, D., 39, 50
Carnelley, K. B., 78, 79, 91, 93, 382, 386, 388, 437, 445
Carpenter, K. E., 121, 129, 133
Carpenter-Theune, K. E., 122, 130, 133, 157, 172, 187, 193
Carr, A. N., 236, 241, 242, 247, 257, 258, 264
Carson, C. L., 414, 415, 420, 421
Carstensen, L., 76, 90, 91
Carter, C. S., 316, 332
Carter, S., 262, 263, 286, 290
Carter, S. R., III, 415, 424
Carver, V. H., 355, 367
Cascio, C., 327, 333, 336
Casella, D. F., 38, 51
Cash, T. F., 43, 50
Cashdan, E., 58, 64, 68
Casillias, A., 275, 284, 287
Caspi, A., 64, 66, 71, 324, 332
Cassidy, J., 21, 24, 77, 82, 91, 93
Castro-Martin, T., 396, 403, 406
Catanese, K. R., 139, 149
Cate, R. M., 3, 176, 192, 307, 312, 377, 379, 382, 388, 418, 420, 518
Caughlin, J. P., 158, 171, 326, 334, 341, 351
Caulkins, R. S., 280, 281, 293
Cervone, D., 364, 367
Chadiha, L. A., 454, 455, 458, 462, 464, 469, 470
Chagnon, N. A., 61, 68
Chaikin, A. L., 40, 41, 51, 154, 157, 158, 162, 164, 171, 237, 246
Chambless, D. L., 430, 440, 446, 447
Chambliss, W. J., 14, 16, 24
Chan, C-N., 180, 192
Chan, D. K-S., 33, 50, 155, 165, 166, 171
Chang, S-C., 180, 192
Chapdelaine, A., 219, 226, 232
Chaplin, W., 434, 436, 448
Chapman, J. F., 63, 68, 71
Chappell, K., 79, 91
Chartrand, T. L., 21, 24, 26, 203, 213
Chavez, A. M., 176, 179, 180, 183, 187, 188, 189, 190, 192
Cheek, J. M., 364, 367
Chelune, G. J., 164, 171
Chen, F. F., 274, 286
Chen, J. B-S., 410, 422
Chen, J. Y., 63, 72
Chen, M., 23, 24
Cheng, C. M., 21, 26
Cheng, G. H-L., 33, 50, 155, 165, 166, 171
Cherlin, A., 8, 24, 84, 91, 402, 406
Cherry, S., 442, 448
Chipuer, H. M., 363, 367
Chisholm, J. S., 65, 66, 68
Chiu, C., 478, 483
Cho, W., 321, 332
Choo, P., 322, 332
Christ, W. G., 79, 80, 94, 282, 287, 294
Christensen, A., 298, 312
Christiansen, A., 271, 272, 292

Christopher, F. S., 176, 192
Chu, L. C., 273, 292
Chuan, S. L., 241, 246
Cialdini, R. B., 104, 112, 115, 117
Ciceri, R., 361, 362, 367
Clair, R. P., 416, 420
Clandos, R., 396, 405
Clark, C. L., 7, 17, 22, 24, 79, 91, 280, 282, 290, 362, 367, 410, 420, 429, 445, 454, 455, 458, 459, 461, 462, 469, 474, 483
Clark, D. M., 428, 431, 433, 440, 445, 448, 449
Clark, J. V., 431, 445
Clark, L. A., 363, 370, 441, 442, 450
Clark, M. S., 36, 49, 154, 156, 161, 162, 171, 173, 272, 275, 281, 283, 290, 292, 355, 367
Clark, R. A., 40, 50
Clark, R. D., 55, 56, 58, 68, 103, 108, 109, 114, 115
Clark, R. E., 413, 420
Clarke, J. C., 432, 448
Clarke, S. C., 395, 403, 407
Clatterbuck, G. W., 128, 132
Cleary, J., 143, 150
Cline, R. J. W., 143, 144, 150
Clingempeel, W. G., 395, 396, 400, 401, 406, 407
Clore, G. L., 40, 42, 272, 290, 297, 299, 300, 310, 312
Clutton-Brock, T. H., 56, 57, 69
Clydesdale, T., 387, 388
Coates, L., 154, 170
Cochran, C. C., 416, 420
Coe, C., 415, 422
Coffelt, T. T., 391, 518
Cohen, B., 327, 334
Cohen, C., 84, 85, 93
Cohen, D., 478, 479, 480, 484
Cohen, J., 410, 413, 422
Cohn, D., 81, 91
Cole, J., 410, 422
Cole, S. W., 482, 483
Coleman, L. M., 144, 150
Coleman, M., 395, 398, 401, 402, 406
Coles, M. E., 430, 431, 439, 441, 445, 446
Collins, B. C., 358, 367
Collins, N. L., 22, 25, 40, 50, 77, 91, 226, 233, 240, 246, 471, 474, 475, 482, 483, 490, 498
Collins, W. A., 77, 78, 80, 94, 316, 332, 377, 388, 390
Comer, R., 64, 73
Condon, J. W., 14, 25
Conger, A. J., 430, 449
Conger, J. C., 274, 277, 295
Connolly, J. A., 385, 388
Conrad, L. M., 400, 407
Contreras, R., 322, 332, 344, 350
Cook, M., 38, 39, 49, 50
Cook, M. W., 112, 118
Cook, T. D., 269, 274, 294
Cook, W. L., 47, 48, 52, 281, 292
Cooksey, E. C., 377, 388
Cooley, M. R., 442, 450
Coombs, R. H., 256, 263
Coontz, S., 7, 8, 25
Cooper, A., 259, 260, 263
Cooper, J., 271, 290
Cooper, M. L., 382, 388
Corcoran, D., 76, 77, 94
Cornelius, J., 475, 484

Cortese, A., 304, 305, 307, 309, 311, 313, 317, 320, 321, 323, 324, 336, 413, 424
Cosmides, L., 20, 25, 501, 512
Costa, P. T., Jr., 346, 350
Costanzo, P., 355, 367
Cottle, N. R., 520, 522, 523, 527, 535, 538
Couden, A., 59, 73
Cousins, A. J., 12, 25, 63, 64, 67, 69
Cousins, A. V., 410, 424
Covell, N. H., 143, 146, 151
Cowan, C., 81, 82, 91
Cowan, P. A., 81, 82, 91, 457, 469
Cox, M., 80, 83, 93
Coyne, J. C., 84, 91, 434, 436, 437, 445, 446, 449
Cozby, P. C., 41, 50, 253, 265
Cozzarelli, C., 105, 115
Craig, J. M., 105, 119, 139, 151
Crandall, C. S., 274, 278, 290
Crano, W. D., 14, 25
Crawford, A., 243, 247
Crawford, C. B., 58, 59, 74, 110, 120
Crawford, M., 272, 290
Creasey, G., 14, 22, 75, 77, 80, 81, 84, 88, 89, 90, 91, 92, 93, 136, 208, 210, 429, 518, 523, 524, 527, 529, 531, 534
Creekmore, C. R., 31, 50
Creswell, J. W., 404, 406
Crispi, E., 84, 92
Crnic, K., 83, 92
Crocker, J., 510, 512
Cronk, L., 61, 69
Cross, S. E., 163, 167, 171, 172, 321, 332
Crowe, P. A., 376, 390
Crowell, J., 77, 78, 80, 81, 82, 89, 92, 94
Crozier, W. R., 364, 365, 367
Cue, K., 87, 92
Culler, R. E., 31, 52
Cummings, J., 243, 247
Cunningham, L. H., 114
Cunningham, M. R., 14, 16, 17, 21, 25, 59, 69, 97, 98, 100, 101, 102, 103, 104, 106, 107, 108, 109, 110, 116, 118, 119, 120, 255, 264, 274, 275, 276, 277, 279, 281, 283, 288, 289, 290, 292, 293, 298, 300, 303, 312, 313, 414, 420, 518, 522, 524, 526, 527, 529, 531, 532
Cupach, W. R., 39, 54, 190, 192, 255, 264, 286, 294, 301, 313, 315, 332, 409, 410, 411, 412, 413, 414, 415, 416, 418, 419, 420, 421, 422, 521, 523, 524, 525, 528, 534
Cupach, W. W., 355, 367
Curran, J. P., 430, 431, 439, 446
Curran, M., 83, 92
Curry, T. J., 43, 44, 50
Curtis, J. T., 327, 331
Curtis, R. C., 17, 18, 25, 40, 50
Custer, L., 3, 301, 311, 453, 518, 523, 532, 533, 535

D

Dabbs, J. M., Jr., 63, 69, 159, 173
Dabbs, M. G., 63, 69
D'Agostino, P. R., 36, 50
Dainton, M., 188, 192

Dalrymple, K., 440, 442, 447
Daly, J. A., 410, 415, 420, 421, 424
Daly, M., 57, 64, 69
Dancu, C. V., 430, 431, 434, 445, 450
Darcy, K., 433, 446
Darley, J. M., 35, 50
Darwin, C. R., 55, 56, 59, 65, 67, 69, 98, 116
Davidson, R. J., 355, 368
Davies, G. M., 417, 423
Davila, J., 81, 82, 92, 433, 444, 446, 474, 482, 483
Davis, A., 169, 171
Davis, C. G., 436, 448
Davis, D., 39, 42, 44, 50, 51, 161, 162, 171
Davis, J., 377, 389
Davis, J. A., 55, 69
Davis, J. D., 164, 171
Davis, J. L., 207, 215, 219, 233
Davis, K., 79, 89, 91, 93
Davis, K. E., 178, 192, 271, 291, 317, 324, 332, 343, 350, 410, 413, 415, 421, 509, 513, 527, 537
Davis, K. L., 175, 179, 181, 187, 193
Davis, M. K., 87, 93, 534, 538
Davis, M. S., 4, 5, 7, 8, 9, 14, 17, 25, 415, 421
Davis, R. N., 436, 446
Davis, S., 454, 470
Davison, K. P., 239, 246
Dawson, B. L., 59, 69
Dean, G. O., 17, 26
DeBord, K., 79, 92
Decker, B. P., 229, 233
DeCoster, J., 510, 514
Degler, C. A., 5, 25
de Jesus Mari, J., 441, 446
De Jong Gieveld, J., 519, 523, 537
De La Ronde, C., 15, 27
DeLucia, J. L., 185, 192
De Mello, M. F., 441, 446
Demo, D. H., 395, 399, 405, 406
Denizet-Lewis, B., 380, 388
Dennet, D. C., 510, 512
Denney, N. W., 382, 390
Dennison, S. M., 415, 421
Denrell, J., 37, 38, 51
DePaulo, B. M., 109, 110, 116, 242, 246
Derlega, V. J., 17, 22, 40, 41, 43, 50, 51, 153, 154, 157, 158, 161, 162, 163, 164, 171, 172, 174, 237, 240, 246, 358, 371, 523, 524, 526, 528, 532, 534, 535
Dermer, M., 36, 50, 219, 232, 273, 280, 289, 290, 472, 483
Deschamps, J., 320, 321, 335
Desmond, J. E., 319, 331
Detenber, B. H., 241, 246
Deutsch, R., 510, 514
Devine, P. G., 168, 171, 273, 290
DeVries, A. C., 316, 332
Deyo, Y., 217
Diamond, G. S., 442, 449
Diamond, L. M., 79, 90, 92, 319, 330, 332, 333
diBattista, P., 124, 132
Dicke, A., 343, 346, 350
Dickerson, S. S., 239, 246
Dickson, J. W., 385, 389
Dickstein, S., 80, 92
Diehl, M., 492, 497
Dijksterhuis, A., 281, 286, 290
Dijkstra, P., 58, 68

Dillard, J. P., 356, 367, 410, 421, 435, 446
Dillman, L., 184, 192
Dillow, M. R., 143, 147, 149, 410, 413, 420
Dillworth, D., 281, 293
Dindia, K., 153, 154, 164, 171, 188, 192, 531, 537
Dinwiddie, S. H., 64, 69
Dion, K., 38, 51, 528
Dion, K. K., 12, 22, 25, 26, 47, 51, 236, 246, 317, 320, 322,
            323, 324, 332
Dion, K. L., 22, 26, 317, 320, 322, 323, 324, 332
DiPaula, A., 414, 421
Dishion, T. J., 205, 213
Dobbins, S. E., 430, 448
Dobson, K. S., 436, 440, 446
Docherty, L., 302, 311
Dockum, M., 40, 50
Dodge, C. S., 336, 431, 446
Dodge, K. A., 79, 92, 98, 116
Doherty, R. W., 322, 332
Donchi, L., 33, 51
Donn, J. E., 251, 252, 254, 263
Donnerstein, C., 185, 191, 193
Donovan-Kicken, E., 128, 133
Doobs, L. K., 127, 132
Douglas, W., 18, 25, 124, 125, 132, 136, 137, 138, 149, 150
Dowdy, B. B., 202, 213
Downey, G., 14, 17, 18, 25, 148, 149, 150
Dozier, M., 87, 90, 92
Dransfield, M., 81, 92
Draper, K. K., 382, 388
Draper, P., 65, 66, 68
Dreyer, C. S., 380, 383, 386, 390
Drigotas, S. M., 199, 200, 213, 221, 222, 232, 472, 483
Driscoll, D. M., 128, 132
Driscoll, R., 324, 332, 527, 537
Druen, P. B., 59, 69, 102, 104, 110, 116, 119, 274, 276, 277,
            281, 290, 293, 298, 303, 312
Druen, P. D., 255, 264
Drumm, P., 409, 421
Dubner, S. J., 255, 257, 264
Dubois, S. L., 11, 28
Ducharme, J., 436, 446
Duck, S., 41, 47, 51, 53, 158, 160, 163, 168, 172, 173, 218,
            220, 221, 234, 285, 286, 290, 300, 301, 310, 313,
            520, 525, 537, 538
Dugan, E., 31, 51
Dugas, M. J., 127, 132
Dugatkin, L. A., 103, 104, 116
Duggan, E. S., 433, 446
Dun, T., 158, 165, 170
Duncan, T., 415, 422
Dunkel-Schetter, C., 164, 174
Dunn, J. L., 410, 411, 413, 414, 421
Dunne, M. P., 63, 64, 67, 69
Duntely, J., 56, 73
Duran, R. L., 38, 54
Durvasula, R., 317, 335
Dutton, D. G., 12, 25, 46, 49, 206, 213, 226, 229, 231, 232,
            297, 298, 299, 302, 303, 304, 305, 307, 309,
            311, 312, 315, 316, 317, 318, 322, 323, 324, 325,
            331, 333
Dutton-Greene, L. B., 415, 417, 419, 421
Dutton, L. B., 410, 412, 421
Dweck, C. S., 478, 483
Dyer, M. A., 280, 281, 293

Dykman, B. M., 436, 446
Dykman, B. S., 436, 446
Dykstra, P., 88, 93

E

Eagly, A. H., 38, 51, 103, 116, 275, 277, 290
Easton, J., 410, 417, 421
Eastwick, P. W., 6, 209, 217, 218, 219, 222, 224, 226, 227,
            228, 229, 231, 232, 261, 262, 269, 271, 272, 286,
            290, 518, 522, 523, 526, 530, 532, 533, 534, 535
Ebbesen, E. B., 32, 51
Edelstein, R. S., 168, 172
Edgar, T., 143, 144, 150
Edwards, J. R., 273, 290
Egeland, B., 77, 78, 80, 94
Eggert, L. L., 34, 35, 53, 198, 215
Egland, K. L., 138, 150, 410, 421
Ehlers, A., 440, 445
Eibl-Eibesfeldt, I., 105, 116
Eidelson, R. J., 471, 477, 483
Eisenberg, N., 203, 214
Ekman, P., 355, 368
Elder, G. H., Jr., 393, 406
Elie, R., 439, 449
Ellis, B. J., 18, 25, 55, 56, 58, 61, 64, 66, 69, 73, 98, 116,
            496, 497
Ellis, C., 454, 469
Ellis, D. G., 30, 52
Ellison, N., 148, 150
Ellison, N. B., 110, 117, 148, 150, 396, 397, 406
Ellison, P. T., 63, 68, 70
Eloy, S. V., 189, 192, 415, 421
Ember, C., 55, 64, 71
Ember, M., 55, 64, 71
Emerson, R. E., 411, 413, 418, 421
Emerson, T., 431, 450
Emmelkamp, P. M., 439, 448, 477, 483
Eng, W., 430, 433, 439, 441, 446
Enns, V., 475, 482, 483
Epley, N., 508, 512
Epstein, J. A., 242, 246
Epstein, N., 471, 477, 483
Epstein, W., 281, 284, 295
Erbert, L. A., 157, 169, 170
Erev, I., 159, 173
Erikson, E. H., 376, 377, 383, 388, 389
Eriksson, C. J. P., 102, 119
Ervin, C. R., 220, 221, 232, 249, 263
Erwin, C. R., 300, 312
Erwin, P. G., 42, 51
Etcheverry, P. E., 200, 207, 213
Evans, D., 256, 263
Evans, K., 415, 422
Evans, P. L., 405, 406
Evans, S. M., 508, 514

F

Falk, E., 501, 512
Fallon, B. A., 434, 449

Fannin, A. D., 17, 25
Faravelli, C., 430, 446
Farrell, M. P., 33, 51
Faulkner, S. L., 183, 191
Fay, M., 327, 334
Fazier, P. A., 416, 420
Fazio, R. H., 229, 233, 302, 313
Fedoroff, I. C., 439, 446
Feeney, B. C., 275, 281, 283, 292, 474, 483, 484
Feeney, J. A., 342, 345, 350, 429, 446
Fehr, B., 29, 42, 44, 51, 158, 172, 197, 298, 305, 313, 316,
      318, 319, 333, 342, 345, 350, 357, 368, 410, 424,
      475, 482, 483, 525, 526, 527, 528, 529, 530
Fein, E., 109, 116
Feingold, A., 38, 51, 58, 59, 69, 224, 232
Feldman, A., 83, 92
Feldman, R. S., 365, 369
Felmlee, D. H., 46, 108, 116, 136, 179, 180, 199, 200, 213,
      214, 256, 260, 264, 269, 287, 294, 297, 305, 306,
      307, 308, 309, 312, 313, 324, 336, 365, 368, 410,
      424, 466, 470, 496, 497, 523, 524, 527, 530, 533,
      534, 535, 536
Feng, T., 316, 319, 322, 327, 328, 336
Fennell, M., 440, 445
Fenney, J., 84, 92
Ferrara, M. H., 410, 419
Ferris, K. O., 411, 413, 418, 421
Feske, U., 440, 446
Festinger, L., 31, 51, 103, 116, 198, 214, 300, 312
Fields, J. M., 396, 407
Fiese, B. H., 456, 457, 469
Figley, C. R., 15, 19, 25
Filipczak, B., 394, 407
Filman, G., 325, 331
Finch, J. F., 59, 70, 280, 291
Fincham, F. D., 211, 213, 339, 350, 398, 407, 477, 478, 483,
      510, 511, 512
Findlay, C., 478, 484
Findley-Klein, C., 147, 151
Fine, G. A., 33, 51
Fine, M. A., 391, 397, 399, 406, 518, 524, 525, 527, 532,
      534, 535
Fingerman, K. L., 285, 293
Fink, B., 63, 70
Fink, E. L., 143, 144, 150
Finkel, E. J., 6, 209, 217, 218, 219, 222, 224, 226, 227, 228,
      229, 231, 232, 261, 262, 269, 271, 272, 286, 288,
      290, 518, 522, 523, 526, 530, 532, 533, 534, 535
Finkenaauer, C., 158, 172
Firestone, J. M., 416, 421
Fischer, A., 79, 92
Fischer, A. H., 355, 356, 361, 369
Fischer, B., 103, 117
Fischer, C. S., 30, 32, 51
Fischer, D., 33, 34, 53
Fischer, E. F., 315, 334
Fishbein, M., 180, 192
Fishbein, S., 12, 28
Fisher, H. E., 55, 61, 69, 250, 315, 316, 317, 319, 320, 322,
      326, 327, 328, 329, 330, 331, 333, 335, 336
Fisher, J. D., 143, 146, 151
Fisher, M., 59, 71
Fisher, M. L., 56, 73, 109, 120
Fisher, W. A., 143, 146, 151
Fishkin, S. A., 99, 118, 330, 335

Fiske, S. T., 210, 232, 236, 241, 246, 481, 484
Fisman, R., 218, 221, 232, 233
Fitness, J., 356, 366, 368, 370, 482, 484
Fitzberald, F. A., 5, 25
Fitzgerald, N. M., 307, 312
Fitzsimons, G. J., 237, 240, 241, 246
Fitzsimons, G. M., 165, 166, 167, 170, 482, 484
Flament, M. F., 327, 333
Flanagan, A., 377, 389
Fleming, A. T., 6, 25
Fleming, K., 6, 25
Fletcher, G. J. O., 11, 16, 25, 102, 116, 220, 221, 232, 298,
      299, 304, 312, 316, 333, 339, 350, 379, 389, 471,
      472, 473, 476, 482, 483, 484, 485, 487, 488, 489,
      490, 491, 492, 493, 494, 497, 498, 501, 503, 513,
      524, 526
Flinn, M. V., 59, 69
Flora, J., 354, 368, 434, 449
Floyd, K., 131, 133, 155, 165, 166, 173, 237, 239, 252, 258,
      264, 361, 370
Flynn, H., 306, 307, 309, 312
Foa, E. B., 431, 440, 445, 446, 447
Folkes, V. S., 190, 192, 410, 413
Fonagy, P., 82, 92
Fong, C., 465, 469
Ford, L. A., 127, 131
Forgas, J. P., 135, 150
Forman, R., 31, 50
Fortes, C., 309, 312
Foster, C. A., 324, 333
Foster, G., 32, 43, 46, 51
Fowles, J., 3, 4, 25
Foxman, B., 385, 389
Fraley, B., 18, 25, 42, 47, 51, 108, 117, 458, 469
Fraley, R. C., 78, 88, 89, 92, 217, 232, 359, 368, 474, 484
Fraley, W. C., 429, 446
Franche, R-L., 436, 446
Francis, K., 127, 132
Francis, M. E., 457, 470
Franck, K. A., 30, 51
Franco, N., 415, 422
Franiuk, R., 478, 479, 480, 484
Frank, E. C., 442, 449
Franklin, M. E., 63, 70, 431, 446
Frayser, S., 55, 64, 69
Frazier, L., 85, 92
Frazier, P., 79, 92
Frederick, D., 63, 69
Fredman, L., 434, 446
Fredrickson, B. L., 360, 368
Freeman, K. E., 143, 144, 150
Freeman, S., 112, 115
Frei, J. R., 345, 350
Freimuth, V. S., 143, 144, 150
Freitas, A. L., 14, 17, 18, 25, 148, 150
French, R. D., 436, 445
Freund, S., 315, 333
Friedman, H. S., 38, 51, 365, 368
Friese, I. H., 358, 370
Friesen, J., 49
Friesen, M., 11, 25, 102, 116, 491, 494, 497
Friesen, W. V., 355, 368
Frieze, I. H., 158, 169, 174, 410, 423, 424, 458, 462, 469, 470
Frijda, N. H., 355, 368
Fritz, J. M. H., 416, 421

Frone, M. R., 382, 388
Frost, J. H., 129, 133, 256
Fuetsch, M., 434, 450
Fuhrman, R. W., 168, 171
Furman, W., 39, 50, 54, 77, 86, 92, 285, 290, 377, 384, 385, 388, 389
Fustenberg, F., 84, 91
Fyer, A. J., 442, 448

G

Gable, S. L., 83, 92, 536, 537
Gagne, F. M., 490, 497
Gagnon, J. H., 66, 71, 323, 334
Gaines, B., 14, 15, 16, 27
Gaines, S. O., 465, 469
Gallup, G. G., 55, 63, 69, 70
Gangestad, S. W., 11, 12, 25, 27, 55, 56, 57, 58, 60, 61, 62, 63, 64, 66, 69, 70, 71, 73, 99, 100, 117, 119, 138, 151, 224, 234, 277, 278, 279, 281, 282, 283, 290, 291, 294, 380, 389, 488, 490, 491, 492, 495, 497, 502, 513
Ganong, L. H., 395, 398, 401, 402, 406, 476, 485
Garber, J., 64, 66, 69
Garcia, S., 165, 166, 172, 364, 368
Gardner, C. B., 411, 413, 418, 421
Gardner, R. C., 273, 291
Garfinkel, R., 434, 449
Garske, J., 87, 93
Garske, J. P., 534, 538
Garver-Apgar, C. E., 12, 25, 63, 67, 69, 282, 283, 290
Gary, A. L., 19, 28
Gasper, K., 147, 150, 358, 368
Gaudiano, B. A., 440, 442, 447
Gaulin, S., 58, 67
Gavin, J., 260, 264
Gawronski, B., 510, 513
Geary, D. C., 57, 69
Gefen, D., 33, 53
Geis, G., 24
Gelissen, J., 403, 406
Gentzler, A. L., 386, 389
George, C., 77, 92
George, L. J., 326, 334, 341, 351
Geraci, R. L., 39, 49
Gerard, H. B., 472, 485
Gergen, K. J., 453, 454, 457, 469
Gergen, M. N., 453, 454, 457, 469
Gerrard, M., 382, 390
Gerson, K., 32, 51
Gest, S. D., 39, 51
Getz, L. L., 316, 332
Giaudrone, L., 81, 92
Gibbons, B. S., 410, 414, 415, 421
Gibbs, J. L., 110, 117, 396, 397, 406
Gibbs, R. W., Jr., 356, 368
Gibson, R. M., 103, 117
Gierveld, J. D. J., 400, 406
Gifford-Smith, M. E., 32, 33, 36, 39, 42, 51
Gilbert, D. T., 511, 513
Gilbert, L. A., 358, 368
Gilbert, P., 433, 450
Gilboa-Schechtman, E., 431, 447

Gilding, M., 33, 52
Giles, L., 316, 333, 471, 473, 476, 484, 487, 488, 489, 491, 492, 494, 497, 501, 503, 513
Giles-Sims, J., 402, 406
Gillath, O., 386, 388
Gilligan, C., 85, 92
Gilovich, T., 508, 512
Gingrich, B., 327, 333, 336
Giordano, P. C., 159, 164, 165, 172, 377, 389
Gitow, A., 434, 449
Givens, D. B., 97, 103, 104, 105, 106, 117
Givetz, M., 439, 449
Gladue, B. A., 58, 67
Glaser, J., 283, 292
Glass, C. R., 427, 431, 447
Gleason, K., 82, 93
Gleason, M. E. J., 33, 53, 165, 166, 173, 237, 238, 239, 240, 241, 242, 247
Glick, P., 12, 27, 79, 94, 281, 294, 365, 366, 370
Glover, G. H., 319, 331
Godfrey, D. K., 39, 51
Goethals, G. R., 271, 290
Goffman, E., 19, 25, 161, 165, 172, 261, 263, 359, 368
Goldman, A. I., 505, 508, 513
Goldsmith, D., 381, 382, 389
Goldsmith, D. J., 131, 132
Goldstein, N. J., 104, 117
Goldwyn, R., 77, 85, 88, 90, 93
Gollwitzer, P. M., 490, 497, 511, 513
Gonso, J., 39, 51
Gonzaga, G. C., 286, 291, 316, 319, 328, 331, 333
Goodall, J., 326, 333
Goode, W. J., 325, 333
Goodfriend, W., 197, 207, 209, 213, 214
Goodman, G. S., 21, 26
Goodman, M. R., 398, 406
Goodwin, R., 107, 117, 478, 484
Goodwin, S. A., 219, 232
Gordon, E. M., 161, 172
Gordon, R. A., 15, 16, 25
Gore, J. S., 163, 167, 172
Gorman, J. M., 327, 334
Gorman, L. L., 441, 448
Goslin, S. D., 206, 214
Gotlib, I. A., 436, 446
Gotlib, I. H., 427, 435, 437, 447, 449
Gottlieb, L., 257, 258, 261, 263
Gottman, J. M., 39, 51, 222, 232, 345, 350, 527, 537
Gouldner, A. W., 137, 150
Gouldner, H., 37, 51
Grady, K., 32, 53
Graff-Dolezal, J., 430, 450
Graham-Bermann, S. A., 39, 51
Grammer, K., 63, 64, 69, 70, 72, 103, 105, 117
Grant, V. J., 64, 70
Grant, V. W., 315, 325, 333
Gray, C. R., 520, 522, 523, 527, 535, 538
Gray, P. B., 63, 68, 70, 71
Graziano, W. G., 12, 36, 50, 59, 70, 103, 117, 136, 203, 214, 219, 232, 269, 271, 273, 274, 278, 279, 280, 281, 282, 284, 285, 287, 289, 291, 293, 297, 323, 472, 483, 487, 497, 517, 520, 523, 524, 527, 530, 531, 532, 537
Green, A. S., 33, 53, 165, 166, 173, 237, 238, 239, 240, 241, 242, 247

Green, J. D., 324, 333
Greenberg, R., 41, 54
Greene, D., 508, 514
Greene, K., 17, 153, 154, 161, 163, 172, 174, 240, 523
Greene, L., 377, 389
Greene, R. W., 357, 368
Greene, S. J., 55, 56, 68
Greer, A. E., 59, 70, 459, 469
Greiling, H., 60, 64, 70, 380, 381, 383, 387, 389
Greitemeyer, T., 100, 117, 286, 291
Grello, C. M., 385, 389
Grey, N., 440, 445
Grey, S., 439, 449
Griffeth, R. W., 32, 53
Griffin, A. M., 271, 274, 291
Griffin, D. W., 16, 22, 25, 27, 221, 226, 233, 479, 485, 490, 492, 494, 498
Griffin, E., 31, 52
Griffin, J. J., Jr., 14, 15, 16, 27
Griffith, J. D., 400, 407
Griffitt, W., 198, 214, 522, 537
Griskevicius, V., 104, 117
Griswell, M. L., 510, 513
Gross, J., 325, 328, 331
Grote, N. K., 458, 469
Groth, G., 20, 26, 56, 57, 70, 99, 108, 118, 502, 513
Grove, T. G., 122, 132
Gruenfeld, D. H., 135, 151
Grunbaum, J., 377, 389
Gruter, M., 58, 71
Grzelak, J., 153, 171
Gudykunst, W. B., 121, 122, 123, 125, 126, 128, 129, 132, 133, 169, 172
Guerrero, L. K., 136, 157, 170, 175, 176, 177, 179, 180, 183, 184, 186, 187, 188, 189, 190, 191, 192, 353, 354, 366, 368, 379, 415, 419, 421, 518, 519, 521, 523, 524, 527, 528, 531, 534, 535
Gulledge, A., 113, 117
Gulledge, M., 113, 117
Gurung, R. A. R., 465, 469
Gutierre, R., 64, 73
Guttentag, M., 64, 65, 70
Gydrich, T., 430, 447

H

Haar, T., 147, 150
Haas, S. M., 127, 132
Haase, A. Q., 243, 247
Hackmann, A., 440, 445
Hadley, C., 61, 70
Hagans, C., 86, 94
Hagel, R., 63, 70
Hahn, J., 343, 350
Haig, J., 275, 284, 287
Haigh, M., 180, 193
Hair, E. C., 279, 291
Haldeman, D., 203, 214
Hale, J. L., 183, 184, 185, 192, 193, 194
Hall, J. H., 398, 407
Hall, M., 391, 396, 407
Hallahan, M., 273, 289
Hallam, M., 12, 26, 38, 47, 52, 275, 276, 292

Hallinan, M. T., 32, 52
Ham, J., 507, 509, 511, 514
Ham, L., 434, 447
Hamburg, B. A., 113, 115
Hamilton, D. L., 128, 132
Hamilton, P. A., 112, 113, 118
Hamm, J. V., 43, 45, 52
Hammen, C., 434, 438, 442, 447, 474, 482, 483
Hammer, M. R., 125, 133
Hammon, D., 415, 422
Hammond, S. L., 143, 144, 150
Hampton, K., 243, 247
Hancock, J. T., 242, 246
Handley, I. M., 360, 368
Haney, C., 219, 232
Hankin, B. L., 437, 438, 447
Hanna, S. E., 128, 134
Hannett, C. A., 58, 73
Hannon, P. A., 207, 215, 219, 233
Hans, J., 398, 401, 402, 406
Hansen, A., 311, 312
Hansen, K. A., 278, 294
Hansen, S. L., 107, 117
Hara, K., 155, 174
Harasymchuk, C., 29, 49, 51, 357, 368
Harber, K., 454, 470
Haring, M., 87, 91
Harlow, T. F., 414, 422
Harmon, A., 254
Harnish, R. J., 105, 115
Harper, M. S., 385, 389
Harré, R., 356, 369
Harris, B. A., 298, 313
Harris, D. W., 169, 172, 523, 537
Harris, P. B., 206, 214
Harris, R. J., 416, 421
Harris, T. M., 206, 214
Harrison, A. A., 224, 233
Hart, T. A., 433, 446
Harter, K., 83, 93
Harton, H. C., 229, 233
Hartup, W. W., 39, 42, 43, 44, 45, 51, 52
Harvey, J. H., 7, 165, 169, 178, 201, 203, 214, 230, 237, 249, 271, 272, 292, 298, 311, 312, 375, 391, 396, 397, 399, 406, 419, 429, 447, 454, 470, 504, 513, 517, 519
Harvey, O. J., 219, 234
Harwood, B. T., 46, 52
Hasegawa, T., 280, 293
Haselager, G. J. T., 42, 43, 44, 45, 52
Haselton, M. G., 55, 63, 64, 66, 69, 70, 502, 503, 507, 510, 513
Hassebrauck, M., 158, 172
Hatfield, E., 7, 55, 56, 58, 59, 68, 73, 103, 108, 109, 114, 115, 165, 177, 193, 223, 224, 230, 233, 234, 235, 236, 237, 244, 246, 249, 259, 260, 263, 273, 274, 277, 286, 291, 299, 300, 304, 305, 307, 309, 311, 312, 313, 315, 316, 317, 319, 320, 321, 322, 323, 324, 325, 332, 333, 334, 336, 340, 342, 350, 351, 396, 413, 424, 475, 484, 502, 504, 506, 514, 519
Hathaway, J. E., 377, 390
Haugaard, J. J., 410, 411, 421
Hause, K. S., 183, 186, 189, 193
Hawkins, L. B., 282, 291, 292, 365, 366, 369

Hay, J., 299, 312
Hayes, A., 378, 379, 380, 381, 382, 383, 385, 386, 390
Hayes, K. A., 178, 194
Hayes, S. A., 434, 447
Hayhurst, H., 441, 449
Hays, R. B., 31, 42, 46, 52, 156, 158, 160, 167, 172
Haythorne, W. W., 206, 213
Hazam, H., 158, 172
Hazan, C., 14, 22, 25, 27, 77, 79, 80, 85, 90, 92, 210, 214,
    273, 274, 291, 315, 319, 320, 329, 330, 333, 335,
    342, 350, 429, 447, 474, 475, 484, 518, 537
Hazen, N., 83, 92
Hazeu, H., 40, 50
Heath, K. M., 61, 70
Heckelman, L. R., 434, 449
Hedayati, M., 127, 132
Heerey, E. A., 200, 214
Heidenreich, T., 440, 449
Heider, F., 122, 133, 271, 275, 291, 454, 469, 478, 484,
    500, 509, 510, 513
Heimberg, R. G., 336, 430, 431, 433, 439, 440, 441, 442,
    443, 446, 447, 449
Heinemann, G. D., 405, 406
Heino, R. D., 110, 117, 396, 397, 406
Heinrichs, N., 431, 447
Helb, M. R., 100, 117
Helgeson, V. S., 200, 214, 243, 247
Helmreich, R., 106, 118
Henderson, S., 33, 52
Hendrick, C., 12, 175, 193, 306, 316, 317, 318, 320, 321,
    322, 326, 329, 332, 333, 334, 337, 340, 341,
    343, 344, 345, 346, 350, 351, 353, 366, 391, 517,
    518, 522, 529, 531, 534, 535
Hendrick, S. S., 12, 175, 193, 306, 317, 318, 322, 326, 332,
    334, 337, 339, 340, 341, 343, 344, 345, 346,
    350, 351, 353, 366, 391, 517, 518, 522, 529, 531,
    534, 535
Henningsen, D. D., 139, 150
Henningsen, M. L. M., 175, 179, 181, 187, 193
Henson, M., 169
Hepburn, C., 481, 484
Herbener, E. S., 324, 332
Herbert, J., 327, 334
Herbert, J. D., 431, 440, 442, 446, 447
Herman, E., 41, 54
Herold, E. S., 143, 150, 378, 379, 380, 382, 383, 389, 390
Herringer, T. M., 365, 368
Hersen, M., 427, 439, 445, 447
Hess, J. A., 17, 25
Hesse, E., 77, 85, 88, 90, 92, 93
Hesson-McInnis, M., 75, 91, 510, 513
Hetherington, E. M., 395, 396, 399, 400, 401, 402, 406,
    407
Hewitt, J., 104, 120
Hewitt, L. E., 107, 118
Heyman, R. E., 222, 233, 330, 331
Heyns, R. W., 528, 537
Hian, L. B., 241, 246
Higgins, E. T., 236, 246, 274, 291, 481, 482, 484
Higgitt, A., 82, 92
Hill, C. A., 409, 410, 413, 421
Hill, C. T., 43, 52, 164, 174, 199, 213, 222, 232, 382, 390
Hill, R., 465, 470
Hillis, J. D., 185, 193
Himmelhoch, J. M., 439, 447

Hinde, R. A., 518, 537
Hinsz, V. B., 102, 118
Hirsch, J. S., 345, 351
Hirsch, L. R., 58, 70
Hitsch, G., 241, 246, 255
Hixon, G., 15, 27
Hochschild, A. R., 355, 368, 393, 406
Hodges, S. D., 500, 509, 513
Hodgins, H. S., 106, 120, 274, 280, 295
Hodson, G., 127, 134
Hoeglund, J., 103, 117
Hofer, B., 101, 118
Hoff, T., 377, 389
Hofhansl, A., 109, 120
Hofmann, S. G., 431, 447
Hofstee, W. K. B., 274, 291
Hohaus, L., 84, 92
Hojjat, M., 329, 336, 338, 351
Hokanson, I. E., 435, 447
Hokanson, J. E., 435, 445
Holahan, C. J., 31, 52, 437, 448
Holaway, R. M., 440, 442, 449
Hollabaugh, L. C., 413, 423
Hollander, E., 327, 334
Hollon, S. D., 440, 447
Holmann, N., 64, 68
Holmberg, D., 3, 301, 302, 313, 357, 368, 379, 389, 453,
    454, 455, 456, 457, 459, 460, 461, 463, 464,
    466, 469, 470, 518
Holmes, J. G., 16, 18, 19, 26, 27, 28, 29, 128, 134, 161, 162,
    173, 197, 200, 202, 203, 204, 205, 206, 207, 208,
    209, 212, 214, 219, 221, 226, 233, 272, 280, 288,
    292, 359, 362, 363, 369, 370, 455, 460, 469,
    479, 485, 490, 498
Holms, J., 212
Holt, C. S., 41, 54, 443, 450
Holton, B., 141, 150
Holty, S., 111, 119
Homans, G. C., 18, 25, 210, 214, 281, 291
Homant, M, 33, 34, 53
Honda, M., 105, 117
Honeycutt, J. M., 122, 129, 130, 133, 140, 151, 181, 194,
    357, 368
Hong, Y., 478, 483
Hood, W. R., 219, 234
Hoogland, J. L., 55, 67
Hooker, K., 85, 92
Hooper, C. H., 159, 173
Hope, D. A., 336, 427, 428, 430, 431, 433, 434, 443, 446,
    447, 448, 450
Hopper, J., 398, 406
Horesh, N., 22, 26
Horner, C., 273, 292
Horney, K., 416, 421
Horowitz, L. M., 14, 24, 78, 91, 101, 115, 168, 170, 429,
    433, 436, 445, 446, 474, 483
Hortaçsu, A., 241, 246, 255, 257
Horton, R. S., 38, 52
Hotra, D., 61, 68
Houran, J., 261, 263
House, P., 508, 514
Houts, R. M., 326, 334, 341, 351
Howard, J., 279, 291
Howard, R. D., 55, 67
Howell, L., 317, 335

Howes, C., 41, 44, 52
Hoyt, D. R., 200, 206, 215
Hrdy, S. B., 60, 70
Hsieh, E., 131, 132
Hu, Y., 33, 52
Huang, M., 40, 50
Hughes, D. K., 307, 309, 310, 313
Hughes, M., 178, 180, 183, 379, 389
Hughes, S. M., 63, 70
Hull, J. G., 382, 389
Hullett, C. R., 360, 368
Hunter, P. A., 130, 132
Hunter, S., 164, 171
Huston, T. L., 3, 8, 12, 13, 14, 18, 25, 26, 271, 272, 273,
        280, 284, 289, 291, 292, 293, 298, 307, 312, 315,
        326, 334, 335, 341, 351, 518, 533, 537
Hutchinson, G., 250, 252, 257, 264
Hyde, J. S., 55, 71, 179, 193, 320, 334, 386, 390

I

Ickes, W., 165, 166, 172, 364, 368, 501, 513
Imahori, T. T., 169, 174, 413, 422
Imperato, N., 106, 119
Ingham, R., 144, 150
Ingoldsby, B., 323, 334
Ingram, R. E., 428, 436, 447
Inman-Amos, J., 344, 351
Insel, T. R., 316, 327, 333, 336
Insko, C. A., 199, 215, 224, 230, 233, 234
Ironside, R. G., 30, 53
Irvine, M., 167, 172
Irving, S., 398, 405
Isbell, L. M., 147, 150
Iverson, A., 46, 49, 181, 189, 191, 226, 231, 297, 298, 302,
        303, 304, 305, 307, 309, 311, 316, 317, 318, 322,
        323, 324, 325, 331
Iyengar, S. S., 218, 221, 232, 233
Izard, C. E., 355, 360, 369

J

Jaccard, J., 382, 383, 389
Jackson, R. M., 32, 51
Jacobsen, J., 185, 191, 193
Jacobson, C. K., 229, 233
Jacobson, N. S., 435, 447
Jacobvitz, D., 83, 90, 92, 93
Jacquet, S., 307, 310, 313
Jaffe, K., 437, 445
James, W., 316, 334
Jamieson, D. W., 282, 291
Janes, J., 61, 70
Jankowiak, W. R., 315, 334
Janoff-Bulman, R., 78, 91, 382, 386, 388
Jarrett, R. B., 441, 442, 450
Jarvis, M. L., 523, 538
Jarvis, P., 14, 22, 75, 84, 93, 136, 208, 210, 429, 518, 523,
        524, 527, 529, 531, 534
Jarvis, W. B. G., 274, 293
Jason, L. A., 410, 412, 417, 421

Jefferis, V. E., 21, 26
Jensen, M., 520, 527, 538
Jensen-Campbell, L. A., 59, 70, 100, 103, 117, 118, 279,
        280, 282, 284, 285, 288, 291
Jerrome, D., 32, 41, 52
Jesser, C. J., 414, 422
Jobling, I., 59, 71
Jodl, K. M., 401, 407
John, O. P., 363, 367
Johnson, A. J., 47, 52, 180, 193
Johnson, A. L., 441, 449
Johnson, B. R., 229, 233
Johnson, D. W., 281, 294
Johnson, J. M., 416, 422
Johnson, K., 81, 92
Johnson, K. L., 185, 193
Johnson, M. A., 43, 44, 52
Johnson, M. L., 138, 149
Johnson, M. P., 527, 537
Johnson, R., 281, 294
Johnson, R. M., 276, 292
Johnson, S. J., 143, 144, 150
Johnson, T., 154, 170
Johnson, W. R., 465, 466, 470
Johnston, V., 63, 70
Joiner, T., 360, 368
Joiner, T. E., 434, 437, 443, 447, 448
Joinson, A. N., 236, 240, 247, 249, 263
Jones, A. J., 21, 26, 112, 118
Jones, B. C., 56, 72
Jones, B. L., 169, 172
Jones, D., 58, 70
Jones, D. C., 42, 52
Jones, E. E., 15, 16, 19, 26, 39, 51, 161, 172, 271, 291, 509,
        510, 513
Jones, L. M., 32, 51
Jones, M., 57, 70, 100, 118, 365, 369
Jones, S., 165, 172
Jones, S. M., 177, 184, 191, 192
Jonet, C. J., 378, 389
Jonsson, G. K., 280, 293
Jordan, J. M., 124, 132
Jorgensen, P. F., 415, 421
Jost, J. T., 283, 292
Joubert, S., 319, 334
Juette, A., 105, 117
Jung, C. G., 308, 312, 316, 334

K

Kahlenberg, S. M., 63, 70
Kahn, G. M., 19, 28
Kahn, M. L., 164, 172
Kahneman, D., 142, 150
Kalakanis, L., 12, 26, 38, 47, 52, 275, 276, 292
Kalbfleisch, P. J., 206, 214
Kalick, S. M., 276, 292
Kam, J. A., 414, 422
Kamenica, E., 218, 232
Kamenov, Z., 85, 93
Kandel, D. B., 42, 52
Kann, L., 377, 389
Kanoy, K., 83, 93

Kaplan, D. L., 324, 334
Kaplan, H. S., 55, 70
Kaplan, N., 77, 82, 92, 93
Karama, S., 319, 334
Karavidas, A., 127, 132
Karis, T., 465, 470
Karney, B., 81, 82, 92
Karney, B. R., 222, 233, 339, 351, 499, 513
Karol, S. H., 124, 132
Kasch, C. R., 127, 131
Kashdan, T. B., 18, 24, 274, 275, 284, 289, 324, 330, 332,
        363, 425, 431, 432, 434, 447, 523, 528, 530, 531,
        533, 534, 535, 537
Kashy, D. A., 47, 48, 52, 100, 109, 110, 116, 117, 169, 172,
        219, 220, 232, 233, 242, 246, 273, 281, 292, 476,
        483, 489, 492, 494, 497, 523, 537
Kassel, J. D., 427, 437, 438, 447, 449
Katz, J., 16, 26, 434, 437, 447
Kavanagh, K., 205, 213
Kawada, C. L. K., 511, 513
Kay, A. C., 203, 214
Kean, K. J., 113, 115
Keefe, R. C., 58, 70
Keelan, J. P., 22, 26
Keelan, J. P. R., 14, 24, 475, 482, 483
Keffe, R. C., 279, 283, 292
Keiter, E. J., 282, 293
Kellermann, K. A., 19, 24, 121, 124, 126, 128, 129, 132,
        133, 136, 137, 138, 149, 150, 410, 415, 422
Kelley, H. H., 13, 18, 19, 25, 26, 27, 29, 122, 126, 133, 197,
        200, 201, 202, 203, 204, 205, 206, 208, 209,
        210, 212, 214, 219, 233, 271, 272, 280, 288, 292,
        298, 299, 310, 312, 313, 328, 334, 496, 497, 507,
        508, 509, 513
Kelley, K., 185, 193
Kellner, H., 454, 469
Kelly, E. L., 478, 484
Kelly, J., 399, 406
Kelly, R. L., 57, 64, 70
Keltner, D., 200, 214, 316, 319, 328, 331, 333, 363, 367
Kemper, D., 281, 293
Kemper, T. D., 310, 312, 355, 369
Kendall, P. C., 428, 447
Kenkel, W. F., 256, 263
Kennedy, L. W., 30, 53
Kenny, D. A., 17, 26, 43, 44, 47, 48, 50, 52, 219, 222, 226,
        232, 233, 236, 246, 247, 272, 273, 281, 286, 289,
        292, 409, 423
Kenrick, D. T., 11, 20, 26, 56, 57, 58, 59, 60, 66, 68, 70, 71,
        99, 100, 101, 104, 108, 117, 118, 272, 273, 274,
        276, 277, 279, 283, 286, 292, 293, 323, 334,
        502, 504, 506, 512, 513
Kenski, K., 501, 512
Kenyon, D. Y. B., 401, 407
Kephart, W. M., 320, 334
Kerckhoff, A. C., 12, 26
Kerns, K. A., 80, 86, 89, 91, 94, 386, 389
Kerr, N. L., 19, 26, 29, 197, 200, 202, 203, 204, 205, 206,
        208, 209, 212, 214, 272, 280, 288, 292
Keys, C. B., 324, 334
Keys, D. J., 434, 450
Keysar, B., 508, 512
Khatib-Chahidi, J., 465, 470
Khouri, H., 14, 17, 18, 25, 148, 150
Kiecolt-Glaser, J. K., 391, 406

Kiefer, A., 286, 292
Kiesler, S., 243, 247
Killian, K. D., 454, 465, 470
Kilmann, P. R., 59, 73, 378, 389
Kim, J., 320, 322, 334
Kimble, D. L., 143, 146, 151
Kinchen, S. A., 377, 389
Kininmonth, L. A., 476, 484
Kinnery, R. F., 490, 497
Kinney, T., 431, 449
Kipnis, O., 384, 390
Kirk, K. M., 63, 64, 67
Kirkendol, S. E., 242, 246
Kirkpatrick, L. A., 11, 24, 61, 66, 70, 89, 93
Kirson, D., 318, 328, 335
Kitson, G. C., 398, 406
Kivett, V. R., 31, 51
Kjos, G. L., 32, 51
Kleck, R. E., 38, 52
Klein, D. N., 434, 448
Klein, J. F., 443, 447
Kleinfeld, N., 251, 263
Kleinke, C. L., 17, 26, 107, 112, 118, 120, 164, 172
Klerman, G. L., 441, 442, 450
Kliewer, W., 202, 213
Klineberg, D., 159, 160, 169, 172
Klohnen, E., 79, 81, 93, 280, 292
Klohnen, E. C., 275, 284, 287
Klusmann, D., 56, 70
Knapp, C. W., 46, 52
Knapp, M. L., 4, 26, 30, 52, 176, 177, 179, 193, 356, 369,
        518, 537
Knee, C. R., 280, 288, 292, 471, 478, 479, 480, 484, 493,
        494, 496, 497, 511, 524, 525, 532, 533, 535
Knight, J. A., 35, 52
Knobloch, L. K., 18, 121, 122, 126, 128, 129, 130, 131, 133,
        134, 136, 140, 141, 150, 151, 157, 172, 181, 182,
        183, 187, 190, 193, 194, 198, 202, 215, 361, 410,
        421, 425, 521, 522, 524, 527, 531, 532, 533, 534
Knodel, J., 59, 70
Knox, D., 395, 406
Knutson, B., 356, 369
Ko, S. J., 206, 214
Kobak, R., 78, 88, 89, 93
Kochman, T., 463, 470
Koerner, A., 518, 538
Koerner, S. S., 401, 407
Koester, N. H., 430, 449
Koestner, R., 300, 312
Koh-Rangarajoo, E., 475, 482, 483
Konarski, R., 385, 388
Konecni, V. J., 32, 51
Koo, H. P., 400, 407
Koopman, J. S., 385, 389
Koralewski, M. A., 410, 423
Korn, M., 401, 407
Kortet, R., 102, 119
Kowalski, R. M., 429, 430, 448
Kraaimaat, F., 439, 450
Kramer, M. W., 131, 133
Kraut, R., 243, 247
Krawchuk, A., 106, 119
Kreider, R. M., 396, 407
Kreiser, P. O., 410, 421
Krol, B., 477, 483

Krones, J. M., 59, 70
Kruger, D. J., 59, 71
Kruglanski, A. W., 127, 128, 133, 283, 292
Krull, D. S., 16, 27
Kubitschek, W. N., 32, 52
Kühlberger, A., 511, 513
Kuiper, N. A., 435, 448
Kunkel, A. D., 359, 369
Kunkel, A. W., 44, 45, 50
Kurdek, L. A., 204, 214, 466, 470
Kurzban, R., 218, 233
Kwavnick, K. D., 147, 151

L

La Voie, L., 17, 26, 226, 233, 273, 292
Labeff, E. E., 413, 420
Lackenbauer, S. D., 16, 24, 338, 350
Ladd, A., 77, 80, 81, 89, 92
LaFontana, K. M., 219, 226, 232
Lakin, J. L., 21, 26
Lalumiere, M. L., 58, 61, 71
Lambert, L. S., 273, 290
Lamberth, J., 220, 221, 232, 249, 263, 300, 312
Lamme, S., 88, 93
Lampard, R., 395, 400, 403, 407
Lampe, C., 148, 150
Lancaster, J. B., 56, 71
Lancaster, L. C., 394, 407
Land, D., 78, 80, 85, 90, 91
Land, R. D., 147, 151
Landau, M. J., 18, 27, 45, 53
Landolt, M. A., 58, 61, 71
Landrum, G. C., 435, 447
Laner, M. R., 176, 193, 358, 369, 501, 513
Langan, E., 188, 192
Lange, R., 261, 263
Langer, G., 519, 537
Langhinrichsen-Rohling, J., 410, 412, 413, 422
Langlois, J. H., 12, 26, 38, 47, 52, 274, 275, 276, 277, 291, 292
Langston, C. A., 207, 213
Lantz, H. R., 477, 484
Larose, S., 86, 93
Larsen, K. H., 427, 431, 447
Larsen, R. J., 11, 24, 64, 73, 276, 294
Larson, A., 12, 26, 38, 47, 52, 275, 276, 292
Larson, R., 376, 390
Larson, R. W., 29, 52
Lassiter, G. D., 35, 53, 360, 368
Latham, G. P., 414, 422
Latty-Mann, H., 343, 350
Laumann, E. O., 66, 71, 323, 334
Laurenceau, J. P., 19, 26, 154, 163, 172, 219, 233, 240, 247
Lauterbach, W., 440, 449
Lawrence, M., 507, 509, 511, 514
Lawrence-Lightfoot, S., 345, 351
Lawton, M. P., 32, 53
Layton, B. D., 224, 234
Lazarus, R. S., 354, 369, 370, 415, 422
Le, B., 199, 214
Le, T. N., 316, 334
Lea, M., 396, 407

Leader, J. B., 434, 448
Leaf, P. J., 434, 446
Leary, M. R., 14, 26, 168, 174, 338, 350, 355, 369, 410, 415, 422, 426, 429, 430, 431, 448, 449
Leber, D., 454, 464, 469, 470
LeBlanc, G. J., 55, 73
Leck, K., 282, 292, 365, 366, 369
Lecours, A. R., 319, 334
Ledley, C., 42, 48, 53
Lee, C. M., 415, 422
Lee, E., 410, 419
Lee, J., 106, 119
Lee, J. A., 12, 26, 316, 317, 321, 342, 351, 522, 537
Lee, J. W., 410, 416, 419
Lee, K. J., 63, 72
LeFan, J., 106, 118
Lefebvre, L., 39, 49
Legendre, A., 30, 31, 53
Lehman, D., 87, 91
Lehmiller, J. J., 15, 197, 200, 210, 213, 214, 522
Leites, N., 6, 28
Lemay, E. P., 275, 281, 283, 292
Lenhart, A., 251, 252, 254, 255, 261, 264
Leonard, K., 80, 81, 94
Leone, C., 282, 291, 292, 365, 366, 369
Leonhardt, D., 249, 263
Leroux, J. M., 319, 334
Leslie, L. A., 32, 53, 404, 407, 527, 537
Leung, C., 377, 390
Levenson, M. R., 316, 334
Levesque, G., 86, 93
Levesque, M. J., 42, 48, 53, 139, 151
Levin, L., 56, 57, 72
Levine, R., 322, 334
Levine, S. P., 365, 369
Levine, T. R., 410, 419
Levinger, G. A., 12, 26, 157, 172, 257, 263, 264, 271, 272, 292, 298, 312, 382, 389, 519, 529, 538
Levinson, R. A., 382, 383, 389
Levinson, S., 418, 420
Levitskaya, A., 304, 305, 307, 309, 311, 313, 317, 320, 321, 323, 324, 336, 413, 424
Levitt, M. J., 415, 422
Levitt, S. D., 255, 257, 264
Lewandowski, G. W., 324, 334
Lewin, K., 212, 275, 287, 292, 527, 538
Lewinsohn, P. M., 377, 390, 434, 436, 438, 439, 440, 442, 448, 449, 450
Lewis, C., 412, 423
Lewis, R. A., 177, 193, 520, 538
Lewis, S. A., 113, 115
Li, H., 316, 317, 319, 322, 326, 327, 328, 330, 331
Li, N., 11, 26
Li, N. P., 59, 60, 71, 99, 100, 118, 323, 334
Lichter, D. T., 530, 537
Lichtman, R. R., 454, 470
Liebowitz, M. R., 327, 334, 433, 434, 446, 450
Lim, M. M., 316, 334
Lin, Y., 465, 469
Lindberg, L. D., 377, 390
Lindblade, K., 385, 389
Lindsey, E., 202, 215
Lindstrom, T., 88, 93
Linehan, M. M., 442, 448
Linsenmeier, J. A. W., 11, 26, 59, 71, 99, 118

Linville, P. W., 481, 484
Lipetz, M. E., 324, 332, 527, 537
Lipkus, I., 316, 335
Lippa, R. A., 59, 66, 71
Lipson, S. F., 63, 68, 70
Lipton, J. E., 56, 68
Litowitz, D. L., 280, 281, 293
Little, A. C., 12, 26, 56, 59, 71, 72, 102, 118, 325, 335
Liu, J., 86, 94
Liu, Y., 327, 333, 336
Livingston, K. R., 129, 133
Livingston, R. W., 12, 26
Lloyd, B. B., 55, 57, 67
Lloyd, S. A., 176, 192, 377, 379, 388, 418, 420
LoboPrabhu, S., 84, 93
Lockard, J. S., 357, 360, 369
Locke, E. A., 414, 422
Locksley, A., 481, 484
Logan, T., 410, 422
Lohmann, A., 197, 207, 213, 214
Lomax, J., 84, 93
Lombardi, W., 481, 482, 484
Londahl, E. A., 316, 319, 328, 331, 333
Long, A. E., 18, 27, 45, 53
Long, E., 382, 388
Longmore, M. A., 159, 164, 165, 172, 377, 389
Longo, L. C., 38, 51, 275, 277, 290
Lonsbary, C., 471, 478, 484
Lord, C. G., 39, 51
Lorenz, K., 101, 118
Losow, J. I., 355, 367
Lott, A. J., 299, 312
Lott, B. E., 299, 312
Loving, T. J., 200, 213, 222, 233, 472, 483
Low, B. S., 55, 57, 59, 65, 70, 71
Lowe, C. A., 139, 151
Lowry, R., 377, 389
Lucas, A. A., 13, 135, 175, 181, 187, 518, 519, 521, 522, 524, 527, 528, 532, 533
Lucas, R., 59, 70
Luce, R. D., 219, 233
Lugaila, T. A., 8, 27
Luis, S., 278, 294
Luker, K., 8, 26
Luna, Y., 416, 422
Lundgren, S., 103, 117, 282, 284, 291
Lundy, D. E., 104, 106, 108, 116, 118, 276, 292, 300, 313
Luo, N., 40, 50
Luo, S., 79, 81, 93, 280, 292
Lydon, J. E., 282, 291, 490, 497
Lykken, D. T., 284, 285, 292
Lyman, S., 454, 470
Lyons-Ruth, K., 90, 93
Lyubomirsky, S., 428, 436, 448

M

MacCormack, T., 143, 150
MacFarquhar, N., 169, 173, 218, 233
Macho, m., 430, 450
Machung, A., 393, 406
MacKenzie, S., 357, 368, 379, 389
Macrae, C. N., 38, 54

Madden, M., 251, 252, 254, 255, 261, 264
Madey, S. F., 281, 293
Magai, C., 84, 85, 93
Main, M., 76, 77, 82, 85, 88, 90, 92, 93
Makhijani, M. G., 38, 51, 275, 277, 290
Malamuth, N. M., 58, 71
Malhotra, A., 203, 214
Malle, B. F., 499, 500, 507, 509, 513
Mallinckrodt, B. S., 169, 174
Malloy, T. E., 236, 246
Maner, J. K., 101, 118
Mann, L., 41, 53
Mannarelli, T., 206, 214
Manning, J. T., 63, 71
Manning, W. D., 159, 164, 165, 172, 377, 389
Mannion, H., 59, 71
Mannone, S. F., 122, 129, 133
Manoogian-O'Dell, M., 85, 92
Mansell, W., 431, 448
Manstead, A. S. R., 355, 356, 361, 369
Marcus, D. K., 277, 293
Margand, N., 83, 93
Margulis, S. T., 157, 173, 240, 246
Markman, H. J., 345, 351
Markowitz, J. C., 442, 448
Marks, G., 35, 53
Marks, M., 78, 92, 359, 368
Marks, S. R., 404, 407
Markstrom-Adams, C., 203, 214
Markus, H. R., 345, 351
Marshall, D. S., 98, 118
Marshall, S. K., 203, 214
Martens, L., 49
Martin, D., 87, 93
Martin, D. J., 534, 538
Martin, L. L., 414, 415, 422
Martin, N. G., 63, 64, 67, 69
Martz, J. M., 272, 293
Mashek, D., 316, 317, 319, 322, 326, 327, 328, 329, 330, 331
Mathews, A., 154, 163, 172
Maticka-Tyndale, E., 379, 382, 383, 389
Matsumoto, D., 169, 174
Matthews, J., 218, 219, 222, 224, 231, 232, 271, 272, 286, 290
Mattick, R. P., 432, 448
Matz, D. C., 102, 118
Maxwell, G. M., 112, 118
May, J. L., 112, 113, 118
Mazur, A., 63, 71
Mazure, M., 47, 52, 180, 193
McArthur, L., 280, 293
McAuslan, P., 139, 149
McCabe, D. B., 111, 120, 397, 407
McCabe, M. P., 60, 67
McCabe, S. B., 435, 448
McCain, T. A., 177, 193
McCall, P. L., 410, 416, 423
McCallum, R., 325, 331
McCary, L., 97, 120
McClain, D., 256, 264
McClasky, C., 79, 92
McCloud, B., 255, 263
McClure, J., 509, 514
McCormick, N. B., 14, 21, 26, 112, 118, 414, 422

McCown, J. A., 33, 34, 53
McCrae, R. R., 346, 350
McCroskey, J. C., 177, 193
McDonald, D. A., 143, 144, 150
McFadyen-Ketchum, S., 98, 116
McFall, R. M., 430, 450
McGillis, D., 510, 513
McGoun, M. J., 416, 420
McGowan, M. G., 412, 423
McGuire, M., 58, 71
McGuire, W., 287, 288, 293
McHale, J., 83, 93
McIntosh, W. D., 59, 69, 414, 415, 422
McIntyre, M. H., 63, 68, 71
McKenna, C., 330, 331
McKenna, K. Y. A., 7, 33, 34, 53, 165, 166, 167, 170, 173,
        235, 236, 237, 238, 239, 240, 241, 242, 244,
        246, 247, 258, 396, 397, 522, 523, 526, 528, 536
McKinney, K., 261, 264
McKinney, S., 358, 368
McLaughlin, K., 105, 115
McLean, K. C., 282, 285, 293
McManus, B., 378, 379, 383, 385, 386
McManus, F., 440, 445
McNeely, C. S., 377, 390
McNeil, D. W., 428, 448
McNulty, J. K., 499, 513
McPherson, M., 75, 93, 159, 173
McQuinn, R. D., 156, 167, 171
Mead, G. H., 454, 470
Mead, M., 315, 335
Mealey, L., 56, 71
Medina, P., 64, 73
Meeker, F. B., 107, 118
Meeks, B. S., 340, 346, 351
Mehrabian, S., 528, 538
Meier, V. J., 427, 428, 431, 448
Melby, C., 106, 115
Melchior, L. A., 364, 367
Meleshko, K. G. A., 438, 445
Melinat, E., 40, 49, 167, 168, 169, 170, 240, 246, 518, 537
Mellings, T. M. B., 432, 434, 445, 448
Meloy, J. R., 315, 335, 410, 412, 422
Meloy, R., 412, 423
Mendelson, M. J., 45, 49
Mendoza-Denton, R., 148, 149
Merbach, N., 454, 470
Merker, B., 112, 118
Merkle, E. R., 254, 255, 258, 259, 260, 264
Merkowitz, J. C., 441, 442, 450
Merluzzi, T. V., 427, 431, 447
Mersch, P. P., 439, 448
Mesquita, B., 355, 368
Messenger, J. C., 98, 99, 118
Messer, S. C., 442, 450
Messman, S. J., 183, 186, 189, 193
Meston, C., 274, 282, 293
Metalsky, G. I., 437, 443, 447
Metts, S., 14, 18, 22, 175, 184, 185, 191, 193, 240, 246, 251,
        264, 301, 305, 313, 353, 355, 356, 357, 361, 364,
        366, 367, 369, 410, 413, 420, 422, 424, 471, 477,
        484, 485, 521, 522, 523, 524, 528, 529, 531, 534
Mewhinney, D., 379, 382, 383, 389
Meyers, D. J., 501, 512
Meyers, S. A., 317, 335

Miceli, M., 415, 422
Michael, R. T., 66, 71, 323, 334
Michaelieu, Q., 275, 282, 294
Michaelis, B., 14, 17, 18, 25, 148, 150
Michaels, S., 66, 71, 323, 334
Michalski, R. L., 64, 71
Miell, D. E., 41, 47, 51, 53, 158, 160, 163, 173
Mikach, S. M., 61, 71
Mikucki, S. L., 14, 18, 22, 353, 366, 369, 521, 522, 523,
        524, 529, 531, 534
Mikulincer, M., 21, 22, 26, 27, 80, 85, 86, 159, 173, 329,
        331, 386, 388, 471, 475, 485
Milardo, R. M., 179, 197, 203, 214, 519, 527, 538
Miles, M. G., 282, 293
Millar, M. G., 273, 293
Miller, D. T., 345, 351
Miller, G. F., 55, 61, 63, 64, 70, 71, 329, 335
Miller, K., 17, 18, 25, 40, 50
Miller, L. C., 39, 40, 50, 53, 99, 118, 159, 161, 163, 165,
        173, 240, 246, 330, 335, 500, 507, 509, 511, 513
Miller, L. E., 18, 121, 122, 129, 131, 133, 136, 140, 141,
        181, 182, 187, 361, 425, 521, 522, 524, 527, 531,
        532, 533, 534
Miller, N., 35, 53
Miller, P. J. E., 280, 284, 293, 326, 335, 511, 513
Miller, R. S., 288, 300, 313, 355, 369
Miller, S. C., 229, 233
Mills, J., 161, 171, 272, 283, 290
Mischel, W., 148, 149, 434, 436, 448
Misovich, S. J., 113, 115
Miyake, K., 106, 120, 274, 280, 295
Mize, J., 202, 215
Mochon, D., 218, 226
Moffit, T. E., 64, 66, 71
Mogg, K., 428, 431, 436, 448
Mogilner, C., 221, 233
Mohandie, K., 412, 423
Molinari, V., 84, 93
Monahan, D., 85, 92
Monarch, N. D., 200, 214
Money, J., 325, 335
Mongeau, P. A., 6, 27, 136, 175, 178, 179, 181, 185, 187, 191,
        193, 194, 358, 369, 379, 381, 382, 390, 518, 519,
        521, 523, 524, 527, 528, 531, 534, 535
Monroe, S. M., 377, 390
Monroe, W. S., 536, 538
Monson, T., 36, 50, 219, 232, 280, 289, 472, 483
Montgomery, B. M., 129, 131, 157, 173, 308, 311, 399, 405
Montgomery, M. J., 395, 396, 400, 401, 407
Moore, D., 130, 132
Moore, J. S., 273, 293
Moore, M. M., 104, 105, 106, 118, 119, 357, 369
Moore, S., 33, 51, 377, 390
Moorman, S. M., 285, 293
Morahan-Martin, J., 34, 53
Moran, G., 82, 92, 93
Morewitz, S. J., 410, 423
Morgan, D. L., 519, 538
Morgan, H. J., 328, 335
Morison, V., 402, 406
Morr, M. C., 179, 185, 194, 358, 369
Morris, M. E., 206, 214
Morris, M. L., 163, 167, 171, 172
Morrision, K., 178, 180, 183
Morrison, K., 379, 389

Morse, C., 143, 147, 149
Mortensen, C. R., 104, 117
Morton, T. L., 154, 173
Moser, G., 30, 31, 53
Moskowitz, G. B., 481, 482, 485
Moss, J. J., 520, 527, 538
Motley, M. T., 190, 194, 410, 423
Mott, F. L., 377, 388
Mucci, I. A., 377, 390
Mudar, P., 382, 388
Muehlenhard, C. L., 410, 413, 423
Mueller, U., 63, 71
Muise, A., 16, 24
Mullen, P. E., 410, 412, 414, 423
Müller, N., 434, 450
Mullett, E., 320, 321, 335
Munholland, K., 76, 90, 91
Munoz, R. F., 439, 440, 450
Munroe, R. H., 57, 71
Munroe, R. L., 57, 71
Murnen, S. K., 410, 423
Murphy, A. Z., 316, 334
Murphy, M. M., 355, 367
Murray, A. D., 355, 369
Murray, S. L., 16, 27, 142, 151, 202, 221, 215, 226, 233,
    362, 363, 369, 479, 485, 490, 492, 494, 497, 498
Murstein, B. I., 5, 27, 177, 194, 520, 538
Muscarella, F., 103, 119
Musselman, L., 276, 292
Muthén, B., 158, 173
Muthén, L., 158, 173
Myers, B. J., 84, 93
Myers, V. H., 440, 442, 447

N

Nachshon, O., 22, 27, 159, 173
Nadel, L., 147, 151
Nagin, D. S., 169, 172
Nagy, G., 12, 13, 27
Nahemow, L., 32, 53
Nail, P. R., 229, 233
Nakanishi, M., 158, 173
Nanayakkara, A., 478, 479, 480, 484, 493, 494, 497
Nave, C. S., 139, 151
Nazer, N., 519, 539
Neal, A., 410, 417, 421
Negel, L., 415, 422
Neidig, J. L., 127, 132
Neighbors, C., 478, 479, 480, 484, 493, 494, 497
Nelson, G., 284, 289
Nelson, T. D., 273, 293
Neto, F., 320, 321, 335
Netting, N. S., 203, 215
Nettle, D., 71
Neubauer, S. A., 377, 388
Neuberg, S. L., 59, 70
Neugebauer, R., 441, 446
Newcomb, T. M., 271, 293, 299, 300, 313, 324, 335, 527, 538
Newton, K. J., 143, 146, 151
Newton, T. L., 391, 406
Nicastro, A. M., 410, 424
Niedenthal, P. M., 78, 92, 359, 368

Niehuis, S., 280, 284, 293, 326, 335, 533, 537
Niemeyer, G. J., 44, 53, 86, 94
Niemeyer, R. A., 44, 53
Nisbett, R. E., 221, 225, 233, 301, 313
Nishida, T., 121, 125, 128, 129, 133, 169, 172
Noar, S. M., 143, 151
Nolan, E. M., 440, 442, 447
Nolen-Hoeksema, S., 428, 436, 438, 446, 448
Noller, P., 342, 345, 350, 429, 438, 446, 449
Noonan, K. M., 55, 57, 67
Norman, C. C., 330, 331
Norton, M. I., 129, 133
Norton, P. J., 427, 430, 448
Nunez, J., 64, 73
Nunez, M., 64, 73
Nyrop, R. E., 325, 335

O

O'Brien, K., 86, 93
O'Connor, C., 318, 328, 335
Oemig, C., 200, 214
Oettingen, G., 511, 513
Ogden, J. K., 164, 165, 174
O'Hair, H. D., 410, 4113, 420, 423
O'Hara, M. W., 441, 448
Oishi, S., 415, 423
Okami, P., 56, 71
Oldenburg, C., 86, 94
Oliphant, J. A., 377, 390
Oliver, M. B., 55, 71, 179, 193, 386, 390, 503, 504, 514
O'Loughlin, C., 11, 25, 102, 116, 491, 494, 497
Olsen, N., 207, 215, 219, 233
Olson, A. M., 416, 420
Olson, L. N., 391, 518
Olson, M. A., 229, 233
Olufowote, J., 359, 369
Omarzu, J., 504, 513
O'Meara, D., 180, 182, 183, 194
Omoto, A. M., 167, 171
Onizuka, R. K., 316, 335
Oppermann, M., 379, 389
Oppong, J. R., 30, 53
Orbuch, T. L., 3, 256, 260, 264, 301, 302, 313, 324, 336,
    398, 402, 407, 453, 454, 455, 456, 457, 459,
    460, 461, 463, 464, 470, 518
Orenstein, S., 258, 259, 264
Oriña, M., 501, 513
Orlofsky, J. L., 376, 377, 390
O'Rouke, M. T., 63, 71
Orpaz, A., 386, 388
Ortega, R. M., 455, 458, 462, 464, 470
Osborn, D. R., 102, 119
Oskamp, S., 36, 53
Otsubo, Y., 127, 134
Overall, N., 11, 25, 102, 116, 491, 493, 494, 497, 498
Oxley, D., 42, 52

P

Page, R., 33, 34, 53

Paine, C. B., 236, 247
Paionni, A., 430, 446
Palarea, R. E., 410, 413, 422
Paley, B., 80, 83, 93
Palmer, C. T., 61, 73
Papsdorf, M. P., 432, 448
Paris, M., 221, 231, 316, 325, 330, 331
Park, L. E., 17, 27, 510, 512
Parke, R., 84, 94
Parker, G., 441, 448
Parker, H. S., 410, 422
Parker, I., 441, 448
Parker, K., 84, 91
Parker, S. R., 33, 53
Parkes, C., 88, 93
Parkinson, B., 354, 356, 369
Parks, M. R., 7, 27, 34, 35, 53, 123, 125, 131, 133, 140, 151,
        155, 165, 166, 173, 179, 180, 194, 197, 198, 205,
        215, 237, 239, 252, 258, 259, 264, 381, 382, 389,
        390, 527, 538
Parmelee, P., 42, 43, 44, 54
Parrott, W. G., 356, 369
Parvez, R. A., 55, 69
Pasternak, B., 55, 64, 66, 71
Pasveer, K. A., 160, 171
Pataki, S. P., 272, 283, 290, 355, 367
Pathé, M., 410, 412, 414, 423
Patience, R. A., 102, 118
Paton, R., 465, 470
Patrick, B. C., 154, 161, 162, 163, 173
Patrick, H., 471, 478, 479, 480, 484, 493, 494, 497
Patterson, B., 413, 423
Patty, J., 429, 446
Patzer, G., 38, 53
Paul, E. L., 178, 194, 201, 375, 378, 379, 380, 381, 382,
        383, 384, 385, 386, 387, 390, 517, 518, 523, 526,
        527, 528, 529, 533, 534
Paul, L., 58, 70
Paulhus, D. L., 221, 233
Paulson, G. D., 410, 423
Pawlins, W., 182, 194
Paykel, E. S., 441, 449
Payne, C., 80, 93
Peake, P. K., 148, 149
Pearce, D. G., 18, 28, 359, 370
Pearce, W. B., 154, 173
Pearl, L., 431, 445
Pearson, J., 81, 91
Pedersen, F. A., 56, 64, 65, 72
Pederson, D., 82, 93
Pegalis, L. J., 165, 174
Peggs, K., 395, 400, 403, 407
Peitz, M., 440, 449
Pelham, B. W., 16, 27
Pennebaker, J. W., 239, 246, 280, 281, 293, 454, 457, 470
Penton-Voak, I. S., 12, 26, 56, 63, 72, 102, 118, 325, 335
Peplau, L. A., 164, 174, 199, 213, 222, 232, 382, 390, 410,
        413, 421
Perella, A., 281, 293
Perez, M., 18, 24, 274, 275, 284, 289, 324, 330, 332, 530, 537
Perez, S., 147, 151
Perkins, J. W., 136, 150
Perkowitz, W. T., 39, 51, 161, 162, 171
Perlman, D., 36, 53, 298, 300, 313, 517, 519, 520, 524, 525,
        537, 538

Perner, J., 311, 313
Perone, A., 430, 446
Perot, A., 410, 423
Perper, T., 17, 27, 97, 106, 112, 119, 357, 370, 462, 470
Perrett, D. I., 12, 26, 56, 63, 72, 102, 118
Perry, K. J., 430, 431, 446, 447
Perry, T., 416, 423
Pert, R., 414, 423
Perusse, D., 220, 233
Peter, J., 34, 53
Petronio, S., 145, 151, 154, 157, 158, 161, 167, 172, 173,
        240, 246, 393, 396, 399, 403, 407, 415, 420
Pettit, G. S., 79, 92, 98, 116, 202, 215
Petty, R. E., 271, 274, 293
Pfaff, D., 328, 335
Philhower, C., 100, 101, 109, 116
Philippot, P., 428, 431, 448
Phillips, D., 79, 80, 94
Phillips, N. A., 127, 132
Phillips, R., 519, 538
Phillips, S., 32, 51
Philpott, J., 410, 419
Pierce, C. A., 61, 72
Pieters, R., 414, 415, 419
Pietromonaco, P. R., 19, 26, 79, 93, 154, 163, 172, 219, 233,
        240, 247, 437, 445
Pike, C. L., 102, 116, 276, 290
Pilchowicz, E., 185, 193
Piliavin, J., 226, 234
Pilkonis, P. A., 431, 448
Pinel, E. C., 18, 27, 45, 53
Pines, A. M., 309, 313, 323, 335
Pinney, E. M., 382, 390
Pittman, T. A., 15, 16, 19, 26
Planalp, S., 41, 53, 122, 129, 130, 133, 140, 151, 181, 194,
        356, 369, 370, 472, 485
Polan, M. L., 319, 331
Pollom, L., 17, 25
Pomerantz, E. M., 415, 423, 478, 479, 480, 484
Pope, L. K., 354, 370
Potapova, E., 304, 305, 307, 309, 311, 313, 317, 320, 321,
        323, 324, 336, 413, 424
Potthoff, J. G., 437, 448
Pouli, N., 465, 469
Powell, M. C., 272, 283, 290
Powell, R. R., 465, 470
Prager, K. J., 162, 173, 177, 194
Pratto, F., 66, 72
Predmore, S. C., 14, 15, 16, 27
Prezioso, M., 86, 91
Priester, J. M., 274, 293
Proffitt, D. R., 281, 284, 295
Pruett-Jones, S., 103, 119
Pryor, J. B., 510, 513
Purcell, R., 410, 412, 414, 423
Purvis, J. A., 159, 173
Puts, D. A., 63, 72
Pyszczynski, T., 18, 27, 45, 53, 141, 150

Q

Qian, Z., 530, 537
Quinlan, R. J., 64, 66, 72

Quinn, D. M., 203, 215
Quinsey, V. L., 58, 61, 71

R

Radvansky, G. A., 500, 514
Rafaeli, E., 169, 171
Raiffa, H., 219, 233
Raines, C., 394, 407
Raj, A., 377, 390
Ramirez, A., Jr., 36, 54, 122, 127, 128, 134, 156, 174, 175, 178, 193
Ramsey, J., 40, 50
Ramsey, R. E., 378, 389
Rankin, L. A., 401, 407
Rantala, M. J., 102, 119
Rapoport, J. L., 327, 333
Rapson, R. L., 177, 193, 259, 260, 263, 315, 316, 319, 320, 321, 333, 342, 350
Rasmussen, B., 39, 51
Ratiu, E., 30, 31, 53
Ratner, R. K., 12, 28, 138, 139, 151, 359, 370, 528, 539
Rauch, S. A. M., 440, 446
Rawlins, W. K., 29, 53
Ray, G. B., 361, 370
Ray, J. M., 276, 289
Rea, M., 317, 335
Read, S., 77, 91
Read, S. J., 22, 25, 471, 474, 483, 500, 507, 509, 511, 513
Reed, J., 209, 213
Reeder, G. D., 8, 12, 499, 503, 504, 507, 508, 509, 510, 511, 513, 514, 522, 532, 535
Reeder, H. M., 177, 189, 190, 194, 209, 409, 410, 423
Regan, P. C., 56, 57, 59, 63, 72, 175, 193, 301, 312, 317, 335, 336, 339, 340, 341, 350, 380, 383, 386, 390, 489, 491, 498
Reichert, T., 121, 130, 131
Reichler, A., 410, 417, 421
Reid, M. T., 310, 312
Reik, T., 271, 274, 284, 293
Reinecke, M. A., 437, 438, 449
Reis, H. T., 19, 26, 29, 39, 50, 154, 161, 162, 163, 164, 173, 197, 200, 202, 203, 204, 205, 206, 208, 209, 210, 212, 214, 215, 219, 226, 232, 233, 259, 262, 263, 264, 270, 272, 280, 287, 288, 292, 293, 298, 301, 312, 323, 324, 325, 332, 386, 388, 472, 483
Reise, S. P., 100, 119
Reiss, I. L., 520, 538
Rempel, J. K., 200, 207, 209, 213, 219, 233, 511, 513
Renninger, L. A., 64, 69, 103, 117
Renshaw, P. D., 39, 49
Rentfrow, J. P., 261, 263
Resnick, M., 377, 390
Reyes, M., 106, 119
Reynolds, R. A., 121, 126, 128, 129, 133, 410, 422, 423
Reynolds, V., 66, 72
Reysen, S., 361, 370
Rheingold, A. A., 440, 442, 447
Rhode, P., 377, 390
Rhodes, G., 276, 293
Rholes, W., 79, 80, 82, 83, 94
Richards, M. H., 376, 390

Richardson, R. A., 254, 255, 258, 259, 260, 264
Richardson, S. A., 38, 52
Richeson, J. A., 229, 232
Ridings, C. M., 33, 53
Ridley, M., 63, 72
Riela, S., 315, 316, 317, 321, 322, 323, 324, 335
Ries, B. J., 428, 448
Riggio, R. E., 38, 39, 51, 53
Rikowski, A., 64, 72
Riksen-Walraven, J. M. A., 42, 43, 44, 45, 52
Riordan, C. M., 32, 53
Rios, J. D., 100, 118
Rischer, B., 64, 69
Roberto, K. A., 32, 34, 38, 42, 47, 50, 53
Roberts, A. F., 256, 264
Roberts, A. R., 102, 116, 277, 290
Roberts, J. E., 427, 431, 434, 437, 447, 449
Roberts, L. D., 165, 173, 252, 258, 264
Roberts, L. J., 162
Roberts, N., 342, 350
Roberts, R., 59, 69
Roberts, R. L., 316, 332
Robinson, C., 410, 416, 423
Robinson, J. D., 131, 134
Robinson, L. A., 435, 447
Robinson, M. D., 358, 368
Robson, S., 359, 369
Rodebaugh, T. L., 440, 442, 449
Rodgers, R. H., 400, 407
Rodin, M. J., 37, 53, 528, 538
Rodrigues, A. E., 398, 407
Rodriguez, B. J., 432, 450
Rodriguez, M., 148, 149
Rodriguez, N., 316, 322, 323, 324, 335
Roeder, K., 169, 172
Rogers, G. M., 437, 438, 449
Rogers, P. A., 415, 422
Roggman, L., 276, 292
Rohde, P., 438, 442, 449
Rohling, M. L., 410, 412, 413, 422
Roisman, G., 77, 79, 86, 94
Roloff, M. E., 410, 423
Ronald, L., 38, 52
Roney, C. J. R., 127, 134
Ronk, M. J., 507, 509, 511, 514
Rosanowski, J., 482, 484
Rose, P., 226, 233
Rose, S., 158, 159, 160, 169, 172, 174, 358, 370, 371, 462, 470
Rose, S. M., 177, 194
Roseman, I. J., 355, 370
Rosen, L. D., 219, 232
Rosenbaum, M. E., 274, 293, 324, 335, 528, 538
Rosenblatt, P. C., 465, 470
Rosenfeld, B., 412, 423
Rosenfeld, L. B., 153, 174
Rosenkrantz, P. S., 501, 504, 514
Rosenthal, A. M., 219, 232
Rosenthal, D., 414, 423
Rosenthal, R., 218, 231, 273, 289
Ross, L., 203, 214, 508, 510, 514
Ross, L. T., 139, 149
Ross, M., 356, 370, 478, 485
Ross, M. A., 301, 313
Ross, R. J., 377, 389
Rosselli, M., 100, 118

Rotenberg, K. J., 41, 53
Rothbard, J. C., 474, 485
Rottman, L., 113, 120, 249, 256, 264, 299, 300, 313, 315, 336
Rottmann, L., 218, 219, 220, 224
Rousar, E. E., 328, 335
Rovine, M. J., 163, 172
Rowatt, T. J., 107, 110, 119
Rowatt, W. C., 255, 264, 281, 293
Rowe, D. C., 64, 72
Rowland, D. R., 63, 72
Rubenstein, A. J., 12, 26, 38, 47, 52, 275, 276, 292
Rubin, M., 360, 370
Rubin, Z., 41, 54, 164, 174, 237, 247, 273, 293, 315, 317, 335, 382, 390, 410, 413, 421
Rudnick, J. R., 415, 424
Ruffin, K., 302, 311
Ruphan, M., 477, 483
Rusbult, C. E., 19, 20, 26, 27, 29, 197, 199, 200, 202, 203, 204, 205, 206, 207, 208, 209, 212, 213, 214, 215, 219, 221, 222, 232, 233, 272, 274, 280, 288, 292, 293, 316, 335, 363, 370, 392, 407
Rushton, J. P., 45, 54, 323, 335, 530, 538
Russell, D. W., 158, 159, 174, 438, 450
Russell, J. A., 127, 132, 318, 333, 342, 345, 350
Russell, M., 382, 388
Rutherford, D. K., 122, 129, 130, 133, 140, 151
Rutstin, J., 12, 28
Rynn, M., 442, 449

S

Sabatelli, R. M., 360, 370, 503, 514
Sabini, J., 101, 120, 410, 423
Sacco, W. P., 435, 447
Sachau, D., 206, 214
Sachdev, M., 161, 174
Sadalla, E. K., 20, 26, 56, 57, 70, 99, 108, 118, 279, 293, 502, 513
Saeed, L., 224, 233
Saengtienchai, C., 59, 70
Saferstein, J., 86, 94
Safran, S. A., 430, 439, 441, 446
Sahlstein, E., 158, 165, 170
St. Andre, M., 80, 92
Sakaguci, K., 280, 293
Sakai, R., 106, 119
Salmon, C., 59, 72
Salmoria, R., 430, 446
Saluter, A. F., 8, 27
Salzinger, L. L., 35, 54
Sameroff, A., 456, 457, 469
Samter, W., 39, 41, 54
Sancho, M., 64, 73
Sanderman, R., 477, 483
Sanderson, C. A., 282, 293, 508, 514
Sangrador, J. L., 316, 322, 335
Santelli, J. S., 377, 390
Santisi, M., 100, 118
Saucier, G., 101, 119
Saxon, J. L., 415, 423
Scandura, T., 86, 94
Sceery, A., 78, 88, 89, 93
Schachter, S., 31, 51, 198, 214, 299, 300, 312, 313

Schank, R. C., 500, 514
Scharf, M., 284, 294
Scharfe, E., 474, 485
Scharlott, B. W., 79, 80, 94, 282, 287, 294
Scheflen, A. E., 97, 112, 119, 357, 370
Schiaffano, K., 84, 92
Schiller, M., 80, 92
Schlenker, B. R., 426, 430, 431, 449
Schmidt, C. J., 415, 421
Schmidt, D. P., 11, 27
Schmidt, K. L., 125, 133
Schmidt, L., 226, 234
Schmidt, L. A., 364, 370
Schmidt, N. B., 437, 447
Schmitt, A., 105, 117
Schmitt, D. P., 11, 20, 21, 24, 55, 56, 57, 58, 59, 60, 61, 63, 65, 66, 67, 68, 72, 73, 98, 99, 100, 103, 115, 119, 210, 231, 232, 269, 272, 273, 277, 278, 285, 289, 294, 299, 312, 329, 332, 338, 380, 381, 387, 390, 462, 489, 491, 495, 497, 498, 502, 522, 524, 532, 533, 535
Schmitt, R. L., 477, 484
Schneider, C. S., 409, 423
Schneider, D. J., 415, 424
Schneider, S., 109, 116
Schneier, F. R., 433, 434, 446, 449
Schoenfeld, E., 24
Schouten, A. P., 34, 53
Schrodt, P., 122, 130, 131
Schulman, S., 284, 294
Schultheiss, D., 86, 91
Schultz, W., 327, 335
Schumacher, P., 34, 53
Schut, H., 88, 94
Schützwohl, A., 55, 73
Schvaneveldt, P., 323, 334
Schwartz, J. C., 318, 325, 328, 335
Schwartz, L., 260 264
Schwartz, P., 7, 165, 230, 237, 249, 250, 279, 291, 311, 396, 519
Schwarz, N., 147, 151
Scott, J., 441, 449
Scott, J. P., 32, 34, 53
Scott, M. B., 454, 470
Seal, D. W., 58, 73
Sears, D. O., 35, 54, 191, 194, 534
Secord, P. F., 40, 49, 64, 65, 70, 73
Sedikides, C., 168, 171, 363, 370, 503, 504, 514
Seeley, J. R., 377, 390, 438, 442, 449
Segal, M. W., 32, 54
Segrin, C., 354, 363, 368, 370, 429, 430, 431, 434, 435, 438, 439, 449
Seidman, G., 235, 238, 247
Seifer, R., 80, 92
Seiffge-Krenke, I., 385, 390
Sekequaptewa, D., 286, 292
Seki, K., 169, 174
Seligman, C., 302, 313
Selton, A. W., 101, 118
Senchak, M., 80, 81, 94
Serewicz, M. C. M., 175, 179, 181, 185, 187, 193, 381, 382, 390
Seri, L. G., 410, 411, 421
Seto, M. C., 61, 71
Shackelford, T. K., 11, 24, 27, 55, 56, 59, 64, 68, 71, 73, 269, 274, 276, 282, 285, 294, 324, 332, 491, 498

Shadish, W. R., 269, 274, 294
Shaffer, D. R., 164, 165, 174
Shaffer, L., 377, 389
Shamblen, S. R., 102, 116, 283, 290
Shannon, C. E., 121, 122, 134
Shannon, L., 410, 422
Shanteau, J., 12, 13, 27
Shapiro, J. R., 398, 406
Sharkey, W. F., 415, 423
Sharp, A., 128, 134
Sharp, S. M., 154, 173
Shaver, P. R., 7, 14, 17, 21, 22, 24, 25, 27, 39, 54, 77, 79, 80,
          85, 86, 88, 89, 91, 92, 154, 161, 162, 163, 168,
          172, 173, 210, 212, 214, 219, 233, 270, 273, 274,
          280, 282, 290, 291, 294, 315, 318, 319, 320, 325,
          328, 329, 331, 333, 335, 336, 342, 345, 350,
          362, 367, 410, 420, 429, 445, 447, 454, 455, 458,
          459, 461, 462, 469, 474, 475, 483, 484, 485
Shaw, C., 179, 193
Shaw, J. I., 38, 54
Shebilske, L., 103, 117, 282, 284, 291
Sheese, B., 274, 278, 291
Shelley, D., 106, 119
Sheppard, J. A., 147, 151, 364, 370
Sherblom, J., 126, 134
Sheridan, L., 417, 423
Sherif, C. W., 219, 234
Sherif, M., 103, 119, 219, 234
Sherman, P. W., 55, 67
Sherman, R. C., 251, 252, 254, 263
Sherwin, B. B., 63, 67
Shifren, K., 85, 92
Shimizu, H., 321, 322, 336
Shoda, Y., 280, 295
Shotland, R. L., 105, 119, 139, 151, 255, 264
Shulman, N., 32, 34, 54
Shulman, S., 384, 390
Shuper, P. A., 127, 134
Shuster, S. M., 55, 73
Sias, P. M., 416, 423
Sibley, C., 86, 94
Siebenbruner, J., 377, 390
Sieving, R. E., 377, 390
Silva, P. A., 64, 66, 71
Silver, D., 81, 91
Silver, M., 410, 423
Silver, M. E., 415, 422
Silverman, J. G., 377, 390
Simmel, M., 500, 513
Simmons, C. H., 321, 322, 336
Simms, E. N., 275, 284, 287
Simon, M., 281, 293
Simon, V., 77, 92
Simon, V. A., 285, 290
Simonson, I., 218, 221, 232, 233
Simpson, J. A., 11, 12, 16, 25, 27, 56, 57, 58, 61, 62, 63, 64,
          67, 69, 73, 79, 80, 82, 83, 94, 99, 100, 117, 119,
          138, 151, 199, 215, 219, 220, 221, 232, 234, 274,
          276, 282, 283, 290, 292, 294, 298, 313, 316, 333,
          339, 350, 365, 366, 369, 370, 379, 380, 389, 471,
          473, 475, 476, 483, 484, 485, 487, 488, 489, 490,
          491, 492, 493, 494, 495, 496, 497, 498, 501, 502,
          503, 513, 524, 526
Sinclair, H. C., 410, 423
Sindberg, R. M., 256, 264

Singer, I., 351
Singer, J. D., 169, 174, 227, 234
Singh, D., 58, 73, 274, 277, 278, 294
Sinnett, E. R., 31, 50
Siqueland, L., 442, 449
Skaggs, M. J., 401, 407
Skolnick, A. S., 325, 336
Skowronski, J. J., 272, 290
Slade, A., 75, 87, 89, 94
Sloan, L. R., 112, 115
Slutske, W. S., 64, 69
Smith, A. C., 366, 369
Smith, C. A., 354, 355, 370
Smith, D., 84, 91
Smith, E. R., 510, 514
Smith, J. E., 107, 119
Smith-Lovin, L., 75, 93, 159, 173
Smith, M. D., 316, 319, 328, 331, 333
Smith, R. L., 60, 73
Smith, S. E., 326, 334, 341, 351, 533, 537
Smith, V., 33, 52
Smollan, D., 167, 170
Smoot, M., 12, 26, 38, 47, 52, 275, 276, 292
Snapp, C. M., 168, 174
Snell, J. L., 358, 368
Snoek, J., 519, 529, 538
Snoek, J. D., 157, 172, 257, 264
Snow, C., 262, 263, 286, 290
Snow, D. A., 410, 416, 423
Snyder, E. C., 477, 484
Snyder, M., 12, 17, 27, 79, 94, 167, 171, 236, 247, 281, 282,
          291, 294, 365, 366, 370, 472, 485
Solano, C. H., 430, 449
Soler, C., 64, 73
Solomon, A., 319, 331
Solomon, D. H., 121, 126, 128, 129, 130, 131, 133, 134,
          141, 150, 182, 183, 190, 193, 194, 198, 202, 215
Solomon, J., 76, 82, 88, 93
Sommer, K. L., 409, 413, 420
Sonnega, J., 87, 91
Sonntag, H., 434, 450
Sorrentino, R. M., 127, 128, 132, 134
Soucy, N., 86, 93
Spanier, C., 442, 449
Sparks, G. G., 31, 52
Spears, R., 396, 407
Speed, A., 224, 234
Spence, D., 454, 470
Spirek, M. M., 416, 420
Spitzberg, B. H., 39, 54, 138, 150, 190, 192, 255, 264, 286,
          294, 315, 332, 409, 410, 411, 412, 413, 414, 415,
          416, 417, 418, 419, 420, 421, 422, 423, 424, 435,
          446, 521, 523, 524, 525, 528, 534
Sportolari, L., 259, 260, 263
Sprecher, S., 7, 33, 46, 54, 59, 73, 136, 165, 169, 175, 179,
          180, 193, 199, 214, 218, 220, 221, 223, 224, 225,
          230, 233, 234, 235, 236, 237, 241, 243, 244,
          246, 249, 251, 256, 260, 261, 264, 269, 274, 277,
          286, 287, 291, 294, 297, 298, 299, 300, 301, 302,
          304, 305, 306, 307, 309, 310, 311, 312, 313, 316,
          317, 320, 321, 323, 324, 325, 333, 336, 396, 410,
          413, 419, 424, 466, 470, 471, 477, 485, 496, 502,
          503, 504, 506, 513, 514, 519, 523, 524, 527, 529,
          530, 531, 533, 534, 535, 536
Springer, C., 415, 422

Spurr, J. M., 431, 449
Sroufe, L. A., 77, 78, 80, 94
Srull, T. K., 510, 511, 514
Stafford, L., 188, 194
Stahelski, A. J., 508, 513
Stahmann, R., 113, 117
Staneski, R. A., 107, 118
Stangier, U., 440, 449
Stanley-Hagan, M., 402, 406
Stanley, S. M., 345, 351
Staples, B., 207, 213
Statham, D. J., 64, 69
Steca, P., 364, 367
Steciuk, M., 42, 48, 53
Steele, H., 82, 92
Steele, J., 274, 275, 284, 289
Steele, J. L., 18, 24, 324, 330, 332, 530, 537
Steele, M., 82, 92
Steers, W. N., 38, 54
Stein, J., 416, 422
Steinberg, L., 65, 66, 68
Steinfield, C., 148, 150
Stendhal,, 315, 336
Stephan, F. K., 327, 331
Stephenson, B., 432, 449
Stern, L. A., 184, 192
Sternberg, R. J., 177, 194, 199, 215, 315, 317, 318, 329, 336,
    338, 341, 351, 458, 470
Stetzenbach, K. A., 122, 132
Stewart, A., 415, 421
Stewart, M. O., 440, 447
Stiff, C., 272, 290
Stillion, J., 88, 94
Stillman, D., 394, 407
Stillwell, A. M., 189, 190, 192, 316, 322, 332, 409, 419
Stinson, L., 165, 166, 172, 364, 368
Stivers, T., 131, 134
Stockwell, M. L., 55, 69
Stoebe, M., 88, 94
Stoebe, W., 88, 94
Stone, E. A., 274, 282, 294
Stopa, L., 431, 449
Storms, M. D., 310, 313
Stovall, K. C., 90, 92
Strack, F., 510, 514
Strack, S., 434, 449
Strahan, E. Y., 430, 449
Strassberg, D. S., 111, 119
Stravynski, A., 430, 439, 449
Strodl, E., 438, 449
Stroebe, W., 224, 234
Strong, G., 315, 316, 317, 319, 322, 326, 327, 328, 329, 330,
    331
Strong, M. S., 37, 51
Strunk, D., 440, 447
Stuart, S., 441, 448
Stueve, C. A., 32, 51
Stull, D. E., 43, 52
Suchindran, C. M., 400, 407
Suitor, J. J., 519, 538
Sullivan, Q., 300, 313, 502, 504, 506, 514
Sullivan, W., 59, 73, 224, 234
Sulloway, F. J., 283, 292
Sumich, A., 276, 293
Sundis, M. J., 66, 70

Sunnafrank, M., 36, 54, 121, 122, 126, 127, 128, 129, 100,
    134, 141, 151, 156, 174
Surra, C. A., 307, 309, 310, 312, 313, 520, 522, 523, 527,
    535, 538
Sussman, D., 519, 537
Sutherland, L., 454, 455, 458, 462, 464, 469, 470
Sutton, R. M., 509, 514
Swami, V., 278, 294
Swann, W. B., Jr., 14, 15, 16, 27
Swarr, A., 376, 390
Sweeney, M. M., 403, 407
Sweet, J., 396, 402, 403, 406
Swidler, A., 310, 313
Sykes, R. E., 32, 54
Symons, D., 55, 56, 57, 58, 59, 60, 63, 69, 72, 73, 101, 120
Szolwinski, J. B., 44, 45, 50

T

Tan, J., 106, 108, 118, 276, 292, 300, 313
Tanke, E. D., 17, 27, 236, 247, 472, 485
Tanner, R. E. S., 66, 72
Tassinary, L. F., 278, 294
Taylor, C. T., 430, 432, 445
Taylor, D. A., 19, 24, 30, 40, 49, 122, 126, 131, 154, 155,
    158, 170, 174, 176, 177, 186, 191, 203, 206, 210,
    213, 259, 263, 297, 311, 382, 388, 399, 405
Taylor, S. E., 236, 241, 246, 454, 470, 490, 498
Taylor, S. T., 439, 446
Taymans, S. E., 316, 332
Teachman, J., 391, 396, 407
Teasdale, J. D., 441, 449
Teboul, J. B., 127, 134
Tedrow, L., 391, 396, 407
Tellegen, A., 284, 285, 292
Tennant, A., 97, 120
Tennov, D., 223, 227, 234, 315, 323, 324, 325, 327, 410,
    424
Tesser, A., 113, 120, 414, 415, 422, 530, 538
Teubner, G., 178, 179, 194
Thagard, P., 509, 511, 514
Theiss, J. A., 121, 129, 134
Therrien, L. F., 185, 381, 382, 390
Thibaut, J. W., 13, 18, 27, 122, 126, 133, 200, 204, 209,
    212, 214, 219, 233, 271, 292, 299, 310, 313, 328,
    334
Thiel, R., 273, 290
Thoennes, N., 411, 412, 417, 424
Thomas, G., 221, 232, 316, 333, 339, 350, 471, 472, 473,
    476, 484, 487, 488, 489, 491, 492, 494, 497, 501,
    503, 513
Thompson, K., 322, 332
Thompson, M., 250, 252, 257, 264
Thompson, R., 76, 89, 94
Thompson, T. R., 130, 132
Thompson, V. D., 224, 234
Thoren, P., 327, 336
Thorne, A., 112, 115, 275, 282, 285, 293, 294
Thornhill, R., 55, 56, 60, 61, 62, 63, 64, 69, 73, 277, 278,
    279, 291
Thornton, A., 8, 24
Thurstone, L. L., 217, 234
Tice, D. M., 61, 68

Tiddeman, B. P., 56, 72
Tillmann-Healy, L. M., 454, 469
Tindall, D., 519, 539
Ting-Toomey, S., 169, 174
Tinsley, B., 84, 94
Tither, J. M., 11, 25, 102, 116, 491, 494, 497
Tjaden, P., 411, 412, 417, 424
Tjosvold, D., 281, 294
Tobin, R. M., 274, 278, 281, 291
Toczynski, S., 281, 293
Todd, M. J., 59, 70, 178, 192, 280, 291, 317, 332
Tolhuizen, J. H., 160, 174, 362, 370, 410, 424
Tolmacz, R., 386, 390
Tomlinson, J. M., 285, 294
Tong, P. Y., 33, 50
Tooby, J., 20, 25
Tooke, W., 56, 58, 59, 73, 109, 120
Tormala, Z. L., 274, 293
Toro-Morn, M., 320, 336
Tovee, M. J., 278, 294
Townsend, J. M., 58, 59, 73, 224, 234
Tracey, T. J. G., 165, 166, 174, 364, 370
Trafimow, D., 472, 485, 499, 504, 507, 508, 514
Tran, S., 11, 16, 82, 83, 94, 476, 482, 487, 503, 524, 525, 526, 528, 535
Traupmann, J., 271, 273, 291, 295, 299, 312, 316, 320, 333, 336, 340, 351
Treboux, D., 77, 78, 80, 81, 82, 89, 92, 94
Trembath, D. L., 107, 119
Trevor, T. M. K., 241, 246
Treyens, J. C., 472, 483
Trillin, C., 3, 4, 27
Trivers, R. L., 56, 57, 58, 60, 62, 63, 65, 73, 98, 120, 279, 294, 329, 336, 338, 351
Trost, M. R., 20, 26, 56, 57, 66, 70, 99, 108, 118, 502, 513
Trotta, M. R., 362, 367
Trower, P., 433, 450
Tsai, F., 210, 215
Tsai, M., 31, 54
Tsapelas, I., 315, 320, 333
Tucker, P., 340, 351
Tuckey, M. R., 481, 485
Tudor, M., 284, 289
Turk, C. L., 428, 448
Turke, P., 56, 73
Turner, F., 5, 27
Turner, L. H., 122, 134
Turner, S. M., 427, 430, 431, 434, 442, 445, 450
Tweed, R., 87, 91
Twenge, J. M., 66, 68
Twentyman, C. T., 430, 450
Tyler, T. R., 34, 35, 54

U

Udry, J. R., 63, 73
Umana-Taylor, A. J., 398, 407
Urbaniak, G. C., 59, 73
Ureño, O., 317, 335
Uribe, C., 323, 334
Usher, M., 436, 446
Utne, M., 273, 291, 299, 312

V

Vaillant, C. O., 341, 351
Vaillant, G. E., 341, 351
Vainikka, A., 102, 119
Valencia, A., 61, 70
Valkenburg, P. M., 34, 53
Vallacher, R. R., 35, 52
Vallone, R. D., 40, 49, 167, 168, 169, 170, 240, 246, 518, 537
Valsiner, J., 198, 199, 215
Van Boben, L., 508, 512
Van Dam-Baggen, R., 439, 450
van Der Molen, H. T., 364, 370
Van der Sleen, J., 439, 448
Van Egeren, L., 83, 94
van Ijzendoorn, M., 82, 90, 94
Van Kerkwijk, C., 379, 389
Van Lange, P. A. M., 19, 20, 26, 27, 29, 197, 200, 202, 203, 204, 205, 206, 207, 208, 209, 212, 213, 214, 215, 272, 280, 288, 292
van Leeuwen, M. L., 38, 54
van Lieshout, C. F. M., 42, 43, 44, 45, 52
van Olden, Z., 281, 286, 290
Van Orden, G. C., 356, 368
Van Rheenen, D. D., 126, 134
Van Vliet, W., 30, 54
Vangelisti, A. L., 176, 177, 179, 193, 356, 369, 415, 424, 472, 485, 518, 537
Vanlear, C. A., 157, 174, 518, 538
Vanni, D., 305, 313, 410, 424
Vaughan, D., 413, 424
Ventrone, N. A., 176, 193, 358, 369
Verbrugge, L. M., 43, 54
Verdeli, H., 441, 446
Verette, J., 363, 370
Veroff, J., 302, 313, 357, 368, 454, 455, 456, 457, 458, 460, 461, 462, 463, 464, 469, 470, 528, 537, 4455
Vershure, B., 279, 293
Vicary, A., 78, 92, 359, 368
Vietor, N., 478, 479, 480, 484
Villagran, M. M., 47, 52, 180, 193
Villagran, P., 47, 52, 180, 193
Vinsel, A., 154, 156, 157, 170
Vittengl, J. R., 41, 54, 441, 442, 450
Viviani, B., 430, 446
Vogel, D. M., 501, 504, 514
Vohs, K. D., 139, 149
vom Kolke, A., 321, 322, 336
Vonk, R., 16, 28, 507, 509, 511, 514
Voracek, M., 109, 120
Vorauer, J. D., 12, 18, 28, 138, 139, 151, 356, 359, 370, 528, 539
Vorell, M., 175, 178, 193

W

Wabnik, A. I., 189, 192
Wade, M. J., 55, 73
Walby, S., 417, 424
Wald, J., 97, 120
Waldorf, V. A., 107, 119
Walker, A. M., 127, 134

Walker, D., 147, 151
Walker, M. R., 112, 115
Walker, R., 410, 422
Walker, S. J., 358, 368
Wall, S., 76, 77, 82, 91, 473, 483
Wallace, S. T., 427, 429, 431, 432, 450
Waller, N. G., 429, 446, 474, 484
Waller, W., 520, 525, 526, 539
Walsh, A., 61, 73
Walsh, D. G., 104, 120
Walster, E. H., 12, 25, 38, 40, 45, 50, 51, 113, 120, 218,
        219, 220, 224, 226, 232, 236, 246, 249, 256,
        264, 270, 271, 272, 273, 274, 283, 289, 295, 299,
        300, 312, 313, 315, 323, 336, 341, 350, 458, 470,
        522, 528, 537
Walster, G. W., 226, 234, 271, 273, 283, 295, 323, 336,
        458, 470, 528
Walters, E., 473, 483
Walters, K. S., 427, 430, 433, 450
Walters, S., 58, 59, 72, 74, 110, 120
Walther, J. B., 237, 240, 241, 247, 259, 264
Wamboldt, F. S., 454, 455, 456, 457, 470
Wang, C-C. D. C., 169, 174
Wang, Z., 316, 327, 331, 333, 336
Ward, A., 510, 514
Ward, C. C., 165, 166, 174, 345, 350, 364, 370
Waring, E. M., 154, 174
Warntjes, A., 58, 68
Warren, D. M., 465, 466, 470
Warren, N. C., 250, 262
Wasserman, T., 58, 59, 73, 224, 234
Watchravesringkan, K., 111, 120, 397, 407
Waters, E., 76, 77, 78, 80, 81, 82, 89, 91, 92, 94
Watson, D., 275, 284, 287, 363, 370
Waugh, C. E., 61, 70
Weaver, S. E., 476, 485
Weaver, S. J., 378, 380, 382, 390
Weaver, W., 121, 122, 134
Weber, A. L., 454, 470
Webster, D. M., 127, 128, 133
Webster, G. D., 61, 70
Weeden, J., 101, 120, 218, 233
Wegner, D. M., 415, 424
Wehner, E. A., 384, 385, 389
Wei, M., 158, 159, 174, 438, 450
Weimer, B., 86, 94
Weiner, B., 457, 470
Weiner, J. L., 127, 129, 131, 141, 142, 143, 144, 149, 187,
        190, 191
Weis, D., 97, 119
Weiss, L. H., 143, 146, 151
Weiss, R., 88, 93
Weissman, M. M., 441, 442, 450
Weissman, M. W., 434, 446
Wellman, B., 32, 54, 239, 243, 246, 247, 519, 526, 537,
        538, 539
Wells, A., 428, 431, 433, 440, 445
Welsh, D. P., 385, 389
Weng, W., 316, 319, 322, 327, 328, 336
Wenzel, A., 169, 178, 201, 363, 375, 419, 425, 429, 430,
        431, 432, 433, 434, 441, 443, 444, 447, 448,
        450, 517, 523, 528, 531, 533, 534, 535
Werkman, D. L., 122, 132
Werner, C., 42, 43, 44, 54
Werner, C. M., 207, 213

West, A. R., 520, 522, 523, 527, 535, 538
West, C., 356, 371
West, D. V., 359, 367
West, M. O., 378, 389
West, S. G., 59, 70, 279, 280, 291
Westbay, L., 318, 319, 332
Westbrook, N., 33, 52
Wetzel, C. G., 199, 215
Wheeler, L., 158, 174, 203, 206, 213, 262, 264, 300, 312
Wheeler, S. C., 203, 214
Whitbeck, L. B., 200, 206, 215
White, B. J., 219, 234
White, C. H., 110, 115
White, G. L., 12, 28, 130, 134
White, J. K., 346, 351
White, K. M., 383, 390
White, T. L., 415, 424
Whitley, B. E., Jr., 146, 151, 318, 336
Whitte, J., 236, 241, 242, 243, 247
Whitton, S. W., 221, 222, 232
Whitty, M. T., 257, 258, 260, 264
Wickland, R. A., 432, 449
Widenmann, S., 169, 170, 203, 213
Wiederman, M. W., 11, 28, 58, 59, 60, 74, 146, 151
Wierzbicki, M., 434, 450
Wieselquist, J., 221, 222, 232
Wiggins, J., 274, 277, 295
Wigley, S., 180, 193
Wilbur, C. J., 101, 118
Wilcox, B. L., 31, 52
Wildermuth, S. M., 255, 258, 264
Wilensky, R., 500, 514
Wilkinson, S., 457, 470
Willett, J. B., 169, 174, 227, 234
Willetts, M. C., 256, 260, 264, 324, 336
Williams, B., 377, 389
Williams, B. A., 30, 52
Williams, E., 86, 94
Williams, G. P., 112, 120
Williams, J., 412, 423
Williams, J. M. G., 436, 450
Williams, J. R., 316, 332
Williams, K. D., 285, 295
Williams, S. L., 410, 424
Williams, S. S., 143, 146, 151
Wilmot, W. W., 130, 132, 139, 140, 143, 149, 155, 159, 170,
        176, 179, 181, 182, 186, 187, 188, 192, 399, 405,
        410, 413, 420
Wilson, B. F., 395, 403, 407
Wilson, C. L., 56, 73, 82, 83, 94
Wilson, J., 162, 171
Wilson, J. E., 199, 212, 272, 287, 289
Wilson, M., 57, 64, 69, 230, 233, 410, 417, 421
Wilson, S. R., 359, 369, 410, 424
Wilson, T. D., 221, 225, 233, 301, 313
Winch, R. F., 520, 530, 539
Wineberg, H., 413, 424
Winstead, B. A., 17, 153, 161, 164, 171, 174, 358, 371, 410,
        412, 417, 419, 421, 523, 2240
Winterheld, H. A., 56, 73
Wise, R. A., 327, 336
Witt, J. K., 281, 284, 295
Wittchen, H. U., 434, 450
Wittenberg, E., 47, 52, 180, 193
Wittenberg, M. T., 39, 50

Wohl, M. J. A., 510, 513
Wolfenstein, M., 6, 28
Woll, S. B., 253, 256, 257, 264, 265
Won-Doornink, M. J., 162, 174
Wong, D. T., 102, 120
Wong, P. T. P., 164, 171, 317, 336
Wong, R. Y., 519, 539
Wood, J. F., 33, 52
Wood, J. T., 394, 407
Woods, W., 103, 116
Woody, S. R., 431, 432, 442, 450
Workman, K. A., 100, 118
Worman, S. R., 189, 190, 192
Worthy, M., 19, 28
Wortman, C. B., 41, 54, 87, 91
Wotman, S. R., 316, 322, 332, 409, 419
Wright, C. P., 302, 311
Wright, D., 79, 92, 285, 294
Wright, T. M., 100, 119, 120
Wticher, B. S., 324, 333
Wu, C., 59, 69
Wu, C. H., 102, 116, 277, 290
Wu, S., 325, 328, 335, 336
Wyer, M. M., 242, 246
Wyer, R. S., Jr., 135, 151, 472, 485, 510, 511, 514
Wysocki, D. K., 258, 259, 265, 396, 407

X

Xu, X., 316, 319, 322, 325, 327, 328, 331, 336

Y

Yan, L., 327, 331
Yang, S. M., 121, 125, 128, 129, 133
Yeadon, C., 510, 513
Yeazell, M., 185, 194
Yela, C., 316, 322, 335
Yeo, R. A., 278, 279, 291
Yep, G. A., 161, 172
Yopyk, D. J., 282, 293
Yoshikawa, S., 63, 72
Young, L. J., 55, 74, 316, 334, 336
Young, R. C., 200, 214
Younghans, C. M., 410, 414, 415, 421
Yovetich, N. A., 208, 215, 363, 370
Yu, G., 327, 336
Yum, Y.-O., 155, 174
Yung, J., 465, 469
Yurchisin, J., 111, 120, 397, 407

Z

Zaalberg, R., 356, 361
Zadny, J., 472, 485
Zajonc, R. B., 36, 54, 271, 295, 323, 336, 510, 514
Zakahi, W. R., 38, 54
Zakalik, R. A., 158, 159, 174, 438, 450
Zand, D., 159, 169, 174
Zanna, M. P., 271, 282, 290, 291, 302, 313
Zappieri, M. L., 55, 69
Zawacki, T., 106, 115
Zayas, V., 280, 295
Zebrowitz, L. A., 276, 292
Zeifman, D., 80, 92, 518, 537
Zeiss, A. M., 439, 440, 450
Zeki, S., 316, 319, 327, 328, 332
Zelley, E., 188, 192
Zemke, R., 394, 407
Zierk, K. L., 59, 70
Zillman, D., 112, 120
Zimbardo, P. G., 219, 232, 250, 252, 257, 264, 525, 539
Zimmer-Gembeck, M. J., 377, 390
Zimmerman, D. H., 356, 371
Zimmerman, R. S., 143, 151
Zormeier, M. M., 138, 150, 410, 421
Zucchi, T., 430, 446
Zuckerman, M., 106, 120, 274, 280, 295
Zusman, M. E., 395, 406
Zwaan, R. A., 500, 514

Subject Index

A

Abstinence-only program, 499–500
Accuracy motives, 490
Acquaintanceship, 176–177
Active sexual information seeking, 143
Active strategies, 124
Acts of devotion, 184
Adolescence
  casual sexual hookups, 378
  developmental significance of, 376–377
  intimacy vs. isolation crisis, 377
  subjective experience of hookups, 381–382
  youth sexual/relationship experience, 377–378
Adult Attachment Interview (AAI), 77, 82, 88
Adult attachment theory, 21–22, 65–66
Affect-as-information model, 147
Affiliation, two-factor model of, 13
Affiliation/affiliate responses, 360–361
Affinity-testing strategies, 137
Agape (selfless love), 318, 320, 342–343
Agency, 393, 399–400
Agreeableness, 101
Ambiguous language, 124
Ambivalent individuals, 76, 78, 319
Anticipated interactions, 123, 198
Anxious adults/anxious-ambivalent styles, 78, 319
Approaching, 137–138
Arousal, 299
Arousal-attraction effect, 315, 324
Arranged relationships, 168–169
Assertiveness training, 439
Attachment anxiety, 18
  partner-specific, 226–228
Attachment insecurity, 76
Attachment relationships, 77, 89
Attachment styles, 14, 22
  falling in love, 319–320
  hookups and, 386
  mating and, 100–101
  parasite, 101
  partner, 101
  player, 101
  predator, 101
Attachment theory, 429
  adult love, 315
  advances in theory/research, 77–78
  client-therapist relationships, 87
  contemporary research, 76–83
  co-parenting, 83
  dating relationships, 78–80
  depression and, 437
  family caregiving, 84–85
  friendships and, 85–86
  grandparent-grandchild relationships, 83–84
  human mating and, 65–66
  infant-parent relationships, 82–83
  intergenerational relationships, 83–85
  loss and subsequent relationship initiation, 87–89
  love as attachment, 329
  mentoring relationships, 86–87
  newlywed relationships, 80–82
  parenthood and, 82–83
  relationship initiation and, 75–76, 210
Attract attention stage, 101–104, 113
  expressive features, 102
  grooming, 102–103
  neonate/sexually mature features, 101–102
  peer esteem and male copying, 103–104
  possessions and extrapersonal displays, 103
Attraction
  affiliation/affiliative responses, 12–14, 360–361
  desirable characteristics, 309
  determinants of, 298–299, 530
  fatal attraction, 308–309
  future research directions, 309–311
  initial attraction, 11–12
  intense attraction predictors, 303–305
  interpersonal attraction, study of, 520–521
  later relationship outcomes, 307–309
  methodological issues, 300–303
  online vs. offline predictors, 259–260
  perspectives on, 287
  prediction on, 298
  reinforcement theories, 287–288
  research on predictors of, 305–306
  self-reports of predictors, 300–303, 307
Attraction-related information, 137–138
  perceived romantic interest, 138–139
  seeking information, 137–138
  sending information, 138
Authentic self, 166, 242
Automatic thoughts, 428
Availability, friendship formation and, 36–37
Avoidant people/behaviors, 22, 76, 78, 364

B

Behavioral intervention, 439–440
Behavioral tradition
  depression and, 434–435
  relationship functioning, 427–428
Behavioral uncertainty, 122, 192
Behaviors, as attractive/unattractive, 279
Belief frameworks, 471–472
Belonging need, 338
Biological sex, 403
Birth control, 6

C

Calling system, 5
Casual sex, *see* Hookups

Celebrity effect, 104
Charm behavior, 109
Chemistry.com, 250, 258
Classical realist research, 274
Cleared for encounter, 4, 7, 13
Clicking model, 156
Client-therapist relationships, attachment theory and, 87
Closed-field encounters/partnering, 5, 177
Closeness condition, 167–168
Close relationships, 286
CLUES scale, 128
Cognition, 488
Cognitive-behavioral therapy/group therapy, 440
Cognitive consistency and balance, 299
Cognitive content, 428
Cognitive interventions, 440–441
    emotional disturbances, 440–441
Cognitive restructuring, 440
Cognitive tradition
    depression, 435–437
    relationship functioning, 428
    social anxiety, 431–432
Cognitive uncertainty, 121
Come-on self, 4, 7, 19
Commercial dating sites, 5–7; *see also* Internet matching
        services
Commitment, 307–308
    exchange theory and, 19
Common interests, 4
Communal vs. exchange relationships, 283
Communication; *see also* Opening gambits
    in cross-sex friendships, 186–190
    dynamics of, 97–98
    hookups and, 382
    online communication, 244
    relational maintenance behavior, 188–190
    secret tests, 187–188
    topic avoidance, 186–187
    uncertainty and, 123, 125–126
Communication network proximity, friendship formations,
        34–35
Communication privacy management (CPM) theory, 393
Companionate love, 341–342
Compatibility/ compatibility matching, 262, 501
Competent loners, 399
Competitor derogation, 59
Computer dates, 249
Computer-mediated communication (CMC), 396
    cyberspace proximity, 48
    friendship formation, 30, 33–34
Confronting, 138
Constraint satisfaction model, 509–510
Constructivist research, 275
Content responsiveness, 161–162
Context, 393–399
Conversational openers, 17
    direct approach, 107
    opening gambits, 97, 107
Conversational responsiveness, 162
Co-parenting, 75, 83
Core beliefs, 428
Correspondence of outcomes, 20, 202
Couples, placemaking, 207
Couples counseling, 347–348
    respect toward partner scale, 349

Couples orientation, 458
Courtship attraction, 326
Courtship behavior
    culture and, 98
    gender and, 98–99
    mating and attachment styles, 100–101
    relationship aspirations, 99–100
    research toward universal topics, 522–523
    sociosexuality, 100
Cross-sex friendships, 189
Culture
    courtship behavior and, 98
    falling in love and, 320–322
    interaction scripts, 158
    intercultural couples, 465–466
    relationship prototypes, 158
    self-disclosure and, 158
    unwanted relationship pursuit, 412–414
    youth sexual/relational experiences, 387
Cute-flippant approach, 107
Cyberspace proximity, 48

D

Dance, 113
Darwinian principles, 11, 20, 299
Dating relationships, 78–80
Dating system, 5–6; *see also* Speed-dating
    historical context of, 3
Dating websites, 249–250
Deception, 109–110
Decide and approach stage, 104–106, 114
    moving closer, 106
    nonverbal solicitation, 104–105
    signal (mis)perception, 105–106
Defeated, 399
Definitional uncertainty, 182
Depression, 363, 427
    behavioral tradition, 434–435
    cognitive tradition, 435–437
    excessive reassurance seeking, 437
    interpersonal tradition, 437–438
    relationship initiation and, 434–438
Depressive realism, 436
Descriptive disclosures, 154
Destiny beliefs, 478–479, 493
Developmental-attachment theory, 66
Deviance, 123
Diminishing self, 137–138
Direct accounts, 140
Direct approach/direct propositions, 107–109
Directness tests, 139
Disappointment, 362–363
Disclaimers, 124
Disclosure strategy, 136–137
Disjunctive relationships, 409
Dislike criteria, 37
Dismissing individuals, 22, 77–78, 88
Disorganized-disoriented infants, 76, 88
Display rules for emotion, 355
Disregard criteria, 37
Diversity, 394, 402–403
Divorce initiator, 397
Dominance, 279
Dyadic Adjustment Scale (DAS), 456

Dyadic reciprocity, 226
Dysfunctional beliefs, 477–478

E

Early relationship development, ideal standards in, 494
Early Years of Marriage (EYM) program, 455, 460–461, 464
Effectiveness, 154
Efficacy, influence of, 147–148
eHarmony.com, 6–7, 250, 258–259
Emergent research, 275
Emotional availability, 358–360
Emotional baggage, 380, 396, 398
Emotional bond challenge, 183
Emotional contagion, 434
Emotional disturbances
    behavioral intervention, 439–440
    cognitive intervention, 440–441
    future research, 443–445
    interpersonal intervention, 441–442
    intervention, 439–442
Emotional expression, 355
    display rules, 355
    feeling rules, 355
    as spontaneous and symbolic, 355
Emotions
    emotional realities of hookups, 382–383
    hope and disappointment, 362–363
    individual differences, 363–366
    negative affective states, 358–359
    poise and emotional availability, 358–360
    positive affective states, 360
    in relationship initiation, 353
    relationship initiation enactment, 358–363
    relationship schemas and scripts, 356–358
    sociofunctional approach to, 354–356
Empathy, 346
Encounters, *see* Romantic encounters
Endurance tests, 139, 188
Enhancement motives, 490
Enhancers, 399
Environment, defined, 201
Equity theory, 299
Eros (romantic, passionate love), 317–318, 342
Erotic love, 12
Ethnicity, narrative style and content, 463–464
Evaluative disclosures, 154
Evolutionary-based theories, research on, 277–285
Evolutionary principles, 299
Evolutionary psychology, 66
Evolutionary social psychological theory, 20–21
Evolutionary theory
    love and, 329
    relationship initiation, 338
Excitement, 507
Exclusion criteria, friendship formation, 37–39
Expectancy violations theory (EVT), 183–185
Expectations
    anticipated interactions, 198–199
    interactions not experienced, 199
    physical/social influences on, 199–200
Experiences in Close Relationships Scales, 474
Experimenting stage, 4
Exposure effects, 324

Expressive features, 102
Extrapersonal displays, 103–104
Eye contact, 112

F

Facebook, 148, 242
Falling in love, 315–318, 517
    biological basis of, 326–328
    cultural context, 320–322
    defined, 316–317
    effects of, 325–326
    future research on, 330–331
    gender, 320
    how it works, 328–330
    as motivational stage, 328
    narratives of, 189
    onset of sexual desire, 319
    personality, 319–320
    rates of, 322
    readiness effect, 324–325
    reciprocity and, 322–323
    social appropriateness of, 324
    variations in, 319–323
Family caregiving, 84–85
Family Narrative Consortium, 455
Fatal attraction, 308–309
Favoritism, 326
Fearful adults, 22, 78
Fear of rejection, 359, 363
Feeling rules, 355
Female choice, 326
Field of availables, 12
Filling needs, 324
First date goals, 185
First date scripts, 357–358
First impressions, 236, 472
First meeting scripts, 357
Flattery, 16
Flirtation, 413
Follow the heart, 477
Formal marriage market intermediary, 255–256
Frequency of exposure/familiarity, 35–36
Friends with benefits, 178, 379
Friendship, defined, 29–30
Friendship attraction, 177
Friendship-based intimacy, 177
Friendship formation, 29–30
    attachment and, 85–86
    availability, 36–37
    convergence of factors, 46–47
    dyadic factors, 39–46
    environmental factors of, 30–35
    exclusion criteria, 37–38
    frequency of exposure/familiarity, 35–36
    inclusion criteria, 38–39
    individual factors, 37–39
    online friendships, 33–34
    outcome dependency, 36
    physical attractiveness, 38
    population density, 30–31
    probability of future interaction, 35
    reciprocity of liking, 40
    research, future directions of, 47–48
    residential proximity, 31–32

self-disclosure in, 30, 40–41
shared fun and humor, 41–42
similarity and, 42–46
situational factors, 35–37
social networks, 34–35
social skills, 38–39
workplace/school settings, 32–33
Friendship-to-romance transition
communication in, 186–190
expectancy violations theory, 183–185
friends with benefits, 178
future research, 190–191
platonic relationship, 177–178
relational maintenance behavior, 188–190
relationship history, 178–179
secret tests, 187–188
social network, 179–180
stage theories, 176–180
theoretical perspectives on, 176–185
topic avoidance, 186–187
traditional trajectory, 176–177
turning point approach, 180–181
uncertainty reduction theory, 181–183
Functional distance, 31
Fun qualities, 108
Future uncertainty, 182

G

Gender
courtship behavior and, 98–99
falling in love, 320
narratives and well-being, 463
relationship initiation, 461–463
self-disclosure and, 159, 164–165
Gender stereotypes, 501–503
Generalized attachment representations, 76
Generalized reciprocity, 226
Generational time, 394
Gestures of inclusion, 185
Girl next door type, 102
Global uncertainty, 125
Goodenoughs, 399
Grandparent-grandchild relationships, 83–84
Greeting ritual, 357
Grooming, 102–103
Group dating, 5–6, 179
Growth beliefs, 478–479, 493
Guilt, 355

H

Hanging out, 5–6, 179
Hazing, 137–138
Hedging, 124
High openers, 159
Historical time, 394
Hitting it off, 473
Homework assignments, 439
Hookup buddy, 379
Hookups, 5, 178, 385
alcohol and, 378, 381
emotional realities of, 382–383
future research, 387–388
individual attachment style and, 386
initiating relationships and, 378–380
intimacy development and, 383–386
motivations for, 380–381
relationship initiation and, 375–376
subjective experience of, 381–382
youths/young adults, 378
Hope, 362–363
Humor, 107–108

I

Ice princess type, 102
Ideal vs. current partner comparisons, 492
Idealization, 477
Ideal partners, 503
Ideal relationship, 503
Ideal standards model, 487–491
consequences of discrepancies, 490–491
early relationship development, 494
empirical evidence for, 491–494
enhancement and accuracy motives, 490
evaluative dimensions, 488–489
functions of, 489–490
future research, 495–497
growth and destiny beliefs, 493
ideal vs. current partner, 492
partner and relationship ideals, 491–492, 503
regulation functions of, 493–494
Identifiability, online relationships, 237–238
Implicit theories of relationships, 478
Inclusion criteria, friendship formation, 38–39
physical attractiveness, 38
responsiveness, 39
social skills, 38–39
Inclusion of Others in the Self Scale, 167
Indirect suggestion, 139, 188
Individual factors, friendship formation and, 37–39
Individual preference, 326
Infant-parent attachment relationships, 82–83
Information seeking, 124
attraction-related information, 137–138
in developing relationships, 139–142
direct accounts, 140
directness tests, 139
disclosure strategy, 136–137
endurance tests, 139
general information, 136–137
impact of technology, 148–149
indirect suggestion, 139
initial interactions, 136–139
interrogation, 136
public presentation, 139
relaxing the target, 136–137
separation, 140
sexually related information, 143–146
theory of motivated information management (TMIM), 141–142
third party, 140
triangle tests, 140
typologies of strategies, 139–141
uncertainty and, 124
Informativeness, 154
Initial encounters; see also Relationship initiation
attract attention stage, 101–104

attraction-relation information, 137–138
decide and approach stage, 104–106
future research direction, 113–114
information seeking in, 136–139
prioritize desires stage, 98–101
rapport in, 16–18
talk and reevaluate stage, 101
touch and synchronize, 112–113
Initiating stage, 4
Innocuous approach, 107
Integration phase, 271
Integrative topic, 4, 14, 17
Intense attraction, 303–305
Intensifying vs. restricting scripts, 159–160
Interaction
continuing interactions, 208
generic qualities of partners, 201
given situation, 200–201
inferring partner motives, 209
physical features, 202–204
physical properties and, 206–207
social networks/network members and, 202–206
social personality, 205
theoretical background, 200–205
transformed responses, 207–208
transforming a given situation, 204–205
Interaction motives
partner motives, 209
situation's physical properties and, 206–207
social network members and, 205–206
Interaction scripts, 158
Interactive sexual information seeking, 144
Interactive strategies, 124
Intercultural couples, 465–466
Interdependence theory, 19–20, 209–211
correspondence of outcomes, 20
future research, 211–212
personality traits, 210
Interfaith dating, 203
Intergenerational relationships, 83–85
family caregiving, 84–85
grandparent-grandchild relationships, 83–84
Internet matching services, 5, 6–7, 249–260
attraction to, 253–254
barriers to, 254–255
as formal marriage market intermediary, 255–256
future research, 261–262
matching assistance, 258
member-initiated matches, 257–258
other commercial means vs., 260–261
overview of, 249–250
process of, 256–257
profile of users, 252–253
reasons for use, 253–255
relationship formation at, 259–261
relationship initiation, 251–252, 255–259
social networks/friends vs., 260
Internet relationships
online friendships, 30, 33–34
self-disclosure and, 165–167
Interpersonal attraction
new methodological tools for, 272–273
research literature review of, 270, 272
shifting research methodologies, 523
shifting theoretical perspectives, 524–525

study of, 520–521
Interpersonal intervention, emotional disturbances, 441–442
Interpersonal psychotherapy (IPT), 441
Interpersonal tradition
depression, 437–438
relationship functioning, 429
social anxiety, 432–433
Interrogation strategy, 138
Intimacy, 507
hookups and, 383–386
interpersonal process model, 162–163
isolation crisis vs., 377
Investment model, 392
Involuntary relationships, 168–169
I-sharing, 45

J

Joint storytelling, 456

K

Knapp's stage theory, 176–177

L

Life course perspective, 393
relevant findings of, 394–403
Life span model, 65
Linked lives, 393, 400–401
Living apart together, 400
Long-distance relationships, 200, 207
Long-term mating, 56, 58
features of, 62
qualities for, 11
sex differences in, 58–60
Loss of attachment relationship, 87–89
Love; see also Falling in love
ages and stages, 343–344
as attachment, 329
as emotion, 328
evolutionary approaches, 329–330
matching and satisfaction, 343
people's understanding of, 318–319
recent research on, 344
respect and, 346–347
self-expansion model, 330
as a story, 329
types of love, 317–318, 341–342
Love at first sight, 23, 342, 477
Love experience, 12
Love finds a way, 477
Love Scale (Rubin), 317
Love styles, 317–318, 321, 342–343
Low openers, 159
Ludus (game-playing love), 318, 320, 342
Lying, 109–111

M

Mania (possessive, dependent love), 318, 342–343
Manipulate mating style, 109
Marital satisfaction, 339

Marriage market, 396
Marriage market intermediaries, 256
Marriage trends, 8
Match.com, 6, 110, 250, 252, 259
Matching hypothesis, 299
Mate choice, 326
    attachment and mating, 65–66
    cultural differences in, 64–66
    evolutionary perspective/theories on, 55–58
    individual differences in, 61–64
    long-term/short-term mating, 56
    men and mating differences, 61–63
    sex differences in, 58–60
    sex ratios and mating, 64–65
    women and mating differences, 63–64
Mate copying, 103–104
Mate poaching, 59
Mate preference, 326
Mating attachment styles, 100–101
Mating preferences, 502–503
Mating systems, 55
    sex differences in, 58–61
Mating tactics, 101, 109–112
    charm, 109
    manipulate, 109
    seduce, 109
    support, 109
Meaning, 393, 402
Mentoring relationships, attachment and, 86–87
Modeling, 103, 439
Modern partnering, 6–7
Monogamous mating system, 55
Motives
    constraint satisfaction model, 509–510
    inferring motives, 509–511
    logic of covariation, 509
    relationship beginnings, 11–12
Moving against tactics, 416
Moving away, 416
Moving inward, 416
Moving outward, 416
Moving with tactics, 416
Music, 112
Mutuality uncertainty, 182
Mutual romance friendships, 189
MySpace, 148, 242

N

Naïve realism, 510
Narrative consistency, 460–461
Narratives/narrative approach, overview of, 453–455
Narrative truth, 454
Naturally forming relationships, 240–241
Need for closure, 127
Need to belong, 338
Negative affective states, 358–359
Neonate and sexually mature features, 101–102, 275
Networked relationships, 242–243
Networking, 137
Newlywed relationships, 80–82
New romantic relationships, 391
Newspaper ads, *see* Personal ads
Nonfamilial affiliations, 77
Nonmarital sexual behavior, 8

Nonpersonalistic self-disclosure, 154
Nontalkers, 144
Nonverbal behavior, 113–114; *see also* Physical appearance
Nonverbal communication, 138
Nonverbal cues, 21, 280
Nonverbal solicitation, 104–105
Nonverbal stimuli, 101
Nonverbal synchrony, 112
Northwestern Speed-Dating Study, 218, 220, 224–229, 262

O

Obligatory love, 321
Offering, 137
One-night stands, 378
One and only belief, 477
Online dating, 6–7
    divorced individuals, 396–397
    gay participants, 467
Online discussions, 235–236
Online friendships, 30, 33–34
Online personals, 250
Online relationships
    absence of gating features, 236–237
    control, 238
    discovering similar others, 238–239
    factors for, 236–239
    future research, 243–246
    identifiability, 237–238
    knowing the other, 239
    naturally forming relationships, 240–241
    networked relationships, 242–243
    other commercial means vs., 260–261
    relationship formation, 239–234
    self-disclosure in, 242, 245
    self-presentation in, 110–111
    targeted relationships, 241–242
Ontogenetic time, 394
Openers, 4, 17
Opener Scale, 159
Open field, 177
Opening gambits, 97, 107
    cute-flippant approach, 107
    direct approach, 107
    innocuous approach, 107
Openness-closedness contradiction, 157
Operation Match, 249
Outcome dependency, friendship formation, 36
Overture, decision of, 12–14

P

Parasite, 101
Parental investment-based models, 20–21
Parental investment theory, 62
    mate choice and relationship initiation, 56–58
Parenthood, 82–83
Partnering
    commercialized methods of, 5–7
    modern partnering, 6–7
Partner and relationship ideals, 491–492
Partners, sexually related information, 143–146
Partner-specific attachment anxiety, 226–228

Passionate Love Scale (PLS), 317
Passion-based intimacy, 177
Passive sexual information seeking, 143
Passive strategies, 124
Peer esteem, 103–104
Perceived affinity, 137
Perceived regard, 226–227
Perceived romantic interest, 138–139
Perceived unselectivity, 226
Perceiver bias, 512
Perceiver dispositions, 281–282
Perfectmatch.com, 250, 258
Persistence, unwanted relationship pursuit, 410–412
Personal ads, 5, 250
    rhetoric of responses, 111–112
    self-presentation in, 110–111
Personalistic self-disclosure, 154
Personality traits, 210, 501
    falling in love and, 319–320
Perspective taking, 346, 508
Pew Internet and American Life project, 251–253
Phenomenology of attraction, 300
Physical appearance, 11, 14
    attract attention stage, 101–104
    expressive features, 102
    friendship formation, 38
    as gating feature, 236
    grooming, 102–103
    neonate and sexually mature features, 101–102
    peer esteem and mate copying, 103–104
    possessions and extrapersonal displays, 103
    relationship aspirations and, 99–100
    research literature on, 275–277
    sex differences in preferences, 224–225
Physical context, 394
Physical environment
    defined, 198
    expectation influences and, 199–200
    initial interaction and, 203
    overview of, 197–198
    relationship initiation and, 197–198
Physical-sexual attraction, 177
Physiological arousal, 354
Placemaking, 207
Planning, uncertainty and, 124
Platonic relationships, 130–131
Player, 101
Play the field, 5
Playful love, 12
Playing hard to get, 413
Pleasure principal, 18
Poise, 358
Political ideology, 229
Polygynous mating, 55
Population density, friendship formation, 30–31
Positive affective states, 360
Positive illusions, 363
Possessions and extrapersonal displays, 103
Postdivorce adjustments, 399
Pragma (logical, shopping-list love), 318, 342
Predator, 101
Predicted outcome value theory, 36, 126–127
    assumptions of, 126–127
    empirical tests of, 127
Predicted outcome value theory (POVT), 121–122, 156

Premarital sex, 8
Preoccupied individuals, 22, 77
Prioritize desires stage, 98–101, 113
    gender, 98–99
    mating and attachment styles, 100–101
    relationship aspirations, 99–100
    sociosexuality, 100
Privacy regulations, 154, 156–158
Probability of future interaction, 35
Proceptivity, 326
Process, 393, 401–502
Processes of Adaptation in Intimate Relationships (PAIR)
    Project, 8
Projection bias, 167
Propinquity, 30, 32–33, 324
Prospective partners
    attributing motives for specific actions, 507–511
    goals and motives of, 500–501
    inferring motives, 509–511
    simulation, 508
Proximity
    cyberspace proximity, 48
    friendship formation, 30, 32–33
Psychological context, 397
Public presentation/presentation tests, 139, 188

Q

Qualifiers, 4, 5, 7

R

Race, 229, 402–403
    narrative style and content, 463–464
Rapport
    in initial encounters, 16–18
    self-disclosure and, 17
Readiness effect, 324–325
Realism, 275–276
Real self, 166
Reciprocal liking, 226
Reciprocity, 12, 23, 137, 162
    establishing trust, 41
Reciprocity of liking, 40
Recreational sex, 5
Reinforcement theories, 287–288
Rejection, 189, 528
Relational goal pursuit theory, 414–415
Relational Interdependent Self-Construal Scale, 163
Relational maintenance behavior, 188–190
Relational responsiveness, 161
Relational self-disclosure, 154
Relationship aspirations, courtship behavior and, 99–100
Relationship-based knowledge structures, 488
Relationship beginnings model, 9–18
    building rapport, 16–18
    flow chart of, 9
    motives and initial attraction, 11–12
    overture decision, 12–14
    overview of, 9–11
    presentation of self, 14–16
Relationship beliefs
    conceptual model, 472–473
    destiny belief, 478–479

dysfunctional beliefs, 477–478
future research, 480–482
growth beliefs, 478–479
implicit theories of, 478–480
initial impressions, 472
internal working models, 473–475
relationship ideals, 476
romantic beliefs, 476–477
Relationship development, study of, 520; *see also*
       Friendship formation
Relationship dispositions, 207
Relationship escalation, 184
Relationship experience, youths/young adults, 377–378
Relationship formation
Internet matching services, 259–261
online relationships, 239–234
Relationship functioning
behavioral tradition, 427–428
cognitive tradition, 428
interpersonal tradition, 429
theoretical frameworks for, 427–430
Relationship goals
empirical investigation and findings, 503–507
gender stereotypes, 501–502
ideal partners/relationships, 503
mating preferences, 502–503
perception of goals, 506–507
Relationship history, influence of, 178–179
Relationship ideals, 476
Relationship initiation; *see also* Friendship-to-romance
       transition
after loss, 87–89
arranged marriages, 203
attachment theory and, 75–76
attracting others, 360–361
closed-field partnering, 5
core processes, 530–531
cultural differences in, 64–66
dating system, 5–6
decision to initiate, 13
depression and, 434–438
describing the phenomena, 517–518
emotional disturbances in, 425–427
emotion in, 353
empirical literature review, 269–270
enactment, 358–363
evolutionary theories of, 55–58
expectations/anticipated interactions, 198–199
first meeting scripts, 357
as formative process, 338
gender and, 465
historical perspective on, 5–7
hookups and, 375–376, 378–380
hope and disappointment, 362–363
ideal paradigm for study of, 218–222
ideal standards in, 487–497
individual differences in, 61–64
interdependence analysis, 209–211
Internet matching services, 251–252, 255–259
managing risks of, 160–161
modern partnering, 6–7
motives for forming, 7–8
narratives of, 453
openness-closedness contradiction in, 157
as phase or stage, 518–519

prevalence of, 519
processes following, 496
reasons for entering, 306–307
reducing uncertainty, 361–362
relationship beliefs, 471–472
self-monitoring, 365–366
sequelae of, 532–533
sex differences in, 58–60
shyness, 364–365
social anxiety, 430–433
social and physical environments of, 197–198
stages/phases of, 531
systematic differences in, 531–532
uncertainty and, 121–126, 127–131
when relationships begin, 529
Relationship initiation, empirical literature review,
       269–270
attraction and perceivers, 280–282
behaviors as attractive/unattractive, 279–280
classical realist research, 274
communal vs. exchange relationships, 283
constructivism approach, 275, 280–282
emergent processes, 275, 283–285
evolutionary-based theories, 277–285
future directions, 286–288
missing areas for study, 285–286
new theoretical approaches, 273–274
1985 as starting point, 270
overview of, 274–275
post-1975, 272
properties of targets, 275–277
research prior to 1985, 270–272
sex differences in, 282–283
twin studies, 284–285
Relationship initiation narratives
coherence, 456–457
consistency, 460–461
content of, 458–459
content and well-being, 459
couple orientation, 458
drama and emotion, 457–458
future research, 468–469
gender and, 461–463
initiators and facilitators, 459
intercultural couples, 465–466
joint storytelling, 456
key aspects of, 455–461
less traditional couples, 464–4468
race and ethnicity in, 463–464
same sex couples, 466–468
strategies and goals, 458–459
style, 455–456
Relationship initiation, post dissolution of prior
       relationship, 392–394
age, 403
agency, 393, 399–400
biological sex, 403
children and, 395
context, 393–399, 404
diversity, 394, 402–403
divorce initiator, 398
feminist perspective, 392–393
future research agenda, 403–405
investment model, 392–393
life course perspective, 393–403

linked lives, 393, 400–401
meaning, 393, 402
online dating and, 396–397
partners with children, 395
process, 393, 401–402
psychological characteristics of individuals, 398
rage, 402–403
social context, 396
socioeconomic status, 403
theoretical perspectives on, 392–394
time, 393–394
Relationship initiation research
future directions of, 533–536
historical roots of, 520–521
peers and networks, 527–528
rejection, 528
shifting methodologies of, 523
shifting substantive foci, 525–528
societal change and new topics, 526–527
in various disciplines, 521–522
Relationship intimacy, 161–163
Relationship outcomes
commitment, 307–308
predictors of attraction and, 307–309
Relationship prototypes, 158
Relationships
naturally forming relationships, 240–241
networked relationships, 242–243
why firmed, 529–530
Relationship satisfaction, 337, 339, 347–348
different stages of, 340
recent research on, 340–341
Relationship schemas and scripts, 356–358
Relationship-specific representations, 77
Relationship uncertainty, 128, 182
Relax the target strategy, 136–137
Religious influences, 66
Repartnering, 400–401
age, 403
biological sex and, 403
race and, 402–403
socioeconomic status and, 403
Researcher (outsider) perspective on attraction predictors, 300
Residential proximity, friendship formation, 31–32
Resistant infants, 76
Respect, 344–345
couples and, 347–348
importance of, 345
love and, 346–347
recent research on, 345–346
satisfaction and, 346–347
Respect toward partner scale, 349
Responsiveness, 154
friendship formation, 39
Retrospective account (report) on attraction, 300
Reward value/rewardingness, 184, 299
Rhetoric of responses, 111–112
Role playing, 439
Role taking, 346
Romantic attraction, 177, 323–325
exposure/propinquity effects, 324
filling needs, 324
Romantic beliefs, 476–477
Romantic encounters, conceptual model of, 3

adult attachment theory, 21–22
evolutionary social psychological theory, 20–21
interdependence theory, 19–20
social exchange theory, 18–19
tasks of successful encounters, 4–5
theoretical perspectives on, 18–22
Romantic love, 315, 321, 477
scientific and scholarly delineation, 317–318
Romantic relationships
acquaintanceship and, 176–177
evolutionary theory, 338
goals and motives in, 499–500
need to belong, 338
respect and, 344–349
satisfaction, 338–341
satisfaction in, 337–339
Romantic relationship transition (RRT), 181
Romeo and Juliet effect, 324
Rule of homogamy, 42
Rules, The (Fein and Schneider), 109

S

Safer-sex talkers, 144
Same-sex couples, 466–467
Satisfaction, 337–339
context of, 339
defined, 339
hookups and, 382
recent research on, 340–341
relationship stages and, 340
respect and, 346–347
Schemas, 356–358
School settings, friendship formation, 32–33
Screening pattern, 495
Scripts, 357
first date scripts, 357–358
first meeting scripts, 357
Second encounter, 4
Secret tests, 140, 187–188
Secure individuals, 22, 76
attachment theory, 76–78
coping with loss, 88–89
dating relationships, 79–80
newlywed relationships, 81–82
self-disclosure and, 159
Seduce behavior, 109
Seductive voice, 361
Seekers, 399
Selective proceptivity, 326
Selectivity, 281
Self-disclosure, 17
acquaintance exercise, 167–167
background factors affecting, 158–159
clicking model, 156
defined, 153–154
dialectical and privacy perspectives, 156–157
in friendship, 30
friendship formation, 40–41
future research, 168–169
gender and, 159, 164–165
hookups and, 382
intensifying vs. restricting scripts, 159–160
Internet communication, 165–167
interpersonal skills and, 159

managing risk of, 160–161
online relationships, 242, 245
relational responsiveness, 161–163
social exchange theory and, 19
social penetration theory, 154–155
as start of relationship, 154–158
temporary closeness, 167–168
Self-disclosure voice, 361
Self-esteem, 507
Self-expansion theory, 284, 330
Self-expression, 162
Self-monitoring, 365–366
Self-presentation, 110–111, 359
in first encounters, 14–16
in newspaper ads/online, 110–111
self-expressive vs. strategic motives, 14–15
Self-promotion, 16, 59
lying and, 109–110
Self-reports of attraction predictors, 300–303
disadvantage of, 301–302
primer on method, 302–303
Separation/separation tests, 140, 188
Sex differences
attraction/initiation process, 282–283
ideal partner preferences, 224–225
long-term mating, 58–60
short-term mating, 60–61
Sex ratios, human mating and, 64–65
Sexual challenge, 183
Sexual choice, 326
Sexual coyness, 65
Sexual desire, 319
Sexual experience, youths/young adults, 377–378
Sexuality, changing trends in, 8
Sexually mature features, 101–102
Sexually related information, 143–146
active sexual information seeking, 143
impact of technology, 148–149
influence of efficacy, 147–148
information seeking about, 144–136
interactive sexual information seeking, 144
passive sexual information seeking, 143
research study and findings on, 144–146
role of emotions in, 147
sexual health information, 144–146
Sexual selection theory, 55, 65, 67
Sexual strategies theory (SST), 58
Shaky bridge study, 324
Shared fun/humor, 41–42
Short-term mating, 16, 56, 58
features of, 62
sex differences in, 60–61
Shyness, 364–365
Signal amplification, 359
Signaling/signal perception, 105–106, 138
Similarity, friendship formation, 42–46
Situational factors, friendship formation, 35–37
Social anxiety, 444
behavioral tradition, 430–431
cognitive tradition, 431–432
interpersonal tradition, 432–433
Social anxiety disorder, 426–427
Social context, 396
Social cues, 362, 365
Social environment

defined, 197
expectation influences and, 200
overview of, 197–198
relationship initiation and, 197–198
Social exchange theory, 18–19, 299
commitment and, 19
pleasure principal, 18
self-disclosure and, 19
Social Interaction Anxiety Scale (SIAS), 432
Social networks, 15, 148
falling in love and, 324
friendship formations, 30, 34–35
hookups and, 382
influence of, 179–180
interaction motives, 205–206
Internet matching vs., 260
online networking, 243
Social penetration theory, 154–155, 158, 177, 186
wedge-shaped pattern to disclosure, 155
Social personality, 205
Social proximity effects, 198
Social psychological theory, 376
Social skills, 427
friendship formation, 38–39
Socioeconomic status (SES), 100, 403
Sociofunctional approach, to emotions, 354–356
Sociosexuality, courtship behavior and, 100
Sociosexuality Orientation Inventory (SOI), 100
Soul mates, 14
Speed-dating, 6, 203, 209, 261, 518
attachment anxiety, 226–228
background to, 217–218
future research, 230–231
ideal paradigm for study, 218–224
Northwestern study, 224–229
partner preferences, 224–226
race and political ideology, 229
reciprocity/reciprocal liking, 226
relationship initiation and, 222–224
Stage theories of relationship development, 176–180
Stalking, 411–412, 417–419
Status resources, 31, 507
Storge (friendship love), 318, 342
"Strangers on a train" phenomenon, 237
Strange situation procedure, 76
Strategic pluralism theory, 62
Strategic self-presentation, 21
Strictly platonic friendships, 189
Subjective Closeness Index, 167
Support mating behaviors, 109
Sustaining, 137–138
Swingers, 399
Synchrony, 473

T

Taboo topics, 399
Talk and reevaluate stage, 106–112, 114
direct propositions, 108–109
humor, 107–108
lying to date, 109–110
mating tactics, 109–112
opening gambits, 107
rhetoric of responses, 111–112
self-presentation, 110–111

Targeted relationships, 241–242
Temporary closeness, 167–168
Theory of motivated information management (TMIM), 141–142
Theory of self-expansion, 284
Third party, 140
Third-party tests, 188
Time, 393–394
Tolerance for uncertainty, 127
Topic avoidance, 186–187
Touch and synchronize stage, 112–114
Traditional romantic trajectory, 176–177
Triangle tests, 140, 188
Triangular theory of love, 315
True love conquers all belief, 477
True self, 166
Trust, 219
Truthfulness, 154
Turning point approach, 180–181

U

Uncertainty
    CLUES scale, 128
    communication and, 123, 125–126
    future research on, 130–131
    global uncertainty, 125
    hedging and, 124
    management of, 124
    nature of, 121–122
    personality predictors of, 127
    planning and, 124
    predictors of, 125
    reduction of, 361–362
    relationship initiation, 127–131
    relationship uncertainty, 128
    as rewarding vs. costly, 129
    seeking information, 124
    strategically increased/maintained/reduced, 129–130
Uncertainty orientation, 127
Uncertainty reduction theory (URT), 121–126, 136
    assumptions of, 122–123
    empirical tests, 125–126
    friendship-to-romance transition, 181–183
    hedging and, 124
    planning and, 124
    seeking information, 124
Uncharacteristic relational behavior, 184
Unilateral dependence, 202
Unwanted relationship pursuit
    cultural/contextual catalysts of, 412–414
    factors that contribute to, 412–415
    future research on, 418–419
    mild persistence, 411
    moderate persistence, 411
    origins of, 409–410
    persistence of, 410–412
    pre-stalking behaviors, 411
    relational goal pursuit theory, 414–415
    responses to, 415–418
    severe persistence, 411
    stalking, 411–412, 417–419

V

Vocal cues, 362

W

Waist-to-hip ratio (WHR), 277–278
Want-to-be talkers, 144
Withdrawing, 137–138
Workplace, friendship formation, 32–33

Y

Yahoo! Personals/Premier, 250, 252
Young adulthood, *see* Adolescence
Youth sexual/relational experiences, 387
Yuan belief, 478

Z

Zero acquaintance, 272